2019 YEARBOOK OF THE PRESBYTERIAN CHURCH IN AMERICA

VOLUME 2

Part V   MINISTERIAL DIRECTORY 3
ABBREVIATIONS 704

PREFACE

The forty-fourth edition of the *Yearbook of the Presbyterian Church in America* carries the designation 2019, the year of its publishing. Data in the two volumes represent a historical record of the year 2018. Volume I includes Parts I – IV; Volume II comprises Part V.

Part I of the *Yearbook* records the members of General Assembly committees for 2018-2019 (July to June). The Presbytery Directory (Part II) and the Church Directory (Part III) reflect reported information as of December 31, 2018, with one exception. Names of presbytery stated clerks and their contact information (Presbytery Directory) are current as of the publication of the Yearbook. The Statistical Report (Part IV) primarily reflects church data for the year ending December 31, 2018, or the latest reported information. Some data, however, may be shown from churches operating on a fiscal rather than a calendar year. The Ministerial Directory (Part V) reports information as of December 31, 2018.

The Stated Clerk's Office is dependent upon those who report the information compiled in these volumes. Therefore, we wish to thank the Clerks of Presbytery and Clerks of Session who have faithfully reported in a timely and orderly manner.

                                        L. Roy Taylor
                            Stated Clerk of the General Assembly

PART V

MINISTERIAL DIRECTORY

Abel, Matthew Paul – O Mar 8, 15, MetAtl Pby; astp Trinity P Ch, Covington, GA, 15-

11171 Highway 278, Covington, GA 30014 – 813-541-7273   Metro Atlanta
E-mail: Matt@trinitypca.net
Trinity Presbyterian Church – 770-787-7493

Abendroth, Douglas – op Christ Church Presbyterian, Irvine, CA, 06-07; astp Aliso Creek P Ch, Aliso Viejo, CA, 10-s

2936 Penman, Tustin, CA 92782   South Coast
Aliso Creek Presbyterian Church – 949-460-0080

Abidoye, Jameson – Chap US Army, 15-

9840 NW 31st Place, Sunrise, FL 33351   South Florida
E-mail: jamesonab@gmail.com
United States Army

Abney, Dave – astp Lake Baldwin Comm Ch, Orlando, FL, 10-11; astp Christ Ch Mandarin, Jacksonville, FL, 11-13; ascp 13-14; op Christ Ch, Intown, Jacksonville, FL, 14-17, p 17-

1237 Norwich Road, Jacksonville, FL 32207   North Florida
E-mail: dabney@christchurchintown.org
Christ Church, Intown – 904-517-2297

Abreu, Ezequias – astp Key Biscayne P Ch, Key Biscayne, FL, 15-

E-mail: ezequiasd_abreu@hotmail.com   South Florida
Key Biscayne Presbyterian Church – 305-361-2058

Accardy, Christopher Blake – b Manchester, NH, Jun 11, 65; w Shelley, Newbury, VT, Jun 12, 93; chdn Elizabeth Anne (Rhodes), Hannah Lynne, Elisabeth Grace, Matthew Blake; Plymouth 94, BA; GCTS 97-98; CTS 00, MDiv; UMemp 11, BS; O Nov 10, 00, OPC; staff New England Fell of Evan, 91-94; ip First Christian Ch, Elsberry, MO, 95-96; ascp Newbury Bible Ch, Newbury, VT, 96-97; p Calvary P Ch, Volga, SD, 00-03; op All Nations P Msn, Wilder, VT, 03-07; astp East Lanier Comm Ch, Buford, GA, 09-13; ss Grace P Ch, Grenada, MS, 15-16, p 16-

588 Robin Road, Grenada, MS 38901   Covenant
E-mail: coachchris2915@yahoo.com
Grace Presbyterian Church – 662-219-3727

Acevedo, Joel – astp Alexandria P Ch, Alexandria, VA, 08-17; op Iglesia Presbiteriana Gracia y Paz, Alexandria, VA, 08-15; astp Briarwood P Ch, Birmingham, AL, 18-; op Briarwood Hispanic, 18-

E-mail: jacevedo@briarwood.org   Evangel
Briarwood Presbyterian Church – 205-776-5200
Briarwood Hispanic

Acheson, Brandon – O Sept 20, 15, ChiMet Pby; ascp Westminster P Ch, Elgin, IL, 15-17

151 Glenbrook Circle, Gilberts, IL 60136 – 406-371-5217   Chicago Metro

Acker, William Blanton III – b Bessemer, AL, Aug 18, 47; f William Blanton, Jr.; m Henrietta Marie Sharpe; w Martha Westover, Everett, WA, Aug 8, 69; chdn Stephanie Anne (Van Engen), David William, Michelle Christine (Luchenbill), Gretchen Elizabeth (Wood); CC 69, BA; CTS 73, MDiv, 05, DMin; O Nov 7, 73, RPCES; astp Shannon Forest P Ch, Greenville, SC, 73-75; p Trinity P Ch, Kenner, LA, 75-84; p Covenant P Ch, Cedar Falls, IA, 84-90; p Apple Valley Ch, WI, 91-09; ip Bethel Ref Ch, Freeman, SD, 10-11; astp Jacobs Well P Ch, Green Bay, WI, 11-13; staff Emmaus Road Ch, Appleton, WI, 13-; mal LAMP Theo Sem, 13-

1417 Julie Court, Neenah, WI 54956   Wisconsin
E-mail: billacker@jacobswellgb.org
Emmaus Road Church – 303-520-5988
LAMP Theological Seminary

Acton, K. Hugh – b Jackson, MS, Mar 23, 76; w Rachel Rene Starnes, Dec 29, 99; chdn Hugh Arthur, Eleanor Rose, Jane Ivy, William Henry Alfred; BelC 98, BA; GPTS 01, MDiv; L 01, Cal Pby; O Sept 02, Gr Pby; p Ellisville P Ch, Ellisville, MS, 02-04; p Pearl P Ch, Pearl, MS, 04-05, srp 05-06; p Heidelberg P Ch, Heidelberg, MS, 06-

PO Box 691, Heidelberg, MS 39439 – 601-787-0122   Grace
E-mail: rev.acton@mac.com
Heidelberg Presbyterian Church – 601-787-3483

Adair, Matthew Christopher – f William Gregg; m Deanna Lynn Bandelier; w Lindsey Paige Anderson; SamU 97, BS; BDS 01, MDiv; L Jan 22, 01, Evan Pby; O Feb 24, 02, Evan Pby; astp Faith P Ch, Birmingham, AL, 02-04; p Christ Comm Ch, Watkinsville, GA, 04-

1041 Taylors Court, Watkinsville, GA 30677 – 706-424-1260   Georgia Foothills
E-mail: madair@missionathens.com
Christ Community Church – 706-769-4301

Adams, Aubrey Earl – b Selma, AL, May 26, 46; f Grady Earl; m Georgia Elizabeth Duke; w Rosita Adelaida Antonio, Selma, AL, Dec 10, 71; chdn Elizabeth Leilani, Carla Graciela; MBC 64-65; UAL 65-66; MBC 70-73, BS; RTS 85-88, MDiv; L Oct 18, 88, War Pby; O May 7, 89, War Pby; int Crescent Hill P Ch, Selma, AL, 88-89; lang stdy EICR, 89-90; chp MTW, Cusco, Peru, 90-92; HMA 93-94; chp Hinterland Ch, Satipo, Peru, 94-96; chp Hinterland Ch, Cusco, Peru, 96-99; astp Trinity P Ch, Jackson, MS, 99-03; p Grace P Ch, Madison, FL, 03-04; chp, ev MTW, Hinterland Ministry, Bolivia, 06-12; astp Trinity P Ch, Jackson, MS, 13-

33 Raintree Place, Jackson, MS 39211   Mississippi Valley
E-mail: eadams@tpcjackson.org
Trinity Presbyterian Church – 601-977-0774

Adams, George Andrew – b Chicago, IL, Nov 26, 54; f William Richard; m Charline June Adcox; w Barbara Katherine Johnson, Memphis, TN, Jul 5, 86; chdn Abigail Emma; WRHCC 72-74; SIU 74-76, BS; CBapTS 84-85; CTS 89, MDiv; L Mar 11, 89, GrLks Pby; O Apr 20, 90, GrLks Pby; ap Tates Creek P Ch, Lexington, KY, 89-90; ev, op Dayspring P Ch (Msn), Lexington, KY, 90-93; p Covenant P Ch, Macomb, IL, 93-98; ascp Faith Comm Ch, Pearland, TX, 98-03; p Covenant P Ch, Milledgeville, GA, 03-16, astp 16-18; wc

108 Short Cut Road NE, Milledgeville, GA 31061 – 478-452-6230   Central Georgia
E-mail: adamsrev1@yahoo.com

Adams, Jon Christian – b Freeport, IL, May 7, 60; f Neil Arthur; m Joye Helene Wardecker; w Anne Elizabeth DiVirgilio, Ellicott City, MD, Jul 12, 86; WheatC 78-82, BA; WTS 83-85, MAR; ChTS 86, MDiv; RTS 00-02, DMin; L Jun 85, Pac Pby; O Jul 86, Delmarva Presbytery; ap Chapelgate P Ch, Marriottsville, MD, 86-90; ap Parkview Ch, Lilburn, GA, 90-91; srp 91-01; astp Perimeter Ch, Duluth, GA, 01-02; op The Vine Comm Ch, Alpharetta, GA, 02-04, srp 04-

4655 Bethelview Road, Cumming, GA 30040 – 678-455-0408   Metro Atlanta
E-mail: jadams@thevinecommunitychurch.com
The Vine Community Church – 678-990-9395

Adams, Matthew Dallas – b Marion, SC, Jun 9, 90; f Ernest, Jr.; m Mary Stephenson; w Anna Elizabeth McDonald, Florence, SC, Jul 26, 14; chdn Brooks Dallas; LibU 13, BS; ErskTS 17, MDiv; O Jan 22, 17, PD Pby; p First P Ch, Dillon, SC, 17-

200 East Harrison Street, Dillon, SC 29536   Pee Dee
E-mail: matt.d.adams90@gmail.com
First Presbyterian Church – 843-774-8351

Adams, Peter – p Christ the King PCA, Hastings, MI, 14-

6274 Tischer Road, Lake Odessa, MI 48849 – 616-374-0872   Great Lakes
E-mail: peteradams@juno.com
Christ the King PCA

Adams, Philip Joseph – b Windsor, VT, Jun 26, 50; f Joseph Enos; m Marjorie Holmes; w Regina Moore, Weathersfield, VT, Jun 5, 71; chdn Sarah Joy, John Philip, Seth David, Daniel Alan; UVT 68-72, BA; WTS 74-77, MDiv; L Jan 77, Philadelphia Presbytery (RPCES); O Oct 22, 77, MidAtl Presbytery (PCA); op Christ P Ch, Nashua, NH, 77-81; wc 81-91; sc NoE Pby, 86-95; ev Westminster P Ch Msn, Worcester, MA, 92-06; hr 13

660 US Route 5, North Hartland, VT 05052 – 802-295-2056   Southern New England
HR

Adams, Trey – mis MTW, 11-

c/o Mission to the World   Mississippi Valley
E-mail: archadams@gmail.com
PCA Mission to the World

Adamson, Dan – b Chicago, IL, Apr 6, 70; f James; m Peggy; w Lynda, Homewood, IL, Aug 10, 96; chdn Emily Kathrin, Benjamin David, Joey James, Lucy Cheryl; MBI 93, BA; CTS 04, MDiv; O Aug 8, 04, NoIL Pby; astp All Souls Flwsp, Decatur, GA, 04-09; p Cityview P Ch, Chicago, IL, 09-15; ascp Covenant P Ch, Chicago, IL, 16-

3134 North Leavitt #2, Chicago, IL 60618 – 312-618-6060   Chicago Metro
E-mail: dadamson@covenantchicago.org
Covenant Presbyterian Church – 773-486-9590

Addington, Douglas A. – b Winchester, IN, Jan 31, 62; f Danny L; m Carol L.; w Mona Olivia Rumph, Charlotte, NC, May 17, 86; chdn Daniel J.; BallSU 80-81; CBC 81-84, BA; CBS 89-93, MDiv; O Oct 1, 95, Christ Ind Bible Ch; staff IVCF, 84-88; ascp Christ Ind Bible Ch, Perkasie, PA, 94-96; p West Hills P Ch, Henderson, NC, 96-17

2535 Westover Drive, Henderson, NC 27536 – 252-430-0778   Eastern Carolina
E-mail: dougadd@centurylink.net

Aeschliman, Richard A. – b Memphis, TN, Feb 28, 39; f Louis F; m Evelyn Eichler; w Sandra Matthews, Grenada, MS, Jun 17, 62; chdn Mary E. (Lochstampfor), Elizabeth A. (Dunahoo), Richard A., Rachel A. (McVey); BelC 57-61, BA; CTS 64, BD, 72, MDiv; L 64, Central Presbytery (EPC); O 64, Central Presbytery (EPC); p Hazelwood RP Ch, MO, 64-68; p Westminster P Ch, Elgin, IL, 68-74; admin LOGOS Bkstr, 75-76; dir Ch rel CTS, 76-80; dir dev National P Missions Inc, 80-82; Dir FMF, 82-83; admin CEP, 83-10; hr 10

1388 Keyhaven Court, Lawrenceville, GA 30045 – 770-277-4372   Metro Atlanta
E-mail: aesch@bellsouth.net
HR

Agan, Clarence Dewitt III (Jimmy) – b May 7, 70; f Clarence Jr. "Buddy"; m Jeannie; w Tricia Lee; chdn Sarah, Caroline, Patrick, Abby; ClemU 92, BA; CTS 95, MDiv; AberU 99, PhD; ob prof ErskTS, 01-07; ascp Greenwood P Ch , Greenwood, SC, 02; srp Clemson P Ch , Clemson, SC, 03-07; prof CTS, 07-15; srp Intown Comm Ch, Atlanta, GA, 15-; "Deacons, Deaconesses, and Denominational Discussions: Rom. 16:1 as a Test Case," *Presbyterion*, 08; "Toward a Hermeneutic of Imitation: The Imitation of Christ in the Didascalia Apostolorum," *Presbyterion*, 11; "History, Revelation, Assurance: Three Perspectives on Luke's Gospel," *Presbyterion*, 12; "Like the One who Serves: Growing in Christlike Love for God and Others," *Presbyterian and Reformed*, 13; "Departing from—and Recovering—Tradition: John Calvin and the Imitation of Christ," *JETS*, 13; "Repairing the Hole in Our Holiness: A Review Essay in Dialogue with Kevin DeYoung's The Hole in Our Holiness," *Presbyterion* 40/1-2(2014), 27-46

2938 Pine Orchard Drive, Tucker, GA 30084   Metro Atlanta
E-mail: jagan@intown.org
Intown Community Church – 404-633-8077

Agnew, Douglas Dewitt – b Greenville, SC, Mar 10, 50; f Arthur S.; m Evelyn Anne Jones; w Cindy; chdn Kevin Jacob, Mitchell Stephen, Elizabeth Anne, Seth Coley Johnson, Adrienne Johnson Epting ; ClemU 72, BA; SEBTS 81, MDiv; L 77, Calvary Bap; O 79, Calvary Bap; p Olive Grove Bap, Creedmore, NC, 79-80; p Southside Bap, Charlotte, NC, 80-88; p Grace Ch, Harrisburg, NC, 88-

6565 River Hills Drive, Harrisburg, NC 28075 – 704-567-8534   Catawba Valley
E-mail: brodoug1240@yahoo.com
Grace Church – 704-455-9312

Agnew, R. Parker – b Anderson, SC, Jul 28, 58; f E. Harry; m Frances Leonard; w Anne Rogers, Goodwater, AL, Jun 13, 80; chdn Mary Frances, Susanna; ClemU 76-80, BA; RTS 85-88, MDiv, 85-88, MCE; L Jun 88, CentGA Pby; O Jul 89, CentGA Pby; Recd PCA Jul 18, 95, SEAL Pby; astp Perry P Ch, Perry, GA, 89-91; p Cleveland Street (ARP), New Albany, MS, 91-95; astp First P Ch, Dothan, AL, 95-00; astp Perry P Ch, Perry, GA, 00-05, ascp 05-09; srp 09-

1500 Windsor Avenue, Perry, GA 31069 – 478-293-7636   Central Georgia
E-mail: pagnew@comsouth.net
Perry Presbyterian Church – 478-987-1403

Ahlberg, Michael John – b Denver, CO, Jul 2, 56; f Phillip; m Coralee; w Jeanne Ropp, Mar 15, 86; chdn Daniel Enoch, Michael Carothers; UCO 74-78, BA; RTS 79-82, MDiv, 93-95, DMin; O Jul 25, 82, Cov Pby; ap Carrollton P Ch, Carrollton, MS, 82-83; ap First P Ch, Clarksdale, MS, 83-87; p First P Ch, Union, MS, 87-99; p Faith P Ch, Cheraw, SC, 99-03; p Sharon P Ch, Magee, MS, 03-

617 Simpson Highway 28 East, Magee, MS 39111 – 601-849-2007   Grace
E-mail: mikejahlberg@gmail.com
Sharon Presbyterian Church – 601-849-3551

Ahn, Daniel Sangdo – ob WashTS

10534 Oak Bluff Court, Burke, VA 22015 – 703-665-4147   Korean Capital
E-mail: dahn1957@gmail.com
Washington Theological Seminary

MINISTERIAL DIRECTORY

Ahn, Joseph HyungJun – b Seoul, Korea, Sept 7, 62; f Ki Chul Ahn; m Eun Ae Kim; w Susan Yun, Baltimore, MD, Nov 22, 91; chdn Justin, Joanna, Paul; AvC 91, BA; BibTS 95, MDiv, 95, MA; ChShCS 00, ThM; L Nov 21, 95, KorE Pby; O Apr 9, 96, KorE Pby; astp Antioch Ch, PA, 91-93; astp Nak Won P Msn, Dresher, PA, 94-96; p Inat'l min, 97-00; op Grace Comm, Centreville, VA, 05-

6102 Grogans Court, Centreville, VA 20121 – 703-818-2393   Korean Capital
E-mail: ahnJoseph30@hotmail.com
Grace Community – 703-818-2393

Ahn, Peace Song Sik – b Seoul, Korea, Jun 7, 61; f Chi Jo; m In Ja Kim; w Seon Kyun Kim, Korea, Mar 9, 91; chdn Florence Y; GMCUVA 85, BA; CapBS; L Oct 88; O Oct 89; sec gen GMF, 89-90; ob mis CMF, 90-93; astp Korean Central P Ch of Wash, Vienna, VA, 91-93; op Mok Yang P Ch Msn, Fairfax, VA, 93-

5405 Black Oak Drive, Fairfax, VA 22032 – 703-764-0470   Korean Capital
E-mail: peaceahn@hotmail.com
Mok Yang Presbyterian Church Mission – 703-383-1545

Aikens, Andy – Recd PCA Feb 12, 13, GulCst Pby; astp Grace Comm Ch, Mobile, AL, 13-15; p First P Ch, Crossville, TN, 16-

224 Wycliffe Lane, Crossville, TN 38558   Tennessee Valley
E-mail: andyaikens@gmail.com
First Presbyterian Church – 931-484-4644

Aitcheson, Mike – astp Lake Baldwin Ch, Orlando, FL, 13-; op Christ United Flwsp Orlando, Orlando, FL, 14-

2801 Vine Street, Orlando, FL 32806   Central Florida
E-mail: maitcheson72@gmail.com
Lake Baldwin Church – 407-895-4748
Christ United Fellowship Orlando

Alaniz, Manny – O Sept 13, 15, SoTX Pby; astp Redeemer P Ch, San Antonio, TX, 15-18

9422 Maverick Pass, San Antonio, TX 78240 – 210-241-5969   South Texas
E-mail: manny@stephenchapel.org

Albano, John – O Oct 9, 16, CentGA Pby; p Northgate P Ch, Albany, GA, 16-

1826 Lullwater Road, Albany, GA 31707 – 540-250-6165   Central Georgia
E-mail: johnm.albano@gmail.com
Northgate Presbyterian Church – 229-883-6946

Albee, Troy – b Asheville, NC, Aug 2, 77; f James Wayne; m Gail Sowell; w Krista Louise Deutschmann, Greenville, SC, Aug 23, 03; chdn Jack, Josiah, Natalie, David; FurU 95-99, BA; RTSFL 99-02, MDiv; O Oct 27, 02, Cal Pby; astp, mp Mitchell Road P Ch, Greenville, SC; astp Ch of the Good Shepherd, Durham, NC, 06-09; ascp 09-10; astp Christ the King P Ch, Boston, MA, 10-; chp Grace P Ch, Hanover, MA, 11-

3 Macomber Lane, Pembroke, MA 02359   Southern New England
E-mail: troy@gracesouthshore.org
Christ the King Presbyterian Church – 617-354-8341
Grace Presbyterian South Shore

Alder, Jeremy – Chap Chapelgate Acad, 11-

1434 Becket Road, Eldersburg, MD 21784 – 410-795-0217   Chesapeake
E-mail: jalder@chapelgateacademy.org
Chapelgate Christian Academy

Aldin, Don – b Bryn Mawr, PA, Nov 16, 63; f Eugene Roger; m Barbara Young, Jennifer Spearman Aldin, Nov 27, 93; chdn Margaret Kay, Scott Ryan, Mark Keegan, Nathaniel Tucker; VATech 86, BS; WTS 92, MDiv; O Feb 15, 04, NGA Pby; ascp Redeemer P Ch, Athens, GA, 04-10; op Resurrection P Ch, Athens, GA, 10-15; p 15-17; admin RBI, 17-

1041 Cold Tree Lane, Watkinsville, GA 30677 – 706-338-0987   Georgia Foothills
E-mail: clerkgafoothills@gmail.com
PCA Retirement and Benefits, Inc. – 678-825-1260

Aldrich, John E. – b Houston, TX, Mar 9, 61; f Stephen; m Sandra Seltzer; w Pamela Jo Pitts, Ozark, MO, Jun 16, 84; chdn Andrew John, Matthew Stephen; IUP 79-81; CalBC 81-83, BS; CTS 89-95, MDiv; L Sept 5, 96, GrLks Pby; O Jun 29, 97, GrLks Pby; p North Dupo Bible Ch, Dupo, IL, 87-89; MO Bapt Med Cntr, St. Louis, MO, 89-94; Chap St. Joseph Hospital, Lexington, KY, 94-98; astp Covenant of Gr P Ch, Reisterstown, MD, 98-99, ascp 99-

1963 Barley Road, Marriottsville, MD 21104-1121 – 443-609-4063   Chesapeake
E-mail: jealdrich@comcast.net
Covenant of Grace Presbyterian Church – 410-833-2160

Aldrich, Kenneth A. – b Hornell, NY, Aug 10, 70; f Carol Kenneth; m Carole Ann Seaman; w Amy Jo Guillaume, Grand Rapids, MI, Jun 13, 98; chdn Noel Courage, Benjamin Zeal, Molly Joy; JMU 88-92, BA; RTS 92-95, MDiv; L Jan 11, 03, BlRdg Pby; O Jan 12, 03, BlRdg Pby; ascp Thornapple Evan Cov Ch, Grand Rapids, MI, 99-02; ascp Covenant P Ch, Harrisonburg, VA, 02-06; srp 06-11; p Covenant Life P Ch, Sarasota, FL, 11-

8273 Barton Farms Boulevard, Sarasota, FL 34241 – 540-908-7652   Southwest Florida
E-mail: ken@covenantlifepca.com
Covenant Life Presbyterian Church – 941-926-4777

Alexander, David – b Ballymoney, Northern Ireland, Sept 25, 31; f David; m Annie McAfee; w Elaine Hlavin, St. Louis, MO, May 27, 60; chdn David Jonathan, Brian Andrew; NWC 56, BA; CTS 59, MDiv; O Jun 60, BPC (Columbus Synod); p Crestwood P Ch, Edmonton, AB, 60-66; p Second Street P Ch, Albemarle, NC, 66-84; p Mount Cal P Ch, Roebuck, SC, 84-92; p Second Street P Ch, Albemarle, NC, 92-00; hr 00; ss Mount Carmel P Ch, Ellerbe, NC, 01-10; Chap Stanly Reg Med Cntr, 01-10

c/o Brian Alexander, 817 Loch Island Drive, Chesapeake, VA 23320 – 757-549-6131   Central Carolina
E-mail: alexfamily5@cox.net
HR

Alexander, James Julian – b Asheville, NC, Oct 21, 44; f Bryan W; m Helen Ingle; w Tari Beardslee, El Dorado, AR, Aug 5, 74; chdn Amy Susan (Curtis), Jennifer Lee (Medlin), Vanessa Janette (Sanders), Matthew James (d), Gretchen Rebecca (Newton), Rachel Cristina; BerC 63-67, BA; UKY 67; UNC 70-71; RTS 71-74, MDiv; SUNY 85-87, MS; O Feb 75, CentGA Pby; p Berachah Comm Ch, Augusta, GA, 75-76; Dir Christ for the Inner City, Augusta, GA, 75-78; p First P Ch, Troy, AL, 78-83; chp Rochester, NY, 84-86, t 85-89; ev PEF, 89-94; p Faith P Ch, Florence, SC, 95-06; ev PEF 06-07; p Grace P Ch, Baton Rouge, LA, 07-11; hr 11; ev PEF 11-

413 Poplar Street, Florence, SC 29501   Southern Louisiana
E-mail: jjxan777@gmail.com
HR

Alexander, Jim – O Oct 11, 09, RMtn Pby; p Cheyenne Mountain P Ch, Colorado Springs, CO, 09-17; astp Briarwood P Ch, Birmingham, AL, 17-

505 Bayhill Road, Birmingham, AL 35244 – 205-842-2907   Evangel
E-mail: jalexander@briarwood.org
Briarwood Presbyterian Church – 205-776-5200

MINISTERIAL DIRECTORY

Alexander, John – w Karen Beth Rizzuti, May 20, 06; chdn Molly Grace (d), Charles Lawrence; TempU 05, BA; WTS 10, MDiv; O May 11, Phil Pby; Liberti Ch of the River Wards, Philadelphia, PA, 11-

1251 Marlborough Street, Philadelphia, PA 19125   Philadelphia
E-mail: john@liberti.org
Liberti Church of the River Wards – 215-291-4248

Alexander, John – O Sept 9, 18, War Pby; p First P Ch, Greensboro, AL, 18-

First Presbyterian Church – 334-624-3963   Warrior

Alexander, Paul Harrison – b Ithaca, NY, Jan 29, 33; f Fred A; m Anne Shattuck; w Lorraine Johnson, Sandstone, MN, Aug 24, 56; chdn Junia (Haas), Charysse, DeAnn, Gregory; BJU 50-54, BA; FU 53; TempU 55; FTS 54-56; CTS 56-58, BD; L Aug 58, BPC (Evangelical Synod); O Sept 58, BPC (Evangelical Synod); srp Westminster P Ch, Huntsville, AL, 58-01; fndr WestmCAc, Hunstville, AL, 64; mod RPC, 75; dir MTW, Ukraine, 01-03; pastoral resource, 03-05; mis, 05-12; astp Trinity P Ch, Union, MO, 12-16, min/fam

14 Worthington Drive, Union, MO 63084 – 636-744-0023   Missouri
E-mail: paul.7alexander@gmail.com

Alford, James Weston – b Rome, GA, Jul 16, 65; f James Gibson; m Nancy Estelle Bruner; w Elizabeth Oldham, Jun 22, 02; chdn James Gibson, Christopher Beckwith, Elizabeth Abigail, Nancy Estelle, Weston Oldham; Timothy Eugene; WinC 87, BA; CTS 93, MDiv; L 99, Nash Pby; O May 7, 00, Nash Pby; yp Faith P Ch, Anniston, AL, 94-95; ss Willow Woods P Ch, Snellville, GA, 97-98; ascp, yp Faith P Ch, Goodlettsville, TN, 99-03; p Christ P Ch, Sweetwater, TN, 03-

102 Chapel Avenue, Sweetwater, TN 37874 – 423-351-7841   Tennessee Valley
E-mail: alfamseven@gmail.com
Christ Presbyterian Church – 423-337-5058

Alford, Michael Rives – b Oxford, NC, Aug 23, 38; f David Wilson; m Christine Gladys Cox; w Diana Myers Jennings, Schenectady, NY, Mar 10, 62; chdn Michael Andrew, Peter Mekeel, Mary Beth; NCSt 60, BS; RPI 61; GCTS 63, MDiv; SBTS 66; L Feb 64, Calvary Bap Ch, Framingham, MA; O May 65, St. Matthews Council, Louisville, KY; Recd PCA Jul 89, NoE Pby; p New Colony Bap Ch, Billerica, MA, 66-71; p Nashua Bap Ch, NH, 70-74; ap First P Ch, Schenectady, NY, 74-79, p 80-02; hr 02; p em First P Ch, Schenectady, NY; ss Hope Ch, Ballston Spa, NY, 06-07

107 Nott Terrace, Apt. 710, Schenectady, NY 12308 – 518-346-2142   New York State
HR

Alford, Ryan – O Oct 11, 16, GulfCst Pby; astp Grace Redeemer PCA, Crestview, FL, 16-17; chp 18-

6263 Lausanne Drive North, Mobile, AL 36608 – 251-654-3562   Gulf Coast

Allebach, Jerrett – astp Christ Comm P Ch, West Hartford, CT, 08-11; astp Trinity P Ch, Providence, RI, 13-; op Grace P Ch Worcester, Worcester, MA, 14-

21 Monadnock Road, Worcester, MA 01609   Southern New England
E-mail: jarrett@graceworcester.org
Trinity Presbyterian Church – 401-272-0766
Grace Presbyterian Church Worcester

Allen, Andrew, Jr. – b Tacoma, WA, Dec 17, 70; w Amy, Tacoma, WA, Feb 5, 05; chdn Katherine Elizabeth Grace ; CTS 12, MDiv; O Aug 15, 15, PacNW Pby; astp Faith P Ch, Anchorage, AK, 15-18; op Redeemer P Msn, Kenai, AK, 15-18; "An Old Testament 'Extra Indwelling,'" *The Bantam Review*, 15

PO Box 3758, Soldatna, AK 99669 – 253-223-4041   Pacific Northwest
E-mail: mr.aalen@gmail.com

Allen, Doyle – p Faith Ref P Ch, Fairmont, WV, 06-09; p First P Ch, Ft. Oglethorpe, GA, 10-17; chap USN, 17-

203 Fuller Street, Oceanside, CA 92058 – 423-762-3340   Tennessee Valley
E-mail: pastordoyleallen@gmail.com
United States Navy

Allen, J. Patrick – astp Chapelgate P Ch, Marriottsville, MD, 12-

17 Six Notches Court, Catonsville, MD 21228 – 443-310-1622   Chesapeake
E-mail: pallen@chapelgate.org
Chapelgate Presbyterian Church – 410-442-5800

Allen, Kevin – b Detroit, MI, Apr 23, 68; f Frank Jr.; m Joan Elizabeth Ellsworth; w Elizabeth Rae Troupe, Eugene, OR, Jun 1, 91; chdn Bradley Frank, Emily Jean Rae; UOR 87-91, BS; NGTS 97-00, MDiv; L Jan 28, 00, RMtn Pby; O Oct 8, 00, RMtn Pby; staff CCC, WWAU, 92-95; staff CCC, UUT, 95-97; astp Village Seven P Ch, Colorado Springs, CO, 00-08; ascp 08-16; sc RMtn Pby, 05-17; ob Christianity Explored, 16-

4744 Telephone Road #3-153, Ventura, CA 93003 – 719-277-0293   Pacific
E-mail: kevin.allen@christianityexplored.org
Christianity Explored

Allen, Michael – Jackson, MS, Nov 3, 81; f Robert Martin, Jr.; m Carrye McQuinn; w Emily Petersen, Spartanburg, SC, Jun 11, 05; chdn Jackson Thomas, William Gregory; WheatC 04, BA, 05, MA, 07, PhD; O May 10, EPC; Recd PCA Jan 17, 17, CentFL Pby; prof KTS, 09-14; ob prof RTSFL, 14-

892 North Lake Claire Circle, Oviedo, FL 32765   Central Florida
E-mail: mallen@rts.edu
Reformed Theological Seminary, FL – 407-366-9493

Allen, Rick – ascp Hickory Grove P Ch, Mt. Juliet, TN, 06-

4929 John Hagar Road, Hermitage, TN 37076 – 615-885-2926   Nashville
Hickory Grove Presbyterian Church – 615-754-8337

Allen, Robert Martin Jr. – b Bucyrus, OH, Sept 26, 51; f Robert Martin; m May G. Malone; w Carrye B. McQuinn, Jackson, MS, Aug 19, 72; chdn Jennifer Rebecca, Robert Michael, Jonathan David; UMS 73, BBA, 75, JD; RTS 86, MDiv; O Aug 6, 89, EPC; Recd PCA Oct 19, 95, SFL Pby; exec p Second P Ch, Memphis, TN, 88-95; srp Immanuel P Ch, Miami, FL, 95-99; exec p Coral Ridge P Ch, Ft. Lauderdale, FL, 99-01; ascp, exec p Park Cities P Ch, Dallas, TX, 01-09; wc; ss Carthage P Ch, Carthage, MS, 15-17; hr 17

103 South Branch Street, Madison, MS 39110 – 601-397-8627   North Texas
E-mail: robertallenjr@gmail.com
HR

Allen, Steve – O Jun 1, 08; campm RUF, 12-15; ascp Gr Chapel, Lincoln, NE, 15-18

3615 South 37th Street, Lincoln, NE 68506   Platte Valley
E-mail: steve30allen@gmail.com

Allen, Todd Wardsworth – b Cleveland, OH, Aug 25, 24; f Howard Wardsworth A; m Martha Todd; w Judith Lynn Akin, Acworth, GA, Dec 22, 57; chdn Deborah Deldee, Rebekah Lynn & Rachel Davina (twins), Todd Wardsworth Jr; UGA 60-61; ColTS 56-59, dipl; O Dec 20, 59, Chero Pby (PCUS); p Midway P Ch, Powder Springs, GA, 59-62; p Mars Hill P Ch, Cobb Cnty, GA, 59-62; p Eastern Height P Ch,

Allen, Todd Wardsworth, continued
Savannah, GA, 62-74; p Shenandoah P Ch, Miami, FL, 74-81; World Home Bible League, 81-83; srp Midway P Ch, Powder Springs, GA, 83-96, p em 96; p First P Ch, Villa Rica, GA, 00-09; *Revelation Confidential*

4780 Deer Run, Kennesaw, GA 30152-5711 – 770-426-6324　　　　　　　　Northwest Georgia
E-mail: toddwallen@comcast.net
HR

　　Allison, Bradford Eugene – b Chattanooga, TN, Sept 21, 56; f George Rudder Jr; m Betty Jo Maddox; w Wendy Strassner, Philadelphia, PA, Dec 20, 80; chdn Matthew Rudder, Meredith Miller, Kathryn Davis; MidSoBC 74-78, BA; WTS 78-80, MAR, 80-81, MDiv; L 82, Phil Pby (RPCES); O 82, Phil Pby (RPCES); ap Tenth P Ch, Philadelphia, PA, 81-84; p Glen Burnie Evangelical P Ch, Glen Burnie, MD, 84-93; p Altadena Valley P Ch, Birmingham, AL, 93-

4660 Caldwell Mill Road, Birmingham, AL 35243　　　　　　　　　　　　　　　　Evangel
E-mail: brad@avpc.org
Altadena Valley Presbyterian Church – 205-967-0680

　　Allman, Robert B. III – b Statesboro, GA, Jan 2, 71; f Robert B. Jr.; m Betty Jo McAdory; w Lori M. Venable, Winter Park, FL, Jul 30, 94; chdn Emma Katherine; UCF 89-92; SamU 92-93, BA; BDS 94-97, MDiv; CPE 04-05; ErskTS 08, DMin; L Sept 28, 99, Evan Pby; O Feb 13, 00, Evan Pby; stus First P Ch, Russellville, AL, 99-00, p 00-01; Chap USAR, 00-01; Chap USArmy, 01-

14 Staunton Court, Columbia, SC 29229　　　　　　　　　　　　　　　　　　　Evangel
E-mail: robert.b.allman2.mil@mail.mil
United States Army

　　Allred, Brian J. – astp Good Shepherd P Ch, Valparaiso, IN, 07-; op Trin P Msn, DeMotte, IN, 07-09; astp New Life P Ch, Yorktown, IN, 09-11; ascp 11-

308 South Buckingham Road, Yorktown, IN 47396 – 765-759-5721　　　　　Central Indiana
E-mail: bjallred@newlifepca.org
New Life Presbyterian Church – 765-759-9189

　　Allums, Robert M. – b Shreveport, LA, Oct 7, 57; f William Mims; m Barbara Bennett Johnston; w Helen Gates, Shreveport, LA, Aug 9, 80; chdn Robert Benjamin, Lydia Erin, Mary Emily; OKBU 75; LATU 76-79, BA; SWBTS 81-85, MDiv; L Apr 97; O Oct 97, NoIL Pby; p Tyler Creek Ch, IL, 97-02; Crossway Books; ascp Spring Valley P Ch, Roselle, IL, 04-08; ob seeJesus, 09-

6039 Cypress Gardens Boulevard #221, Winter Haven, FL 33884 – 847-458-8625　　Chicago Metro

　　Almond, James Richard – b Ft. Rucker, AL, Jan 21, 83; f Coy Rickie; m Teresa Gail; w Amanda Joy, Oct 12, 12; CIU 03, BS; RTS 05, MATS, 09, MDiv; O Mar 4, 12, CentCar Pby; astp Carolina P Ch, Locust, NC, 12-14; p Goshen P Ch, Belmont, NC, 14-

1885 Perfection Avenue, Belmont, NC 28012 – 704-467-3216　　　　　　　Central Carolina
E-mail: teacherjra@gmail.com
Goshen Presbyterian Church – 704-827-6280

　　Almquist, Per – b Wright-Patterson AFB, OH, Oct 03, 74; f Kenneth C.; m Janell K.; w Elizabeth Joan, Providence, RI, Sept 02 95; chdn Per Kyle, Jason Christopher, Scott Kenneth Paul; JHU 96, BA; CTS 99, MDiv; O Feb 06, NNE Pby; ascp Christ the Redeemer Ch, Portland, ME, 06-11; op Free Gr P Ch, Lewiston, ME, 08-11; p 11-

160 Canal Street, Lewiston, ME 04240 – 207-333-3588　　　　　　　　Northern New England
E-mail: per.almquist@freegrace.us
Free Grace Presbyterian Church – 207-513-1355

Almy, Logan Patrick – b Decatur, GA, Apr 20, 82; w Natalie Yorg, Stone Mountain, GA, Aug 6, 05; chdn Caleb Logan, Josiah James; UGA 05, BA; CTS 08, MDiv; Recd PCA Jun 10, 10, Siouxl Pby; p Grace P Ch, Duluth, MN, 10-14; p First P Ch, Waynesboro, GA, 14-

223 Pine Cone Road, Waynesboro, GA 30830   Savannah River
E-mail: loganalmy@charter.net
First Presbyterian Church – 706-554-2552

Alphin, Ruffin – b Suffolk, VA, Sept 24, 54; f Robert; m Juanita Powell; w Dorothy Ballard, Ivor, VA, Aug 21, 76; chdn Allison, Adam, Anna; VPI 77, BS; GrTS 84, MDiv; WTS 97, DMin; O 90; Recd PCA Apr 9, 94, JR Pby; p Dutchtown Brethren Ch, Warsaw, IN, 83-85; p Maranatha Bible Ch, New Kinsington, PA, 85-94; p Westminster Ref P Ch, Suffolk, VA, 94-

3488 Godwin Boulevard, Suffolk, VA 23434 – 757-934-3886   Tidewater
E-mail: ruffrocket@wrpca.org
Westminster Reformed Presbyterian Church – 757-539-0540

Alsup, Michael J. – b Japan, Apr 20, 61; f C. F; m Martha Weeks; w Kelly Bullock, Fairhope, AL, Feb 25, 89; chdn Katherine Rene; AU 79-83, BS; RTS 89-92, MDiv; O Nov 29, 92, SEAL Pby; ascp Trinity P Ch, Opelika, AL, 92-00, srp 00-03; p First P Ch, Troy, AL, 03-

105 George Wallace Drive, Troy, AL 36081 – 334-566-3020   Southeast Alabama
E-mail: Michael.alsup.email@gmail.com
First Presbyterian Church – 334-566-0817

Altman, Blake Ashley – b Wichita Falls, TX, Aug 18, 77; f William Kean; m Doris Elaine; w Lauren Marie; chdn Andrew Wayne, Anne Elaine, Bennett Austin, August William; TXA&M 00, BS; DTS 04, ThM; O Oct 1, 06, MNY Pby; ob campm Manna Christian Fell, Princeton, 06-11; astp Hope P Ch, Lawrenceville, NJ, 09-11; op, chp Trin P Ch of Owasso, OK, 11-13, p 13-

9210 North Garnett Roads, Owasso, OK 74055 – 918-805-4269   Hills and Plains
E-mail: blake@trinityowasso.com
Trinity Presbyterian Church of Owasso

Altork, Richard Farley – b New York, NY, Jul 22, 43; f William Abraham; m Elizabeth Evans Price; w Barbara Gail Jinright, Thomasville, GA, Sept 25, 71; chdn Leila (Adams), Susan Rachel, Marcy (Krenzin), Robert Jinright, Daniel Abraham; MonC 63, AA; BelC 67, BA; ColTS 71, MDiv; O Apr 71, SWGA Pby (PCUS); ap First P Ch, Thomasville, GA, 71-72; p Courtland P Ch, 72-73; p Dawson Ch, GA, 73-75; p Mtn City Ch, Mtn City, TN, 75-80; p Clinton Ch, Mtn City, TN, 75-80; p Fuquay-Varina Ch, NC, 80-84; p Village Chapel P Ch, 84-86; p First P Ch, Plantation, FL, 86-88; mis WBT, Philippines, 90-15; ss Prosperity P Ch, Charlotte, NC, 15-16; *Believer Basics - The Believer's Basic Training Manual*, 05; email subscription publication "Soul Food" 95-

515 West End Drive, Monroe, NC 28112 – 704-221-7945   Catawba Valley
E-mail: richard_altork@sil.org

Alwinson, Peter A. – b Pomona, CA, Apr 11, 55; f Peter G. (d); m Ruth M. Broad; w Caron Diane Covalt, Orange, CA, Jun 9, 79; chdn Joel Peter, Jon Michael, Jessie Marie; BIOLA 79, BA; TEDS 81, MDiv; RTSFL 96, DMin; O Jan 4, 87, CentFL Pby; p Willow Creek Ch, Winter Springs, FL, 87-12; ob VP KeyLife Network, Maitland, FL, 12-16

426 Woodcrest Street, Winter Springs, FL 32708 – 407-542-3262   Central Florida

Amaismeier, Philip – O Nov 11, 18, Pitts Pby; ascp Washington P Ch, Washington, PA, 18-

12 College Street, Box 45, West Middletown, PA 15379 – 724-288-5183   Pittsburgh
E-mail: phil@amaismeier.com
Washington Presbyterian Church – 724-228-4776

Ames, Arthur Gordon – b Niskayuna Cty, NY, Nov 3, 42; f Gordon Arthur; m Levia Cuoco; w Penny Lea Hamaker (d); (2) Catherine Moira Webel, St. Louis, MO, Oct 29, 16; chdn Kimberly Ruth, David Arthur, Coray June; HougC 64, BA; WTS 70, BD, 76, MDiv; CTS 93, DMin; L May 70, Phil Pby (OPC); O May 71, NCA Pby (OPC); Recd PCA Apr 83; ap First Ch, Sunnydale, CA, 71-73; p Trinity Ch, Newburg, OR, 73-76; p Grace Ch, Carson, CA, 76-83; p Colfax Center P Ch, Holland, IA, 83-87; ascp Village Seven P Ch, Colorado Springs, CO, 87-94; p Glen Burnie Evangelical P Ch, Glen Burnie, MD, 94-99, wc 99-00; ascp Grace P Ch of the W Reserve, Hudson, OH, 00-03; astp Harvest Ch of Medina, Medina, OH, 03-05, ascp 05-10; hr 10

1441 Glenpeak Drive, Maryland Heights, MO 63043 – 314-753-3133   Missouri
E-mail: artames@att.net
HR

Ames, John Brewer III – O Sept 11, 16, SEAL pby; Pea River P Ch, Clio, AL, 16-

3244 Louisville Street, Louisville, AL 36017   Southeast Alabama
E-mail: amesjoh@gmail.com
Pea River Presbyterian Church

Ammen, Chris – w Sarah; chdn Jake, Caleb; astp Trinity P Ch, Tuscaloosa, AL, 12-15, ascp 15-

908 Monarch Way, Northport, AL 35473   Warrior
E-mail: cammen@trinitytuscaloosa.org
Trinity Presbyterian Church – 205-391-2111

Amsler, Robert L. – w Julie Trenis, ascp Heritage P Ch, Warrenton, VA, 08-; op Cristo Redentor, Warrenton, VA, 13-18

9252 Elk Run Road, Catlett, VA 20119-2026   Potomac
E-mail: rlamsler@gmail.com
Heritage Presbyterian Church – 540-347-4627

An, Daniel Changil – O May 02, KorCent Pby; p Immanuel P Ch, IL, 02-

104 Lilac Lane, Buffalo Grove, IL 60089 – 847-215-7591   Korean Central
E-mail: jesaja4031@hotmail.com
Immanuel Presbyterian Church

An, Joseph Hyosung – WSCAL; O Apr 11, 00, KorSW2Pby; ob astp First PC of Or Co, Midway City, CA, 00-03; op The Humbled One Church, CA, 03-14; p Il Shin P Ch, Downey, CA, 12-

5404 Rome Avenue, Cypress, CA 90630 – 714-726-0235   Korean Southwest Orange County
E-mail: hyosungan@hotmail.com
Il Shin Presbyterian Church – 562-401-0191

An, Sung Tag – Recd PCA Sept 14, 86; p Dallas Korean P Ch, Carrollton, TX, 86-96; hr; astp Dallas Korean P Ch, Carrollton, TX, 94-

106 West Avenue G, Killeen, TX 76541 – 254-501-9058   Korean Southern
HR

Anderegg, David Jr. – b Cincinnati, OH, Aug 15, 58; f David L., Sr.; m Patricia Ann Butler; w Tee Andrea Adams, Royston, GA, Sept 4, 82; chdn David L. III, Laura Anne, Emma Katherine, Virginia Erin, Benjamin Turretin; BrPJC 79, AA; UGA 83, BA; AU 87, MBA; RTS 97, MDiv; L Nov 2, 97; O Nov 2, 97, GulCst Pby; staff WDA, AU, 83-86; int Trinity P Ch, Jackson, MS, 95-97; astp First P Ch, Panama City,

Anderegg, David Jr, continued
FL, 97-01; p Pinewoods P Ch, Cantonment, FL, 01-11; admin RBI, 11-; contr, co-ed *PCA Call Package Guidelines,* contr *PCA RBI Retirement Plan Review, PCA RBI Benefit Bulletin*

3957 Fellowship Drive, Buford, GA 30519 – 678-743-3956   Gulf Coast
E-mail: danderegg@pcanet.org
PCA Retirement & Benefits, Inc. – 678-825-1260

Anderson, Aaron – astp Providence P Ch, York, PA, 09-15; op City Ch York, York, PA, 09-15; ob LOGOS Acad, York, PA, 15-

604 Madison Avenue, York, PA 17404 – 717-764-0292   Susquehanna Valley
E-mail: anderson.aaronjames@gmail.com
LOGOS Academy, York, PA

Anderson, Brad Alan – b Joplin, MO, Nov 12, 66; f William Lee; m Nancy Gale Robson; w Dana Leigh Bell, St. Joseph, MO, Sept 5, 92; chdn Katherine, Abigale, William, Joshua; UMOC 90, BS; CTS 99, MDiv; O Apr 18, 99, Hrtl Pby; staff Navs, 90-95; ascp Zion Ch, Lincoln, NE, 98-02; srp Faith Covenant OPC, Kalispell, MT , 02-06; prof CTS, 07-11; astp Valley Springs P Ch, Roseville, CA, 12-13, ascp 13-15, srp 15-

9578 Windrose Lane, Granite Bay, CA 95746   Northern California
E-mail: brada@valleysprings.org
Valley Springs Presbyterian Church – 916-786-7940

Anderson, Chad – b Holdrege, NE, Jul 1, 76; w Deborah Korb; chdn Barnabas Samuel, Stephen Thomas; CTS 04, MDiv; O May 08, PlVall Pby; ascp Trinity P Ch, Kearney, NE, 06-09, srp 09-

415 East 32nd Street, Kearney, NE 68847   Platte Valley
E-mail: chad@tpckearney.org
Trinity Presbyterian Church – 308-234-3142

Anderson, Charles – O 17, CentInd Pby; p Redeemer P Ch, Indianapolis, IN, 17-

1505 North Delaware Street, Indianapolis, IN 46202   Central Indiana
E-mail: charles@redeemindy.org
Redeemer Presbyterian Church – 317-238-5487

Anderson, Charles William – b Chicago, IL, Aug 1, 25; f Clarence P; m Edith M. Linden; w Florence M. Chisholm, Long Beach Island, NJ, Aug 26, 49; chdn Nancy, William L; WheatC 49, BA; FTS 52, BD; USo 72, STM; L Jan 52, Phil Pby (BPC); O May 22, 52, BPC; p Christ BPC, Philadelphia, PA, 52-53; p Boothwyn RP, Boothwyn, PA, 54-64; prof CC, 64-93, Chap 86-90; hr 93; ip Chattanooga Valley P Ch, Flintstone, GA, 92-94; prof African Bible College, Malawi, 97-98

508 Fortwood Place, Chattanooga, TN 37403 – 706-820-1672   Tennessee Valley
E-mail: anders1925@aol.com
HR

Anderson, Daniel Sean – chp Little Rock, AR, 15- 16; op Central P Msn, Little Rock, AR, 16-

1300 North Hughes Street, Little Rock, AR 72207-6111 – 501-352-0455   Covenant
E-mail: anderson.danielsean@gmail.com
Central Presbyterian Mission

Anderson, David Holland – b Danville, VA, Apr 23, 51; f Ezra; m Elma Lee Mays; w Patricia Ann Austin, Cleveland, TN, Aug 1, 70; chdn Amanda Marie (Rollins), Elizabeth Anne, Susanna Lee, David H. II

Anderson, David Holland, continued
Sarah Jane; TomlinsonC, AA; UTC, BS; RTSFL 96-98, MDiv; L Jul 98, TNVal Pby; O Aug 30, 98, TNVal Pby; p Trinity P Ch, Maryville, TN, 98-

1063 Southwick Drive, Alcoa, TN 37701 – 865-380-9253 Tennessee Valley
E-mail: DavenPatA@charter.net
Trinity Presbyterian Church – 865-982-6932

Anderson, David Sean – b Milwaukee, WI, Jul 20, 71; f Raymond John; m Mary Kathleen Bronesky; w Kari Lynn Shook, Cleveland, OH, Nov 5, 95; chdn Elisa, Benjamin, Ian, Emma Kate; WittU 93 BArch; CTS 00, MDiv; O Sept 01, NoIL Pby; astp Wheatland P Ch, Lancaster, PA, 02-04, ascp 04-07; ob p Grace Flwsp Ch, Freeport, IL, 07-10; astp Grace Redeemer Ch, Teaneck, NJ, 10-11; ascp 11-12; astp Crossroads P Flwsp, Maplewood, MO, 13-16

3515 Cambridge Avenue, Maplewood, MO 63143 – 201-312-8992 Missouri

Anderson, Jason Ryan – b Atlanta, GA, May 31, 72; f James Hoyt; m Pamela Dianne Sousa; w Cristy, Gainesville, GA, Oct 8, 91; chdn Aeryn Elizabeth; NGA 94, BS; AUM 03, MS; ABD, AU 05; RTS 17, MDiv; O Jun 18, Flwsp Pby; stus Old Lebanon P Ch, Ackerman, MS, 14-18; p Hopewell P Ch, Rock Hill, SC, 18-

1891 Springsteen Road, Apt 214, Rock Hill, SC 29730 Fellowship
E-mail: jasonryananderson@hushmail.com
Hopewell Presbyterian Church – 803-324-1066

Anderson, John Boyce – w Carey Elizabeth Henderson; chdn Jason Luke, Jennifer Paige; RTS 76-78; WTS 79-81, MDiv; USF 88-94, MBA; op Calvin P Ch, Phoenix, AZ, 81, srp 81-86; astp Covenant P Ch, Naples, FL, 03-04; op Bay P Ch, Bonita Springs, FL, 05-07; p 07-

9694 Litchfield Lane, Naples, FL 34109 – 239-280-8407 Suncoast Florida
E-mail: baypres@msn.com
Bay Presbyterian Church – 239-498-9055

Anderson, Jon Christopher – b Fairfax, VA, Oct 7, 71; f James William; m Carol Jean McDonald; w Rachel Christine Scott, Glasgow, KY, Aug 6, 94; chdn Anne Michal, Elizabeth Austen, Emma Claire, Jon Patrick (Jack), Matthew Knox (d), Simeon Creed, Mallory Jane; UVA 89-94, BA, MEd; RTS 96-00, MDiv; O Oct 22, 00, Cov Pby; astp Carthage P Ch, Carthage, MS, 97-00; astp Grace P Ch, Starkville, MS, 00-02, ascp 02-05; astp Westminster P Ch, Bryan, TX, 05-06; ascp 06-

1518 Bluefield Court, College Station, TX 77845-7956 – 979-450-5208 South Texas
E-mail: jon@wpc-bryan.org
Westminster Presbyterian Church – 979-776-1185

Anderson, Joshua – b Richmond, VA, Jul 8, 80; w Ami Giancoli, Smithfield, VA, May 3, 03; chdn Cael Joshua, Gillian Mae, Judah Barry, Tristan Patrick; UVA 03, BA; CTS 08, MDiv; O Aug 3, 08, MO Pby; astp Providence Ref P Ch, St. Louis, MO, 08-09; ascp 09-14; p Colleyville P Ch, Colleyville, TX, 14-

715 Cheek Sparger Road, Colleyville, TX 76034 – 817-501-9015 North Texas
E-mail: josh@cpcpca.org
Colleyville Presbyterian Church – 817-498-2626

Anderson, Peter William – b Clinton, SC, Aug 2, 49; f George Andrew; m Mary Katharine Ballard; w Martha Blackwell Hanna, Hopewell, VA, Nov 29, 74; chdn Sarah Katharine, Carrie Elizabeth; KgC 67-70, BA; ETSU 72; UNC 72-73, MEd; WTS 73-77, MDiv; IST 90, DMin; O Jul 17, 77, Westm Pby; op Trinity P Ch Windward, Kailua, Oahu, HI, 77-80, p 80-94; op Trinity Ch Central Oahu, Mililani, HI, 91-95, p 95-14

199 Twin Fawns Trail, Dahlonega, GA 30533 – 808-625-0614 Metro Atlanta

Anderson, Ryan Clark – b Knoxville, TN, Setp 29, 77; w Laura Sommer, St. Louis, MO, Sept 8, 07; chdn Audrey Clark, Evangeline Sommer, Iris Hope; UT 99, BS; CTS 07, MDiv; O Jan 31, 09, EPC; Recd PCA May 7, 11, NoTX Pby; campm RUF, TCU, 11-

4200 South Drive, Ft. Worth, TX 76109 – 817-818-9032   North Texas
E-mail: ryan.anderson@ruf.org
PCA Reformed University Fellowship

Anderson, Scotty Shane – w Kerry; chdn Clay, Avery, Grace; USAFA 94, BS; GPTS, MDiv; O Aug 7, 05, Cal Pby; astp Woodruff Road P Ch, Simpsonville, SC, 05-18, ascp 18-

461 River Way Drive, Greer, SC 29651 – 864-363-4632   Calvary
E-mail: scotty@woodruffroad.com
Woodruff Road Presbyterian Church – 864-297-5257

Anderson, Seth – b Danvers, MA, Jun 16, 77; f Peter David; m Sharon Litchfield; w Karen Morrison, Winchester, MA, Mar 24, 78; chdn Anna, Joshua, Mary Grace, Caroline, Andrew; GordC, BA; CTS 06, MDiv; O Nov 9, 08, NNE Pby; stus Trinity P Ch, St. Albans, VT, 07-08, p 08-

11 Maple Grove Estates, Swanton, VT 05478 – 802-752-5775   Northern New England
E-mail: tpc_stalbans@yahoo.com
Trinity Presbyterian Church – 802-527-7221

Anderson, Sidney Ballard – b Decatur, GA, Oct 7, 46; f George Andrew A; m Katharine Ballard; w Louise Stembridge, Zephyrhills, FL, Jun 5, 73; chdn Beth Ann (Nedelisky), Paul Sidney; KgC 64-68, BA; ColTS 68-69; PTS 69-71, MDiv; O Jul 71, PCUS; p Jewell Rdge & Jewell Vly Ch, Whitewood, VA, 71-73; p Swannanoa Valley P Ch, 73-75; mis Nigeria, 75-88; MTW, 88-92; mis MTW 93-12; hr 12

85 Cypress Circle, Barboursville, VA 22923   Western Carolina
E-mail: sidneybanderson@gmail.com
HR

Anderson, Stephen (Chip) – Recd PCA Sept 16, 17, SNE Pby; astp Christ P Ch, New Haven, CT, 17-

227 Hansen Avenue, Bridgeport, CT 06605   Southern New England
E-mail: Chip.Anderson@CPCNewHaven.org
Christ Presbyterian Church – 203-777-6960

Anderson, Thomas Edward Jr. – b Birmingham, AL, Jan 29, 53; f Thomas E; m Mary Shepherd; w Sara Miller, Birmingham, AL; chdn Malcom Edward, Owen Thomas; TNTC 71-74, BA; RTS 78-81, MDiv; L Apr 28, 81, Evan Pby; O Jun 21, 81, Evan Pby; op Presbyterian Ch East, Birmingham, AL, 81-86; ap Christ P Ch, Nashville, TN, 86-91; p Trinity P Ch, Orangeburg, SC, 91-95; astp Arden P Ch, Arden, NC, 95-00; astp First P Ch, Macon, GA, 00-11; op Strong Tower Fell, Macon, GA, 09-16; hr 16

1860 Rockwood Road, Vestavia Hills, AL 35216 – 478-550-8806   Central Georgia
E-mail: pastortomanderson@gmail.com
HR

Anderson, Whitney – b San Antonio, TX, Mar 19, 66; f Clif; m Margaret King; w Heather Gail Pauer, Temple, TX, Sept 7, 96; SWU 88, BBA; RTS 00, MDiv; L Jan 01, SoTX Pby; O Oct 01, SoTX Pby; ascp Cross Pointe Ch, Austin, TX, 01-08; op Christ P Ch of Georgetown, Round Rock, TX, 08-12; p 12-

3644 Fossilwood Way, Round Rock, TX 78681 – 512-784-5868   South Texas
E-mail: whit@cpcgeorgetown.org
Christ Presbyterian Church – 512-966-9644

MINISTERIAL DIRECTORY

Andrade, Joabe S. – b Recife, Brazil, Mar 30, 62; f Joao Pereira; m Marta Sena; w Amy Mowry, England, May 23, 92; chdn Joabe Sena II, Elizabeth Rose Mowry; SemPresNorteBrasil 85, BA; FFP de Vitoria 88; L Jan 18, 00, SFL Pby; O Jun 18, 00, SFL Pby; op Brazilian Ch of Ft. Lauderdale Msn, Coral Springs, FL, 95-04; astp Covenant P Ch, Ft. Lauderdale, FL, 01-04; ob Brazilian PC, Brazil, 06-

Address Unavailable   South Florida

Andreades, Sam A. – w Marika; chdn Thaddaeus, Jeremy, Veronica, Enoch; YU, BS; NYU, MS; RTSFL, MDiv; CTS 13, DMin; p The Village Ch, New York, NY, 02-13; srp Faith Ref P Ch, Quarryville, PA, 14-18; wc

331 Stony Hill Road, Quarryville, PA 17566   Susquehanna Valley
E-mail: sam@affirminggender.com

Andress, Geoffrey – b West Chester, PA, Jun 8, 51; f Arthur; m Muriel Cook; w Rose Marie Miller, Lebanon, Aug 4, 73; chdn Matthew James, Mark Edward; WChSC 69-73, BS; GPTS 89-93, MDiv; L Nov 89, Wcar Pby; O Aug 8, 93, Wcar Pby; stus Fellowship P Ch, Newport, TN, 91-93, p 93-96; p Grace P Ch, Norman, OK, 96-98, wc 98-00; p First Bapt Ch, Wallingford, VT, 01-02; hr 05; ip Immanuel PCA, Mesa, AZ, 08-09; astp Sherwood Shores Chapel, Gordonville, TX, 13-15; hr 15; ip Immanuel P Ch, Mesa, AZ, 18; ob Shadow Ministries

2121 North Center Street, Lot 211, Mesa, AZ 85201   Southwest
E-mail: geoffreyandress@yahoo.com
HR

Andrews, Timothy Stephen – b Syracuse, NY, Mar 15, 68; f Wesley; m Loretta; w Janice Mlynar, Rochester, NY, Sept 24, 94; chdn Joshua Timothy, Amy Lori, Nathan John, Benjamin Mark; HougC 91, BA; GCTS 00, MDiv; L Sept 23,00, NoE pby; O Feb 24, 01, NNE Pby; p Christ P Ch, Nashua, NH, 00-04; p Redeemer P Ch, Concord, MA, 04-05; ob Evan Cong Ch, Lancaster, MA

47 Groton Shirley Road, Ayer, MA 01432 – 978-772-5767   Southern New England
Evangelical Congregational Church, Lancaster, MA

Andrews, Wesley Ryan – O Mar 24, 13, CentCar Pby; astp Uptown Ch, PCA, Charlotte, NC, 13-15; ascp 15-

1117 Robinhood Circle, Charlotte, NC 28227 – 704-999-5233   Central Carolina
E-mail: wesandrews@uptownchurch.org
Uptown Church, PCA – 704-375-7355

Angert, Morgan – O Jan 14, 17, GAFH Pby; astp Good Shepherd P Msn, Athens, GA, 17-

404-944-7545   Georgia Foothills
E-mail: moran@gracefc.net
Good Shepherd Presbyterian Mission – 803-604-7691

Angle, Steven L. – b Charlotte, NC, Oct 27, 59; f Robert Bruce; m Claire Frank; w Christy Grimes, Greensboro, NC, May 3, 82; chdn Rebecca Lanier, Molly Hughes; ASU 78-81, BS; ColCU 90, MA; RTSFL 91-93, MDiv; L Jan 22, 94, CentCar Pby; O Feb 20, 94, CentCar Pby; IVCF, 82-89, couns 90-91; chp, op Grace P Ch, Kernersville, NC, 94-96, p 96-03; astp Redeemer P Ch, Winston-Salem, NC, 03-; op Southside Comm Msn, Winston-Salem, NC, 05-11; p 11-

1309 Waughtown Street, Winston Salem, NC 27107 – 336-749-4365   Piedmont Triad
E-mail: stevenlangle@gmail.com
Southside Community Church – 336-734-6914

Aoyagi, Seima – b Japan, Oct 9, 73; w Naoko Aoyagi; chdn Senri, Towa, Satoki, Akari; Sophia 92-96, BA; CTS 04-08, MDiv; O Oct 4, 09, MO Pby, mis 09-

1811711 Tsukishima, Chuoku, Tokyo, 1040052 JAPAN   Missouri
E-mail: aoyagifamily@gmail.com

Aquila, Dominic Anthony – b Ancon, CZ, Jul 19, 46; f Dominick; m Marta McInnis; w Davileen Jennings, Tutwiler, MS, Jul 5, 68; chdn Dominic II, Laura, Jason, Virginia; BelC 68, BA; RTS 72, MDiv; WTS 78, DMin; L 72, DMV Pby (RPCES); O 72, DMV Pby (RPCES); p Stony Point Ref P Ch, Richmond, VA, 72-78; p Cerritos Valley OPC, Artesia, CA, 78-83; DnStu RTS, 84-86; p Forestgate P Ch, Colorado Springs, CO, 87-88; srp Kendall P Ch, Miami, FL, 88-00; adj prof KTS, 90-00; adj prof TEDS, Miami, 90-; adj prof NGTS, 93-01; AC, ed, pcanews.com, 00-04; pres NGTS, 01-; ed *byfaithonline* nwsltr, 04-07; int srp Village Seven P Ch, CO Springs, 05-07; ss Cornerstone P Ch, Castle Rock, CO, 09-10; mod 34th PCA GA 06; chmn GA SJC, 06-09; ed The Aquila Report, 08-; int Pres Prov Christian C, Pasadena, CA, 12-14; ip High Plains Flwsp, Falcon, CO, 13-14; ip Covenant Ref P Ch, Pueblo West, CO, 14-15; "The Idea of the Seminary" in *Interpreting and Teaching the Word of Hope*; "Law, Grace, and Liberty: Ministering the Whole Gospel to the Whole Person" in *The Assembling of Ourselves Together;* "Redemptive History and the Regulative Principle of Worship" in *The Hope Fulfilled: Essays in Honor of O. Palmer Robertson*

7962 Horned Lark Circle, Port Saint Lucie, FL 34952 – 719-282-8755   Rocky Mountain
E-mail: daquila6@aol.com
New Geneva Theological Seminary – 719-573-5395

Arakelian, Brad – b San Diego, CA; f Haigaz; m Iola Mae Nelson; UCSD, BA; FulTS 97, MDiv; O Mar 01, SoCst Pby; ob mis BEAMM, 02-12; astp North City P Ch, Poway, CA, 12-

2331 Cordero Road, Del Mar, CA 92014 – 619-755-3527   South Coast
E-mail: Bradley@northcitychurch.com
North City Presbyterian Church – 858-748-4642

Archer, J. Andrew – w Lindsey; chdn Celia, Joel, Audrey; VSC 01, BFA; RTSA 16, MDiv; O Oct 22, 17, MetAtl Pby; astp Ponce P Ch, Atlanta, GA, 17-

592 Timberlea Lake Trace, Marietta, GA 30067 – 478-714-6189   Metro Atlanta
 E-mail: jdrewarcher@gmail.com
Ponce Presbyterian Church – 404-709-2264

Arciaga, Daniel E. – b Manila, Philippines, Jan 24, 46; f Nicanor F; m Cecilia P. Estole; w Katherine Ann McInnes, Centerville, IA, Dec 16, 78; chdn Hannah Leah, Sarah Kathleen, Jonathan Daniel; cert, FeatiU 65; PhilChrU 73, BA; RTS 77, MDiv, 77, MCE; LTS, doct stu; TTS, doct stu; O Nov 26, 78, GulCst Pby; Recd PCA Jan 18, 97, NoIL Pby; mis Philippines, 79-82; p 1st Christian Ch, Cumberland, MD, 84-90; ip St. Matthews Ch, Cumberland, MD, 90-93; Chap Memorial Hosp, Cumberland, MD, 90-93; p Filipino Comm Ch, Forest Park, IL, 93-96, ev, chp 96; op Living Waters P Msn, Addison, IL, 97-17; hr 17

969 South Michigan, Addison, IL 60101-4832 – 630-740-4878   Chicago Metro
E-mail: lwpc126@gmail.com
HR

Arjona-Todd, Juan Jose – b Veracruz, Mexico, Aug 30, 59; f Carlos; m Violeta; w Martha Garzon-Castro, Hermosillo, Mexico, Oct 11, 91; chdn Lillian, Jose-Andres, Ricardo-Gilberto; URegionmontana 87; WSCAL, MDiv; L Sept 16, 00, SoCst Pby; O Feb 11, 01, SoCst Pby; staff CE in Monterrey, Mexico, 90-91; IVCF of Mexico, 92-96; chp Escondido, CA, 01; op Msn Vida Nueva, Escondido, CA, 01-

2062 Ginny Lane, Escondido, CA 92025 – 760-500-9327   South Coast
E-mail: juanjosearjonatodd@gmail.com
Mision Vida Nueva – 760-500-9327
E-mail: pastor@misionvidanueva.org

MINISTERIAL DIRECTORY

Arkema, Ryan – O Oct 23, 11, Siouxl Pby; p Lennox Ebenezer P Ch, Lennox, SD, 11-14; astp Redeemer P Ch, Parker, CO, 14-16; p Arlington P Ch, Arlington, TX, 16-

4503 Moores Landing, Arlington, TX 76016 – 817-229-8837 North Texas
E-mail: ryan.arkema@apcweb.org
Arlington Presbyterian Church – 817-261-8938

Armel, Adrian – astp Pioneer P Ch, Ligonier, PA, 06-08; p Laurel Highlands P Ch, Bovard, PA, 08-

182 Bennetts Road, Greensburg, PA 15601 – 724-830-0138 Pittsburgh
E-mail: adarmel@ixpres.com
Laurel Highlands Presbyterian Church – 724-834-4595

Armes, Stanley Byram – b Philadelphia, PA, May 1, 47; f John G; m Laura Bell Byram; w Donna Rae Sinclair, Springfield, IL, Jun 30, 73; chdn Sarah Rae, Andrea Jean, Deborah Ann; CC 65-69, BA; CTS 69-73, MDiv; MINTS 18, DMin; L Jan 77, NoE Pby; O May 78, NoE Pby; mis MTW, Kenya, 78-88; MNA, 89-91; p Pulaski P Ch, 91-96, wc 96; mis MTW, South Africa, 97-10; Bible Inst Eastern Cape, 10-14; hr 14; "Biblical Foundations Marriage"; *The True Cost of Worship; Biblical Foundations of Marriage; Introduction to the Old Testament; Biblical Ethics; Pastoral Counseling; The Doctrine of the Holy Spirit in the Old Testament*

1306 Timberlane Drive, Sterling, IL 61081 Tennessee Valley
E-mail: stan.armes@gmail.com
HR

Arms, Randall – astp Grace Ref Ch, Omaha, NE, 04-05, ascp 05-08; ascp New Song Ch Gretna, Gretna, NE, 08-18, p 18;

19813 Hazelnut Drive, Gretna, NE 68028 – 402-332-3503 Platte Valley

Armstrong, Chuck – astp Redeemer P Ch Westside, New York, NY, 18-

101 West End Avenue, Apt. 10K, New York, NY 10023 Metropolitan New York
E-mail: chuk.armstrong@gmail.com
Redeemer Presbyterian Church Westside – 212-808-4460

Armstrong, John Franklin Jr. – b Dallas, TX, Jul 29, 63; f John F.; m Mary Eileen Farrior; w Cynthia Ann Bickel, Woodlands, TX, Dec 30, 84; chdn John III, Jennette Faith; TXA&M 85, BS; MAMFT, RTS 00, 00, MDiv; L Aug 7, 01, MSVal Pby; O Aug 12, 01, MSVal Pby; astp First P Ch, Kosciusko, MS, 01-02, ascp 02-05; p Faith Ref P Ch, Frederick, MD, 05-

8909 Yellow Springs Road, Frederick, MD 21702 – 301-663-9253 Potomac
E-mail: john@faithreformed.org
Faith Reformed Presbyterian Church – 301-662-0662

Armstrong, Matthew – b Mar 21, 76; w Stacey; chdn Zoe, Cameron, Noah; GATech 00, BS; WTS 06, MDiv; O Feb 25, 07; astp All Souls Flwsp, Decatur, GA, 06-10; op Village Ch of East Atlanta, Atlanta, GA, 10-17, p 17-

1231 Glenwood Avenue, Suite B, Atlanta, GA 30316 Metro Atlanta
E-mail: matt@villagechurchofeastatlanta.org
Village Church of East Atlanta – 404-865-1443

Armstrong, Scott – w Kerstin; chdn Karis, Carlie, Camille; FurU 94, BA; RTS 98, MA, 05, MDiv; O Feb 06, NGA Pby; astp Perimeter Ch, Duluth, GA, 05-09; op City Ch - Eastside, Atlanta, GA, 07-11; p 11-

405 Clifton Road NE, Atlanta, GA 30307 Metro Atlanta
E-mail: scott@citychurcheastside.org
City Church - Eastside – 404-856-0183

Arnold, Joseph Wayne – p Covenant PCA Ch, Rockingham, NC, 13-14; p Faith P Ch, Cheraw, SC, 14-

121 Belmont Lane, Cheraw, SC 29520   Pee Dee
E-mail: revjoe.faithpca@gmail.com
Faith Presbyterian Church – 843-537-7264

Arnoult, Jonathan Blake – astp Christ the King P Ch, Houston, TX, 12-; campm RUF, UHous, 12-

8014 Meadowvale Drive, Houston, TX 77063   Houston Metro
E-mail: blake.arnoult@ruf.org
Christ the King Presbyterian Church – 713-892-5464
PCA Reformed University Fellowship

Arthur, David Lee – b Guadalajara, Mexico, May 17, 67; f Jack; m Kay Lee; w Margaret McGown, Columbia, SC, Jul 11, 87; chdn Jesse, Abigail, Ann; CC 98, BS; RTS 99, MATS; L Sept 99, TNVal Pby; O Nov 14, 99, TNVal Pby; astp Lookout Mountain P Ch, Lookout Mountain, TN, 99-04, astp 08-; co-auth *Desiring God's Own Heart*, 97; *Lord, Help Me Grow Spiritually Strong*, 09; *The New How to Study Your Bible*, 11; *Experiencing the Life Changing Power of Faith* – Romans Study, 11; *Jesus: Experiencing His Touch Mark 1-6*, 15; *Jesus: Listening for His Voice Mark 7-13*, 15; *Jesus: Understanding His Death and Resurrection Mark 14-16*, 15

207 Wendy Trail, Lookout Mountain, GA 30750 – 706-820-9117   Tennessee Valley
E-mail: darthur@precept.org
Lookout Mountain Presbyterian Church – 423-821-4528

Ashbaugh, Mark – O Nov 17, 13, Flwsp Pby; astp Bethel P Ch, Clover, SC, 13-14; campm RUF, Winthrop, 14-

668 Bancroft Drive, Rock Hill, SC 29730   Fellowship
E-mail: markashbaugh1@gmail.com
PCA Reformed University Fellowship

Ashley, Eric – b Tifton, GA, Jul 14, 77; w Annette Fortney, Griffin, GA, May 3, 03; chdn Nathan Mitchell, Naomi Elizabeth, Daniel Jude, Samuel Joseph; MerU 99, BS; CTS 07, MDiv; O Sept 07, CentGA Pby; astp First P Ch, Macon, GA, 07-13; astp West End Comm Ch, Nashville, TN, 13-; op Parks Ch PCA, Nashville, TN, 18-

329 53rd Avenue North, Nashville, TN 37209 – 478-787-5525   Nashville
E-mail: eric@parkschurchpca.com
West End Community Church – 615-463-8497
Parks Church PCA

Askew, Charles – b Atlanta, GA; w Lauren; chdn Charles, Eleanor, Samuel; UFL 00, BA; RTS 05, MDiv; O Dec05, PalmPby; campm RUF, CoastCar, 05-09; campm RUF, NCSt, 09-

3617 Dade Street, Raleigh, NC 27612 – 919-559-2762   Eastern Carolina
E-mail: caskew@ruf.org
PCA Reformed University Fellowship

Assis, Eliel – b Rio de Janeiro, Nov 25, 64; f Nathan Dantas; m Marlene Pinto; w Raquel Carvalho de Assis, Sao Paulo, Jul 9, 88; chdn Davi, Andre', Debora; Jose Manoel da Conceicao TS 93, ThB; L Dec 11, 93, PC of Brazil; O Mar 13, 94, PC of Brazil; Recd PCA 99, MNY Pby; p P Ch, Sao Paulo, Brazil, 93-97; p Redentor P Ch, South River, 98-04; astp Christ Cov Ch, Southwest Ranches, FL, 04-; op Brazilian Ch of Ft. Lauderdale Msn Coral Springs, FL, 04-06; ob p The Comm Bible Church, 06-14; wc

408 Sierra Vista Lane, Valley Cottage, NY 10989 – 631-594-2290   Metropolitan New York
E-mail: epassis@aol.com

MINISTERIAL DIRECTORY

Assis, Felipe – p Crossbridge Ch Miami, Miami, FL, 07-

6605 SW 88th Street, Miami, FL 33156 – 305-661-9900   South Florida
E-mail: felipe@crossbridgemiami.com
Crossbridge Church Miami – 305-661-9900

Assis, Marcus – O Nov 14, SFL Pby; astp Crossbridge Ch Miami, 14-

6605 SW 88th Street, Miami, FL 33156   South Florida
E-mail: marcus@crossbridgemiami.com
Crossbridge Church Miami – 305-661-9900

Athey, Vincent Philip – O 17, Prov Pby; campm RUF, UALHunts, 17-

2614 Pansy Street SW, Huntsville, AL 35801 – 571-212-8567   Providence
E-mail: vincent.athey@ruf.org
PCA Reformed University Fellowship

Atkinson, Stephen – astp Covenant Ch, Fayetteville, AR, 13-17; ob Christian Witness to Israel, 17-

6401 South 50th Street, Rogers, AR 72758   Hills and Plains
E-mail: sgt.atkinson@gmail.com
Christian Witness to Israel

Atkisson, David Thell – b Louisville, KY, Feb 17, 60; f Alfred B. (d); m Nona Jean Boatright (d); w Cheryl Lynn Wheeler, Berea, KY, Dec 19, 80; chdn Hilary Aileen (Normanha), Jacob Thell, Taylor Meredith (Skaggs), Jessica Griffith; BerC 78-82, BA; RTS 95-99, MDiv; L Jan 13, 01, Westm Pby; O May 6, 01, Westm Pby; mis, chp MTW, Brazil, 01-08; p Grace Ch Elizabethtown, KY, 08-

243 West Dixie Avenue, Elizabethtown, KY 42701   Ohio Valley
E-mail: pastor@gcepca.org
Grace Church Elizabethtown – 270-769-0173

Aubrey, Imad – O May 11, 14, NoTX Pby; astp Town North P Ch, Richardson, TX, 14-

836 Arbor Downs Drive, Plano, TX 75023   North Texas
E-mail: imad.aubrey@tnpc.org
Town North Presbyterian Church – 972-235-1886

Aucker, Brian – b Baltimore, MD, Feb 23, 60; f William Gilbert; m Carolyn Catherine Wunder; w Pamela Huffington, Churchville, MD, Mar 18, 83; chdn Erin Christine (Hutchinson), Nathan Timothy, Rachael Marie; McDanC 82, BA; CTS 96, MDiv; UEdin 01, PhD; O Sept 8, 02, MO Pby; adj prof CTS, 00-01; astp Covenant P Ch , St. Louis, MO, 01-04; ob Westminster Ch Acad, St. Louis, 04-07; asst prof CTS, 07-; Thesis: "Putting Elisha in His Place: Genre, Coherence, and Narrative Function in 2 Kings 2-8"; co-ed *Reflection and Refraction: Studies in Biblical Historiography in Honour of A. Graeme Auld*; "Joel," "Micah," "Haggai," intro and notes, ESV Study Bible; OT consultant, ESV Study Bible

942 Twinpine Drive, St. Louis, MO 63131 – 314-965-0835   Missouri
Covenant Theological Seminary – 314-434-4044

Aucremann, David McIver Snipes – b Durham, NC, May 3, 70; f David McIver Snipes; m Janet Nance Aucremann; w Sue Ellen DeStefani, Charlotte, NC, May 4, 96; chdn Madolyn Grace, David McIver Snipes Jr.; PC 88-92, BA; RTSNC 96-99, MDiv; L Oct 98, CentCar Pby; O May 99, CentCar Pby; p Freedom P Ch, Charlotte, NC, 99-01; astp Wellington P Ch, Wellington, FL, 01-02, ascp 02-06; op Christ Ch, West Palm Beach, FL, 05-06; astp Good News Ch, St. Augustine, FL, 06-07; ascp 07-

353 Valverde Lane, St. Augustine, FL 32086 – 904-794-5108   North Florida
E-mail: dave@goodnewsloves.com
Good News Church – 904-819-0064

Auffarth, Mark – w Anne; chdn Robert, Samuel, Kimberly, Agustin, Lydia, Megan; astp Willow Creek Ch, Winter Springs, FL, 03-04; srp Iglesia Presbiteriana Cristo Rey, Santiago, Chile, 04-10; srp Eastside P Ch (formerly Shannon Forest), Greenville, SC, 10-

9 Suffolk Downs Way, Greenville, SC 29615 – 864-569-3994   Calvary
E-mail: mark@eastsidepres.com
Eastside Presbyterian Church – 864-678-5100

Augustine, Todd – b Buffalo, NY, May 28, 63; WheatC 96, BA, 97, MA; SBTS 00, MDiv; O May 28, 17, SucstFL Pby; College Ch, Wheaton, IL, 02-16; astp Covenant Ch of Naples, Naples, FL, 17-

8203 Wilshire Lakes Boulevard, Naples, FL 34109   Suncoast Florida
Covenant Church of Naples – 239-597-3464

Austin, A. Kenneth – w Joyce A; p Chattanooga Valley P Ch, Flintstone, GA, 82-86; prof CC, 72-94; hr 94

171 Vinita Trail, Flintstone, GA 30725 – 706-820-1162   Tennessee Valley
HR

Austin, Bryan W. – b Enid, OK, Aug 12, 59; f Dorsey Wayne; m Carolyn Sue Sipes; w Kathryn Irene Gehr, Maryland, Jun 29, 84; chdn Joshua James, Amy Sue, Jonathan Lee; UMD 81, BS; RTS 95, MDiv/CE; O May 26, 96, Cal Pby; astp Westminster P Ch, Clinton, SC, 96-98, wc 98-00; ob t Washington Christian Acad, 00-14; astp Wallace P Ch, Hyattsville, MD, 00-08; ss Faith Ref P Ch, Frederick, MD, 05; ss Harvest Fell P Ch, Lusby, MD, 06-07; ss Grace Ref P Ch, Manassas, VA, 07; ss Spriggs Road P Ch, Manassas, VA, 07; wc 14-

865 Windrush Loop, Chattanooga, TN 37421 – 240-988-7584   Potomac
E-mail: rev.austin7@verizon.net

Austin, Kenneth S. – b Springfield, MA, Jul 27, 57; f James L.; m Helen Park McPherson; UWFL 86, BS; RTS 91, MDiv; CPE 7 Units, Chaplain I and II, 08-10; L Jan 23, 01, Evan Pby; O Jun 3, 01, Evan Pby; chp, mis MTW, New Zealand, 99-04; wc; chap trn, CPE, B'ham, AL; stu ACBC cert

3201 Spring Aire Court #C, Birmingham, AL 35216 – 205-823-6362   Evangel
E-mail: ksaaustin5@gmail.com

Austin, Rhett – b Birmingham, AL, Sept 16, 83; f Ricky Jo; m Carol Ann Bailey; w Valerie Christine Kepner, Birmingham, AL, Jan 17, 09; chdn Charles Rhett; SEBC 07, BA; WheatGrS 12, MA, 14, MA; ascp Faith Comm Ch, West Chicago, IL, 18-

880 Main Street, West Chicago, IL 60185   Chicago Metro
E-mail: rhett.austin@faithchurchwc.org
Faith Community Church – 630-231-8230

Austin, Thomas Lee – b Kingsport, TN, Jul 7, 47; f Dale J., Sr; m Margaret D. Beaty; w Ann N. Reid, Columbia, SC, Jul 16, 83; chdn Anna Lynn, Rebecca Ann; KgC 70, BA; TNSU 80, MBA; CIU 83, MDiv; WTS 92, DMin; L 83, Cal Pby; O 83, Cal Pby; mis MTW, Nairobi, Kenya, 83-99; mis MTW, Cape Town, South Africa, 99-10; mis MTW, Global Training/Development, 11-; "Urban Ministry and Theological Education," *East Africa Journal of Evangelical Theology* (EAJET), 8:2, 1989; "Integrating City and Seminary," *Urban Mission*, 92; "The Glory of God," *Reformation and Revival Journal*, 95; "On the Demonization of Believers," *Reformation and Revival Journal*, 95; contr *Evangelical Dictionary of World Missions*

3246 Indian Valley Trail, Atlanta, GA 30341 – 404-474-3734   Palmetto
E-mail: taustin@mtwafrica.org
PCA Mission to the World

Aven, Donald Webster – b Memphis, TN, Feb 10, 47; f Allen W (d); m Christine S. Rhodes; w (1) Edwina M. Calvert (d), (2) Cecile O. Smith, St. Louis, MO, Aug 4, 90; UMS 65-69, BA; CTS 74-78, MDiv, 79, ThM; L Oct 20, 78, So Pby (RPCES); O Sept 28, 80, So Pby (RPCES); Chap USN, 80-96; Chap Deaconess Hospital, Cincinnati, OH, 97-05; astp Faith P Ch, Cincinnati, OH, 98-04; Chap Drake Hosp, Cincinnati, 05-11; op Gr Flwsp Middlesboro, Middlesboro, KY, 11-16; hr 16

5404 Heritage Lane, Kingsport, TN 37664 – 423-869-4576　　　　　　　　　　　　　　Ohio Valley
E-mail: gumbeda@aol.com
HR

Awtry, Michael – astp North City P Ch, Poway, CA, 18; ascp Redeemer P Ch, Santa Rosa, CA, 18-

714 Charles Street, Santa Rosa, CA 95404　　　　　　　　　　　　　　　　　Northern California
E-mail: mwawtry@gmail.com
Redeemer Presbyterian Church – 707-539-9794

Ayllon, Pablo – O Feb 8, 15, TNVal Pby; astp Grace P Ch, Dalton, GA, 15-

1901 Mountain Brook Drive, Dalton, GA 30720　　　　　　　　　　　　　　　Tennessee Valley
E-mail: pablodi3760@yahoo.com
Grace Presbyterian Church – 706-226-6344

Bae, Benjamin – O 18, SNE Pby; astp Citylife P Ch of Boston, Boston, MA, 17-

62 Green Street #2, Newton, MA 02458　　　　　　　　　　　　　　　　Southern New England
Citylife Presbyterian Church of Boston – 617-292-0990

Bae, Hyung Min David – astp Korean P Ch of Wash, Fairfax, VA, 18-

6323 Millwood Court, Springfield, VA 22152　　　　　　　　　　　　　　　　　Korean Capital
E-mail: David.H.Bae@gmail.com
Korean Presbyterian Church of Washington – 703-321-8090

Bae, John H. – w Sarah; UNC, BS; WTS, MDiv; GCTS, ThM; yp Kor Phil Ch, Philadelphia, 01-04; astp CrossPoint Green Lake, Seattle, WA, 05-08; ob New Creation Fell, Jackson Heights, NY; ob ascp Korean Ch of Queens, 10-

1664 Bell Boulevard 2nd Floor, Bayside, NY 11360　　　　　　　　　　　　Metropolitan New York
E-mail: pastorjbae@gmail.com
Korean Church of Queens

Bae, Sang Ho – b Kim Je, South Korea, Aug 5, 52; f Jong Soo Bae; m Jum Nyu Nah; w In Kyo Oh, Seoul, Korea, Apr 16, 77; chdn Hannah, Peter, Andrew; ChShC 72-76; PGATCS 76-79; L Feb 12, 79, Kim Je pby, Korea; O Feb 12, 79, Kim Je pby; Chap Rep of Korea Army, 79-82; srp Chungnong P Ch, Korea, 82-85; mis Philippines, 85-96; srp Elim P Ch, San Jose, CA, 96-06; mis Philippines, 06-

15-A Quezon St. Bankers Village, Antipolo City, Rizal Philippines　　　　　　　Korean Northwest
E-mail: sanghobae@yahoo.com

Bae, Stephen Go Soon – b Seoul, Jan 20, 60; f Uo Jin; m Uu Jae Chi; w Mi Jeoung; chdn Eunice; STC 85-89, BA; ChShTS 78-85, ThM; L Aug 22, 87; O Aug 22, 87, Kim Yoon Sun (Korean Denom); Recd PCA, KorS Pby; ob astp Korean P Ch, Houston, TX, 91-10; srp Peace P Ch of Houston, Houston, TX, 13-18; wc

14479 Still Meadow Drive, Houston, TX 77079　　　　　　　　　　　　　　　Korean Southern
E-mail: stephenbae@yahoo.com
Peace Presbyterian Church of Houston – 713-825-2864

Bae, Young Hoon – ob 18-

11042 Aristotle Drive, Fairfax, VA 22030 – 757-397-7063 Korean Capital
E-mail: younghoonbae3@gmail.com

Baeq, Daniel Shinjong – b Seoul, Mar 9, 71; f Seung Won; m Myung Sook; w Esther Kang; chdn Joshua Jiwon, Rachel Jimin, Samuel Jiwu, Hannah Jisue; ChoongAngU 95, BA; ChShTS 99, MDiv; FulTS 05, ThM; O Oct 14, 02, KorCap Pby; Korean Central P Ch of Wash, Centreville, VA, 01-04; mis Cambodia, 04-10; TIU, dir reasearch, 11-13; srp Bethel Korean P Ch, Ellicot City, MD, 15-; "Spirit House," International Journal of Frontier Mission, 29(1), 12; "Contextualizing Religious Form and Meaning," IJFM, 27(4), 10

3512 North Chatham Road, Ellicott City, MD 21042 Korean Capital
E-mail: danbaeq@gmail.com
Bethel Korean Presbyterian Church – 410-461-1235
3165 St. Johns Lane, Ellicott City, MD 21042

Bagby, Norman Anderson Jr. – b Autauga Cty, AL, Apr 9, 39; f Norman A B; m Katherine Shull; w Frances Crymes, Camden NJ, May 15, 65; chdn Robyn Michelle, Dent Anderson, Sandra Ruth, Grace; MSSC 57-60; BelC 62, BA; WTS 66, BD; O Nov 13, 66, SMS Pby (PCUS); p First P Ch, Taylorsville, MS, 66-70; p Calvary P Ch, Mize, MS, 66-70; p Sharon P Ch, Magee, MS, 67-76; p Collins P Ch, Collins, MS, 76-81; sc Gr Pby, 73-82, wc 81-84, fun dir 84-90; ss Trinity P Ch, Slidell, LA, 85-87; ss First P Ch, Picayune, MS, 88-89, wc 89-90; ss Moss Point P Ch, Moss Point, MS, 90, p 90-00; rc Gr Pby, 91-00, wc 00-01; astp First P Ch, Hattiesburg, MS, 01-15; hr 15; p/t hospice chap & funeral dir, 15-

162 Oak Grove Place, Biloxi, MS 39530 – 601-606-0690 Grace
E-mail: nbag@cableone.net
HR

Baggett, David – chp, ev 09-12; op Christ Redemption Flwsp, Havertown, PA, 12-13

111 Lake Ridge Drive, Forest, PA 24551 – 434-420-4671 Blue Ridge
E-mail: drbaggett@yahoo.com

Baik, Chang Ho – p Orange Hill P Ch, Orange, CA, 08-

27 Riverstone, Irvine, CA 92606 – 949-857-0824 Korean Southwest Orange County
E-mail: pch3927@hotmail.com
Orange Hill Presbyterian Church – 714-633-3104

Baik, Johan – b Incheon, Korea, Jun 8, 72; f Peter Byeongsu; m Susan Jeongsuk; w Yoonha; chdn Anna, Aaron, Andrew; LeTourneau 95, BA; CTS 98, MDiv, 00, ThM; O Aug 00, KorNW Pby; astp Elim P Ch, Campbell, CA, 00-01; Chap USN, 02-14; astp Inland Korean P Ch, Pomona, CA, 14-16; Chap USNR, 14-; Chap US Federal Prison, 16-

7006 Piedmont Street, Chino, CA 91710 – 951-294-0044 Korean Southwest
E-mail: rev.johan.baik@gmail.com
United States Navy Reserve

Baik, Seoung Yul – op Bethel Korean P Msn, Evans, GA, 07-11

Address Unavailable Korean Southeastern

Baile, Charles A. – b Washington, DC, Dec 13, 69; f Robert James; m Shirley Ann Webb; w Kimberly Ann Cotter, Greenville, SC, Oct 7, 95; chdn Haddon James, Anna Elise, Karis Noel CatCC 87-88; NyC

Baile, Charles A., continued
88-91, BA; GPTS 93-94; RTS 94-97, MDiv; L Oct 23, 97; O Feb 15, 98, Cal Pby; astp Mitchell Road P Ch, Greenville, SC, 98-02; p Shady Grove P Ch, Derwood, MD, 02-

202 Oakton Road, Gaithersburg, MD 20877 – 301-947-4174   Potomac
E-mail: charliebaile@comcast.net
Shady Grove Presbyterian Church – 301-330-4326

Bailey, Chad T. – w Rebecca; chdn Hannah, Samuel, Andrew, Michael; O Feb 8, 04, Cov Pby; astp College Hill P Ch, Oxford, MS, 03-06; p The Rock P Ch, Stockbridge, GA, 07-16; astp Second P Ch, Greenville, SC, 16-

112 Birnam Court, Greenville, SC 29615   Calvary
E-mail: ctbailey@me.com
Second Presbyterian Church – 864-232-7621

Bailey, Craig B. – b Bluefield, WV, Aug 24, 63; f Robert H; m Mary Elizabeth Collier; w Kathryn Jean Cottle, Virginia Bch, VA, Jun 6, 87; chdn KathrynElizabeth, Brooke, Adam, Claire, Anna Ruth; ConcU 81-82, 85-87, BS; KgC 83-85; CBS 90-93, MDiv; L Nov 93, NR Pby; O Aug 7, 94, NR Pby; int Friendship P Msn, Princeton, WV, 93-94, p 94-97, op 97; chp Palm Pby, Charleston, SC, 97-98; op Redeemer P Ch, Charleston, SC, 99-00; p 00-

479 Wade Hampton Drive, James Island, SC 29412-9147 – 843-762-7583   Lowcountry
E-mail: craig@redeemer-charleston.org
Redeemer Presbyterian Church – 843-762-1093

Bailey, Donald Lloyd Jr. – b Orlando, FL, May 24, 59; f Don; m June McRorie; w Tracey Priebe, Clermont, FL, Jul 30, 88; chdn Luke Samuel, Roxanne; FSU 81, BS; CTS 99, MDiv; L Apr 01, MO Pby; O Apr 01, MO Pby; ydir Old Orchard Ch, Webster Groves, MO, 99-01, ascp 01-03; op Comm P Ch, Orlando, FL, 03-13; ob astp Saint Andrews Chapel, Sanford, FL, 14-

5525 Wayside Drive, Sanford, FL 32771   Central Florida
E-mail: mosteen@sachapel.com
Saint Andrews Chapel – 407-328-1139
5525 Wayside Drive, Sanford, FL 32771

Bailey, Hunter M. – w Abbie; chdn Hunter Mitchell Jr. "Hutch," Nola Grace, Robert Joseph "Bo"; UAR 98, BA; RTS 02, MDiv; UEdin 03, ThM, 08, PhD; int First P Ch , Jackson, MS, 99-02; int MTW, Scotland, 02-06; campm RUF, Emory, 06-13; op Christ Comm Ch, Fayetteville, AR, 13-

193 West Lafayette Street, Fayetteville, AR 72701   Hills and Plains
E-mail: hunter@cccfay.com
Christ Community Church

Bailey, James R. – b Hudson, NY, Aug 19, 41; f Kenneth Jerome; m Naomi Isabel Baldwin; w Kathryn Jo Amundson, Minden, NV, Jan 13, 84; chdn Alesia (Booth), Matthew Radtke, Timothy; MISU 60; RTSFL 98, MDiv; O Feb 10, 02, Pac Pby; astp Christ P Ch, Santa Barbara, CA, 02; ob Dir Cloudhaven Retreat Center, 03-; mod SW pby, 06

30 Lakeview Drive, Cloudcroft, NM 88317 – 575-682-2670   Southwest
E-mail: jim@cloudhaven.org
Cloudhaven Retreat Center

Bailey, Leonard – w Amy; chdn Rae, Jakob, Ilona, Maire; TowU 94, BS; RTS 04, MABS; O May 05, Ecar Pby; astp Redeemer P Ch, Raleigh, NC, 06-07; astp New Life in Christ Ch, Fredericksburg, VA, 07-10; op Hope of Christ P Ch , Stafford, VA, 08-10; p 10-

19 Silverton Court, Stafford, VA 22554 – 540-645-2880   James River
E-mail: leonard.bailey@hopeofchrist.net
Hope of Christ Presbyterian Church – 540-645-2880

Bailey, Richard Dunwody – b Montgomery, AL, Dec 20, 57; f George F. Jr.; m Mary Gene Dunwody; w Teresa Ann Rogers, Columbus, GA, May 24, 80; chdn Richard D. Jr., Wilson Rogers, George Duncan; UAL 80, BA; RTS 02, MABS; O Nov 10, 02, SELA Pby; astp Plains P Ch, Zachary, LA, 02-10; chp, mis MTW, Perth, Australia, 10-

3543 Cherry Street, Zachary, LA 70791　　　　　　　　　　　　　　　　Southern Louisiana
E-mail: rbplains@gmail.com
PCA Mission to the World

Bailey, Robert – b Augusta, GA, Feb 23, 63; f Robert Henry (d); m Jo Anne Varner; w Martha Scovill Polhill, Birmingham, AL, Aug 5, 89; chdn Robert Dabney, Rankin Alexander, Nikolas Andrew; AU 81-82; UGA 82-85, BA; RTS 90-95, MDiv; O Nov 3, 96, Evan Pby; astp Decatur P Ch, Decatur, AL, 96-01; chp, op Providence P Msn, Lubbock, TX, 01-04; ss Decatur P Ch, Decatur, AL, 08-09; ss Providence P Ch, Lubbock, TX, 12-13; srp Southside Comm Ch, Corpus Christi, TX, 14-

4602 Jarvis Street, Corpus Christi, TX 78412　　　　　　　　　　　　　　　South Texas
E-mail: moonnerd@yahoo.com
Southside Community Church – 361-992-4977

Bainton, Gary A. – b Milford, CT, Mar 30, 52; f Warren Herbert; m Audrey May Wickett; w Mary Ellen Eaton, Richmond, VA, Mar 12, 77; chdn Sarah Noelle, Matthew Warren; CWM 70-72; AugC 79-82, BA; ErskTS 88-92, MDiv; L Jan 93, CentGA Pby; O Jul 31, 94, CentGA Pby; fndr, Dir Greater Augusta P Min, 80-89; fndr, Dir Assoc for Greater Augusta P Ev Min, 89-94; p South Liberty P Ch, Sharon, GA, 94; p Rose Hill P Ch, Columbia, SC, 94-97; srp 97-05; susp 05-13; ss Longtown P Ch, Ridgeway, SC, 13-18; wc

8010 Longtown Road, Ridgeway, SC 29130 – 803-361-2217　　　　　　　　　　Palmetto
E-mail: gabainton@juno.com

Bair, Ross A. – b Mt Vernon, OH, Mar 18, 28; f Simon Henry B; m Beulah Shryock; w Helen Beal, Marion, OH, Sept 1, 50; chdn Deborah Ann, Claudia Jean, Kathryn Sue; MUOH 46-49; UMiami 63-64, BA; ColTS 67, MDiv; WTS 81, DMin; O Jul 67, Evgld Pby (PCUS); ap Coral Ridge P Ch, Ft. Lauderdale, FL, 67-69; p First P Ch of Coral Springs, Margate, FL, 69-92; hr 92; p Grace Comm P Ch, Blairsville, GA, 93-03

761 McClure Road, Hayesville, NC 28904-7265 – 828-321-5171　　　　　　Georgia Foothills
E-mail: rosshelenbair2@aol.com
HR

Baird, Charles Knox – b Jackson, MS, Sept 18, 57; f James McKenzie; m Jane Elizabeth McMillian; w Debra; chdn Alexandria Elizabeth, James Knox; BelC 76-80, BA; RTS 84-88, MDiv; O Jan 21, 90, Gr Pby; moya First P Ch, Macon, GA, 87-88; astp, moy First P Ch, Hattiesburg, MS, 88-91, ascp 91-93; astp First P Ch, Dothan, AL, 93-97, wc 98-03; astp First P Ch, Hattiesburg, MS, 03-

6 Columbus Road, Hattiesburg, MS 39402 – 601-296-2395　　　　　　　　　　Grace
E-mail: Knoxbaird@fpcpca.net
First Presbyterian Church – 601-268-0303

Baird, Geren McLemore III – b Memphis, TN, Nov 15, 50; f Geren McLemore Jr.; m Evelyn Virginia Guthery; w Janice Margie Herring (d), Donna Jarvis, Apr 8, 10; chdn Geren McLemore IV; CFLCC 71, AA; FAU 73, BA; RTS 78, MDiv; CPE Residency, 4 units Florida Hospital, Orlando, FL 97-98; O Oct 78, MSVal Pby; p Scooba P Ch, Scooba, MS, 78-82; p Shuqualak P Ch, Shuqualak, MS, 78-82; p Raymond P Ch, Raymond, MS, 82-86; Women's Pregnancy Cent, 86-87; Divested w/out censure, 89; Chap Vitas Hospice, 98-06; Chap Cornerstone Hospice, 06-12; Chap Dr. Phillips Hospital, Orlando, FL, 12-

3608 Sanctuary Drive, St. Cloud, FL 34769 – 407-572-9246　　　　　　　　Central Florida
E-mail: gerenb@aol.com
Dr. Phillips Hospital

Baird, James M. – b Carteret, NJ, Aug 11, 28; f James M B; m Cristina Milligan; w Jane McMillan, Acworth, GA, Mar 19, 52; chdn James McKenzie III, Charles Knox, David McMillan, John Mark Darden; MaryvC 46-50, BS; ColTS 54-57, BD; BelC 78, DD; L May 3, 56, Chero Pby; O Jul 9, 57, CMS Pby (PCUS); p Mount Salus P Ch, Clinton, MS, 57-60; p First P Ch, Brewton, AL, 60-64; p First P Ch, Gadsden, AL, 64-72; p First P Ch, Macon, GA, 72-80; p Granada P Ch, Coral Gables, FL, 80-83; srp First P Ch, Jackson, MS, 83-95; hr 95

14 Carriage Court Place, Brandon, MS 39047 – 601-992-9950 Mississippi Valley
E-mail: baird2830@comcast.net
HR

Baker, Allen M. III – b Birmingham, AL, Mar 21, 52; f Allen M. Jr.; m Betty Chism; w Wini Owings, Birmingham, AL, Aug 16, 75; chdn Andrew, Allen, Jeffrey; UAL 74, BS; RTS 81, MDiv; O Jul 12, 81, MidAtl Pby; op Sycamore P Ch, Midlothian, VA, 81-82; ap Perimeter Ch, Duluth, GA, 82-84; op Christ P Ch, Marietta, GA, 84-89; srp Golden Isles P Ch, St. Simons Island, GA, 93-03; ob ev PEF, 89-; op Christ Comm P Ch, West Hartford, CT, 03-06; p 06-11; *Seeking a Revival Culture: Essays on Fortifying an Anemic Church, Revival Prayer: A Needed Paradigm Shift in Today's Church, Essays on Revival: In Wrath May God Remember Mercy; Evangelistic Sermons on WDRC FM, Hartford, Connecticut*

127 Trillium Drive, Birmingham, AL 35210 Evangel
E-mail: al.baker1952@gmail.com
Presbyterian Evangelistic Fellowship – 276-591-5335

Baker, Brent – astp Park Cities P Ch, Dallas, TX, 12-

5150 Rexton Lane, Dallas, TX 75214 North Texas
E-mail: brent.baker@pcpc.org
Park Cities Presbyterian Church – 214-224-2500

Baker, Carl Christian – b Libertyville, IL, Nov 22, 50; f Carl C. Sr; m Patricia Decker; w Marilyn L. Elliott, Long Grove, IL, Feb 3, 73; chdn Sarah, M. Scott; SIU 78, BS, 83, MS; CTS 91, MDiv; L Dec 7, 91, NoE Pby; O May 31, 92, NoE Pby; p Reformed P Ch, Duanesburg, NY, 92-98; ob instr, admin Wildwood CS/Heritage Class CS, Manchester, MO, 98-13; astp Heritage P Ch, Wildwood, MO, 01-13; ob Interim Pastor Min, 13-; ss Southlake P Ch, Huntersville, NC, 15-17

7005 Eichelberger Drive, Saint Louis, MO 63123 Missouri
E-mail: c.c.baker2@gmail.com

Baker, Derek – b Bay City, TX, Feb 14, 77; f Walter August; m Nancy Kay Elmore; w Stefani Brooke Anderson, Lubbock, TX, Jul 2, 99; chdn Haley, Haddon, Hudson, Holden; UTXAu 99, BS; GCTS 08, MDiv; O May 10, OPC; Recd PCA Jan 21, 17, SNE Pby; ascp First P Ch North Shore, Ipswich, MA, 10-; op First P Ch Danvers, Danvers, MA, 18-

4 Adeline Road, Ispwich, MA 01938 Southern New England
First Presbyterian Church North Shore – 978-356-7690
First Presbyterian Church Danvers

Baker, Hubert Roy – b Hopewell, VA, Jul 30, 38; f Green; m Alexandrenia Smith; w Joan Juanita Collins, Hopewell, VA, Jun 4, 60; chdn David Roy, Jonathan Paul, Timothy Alan; NTSU 70, BA; CTS 75, MDiv; O Jun 19, 75, MidW Pby (RPCES); Chap USArmy, 75-; ACM, First Oak Leaf Cluster; MSM, ACM 2nd Oak Leaf Cluster

424 Chippewa Trail, Browns Mills, NJ 08015-6458 – 609-893-0008 Missouri
United States Army

Baker, R. Aaron – b Baltimore, MD, Jul 12, 72; f Ronald Lee; m Mary Lou Postlewait; w Allison Mary Ryan, Chicago, IL, Jun 22, 96; chdn Eleanor Mary, Sarah Virginia, Cora Catherine; MBI 94, BA; TEDS 99, MA; L Oct 27, 00, NoIL Pby; O Sept 9, 01, NoIL Pby; astp Covenant P Ch, Chicago, IL, 01-05; srp 05-

2538 North Monticello Avenue, Chicago, IL 60647 – 773-270-1615   Chicago Metro
E-mail: abaker@covenantchicago.org
Covenant Presbyterian Church – 773-486-9590

Baker, Ryan – MTW Chiba Team, Chiba, Japan, 98; campm RUF, CSU, 07-13; p Grace Ch Stillwater, Stillwater, OK, 14-

4718 West Country Club Drive, Stillwater, OK 74074   Hills and Plains
E-mail: rbakerruf@gmail.com
Grace Church Stillwater – 405-612-5299

Baker, S. Wesley Jr. – b Ft. Sam Houston, TX, Oct 31, 67; f Sherman Wesley Sr; m Elaine Yaws; w Jami Maree Vaden, Sequin, TX, Aug 27, 88; chdn Lauren, Cullen, Noah, Abigail, Katheryn, Olivia, Emily Caroline; TXA&M 86-90, BA; RTS 93-96, MDiv; L Feb 94; O Jul 7, 96, MSVal Pby; ss Lebanon P Ch, Learned, MS, 94-96, p 96-00; ob ev, mis PEF, Peru, 00-04; mis Peru Mission, 04-

El Floral 446 #301A, Trujillo, PERU – 011-947-735-152   South Texas
518 Raven Ridge, New Braunfels, TX 78130
E-mail: wesbaker@perumission.org
Peru Mission

Baker, Stephen Barrett – b Chattanooga, TN, Sept 9, 57; f George K; m Pauline Thompson; w Kathleen Mary Oesch, St. Louis, MO, May 15, 82; chdn Charissa Lynn (Sethman), Mark Wesley, Paul Stephen; CBC 75-79, BA; WKU 79-80, MA; CTS 80-84, MDiv; L May 83; O May 84, CentCar Pby; ap First P Ch, Stanley, NC, 84-86; p Walnut Hill P Ch, Bristol, TN, 86-90; ob Dir AACPC, 90-12; ip Bellemont P Ch, Bristol, TN, 03-07; p Coeburn P Ch, Coeburn, VA, 12-; "Theological Journeys," *Contra Mundum,* Fall 92; "How to Help Your Local Crisis Pregnancy Center," *Today's Christian Doctor,* Summer 96

290 Davis Avenue SE, Coeburn, VA 24230   Westminster
E-mail: mtnman@e-bakers.com
Coeburn Presbyterian Church – 276-395-2866

Baldanza, Chad – O 16, SNE Pby; astp Christ the King JP/Roxbury, Jamaica Plain, MA, 16-18

25 Driscoll Drive, Dorchester, MA 02124   Southern New England
E-mail: chadbaldanza@gmail.com

Baldini, Charles J. – b Brooklyn, NY, Sept 21, 56; f Anthony John; m Michelena DeStefano; w Leslie Celeste Hug, Venice, FL, Dec 7, 85; chdn Rebekah Elaine, Sarah Patricia, Jonathan Paul, Benjamin Calvin; CBC 83-87, BS; CTS 89-91, MDiv; L May 91, Ecar Pby; O Jun 13, 93, GrLks Pby; op Jacksonville, NC, 91-93; chp, op GrLks Pby, 93-94, wc 94; p Providence P Ch, Royal Palm Beach, FL, 95-97; p Covenant P Ch, Cape May, NJ, 97-98, wc 98-99; ss Cornerstone P Ch, Palm Beach Gardens, FL, 99; ob p Immanuel Union Ch, Staten Island, 00-

Address Unavailable – 718-370-2124   Metropolitan New York
E-mail: tecjb@aol.com
Immanuel Union Church, Staten Island

Baldwin, Allan McDonald – b Brooklyn, NY, Apr 28, 34; f Arthur; m Margaret Price; w (1) Claude-Marie Halbritter, (dv); (2) Diane MacDonald, Wayland, MA, Nov 5, 89; chdn Timothy Arthur, Peter Hugo, Claire-Lise, Nichole Lanza; YU 52-56, BS; New College, Edinburgh 57-58; UTSNY 56-59, MDiv; O Sept 59, UPCUSA; p Yorkville Ch, Yorkville, NY, 59-63; stu L'Abri, 63-66; p Fifth RPC, Phila, PA, 66-67;

Baldwin, Allan McDonald, continued
p Christ Ch, Grand Rapids, MI, 67-84; bd mbr CTS, 68-87; Chap Pinerest Chr Hosp, Grand Rapids, MI, 85-86; Chap Bronson Meth Hosp, Kalamazoo, MI, 86-87; Chap Carleton-Willard Vlg, Bedford, MA, 88-12; astp Trinitarian Congr Ch, Wayland, MA, 89-90; fel College of Chap, 91; treas MA Chap Assoc, 92-99; p/t chap 13-14; hr 14; ip past care, Trinitarian Cong Ch, Wayland, MA, 15-

11 Anthony Road, Wayland, MA 01778-3001 – 508-655-2885   Southern New England
E-mail: abaldwin.11@verizon.net
HR

Baldwin, Rich – O May 29, 16, PlVall Pby; astp Grace Central Ch, Omaha, NE, 16-18

10923 Sahler, Omaha, NE 68164   Platte Valley
E-mail: rich.baldwin.310@gmail.com

Baldwin, Stephen Conner – b Little Rock, AR, Dec 14, 50; f Phill B; m Elizabeth Scheirer; w Karen Chaffin, Little Rock, AR, Dec 26, 75; chdn Kelsey Leigh, Stephen David, Rachel Jean; PhU, BA; CTS, MDiv, DMin; L Mar 26, 82, MidW Pby (RPCES); O Oct 3, 82, DMV Pby (PCA); ap McLean P Ch, McLean, VA, 82-84; p Reston P Ch, Reston, VA, 84-90; ev, chp WHM, 90-95; ev, op Cornerstone P Ch, Castle Rock, CO, 95-02; op Providence P Ch, Concord, NC, 02-05; srp 05-08; astp Crossroads P Flwsp, Maplewood, MO, 11- 13; pres Provisions Group, Inc., Castle Rock, CO, 14-18; astp Valley Springs P Ch, Roseville, CA, 18-

Valley Springs Presbyterian Church – 916-786-7940   Northern California

Bales, John G. – ascp New Life P Ch, Escondido, CA, 12; ob exec dir Life Net of Missoula, 12-15

66 Daughtrey Avenue #505, Waco, TX 76706 – 254-710-4608   North Texas
E-mail: John_G_Bales@baylor.edu

Ball, Kevin John – b Dodge City, KS, Jul 4, 73; w Erin; chdn Doran John, Marilla Suzanne, Elizabeth Anne Naomi; KSU 96, BS; CTS 04, MDiv; CathUAm 16, MA; O Nov 13, 05, War Pby; p Marion P Ch, Marion, AL, 05-07; astp Grace Evangelical P Ch, Davidsonville, MD, 07-11, ascp 11-18

3583 2nd Avenue, Edgewater, MD 21037 – 443-607-6337   Chesapeake
E-mail: kevinjball@verizon.net

Ball, Larry Edward – b Cabin Creek, WV, Nov 5, 47; f Clennie James B; m Thelma Shamblin; w Brenda Cooper, Winifrede, WV, Nov 25, 71; chdn Titus Benjamin, Timothy Brooks, Sarah Alta; WVTech 65-69, BS; WTS 69-72, MDiv; O Jul 72, PCUS; p Hurley Ch, Hurley, VA, 72-73; p Meadow Creek P Ch, Greeneville, TN, 73-77; ss Grace Ch, Greeneville, TN, 76-77; sc Westm Pby, 76-99; p Bridwell Heights P Ch, Kingsport, TN, 81-12; CPA; hr 12; *Blessed Is He Who Reads – A Primer on the Book of Revelation; Unto You and Your Children – The Promises of the Covenant – A Primer*

329 Stone Court, Kingsport, TN 37664 – 423-292-5186   Westminster
E-mail: larryeball1947@gmail.com
HR

Ball, Warren Herbert – b Syracuse, NY, Apr 15, 29; f Joseph Emil; m Louise Schmuck; w Gwendolyn Newkirk, Philadelphia, PA, Sept 12, 53; chdn David Joseph, Stephen Warren, Mary Louise, Beth Anne; HougC 45-49, BA; PTS 49-52, BD, 52-53, ThM; EBapTS 73-76, DMin; O Sept 20, 52, Syracuse Pby (PCUSA); p Latta Mem Ch, Christiana, PA, 53-57; op Highland Ch, Lancaster, PA, 57-59; p Chambers Mem Ch, Rutledge, PA, 59-78; p P Ch of Coatesville, PA (Ind), 78-85, wc 85-89; admin WTS, 89-91, wc 91-93; hr 93; astp Reformed P Ch, West Chester, PA

511 Reservoir Road, West Chester, PA 19380 – 610-430-1636   Philadelphia Metro West
HR

Ballard, Matt – astp Perimeter Ch, Duluth, GA, 09-10; op Southpointe Comm Ch, Nolensville, TN, 10-14; p 14-

4544 Sawmill Place, Nolensville, TN 37135 – 314-397-3383   Nashville
E-mail: matt.ballard@southpointecommunity.org
Southpointe Community Church

Balzer, David – w Laura; chdn Benjamin Ewing, Catherine Reed; campm RUM, KingC, 03-06; camp RUM, ETSU 03-11; ss Grace P Chelsea, Chelsea, AL, 12-14; p Grace Ch for all Nations, Stone Mountain, GA, 14-

1777 Grandeus Lane SW, Stone Mountain, GA 30087   Metro Atlanta
E-mail: david.joseph.balzer@gmail.com
Grace Church for all Nations – 404-292-5514

Bamberg, Stanley W. – b Marion, AL, Sept 29, 52; f Alvin W.; m Anne Barnette; w Julianna Rankin, Marion, AL, Jun 1, 74; chdn Brian Joe, William Rankin; UMonte 74, BA; RTS 77, MDiv; FrUAmst 87, Doct; O 77, Tusca Pby; Bethel P Ch, Northport, AL, 77-84; First P Ch, Phenix City, AL, 87-94; Chap Operation Desert Storm, 90-91; asst prof MonC, 94-00; p Linden P Ch, Linden, AL, 00-03; Chap AL Nat'l Guard, 04-12; chap Op Iraqi Freedom, 04-07; instr Marion Military Acad, 07-; "Our Image of Warfield Must Go," *Journal of the Evangelical Theological Society*, 34.2, June 91; A Footnote to John Adams' Political Theory: Vindiciae contra Tyrannos," *Premise*, III.8 Aug 96; "B. B. Warfield: Apostle to the Children of the New Age," *Premise*, IV.3, Oct 97; trans *A Book of Reformed Prayers*, 98; "Why Do We Ask Why?" *Premise*, IV.4

PO Box 28, Marion, AL 36756 – 334-683-2345   Warrior
E-mail: sbamberg@marionmilitary.edu
Marion Military Academy

Ban, Martin Richard – b Los Angeles, CA, May 15, 60; f Joseph John; m Veronica Bernyce Rowley; w Marilee Anne Blevins, Sherman, TX, Aug 13, 83; chdn Joseph, Rani Kate, Trevor, Austin, Mollie; AusC 82, BA; WSCAL 89, MDiv; L Oct 87, NorthCA OPC; O Oct 89, NorthCA OPC; Recd PCA 00, Hrtl Pby; chp, p Delta Oaks OPC, Antioch, CA, 89-00; srp Westhills Ch, Lenexa, 00-02; op, chp Christ Ch Santa Fe PCA, Santa Fe, NM, 02-06; p 06-15; pres Redeemer sem, Dallas, TX, 15-17, chp 17-18; op St. Jude P Ch Oak Cliff Msn (PCA), Dallas, TX, 18

1614 Oak Knoll Street, Dallas, TX 75208   North Texas

Bancroft, Josiah Dozier IV – b Birmingham, AL, Sept 22, 52; f Dr. Joe D; m Paula Barber; w Barbara Cochran, Birmingham, AL, Dec 20, 75; chdn Elizabeth Ann, Josiah V., Jesse Rebekah; SamU 71-74; CC 75, BA; RTS 78-81, MDiv; O Sept 81, LA Pby; p Abundant Life P Ch, Jonesville, LA, 81-85; op Christ P Ch, Mobile, AL, 85-86, p 86-92; mis WHM, MTW, Dublin, Ireland, 92-96; WHM, US Director, 96-98; WHM, Assoc Dir, Ireland Team Ldr, 99-02; WHM, Dir Renewal, Ireland Field Dir, 02-05; p Grace Comm Ch, Fletcher, NC, 05-10; ob Dir of Mission Serge (form WHM), 10-

1425 Stephen Road, Jenkintown, PA 19046 – 828-551-0784   Eastern Pennsylvania
E-mail: jbancroft@serge.org
Serge

Baney, Gregory D. – astp Hixson P Ch, Hixson, TN, 16-18, ascp 18-

187 Hidden Harbor Road, Hixson, TN 37343   Tennessee Valley
E-mail: gregb@hixsonpres.org
Hixson Presbyterian Church – 423-875-0616

MINISTERIAL DIRECTORY

Bang, Duk Soo – op Hope P Ch of Dallas Msn, Carrollton, TX, 91-97; sc KorS Pby, 93-97; op Sung San P Msn, Carrollton, TX, 97-

2636 Cedar Falls Drive, Little Elm, TX 75068   Korean Southern
E-mail: sungsandallas@yahoo.co.kr
Sung San Presbyterian Mission – 972-416-8954

Bang, Jin Won – p New Orleans Onnuri P Ch, Metairie, LA, 04-06; p Pilgrim P Ch of Dallas, Carrollton, TX

2021 Chalfont Drive, Carrollton, TX 75007 – 469-366-7989   Korean Southern
E-mail: Jwbang99@hotmail.com

Bang, Paul J. – astp Korean P Ch of Wash, Fairfax, VA, 10-

6324 Drill Field Court, Centreville, VA 20121   Korean Capital
E-mail: pauljbang@gmail.com
Korean Presbyterian Church of Washington – 703-321-8090

Bankson, Paul L. – b Birmingham, AL, Aug 2, 63; f H. Levoy; m Wanda Taylor; w Connie Anderson, Ft. Lauderdale, FL, Aug 6, 88; chdn Andrew, Stephen, Matthew; AU 86, BS; RTS 88-91, MDiv; RTSFL 15, DMin; L Jan 90, Gr Pby; O Jun 92, Cov Pby; stus Geneva P Ch, Matherville, MS, 89-91; campm RUM, UTN-Martin, 91-96; campm RUM, MerU, 96-99; astp First P Ch, Macon, GA, 99-04; op Houston Lake P Ch, Warner Robins, GA, 04-07, p 07-

101 O'brien Drive, Kathleen, GA 31047 – 478-737-2970   Central Georgia
E-mail: pbankson@gmail.com
Houston Lake Presbyterian Church – 478-987-7503

Banner, Luke Alexander – O Sept 3, 17, Nash Pby; astp Christ P Ch of Clarksville, Clarksville, TN, 17-

852 Cherry Blossom Lane, Clarksville, TN 37040 – 615-400-5910   Nashville
E-mail: lukebanner14@gmail.com
Christ Presbyterian Church of Clarksville – 931-906-6650

Baral, William – w Kate; chdn Grace, Elijah, Samuel; TNTC 88, BRE; TBTS, MDiv; BibTS 05, ThM; O Feb 26, 06, SusqV Pby; ob p Canadochly Evangl & Ref Ch, York, PA, 06-

4843 East Prospect Road, York, PA 17406 – 717-755-1691   Susquehanna Valley
E-mail: wbaral@juno.com
Canadochly Evangelical & Reformed Church

Barbee, Brett – O Feb 5, 12; op Living Hope Church, Anderson, SC, 12-15, p 15-18; p Strong Tower Flwsp Msn, Macon, GA, 18-

Strong Tower Fellowship Mission – 478-742-7379   Central Georgia

Barber, Chad – b Elon, NC, May 28, 75; f Thomas Glen; m Sandra Foster; w Brooke Sherrod, Charlotte, NC, Dec 20, 03; chdn Savannah Rose, Luke Dillon, Ryan Aaron; UNCC 99, BS; RTSNC 05, MDiv; O Feb 9, 14, Flwsp Pby; dir disc Westminster P Ch, Rock Hill, SC, 13-14, astp, modis 14-

5583 Morris Hunt Drive, Fort Mill, SC 29708   Fellowship
E-mail: cbarber@wpcgo.com
Westminster Presbyterian Church – 803-366-3107

Barber, John J. – b New York, NY, Aug 2, 55; f John Frederick; m Anna Mary McWilliams; w Bonnie Howard, Springfield, VA, Jan 30, 90; FAU, BFA; WTS, MAR; YDS, MDiv; O Nov 21, 90, Pot Pby; ob ev PEF, 90-93; ob American Revival Ministries, Orlando, FL, 93-06; p Cornerstone P Ch, Palm Beach Gardens, FL, 06-16

3771 Timberline Drive, Orange Park, FL 32065   Gulfstream
E-mail: drjjb@hotmail.com

Barber, Michael – b Sparta, IL, May 21, 71; w Gretchen Leigh; chdn Samuel Hewitt, Joseph Warren Harvester, Caroline Ruth; CTS 08, MDiv; O May 27, 12, SoTX Pby; Chap St. David's Med Ctr, Austin, TX, 10-

9900 Michael Dale, Austin, TX 78736   South Texas
E-mail: maikelbaba@gmail.com
St. David's Medical Center, Austin, TX

Barber, W. Scott – b Athens, GA, Oct 1, 70; f William Carter; m Scottie Rebecca; w Elizabeth Leesa Tanner, Carrollton, GA, Jul 23, 94; chdn Elizabeth, Sydney, Caroline; SamU 93, BS; UGA 96, JD; CTS 09, MDiv; O Aug 23, 09, Prov Pby; p Redeemer P Ch, Florence, AL, 09-

330 Nottingham Road, Florence, AL 35633   Providence
E-mail: scott.barber@redeemershoals.com
Redeemer Presbyterian Church – 256-766-3414

Barcley, William – prof RTS, 01-07; p Lebanon P Ch, Learned, MS, 04-06;sr p Sovereign Gr P Ch, Charlotte, NC, 07-; adj prof RTSNC, 07-; *1 and 2 Timothy*; *Christ in You: A Study in Paul's Theology and Ethics*; *The Secret of Contentment*; *Gospel Clarity: Challenging the New Perspective on Paul*

133 Chaphyn Lane, Matthews, NC 28105 – 704-321-4583   Central Carolina
E-mail: bill.barcley@sovereigngrace.org
Sovereign Grace Presbyterian Church – 704-553-9600
Reformed Theological Seminary, NC – 704-366-5066

Barcroft, Douglas Morgan – b Memphis, TN, May 10, 58; f Ben Douglas; m Dorothy Nell Birchett; w Derenda Lynn Hosse, Memphis, TN, Aug 8, 81; chdn Benjamin Douglas Kim, Sarah Grace, Charley Kate Mao; UTMartin 80, BS; UTMemphis 93, BS, 95, MS; MidABTS 87, MDiv; O Sept 84, Covington Pike Bapt Ch; Recd PCA Oct 00, Cov Pby; p Fellowship Bapt Ch, Batesville, AR, 87-88; p Covington Pike Bapt Ch, Memphis, TN, 88-94; astp St. Andrews P Ch, Cordova, TN, 00-03, ascp 03-08; wc 08-10; astp Hickory Withe P Ch, Eads, TN, 10; ascp 10-11; srp 11-

12173 Dargie Drive, Arlington, TN 38002 – 901-299-4025   Covenant
E-mail: dougpca@bellsouth.net
Hickory Withe Presbyterian Church – 901-465-8682

Barczi, Nathan – O Oct 4, 15, SNE Pby; astp Christ The King P Ch, Cambridge, MA, 15-16; ascp 16-

37 Avon Street, Somerville, MA 02143 – 617-320-1346   Southern New England
E-mail: nbarczi@gmail.com
Christ The King Presbyterian Church – 617-354-8341

Barham, Cameron – O Aug 30, 14, NWGA Pby; p Christ Comm Ch, Kennesaw, GA, 14-

3459 Acworth Due West Road, Suite 440, Acworth, GA 30101 – 478-718-7957   Northwest Georgia
E-mail: cameron@christcommunitycobb.org
Christ Community Church – 770-529-2600

Barker, David George – b Dallas, TX, Nov 21, 53; f Merritt A.; m Anne L. Warne; w Janet M. Keys, Hatboro, PA, Aug 1, 81; chdn Matthew, Stephen, Joshua, Aaron; MaryvC 75, BA; WTS 83, MDiv;RPTS 14, DMin; L 83, DelMarva; O Aug 86, OPC; Recd PCA 01, Pot Pby; astp Calvary OPC, Schenectady, NY, 86-88; p Covenant OPC, Amsterdam, NY, 88-01; p New Cov P Ch, Abingdon, MD, 01-

918 Shelburne Road, Bel Air, MD 21015-6335 – 410-420-0632   Chesapeake
E-mail: david.barker@ncpres.org
New Covenant Presbyterian Church – 410-569-0289

Barker, Frank Morehead Jr. – b Birmingham, AL, Jan 31, 32; f Frank M B Sr; m Annie Lee; w Barbara Brown, Birmingham, AL, Nov 3, 61; chdn Anita Lee, Frank M III, Margaret Ann; AU 53, BS; ColTS 60, BD, 60, ThM; RTS 88, DD; O Jun 60, Bham Pby; srp Briarwood P Ch, Birmingham, AL, 60-99, p em 99-; *A Living Hope, Encounters with Jesus, First Timothy*

PO Box 43446, Birmingham, AL 35243 – 205-790-0268   Evangel
E-mail: fbarker@briarwood.org
Briarwood Presbyterian Church – 205-776-5200

Barker, William Shirmer II – b St. Louis, MO, Dec 15, 34; f Theodore R; m Nancy Edwards; w Kathryn Gail Kern, St. Louis, MO, Dec 28, 57; chdn Anne Kathryn, Matthew Woods; PU 56, BA; CornU 59, MA; VandU 70, PhD; CTS 60, BD; L Jun 60; O Jun 60, MidSo Pby (BPC); p Hazelwood Ref P Ch, Hazelwood, MO, 60-64; prof CC, 64-72; DnFac CTS, 72-77, pres 77-84; ob prof WTS, 87-00, ob AcadDn 91-00, prof em 00-; hr 00; adj prof CTS, 02-; Mod RPC, 73; Mod PCA GenAs 94; brd CC, 73-91; PCA AC, 82-86; IRC 92-00; Days/Creation, 99-01; sub-co Hist Cen, 01-; SJC 13-17; Ed-pub, *Presbyterian Journal*, 84-87; contr ed, *Theonomy: A Reformed Critique*; *Puritan Profiles: 54 Influential Puritans at the Time When the Westminster Confession of Faith was Written*, 96; (with Samuel T. Logan Jr.) *Sermons That Shaped America: Reformed Preaching 1630-2001*, 03; *"In All Things..." The Preeminence of Jesus Christ in the History of Covenant College, 1955-2005*, 05; *Word to the World: The Collected Writings of William S. Barker*, 05; "The Heresy Trial of Samuel Hemphill (1735)" in *Colonial Presbyterianism: Old Faith in a New Land*, ed. S. Donald Fortson III, 07; "The Historical Context of the *Institutes* as a Work in Theology," Chapter 1 in *A Theological Guide to Calvin's Institutes: Essays and Analysis*, 08

508 Sunnyside Avenue, Webster Groves, MO 63119-2649 – 314-327-1323   Philadelphia
E-mail: wmsbarker@gmail.com
HR

Barkhouse, Jeffrey – O Jun 30, 13, CentGA Pby; astp St. Andrews P Ch, Midland, GA, 13-15, ob 15-

92337 Camille Drive, Columbus, GA 31906   Central Georgia
E-mail: jeffreybarkhouse@hotmail.com

Barkley, Brett – O Jan 12, 14, Ohio Pby; p Zion Ref Ch, Winesburg, OH, 14-

1809 Township Road 675, Dundee, OH 44624   Ohio
E-mail: brett@zcpca.org
Zion Reformed Church – 330-359-5733

Barlett, Hugh Meredith – b Park Ridge, IL, Aug 2, 60; f Joe M; m Miriam M. Morgan; w Judith L. Henkle, Lincoln, NE, Feb 13, 82; chdn Sarah Elizabeth, Katherine Betty; Daniel Douglas; WheatC 78-81, BA; CTS 87-89, MDiv; CTS 10, DMin; L 84, SiouxI Pby; O Aug 20, 89, Hrtl Pby; p Zion Ch, Lincoln, NE, 89-92; p Chesterfield P Ch, Chesterfield, MO, 92-

246 Aspen Trail, Ballwin, MO 63011 – 636-394-4391   Missouri
E-mail: hughb@chespres.org
Chesterfield Presbyterian Church – 636-394-3337

Barnard, Craig – b Atlanta, GA, Nov 4, 65; f Robert Dean; m Georgia Ursula; w Mary Beth Bryan, Greenwood, MS, Jul 8, 89; chdn Mary Claire, Margaret Ellen, Nathan Craig; BelC 89, BA; CTS 96, MA; astp Main Street P Ch, Columbus, MS, 07-10; wc 10-16; p Spout Springs P Ch, Ripley, MS, 16-

822 Oxford Loop, New Albany, MS 38652   Covenant
E-mail: craidebarnard@gmail.com
Spout Springs Presbyterian Church

Barnes, Andrew J. – b Rock Island, IL, May 24, 82; f Christopher Paul; m Debra Lynn; w Dena Michelle Powell; chdn Oliver Abraham, Ezekiel Christopher; TIU 04, BA; RTS 08, MDiv; O Aug 24, 08, MSVal Pby; p Tchula P Ch, Tchula, MS, 08-10; p Christ P Ch, Kansas City, MO, 11-18

11908 West 68th Street, Shawnee, KS 66216   Heartland
E-mail: barnesaj@gmail.com

Barnes, Bradley – b Minneapolis, MN, Jun 27, 71; f John Heenry; m Janette Lucille LeRoy; w Meda Webster Tilman, Charlottesville, VA, Dec 17, 94; chdn Benjamin Henry, Jacob McNeir, Louisa Webster; WFU 93, BS; GCTS 04, MDiv; O Jan 17, 04, SNE Pby; astp Christ The King P Ch, Cambridge, MA, 04-; campm RUM, Harvard, 04-10; p Christ the King Newton, Newton, MA, 11-

447 Brookline Street, Newton, MA 02459   Southern New England
E-mail: bradleyjbarnes@gmail.com
Christ The King Presbyterian Church – 617-354-8341
Christ the King Newton – 617-213-0817

Barnes, Jack William – b Birmingham, AL, Apr 19, 58; f Robert E.; m Barbara Childers; w Anita Barker, Birmingham, AL, Aug 19, 88; chdn William Taylor, Frances Barbara, Richard Frank, Robert Lee; UAL 81, BS; BhamTS 95; O Nov 5, 95, Evan Pby; astp, ms/sa Briarwood P Ch, Birmingham, AL, 88-96, ascp 97-99; op Covenant Comm Ch, Scottsdale, AZ, 99-02, p 02-13; astp Covenant P Ch, Nashville, TN, 13-

33 Burton Hills Boulevard, Nashville, TN 37215   Nashville
E-mail: billy@covenanntpres.com
Covenant Presbyterian Church – 615-383-2206

Barnes, James Haskins – b Clarksdale, MS, Feb 19, 52; f Harris H. Jr.; m Jamye Alice Haskins; w Jane Ellen Thompson, Jackson, MS, May 18, 74; chdn David, Beth, Brad; MSU 70-74, BA; RTS 74-77, MDiv; O Jul 17, 77, Cong Pby (PCUS); ap First P Ch, Columbia, SC, 77-84; p First P Ch, Kosciusko, MS, 84-94; op Christ Cov P Ch, Knoxville, TN, 94-95, srp 95-17; hr 17

417 Battle Front Trail, Knoxville, TN 37922 – 865-675-0040   Tennessee Valley
HR

Barnes, Lonnie Wayne – b Roanoke Rapids, NC, May 14, 52; f Claude Floyd; m Margaret L.; w Ella Cheryl Lee, Burlington, NC, May 24, 75; chdn Edward Wayne, Janet Leigh, John Michael, David Lee; CC 70-74, BA; CTS 76-77; RTS 77-79, MDiv; RTSNC, DMin cand; L Jun 77, Car Pby; O Sept 22, 79, Ecar Pby; op Greenville, NC, 79-80; p White Oak P Ch, Fremont, NC, 80-82; p Westminster P Ch, Roanoke, VA, 82-93; ob Dir Patrick Henry Boys/Girls Plantation, Brookneal, VA, 93-94; p Shearer P Ch, Mooresville, NC, 94-07; astp Northside P Ch, Burlington, NC, 07; p Fellowship P Ch, Newland, NC, 07-

1282 Walt Clark Road, Newland, NC 28657 – 828-733-9866   Western Carolina
E-mail: barneslon9@cs.com
Fellowship Presbyterian Church – 828-733-0859

Barnes, Robert Frank – b New Orleans, LA, Sept 15, 66; w Kimberly Owen, Apr 14, 90; chdn Bethany, Noah; BelC 88, BA; RTS 94, MDiv; L 04, CentFL Pby; ed Tabletalk Magazine, 95-01; ed Spirit

MINISTERIAL DIRECTORY

Barnes, Robert Frank, continued
of the Reformation Study Bible, 01-03; ed Discover God Study Bible, 02-06; ed ESV Study Bible, 06-07; p DaySpring Ch, Spring Hill, FL, 07-

8369 Annapolis Road, Spring Hill, FL 34608-6702 – 352-556-8706   Central Florida
E-mail: rfbarnes@gmail.com
DaySpring Church – 352-686-9392

    Barnes, Roland Sanders – b Macon, GA, Apr 1, 52; f Dr. Walter Prothro; m Mary Evelyn Norton; w Georgia "Peaches" Emily Chappas, Atlanta, GA, Aug 17, 74; chdn Charlotte Emily, Jennifer Evelyn, Christopher Roland, Jordan Knox; UGA 70-74, BA; TEDS 74-78, MDiv; O Apr 22, 79, CentGA Pby; ap First P Ch, Macon, GA, 79-81; op Trinity P Ch, Statesboro, GA, 81-84, p 84-98, srp 98-; bklts: "Truth That Will Change Your Life," "Selecting God's Men," "The Miraculous Gifts of the Spirit, Have They Ceased?" "Knowing Your Creator," "Can Our Churches Grow?" "A Rationale for Evening Worship on the Lord's Day," "Men and Women in the Church"

119 College Boulevard, Statesboro, GA 30458-5203   Savannah River
E-mail: rsbarnes@frontiernet.net
Trinity Presbyterian Church – 912-489-8186

    Barr, Daniel Franklin – b Bristol, VA, Dec 25, 46; f Dr Kyle Edward B; m Jane Graham; w Maryellen Selleck, Chester, PA, Aug 14, 71; chdn Jeffrey Wayne, Esther Jane, Frederick Kyle; GBibC 69, BA; FTS 69-71; BST 72, MDiv; L Jan 19, 74; O Jan 27, 74, Westm Pby; ap Bellemont Ch, Bristol, TN, 67-69; ip Beidleman Ch, Bristol, TN, 74-75; ss Eastern Heights P Ch, Bristol, TN, 75, p 75-86, wc 86; p Covenant Bible Ch, Cape May, NJ, 86-96, wc 96-99; op Shore Points P Flwsp, Marmora, NJ, 99-01; p Shore Points P Ch, Marmora, NJ, 01-

806 Shunpike Road, Cape May, NJ 08204-4407 – 609-884-1794   New Jersey
E-mail: dfmsbarr@comcast.net
Shore Points Presbyterian Church – 609-884-1794

    Barr, Rick – w Beth; ascp Grace Ch PCA, Dover, DE, 08-

1144 Yearsley Drive, Dover, DE 19904 – 302-677-0326   Heritage
E-mail: rbarr@gracedover.com
Grace Church PCA – 302-734-8150

    Barrett, Charles – astp Wayside P Ch, Signal Mountain, TN, 15-16; ascp 16-

2506 Fairmount Pike, Signal Mountain, TN 37377   Tennessee Valley
E-mail: chuck@waysidechurch.org
Wayside Presbyterian Church – 423-886-1181

    Barrett, John – Jul 10, 75; f Robert; m Eileen; w Amber Michelle, Nov 24, 02; chdn Creed Johnson, Jack Maddox, Cody James; NCSt 97, BS; ErskTS 12, MATS; O Feb 10, 13, SavRiv Pby; ascp First P Ch, Augusta, GA, 13-

642 Telfair Street, Augusta, GA 30901   Savannah River
E-mail: jbarrett@firstpresaugusta.org
First Presbyterian Church – 706-262-8900

    Barrett, Ray – Chap USArmy, 02-10; hr 18

5608 Weldon Road, Tallassee, AL 36078 – 660-232-0764   Evangel
E-mail: raybarrett3@hotmail.com
HR

Barrie, Jason Wade – b Parma, OH, Oct 22, 71; f Robert; m Darlynn Brown; w Kristin Obenchain, West Point, NY, Jun 4, 94; chdn Emily, Adam, Kendall; USMA 94, BS; WSCAL 03, MDiv; WTS 13, DMin; O Jun 29, 03, RMtn Pby; ascp Rocky Mountain Comm Ch, Billings, MT, 03-

922 South 48th Street West, Billings, MT 59106 – 406-855-0020   Rocky Mountain
E-mail: jason@rmccmontana.org
Rocky Mountain Community Church – 406-259-7811

Barrs, Jerram – prof CTS, 89-

280 Amber Jack Drive, Ballwin, MO 63021-5013 – 636-394-9865   Missouri
Covenant Theological Seminary – 314-434-4044

Barry, David – astp Midway P Ch, Powder Springs, GA, 17-

4809 West McEachern Wood Drive, Powder Springs, GA 30127   Northwest Georgia
E-mail: david.barry@midwaypca.org
Midway Presbyterian Church – 770-422-4974

Barson, Deryck – astp Tenth P Ch, Philadelphia, PA, 16-

2086 Jenkintown Road, Glenside, PA 19038   Philadelphia
E-mail: dbarson@tenth.org
Tenth Presbyterian Church – 215-735-7688

Barth, Allan M. – b Minneapolis, MN, Sept 30, 53; f Merwin; m Betty Langmade; w Rene, Boca Raton, FL, Nov 29, 74; chdn Peter Allan, Rebecca Patience, Casey Ann; FAU 74, BA; TEDS 75-77; RTS 82, MDiv, 83, MEd; RTSFL 14, DMin; O Mar 83, TNVal Pby; ap Cedar Springs P Ch, Knoxville, TN, 82-85; op River Ridge P Ch, New Port Richey, FL, 85-89, p 89-95; op, ev North Shore Comm Ch, Oyster Bay, NY, 95-99, p 99-01; ob ev Redeemer ChPlant Cent/Redeemer City to City, 01-; Dir Europe, Afr, MidEast, Nam; ob VP Redeemer City-to-City, Global Catalyst for North America, Europe, Middle East and Africa, Executive Director of City to City North America, 15-

3531 Pine Haven Circle, Boca Raton, FL 33431   Metropolitan New York
E-mail: alb@redeemercitytocity.com
Redeemer City to City

Bartmess, Aaron – b Chambersburg, PA, Feb 4, 70; f William; m Jean Anne Knepp; w Teri Ellen Albertson, Forks, PA, Jun 19, 93; chdn Caleb Josiah, Sarah Grace, Joel Abram; ShSU 92, BA; CTS 01, MDiv; O Feb 16, 02, NJ Pby; astp, ydir Covenant P Ch, Cherry Hill, NJ, 01-08; p Edgemont P Ch, Bristol, TN, 08-

126 Churchill Circle, Bristol, TN 37620 – 423-573-3416   Westminster
E-mail: sarahbob@btes.tv
Edgemont Presbyterian Church – 423-652-2213

Barton, Rodney – p Arcadia P Ch, Kingsport, TN, 13-

2010 Bruce Street, Kingsport, TN 37664   Westminster
E-mail: rnjbarton@gmail.com
Arcadia Presbyterian Church – 423-323-1444

Barton, Timothy, Jr. – astp Grace Ch of Utah, Layton, UT, 09-16; astp The Vine Comm Ch, Cumming, GA, 16-

4255 Doubletree Court, Cumming, GA 30040   Metro Atlanta
E-mail: tbarton@thevinecommunitychurch.com
The Vine Community Church – 678-990-9395

MINISTERIAL DIRECTORY 37

Bartuska, Peter Anthony – b Camden, NJ, Aug 12, 64; f Peter Moses; m Beverly Ann Scribner; w Terri Denise Johnson, Knoxville, TN, Aug 13, 88; chdn Taylor Christine, Andrew Peter, Shelby Ann; TayU 86, BA; WTS 87-88; RTS 90-92, MDiv; L Jul 93, SFL Pby; O Oct 30, 94, GrLks Pby; op Grace P Ch, Danville, KY, 94-95, p 95-05; astp Treasure Coast P Ch, Stuart, FL, 05-06; op Faith Ch, Port St. Lucie, FL, 05-06; p Treasure Coast P Ch, Stuart, FL, 06-10; astp Wellington Presbyterian Church, Wellington, FL 12-14; p Christ Comm Ch (form Wellington), Wellington, FL, 14-

14515 Horseshoe Trace, Wellington, FL 33414 – 772-341-4561   Gulfstream
E-mail: peterabart@gmail.com
Christ Community Church

Basham, Dwight – w Pepper; chdn Benjamin, Aaron, Lydia, Samuel, Phoebe; VATech 90, BA, 99, MA; RTS 03, MDiv; O 06, WCar Pby; astp Drapers Valley P Ch, VA,03-06; p Memorial P Ch, Elizabethton, TN, 06-13; wc 13- 14; asp Arden P Ch, Arden, NC, 14-

9 Cedar Trail, Asheville, NC 28803 – 828-551-8705   Western Carolina
E-mail: ardenmusicmin@gmail.com
Arden Presbyterian Church – 828-684-7221

Basie, John A. – astp Westminster P Ch, Rock Hill, SC, 06-14; hr 14

1525 Bayberry Place, Clover, SC 29710 – 803-493-7272   Fellowship
E-mail: j.basie3@gmail.com
HR

Basile, Christopher – O 15, MNY Pby; p Grace Comm Ch, Bridgewater, NJ, 15-

202 Capricorn Drive, Apt.11, Hillsborough, NJ 08844   Metropolitan New York
E-mail: crb593@msn.com
Grace Community Church

Bates, Derek Alan – w Luda; chdn Caleb, Abiel, Elisea; O Sept 21, 08, Pitts Pby; campm RUF, Pitt, 08-

6527 Aylesboro Avenue, Pittsburgh, PA 15217 – 412-422-4179   Pittsburgh
E-mail: dbates@ruf.org
PCA Reformed University Fellowship – 314-229-0218

Bates, James Charles – b Oceanport, NJ, Apr 7, 65; f Calvin; m Bette Randle; w Joyce Frances Haines, Asbury Park, NJ, Jan 2, 88; chdn Stephen, Erika, Shannon, Jesse, Veronica; CIU 89, BS; BibTS 97, MDiv; O Jan 24, 99, EPC; Recd PCA 01, SusqV Pby; Ashland Evan Ch, Voorhees, NJ, 98-00; p Kirkwood P Ch, Kirkwood, PA, 01-03; sc SusqV Pby, 03-08; astp Faith Ref P Ch, Quarryville, PA, 05-09; ascp 09-15; CCEF, Intro to Counseling Cert

1175 Elm Avenue, Lancaster, PA 17603   Susquehanna Valley
E-mail: jbates01@mac.com

Bates, Marvin James III – b Birmingham, AL, Jun 21, 61; f Marvin James Jr.; m Nan Allison; w Patricia Hannaford, Jackson, MS, Jul 26, 86; chdn Allison Kayleigh, Ashley Elisabeth, Anna Katherine; GATech 79-80; UAL 80; BryC 81-83, BA; RTS 83-87, MDiv; L Jul 85, NGA Pby; O Aug 30, 87, CentFL Pby; ap Orangewood P Ch, Maitland, FL, 87-91; op University P Ch, Orlando, FL, 91-94; p 94-07; srp Village Seven P Ch, Colorado Springs, CO, 07-

2350 Pin High Court, Colorado Springs, CO 80907   Rocky Mountain
E-mail: mbates@v7pc.org
Village Seven Presbyterian Church – 719-574-6700

Bates, Stephen – O Nov 13, 16, Wcar Pby; astp Trinity P Ch, Asheville, NC, 16-

41 Cloyes Street, Asheville, NC 28806   Western Carolina
E-mail: stephenjamesbates@gmail.com
Trinity Presbyterian Church – 828-299-3433

Bathurst, Timothy A. – b Pottstown, PA, Jan 2, 64; f James Bathurst; m Jo Ann Schumacher; w Amy Thomas, Warren, PA, Jun 14, 86; chdn Rachel Joann, David James, Samuel Thomas; GroCC 82-86, BA; GCTS 86-88; WTS 88-91, MDiv; L Mar 93; O Oct 29, 95, Phil Pby; ascp New Life Ch of Phil, Philadelphia, PA, 91-00, ascp 16-

6103 North 8th Street, Philadelphia, PA 19120 – 215-224-2696   Philadelphia
New Life Church of Philadelphia – 215-324-4566

Batusic, John S. – b Charleston, WV, Oct 11, 56; f Richard Alvin; m Betty Lou Sims; w Rebecca Jo McNutt, Burlington, NC, May 20, 78; chdn John William, Richard David; WVU 74-77, BS; GCTS 78-81, MDiv; L Nov 81, MidAtl Pby; O Nov 81, MidAtl Pby; ap Rivers Edge Bible Ch, Hopewell, VA, 81-83, p 83-87; p Chestnut Mountain P Ch, Chestnut Mountain, GA, 87-

3933 Kilgore Falls Drive, Gainesville, GA 30507 – 770-967-3403   Georgia Foothills
E-mail: batusic@juno.com
Chestnut Mountain Presbyterian Church – 770-967-3440

Batzig, Nicholas – O Feb 1, 09, SavRiv Pby; op New Cov P Msn, Richmond Hill, GA, 09-15; p 15-18

132 Mill Hill Road, Richmond Hill, GA 31324 – 215-510-5615   Savannah River
E-mail: nbatzig@gmail.com

Baucum, Todd Douglas – w Mary; chdn Suzanne, Anna, Caroline, Lauren; LibU 83, BS; MempTS 87, MDiv; TrinSchMinPA, DMin; PurRefSem, stu; p Oakland P Ch, Topeka, KS, 90-93; ascp First P Ch, Topeka, KS, 93-96; chap KS State House, 93-94; p Kanawha United P Ch, Charleston, WV, 96-01; p Green Hill P Ch, Enterprise, AL, 01-04; p First P Ch, Enterprise, AL, 04-; adj prof BhamTS, 08-; "Innate Knowledge in Wilhelmus a Brakel," *Puritan Reformed Journal*, July 14

619 Wildwood Drive, Enterprise, AL 36330 – 334-475-6683   Southeast Alabama
E-mail: tbaucum@centurytel.net
First Presbyterian Church – 334-347-9515

Baudhuin, Chad – w Bliss; chdn Cadence, Colson, Charles; AndersonU 95, BA; WheatC 00, MA; CTS 10, MDiv; O May 31, 15, Wisc Pby; ascp Jacob's Well P Ch, Green Bay, WI, 15-17; op All Saints Ch, Green Bay, WI, 18-

352 Orchard Lane, Green Bay, WI 54311   Wisconsin
E-mail: ardenmusicmin@gmail.com
All Saints Church

Baugus, Bruce – b Easton, MD, Nov 9, 74; f Albert D.; m Diane Watson; w Tricia Apple, Jun 22, 96; chdn Nathanael, Bryant; PSU 96, BS; SBTS 99, MDiv; CTS 09, PhD; O May 98, Bapt; O May 14, MSVal Pby; p Bedford Rd. Bapt Ch, Cumberland, MD, 98-02; adj prof Cornerstone University, Grand Rapids, MI, 03-08; adj prof BelC, 12-; asst prof RTS, 08-12, assoc prof 12-; *China's Reforming Churches: Mission, Polity, and Ministry in the Next Christendom*, 14

439 Shadowood Drive, Ridgeland, MS 39157   Mississippi Valley
E-mail: bpbaugus@gmail.com
Belhaven University – 601-968-5930
Reformed Theological Seminary – 601-923-1600

MINISTERIAL DIRECTORY

Baxley, Andrew – O 17, TNVal Pby; mis MTW, 17-

218D Leslie Lane, Ballwin, MO 63021 Tennessee Valley
E-mail: andrewbaxley@gmail.com
PCA Mission to the World

Baxley, Terry Randall – b Hemingway, SC, Nov 23, 58; f Thomas Orin (d); m Lillian Hanna (d); w Elizabeth (Beth) Lodge, Virginia Beach, VA, Sept 11, 82; chdn Angell Anne, Andrew Marshall, Allison McClease, Carey Elizabeth, Daniel Thornwell; ClemU 77-78; CBC 79-82, BA; CTS 83-86, MDiv; L Apr 24, 86, Cal Pby; O May 3, 87, Cal Pby; ap Westminster P Ch, Clinton, SC, 87-91; op Cornerstone P Ch, California, MD, 91-92, p 92-09; ascp 09-11; p em 11

256 Fieldgate Circle, Pawleys Island, SC 29585 – 843-314-0687 Pee Dee

Baxter, Dave – O Jun 29, 14, CentCar Pby; astp Christ Cov Ch, Matthews, NC, 14-

2510 Connemara Drive, Matthews, NC 28105 – 864-923-3956 Central Carolina
E-mail: davejbaxter@gmail.com
Christ Covenant Church – 704-847-3505

Baxter, James A. – b Redwood Falls, MN, Jun 24, 64; f Robert E; m Goodmanson; w Wendy Skogen, Othello, WA, Sept 1, 90; chdn James Aaron, Sarah Marie, Jonathan Robert, Marylynn Dana; MidANU 82-84; CC 84-86, BA; CTS 86-90, MDiv; L 91, NoCA Pby; O Sept 6, 92, NGA Pby; ydir Covenant P Ch, St. Louis, MO, 86-90; astp Trinity P Ch Windward, Kailua, Oahu, HI, 90-91; astp Smyrna P Ch, Smyrna, GA, 92-98; p First P Ch, Enterprise, AL, 98-03; p New Hope P Ch in America, Olathe, KS, 04-

113310 S Black Bob Rd, Olathe, KS 66062 – 913-390-8788 Heartland
E-mail: jim-newhope@sbcglobal.net
New Hope Presbyterian Church in America – 913-782-7325

Baxter, Robert Edgar – b Sioux City, IA, Aug 8, 31; f E.W.; m Margaret M Helson; w Mary Lucile Goodmanson, Sioux City, IA, Jan 3, 56; chdn Robert Mark, Mary Beth, James Allen; MCSC, BA; MTS, MDiv; O May 12, 57, SiouC Pby (UPCUSA); p First Ch, Sanborn, IA, 57-61; p First Ch, Redwood Falls, MN, 61-67; p First Ch, Olathe, KS, 67-77; p New Hope P Ch in America, Olathe, KS, 78-93; srp Mount Cal P Ch, Roebuck, SC, 93-00; ascp First P Ch, Dothan, AL, 01- 14; p First P Ch, Florala, AL, 14-15; *Aim High* 78

13350 S. Greenwood Street, Apt 121, Olathe, KS 66062 – 334-648-1951 Southeast Alabama
E-mail: bob.baxter@gmail.com

Bayer, Hans F. – b Stuttgart, Germany, Oct 27, 54; f Walther; m Ilse; w Susan E. Vineyard, Mansfield, OH, Apr 8, 76; chdn Christopher N., Benjamin D., Katharine L.; AshTS 77, MA, 79, MDiv; AberU 84, PhD; L Jan 97, NoIL Pby; O May 25, 97, NoIL Pby; lect German TS, Giessen, Germany, 84-94; chp Wetzlar, Germany, 87-94; prof CTS, 94-

8808 Paragon Circle, St. Louis, MO 63123 – 314-849-1493 Chicago Metro
Covenant Theological Seminary – 314-434-4044

Bayly, David Jeremy – srp Christ the Word Ch, Toledo, OH, 02-

6944 North River Road, Waterville, OH 43566 Ohio
E-mail: djbayly@christtheword.com
Christ the Word Church – 419-329-1100

Baysinger, James Curtis – astp Desert Palms Ch, Chandler, AZ, 14-17, ascp 17-

1369 East Chestnut Lane, Gilbert, AZ 85298 – 925-784-8760 Southwest
E-mail: jcbaysinger@dpc-pca.org
Desert Palms Church – 480-422-2499

Beach, Justin – O Feb 14, 16, ChiMet Pby; astp Ethos P Msn, Chicago, IL, 16-17; astp Fellowship of Gr, Peoria, AZ, 17-

3742 East Kristal Way, Phoenix, AZ 85050   Southwest
E-mail: justinmbeach@gmail.com
Fellowship of Grace – 623-979-3514

Beach, Stanley – b Gagetown, MI, Jun 15, 35; f Leslie; m Inez M. Crawford; w Ellen L. Sickler, Cass City, MI, Dec 30, 55; chdn Randal J., Laurie E. (Dewey); TayU 58, BA; CTS 58-61, MDiv; UTSVA 72-74, DMin; O May 19, 61, MSVal Pby; Recd PCA 97, CentFL Pby; Chap USN, 60-87; sp various pulpits, 88-90; re New Hope P Ch, Eustis, FL, 91-96, astp 97-99; assoc, Dir PRJC, 98-; hr 99

10950 Temple Terrace # W-315, Seminole, FL 33772 – 352-365-2406   Central Florida
E-mail: stanbeach@aol.com
HR

Beachy, Grant M. – w Sara, Jul 22, 00; chdn Anna Catherine, Colin Creed, Samuel Patton (d), Bailey Grace; FurU 00, BA; CTS 04, MDiv; O May 15, 05, Cal Pby; astp Redeemer P Ch, Travelers Rest, SC, 05-11; p Harvest P Ch, Jacksonville, NC, 11-

921 Lynchburg Drive, Jacksonville, NC 28546 – 910-650-0898   Eastern Carolina
E-mail: gmbeachy@gmail.com
Harvest Presbyterian Church – 910-353-9888

Beale, Joseph Daniel – b Fulton, AR, Sept 27, 23; f Ernest Penny B. Sr.; m Corinne Humphries; w Annette Crouch, Cayce, SC, Aug 21, 59; chdn Gwendolyn B. (Blount), Catherine B (Bagley), Ruth B. (Bloxham), Joseph Daniel Jr.; LSU 43; PC 46-50, BA; ColTS 50-53, MDiv; L Apr 14, 53, Hrmny Pby; O Apr 26, 53, Hrmny Pby; ss Trinity Ch, Travelers Rest, SC, 49-51; ss Wee Kirk P Ch, Lithonia, GA, 51-53; p McDowell Ch, Greeleyville, SC, 53-55; p Union P Ch, Salters, SC, 53-55; ss Lane Ch, Lane, SC, 53-55; p Aimwell P Ch, Ridgeway, SC, 55-65; p Longtown Ch, Ridgeway, SC, 55-65; ss Mt. Olivet Ch, Winnsboro, SC, 63-65; p Little Chapel on Boardwalk, Wrightsville Beach, NC, 65-68; ap, medu First P Ch, Anderson, SC, 68-72; p Reidville P Ch, Reidville, SC, 72-82; p Antioch P Ch, Woodruff, SC, 72-85; ss Union P Ch, Abbeville, SC, 85-87; p Lebanon P Ch, Winnsboro, SC, 87-91, p em 91-; hr 91; ss Concord Ch, Blackstock/New Hope ARP, Douglass, SC, 91-02

242 Griffin Mountain Trail, Conyers, GA 30013 – 803-794-0078   Palmetto
E-mail: revbeale@bealebagley.com
HR

Beall, William Jackson – b Florence, SC, Sept 30, 55; f Charles R. Jr.; m Betty Jane Crowther; w Martha K. Collier, Gadsden, AL, Aug 8, 81; chdn Rebecca Jane, Scott Collier; ClemU 77, BA; RTS 82, MDiv; O Sept 82, Wcar Pby; ap Arden P Ch, Arden, NC, 82-85; p Grace Cov P Ch, Brevard, NC, 85-87; ascp Westminster P Ch, Gainesville, GA, 87-00; Dir MTW/Internship and Two Year, 00-07; Dir MTW/Church Resourcing, 07-17; astp Mitchell Road P Ch, Greenville, SC, 17-

205 Meritta Trail, Greenville, SC 29615 – 678-557-3533   Calvary
E-mail: jackbeall@gmail.com
Mitchell Road Presbyterian Church – 864-268-2218

Beam, Justin – ob p New Pres Ch, Wilton Manors, FL, 16-

6015 NW 45th Way, Coconut Creek, FL 33073   South Florida
New Presbyterian Church, Wilton Manors, FL

Bean, Charles Dawson – b Dallas, TX, Jul 24, 76; f Kenneth Charles; m Marikay Morton; w Shanna Jane Hymes, Weston, TX, May 26, 01; chdn Joshua, Caleb, Mary Beth; TXTU 01, BS; CTS 10, MDiv; O

MINISTERIAL DIRECTORY

Bean, Charles Dawson, continued
Mar 25, 12, Cov Pby; campm CCC, LSU, 01-06; campm RUF, UTMartin, 11-15; clin past ed; chap res, Covenant Med Cent, Lubbock, TX, 16-17

7408 80th Street, Lubbock, TX 79424   Covenant
E-mail: dawson.bean@gmail.com

Beane, Jonathan – astp West Boca P Ch, Boca Raton, FL, 05-07; campm RUF, ArmSU, 07-11; srp Covenant P Ch at Greenville, Greenville, MS, 11-15; p New Cov P Ch, Manning, SC, 15-

2833 Alex Harvin Hwy, Manning, SC 29102   Pee Dee
E-mail: jpbeane@gmail.com
New Covenant Presbyterian Church – 803-473-3677

Beans, Frank W. III – O Jun 14, 14, SusqV Pby; campm RUF, Millersville, 14-

1229 Colonial Road, Lancaster, PA 17603   Susquehanna Valley
E-mail: trip.beans@ruf.org
PCA Reformed University Fellowship

Beates, Michael Scott – b Westfield, NY, Jul 27, 56; f Cdr. James K.; m Marjorie A.; w Mary Diane Schreck, Naples, FL, Nov 24, 79; chdn Jessica Sherrise, Jameson Edwin (Jeb), Abraham Michael, Abigail Mary, Shoshanah Mercy, Elias Calvin Augustine, Josiah Campbell; ClemU 78, BA; BibTS 87, MDiv, 88, STM; RTSFL 03, DMin; L Jul 16, 91, CentFL Pby; O Sept 8, 91, CentFL Pby; Young Life, Buffalo, NY, 80-83; BibTS, tch asst, 86-88; ob LigMin, dir edtl, assoc ed, Tabletalk, Orlando, FL, 89-96; ascp Covenant P Ch, Oviedo, FL, 91-08; ob DnStu RTSFL, 96-02; ob headm Covenant CS, 02-03; adj prof FSC, 98-01; adj prof Belhaven C, Orlando, 99-14; adj prof Ref Bib C, Sanford, FL, 14-; BdDir Joni and Friends, 00-; contr *Discover God Study Bible*, 04-06; *Beyond Suffering Bible* Project 14-16; ob fac, DnStu The Geneva School, Winter Park, FL, 08-; "God's Sovereignty and Genetic Anomalies" in *Genetic Ethics: Do the Ends Justify the Genes?* 96; "Of Doctors and Other Priests" and "Can You Clone a Soul?" in *Playing God: Dissecting Medical Ethics & Manipulating the Body*, 97; "The Father as Priest" in *Family Practice: God's Prescription for a Healthy Home*, 00; "The Church and Disability" in *Beyond Suffering: A Christian View on Disability Ministry*, 11; *Disability and the Gospel: How God Uses Our Brokenness to Display His Grace*, 12

3043 Nicholson Drive, Winter Park, FL 32792 – 407-247-5843   Central Florida
E-mail: msbeates@genevaschool.org
The Geneva School – 407-332-6363
Reformation Bible College, Sanford, FL

Beatty, Robert – b Louisville, KY, Mar 1, 63; f Robert William Sr.; m Cova B. Heath; w Alisa Faye Dean, Louisville, KY, Mar 14, 92; WhTS 01, MDiv; L May 96, GrLks Pby; O May 01, GrLks Pby; p Christ Cov P Ch, Lexington, KY, 96-

324 North Homestead Lane, Lancaster, KY 40444 – 859-548-2395   Ohio Valley
E-mail: bbeatty@windstream.net
Christ Covenant Presbyterian Church – 859-333-8950

Beauchamp, Tim R. – Recd PCA Aug 25, 15, SEAL Pby; op Trinity Ch Guam, Yigo, GU, 15-

PO Box 12051, Ygo, GU 96929   Southeast Alabama
E-mail: tim.r.beauchamp@gmail.com
Trinity Church Guam – 671-864-6032

Beaulieu, Henry Hamilton – b Montgomery, AL, Jan 6, 63; f Francis; m Margaret Smith; w Gretchen Gordon, Montgomery, AL, Dec 15, 91; chdn Faith, Grace, Jonathan, Jackson; WheatC 81-85, BA; RTS 92-95, MDiv; L Oct 94, SEAL Pby; L Jun 95, MSVal Pby; O Dec 16, 95, SEAL Pby; Chap USArmy, 46th Eng

Beaulieu, Henry Hamilton, continued
Btn, Ft. Polk, LA, 96-99; astp Eastwood P Ch, Montgomery, AL, 99-01; p Chapel Woods P Ch, Snellville, GA, 01-02; astp Eastwood P Ch, Montgomery, AL, 02-14; Chap ALARNG, JFHQ, ALARNG- State Chaplain, Montgomery, AL; astp Trinity P Ch, Statesboro, GA, 14-

125 Pine Bluff Drive, Statesboro, GA 30458 – 912-515-4106　　　　　　　　　　Savannah River
E-mail: henry.beaulieu2@gmail.com
Trinity Presbyterian Church – 912-489-8186

Bech, Niel W. Jr. – b Philadelphia, PA, May 8, 47; f Niel W.; m Charlotte Weyman; w Karen J. Keller, Philadelphia, PA, Dec 18, 71; chdn Heather Jean, Judith Lynn, Niels Joshua, Noah Christian; TempU 70, AS; GenC 85, BA; REpS 85, MDiv; O May 85, RefEpis; Recd PCA Sept 11, 93, Phil Pby; REpS, 79-89; ss RefEpis, 83-89; astp Covenant P Ch, Hatboro, PA, 93-00; astp Third Ref P Ch, Philadelphia, PA, 01-07; hr 13; ss Covenant OPC, Vineland, NJ, 14-; "Where to Prepare" in several ed, *Great Commission College & Graduate School Guide*

4417 Tyson Avenue, Philadelphia, PA 19135 – 215-333-1405　　　　　　　　　　Philadelphia
E-mail: dpmprompt@aol.com
HR
Covenant OPC, Vineland, NJ

Bechtel, Christopher – p Evergreen P Ch, Salem, OR, 12-

1110 5th Street NE, Salem, OR 97301　　　　　　　　　　　　　　　　　　Pacific Northwest
E-mail: bechtelcr@gmail.com
Evergreen Presbyterian Church – 503-371-1177

Beck, Stephen Paul – b Goshen, NY, Sept 18, 55; f William; m Ruth Snyder; w Susan Baber, Richmond, VA, Jul 24, 76; chdn Sarah A. (Fullerton), Rachel L. (Chancellor), Elizabeth R. (Chen), Hannah J. (Green); PhilBibU 73-77, BS; TEDS 77-80, MDiv; WTS 94, PhD; O Mar 83, Dmv Pby; ap Valley P Ch, Lutherville, MD,81-83; p Reformed P Ch, Ephrata, PA, 83-86, srp 86-93; ev Ecan Pby, 93; op Gr Toronto Msn, Toronto, ON, 93-97, srp 97-03; op Grace West Ch, Oakville, ON, 03-05; ob prof Freie Theologische Hochschule, Giessen, Germany, 05-; ob Redeemer Church Planting Center, New York, 05-06; Dir, City Mentoring Programm, Frankfurt, Germany 06-; ob op Mosaik Kirche, Frankfurt, Germany, 11-; *klug_bauen* 07; *Mit Gott auf den Geschmack kommen* 08; *Smartbuilder: A God-centered Spirituality in a Me-centered World*, 11; *Mission MosaikKirche: Wie Gemeinden sich fuer Migranten und Fluechtlinge oeffnen*, 17

Bruhlstrasse 22, 60439 Frankfurt-Heddernheim, GERMANY – 011-49-69-97767667　　Eastern Canada
E-mail: Stephen.beck@fthgiessen.de
Freie Theologische Hochschule, Giessen, Germany

Becker, Jonathan – b Syracuse, NY, Jun 20, 69; f John Irving; m Eleanor Ruth; w Tracie Kaye Thomsen, Continental, OH, Aug 5, 95; chdn Jonathan Taylor Thomsen, John Caedmon Triumph, Thymian Heidi Noelle, Tatiana Abella Xaris; PenCC 93, BA; TEDS 93-95; LCC 96, PhD; SWBTS 03, cert; O Oct 15, 08, EPC; O Apr 19, 11, GulCst Pby; int The Campus Ch, Pensacola, FL, 92; int Willow Creek Comm Ch, S. Barrington, IL, 93-95; ap N Mt Zion Ch, Continental, OH, 93-96; ap Bapt Temple Ch, McAllen, TX, 96-99; p First Bapt Ch, Weslaco, TX, 99-06; p First Bapt Ch, McAllen, TX, 06-07; ap Second P Ch, Memphis, TN, 07-11; p Concord P Ch, Gulf Breeze, FL, 11-; *Leadership: Shaped by the Gospel*; *Living, Sharing, Leading: A Journal for Evangelism*

8573 Gulf Boulevard Unit 1101, Navarre, FL 32566-6836 – 850-932-0135　　　　　Gulf Coast
E-mail: drjonbecker@me.com
Concord Presbyterian Church – 850-932-6243

Becker, Robert M. – b Buffalo, NY, Mar 25, 57; f Clayton Charles; m Josephine M. Murano; w Carol J. Jakielaszek, Buffalo, NY, Sept 1, 79; chdn Melody L., Gretchen E., Nicholas Aaron, Grace

Becker, Robert M., continued
Elizabeth; GenC 75-78; SUNY 78-79, BA; WTS 81-84, MDiv; O Jun 1, 86, JR Pby; ob ascp New Life in Christ Ch, Fredericksburg, VA, 84-94; op New City Flwsp, Fredericksburg, VA, 94-96, p 96-

6703 Plantation Forest Drive, Spotsylvania, VA 22553-7784 – 540-765-5272   James River
E-mail: bobbecker@newcityfellowship.org
New City Fellowship – 540-899-5349

    Bedell, Casey – O Jun 28, 15, Pot Pby; ob admin Ministry to State, Washington, DC, 13-16; astp Covenant P Ch, Issaquah, WA, 16-17, ascp 17-

1118 7th Avenue NW #A127, Issaquah, WA 98027 – 425-999-1127   Pacific Northwest
E-mail: caseyb@cpcissaquah.org
Covenant Presbyterian Church – 425-392-5532

    Beesley, Richard Vernon – b Vincennes, IN, Jan 27, 31; f Oscar Vernon; m Ruth Irene Reel; w Naomi Ruth Rehwald, Knox Co, IN, Sept 4, 53; chdn Bruce Allyn, Brian Keith; VinU 51, AS; INStU 53, BS, 55, MS; LPTS 60, MDiv; UMO 64, PhD; OakCC 74, DD; BethS 88, DLitt; O May 22, 60, Vincennes Pby (UPCUSA); p First Ch, Mt. Vernon, IN, 57-60; p Westminster Ch, Versailles, MO, 60-65; WheatC, 65-68; AcadDn OakCC, 68-75, prof, VP 78-88; ob p Northside Cong Ch, Evansville, IN (Ind), 85-96; hr 96

627 Maryland Place, Vincennes, IN 47591-6431 – 812-882-0277   Illiana
HR

    Beham, Matt – O Mar 1, 16, SoTX Pby; astp Redeemer P Ch, San Antonio, TX, 16-

636 West Hollywood Avenue, San Antonio, TX 78212 – 210-508-7662   South Texas
E-mail: matthew.beham@gmail.com
Redeemer Presbyterian Church – 210-930-4480

    Beier, Brad – w Shannon; chdn Elianna, Mikayla, Olivia, Susanna; ydir Korean Ch in Jackson Msn, Raymond, MS, 99-00; chp, int Faith Christian Flwsp Ch, Baltimore, MD, 02-03; ob astp Bethel Christian Ch Msn, Chicago, IL, 03-; op Living Hope Ch, Chicago, Chicago, IL, 10-

6352 South Ingleside Avenue, Apt. 2, Chicago, IL 60637-3662   Chicago Metro
E-mail: bradbeier@gmail.com
Bethel Christian Church – 773-202-7900
Living Hope Church, Chicago – 708-280-8779

    Belcher, George D. III (Del) – w Nancy Garrison; chdn George D IV, Stephanie Klomsten Belcher, Tom Shemanski, Marjorie Belcher Shemanski, Breaden Belcher, Noah Thorne, Audrey Belcher Thorne, Julia; WheatC 79, BS; RTSFL 95, MDiv, 11, DMin; O 96; Recd PCA 06; p Pathway Comm Ch, Brighton, MI, 07-; adj prof CornerstoneU, ConcordiaU; mod GrLks Pby, 18

PO Box 1198, Brighton, MI 48116   Great Lakes
E-mail: belcher07@sbcglobal.net
Pathway Community Church – 810-623-0144

    Belcher, Jim – op Redeemer P Ch, Newport Beach, CA, 02-10; ob Providence Christian College

990 Atchison Street, Pasadena, CA 91104   South Florida
Providence Christian College

    Belcher, Richard P. Jr. – b Glen Ellyn, IL, Mar 29, 55; f Richard P; m Mary Anne Casner; w Lu Ingelse, Oostburg, WI, May 15, 76; chdn Nikki, Danielle, Alisha; CC 73-77, BA; CTS 77-80, MDiv; ConcS 87, STM; WTS 91-95, PhD; L Oct 79, RPCES; O Nov 81, Indep Council; Recd PCA Sept 21, 95, Flwsp Pby; p Comm Bib Ch, Rochester, NY, 81-91; ob prof RTSNC, 95-; *The Messiah and the Psalms,* 06;

Belcher, Richard P. Jr., continute
"Suffering" and "Thanksgiving, Psalms of," in *Dictionary of the Old Testament: Wisdom, Poetry, & Writings*, 08; "The King, the Law, and Righteousness in the Psalms," in *The Law is Not of Faith*, 09; *Genesis: The Beginning of God's Plan of Salvation*, 12; "Job," "Ecclesiastes," and "Daniel" in *A Biblical-Theological Introduction to the Old Testament*, 15; *Prophet, Priest, and King: The Roles of Christ in the Bible and Our Roles Today*, 15; *Job: The Mystery of God's Sovereignty*, 17; *Ecclesiastes: A Mentor Commentary*, 17; "Supernatural Creation of Man: The Historicity of Adam and Eve," in *Creation and Change*, 17; *Finding Favour in the Sight of God: A Theology of Wisdom Literature*, 18

227 Annatto Way, Tega Cay, SC 29708   Fellowship
E-mail: rbelcher@rts.edu
Reformed Theological Seminary, NC – 704-688-4226
2101 Carmel Road, Charlotte, NC 28226

Belk, Hudson Gregory – O Jun 8, 14, CatVal Pby, ob 14-

19108 Kanawha Drive, Cornelius, NC 28031 – 843-696-3594   Catawba Valley
E-mail: hudsonbelk2@hotmail.com

Bell, Eugene C. – b Denver, CO, Mar 8, 71; CC 89-95, BA; CTS 95-99, MDiv; O Apr 9, 00, NoCA Pby; astp Redeemer P Ch, Santa Rosa, CA, 00-01; ev Longmont, CO, 01-02; op St. Vrain P Msn, Longmont, CO, 02-08; astp Evergreen P Ch, Beaverton, OR, 08-10; chp, op Chehalem Valley P Ch, Newberg, OR, 09-10, p 10-

1006 Madison Drive, Newberg, OR 97132   Pacific Northwest
E-mail: ecbell@cvpchurch.com
Chehalem Valley Presbyterian Church – 503-476-4649

Bell, Loren D. – O Mar 16, MO Pby; astp New Creation P Ch, Wentzville, MO, 16-17; ascp 17-

25 Quail Meadows Court, Lake Saint Louis, MO 63367   Missouri
E-mail: Ecbell91@gmail.com
New Creation Presbyterian Church – 636-791-0201

Bell, Mark Alan – b Butler, PA, Jul 15, 68; f Dean Leroy (d); m Margaret Louise McKenzie; w Claudia Michels, Butler, PA, Jun 11, 94; chdn Elizabeth Joy, Philipp Joseph, Joanna Hope, Rebekah Faith; GroCC, BA; GCTS, MDiv; L Jan 95, Asc Pby; O Oct 17, 98, NoE Pby; int Hillcrest P Ch, Volant, PA; ip Faith Ref, Butler, PA; srp Redeemer Ref P Ch, Queensbury, NY, 98-09; p Cornerstone P Ch, Youngstown, OH, 09-

6332 Tara Drive, Poland, OH 44514 – 330-953-1324   Ohio
E-mail: malanbell@gmail.com
Cornerstone Presbyterian Church – 330-758-5628

Bell, Robert Earl – b Toronto, Ont, Can, Apr 4, 51; f R. Henry; m Pauline F. Rockwell; w Melody A. Peterkin, Brookhaven, PA, Jun 15, 74; chdn Alison Ruth, R. Andrew, Aaron R.; PhilCB 69-73, BS; WheatGrS 73-74, MA; WTS 78; CTS 81-84, MDiv; O Jan 85, LA Pby; ap Westminster P Ch, Lancaster, PA, 75-78; admin Westminster Reformed P Ch, Ballwin, MO, 81-83; p John Knox P Ch, Ruston, LA, 85-87; ap Kirk of the Hills P Ch, St. Louis, MO, 87-90; p Cornerstone P Ch, O'Fallon, MO, 87-93, wc 93; VP New Hope Pastoral Ministries, Inc., Timonium, MD, 93-; p Aisquith P Ch, Baltimore, MD, 94-

3003 Oakcrest Avenue, Baltimore, MD 21234-6919 – 410-444-5111   Chesapeake
E-mail: bob@aisquith.org
Aisquith Presbyterian Church – 410-444-4598

MINISTERIAL DIRECTORY

Belonga, Mark A. – b Detroit, MI, May 5, 75; f Michael; m Cynthia; w Andrea Van Eck, South Holland, IL, Aug 17, 96; chdn Joshua Michael, Caleb Jonathan, Rebekah Faith, Jocelyn Hope; WheatC 96, BS; WTS 10, MDiv; O Oct 7, 12, NoTX Pby; astp Redeemer P Ch, McKinney, TX, 12-14; ascp 14-

980 Mystic Way, Prosper, TX 75078 – 214-547-8698   North Texas
E-mail: mark@redeemer-mckinney.org
Redeemer Presbyterian Church – 972-529-1502

Belz, Sam – O Aug 15, Iowa Pby; p Bethany Evangelical & Ref Ch, Ledyard, IA, 15-18; astp Westminster P Ch, Atlanta, GA, 18-

1438 Sheridan Road, Atlanta, GA 30324 – 828-545-4606   Metro Atlanta
E-mail: s.belz@wmpca.org
Westminster Presbyterian Church

Ben-Ezra, Hyman Leon – b Brooklyn, NY, Jan 28, 51; f Leon; m Eloise; w Linda G. Anderson (d); chdn Seth Andrew, Jonathan Mark, Elizabeth Ann, Adiel Ivah, Gabrielle Noel; RutgU 73, BA; WTS 79, MDiv; L 79, Phila Pby (RPCES); O 80, Phila Pby (RPCES); ap Calvary Ch, Warminster, PA, 80-81; headm American Christian School, 81-85; p Faith Ref Ch, Erie, PA, 85-

1072 Priestley Avenue, Erie, PA 16511 – 814-899-4866   Ascension
E-mail: FaithReformedChurch@gmail.com
Faith Reformed Church – 814-899-3037

Bender, Mark John – b Pittsburgh, PA, Jul 18, 62; f Alfred A.; m June F. Foote; w Marlene Lyn Myers, Pittsburgh, PA, Jun 1, 85; chdn Johanna Lee, Caroline Hope, Alexandra Nicole, John David; GenC 81-85, BA; RPTSW, MDiv; O Nov 19, 89, DMV Pby; ap Timonium P Ch, Timonium, MD, 89-91; p Calvary P Ch, Norfolk, VA, 91-

6110 Ivor Avenue, Norfolk, VA 23502-5309 – 757-461-2599   Tidewater
E-mail: markjbender@cox.net
Calvary Presbyterian Church – 757-461-7043

Benfer, Max Ryan – b Washington, DC, Oct 8, 73; w Michelle, Feb 24, 01; chdn Luke Jackson, Andrew Charles, Isaac Ryan, Miriam Patricia Marie, James Owen, Eva Mae; WTS 06, MAR; O Mar 8, 09, Chspk Pby; astp Severna Park Evangelical P Ch, Pasadena, MD, 09-12; ob 12-13; p Meadowcroft P Ch, West Chester, PA, 13-; "A Heart Full of Pride," *The Journal of Biblical Counseling*, Spring 05

1050 Ridgewood Lane, West Chester, PA 19382 – 443-816-1533   Philadelphia Metro West
E-mail: mbenfer@meadowcroftchurch.org
Meadowcroft Presbyterian Church – 610-455-0455

Bennett, Alfred Wendell Jr. – b Marion, AL, Aug 5, 51; f Alfred Wendell; m Maxine Creel; w Diann Inman, Marion, AL, Jun 1, 74; chdn Matthew David, Rebecca Joy; MarI 69-71, AA; UMonte 73, BA; RTS 77, MDiv; O Sept 18, 77, JohnKnox Pby (PCUS); ap First P Ch, Dothan, AL, 77-81; ap First P Ch, Johnson City, TN, 81-83; p Midway P Ch, Jonesborough, TN, 83-87; p Covenant P Ch, Sebring, FL, 87-98; t/tr CEP, 90-97; adj prof philosophy, NT, world rel, SouthFLCC, 92-98; p Millbrook P Ch, Millbrook, AL, 98-05; reg train CEP 06-; min dir RH, 07-09; wc; hr 13

3865 Buster Sealy Road, Uniontown, AL 36786 – 334-285-9348   Southeast Alabama
HR

Bennett, Bill – b Fort Valley, GA, Sept 3, 68; w Jill Blankenship, Feb 12, 94; chdn Chet, Jane, Jake, Tate, Knox, Ty; CC 07; RTSA 12, MDiv; O Apr 15, 14, GAFH Pby; astp East Lanier Comm Ch, 14-16; op Jefferson Mission, 15-

6304 Flat Rock Drive, Flowery Branch, GA 30542 – 770-945-7800   Georgia Foothills
E-mail: bbennett@jeffersonpca.org
Jefferson Mission – 678-979-5200

Bennett, Christopher Michael – New London, CT, Aug 17, 89; f Jay; m Michelle Hunter Fuquay; w Amy Frances Cooper, Dallas, TX, May 28, 16; UNFL 11, BA; CTS 16, MDiv; O Jun 4, 17, CentFL Pby; astp First P Ch, Macon, GA, 16-

556 Marjorie Place, Macon, GA 31204   Central Georgia
E-mail: cbennettm@gmail.com
First Presbyterian Church – 478-746-3223

Bennett, Christopher P. – b Bethesda, MD, Jun 29, 50; f Fred G. (d); m Nancy (d); w Frances P.; chdn Audrey Claire; LehU 72, BS; PSCE 87, MA; CTS 78, MDiv; L 78, DMV Pby (RPCES); O 78, DMV Pby (RPCES); op Providence RP Ch (RPCES), 79-82; Chap USN, 82-05; ascp Crossroads P Ch, Woodbridge, VA, 05-10; astp Faith Ref P Ch, Quarryville, PA, 10-14; hr 14; sc Lowc pby

129 Northview Lane, Quarryville, PA 17566 – 717-224-0257   Lowcountry
E-mail: allofgrace@att.net
HR

Bennett, David E. – b Bourne, MA, Sept 17, 53; f Edward L; m Dotson; w Anne L. Pulliam, San Diego, CA, Dec 1, 73; chdn Heather, Julie, Jon; CPStU 71-76, BS; SJSU 81, BA; WTS 81-84, MDiv; L Jan 87, Pac Pby; O Jun 87, Pac Pby; ap Christ Community, 86-88; ap Canyon Creek P Ch, San Ramon, CA, 88-89; op Oak Hills P Ch, Concord, CA, 89-92, p 92-94; p Desert Palms P Ch, Chandler, AZ, 94-06; op New City Ch Phoenix, Phoenix, AZ , 07-

20320 West Baseline Road, Suite 182-212, Phoenix, AZ 85041 – 480-236-1400   Southwest
E-mail: newcityphoenix@mac.com
New City Church Phoenix – 602-358-8212, www.newcityphoenix.com

Bennett, Dennis Gene – b Brooklyn, NY, Sept 19, 50; w Cynthia Louise Jones, Apr 6, 91; chdn Steven William Haynie, Dustin Baker, Innocent Rwagasore, Benadette Kaitese; SUNY 72, BA; CTS 79, MDiv; TTS 07, DRS; O Oct 3, 81, ECA; Recd PCA Apr 18, 95, NGA Pby; IVBI, 80-83; assoc prof AUBS, 83-86; CEP, 86-97; mis MTW, 97-04; prof. Bible Inst. of South Africa, 97-06; ob Equipping Pastors Int, Inc., Winter Springs, FL, 04-06; PCA CDM, 06-; AcadDn Metro Atlanta Seminary, 06-

2812 Marcia Drive, Lawrenceville, GA 30044 – 678-313-6534   Metro Atlanta
E-mail: dbennett@pcanet.org
PCA Committee on Discipleship Ministries – 678-825-1158
Metro Atlanta Seminary

Bennett, Drew – ascp Trinity P Ch, Lakeland, FL, 05-08; op Church of the Redeemer, Winter Haven, FL, 09-11; p Redeemer P Ch, Lakeland, FL, 11-

156 Lake Mariam Road, Winter Haven, FL 33884 – 863-286-2310   Southwest Florida
E-mail: drew@redeemerwinterhaven.org
Redeemer Presbyterian Church – 863-660-5448

Bennett, Jacob A. – O Aug 15, 12, MO Pby; Chap Friendship Village, St. Louis, MO, 12-17; astp Covenant P Ch, Chattanooga, TN, 17-18, ascp 18-

8451 East Brainerd Road, Chattanooga, TN 37421 – 314-608-9234   Tennessee Valley
E-mail: tvpclerk@gmail.com
Covenant Presbyterian Church – 423-899-5377

Bennett, John – Recd PCA Oct 31, 15, SoTX Pby; campm RUF, 15-18; astp Christ P Ch, New Braunfels, TX, 18-

302 Branch Road, New Braunfels, TX 78130   South Texas
E-mail: jbennettcpcnb@gmail.com
Christ Presbyterian Church – 830-629-0405

Bennett, Roy Robert – b Artesia, CA, Mar 13, 53; f Robert Calvin; m Donna Lou Wilmore; w Norma Jean Nielsen, Red Deer, AB Canada, Dec 28, 83; chdn Megan Makaria, Bronwyn Kardia; PBI 84-88, ThB, 84-88, BRE; DipCS, RegC 88-89; RTS 94-97, MA; L Jun 1, 89, EFC of Canada; O May 12, 01, Pac Pby; ascp Lethbridge, AB, Canada, 89-94; p Santa Cruz, CA, 97-00; op Christ Ch Ojai, Ojai, CA, 01-06; op Christ Ch Ventura, Ventura, CA, 05-07; p Christ Ch Ojai, Ojai, CA, 06-07; p Christ Ch Ventura, CA, 08-

809 Mountain View Avenue, Ojai, CA 93023 – 805-646-3227   Pacific
E-mail: ojairoyb@gmail.com
Christ Church Ventura – 805-646-5101; www.christchurchventura.org

Benson, Edward Hunter – O Aug 19, 12, SoCst Pby; ascp Harbor P Ch North Co, 12-13; astp Redeemer P Ch of San Diego, 13-

189 North Vulcan Avenue, Encinitas, CA 92024   South Coast
E-mail: hunterbenson11@gmail.com
Redeemer Presbyterian Church of San Diego – 760-753-2535

Benton, Woodrow Wilson Jr. – b Jackson, MS, Apr 25, 41; f Woodrow Wilson, Sr.; m Elizabeth Wilson; w Pamela Woodward, Kosciusko, MS, Jun 16, 63; chdn Louis, Paige, Laura; BelC 63, BA; ColTS 66, BD; UEdin 69, PhD; O Jun 26, 66, StAnd Pby (PCUS); prof BelC, 66-67, prof 69-70; First Ch, Cleveland, MS, 70-82; p Covenant P Ch at Cleveland, Cleveland, MS, 82-85; srp Kirk of the Hills P Ch, St. Louis, MO, 86-06; ip Christ P Ch, Nashville, TN, 07-12, p em 13

2752 Rock Wall Road, Nashville, TN 37221   Missouri
E-mail: pbenslu@aol.com

Bentz, David Earl – b Harrisonburg, VA, Aug 18, 67; f Robert E.; m Fay LaRue Beeghly; w Christine DellaVecchia, Harrisonburg, VA, Nov 21, 92; chdn Joseph, Katie, Kellie, Timothy; JMU 88, BS, 92, BS; RTS 99, MDiv; L Oct 9, 99, JR Pby; O Feb 6, 00, JR Pby; ascp New Life in Christ Ch, Fredericksburg, VA, 99-02; op Grace P Ch, King George, VA, 02-06; p 06-

PO Box 1538, King George, VA 22485 – 540-775-2975   James River
E-mail: dave@gracekg.com
Grace Presbyterian Church – 540-775-9990

Berg, Andrew Christman – b Coral Gables, FL, Nov 6, 60; f Charles F. Jr.; m Marjorie Watson; w Carol Sue Franklin, Greenville, SC, May 21, 83; chdn Jessica Erin, Lindsey Elise, Chelsea Eden, Reece Christman; OHWU 78-79; FurU 79-82, BA; CTS 82-86; L 84, SFL Pby; O Sept 86, Gr Pby; ascp First P Ch, Hattiesburg, MS, 86-88; ss Columbia P Ch, Columbia, MS, 88-89, p 89-95, wc 95-; ob Harvest Ministries Camp & Conference, 96-00, wc 00-10; ascp Grace P Ch, Cookeville, TN, 11-

610 Rolling Meadows Lane, Rickman, TN 38580 – 931-397-9952   Nashville
E-mail: acberg@ymail.com
Grace Presbyterian Church – 931-537-6400

Berger, Keith H. – b Wilmington, DE; f Howard P.; m Katherine Louise Young; w Mary Paige Vann, Corinth, MS, Jan 3, 98; DukeU 90, BS; RTS 99, MDiv; O Jun 27, 99, SELA Pby; campm RUF, 99-

2913 Hartwood Drive, Fort Worth, TX 76109-1238 – 225-819-9561   Southern Louisiana
E-mail: kberger@ruf.org
PCA Reformed University Fellowship – 225-336-0072

Bergey, Ronald L. – b Sellersville, PA, Jan 27, 48; f Lester L; m Edna Gehman; w Francine M. Bejrach, Jerusalem, Israel, Sept 2, 76; chdn Natacha Nicole, Danya Carole, David Christian, Caroline Rebecca, Jérémie Nathan; PhilCB 71-75, BS; IHLS 75-78, MA; HebUJ 76-78; UPA 79; DrU 79-83, PhD; O Apr 24, 87, PacNW Pby; adj prof IHLS, 78-79; adj prof FTS, 80-82; assoc prof, AcadDn WRS, 83-87;

Bergey, Ronald L., continued
mis MTW, Aix-en-Provence, France, 88-16; prof formerly FLTR now FacJeanCalvin 91-17; contr *NAS Study Bible*, Introd and Notes to Micah and Song of Solomon; *The Book of Esther's Position in the Linguistic Milieu of Post-Exilic Biblical Hebrew Prose*, 83, "Late Linguistic Features in Esther," 84, "Post-Exilic Hebrew Linguistic Developments in Esther," 88; "La Prophecie d'Esaie 7:14-16," 95; "The Rhetorical Role of Reiteration in the 4th Servant Song, Is 52:13-53:12," 97; "Litterature et Theologie dans le Pentateuque," 99; contr *English Standard Version*; "Le Role de la famille dans L'Ancien Testament," 01; :L'Ancien Testament: evolutinos majeures au XXe siecle et perspective d'avenir au XXIe siècle," (Pentateuque et Prophetes), 01; "Livres historiques et Ecrits," 02; "The Song of Moses (Dt 32) and Isaianic Prophecies: A Case of Early Intertextuality," 02; "La conquête de Canaan: un génocide?" RR, 03; "L'unité des frères: une méditation sur le Ps 133," RR, 03; "Le cantique de Moïse: son reflet dans le prisme du canon des Ecritures," RR, 03; "Sang," "Dictionnaire de Théologie Biblique" Excelsis, 06; *English Standard Version Study Bible*: Introd and Notes on Ruth; "Le credo de Jonas dans le récit de la tempête sur a mer, une analyse structurelle de Jonas 1, 4-16," "Texte et historicité, Récit biblique et histoire," 06; "La célébration de la sexualité: le Cantique des cantiques," "Bible et sexualite," 05; "Des méditations sur la pertinence du sabbat pour le Chrétien" *RR*, 58:2 (07); Bible translation, *Segond 21*, 07; translation consultant for the OT; *Segond 21* Bible d'étude (Study Bible) 07, study notes for some OT books; "'Qu'il habite dans les tentes de Sem' (Gn 9.27) et la promesse tripartite," *RR*, 08; Election dans le Deutéronome, *RR*, 08; "Ps 23: réactualisation de la grande redemption," *RR*, 08; *Grand Dictionnaire Biblique*: "Pentateuque," 09; "Pathologie et guérison spirituelle," *RR*, 10; "La confession des péchés dans les lois sur les sacrifices,'' *RR*, 12; 'Les parents comme médiateurs de l'alliance dans le Deutéronome,'' *RR*, 12; 'Vrais et faux prophètes,'' *RR*, 12; "Jonah, Prophet Struggling with YHWH's Mercy" in *The Lion Has Roared, Theological Themes in the Prophetic Literature of the Old Testament*, 12; "Joseph et ses frères," 13; "La fin cauchemardesque du livre d'Esaïe" RR, 14; "Les grandes lignes unissant l'Ancien et le Nouveau Testament" RR, 15; "Dieu peut-il commander d'aimer"? RR, 16; *Découvrir Dieu à travers le Pentateuque*, 16

4 Rue Reine Jeanne, 13100 Aix-en-Provence, FRANCE – 011-442-66-13-08 Pacific Northwest
E-mail: Ronald.bergey@orange.fr
HR

Bergman, Brent Allen – ORU 99, BA; CTS 02, MDiv; astp Covenant P Ch, Sebring, FL, 06; p Grace Comm Ch, Palm Harbor, FL, 07-

1312 Vermont Avenue, Tarpon Springs, FL 34689 Southwest Florida
E-mail: faithkeeper77@juno.com
Grace Community Church – 727-789-2124

Berman, Beau Jason – b Orange County, CA, Aug 23, 73; f Bruce; w Shannon Sivertsen, Nov 3, 01; chdn Brodie Jacob, Sutton Elizabeth, Scout Marie; UAR 96, BA; DTS 04, MA, 09, ThM; O Nov 10, NoTX Pby; ascp RiverOaks P Ch Tulsa, OK, 10-15; op Ethos P Msn, Tulsa, OK, 14; p 14-

7122 East 86th Street, Tulsa, OK 74133 – 918-494-2626 Hills and Plains
E-mail: bberman111@gmail.com
Ethos Presbyterian Church

Bernard, Brandon – w Aimee; chdn Flora, Owen, Violet; BayU 98, BBA; WSCAL 05, MDiv; O Sept 27, 15, SLA Pby; p Westminster P Ch, Baton Rouge, LA, 15-

3701 Jones Creek Road, Baton Rouge, LA 70816 Southern Louisiana
E-mail: bbernard1517@gmail.com
Westminster Presbyterian Church – 225-753-0600

Bernardes, Renato DeSouza – b Brazil, Mar 24, 49; f A.; m E. DeSouza; w Claudia DaSilva Lopes, Rutherford, NJ, Jul 7, 73; chdn Rebecca, Renato, Rachel; MonSC, BA; PTS 83, MDiv; L Sept 80, Pby of Newark (PCUSA); O Oct 29, 85, Pby of Newark (PCUSA); Recd PCA Nov 18, 89; ydir St. Paul's P Ch, Newark, NJ, 79-81, ap 84-87; astp Comunidade Crista Presbiteriana, Newark, NJ, 89-93, srp 93-

152 High Street, Perth Amboy, NJ 08861-4711 – 732-826-3909 Metropolitan New York
E-mail: renato@ccpnewark.com
Comunidade Crista Presbiteriana – 973-465-2126

MINISTERIAL DIRECTORY

Berry, Chuck – b Wilmington, DE, Dec 6, 59; f Albert Charles; m Freida Hull; w Amy Lynn Harrington, Columbia, SC, Aug 11, 90; chdn Addi Melissa, Emily Michele, Anna Elisabeth; UDE, BS; CBS 97, MDiv; O Jul 15, 98, CentFL Pby; int Cornerstone P Ch, Columbia, SC, 86-90; ydir New Cov P Ch, Manning, SC, 87; ydir Seven Rivers P Ch, Lecanto, FL, 92-98, astp 98-99; op Nature Coast Comm Ch, Homosassa, FL, 99-01, wc 01-02; astp Orangewood P Ch, Maitland, FL, 03-07; p CrossPoint Comm Ch, Boone, NC, 08-18; astp Orangewood P Ch, Maitland, FL, 18-

170 Nestle Road, Boone, NC 28607 – 828-355-9387   Central Florida
Orangewood Presbyterian Church – 407-539-1500

Berry, Mark – w Lori; chdn Emmett, Anna, Taylor, Abigail, Hadassah; VandU 88, BA, 90, MBA; CTS 99, MDiv; O Jul 00, Nash Pby; mis MTW, Peru, 01-16; HMA 10-11; ob16-

17015 Lakota Drive, Spring Hill, TN 37174 – 615-939-0723   Nashville
E-mail: mberry@serge.org

Bert, Luke Barnabas – O Oct 20, 17, Ecan Pby, ob 17-

726 113e Rue, Shawinigan-Sud, QC G9P 2W7 Canada – 819-852-8262   Eastern Canada
E-mail: Lukeb.bert@gmail.com

Bertalan, Edward Frank – b Washington, DC, Mar 22, 48; f Frank J.; m Helen Scheck; w Raby, Knoxville, TN, Dec 14, 74; chdn Marianne, Amy, Virginia; USNA; UOK 71, BME; DTS; RTS 81, MDiv; O Aug 15, 81, SoTX Pby; op, p Heritage P Ch, Corpus Christi, TX, 81-83, wc 84; op, p Arlington P Ch, Arlington, TX, 85-88; op Chaparral Hills P Ch, San Diego, CA, 88-91, wc 91-92; op, p Lakeside P Ch, North Richland Hills, TX, 92-96; ascp Second P Ch, Memphis, TN, 96-00; op King of Glory Ch, Miami, FL, 00-02; astp Granada P Ch, Coral Gables, FL, 01-02; astp Christ Cov P Ch, Knoxville, TN, 02-04; p Christ Comm P Ch, Clearwater, FL, 04-06; hr 09; ascp Centerpoint Comm Ch, Ocala, FL, 11-

6859 SE 12th Circle, Ocala, FL 34480   Central Florida
E-mail: EdBertalan@yahoo.com
Centerpoint Community Church – 352-369-4422
HR

Bertrand, J. Mark – b Lake Charles, LA; f David P.; m Judith C. Cossey; w Laurie Ann Bertrand, Houston, TX, Mar 16, 96; UnU 91, BA; UHou 00, MA; O Feb 14, 17, Siouxl Pby; p Grace P Ch, Sioux Falls, SD, 17-; *Rethinking Worldview*, 07

2007 South Phillips Avenue, Sioux Falls, SD 57105 – 605-271-6323   Siouxlands
E-mail: jmb@jmarkbertrand.com
Grace Presbyterian Church – 605-201-6444

Best, Louis – w Shirley; chdn Philip, Deborah; MITech 70, BS; Middlebury 85, MA; Argentine Defense 97, MA (ABT); CTS 04, MDiv; O Feb 5, 05, NoTX Pby; op Hill Country P Msn, Harker Heights, TX, 05-18; hr 18

3907 Bella Vista Loop, Harker Heights, TX 76548 – 254-698-4950   North Texas
E-mail: LNSBEST@embarqmail.com
HR

Betters, Charles F. – b Pittsburgh, PA, Jan 16, 48; f Lawrence; m Florence Ginand; w Sharon Watts, Red Lion, DE, Jan 25, 69; chdn Heidi, Charles, Daniel, Mark (d); UDE 65-69, BA; ETS 69-72, MDiv; CTS 98, DMin; O Jul 70, EPA Conf; Recd PCA Feb 86, DMV Pby; p Wissahickon Ch, 69-72; p Logan Ch, 72-76; p Red Lion Evan Ch, 76-86; srp Reach Ch Summit Bridge Road, Bear, DE, 86-14; fndr MARCINC

Betters, Charles F., continued
Ministries; p CenterPoint Ch, Clayton, DE, 09; ascp Reach Ch Summit Bridge Rd, Bear, DE, 14-; op Reach Ch Fair Hill, Elkton, MD, 15-; *Treasures of Faith*, P&R Pub, 98

5 Chesapeake Drive, Bear, DE 19701-1608 – 302-834-8564   Heritage
E-mail: drbetters@grpc.org
Reach Church Summit Bridge Road – 302-834-4772
Reach Church Fair Hill – 443-406-3209

Betters, Charles L. – O Oct 14, Hrtg Pby; srp Reach Ch Summit Bridge Rd, Bear, DE, 14-; op Reach Ch Red Lion, Bear, DE, 15-

Reach Church Summit Bridge Road – 302-834-4772   Heritage
Reach Church Red Lion

Betters, Daniel Andrew – b Philadelphia, PA, Nov 19, 75; f Charles ; m Sharon Eleanor Watts; w Laura Elizabeth Gould, Bear, DE, Jun 10, 00; chdn Emma, Caleb, Evangeline, Miriam Siddhi, Jovan; UDE 98, BA; RTS 07, MAR; O Mar 25, 07, Hrtg Pby; yp Glasgow Ref P Ch, Bear, DE, 98-10, ascp 07-10; p The Town (form Stone's Throw), Middletown, DE, 11-

105 Brooks Drive, Middletown, DE 19709 – 302-547-4498   Heritage
E-mail: dan@thetown.org
The Town – 302-464-5782

Bianco, Joseph – w Camden; chdn Elisha John, Elorah Joy; O Aug 21, 16, Pitts Pby; astp City Ref P Ch, Pittsburgh, PA, 16-

2147 Fairland Street, Pittsburgh, PA 15210 – 412-651-2681   Pittsburgh
City Reformed Presbyterian Church – 412-720-7014

Bick, Sung Bong – p Atlanta Nam Yang Ch, Snellville, GA, 04-

Atlanta Nam Yang Church – 770-982-2964   Korean Southeastern

Bickley, Stephen P. – b Chicago, IL, Nov 22, 52; f Edward Arthur; m Phyllis Marian; w Maureen Anne O'Rourke, South Holland, IL, Aug 27, 77; chdn Erin Jean, Will Edward, Hugh Francis; TayU; ILSU 74, BS; TEDS 78, MDiv; L Sept 78; O Mar 81; p Internat'l P Ch, London, 80-86; The Proclamation Trust, London, 86-88; op Lakeside P Ch, Wales, WI, 88-91, p 91-92; p Trinity P Ch, Rochester, MN, 93-00; op Providence Comm Ch, Victoria, BC, 09-10; srp 10-17

12823 Arbor Lakes Parkway N, Maple Grove, MN 55369 CANADA – 250-686-7316   Western Canada
E-mail: spbickley@hotmail.com

Biese, Ryan F. – b St. Louis, MO, Aug 22, 86; f Charles; m Shawn; w Ann Catherine Howard, May 14, 11; chdn Dabney Virginia Caroline, Thornwell Charles Hugh; GroCC 09, BA; RTS 13, MDiv; L Gr Pby Sept 12, MSVal Pby May 13; O Aug 11, 13, MSVal Pby; p First P Ch at Winona, Winona, MS, 13-

501 Whitehead Drive, Winona, MS 39867 – 769-610-5132   Mississippi Valley
E-mail: rfbiese@gmail.com
First Presbyterian Church at Winona – 662-283-2487

Biggs, Martin S.C. (Mike) – b Jackson, MS, May 28, 59; f Robert A. Jr.; m Lady Rachel Conner; w Janna Lynn Weeks, Canton, MS, Jul 12, 86; UMS 81, BA; RTS 87, MDiv, 87, MCE; L Sept 17, 84, MSVal Pby; O Sept 13, 87, Cov Pby; campm RUM, UAR, 87-94; campm RUM, NMSU, 94-01; chp, op Christ the King P Ch, Norman, OK, 01-05, p 05-

PO Box 720552, Norman, OK 73070 – 405-701-3014   Hills and Plains
E-mail: mbiggs@ctknorman.com
Christ the King Presbyterian Church – 405-364-6722

MINISTERIAL DIRECTORY   51

Billings, Oliver George – b Long Branch, NJ, Sept 20, 55; f Robert Edward; m Elizabeth Quinn; w Debra Dawn Cook, Haddonfield, NJ, Jun 29, 85; chdn Joshua George, Jenna Louise; RoC 78, BA; REpS 85, MDiv; L Nov 85; O Apr 86, NJ Pby; ap Kresson Bib Ch, Voorhees, NJ (Ind), 86-88; Chap Intern DSH, New Castle, DE, 88; Chap Resident PMC, Phil, PA, 88-89; Sr. Chap CCHS, Christiana Hosp, Newark, DE, 89-; mbr College of Chaplains, Mar 92; Boad Cert Chap Assoc of Prof Chap, Feb 96; Mod Her Pby, 96

130 Wortham Lane, Bear, DE 19701 – 302-836-0511   Heritage
E-mail: gbillings@christianacare.org
CCHS, Christiana Hospital, Newark, DE

Billingslea, David – O Sept 30, 18, NoTX Pby; campm RUF, 18-

501 South Weathered Drive, Richardson, TX 75080 – 719-640-5029   North Texas
E-mail: david.billingslea@gmail.com
PCA Reformed University Fellowship

Bills, Dennis – b Huntington, WV, Dec 7, 70; w Kathi Jo Scarlett; chdn Josiah Eldon, Adoniram Taylor, Spencer Thomas; BJU 93, BA, 95, MA; CC 08, MEd; O Oct 25, 08, NR Pby; p Winifrede P Ch, Winifrede, WV, 08-12; p Trinity P Ch, New Martinsville, WV, 12-

716 Park Avenue, New Martinsville, WV 26155 – 304-398-4173   New River
E-mail: dbills@adoniram.net
Trinity Presbyterian Church – 304-455-3690

Bindewald, David Anthony – b Greenville, SC, Dec 8, 51; f Richard A.; m Jane Hunter Simpson; w Barbara Jane Bly, Durham, NC, Dec 29, 73; chdn David A., Erin Elizabeth; UNC 73, BA; CBS 86, MDiv; L Jul 23, 85, Palm Pby; O Aug 2, 87, Palm Pby; ap Northeast P Ch, Columbia, SC, 87-88; ob mis SEND Int, Tokyo, Japan, 88-95; mis MTW, 95-98; astp Lexington P Ch, Lexington, SC, 98-02, ascp 02-12; mis MTW 12-14; astp Lexington P Ch, Lexington, SC, 14-17; hr 17

116 York Road, Cranberry Township, PA 16066 – 803-354-6254   Palmetto
E-mail: davidbindewald1@gmail.com
HR

Binion, Robert Ernest, Jr – Atlanta, GA, Feb 19, 87; w Michelle Elizabeth; chdn Elizabeth Belle; astp McLean P Ch, McLean, VA, 15-17; p New Song P Ch, Salt Lake City, UT, 17-

443 East Hollywood Avenue, Salt Lake City, UT 84115 – 404-513-5761   Northern California
E-mail: binion.robert.e@gmail.com
New Song Presbyterian Church

Binnie, Phillip Baird – b Chicago, IL, Jun 19, 52; f George P.; m Mina Cumming; w Deborah Wallis, St. Louis, MO, Jul 31, 82; chdn Alexina Alonso, Naomi Marie, Thomas Baird, Emily Ruth; USF 74, BA; CTS 81, MDiv, 97, DMin; L 81, MO Pby (RPCES); O 83, St. Louis Pby; Swiss L'Abri, 74-77; Dutch L'Abri, 83-84; Swiss L'abri, 84-86; Chap VAMC, Tampa, FL, 86-88; Chap Supvsr Miami VA Healthcare System, 89-; astp Granada P Ch, Coral Gables, FL, 02-

5801 SW 63rd Court, Miami, FL 33143-2151 – 786-247-9200   South Florida
E-mail: phil@granadapca.org
Miami VA Healthcare System – 305-575-7000 ext. 4079
Granada Presbyterian Church – 305-444-8435

Birch, Jeffrey Richard – b Queens, NY, Mar 4, 62; f Richard; m Dana Dodge; w Evelyn Powell, Thornton, PA, Jun 25, 88; chdn Joel Andrew; WChSC 84, BA; WTS 90, MDiv; O Jun 10, 90; Recd PCA May 8, 93, Phil Pby; ob astp Church of the Good Shepherd, Yeadon, PA (ind), 86-90; ob ascp Church of

Birch, Jeffrey Richard, continued
the Good Shepherd, Yeadon, PA, 90; ob srp Church of the Good Shepherd, Yeadon, PA, 91-96; astp Heritage P Ch, Edmond, OK, 96-98, ascp 98-02; op Edmond Comm Ch, Edmond, OK, 01-02; p Spruce Creek P Ch, Port Orange, FL, 02-

1705 Taylor Road, Port Orange, FL 32128 – 386-761-2902   Central Florida
E-mail: jeff.birch88@gmail.com
Spruce Creek Presbyterian Church – 386-761-2902

Birchler, George – b Sparta, IL, Jan 20, 48; f Robert O.; m Gertrude Woodside; w Darlene Boenker, Youngstown, OH, Dec 29, 70; chdn Jonathan Bruce, Daniel Kurt, Timothy Robert, Heidi Joy; CC 70, BA; WTS 73, MDiv; L Apr 73, Phil Pby (RPCES); O Jun 74, FL Pby (RPCES); p Grace P Ch, Pinellas Park, FL, 74-81; ob AcadDn, instr ConoCS; ascp Bible P Ch of Cono Center, Walker, IA, 01-02; p Woodland Heights P Ch, Selma, AL, 02-13; sc War Pby, 04-08; hr 14

1300 Sherwood Street SE #114, Hutchinson, MN 55350 – 334-327-6821   Siouxlands
E-mail: georgebirchler@att.net
HR

Birkett, John O. – TCC 90, BA; CTS 93, MDiv; L Apr 24, 93, PacNW Pby; O Aug 28, 94, Ill Pby; int Faith P Ch, Tacoma, WA, 93-94; p Christ P Ch, Owensboro, KY, 94-

3100 Hill Gail Court, Owensboro, KY 42303 – 270-684-0597   Illiana
E-mail: christpca@juno.com
Christ Presbyterian Church – 270-685-3055

Bisgrove, David – astp Redeemer P Ch of New York, New York, NY, 04-11; ascp 11-17; srp Redeemer P Ch Westside, New York, NY, 17-

130 West 86th Street #2A, New York, NY 10024   Metropolitan New York
E-mail: david@redeemer.com
Redeemer Presbyterian Church Westside – 212-808-4460

Bishop, Curran – b Gainesville, GA, Dec 14, 79; f Robert M.; m Christine Matta; w Abigail Hudson, Brevard, NC, Mar 23, 03; chdn Eleanor Rose, Hudson Davis, John Curran, Peter Knox; CC 02, BA; CTS 10, MDiv; ConcS, PhD cand; O Feb 13, Ill Pby; p Grace P Ch, Carbondale, IL, 13-17; astp Christ P Ch, New Haven, CT, 18-, op Christ P Ch, Milford, CT, 18-

51 Housatonic Avenue, Milford, CT 06460 – 203-812-9928   Southern New England
E-mail: curran.bishopo@cpcmilford.org
Christ Presbyterian Church – 203-777-6960
Christ Presbyterian Church

Bissell, Brad Thomas – b Barrington, IL, Feb 26, 91; f Robert; m Ruth Mary O'Donnell; w Allison Laura Bissell, Rochester, NY, Dec 21, 13; chdn Caleb Thomas; GetC 12, BA; CTS 17, MDiv; O Feb 26, 17, MNY Pby; astp Redeemer Ch of Montclair, Montclair, NJ, 16-

23 N Willow Street, Montclair, NJ 07042 – 732.440.7547   Metropolitan New York
E-mail: Brad@RedeemerMontclair.com
Redeemer Church of Montclair – 973-233-0388

Bitterman, Chris – b Lancaster, PA, Jan 21, 63; f Chester Allen, Jr.; m Mary Herr Witmer; w Ginger Lopp; chdn Lynette Kay, Chris Edward, Jr., William Elliot, Valerie Ann; CBC 86, BA; RTSNC 06, MATS; L Mar 07, PTri Pby; astp Meadowview Ref P Ch, Lexington, NC, 07-08, srp 08-

1 Graceway Drive, Lexington, NC 27295 – 336-357-2914   Piedmont Triad
E-mail: CBitterman@meadowviewpca.org
Meadowview Reformed Presbyterian Church – 336-249-2680

MINISTERIAL DIRECTORY 53

Bitzer, Richard Paul – b Baltimore, MD, May 2, 47; f William Jennings; m Cora Rebecca Anderson; w Lynda Sue Vincent, Baltimore, MD, Jun 19, 71; chdn Lindsay Rebecca, Alexander James; UB 70, BA; GCTS 79, MDiv; L Mar 31, 79, DMV Pby; O Nov 11, 79, DMV Pby; ap Evangelical P Ch, Baltimore, MD, 79-82; p Munson Hill Ch, Falls Church, VA, 82-88; ob t AAChSc, 88-, wc 88-95

314 Hilltop Drive, Huddleston, VA 24104-3127 – 410-980-3515   Chesapeake
Annapolis Area Christian School

Bivans, William John – b Miami, FL, Feb 17, 50; f Ernest L.; m Marjorie Burns; w Peta Joan Gudgeon, Key Biscayne, FL, Feb 19, 71; chdn Sarah Nell, Stephen Matthew, Ruth Marion, Joshua Edward, John Calvin, Anna Elizabeth; UFL 74, BS; GCTS 77, MDiv; O Dec 18, 77, Congaree Pby (PCUS); p Richland Ch, Eastover, SC, 77-80; ap Covenant P Ch, Columbia, SC, 80-81; p Fellowship P Ch, Greer, SC, 81-88; ac dir Bethany Christian Services, SC, 88; p Countryside P Ch, Cameron, NC, 88-94; op Sandhills P Ch, Southern Pines, NC, 90-93; op Christ Comm P Msn, Cameron, NC, 94-00; chp Brunswick Co, NC, 00-03; astp Cross Creek P Ch, Fayetteville, NC, 03-16; hr 16

1241 U.S. Highway 1, Cameron, NC 28326-7965 – 910-245-3357   Central Carolina
E-mail: billbivans@gmail.com
HR

Bjerkaas, Robert A. – b Champaigne, IL, Jul 10, 68; f Allan Wayne; m Judith Louise Egstad; w Kerrie Beth Williams, Columbia, MD, May 31, 97; chdn Christopher Jay, Margaret Elizabeth, Timothy James, Nathaniel Robert; UMD 90, BA, 96, BA; ChTS 98, MDiv; RTSFL 05, ThM; L Dec 3, 94, OPC; O Sept 17, 99, NoE pby, PCA; p Trinity P Ch, St. Albans, VT, 99-06; p Church in the Canyon, Calabasas, CA, 07-; "'And Adam Called His Wife's Name Eve:' A Study in Authentic Biblical Manhood," *Journal for the Biblical Study of Manhood & Womanhood*, Spring (07)

6266 Tamarind Street, Oak Park, CA 91377   Pacific
E-mail: pastor@churchinthecanyon.org
Church in the Canyon – 818-880-2060

Bjerke, Aaron – asrp Redeemer P Ch of New York, New York, NY, 13-

110 East End Avenue, Apt. 10A, New York, NY 10028   Metropolitan New York
E-mail: aaron.bjerke@redeemer.com
Redeemer Presbyterian Church of New York – 212-808-4460

Black, John – RTSNC 04, MDiv; O May 05, Palm Pby; p Andrews P Ch, Andrews, SC, 05-06; p Second Street P Ch, Albemarle, NC, 06-

522 Lynn Road, Oakboro, NC 28129-7760 – 704-485-8257   Central Carolina
E-mail: jcblack@hotmail.com
Second Street Presbyterian Church – 704-982-6824

Blalack, Mark Jerome – b Kennesaw GA, Dec 26, 70; f Jerome Blalack; m Daisy Ellen Blackwell; w Amy Dianne Barksdale, Marietta GA, Jan 4, 97; chdn Patrick Robert, Caroline Joy; KSU, BS; RTSNC 98-02, MDiv; O Jul 20, 03, TNVall Pby; astp West Hills P Ch, Knoxville, TN, 03-05; p Harmony P Ch, Kingsport, TN, 07-

1601 Fairfield Avenue, Kingsport, TN 37664   Westminster
E-mail: mjblalack@hotmail.com
Harmony Presbyterian Church – 423-288-4021

Bland, James Christian III – b Washington, DC, Jul 27, 41; f James C. Jr; m Isabel Marshall; w Linda McGeary, Hyattsville, MD, Dec 21, 68; chdn Cynthia Elisabeth(Smith), Karen Melissa(Drake), Geary Christian; UMD 59-64, BS, 65-67, grad wk; GCTS 67-70, MDiv; WTS 86, DMin; O Sept 13, 70, Evgld Pby (PCUS); ap Coral Ridge P Ch, Ft. Lauderdale, FL, 70-73; p First P Ch, Gadsden, AL, 73-78;

Bland, James Christian III, continued
p Kendall P Ch, Miami, FL, 78-87; op Bay Area P Ch, Webster, TX, 87-88, srp 88-98; bd trust WTS, 80-; coord MNA, 98-16; lect WTS, 07-; adj prof Redeemer Sem, 12-; hr 18; astp Grace Comm Ch (Mission), Buford, GA, 18-; contr ed, *This is the Life*; *Miracles of Christ and Their Spiritual Application*; contr *Pastor/Evangelist; Studies in the Miracles of Christ*

1998 American Way, Lawrenceville, GA 30043 – 678-376-0165   Georgia Foothills
E-mail: jcblandiii@outlook.com
Grace Community Church Mission – 678-699-0586
HR

 Blankenship, Kirk Mitchell – w Michelle; chdn Kenny, Naomi, Lydia, Jason; MaryWashC 98, BS; RTS 06, MDiv; astp Meadowview Ref P Ch, Lexington, NC, 09-12; ascp 13-18; p Pilgrim P Ch, Martinsburg, WV, 18-

110 Peregrine Road, Martinsburg, WV 25405   Potomac
E-mail: kblank@pilgrimpca.org
Pilgrim Presbyterian Church – 304-263-5362

 Bledsoe, Allan – astp First P Ch, Prattville, AL, 14-18; ascp 18-

171 Twelve Oaks Lane, Prattville, AL 36066   Southeast Alabama
E-mail: allan@fpcministries.org
First Presbyterian Church – 334-365-6387

 Bledsoe, Richard William – b Tacoma, WA, Sept 13, 49; f Marx Arba; m Irma Lucille McCart; w Carla Brahe, Boulder, CO, Apr 24, 76; chdn Alwen Grace, Ian Owen, Jamie Richard Luke; CSU 72, BA; WTS, MDiv; L Sept 85, SW Pby; O Sept 86, SW Pby; p Tree of Life P Ch, Boulder, CO, 86-06; hr 18

4680 Ashfield Drive, Boulder, CO 80301-4014 – 303-530-4251   Rocky Mountain
E-mail: revbledsoe@yahoo.com
HR

 Blevins, John, III – O Nov 15, 15, TNVal Pby; ascp Covenant P Ch, Oak Ridge, TN, 15-

2613 Silent Springs Lane, Knoxville, TN 37931   Tennessee Valley
E-mail: john.blevins.3rd@gmail.com; www.johnblevinsiii.com
Covenant Presbyterian Church – 865-483-9888

 Blevins, Philip Reid – b Bristol, VA, Jun 27, 49; f Denver L.; m Ann Czarnocki; w Carlen R. Davis, Jackson, MS, Sept 23, 78; chdn Philip Nathan, Clinton Rowntree, Seth Upham, Knox Denver; GBibC 75, BA; RTS 79, MDiv, 79, MCE; ConcS; RTS 86, ThM; EvCU 94, DMin; L Oct 80; O Feb 81, So Pby (RPCES); p Carolina P Ch, Philadelphia, MS, 83-95, wc 95-; ss Concord P Ch, Pickens, MS, 96-97; pres GBibC, 97-15; hr 15

57 Abbie Lane, Bristol, TN 37620-3101 – 423-652-0828   Westminster
HR

 Bloodworth, Marion Lee Jr. – b Durham, NC, Dec 1, 54; f M. L. Sr; m Lillian Rollins; w Eliana Blackwell, Jackson, MS, Jun 28, 86; chdn Adriana Lee, Alyse Eliana; NCSt 79, BEd; RTS 85, MDiv; L Feb 86, MSVal Pby; O Jun 25, 89, Gr Pby; int Independent P Ch, Savannah, GA, 86-87; ss Philadelphus P Ch, Waynesboro, MS, 88-89, p 89-96; p First P Ch, Indianola, MS, 96-02; ss Covenant P Ch, Montgomery, AL, 02-03, p 03-; prof BhamTS, 06-

509 Wakefield Drive, Montgomery, AL 36109 – 334-244-2454   Southeast Alabama
E-mail: covenantpcmgm@bellsouth.net
Covenant Presbyterian Church – 334-272-1133

MINISTERIAL DIRECTORY

Blosser, Greg – op Grace Central P Msn, Columbus, OH, 04-08; p Grace Central P Ch 08-

372 East Weber Road, Columbus, OH 43202 – 614-447-9744   Columbus Metro
E-mail: Greg@gracecentral.org
Grace Central Presbyterian Church – 614-299-0919

Bluhm, Luke – O Aug 14, 16, Pitts Pby; ascp Kiski Valley P Ch, Leechburg, PA, 16-

434 1/2 Pitt Street, Leechburg, PA 15656 – 440-591-2561   Pittsburgh
Kiski Valley Presbyterian Church – 724-845-1280

Bobell, Michael – w Sarah, Aug 26, 06; ILSU 01, BS; CTS 08, MDiv; O Nov 08, MNY Pby; astp Grace Redeemer Ch, Glen Rock, NJ, 08-10; p New Life P Ch, Maryland Heights, MO, 18-

10640 Clarendon Avenue, St. Louis, MO 63114   Missouri
E-mail: pastornlpc@gmail.com
New Life Presbyterian Church – 314-205-1225

Bobo, Jason – b Houston, TX, Nov 17, 77; f Donnie; m Zuma Brinkman; w Tiffany D. Fraser, Gridley, CA, Jun 9, 76; chdn Cason Staples, Justus Ryle Reuel, Shaylee Preston, Garrison Keith; GrCC 00, BA; 08, MDiv; O, SoBapt; Recd PCA 10, SW Pby; campm RUF, AZSt, 10-12; ob VP Redeemer Sem, Dallas, TX, 12-14; astp Christ P Ch, Tulsa, OK, 14-16, ascp 16-

5120 South Columbia Place, Tulsa, OK 74105 – 214-862-2861   Hills and Plains
E-mail: jasonlbobo@gmail.com
Christ Presbyterian Church – 918-749-1629

Bobo, Jesse Ray – b Atlanta, GA, Jun 30, 46; f Thomas Watson Sr.; m Frances Denman; w Wanda Marie Casey, Roswell, GA , Nov 22, 80; BJU 66-71, BA; UHH 72; HLC 73; MSC 87; RTS 86-90, MDiv; L 84, NGA Pby; O Jan 20, 91, Gr Pby; ip Marshville, NC , 71-72; prin HICS, 73-76; fndr, exec dir Salacoa Refuge, Inc., Salacoa, GA, 89-11; p Heidelberg P Ch, Heidelberg, MS, 90-05; p Roebuck P Ch, Roebuck, SC, 05-15; hr

313 Abbey Court, Canton, GA 30115 – 770-213-8866   Northwest Georgia
E-mail: raybobo@juno.com
HR

Bobos, Kyle – O May 17, 09, HouMet Pby; astp Grace P Ch, The Woodlands, TX, 09-

14203 Irvine Ranch Trail, Conroe, TX 77384 – 936-520-8347   Houston Metro
E-mail: kyle@gracewoodlands.org
Grace Presbyterian Church – 281-296-0911

Boden, Craig Lawrence Woodliff – b Gadsden, AL, Mar 23, 49; f Warren; m Julia Woodliff; w Susan Foster, Gadsden, AL, Apr 8, 71; chdn Brecca Ann (Cleveland), John Bradley; AU 75, BS; BhamTS 84, MDiv; UAB 97, MAC, 98, EdS; L 84, Evan Pby; O 85, TNVal Pby; p West Hills P Ch, Harriman, TN, 85-89; astp Covenant P Ch, Birmingham, AL, 89- 12, hr 12; astp Rainbow P Ch, Rainbow City, AL, 15-16

174 Sandy Shores Lane, Rainbow City, AL 35906 – 256-442-8989   Evangel
E-mail: cbodenlpc@gmail.com
HR

Bogue, Carl W. Jr. – b Vincennes, IN, Dec 8, 39; f Carl W; m Jessie Mae Parker; w Rosalie Ruth Maffett (d); Deborah Ann Feil, Dec 3, 04; chdn Katherine Anne (Chapman), Andrew Jonathan, Elizabeth Lynne, Sarah Suzanne (Coombes); MuskC 57-61, BA; PittsTS 62-65, MDiv; Drs, FrUAmst 65-69, 75, ThD; L Jun 24, 65, Vincennes Pby (UPCUSA); O Nov 2, 69, Cleveland Pby (UPCUSA); p Allenside UPCUSA, Akron, OH, 69-75; p Faith P Ch, Akron, OH, 75-07, hr 07; auth *Jonathan Edwards and the Covenant of*

Bogue, Carl W. Jr., continued
Grace (repub 09); *Hole in the Dike: Critical Aspects of Berkouwer's Theology*; contr *Inerrancy and the Church, The Scriptural Law of Worship*; contr *Soli Deo Gloria: Essays in Reformed Theology* contr *God & Politics: Four Views on the Reformation of Civil Government*; ed *Bible Building Blocks*

16234 North 102nd Way, Scottsdale, AZ 85255-8603 – 480-656-6176   Ascension
E-mail: cwbogue@aol.com
HR

   Bohling, Matt – b Manhasset, NY, Jul 15, 71; f Kenneth T.; m Barbara Jean Jacobson; w Julianne Lee Bauer, San Diego, CA, Jul 20, 96; chdn Jacob, Jesse, Joseph, Joy; Coastal Car U 89-93, BS; WSCAL 96-01, MDiv; L Sept 19, 98, SoCst Pby; O May 19, 02, Pitts Pby; p Laurel Highlands P Ch, Latrobe, PA, 02-08; p Living Hope P Ch , Seattle, WA, 08-18; ob Flourish

3101 SW 105th Street, Seattle, WA 98146 – 206-713-7438   Pacific Northwest
E-mail: matthew.bohling@gmail.com

   Boidock, Robert D. – b Englewood, NJ, Feb 28, 49; f John S (d); m Susan MacDonald (d); w Mary L. Sandbom, Denver, CO, Dec 13, 75; chdn Benjamin, Allison, Katie, Michael; VPI 67-71, BS; RTS 90-93, MDiv; L May 93, War Pby; L Jun 93, Pitts Pby; O Oct 19, 93, Pitts Pby; op Washington P Ch, Washington, PA, 94-97, p 97-01; ascp Cornerstone P Ch, California, MD, 01-09; Chap USArmy; hr

3751 Maroneal Street, Houston, TX 77025   Potomac
E-mail: robert.boidock@gmail.com
HR

   Boland, Mike – astp City Ch - Eastside, Atlanta, GA, 15-

16 Kenyon Street SE, Atlanta, GA 30312   Metro Atlanta
E-mail: mike@citychurcheastside.org
City Church - Eastside – 404-856-0183

   Boland, Thomas J. – b Winthrop, MA, Nov 29, 57; f Thomas Joseph; m Roseann Pascarelli; w Kimberly Sue Waddell, Ft. Lauderdale, FL, Mar 6, 93; chdn Brock Thomas, Jenna Rose, Katie Anne, Zack William; FIU 88, BA; KTS 09, MDiv; O Aug 17, 08, SFL Pby; astp Coral Ridge P Ch, Ft. Lauderdale, FL, 06-12; op Cross Comm Ch of South Florida, Deerfield Beach, FL, 12-17; p 17-; Bible Studies: "David: A Man After God's Own Heart"; "The Beatitudes: Men of the Kingdom"; "Growing to Maturity"; "Focused Faith"

5730 NE 21st Road, Fort Lauderdale, FL 33308 – 954-300-9854   South Florida
Cross Community Church of South Florida – 954-300-9854

   Boles, John Ralph Jr. – b Montgomery, AL, Aug 25, 53; f John Sr; m Frankie McCall; w Janice Sue Kiewel, Santa Ana, CA, Jun 12, 82; chdn David, Jeffrey; AU 71-72; BelC 72-75, BA; CTS 76-77, MA; L Jul 11, 86, SEAL Pby; O Nov 13, 88, MO Pby; t music & Bible, Westminster Christ Acad, St. Louis, 76-79; ydir, mmus First P Ch, Prattville, AL, 80-88; astp/mmus Covenant P Ch, St. Louis, MO, 88-89; mmus Trinity UMC, Opelika, AL, 89-91; p Alta Vista P Ch, Sweetwater, TN, 91-96; p Christ P Ch, Sweetwater, TN, 96-98 (merger w/ 2 chs); ob fndr Primetime International, 98-00; ascp First P Ch, Montgomery, AL, 00-01, ob Ramsay Mem P Ch, Franklin AL, 01-03; p Hayneville P Ch, Hayneville, AL, 03-10; p Good Hope P Ch, Benton, AL, 03-10; p Lowndesboro P Ch, Lowndesboro, AL, 03-10; Chaplain, VistaCare Hospice, Montgomery, AL, 05-10;p First P Ch, Camden, AL, 10-; former ed publ *Ministry Ideas in Smaller Churches* (nwsltr)

416 Pine Street, Camden, AL 36726 – 334-407-0382   Warrior
E-mail: jbolesgsa@hotmail.com
First Presbyterian Church – 334-682-5253

MINISTERIAL DIRECTORY 57

Bolus, Michael David – b Omaha, NE, Jul 25, 36; f William Jack B. (d); m Pauline Tucker(d); w Elizabeth Swartwout, Yonkers, NY, Jun 10, 61; chdn Michael David Jr, Elizabeth Ruth; ETSU 59, BS; CIU 60-61; ColTS 65, MDiv; LRTS 81, DMin; O Jul 25, 65, Cher Pby (PCUS); p Mars Hill Ch, Acworth, GA, 65-67; p Inskip Ch, Knoxville, TN, 67-69; p Calvary Ch, Johnson City, TN, 70-72; ev PEF, 72-74; p Westminster P Ch, Roanoke, VA, 75-81; ap First P Ch, Macon, GA, 81-85; chmn Cred & Exam co, 83-85; p Thomson P Ch, Thomson, GA, 86-95; ob srp Grace Ch (ind), Bainbridge, GA,95-99; sec SJC co, 96-99, wc 99-00; p Hopewell P Ch, Rock Hill, SC, 00-18; TN Nat'l Guard, USAR, 54-63; overseas min India & Jamaica; *Our Wonderful Counselor*; *Living In His Presence*; tv min "The Hour of Hope"

742 Lynville Lane, Rock Hill, SC 29730 – 803-328-3574   Fellowship
E-mail: hopewellpca@comporium.net

Bolze, Mark – b Carlisle, PA; f Kenenth W.; m Norma; PASU 90, BS; RPTS 08, MDiv; O May 31, 09, Hrtg Pby; p Trinity P Ch, Newark, DE, 09-11; wc 11

215 Hillcrest Drive, Carlisle, PA 17013   Heritage
E-mail: mark.bolze@comcast.net

Bond, Harris – w Laura Beth; chdn Thomas, Samuel, Jane Paschal; AubU, BA; RTSNC, MDiv; O Nov 6, 05, MSVall Pby; astp First P Ch, Belzoni, MS, 05-08; p Knollwood P Ch, Sylacauga, AL, 08-

216 South Norton Avenue, Sylacauga, AL 45150 – 256-487-2730   Evangel
E-mail: harris.bond@gmail.com
Knollwood Presbyterian Church – 256-249-2648

Bond, Travis J. – w Sarah; chdn Alayna, Rachel, Sadie, Faith; GroCC, BS; RPTS, MDiv; astp New Hope P Ch, Monroeville, PA, 03-04; p Faith P Ch, Cheraw, SC, 04-10; ob p Medway Comm Ch, Medway, MA, 10-

11 Island Road, Franklin, MA 02038   Southern New England
E-mail: pastor.travis@medwaycc.org
Medway Community Church, Medway, MA

Bonds, Michael Timothy – b Tuscaloosa, AL, Oct 5, 53; f Horace George; m Mary Juanita Williams; w Penny Dianne Black, Tuscaloosa, AL, Jun 14, 80; chdn Michael Timothy Jr., Joanna Nicole, Daniel Luke; TrSU 86, BS; MSC 85, MEd; RTS 86, MDiv; O Oct 26, 86, MSVal Pby; p Wynndale P Ch, Terry, MS, 86-91; p First P Ch, Centreville, AL, 91-

106 Valley Street, Centreville, AL 35042-1233 – 205-926-9001   Warrior
First Presbyterian Church – 205-926-4261

Bone, Dennis – b Pasadena, CA, Sept 3, 54; f Norman; m Violet Purcell; w Deborah Ann Troxell, Warminster, PA, Aug 19, 78; chdn Brian David, Evan Charles; GlenJC 75; CC 78, BA; WTS 80, MAR, 81, MDiv; O Nov 82; Recd PCA 03, SoCst Pby; ob p Grace Covenant Church, Vista, CA, 96-

754 Lazy Circle Drive, Vista, CA 92081 – 760-726-2617   South Coast
E-mail: djbone4@cox.net
Grace Covenant Church, Vista, CA

Bonham, Nathaniel – mis MTW, 11-

130 Deer Haven Drive, Madison, MS 39110   Mississippi Valley
E-mail: nbonham@gmail.com
PCA Mission to the World

Bonkovsky, Erik – b Hanover, NH, Jul 14, 76; f Herbert Lloyd; m Marilyn Louise Cahoon; w Sarah Lorayn Reed, Cranbury, NJ, Aug 19, 01; chdn Reed Winder, Leland Mae, Lorayn Grace; PU 98, BA; WTS 01, MDiv; CTS 17, DMin; O Oct 29, 06, JR Pby; astp Grace Comm P Ch, Mechanicsville, VA, 06-08; op City Ch of Richmond, 08-11; p 11-

1705 Hanover Avenue, Richmond, VA 23220 – 804-516-7646   James River
E-mail: erik@citychurchrva.com
City Church of Richmond – 804-767-8038

Bonomo, Jonathan – O Oct 9, 11, GrLks Pby; ascp Michiana Cov Ch, South Bend, IN, 11-16; astp Calvary P Ch, Willow Grove, PA, 16-17; ascp 17-

500 Grant Avenue, Willow Grove, PA 19090 – 267-307-9958   Eastern Pennsylvania
E-mail: jb4calvin@gmail.com
Calvary Presbyterian Church – 215-659-0554

Boomer, George S. – astp Westminster Ref P Ch, Suffolk, VA, 07-10; op Hope P Ch, Smithfield, VA, 08-10; p 10-

1100 Gatling Pointe Parkway, Smithfield, VA 23430 – 757-357-0717   Tidewater
E-mail: george@hopepca.com
Hope Presbyterian Church – 757-771-2243

Bootsma, David – b Burnaby, BC, May 9, 65; f Albert; m Ann VanderPlas; w Shari Hartzler, Carstairs, AB, Aug 8, 92; chdn Kourtney, fvc Kierra, Alyssa; NBTS 86-90, BRE; ACTS 90-92, STM; O Jun 94, NA Bapt; Recd PCA Apr 25, 97, PacNW Pby; p Mary Hill Bapt Ch, Coquitlam, BC, 92-96; chp British Columbia, 96-98; op New Beginnings Comm Ch Msn, Vernon, BC, 98-06, p 06-10; p Free Grace Pres Ch, Vernon, BC, 13-

3702 13th Street, Vernon, BC V1T 3T4 CANADA – 250-558-5513   Western Canada
E-mail: davenbcc@telus.net
Free Grace Presbyterian Church

Bopp, John R. – p Westminster P Ch, Vincennes, IN, 06-14; p New Life P Ch, Mineola, FL, 14-

New Life Presbyterian Church – 352-241-8181   Central Florida

Borden, Jeffrey A. – b Baltimore, MD, Mar 21, 57; f Noel M; m Kay Francis Byers; w Patricia Morosky, Morgantown, WV, Jun 4, 83; chdn Daniel Ray, Matthew Amos, Lydia Joy; WLibStC 79, BS; CaBS 88, MDiv; Stellenbosch U, South Af 03, ThM; O May 13, 90, JR Pby; ap New Cov P Ch, 88-91; mis MTW, 91-16; coord MINTS Africa, 11-18; dir Africans teaching Africans, 18-

3596 Dry Hollow Road, Dayton, VA 22821 – 540-908-3102   Blue Ridge
E-mail: bordenjp83@gmail.com
Africans Teaching Africans

Borger, Justin – astp St. Pauls P Ch, Orlando, FL, 13-

707 Timor Avenue, Orlando, FL 32804 – 423-718-6271   Central Florida
E-mail: justin.borger@gmail.com
St. Paul's Presbyterian Church – 407-647-7774

Borger, Robert James – b Parkersburg, WV, Jul 25, 53; f Philip E.; m Jane Vincent Smyth; w Janice Lea Cross, Greenville SC, Oct 9, 82; chdn Benjamin Paul, Justin Loudon, Joan Williams, Kim Borger Backus; WVU 75, BS; WTS 79, MDiv, 11, DMin; L Mar 79, Mid Pby (OPC); O Oct 10, 80, Mid Pby (OPC); ev Lighthouse Gospel Chapel, Milwaukee, WI, 79-80; p Griggs OPC, Grand Rapids, MI, 81-86; Dir

Borger, Robert James, continued
CAC, 87; coord RLMI, 87-88; p Reformed P Ch, Lookout Mountain, GA, 88-91; p First P Ch, Ft. Oglethorpe, GA, 92-02, srp 02-04; astp Highlands P Ch, LaFayette, GA, 05-07, ascp 07; astp Evangelical P Ch, Annapolis, MD, 07-09; ascp 09-14; ob 14-15; astp Highlands P Ch, LaFayette, GA, 15-; contr *Election Day Sermons*, 96

144 Avenue of the Oaks, Rock Spring, GA 30739 – 706-671-5564   Tennessee Valley
borger.7@gmail.com
Highlands Presbyterian Church – 706-638-8940

Borges, Glauber – astp Comunidade Crista Presbiteriana, Newark, NJ, 07-14; wc

2019 Balmoral Avenue, Union, NJ 07083   Metropolitan New York

Borggren, Erik – b Phoenix, AZ, Jun 14, 77; f Larry; m Karen; w Erica, Jun 15, 02; chdn Ethan, Liliana; USMA 99, BS; NPTS 12, MDiv; O May 19, 13, ChiMet Pby; astp Lincoln Square P Ch, Chicago, IL, 13-18; "Menus, Trees, and Thrones: Reimagining Education in the Liturgical Classrooms of Scripture" *Common Ground Journal* V11 N2, Spr 14; "Romans 13:1-7 and Philippians 3:17-21: Paul's Call to True Citizenship and to Gaman" *The Covenant Quarterly* V73 N2, 15

4748 North Virginia Avenue, Chicago, IL 60625 – 773-580-7878   Chicago Metro

Boroughs, Thaddeus Calhoun III – b Greenville, SC, Aug 6, 50; f Thaddeus C. Jr.; m Eleanor Armstrong; w Susan Manning, St. Louis, MO, Jun 14, 75; chdn Abigail, Megan (Bingham); CC 68-72, BA; CTS 72-74, 76-78, MDiv; L Jan 10, 78, Midw Pby (RPCES); O Jul 9, 78, MidW Pby (RPCES); cop Murphy-Blair Comm Ch, 78-84, wc 84-89; ap Mitchell Road P Ch, Greenville, SC, 89-90; p St. Elmo P Ch, Chattanooga, TN, 90-

4411 Tennessee Avenue, Chattanooga, TN 37409-1645 – 423-825-6042   Tennessee Valley
E-mail: sepccal@comcast.net
St. Elmo Presbyterian Church – 423-821-1424

Bosserman, Brant – b Edmonds, WA, Dec 22, 81; w Heather, Kirkland, WA, Jan 3, 04; chdn Chalcedon Mariah, Nicea Zion, Augustine Luke; NorthWU 04, BA; FulTS 07, MA; BangorU 11, PhD; op Trinitas P Ch, Bothell,WA, 13-

12916 15th Place West, Everett, WA 98204   Pacific Northwest
E-mail: brant@trinitaschurch.com
Trinitas Presbyterian Church

Bossom, Ronald LeRoy – b Baltimore, MD, Feb 14, 46; f Charles A; m Dorothy Sullivan; w Susan Sauter, Baltimore, MD, Jun 21, 69; chdn Elizabeth Joy, Matthew Amos, Deborah Hope, Marianna Priscilla, Stephen Paul; TowU 68, BS; RTS 75, MDiv; L Jul 22, 75; O Aug 4, 75, MidAtl Pby; ev WADC, 75-77; p Harvester P Ch, Springfield, VA, 77-15; hr 15

5923 Sherborn Lane, Springfield, VA 22152-1035 – 703-451-1496   Potomac
HR

Bostrom, Matt Joseph – astp Coram Deo P Ch, Spokane, WA, 17-18

408 Erika Lane, Wenatchee, WA 98801 – 719-494-7611   Pacific Northwest
E-mail: mjbostrom@gmail.com

Bostrom, Stephen David – b Colorado Springs, CO, Jan 11, 51; f Warren A.; m Ruby Luco; w Virginia Pettit, Colorado Springs, CO, May 29, 76; chdn Jared Samuel, Jordan Michael, Rachel Ariel, Zachary Gabriel, Micah Elliot, Noah Daniel, Jesse Nathaniel, Isaac Joel; WestC 73, BA; CBTS 74-76; CTS 77, MDiv; L Sept 77, RMtn Pby (RPCES); O Mar 5, 78, So Pby (RPCES); ap Shannon Forest P Ch,

Bostrom, Stephen David, continued
Greenville, SC, 77-82; chmn BethCS, Greenville, SC, 81-86; op Covenant P Ch, Easley, SC, 81-82, p 82-88; srp Peace P Ch, Cary, NC, 88-06; chp Helena, MT, 06-08; op All Souls Comm Ch, Helena, MT, 08-11; pastor-at-large, Helena, 12-; MNA MTS, MT, 14-; Field Rep for BGEA, 16-; contr *Rulers: Gospel and Government*, 14

5975 North Slope, Helena, MT 59602 – 406-461-8529 Rocky Mountain
E-mail: stevebostrom@gmail.com
Mission to North America Ministry to State

Boswell, Andrew Hemphill Jr. – b Greenwood, MS, Nov 14, 46; f Andrew Hemphill; m Marian Mills; w Dena Schwarz, Winter Haven, FL, Aug 23, 69; chdn Ruth Marie, David Andrew, Sarah Anna, Esther Elizabeth, Hannah Maria, Jonathan James, Deborah Susanna; MSU; DSU 69, BS; MSC; RTS 74, MDiv; LRTS 78, DMin; RTS 03, DMin; O Aug 3, 80, NGA Pby; couns, t TPCDRC, Pompano Bch, FL, 74-76; ydir Covenant P Ch, Winter Haven, FL, 76-77; couns ABCC, Decatur, GA, 78-80; couns First P Ch, Macon, GA, 79-80; dean AUBS, 78-80; ascp Coral Ridge P Ch, Ft. Lauderdale, FL, 80-02; VP Coral Ridge Min, Inc, 90-92, wc 02-03; ascp Christ P Ch, Nashville, TN, 03-05; ob dir Crisis Marriage Division, Family Dynamics Inst, 05-

5841 North Lick Creek Road, Franklin, TN 37064 – 615-790-6509 Nashville
E-mail: aboswell@familydynamics.net
Family Dynamics Institute

Boswell, Frank D. – b Louisville, KY, Jan 22, 51; f Frank G; m Jacqueline Johnson; w Jean M Potter, Niles, MI, Jun 5, 71; chdn Jonathan James, Sarah Elizabeth, Lauren Meredith; UMI 73, BA; GCTS 76, MDiv; FulTS 11, DMin; O Nov 28, 76, MidAtl Pby; ap West End P Ch, Hopewell, VA, 76-78; p Westminster P Ch, Jacksonville, FL, 78-84; op Cross Pointe Ch, Austin, TX, 84-87, p 87-92; p Hunt Valley Ch, Hunt Valley, MD, 92-

1107 Walnut Wood Road, Hunt Valley, MD 21030-5403 – 410-527-1690 Chesapeake
E-mail: pastors@huntvalleychurch.org
Hunt Valley Church – 410-771-0690

Bottomley, Evan Arnold – b Lloydminster, Saskatchewan, Canada, Feb 12, 47; f John F.; m Edith M. Ferguson; w Marilynn J. Smith, Lloydminster, Aug 22, 70; chdn Mark Anthony, Michael Andrew, Jay Timothy, Dean Thomas; USask 71, BEd; WTS 74, MDiv; L 74, PCC; O 74, PCC; p St. James Ch, Newcastle, NB, 74-78; p Chalmers Ch, Calgary, 78-80; p Cov Evangelical P, Calgary, AB, 80-88; op/p North Ridge P Ch, Calgary, AB, 88-02; Ministerios de Amour, Mex, 02-05; Grace Network, Canada, 05-

1426 Nelson Place, Kelowna, BC V1Y 9H5 CANADA – 250-861-1189 Western Canada
E-mail: evanab@gmail.com
Grace Network

Bottomley, Michael – astp Harbor P Ch, San Diego, CA, 11-14; ascp Harbor P Ch UTC, 12-14; p 14-

E-mail: michaelb@harborpc.org South Coast
Harbor Presbyterian Church UTC – 858-523-8738

Bottoms, C. Benson III – b Miami, FL, Jul 26, 59; f Charles Benson Jr.; m Sandra Hardin; w Lynne Weston, Athens, GA, Mar 28, 92; chdn Charles Benson IV "Bo," Mary Hamilton; UGA 82, BA; GCTS 97, MDiv; L Jan 99, NGA Pby; O Jan 99, NGA Pby; ascp Redeemer P Ch, Athens, GA, 97-01, chap Hospice

165 University Drive, Athens, GA 30605 – 706-353-9476 Georgia Foothills
E-mail: bensonbottoms@gmail.com

MINISTERIAL DIRECTORY 61

Bourgeois, L. John, IV – O Oct 27, 13, JR Pby; ascp City Ch of Richmond, Richmond, VA, 13- 15; campm RUF, WFU, 15-

652 Friar Tuck Road, Winston Salem, NC 27104 – 804-767-0123   Piedmont Triad
E-mail: bourgeois.john@gmail.com
PCA Reformed University Fellowship

Bowen, Charles Gregory – RTSNC; O Feb 3, 13, Palm Pby; p Grace P Ch, Aiken, SC, 13-18

111 Kelly Drive, Aiken, SC 29803 – 803-226-4390   Palmetto
E-mail: cgbowen@msn.com

Bowen, Christopher L. – b Chattanooga, TN, Jun 29, 78; w Jennifer; chdn Phoebe Fay, Hadley Grace, Leland Mae; UT 00, BS; DTS 05, ThM; int Park Cities P Ch, Dallas, TX, 04-06; campm RUF, KennSt, 06-13; ip East Cobb P Ch, Marietta, GA, 13; campm RUF, Winthrop, 13-14; astp First P Ch, Chattanooga, TN, 14-18; astp Hilton Head P Ch, Hilton Head Island, SC, 18-

235 William Hilton Parkway, Hilton Head Island, SC 29926   Lowcountry
Hilton Head Presbyterian Church – 843-689-6362

Bowen, James M. Jr. – b Roanoke, VA, Mar 1, 40; f James M. (d); m Julia F Dalton (d); w Jan C Jackson, New Providence, TN, Jun 28, 64; chdn James Michael, William Dalton; UFL 58-62, BS; MSC 71-72; RTS 71-75, MDiv; O Jul 15, 75, SFL Pby; op Grace P Ch, Stuart, FL, 75-79, p 79-05; hr 05; p em Grace P Ch, Stuart, FL, 07

2160 Island Creek Drive, Hillsville, VA 24343-4718   Gulfstream
E-mail: bowenjimandjan@charter.net
HR

Bowen, Kevin Michael – b Ridgewood, NJ, Dec 9, 61; f Edward Joseph Jr.; m Isabelle Julia Helbig; w Ruth Ann Lutzweiler, Nashville, TN, Oct 29, 94; chdn Jason Michael; RBC 90, BRE; CTS 00, MDiv; O Feb 4, 01, MO Pby; ascp Heritage Ref P Ch, Eureka, MO, 00-02, wc 02; p Middlesex P Ch, Butler, PA, 02-

120 Church Road, Butler, PA 16002 – 724-586-2340   Ascension
Middlesex Presbyterian Church – 724-586-7096

Bowen, Michael David – b Bradford, PA, May 4, 65; f Leland G.; m Juanita M. Dorsey; w Cheri L. Burkette, Ewa, HI, Sept 29, 90; chdn Michaela, Marie, David William, Nathan; WLU 87, BA; DTS 97, ThM; O Aug 20, 00, NoTX Pby; astp Fifth Street P Ch, Tyler, TX, 00-04, ascp 04-12; p Covenant P Ch, Cynthiana, KY, 12-

3346 KY Highway 392, Cynthiana, KY 41031 – 859-954-8038   Ohio Valley
E-mail: mikebowen1965@gmail.com
Covenant Presbyterian Church – 859-234-5786

Bowen, Randall E. – b Glendale, CA, Jun 7, 65; f William E.; m Joan E. Kipper; Master'sC 95, BBE; WSCAL 98, MDiv; L Jan 24, 98, SoCst Pby; O Nov 8, 98, SoCst Pby; Chap USAR, 98-

8115 Dalton Way, Hanover, MD 21076   South Coast
E-mail: randall.bowen777@gmail.com
United States Army Reserve

Bowen, Stephen Todd – b Columbus, GA, Aug 2, 65; f Chester Edward; m Linda Carolyn Polston; w Jacqueline Elizabeth Townsend, Lincoln, NE, Jan 14, 95; chdn Spencer Dylan, Jasmine Renee, Reagan Elizabeth, Braden Andrew, Jordan Michelle; VandU 86, BS; CTS 93, MDiv; L 93, Hrtl Pby; O May 15, 94,

Bowen, Stephen Todd, continued
Hrtl Pby; ascp Zion Ch, Lincoln, NE, 94-97; op Grace Cov Ch, Grand Island, NE, 97-04; sc Hrtl Pby, 00-07; p Grace Cov Ch, Grand Island, NE, 04-; sc PlVal Pby, 07-

1705 Gretchen Avenue, Grand Island, NE 68803 – 308-383-4343   Platte Valley
E-mail: tbowen@gracegi.org
Grace Covenant Church – 308-384-5625

   Bower, Nathaniel – O Sept 21, 14, Ohio Pby; campm RUF, 14-

5508 Norton Court, Stow, OH 44224 – 330-998-4279   Ohio
E-mail: nate.bower@ruf.org
PCA Reformed University Fellowship

   Bowers, Bruce – RutgU 90, BA; RTSNC 03, MATS; UEdin 05, ThM; O Feb 15, 09, SEAL Pby; int Sovereign Gr P Ch, Charlotte, NC, 05-06; astp Trinity P Ch, Opelika, AL, 07-09, ascp 09-; t Trinity C School, 07-; rvw "Divine Poetry for the Postmodern Church: Review of *The Book of Psalms for Worship*," *Expository Times*, May 10

1100 India Road, Apt. B, Opelika, AL 36801 – 334-750-7067   Southeast Alabama
E-mail: associate@tpcopelika.org
Trinity Presbyterian Church – 334-745-4889

   Bowers, Perry A. – b Ann Arbor, MI, Feb 13, 53; f Gerald Miles; m Margreta Alice Skog; w Janet Logan, Bethesda, MD, Sept 13, 75; chdn Joy Helene, Megan Alyse; UMD 75, BS; WCBS 79, MDiv; CBS&SM 92, DMin; O Aug 1, 88, Palm Pby; p Nursery Road P Ch, Columbia, SC, 88-93; ob pres Focused Living Ministries, 93-; *Each One Reach One*, 92; *Each One Teach One: Discipleship, Making Christ's Last Command our First Concern*

805 Shelter Cove Court, Columbia, SC 29212 – 803-732-3339   Palmetto
Focused Living Ministries – 803-732-3339

   Bowles, Matteson Todd – astp West Hills P Ch, Knoxville, TN, 08-09; campm RUFI, GMU, 13-

7631 Pine Street, Manassas, VA 20111 – 865-384-0299   Potomac
E-mail: mattesonbowles@yahoo.com
PCA Reformed University Fellowship International

   Bowlin, Lawrence – O May 29, 05, Pitts Pby; astp First Ref P Ch, Pittsburgh, PA, 05-07; p Providence P Ch, Murphy, NC, 07-12; ascp Presbyterian Ch of Coventry, Coventry, CT, 12-18; srp Tyrone Cov P Ch, Fenton, MI, 18-

10235 White Lake Road, Fenton, MI 48430   Great Lakes
E-mail: Pastorbowlin@hotmail.com
Tyrone Covenant Presbyterian Church – 810-629-1261

   Bowling, Jack W. – b Thayer, MO, Jun 8, 42; f James Lee B; m Virginia Wishard; w Mary Hurley, Greeneville, TN, Dec 18, 66; chdn Jack Wayne Jr, David Michael; KgC 64, BA; ColTS 67, MDiv; O Jun 67, Bham Pby (PCUS); p First P Ch, Jasper, AL, 67-69; p Bridwell Heights P Ch, Kingsport, TN, 69-73; couns, Dir TPCDRC, Pompano Beach, FL, 73-75; p South Point P Msn, Gastonia, NC, 75-78; p East Belmont P Ch, Belmont, NC, 79-85; ss Second Street P Ch, Albemarle, NC, 86; ss Castanea P Ch, Stanley, NC, 87, wc 87-89; ss First P Ch, Stanley, NC, 89; astp West End P Ch, Hopewell, VA, 89-94; prin West End CS, Hopewell, VA, 89-94; p Harmony P Ch, Kingsport, TN, 94-01; p Countryside P Ch, Cameron, NC, 01-06; ss Norman P Ch, Norman, NC, 06-09; p 09-

905 Glendale Drive, PO Box 726, Aberdeen, NC 28315 – 910-637-0415   Central Carolina
E-mail: jwbowling42@yahoo.com
Norman Presbyterian Church – 919-770-2431

MINISTERIAL DIRECTORY

Bowman, Thomas Brannon – b Montgomery, AL, Dec 27, 65; f Clarence S.; m Susan Fay Shelton; w Carol Annette New, Hueytown, AL, Feb 16, 90; chdn Thomas Brannon Jr.; BhamSoC 88, BS; U 99, MMus; BhamTS 00, MDiv; L Jul 97, SEAL Pby; O Dec 17, 00, SEAL Pby; mmus Southwood P Ch, Huntsville, AL, 90-95; mmus, modis Young Meadows P Ch, Montgomery, AL, 95-00; p Monroeville P Ch, Monroeville, AL, 00-05; prof BhamTS, 01-05; p Grace Ch of the Islands, Savannah, GA, 06-12; Chap USAF, 13-16; p Millbrook P Ch, Millbrook, AL, 16-

731 Cantabury Lane, Millbrook, AL 36054 – 334-285-4031   Southeast Alabama
E-mail: brannonbowman@yahoo.com
United States Air Force
Millbrook Presbyterian Church – 334-285-4031

Bowsher, Herbert James – b Chester, PA, Jul 27, 49; f Herbert Miller; m Vera Polishuk; w Julia Ann Stephens (dv); Paula Watkins (2); chdn Sarah Elizabeth, Herbert James Jr.; DicC 71, BA; RTS 78, MDiv; O Nov 80, Evan Pby; p Reformed Hrtg P Ch, Birmingham, AL, 79-88, wc 88-99; ss Reformed Hrtg P Ch, Birmingham, AL, 99-04; astp Lake Crest P Ch, Birmingham, AL, 10-17; hr

5921 Shades Run Lane, Birmingham, AL 35244 – 205-424-9800   Evangel
E-mail: herb@cromcheck.com
HR

Box, Darwin W. – b Kingsville, TX, Dec 24, 46; f Wayne Henry; m Darlene Cox; w Linda Lee Johnson, Columbus, GA, Apr 1, 66; chdn Dawn Renee (Givens), Denise Rochelle (Williams); ColC 65-67; AugC 72-76; OgleU 84-86; RTS 90-93, MDiv; L Nov 9, 93, Pot Pby; O Sept 11, 94, CentFL Pby; exec p Reston P Ch, Reston, VA, 93-94; op Cypress Creek P Msn, Lutz, FL, 94-97; astp Wildwood P Ch, Tallahassee, FL, 97-99, ascp 99-03; op NorthPointe Comm Ch, Tallahassee, FL, 03-04; ob Chap Big Bend Hospice, 04-

2839 Fitzpatrick Drive, Tallahassee, FL 32308 – 850-894-9775   Gulf Coast

Boxerman, David Stewart – b St. Louis, MO, Mar 20, 52; f Stanley L.; m Bettie Alice Rice; w Donna Joy Allen, Mesa, AZ, May 21, 82; chdn Tabitha Joy (Columbare), Ariel Elizabeth Joy (Bealer), Lydia-Marie Joy (Standley), Johnathan-David James Stanley; UMO 70-74, BS; CTS 77-81, MDiv; L Mar 21, 81, MidW Pby (RPCES); O Oct 25, 81, FL Pby (RPCES); op Immanuel RP Ch, DeLand, FL, 81-82; p Immanuel P Ch, DeLand, FL, 82-95; op Grace P Ch, Palm Coast, FL, 95-97; sc CentFL Pby, 97; p Lakeside P Ch, Southlake, TX, 97-; mem, Ad Hoc Committee to Revise Standing Rules, 03-05, 07-09; Chairman, Candidates Committee, 04-15; GA Overtures Co, 10-13; mem Pby Sess Rec Rev co, 12-; ed *News and Notes*, 87-92

2701 West Southlake Boulevard, Southlake, TX 76092 – 817-456-1357   North Texas
E-mail: revdavebox@sbcglobal.net
Lakeside Presbyterian Church – 817-431-0151

Boyce, William Evan – b Oct 13, 84; w Melynda Ann, Jun 21, 08; chdn Samuel James, Luke Jonathan; O Dec 2, 12, Pot Pby; astp Christ Ch of Arlington, Arlington, VA, 12-14; ascp 14-

1313 South Buchanan Street, Arlington, VA 22204   Potomac
E-mail: billy@ccapca.org
Christ Church of Arlington – 703-527-0420

Boyd, Paul – campm RUF, U NoFL, 04-07; campm RUF, MidTNSt, 07-13; op Redeemer Ch Murfreesboro, Murfreesboro, TN, 13-17; p 17-

2221 Scout Drive, Rockvale, TN 37153 – 615-796-5050   Nashville
E-mail: paul.boyd@redeemermurfreesboro.org
Redeemer Church Murfreesboro – 615-796-5050

Boyd, Richard – b Apr 23, 76; w Kristi Lea, Jun 8, 02; chdn Elizabeth, Joshua, Susanna; astp Lakeside P Ch, Southlake, TX, 09-10; Chap USAF, 10-

2671 Pebble Dawn, San Antonio, TX 78232 – 817-733-5823   North Texas
E-mail: richandkristi@hotmail.com
United States Air Force

Boyd, William Le Roy – Lake Charles, LA, Sept 13, 61; f James Le Roy; m Charlotte Elliott; w Kristy, Chestnut Mountain, GA, Sept 16, 06; chdn Matthew Tair Le Roy; CC 85, BA; CTS 03, MDiv; O Feb 24, 08, MetAtl Pby; mis chp asst IMPACT, Japan, 93-96; campm ISI, 02-07; int MetAtl Pby, 06-08; mis MTW, South & SE Asia, 07-10; mis MTW, NA, 10-16

447 Cole Drive SW, Lilburn, GA 30047 – 678-401-2861   Metro Atlanta
E-mail: wlroy@acleaders.org

Boyd, William Luther – b Birmingham, AL, Dec 30, 67; f Luther Rhinehart; m Frances Edge; w Martha Stansel, Greenwood, MS, Aug 21, 93; chdn William Stansel, Augustus Couch, Elizabeth Farrow; UMS 85-89, BS; CTS 91-95, MDiv; L Jul 95, SoTX Pby; O Oct 95, SoTX Pby; Alpine Camp for Boys, 89-91; int Kirk of the Hills P Ch, St. Louis, MO, 93-95; campm RUM, UTXAu, 95-03; op All Saints P Ch, Austin, 03-07; p 07-10; srp Covenant P Ch, Birmingham, AL, 12-17

3424 Brookwood Trace, Birmingham, AL 35223   Evangel
E-mail: williamlboyd@gmail.com

Boyer, R. Eugene – mis MTW, FRANCE

c/o MTW   Chesapeake
PCA Mission to the World

Boykin, Burton Haldane Jr. – b Tallahassee, FL, May 6, 59; f Burton Haldane Sr.; m Eleanor Lewis; w Anita New, Lyons, GA, Aug 21, 83; chdn Burton Haldane III, Wilbur Addison, Seth Harrison, Yates Lewis, Cobi William, Tanner Charles, Griffith New; OCEU 77-79, AA; EmU 79-81, BBA; BhamTS 85-89, MDiv; L Sept 24, 86, Evan Pby; O Oct 15, 89, Evan Pby; ydir Third P Ch, Birmingham, AL, 86, astp 86-89; ascp Comm P Ch, Moody, AL, 89-95, p 95-

3308 Highfield Drive, Moody, AL 35004-2658 – 205-640-5037   Evangel
E-mail: burt@communitypca.net
Community Presbyterian Church – 205-640-5698

Boyte, John K. Jr. – ClemU 87, BS; ErskTS 02, MDiv; O Aug 02, Cal Pby; ascp New Cov P Ch, Anderson, SC, 02-09; campm RUF, AndersonC, 02-

103 Wiltshire Court, Anderson, SC 29621 – 864-224-8729   Calvary
E-mail: jboyte@ruf.org
PCA Reformed University Fellowship

Bradbury, Robert Walter – b Camden, NJ, Mar 8, 32; f Burke; m Velma Badger; w Beverly Saft, Syracuse, NY, Jun 7, 58; chdn Nancy Jo (Celmo), Matthew, Rebekah (O'Connor), Douglas, Ruth (Ungerer); NYSCF 50-54, BS; BibS 54-55; PXTS 55-57, BD; NYTS 68-70, ThM; L Jun 26, 56, Caledonia Pby (UPNA); O Aug 16, 57, Caldedonia Pby (UPNA); p Second UP Ch, Jersey City, NJ, 57-60; p Central Ch, Huntington, NY, 60-62; p Broughton Ch, Bloomfield, NJ, 62-77; p New Life P Ch of Hopewell Twnsh, Aliquippa, PA, 77-97; hr

4716 Deer Crossing Court, Flowery Branch, GA 30542 – 770-965-9529   Georgia Foothills
E-mail: rwbradbury@aol.com
HR

MINISTERIAL DIRECTORY

Braden, James L. – b Toledo, OH, Mar 22, 43; f James L.; m Miriam Palmer; w Phyllis Miller, Nyack, NY, Jun 8, 68; chdn James Berkeley, Heather Elizabeth; CBC 62-65; NyC 65-68, BA; BethlTS 68-72, MDiv; CTS 85-87, ThM; O Oct 76, C&MA; p Pitman C&MA, Pitman, NJ, 73-79; p Fremont C&MA, Fremont, OH, 79-85; op Cross Creek P Ch, Fayetteville, NC, 87-90, p 90-11; hr 11

227 Penwood Lane, Lexington, SC 29072 – 910-728-1379   Palmetto
E-mail: jpbraden6868@gmail.com
HR

Bradford, Geoffrey Todd – b Nashville, TN; f Jim; m Susan; w Susan Langford, Davidson, NC, Jun 4, 94; chdn Garrison, Samuel, Henry, Clay, Ezra, Asher; DavC, BA; WTS, MDiv; L Sept 98, Phil Pby; O Jun 4, 00, Phil Pby; ascp New Life P Ch, Dresher, PA, 97-02; chp, op liberti Ch, Philadelphia, PA, 02-06; srp 06-09; p liberti Fairmount, Philadelphia, PA, 09-11; p Christ The King P Ch, Raleigh, NC, 11-

2405 Stafford Avenue, Raleigh, NC 27607 – 919-836-0533   Eastern Carolina
E-mail: gbradford@ctkraleigh.org
Christ The King Presbyterian Church – 919-546-0515

Bradford, Henry C. III – b Jacksonville, FL, Jan 12, 57; f Henry C. Jr.; m Eula Thomas; w Katherine Lee Veenstra, Jacksonville, FL, Feb 23, 80; chdn H.C. IV "Heath," Richard Caleb, Noah Steele, Joshua Taylor; FLColl; Flagler; RTSFL 01, MDiv; L Sept 98, NFL Pby; O Sept 9, 01, SFL Pby; srp Kendall P Ch, Miami, FL, 01-03; p Evergreen P Ch, Sevierville, TN, 03-14; wc 14-

1212 Edgewater Drive, Saint Johns, FL 32259   Tennessee Valley

Bradford, Steven Thomas – b Front Royal, VA, May 22, 43; f William E; m Dolores Bossler; w Helen Dilley, Ft. Lauderdale, FL, Mar 21, 69; chdn Jonathan Lael, Stephani Elizabeth, Joshua Lemuel, Christopher William; TulU 61-62; CBC 64-67, BA; WTS 67-71, MDiv; L Oct 18, 72, Pby of the South (OPC); O Feb 1, 78, SFL Pby; mout/evan Shenandoah P Ch, Miami, FL, 77-80; p Wildwood P Ch, Tallahassee, FL, 80-85; p Trinity P Ch, Kenner, LA, 86-87, wc 87-92; ob instr Tallahassee Bible Inst, 91; ob ss Gateway P Ch (Indep), Lake City, FL, 92-93; ob instr Advent Epis Ch, Tallahassee, FL, 92-94; wc 95-98; instr Tallahassee Bible Inst, 96-99; vis lect/prof Reformed Theo College, Uganda, 96-99; ob assoc, mis Church Planting Int, Ref PC Uganda, Pensacola, FL, 98-05; coord Church Plant Int, dir African Ministries, 02-18

77 Strattonwood Place, Crawfordville, FL 32327-5369 – 850-385-7371   Gulf Coast

Bradford, William – w Allen; chdn Mollie, William, Hannah, Andrew; UMS 90, BA; RTS 96, MDiv, 98, ThM; O 98, MSVal Pby; ob ev Peru Mission, PEF, 99-03; ob ev Peru Mission, Christian Missionary Society, 03-09; srp Lawndale P Ch, 09-

2115 Applewood Street, Tupelo, MS 38804   Covenant
E-mail: billbradford@lawndalepc.com
Lawndale Presbyterian Church – 662-844-6795

Bradham, Mike – w Laura; chdn Faith, Jessica, David; TXA&M 88, BS, 93, MS; CTS 99, MDiv; ascp Redeemer P Ch, Indianapolis, IN, 03-08; wc 08-

6411 Woodbrook Lane, Houston, TX 77008 – 281-343-9131   Central Indiana
E-mail: mikebradham@gmail.com

Bradley, Gary Brent – b North Hollywood, CA, May 13, 48; f Edgar Eugene B; m Margaret Martin; w Esther Mucher, Castile, NY, Jul 18, 70; chdn Kimberly May, Robert Brent, Alondra Kay, Calvin Rhett, Jonathan Knox; BJU 70, BA; BST 73, MDiv; L Sept 9, 74; O Sept 15, 74, Pac Pby; moy Calvary P Ch, Glendale, CA, 73-76; op, p Covenant P Ch, Bakersfield, CA, 76-82; p Westminster P Ch, Kingsport, TN, 82-; contr *The Presbyterian Witness, Counsel of Chalcedon, Tabletalk*

676 Harrtown Road, Blountville, TN 37617-3826 – 423-323-1078   Westminster
E-mail: westmin@embarqmail.com
Westminster Presbyterian Church – 423-247-7341

Bradley, Matthew Todd – b Bryan, TX, Jan 27, 74; f Ray Todd; m Pamela Carol; w Leslie Gail Bradley; chdn Ian Timothy, Xavier Nathaniel; ETSU 96, BA; DTS 06, ThM; O Feb 18, 09, Nash Pby; intern Park Cities P Ch, Dallas, TX, 07-08; astp Covenant P Ch, Nashville, TN, 09-10; ascp 10-15; sc Nash pby, 13-16; op All Saints P Ch, Brentwood, TN, 15-

221 Heathstone Circle, Franklin, TN 37069 – 615-886-0795   Nashville
E-mail: mbradley@allsaintspres.net
All Saints Presbyterian Church – 615-886-0795

Bradley, Zachary – b Roanoke, VA, Apr 1, 80; w Robin; WFU 02, BA; GCTS 05, MDiv; astp Evergreen P Ch, Sevierville, TN, 08-10; astp Perimeter Ch, Johns Creek, GA, 10-17; op Brookhaven P Ch, Atlanta, GA, 13-17, p 17-

1844 Tobey Road, Atlanta, GA 30341 – 678-982-0095   Metro Atlanta
E-mail: zachbradleywfu@yahoo.com
Brookhaven Presbyterian Church – 678-982-0095

Bradshaw, Jere Scott – O Aug 22, 12, SEAL Pby; ob astp Comm EFC, Elverson, PA, 12-15; srp Covenant P Ch, Auburn, AL, 15-

445 Shelton Mill Road, Auburn, AL 36830   Southeast Alabama
E-mail: jerescottbradshaw@gmail.com
Covenant Presbyterian Church – 334-821-7062

Bradshaw, Wade – b Houston, TX, Jul 24, 57; w Chryse; chdn Ethan, Gordon, Gillian, Fiona; TXA&M; TEDS, MA; TXA&M, DVM; O 07, BlRdg Pby; p IPC, Liss, England, 05-06; astp Trinity P Ch, Charlottesville, VA, 07-

106 Kerry Lane, Charlottesville, VA 22901   Blue Ridge
E-mail: wade.bradshaw@trinitycville.org
Trinity Presbyterian Church

Bradsher, David – b Washington, DC, Jun 10, 74; w Jennifer Lynn Carrier, Maryland, Aug 22, 98; chdn Ruth, Samuel, Lydia, Ethan; RTSFL 05, MDiv; O Aug 2, 09, NFL Pby; op Gr Comm Msn, Fernandina Beach, FL, 09-10; p 10-

86126 Fieldstone Drive, Yulee, FL 32097   North Florida
E-mail: dave.bradsher@gmail.com
Grace Community Church – 904-491-0363

Brady, Ronald J. – b Chetek, WI, Mar 7, 38; f John H.; m Melva L. Stensby; w Martha Grimm, Ft. Lauderdale, FL, Sept 21, 68; chdn Dawn Lyn (Sparks), Christy Leigh (Smith), Holly Anne (Welch); MBI 56-59, dipl; UDub 59-61, BA; WheatGrS 61-63, MA; MTS 63-65, MDiv; WTS 78, DMin; O Jun 27, 65, Chippewa Pby (UPCUSA); ap First Ch, Plantation, FL, 65-70; t JBC, 71-78; p North Miami Beach Ch, FL, 79-81; ap Old Cutler P Ch, Miami, FL, 81-83; p Shenandoah P Ch, Miami, FL, 83-87; srp Fifth Street P Ch, Tyler, TX, 88-03; ob ss Hanna City P Ch, Hanna City, IL, 04, p 04-08; hr 08; astp Fifth Street P Ch Tyler, TX, 12-13

8327 Whitesburg Way #1318, Huntsville, AL 35802 – 256-964-7478   North Texas
E-mail: revron38@gmail.com
HR

Brandenstein, Mike – wc

Address Unavailable   Missouri

MINISTERIAL DIRECTORY

Brannan, Carl Dyess Jr. – b Jackson, MS, May 10, 56; f Carl Dyess; m Martha Witherspoon; w Janet Elizabeth Price, Jackson, MS, Jul 10, 82; chdn Rachel Elizabeth, Sarah Rebecca, Cealia Jane, Robert Price; VandU 78, BA; RTS 82, MDiv, 92, DMin; O Aug 82, StAnd Pby (PCUS); p Saltillo PCUS Ch, Saltillo, MS, 82-85; p First P Ch, Indianola, MS, 86-92; srp Christ P Ch, Winterville, NC, 92-03; srp Grace P Ch, Ocala, FL, 03-18

1715 Myrtle Street, Jackson, MS 39202   Central Florida
E-mail: seniorpasto1r@cox.net

Brannen, Jeffrey – O Feb 12, 12, CentGA Pby; p St. Andrews P Ch, Americus, GA, 12-15; wc 15-18; chap USArmy, 18-

2012B Tulip Ct., Ft. Gordon, GA 30905 – 478-747-4060   Central Georgia
E-mail: jeffrey_brannen@yahoo.com
United States Army

Branscomb, Joel – O May 7, 17, PTri Pby; astp Trinity Ch, Winston-Salem, NC, 17-18; ascp 18-

237 Karen Circle, Winston-Salem, NC 27105 – 336-413-6717   Piedmont Triad
Trinity Church – 336-701-6030

Branson, Craig Lee – b Washington, MO, May 15, 48; f Irvin; m Collier; w Flottman, Gerald, MO, Feb 17, 68; PBJC 77; BelC 78-80, BA; RTS 80-83, MDiv; O Jul 31, 83, SFL Pby; ap Lake Osborne Continuing P Ch, Lake Worth, FL, 83-89, op 89-92; astp Spring Meadows P Ch, Las Vegas, NV, 92-93; srp Bellewood P Ch, Bellevue, WA, 93-98; ascp Old Cutler P Ch, Miami, FL, 99-15

28918 Fairs Gate, Fair Oaks Ranch, TX 78015 – 786-293-3400   South Florida
HR

Bratt, Daniel Lee – b Lansing, MI, Jul 1, 48; f Daniel; m Elizabeth Margaret Klein; w Kathleen Ann Montague, Clio, MI, Jun 18, 77; chdn Elizabeth Margaret, Jonathan Daniel, David Montague, Jedidiah Joshua, Nathan Paul, Micah Joseph; CalvC 70, BS; MISU 72, MS; CalvS 83, MDiv; O 83, CRC; O Sept 30, 07, GrLks Pby; staff IVCF, 73-78; p Franklin Lks CRC, Franklin Lks, NJ, 83-96; p Franklin Lks Ref Bib Fell, Franklin Lks, NJ, 96-03, wc 03-07; astp Christ Cov Ch, Midland, MI, 07-17; op Providence PCA of Lans, East Lansing, MI, 12-17; hr 17

2323 Hampshire Road, Lansing, MI 48911   Great Lakes
E-mail: dkbratt@sbcglobal.net
HR

Brauer, Eric – b Milford, CT, Sept 18, 56; f Ellwood A.; m Eleanor A. Mingrone; w Karen Beth Yelenik, Lorain, OH , May 10, 80; chdn Talitha Kay, KarisTina, Corban Alex, Laurel Erin, Joanna Beth, Elyssa Joy, Emily Renee; UCin 79, BS; WTS 88, MDiv; L Mar 89; O Feb 4, 90, Phil Pby; ev, mis IVCF, Ireland; ev, mis WHM, Ireland; chp Serge, Dublin, IR, 95-17, Austria, 17-

Johann Strauss-Gasse 33/37, 1040 Vienna AUSTRIA – 43-677-62427451   Eastern Pennsylvania
E-mail: ericandkarenbrauer@yahoo.com
Serge

Brauning, Wayne Frank – b Grafton, NE, Mar 9, 34; f Ruben Jacob; m Vera; w Marilyn Joan, Wichita, KS, Aug 11, 56; chdn Daniel W., Stephen M., Kathleen J.; UNE, BA; WTS 60, MDiv, 93, DMin; O Oct 60, Phil Pby (RPCES); p 5th RP Ch, Philadelphia, PA, 60-66; wc soc wk, prob off, 66-70; headm PACS, 70-74; sp Hope RP msn, Philadelphia, PA, 74-79; wc soc wk, prob off, 74-92; ss Hope Ch, New Hope, PA, 92-93; p Immanuel P Ch, Exton, PA, 93-05; ss Trin Ref P Msn, Ramstein, Germany, 05; ss Covenant Msn, Okinawa, 06; ss Dovedale Ref Ch, Christchurch, NZ, 07; mod PhilMetW Pby, 09-10; hr

36 Valley Heights Drive, Williamsport, PA 17701 – 610-304-9121   Philadelphia Metro West
E-mail: wfbrauning@yahoo.com
HR

Brawner, Thomas Frederick – b Tuscaloosa, AL, Aug 28, 55; f Judson Frederick Jr; m Mary Louise Tremer; w Edna Elizabeth Hill, Mt. Pleasant, SC, Aug 4, 79; chdn Andrew Frederick, Philip Hill, Melody Louise; ClemU 73-77, BA; CBS 77-80; SWBTS 81-83, MDiv; O May 22, 83, So Bapt; Recd PCA Oct 27, 88, Cal Pby; ydir First Bap Ch, Bishopville, SC, 78-79; campm UMI, 83-88; campm EMIU, 83-88; campm RUF, ClemU, 89-; RUFI, ClemU, 89-

133 Windy Hill Road, Central, SC 29630-9423 – 864-654-5117   Calvary
E-mail: rbrawner@ruf.org
PCA Reformed University Fellowship – 864-624-9100
Reformed University Fellowship International

Breed, Daniel – chp Wisconsin, 11-12; Emmaus Road Ch, Appleton, WI, 12-16, srp 16-

722 South Story Street, Appleton, WI 54914   Wisconsin
E-mail: daniel.breed@gmail.com
Emmaus Road Church – 303-520-5988

Breeden, Gavin – b Union City, TN, Mar 27, 85; f Ronald; m Sheryl Farmer; w Shalaine, Jun 10, 06; chdn Addie Pearl, Miles; UTMartin 06, BA; RTSNC 11, MDiv; O Nov 13, 11, MSVal Pby; astp Northpointe P Ch, Meridian, MS, 11-15; campm RUF, TNTech, 15-

326 Linnaeus Avenue, Cookeville, TN 38501 – 704-689-5808   Nashville
E-mail: gavinbreeden@gmail.com
PCA Reformed University Fellowship

Breeden, Tom – b Charlottesville, VA, Aug 25, 90; UVA 12, BS; RTS 16, MDiv; O Jun 11, 17, BlRdg Pby; astp Grace Comm Ch, Charlottesville, VA, 17-; *Can I Smoke Pot? Marijuana in Light of Scripture*, 16

5146 Dickerson Road, Charlotesville, VA 2911   Blue Ridge
E-mail: tom@cvillegrace.org
Grace Community Church – 434-975-2259

Breitkreuz, Al – O Feb 27, 00, PacNW Pby; p Faith P Ch, Vancouver, BC, 00-07; astp Bedford P Ch, Bedford, NS, 08; ascp 08-09; p 09-13; wc 13-15; ob Salvation Army, 15-

5935 165 A Street, Surrey, BC V3S 4N9 CANADA   Western Canada
E-mail: breitkreuzal@gmail.com
Salvation Army

Bresson, Brad Lee – b Dayton, OH, Mar 16, 66; f Richard; m Marlen Davis; w Lynn Carley, Palm Bay, FL, May 27, 95; chdn Christina, Reese, Emma, Noah; CedC, BBA; RTSFL 99-02, MDiv; O Jun 2, 02, CentFL Pby; op Nature Coast Comm Ch, Homosassa, FL, 02-

6201 West Craft Lane, Homosassa, FL 34448 – 352-382-7244   Central Florida
E-mail: brad@n3c.org
Nature Coast Community Church – 352-628-6222

Brevick, Arnold – p First P Ch, North Port, FL, 04-

5414 Gabo Road, North Port, FL 34287 – 941-240-1715   Southwest Florida
E-mail: abrev@comcast.net
First Presbyterian Church – 941-426-1230

Brewer, Chad – b Westminster, MD, Apr 27, 72; f Marvin; m Linda May Buffington; w Christie, New Windsor, MD, Aug 3, 01; chdn Charis Jane, Chara Ansley; ShSU 94, BA; CTS 00, MDiv; L May 13, 01,

Brewer, Chad, continued
MO Pby; O May 13, 01, MO Pby; campm RUF, UMO, 99-03; campm RUF, PennSt, 03-08; campm RUF, UMN, 08-15; campm RUF, UCIrvine, 15-

12 Twain, Irvine, CA 92617 – 814-237-2739　　　　　　　　　　　　　　　　　South Coast
E-mail: chadbrewer1@yahoo.com
PCA Reformed University Fellowship

Brewer, David John – b Putnam, CT, Oct 26, 44; f David Joseph; m Barbara Ellen Gallop; w Nancy Carol Trumbore, Hatfield, PA, Aug 27, 66; chdn Rebecca, Christina, David; BJU 66, BA; FTS 69; WTS, stu; EasternU 03, MBA; O Jul 27, 69, Berean Bap; ap Ch of the Open Door, Ft. Washington, PA, 75-77; ev Phil Pby, 79-83; p Covenant P Ch, Harleysville, PA, 83-88, wc 88-03; ob ACTS Retirement Life Communities, 03-11; hr 11

915 Woodlawn Drive, Lansdale, PA 19446-4545 – 215-368-9212　　　　　　Eastern Pennsylvania
E-mail: djhbrewer@verizon.net
HR

Brewer, Hunter Townsend – b Gadsden, AL, Aug 19, 74; f Sam; m Cindy Jane Martin; w Vicki Linn Klauser, Birmingham, AL, Dec 4, 99; SamU, BS; RTSFL 03, MDiv; O Nov 23, 03, MSVal Pby; int Rainbow P Ch, Rainbow City, AL, 98-99; int Orangewood P Ch, Maitland, FL, 00-02; astp Lakeland P Ch, Flowood, MS, 03-05; op Madison Heights P Msn, Madison, MS, 05-07; p 07-13; wc 13-14; ob 14-18; chp 18-; *So You Want To Be A Leader*

801 Brentwood Lane, Oxford, MS 8655 – 601-624-2282　　　　　　　　　　Mississippi Valley
E-mail: midsouthnetworkpca@gmail.com

Brewer, Jason Elliott – b Marietta, GA, Jan 31, 70; f Raymond G.; m Margaret Louise Bussey; w Claudia Anne Rogers, Mullins, SC, Aug 14, 93; chdn Thomas Ryan; USC, BA; RTS, MDiv; L Oct 95; O Nov 2, 97, Palm Pby; p Mullins P Ch, Mullins, SC, 97-

1209 South Main Street, Mullins, SC 29574 – 803-464-8911　　　　　　　　　　　　Pee Dee
E-mail: jgamecock@aol.com
Mullins Presbyterian Church – 843-464-9593

Brewer, Thomas – ob LigMin, Sanford, FL, 18-

421 Ligonier Ct, Sanford, FL 32771　　　　　　　　　　　　　　　　　　　　Central Florida
E-mail: tbrewer@ligonier.org
Ligonier Ministries – 407-333-4244

Brewton, Clifford H. – b Mershon, GA, Feb 14, 32; f Charles Russell; m Inetta Williams; w Rachael Anne Meadors, Ridgeland, SC, Jul 21, 56; chdn Rebekah Elaine (Chromi), Clifford Daniel, Laura Anne (McCurdy); MerU 52-53; CC 56, BA; ColTS 56-59, BD; O Aug 2, 59, Sav Pby; p Greenville Ch,Greenville, GA; p Friendship Ch, Concord, GA, 57-58; p Lithonia Ch, Lithonia, GA, 58-59, p Hull Mem P Ch, Savannah, GA, 59-67; p Emmanuel P Ch, Jonesboro, GA, 77-03; astp Grace Comm P Ch, McDonough, GA, 03-05; hr 05; Governor's Staff, State of GA, 68-76

219 Country Lake Drive, McDonough, GA 30252-2682 – 770-914-3097　　　　　Metro Atlanta
E-mail: hellogeorgia@bellsouth.net
HR

Brice, Adam L. – b Richmond, IN, Aug 15, 66; f Jon Nelson; m Martha Lee Goode; w Elizabeth Anne Stockmeyer, Ann Arbor, MI, May 4, 91; chdn Isabelle Marie, Noah Branden, Emily Sara; INU 88, BA; WTS 94, MDiv, 05, ThM; L Nov 96, Phil Pby; O Jan 17, 99, Phil Pby; astp Tenth P Ch, Philadelphia,

Brice, Adam L., continued
PA, 99-00; op Christ the King P Ch, Conshohocken, PA, 99-00, p 00-08; op Resurrection P Ch, West Lafayette, IN, 08-11; p 11-

100 Trowbridge Drive, Lafayette, IN 47909 – 765-807-5288   Central Indiana
E-mail: adambrice815@gmail.com
Resurrection Presbyterian Church

Bridgeman, A. Warren – Chap USAF, 02-09; hr 09

1131 Emerald Dunes Drive, Sun City Center, FL 33573 – 813-685-4447   New Jersey
E-mail: awbridgeman@hotmail.com
HR

Bridgeman, Lee Gregory – op New Hope Comm Ch of Richardson, Richardson, TX, 14-18

1321 Northlake Drive, Richardson, TX 75080   North Texas
E-mail: leegb1@msn.com

Bridges, Scott A. – b Oklahoma City, OK, Apr 2, 63; f Dr. D. W. Jr.; m Joyce McCarter; w Julie Allison Pollard, Franklin, TN, May 27, 89; chdn Emily Anne, Jonathan Hanson; OKSU 85, BS; CTS 92, MDiv; L Aug 9, 92, MO Pby; O Aug 9, 92, MO Pby; astp Covenant P Ch, St. Louis, MO, 92-96; op Christ P Ch, Santa Barbara, CA, 96-00, p 00-08; srp Wallace P Ch, College Park, MD, 08-18; admin PCA MNA, 18-

E-mail: sbridges@pcanet.org   Potomac
PCA Mission to North America

Brieaddy, Timothy – astp Grace P Ch, Kernersville, NC, 06-09; p Gr Flwsp P, Asheboro, NC, 11-15; wc

1109 Century Park Drive, Kernersville, NC 27284   Piedmont Triad
E-mail: tbrieaddy@triad.rr.com

Brignac, James – w Cullen; chdn Samuel, Ryan, Abigail; RTS 14, MDiv, 14, MAMFT; O MSVal Pby; astp First P Ch, Yazoo City, MS, 14-16; astp Ponte Vedra P Ch, Ponte Vedra Beach, FL, 17-

6527 Ginnie Springs Road, Jacksonville, FL 32258   North Florida
E-mail: jamesbrignac@gmail.com
Ponte Vedra Presbyterian Church – 904-285-8225

Brinkerhoff, Timothy J. – b Paterson, NJ, Aug 20, 62; f John Soley; m Joan Wilson; w Lori Jean DeVries, Midland Pk, NJ, Jun 13, 87; chdn Kimberly Joy, Joshua Timothy, Jonathan Christian, Alisha Faith, Stephen Henry; HougC 80-84, BA; WTS 86-90, MDiv; L Oct 28, 91, NJ Pby; O Nov 29, 92, NJ Pby; int Hope Ch, New Hope, PA, 91; astp Knowlton P Ch, Columbia, NJ, 92-93, ascp 93-95; ob p LaFayette Federated Ch (non-PCA), Lafayette, NJ, 95-10; ob Chap, t Veritas Christian Acad, NJ, 12-

27 Broad Street, Branchville, NJ 07826-5603 – 973-948-0922   Metropolitan New York

Briones-Silva, Oscar – Recd PCA Sept 18, SWFL Pby; op Iglesia Del Redentor Msn, Winter Haven, FL, 18-

1550 11th Street NE, Apt. G1, Winter Haven, FL 33881 – 631-276-9138   Southwest Florida
E-mail: oscarmbriones@gmail.com
Iglesia Del Redentor Mission – 631-276-9138

Broadwater, Daniel Charles – b Frostburg, MD, May 1, 47; f Charles Wesley; m Gladys Virginia Wilson; w Dr. Katherine Mary Arwady, Timonium, MD, Mar 4, 78; chdn Luke William, Benjamin Joseph, Andrew Charles, Alex Daniel; AllgCC 70-71, AA; TowU 71-73, BS; WTS 74-76, MA, 77-78, MDiv; GCTS 94, DMin; L Dec 78, DMV Pby (RPCES); O Nov 19, 79, DMV Pby (RPCES); Glen Arm Fellowship, Glen Arm, MD, 76-77; Timonium P Ch, Timonium, MD, 78-79; op Grace Ref P Ch, Relay, MD, 79-82, p 82-; *Getting Your Congregation Involved in Applying the Weekly Messsage*; contr *Ideas*; hymns/worship songs: "Come Before the Lord of Glory," "I Take Joy," "Face to Face," "Let It Ring - A Christmas Album," contr "Mary Had a Baby"

29 Holmehurst Avenue, Baltimore, MD 21228-4631 – 410-744-2447   Chesapeake
E-mail: broadwaters@comcast.net
Grace Reformed Presbyterian Church – 410-247-4088

Broadwick, Arthur Clyde – b Philadelphia, PA, Mar 30, 36; f C G Arthur; m Margaret Hemphill; w Lois Louise Randall, Allentown, PA, Dec 7, 57; chdn Arthur David, Timothy Scott, Bonnie Sue; MuhC 53-57, BS; WTS 63-66; PittsTS 66-67, MDiv; O Jul 16, 67, WJersey Pby (UPCUSA); p Center UP Ch, New Castle, PA, 67-69; p Union UP Ch, Robinson Township, PA, 69-75; p Providence P Ch, Robinson Township, PA, 75-92; ob ascp Independent P Ch, Savannah, GA, 92-01; hr 01

108 Rose Dhu Way, Savannah, GA 31419-3353 – 912-927-6075   Savannah River
E-mail: abroadwick@ipcsav.org
HR

Brock, Christopher Paul – O Jan 6, 13, CentCar Pby; mis MTW, 12-

32 Boulevard des Capelles, Plaisance du Touch 31830 FRANCE– 704-281-0115   Central Carolina
E-mail: chrisbrock78@gmail.com
PCA Mission to the World

Brock, Cory – O Aug 5, 17, MSVal Pby, ob 17-18; astp First P Ch, Jackson, MS, 18-

4430 Brook Drive, Jackson, MS 39206   Mississippi Valley
E-mail: brock.cory@gmail.com
First Presbyterian Church – 601-353-8316

Brock, James – b St. Paul, MN, May 28, 83; f Gerald; m Ruth; w Suzanne Bryan, Dillwyn, VA, Jul 23, 05; chdn Nathan, Isaac, Toby, Zachary, Asher; ClaremontMcKC 05, BA; CTS 12, MDiv; astp Church of the Redeemer, Atlanta, GA, 13-17; chp Virginia Beach, VA, 17-18; op Princess Anne Msn, Virginia Beach, VA, 18-

1189 Kenwood Court, Virginia Beach, VA 23936 – 314-443-0245   Tidewater
E-mail: jimmy@princessannemission.org
Princess Anne Mission – 757-219-2716

Brock, Michael – b Ashland, KY, Jan 19, 67; f Michael; m Helen Hackney; w Lisa Bryant, Marietta, GA, Jul 29, 89; chdn Ragan Elizabeth, Tabitha Erin, Priscilla Ruth, Charles Gregory, Bryant Lee; SamU 89, BS; BhamTS 02, MDiv; O Jul 91, SoBapt; astp Trinity P Ch, Montgomery, AL, 02-03; p Redeemer P Ch, Florence, AL, 03-08; astp Midway P Ch , Powder Springs, GA, 08-11; sc NWGA Pby, 08-11; srp Eastern Shore P Ch, Fairhope, AL, 11-; pres MSS, 10-

517 Richmond Circle, Fairhope, AL 36532   Gulf Coast
E-mail: mbrock@easternshorepca.org
Eastern Shore Presbyterian Church – 251-928-0977
Mission Sending Service

Broderick, William D. – b Framington, MA, Nov 27, 68; f Robert E.; m Helen T. Driscoll; w Michelle Jeanette Kilpatrick, Ft. Lauderdale, FL, May 23, 98; FLTechU 92, BS; KTS 98, MDiv; KTS 04, DMin; Holy Apostles C/TS 10, MA; L Jan 99, PacNW Pby; O Oct 98, Ind; Recd PCA Jan 00, PacNW Pby;

Broderick, William D., continued
yp West Broward Comm Ch RCA, Ft. Lauderdale, 95-98; ob srp Valley Bible Church, Arco, ID (ind), 99-01; astp Inverness P Ch, Baltimore, MD, 01-03; ob p Second Cong Ch, Douglas, MA, 03-13; chap 13-18; ob p Safe Harbor Comm Ch, Ft. Myers, FL, 18-

8088 Breton Circle, Fort Myers, FL 33912-4648 – 508-498-3481 Suncoast Florida
E-mail: billbrod@aol.com
Safe Harbor Community Church, Ft. Myers, FL

Brodine, Luke William – b Salt Lake City, UT, Jul 10, 79; f William; m Susan; w Sarah Connor Mathias, Columbia, SC, Jul 31, 04; MTSU 02, BS; ErskTS 08, MDiv; CTS 16, DMin; int RUF, UW, 03-05; int Clemson P Ch, Clemson, SC, 05-08; astp Grace P Ch of Silicon Valley, Palo Alto, CA, 09-18; astp Intown Comm Ch, Atlanta, GA, 18

E-mail: luke@intown.org Metro Atlanta
Intown Community Church – 404-633-8077

Brogan, Anthony – O 16, Evan Pby; astp Altadena Valley P Ch, Birmingham, AL, 16-17; ascp Christ Ch Greensboro, Greensboro, NC, 17-

801 Coronado Drive, Greensboro, AL 27410 – 205-276-6470 Piedmont Triad
E-mail: anthony@christchurchgreensboro.org
Christ Church Greensboro – 336-209-5659

Brokaw, Adam Michael – O May 29, 16, Cov Pby; astp Covenant P Ch at Cleveland, Cleveland, MS, 16-

109 N Victoria, Cleveland, MS 38732 Covenant
E-mail: brokawam@gmail.com
Covenant Presbyterian Church at Cleveland – 662-843-9598

Brom, Hubert Ben – b Oskaloosa, IA, Jul 18, 23; f Ben; m Coulter; w Mary Standley, Los Angeles, CA, Sept 6, 52; chdn Stephen, Jeffrey, James, Marcia (Carlson); UIA 48, BA; FulTS 52, MDiv; FrUAmst 53-54; MTS 54-56; UIA 60, PhD; O Jan 26, 56, PCUSA; Recd PCA Apr 27, 91, SoCst Pby; srp McArthur Comm P Ch, 54-56; srp Blairstown P Ch, 56-59; srp St. Andrew P Ch, 59-69; srp Beulah P Ch, 69-75; srp Glendale P Ch, 75-80; Comm Ch of Vista, Vista, CA , 81-90; ip Calabasas P Ch, Calabasas, CA, 90-91; ev SoCst Pby, 91-98; ip Redeemer P Ch, Torrance, CA, 91-92; ip Oak Springs P Msn, Temecula, CA, 92-93; hr 98

2124 B Ronda Granada, Laguna Hills, CA 92653 – 949-855-4355 South Coast
E-mail: hughbrom@juno.com
HR

Bromhead, Jonathan Adam – Fairfax, VA, Oct 5, 82; f Rob; m Nancy Geiger; w Julie Phillip, Lake Geneva, WI, Jul 5, 06; chdn Caden, Noah, Luke, Isabella; WheatC 05, BA; GCTS 08, MDiv; O Jan 18, 09, PCUSA; Recd PCA May 20, 17, NJ Pby, chp 17-18; op King's Cross Ch, Trenton, NJ, 18-

21 Windswept Drive, Trenton, NJ 08690 – 540-209-4600 New Jersey
E-mail: jonathan.bromhead@gmail.com
King's Cross Church – 540-209-4600

Bronson, Andrew – b Baltimore, MD, Feb 7, 78; f William R.; m Jean C.; w Rebecca Rogers; chdn Ryder Matthew; VandU 00, BA; CTS 11, MDiv; mis MTW, Bangkok, Thailand, 11-

c/o MTW North Texas
PCA Mission to the World

Brooker, Darrell – KTS 97, MDiv; p Monarch Reformed Church (RCA), Monarch, AB, 97-01; Westm Chapel, Lethbridge, AB, 01-04; p Redeemer P Ch, Santa Rosa, CA, 05-

4930 Newanga Avenue, Santa Rosa, CA 95405 – 707-318-6605   Northern California
E-mail: dsbrooker@gmail.com
Redeemer Presbyterian Church – 707-539-9794

Brooks, Steven Joseph – b Sunbury, PA, Oct 12, 78; f Alan; m Ruth; w Kelly Dugger, Tallahassee, FL, Aug 7, 99; chdn Emily Grace, Micah Russ, Carter Joseph, Randy Wyatt; FSU 00, BS; RTSFL 05, MDiv; O Apr 07, GulCst Pby; astp CenterPoint Ch, Tallahassee, FL, 07-09; ascp Faith P Ch, Watkinsville, GA, 09-

2191 Mars Hill Road, Watkinsville, GA 30677 – 706-248-5151   Georgia Foothills
E-mail: stevenb@faithpcachurch.org
Faith Presbyterian Church – 706-769-8315

Brown, Alexander – b Dundee, UK, Nov 25, 81; f James S.; m Sandra W.; w Sara Allen, St. Louis, MO, Nov 10, 07; chdn Ada, Campbell; UDund 03, MA; UGlasg 07, ThB; L Oct 20, 09, SavRiv Pby; O Jun 6, 10, SavRiv Pby; p Golden Isles P Ch, St. Simons Island, GA, 10-

413 Couper Avenue, St. Simons Island, GA 31522 – 912-577-3890   Savannah River
E-mail: abrown@gipc-pca.org
Golden Isles Presbyterian Church – 912-638-2563

Brown, Brian – O Nov 20, 16, PlVall Pby; campm RUF, 17-

1917 Prospect Street, Lincoln, NE 68502   Platte Valley
E-mail: brian.brown@ruf.org
PCA Reformed University Fellowship

Brown, Bruce – O Jun 26, 16, CatVal Pby; p Prosperity P Ch, Charlotte, NC, 16-

14329 Eastfield Road, Huntersville, NC 28078 – 704-698-8009   Catawba Valley
E-mail: christshousehold@yahoo.com
Prosperity Presbyterian Church – 704-875-1182

Brown, Bryan – ob campm 09-; astp Perimeter Ch, Johns Creek, GA, 14-

11205 Linbrook Lane, Johns Creek, GA 30097   Evangel
E-mail: bbrown@campusoutreach.org
Perimeter Church – 678-405-2000

Brown, Carter – O Aug 14, SFL Pby; astp Rio Vista Comm Ch, Ft. Lauderdale, FL, 14-17; astp Crossbridge Ch Miami, Miami, FL, 17-

Crossbridge Church Miami – 305-661-9900   South Florida

Brown, Christopher – astp Covenant Ref P Ch, Asheville, NC, 18-

290 Woody Lane #A, Asheville, NC 28804   Western Carolina
E-mail: Christopher1j1brown1@gmail.com
Covenant Reformed Presbyterian Church – 828-253-6578

Brown, Christopher D. – b Greenville, SC, Feb 75; w Patricia Louise Mills, Charleston, SC, Feb 14, 09; ErskC 97, BA; RTSNC 00, MDiv; O May 1, 05, Palm Pby; Chap Heartland Hospice, Charleston SC,

Brown, Christopher D., continued
05; Chap Winyah Hospice, Charleston, 06-07; Chap Medical U of South Carolina Hosp, 07-; Chap USAR, 08-16

1140 Waters Inlet Circle, Charleston, SC 29492 – 843-870-2378 Lowcountry
E-mail: brownchd@musc.edu
Medical University of South Carolina Hospital, Charleston

Brown, Christopher William – astp Harvester P Ch, Springfield, VA, 13-17; op Iglesia Harvester, Springfield, VA, 13-17; astp Comunidade Crista Presbiteriana, Newark, NJ, 17-

45 McWhorter Street, Newark, NJ 07105 New Jersey
E-mail: chris@ccpnewark.com
Comunidade Crista Presbiteriana – 973-465-2126

Brown, Craig Thornton – b Dallas, TX, Apr 15, 68; f Jack P. Jr.; m Deanna Louise Reidell; w Jana Lynn Bunn, Franklin, TN, Jun 15, 96; chdn James Travis, Clark Tennent, Annalise Marie, Simon Cole, Yasmeen Phillips; VandU 90, BS; CTS 99, MDiv; L Jul 99, Nash Pby; O Jul 99, Nash Pby; astp Christ Comm Ch, Franklin, TN, 99-03, ascp 03-04; op City Ch of East Nashville, Nashville, TN, 04-06; p 06-14; Church Mult Min, 14-18; op Redeemer Flwsp of Nashville, TN, 18-

1406 Woodland Street, Nashville, TN 37206 – 615-642-7426 Nashville
E-mail: ccenbrown@gmail.com
Redeemer Fellowship of Nashville

Brown, Dennis L. – w Kay; O Meth; Recd PCA Nov 12, 94, Phil Pby; srp Springton Lake P Ch, Newtown Square, PA, 94-09; ob Friendship P Ch, Taiwan, 09-18

140 Summitville Court, Lancaster, PA 17603 – 717-696-9596 Philadelphia Metro West
E-mail: dennis.brown.pca@gmail.com

Brown, Howard A. – b Charleston, SC, Jan 29, 72; f Alphonso; m LaQuines Goodwin; w Kellie D. Gordon, Charleston, SC, Dec 20, 97; chdn Harrison, Clark; ClemU 89-93, BA; CTS 94-98, MDiv; L Feb 12, 99, NGA Pby; O Feb 12, 99, NGA Pby; astp Redemption Flwsp P Ch, Fayetteville, GA, 98-01; p Forest Park Community Ch, Baltimore, MD, 01-03; astp Uptown Christ Cov Ch, Charlotte, NC, 03-08; op Christ Central Ch, Charlotte, NC, 03-08; p 09-

10502 Ivy Close Road, Huntersville, NC 28078 – 704-609-5493 Central Carolina
E-mail: hbrown@christcentralchurch.com
Christ Central Church – 704-608-9146

Brown, James Harold – b Gadsden, AL, May 13, 62; f George M. Silvey Jr.; m Nancy Stimpson; w Robin Brown, Hattiesburg, MS, Jun 1, 85; chdn Joshua McIntyre, Evan Porter, Dori Elizabeth, Jayme Catherine; BelC 84; CTS 89, MDiv; L Oct 90, SFL Pby; O Sept 8, 91, SFL Pby; ydir Bay Street P Ch, Hattiesburg, MS, 84-86; ydir Westminster Ref P Ch, Ballwin, MO, 86-89; astp Granada P Ch, Coral Gables, FL, 89-95; astp, moy St. Andrews P Ch, Columbia, SC, 95-99, wc 99-00; ob couns Lake Murray Couns Cent, 00-; adj prof CIU, 03-

PO Box 2647, Irmo, SC 29063 – 803-917-8773 Palmetto
Lake Murray Counseling Center
Columbia International University – 803-754-4100

Brown, James Oliver Jr. – b Philadelphia, PA, Apr 25, 46; f James Oliver; m Alberta Bryant; w Patricia May Page, China, ME, Jun 21, 69; chdn Robyn Beth (Flemer), Rebecca Gail (Roosma); TrenSC 68, BA; BJU 72, MDiv; UNC 79-85; O 73, Ecar Pby; p Emmanuel Ch, Wilmington, NC, 73-85; ap Faith P Ch, Wilmington, DE, 85-87, srp 87-12; astp 12-; mod Hrtg pby, 00

604 Whitby Drive, Wilmington, DE 19803 – 302-658-2687 Heritage
E-mail: patbrown35@hotmail.com
Faith Presbyterian Church – 302-764-8615

Brown, Joseph E. – Beaumont, TX, Dec 16, 77; w Blair; chdn Jeb, Anna Roe, Jane Martin, Catherine; O Feb 28, 09, JR Pby; astp West End P Ch, Richmond, VA, 09-13; ascp 13-

9205 Lyndonway Drive, Richmond, VA 23229 – 804-543-7116   James River
E-mail: joe@wepc.org
West End Presbyterian Church – 804-741-6562

Brown, Kenneth N. – b Sylvia, TN, Jul 24, 48; f Raymond A.; m Margaret W. Dowdy; w Cynthia Jan Hantman, Albany, GA, Sept 11, 71; chdn Kara, Joel, Erin, David; ShorterC 75, BS; SEBTS 78, MDiv; L Jan 74, Byne Mem Bapt Ch; O Mar 10, 74, Byne Mem Bapt Ch; Recd PCA Oct 98, GrLks Pby; p Corinth Bapt Ch, Oxford, NC, 74-77; p First Bapt Ch, Colquitt, GA, 78-80; p Lakewood Bapt Ch, Nashville, TN, 80-83; Chap USArmy, 83-10; astp Redeemer P Ch, Dickson, TN, 10-14; ascp 14-16; hr 16

1004 Polly Willey Road, Dickson, TN 37055 – 615-789-4884   Nashville
HR

Brown, M. Marshall – b Dallas, TX, Nov 11, 73; f M. M. "Buster"; m Anne Terrell Blackburn; VandU 96, BA; RTS 02, MDiv; O Nov 02, War Pby; campm RUF, UAL, 02-09; astp Pacific Crossroads Ch, Los Angeles, CA, 09-14; srp Grace P Ch of the North Shore, Winnetka, IL, 14-

311 Rosewood Avenue, Winnetka, IL 60093   Chicago Metro
E-mail: marshall@gracenorthshore.org
Grace Presbyterian Church of the North Shore – 847-920-9517

Brown, Mark T. – O Aug 9, 09, PTri Pby; astp Redeemer P Ch, Winston-Salem, NC, 09-; op Redeemer Yadkin Valley, Yadkinville, NC, 09-

616 North Peace Haven Road, Winston Salem, NC 27104   Piedmont Triad
E-mail: mtbrown@triad.rr.com
Redeemer Yadkin Valley – 336-426-8371

Brown, Michael – O Aug 19, 18, SavRiv Pby; ascp First P Ch, Pooler, GA, 18-

105 Tahoe Drive, Pooler, GA 31322   Savannah River
E-mail: michael@firstprespooler.com
First Presbyterian Church – 912-330-9415

Brown, Michael S. – w Debbie; chdn Grace, David; CIU 93, BMus, 93, Bbib; RTSNC 11, MDiv; O Apr 26, 12, Palm Pby; p New Harmny P Ch, Alcolu, SC, 12-16; p Mouzon P Ch, Kingstree, SC, 17-

124 Lynchburg Road, Kingstree, SC 29556 – 803-410-8328   Pee Dee
E-mail: cbcgrad@aol.com
Mouzon Presbyterian Church – 843-201-6600

Brown, Paul A. – w Mai; chdn Aaron, Bethany; TayU 78, BA; DTS 82, ThM; BethTS 95, DMin; O Jul 82, Midw Pby, EPC; p EPC, Lake City, MI, 82-87; p Dundalk EPC, Dundalk, MD, 87-04; p New Cov P Ch, Dallas, TX, 04-

11342 Country Ridge Lane, Forney, TX 75126 – 972-564-0354   North Texas
E-mail: NCPCDallas@aol.com
New Covenant Presbyterian Church – 214-321-6435

Brown, Ronald Earl – b Ft. Lauderdale, FL, Oct 11, 59; f Jim; m Ruth Haase; w Susan Radcliffe, Jackson, MS, May 24, 86; GenC 82; RTS 87, MDiv; O Nov 88, GulCst Pby; campm FSU, 88-95; astp Seven Rivers P Ch, Lecanto, FL, 95-02; astp First P Ch, Chattanooga, TN, 02-06; campm CC, 06-14; astp First P Ch, Panama City, FL, 14; p 14-16, srp 16-

1609 Inverness Road, Lynn Haven, FL 32444 – 850-589-7993   Gulf Coast
E-mail: ron.brown@firstprespc.org
First Presbyterian Church – 850-785-7423

Brown, Ryan – b Duluth, GA, Jan 12, 85; w Marianne; GASoU 07, BBA; CTS 14, MDiv; O Nov 1, 14, MetAtl Pby; astp Perimeter Ch, Johns Creek, GA, 14-

3080 Abbotts Pointe Drive, Duluth, GA 30096 – 404-374-5345   Metro Atlanta
E-mail: ryanb@perimeter.org
Perimeter Church – 678-405-2000

Brown, Sam – O Oct 30, 11, Ecar Pby; p Grace P Ch, Fuquay-Varina, NC, 11-18; astp Trinity P Ch, Cleveland, TN, 18-

2045 Tomahawk Circle NW, Cleveland, TN 37312   Tennessee Valley
E-mail: imsambrown@gmail.com
Trinity Presbyterian Church – 423-559-9595

Brown, Scott – b W. Lafayette, IN, Mar 12, 67; f Don; m Joyce Dayvolt; w Rebecca Lynne Roost, Indianapolis, Jun 12, 93; chdn Jacob Austin, Carter William, Zachary Scott; Purdue 89, BA; AsbTS 94, MDiv; O Oct 94, Christian Ch; Recd PCA Nov 97, GrLks Pby; int East 91st St Chr Ch, Indianapolis, 90-91; ascp Hill n Dale Chr Ch, Lexington, KY, 94-97; astp North Cincinnati Comm Ch, Mason, OH, 97-00, ascp 00-03; op New Valley Ch, Tempe, AZ, 03-07; p 07-

141 West Pecan Place, Tempe, AZ 28584 – 480-831-0383   Southwest
E-mail: scottybrown@cox.net
New Valley Church – 480-296-5900

Brown, Stephen Webb – b Asheville, NC, Dec 16, 40; f Newton Webb; m Launia Cole; w Anna Williamson, Hendersonville, NC, Dec 18, 60; chdn Robin Leigh, Jennifer Lee; BreJC, AA; HPtC, BA; BosUST, STB; O Jun 15, 65, Meth; p Dennis Comm Ch, Cape Cod, 64-68; p First Ch, Quincy, MA, 68-74; p Key Biscayne P Ch, Key Biscayne, FL, 74-90; prof RTSFL, 90-09; ob Key Life Network, Maitland, FL, 85-; prof em RTSFL, RTSDC, RTSA, 09-14; *Where the Action Is*; *So Now You Are a Christian*; *If God is in Charge*; *Heirs with the Prince*; *No More Mr. Nice Guy*; *When Your Rope Breaks*; *When Being Good Isn't Good Enough*; *Jumping Hurdles*; *How To Talk So People Will Listen*; *Born Free*; *Living Free*; *Approaching God*; *Follow the Wind*; *A Scandalous Freedom: The Radical Nature of the Gospel*; *What Was I Thinking: Things I've Learned Since I Knew It All*; *Three Free Sins, God's Not Mad at You*; *Hidden Agendas: Dropping the Masks that Keep Us Apart*

c/o Key Life Network, PO Box 945000, Maitland, FL 32794   Central Florida
E-mail: steve@keylife.org
Key Life Network – 407-539-0001

Brown, Thomas – b Hayward, CA, Jul 30, 70; f Rev. David Richard; m Jeanette Christine Phoenix; w Sara Christine Biggs, Mar 15, 08; USCA, BA; RTSNC, DMin; L Oct 01, CentCar Pby; O Oct 1, 02, NoCA Pby; p Grace Ch of Pleasanton, Pleasanton, CA, 02-09; p Grace Ch PCA, Livermore, CA, 09-12; astp Danville P Ch, Danville, CA, 12-

2455 Talavera Drive, San Ramon, CA 94583   Northern California
E-mail: tom_sara@att.net
Danville Presbyterian Church – 510-792-7755

Brown, Travis Joshua – astp Chestnut Mtn P Ch, Flowery Branch, GA, 18-

PO Box 7280, Chestnut Mountain, GA 30502 – 615-509-6187   Georgia Foothills
E-mail: travis.brown@cmpca.org
Chestnut Mountain Presbyterian Church – 770-967-3440

Brown, Walter Eddie Jr. – b Goldsboro, NC, Nov 3, 50; f Walter E; m Elsie Troutman; w Gail Campbell, W Orange, NJ, Mar 5, 77; chdn Katie, Alan; WCU 75, BA; RTS 83, MDiv; L 77, TN Pby;

Brown, Walter Eddie Jr., continued
O Feb 84, NoE Pby; op Chapel Fellowship, Irvington, NJ, 84-89; ascp Peace P Ch, Cary, NC, 92-99; mis WHM, Nairobi, Kenya, 99-04; ev Christ Our Redeemer Msn, Cary, NC, 04-11; p 11-16; ob dir Together in Grace, 16-

2024 Battlewood Road, Apex NC 27523   Eastern Carolina
E-mail: eddie4cor@gmail.com
Together In Grace

    Browne, John – b Northern Ireland, Jan 29, 53; f David Browne (d); m Norah Borland; w Betsy Ward, California, Aug 18, 79; chdn David C, Kathleen E, Daniel J; WhitBC 81-82; BelC 82-85, BA; RTS 85-89, MDiv; L Oct 89; O Feb 10, 91, CentGA Pby; int Dayspring P Ch, Forsyth, GA, 89-91, p 91-95; op Gr Cov Msn, Elon College, NC, 95-00; ascp Metrocrest P Ch, Carrollton, TX, 00-11; wc; MNA, disaster response, 15-

2301 Castle Rock Road, Carrollton, TX 75007 – 972-306-5886   North Texas
PCA Mission to North America – 678-825-1200

    Browning, Robert – b Jackson, TN, May 25, 72; f Bob R.; m Linda Sue Odell; w Natalie Susan Isbell, Memphis, TN, Nov 15, 97; chdn Richard Thomas, Margaret Ann; RhC 94, BA; RTSNC 02, MDiv; O Nov 3, 02, Cov Pby; campm RUF, UMemp, 02-05; p Christ P Ch, Olive Branch, MS, 05-18; astp, exec p Independent P Ch, Memphis, TN, 18-; sc Cov pby, 09-

4738 Walnut Grove Road, Memphis, TN 38117   Covenant
E-mail: covpressc@gmail.com
Independent Presbyterian Church – 901-685-8206

    Browning, Thomas Rufus – b Dallas, TX, Apr 20, 52; f Thomas James; m Barbara Kathleen Burkett; w Beverly Ann Thyer, Arlington, TX, Feb 16, 72; chdn Thomas Gage, Aaris (Jackson); UTXA; Arlington BaptC, BS; DTS, ThM; L 99, NoTX Pby; O Oct 01, NoTX Pby; astp Bible Chapel, Ft. Worth, 83-86; yp Arlington P Ch, Arlington, TX, 99-01, ascp 01-10; astp Grace Comm P Ch, Fort Worth, TX, 10-

701 Drummond Drive, Arlington, TX 76012 – 817-795-1618   North Texas
E-mail: thomasbrowning@sbcglobal.net
Grace Community Presbyterian Church – 817-847-7766

    Brubaker, Bob – p Christ Comm P Ch, Clearwater, FL, 08-

19029 US Highway 19 North #20E, Clearwater, FL 33764 – 727-539-1434   Southwest Florida
E-mail: bob@bobbrubaker.com
Christ Community Presbyterian Church – 727-530-1770

    Bruce, James – ob prof JohnBrownU

603 North Madison Street, Siloam Springs, AR 72761   Hills and Plains
John Brown University

    Brudenell, Victor E. – O Feb 7, 99, SFL Pby; op The Ch for Today Msn, Ft. Lauderdale, FL, 99-06; hr 06

1712 Poinsettia Drive, Ft. Lauderdale, FL 33305 – 954-561-2943   South Florida
HR

    Bruhn, Robert Paul – b Casper, WY, Aug 7, 52; f Otto; m Lillian Huber; w Ellie Steele, Colorado Springs, CO, Dec 30, 78; chdn Sarah, Benjamin, Nathaniel, Charissa; WSC 70-73; ETXSU 75-78, BA; TEDS 82-85, MDiv; L Jan 85, NoIL Pby; O Oct 87, PacNW Pby; op Good Shepherd P Msn, Kent, WA, 87-90; ip Hillcrest P Ch, Seattle, WA, 90, p 91-07; wc 07-

1612 Fairy Dell Trail, Lookout Mountain, GA 30750 – 307-797-3501   Pacific Northwest
E-mail: bruhnbob@yahoo.com

Bruner, David – astp Harbor P Ch UTC, San Diego, CA, 14-16; astp All Souls Ch of Seattle, Seattle, WA, 16-

E-mail: dbruner23@gmail.com   Pacific Northwest
All Souls Church of Seattle – 206-829-8349

Brunjes, Michael – O Feb 16, Glfstrm Pby; astp Christ Comm Ch PCA Palm Beach, Wellington, FL, 16-17; astp Christ P Ch, New Haven, CT, 17-

417 South Main Street, Wallingford, CT 06492   Southern New England
E-mail: mike@cpcwallingford.org
Christ Presbyterian Church – 203-777-6960

Brunson, Robert F. – b Gadsden, AL, Dec 25, 57; f Theo R.; m Kathryn E. Lindsey; w Karen A. Edwards, Gadsden, AL, Dec 22, 78; chdn David Samuel, Lindsey Claire; UAL 76-79, BA; RTS 83-86, MDiv; L 85; O 87, GulCst Pby; ap Warrington P Ch, Pensacola, FL, 87; IVCF, 87-88; couns Big Oak Ranch for Boys, Glencoe, AL, 88-89; p Thomson Mem P Ch, Centreville, MS, 89-93; p First P Ch, Camden, AL, 93-97; ascp Covenant P Ch, Lakeland, FL, 97-99; astp Village Seven P Ch, Colorado Springs, CO, 99-00; ascp 00-04; ob astp Church of the Apostles, Atlanta, GA, 04-05; astp Highlands P Ch, Ridgeland, MS, 05-07; ascp 07-10; srp Westminster P Ch, Ft. Myers, FL, 10-; astp Westminster P Ch, Huntsville, AL, 16-18; astp ChristChurch P, Atlanta, GA, 18-

625 Piedmont Avenue NE, Apt 3003, Atlanta, FL 30308   Metro Atlanta
E-mail: robertbrunson8669@gmail.com
ChristChurch Presbyterian – 404-605-0505

Bryan, Chris – Chap USArmy, 10-

2409 Danbury Place, Lawrence, KS 66049 – 785-393-7427   Missouri
United States Army

Bryan, David – b Pittsburgh, PA, Mar 9, 80; w Beth Kane Kilmartin, Oreland, PA, Nov 23, 02; chdn Lucas David; JMU 02, BA; TEDS 06, MDiv; O Aug 12, 07, ChiMet Pby; mis MTW, Spain, 08-12; ob 12-

942 Waukegan Road, Apt. B, Deerfield, IL 60015 – 651-315-6695   Chicago Metro
E-mail: dbryansurf@gmail.com

Bryan, Kreg – w Julie; chdn Jessica, Jonathan, Kaitlin, Sarah; p Kirk O the Isles P Ch, Savannah, GA, 03-05; p Grace P Ch of the W Reserve, Hudson, OH, 05-09; wc 09-12; ascp Woodland Ridge P Ch, Overland Park, KS, 13-14; srp 14-16; srp Covenant P Ch, Milledgeville, GA, 16-

521 West Thomas Street, Milledgeville, GA 31061   Central Georgia
Covenant Presbyterian Church – 478-453-9628

Bryant, James Anthony – b Ft. Sill, OK, Sept 15, 52; f James Carlton; m Shirley Carole Albea; w Leigh Ann McCleskey, Columbia, SC, Feb 22, 74; chdn Leslie Ann, Lauren Elizabeth, Benjamin Curtis, James Matthew; USC 70-74; RTS 74-77, dipl; L Apr 18, 77; O Apr 18, 77, Evan Pby; ap Covenant P Ch, Montgomery, AL, 77-78; op Clinton, SC, 78-81; op Savannah, GA, 81-84, wc 84-86; p Zion P Ch, Chester, SC, 86-88; sp Central P Ch, Kingstree, SC, 88-89; ss 90, p 91-94, wc; astp New City Fell P Ch, Fredericksburg, VA, 07-08; wc 08-

313 Dove Park Road, Columbia, SC 29223-1409 – 540-891-7961   James River

Bryant, Jared – astp Resurrection P Ch, Athens, GA, 11-

4031 Whitlow Creek Drive, Bishop, GA 30621 – 706-461-1134   Georgia Foothills
E-mail: jbryant@resurrectionathens.com
Resurrection Presbyterian Church – 706-255-6492

MINISTERIAL DIRECTORY 79

Bryant, Jeff – w Amanda, Oct 29, 11; chdn Eleanor, Nathaniel; AndU 07, BA; ErskTS 09, MATS, 17; O Jun 1, 18, War Pby; p First P Ch, Demopolis, AL, 18-

1903 Vine Avenue, Demopolis, AL 36732 – 864-554-1464　　　　　　　　　　Warrior
E-mail: jef.alan.bryant@gmail.com
First Presbyterian Church – 334-289-3895

Bryant, Robert – w Betsy; chdn Katie, Ashlyn, Mackenna, Emma; ClemU 90, BS; LAMP 17, MDiv; WTS, DMin cand; O Aug 24, 18, Palm Pby; astp St. Andrews P Ch, Columbia, SC, 18-

17 Lake Front Court, Columbia, SC 29212 – 803-422-6697　　　　　　　　　Palmetto
E-mail: bob@sapc.net
St. Andrews Presbyterian Church – 803-732-2273

Bryars, James Arthur – b Mobile, AL, Sept 19, 57; f Jimmy; m Frances A. Brown; w Rebecca Lynn Newby, Hopkinsville, KY, May 19, 84; chdn James, Catherine, Jennifer, Caroline; USNA 75-77; UAL 77-79, BS; DTS 85-89, MABS; O Jan 96, Bapt Ch, Mobile, AL; Recd PCA Feb 01, GulCst Pby; campm CCC, UAR, 80-83; campm CCC, UNTX, 83-85; staff CCC, DTS, 85-89; mis CCC, Czech Rep, 90-94; staff CCC, Nashville, TN, 94-95; ascp Dauphin Way Bapt Ch, Mobile, AL, 95-00; ip Eastern Shore P Ch, Fairhope, AL, 00-01; op Grace Comm Ch, Mobile, AL, 01-03, srp 03-

6520 Charingwood Drive North, Mobile, AL 36695 – 251-660-5019　　　　　Gulf Coast
E-mail: office@gracemobile.org
Grace Community Church – 251-345-3303

Buchner, Eric Todd – astp Seacrest Boulevard P Ch, Delray Beach, FL, 02-05; p Reidville P Ch, Reidville, SC, 05-

125 Wofford Circle, Woodruff, SC 29388　　　　　　　　　　　　　　　　Calvary
E-mail: reidvillepres@bellsouth.net
Reidville Presbyterian Church – 864-433-9965

Buck, Bryan – astp City Church - Eastside, Atlanta, GA, 10-14; op Oaks Parish, Portland, OR, 14-

4914 SE 52nd Avenue, Portland, OR 97206　　　　　　　　　　　　　Pacific Northwest
E-mail: bryansbuck@gmail.com
Oaks Parish – 503-974-6611

Buckner, James L. Jr. – b Asheville, NC, May 19, 52; f James L., Sr.; m Geneva Carter; w Bonnie Lyall, Asheville, NC, Aug 23, 80; chdn Joseph Lyall, Ruth Lyall, David Lyall; Citadel 70-74, BA; GSU 77-79, MEd; CIU 79-82, MDiv; O Jul 28, 83, Cal Pby; mis MTW, Hong Kong, 84-09; ob p EFCC Discovery Bay Int Comm Ch, 09-18

E-mail: jbuckner@psmail.net　　　　　　　　　　　　　　　　　　　　Palmetto

Buerger, John Martin – astp New St. Peters P Ch, Dallas, TX, 13-14; ascp 14-

9505 Larchwood Drive, Dallas, TX 75238　　　　　　　　　　　　　　　North Texas
E-mail: john.buerger@newstpeters.org
New St. Peter's Presbyterian Church – 214-438-0120

Buffaloe, Kelley Lee – p Antioch P Ch, Goldsboro, NC, 08-

117 Brookside Way, Pikeville, NC 27863 – 919-709-4038　　　　　　　Eastern Carolina
E-mail: kbuffaloe@juno.com
Antioch Presbyterian Church – 919-735-3623

Bulkeley, Craig Smith – b Chicago, IL, Dec 29, 56; f Lewis Edwards; m Mary Johnson Smith; w Tracie Lynne Halfacer, Coral Gables, FL, Apr 29, 95; chdn Mary Rachel, Charlotte Ann; MUOH 77, AB; WTS 79, MAR, 80, ThM; UMiami 85, JD; L, Wcar Pby; O Apr 22, 01, Wcar Pby; p Friendship P Ch, Black Mountain, NC, 01-15; "Christianity and Religious Liberty" in *Christianity and Civilization*, Vol 1, Spr 82; *The Book of Church Order Outline*; *Hope for the Children of the Sun*, 07

PO Box 776, Black Mountain, NC 28711 – 828-669-0872   Western Carolina
E-mail: Bulkeley@Bellsouth.net

Bull, Scott – O Feb 12, 17, GAFH Pby; op Grace Comm Ch (Mission), Buford, GA, 16-

1780 Heatherton Road, Dacula, GA 30019 – 678-699-0586   Georgia Foothills
E-mail: sbull@gccb.org
Grace Community Church – 678-699-2586

Bullock, Dennis – astp All Saints Ref P Ch, Richmond, VA, 04-05, ascp 05-07, p 07-

7524 Comanche Drive, Richmond, VA 23225 – 804-272-4773   James River
E-mail: asrpc.dbullock@verizon.net
All Saints Reformed Presbyterian Church – 804-353-7321

Bullock, Nicholas – O Jan 10, 16, MSVal Pby; p Second P Ch, Yazoo City, MS, 16-

930 Belle Air Circle, Yazoo City, MS 39194   Mississippi Valley
E-mail: revnsbullock@gmail.com
Second Presbyterian Church – 662-746-8852

Bumgardner, John Owens Jr. – b Columbia, SC, Mar 22, 49; f John O; m Julia Anne Salley; w Kathryn Anne Perry, Nashville, GA, Jan 26, 80; chdn Kathryn Anne, Salley Payne, John Owens III; USC, BA; GCTS, MDiv; RTS 95, DMin; O Feb 78, PCUS; p Rose Hill P Ch, Columbia, SC, 78-82; p First P Ch, Dillon, SC, 82-17; hr 17

422 Johnson Drive, Dillon, SC 29536-2120 – 843-774-3825   Pee Dee
E-mail: johnbumgardner@live.com
HR

Bumpas, William Wallace Jr. – b Batesville, MS, Mar 14, 62; f William Wallace Sr.; m Kennie Ruth Robison; w Reni Dorizas, Jackson, MS, Jun 17, 89; chdn Will, Elizabeth, Walker, Ian; UMS 84, BA; RTS 92, MDiv; L Feb 19, 91; O Jun 27, 93, MSVal Pby; int Bethel P Ch, Clover, SC, 92-93; p DeKalb P Ch, DeKalb, MS, 93-98; p Pleasant Springs P Ch, DeKalb, MS, 93-98; p First P Ch, Dyersburg, TN, 98-17; ob FCAc, French Camp, MS, 17-

One Fine Place, French Camp, MS 39745 – 731-334-8378   Covenant
E-mail: wallybumpas@gmail.com
French Camp Academy – 662-547-6482

Bunderick, Trey – campm RUF, 12-15

1112 Hermitage Avenue SE, Huntsville, AL 35801-2530 – 706-255-2707   Covenant

Bunn, Max – O Nov 13, 18, Evan Pby; astp Briarwood P Ch, Birmingham, AL, 18-

Briarwood Presbyterian Church – 205-776-5500   Evangel

Burch, John Stuart – b Rome, NY, Jul 29, 46; f Colin F.; m Audrey Elaine Weibel; w Susan Hollister Kirkpatrick, Bethesda, MD, Nov 24, 78; chdn Rebekah Elizabeth, Ruthanne Clare; VPI 64-68, BS; GCTS 82, MDiv; WTS 96, DMin; ACT 05, ThM; L 82, Natl Capitol Pby; O 85, Fayetteville Pby; ap Fourth P Ch,

Burch, John Stuart, continued
Bethesda, MD, 82-84; p Cameronian P Ch, Rockingham, NC, 85-88; mis MTW, Brisbane, Aust, 91-04; MTW, Spiritual Life Dept, 04-08; MTW iLead prog, San Juan, PR, 08-10; mis MTW, Member Care & Development, 10-18; hr 18

2100 Willow Chase Court, Tucker, GA 30084 – 770-558-6028   Metro Atlanta
E-mail: johnsburch@gmail.com
HR

Burchette, Mark Haydon – b Hartford, CT, May 16, 58; f Herb; m Jayne Scilley; w Denise Lombardi, Boca Raton, FL, Aug 3, 85; chdn Jillian Lee; CBC, AA; FAU, BS; RTSFL 95, MDiv; L Apr 95, CentFL Pby; O Jan 14, 96, CentFL Pby; astp Northside P Ch, Melbourne, FL, 96-98; ascp New Cov P Ch, Anderson, SC, 98-

616 Pinehollow Drive, Anderson, SC 29621 – 864-224-8724   Calvary
New Covenant Presbyterian Church – 864-224-8724

Burden, David – O Mar 10, 13, Nash Pby; astp Midtown Flwsp Ch, Nashville, TN, 13-

4413 Scenic Drive, Nashville, TN 37204 – 615-456-6676   Nashville
E-mail: dave@midtownfellowship.org
Midtown Fellowship Church – 615-269-9015

Burden, Timothy Bryce – b Ft. Worth, TX, Dec 27, 76; f Gary; m Frances; w (dv); chdn Myra Elizabeth; LibU 98, BS; CTS 04, MDiv; O Aug 07, Ecar Pby; int Gr & Peace Flwsp, St. Louis, MO, 04-06; astp Peace P Ch, Cary, NC, 06-08; wc 09-10; ss Eau Claire P Ch, Columbia, SC, 10-11, p 11-14; wc 14-

625 Wildwood Avenue, Columbia, SC 29203   Palmetto
E-mail: timburden76@gmail.com

Burdette, Drew – campm RUF, 13-

6207 38th Avenue NE, Seattle, WA 98103 – 314-448-7550   Pacific Northwest
E-mail: drew.burdette@ruf.org
PCA Reformed University Fellowship

Burdette, Joshua – O ChiMet Pby; ascp Ethos P Msn, Chicago, IL, 14-15; astp Ethos P Ch, Tulsa, OK, 15-18; astp Christ P Ch, Santa Barbara, CA, 18-

Christ Presbyterian Church – 805-957-4200   Pacific

Burguet, Richard Lamar – b Jackson, MS, Dec 11, 54; f Jorge E.; m Irma Richardson; w Anne Patricia Dodson, Jackson, MS, Aug 19, 78; chdn Iain Douglas, Elizabeth Anne, Suzanna Maria, Mary Claire; MSU 72-74; BelC 74-77, BA; RTS 78-82, MDiv; L 82; O 82, Cal Pby; ap Second P Ch, Greenville, SC, 82-85; p Thomson Mem P Ch, Centreville, MS, 85-88; op Golden Isles P Ch, St. Simons Island, GA, 88-92; p Southeast P Ch, Columbia, SC, 93-97; ascp Rose Hill P Ch, Columbia, SC, 97-99; p Loch Raven P Ch, Baltimore, MD, 99-06; p New Hope P Ch, Eustis, FL, 06-; *Covenant Disciples Students' Workbook,* 08; *Covenant Disciples Parents' Handbook,* 08; month contr Lake County's *Healthy Living*: Mencouragement, 12-

36448 Clara Street, Eustis, FL 32736-8485 – 352-357-5737; 352-434-5331   Central Florida
E-mail: rlburguet@gmail.com, office@newhopepca.com
New Hope Presbyterian Church – 352-483-3833

Burke, David L. – b St. Louis, MO, Oct 10, 48; f John R; m Opal L. Shockley; w Vickie L. McKissick, Minneola, KS, May 29, 71; chdn Sarah Lee, John Owen, Nathaniel David, Timothy James; WichSU, BS; RPTS 73-76, MDiv; L Feb 76; O Jul 21, 76, RPCNA; p Hetherton Ref P Ch, Johannesburg,

Burke, David L., continued
MI, 76-77; p Quinter Ref P Ch, Quinter, KS, 84-87; ascp Evangel P Ch, Wichita, KS, 89-96; p Ortega P Ch, Jacksonville, FL, 96-17; sc NFL pby, 17-; tutor Providence Ext Prog, 09-14, 17-; hr 17

7183 Hanson Drive North, Jacksonville, FL 32210 – 904-387-3747   North Florida
E-mail: dburke@ortegapres.org
HR

Burns, Bill – ascp Trinity Harbor Ch, Rockwall, TX, 10-14; wc 14-

7136 Blackwood Drive, Dallas, TX 75231   North Texas

Burns, Robert W. – b Omaha, NE, Jul 21, 50; f George R.; m Eleanore Maude Wallace; w Janet Sue Alcorn, Bethesda, MD, Jul 15, 77; chdn Robert W. II, Christopher Wayne; VMI 68-70; UMD 70-72, BA; CTS 77, MDiv; WTS 85, DMin; UGA 01, PhD; L Jul 78, CentGA Pby; O Oct 19, 79, FL Pby (RPCES); op Evangelical P Ch, Cape Coral, FL, 79-80; ms/sa Ch of the Savior, Wayne, PA, 80-85; astp Perimeter Ch, Johns Creek, GA, 85-04; fndr Fresh Start Seminars, Paoli, PA; Dir CTS, Cent for Min Leadership, 04-09, assoc prof 04-09; dean CTS, Lifelong Learning; astp Seven Hills Flwsp, Rome, GA, 15-17; ascp Church of the Good Shepherd, Durha, NC, 17-; *Recovery from Divorce; The Adult Child of Divorce; A Recovery Handbook; The Fresh Start Divorce Recovery Handbook; Resilient Ministry; The Politics of Ministry*

7007 Knotty Pine Drive, Chapel Hill, NC 27517   Eastern Carolina
E-mail: bobburns@cgsonline.org
Church of the Good Shepherd – 919-490-1634

Burns, Robert Nicholas Jr. – b Pompten Plains, NJ, Mar 4, 65; f Robert N. Sr.; m Reinhilda Ann Tafelmeir; w Melissa Lea Barber, Tokyo, Sept 28, 91; chdn Priscilla Leigh; USNA 87, BS; RTS 01, MDiv; CTS 14, DMin; O Feb 23, 03, CentFL Pby; Chap USN, 03-

31 Upshur Road, Annapolis, MD 21402 – 910-478-8181   Central Florida
E-mail: riflesmith87@gmail.com
United States Navy

Burns, Terrance Timothy – b Wyandotte, MI, Jul 7, 55; f James V.; m Kathryn Hohloch; w Cynthia Diane Felix, Ft. Polk, LA, Apr 8, 89; chdn Kevin Michael, Brian Patrick, Alan Christopher; CSU 77, BA; USACGS 91, dipl; USNCSC 93, dipl; RegU 01, MA; O Oct 17, 04, BlRdg Pby; admin, astp Trinity P Ch, Charlottesville, VA, 04-08; ob p Nicosia Comm Ch, Cyprus, 09-16; St. Andrews Scots P Ch, Rome, 16; Scots Kirk Paris, 16-17; p Culbokie, Scotland, 17-

The Manse, Smithfield, Culbokie, Dingwall, Scotland   Blue Ridge
E-mail: terrance.burns1955@yahoo.com

Burrell, Kevin L. – b Canandaigua, NY, Apr 2, 69; f Lynn; m Lennie Alison Henderson; ErskC 91, BS; RTSFL 96, MDiv; L Jan 97, NGA Pby; O Jun 1, 97, NGA Pby; ascp Faith P Ch, Watkinsville, GA, 97-04; astp St. Pauls P Ch, Orlando, FL, 04-08; astp Stone Bridge Ch Comm, Charlotte, NC, 08-; "The Ethics of Environmentalism," *Faith and Practice*, Fall (96)

9318 Golden Pond Drive, Charlotte, NC 28269 – 704-323-5871   Catawba Valley
E-mail: burrell@mac.com
Stone Bridge Church Community – 704-549-8272

Burridge, Robert N. Jr. – BibTS, MDiv; O Jan 20, 87, CentFL Pby; p Grace P Ch, Pinellas Park, FL, 87-13; exec dir Genevan Inst for Ref Studies

8245 Parkwood Boulevard, Seminole, FL 33777 – 727-398-6078   Southwest Florida
E-mail: editor@girs.com
Genevan Institute for Reformed Studies

Bush, Kenneth Wayne – b Ota-shi, Japan, Jun 25, 55; f Kenneth J.; m Miyoko Takahashi; w Kathryn T. Kummer, Doylestown, PA, May 31, 86; chdn Bethany Marie, Susannah Joy, Amanda Hope, Leah Faith; PASU 78, BA; BibTS 86, MA, MDiv; DukeU 97, ThM; USAWC, MSS, 07; RTS, DMin cand; L 86, Phil Pby; O 86, Phil Pby; ap Christ P Ch, Doylestown, PA, 86-88; Chap USAR, 88; Chap USArmy, Ft. Leonard Wood, MO, 89-91; Chap USArmy, Korea, 91-92; Chap USArmy, Ft. Jackson, SC, 92-96; Chap USArmy, stu, DukeU, 97; Chap USArmy, Ft. Leavenworth, KS, 97-00; Chap USArmy, Germany, 00-03; Chap USArmy, Chief, Training Development, USACHCS, 03-08; Chap USArmy, Director of Training and Leader Development, USACHCS, 08-17; hr 17; ACM (5OLC); AAM; MSM (3OLC); "Military Worship Wars: Blended Worship as a Pastoral Response;" *The Army Chaplaincy*, Winter-Spring 03; "Giving Voice to the Sacred Story: Developing Military Homileticians," *The Army Chaplaincy*, Summer-Fall 10

4480 North Waterside Drive, Lenexa, VA 23089 – 804-966-5239   Eastern Pennsylvania
E-mail: kwbush55@verizon.net
HR

Bustamante, Roberto – astp New Life Msn Ch of Buena Park, Buena Park, CA, 08-15; astp Lamp P Ch of Los Angeles, Gardena, CA, 15-

2529 Cypress Point Drive, Fullerton, CA 92833 – 714-213-8137   Korean Southwest
E-mail: rs_bustamante@yahoo.com
Lamp Presbyterian Church of Los Angeles – 310-327-8778

Butler, John Owen – b Junction City, KS, Jun 5, 57; f Jack Davis; m Catherine Ann Mulkey; w Marie L. Gruezke, Greenville, TX, Jun 20, 81; chdn Joshua, Beth, Stephen; TXA&M-Comm 75-78, BS; RTS 82-85, MDiv; GPTS; L Jul 27, 85, SoTX Pby; O Nov 15, 86, MSVal Pby; Westminster P Ch, dir evan, Greenville, TX, 81-82; int Covenant P Ch, Houston, TX, 85-86; p Tchula P Ch, Tchula, MS, 86-89; p Beal Heights P Ch, Lawton, OK, 89-12; Chap OKARNG, 89-98; sc MidA Pby, 92-01; p Heritage P Ch, Edmond, OK, 12-15; wc; adj inst Equip Gospel Min/Malaysia Bib Sem, Kuala Lumpur, MY, 13-; mis MTW, 16; prin. lect Sunshine Coast TheoC, Queensland, 16; ob srp Grace Christian Ch (WPCA), Buderim, Queensland,17-

17/14-16 Toral Court, Buderim, QLD 4556 AUSTRALIA   North Texas
E-mail: okcalvin@gmail.com
Grace Christian Church

Butler, Timothy – astp Grace P Ch of St. Charles Co, St. Charles, MO, 12-17; ascp 17-

2947 Plum Leaf Circle, St. Peters, MO 63303   Missouri
Grace Presbyterian Church of St. Charles County – 636-926-2955

Butterfield, Michael J. – b Honolulu, HI, May 26, 59; f Eldred Marshall; m Mary Katherine; w Barbara Annette Lewis, Wales, Jul 18, 87; chdn Katherine Margret, Hannah Michelle, Megan Shân, Michael John, II, Richard Cameron; RBC/KuperC 93, BRE; RTS 08, MDiv; L Oct 7, 09, Cov Pby; O Jun 11, 10, Ecan Pby; p Westminster Bible P Ch, Sydney, NS, 11-14; p Macon P Ch, Macon, MS, 18-

457 Washington Street, Macon, MS 39341 – 662-788-2001   Mississippi Valley
E-mail: hilasterion.rom.3.25@gmail.com
Macon Presbyterian Church – 662-726-5184

Byers, James Simons – b Columbia, SC, Aug 26, 60; f Charles C.; m Frances Talbert; w Carmin Elizabeth Aiken, Greenville, SC, Dec 8, 84; chdn Josiah Simons, Victoria Abigail; ClemU 82, BME; RTS 00, MDiv; L Oct 28, 00, CentCar Pby; O Feb 18, 01, CentCar Pby; mis MTW, Lyon, France, 01-03; p New Hope P Ch, China Grove, NC, 04-

790 Mt. Moriah Church Road, China Grove, NC 28023 – 704-857-8707   Catawba Valley
E-mail: byersjc@gmail.com
New Hope Presbyterian Church – 704-857-3211

Byrd, Charles – ob p Ref Heritage Comm Ch, Holland, MI, 04-12; p Redeemer P Ch, Holland, MI, 12-

329 Roosevelt Avenue, Holland, MI 49424 – 616-994-9984   Great Lakes
Redeemer Presbyterian Church – 616-994-9984

Byrd, Jeremy – b Gross Pointe, MI, Dec 27, 78; f Sam; m Mary Ellen Vanni; w Heather Lynn Smith, Shelby Township, MI, Aug 3, 01; chdn Robert, Zacharais, Haddon; Ambassador 01, Bbib; BhamTS, MABS; O Sept 23, 18, GrLks Pby; p Christ Ch Ann Arbor, Ann Arbor, MI, 18-

1225 Maryland Street, Grosse Point Park, MI 48230   Great Lakes
Christ Church Ann Arbor – 734-276-6119

Byrd, Scott Aaron – O Mch 18, 18, Cov Pby; ascp Christ P Ch at Oxford, Oxford, MS, 18-

1400 Melanie Drive, Oxford, MS 38655   Covenant
Christ Presbyterian Church at Oxford – 662-234-3399

Byrne, Robert D. – b Kingston, NY, Mar 4, 52; f David Matthew; m Mary Evelyn Douglas; w Geraldine Kurtas, Philadelphia, PA, May 17, 75; chdn Chandler, Rebekah, Ethan, Patrick, Emilie; CC 70-74, BA; GRBS 77; RTS 78-81, MDiv; O Nov 9, 81, Gr Pby; p Leakesville P Ch, Leakesville, MS, 81-85; New Hope ARP, 86-88; p N. Rome P Ch, Tampa, FL, 88-92; Chap Veterans Administration Hospital, Tampa, FL, 89-10; sc SWFL Pby, 93-94; ascp Seminole P Ch, Tampa, FL, 01-03, ss 03-05; ss Cornerstone P Ch, Lutz, FL, 09-10, p 10-18; hr 18

17520 Marsh Road, Lutz, FL 33558 – 813-966-0027   Southwest Florida
E-mail: pastorbyrne@gmail.com
HR

Cabinte, Reyn – b Newport Beach, CA, Sept 13, 74; w Esther Lee, New York, NY, Feb 23, 02; chdn Soren Juin Yoshiharu; ColU 92, BA; ATS 06, MDiv; L Jan 07, MNY Pby; astp Emmanuel P Ch, New York, NY, 07; op Uptown Comm Ch, New York, NY, 07-

114 Bennett Avenue #3A, New York, NY 10033   Metropolitan New York
E-mail: reyn@uptowncommunitychurch.com
Uptown Community Church – 917-310-0871

Cadman, Bailey Charles – b Pittsburgh, PA, Jun 6, 49; f William; m Geraldine Gray; w Roberta Ann Michalka, Pittsburgh, PA, May 22, 76; chdn Rebekah Autumn, Matthew Henry; UPitt 72, BA, 74-76, AB; PASU 74, MA; PittsTS 81, MDiv; L Feb 24, 81, Asc Pby; O Jul 12, 81, Asc Pby; ap Gospel Flwsp P Ch, Valencia, PA, 81-89, srp 89-92; srp Faith Comm Ch, Pearland, TX, 92-01; srp Providence P Ch, Robinson Township, PA, 01-10; hr 10

Shady Grove Ranch, 549 Shady Grove Road, Jefferson, TX 75657 – 903-601-1065   Pittsburgh
E-mail: cadmanb2003@gmail.com
HR

Cadora, Matthew Allen – b Atlanta, GA, 63; w Lisa M.; UGA 87, BBA; GATech 89, MS; WestTS 00, MDiv; L & O Aug 6, 00, NGA Pby; int Grace Ch Seattle, Seattle, WA, 97-00; astp Intown Comm Ch, Atlanta, GA, 00-04; srp Faith P Ch, Cincinnati, OH, 05-

786 Elderwood Drive, Cincinnati, OH 45255 – 513-939-9300   Ohio Valley
E-mail: matt@faithpca.org
Faith Presbyterian Church – 513-231-1399

Cain, Benson – b Birmingham, AL, Apr 21, 26; f Joseph Bibb; m Marie Brooks; w Coline Gunn (d), Kobe, Japan, Oct 7, 55; chdn Colin Benson, Bibb Randall, Walter McDuffie, Marie Irene (Simoneaux),

Cain, Benson, continued
Donald Gunn; PC 50, BA; ColTS 52, BD; KSJL 53-56; ColTS 59, ThM; NOBTS 64-66; FulTS 78; RTS 87, DMin; L Jun 24, 52, EAL Pby (PCUS); O Jul 6, 52, EAL Pby (PCUS); p Millbrook P Ch, Millbrook, L, 52; mis Japan, 53-69; instr Shikoku ChrC, 54-55; prof KRTS, 61-69; ap First Ch, Hendersonville, NC, 68-69; p Forest-Covenant P Ch, Forest, MS, 69-72; Columbia P Ch, Columbia, MS, 72-73; p Hopewell Ch, Florence, SC, 73-78; prof KRTS, 78-80; prof Tokyo ChTS, 82-89; hr 89; ev PEF, 89-07; ip Faith OPC, Ocala, FL, 89-90; op Comm P Ch, McIntosh, FL, 91-92, ss 92-95; Faith P Ch, honorary ascp, Gainesville, FL, 89-07; t Wesley Commons Retire Home, New Hope PC, Abbeville, SC; *The Priesthood of All Believers in the New Testament*; contr *Reformed Theology* 9 & 16; *Gospel History and Apostolic History Syllabus*; bklts "The Law in the New Testament," 90; "Post WW 2 Evangelism in Japan," 09; "The Preeminence of Christ," 13; "The Lordship of Christ," 13

1110 Marshall Road, Greenwood, SC 29646 – 864-227-7318   North Florida
HR

    Cain, Brooks – mis MTW, Japan, 12-

c/o Mission to the World   Blue Ridge
E-mail: cain.brooks@gmail.com
PCA Mission to the World

    Cain, Richard Glenn – b Lumberton, NC, Jan 12, 62; f Glenn; m Betty Jo Vaught; w Helen Scott Austin, Chattanooga, TN, May 24, 86; chdn Elizabeth, Katherine, Rachel, Austin; UNC 80-84, BA; DTS 84-88, ThM; RTSNC 07, DMin; O Feb 89, 1st Evang Ch, Memphis; Recd PCA Oct 97, North GA; yp 1st Evan Ch, Memphis, TN, 88-91; fm Overseas Crusades, Buenos Aires, Argentina, 91-94; astp Grace Covenant Ch, Charlotte, NC, 94-96; astp Intown Community Ch, Atlanta, GA, 97-00; chp, op Grace P Ch, Douglasville, GA, 01-02; p Trinity P Ch, Tuscaloosa, AL; p Rainbow P Ch, Rainbow City, AL, 18-

3220 Rainbow Drive, Rainbow City, AL 35906 – 251-215-0256   Evangel
E-mail: dickcain@rainbowpca.org
Rainbow Presbyterian Church – 256-442-3440

    Caines, John Render – b Trenton, NJ, Feb 23, 47; f H. Lennon; m Mary L. McCutchen; w Linda R. Jackson, Scranton, PA, May 18, 68; chdn John Render Jr., Heather Erin; Philip Lennon, Gretchen Esther, David William, Ruth Allie; CC 69, BA; WTS 72, MDiv; CTS 87, DMin; L Dec 71, NJ Pby (RPCES); O Jul 72, NJ Pby (RPCES); p Evangelical Ch, Grand Cayman Is, 72-73; p Bethel Ref P Ch, Sparta, IL, 73-80; op, p Davenport Rd P Ch, Simpsonville, SC, 80-83; p East Ridge P Ch, East Ridge, TN, 83-88; op, srp Covenant P Ch, Chattanooga, TN, 88-; bd mbr CC, 85-93, 94-03, 04-12, 13-1, p em, 15; sc TNVal Pby, 96-00; hr 15

492 Larry Drive, Ringgold, GA 30736-8701 – 706-891-9387   Tennessee Valley
E-mail: jcaines@covenantchattanooga.org
HR

    Caines, John Render, Jr. – b Princeton, NJ, Oct 31, 71; f John Render; m Linda Ruth Jackson; w Shonda Evearitt, May 27, 95; chdn Emma Moriarity Pannkuk (Jay), John Render III, Louis Cedric; CC 93, BA; CTS 98, MDiv; p East Ridge P Ch, East Ridge, TN, 03-

4909 Florida Avenue, Chattanooga, TN 37409 – 423-822-7323   Tennessee Valley
E-mail: jrcaines@gmail.com
East Ridge Presbyterian Church – 423-867-7295

    Caines, Philip – b Sparta, IL, Jul 26, 74; f John Render; m Linda Ruth Jackson; w Sarah Lowe, Chattanooga, TN, May 31, 96; chdn Abigail Mae, Thomas Lennon, Jacob Render, Hannah Marie; CC 96, BA; CTS 01, MDiv; astp Covenant Ref P Ch, Asheville, NC, 03-06, ascp 06-08; p Trinity P Ch, Cleveland, TN, 08-

1780 Stuart Road NE, Cleveland, TN 37312   Tennessee Valley
E-mail: philip@trinityprescleveland.com
Trinity Presbyterian Church – 423-559-9595

Caires, Darcy Jr. – b Sao Paulo, Brazil, Apr 25, 63; f Darcy; m Deise Machado; w Christina Mello, Harrison, NJ, Jan 12, 91; SPS, ThB; L Jul 31, 86, Norte-Paulistano Pby; O Aug 30, 86, North-Paulistano Pby (IPB); Recd PCA Feb 29, 92, NJ Pby; astp Comunidade Crista Presbiteriana, Newark, NJ, 92-93, wc 93-94; ob chp Mineola, NY, Cliffside Park, NJ, 94-95; op Comunidade Crista Presbiteriana, Mineola, NY, 95-98, p 98-01; astp, ev Astoria Comm Ch, Astoria, NY, 01-05, ascp 05-13; op Queens P Ch, Long Island City, NY, 10-13; srp 13-15

2028 41st Street, Astoria, NY 11105-1614 – 718-728-1696 Metropolitan New York
E-mail: CairesJr@aol.com

Cairns, Robert Steven – b Amarillo, TX, Jan 4, 54; w Paula Fay, Dec 21, 74; chdn Jennifer, Ben, Michael; WTSU 77; WTS 84, MDiv; L Apr 85, OPC; O Apr 25, 86, OPC; Recd PCA Oct 26, 91, SoTX Pby; Young Life, Amarillo, TX, 84-89; couns, ev Christ Cov OPC, Amarillo, TX, 86-91; ascp, couns Bay Area P Ch, Webster, TX, 91-98; WTS, dir, TX Development, 99-08; WTS Dir Church Rel & Reg Dev, 09-12; WTS Partnership Mgr, 12-15; WTS Sr. Admiss Couns, 16-

43 Spring Creek Road, Boerne, TX 78006 – 830-537-6120 South Texas
E-mail: scairns1221@gmail.com

Calabretta, Robert – O Feb 12, 17, MNY Pby; astp Living Faith Community Ch, Flushing, NY, 16-18; op King's Cross Ch, Flushing, NY, 18-

144-67 41st Avenue, Apt. 623, Flushing, NY 11355 – 716-812-2488 Metropolitan New York
E-mail: Robert@kingscrossnyc.org
King's Cross Church

Calderazzo, James – b Norristown, PA, Dec 7, 65; f Franklin James; m Janet Hamilton; w Susan Lewis, Orlando, FL, Jan 21, 95; chdn Hannah; DukeU 84-88, BS; CTS 91-95, MDiv; O Mar 2, 97, Cov Pby; astp Main Street P Ch, Columbus, MS, 95-98; p Christ P Ch, Sweetwater, TN, 98-03; p Grace P Ch, Baton Rouge, LA, 03-06; p Safe Harbor P Ch, Destin, FL, 06-

47 Talon Way, Santa Rosa Beach, FL 32459-8319 – 850-654-9337 Gulf Coast
E-mail: jmcldrzz@bellsouth.net
Safe Harbor Presbyterian Church – 850-837-2133

Call, Raymond E. III – b Los Alamitos, CA, Apr 21, 72; w Michele; chdn Rebecca, Jeremiah, AnnaGrace, John, Daniel, Christina, Peter, Lucas; CSULB 95, BA; CTS 06, MDiv; O 07, MO Pby; mis MTW, BEAMM, US/Mexico Border, 06-13; mis MTW/Uruguay Mission OPC, 13-

c/o MTW – +59891357523 South Coast
E-mail: rcall@mtwla.org
Mission to the World

Callison, Robert A. – b Grand Junction, CO, May 17, 56; f Gerald; m Wilma Rettig; w LoAn Neaves (d), San Diego, CA, Jan 10, 87; MesaC 78, BS; WTS 89, MDiv; RTSFL 12, DMin; L Apr 90, SoCst Pby; O Mar 3, 91, SoCst Pby; vol pris min, 89-91; ev SoCst Pby, 91; Chap USNR, USS Denver LPD-9, 92-94; Chap USNR, 1st Btn 12th Marines, 94-96; Chap USNR, 1 Btn 3rd Marines, 96-97; Chap USNR, MCBH Kaneohe Bay, HI, 97-01; Chap USN, USS Nassau LHA-4, 01-03; Chap USN, Quantico, VA, 03-06; Chap USN, Jacksonville, NC, 06-08; Chap USN, Millington, TN, 08-15; astp Riveroaks Ref P Ch, Germantown, TN, 15-; Lt. CHC, USNR, 92; LCDR CHC, USNR, 99

4532 East Woodlawn Circle, Collierville, TN 38017 – 901 483-8522 Covenant
E-mail: localrob504@gmail.com
Riveroaks Reformed Presbyterian Church – 901-755-7772

Calton, Wes – w Kelly; chdn Walker, Pack, Whitley, Ann McClain; DavC 10, BA; RTSNC 13, MDiv O Sept 8, 13, NWGA Pby; campm RUF, KennStU, 13-

2805 Pine Hill Drive NW, Kennesaw, GA 30144   Northwest Georgia
E-mail: wes.calton@ruf.org
PCA Reformed University Fellowship

Calvert, Michael – w Carol; chdn Benjamin, Joseph, Brooke; SamU 81, BA; SWBTS 84, MDiv; NWU, South Africa 14, PhD; p Christ P Ch, Owens Cross Roads, AL, 05-

2616 Elderdale Drive, Hampton Cove, AL 35763 – 256-532-5134   Providence
E-mail: mcalvert256@comcast.net
Christ Presbyterian Church

Calvert, Paul – b Troy, OH, Feb 3, 66; f Richard Lee; m Rosalie Sue Kroger; w Michelle Denise Minnich, Vail, CO, Jan 13, 95; chdn Jordan DeAnn, Jacob Paul; WLBI 85-86; CedC 98, BA; DTS 89; RTS 93-95; CinBibSem 93-96, MDiv; O 10, OHVal Pby; yp First Bapt Ch, Troy, OH, 86-88; p Mt. Pleasant Bapt Ch, St. Paris, OH, 96-99; p Cove Spring Ch, Elizabeth Twsp, OH, 99-07; Grace Bapt Ch, Troy, OH, 07; The Meadows Comm Ch, Dayton, OH, 07-10; op Centerpoint Christ Comm Ch, Troy, OH, 10-17

1597 North Road, Troy, OH 45373 – 937-339-7325   Ohio Valley
E-mail: paulcalvert@mac.com

Camenisch, Glenn Davis – b Stanford, KY, Jan 4, 50; f Robert H; m Martha May Davis; w Mary Frances Taylor, Miami, FL, Aug 27, 73; chdn Joel Glenn, Andrew Taylor, Sara Marie; KgC 72, BA; RTS 76, MDiv; O Jun 27, 76, Evan Pby; ap First P Ch, 76-78; mis MTW, Portugal, 78-17; hr 17

c/o MTW   Evangel
E-mail: GDCamenisch@usa.net
HR

Camera, David – w Gwendolyn Gay, Jul 8, 95; chdn Owen, Ethan, Aria; KStU 92, BA; WheatC 95, MA; TEDS 98, MDiv; O Aug 06, Evan Pby; astp Briarwood P Ch, Birmingham, AL, 06-09; astp River Oaks P Ch, Lake Mary, FL, 10-

385 Washington Avenue, Lake Mary, FL 37066   Central Florida
E-mail: cameradavid1@gmail.com
River Oaks Presbyterian Church – 407-330-9103

Campbell, James P. Jr. – b Tuscaloosa, AL, Sept 4, 42; f James P C Sr; m Minnie Spencer; w Cheryl Woodham, Trussville, AL, Sept 4, 65; chdn James P III, Shawn, Jonathan, Knox; UAL 63, BS; GCTS 74, MDiv; L Aug 15, 74; O Nov 16, 74, CentGA Pby; op Columbus, GA, 74-77; p Westminster P Ch, Columbus, GA, 77-86; p First P Ch, Ft. Oglethorpe, GA, 86-91, wc 91-01; hr 01; *Expository Commentary on Hebrews*; pamp *A Basic Guide to Bible Commentaries; Romans Chapter One-Eight, The Necessity of the Gospel*

PO Box 23, Signal Mountain, TN 37377 – 423-400-4600   Tennessee Valley
HR

Campbell, John Thomas Jr. (Jack) – b Midland, MI, Jul 11, 49; f John T.; m Rose Mary Eden; w Sherri Rae Cate, Raymond, NH, Jul 5, 80; chdn John Thomas III, Caleb Benjamin (d), Jessica Ann, Judith Michelle, Julia Grace, Joshua Daniel; USMC 69-70; MarU 71-72; AldBC 73-77, BS; CIU 82, MDiv; O Dec 83, Cal Pby; p Davenport Rd P Ch, Simpsonville, SC, 83-89; mis MTW, Madrid, Spain, 89-95; mis RMI, Madrid, Spain, 95-04; RMI Intnat'l, 04-

104 Hillandale Road, Pendleton, SC 29670 – 864-646-8956   Calvary
Reformed Ministries International

Campbell, Ken – b Salem, MA, Feb 7, 43; f James; m Eleanor Malcolmson; w Cathy, Burlington, MA, Jan 25, 69; chdn David, Bethany (Skillen); SuffolkU 68, BS; GCTS 71, MDiv; FairDickU 83, MBA, 10, DMin; O Sept 29, 96; ascp Hope Ch, Wilton, CT, 95-97; p Faith Comm Ch, Edgartown, MA, 97-06; astp Redeemer P Ch, Austin, TX, 10-17; MNA/SMN 13-; astp Emmanuel P Ch, Cedar Park, TX, 17-; *That My House May Be Filled: Implementing a Church Ministry with People Impacted by Disability*, 10

1328 Pasa Tiempo, Leander, TX 78641   South Texas
Emmanuel Presbyterian Church – 512-690-2577

Campbell, Michael A. – b Germany, Jun 17, 64; f George Albert III; m Shelby Jean Lilly; w Keren Anne Thompson, Miami, FL, Jun 27, 87; chdn Katherine Lilly, Matthew John, Elisabeth Rose; KgC 82-86, BA; CTS 94, MDiv; 14, DMin; O May 11, 97, SFL Pby; medu Sunshine Mission Minister, St. Louis, MO, 90-92; admin Ministries in Action, 92-97; p Pinelands P Ch, Miami, FL, 97-04; op Redeemer P Ch, Jackson, MS, 04-05; srp 05-15; srp Old Cutler P Ch, Palmetto Bay, FL, 15-

E-mail: mike@ocpc.org   South Florida
Old Cutler Presbyterian Church – 305-238-8121

Campbell, Thomas Milton – b Charlotte, NC, Jan 4, 49; f James Edward; m Fanny LaRue; w Helene Anne, McKeesport, PA, Jun 19, 71; chdn Daniel, Susan; US MerchMarAcad 71, BS; VPI 76, BS; ORSU 84, MF; CIU 97, MDiv; L Jan 28, 99, Palm Pby; O Jun 13, 99, Palm Pby; astp Cornerstone P Ch, 99-04; mis MTW, 04-07; mis CCI, 07-16; hr 16

50 Keoway Drive # B2, Seneca, SC 29672   Palmetto
E-mail: tomnhelene@swissmail.com
HR

Campo, Theodore Joseph – b Mineola, NY, Jun 26, 62; f Theodore John; m Josephine Marie Burke; w Michelle Ann Contois, Stuart, FL, Mar 8, 86; chdn Hannah Catherine, Theodore Joseph Jr., Madeline Michelle; SEC 86, BA; CBS 86, MDiv; L Aug 89, SFL Pby; O Sept 15, 91, SFL Pby; astp, moy St. Andrews Park Road P Ch, Hollywood, FL, 89-93, ascp 93-94; srp 94-

5500 Harrison Street, Hollywood, FL 33021 – 954-963-8111   South Florida
E-mail: tj@standrewspca.com
St. Andrews Park Road Presbyterian Church – 954-989-2641

Candell, Jeffrey M. – b West Covina, CA, Jun 13, 64; f Lloyd M; m Sharon K. Cookman; w Robyn M. Bagby, Jackson, MS, May 19, 90; chdn Emily Nichole, Christopher Lloyd, Kathryn Elizabeth, Dennis Anderson; UCSB 88, BA; RTS 91, MDiv; O Nov 10, 91, CentGA Pby; int First P Ch, Aliceville, AL, 89-90; astp Perry P Ch, Perry, GA, 91-98; ascp Spring Cypress P Ch, Spring, TX, 98-05; ascp Providence Comm Ch, Victoria, BC, 05- 15; ascp Lighthouse P Msn Ch, Victoria, BC, 15-

PO Box 46026, RPO Quadra Village   Western Canada
Victoria, BC, V8T 5G7 CANADA – 250-483-5583
E-mail: jeff@lighthousechurch.ca
Lighthouse Presbyterian Mission Church – 250-818-9252

Cangelosi, Caleb G. – b Zachary, LA, Jan 12, 76; f Dale Douglas; m Melanie Johnston; w Elizabeth Smith, Mar 3, 01; chdn Daniel Johnston, Laura Grace, Elizabeth Ann, Caroline Leslie, Ezra Paul; LSU 98, BS; RTS 03, MDiv; PurRefTS 18, ThM; O Jun 15, 03, Gr Pby; p Columbia P Ch, Columbia, MS, 03-07; p Grace P Ch, Cookeville, TN, 07-14; ascp Pear Orchard P Ch, Ridgeland, MS, 14-; fndr Log College Press; *Family Mealtime Prayers;* "The Church Is a Missionary Society, and the Spirit of Missions Is the Spirit of the Gospel: The Missional Piety of the Southern Presbyterian Tradition," *Puritan Reformed Journal 5:1* (2013); "William Swan Plumer's Defense of the Impeccability of Jesus Christ," *The Confessional Presbyterian*, Vol. 9, 13; "The Mouth of the Morningstar: John Wycliffe's Preaching and the Protestant Reformation," *Puritan Reformed Journal*, 6:2, 14

92 Cotton Wood Drive, Madison, MS 39110 – 601-720-7201   Mississippi Valley
E-mail: caleb@pearorchard.org
Pear Orchard Presbyterian Church – 601-956-3283

Cannada, Robert Cox Jr. – b Jackson, MS, Apr 4, 48; f Robert C; m Inez Chisolm; w Rachel Earhart, Pine Bluff, AR, Jun 6, 70; chdn Christy (Burrow), Cecilia (Rutledge); VandU 70, BA; RTS 73, MDiv, 95, DMin; O, SC Pby (PCUS); ap First Ch, Clinton, SC, 73-76; p Covenant P Ch, Little Rock, AR, 76-86; srp First P Ch, Macon, GA, 86-93; ob admin, VP RTSNC, 93-01; ob exec vp RTS, all campuses, 98-01; ob pres RTS, 02-04; ob Chan RTS, 04-12; ob Chan Emeritus 12; hr 18

111 Mississippi Street, Madison, MS 39110 – 769-798-6617   Mississippi Valley
E-mail: rcannada@rts.edu
HR

Cannata, Raymond Douglas Fortier – b East Meadow, NY, Oct 14, 68; f George Augustus; m Audrey Martin Crowson; w Katharine Marie Fortier, Winston-Salem, NC, Apr 20, 91; chdn Andrew Calvin, Rachel Grace; WFU 90, BA; PTS 94, MDiv, 95, ThM; WTS 10, DMin; L May 18, 96, NJ Pby; O Nov 9, 97, MNY Pby; astp Grace Comm Ch, Bridgewater, NJ, 97-99, ascp 99-00, srp 00-05; srp Redeemer P Ch, New Orleans, LA, 05-; mod MNY pby04; mod SELA pby 09; co-fndr *Princeton Theological Review, Signs and Seals Amid the Rubble: Kingdom Ministry in New Orleans*, 10, *Rooted: The Apostles' Creed*, 13, *The Man Who Ate New Orleans* (film), 12

737 Henry Clay Avenue, New Orleans, LA 70118   Southern Louisiana
E-mail: redeemer_nola@yahoo.com
Redeemer Presbyterian Church – 504-894-1204

Cannon, Thomas K. – b Norristown, PA, Mar 4, 58; f Joseph John; m Elizabeth Louise Kenny; w Dawn James, Florence, SC, Dec 29, 85; chdn Grace Elizabeth, James Andrew, Noah Zachary; USC 82, BA; WTS; RTS 88, MDiv; O Sept 4, 88, Palm Pby; ob mis Australia (P Ch of Australia), 88-97; ascp The Village Ch, New York, NY, 97-98; campm RUF, NYU, 97-01; RUM, NE area coord, 00-01; campm RUF, SCAD, 01-07; p Red Mtn Ch, Birmingham, AL, 07-08; srp 08-14; coord RUF, 14-18

98 Saluda Way, Beaufort, SC 29906   Evangel

Cano, Carlos – op Iglesia La Vid, 06-

3516 Salinas Avenue, Laredo, TX 78041   South Texas
E-mail: lavidlaredo@aol.com
Iglesia La Vid

Cantu, Jahaziel – b Monterrey Mexico, Sept 18, 79; f Leonel; m Minerva Tamez; w Ann, Dallas, TX, Jun 20, 09; chdn Elijah Jahaziel, Elizabeth Grace; UNuevoLeón 03; WTSTX 09, MDiv; O Feb 13, 13, NoTX Pby; ip Cristo Rey, Dallas, TX, 05-12; ascp Christ P Ch, Flower Mound, TX, 13-17; chp 18-; contr *All Are Welcome: Toward a Multi-Everything Church*

2517 Sycamore Leaf Lane, Flower Mound, TX 75022 – 214-243-9321   North Texas
E-mail: jahazielct@elbuenpastorpca.org

Capen, Todd – b Barstow, CA, Feb 21, 58; f Phil A.; m Marie Nina Johnson; w Mary Ann Fellows, San Mateo, CA, Jan 8, 83; chdn Aubree, Amaris; BIOLA 82, BS; RTS 93, MDiv; L Mar 96, NoCA Pby; O Oct 27, 96, NoCA Pby; p Trinity P Ch Windward, Kailua, Oahu, HI, 96-

875 Auloa Road, Kailua, HI 96734 – 808-263-1198   Northern California
E-mail: todd@trinitychurchkailua.org
Trinity Presbyterian Church – 808-262-8587

Capitano, Sam – b Wilkes-Barre, PA, Dec 19, 65; f Samuel; m Josephine Schifano; w Lisa Craye, Fredericksburg, VA, Jn 8, 91; chdn Taniya (Puig), Amanda (Murray), Zarina (Prevost), Samantha, Joseph, James; UScranton 87, BS; NGTS 17, MDiv; O Ja 17, JR Pby; astp New Life in Christ Ch, Fredericksburg, VA, 17-

1010 Roberts Court, Fredericksburg, VA 22401 – 540-373-0053   James River
E-mail: sam@nlicc.orgNew Life in Christ Church – 540-786-4848

Capper, LeRoy S. – b Chicago, Il, Aug 27, 56; f LeRoy; m Marilyn Jane Freer; w Nancy Ann Smith, Ypsilanti, MI, Jul 14, 79; chdn LeRoy Scott Jr., Laura Anne, Mary Beth, Mark Andrew; MISU 74-78, BA; CTS 81-85, MDiv; L Oct 19, 85, MO Pby; O May 24, 87, Asc Pby; p Faith P Ch, LaVale, MD, 87-; sc Pitts Pby, 97-; op WCI P Ch, Cumberland, MD, 01-; instr Ukraine Bib Sem, 10-

1620 Bedford Street, Cumberland, MD 21502-1052 – 301-777-3458   Pittsburgh
E-mail: fpc@atlanticbbn.net
Faith Presbyterian Church – 301-729-0100
WCI Presbyterian Church – 301-729-0100

Caradine, Thomas R. Jr. – b Birmingham, AL, May 23, 53; f Thomas R.; m Francis Gilliam; w Cynthia Ann Persons, Atlanta, GA, Aug 21, 76; chdn Kathryn Ryan, Holly Ann, Barbara Cameron; SamU 76, BS; BhamTS 84, MDiv; L Sept 84, Evan Pby; O Sept 84, Evan Pby; astp Briarwood P Ch, Birmingham, AL, 84-85, ascp 85-99; ascp Oak Mountain P Ch, Birmingham, AL, 03-

2508 Magnolia Place, Birmingham, AL 35242 – 205-991-0445   Evangel
E-mail: tcaradine@ompc.org
Oak Mountain Presbyterian Church – 205-995-9265

Carden, Zachary F. III – astp Hope P Ch, Marietta, GA, 03; astp Covenant P Ch, Chattanooga, TN, 03-08; astp Christ Comm Ch, Kennesaw, GA, 08-11; ob astp Ch of the Apostles, Atlanta, GA, 11-

2061 Sanderlings Drive, Kennesaw, GA 30152 – 770-726-9209   Northwest Georgia
Church of the Apostles – 404-842-0200
3585 Northside Parkway NW, Atlanta, GA 30327

Carey, Robert Josiah Hereford – w Megan Kelley Schwartz; CTS 14, MDiv; O 15, SLA Pby; campm RUF, Tulane, 15-

2621 Robert Street, New Orleans, LA 70115   Southern Louisiana
E-mail: josiah.carey@ruf.org
PCA Reformed University Fellowship

Cargo, Hace – b Atlanta, GA, Mar 16, 87; f Robert Augustus; m Margaret Anne; w Sally Smith, Lagrange, GA, Jun 6, 09; chdn Robert Clifton; UGA 09, BA; CTS 14, MDiv; O Nov 16, 14, MetAtl Pby; astp Brookhaven P Ch, Atlanta, GA, 14-

2252 Capehart Circle NE, Atlanta, GA 30345 – 404-538-9902   Metro Atlanta
E-mail: hace.cargo@brookhavenpres.com
Brookhaven Presbyterian Church – 678-982-0095

Cargo, Robert Augustus – b Gadsden, AL, Nov 4, 54; f Hace Clemons; m Martha Lorena King; w Margaret Anne Ruff, Tupelo, MS, Aug 4, 84; chdn Hace Clemons II, Myra Elizabeth, Robert Eason, Margaret Claire; SamU 73-77, BA; TEDS 79-82, MDiv; O Oct 24, 82, Cov Pby; op Oxford, MS, 82-85; ap Perimeter Ch, Duluth, GA, 85-90; srp Intown Comm Ch, Atlanta, GA, 90-98; srp Orangewood P Ch, Maitland, FL, 98-02; astp, DChPl Perimeter Ch, Johns Creek, GA, 02-

4243 Ridgegate Drive, Peachtree Corners, GA 30097 – 678-417-6858   Metro Atlanta
E-mail: bobcargo@perimeter.org
Perimeter Church – 678-405-2104

Carl, Brett William – b Chicago, IL, Apr 13, 72; f James M.; m Susan Lynn White; w Debra Lynn Enlow, Fairhope, AL, Jun 19, 99; chdn Caitlin MacKenzie, Riley Elizabeth, Addison Claire; HDC 94, BA; RTSFL 97, MDiv; L May 99, GulCst Pby; O Mar 5, 00, JR Pby; ydir Eastern Shore P Ch, Fairhope, AL, 97-99; astp, ydir Westminster Ref P Ch, Suffolk, VA, 99-09; ascp 09-

104 Pelham Place, Suffolk, VA 23434 – 757-613-0200   Tidewater
E-mail: brett@wrpca.org
Westminster Reformed Presbyterian Church – 757-539-0540

Carlton, Oscar Jefferson III – b Birmingham, AL, Sept 14, 56; f O. J. Jr.; m Ann Noble; w Bonnie Dorough, Birmingham, AL, Aug 18, 79; chdn Jay, Kyle, Ann Noble; CBC 74-78, BA; CBS 79-82, MDiv; O Feb 85 & Jun 06, SEAL Pby; First P Ch, Dothan, AL, 85-88; op Christ P Ch, New Braunfels, TX, 88-91; op Lake Crest P Ch, Birmingham, AL, 91-93, p 93-95; p Providence P Ch, Montgomery, AL, 06-13; ob Chap University Hosp, Birmingham, AL, 12-14

405 Amelia Lane, Santa Rosa Beach, FL 32459　　　　　　　　　　　　Southeast Alabama
E-mail: jcarlton112@gmail.com

Carmichael, Joseph Van (Josh) – w Betsy; chdn Fulton, Morris, Milledge, Henry, Thomas, Joseph; UAL 93, BS, 95, MBA; RTS 01, MDiv; SBTS 12, PhD; O Sept 7, 03, Palm Pby; astp Trinity P Ch, Orangeburg, SC, 03-05; astp Redeemer P Ch, Louisville, KY, 06-11; assoc dir CMDA, ULouv, 09-11; p First P Ch, Greensboro, AL, 11-15; p Newbern P Ch, Newbern, AL, 11- 15; ss New Cov P Ch, Selma, AL; prof BhamTS, 14-; t Eastwood CS, 16-; p Little Sandy Ridge P Ch, Fort Deposit, AL, 18-; chap res Princeton Bapt Med Cntr, Birmingham, AL; "The Hymns of Anne Steele in John Rippon's Selection of Hymns: The Sung Theology of the English Particular Baptist Revival" in *Baptists and Revival*, 18; "William Tyndale" – *Reformation Today* July-Aug 17

1830 Croom Drive, Montgomery, AL 36106　　　　　　　　　　　　　　　　Warrior
E-mail: jvcarmichael@gmail.com
Birmingham Theological Seminary
Little Sandy Ridge Presbyterian Church – 334-382-6568
Princeton Baptist Medical Center, Birmingham, AL

Carmody, Jack – b Atlanta, GA, Feb 28, 81; w Carrie; chdn Chase, Caroline; O Aug 21, 11, Palm Pby; astp Chapin P Ch, Chapin, SC, 11-

297 Foxport Drive, Chapin, SC 29036 – 803-760-8003　　　　　　　　　　Palmetto
E-mail: jackc@chapinpres.com
Chapin Presbyterian Church – 803-345-0500

Carpenter, Brad – astp Valley Springs P Ch, Roseville, CA, 06-11; ob Church of the Shepherd, IL, 11-13, chp 13-15; p City of Grace, Sacramento, CA, 16-

8248 Rensselaer Way, Sacramento, CA 95826-2959 – 916-437-8360　　Northern California
E-mail: brad@cityofgracechurch.org
City of Grace – 916-437-8360

Carpenter, Brian – b St. Louis, MO, Apr 21, 69; f Robert L.; m Ellen S. Tillman; w Laura Ann Greinger, Atlantic, IA, Jul 10, 92; chdn Evelyn Grace, Jordan Elizabeth; UMO 91, BS; LPTS 99, MDiv; O Nov 7, 99, PCUSA; Recd PCA May 3, 02, OHVal Pby; stus St. Andrews P Ch, Evansville, IN, 96-97; stus Laurel P Ch, Hager City, WI, 97-98; stus Parke Mem P Ch, Evansville, IN, 98-99; p Georgetown P Ch, Georgetown, OH, 99-01; astp Faith P Ch, Cincinnati, OH, 02-04; p Foothills Comm Ch, Sturgis, SD, 04-18; wc

1107 Creighton Road, Papillion, NE 68046 – 605-720-3330　　　　　　　Siouxlands
E-mail: bouletheou@hotmail.com

Carpenter, Thomas – w Ashley; chdn Natalie; O May 10, 05, CentFL Pby; astp CityChurch, Ft. Lauderdale, FL, 06-07; ob mis London, 07-09; astp CityChurch, Ft. Lauderdale, FL, 09-16

1539 SW 23rd Terrace, Deerfield Beach, FL 33442-7521 – 305-361-9305　　South Florida
E-mail: thomastcarpenter@hotmail.com

Carper, Tim – O Jul 11, 15, NFL Pby; campm RUF, UFL, 15-17

915 Walnut Street SW, Winston-Salem, NC 27101 – 757-470-1796　　　　North Florida
E-mail: tim.carper123@gmail.com

Carr, Billy Clifford – b Greeneville, TN, Aug 4, 55; f Clifford Roy; m Alta Leota Pierce; w Patricia Susan Arnold, Bristol, TN, Dec 10, 77; chdn Vanessa Christine, Rebekah Susan; ETSU 77, BS, 82, MEd; GPTS 98, MDiv; L Jan 9, 93, Westm Pby; O Jul 10, 99, Westm Pby; mis MTW, Johannesburg, South Africa, 99-10; mis MTW, Bemidji, MN, 10-

c/o Mission to the World   Siouxlands
PCA Mission to the World

Carr, Kevin C. – b Buffalo, NY, Feb 13, 51; f Wilfred Hermon; m Comstock; w Krehl, Buffalo, NY, Jun 24, 72; chdn Matthew, Steven; ErCC 69-71, AD; SUNY 73-75, BS; BibTS 75-78, MDiv; CGST 78, grad wk, 88, DMin; L Sept 78, Pac Pby; O Feb 79, Pac Pby; ap Calvary P Ch, Glendale, CA, 79-80; p Comm Bib Ch, Window Rock, AZ, 80-89; p First P Ch, Hinckley, MN, 89-; *Keeping the Church on Target*; *The Wonderful Grace of Jesus*; *Lord, Teach Us to Pray! The Book of Books; Seeing is Believing*

PO Box 157, Hinckley, MN 55037-0157 – 320-384-0383   Siouxlands
E-mail: kevincarr1@juno.com
First Presbyterian Church – 320-384-6440

Carr, Robert Lee – b Philadelphia, PA, Jul 4, 48; f Frederick B.; m Johnson; w Lois Chantz, Philadelphia, PA, May 22, 76; chdn Rebekah, Jessica, Stephen, Andrew; FulJC, AA; TempU, BA; WTS, MAR, MDiv; CIU, DMin; O Apr 23, 89, Phil Pby; p Community of Christ, Philadelphia, PA, 74-78; ob ev WHM, Uganda, 85-92; ob Dir WHM, African Svcs, 92-95; ob chp, t/tr Kenya, 95-13; church mobilization US, Serge, 13-15; chpl coach, asst coor Metro Phily ChPlant, 15-

2936 Elliott Avenue, Willow Grove, PA 19090   Eastern Pennsylvania
E-mail: kenyaplant@gmail.com
Metro Phily Church Planting Partnership

Carr, Thomas Ray – b Panama City, FL, Sept 15, 49; f Buell Edward; m Gladys Peacock; w Alison Elaine Cook, Panama City, FL, Jun 21, 74; chdn Matthew Jared, Erin Amanda; GCCC 69, AA; UWFL 71, BA; RTS 82, MDiv; O Jun 82, GulCst Pby; p New Phil P Ch, Quincy, FL, 82-85; p Chapel In The Gardens P Ch, Garden City, GA, 85-93; p First P Ch, Demopolis, AL, 93-17; sc War Pby, 94-03; hr 17

1113 Dow Street, Demopolis, AL 36732-3560 – 334-289-9935   Warrior
E-mail: trcarr@bellsouth.net
HR

Carrico, John – b Temple, TX, Mar 6, 65; f John David; m Marilyn Joyce; w Pamela Rene Hennessey, Little Rock, AR, Jun 24, 95; chdn John David III, Kailey Grace; UARLR 91, BA; CTS 03, MDiv; O Nov 11, 08, Evan Pby; Mitchell Road PCch, child dir, Greenville, SC, 03-06; North Cincinnati Comm Ch, child dir, Mason, OH, 06-07; astp First P Ch, Tuscumbia, AL, 07-11; ob 13-

1 Ohio Cove, Little Rock, AR 72227   Providence
E-mail: jdcarrico2@gmail.com

Carroll, Charles S. III – b Jackson, MS, Jul 31, 45; f Charles S.; m Clara Johnson; w Becky Bartholomew (d); Jean Bivens Oct 15, 06; chdn Shannon, Imes, Joshua, Caleb, Stephanie (Collier), Stephan Bivens; HJC 63-65; MSU 65-67, BS; RTS 72-75, MDiv; L Jul 74; O Jul 27, 75, Gr Pby; p Mount Olive P Ch, Mount Olive, MS, 75-79; p Lawndale P Ch, Tupelo, MS, 84; admin FCAc, French Camp, MS, 84-17; mgr WFCA Radio, 84-17; ss Spout Springs P Ch, Ripley, MS, 85-05; ss Carrollton P Ch, Carrollton, MS, 05-17; hr 17

127 Quail Circle, Houston, MS 38851   Covenant
E-mail: carr1015@att.net
HR

MINISTERIAL DIRECTORY

Carroll, Grant – astp First P Ch, Kosciusko, MS, 08-12; campm RUF, HolmesCC, 08-12; campm RUF, Jksnville St, 12- 17; ascp Faith P Ch, Anniston, AL, 17-

1405 George Douthit Drive SW, Jacksonville, AL 36265   Evangel
E-mail: gbcarroll@gmail.com
Faith Presbyterian Church – 256-238-8721

Carroll, John Allen – b Mount Vernon, NY, Feb 28, 45; f John M (d); m Dorothy Trout (d); w Mary E. Lackey, Roanoke, VA, Jun 5, 71; chdn Paula (Acker), Alicia (Henn), Ana Maria (Hasbrouck) ; VPI 66, BS; UPI 68-70, grad wk; CBS 94, MDiv; RTSNC 04, DMin; O Aug 13, 95, Palm Pby; Navs, Philippines, Argentina, 68-95; p Central P Ch, Kingstree, SC, 95-00; Christ Ch, dir admin & outreach, Katy, TX, 00-01, astp 01-02, ascp 02-11; p em, 11; sc HouMet Pby, 07-10; hr 11; mod BlRdg pby, 17; contr *NIV Collegiate Devotional Bible*, 98; *Cover to Cover: Through the Bible in 365 Days*, 14

1186 Camp Jaycee Road, Blue Ridge, VA 24064 – 540-494-2832   Blue Ridge
E-mail: jacarroll71@gmail.com; ThistleDewFarm.us
HR

Carroll, Timothy J. – b Woodbridge, VA, Jan 2, 80; f John (d); m Pierangela; w Dorothy; chdn Amelia; CTS 11, MDiv; O Feb 17, 13, Pot Pby; astp Crossroads P Ch, Dumfries, VA, 13-16; astp Chinese Christian Ch, Falls Church, VA, 16-

3318 Glenmore Drive, Falls Church, VA 22041   Potomac
E-mail: mr.tim22@gmail.com
Chinese Christian Church – 703-820-1010

Carson, Daniel Worth – b Miami Beach, FL, Jul 30, 59; f Joseph Edwin III; m Jean Bradley; w Sandra Elaine Enyeart, Miami, FL, Jun 4, 83; chdn Rachel Elaine, Andrew Worth, Nathan Benjamin; GWC 81, BA; UEdin 82; PTS 85, MDiv;CTS 05, DMin; O Nov 5, 85, NJ Pby; ap Princeton P Ch, Princeton, NJ, 85-86; op Grace Comm Ch, Bridgewater, NJ, 86-89, p 89-99; srp Granada P Ch, Coral Gables, FL, 99-

14541 Tarpon Drive, Coral Gables, FL 33158 – 305-378-0751   South Florida
E-mail: wcarson@granadapca.org
Granada Presbyterian Church – 305-444-8435

Carter, J. Alan – b Meridian, MS, Jul 4, 49; f E G Carter; m Margaret; w Sally Hogan, Jackson, MS, Jul 22, 72; chdn Nathan, Tim; MSU 71, BS; RTS 76, MDiv, 80, MCE; WKU 81-82, MA; UNotD 87, PhD; O Jun 27, 76, MSVal Pby; p Mt. Hermon Ch, Madison, MS, 76-80; ss Round Pond (PCUS), Franklin, KY, 80-81; srp Faith P Ch, Birmingham, AL, 86-16; ob 18-; brd GCP 91-95; CEP Co 91-95; IRC Co 07-09; AL JointCo CampMin

3050 Roxbury Drive, West Linn, OR 97068 – 205-821-3586   Evangel
E-mail: alancarter1949@gmail.com

Carter, James Richard – b Monroeville, AL, Oct 30, 60; f Harris R.; m Evelyn S. Kelley; w Terri L. Ganey, Mullins, SC, Aug 21, 82; chdn Sarah Elizabeth, David Matthew; BelC 83, BA; RTS 85, MA, 88, MDiv; ErskTS 16, DMin; L Jun 86; O Jun 2, 88, MSVal Pby; Chap USArmy, 88-11; ob srp New P Ch, Wilton Manors, FL, 11-17; admin MNA, Chaplains Ministry, 17-

3600 NW 23rd Terrace, Boca Raton, FL 33431 – 561-367-3168   South Florida
PCA Mission to North America – 678-825-1200

Carter, Mitchell – b Ft. Wayne, IN, Feb 20, 90; f Mark; m Lynetta; w Lauren Williams, Jun 8, 13; chdn Hadley, Madison, Audrey; HU 13, BA; CTS 16, MDiv; O Jan 7, 18, Nash Pby; astp City Ch of East Nash, Nashville, TN, 18-

3016 Rich Acres Dr., Nashville, TN 37207   Nashville
E-mail: mitchell.carter@citychurcheast.org
City Church of East Nashville – 615-262-3246

Carter, Paul Ray – b Richmond, VA, May 21, 53; f Ray Malcolm; m Hellen Inez Spicer; w Julie Anne Reil, Richmond, VA, Dec 20, 75; chdn Matthew Reil, Nathan Andrew, Michael Ryan, Jonathan Paul; VPI 71-75, BA; RTS 81-84, MDiv; CTS 02, DMin; O Jul 84, NR Pby; staff CCC, TXA&M, 76-81; p Grace P Ch, Lexington, VA, 84-

40 Village Way, Lexington, VA 24450 – 540-463-3524   Blue Ridge
E-mail: pcarter@adelphia.net
Grace Presbyterian Church – 540-463-2374

Carter, Robert G. – b Atlanta, GA, Dec 30, 56; w Deborah, Nov 11, 78; chdn Anna, Andrew, William; astp, DPC Perimeter Ch, Johns Creek, GA, 86-

1070 Tuxedo Drive, Roswell, GA 30075 – 678-405-2220   Metro Atlanta
E-mail: bobc@perimeter.org
Perimeter Church – 678-405-2000

Caruncho, Janas – ob ascp Chinese Christian Ch of NJ, 10- 17; srp Redeemer Sugar Land, Sugar Land, TX, 17-

1723 Jourdan Way, Sugar Land, TX 77479 – 973-335-0183   Houston Metro
E-mail: janas@redeemersl.org
Redeemer Sugar Land – 832-576-2216

Cary, Mark David – b Texas, Feb 17, 60; f David H; m Betty Williamson; w Sarah Lucille Swift, Phil, PA, Aug 25, 84; chdn Elisabeth Augusta, Paul Mark; PhilCC 83-85; REpS 83-86; SCS 87-89; TC, BA; SCS, MDiv; L Jan 26, 90, SW Pby; O May 27, 90, SW Pby; p Sangre de Cristo Ch, Westcliffe, CO, 87-89; op Faith P Ch, Las Cruces, NM, 90-92; astp University P Ch, Las Cruces, NM, 92; South Valley P Ch, Chandler, AZ, 92-93; chp, op Dayspring Comm Ch (Msn), Pueblo, CO, 93-95; ob p Wetmore Comm Ch, Wetmore, CO, 95-97; astp Chapelgate P Ch, Marriottsville, MD, 97-00; mis MTW/Impact, 01-02; ascp First P Ch, Gadsden, AL, 02-04; p South Dayton P Ch, Dayton, OH, 04-17

2757 Harris Avenue, Apt 1, Norwood, OH 45212   Ohio Valley
E-mail: 1mark.cary@gmail.com

Case, Eugene Cliff – b Cincinnati, OH, Dec 26, 47; f Coburn C C; m Stella Hamm; w Rachel Esther Wilson, Charlotte, NC, May 31, 97; chdn Thomas Jonathan Jackson, Laura Elisabeth, Emilie Kathleen, Preston Brooks, Robert Lewis Dabney; MhdSU 70, BA; ColTS 70-71; CalvS 71; RTS 74, MDiv; O Aug 12, 74, Gr Pby; p First P Ch, Woodville, MS, 74-16; p Bethany P Ch, Centreville, MS, 77-16; sc Gr Pby, 91-14; hr 16

PO Box 851, Woodville, MS 39669-0851 – 601-888-4837   Grace
E-mail: ecase14507@yahoo.com
HR

Casoria, Anthony J. – b Trenton, NJ; f Michael; m Rose Marie; w Nancy Jean Lyman, Ft. Lauderdale, FL, Dec 13, 80; chdn Joy Marie (Casper), Elizabeth Ann (Myers); BelC 68-72, BA; RTS 72-76, MDiv; O Oct 17, 76, Evgld Pby (PCUS); ascp Palmetto Ch, Miami, FL, 76-77; ascp First Ch West, Plantation, FL, 77-88; p Center Grove P Ch, Edwardsville, IL, 88-05, srp 05-15; hr 15; p em Center Grove P Ch, 15; 1980 Geo Washington Hon Medal, Freedoms Found, Valley Forge

674 Salisbury Road, Hendersonville, NC 28792 – 618-580-3147   Illiana
E-mail: tony.casoria@gmail.com
HR

Cass, Gary – b Las Vegas, NV, Jul 25, 59; w Sandy, San Diego, CA, Aug 29, 82; chdn Isaac Benjamen, Joshua Daniel, Sharaya Lynn; Vanguard 85, BA; WSCAL 90, MA, 02, DMin; O Aug 05, SFL

Cass, Gary, continued
Pby; ob exec dir Coral Ridge Ministries, Fort Lauderdale, FL, 04-07; ob chmn Christian Anti-Defamation, 07-; *Gag Order*; *The Bible and the Black Board*; *Christian Bashing*

PO Box 1115, Vista, CA 92085-1115 – 954-551-9770   South Coast
E-mail: pastorgarycass@gmail.com

Casselli, Stephen J. – b Columbus, OH, May 27, 64; f Joseph; m Evelyn; w Melissa Riester, Mansfield, OH, Dec 6, 86; chdn CJ, Daniel, Katie; DenU 86, BA; WTS 94, MDiv, 07, PhD ; L May 94, Phil Pby; O Nov 98, SWFL Pby; op Holy Trin P Ch, Tampa, FL, 98-01, srp 01-; "Jesus as Eschatological Torah," *Trinity Journal 18.1* (1997); and "The Threefold Division of the Law in the Thought of Aquinas," *Westminster Theological Journal 61:2* (Fall 1999); "Anthony Burgess' Vindiciae Legis and the 'Fable of Unprofitable Scholasticism': A Case Study in the Reappraisal of Seventeenth Century Reformed Scholasticism," PhD diss.

465 Lucerne Avenue, Tampa, FL 33606 – 813-254-4238   Southwest Florida
E-mail: s.casselli@verizon.net
Holy Trinity Presbyterian Church – 813-831-8331

Cassidy, David – b Freeport, IL, Sept 27, 59; f Patrick Gerald; m Dolores Ann Saunders; w Toni Aline Felean, Paducah, Sept 13, 80; chdn Sean, Claire; UEvansville; OxU; TC; CTS; O Nov 9, 02, Nash Pby; CollD Oxford U, 79-81; Maranatha Ch, London, 81-83; p Capital Comm Ch, London, 84-87; p Cornerstone Ch, Paducah, KY, 87-95; ob p New Covenant Ch, Paducah, KY, 96-05; p Redeemer P Ch, Austin TX 05-14; srp Christ Comm Ch, Franklin, TN, 14-

3817 Old Charlotte Pike, Franklin, TN 37069 – 512-422-0111   Nashville
E-mail: david.cassidy@christcommunity.org
Christ Community Church – 615-468-2200

Cassis, Robert H. Jr. – b Nyack, NY, Jun 5, 40; f Robert H Sr.; m Eleanor Boggiano; w Kathy Lee Webster, Spring Valley, NY, Jun 10, 61; chdn Terry Lee (Pinnix), Robert H III; USCGA 57-61, BS; USNPGS 64-66, BS; NYU 66-72, MBA; RTS 87-90, MDiv; L Jun 1, 90; O Nov 18, 90, PacNW Pby; chp, ev PacNW Pby, 90-98; ev, op South Sound P Msn, Olympia, WA, 91-98, wc 98-99; ob exec dir West Puget Sound YFC, Poulsbo, WA, 99-09; ob ev Olympia CRC, 00; astp Grace Comm P Ch, Bremerton, WA, 15-

14902 NW Eagles View Drive, Seabeck, WA 98380 – 360-830-5150   Pacific Northwest
E-mail: rhcassis@gmail.com
Grace Community Presbyterian Church – 360-930-9194

Castaneda, Benjamin E. – astp Rincon Mtn P Ch, Tucson, AZ, 14-

8982 East Kirkpatrick Circle, Tucson, AZ 85710 – 520-444-9135   Southwest
E-mail: bcastaneda@rinconpres.org
Rincon Mountain Presbyterian Church – 520-327-2390

Castleberry, Curtis – astp Oaklawn P Ch, Houston, TX, 17-18; campm RUF, 18-

6338 Regency Court, San Antonio, TX 78249   South Texas
E-mail: curtis.castleberry@ruf.org
PCA Reformed University Fellowship

Casto, Trent – b Buckhannon, WV; f Jerald; m Vickey; w Emily Johnstone, Roanoke, WV, Jan 3, 04; chdn Hudson, Anna Katherine, William; WVU 04, BS; CTS 09, MDiv; GCTS 15, DMin; O Jun 13, 10, SucstFL Pby; mis ESI, Czech Republic, 04-05; p Eng Hope Comm Ch, St. Louis, MO, 05-08; int Park Cities P Ch, Dallas, TX, 09-10; astp Covenant Ch of Naples, Naples, FL, 10-12; ascp 12-16, srp 17-; Mod SucstFL Pby 14

7544 Cordoba Circle, Naples, FL 34109 – 239-595-9469   Suncoast Florida
E-mail: Trent.casto@covenantnaples.com
Covenant Church of Naples – 239-597-3464

Caston, R. McKay – b Memphis, TN, Dec 18, 68; w Kristy Davis, Jackson, MS, Jun 6, 92; chdn Ann Ferris, Schaeffer, Sarah Wynn; UMS 91, BA; CTS 95, MDiv, 05, DMin; TTS, PhD; O Mar 19, 95, Cov Pby; int Kirk of the Hills P Ch, St. Louis, MO, 93-94; ob astp, medu, moya Independent P Ch, Memphis, TN, 95-98; astp Lawndale P Ch, Tupelo, MS, 99-03; p Westminster P Ch, Greenwood, MS, 03-07; chpres Perimeter Ch, Duluth, GA, 07-09; op Creekstone Ch, Dahlonega, GA, 09-17, p 17-; fac MetAtl Sem; *The Bronze Serpent: Prayers for Living All of Life in View of the Cross; A+ for an F: A Primer in the Gospel for Ordinary Folks*

59 Amy Trammel Court, Dawsonville, GA 30534 – 678-651-5551 Metro Atlanta
E-mail: mckaycaston@gmail.com
Creekstone Church – 678-651-5557

Castro, Christian – b Sao Paulo, Brazil; w Elizabeth; chdn CJ, Caleb Daniel, Isaac Jeremy; CentBC 01, BA; WTS 04, MDiv; O Aug 8, 04, MNY Pby; op Proclamation Comm Ch, Port Chester, NY, 04-06; astp Comunidade Crista Presbiteriana, Newark, NJ, 06-11; astp Harbor P Ch, San Diego, CA, 11-13; ascp Harbor P Ch West Chula Vista, Chula Vista, CA, 13-14; p Grace Renewal Ch, Chula Vista, CA, 14-

706 Marbella Circle, Chula Vista, CA 91910 – 619-734-5140 South Coast
E-mail: cmcastro79@gmail.com
Grace Renewal Church – 619-851-6465

Castro, William – b Trujillo, Peru; w Judith; chdn Grace, Laura, Camila; GPTS, ThM; O Jun 6, 10, Cal Pby; astp Mitchell Road P Ch, Greenville, SC, 10-17; op Emmanuel P Msn, Greenville, SC, 16-; "Deconstructing the Racialist Framework" in *Heal us Emmanuel; "Igniting your Heart for Integrated Ministry,"* pcamna.org

305 Mitchell Road, Greenville, SC 29615 Calvary
E-mail: wcastro@emmanuelupstate.org
Emmanuel Presbyterian Mission

Caswell, R. Lyle Jr. – b Carrollton, GA, Sept 16, 71; f R. L. Sr.; m Betty Sue Anderson; w Gretchen Luchrysta Sweet, Lakeland, FL, Dec 16, 95; chdn R. Lyle III "Jack", Mary Franklin, Ethan Elliott, Gretchen May; SamU 93, BA; BDS 96, MDiv; L Jan 99, Queensland pby; O Jan 99, Queensland pby; Recd PCA 00, NGA Pby; campm Covenant P Ch, Birmingham, AL, 94-97; campm MTW, Australia, 98-00; MTW, dir mobilization, 00-02; ascp East Lanier Comm Ch, Buford, GA, 02-03; astp Trinity P Ch, Lakeland, FL, 04-08; op Christ Comm Msn, Lakeland, FL, 04-08; p 08-

5625 Stratford Lane, Lakeland, FL 33813 Southwest Florida
E-mail: lyle@ccpclakeland.org
Christ Community Church – 863-644-7717

Cates, Martin – b Petersburg, VA, Dec 27, 82; f Clarence Lee, Jr.; m Brenda Lynn Roach; w Meredith Grace Ford, Blacksburg, VA, May 19, 07; chdn Hatley-Grace, Mary-Margaret; VPI 05, BA; CTS 13, MDiv; O Jan 28, 18, JR Pby; astp Sycamore P Ch, Midlothian, VA, 16-

11919 Heathmere Cres, Midlothian, VA 23113 – 757-620-7567 James River
E-mail: mcates@sycamorepres.com
Sycamore Presbyterian Church – 804-794-0238

Cathcart, Robert Dean Jr. – b Augusta, GA, Aug 21, 72; f Robert Dean Sr.; m Martha Lily Elmore; w Sarah Elizabeth Ropp, Sumter, SC, Aug 5, 95; chdn Robert Dean III, Sarah Anna, Margaret Lorraine, Charles Ropp; USC 90-94, BMusEd; SETS 95-96; RTS 96-98, MDiv; ErskTS Inst for Ref Worship 07, DMin; L Dec 98, Palm Pby; O May 9, 99, Palm Pby; astp, yp Hilton Head P Ch, Hilton Head Island, SC, 98-01; p Friendship P Ch, Laurens, SC, 01-; "From Cassian to Cranmer: Singing the Psalms from Ancient Times Until the Dawning of the Reformation," *Sing a New Song*, 10

236 Hickory Forest Drive, Laurens, SC 29360 – 864-575-2521 Calvary
E-mail: fpc@prtcnet.com
Friendship Presbyterian Church – 864-575-2257

MINISTERIAL DIRECTORY

Cathey, Walter H. Jr. – b Charlotte, NC, Feb 2, 45; f Walter H; m Frances Nell Martin; w Helen Drummond, Jackson, MS, Apr 5, 69; chdn Jennifer Helen (Stevens), Bethany Anna (Donaldson), David Benjamin, Stephen Drummond; CBC 64-67; BryC 67-68, BA; RTS 72-75, MDiv; L 73, MSVal Pby; O Oct 26, 75, CentGA Pby; mis Ethiopia, 69-72; p Westminster P Ch, Martinez, GA, 75-78; prof BelC, 78-80; mis Taiwan, 80-84; p Brent P Ch, Brent, AL, 84-93; srp First P Ch, Panama City, FL, 93-03; hr 03

7702 Compton Court, Charlotte, NC 28270 – 704-541-5553   Gulf Coast
E-mail: helencathey@gmail.com
HR

Cauble, Scott – b Salisbury, NC, Dec 28, 68; f Charles W.; m Janet G.; w Nancy; chdn Katie, Peter, Virginia, Seth; MBI 97, BA; TEDS 01, MDiv, 15, ThM; L Jun 7, 03, OHVal Pby; O Nov 16, 03, OHVal Pby; Chap USN, Destroyer Squadron Six, 03-05; Chap USN, Marine Corps Base Quantico, VA, 05-09; Chap USN, 2d Marine Division, 09-11; Chap USN, Naval Air Station Sigonella, 11-14; Chap USN, Naval Chap School/Center, 15-18; Chap USN, USS Nimitz, Bremerton WA, 18-

PO Box 2971, Silverdale, WA 98383   Ohio Valley
E-mail: scottcauble@hotmail.com
United States Navy

Causey, Raymond – ev Perimeter Ministries, Atlanta, GA, 02-05; op South Atlanta Comm Msn, Fayetteville, GA, 05-08; p 08-16; p Redemption Flwsp P Ch, Fayetteville, GA, 16-

7727 Briar Forest Lane, Riverdale, GA 30296   Metro Atlanta
Redemption Fellowship Presbyterian Church – 770-460-1220

Cavallaro, Steven Paul – w Amie Beth Cavallaro; chdn Jadon Beth, Elijah Paul Huanan, Micah Beth Marina, Asher Paul Merve ; RTSFL 94, MDiv, 99, MAC; p Good Shepherd ARP, 98-08; p Desert Springs P Ch, Tucson, AZ, 10-; "The Waiting," *Never Alone*, 15

7877 North Chainfruit Cholla Drive, Tucson, AZ 85741 – 520-395-0661   Southwest
E-mail: steve@desertspringspca.org
Desert Springs Presbyterian Church – 520-742-8990

Cavalli, Frank – p New Life P Ch, Clermont, FL, 03-06; p St. Pauls P Ch, Orlando, FL, 08-18

4917 Eli Street, Orlando, FL 32804   Central Florida

Caviness, Donald Keith – b Burlington, NC, Feb 19, 52; f Jasper T.; m Audrey Violet McLaughlin; w Velma Howell, Jackson, MS, Jul 5, 74; chdn Kerry Lynn, Susannah Leigh; BelC 76, BA; RTS 82, MDiv, 93; L Oct 81; O Jun 2, 82, MSVal Pby; mis GEM Italy, 73-74; mis MTW, Taiwan, 76-79; ydir McIlwain Mem P Ch, Pensacola, FL, 79; ss Smyrna P Ch, Kosciusko, MS, 81-82; mis MTW, Portugal, 82-91; cop Igreja Evangelica de Portela, 83-86; chp Igreja Evangelica de Telheiras, 87-91; int MTW, 91-94; ob prof Sch of Intercultural Studies, 94-97; op Redeemer P Msn, Rutherfordton, NC, 97-02; p Story Mem P Ch, Marion, NC, 04-05; p First P Ch, Philadelphia, MS, 06-

503 Poplar Avenue, Philadelphia, MS 39350   Mississippi Valley
E-mail: athike1@yahoo.com
First Presbyterian Church – 601-656-4312

Cecil, Dann – p North Ft. Myers P Ch, Ft. Myers, FL, 05-

1409 NE 17th Avenue, Cape Coral, FL 33909   Suncoast Florida
E-mail: danncecil@excite.com
North Ft. Myers Presbyterian Church – 239-826-8806

Cepeda, Jesus – chp Brownsville, TX, 06-08; Dios Con Nosotros Ch, Edinburg, TX, 08-16; wc

3626 Mina De Oro, Edinburg, TX 78541 — South Texas
E-mail: revjesuscepeda@yahoo.com

Cerveny, Billy – astp Midtown Flwsp Ch, Nashville, TN; wc

908 Cadillac Avenue, Nashville, TN 37204 — Nashville

Ceselsky, John Edward – b Baltimore, MD, Dec 28, 67; f John Emmanuel; m Mary Janet Voelker; w Julie Deanne Tiemann, Baltimore, MD, Oct 9, 99; UB 94, BA; CTS 98, MDiv; O Feb 27, 00, Pot Pby; astp Aisquith P Ch, Baltimore, MD, 98-

131 German Manor Road, Forest Hill, MD 21050 – 410-836-6655 — Chesapeake
E-mail: john_ceselsky@verizon.net
Aisquith Presbyterian Church – 410-444-4598

Cha, Damon – astp New Life Msn Ch, Fullerton, CA, 08-11; astp Redeemer P Ch, Los Angeles, CA, 11-

PO Box 1206, Simi Valley, CA 93062 — Korean Southwest
E-mail: damoncha@gmail.com
Redeemer Presbyterian Church – 213-447-1187

Cha, Paul Jay – O Apr 9, 13, KorSE Pby; op Open Kingdom PCA of Melbourne, Melbourne, FL, 13-

8517 Ivanhoe Drive, Melbourne, FL 32940 – 951-870-0113 — Korean Southeastern
E-mail: pauljaycha@yahoo.com
Open Kingdom PCA of Melbourne – 951-870-0113

Cha, Yong Ho – op Korean P Ch of Centreville, Chantilly, VA, 98-; sc KorCap Pby

14556 Battery Ridge Lane, Centreville, VA 20120 – 703-830-7809 — Korean Capital
E-mail: chayongho@hotmail.com
Korean Presbyterian Church of Centreville – 703-327-6779

Chai, Yong Ho – Recd PCA Apr 15, 13, KorS Pby; p Na Nu Rie P Ch of Lawton, 13-

Na Nu Rie Presbyterian Church of Lawton – 512-801-2876 — Korean Southern

Chambers, Phil – b Athens, GA, Oct 6, 68; f Alfred; m Martha White; w Jennifer; chdn Lily, Kate; SamU, BS; BDS 94-97, MDiv; O Sept 28, 97, Evan Pby; ms/sa Oak Mountain P Ch, Birmingham, AL, 91-97; mis MTW, 97-00; ascp, mout Oak Mountain P Ch, Birmingham, AL, 01-10; op Christ Comm Ch, Helena, AL, 10-

105 Rosebury Circle, Helena, AL 35080 – 205-991-7478 — Evangel
E-mail: philchambers@me.com
Christ Community Church

Champagne, Marc A. – b Pullman, WA, Oct 26, 71; f Edward Arthur; m Margaret Lynn Bowers; w Jill Anne Riddiford, Copley, OH, Aug 31, 96; chdn Noelle Anne, Micah Aaron, Sophia Lynn, Noah Charles; GroCC 90-94, BA; RTS 98-01, MDiv; L Oct 13, 01, OHVal Pby; O Oct 13, 01, OHVal Pby; astp North Cincinnati Comm Ch, Mason, OH, 01-11, ascp 11-12; op Redeemer Ch, Cincinnati, OH, 12-

5223 Farmridge Way, Mason, OH 45040 – 513-237-4717 — Ohio Valley
E-mail: marc@redeemercincy.com
Redeemer Church

MINISTERIAL DIRECTORY

Champion, Charles Edward – b Chattanooga, TN, Mar 6, 34; f Charles J; m Leona Rose; w Raedean Brown, Chattanooga, TN, Aug 28, 53; chdn Charles Michael, Mickey Raedean; BelC; RTS 73-75, dipl; L Oct 74, MSVal Pby; O Dec 17, 75, Cov Pby; p Houston P Ch, Houston, MS, 75-81; p Mount Cal P Ch, Roebuck, SC, 81-83; p New Hope P Ch, Abbeville, SC, 83-94; p Antioch P Ch, Woodruff, SC, 94-; sc Cal Pby, 91-

712 Harrison Grove Road, Roebuck, SC 29376 – 865-342-6016   Calvary
E-mail: cechampion@me.com
Antioch Presbyterian Church

Chan, Wade – O Nov 19, 17, NoCA Pby; astp Indelible Grace Ch, Castro Valley, CA, 17-

Indelible Grace Church – 510-274-1199   Northern California

Chaney, Bradley Lawrence – b Columbia, SC, Oct 7, 76; f Dale Smith; m Georgia Carol; w Erin Renee Floyd, Phoenix, AZ, Aug 15, 97; chdn Hannah Charis, Alethea Joy, Cora Elizabeth, Kiah Bradley, Anya Maria; UAZ 98, BS; RTS 02, MDiv; O Nov 3, 02, PacNW Pby; p All Saints P Ch, Boise, ID, 02-

677 West Cagney Street, Meridian, ID 83646 – 208-994-6423   Pacific Northwest
E-mail: bchaney@allsaintspca.org
All Saints Presbyterian Church – 208-658-0670

Chang, Dong Won – p Philippoi P Ch, Suwanee, GA, 07-17

Address Unavailable   Korean Southeastern

Chang, Jin Myung – b Seoul, Jul 18, 55; f Ik Sung; m Ung Moon Choi; w Young Joo Yoo, Seoul, Nov 23, 85; chdn Phillip Ueachan, Gloria Yeayoung, Patrick Yeajong; KorU 81, BA; CapBS 95, MDiv; L Apr 3, 95; O Apr 1, 96, KorCap Pby; astp, medu Korean Central P Ch of Wash, Vienna, VA, 95-09; srp Faithful Life Ch Msn 09-

10107 Ebenshire Court, Oakton, VA 22124 – 703-319-1965   Korean Capital
E-mail: rev.jmc@hotmail.com
Faithful Life Church Mission

Chang, Jungsun – wc

722042, C. Ak-suu, Gvardeiskaya st. 23 Kyrgyzstan   Korean Southeastern
E-mail: p094501@gmail.com

Chang, Simon Jinhee – w Heekyoung; chdn Raymond, William, Frederick; UScranton, MA; BibTS 04, MDiv; O May 2, 04, KorCent Pby; astp Korean Ch of Chicago, Hoffman Estates, IL, 04; Chap USArmy, Ft. Drum, NY, 04-07; Chap USArmy, Bamberg, Germany, 07-10; chap USArmy 10-

E-mail: jinhee.chang@us.army.mil   Korean Central
United States Army

Chang, Song Kyun – b Seoul, Feb 4, 59; f Yi Kyung; m Eun Do Chun; w Ae Ran Chung, Virgina, Dec 29, 84; chdn Timothy, Lois JiYoon; GMCUVA 88, BS; CapBS 96, MDiv; L Apr 1, 96, KorCap Pby; O Apr 7, 97, KorCap Pby; admin, astp, moya Korean Central P Ch of Wash, Vienna, VA, 94-05; Koinos Fell Ch, 05-10

610/148 M4 Sinthanee, 10 T.Rimkok, A.Meuang Chiangrai 57100 Thailand   Korean Capital
E-mail: skc5924@gmail.com

Chang, Stephen Wanki – b Seoul, Korea, Apr 29, 56; f Song Dal; m Kyong Bok Whang; w Suck-Ran Kang, Maryland, Aug 1, 81; chdn Stephen Jr., Sharon; MBI 83, BS; TEDS 87, MDiv, 87, MCE; CTS 05, DMin; L Apr 12, 88, KorCent Pby; O Oct 29, 89, KorCent Pby; DCE Korean Bethel P Ch, Chicago, IL,

Chang, Stephen Wanki, continued
84-88, ap 88-92; op Korean Central P Ch of Cincinnati, Cincinnati, OH, 92-97; op Christ P Msn, Lincolnwood, IL, 97-99; ascp Sung Min P Ch, Chicago, IL, 99-01; Chap Swedish Covenant Hosp, 01-15; Chap Vitas Hospice, 03-

3865 West Pratt Avenue, Lincolnwood, IL 60712 – 847-675-3901   Korean Central
E-mail: schang2956@gmail.com
Vitas Hospice

    Chang, Thomas – Recd PCA Nov 15, 16, EPA Pby; astp Gracepoint Ch, Erdenheim, PA, 16-

206 Brookwood Drive, Ambler, PA 19002 – 201-240-9228   Eastern Pennsylvania
Gracepoint Church – 215-326-9155

    Chang, Timothy – O Jul 7, 13, SNE Pby; astp Citylife P Ch of Boston, Boston, MA, 13-18; ascp 18-

125 Lexington Street #23, Auburndale, MA 02466   Southern New England
E-mail: tim@citylifeboston.org
Citylife Presbyterian Church of Boston – 617-292-0990

    Chang, William – astp New Life Mission Church of Fullerton, CA, 14-

921 Tracie Drive, Brea, CA 92821   Korean Southwest Orange County
E-mail: willchang77@gmail.com
New Life Mission Church of Fullerton – 714-526-6562

    Channell, Wesley – b Atlanta, GA, Jan 31, 54; f Wesley, Sr.; m Lucile Mann; w Margaret Louise, Indianapolis, IN, Dec 31, 77; chdn Caitlin, Megan, Wynne, Wesley; GPCT 75, BA, 76, MS; AmCLU 87; BDS 98, MDiv; L 99, Evan Pby; O Nov 8, 99, GulCst Pby; asst Briarwood P Ch, Birmingham, AL, 99; ip Lakewood P Ch, Pell City, AL, 99; p First P Ch, Atmore, AL, 00-06; hr 10

6640 Castleton Drive, Sandy Springs, GA 30328 – 404-845-0117   Gulf Coast
E-mail: chanpoet@aol.com
HR

    Chapell, Bryan Scott – b St. Louis, MO, Nov 18, 54; f Wayman G; m Elizabeth M. Freels; w Kathleen Beth Gabriel, Woodburn, IL, May 27, 78; chdn Colin Brett, Jordan Blake, Corinne Elisabeth, Kaitlin Bryanna; NWU 75, BSJ; CTS 78, MDiv; SIU 87, PhD; L, Midw Pby (RPCES); O Oct 76, Woodburn P Ch (Ind); ydir Chesterfield P Ch, Chesterfield, MO, 75-76; p Woodburn Ch, IL, 76-79; dirStSvs CTS, 78-81; p Bethel Ref P Ch, Sparta, IL, 81-86; prof CTS, 86-, VP, DnFac 88-94, pres 94-12; Chan CTS, 12-13; srp Grace P Ch, Peoria, IL, 13-; contr various publ; *Standing Your Ground*; *In the Grip of Grace*, *Using Illustrations to Preach with Power*; *Christ-Centered Preaching*; *Preparing for Licensure and Ordination Exams*; *Each For the Other*, 99; *The Wonder of It All*, 99; *1 & 2 Timothy and Titus*, 00; *Holiness by Grace*, 02; *Praying Backwards*, 05; *Why Do We Baptize Infants?*, 06; *Christ-Centered Worship*, 09; *Ephesians*, 09; *The Hardest Sermons You'll Ever Have to Preach*, 11; *The Gospel According to Daniel*, 14; *Unlimited Grace*, 16

Grace Presbyterian Church, 8607 Illinois 91, Peoria, IL 61615   Northern Illinois
E-mail: bchapell@gracepres.org
Grace Presbyterian Church – 309-693-3641

    Chaplain, Scott Paul – ob p Grace Fell Ch, 12-13; wc 13-

2110 Iris Drive, Columbia, MO 65202   Missouri
E-mail: chappy74@aaahawk.com

MINISTERIAL DIRECTORY

Chaplin, Carl Dean – b Richmond, KY, Jan 28, 49; f Thomas Graham Jr.; m Betty Ellis; w Rebecca Ann Duhs, Bartow, FL, Feb 11, 78; chdn Ellis Dean, Robert Albert, Mary Carolann; EKYU 73, BS; RTS 82, MDiv, 13, DMin; O Oct 82, Cov Pby; p Grace P Ch, Jackson, TN, 82-89; mis MTW and African Bible Colleges regional rep, 90-91; mis chp MTW, Prague, Czech Republic 91-06, mis MTW, Europe RAP Director 06-08, mis chp MTW, Riga, Latvia, 08-13; min dev lead, MTW 13-15; Global Project Specialist, MTW, 15-17; coo MTW 18.26 Network-Vocational Missions, MTW, 17-; ed *Kingdom Pursuit: Exploring the Many Facets of Missions,* 17

4630 Chattanooga Valley Road, Flintstone, GA 30725 – 678-458-2844   Covenant
E-mail: cdc2849@gmail.com
PCA Mission to the World

Chapman, Alton Craig – b Austin, TX, Sept 13, 60; f George C.; m Gayla Craig; w Dru; chdn Carolyn McKinnon, Garrett Aldridge; UTXAu 83, BA; St. MarysU 86, JD; WTS 03, MDiv; O Oct 19, 03, MNY Pby; Park Cities P Ch, astDir Evang/Miss, Dallas, TX, 96-99; Park Cities P Ch, Dir Singles, Dallas, TX, 99-01; ascp Trinity P Ch, Rye, NY, 03-16; astp All Saints P Ch, Austin, TX, 17-

7808 Rialto Boulevard, Austin, TX 78735 – 914-967-6996   South Texas
E-mail: cchapman@allsaintsaustin.org
All Saints Presbyterian Church – 512-732-8383

Chapman, David – b Lafayette, LA, Mar 25, 66; f Cecil V.; m Mabel Ann Thweatt; w Tasha Dawn Neeper, Los Alamos, NM, Nov 26, 88; chdn Leela Anne, Karis Dawn; RU 84-88, BA; TEDS 92-96, MA, 92-96, MDiv; UCam 96-00, PhD; L Apr 96, NoIL Pby; O Nov 12, 00, NoIL Pby; CCC, 89-93; Student Ministries, Inc, 93-96; prof CTS, 00-; contr various publ; *Ancient Jewish and Christian Perceptions of Crucifixion,* 08; NT Archaeology Editor & Hebrews in *ESV Study Bible,* 08; *Philippians: Rejoicing and Thanksgiving (Focus on the Bible),* 12; *Trial and Crucifixion of Jesus: Texts and Commentaries,* 15; NT Editor & Contributor in *ESV Archaeology Study Bible,* 18; "1 & 2 Thessalonians" in *ESV Expository Commentary,* 18

911 Dinard, Manchester, MO 63021 – 636-861-4585   Chicago Metro
E-mail: dchapman@covenantseminary.edu
Covenant Theological Seminary – 314-434-4044

Chapo, Frank K. – b Hungary, Oct 16, 21; f Joseph C.; m Mary Csermak; w Lela Hise (d), (2) Carolyn King Enkema, McMinnville, TN; MaryvC 57, BA; ColTS 57-60, BD; O Oct 1, 60, Hlst Pby (PCUS); p Micaville, NC, 60-63; p Gate City, VA, 63-71; p Asbury P Ch, Johnson City, TN, 71-81; p Faith Ch, Johnson City, TN, 81-85; ss 85-86; hr 96

911 Grady Drive, Johnson City, TN 37604-2940 – 423-926-9370   Westminster
HR

Chappell, Eric – O Oct 27, 13, SoCst Pby; astp New Life P Ch, Escondido, CA, 13- 18; astp Trinity P Ch of Or Co, Orange, CA, 18-

536 E. Jefferson Avenue, Orange, CA 92866   South Coast
E-mail: eric.c@trinitypresoc.org
Trinity Presbyterian Church of Orange County – 714-515-4686

Chappell, Justin – O Mar 15, 15, SWFL Pby; astp Cornerstone of Lakewood Ranch, Bradenton, FL, 15-17; astp The Table Ch, Lafayette, CO, 18-

803 Francis Street, Longmont, CO 80501   Rocky Mountain
E-mail: justin.r.chappell@gmail.com
The Table Church – 720-772-8322

Charette, Joshua – astp Rocky Mountain Comm Ch, Billings, MT, 10-; op Great Plains Gathering, Billings, MT, 14-

2423 Cascade Avenue, Billings, MT 59101   Rocky Mountain
E-mail: joshuacharette@hotmail.com
Rocky Mountain Community Church – 406-259-7811
Great Plains Gathering – 406-855-8755

Chase, Charley Lynn – b Franklin, LA, Dec 30, 46; f Edward Earl C; m Verna Savoy; w Susan West, New Orleans, LA, Jun 8, 68; chdn Andrea Lynn, Christine Ruth, Peter Gary Edward, Nathan Wade; BelC 68, BA; RTS 71, MDiv; O Feb 6, 72, CMS Pby (PCUS); p Durant, MS, 72-73; p Forest, MS, 74-78, op 74-80; p Clinton, MS, 80-83; p Heritage P Ch, Corpus Christi, TX, 83-88; p New Cov P Ch, Dallas, TX, 88-90; srp Vineville P Ch, Macon, GA, 90-96; astp Highlands P Ch, Ridgeland, MS, 96-98; p Second P Ch, Yazoo City, MS, 98-01; srp First P Ch, Dothan, AL, 01-07; hr 08; ev 10-; op Providence Ch, Thomaston, GA, 10-16

5369 Rivoli Drive, Macon, GA 31210-1599   Central Georgia
E-mail: charleylchase@aol.com
HR

Chavis, Cyril – O Mch 4, 18, MSVal Pby; campm RUF, JackSt, 18-

730 Avalon Road, Jackson, MS 39206   Mississippi Valley
E-mail: cyril.chavis@ruf.org
PCA Reformed University Fellowship

Cheatham, Andrew – w Cindy; VandU 95, BS; UMD 99, MBA; GPTS 07, MDiv; O 08, OPC; Recd PCA 14, Ill Pby; p Covenant OPC, Cedar Falls, IA, 08-14; p Concord P Ch, Waterloo, IL, 14-

324 Thomas Lane, Waterloo, IL 62298 – 618-939-6533   Illiana
E-mail: pastoracheatham@gmail.com
Concord Presbyterian Church – 618-939-7116

Chedid, Bassam – w Norma; chdn Chad, Ana, Dora; SimpC, BA; RTS, MDiv, DMiss; L Nov 12, 02, MSVal Pby; O Mar 30, 03, MSVal Pby; ascp San Francisco, 81-84, mis 81-90; ob pres Children of Abraham, 97-; *Islam: What Every Christian Should Know*

3640 Sand Tail Court, Colorado Springs, CO 80908   Mississippi Valley
E-mail: chedid@cs.com
Children of Abraham

Cheezum, Jeremy – b Bethlehem, PA, Jan 13, 79; f John; m Anne; w Kimberly, Fayetteville, AR, Jul 14, 01; chdn James Fletcher, Bailey Ruth, Philip Logan, Lydia Kate; Mansfield U 01, BA; RTS 05, MDiv; O Nov 6, 05, MSVal Pby; astp Providence P Ch, Clinton, MS, 05-08; p Forreston Grove Ch, Forreston, IL, 08- 15; p Trinity Ref P Ch, Montrose, CO, 15-

2223 Cambridge Street, Montrose, CO 81401   Rocky Mountain
E-mail: jeremycheezum@yahoo.com
Trinity Reformed Presbyterian Church – 970-249-1053

Chen, Allen – astp Cross Park Ch, Charlotte, NC, 17-; op Cross Cov Chinese Ch, Matthews, NC, 17

12434 Stratfield Place Circle, Pineville, NC 28134 – 765-276-7743   Central Carolina
E-mail: yinxinchengyi@gmail.com
Cross Park Church – 980-285-7020
Cross Covenant Chinese Church – 765-276-7743

MINISTERIAL DIRECTORY

Chen, Biao – b Lanzhou, China, Nov 14, 62; f Qian; m Zhengling Wang; w Xuguang Pan; chdn Qingyun (Jessica), Jerry Jielei; Nanjing Inst. of Meteorology 82, BS; China Acad 84, MS; TXA&M 94, PhD; RTSFL 04, MDiv; Recd PCA Jan 24, 09, CentFL Pby; coord Chinese IIIM Min, FL, 03-; ob p Orlando Chinese Evan Christian Ch, 04-15

1113 Parker Canal Court, Oviedo, FL 32765 – 407-971-8923   Central Florida
E-mail: biaochen_2000@yahoo.com

Chen, Kevin – O Nov 1, 15, GrLks Pby; astp Christ Ch Ann Arbor, Ann Arbor, MI, 15-17; ascp 17-18

1590 Latham Street, Mountain View, CA 94041 – 240-274-7113   Great Lakes

Chen, Mike – O Sept 23, 12, Phil Pby; astp City Ch, Philadelphia, PA, 12-15

Address Unavailable   Philadelphia

Cheng, David – O Jun 10, 18, Pac Pby; astp King's Ch, Long Beach, CA, 18-

King's Church – 562-424-1205   Pacific

Cheng, Wilson – astp Covenant Ch, Whitestone, NY, 98-06; op Cov of Grace Ch, Briarwood, NY, 98-06, p 06-08; srp 08-

102 Madison Avenue, Garden City Park, NY 11040 – 516-877-2190   Metropolitan New York
E-mail: wilsch810@hotmail.com
Covenant of Grace Church – 718-352-8646

Cheon, Caleb Seung – astp Briarwood P Ch, Birmingham, AL, 09-12; mis MSS, Taiwan, 12-

2200 Briarwood Way, Birmingham, AL 35243 – 205-413-2635   Evangel
E-mail: omy3535@hotmail.com
Missionary Sending Service

Cherry, Elliott – astp Midtown Flwsp Ch, Nashville, TN, 18-

948A Battlefiled Drive, Nashville, TN 37204 – 615-974-8346   Nashville
Midtown Fellowship Church – 615-269-9015

Chesnutt, James Randall – b Bristol, TN, Aug 28, 55; f James Harold; m Wanda Burgan; w Laura Pletscher, Lansdale, PA; chdn Samuel Timothy, David Benjamin, Mary Elizabeth; GBibC 80-84, BCE; BibTS 80-84, MA, 80-84, MDiv; L May 11, 85, Phil Pby; O Feb 7, 88, NJ Pby; Dir His Place Christian Coffeehouse, Bristol, TN, 76-80; Dir BarMin, Wildwood, NJ; int St. Paul's Ref Ch & Pleasant Hill Ref Ch, 81-82; p Evangelical P Ch of Star Cross, Williamstown, NJ, 88-16

5 Woodside Drive, Milford, DE 19963 – 302-491-4804   New Jersey
E-mail: rchesnutt@comcast.net

Chester, David – O Aug 14, 18, Evan Pby; astp Christ Comm Ch, Helena, AL, 18-; *A Chord in Time*

5106 Beacon Drive, Irondale, AL 35210 – 203-213-4167   Evangel
E-mail: dchester@student.wts.edu
Christ Community Church – 205-881-4222

Cheung, Han Sik – astp The Way Ch, Los Angeles, CA, 09-

3731 Danny Street, La Crescenta, CA 91214 – 562-947-4842   Korean Southwest
E-mail: skmdiv@hotmail.com
The Way Church – 323-735-0200

Chi, Daniel – ob OCM Grace Church, Ridgefield Park, NJ, 10-13; op Beloved P, Norwood, NJ, 13-

310 Mountain Way, Rutherford, NJ 07070   Korean Northeastern
E-mail: danielchi@gmail.com
Beloved Presbyterian

Chi, Joseph – b Lansdale, PA, Apr 30, 72; w Sunny Park; chdn Benjamin Joseph, Emily Abigail, Ewan Gabriel; WTS 99, MDiv; UEdin 09, PhD; O 99, KAPC; Recd PCA 09, KorE Pby; Peniel Korean P Ch, Willow Grove, PA, 98-04; astp Cornerstone P Ch, Lansdale, PA, 09-11, p 11-13

400 Amy Court, North Wales, PA 19454 – 215-808-4247   Korean Eastern
E-mail: sunjoechi@yahoo.com

Chi, Paul – op Harvest Ch of Madison, Madison, WI, 08-

30 North Spooner Street, Madison, WI 53705   Korean Central
E-mail: pastorpaul@gmail.com
Harvest Church of Madison

Chiarot, Kevin – astp Westminster P Ch, Rock Tavern, NY, 04-06; p Covenant P Ch at Jackson, Jackson, TN, 06-13; p Westminster P Ch, Rock Tavern, NY, 13-

560 Station Road, Rock Tavern, NY 12575 – 845-496-7910   New York State
E-mail: kchiarot@frontier.com
Westminster Presbyterian Church – 845-496-7971

Chiarot, Timothy – p First P Ch, Unionville, NY, 14-17

PO Box 211, Montgomery, NY 12549 – 845-457-3606   New York State
E-mail: timchiarot@gmail.com

Childers, Steven Lee – b Tokyo, Japan, Jan 24, 55; f Lyon B.; m Ona Jean Hardy; w Rebecca Heath, Oklahoma City, Aug 9, 80; chdn Angela Christine; Cara Elizabeth, Laura Anne; OKSU, BS; CTS, MA; TEDS, MDiv; FulTS 96, DMin; O Apr 78, RPCES; op, p Heritage P Ch, Edmond, OK, 77-82; TEDS, 84-85; op, p Trinity P Ch, Plano, TX, 85-87, srp 87-95; fndr, Dir Trinity Inst for Church Planting, Plano, TX, 92-95; lect CTS, 86; lect RTS, 90-95; instr MNA, Church planting, 86-95, wc 95; asst prof, admin RTSFL, 96-; *Church Planting & Development*; contr *Laying Firm Foundations*; auth various seminar training manuals

122 Hamlin T. Lane, Altamonte Springs, FL 32714 – 407-682-6949   Central Florida
Reformed Theological Seminary, FL – 407-366-9493
1231 Reformation Drive, Oviedo, FL 32765

Childress, Leroy – O Mar 4, 18, ChiMet Pby; p Grace Ch, Lansing, IL, 18-

2740 Indiana Avenue, Lansing, IL 60438   Chicago Metro
E-mail: pc@gracechurchlansing.org
Grace Church – 708-474-0180

Chin, Anthony Xavier – b Jamaica, Feb 18, 47; f Joseph Victor; m Lurline M. Wong; w Winsome M. Newman, Jamaica, Nov 28, 70; chdn Gregory Joseph Anthony, Nicole Anne-Marie, Patrice Alicia; SoTC 65; KTS 95, MDiv; L Jan 18, 94, SFL Pby; O May 14, 95, SFL Pby; int Immanuel P Ch, Miami, FL, 94-95, astp 95-98; coord MNA, multicultural min, FL & Caribb, 98-99, wc 99-04; hr 04

11200 Cypress Tree Circle, Ft. Myers, FL 33913   Suncoast Florida
E-mail: tonyxchin@embarqmail.com
HR

MINISTERIAL DIRECTORY

Chin, Daniel – ascp Global Msn Ch, Diamond Bar, CA, 16-

44 Rue Du Chateau, Aliso Viejo, CA 92656 – 909-396-4441   Korean Southwest
E-mail: danchin616@gmail.com
Global Mission Church – 909-396-4441

Chin, Son Kwan – w Kyong Ok; chdn Hanna, Hankook; O Oct 89; op Hope P Ch of Dallas Msn, Carrollton, TX, 99-02; p Manna P Ch, Plano, TX, 03-05; mis

4020 221st Street, Bayside, NY 11361 – 972-690-8913   Korean Southern
E-mail: sonchin@hotmail.com

Chinchen, John William – b Detroit, MI, Jun 30, 24; f Arthur Samuel C; m Beth Crummey; w Nell Robertson, San Jose, CA, Nov 5, 45; chdn Bill, Vann, Delbert, Lisa, Paul, Palmer, Marion Susan; VCSTC; ColU; SJSU 47, BA; SFTS 61, BD; BIOLA 92, LLD; O Jun 61, SanJose Pby; p Clallam Bay Ch, Clallam Bay, WA, 61-65; Dir, ev VlyCS, Los Gatos, CA, 65-67; p First P Ch, Picayune, MS, 67-69; ob ENI Mission, Liberia, 70-76; ob fndr, pres AfrBC, 76-

c/o African Bible College, PO Box 103, Clinton, MS 39060   Grace
African Bible Colleges, Inc.

Chinchen, Paul David – b Port Angeles, WA, Nov 1, 63; f Jack; m Nell; w Laura Bonjorno; chdn Ashley, Annabelle, Levi, Bess, Vanndel; BIOLA 86, BA; RTS 92, MDiv; UStel 98, ThM, 01, ThD; O Apr 29, 07, War Pby; mis African Bible Colleges, Inc., 89-

E-mail: paulchinchen@yahoo.com   Warrior
African Bible Colleges

Chinn, Daniel Kevin – w Sue, Dec 23, 88; chdn Calvin, Jessica, Katie, Shiloh; OK Wesl U 97, BS; WSCAL 01, MDiv; CTS 10, DMin; L Jan 26, 01, SoCst Pby; L Jan 26, 02, SoCst Pby; p Sovereign Grace Bapt Ch, San Antonio, 89-91; ascp Grace Bapt Ch, Bartlesville, OK, 91-97; ascp Escondido United Ref Ch, 97-99; Chap Calipatria Fed Prison, CA, 98-99; int New Life P Ch, Escondido, CA, 99-01; ob Chap COz, 01-

1189 Newport Road, Walnut Shade, MO 65771 – 417-348-1173   Missouri
E-mail: chinn@cofo.edu
College of the Ozarks

Chinnavan, Jegar – O Aug 24, 14, Cal Pby; astp Woodruff Road P Ch, Simpsonville, SC, 14-15; astp Spriggs Road P Ch, Manassas, VA, 15-; op First Asian Indian P Ch, Centreville, VA, 15-

13103 Rose Petal Circle, Herndon, VA 20171   Potomac
E-mail: jegarchinnavan@gmail.com
Spriggs Road Presbyterian Church – 703-791-5555
First Asian Indian Presbyterian Church – 864-381-3173

Chitty, Steven Christopher – astp Redeemer Ch Murfreesboro, Murfreesboro, TN, 14-16; astp Grace P Ch of Silicon Valley, Palo Alto, CA, 16- 18; p Grace South Bay - Msn, San Jose, CA, 18-

643 South Clover Avenue, San Jose, CA 95128   Northern California
E-mail: stevenchitty@gmail.com
Grace South Bay - Mission

Chizek, James Gary – b Milwaukee, WI, Dec 7, 60; MATC 84-85, AA (2); ConcU 87, BA; RTS 91, MDiv/Missions; L Apr 20, 94; O Nov 20, 94, MO Pby; Chap cand USAFR, Grand Forks AFB, ND, 91; Chap cand USAFR, McChord AFB, WA, 92; Chap cand USAFR, KI Sawyer AFB, MI, 92-94; Chap USAFR, Whiteman AFB, 94-95; int BPC, Merrill, WI 92-93; p Westminster P Ch (PCA), Boonville, MO,

Chizek, James Gary, continued
94-96; Chap USAF, Dover AFB, DE, 96-97; Chap USAF, Ramstein, Germany, 97-00; Chap USAF Zagreb, Croatia 98, Chap USAFR, Langley AFB, 00-03; sp Christ Ch of Arlington, Arlington, VA, 04; ss Trin Ref P Msn (PCA) Landstuhl, Germany, 05; sp Eastminster P Ch (PCA), Virginia Beach, VA, 05; Wing Chap WI Air Nat Guard, Madison, WI 08-12; Chap Undisclosed Location in Middle East 11; Chap USAFR Joint Base Elmendorf-Richardson, AK

29030 Rheault Road, Lake Linden, MI 49945 – 906-369-4763   Wisconsin
E-mail: ilovechrist@hotmail.com
United States Air Force Reserve

 Cho, Abraham – astp Redeemer P Ch of New York East Side, New York, NY, 07-17, srp 17-

530 West 45th Street # 9H, New York, NY 10036   Metropolitan New York
E-mail: abe@redeemer.com
Redeemer Presbyterian Church of New York East Side – 212-808-4460

 Cho, Brian – astp Exilic Ch, New York, NY, 18-

Exilic Church – 917-705-0048   Korean Northeastern

 Cho, Daniel Byong Il – p Eden Korean P Ch, Castro Valley, CA, 13-

23189 Canyon Terrace Drive, Castro Valley, CA 94552   Korean Northwest
E-mail: cho820@hotmail.com
Eden Korean Presbyterian Church – 510-538-1853

 Cho, Daniel Han – p Tree of Life PCA, Plano, TX, 08-15; p Peniel P Ch, Los Angeles, CA, 15-17; astp Yea Hyang P Ch, Raleigh, NC, 17-18, srp 18-

126 Cove Creek Drive, Cary, NC 27519 – 214-714-5865   Korean Southeastern
E-mail: pastordaniel214@gmail.com
Yea Hyang Presbyterian Church – 919-694-5291

 Cho, David – astp Citylife P Ch of Boston, Boston, MA, 10-18, ascp 18-

46 Sydney Street #2, Dorchester, MA 02125   Southern New England
E-mail: david@citylifeboston.org
Citylife Presbyterian Church of Boston – 617-292-0990

 Cho, Denny Jooyun – O Oct 31, 10, KorE Pby; astp Emmanuel Ch in Phil, 10-

Emmanuel Church in Philadelphia – 215-476-0330   Korean Eastern

 Cho, Hwi – ob Korea

E-mail: may5_2001@yahoo.com   Korean Capital

 Cho, Hyung Soo – b Seoul, Aug 13, 56; f Gae Do; m Hyun Hee Lee; w Jung Sook Lee, Seoul, Sept 7, 85; chdn Rachel, Nathan; HUFS, BA; WSCAL 88-93, MDiv; L Apr 93; O Apr 12, 94, KorSW Pby; astp, medu Sa Rang Comm Ch, Anaheim, CA, 94-97, wc; ob p Abundant Ch, Anaheim, 98-

1700 West Cerritos Avenue Unit 357, Anaheim, CA 92804-6188 – 714-226-0531   Korean Southwest
E-mail: josephhscho@hotmail.com
Abundant Church – 714-812-0063

 Cho, Jae Hyun – ob Dream Church

E-mail: chojh222@yahoo.com   Korean Capital
Dream Church

Cho, Jinmo Timothy – p Korean United Ch of Phil, Philadelphia, PA, 12-

1200 West Cheltenham Avenue, Philadelphia, PA 19126 – 215-646-2928   Philadelphia
E-mail: covenantcho@yahoo.com
Korean United Church of Philadelphia – 215-927-0630

Cho, Jongmoon – astp Sa Rang Comm Ch, Anaheim, CA, 08-14

11710 Triple Notch Terrace, Henrico, VA 23233   Korean Southwest
E-mail: pdavidcho@gmail.com

Cho, Joshua – astp Sae Han P Ch, Alpharetta, GA, 07-11; p Open Door Comm Ch, Alpharetta, GA, 11-

2665 Vistoria Drive, Cumming, GA 30041 – 678-772-3340   Georgia Foothills
E-mail: joshuacho@yahoo.com
Open Door Community Church – 678-812-4578

Cho, Kyung Joon – op, ev Gr Han-Mee P Msn, Lawrenceville, GA, 92-

1640 Hemingway Court, Lawrenceville, GA 30043 – 770-921-2993   Metro Atlanta
Grace Han-Mee Presbyterian Mission – 770-921-2993

Cho, Milo – mis 17-

Address Unavailable   Korean Central

Cho, Nam – ap Immanuel Korean P Ch, Chatsworth, CA, 91-92, wc; ob p Simi Valley First P Ch (non-PCA), 97-00; sc KorSW Pby, 99-01; srp Valley Bethel P Ch, Chatsworth, CA, 00-

10209 De Soto Avenue, Chatsworth, CA 91311 – 818-349-2096   Korean Southwest
E-mail: namchobethel@hotmail.com
Valley Bethel Presbyterian Church – 818-407-1234

Cho, Nam Hunn – p Ju-An P Ch, Wonjusi, Gangwon-do, 10-

1630-10 Dangudong, Wonjusi ganhwondo 91311, KOREA   Korean Southwest
E-mail: namhunn@hanmail.net
Ju-An Presbyterian Church

Cho, Paul Eun Sung – p Eunhye Korean P Ch, Indianapolis, IN, 05-

13049 Dekoven Drive, Fishers, IN 46037   Korean Central
E-mail: paulcho7@hotmail.com
Eunhye Korean Presbyterian Church – 317-722-0372

Cho, Sang Woo James – astp Korean Central P Ch of Wash, Centreville, VA, 11-

5812 G Post Corners Trail, Centreville, VA 20120   Korean Capital
E-mail: swcho@kcpc.org
Korean Central Presbyterian Church of Washington – 703-815-1200

Cho, Shin Min – wc 14-

4309 Brintons Cottage Street, Raleigh, NC 27616   Korean Southeastern
E-mail: semin52@hotmail.com

Cho, Yong Joong – b Korea, Dec 29, 53; f Tong Keun; m Eui Soon Kim; w Kyoung Lyoun Choi, Seoul, Apr 5, 77; chdn Stephen Joon, Paul Young, Timothy Sung; TC 83, BA; TEDS 85, MDiv, 87, ThM, 97, PhD; O Apr 17, 87, KorCent Pby; ob mis Philippines, 91-; ob Global Partners; *A Comparison of the Nature of Community in Grace Bible Church and the Bread of Life Ministry in Metro Manila, Philippines*, 97

Philippines, Global Partners   Korean Central

Cho, Young Ho – b Sou Kor, Jun 27, 52; f Hee-Joong; m Nan-Soon Kang; w Ester, Seoul Kor, Jan 5, 82; chdn Grace E, Gloria E, David S; ChShCS 79, BA; HPTS 82, MDiv; RTS 88, ThM; L Jun 82; O Oct 83, RPCKor; p Kor Ch of Tuscaloosa, AL, 87-89; mis Asia, 90-91; p Korean Ch of A & M, College Station, TX, 91-93; mis China, 94-

Address Unavailable   Korean Southern

Cho, Young Ik – b Chun-Nam, Kor, Jun 9, 35; f Saehyun Cho; m Kuikyung Noh; w Ayoung, Chicago, IL, Sept 25, 72; chdn Daniel, Paul; TPC 58-62, BA; PTS 62-64, MDiv; MTS 68-75, STM; L 79; O 79, Disc of Christ, Christian Ch; Recd PCA Apr 93, KorCent Pby; p Highland Korean P Ch, Vernon Hills, IL, 93-00; hr 00; p em Highland Korean P Ch, Vernon Hills, IL, 00-

3107 Via Serena South Unit Q, Laguna Woods, CA 92537 – 847-680-9126   Korean Central
HR

Cho, Young Je – p Living Hope Ch, Palisades Park, NJ, 03-

28 Strawberry Hill Lane, West Nyack, NY 10994 – 845-353-1473   Korean Northeastern
E-mail: sansomang@gmail.com
Living Hope Church – 201-725-8776

Cho, Young Pal – b Seoul, Korea, Jul 24, 53; f Kyung-Ha; m Cheong-Ja Cheon; w Sung-Eun Lee, Seoul, Jun 28, 84; chdn Hyun-Jin, Yu-Jin; KorPTS 72-78, BD; BibTS 80-84, MDiv, 83-86, STM; WTS; RTS 10, DMin; L Feb 5, 85; O Sept 3, 85, NY Pby/KorPC Synod/USA (Hapdong GA); p Back-Min (Kor) P Ch, 85-86; ap Bethel (Kor) P Ch, 86; ap Choong Hyeon (Kor) P Ch, 86-89; p Arumdawn P Ch, Village of Palmetto Bay, FL, 89-94, wc 94; ev Suwanee P Msn, Suwanee, GA, 95-02; sc KorSE Pby, 00-02; Orlando Korean P Ch in America, Apopka, FL, 03-06; p Columbus P Ch, Columbus, GA, 06-16; p Hanmaum P Ch, Duluth, GA, 16-; trans com, Korean *BCO;* St. Francis Hosp, chap int 12, chap res, 13-

495 Johnson Road, Suwanee, GA 30024   Korean Southeastern
E-mail: jlovesu2011@yahoo.com
Hanmaum Presbyterian Church – 770-442-9809

Choe, Daniel Pyongsu – b Seoul, Korea, Nov 20, 49; f Chang Koo; m Soon Nim Kim; w Chae Sook Lee, Seoul, Korea, Mar 2, 76; chdn Grace, David; DHTS, ThB; NPTS, MDiv; L Jul 12, 85; O Jul 12, 86, KorCent Pby; p Korean Bethel P Ch, Chicago, IL, 90-98; sc KorCent Pby, 90-94; p Inland Korean P Ch, Pomona, CA, 98-11; hr 11; Bethel P Ch of Chicago, Palatine, IL, 16-

942 East Kings Row #8, Palatine, IL 60074 – 909-620-9102   Korean Central
E-mail: pyongsuchoe@gmail.com
HR
Bethel Presbyterian Church of Chicago

Choi, Alex – ob p Sovereign Gr Ch, Los Angeles, CA, 16-

1920 Fletcher Avenue, South Pasadena, CA 91030   Pacific
E-mail: alex@sovereigngracela.com
Sovereign Grace Church – 213-617-0469

Choi, Bong Ho – b Kyung Nam, Korea, Dec 20, 52; f Kyu Seup Choi; m Yun Ju Choi; w Nan Hee Choi, Seoul, Apr 27, 82; chdn Yushin, Jee Hyun; ChShC 75, BA; ChShTS 80, ThB; L Oct 81; O Oct 82, Sudo Pby; astp Chung Hyun Ch, Seoul, 80-85; srp Koean Union Ch, Manila, 85-88; mis Philippines, 88-94; srp Burbank Korean P Ch, Burbank, CA, 94-04, ascp 04-

9507 Via Venezia #62, Burbank, CA 91504 – 818-358-4431   Korean Southwest
E-mail: bongchoi777@yahoo.com
Burbank Korean Presbyterian Church – 818-840-0668

Choi, Byung Hak – p Choongmanhan P Ch, Austin, TX, 02-10; p Na Nu Rie P Ch of Lawton, Lawton, OK, 10-13; op Austin Gr P Ch, Pflugerville, TX, 13-

11920 Shropshire Blvd., Austin, TX 78753 – 580-248-6771   Korean Southern
Austin Grace Presbyterian Church – 512-801-2876

Choi, Calvin Woosung – w Jean; chdn Elisha, Isabel, Abigail; BosU 97; WTS 02, MDiv; GCTS 07, ThM; LonSchTheo 13, PhD; ob Gordon-Conwell Theological sem, South Hamilton, MA, 10-13; srp Watertown Evan Ch, 12-

2607 Stearns Hill Road, Waltham, MA 02451   Korean Northeastern
E-mail: praisechrist@hotmail.com
Watertown Evangelical Church

Choi, Chun Yong – O Oct 97; p First Korean P Ch of Springfield, Nixa, MO, 97-06; wc 06-

PO Box 1259, Nixa, MO 65714   Korean Central

Choi, David – astp Disciple Msn Ch, Denver, CO, 10- 16; astp Skyview P Ch, Centennial, CO, 16-

3328 West 114th Place, Westminster, CO 80031 – 303-564-2537   Rocky Mountain
E-mail: davidchoi105@gmail.com
Skyview Presbyterian Church – 303-797-9000

Choi, Deokjun – p El Centro Korean P Ch, El Centro, CA, 14-

1107 Fieldview Avenue, El Centro, CA 92243   Korean Southwest Orange County
E-mail: paulo70@hanmail.net
El Centro Korean Presbyterian Church

Choi, Doug Sung – b Hadong, Korea, Aug 22, 48; f Wu-Yong; m Soon-Mal Chung; w Min Joo Lee, Pusan, Korea, May 31, 77; chdn Paul Pyungwha, G'Heh Esther, Hankook Moses; KosU 75, BA; RTS 79, MDiv, MCE; UNC 81; YDS 85, STM; EmU 87-92, PhD; O Oct 81, Pusan Pby (KPC); p Korean P Ch, Fayetteville, NC, 83-86; op Korean Msn, Fayetteville, NC, 86-87; ob prof KosU, 90-

KOREA – 0417-555-8171   Central Carolina
Kosin University

Choi, Eun Soo – w Sue; chdn Stephen, Hannah; ATS; O Nov 18, 01, KorE Pby; astp Hudson Korean P Ch, Union City, NJ, 03-05; srp Hosanna Comm Ch, NJ, 05- 13; p Gospel P Ch, Parsippany, NJ, 13-

714 7th Street #2, Carlstadt, NJ 07072 – 973-439-0386   Korean Northeastern
E-mail: eunsoo61@yahoo.com
Gospel Presbyterian Church – 201-232-2285

Choi, Ho Nyun –

Address Unavailable   Korean Central

Choi, Hyung Joon – astp New Life Comm Ch, Fayetteville, NC, 11-14; Chap 14-

PSC 560, Box 293, APO, AP 96376   Korean Southeastern
E-mail: hjchoi78@gmail.com

Choi, Hyung Kwan – b Pusan, South Korea, Jan 22, 55; f Yong Gil; m Wan Sook Yoon; w Young Ryo Choi, Seoul, Korea, Aug 20, 83; chdn Grace, Aaron, Paul; ChShC 83, BA; BibTS 89, MAR, 90, MDiv; L Jun 15, 89; O Nov 89, KorE Pby, op 89-94; p Nak Won P Msn, Dresher, PA, 94-

1300 Cedar Road, Ambler, PA 19002 – 215-540-5866   Korean Eastern
E-mail: hyungkwanchoi@yahoo.com
Nak Won Presbyterian Mission – 215-646-3887

Choi, James – O 16, Pot Pby; astp McLean P Ch, McLean, VA, 16-

7310 Leesville Boulevard, Springfield, VA 22151 – 703-434-2191   Potomac
E-mail: prostrate@gmail.com
McLean Presbyterian Church – 703-821-0800

Choi, Jea Huy – op Wheat Msn in Atlanta, Norcross, GA, 07-

Wheat Mission in Atlanta – 770-717-0790   Korean Southeastern

Choi, Jeffrey – O MNY Pby; astp Queens P Ch, Astoria, NY, 14-17; ascp Astoria Comm Ch, Astoria, NY, 17-

10-49 49th Avenue Apt. 3, LIC, NY 11101   Metropolitan New York
E-mail: jeffrey.choi@gmail.com
Astoria Community Church – 718-721-3440

Choi, Jeong Hoon – astp Light of the Gospel Ch, Columbia, MD, 18-

3105 Wheaton Way Apt #D, Ellicott City, MD 21043   Korean Capital
E-mail: nad007@hanmail.net
Light of the Gospel Church

Choi, Jinkyu Boaz – ascp Inland Korean P Ch, Pomona, CA, 16-

123 South Vermont Avenue, Fullerton, CA 92833 – 909-622-2324   Korean Southwest
E-mail: bcmc.pastor@gmail.com
Inland Korean Presbyterian Church – 909-622-2324

Choi, Jong Ug – p Saesoon P Ch of Virginia, Norfolk, VA, 08-

5135 Stanart Street, Norfolk, VA 23462 – 757-687-6550   Korean Capital
E-mail: juservant@hanmail.net
Saesoon Presbyterian Church of Virginia – 757-455-5565

Choi, Jung Sun – b Pyung-book, Korea, Jan 11, 23; f Sung Joo; m Deuk Shin Ahn; w Myung Sook Yoon, Shunyang, China, Dec 6, 46; chdn Kong Eun (Cho), Kong Mee (Hwang), Kong Chan, Kong Chil, Kong Sam, Kong Ock (Baek); KorPTS 45-51, 75-77, MDiv; O Sept 11, 53, Korea; Recd PCA Dec 12, 92, NoE Pby; p Joongdong P Ch, Kor, 76-86; p Central Ch of Wakayama, Japan, 89; cop Queens Japanese Ch, NY, 91-92; p Faith Ch of Westchester, White Plains, NY, 92-94; hr 94

Address Unavailable   New York State
HR

MINISTERIAL DIRECTORY

Choi, Kil dong – p Arumdawn P Ch, Village of Palmetto Bay, FL, 93-98, wc 98-05; hr 05

13370 Hillsborough Drive #201, La Mirada, CA 90638   South Florida
HR

Choi, Paul Byoungchan – p Madison Sah-lang Ch, Madison, WI, 16-

1 Raskin Circle, Madison, WI 53719   Korean Central
E-mail: cbc129@hotmail.com
Madison Sah-lang Church – 608-395-4205

Choi, Paul Dong Pil – op Korean Gr P Ch of Corpus Christi, Corpus Christi, TX, 09-12; hr 12

2507 Barret Drive, Frisco, TX 75033 – 361-992-0321   Korean Southern
E-mail: dongpchoi@sbcglobal.net
HR

Choi, Sahng-Deok – b Seoul, Sept 11, 57; w Yesun Kim, Seoul, Oct 3, 84; chdn Jin Sung, Bomee; ChShC 80, BA; GATS 83, MDiv; LBTS 93, ThM; CalvS 96, ThM; O Mar 28, 83, GenAssembPresbyterian; Recd PCA Jun 21, 99, KorCent Pby; p Dong Kwang P Ch, Seoul, 96-98; p P Ch of St. Peter, NJ, 98-99; p Korean P Ch of Milwaukee, Whitefish Bay, WI, 99-03; p Hebron P Ch, Prospect Heights, IL, 03-05

3117 Elm Street, Apt 2N, River Grove, IL 60171 – 773-977-9830   Korean Central

Choi, Soon Chul – O Oct 2, 89, KPC; Recd PCA Apr 3, 95, KorCap Pby; srp Rothem Risen Sun P Ch, Springfield, VA, 95-

8621 Reseca Lane, Springfield, VA 22152-1458 – 703-866-6323   Korean Capital
E-mail: rothemchoi@hotmail.com
Rothem Risen Sun Presbyterian Church

Choi, Soon Sung – ascp Korea SaeHan Ch of Louisville, KY, 08-09; astp Sa Rang Comm Ch, Anaheim, CA, 09-

1840 Brea Boulevard #7, Brea, CA 92835 – 714-318-4526   Korean Southwest
E-mail: sschoi@sarang.com
Sa Rang Community Church – 714-772-7777

Choi, Sung Hee – b Korea, Mar 14, 55; m Song Ah Lee; w Hye Sun Hyun, Korea, Dec 17, 90; RckmC 82, BA; WTS 86, MDiv; L 86; O Oct 4, 88, KorSE Pby; ap Korean P Ch of Wash, Fairfax, VA, 86-91; p Korean Shinjung P Ch, Atlanta, GA, 91-92; Chap LTJG, USN, CHC, USNR, 92-93; Chap USNR, active duty, 93-

2582 Associated Road #2, Fullerton, CA 92835   Korean Southeastern
United States Navy Reserve

Choi, Woo Shik – Jung Hee Choi; chdn So Jung, So Hyun; srp Church of the Nations, Chicago, IL, 98-07; ob mis Youth With a Mission, 07-

1026 Kingsport Drive, Wheeling, IL 60090 – 847-403-3304   Korean Central
E-mail: wchoi3@hotmail.com
Youth With a Mission

Choi, Young Kyu – ev 04-07; astp Korean First P Ch, Tucker, GA, 07-17; op Christ Cov P Ch, Peachtree Corners, GA, 17-

3583 Willow Glen Trail, Suwanee, GA 30024   Korean Southeastern
Christ Covenant Presbyterian Church – 770-880-5159

Choi, Younghyun – astp Sa Rang Comm Ch, Anaheim, CA, 08-

226 Pointe Drive, Brea, CA 92821   Korean Southwest Orange County
E-mail: pastorfanny@gmail.com
Sa Rang Community Church – 714-772-7777

Choi, Yun S. – op New Life Comm Ch, Palatine, IL, 03-17; ob 17-

1329 Evergreen Drive #1, Palatine, IL 60074 – 847-358-0812   Korean Central
E-mail: yunchoi@wantanewlife.org

Chon, David DongSik – b Seoul, Korea, Feb 12, 37; w Young Ag Chon, Seoul, Kor, Sept 20, 59; chdn Hye-Ran, Bong-Yong; DKU, BA; Naval Ac, KOR; PGATCS, MDiv; O Apr 21, 61, Mok-Po Pby, KOR; p Rok-Dong P Ch, 61-63; Chap Navy ROKN, 63-84; p Sierra Vista Korean United P Ch, Sierra Vista, AZ, 92-02; misSIM Ethiopia; trans wks of Jay E. Adams into Korean: *The Big Umbrella*; *Pulpit Speech*; *A Theology of Christian Counseling*

3712 Club Rancho Drive, PO Box 127, Palmdale, CA 93551 – 661-886-9513   Korean Southwest
E-mail: davidchon1@yahoo.com

Chong, Andy In Ho – p La Mirada Korean P Msn, La Mirada, CA, 08-

E-mail: inhochong@hotmail.com   Korean Southwest
La Mirada Korean Presbyterian Mission – 562-947-9693

Chong, Byong Kyu – p La Mirada Korean P Msn, La Mirada, CA, 96-08; sc KorSW Pby, 96-97

23109 Meyler Avenue, Torrance, CA 30502 – 562-926-3825   Korean Southwest

Chong, Daniel – w Maria (d) (2) Grace; UCI 99, BA; WSCAL 03, MDiv; astp Redeemer P Ch, Los Angeles, CA, 05-

11442 Santini Lane, Northridge, CA 91326 – 562-822-6550   Korean Southwest
E-mail: pastor.daniel.chong@gmail.com
Redeemer Presbyterian Church – 562-602-2474

Chong, David – b Seoul, Jun 21, 62; w Joanna, CO, Aug 16, 86; chdn Joseph Timothy, Aileen Joy; WSCAL, MDiv; O Oct 93, Christian Pres Ch; op New Life Msn Ch of Colorado, Englewood, CO, 04-

19095 East Bethany Place, Aurora, CO 80013 – 303-617-1005   Rocky Mountain
E-mail: pastor_chong@yahoo.com
New Life Mission Church of Colorado – 303-617-1005

Chong, John Huichu – b Korea, Oct 5, 36; f Chong, Won Il; m Kim, Kan Sung; w Kim, Hyong Cha, Pa Joo, KOR, Sept 26, 61; chdn Shin Ok (Chong), Shin Soon (Cho), Shin Ae (Yoon); GATS 82; O Jul 18, 76, RPCES; ev Jang Pa Ch, KOR, 64-72; ev Young Mee Ch, KOR, 72-73; p Immanuel Korean P Ch, Chatsworth, CA, 75-00; hr 00; p em KorSW Pby

25922 Via Lomas #4, Laguma Hills, CA 92653 – 949-215-9668   Korean Southwest
HR

Chong, Paul Kong Pil – op Las Vegas Presbyterian Ch, Las Vegas, NV, 09-

9672 Cartwheel Street, Las Vegas, CA 89178 – 702-742-3324   Korean Southwest
E-mail: notebookpencilcase@gmail.com
Las Vegas Presbyterian Church – 702-742-3324

MINISTERIAL DIRECTORY

Chrisco, Gerald – b Burlington, NC, Mar 2, 57; NCSt 79, BS; WFU 81, MBA; RTS 09, MAR; O May 10, 10, PTri Pby; ascp New Hope P Ch, Clemmons, NC, 10-

225 Coves End Court, Belews Creek, NC 27009-9220 – 336-462-1307   Piedmont Triad
E-mail: gchrisco@buddgroup.com
New Hope Presbyterian Church – 336-778-1556

Christenson, Timothy James – b Seattle, WA, Mar 27, 53; f James J; m Ruby D. Cook; w Rosalind J. Rohrer, Wheaton, IL, May 30, 76; chdn Carolyn (Broughton), Kathryn, Clayton; WheatC, BS; DTS, ThM; KTS, DMin; Recd PCA Jan 16, 96, SFL Pby; p Wellington P Ch, Wellington, FL, 96-06; p Faith P Ch, Sonoma, CA, 06-16; ob Equipping Pastors, Int, 16-

755 Craig Avenue, Sonoma, CA 95476 – 707-939-8366   Northern California
E-mail: theovisions@gmail.com

Christian, David Kenneth – w Michele; chdn Abigail; RTSFL 03; O May 16, 04, JR Pby; astp New Life P Ch, Virginia Beach, VA, 04-10, ascp 10-15, srp 15-

2526 Entrada Drive, Virginia Beach, VA 23456 – 757-816-1840   Tidewater
E-mail: kenchristian@cox.net
New Life Presbyterian Church – 757-430-0461

Christian, Matthew S. – astp First P Ch, Macon, GA, 99-03; astp Intown Comm Ch, Atlanta, GA, 03-11; astp All Souls Flwsp, Decatur, GA, 11-15

3077 Turman Circle, Decatur, GA 30033 – 770-939-0061   Metro Atlanta

Christiansen, Adam – O May 6, 12, Ecar Pby; p Pamlico P Ch, Oriental, NC, 12-

1009 B Gilgo Road, Pamlico, NC 28571 – 252-876-8928   Eastern Carolina
E-mail: adamchristiansen@gmail.com
Pamlico Presbyterian Church – 252-249-2402

Chu, Benjamin – astp Christ Cov Ch, Southwest Ranches, FL, 07-17; ob astp Abundant Grace Comm Ch, FL, 17-

175 SW 166th Avenue, Pembroke Pines, FL 33027 – 954-885-6398   South Florida
Abundant Grace Comm Ch, FL

Chu, Paul David – b New York, NY, Jul 31, 73; w Pey; chdn Cooper, Sophie, Eva, Soren; UNC 95, BS; WTS 05, MDiv, ob 07-16; astp Naperville P Ch, Naperville, IL, 16-

105 South Birchwood Drive, Naperville, IL 60540 – 980-267-2735   Chicago Metro
E-mail: paul.david.chu@alumni.unc.edu
Naperville Presbyterian Church – 630-961-0579

Chua, Beng Voon – b Malaysia, Jun 27, 71; f Taim Buan; m Yoke Choo Wong; w Su Chu Chen, Malaysia, Sept 18, 99; chdn Stephen; OKCityU 94, BA; DenTS 98, MDiv; O Jan 13, 99, CDI; Recd PCA 01, Pot Pby; ascp Chinese Christian Ch, Falls Church, VA, 01-07; srp 07-

12749 Effie Rose Place, Woodbridge, VA 22192 – 703-730-5231   Potomac
E-mail: jnchua@aol.com
Chinese Christian Church – 703-820-1010

Chuc, Salatiel – b Quintana Roo, Mexico, Aug 3, 70; f Ezequiel; m Elvira Catzin; w Maria M Angulo Munoz, Yucatan, Mexico, Aug 5, 95; chdn Salatiel, Jose; SanPablo Sem 95, BA; RTSNC 17, MDiv; O Feb 2,

Chuc, Salatiel, continued
98, NPCMexico; Recd PCA 17, CentCar Pby; p Moriah PC Merida, Mexico, 98-10; t San Pablo Sem, 98-10; asst Carolina P Ch, Locust, NC, 10-17, astp 17-

111 Simpson Road, Locust, NC 28097 – 704-781-5218   Central Carolina
E-mail: chuc_0870@hotmail.com
Carolina Presbyterian Church – 704-888-4435

    Chun, Dong Sun – b South Korea, Jun 19, 52; f Kyungeol Chun; m Jin Shim Ahn; w Yeon Hee Cho; chdn Ji Hyun, Jin Woong; SNU 78, BA; CapBS 03, MDiv; O Oct 04, KorCap Pby; astp Ch of the Wilderness, Rockville, MD, 01-06, p 07-09; p Seongdo Korean P Ch, Derwood, MD, 10-

7204 Phelps Hill Court, Derwood, MD 20855 – 301-740-3496   Korean Capital
E-mail: dsyhchun@yahoo.com
Seongdo Korean Presbyterian Church – 301-942-5123

    Chun, James Jinsuk – w Helen; FulTS 00, MDiv; Young Nak P Ch, Granada Hills, CA; Ark Msn Ch, Carmichael, CA; astp Korean Central P Ch, Centreville, VA, 11-18; srp The Ch for All Nations, Vienna, VA, 18-

43644 Scarlet Square, Chantilly, VA 20152 Korean   Capital
E-mail: arkmission@gmail.com
The Church for All Nations – 703-573-3767

    Chun, Sung – O May 15, 16, KorSE Pby; astp Sae Han P Ch of Atlanta, Alpharetta, GA, 16-

2289 Tenor Lane, Alpharetta, GA 30009   Korean Southeastern
E-mail: chanee83@gmail.com
Sae Han Presbyterian Church of Atlanta – 770-619-5340

    Chung, Aaron Justice – ob ; op Exilic Ch, New York, NY, 16-

442A Lincoln Street, Palisades Park, NJ 07650 – 760-533-5792   Korean Northeastern
Exilic Church – 917-705-0048

    Chung, Albert – b Montreal, QB, Jun 3, 75; f Dai-Hai ; m In-Sook ; w Linda Ryu , Toronto, Nov 30, 06; chdn Christopher Laeden, Emma Sophia; UTor 97, BS; TEDS 02, MDiv; SBTS 02, DMin; yp Young Nak P Ch, Toronto, 03-14; chp Toronto, 14-

110 Nortonville Drive, Toronto, ON M1T 2G8 CANADA – 416-669-8788   Eastern Canada
E-mail: albert@trinitygrace.ca

    Chung, Daniel – w Gina; chdn Dikaios, Doulos; Chap USN, 10-

4030 Craven Road #26, Oceanside, CA 92057   Korean Southwest Orange County
E-mail: dchung.navy@gmail.com
United States Navy

    Chung, Hwa Soo – astp First Korean P Ch of St. Louis, St. Ann, MO, 06-07

Address Unavailable   Korean Central

    Chung, John – b Fairfax, VA, Jan 10, 80; f Sam; m Song H. Yang; w Saras Y. Kim, St. Louis, MO, Jul 9, 05; chdn Karis, Jaron; UIUC, BA; CTS, MDiv; Recd PCA Oct 18, 09, KorCent Pby; p Korean P Ch of St. Louis, St. Louis, MO, 05-08; MTW, 08- 14; astp Christ Central P Ch of Wash, Centreville, VA, 14-16

8725 Brook Road, McLean, VA 22102   Korean Capital

MINISTERIAL DIRECTORY

Chung, John – mis

2919 Foxcroft Lane, South Daytona, FL 32119   Korean Northwest
E-mail: johnbschung@gmail.com

Chung, Jonathan – astp First Korean P Ch, Glenview, IL, 17-

750 Aspen Drive, Buffalo Grove, IL 60089   Korean Central
E-mail: chung.jonny@gmail.com
First Korean Presbyterian Church – 847-299-1776

Chung, Ku Sang – b Korea, Dec 4, 53; f Soonyong; m Yong Bong Kim; w Eun Kyung Han, Seoul, May 20, 88; chdn Jihoon, Aeeun, Esther; ChShCS 80, BA; HPTS 84, MDiv; LibU 95, ThM; O, KPC-Ref; Recd PCA Jul 8, 97, KorSE Pby; Eden P Ch, Seoul, 84-87; p Aelin P Ch, Suwon, Kor, 87-89; p Sidong P Ch, Seoul, 89-94; ev Orlando Korean P Ch in America, Apopka, FL, 95-03

11792 East Adriatic Place, Aurora, CO 80014-1164 – 407-814-8293   Korean Southeastern

Chung, Maranatha – b Hong Kong, May 22, 68; f Kwong Cho Chung; m Yokho Chung-lo; w Angela L. Chung, Houston, TX, Aug 19, 95; chdn Makarios, Berithen, Eleos; TXA&M 90, BS, 93, MS; WTS 04, MDiv; 17, ThM; O Nov 22, 08, Phil Pby; op Northeast Comm Ch, Philadelphia, PA, 08-

7930 Loretto Avenue, Philadelphia, PA 19111 – 267-240-3326   Philadelphia
E-mail: mchung@nccphilly.org
Northeast Community Church – 215-331-6344

Chung, Michael – srp Indelible Gr Ch, Castro Valley, CA, 13-

19546 Mt. Lassen Drive, Castro Valley, CA 94552   Northern California
E-mail: m.chung@live.com
Indelible Grace Church – 510-274-1199

Chung, Min Joshua – b Seoul, Korea, Aug 22, 64; f Sung Soo Chung; m Jai Hyang; w Geeyun Shin, Des Plaines, IL, Jul 25, 87; chdn Joshua Sun Kyung, Daniel Sun Ho, Ruth Sun Young, Hannah Sun Eun, Sarah Covenant Sun Un; UIL 87, BS; BibTS 90, MDiv, MA, 03, DMin; O Nov 25, 91, KorE Pby; ydir Emmanuel Ch in Phil, Philadelphia, PA, 87-90; op Covenant Flwsp Ch, Champaign, IL, 90-, ob campm 92-03, ob p 03-

502 West Green Street, Apt. 301, Urbana, IL 61801-3988 – 217-344-2237   Korean Central
Covenant Fellowship Church
PO Box 2754, Champaign, IL 61825-2754

Chung, Myong Sick – b Korea, Oct 3, 53; f Young-Man; m Jung-Nyuh Hong; w Shing-Hyang Lee, Daejeon, Korea, Dec 8, 78; chdn Yon-Ju Lydia, Hong-Ju Rebekah, Daniella Seung-Un, Cornelius Eun-Hyun, Anthony Eun-Sup; SNU 75, BS; WTS 88, MDiv; L Oct 30, 89; O Sept 4, 90; Recd PCA Apr 16, 91, NGA Pby; op Onnuree P Msn, Atlanta, GA, 91-97, wc 97-

E-mail: accufast@ix.netcom.com   Korean Southeastern

Chung, Paul Minchul – op New Heart Msn Ch, Manhasset, NY, 10-

37 Barry Park Court, Albertson, NY 11507 – 516-741-2109   Korean Northeastern
E-mail: pastorpaulchung@gmail.com
New Heart Mission Church – 516-627-5700

Chung, Philip Sangjin – astp Korean Central P Ch, Centreville, VA, 17-

13377 Connor Drive, Apt. P, Centreville, VA 20120 – 703-815-1315   Korean Capital
E-mail: philip.chung@kcpc.org
Korean Central Presbyterian Church – 703-815-1200

Chung, Rheeyun D. – p Sacramento First P Ch, Sacramento, CA, 98-02; p Saints Church, Rancho Cordova, CA, 02-

3655 Mulholland Way, Sacramento, CA 95821   Korean Northwest
Saints Church, Rancho Cordova, CA (non PCA)

Cid, Alejandro – b Buenos Aires, Nov 14, 59; Miami Int Sem, DMin; O Feb 16, 14, SFL Pby; astp Old Cutler P Ch, Palmetto Bay, FL, 14-

E-mail: alejandrocid59@yahoo.com   South Florida
Old Cutler Presbyterian Church – 305-238-8121

Cies, Andrew – O Sept 25, 16, NoTX pby; astp Town North P Ch, Richardson, TX, 16-

705 Brentwood Lane, Richardson, TX 75080   North Texas
Town North Presbyterian Church – 972-235-1886

Cinaglia, Damon – O Oct 9, 16, Hrtg Pby; pal CenterPoint Ch, Clayton, DE, 16-

210 Guernsey Court, Middletown, DE 19709   Heritage
E-mail: dcinaglia@centerpointpca.org
CenterPoint Church – 302-293-7010

Cirino, Nicholas Vincent – O Nov 19, 17, EPA Pby; astp Cornerstone P Ch, Center Valley, PA, 17-

4455 Keene Street, Center Valley, PA 18034 – 610-742-1427   Eastern Pennsylvania
E-mail: nvcirino@hotmail.com
Cornerstone Presbyterian Church – 610-282-5683

Clark, Bruce Troy – w Sarah; chdn Lydia, Rosemary, Winston, Julianne; USAFA 00, BS; CTS 08, MDiv; UCam 13, PhD; O Sept 22, 13, Ecar Pby; astp Church of the Good Shepherd, Durham, NC, 13-16; astp Briarwood P Ch, Birmingham, AL, 16-; op Trinity Ch Dorado, Dorado, PR, 16-

Urb. Paseo Los Corales I, 645 Golfo de Alaska, Dorado, PR 00646 – 646-416-4639   Evangel
E-mail: btc.cam@gmail.com
Briarwood Presbyterian Church – 205-776-5200
Trinity Church Dorado – 787-550-6387

Clark, Bryan B. – b Billings, MT, Aug 12, 71; f Rexford; m Marabee Burnham; w Alicia Christine Boroff, Mansfield, OH, Sept 25, 93; chdn Bruce Weston, Brandon Cameron, Brianna Marie, Brooklyn Kay; USAFA 93, BS; UMD 95; CTS 03, MDiv; O Jun 9, 03, RMtn Pby; astp Trinity P Ch, Bozeman, MT, 03-06, p 06-

933 Longbow Lane, Bozeman, MT 59718 – 406-586-2866   Rocky Mountain
E-mail: bryan@trinitybozeman.org
Trinity Presbyterian Church – 406-585-2223

Clark, Danny – campm RUF, Citadel, C of Charleston, 08-

1322 Addykay Place, North Charleston, SC 29406 – 843-261-3146   Lowcountry
E-mail: dclark@ruf.org
PCA Reformed University Fellowship

Clark, David Marion – b Darlington, SC, Mar 6, 55; f J. Franklin, Jr; m Ellen Bryant; w Ginger McGay, Hyannisport, MA, Aug 4, 79; chdn Sarah, Jean; USC 76, BA; GCTS 81, MDiv; O Oct 25, 81, PCUS; Recd PCA Jan 11, 92, Phil Pby; Batesburg-Leesville P Ch, 81-83; Johnston P Ch, 81-84; Garrison Mem ARP, 84-87; ascp Tenth P Ch, Philadelphia, PA, 92-99; p Faith P Ch, Gainesville, FL, 99-05; ascp, exec

Clark, David Marion, continued
p Tenth P Ch, Philadelphia, PA, 05-14; ip Lake Oconee P Ch, Eatonton, GA, 14-15; astp 15-; "Baptism: The Joyful Sign," in *Give Praise to God*; ed *To the Glory of God*; ed *Come to the Waters;* ed *The Problem of Good; Telling the Story of Jesus*

113 Scott Road, Eatonton, GA 31024 – 706-347-8013   Central Georgia
E-mail: dmclark1002@gmail.com
Lake Oconee Presbyterian Church – 706-484-0600

Clark, Doug – Chap USArmy, 15-

United States Army   South Florida

Clark, George S. – b Rehoboth, NM, Jul 30, 35; f Howard A.; m Alma B. Dimmick; w Sherie L. MacKeen, St. Louis, MO, Jun 10, 60; chdn G. Philip, Lauren Edward; ShelC 53-57, BA; FTS 57-60, MDiv; L Jan 60, Phil Pby (BPC); O Jun 60, Phil Pby (BPC); mis Ind Bd, Bethlehem, Jordan, 60-65; mis Ind Bd, Beirut, Lebanon, 65-69; NBS, Window Rock, AZ, 69-71; ob prof, admin BibTS, 71-00; hr 00

4701 Corsage Drive, Lutz, FL 33549 – 813-920-3337   Philadelphia Metro West
E-mail: gnsclark@usa.com
HR

Clark, Joseph William – b Montgomery, AL, Mar 5, 54; f James Monroe; m Mary L. Pouncey; w Cecelia Ann Harden, Montgomery, AL, Oct 15, 83; chdn Andrew William, Joshua Alan, Daniel Joseph; UAL 72-76, BS; GCTS 80-82; CTS 82-85, MDiv; L Oct 83, Evan Pby; O Feb 86, GulCst Pby; ap Westminster P Ch, Ft. Walton Beach, FL, 86-87; p Evangelical P Ch, Carbondale, IL, 87-90; p Malvern Hills P Ch, Asheville, NC, 90-99, wc 99-06; ascp Covenant Ref P Ch, Asheville, NC, 06-18; ip, ss Presbyterian Ch of Coventry, Coventry, CT, 18-

441 South Main Street, Apt 4, Manchester, CT 06040 – 828-299-3257   Western Carolina
E-mail: jclark5@charter.net
Presbyterian Church of Coventry – 860-742-7222

Clark, Raymond Wilson – b Lansing, MI, Jul 24, 39; f Irving Nelson; m Lena Mae Wright; w Penny Ann Sheraton, Seattle, WA; chdn Christopher Raymond, Aaron Thomas, Benjamin Sheraton, Nathan Robert; TynC 62, BRE; CTS 65, BD; TEDS 71, ThM; prof CC, 66-; astp Hixson P Ch, Hixson, TN, 97-99; astp St. Elmo P Ch, Chattanooga, TN, 02-13; hon DD, CTS, 01

499 McFarland Road, Lookout Mountain, GA 30750 – 706-820-1259   Tennessee Valley
Covenant College – 706-820-1560

Clark, Robert Lee Jr. – b Cincinnati, OH, Mar 3, 53; f R.L. Sr; m Alberta Miriam Cahall; w Nedra Marie Houchens, Cincinnati, OH, Mar 18, 78; chdn Aarin Rachel, Andrew Robert, Adam Richard, Arden Rebekah; UCin 85, BA; CTS 89, MDiv; L Jan 88, MO Pby; O Nov 19, 89, NoTX Pby; stus Heritage Ref P Ch, Eureka, MO, 87-89; ascp Town North P Ch, Richardson, TX, 89-95; srp Westminster P Ch, Elgin, IL, 95-02, wc 02-08; astp Christ P Ch, Richmond, IN, 08-10, ascp 10-12; p 12-

2509 South B Street, Richmond, IN 47374 – 765.373.8744   Central Indiana
E-mail: bob@knowingchrist.net
Christ Presbyterian Church – 765-966-4017

Clark, Stephen Morrieson – b Jamaica, West Indies, Jul 26, 50; f Ernest; m Elizabeth Jespersen; w Olivia Arscott, Devon, Jamaica, W.I., Aug 12, 72; chdn Stephen Matthew, Jean-Paul, Alisha Katherine; ULon 72, dipl; GCTS 80, MDiv; PTS 80, ThM; DrewU 81-83, MPhil, 86, PhD; O 74, mis Ch, Jamaica; p Grace mis, 74-77; srp Knowlton P Ch, Columbia, NJ, 81-93; lect WTS, 89-93; srp Wallace P Ch, Hyattsville, MD, 93-07; lect ChTS, 97; lect RTS Metro, 00-07; srp Old Cutler P Ch, Miami, FL, 07-15; hr 15;

Clark, Stephen Morrieson, continued
"Jonathan Edwards: The History of Redemption," *Westminster Theological Journal*, Spring 94; "Jonathan Edwards: The Assurance of Salvation and the Care of the Church" in *The Assembling of the Ourselves Together*, 05; *As Good As it Gets; Life, Love, and Relationships; 50 Days in the Song of Songs*, 11; "Karios And Kingdom" in *A Kairos Moment for Caribbean Theology*, 13

3361 Meander Lane, Safety Harbor, FL 34695 – 727-953-5038   Southwest Florida
E-mail: stephenclark2u@gmail.com
HR

Clark, Taylor – b Hoboken, GA, Aug 21, 87; f Dennis; m Janice; w Anna Marie Ball, Christiansburg, VA, Jan 5, 08; chdn Brayden Luke, Lydia Marie, Ezekiel James; LibU, BS; CTS, MDiv; O Sept 18, 16, GrLks Pby; astp Tyrone Cov P Ch, Fenton, MI, 15-17; ascp Faith Cov P Ch, Kalispell, MT, 17-18

1076 Old Racepond Road, Hoboken, GA 31542 – 406-314-8153   Rocky Mountain
E-mail: pastor.clark.pca@gmail.com

Clarke, Bryan – UWindsor, BEd; RTSNC, MDiv; UAlb, MEd, PhD; O Nov 28, 04; astp Woodgreen P Ch, Calgary, AB, 04-05; campm RUM, UAlb, 05-11; ob GraceFinder Resourcing Network, 11-

1034 East Bend NW, Edmonton, AB T6M 0V6 CANADA – 780-481-1916   Western Canada
E-mail: bclarkegracefinder@gmail.com
GraceFinder Resourcing Network

Clarke, Robert T. III – b Columbia, SC, Mar 26, 49; f Robert T Jr.; m Frances W; w Jane Winburn (d), (2) Kathleen Bearce, Johns Creek, GA, Jan 21, 12; chdn Brittani Lee, Allyson Jane; USo 71, BA; CTS 91, MDiv; O May 24, 92, TNVal Pby; p Sweetwater Valley P Ch, Sweetwater, TN, 92-96; cop Christ P Ch, Sweetwater, TN, 96-98; p Covenant P Ch, Greenville, MS, 98-09; dir Min Relief, RBI, 09-

1700 North Brown Road #106, Lawrenceville, GA 30701-7011   Covenant
E-mail: bclarke@pcanet.org
PCA Retirement & Benefits, Inc. – 678-825-1260

Clarke, Terrance A., Jr. – b Galveston, TX, Sept 5, 51; f Terrance A.; m Mary Louise Hamilton; w Francine Elizabeth Topmiller, Albany, GA, May 12, 90; BelmC 85, BBA; KTS 95, MDiv; UWales 02, PhD; L Jul 20, 93, SFL Pby; O Oct 29, 95, Pby of the Dakotas (OPC); Recd PCA Jul 15, 97, MO Pby; p Trinity OPC, Bridgewater, SD, 95-96; wc; vis lect/prof CTS, 03; mis MTW, Australia, 04-; lect Queensland Theo College, 07-08; lect, prin WTC, 09-; contr, *Dictionary of the Old Testament: Pentateuch*; "Complete v. Incomplete Conquest: A Re-examination of Three Passages in Joshua" in *Tyndale Bulletin*, 09

c/o Mission to the World   Missouri
E-mail: fttaclarke@iinet.net.au
PCA Mission to the World
Sunshine Coast Theological College, Buderim, Australia

Clarkson, Preston D. – O Jul 1, 12, JR Pby; fm MTW, 12-

5848 Hardwood Lane, Prince George, VA 23875 – 804-586-1418   James River
E-mail: pdclar@email.wm.edu
PCA Mission to the World

Clausing, Cameron David – O Aug 25, 13, Nash Pby; astp Parish P Ch, Franklin, TN, 13-

929 Hickory Hills Drive, Franklin, TN 37067   Nashville
E-mail: camclausing@gmail.com
Parish Presbyterian Church – 615-574-1029

MINISTERIAL DIRECTORY

Clay, Daniel Lanier – b Jacksonville, FL, Apr 30, 62; f James G; m Alice M; w Amy Warren, Atlantic Bch, FL, Aug 15, 87; chdn Sterling Adam, Hannah Lanier, Stuart Robert; BreJC 80-82, AA; USAL 82-85, BA; USC 85-87, MATS; CBS 88-89; RTSFL 8992, MDiv; L Apr 21, 91, CentFL Pby; O Feb 21, 93, CentFL Pby; op Grace P Ch, Palm Coast, FL, 92-94; headm Chapel CS, Garden City, GA, 94-99; p Chapel In The Gardens P Ch, Garden City, GA, 94-99; p Church of the Cov, Cincinnati, OH, 99-06; mis MTW West Africa, 06-08; ob t Providence Extension Ministries, Jacksonville, 07-18; ascp Ortega P Ch, Jacksonville, FL, 11- 18; ascp Covenant P Ch, Houston, TX, 18-

24022 Gray Falls Drive, Houston, TX 77077 – 904-415-8766   Houston Metro
E-mail: pastordanclay@gmail.com
Covenant Presbyterian Church – 281-870-0349

Clay, Henry – b Naples, Italy, Jun 18, 54; w Wendy; chdn Walt, Thomas, Annie, Caroline; GATech 78, BME; CBS 05, MDiv; O Aug 17, 06, Palm Pby; staff Navs, 78-; mis Bonn, Germany, 78-80; campm Univ SoCar, 80-83; mis Buenos Aires, 86-01; astp Northeast P Ch, Columbia, SC, 02-08; Area staff Nav 08-11; Dir staff care Nav 11-17; Leadr development, 18-

105 Springlawn Road, Columbia, SC 29223 – 803-233-7859   Palmetto
The Navigators

Clayton, John – O Jun 2, 13, Cov Pby; astp Covenant Ch, Fayetteville, AR, 13; op Covenant P Ch, Fort Smith, AR, 13-

4627 Free Ferry Road, Fort Smith, AR 72903 – 479-650-5117   Covenant
E-mail: jclayton@cpcfs.org
Covenant Presbyterian Church – 479-242-7737

Clegg, Matt – O 17, Evan Pby; astp Red Mountain Ch, Birmingham, AL, 17-

205 Oak Road, Vestavia Hills, AL 35216   Evangel
E-mail: matt@redmountainchurch.org
Red Mountain Church

Clegg, Ronald William – b Logan, WV, Oct 13, 54; f William E.; m Lillian Mae Gallemore; w Frances Gayle Sankey, Montgomery, AL, Aug 21, 82; chdn Mary Lauryn, Matthew William, Anna Kathryn, Andrew Wesley; MarU 72-76, BA; RTS 81-86, MDiv; L Jul 83, CentFL Pby; O Oct 86, SEAL Pby; p Friendship P Ch, Eufaula, AL, 86-89; op New Life P Ch, Tifton, GA, 89-94, p 94-00, mis 00-09; p Parkview Ch, Lilburn, GA, 09-16; astp Southwood P Ch, Huntsville, AL, 16-

2505 Lawson Lake Court SE, Huntsville, AL 35803 – 678-524-5229   Providence
E-mail: ron.clegg@southwood.org
Southwood Presbyterian Church – 256-882-3085

Clelland, David Harry – b Pittsburgh, PA, Oct 19, 42; w Gayle Paton (d), Pittsburgh, PA, Jul 10, 65; chdn Rebecca Lynn (Blasingame), Susan Gayle (Gregory); PASU 64, BS; CTS 79, MDiv; L Jan 78, MidW Pby; O Jun 80, SW Pby (RPCES); p Town North P Ch, Richardson, TX, 80-09; Southwest Ch Planting Network, church planting coach, Dallas, TX, 11-16; hr 16; pRes Providence P Ch, Dallas, TX

2706 Foxboro Drive, Richardson, TX 75082-3052 – 972-669-2817   North Texas
E-mail: david.clelland@sbcglobal.net
HR

Clement, Justin – w Elizabeth; chdn John Huss, Gardner, Eliza Jane; SamU, BA; CTS, MDiv; O Oct 30, 04, SoTX Pby; astp Redeemer P Ch, San Antonio, TX, 04-06; campm RUF, TrinityU, 06-10; campm RUF, UGA, 10- 17; RUF, area coord, GA and NC, 17-

345 Kings Road, Athens, GA 30606 – 210-267-7884   Georgia Foothills
E-mail: jclement@ruf.org
PCA Reformed University Fellowship

Clements, Don Keith – b Detroit, MI, Aug 28, 38; f Russell Carl (d); m Julia Mench (d); w Esther Alexander, Washington, DC, Apr 7, 68; chdn Stephanie Cristin, Susannah Noel, Sarah Elizabeth (Hein); UDet 55-56; WaySU 56-58; GtwnU 59-60; VandU 61-63; DLI 64-65, dipl; CTS 70-74, MDiv; GCTS 89, DMin; L Jan 9, 73, MidW Pby (RPCES); O Jul 21, 74, CentGA Pby; ip Perry P Ch, Perry, GA, 72; op First Ref P Ch, Atlanta, GA, 73-74; p Eastern Heights P Ch, Savannah, GA, 74-75; Chap USN, 76-85; medu New Cov P Ch, Virginia Beach, VA, 80-83; sc MidAtl pby 80-83; p Maple Ave Bap Ch, Newport, RI, 84-85; p Grace Cov P Ch, Blacksburg, VA, 85-92, wc 93; p Valley P Ch, Narrows, VA, 94-03; sc NR Pby, 97-02; ob ev PEF, dir, Metokos Ministries, 00-18; sc BlRdg Pby, 02-11; ss Christ Ch of Arlington, Arlington, VA, 04; ip Draper's Valley P Ch, Draper, VA, 07-08; ip Hope P Ch, Martinsville, VA, 09-10; ss Grace Fell, Middleboro, KY, 11; ss Proclamation P Ch, Pulaski, VA, 12-13; lic Pot pby & GrLks pby; hr 18; *Biblical Church Government; Historical Roots of the PCA; God the Holy Spirit; God the Son*; co-found, pub *The Aquila Report,* 09-12

501 College Street, Narrows, VA 24124 – 540-726-8223   Blue Ridge
E-mail: donclements82838@gmail.com
HR

Click, Caleb – O Jan 14, SavRiv Pby; astp First P Ch, Augusta, GA, 14- 16; astp Perimeter Ch, Johns Creek, GA, 16-

1045 Thimblegate Court, Johns Creek, GA 30097 – 678-575-0855   Metro Atlanta
E-mail: calebc@perimeter.org
Perimeter Church – 678-405-2000

Clifford, Roger L. – chp Grundy, VA, 83-85; p Calvin P Ch, Richmond, VA, 85-94; hr 94

7912 Hermitage Road, Richmond, VA 23228-3735 – 804-266-4205   James River
HR

Clotaire, Raymond – Recd PCA Apr 9, 15, NFL Pby; op Elohim Evangelical Ch, 15-17, p 17-

3288 Horseshoe Trail Drive, Orange Park, FL 32065   North Florida
E-mail: ray.clotaire@ymail.com
Elohim Evangelical Church – 904-248-9599

Cloud, Stephen D. – b Port St. Joe, FL, Jan 7, 58; f Charles W.; m Betty J. Mercer; w Laura Annette Fell, Robertsdale, AL, May 17, 80; chdn Bryant, Ashley, Annalisa, Joshua; UMobile 80, BA; SEBTS 83, MDiv; BDS 96, DMin; L Feb 01, GulCst Pby; O Oct 01, GulCst Pby; admin, prin Faith CS, Robertsdale, AL, 97-03; ss Faith P Ch, Robertsdale, AL, 01, astp 01-03; p Fairfield P Ch, Pensacola, FL, 03-09; op Lillian Fellowship, Lillian, AL, 09-17; astp Briarwood P Ch, Birmingham, AL, 17-

E-mail: scloud1@cox.net   Evangel
Briarwood Presbyterian Church

Clower, Lea Adolph – b Miami, FL, Sept 27, 47; f John T.; m Barbara Lea Honeycutt; w F. Jeane Rhodes, Charlotte, NC, Jun 15, 69; chdn Lea A. Jr., Edward A., Jennifer J.; UNC 69, BA; CTS 83, MDiv; O Nov 6, 83, SFL Pby; ap Covenant P Ch, Naples, FL, 83-86; ap Key Biscayne P Ch, assigned to World Servants, Key Biscayne, FL, 86-88; astp First P Ch, Chattanooga, TN, 88-02; p Rainbow P Ch, Rainbow City, AL, 02-09; hr 09

E-mail: leaclower@bellsouth.net   Tennessee Valley
HR

Cobb, Charles Harold Jr. – b Anderson, SC, Apr 5, 32; f Charles Harold C; m Lucile Cawthon; w (1) Clemmie Hurst (d), (2) Barbara Williams, Dallas, TX, Sept 4, 81; chdn Charles Harold III, Evelyn Lucile, Elizabeth Eloise, Elaine Lee, George Harvard, Steven Lee; KgC 54, BA; UTSVA 57, BD; O Sept 27,

Cobb, Charles Harold Jr., continued
57, ParisPby; p Alpine Ch, Longview, TX, 57-59; mis Brazil, 59-72; p Town East P Ch, Dallas, TX, 72-94; ap New Cov P Ch, Dallas, TX, 94-95, ascp 95-97; hr 97

25 West View, Brevard, NC 28712 – 828-966-9505   North Texas
E-mail: cbcobb81@citcom.net
HR

Cobb, Donald Edward – b Plymouth, MA, Aug 31, 61; f I. Stanley; m Harriet Corinne Briggs; w Claire-Lise Favre-Bulle, La Chaux-de Fonds, Switzerland, Jul 10, 92; chdn Dimitri Alexandre, Lucas Yann; FLTR/Aix, BD, MDiv; L Jan 16, 96, CentFL Pby; O Apr 6, 97, CentFL Pby; prof Ecole Biblique Emmaus, Switzerland, 92-94; mis MTW, 97-; *The Second Helvetic Confession, A New Translation in Modern French*, 01; *The Doctrine of the Church* (Turkish) 02

c/o MTW   Central Florida
E-mail: 495150@worldnet.att.net
PCA Mission to the World

Coburn, Andrew Paul – b Nashua, NH, May 23, 65; f Paul Frederick; m Luiza Pereira Da Cruz; w Kelli Mackin, Demopolis, AL, Aug 8, 93; chdn Anna Caroline, Maggie Elizabeth, Merry Rebecca, Amy Claire; BelC 87, BA; RTS 96, MA, 03, MDiv; O Nov 15, 09, ARP; camplife dir, Jackson, MS YFC, 83-86, 88-91; ydir, Covenant Life P Ch, Sarasota, FL, 91-92; ydir, Lakeside P Ch (EPC), Brandon, MS, 92-94; campm, MTW Guayaquil, Ecuador, 97-00; ydir, Raymond P Ch, Raymond, MS, 01-03; dir intl univ min, MTW, Lawrenceville, GA, 03-07; ascp-youth, New Albany P Ch (ARP), New Albany, MS, 08-12 astp, yp Lawndale P Ch, Tupelo, MS, 12-

505 Rebel Drive, Tupelo, MS 38801 – 662-317-1700   Covenant
E-mail: andycoburn@lawndalepc.com
Lawndale Presbyterian Church – 662-844-6795

Cochell, James – b Portland, OR, Feb 9, 72; f Jim Ray; m Concetta P. Covatta; w Rebekah Mercaldo, Middletown, NY, Aug 20, 94; NyC 94, BS; GCTS 09, MDiv; O May 22, 11, CentCar Pby; Chap USArmy, 11-

8542 SW Sun Valley Drive, Lawton, OK 73505 – 704-773-9312   Catawba Valley
E-mail: jamescochell@yahoo.com
United States Army

Cochet, Alan – O PCUSA; Recd PCA Oct 10, 85; p College Hill P Ch, Oxford, MS, 85-13; hr 13

404 Lakeview Court, Oxford, MS 38655-9693 – 662-234-5370   Covenant
E-mail: 22barnabas@gmail.com
HR

Cockrell, Larry – b Feb 19, 56; w Gloria Dianne Binion; chdn Janelle Patrice, Stephen Donnell; UAL 79, BS; BhamTS 91, MRE; BhamSoC 96; O Bapt; Recd PCA Jan 23, 96, Evan Pby; p Household of Faith Ch, Birmingham, AL, 96-

500 Winterpark Circle, Birmingham, AL 35215 – 205-841-7014   Evangel
E-mail: ldcockrell@aol.com
Household of Faith Church – 205-836-5758

Codling, Donald Alwyn – b Prince Albert, SK, Canada, Oct 16, 41; f Alwyn; m Dorothy Laing; w Lois Hawkes, Bluevale, Ont, Canada, Jun 8, 68; CanSC 63, BS; KCT 70, BD; WTS 74, ThM; FrUAmst 74-77, 80; L 70, ETor Pby (PCC); O 70, ETor Pby (PCC); p Bathurst & Tabusintac, N.B., 70-73; p Mackay

Codling, Donald Alwyn, continued
Ch, Timmins, Ont, Canada, 78-81; p Bedford P Ch, Bedford, NS, 83-09; hr 09; sc ECan Pby, 87-15; *Trinity: What does the Bible Say?*; *Sola Scriptura and Revelatory Gifts: How Should Christians Deal with Present Day Prophecy?*; *Sola Scripura ... - Sola Scriptura e os dons de revelação : como lidar com a atual manifestação do dom de profecia?*

900 Old Sackville Road, Lower Sackville, NS B4E 1R1 CANADA – 902-864-1587   Eastern Canada
E-mail: dcodling@hfx.eastlink.ca
HR

Codling, Douglas Owen – b Melfort, SK, Canada; f Llewelyn E.; m Violet McHarg; w Hellen O. Pollari, Timmins, Ont, Canada, Aug 27, 66; chdn Stephen, Bethany, Deborah, Ruth (d); TchC 58, dipl; USask 63, BA; KCT 66, MDiv, 68, grad wk; O May 12, 68, E Toronto Pby (PCC); ap Scott Mission, Toronto, 66-68; p Little Narrows, NS, 68-71; p Sunny Corner, NB (PCC), 71-77; op Vancouver, BC (RPCES), 77-83; srp Faith P Ch, Vancouver, BC, 83-01, wc 01-03; ob p Grace P Ch, Regina, SK, 03-10

PO Box 21, Cymric, SK S0G 0Z0 CANADA – 306-484-2255   Western Canada
E-mail: dougcodling@hotmail.com

Codling, James Llewellyn – b Saskatchewan, Can, Nov 28, 49; f Llewellyn E.; m Violet McHarg; w Christine Melby, St. Louis, MO; chdn Mattie, Louis Peter; USask 67-71, BEd; KCT 73-76, MDiv; CTS 78-80, ThM; ConcS 90, ThD; MSU 90, Med, SpEd, DEd; L Mar 76, ETor Pby (PCC); O May 76, N Sask Pby; p Elphinstone, Okanais, Rollg Rvr, 76-78; op Cov Comm Ch, Regina, SK, 80-81; p Olive Branch Ch, St. Louis, MO, 83-86; PalmHC, 87-88; ydir First P Ch, Louisville, MS, 88-89; ss Macon P Ch, Macon, MS, 90-91; ob prof MHJC, 91-00; adj prof TTS, 94-16; ob prof MSU, 00-16; ss Bethel P Ch, Epes, AL, 01-09; p Old Lebanon P Ch, Ackerman, MS, 09-15; hr 16; *Creative Arts, Forgotten Foundations of Education; Perceptions of Actresses: Aging Perceptions of Strong Female Characters; Empathic Resonance and Meryl Streep; Ethics, Eschatology, and Education*

505 North 2nd Street, Bay St. Louis, MS 39520 – 662-694-0656   Covenant
HR

Coenen, Jeremy – b Madison, WI, May 10, 77; w Sarah Beth Pilsbury, May 15, 99; chdn Andrew, James; TIU 99, BA; WTS 04, MDiv; O 06; astp First P Ch, Schenectady, NY, 06-08; astp East Ridge P Ch, East Ridge, TN, 08-13; chap 13-

2413 B Sundog Court, Eielson AFB, AK 99702 – 423-240-7213   Tennessee Valley
E-mail: JJamesCoenen@gmail.com

Coffee, Clay – w Hillary; chdn Carson, Cole, Campbell; St. Johns 93; CTS 99; astp, DirCouns Perimeter Ch, Duluth, GA, 99-06; dir Marriage Enrich/Divorce Recovery, Central P Ch, St. Louis (non-PCA), 06-14; wc

3726 Arsenal Street, Saint Louis, MO 63116-4802 – 314-771-7123   Missouri
E-mail: clay.coffee@gmail.com

Coffeen, Richard Lee – w Therese; chdn Galadriel Eve, Caylah Mary, Calvin John, Hannah Abigail, Ransom Isaiah, Eowyn Elizabeth, Xaris Rebekah; astp Chinese Christian Ch, Falls Church, VA, 03-05; ob t Dominion Christian School, 05-12; astp Potomac Hills P Ch, Leesburg, VA, 08-10; ob t Providence Class Acad, Bossier City, LA, 12-13; ob yp North Shore Chinese Christian Ch, Deerfield, IL, 13-; *The Discipline of Mytra*, 09

1131 Camille Avenue, Deerfield, IL 60015 – 224-515-8223   Chicago Metro
E-mail: rich.coffeen@nsccc.org

Coffin, David F. Jr. – b Washington, DC, Jul 18, 52; f David Frank; m Edith Caroline Davis; w Jennifer Pauline Quie, Washington, DC, Aug 17, 74; chdn Andrew Marshall, Rebecca Elizabeth, Sarah

Coffin, David F. Jr., continued
Jacqueline; L'Abri 73-74; LVSC 74-75; StVC 78, BA; PittsTS 78-80; WTS 03, PhD; O Dec 7, 90, Pot Pby; p New Hope P Ch, Fairfax City, VA, 90-17, astp 18-; PhD diss "Reflections on the Life and Thought of Robert Lewis Dabney, with Particular Reference to his Views on Divine Sovereignty and Human Free Agency"

10927 Park Road, Fairfax, VA 22030-5253 – 703-352-4936   Potomac
E-mail: David@NewHopeFairfax.org
New Hope Presbyterian Church – 703-385-9056

    Coggins, Michael – astp Chesterfield P Ch, Chesterfield, MO, 06-15; astp Gr Blue Ridge, Hendersonville, NC, 15-17, ascp 17-

307 Ballayntyne Commons Circle #203, Hendersonville, NC 28792   Western Carolina
E-mail: mcoggin57@yahoo.com
Grace Blue Ridge – 828-393-5147

    Cohee, Daniel – b Portsmouth, VA, Nov 6, 78; f Frank; m Margaret; w Yatang Zhuang, Taipei, Taiwan, Sept 1, 12; chdn Emmeline Claire, Susannah Margaret; CC 01, BA; WTSTX 07, MDiv; O Sept 13, 09, Evan Pby; mis MSS, 09-; ip New Hope Christ Fell, Taipei, 10-16

185 Wild Timber Parkway, Pelham, AL 35124   Evangel
E-mail: daniel.cohee@gmail.com
Missionary Sending Service

    Coho, Frank E. Jr. – b Lancaster, PA, Sept 27, 41; f Frank E; m Margaret Mary Young; w Marcia Jean Dalrymple, Somerville, MA, Sept 17, 66; chdn Cathy Jean, Christine Joy, Daniel William, Kendra Lee; FMC 59-61; WCPA 61-63, BA; FulTS 63-66, MDiv; HarvU 76-77; YDS 81, STM; L Jun 10, 66, Pitts Pby (UPCUSA); O Sept 25, 66, Pitts Pby (UPCUSA); p Rometown and Kerr Hill chs, Titusville, PA, 66-68; p Latta Mem P Ch, Christiana, PA, 68-72; ap, p St. Andrews P Ch, Butler, PA, 73-76; op Stamford, CT, 77-82; p Midland Ref Ch (RCA), 82-89; prof LanBC, 90-07; hr 07

134 East Clay Street, Lancaster, PA 17602-2018 – 717-392-0001   Susquehanna Valley
HR

    Colclasure, William Joseph – b Alton, IL, May 20, 51; f Maurice Samuel; m Rose Marie Edwards; w Mary Katherine Begany, Philadelphia, PA, Dec 22, 73; chdn William Jordan, Robert Cullom; UMO 69-73, BS; WTS 75-78, MDiv; O Jul 23, 78, SFL Pby; ap Rio Vista Comm Ch, Ft. Lauderdale, FL, 78-82; op Pine Ridge P Ch, Orlando, FL, 83-84, p 84-

5421 Baybrook Avenue, Orlando, FL 32819-7134 – 407-295-6183   Central Florida
Pine Ridge Presbyterian Church – 407-293-7298

    Cole, Howard – O May 22, 11, CentCar Pby; astp Ch of Redeemer, Monroe, NC, 11-14; p Metro North P Ch, Goose Creek, SC, 14-

709 Quintan Street, Goose Creek, SC 29483 – 843-214-5577   Lowcountry
E-mail: hcole@metronorthpca.org
Metro North Presbyterian Church – 843-764-0873

    Cole, James Alan Jr. – b Hollywood, FL, Sept 14, 50; f James Alan Sr.; m Dorothy Mary Humphreys; FSU 72, BS; FBC 75, BA; RTS 86, MDiv, 86, MCE; L 86; O 86, FL Pby (ARP); Recd PCA Jul 17, 86; ascp Seven Rivers P Ch, Lecanto, FL, 86-10

Address Unavailable   Central Florida

Coleman, Daniel Carrington – b Elmhurst, IL, Jun 23, 51; f Henry Edmunds; m Isabel Campbell Gennert; w Teresa Dawn Eppler, Greenville, SC, Jun 2, 79; chdn Elizabeth Anne Edmunds, Matthew Henry Thomas, Sarah Gordon Conrad, Benjamin Carrington Connor, Mary Margaret Murray, Anna Lucinda Clark, Martha Catherine Embry, Susannah Grace Eaton; NewbC 70-72; ChSoU 75, BS; BJU 79, MDiv, 81, PhD; L Jan 76, Ind; O Feb 7, 82, Ind; p Trinity Ch (Ind), Orlando, FL, 82-87; prof, admin GPTS, 90-94; p Providence P Ch, Spartanburg, SC, 88-; contr: *Biblical Viewpoint*; *The Southerner*; *Businessgram*; *The Bulletin*

389 Newman Drive, Roebuck, SC 29376 – 864-587-7380   Calvary
Providence Presbyterian Church – 864-579-1665

Coleman, Michael Lee – b Baltimore, MD, Jul 6, 49; f Carroll R.; m Charlotte I. Boone; w Barbara A. Shelton, Baltimore, MD, Sept 11, 71; chdn David, Stephen, Jason; UMD 71, BA; FulTS 82, MDiv; O Jun 83, Ref Epis; Dir Young Life, MD, 71-81; p Grace Ch, Havre de Grace, MD, 83-85; op Reformed P Ch, Bowie, MD, 85, p 86-18, astp 18-

14401 Knoll View Court, Bowie, MD 20720-4842 – 301-464-0565   Potomac
E-mail: rpcb@juno.com
Reformed Presbyterian Church – 301-262-2280

Coleman, Stephen – b Providence, RI, Feb 15, 80; w Carrie; chdn Molly, Oliver, Charlotte, Whitman, Margaret; GroCC, BA; WSCAL, MDiv; CathUAm 10, MA, 16, PhD; O Feb 06, Pac Pby; astp Valley P Ch, North Hills, CA, 06-08; astp Wallace P Ch, College Park, MD, 08-13; ascp 13-17; ob astprof WTS, 17-

1526 Vernon Road, Blue Bell, PA 19422 – 301-412-8331   Potomac
E-mail: colemansm1@gmail.com
Westminster Theological Seminary

Coleman, Wade Francis – b Chattanooga, TN, May 17, 67; f Donald Francis; m Anna Mae Reed; w Marian Ruth Dabney, Virginia Beach, VA, Jun 16, 90; chdn Joshua Wade, Christopher Benjamin, Micah Andrew, Charis Elizabeth, Noah Stephen; KgC 89, BA; RTS 96, MA, 98, MDiv; L Oct 98, MSVal Pby; O Jun 99, MSVal Pby; Edgemont P Ch, Bristol, TN, 90-94; int Providence P Ch, Clinton, MS, 95-99, ascp 99-03; srp Westminster P Ch, Bryan, TX, 03-

4734 Tiffany Park Circle, Bryan, TX 77802 – 979-774-6670   South Texas
E-mail: pastorwade.coleman@gmail.com
Westminster Presbyterian Church – 979-776-1185

Colflesh, Matthew T. – b Abington, PA, March 18, 74; f John Byron; m Barbara Jeanne Lockard; w Monica Lynn Johnson, Lambertville, NJ, May 26, 07; chdn Lily Morgan, Reese Mary, Nora Mae, Mabel Wendy, Miles Pearce, Ralph Matthew; Bloomsburg University of PA 96, BS; WTS 00, MDiv; L Jun 00, Philadelphia Pby (OPC); O Feb 01, Philadelphia Pby (OPC); int Covenant P Ch, Doylestown, PA, 97-99, ascp Covenant P Ch, Doylestown, PA, 01-04; wc 04-

1598 Crested Road, Coopersburg, PA 18036   Philadelphia
Email: mcolflesh@gmail.com

Collins, Calvin – astp Westminster P Ch, Johnson City, TN, 08-10; wc 10-

Address Unavailable   Westminster

Collins, Clifford John – b Knoxville, TN, Aug 29, 54; f James William; m Marjorie Charlene Gimpel; w Diane Marie Postetter, Boston, MA, Jun 9, 79; chdn Joy Marie, Joseph Philip; MIT 78, BS, 78, MS; FELS 85, MDiv; ULvrpl 89, PhD; L Sept 83, PacNW Pby; O Sept 10, 89, PacNW Pby; ev Faith P Ch, Spokane, WA, 89-92; asst prof CTS, 93-95, assoc prof 95-00, prof 00-; fellow, Center for the Renewal of Science and Culture, 98-; Senior Research Fellow, Creation Project at Carl Henry Center for Theological Understanding; Theses: *Homonymous Verbs in Biblical Hebrew*; *Divorce and Remarriage in the Bible: A Problem in*

Collins, Clifford John, continued
Hermeneutics; contr *New International Dictionary of OT Theology and Exegesis*; auth *The God of Miracles: An Exegetical Examination of God's Action in the World*; OT Chair, *English Standard Version*; *Science and Faith: Friends or Foes?* 03; *Genesis 1-4: A Linguistic, Literary, and Theological Commentary*, 06; Old Testament ed, *ESV Study Bible; Did Adam and Eve Really Exist? Who They Were and Why You Should Care*, 11; *Reading Genesis Well: Navigating History, Poetry, Science, and Truth in Genesis 1–11*, 18

1310 Eaglebrooke Court, Ballwin, MO 63021-7549 – 636-225-2595   Missouri
E-mail: jack.collins@covenantseminary.edu
Covenant Theological Seminary – 314-434-4044

   Collins, Richard Benjamin – w Kim; chdn Brianna, Kylie, Mackenzie; TrSU, BS; BDS, MDiv; O Dec 15, 07, Evan Pby; yp Evangel Ch PCA, Alabaster, AL, 08, astp 09-12; ascp , yp, mp; 12-

174 Heritage Trace Parkway, Montevallo, AL 35115 – 205-948-6158   Evangel
E-mail: bennycollins07@gmail.com
Evangel Church PCA – 205-664-0889

   Collins, Rodney Johnston – b Rochester, NH, Dec 5, 54; f Oral E.; m Joyce Irene Towle; w. Eileen Kelleher, Westfield, MA; chdn Jennifer Joyce, Rodney Johnston Jr., Michelle Renée, Brian Christopher (d), Matthew David, Joy Elizabeth; BelC 78, BA; RTS 82, MDiv; L Oct 82; O Mar 83, NoE Pby; op Grace P Ch, Laconia, NH, 83-85, p 85-04; wc 04-08; ascp West Springfield Cov Comm Ch, West Springfield, MA, 08-

303 Southwick Road, Westfield, MA 01085 – 413-221-9564   Southern New England
E-mail: rjcollins73@gmail.com
West Springfield Covenant Community Church – 413-733-2828

   Collins, Roger Gerald – b Natick, MA, Jun 29, 57; f Oral Collins; m Joyce Towle; w Sharon Ann Sievert, Appleton, WI; chdn Kimberly Lynn, Roger Gerald Jr., Rachel Elizabeth, Jason Andrew, Lauren Rebecca; BelC 79, BA; RTS 82, MDiv, 87, ThM; O Jun 20, 82, MSVal Pby; ap Alta Woods P Ch, Jackson, MS, 82-84; p Grace P Ch, Byram, MS, 84-; sc MSVal Pby, 98-

130 Byram Parkway, Byram, MS 39272 – 601 373-7177   Mississippi Valley
E-mail: clerk@msvalley.org
Grace Presbyterian Church – 601-990-7817

   Collins, Wendell Fraser III – O Mar 6, 14, Cov Pby; astp Riveroaks Ref P Ch, Germantown, TN, 14-17; astp Christ Ch Santa Fe PCA, Santa Fe, NM, 17- 18; srp Lakeview P Ch, Vernon Hills, IL, 18-

1105 Hedgerow Drive, Grayslake, IL 60030   Chicago Metro
E-mail: wfctre@gmail.com
Lakeview Presbyterian Church – 847-680-7940

   Collins, Wylly – b Macon, GA, Nov 1, 72; f James T.; m Margaret Elisabeth; w Kristin Ann, Washington, MO, Jun 29, 96; chdn Amelia Grace, Melissa May, William Taylor, Nathaniel Wylly; CC 91-95, BA; RTS 95-99, MDiv; O Jun 00, MSVal Pby; astp First P Ch, Belzoni, MS, 00; p First P Ch, Florala, AL, 00-04; Chap AL ARNG, 05-

PO Box 231362, Montgomery, AL 36123   Southeast Alabama
E-mail: wyllycollins1776@yahoo.com
Alabama Army National Guard

   Colquitt, Chris – campm RUF, Northwestern, 18-

638 Garrett Place, Evanston, IL 60201   Chicago Metro
E-mail: chris.colquitt@ruf.org
PCA Reformed University Fellowship

Colravy, Cory Dean – b Fairbury, IL, Oct 10, 66; f James Edmund; m Marjorie Jane Frye; w DawnMarie Newman, Bradenton, FL, Apr 17, 93; chdn Megan Danae, Alexis Nicole, Andrew James, Georgia Grace; USF 92, BS; RTSFL 03, MDiv; O Aug 20, 03, CentGA Pby; p New Life P Ch, Tifton, GA, 03-08; p Covenant P Ch, Panama City, FL, 08-

3305 South Harbour Circle, Panama City, FL 32405 – 850-640-1424   Gulf Coast
E-mail: cory@covenantpca.net
Covenant Presbyterian Church – 850-769-7448

Colson, Chuck – O Jan 25, 14, NFL Pby p Christ Ch Mandarin, Jacksonville, FL, 14-

724 Piney Place Street, St. Johns, FL 32259   North Florida
E-mail: ccolson@christchurchmandarin.org
Christ Church Mandarin – 904-262-5588

Colvard, Michael – w Lindsay Elizabeth; chdn David, Joshua, Timothy; CTS 09, MDiv; O Feb 9, 14, CatVal Pby; astp Harbor Ch PCA, Mooresville, NC, 14-16, srp 16-

244 Flanders Drive, Mooresville, NC 28117 – 704-799-8453   Catawba Valley
E-mail: mdcolvard@gmail.com
Harbor Church PCA – 704-662-6540

Combs, Billy George – b Santa Ana, CA, Jun 12, 37; f William Estes C; m Mamie Futch; w Lucille Rostron, Ruston, LA, Mar 30, 61; chdn Susan Renee, Barbara Gail, Daniel Philip; UNV 58-59; LATU 59-64, BS, 59-64, MS; RTS 70, MDiv; O Jul 26, 70, SMS Pby; p First P Ch, Picayune, MS, 70-83; admin, asst prof AUBS, 83-86; p Westminster P Ch, Webster, TX, 86-09; hr 09

101 East Wildwinn Drive, Alvin, TX 77511 – 281-824-4575   Houston Metro
E-mail: billycombs@comcast.net
HR

Conant, Jonathan – ascp First P Ch North Shore, Ipswich, MA, 18-

67 Homestead Circle, South Hamilton, MA 01982   Southern New England
First Presbyterian Church North Shore – 978-356-7690

Congdon, Joe – b Houston, TX, Oct 21, 78; w Felicity, Oct 11, 08; chdn Zoey, Jonah, Ramona; WashU 02, BA, 02, BFA; CTS 14, MDiv; O Nov 17, 14; mis MTW, Tokyo, 14-

c/o MTW   Houston Metro
E-mail: joe.congdon@gmail.com
PCA Mission to the World

Conkel, Dean Eric – b Ft. Lauderdale, FL, Jun 1, 62; f Donald; m Carol Rozler; w Pearl Klein, Pompano Bch, FL, Jul 4, 86; chdn Timothy, Michael, Matthew; PBAC; RTS, MDiv; O Apr 17, 94, CentGA Pby; astp Lakemont P Ch, Augusta, GA, 94-96, ascp 96-99; admin, ydir CEP, 99-06; astp Lake Oconee P Ch, Eatonton, GA, 06-08; p Dayspring P Ch, Forsyth, GA, 08-16; astp First P Ch, Panama City, FL, 16-18; p Lillian Flwsp, Lillian, AL, 18-

385 Quigley Road, Pensacola, FL 32506 – 478-994-0133   Gulf Coast
E-mail: conkelhut@bellsouth.net
Lillian Fellowship – 251-215-0256

Conklin, Kenneth James – b Newport, RI, Oct 9, 72; f Ken; m Barbara Wort; w Allyson Kennedy; chdn Janice, Bethany, James, Adah; ClrCC 02, BA; CTS 07, MDiv; O Feb 09, MO Pby; Chap MO Nat'l Guard 09-14; Chap USArmy, Ft. Hood, TX, 14-17; Ft. Polk, LA, 17-

5979A Harrell Place, Ft. Polk, LA 71459 – 314-229-2902   Missouri
E-mail: kennethjconklin@hotmail.com
United States Army

MINISTERIAL DIRECTORY

Conkling, Timothy G. – b Orlando, FL, Jan 1, 62; f Homer C.; m Martha Elizabeth Fort; w Evelyn Charlene Adams, Lancaster, PA, Jun 15, 85; chdn Allison Fay, Martyn Christopher; ESM 83, BMus, 84, MMus; WTS 90, MDiv; UHI 02, MA; L Mar 90; O Jun 7, 92, Phil Pby; ascp New Life P Ch, Dresher, PA, 88-91; t Christ's College, Taipei, Taiwan, 92-94; astp, srp Friendship P Ch, Taipei, Taiwan, 92-02; mis MTW, 92; ob mis ChMI, 92-01; ascp Trinity P Ch, Kailua, Oahu, HI, 99-01; ss Trinity Leeward Cov Ch, Kapolei, HI, 00-01; chp ChMI, Taipei, Taiwan, 01-; adj prof China Reformed Theo Sem, Taipei, 02-; srp New Hope Christ Fell, Taipei, 03-06

PO Box 1574, Titusville, FL 32781 – 321-269-4090   Northern California
E-mail: tconkling@pobox.com
China Ministries International
China Reformed Theological Seminary, Taipei

Connor, Marshall Dreher Jr. – b Columbia, SC, Jan 16, 48; f Marshall D. Sr; m Dorothy C. Stoner; w Linda S. Arrington, West Columbia, SC, Sept 5, 69; chdn Lara, Stephanie, Shannon, Mark, Caroline, Melissa, Bethany, Ryan; USC 74, BS; RTS 81, MDiv; L Mar 10, 81, MSVal Pby (ARP); O Aug 17, 81; Recd PCA Mar 9, 93, Gr Pby; op Union Hills msn, Phoenix, AZ, 81-82; p Edwards Mem, Cayce, SC, 83-93; p First P Ch, Gulfport, MS, 93-04; p Aimwell P Ch, Ridgeway, SC, 08-17; hr 17

301 Forest Lake Drive, Madison, MS 39110 – 769-300-8584   Palmetto
E-mail: mdconnor@truvista.net
HR

Connors, William Thomas – b Boston, MA, Apr 28, 70; f Joseph P., Sr.; m Kathleen Therese; w Michele Marie Gentile, Wilmington, DE, Sept 26, 98; chdn Caleb, Andrew, Brendan, Sydney; RPI 92, BS; CTS 03, MDiv; O Apr 25, 07, RMtn Pby; astp City P Ch, Denver, CO, 07-08; op Denver P Ch, Denver, CO, 08-14, p 14-

8139 East 23rd Avenue, Denver, CO 80238 – 303-993-4912   Rocky Mountain
E-mail: william.connors@comcast.net
Denver Presbyterian Church – 303-495-3345

Conrad, James Andrew – b Irving, TX, Jan 28, 71; f Jim; m Evie Moore; w Michelle Beland, Fredericksburg, VA, Dec 19, 92; chdn Hanan, Riley, Clara, Ethan; CC 89-93, BA; CTS 93-97, MDiv; O Nov 30, 97, JR Pby; astp, moy Sycamore P Ch, Midlothian, VA, 97-99, ascp 99-08; op Spring Run P Ch, Midlothian, VA, 06-08; p 08-

5710 Sandstone Ridge Road, Midlothian, VA 23112 – 804-739-8182   James River
E-mail: andrew@springrunpc.org
Spring Run Presbyterian Church – 804-608-8233

Conrad, James J. Jr. – b St. Louis, MO, Apr 14, 38; f James J.; m Laura Jane DeGrave; w Evelyn Jo Moore, Lookout Mtn, TN, Aug 26, 67; chdn James Andrew, Laura Virginia, John Matthew; CC 62, BA; CTS 66, BD; L 69; O May 17, 70, So Pby (RPCES); ap Ref P Ch, Huntsville, AL, 68-70; p Westminster P Ch, Bedford, TX, 70-74; srp Covenant P Ch, Naples, FL, 74-00; p Providence P Ch, Murphy, NC, 00-06; hr 06; astp Spring Run P Ch of Chesterfield Co, Midlothian, VA, 14-

9612 Brading Lane, Richmond, VA 23236 – 804-608-0797   James River
E-mail: jcon1207@yahoo.com
HR
Spring Run Presbyterian Church of Chesterfield County

Conrad, Nate – b Owatonna, MN, Jul 10, 75; f Arnold; m Sharon; w Kara Veerman, Naperville, IL, Jul 11, 98; chdn Natalie, Amy, Lindsey; WheatC 97, BS, 02, MA; O Oct 15, 08, ChiMet Pby; yp Naperville P Ch, Naperville, IL, 97-06, astp 07-08, ascp 08-15; ascp Northwest P Ch, Dublin, OH, 15-; sc ColMet pby, 15-

6901 Erie Court, Dublin, OH 43017   Columbus Metro
E-mail: nconrad@npcdublin.org
Northwest Presbyterian Church – 614-799-2300

Constable, Steven Nicholas – b London, England, Aug 11, 63; f Adrian; m Thelma Stapleton; w Barbara Weidenbruch, Washington, DC, Aug 8, 87; chdn Benjamin, Christine, John, Emma; USusx 82-85, BA; ClarkU 85-87, MA; TEDS 89-92, MDiv; O Aug 15, 93, NoIL Pby; astp Lakeview P Ch, Vernon Hills, IL, 93-94, ascp 95-96; ob mis International P Ch, London, 96-00; p New Hope P Ch, Vestal, NY, 00-04; p Stony Point Ref P Ch, Richmond, VA, 04-

1707 Pulliam Street, Richmond, VA 23235 – 804-232-6275   James River
E-mail: stevenconstable@stonypointchurch.org
Stony Point Reformed Presbyterian Church – 804-272-8111

Cook, Jonathan – astp Grace Cent Ch, Omaha, NE, 15-

1305 South 95th Street, Omaha, NE 68124   Platte Valley
E-mail: jonathan@gracereformed.net
Grace Central Church – 402-573-1663

Cooke, Bruce – campm Inter-Varsity Christian Flwsp, UDE, Newark, DE, 07-08; ob campm IVCF, Boston U, 08-

479 Boylston Street, Newton, MA 02459-2739 – 302-897-5077   Southern New England
E-mail: abrucecooke@gmail.com
Inter-Varsity Christian Fellowship, Boston University

Cooksey, Harry Stuart – b Mobile, AL, Mar 7, 54; f Stuart; m Martha Ann Gaines; w Kay Cannon, Spartanburg, SC, Jun 3, 78; chdn Elizabeth, Emily; AU 72-76, BS; RTS 84-87, MDiv, 94, DMin; O Jun 26, 88, Evan Pby; CCC, 76-81; ip Shannon Forest P Ch, Greenville, SC, 83-84; astp First P Ch, Gadsden, AL, 88-92, ascp 92-95; ss Eastside P Ch, Gadsden, AL, 95-97; srp Chapel Woods P Ch, Snellville, GA, 97-01, wc 01-05; RBI, Sr. Field Coord, 06-17; CRC cert, 08; hr 17

6450 Jones Creek Court, Suwanee, GA 30024 – 470-297-4353   Metro Atlanta
HR

Cooney, Allen – Huntley; chdn Lauren, Madeleine; CTS 04, MDiv; O Oct 04, SW Pby; astp Catalina Foothills Ch, Tucson, AZ, 04-07; op Dove Mountain Ch, Oro Valley, AZ, 07-09; p 09-11; astp Catalina Foothills Ch, Tucson, AZ, 11-

6625 North Shadow Run Drive, Tucson, AZ 85704 – 520-229-3349   Southwest
E-mail: allenc@cfcpca.org
Catalina Foothills Church – 520-615-8500

Cooper, George Lockard – b Elkton, MD, Apr 9, 31; f Herbert S.; m Mary E. Baugus; w Edith Marie Furr, Concord, NC, Sept 11, 54; chdn V. Beth (Lutz), Janet L. (Cothran), Joyce M. (Campbell); ShelC 51-55, BA; HTC 66-67; FTS 55-56; CTS 58, BD; L 59, GrLk Pby (EPC); O May 6, 59, GrLk Pby (EPC); p RP Ch, Titusville, PA, 58-61; p Olive Branch P Ch, St. Louis, MO, 61-67; t Wilmington CS, DE, 67-86; hr 87

87 B Kenilworth Road, Asheville, NC 28803   Heritage
HR

Cooper, Kurt – astp Lawndale P Ch, Tupelo, MS, 08-11; astp Trinity P Ch, Montgomery, AL, 11-

8741 Will Newton Drive, Montgomery, AL 36117 – 334-523-1924   Southeast Alabama
E-mail: kurtandmarty@gmail.com
Trinity Presbyterian Church – 334-262-3892

Cooper, Richard – O Jul 27, 97, CentFL Pby; astp Ponte Vedra P Ch, Ponte Vedra Beach, FL, 97-99, ascp 99-03, srp 03-

101 Nina Court, Ponte Vedra Beach, FL 32082-2429 – 904-285-8089   North Florida
E-mail: rcooper@pvpc.com
Ponte Vedra Presbyterian Church – 904-285-8225

Cooper, Steven – ascp Harbor P Ch, San Diego, CA, 09-14; p Harbor City Ch, San Diego, CA, 14-

705 16th Street, San Diego, CA 92101 – 619-289-8857   South Coast
E-mail: steven@harborcity.church
Harbor City Church

Cooper, William Henry Jr. – b Portsmouth, VA, Oct 25, 49; f William H. Sr.; m Maebelle Edward; w Regina Lynn Greer, Cornersville, MS, Nov 12, 77; chdn William Greer, Benjamin Edward; ODU 67-71, BA; RTS 73-77, MDiv; CTS 87, DMin; L Jan 75, Car Pby; O Jun 78, Evan Pby; p Comm P Ch, Madison, AL, 78-91; ss Courtland P Ch, Courtland, AL, 91-08; p 08-09; wc 10; hr 13

4855 South Tanager Avenue, Brookline, MO 65619   Providence
E-mail: drwilliamcooper@gmail.com
HR

Coppedge, Benjamin – WTS 13; campm RUF NMStU, 14-17; campm RUF UGA, 17-

115 Lenox Road, Athens, GA 30606 – 706-372-4627   Georgia Foothills
E-mail: ben.coppedge@ruf.org
PCA Reformed University Fellowship

Coppersmith, Walter Alan – b Washington, DC, Mar 7, 61; f Arthur Clinton; m Edelgard Krimhilda Kannchen; w Barbara Jo Hutchison, Williamsport, PA, Jun 20, 92; chdn Tyler Michael; UMD 79-84, BS, 87-89, MBA; RTS 92-95, MDiv; L May 15, 95; O Mar 8, 98, Pot Pby; stus Tollgate Ref Ch, Owings Mills, MD, 96-97; stus Living Hope Ch, Owings Mills, MD, 97-98, p 98-00; wc 00-01; p Covenant P Ch, Steubenville, OH, 01-05; chp Wintersville, OH, 05-06; op New Horizons, Wintersville, OH, 06-08; astp Westminster P Ch, Butler, PA, 09-11; ascp 11-14

PO Box 693, 202 Crowe Avenue #10, Mars, PA 16046 – 412-656-0599   Ascension
E-mail: refandrev@gmail.com

Corbett, Marc – b Florence, SC, Aug 26, 74; f F.M.; m Shirley Tugwell; w Amy Barnett, Dallas, TX, Jun 5, 99; LibU 93-96, BS; DTS 00, ThM; O Oct 14, 01, NoTX Pby; campm RUF, TXTech, 01-08; campm RUF, Liberty, 08-18; wc

305 Cabell Street, Lynchburg, VA 24504   Blue Ridge

Corbin, Brent – campm RUF, UTulsa, 10-18; RUF area coord, 18-

933 Staring Lane, Baton Rouge, LA 70810   Hills and Plains
E-mail: corbin.brent@gmail.com
PCA Reformed University Fellowship

Corey, Thomas Michael – b Baltimore, MD, Feb 19, 47; f Charles Donald; m Kerschner; w Anne Craig Terrell, Philadelphia, PA; chdn Michael, Susannah, Allison, Aaron, Elizabeth; WheatC 69, BA; WTS 73, MDiv; GCTS 10, DMin; L May 6, 74, OPC; O Dec 12, 76, OPC; Recd PCA Jan 14, 94; ev Church of the City, Philadelphia, PA, 76-78; p SW Philadelphia Ref Fell, PA, 78; Church of the Redeemer, Philadelphia, PA, 81-90; Glad Tidings (CRC), Edmonton, AB, 91-94; srp Hope Ch, Ballston Spa, NY, 94-06; wc 06-08; ob astp Terra Nova Ch, Troy, NY, 08-11; ob IVCF SUNY Albany, CornU, Rensselaer, 12-

9 Van Brummel Lane, Ballston Spa, NY 12020 – 518-584-5011   New York State
E-mail: tomcorey47@gmail.com
Inter-Varsity Christian Fellowship

Corley, Kevin – b Birmingham, AL, Jun 21, 80; w Rebecca Cushman; chdn Weston Michael, William Taylor, Jackson Knox; UAL 03, BS; RTS 10, MDiv; O Feb 20, 11, SEAL Pby; astp Grace Flwsp P Ch, Clanton, AL, 11-

1208 Fourth Avenue, Clanton, AL 35045 – 205-601-9110   Southeast Alabama
E-mail: kevcorley@gmail.com
Grace Fellowship Presbyterian Church – 205-755-4150

Cornwell, Jason – O May 5, 13, Cal Pby; astp Eastside P Ch, -13

106 Pronghorn Court, Simpsonville, SC 29680   Calvary

Cortese, Dean Philip – b Miami, FL, Apr 25, 56; f Norman; m Arline Snyder; w Sue Lach, Orlando, FL, Mar 26, 83; chdn Daniel Philip, Jonathan Dean, Mark Steven, Anna Rebecca; CalvC 75-80, BA; RTS 81-85, MDiv, 81-85, MCE; L 84, MSVal Pby; O 85, Wcar Pby; ap Arden P Ch, Arden, NC, 85-91; staff MTW/Impact, 91-92; staff MTW, 92-94; staff MTW/Impact, 94-97; ascp Grace Comm Ch, Fletcher, NC, 97-08; Chap 10-

148 Lake Rugby Drive, Hendersonville, NC 28791 – 828-890-2007   Western Carolina

Cortese, Raymond Allen – b Miami, FL, Dec 17, 57; f Norman Anthony; m Arline Dorothy Snyder; w Diane Joan Guinn, Western Spgs IL, Aug 10, 79; chdn Michael Anthony, Kristen Diane, Amy Elizabeth, Tucker McClain; BelC 79, BA; RTS 82; WTS 83, MDiv; L Feb 82, MSVal Pby; O Jul 83, CentFL Pby; op Seven Rivers P Ch, Lecanto, FL, 83-84, srp 84-

5705 West Lucky Ranch Trail, Homosassa, FL 34448   Central Florida
E-mail: rcortese@sevenrivers.org
Seven Rivers Presbyterian Church – 352-746-6200

Cory, Duane Edward – b Indianapolis, IN, Feb 8, 54; f Paul; m Pauline Blackburn; w Holly Lemaire, Wheaton, IL, Jun 11, 77; chdn Ian James, Morgan Elizabeth, Brittany Lynn, Graham Edward; CC 76, BA; WTS 84, MAR, 84, MDiv; O May 83, SFL Pby; ap Spanish River P Ch, Boca Raton, FL, 83-87; op Deer Creek Comm Ch, Littleton, CO, 87-92, srp 92-

8131 South Pierce Street, Littleton, CO 80128 – 303-979-9266   Rocky Mountain
E-mail: duane@deercreekchurch.com
Deer Creek Community Church – 303-933-9300

Cosby, Brian – astp Carriage Lane P Ch, Peachtree City, GA, 10-11, ascp 11-12; p Wayside P Ch, Signal Mountain, TN, 12-15; srp 15-

2506 Fairmount Pike, Signal Mountain, TN 37377   Tennessee Valley
E-mail: brian@waysidechurch.org
Wayside Presbyterian Church – 423-886-1181

Cosner, Michael – mis MTW, 13-

1244 Charlotte Avenue, Rock Hill, SC 29732 – 803-324-2337   Fellowship
E-mail: cosnersmtw@gmail.com
PCA Mission to the World

Costa, Eric – w Jerilee; chdn Ransom, Justus, Evangeline, Jubilee; GeorgeFoxU 01, BA; MuSB 04, MDiv; O Oct 30, 05, PacNW Pby; astp Intown P Ch, Portland, OR, 05-09; astp Evergreen P Ch, Beaverton, OR, 09-12; op Ascension P Ch, Hillsboro, OR, 12-

1890 SE Maple Street, Hillsboro, OR 97123 – 503-860-3330   Pacific Northwest
E-mail: rev.eric.costa@gmail.com
Ascension Presbyterian Church – 503-893-9272

Cottone, Jeff – O Arp 28, 13, SusqV Pby; astp Hope Ref P Ch, Shippensburg, PA, 13-; op Redeemer P Msn, Chambersburg, PA, 14-

2830 Keefer Road, Chambersburg, PA 17201-9509 – 717 713-4353   Susquehanna Valley
E-mail: Jeff.cottone@gmail.com
Hope Reformed Presbyterian Church – 717-532-8998
Redeemer Presbyterian Mission – 717-713-4345

Counts, Bryan – w Erika; chdn Garrison, Daniel, Caroline, Jonathan; CC 98, BA; CTS 04, MDiv; O Oct 04, RMtn Pby; astp Village Seven P Ch, Colorado Springs, 04-10, ascp 10-

2310 Zane Place, Colorado Springs, CO 80909 – 719-574-6700   Rocky Mountain
E-mail: bcounts@v7pc.org
Village Seven Presbyterian Church – 719-574-6700

Counts, Kenneth D. – b Montgomery, AL, Apr 4, 53; f Malcolm D.; m Zelda Bowland; w Gwendolyn Hard, Montgomery, AL, Nov 27, 76; chdn Nathan Darby, April Grace, Joel Robert; CC 76, BA; RTS 80, MDiv; TEDS 02, ThM; LMFT, 05; L Jun 12, 79, Evan Pby; O Jun 29, 80, LA Pby; ss Geneva P Ch, Matherville, MS, 80; p John Knox P Ch, Ruston, LA, 80-84; ap Town North P Ch, Richardson, TX, 84-85; t Cornerstone Ac, Dallas, TX, 84-85; p Abundant Life P Ch, Jonesville, LA, 85-91; astp Jackson St P Ch, Alexandria, LA, 91-93; Chap USN, Okinawa, Japan, 93-96, 96-99, 99-01; TEDS, 01-02; Chap Marine Corps Recruit Depot, 02-05; Marine Aircraft Group 13, Yuma, AZ, 05-07; USS HARRY S TRUMAN (CVN-75), 07-09; Chap MCBase Camp Lejeune, NC, 09-

207 Quailwood Court, Cape Carteret, NC 28584   Eastern Carolina
E-mail: kengwencounts@msn.com
United States Navy

Counts, King Allen – b Bristol, TN, Apr 22, 56; f Fred D.; m Mary Lou Fields; w Angela E. Clark, Pensacola, FL, Jul 8, 78; chdn Elizabeth Marion, Adam Timothy, Aaron Samuel; GBibC, BCE; RTS 82, MDiv, 85, MA, 92, DMin; LMFT 05-; L Jul 81, Cov Pby; O Jul 4, 82, Westm Pby; p King Mem P Ch, Bristol, VA, 82-84; p Lippincott Chapel, Bristol, TN, 82-83; ss Forest Grove P Ch, Carthage, MS, 84-85; ss McBride Mem P Ch, Camden, MS, 84-85; p Heidelberg P Ch, Heidelberg, MS, 85-89; p Lookout Valley P Ch, Chattanooga, TN, 89-92; adj prof CC, 91-05; p Mountain View P Ch, Chattanooga, TN, 92-05; srp Carlisle Ref P Ch, Carlisle, PA, 05-12; ob LicMFT, assoc dir The Soldier Center, Clarksville, TN, 12-

604 Snowshoe Lane, Clarkesville, TN 39040 – 931-266-9271   Nashville
E-mail: kingcounts1@gmail.com
Soldier Center Institute for Marriage and Family – 931-553-6981

Coverstone, Justin – b Rock Island, IL, Sept 13, 77; f Larry; m Kay; w Brianna Wells, Monroe, WI, Aug 5, 00; chdn Isabella, Gavin, Judson, Asher, Abigail, Eliza, Evangeline; AmbassBibC 97; RTSFL 10, MDiv; O Oct 23, 11, NoIL Pby; p Grace Flwsp Ch, Freeport, IL, 10-

4111 West Becker School Road, Freeport, IL 61032   Northern Illinois
E-mail: Justin.coverstone@gmail.com
Grace Fellowship Church

Covey, Jimmy – b Stafford Co, KS, Jul 21, 49; f Ivan Vernon; m Opal Maxine Stimatze; w Vicki Lee Crumm, Marland, OK, May 18, 69; chdn Mark Richard, Shawn Erin; PhU 67-71, BA, 71-74, MDiv; RTS 93-95, DMin; O Jun 2, 74, Disciples of Christ; Recd PCA Sept 26, 97, RMtn Pby; p Marland, OK,69-72; p Dover, OK, 72-74; p Crescent, OK, 94-96; rep, staff Navs, USAFA, 74-80; Navs, TXTU, 80-83; Navs, USAFA, 83-94; Navs, OKSU,94-96; ob Ref Discipleship Min, Colorado Springs, CO, 96-99; ob ARDM, 99-

2702 Purgatory Drive, Colorado Springs, CO 80918 – 719-534-9621   Rocky Mountain
E-mail: jcoveyusafa@gmail.com
Alliance of Reformed Discipleship Ministries – 719-260-9550
PO Box 63269, Colorado Springs, CO 80962-3269

Coward, Stephen – w Adriane; chdn Grayson, Shepard, Adeline; ArmsAtlU, BA; RTSFL, MDiv; O May 12, 05, Evan Pby; moy Calvary P Ch, Willow Grove, PA, 03-05; astp Decatur P Ch, Decatur, AL, 05-13; astp Reach Ch, Bear, DE, 14-17, ascp 17-

211 Corinthian Drive, Bear, DE 19701   Heritage
E-mail: pastorsteve@reachchurch.online
Reach Church – 302-834-4772

Cox, Gary Ransom – b Yokohama, Japan, Jun 28, 52; f Emmett W Jr; m Istalena R Williford; w Rita, Oct 23, 04; chdn Nathan, Grant, Rachel, Jordan; BJU 70-74, BA; WTSFL 81-82; ColGS 82-83; TTS 83-87, MDiv; RTSNC 07, DMin; L Apr 85, CentCar Pby; O Aug 25, 88, CentCar Pby; ap Pinelands P Ch, Miami, FL, 83-85; op, ss Grace Ch, Harrisburg, NC, 85-88; exec dir Perspective Min, 88-89; Chap USAR, NCARNG; p Meadowview Ref P Ch, Lexington, NC, 89-93, srp 93-01; astp Briarwood P Ch, Birmingham, AL, 01-03; asst Serve Int, Atlanta, 04-05; p Faith P Ch, Gainesville, FL, 05-07; srp 07-08; srp Westminster P Ch, Muncie, IN, 08-14; p Grace P Ch, Madison, FL, 14-

422 NW College Loop, Madison, FL 32340   Gulf Coast
E-mail: 1pastorgary@comcast.net
Grace Presbyterian Church – 850-973-2692

Cox, James Leslie – b Los Angeles, CA, Nov 15, 40; f James L.; m Louise M.; w (1) (d) Sandra Lee Shoop; (2) Mary Ann Syler, Feb 12, 93; chdn Christa Louise, Nathaniel Lewis; UKY 58-59; WKU 59-60; CC 60, BA; CTS 66, BD; L 67, So Pby (RPCES); O 68, So Pby (RPCES); yp RP Ch, Huntsville, AL, 64-65, yp 66-68; dean CC, 68-71; L'Abri, 71-74; prin, supt WestmC Ac, Huntsville, AL, 74-85; ap Westminster P Ch, Huntsville, AL, 85-88; ob t WestmCAc, Huntsville, AL, 88-94; ob t Bowling Green CAc, 95-06; hr 06

7380 Morgantown Road, Bowling Green, KY 42101-4205 – 502-842-6495   Nashville
E-mail: cox111540@gmail.com
HR

Cox, Robert Glenn – b Jacksonville, FL, Sept 23, 70; f William Curtis; m Johanna Charline Fish; w Malinda Stone Williams, Starkville, MS; chdn Robert David, SarahHolland; FSU 92, BS; CTS 98, MDiv; L Feb 28, 99, Palm Pby; O Feb 28, 99, Palm Pby; astp Westminster P Ch, Sumter, SC, 98-01; astp Presbyterian Ch of Coventry, Coventry, CT, 01-05; ascp Trinity P Ch, Providence, RI, 05-10; Chap USArmy, 10-

109 Sigerfoos Road, Ft. Benning, GA 31905   Southern New England
E-mail: rgcox99@gmail.com
United States Army

Cox, Stacey Michael – w Allison; chdn Anna, Seth, Jessi; ClemU 93, BA, 98, MS; SETS 01, MDiv; ErskTS 12, DMin; O Oct 04, CentCar Pby; ascp First Bapt Ch, Bishopville, SC, 01-02; chp Pine Tree Hill Comm Ch, Camden, SC, 02-04; ascp Grace Ch, Harrisburg, NC, 04-07; Rivertown Ch, 07-09; astp Horizon Ch, Greenville, SC, 09-13 ascp 13-14; p Westminster P Ch, Gainesville, GA, 14-; *The Emergence of Gender-based Religiosity for the 21st Century: The Promise Keepers as a Social Movement;* diss *An Old Path for a New Day: A Case for How the Reformed Tradition Speaks to the Masculine Heart*

2719 Water View Circle, Gainesville, GA 30504 – 678-283-8479   Georgia Foothills
E-mail: staceymcox@yahoo.com
Westminster Presbyterian Church – 770-534-1078

Cox, Thomas Mason – b New York, Sept 7, 62; f Dr. Mason Chandler C.; m Verla Elizabeth Marceline Skantz; w Kelli Anne Robinson, Flint, MI, Apr 18, 92; chdn Jacob Thomas, Jenna Anne; USC 84, BA; IST 91, cert; RTSFL 98, MDiv; L Jul 14, 98, Evan Pby; O Oct 18, 98, Evan Pby; astp, mout Faith P Ch, Anniston, AL, 98-99, ascp 99-01; p Evangelical P Ch, Levittown, PA, 01-12; p Malvern Hills P Ch, Asheville, NC, 12-

16 Crestview Court, Asheville, NC 28806   Western Carolina
E-mail: gocox84@juno.com
Malvern Hills Presbyterian Church – 828-258-8624

MINISTERIAL DIRECTORY 133

Coyer, Jeremy James – O Feb 26, 12, Asc Pby; astp Hillcrest P Ch, Volant, PA, 12-15; op Christ Cov Flwsp, Senaca, PA, 12-15, p 15-

2 Duke Street, Franklin, PA 16323   Ascension
E-mail: jcoyer.ccf@gmail.com
Christ Covenant Fellowship – 814-670-9925

Coyle, Derek – O Oct 8, 17, EPA Pby; astp West Valley P Ch, Emmaus, PA, 17-18; ob astp Covenant P Ch at Little Rock, Little Rock, AR, 18-

147A Jefferson Street, East Greenville, PA 18041 – 267-210-5120   Eastern Pennsylvania
Covenant Presbyterian Church at Little Rock – 501-228-5903

Coyle, Doug – astp University P Ch, Las Cruces, NM, 98-02; op Grace Cov Ch, Las Cruces, NM, 04-06, p 06-

5430 Superstition, Las Cruces, NM 88001 – 575-639-7700   Southwest
E-mail: coylecoyle@aol.com
Grace Covenant Church – 575-526-5577

Crabb, Kenneth Wayne – b Monroe, NC, Nov 8, 48; f Leonard M; m Inez P. Pressley; w Susan Lee Baynard, Lexington, SC, Jun 20, 70; chdn Jonathan, Jessica; USC 70, BS; CBS 88, MDiv; L Jul 28, 88, Palm Pby; O May 14, 89, Palm Pby; mis MTW, Chile, 89-00; astp Arden P Ch, Arden, NC, 00-02, ascp 02-13; hr 13

1242 Pattys Chapel Road, Fletcher, NC 28732 – 828-651-8129   Western Carolina
E-mail: pastorcrabb@gmail.com
HR

Craddock, Michael – w Rachel; chdn Ezra, Asher, Caleb; CTS 09, MDiv; astp North Cincinnati Comm Ch, dir stu/child min, Mason, OH, 10-13; ascp 13-15, srp 15-

8410 Timber Lane, Mason, OH 45040   Ohio Valley
E-mail: michael@northcincy.org
North Cincinnati Community Church – 513-229-0190

Craft, James G. – b Miami, FL, Aug 17, 49; f Maurice Whidden; m Sara Blanton Dawkins; w Frances Margaret Stevenson, Atlanta, GA, Jul 16, 72; chdn James Timothy, Emily Sara, Robert Stevenson; UGA 72, BA; RTS 84, MDiv; O Aug 5, 84, CentGA Pby; staff CCC, UMemp, 72-74; Dir CCC, UMS, 74-80; ap First P Ch, Augusta, GA, 84-86; p Westminster P Ch, Tallahassee, FL, 86-

2428 Shalley Drive, Tallahassee, FL 32309-3019 – 850-228-8637   Gulf Coast
E-mail: jgcraft@juno.com
Westminster Presbyterian Church – 850-894-4233

Craft, John – campm RUF, UTChatt, 08-14; campm RUF, 14-

344 Grandview, Memphis, TN 38111   Covenant
E-mail: jcraft@ruf.org
PCA Reformed University Fellowship

Craig, Jonathan Michael – b Flowood, MS, Dec 9, 81; f Michael Richard; m Carol Woleben; w Susannah Perry, Jackson, MS, Aug 9, 08; chdn, Judah Jonathan, Benjamin Michael; VSU, 04, BGenStu; RTS, 09, MDiv; O Jan 23, 11, Gr Pby; int First P Ch, Gulfport, MS, 09-11; Chap USN, Naval District Washington DC, 11-14; Chap USN, Naval Surface Squadron 14, Mayport, FL, 14- 17; Chap USNR, 4th

Craig, Jonathan Michael, continued
Marine Division, 3rd Battalion, 14th Marines, Bristol, PA 17-; astp Westminster P Ch, Tallahasse, FL, 18-
Vive Deo Ut Vivas, A History and Genealogy of the James Craig (1717-1793) Family in America, 14

2917 Giverny Circle, Tallahassee, FL 32309 – 904-252-4397   Gulf Coast
E-mail: jonathanmcraig@yahoo.com
United States Navy
Westminster Presbyterian Church – 850-894-4233

Craig, Michael Richard – b Gulfport, MS, May 26, 57; f Richard Washington; m Catherine Barton; w Carol Woleben, Gulfport, MS, Jun 21, 80; chdn Jonathan Michael, Stephen Andrew; BelC 80, BA; RTS 85, MDiv; ArtInstJax 16, BFA; USNavy CPE, 93; BCC-APC, 96; L 84; O 85, Gr Pby; Chap USN, Philadelphia, PA, 85-87; Chap USN, USS Nitro (AE-23) , 87-90;Chap USN, USCstGd Base, Kodiak, AK, 90-92; Chap USN, Portsmouth Nav Hosp, VA, 92-93; Chap USN, Nav Hosp, Okinawa, JAPAN, 93-96; Chap USN, Naval Sub Grp, Kings Bay, GA, 97-99; Chap USN, NS Pearl Harbor, HI, 99-02; Chap USCG Activities NY, Staten Island, 02-05; First P Ch, Gulfport, MS, 07; Chap AUTEC, Andros Island, Bahamas, 07-; Sr. Chap Orange Park Med Cntr, Orange Park, FL, 09-12; *Runaway Jonah, The Story of the Biblical Prophet*, 08; *How to Master Sin*, 10; *Changing Lives Through Counseling*, 11

3080 Williamsburg Court, Orange Park, FL 32065 – 904-252-4392   Grace
E-mail: michaelrcraig@comcast.net; www.nobodiesartwork.com

Crain, Billy – b Dallas, TX, Jun 27, 74; f Michael; m Martha Elizabeth; w Ashley Joan, Austin, TX, Jan 13, 01; chdn William Hudson, Michael Knox, Jackson Deniger, Parker Anne; UTXAu 96, BA; RTS 03, MDiv; O Mar 30, 08, HouMet Pby; campm RUF, RiceU, 08-14; astp Christ Comm Ch, Fayetteville, AR, 14-

1723 North Charlee Avenue, Fayetteville, AR 72703 – 832-878-0286   Hills and Plains
E-mail: billy@cccfay.com
Christ Community Church

Crain, Tommy Christopher – w Nancy; chdn Miriam, Eden, Malachi; CTS 98, MDiv; StLU 03, PhD; O Aug 20, 06, Palm Pby; astp Covenant P Ch, Columbia, SC, 06-12; Chap USArmy, 12-

31 Virginia Place, Ft. Bragg, NC 28307 – 803-318-9511   Palmetto
E-mail: candncrain@yahoo.com
United States Army

Cramer, Casey – astp Christ Comm Ch, Franklin, TN, 18-

151 Cornerstone Circle, Franklin, TN 37064   Nashville
Christ Community Church – 615-468-2200

Crandall, David H. – w Magda, Miami, FL, Nov 25, 89; chdn Kathryn, Kevin, Sydney; FIU 87-89, BS; KTS, MDiv; O Jan 1, 98, SFL Pby; astp Immanuel P Ch, Miami, FL, 98-99; p Faith P Ch, Miami, FL, 99-01; ascp River of Hope P Ch, Miami, FL, 01; chp Perimeter Ministries, Conyers, GA, Atlanta, GA, 01-03; op Christ Comm Ch, Conyers, GA, 03-06; p 06-16; chp 17-

142 Benjamin Lane, Hendersonville, TN 37075 – 615-596-8303   Nashville
E-mail: dcrandall7@gmail.com

Crane, Frank Parkhurst – b Wilkes-Barre, PA, Jun 24, 41; f John G.; m Barbara Coughlin; w Joy Preston, Sparta, IL, Jan 18, 64; chdn Ben, Gretchen, Adele, Charlotte; CC 63, BA; CTS 67, MA, 73, MDiv, 83, DMin; L 66, MidW Pby; O Jun 67, NE Pby (RPCES); p Westminster Ch, Newburgh, NY, 67-72; p Westminster P Ch, Muncie, IN, 72-79; p Stony Point Ref P Ch, Richmond, VA, 79-07; mpc Stony Point Ref P Ch, Richmond, VA, 07-10; hr 10

10912 Lantern Way, Richmond, VA 23236-3580 – 804-247-3985   James River
E-mail: frank@crane-coaching.com
HR

MINISTERIAL DIRECTORY   135

Crane, Richard – b Talca, Chile, Aug 22, 49; f John G.; m Barbara Coughlin; w Robyn Lutz, Scranton, PA; chdn Janette, Susana, Daniel; CC 73, BA; CTS 77, MDiv; L 77, Midw Pby (RPCES); O 78, DMV Pby (RPCES); mis WPM, Chile, 77-82; mis MTW, Chile, 82-02, Latin America, 02-; *Panorama de la Biblia*

c/o MTW   Heritage
E-mail: rrcrane@comcast.net
PCA Mission to the World

Cranshaw, Brandon – p Eau Claire P Ch, Columbia, SC, 08-09; p First Ref P Ch, Minco, OK, 10-13; astp Grace Cov Ch - PCA, Dallas, GA, 13-16

915 South Wine Street, Gainesville, TX 76240   Northwest Georgia
E-mail: brandoncranshaw@gmail.com

Craven, Charles Eugene – b Hickory, NC, Jul 14, 31; f James Robert; m Genie Warrick; w Isbell Blair, Bartow, FL, May 29, 54; chdn James, Janet, Sarah, John; DavC 53, BS; ColTS 56, BD, 64, ThM; O Jun 56, Westm Pby; p First Ch, Haines City, FL, 56-58; mis Taiwan, 58-68; ap Chattanooga, TN, 69-76; p Westminster P Ch, Rock Hill, SC, 76-84; srp Freedom P Ch, Charlotte, NC, 84-94; hr 95; ss Freedom P Ch, Charlotte, NC, 05-

1330 India Hook Road, Rock Hill, SC 29732 – 704-892-4111   Catawba Valley
HR
Freedom Presbyterian Church

Crawford, Bentley – O Nov 11, 18, MSVal Pby; campm RUF, 18-

1450 Brecon Drive, Jackson, MS 39211   Mississippi Valley
E-mail: bccrawf@gmail.com
PCA Reformed University Fellowship

Crawford, Marty Wayne – b Ft. Payne, AL, Jan 31, 65; f David Ray; m Virginia Carolyn Whitten; w Penny Lynne Robertson, Birmingham, AL, Jul 21, 90; chdn SamuelAlexander, India Rae; UMonte 87, BBA; CTS 96, MDiv; L May 11, 99, Evan Pby; O Jun 27, 99, Evan Pby; asst, Dir Young Business Leaders (min of Briarwood), 96-98; astp, admin Covenant P Ch, Birmingham, AL, 98-

707 Donna Drive, Birmingham, AL 35226 – 205-823-1921   Evangel
E-mail: mcrawford@covpres.com
Covenant Presbyterian Church – 205-871-7002

Creason, Joshua D. – w Stephanie; chdn Elena, Emily, Lily; astp Covenant Comm Ch, Scottsdale, AZ, 11-12, ascp 12-17; astp Uptown Church, PCA, Charlotte, NC, 17; astp South Charlotte P Ch, Charlotte, NC, 17

6801 Bevington Brook Lane, Charlotte, NC 28277 – 704-547-4866   Central Carolina
E-mail: joshua.creason@gmail.com
South Charlotte Presbyterian Church – 704-619-2832

Creech, Joseph Leslie – b Pensacola, FL, Feb 16, 52; f Milton V McCourry; m Carmen Gonzalez; w Marguerite Adams Hogan, Jackson, MS, May 24, 75; chdn Joseph Samuel, Sarah Jane, David Alexander, Jonathan Owen; BelC 74, BA; RTS 78, MDiv, 78, MMiss, 89, MA; O Jun 4, 78, GulCst Pby; mis Mexico, 78-86; astp Orangewood P Ch, Maitland, FL, 86-13, ascp 13-

1175 Charming Street, Maitland, FL 32751 – 407-617-6000   Central Florida
E-mail: jcreech@orangewood.org
Orangewood Presbyterian Church – 407-539-1500

Crenshaw, David Clayton – b Orlando, FL, Oct 18, 39; f H.D.; m Addie Overstreet; w (1) Rossie Elizabeth Parrish (d); (2) Janet Marie Holbrook, Honolulu, HI, Sept 5, 81; chdn Robert L., David Charles, Michael Andrew, Karen Celeste; ChamU 82; WTS 85, MAR, 86, MDiv; L Apr 86, Pac Pby; O Feb 87, Pac Pby; p Covenant P Ch, Bakersfield, CA, 87-95, wc 95-97; astp Grace Ch of Pleasanton, Pleasanton, CA, 97-98, p 98-01, wc 01-03; astp Potomac Hills P Ch, Leesburg, VA, 03-06; astp Fairfield P Ch, Pensacola, FL, 06-08; ascp 08-09; astp Lillian Fell, Lillian, AL, 09-12; ss Faith P Ch, Robertsdale, AL, 12-13, p 13-14; hr 14

1094 Chandelle Lake Drive, Pensacola, FL 32507 – 850-607-7741   Gulf Coast
E-mail: cestlavi@cox.net
HR

Crenshaw, George Carter – b Huntsville, AL, Aug 28, 59; f Joseph Neal; m Julia Newell; w Deborah Raines, Jackson, MS, Apr 16, 83; chdn David Carter, Samuel Joseph, Julia Earline; VandU 81, BA; RTS 87, MDiv; L 86, TNVal Pby; O Feb 2, 92, SEAL Pby; astp First P Ch, Prattville, AL, 92-94; astp Christ Comm Ch, Franklin, TN, 94-97; op West End Comm Ch, Nashville, TN, 97-98; srp 98-

600 Vosswood Drive, Nashville, TN 37205 – 615-353-5919   Nashville
E-mail: carter@westendcommunitychurch.org
West End Community Church – 615-463-8497

Creswell, Andrew Wilson – b Pontiac, MI, Feb 25, 27; f Andrew Sterrett; m Mary Eleanor Wilson; w Margaret Taylor Mehaffey (d), Montrose, CA, Aug 31, 51; chdn MaryKatherine (Trotter); MuskC 49, BS; PXTS 52, ThM; O Jun 22, 52, ARVal Pby (UPCNA); p Minneola UP Ch, KS, 52-57; ob mis Sudan, 58-63; ob mis Jordan, 64-66; ob mis Sudan, 68-69; ob mis Liberia, 71-73; ob mis Sudan, 74-80; ob prof GidTC, 75-80, mis 86-94, ob prof 86-94; hr 94

Address Unavailable   Rocky Mountain
HR

Creswell, N. Bruce – b Baltimore, MD, Aug 16, 54; f Norman Bruce; m Lorraine Hardin; w Carolyn Main, Frederick, MD, Jun 9, 79; chdn Mary Elisabeth, Norman Bruce III, David Jeremiah, Gregory Frederick; BJU 77, BA; RTSNC, MDiv; O Mar 80; Recd PCA, CentCar Pby; t Cross Lanes Ch Sch, Cross Lanes, WV, 80-82; p Bellepoint Bapt Ch, Hinton, WV, 82-92; p Faith Bible Ch, Harrisonburg, VA, 92-01; astp Christ Cov P Ch, Matthews, NC, 01-

7701 Monogramm Lane, Mint Hill, NC 28227-6533 – 704-545-1827   Central Carolina
E-mail: bcreswell@christcovenant.org
Christ Covenant Presbyterian Church – 704-847-3505

Crichton, Iain William – b Edinburgh, Scotland, Mar 16, 50; f William R.; m Dorothy Mitchell; w Arneda Metzler, Marietta, PA, Jun 24, 72; chdn Gregory, Matthew, Megan; CairnU, BS; DTS, MA; WTS, DMin; O May 77, Faith Bible Ch; American Missionary Fell, 78-85; CUTS, 85-89; adj prof WTS, 88-89; InterserveUSA, 89-91; sc Phil Pby, 84-91; p Church of the Redeemer, Philadelphia, PA, 91-97; astp Korean United Ch of Phil, Philadelphia, PA, 97-00, wc 00-03; ob Chap Acts Retirement-Life Comm, 03-17, VP Mission Support, Spritual Life, 17-; hr 16

1507 Tennis Circle, Lansdale, PA 19446   Philadelphia Metro West
Acts Retirement-Life Communities
HR

Cristman, Joe – UIL(Chi) 14, BS; TEDS 17, MDiv; O Nov 12, 17, ChiMet Pby; astp Bethel Christian Ch, Chicago, IL, 17-

4131 West Belmont Avenue, Unit 209, Chicago, IL 60641 – 630-313-9437   Chicago Metro
E-mail: joecristman@gmail.com
Bethel Christian Church – 773-202-7900

Croft, Stacey – campm RUF, VandU, 10- 16; ascp Christ P Ch, Nashville, TN, 16-

1928 Harpeth River Drive, Brentwood, TN 37027   Nashville
Christ Presbyterian Church – 615-373-2311

Crofutt, Richard – O Mch 11, 18, Asc Pby; p Reformed P Ch of Slate Lick, Kittanning, PA, 18-

189 Coal Hollow Road, Sarver, PA 16055 – 724-353-1996   Ascension
E-mail: richcrofutt@yahoo.com
Reformed Presbyterian Church of Slate Lick – 724-545-6441

Crompton, Gordon Douglas – b Buncombe Cnty, NC, Jul 3, 51; f James O.; m Georgia G.; w Deborah Fender, Asheville, NC, May 24, 73; chdn DeeDee, Danny, Jonathan; Old Reliable Univ 76, BA; TempleC; Tab Coll; BethC 80, ThB; BethS 88, MMin; GPTS 97, ThM, 98, ThD; O Feb 10, 83, Bapt; Recd PCA Nov 24, 92, Wcar Pby; p Blessed Hope B Ch, Henderson Cnty, NC, 82-85; t TBC, 82-83; p Kings Grv B Ch, Edneyville, NC, 85-90; dean, prof Grace Bib Inst, 86-89; t FthCS, 88-93; sp Grace Bib Ch, 91; t FthCS, Asheville, NC, 92-96; p New Cov P Ch, Raleigh, NC, 96-01; p Providence P Ch, Harlem, GA, 01-; *The Life and Theology of Thomas Goodwin*

PO Box 1045, Harlem, GA 30814 – 706-556-1010   Savannah River
E-mail: scot1715@juno.com
Providence Presbyterian Church

Crook, Edward Sterling – b Morgantown, WV, Sept 5, 49; f Herbert; m Hazel Lily; w Ellen Steele, Hinton, WV, Jun 4, 71; TRBI 73-75, AB; LibBapC 75-78, BS; CTS 80-82, MA; CIU 81-82, MDiv; LaelU 82-88, ThD; L Sept 82, Ecar Pby; O Sept 82, Ecar Pby; t LaelU, 82; p White Oak P Ch, Fremont, NC, 82-86; p First P Ch, Ellerbe, NC, 86-90; p Walnut Hill P Ch, Bristol, TN, 90-06; p Zion P Ch, Chester, SC, 06-08; ev PEF, 06-13; hr 13; ss Princeton P Ch, Johnson City, TN, 13-14

408 Hawley Meadows Court, Blountville, TN 37617 – 423-574-2939   Westminster
E-mail: ecrook@btes.tv
HR

Crooks, Ian William – b North Ireland, Sept 3, 61; f Robert; m Florence Shepherd; w Rhoda Yvonne Hammond, N. Ireland, May 12, 87; chdn Alison, Joshua, Ben; UUlster 80-83, BS; QUB 87-90, BD; L Jun 90, Tyrone Pby, PCI; O Feb 91, East Belfast Pby, PCI; Recd PCA 00, Ecan Pby; astp Newtown Brkda, 90-93; p Rasharkin P Ch, N. Ireland, 93-00; op Sovereign Comm Ch, Miramichi, NB, 00-04, p 04-05; p Westm Chapel, Lethbridge, AB, 05-

109 Heritage Circle West Lethbridge, AB T1K 7T3 CANADA – 403-394-0934   Western Canada
E-mail: icrooks77@gmail.com
Westminster Chapel – 403-329-1446

Crosby, John – astp Independent P Ch, Memphis, TN, 08-10; astp Lexington P Ch, Lexington, SC; campm RUF, UMemp, 16-

4738 Walnut Grove Road, Memphis, TN 38117   Covenant
PCA Reformed University Fellowship

Crosby, Scott Thomas – b Mt. Lebanon, PA, May 29, 70; w Anne Marie MacKechnie, West Springfield, MA, Jul 30, 94; chdn Ezra Gordon, Honor Elizabeth; Berklee 92, BA; WestTS 07, MAR; O 09, MNY Pby; astp Redeemer P Ch of New York, New York, NY, 09-12; srp Liberti Fairmount, Philadelphia, PA, 12-

2200 Arch Street, Suite 200, Philadelphia, PA 19103 – 212-749-5188   Philadelphia
E-mail: scott@liberti.org
Liberti Fairmount – 215-255-8414

Cross, David Lee – b Dunmore, PA, Feb 23, 42; f Walter G., Sr.; m Myrtle Bainbridge; w Barbara Honan, Scranton, PA, Jun 16, 63; chdn Shannon Lea, Shelly Lynn; CBC 64, BBE; REpS 68, MDiv; L 69, DMV Pby (RPCES); O 69, DMV Pby (RPCES); mis WPM, Australia, 70-81; p Carlisle Ref P Ch, 81-90; mis MTW, England, 90-11; hr

917 Forbes Road, Carlisle, PA 17013 – 717-713-0905   Susquehanna Valley
E-mail: d.cross1942@gmail.com
HR

Cross, Heath Allen – b Blytheville, AR, Mar 9, 81; w Amber Pate, Blytheville, AR, Jan 4, 03; chdn Canaan, Eden; MSU 14, BS; RTS 16, MDifO Feb 12, 17, MSVal Pby; p Edwards P Ch, Edwards, MS, 17-

211 McRee Drive, Clinton, MS 39056   Mississippi Valley
E-mail: heathacross@hotmail.com
Edwards Presbyterian Church – 601-541-9495

Cross, Kenneth Alan – b Richmond, VA, Aug 10, 56; f Oliver Bruce; m Patricia James; w Lynn Johnson, Birmingham, Jun 5, 82; chdn Katherine Grace, Oliver Bruce, Margaret Patricia, Virginia Karen, Rebekah Faith; SEBC 81, BA; RTS 88, MDiv; L Oct 21, 86, MSVal Pby; O Oct 30, 88, CentGA Pby; ap 1st Bap Ch of San Jose, CA, 80-81; ap 1st Bap Ch of Los Gatos, 81-85; p Northgate P Ch, Albany, GA, 88-93; op Sandhills P Ch, Southern Pines, NC, 93-97, p 97-08; op Advent Ch, Charlotte, NC, 08-12; ob exec dir Sports Chaplains Network, Charlotte, NC, 12-17; ss Lakeshore P Ch, Denver, NC, 15-; CedeSports, Charlotte, NC, 17-

49452 River Run Road, Albemarle, NC 28001 – 980-333-1670   Central Carolina
E-mail: kencross@sportschaplains.org
Lakeshore Presbyterian Church
CedeSports

Cross, Raymond George – b Detroit, MI, May 11, 28; f Dudley Wilford; m Ann Francis Spranger; w Jo Adams (d), Sardis, MS, Dec 17, 94; chdn Rev. Randall Raymond, Dr. James W. Adams II, Elizabeth Marie Adams, Joseph Lee Adams; UCA; SJSU; RTS 87, MDiv; L Mar 86, War Pby; L Jun 87, Cov Pby; O Mar 88, Cov Pby; p Sardis P Ch, Sardis, MS, 87-91; Chap MS St Grd, 88-91; chp MTW/Impact, Tokyo/Chiba, JAPAN, 92-94; ss Sardis P Ch, Sardis, MS, 10-15; chap AmerLeg Post 127

313 North Main Street, Sardis, MS 38666-1113 – 662-501-0155   Covenant
E-mail: raycrosstalk@aol.com

Cross, Walter Gerald III – b La Paz, Bolivia, SA, Mar 13, 45; f Walter G. Jr.; m Mary Wilkins; w Margaret Anne Lee, Buffalo, NY, Jun 8, 68; chdn Emily Kay, Sarah Lee; CBC 67, BA; CTS 71, ThM, 93, DMin; L Sept 71, Midw Pby; O May 72, DMV Pby (RPCES); p Ft. Jackson, SC, 63-66; mis WPM, Chile, 73-86, prof 73-76; chp Chile, 77-86; chp MTW, Mexico City, 87-95; dir Mex ChPl center, 95-00; dir Living in Grace prog, Latin Am, 00-16; hr 17; *Vivir en el Poder del Evangelio*, 09

400 Dawn Drive, Nashville, TN 37211   Chesapeake
HR

Crossland, Robert – O Nov 28, 10, NoCA Pby; astp Grace P Ch of Silicone Valley, Palo Alto, CA, 10- 16, p 16- 18; p Grace South Bay - Msn, San Jose, CA, 18-

1288 Dentwood Drive, San Jose, CA 95118 – 650-521-6798   Northern California
E-mail: bob@gracepres.com
Grace South Bay – Mission

Crosswhite, Kenneth Wayne – b Franklin, IN, Sept 2, 52; f Kenneth; m Nell Wright; w Keith Morris, Aiken, SC, Aug 21, 76; chdn Kenneth Yates; USC, BS; RTS 76-78; WTSFL 79-82; O Nov 82, SFL Pby; ap

Crosswhite, Kenneth Wayne, continued
Spanish River P Ch, Boca Raton, FL, 82-83; ap First P Ch, Augusta, GA, 83-85; ap Cornerstone P Ch, Columbia, SC, 85-91; ob Dir Perception Ministries, Inc., Columbia, SC, 91-; ob p Grace Flwsp Ch (Ind), Columbia, SC, 92-99

115 Larkspur Road, Columbia, SC 29212-2047 – 803-732-2110   Palmetto
Perception Ministries, Inc. – 803-749-0606

Crow, George Davis III – b Austin, TX, May 23, 48; f George Davis Jr.; m Eloise Juanita Burtis; w Cathy Wood Grayson, Birmingham, AL, Aug 7, 76; chdn Emily Browning, Daniel Gillespie; USAFA 66-70, BS; CBS 75-79, MDiv; RTS 88-94, DMin; L Oct 25, 79; O Feb 17, 80, Cal Pby; op Northeast P Ch, Columbia, SC, 80, srp 80-

1012 Coldbranch Drive, Columbia, SC 29223-5540 – 803-736-1544   Palmetto
E-mail: crowpreach@aol.com
Northeast Presbyterian Church – 803-788-5298

Crowe, Brandon – ob prof WTS

E-mail: bcrowe@wts.edu   Philadelphia
Westminster Theological Seminary – 215-887-5511

Crowe, Linward Allen – b Nyack, NY, Jun 10, 41; f Ernest L.; m Anne Catherine Hummel; w Janet Elinor Foyle, Philadelphia, PA, Oct 2, 65; chdn Jonathan David, Peter Christian; ShelC 63, BA; TempU 68, MA; WTS 66-67; FTS 67, MDiv; L Mar 82, Phil Pby (RPCES); O Dec 82, Phil Pby; ob asst prof DrexU, 69-98; ap Tenth P Ch, Philadelphia, PA, 81-88; pres PLF, 88-04; ob staff Navs, Philadelphia, 04-; *My America: Her Faith & Freedom;* "Can Urban & Suburban Christians Agree," *Christianity Today, 10/13/13*

1701 Cambridge Drive, Mahneim, PA 17545 – 717-879-9556   Philadelphia
E-mail: l-jcrowe@verizon.net
The Navigators

Crown, Rohan – astp Crestwood P Ch, Edmonton, AB, 04-07; ascp Westm Chapel, Lethbridge, AB, 08-; op Amazing Grace Comm Ch, Lethbridge, AB, 09-

1808-7 Avenue N, Lethbridge, AB T1H 0Y7 CANADA – 403-524-1511   Western Canada
E-mail: AmazingGracePCA@gmail.com
Westminster Chapel – 403-329-1446
Amazing Grace Community Church – 403-329-0822

Crum, David Alan – b Rochester, PA, Feb 11, 49; f William H., Sr.; m Mary Frances Howitt; w Jill Anne Moir, Whippany, NJ, My 31, 75; chdn Peter, Matthew, Benjamin, Jonathan, Nathaniel, Thomas, David, Stephen, Jill Elisabeth, William, Jesse; GordC 75, BA; REpS 82, MDiv; CTS 00, DMin; O Jun 10, 82, RefEpis; Recd PCA Jan 25, 91; p St. Philips REC, Warminster, PA, 79-82; Chap USN, 82-89; p Covenant P Ch, Landisville, PA, 91-94; ob ascp Evan Comm Ch, Bloomington, IN (ind), 94-97; ob exec dir Freedom Through Christ Ministries, Bloomington, IN, 97-01; srp Westminster P Ch, Brandon, FL, 01-05, hr 18

3737 North Collins Drive, Bloomington, IN 47404 – 443-834-5449   Central Indiana
HR

Crumbley, Joseph William – b Buford, GA, Sept 7, 58; f George Morris; m Velma Porter; BelC 76-78; WhitC 78-80, BA; CTS 80-83, MDiv; WTS 07, PhD; L Aug 83, St. Louis Pby; O Jul 85, NGA Pby; p Wee Kirk P Ch, Lithonia, GA, 85-89, wc; astp Westminster P Ch, Gainesville, GA, 09-14; ob 14-

90 Lakeview Drive, Auburn, GA 30011 – 770-962-0765, 678-480-7923   Georgia Foothills
E-mail: josephcrumbley@gmail.com

Crumpecker, William Curtis Jr. – b Sikeston, MO, Aug 27, 52; f William Curtis Sr.; m Alma Jean Davis; w Patricia Kiggins, Pittsburgh, PA, May 27, 78; chdn Leah Grace, Anna Christine, Evan Michael; UMOSL; CTS 80-84, MDiv; L 83, StLou Pby; O May 86, Mid-America; p Calvary P Ch, Stilwell, OK, 86-89; p Trinity P Ch, Union, MO, 89-

603 West Roosevelt Avenue, Union, MO 63084-1116 – 636-583-1570   Missouri
Trinity Presbyterian Church – 636-583-8463

Crusey, Todd – astp Grace P Ch, The Woodlands, TX, 11-

11 Ridgecross Place, The Woodlands, TX 77381 – 832-315-5674   Houston Metro
E-mail: todd@gracewoodlands.org
Grace Presbyterian Church – 281-296-0911

Crutchley, Jesse M. – O Mar 6, 16, Chspk Pby; p Severn Run Evangelical P Ch, Millersville, MD, 16-

7 Admiral Road, Severna Park, MD 21146 – 410-647-5573   Chesapeake
E-mail: jesse.srep@gmail.com
Severn Run Evangelical Presbyterian Church – 410-923-7500

Cruzat, Lester – Recd PCA Oct 21, 14, MO Pby; ob p The Crossing Ch (KAPC), 14-

2039 Silent Spring Drive, Maryland Heights, MD 63043 – 217-721-4445   Missouri
The Crossing Church

Culbertson, Rodney Archer Jr. – b Greenville, SC, Oct 12, 54; f Rodney Archer (d); m Addie Virginia Sample(d); w Catherine Helen Wooten, Columbia, SC, Aug 25, 79; chdn Helen Virginia, Graham Wooten, Hunter Scott, Tyler O'Dell; USC 72-76, BA; CIU 77-80, MDiv; RTS 95-01, DMin; O Oct 5, 80, CentFL Pby; adj prof CBC, 79-80; ap Faith P Ch, Gainesville, FL, 80-84; campm RUM, Gainesville, FL, 80-89; chp Christ Comm P Ch, Clearwater, FL, 90-92, p 92-94; ob dirAdmiss, VP StuDev RTSNC, 94-07; chp, ss Christ the King P Msn, Charlotte, NC, 99-04; ss Second Street P Ch, Albemarle, NC, 05-06; ob assoc prof, Dn StuDev RTSNC, 07-; int AcadDn 09-10, 15; ExecDir 10-12; *So, You Want to Go to Seminary?* 11; "Ministering to the Needs of Small and Declining Churches," www.rts.edu; *The Disciple Investing Life; Do I Love God? The Question That Must Be Answered*, 17; *Christ Changing Lives: Digging Deeper into the Practice of Disciple Investing*; *The Disciple Investing Apostle*; *As The Father Has Sent Me: God's Progress of Redemption/Part One*, 18; *So Send I You: God's Progress of Redemption/Part Two*, 19

7019 Red Lion Road, Charlotte, NC 28211 – 704-651-8831   Southwest Florida
E-mail: rculbertson@rts.edu
Reformed Theological Seminary, NC – 704-688-4227
2101 Carmel Road, Charlotte, NC 28226

Cullen, David James, III – Chap 04-

Address Unavailable   Rocky Mountain

Culley, Jonathan – b Ft. Sill, OK, Nov 22, 73; w Michelle; chdn Josiah, Trenton, Elias, Rylan; VATech 96, BS; RTSFL 05, MDiv; astp Covenant P Ch, Palm Bay, FL, 06-07, ascp 07-

720 Emerson Drive NE, Palm Bay, FL 32907   Central Florida
E-mail: jonathan.culley@gmail.com
Covenant Presbyterian Church – 321-727-2661

Cummings, David B. – b Pittsburgh, PA, Sept 10, 50; f Calvin Knox, Sr.; m Mary; w Carol Bilthouse (d); (2) Anita Richards, Ithaca, NY, Oct 13, 12; DordtC 72, BA; WTS 75, MDiv; O Sept 30, 75, OPC; Recd

Cummings, David B., continued
PCA 11, Westm Pby; p Grace OPC, Hanover Park, IL, 75-86; p Faith OPC, Pole Tavern, 86-07; p Sandlick P Ch, Birchleaf, VA, 11-; *Basis of a Christian School* (ed), *Purpose of a Christian School* (ed)

PO Box 136, Birchleaf, VA 24220   Westminster
E-mail: dbcummings7@gmail.com
Sandlick Presbyterian Church – 274-865-5584

Cuneo, Mike – astp Calvary P Ch, Greenville, SC, 07-17

1320 Butterfield Road, San Anselmo, CA 94960 – 864-268-9880   Calvary
E-mail: mcuneo@integrity.net

Cunningham, David Lee – b Charlotte, NC, Mar 30, 69; f Don; m Evelyn Parker; w Susan Elizabeth Byrd, Griffin, GA, Jan 18, 92; chdn Tyndall Elizabeth, Joshua Parker, Katie Grace, Emma Ruth; SamU 87-91, MA; BDS 94-97, MDiv; L Evan Pby; O Oct 25, 98, Evan Pby; Briarwood P Ch, 93-97; mis MTW, 97-12; p Christ Comm Ch, Helena, AL, 12-

Christ Community Church   Evangel

Cunningham, James C. – b New York City, NY, Oct 30, 56; f Cortlandt; m Betty Small; w Mary Smiraglia, Silver Spring, MD, Nov 22, 80; chdn Alison Margarette, Kelsey Marie, Julie Kate; UMD 78, BA; FulTS 78-79; BibS 91; RTS 91; EBapTS 93, MDiv; L Nov 95; O Jul 14, 96, NJ Pby; YL, 78-98; astp Princeton P Ch, Princeton, NJ, 96-99, wc 99; ob staff YL, 99-; ip Hope P Ch, Lawrenceville, NJ, 05-07

308 Victoria Drive, Bridgewater, VA 22812 – 540-828-2836   Metropolitan New York
E-mail: jimcunningham1@comcast.net
Young Life

Cunningham, John C. Jr. – b Newark, OH; f John, Sr. (d); m Rachel; w Susan; chdn Evan, Elisabeth; BGSU 86, BFA; ColCU 91, MBibCoun; YDS 97, MAR; UVA 16, PhD; astp Trinity P Ch, Charlottesville, VA, 07-15; wc 15-16; asst prof Providence Christ College, Pasadena, CA, 16-

1541 Wesley Avenue, Pasadena, CA 91104-2646   Blue Ridge
E-mail: cunningham@providencecc.edu
Providence Christian College – 909-782-8616
1539 East Howard Street, Pasadena, CA 91104

Cunningham, Jonathon Christian – O Jun 1, 13, Glfstrm Pby; op Christ the King P Ch, Port St Lucie, FL, 13-

2646 SW Acco Road, Port St Lucie, FL 34953 – 561-596-0332   Gulfstream
E-mail: jccunningham0@gmail.com
Christ the King Presbyterian Church – 561-596-0332

Cunningham, Robert – O Feb 21, 16, BlRdg Pby; campm RUF, UVA, 16-

1609 Dublin Road, Charlottesville, VA 22903   Blue Ridge
E-mail: cunningham.rc@gmail.com
PCA Reformed University Fellowship

Cunningham, Robert H. – b Lexington, KY, Oct 12, 79; f Ronald Mac; m Marilynn Holt; w Abby Estes, Almont, CO, Aug 26, 06; chdn Holt, Charlie; MurrayS 02, BS; CTS 06, MDiv; O 08, OHVal Pby; astp Tates Creek P Ch, Lexington, KY, 08-11, ascp 11-12, srp 12-

2136 Broadhead Place, Lexington, KY 40515   Ohio Valley
E-mail: robert@tcpca.org
Tates Creek Presbyterian Church – 859-272-4399

Cureton, Barry S. – b Saratoga Spgs, NY, Jan 25, 61; f Burnett S.; m Anna Heine; w Margaret Johnson, Wayne, PA, Jun 7, 86; chdn Rebecca Jane, Benjamin James, Glenna Katherine; WChSC 86, BA; WTS MDiv, 92; CTS 14, DMin; L Sept 11, 93, Phil Pby; O Nov 20, 94, CentGA Pby; ydir Proclamation P Ch, Bryn Mawr, PA, 92-94; astp Westminster P Ch, Valdosta, GA, 94-97; ascp Liberty Ch PCA, Owings Mills, MD, 97-

11301 Liberty Road, Owings Mills, MD 21117 – 410-566-1829   Chesapeake
E-mail: barry_cureton@libertychurchpca.org
Liberty Church, PCA – 410-655-5466

Cureton, Ray H. – b Landstuhl, Germany, Jul 21, 53; f Herman Ray, Jr.; m Alma Eckart; w Silvana S. DePaulo, Cobb Cty, GA, Jul 1, 77; chdn Chad Wayne, Carrie Jean; CIU 84, BS; CBS 98, MDiv; L Apr 86, Palm Pby; O Oct 98, Palm Pby; p Trinity P Ch, Lancaster, SC, 98-02; srp First P Ch, Prattville, AL, 02-08; ss Clayton P Ch, Clayton, AL, 14-; ss Pleasant View P Ch, Clayton, AL, 14-

1271 Cross Creek Road, Prattville, AL 36067 – 334-361-4632   Southeast Alabama
E-mail: rayjlmtik@aol.com
Clayton Presbyterian Church – 334-775-8584
Pleasant View Presbyterian Church

Curles, Patrick Wesley – b Birmingham, AL, Dec 3, 67; f Wallace Wayne; m Ann Robinson; w Laurie Lee Anchors, Ft. Walton Bch, FL, Aug 17, 91; chdn Wesley Garner, Anna Lee, Mary Frances; AU 90, BA; WTS 94, MDiv; L Sept 27, 94, Evan Pby; O Nov 19, 95, Evan Pby; ascp Faith P Ch, Birmingham, AL, 95-01; astp Trinity P Ch, Montgomery, AL, 01-

2426 Belcher Drive, Montgomery, AL 36111 – 334-263-3691   Southeast Alabama
E-mail: pcurles@trinitypca.org
Trinity Presbyterian Church – 334-262-3892

Curles, W. Wayne – b Camilla, GA, May 21, 39; f Wallace; m Irene Morrell; w Anne Robinson, Camilla, GA, Aug 28, 60; chdn Sheila Frances (Lovelady), Robbie Ann (Wilson), Wallace Wayne Jr., Patrick Wesley; EmU 61, BA; UAB 71, PhD; RTS 79, MDiv; L Oct 17, 78, MSVal Pby; O Jun 10, 79, CentGA Pby; op Albany, GA, 79-80; p Northgate P Ch, Albany, GA, 80-88; mis Austria, 88-92; ob CRM, 88-; ob BEE, 88-

3708 Cumberland Trace, Birmingham, AL 35242 – 205-981-1492   Central Georgia
E-mail: waynecurles@mindspring.com
Church Resource Ministries – 714-779-0370
1240 North Lakeview Avenue, Suite 120, Anaheim, CA 92807
Biblical Education Extension

Curnow, Richard Alexander Jr. – b New York, NY, Sept 2, 39; f Richard A; m Katherine Boude Moore; w Lynn Elzey, Asheville, NC, Feb 21, 64; chdn Daniel Alan, Diane Michele; BelC 64-66, BA; ColTS 66-69, MDiv; O Jul 27, 69, Atl Pby; p Ingleside P Ch, Lawrenceville, GA, 69-72; p Malvern Hills P Ch, Asheville, NC, 72-78; p Faith P Ch, Paris, TX, 78-84; p Covenant P Ch, Chatsworth, CA, 85-96; p Faith P Ch, Morganton, NC, 97-07; ascp 07-09; hr 09

478 Lost Corner Road, Morganton, NC 28655 – 828-438-8071   Western Carolina
E-mail: Curnow@bellsouth.net
HR

Currence, David Alan – b Creston, IA, Mar 18, 44; f Verl A.; m Jean A.; SterC 68, BS; KSU 69-70, grad wk; GCTS; L 76, CCCC; O 78, CCCC; p Westmoreland Bible Ch, NH, 76-87; p Rocky Springs P Ch, Harrisville, PA, 87-93; p Gr P Msn, St. Marys, GA, 93-94, wc 94; p Riverview P Ch, Charleston, WV, 95-10; hr 11

1509 Clement Road, Greer, SC 29650-0914   New River
HR

MINISTERIAL DIRECTORY 143

Currey, Nathan – b Buffalo, NY, Jun 28, 71; f Richard; m Barbara Janet Vail; w Janey Mills, Pitman, PA, Jun 12, 93; chdn Emily, Joshua, Rebekah, Meghan; MBI 93, BA; CTS 97, MDiv; O Aug 1, 99, BPC; astp Grand Island BPC, 97-02; ascp Redeemer P Ch, Overland Park, KS, 02-

15558 Apache, Otathe, KS 66062 – 913-397-6483   Heartland
E-mail: ncurrey@redeemer-pca.org
Redeemer Presbyterian Church – 913-685-2322

Currid, John D. – w Nancy; chdn Elizabeth, David; GCTS, MATS; UChi, PhD; O Jan 05, MSVal Pby; ob prof RTS; astp Providence P Ch, Clinton, MS, 05-07; ARP, 08-17; astp Sovereign Gr P Ch, Charlotte, NC, 17-; Commentaries on Genesis, Exodus, and Leviticus; *Ancient Egypt and the Old Testament*; *Doing Archaeology in the Lands of the Bible*

10112 Buggy Horse Road, Charlotte, NC 28277 – 601-559-8381   Central Carolina
E-mail: jcurrid@rts.edu
Sovereign Grace Presbyterian Church – 704-553-9600

Currie, Matt – astp Redeemer P Ch, Athens, GA, 11-13

221 Falling Shoals Drive, Athens, GA 30605 – 706-340-4896   Georgia Foothills
E-mail: Matthewallancurrie@gmail.com

Currin, Jerry Carl – b Dillon, SC, Jun 16, 51; f Carl Taylor; m Lucille Hayes; w Sandra Marie Hower, Durham, NC, May 6, 72; chdn Elizabeth, Katherine, Carolyn; DukeU 69-73, BA; TEDS 78, MDiv; L Jun 79, EFC; O Jul 86, NGA Pby; staff CCC, 74-78; p EFC, Minneapolis & Atlanta, 78-82; admin Grace Comm Ch, Atlanta, GA, 82-85; t Mt. Vernon ChrAc, Atlanta, GA, 86; ev, op Good Shepherd Msn, Marietta, GA, 86-87; p Dayspring P Ch, Forsyth, GA, 87-88, wc 88-91; ob assoc evan PEF, 87-; astp msns Christ Cov P Ch, Matthews, NC, 99; p North Hills P Ch, Salisbury, NC, 99-02; sr ascp Church of the Good Shepherd, Durham, NC, 02-13; ob Interim Pastor Min, 13- 18; ss, ip Grace Evangelical P Ch, Davidsonville, MD, 18-

E-mail: jerryc@graceep.org   Chesapeake
Grace Evangelical Presbyterian Church – 410-798-5300

Curtis, Byron G. – b Washington, DC, Oct 7, 54; f Robert E.; m Jean Thompson Gilmore; w Sue Ann Heitzenrater, Beaver Falls, PA, Jun 4, 77; chdn Nathan Robert, Naomi Ariel; GenC 76, BA; RPTS 76-78; PittsTS 76-77; RTS 78-80, MDiv; DukeU 83-96; WTS 05, PhD; L Jul 80, Pitts Pby (RPCNA); O Aug 85, Ecar Pby; campm Pittsburgh, PA, 80-83; ap Peace P Ch, Cary, NC, 85-91; ob asst prof GenC, 91-06, ob assoc prof 06-08; ob prof 08-; visit prof Jerusalem U College, 11; *Up the Steep and Stony Road: The Book of Zechariah in Social Location Trajectory Analysis*, 06; "Hosea 6:7 and Covenant-Breaking like/at Adam," in *The Law is Not of Faith*, 09; "Early Christianity: Controversy over Christ," *Reformed Theological Journal* (09); "After the Exile: Haggai and History," in *Giving the Sense: Understanding and Using Old Testament Historical Texts* (Eugene H. Merrill Festschrift); "Orthodoxy and the Enlightenment," *Semper Reformanda* 6 (1998):131-46; "'Private Spirits' in the *Westminster Confession of Faith* §1.10 and in Catholic-Protestant Debate (1588–1652)," *Westminster Theological Journal* 58 (1996); "The Mas'ot Triptych and the Date of Zechariah 9-14" in *Perspectives on the Formation of the Book of the Twelve*, 12

3719 College Avenue, Beaver Falls, PA 15010-3410 – 724-847-3854   Eastern Carolina
E-mail: bgcurtis@geneva.edu
Geneva College – 724-847-6703
3200 College Avenue, Beaver Falls, PA 15010

Curtis, Michael R. – b Spain, Apr, 71; w Kimberly E. Johnson, Kennett Square, PA, Jun 26, 93; chdn Jonathan, Ryan, Daniel; BucknU 89-93, BA; CTS 93-97, MDiv; O Aug 16, 98, MO Pby; staff Young Life, SW St. Louis, MO, 97-99; Chap USAR, 98-99; Chap USArmy, Ft. Campbell, KY, 99-02; Chap USArmy,

Curtis, Michael R., continued
Panmunjom, Korea, 02-03; Chap USArmy, Aberdeen Proving Ground, MD, 03-05; Chap USAF, Tinker AFB, OK, 05-08; Joint BaseMcGuire-Dix-Lakehurst, 08-11; Chap USAF, Ramstein, Germany, 11-14; Chap USAF Joint Base, San Antonio, TX, 14-

508 Grove Bend, San Antonio, TX 78253 – 405-633-2427   Missouri
E-mail: michael.r.curtis12.mil@mail.mil
United States Air Force

    Cushing, Joshua – O Oct 27, 18, PTri Pby; astp Friendly Hills Ch PCA, Jamestown, NC, 18-

3309 Regents Park Lane Unit C, Greensboro, NC 27455 – 443-907-2538   Piedmont Triad
E-mail: josh.cushing@my.wheaton.edu
Friendly Hills Church PCA – 336-292-7788

    Cushman, George Mark – b Chattanooga, TN, Mar 15, 54; f Ernest (d); m Julia Taylor; w Leslie Weston, Macon, GA, Mar 19, 77; chdn Rebecca (Corley), Christopher Weston, Anna (Norris); FurU 76, BA; TEDS 81, MDiv; CTS 04, DMin; L Jan 82, CentGA Pby; O Jan 82, CentGA Pby; ap Vineville P Ch, Macon, GA, 81-85; p Grace P Ch, Dalton, GA, 85-05; astp Briarwood P Ch, Birmingham, AL, 05-

737 Mill Springs Lane, Birmingham, AL 35244 – 205-437-9559   Evangel
E-mail: mcushman@briarwood.org
Briarwood Presbyterian Church – 205-776-5200

    Cutter, Horace – b Rahway, NJ, Jan 15, 61; f Horace; m Williemae; w Shibana, Aug 12, 89; chdn Kenyon, Albert, Kevin, Jehu-Perry, Anastasia; RTSNC 06, MDiv; astp Redemption Flwsp P Ch, Fayetteville, GA, 10-13; ob 13-

Address Unavailable   Metro Atlanta

    D'Arezzo, A. John Jr. – b West Point, NY, Nov 6, 47; f Alfred J.; m Catherine Ann McBride; w Karen Jane Williams, Wauwatosa, WI, Aug 28, 71; chdn Andrew Williams, James John, Daniel Wilkin; UTXAu 75, BA; IHLS 80; TEDS 80, MDiv, 81, ThM; RTS, DMin cand; L Jun 75, GrCovCh, Austin, TX; O Sept 81, TNVal Pby; ap Cedar Springs P Ch, Knoxville, TN, 81-87; p Covenant P Ch, Little Rock, AR, 87-90; couns Minirth-Meier Clinic, Little Rock, AR, 91-93; ss Northside P Ch, No. Little Rock, AR, 93-94; couns Centers for y & Family, Little Rock, AR, 93-; ss First P Ch, Clarendon, AR, 94-96; ss Covenant P Ch, Russellville, AR, 97-98, wc; ss First P Ch, Clarendon, AR, 98-

22522 Dixie Drive, Little Rock, AR 72223-9157 – 501-821-5830   Covenant
E-mail: johndarezzo@hotmail.com
Centers for Youth & Family – 501-666-0254
1509 North Pierce Street, Little Rock, AR 72205
First Presbyterian Church at Clarendon – 870-747-3854

    Daane, Kevin – w Kathy, DeMotte, IN, Jun 6, 87; chdn Madeline, Steven; WSCAL 05, DMin; O Feb 26, 06, SoCst Pby; ascp New Life P Ch, Escondido, CA, 06-

2343 Viewridge Place, Escondido, CA 92026   South Coast
E-mail: Kevin.D@NewLifePCA.com
New Life Presbyterian Church – 760-489-5714

    Dages, William C. – b Philadelphia, PA, Apr 4, 55; f Robert William; m Phyllis Marie Dahlgren; w Stacye Danette Means, Johnson City, TN, Mar 2, 85; chdn Michael Thomas, Bethany Marie, Joanna Caroline; MesC, BCE; GPTS, MDiv; O Apr 13, 97, Wcar Pby; astp Story Mem P Ch, Marion, NC, 97-99, ascp 99-07; srp 07-10; wc 10-13; ob p Mt. Celo P Ch, South Burnsville, NC, 13-

194 Knollwood Drive, Marion, NC 28752 – 828-659-1424   Western Carolina
E-mail: wcdages@charter.net
Mt. Celo Presbyterian Church

MINISTERIAL DIRECTORY

Dahlfred, Karl – mis 14-

27815 Ben Nevis Way, Yorba Linda, CA 92887 — South Coast

Dalberth, Robert – astp Emmanuel P Ch, New York, NY, 10-16; astp Grace and Peace Comm Ch, Philadelphia, PA, 16-

Grace and Peace Community Church — Philadelphia

Dalbey, Mark Lloyd – b Portland, OR, Mar 28, 52; f Lloyd Allen; m Jane Esther Barthel; w Elizabeth Perrin, Butler, PA, Aug 16, 75; chdn Steven Mark, Kristen Beth, Eric Lloyd; TarkC 70-74, BA; PittsTS 74-78, MDiv; CTS 91-99, DMin; O Nov 21, 78, Asc Pby; instr, dean GenC, 77-84; p Church of the Cov, Cincinnati, OH, 84-92; p Christ P Ch, Richmond, IN, 92-99; asst prof, DnStu CTS, 99-09; asst prof, VPres Fac Develop, 09-10; asst prof, VPres Academics & Fac Develop, 10-13; intPres, 12-13; assoc prof, Pres, 13-; "Gospel-Centered Worship and the Regulative Principle" in *All for Jesus* (CTS 50th Anniversary vol)

12289 North 40 Drive, St. Louis, MO 63141 – 314-392-4152 — Missouri
E-mail: mark.dalbey@covenantseminary.edu
Covenant Theological Seminary – 314-434-4044

Daley, Essen G. – b Norfolk, VA, Oct 7, 70; f Ken G.; m Ellen Christine Hancotte; w Cathlene Denise Metzger, Virginia Beach, VA, Aug 15, 92; chdn Rachel, Sarah, Michael, Lydia Chen; JMU 92, BA; RTSFL 96, MDiv, 12, DMin; L Oct 96; O Oct 12, 97, JR Pby; yp First P Ch, Orlando, FL, 94-96; ascp, mout Covenant P Ch, Harrisonburg, VA, 96-02; op Tabernacle P Ch, Waynesboro, VA, 02-03, p 04-

34 Longview Circle, Fishersville, VA 22939 – 540-943-4718 — Blue Ridge
E-mail: essen@tab-pres.org
Tabernacle Presbyterian Church – 540-932-1778

Dallery, James Franklyn – b Sumter, SC, Aug 24, 63; f Edgar L.; m Mary E. Lee; w Tamara Stanley, Danbury, CT, Aug 1, 87; chdn William Manning, Abigail Miller, Stanley Maclean; CIU 87, BS; CTS 91, MDiv; RTS, DMin cand; O Aug 18, 91, Gr Pby; astp Faith P Ch, Brookhaven, MS, 91-93; p St. Matthews P Ch, St. Matthews, SC, 93-98; op Eagles Landing P Ch, McDonough, GA, 98-02; astp Christ Cov P Ch, Knoxville, TN, 04-07; ascp 07-17

329 Russfield Drive, Knoxville, TN 37934 — Tennessee Valley

Dallwig, Steven M. – astp Chapelgate P Ch, Marriottsville, MD, 13-15; ascp 15-

6826 Littlewood Court, Sykesville, MD 21784 – 410-552-5309 — Chesapeake
E-mail: sdallwig@chapelgate.org
Chapelgate Presbyterian Church – 410-442-5800

Dalton, Daniel – b San Francisco, CA, Feb 26, 72; w Jamie, Jul 12, 97; chdn Kaela, Ellenor; AzPU 94, BA; RTSFL 03, MDiv; O Oct 03, SWFL Pby; astp Cypress Ridge P Ch, Winter Haven, FL, 03-05, ascp 05-08; ascp Christ Central P Ch, Tampa, FL, 09-

5903 North Tampa Street, Tampa, FL 33604 – 813-767-7016 — Southwest Florida
E-mail: ddalton@christcentralpca.org
Christ Central Presbyterian Church – 813-774-3881

Dalton, Jason Edward – O May 20, 12, PacNW Pby; astp Evergreen P Ch, Beaverton, OR, 12-15; p New Cov P Ch, Spearfish, SD, 15-18

3916 Ward Avenue, Spearfish, SD 57783 – 503-564-8564 — Siouxlands
E-mail: jasonedalton@gmail.com

Daniel, Christopher Keith – campm RUM,VCU, 03-09; ob exec dir Richmond Center for Christian Study, 09-

2519 Cherrytree Lane, Bon Air, VA 23235 – 804-852-5151　　　　　　　　James River
E-mail: cdaniel@richmondstudycenter.org
Richmond Center for Christian Study

Daniell, Clif – O Jun 11, 12, NWGA Pby; ap Grace P Ch, Douglasville, GA, 11-14; ascp 14-

3907 Lauada Dive, Douglasville, GA 30135 – 678-715-8690　　　　　　　Northwest Georgia
E-mail: cmdaniels@netzero.net
Grace Presbyterian Church – 770-489-6758

Danner, James – f Robert M.; m Jean S.; w Susan B., St. Petersburg, FL, Aug 25, 79; chdn Jillian Ruth, William Jackson; UFL 80, BA; RTS 85, MDiv; O Aug 4, 85, MSVal Pby; p Old Madison P Ch, Canton, MS, 85-87; p Grace Flwsp P Ch, Albertville, AL, 87-99; srp Main Street P Ch, Columbus, MS, 99-07; p Grace Comm Ch, Valdosta, GA, 07-18; hr 18

16720 Henderson Pass, San Antonio, TX 78232 – 210-417-7224　　　　　　Central Georgia
HR

Dare, David Lynn – b St. Louis, MO, Sept 17, 42; f Ned Northcutt; m Christine Feverston; w Mary Lee Weeks, San Mateo, CA, Feb 14, 69; chdn Thena, Marianna, Matt Dare; PhU 65, BA; CTS 75, MDiv; L Feb 77; O Nov 11, 78, CA Pby; couns Meonah Study Fellowship, Union, MO, 77-79; p Fellowship of His People, Berkeley, CA, 77-79; Chap USArmy, Ft. Knox, KY, 79-82; Chap Heilbronn, Germany, 82-85; Chap Ft. Polk, LA, 85-89; Chap USMA, (Stewart Post Chapel), Newburgh, NY, 89-94; POM Chapel-DLI, 94-96, 94-96; ACM, AAM; Maj., 89

6438 Innsbrook Way, Orangevale, CA 95662-3832 – 916-729-0802　　　　Northern California

Darnell, Thomas Lynn – b Mankato, MN, Jul 6, 49; f Homer Wallace (d); m Helen Lucille Kray (d); w Cheryl Ann Mansur, St. Louis, MO, Jun 5, 76; chdn Gabrielle Elyse, Travis Lane; UNIA 71, BA; CTS 90, MA; L Jan 9, 88, JR Pby; O Jun 7, 92, JR Pby; staff Navs, CornU, 73-78; staff NAV, UVA, 78-83; staff Trinity P Ch, Charlottesville, VA, 83-92, ascp 92-97; p Grace Cov P Ch, Williamsburg, VA, 97-05; ascp Midtown Flwsp Ch, Nashville, TN, 05-09; astp City Ch of East Nash, Nashville, TN, 09-15; p Spiritual Form, Nash pby, 15-; astp Covenant P Ch, Nashville, TN, 16-

106 Joshuas Run, Goodlettsville, TN 37072 – 615-226-4194　　　　　　　Nashville
E-mail: tdarnell@bellsouth.net
Covenant Presbyterian Church – 615-383-2206

Das, Adrian – b Pakistan, Dec 28, 65; f Vincent; m Norma Lee; w Kelley Joy, Heartland, MI, Jul 22, 95; chdn Andrew Robert, Norma Grace, Jonathan Vincent; SIUE 89, BS; CTS 06, MDiv; O Nov 13, 06, Ill Pby; staff IVCF, ISU & SIUE, 01-05; p Westminster P Ch, Godfrey, IL, 05-

724 Crestwood Drive, Godfrey, IL 62035 – 618-466-0279　　　　　　　　Illiana
E-mail: adikeldas1@yahoo.com
Westminster Presbyterian Church – 618-466-5756

DaSilva, Nelio – b Corumba-MS, Brazil, Mar 5, 51; f Paulo; m Dirce; w Tereza Gueiros, Recife-PE, Brazil, Nov 20, 76; chdn Leo, Marcus, Michael; Seminario Presbiterianio do Norte 76, BS; L Jan 5, 77; O Apr 7, 77, Campo Grande Pby, Brazil; St. Paul's PCUSA, Newark, NJ, 80-86; fndr, op Comunidade-Crista Presbiteriana, Newark, NJ, 86-92; MNA coord/chp for Brazilian & Portuguese in U.S., 93-; fndr Igreja Presbiteriana Redentor, Greater Newark, NJ, 93-95; ob Brazilian Movement ldr, Orlando, FL, 95-;

DaSilva, Nelio, continued
wc; ob Center for Brazilian Church Planting, 99-00; Serge, 00-; *Turning Failures into Victories, What To Do When My Boat is Sinking*; *Believing in the Impossible*, 98; *Drops of Encouragement*, 98; *Grace: God's Antidoto Against Rejection*

E-mail: bestrong@encorajamento.com   Metropolitan New York
Serge
100 West Avenue #W960, Jenkintown, PA 19046

DaSilva, Paulo Cesar, Jr. – O Aug 7, 16, Glfstrm Pby; astp Emanuel P Ch, Boca Raton, FL, 16-

Emanuel Presbyterian Church – 561-577-2140   Gulfstream

Daughtry, James Harry Jr. – b Ft. Benning, GA, Sept 7, 55; f James H. Sr.; m Ida Jo Ozburn; w Sharon Louise Gregg, Oct 23, 93; chdn Anna Louise, Peterson McKinney, Joseph Carlisle; AU 75-77, BA; RTS 81-85, MDiv; L 84; O 85, CentGA Pby; int Westminster P Ch, Valdosta, GA, 83-84; op, p Covenant P Ch, Milledgeville, GA, 85-87, wc 87-90; ss Ebenezer P Ch, Huntsville, AL, 90; ap Lawndale P Ch, Tupelo, MS, 90-92; p Ebenezer P Ch, Huntsville, AL, 92-14

5726 Jones Valley Drive, Huntsville, AL 35802   Providence
E-mail: jashadaughtry@msn.com

Davelaar, Nicholas – b Sioux Center, IA, Sept 28, 80; w Coralin Den Boer, Dec 21, 01; chdn Noah, Andrew, Millie, Sarah, Hannah, Percy; DordtC 03, BA; CalvS 07, MDiv; PurRefTheoSem 11-13, ThM; O Nov 11, 07, CRC; p First CRC, Hospers, IA, 07-11; Chap USAFR, 08-13; p Covenant P Ch at Russellville, Russellville, AR, 13-

405 Turrentine Way, Russellville, AR 72802   Covenant
E-mail: davelaarfam@gmail.com
Covenant Presbyterian Church at Russellville – 479-967-4889

Davey, Patrick H. – b Pensacola, FL, Apr 17, 57; f Francis H.; m Ernestine Claire Hess; w Anna Britt Harrold, Kosciusko, MS, Jan 7, 84; chdn Jonathan Michael, Aaron James, Stephen Forest; PenJC 75-79; BelC 79-81, BA; RTS, MDiv, MA; O Oct 9, 94, Gr Pby; ydir First P Ch, Kosciusko, MS, 81-89; ydir First P Ch, Madison, MS, 89-94; astp Faith P Ch, Brookhaven, MS, 94-03, ascp 03-11; astp Eastern Shore P Ch, Fairhope, AL, 11-

250 Royal Lane, Fairhope, AL 36532   Gulf Coast
E-mail: pdavey@easternshorepca.org
Eastern Shore Presbyterian Church – 251-928-0977

Davidson, Charles William – b Camp LeJeune, NC, Feb 13, 56; f William C.; m Mary Williard Summers; w Bonita Louise Turner, Columbia, SC, Dec 15, 84; chdn Joy Elise, Anna Ruth, Ila Summers; UNCA 74-76; ClemU 76-78, BS; CBS 82-84, MDiv; CTS 14, DMin; L Jan 85, Palm Pby; O May 86, Westm Pby; ap Edgemont P Ch, 86-89; mis MTW, Lima, Peru, 90-08; mis MTW, BEAMM, El Paso, TX, 08-12; mis MTW, Monterrey, Mexico, 13-

c/o Mission to the World – 915-921-0030   Westminster
E-mail: charlie@cpimonterrey.com
PCA Mission to the World – 678-823-0004

Davidson, Gregory – b Oklahoma City, OK, Dec 27, 57; f Donald Gene; m Patricia Sue Paschall; w Donna Elva Garcia, Mar 20, 82; chdn Mary Grace; UTXAu 80, BBA, 97, MA; APTS 01, MDiv; O 04, PCUSA; Recd PCA 07, SoTX Pby; p Salado P Ch, Salado, TX, 04-05; astp CrossPointe Ch, Austin, TX, 07-13; wc 13-

PO Box 12131, Austin, TX 78711 – 512-228-4223   South Texas
E-mail: stpcastatedclerk@gmail.com

Davidson, Nathaniel – b Silver Spring, MD, May 7, 81; w Shannon Clarke, Harrisonburg, VA, Jul 9, 05; chdn Graham, Kathryn; UMD 04, BS; RTSNC 08, MDiv; O Sept 27, 09, HouMet Pby; astp Bay Area P Ch, Webster, TX, 09-15; astp Grace P Ch, Lexington, VA, 15-

Grace Presbyterian Church – 540-463-2374   Blue Ridge

Davidson, Robert S. – b Youngstown, OH, Jan 15, 49; w Joy Len; chdn Kristen, Kevin; BW 71, BS; PittsTS 75, MDiv; IntSem 94, PhD; O Jun 15, 75; ap First P Ch, St. Clairsville, OH, 75-77; p First P Ch, Moorcroft, WY, 77-79; p Gracewood P Ch, Memphis, TN, 79-89; p First P Ch, Picayune, MS, 89-99; ob t Lake Worth CS, Boynton Beach, FL, 99-00, wc 00-; Trinity Comm Church, FL; RCA; astp Cross Comm Ch of South Florida, Deerfield Beach, FL, 12-14, hr 15

Address Unavailable   South Florida
HR

Davies, Richard Henry – b New Orleans, LA, May 19, 50; f Harry Richard, Jr; m Virginia Riley; w Molly Reed, Tuscumbia, AL, Aug 17, 74; chdn Elizabeth Lauren, Cullen Virginia, Richard Henry, Jr; BelC 73, BA; RTS 76, MDiv; IBCS 86, DMin; L Jan 21, 75, MSVal Pby; O Jun 27, 76, Gr Pby; p Grace P Ch, Metairie, LA, 76-; *The Stories of a Parish Pastor*, 17

3141 Marvland Avenue, Kenner, LA 70065 – 504-454-8905   Southern Louisiana
E-mail: srpastorgrace@yahoo.com
Grace Presbyterian Church – 504-454-8905

Davis, Brian Charles – b Kansas City, MO, Jan 16, 82; f Michael Spencer; m Diana Lynn Mayden; w Jeanette Fisk, Kansas City, MO, May 7, 04; chdn Jack Michael, Dustin Charles, Timothy Samuel; TCU 04, BA; WTS 09, MDiv; O Nov 8, 09, OHVal Pby; campm RUF, Purdue, 09-13; astp Fort Worth P Ch, Fort Worth, TX, 13-14; ascp 14-15; op Trin P, Fort Worth, TX, 15-17, srp 17-

4128 Whitfield Avenue, Fort Worth, TX 76109   North Texas
E-mail: brian@trinitypresfw.org
Trinity Presbyterian

Davis, Brian Howard – b Ridley Park, PA, Sept 29, 64; f Charles Wesley; m Elizabeth Zillah Alshouse; w Kimberly Kaye Matter, Philadelphia, PA, Dec 9, 89; chdn Elise Hannah, Emilie Margaret; DrexU 87, BS; ChTS 96, MATS; L May 94, Hrtg Pby; O Mar 14, 99, Hrtg Pby; ascp Covenant PC, Glen Mills, PA, 99-01; astp Proclamation P Ch, Bryn Mawr, PA, 01-04; p Bay Street P Ch, Hattiesburg, MS, 04-

200 Short Bay Street, Hattiesburg, MS 39401   Grace
E-mail: baystreetpca@megegate.com
Bay Street Presbyterian Church – 601-582-1584

Davis, Carl Judson – b Atlanta, GA, Apr 18, 63; f Carl W. Jr.; m Ermine R. Toney; w C. Lynn Colcord, Avondale, GA, Aug 2, 86; chdn Elise Michelle, Jonathan Richard, Christopher William, Abigail Suzanne, Alexa Grace; UGA 85, BA; TEDS 89, MA; USheffield, Eng 93, PhD; L Apr 15, 97, NGA Pby; O May 17, 98, NGA Pby; op Messiah Flwsp Msn, McDonough, GA, 98-00; astp Alta Woods P Ch, Pearl, MS, 00-03; srp Raymond P Ch, Raymond, MS, 03-05; prof BryC, 05-; *The Name and Way of the Lord: Old Testament Themes, New Testament Christology*, 96

1841 Coffee Tree Lane, Soddy Daisy, TN 37379 – 423-843-0973   Tennessee Valley
Bryan College

Davis, D. Clair – b Washington, IA, Mar 25, 33; f Harvey; m Kathryne Daniel; w Goentje (Lynn) Schargorodsky (d); Carol Moore, Feb 19, 05; chdn Erik V, Jessica G, Emily K., Marc B; WheatC 53, BA, 57, MA; WTS 54-56, BD; Dr.theol, Georg-August Universitaet, Goettingen, Germany 57-60; L Jul 58;

Davis, D. Clair, continued
O May 63, Pby of WI (OPC); prof WTS, 66-04; ap New Life (OPC), Jenkintown, PA, 79-88; ascp New Life P Ch, Dresher, PA, 88-05; astp Gr Vancouver, Vancouver, BC, 06-09; chap, prof Redeemer Sem, Dallas, TX, 09-14; hr 14

1614 Hillcrest Road, Glenside, PA 19038 – 215-836-2032   Philadelphia
E-mail: Carolclair219@gmail.com
HR

Davis, Dale Ralph – b Mercer, PA, Sept 7, 44; f James Daryl; m Mary Ellen Wilson; w Barbara Louise Herron, Scott City, KS, Aug 19, 66; chdn Luke, Seth, Joel; SterC 66, BA; TEDS 66-68; DubTS 69, MDiv; UTSVA 74, ThM; SBTS 78, PhD; O Aug 3, 69, NorKS Pby (UPCUSA); p First P Ch, Czech P Ch, BlueRapids, KS, 69-73; ydir Trinity Ch, Louisville, KY, 74-76; prof BelC, 78-81; prof RTS, 81-84; p Westm Ref P, Westminster, MD, 84-88; srp Aisquith P Ch, Baltimore, MD, 88-94; ob prof RTS, 94-02; p Woodland P Ch, Hattiesburg, MS, 02-10; hr 10; *A Proposed Life Setting for the Book of Judges*; *No Falling Words: Expositions of the Book of Joshua*, 88; *Such a Great Salvation: Expositions of the Book of Judges*, 90; *Looking on the Heart: Expositions of The Book of I Samuel* (2 vols), 94; *2 Samuel: Out of Every Adversity*, 99; *I Kings: The Wisdom & the Folly*, 02; *2 Kings: The Power and the Fury*, 05; *The Word Became Fresh*, 07; *Micah: A Study Commentary*, 10; *The Way of the Righteous in the Muck of Life*, 10; *The Message of Daniel*, 13; *True Word for Tough Times (Jeremiah)*, 13; *Slogging Along in the Paths of Righteousness*, 14; *Faith of Our Father: Genesis 12-25*, 15; *Stump Kingdom (Isaiah 6-12)*, 17

300 Rabbit Run Trail, Simpsonville, SC 29681 – 864-399-6407   Grace
E-mail: leftyehud@gmail.com
HR

Davis, Daryl Robert – b Bellefonte, PA, Dec 12, 50; f Robert F.; m Joan L. Dainowski; w Debra Wolff, Sarasota, FL, May 24, 02; chdn Jenny, Rebecca, John; GroCC 72, BA; WTS 77, MDiv; O Dec 21, 80; Dir CCO, Grove City College, 77-80; astp Providence P Ch, Robinson Township, PA, 80-83, ascp 84-89; ascp Covenant Life P Ch, Sarasota, FL, 90-10; ss Hope P Ch, Bradenton, FL, 10; ss Cornerstone of Lakewood Ranch, Bradenton, FL, 10-13; hr 17

1451 Daryl Drive, Sarasota, FL 34232 – 941-371-5134   Southwest Florida
E-mail: supralapse@gmail.com
HR

Davis, Duane – O Sept 11, Phil Pby; ip liberti- Fairmount, Philadelphia, PA, 11-12; p Trinity P Ch, Asheville, NC, 12-15; astp Christ The King P Ch, Raleigh, NC, 15-; op Renewal P, Raleigh, NC, 16-

3208 Huntleigh Drive, Raleigh, NC 27604   Eastern Carolina
E-mail: ddavis@renewalraleigh.org
Christ The King Presbyterian Church – 919-546-0515
Renewal Presbyterian

Davis, G. William III – b Tupelo, MS, Apr 12, 55; f G. William D; m Jean Marie Smith; w Stacy Brooke Addington, Nashville, TN, Aug 30, 86; chdn George William IV, Katherine Collins, Logan McKinley; UMS 74-77; BelmC 79-80, BBA; RTS 91-94, MDiv; O Jul 17, 94, NGA Pby; astp Intown Comm Ch, Atlanta, GA, 94-96; p River Ridge P Ch, New Port Richey, FL, 96-01; p Covenant P Ch, Naples, FL, 01; chp Nash Pby, 02-03; op Gr Flwsp PCA, Thompson's Station, TN, 03-04; p 04-07; astp Parish P Ch, Nashville, TN, 09-14

1504 Bellafonte Court, Nashville, TN 37221   Nashville

Davis, Glenn – b Sydney, NS, Jan 25, 64; w Brenda; chdn Sarah Kate Anjia, Christy Margaret Chun Mae; Acadia, BA; RTS 89, MDiv; O Dec 5, 04, Ecan Pby; astp Bedford P Ch, Bedford, NS, 04-08; ascp 08-10; wc 10-

3466 Wolfe Crescent, Apt 3, Halifax, NS B3L 3S2 CANADA – 902-564-4725   Eastern Canada
E-mail: Glenn.Davis@forces.gc.ca

Davis, Howard Quitman III – b Cleveland, MS, Sept 3, 74; f Howard "Q." Jr.; m Fran Dearman; w Melissa Kay Ballard, Brookhaven, MS, Jun 6, 98; chdn Ellie Grace, Anna Elizabeth, Rachel Joy, Haven Ballard, Catherine Hope ; BayU 93-97, BBA; CTS 99-02, MDiv; O Jun 30, 02, LA Pby; int Grace P Ch of St. Charles Co, St. Charles, MO, 99-02; p Grace P Ch, Shreveport, LA, 02-; fndr, headm Providence Classical Acad, Bossier City, LA

328 Hunters Hollow Drive, Bossier City, LA 71111 – 318-344-1232 North Texas
E-mail: hqdavis@gmail.com
Grace Presbyterian Church – 318-219-5556

Davis, Ivan – w Ann; chdn Rachel, Matthew, Rebekah; RTS, MDiv; WTS, PhD (ABD); Recd PCA Apr 25, 98, CentCar Pby; p Covenant OPC, Grove City, PA, 80-87; p Emmanuel OPC, Morristown, NJ, 87-93; p Coulwood PC, Charlotte, NC, 96-03; ob Chap Stanley Total Living Center, 05-

350 Hickory Hill Lane, Stanley, NC 28164 – 704-820-0723 Catawba Valley
E-mail: ivankiwi@bellsouth.net
Stanley Total Living Center

Davis, James B. – b Raleigh, NC, Nov 9, 67; f James B., Sr.; m Juni K. Guffin; w Emily Christine Massey, Sale Creek, TN, May 25, 91; chdn Emily Abigail, James Micah, Kayley Anna; BryC 90, BA; DTS 97, MABS, 97, MACE; O Mar 15, 98, GulCst Pby; moy Sale Creek Independent P Ch, Sale Creek, TN, 87-92; ydir Metrocrest P Ch, Carrollton, TX, 92-96; astp, moy McIlwain Mem P Ch, Pensacola, FL, 96-99; ascp Cedar Springs P Ch, Knoxville, TN, 99-07; chp EPC, 07-09; ascp Metrocrest P Ch, Carrollton, TX, 09- 18; p Mountain Flwsp, Signal Mountain, TN, 18-; *Cruciform: Living the Cross-Shaped Life*, 11

110 Woodcliff Circle, Signal Mountain, TN 37377 Tennessee Valley
E-mail: jimmy@mtnfellowship.org
Mountain Fellowship

Davis, Jason – b Vidalia, GA, Dec 2, 81; w Rachel; chdn Bonnie, Gracie; MerU 04, BS; RTS 10, MDiv; O Feb 13, 11, NWGA Pby; astp Smyrna P Ch, Smyrna, GA, 11-12, ascp 12-15; chp Grace Comm P Ch (formerly Vidalia ChPl), 15- 17; p Grace Comm P Ch, Lyons, GA, 17-

700 Jackson Street, Vidalia, GA 30474 Savannah River
E-mail: vidaliacommunity@gmail.com
Grace Community Presbyterian Church – 912-526-6478

Davis, John Michael – b Atlanta, GA, Mqy 22, 89; f John A.; m Crystal Rae Ivy; MerU 11, BBA; CTS 14, MDiv; O Feb 12, 17, CentGA Pby; Chap USAR, 17-; ip Strong Tower Flwsp Msn, Macon, GA, 17-

2193 Vineville Avenue, Macon, GA 31204 – 678-787-0747 Central Georgia
 E-mail: jmdavis522@gmail.com
United States Army Reserve
Strong Tower Fellowship Mission – 478-742-7379

Davis, John Michael – O Nov 14, Evan Pby; astp Christ Ch PCA, Trussville, AL, 17-

3330 Highfield Drive, Moody, AL 35004 Evangel
E-mail: mdavis0@yahoo.com
Christ Church PCA – 205-655-3533

Davis, Jonathan Patrick – b Kansas City, MO, Oct 20, 83; f Michael Spencer; m Diana Lynn Mayden; w Erin Alyce Zimmer, St. Louis, MO, Jan 19, 08; chdn Caroline Hope, Margaret Spencer, Emma Katherine; TCU 05, BBA; CTS 11, MDiv; O Jul 31, 11, OHVal Pby; campm RUF, UKY, 11-17; astp Downtown P Ch, Greenville, SC, 17-

23 Hialeah Road, Greenville, SC 29607 Calvary
E-mail: jdavis@downtownpres.org
Downtown Presbyterian Church – 864-326-0624

Davis, Lamar Bryan – b Athens, GA, Sept 2, 47; f Noah Columbus; m GuyNelle Mitchell; w Elizabeth (Liz) Bradberry, Atlanta, GA, Nov 29, 74; chdn Elizabeth Joy (Mather), Bryan Douglas, Rebecca Faith (Burtoft), Stephen Noah; GATech 71, BCEng; CBS 86, MDiv; L Jul 22, 86, SEAL Pby; O Aug 16, 87, SEAL Pby; ss Clanton P Ch, Clanton, AL, 86-87, p 87-05; Chap ALANG, 89-99; Chap CAP, 91-

1159 Big Cloud Circle, Alabaster, AL 35007   Southeast Alabama
E-mail: lamardavis@gmail.com
Civil Air Patrol

Davis, Luke – b Marysville, KS, Aug 31, 70; f Dale Ralph; m Barbara Louise; w Christina Marie Crowley, Atlanta, GA, Apr 26, 97; chdn Joshua Cameron, Lindsay Jael Herron, Jordan Christopher; CC 92, BA; CTS 96, MDiv; O Aug 8, 04, ARP; yp White Oak ARP, Senoia, GA, 96-97; t WCA, Opelousas, LA, 97-00; t Cov School, Charlottesville, VA, 00-04; DaySpring ARP, Salisbury, NC, 04-06; Chap Wellington ChSch, 06-08; Westminster ChrAcad, St. Louis, 08-; *Litany of Secrets*, 13; *The Broken Cross* 15; *A Shattered Peace*, 17; *Joël: The Merivalkan Chronicles, Book One*, 17

1373 Timothy Ridge Drive, St. Charles, MO 63304-3438 – 636-244-2803   Missouri
E-mail: LDavis@wcastl.org
Westminster Christian Academy, St. Louis

Davis, Marc Bernard – b Abington, PA, Sept 9, 68; f D. Clair; m Lynn Schargorodsky; w Susan Carole Pitt, Fairfax, VA, Jun 13, 92; chdn Nathaniel Clark, Margaret Susan, Owen Christopher; UVA 90, BA; WTS 97, MDiv; O Jan 4, 09, Phil Pby; astp New Life P Ch, Glenside, PA, 07-10, ascp 10-

1413 Arline Avenue, Roslyn, PA 19001 – 215-659-1942   Philadelphia
E-mail: mdavis@newlifeglenside.com
New Life Presbyterian Church – 215-576-0892

Davis, Mark – b Oklahoma, Dec 21, 66; w Kristina Brickey; chdn Kara, Madalyn, Cayden, Esther Kate, Samuel; OKSU; UCOK; CTS 97, MDiv; O MO Pby; astpChesterfield P Ch, Chesterfield, MO, 02; astp, mfam, yp Park Cities P Ch, Dallas, TX, 02-08, srp 08-

3812 Stanford Avenue, Dallas, TX 75225 – 214-521-1566   North Texas
E-mail: mark.davis@pcpc.org
Park Cities Presbyterian Church – 214-224-2500

Davis, Nicholas – astp Christ Ch P, Irvine, CA, 16- 18; srp Redemption Ch, San Diego, CA, 18-

840 Sheridan, Escondido, CA 92026   South Coast
E-mail: nick.davis@redemptionsd.com
Redemption Church – 619-717-2960

Davis, Robert E. – b Springfield, MA, May 4, 57; f Melvin Eugene; m Ruth Eleanor; w Kimberly Beth Greenawalt, Nixon, PA, May 23, 81; chdn Peter, Katherine, Rebekah, Bethany; GroCC 74-79, BA; PTS 87, MDiv; GCTS 96, DMin; O Dec 82; Recd PCA 04, OPC; Recd PCA Oct 08, BlRdg Pby; p Covenant Ch, Millers Falls, MA, 82-08; p Drapers Valley P Ch, Draper, VA, 08-

2800 Barrett Ridge Road, Draper, VA 24324 – 540-980-1099   Blue Ridge
E-mail: robertdavisdvpc@comcast.net
Draper's Valley Presbyterian Church – 540-994-9015

Davis, Scott – Recd PCA Jun 5, 16, Cov Pby; p Hope Ch Hot Springs, Hot Springs, AR, 16-

836 Shady Grove Road, Hot Springs, AR 71901   Covenant
E-mail: scott.davis@hopechurchpca.org
Hope Church Hot Springs – 501-623-1112

Davis, T. William – b Colver, PA, Sept 19, 41; f James S; m Ruth Riddle; w Bessie M. Shutt, Ebensburg, PA, Jul 6, 62; chdn James A, Ruth I, T.W. Jr.; VFCC 59-63, BS; BibTS 84-90, MDiv, 84-90, MA; L Jul 63, E Dist Council AG; O May 81, Gen Council AG; p Faith AG, Curwensville, PA, 63-65; p Adrian, PA AG, 65-66; ss Eldred, PA AG, 75-77; p Cyclone Comm Ch, Cyclone, PA, 78-84; ascp Lansdale P Ch, Lansdale, PA, 89-05; couns Cov Counseling Center, Lansdale, PA, 89-; ob couns CCEF, Lehigh Valley, PA, 90-92; hr 10; campground min, Boulderwoods Campground

PO Box 244, Tylersport, PA 18971 – 267-718-5357   Eastern Pennsylvania
E-mail: davis664@verizon.net
HR

Davis, Thaddeus Vance – Alma, MI, Feb 11, 79; f Burnet; m Karyn Kristina Harmon; w Laura Jean, Sarasota, FL, Dec 28, 02; chdn Lilli Adelyn, Koen Ezekiel; USanDiego 05, BA; GCTS 16, MDiv; O Mar 11, 17, CentCar Pby; Chap USAF, 17-

605 Silversmith Lane, Charlotte, NC 28270 – 704-615-0267   Central Carolina
E-mail: thaddeusdavis@gmail.com
United States Air Force

Davis, Walt – O Nov 29, 16, Evan Pby; campm RUF, SamfU, 16-

2617 BM Montgomery Street, Homewood, AL 35209   Evangel
E-mail: walt.davis@ruf.org
PCA Reformed University Fellowship

Davison, Jason – astp Green Lake P Ch, Seattle, WA, 09-13; op Jubilee Comm Msn, Seattle, WA, 14-15; astp Green Lake P Ch, Seattle, WA, 16-

1805 East Spruce Street, Seattle, WA 98122 – 253-244-9330   Pacific Northwest
E-mail: jason@jubileeseattle.com
Green Lake Presbyterian Church – 206-783-1843

Dawkins, Todd – b Indianapolis, IN, Sept 7, 73; f Phillip; m Beth Kixmiller; w Stacy Shank, Mar 11, 00; chdn Evah, Levi; INU 98, BA; DTS 07, ThM; O Oct 16, 16, CentInd Pby; astp Redeemer P Ch, Indianapolis, IN, 14-

6375 Broadway Street, Indianapolis, IN 46220   Central Indiana
E-mail: todd@redeemindy.org
Redeemer Presbyterian Church – 317-238-5487

Daws, Chase – O May 3, 18, NoCA Pby; campm RUF, Berkeley, 18-

5530 Taft Avenue, Oakland, CA 94618   Northern California
E-mail: chase.daws@ruf.org
PCA Reformed University Fellowship

Dawson, John – b Alliance, OH, Mar 30, 58; f Gilbert; m Patricia Neill; w Sally Joy Haydon, Wichita, KS, Apr 24, 82; chdn Amy, Rachel, James, John Haydon, Annie Laurie; WheatC 80, BS; WTS 85, MAR; VandU 94, MA; p Lakeside Fellowship ARP, Mooresville, NC, 95-09; p Abingdon P Ch, Abingdon, VA, 10-; adj prof GBibC, 12-; chmn NAPARC, Calhan, co, 03-04

18454 Lee Highway, Abingdon, VA 24210 – 276-451-5388   Westminster
E-mail: pastorjohndawson@gmail.com
Abingdon Presbyterian Church – 276-628-9887

MINISTERIAL DIRECTORY 153

Dawson, John Kent – w Rebekah; chdn Oliver, Elliot; MSU, BA; FLTR/Aix; CTS, MDiv; RTS, DMin; O May 14, 05, MSVal Pby; astp Brandon P Ch, Brandon, MS, 05-14; srp 14-

119 Richmond Drive, Brandon, MS 39042 – 601-750-1641   Mississippi Valley
E-mail: jdawson@brandonpres.com
Brandon Presbyterian Church – 601-825-5259

Day, William Lee – b Worcester, MA, Dec 1, 44; f Charles E.; m Edna M. Bernard; w Sharon A. Leavitt, Garden City, SC, Sept 24, 83; chdn Robert, Scott, Brian, Chad, Wade, Chris, Juanaria, Virginia, Estevan, Jacinto; USC Coastal Car 95; CTS; O Jan 26, 02, Palm Pby; mis MTW, WBT, 89-93; chp MTW, Belize, 96-05; MTW, Ethnic Min Coord, USA, 05-15; hr 15

1688 Southwood Drive, Surfside Beach, SC 29575 – 843-215-7181   Pee Dee
E-mail: billday1688@gmail.com
HR

Dayhoff, Allan Jr. – b Baltimore, MD, Jun 19, 61; f Allan Wesley Sr.; m Hope A. Haddaway; w Deborah Lynn Hautt, Dayton, OH, Aug 20, 83; BJU 83, BA, 85, MA, 88, MDiv; CTS 95, DMin; L Sept 88, Cal Pby; L Feb 89, Pot Pby; O Sept 16, 90, Pot Pby; chp, op Grace Flwsp Ch, Chantilly, VA, 90-92, p 92-; *Church in a Blues Bar...Listening to Hear,* 17; *God and Tattoos...Why are People Writing on Themselves?* 17

4206 Mellwood Lane, Fairfax Station, VA 22033 – 703-405-7872   Potomac
E-mail: drallandayhoffsoffice@gmail.com
Grace Fellowship Church – 703-327-5000

Dean, Ryan – astp Redeemer Ch, PCA, Jackson, MS, 11- 16; p First P Ch at Clarksdale, Clarksdale, MS, 16-

900 West 2nd Street, Clarksdale, MS 38614 – 601-813-7242   Covenant
E-mail: ryanmdean@me.com
First Presbyterian Church at Clarksdale – 662-624-2280

Dean, Scott Allen – b Kansas City, KS, Nov 23, 67; f Don; m Judy Dennis; w Laurel Kinzer, Markle, IN, Jun 15, 91; chdn Micah, Jonathan, Madeleine, Grace; TayU 90, BA; TEDS 94, MDiv; L Jun 11, 95, GrLks Pby; O Jun 11, 95, GrLks Pby; astp Christ Comm Ch, Carmel, IN, 94-98; op, chp Crossroads Comm Ch, Fishers, IN, 98-01, srp 01-

9015 Deer Run Drive, Indianapolis, IN 46256   Central Indiana
E-mail: sdean35@aol.com
Crossroads Community Church – 317-485-2175

deAraujo, Talles Farias – Recd PCA Sept 20, 14, SNE Pby; p Bethel P Ch, Marlborough, MA, 14-

96 Washington Street, Hudson, MA 01749   Southern New England
Bethel Presbyterian Church – 508-481-4110

DeBardeleben, Charles Graves – b Nashville, TN, Aug 29, 51; f John T; m Martha Evelyn Graves; w Stacy Renee Mardis, Jackson, MS, Aug 20, 77; chdn Anna Lauren, Ashley Rebekah, Tyler Graves, Chandler Mardis; BelC 73; RTS 78, MDiv; O Nov 5, 78, Evan Pby; ap First P Ch, Montgomery, AL, 78-81; p Grace P Ch, Stone Mountain, GA, 81-91; srp McIlwain Mem P Ch, Pensacola, FL, 91-01; dean PensacolaTheoInst, 91-01; p Westminster P Ch, Gainesville, GA, 01-13; Redeemer Comm Ch PCA, Ocala, FL, 14-

6840 NE 35th Lane, Silver Springs, FL 34488 – 678-897-0129   Central Florida
E-mail: cdebard@att.net
Redeemer Community Church PCA – 352-369-4422

DeBruin, Troy – b Royal Oak, MI, Jan 30, 73; f Charles E.; m Susan M.; w Amy, West Grove, PA, Jul 1, 94; chdn Alayna Mary, Molly Clara, Luke Charles, Lydia Beth, Ella Margaret, Anthony Isaac (d); LanBC 95; BibTS 06, MDiv; ydir Trinity P Ch, Harrisburg, PA, 95-00; astp Westminster P Ch, Lancaster, PA, 00-07, ascp 08-15; op Proclamation P Ch, Mount Joy, PA, 15, p 15-

745 Pinkerton Road, Mount Joy, PA 17552　　　　　　　　　　　　　　　　Susquehanna Valley
E-mail: debruintroy@gmail.com
Proclamation Presbyterian Church – 717-207-8220

Decker, Hans – b Hood River, OR, Feb 16, 87; f Bruce; m LaJuana Klinger; w Melynda Anne Feeney, Philadelphia, PA, Aug 7, 10; chdn Immanuel Dominic, Alastair Lewis, Bram Eliot; UDall 09, BA; WTS 13, MDiv; HDS 15, ThM; O Feb 23, 14, Phil Pby; Chap USAFR, McGuire-Dix-Lakehurst, NJ, 15-17

58 White Road, Oxford OX42JL United Kingdom　　　　　　　　　　　　　　　　Philadelphia
E-mail: hzdecker@gmail.com
United States Air Force Reserve

Decker, Kris Alan – b McPherson, KS, Jun 8, 65; f Merlin Keith; m Beverly Jane Reese; w Mary Carolyn Ellis, Memphis, TN, Dec 18, 92; chdn William Reese, Janie Karen, Anna Kathleen; ButlerCCC 83-85, AA; ESU 85-88, BS; RTS 93-98, MDiv; L Jan 27, 01, CentCar Pby; O Apr 28, 01, CentCar Pby; Second P Ch, Memphis, TN, 90-93; Lakeside P Ch, Jackson, MS, 93-98; ascp Christ Cov P Ch, Matthews, NC, 99-14; Carmel CS 15-17; ob exec dir Camp Lurecrest Min, 17-

1637 Waxhaw Indian Trail Road South, Waxhaw, NC 28173 – 704-604-6946　　　　Central Carolina
E-mail: krisdecker65@gmail.com
Camp Lurecrest Ministries

DeGroat, Charles – b Long Island, NY, Aug 5, 70; f Richard M.; m Carol G. Eckel; w Sara C. Dahm, Pella, IA, Jun 25, 94; DordtC 92, BA; RTS 98, MDiv, 99, MA; O Feb 21, 99, CentFL Pby; astp Willow Creek Ch, Winter Springs, FL, 98-04; adj prof RTSFL, 05-07; wc 07-

Address Unavailable　　　　　　　　　　　　　　　　　　　　　　　　　Central Florida

Deison, Peter Van – b Dallas, TX, Jan 24, 46; f Raymond; m Helen Wood Kirk; w Harriet Jane Schoellkopf (d), Dallas, TX, Jun 15, 68; chdn Mary Virginia, Helen Anne; UTXAu 64-68, BA; DTS 74-78, ThM; FieldI 94, PhD; O Jul 17, 78, TNVal Pby; ap First P Ch, Chattanooga, TN, 78-88; ob Dir CCL, 88-94; astp Park Cities P Ch, Dallas, TX, 92-94, ascp 94-; pres Park Cities P Ch Found, 14-; *The Priority of Knowing God*, 90, rev 00; contr *Christian Educators' Handbook on Spiritual Formation*, 94; contr *Integrity of Heart and Skillfulness of Hands*, 94; *They Walked and Talked With Jesus*, CEP Discipleship Studies; vid *Finding My Purpose; Visits From Heaven*, 16

5858 Farquhar Lane, Dallas, TX 75209 – 214-361-0550　　　　　　　　　　　　　North Texas
E-mail: pete.deison@pcpc.org
Park Cities Presbyterian Church – 214-224-2740

Dekker, Robert William – b Baltimore, MD, Oct 6, 66; f John A.; m Nita I.; w Tracy A. Dold, Maryland, Oct 8, 94; chdn Kaleb Robert, Joshua John, Hannah Josephine; LibU, BA; RTS 91-93, MDiv; BibTS 92; L 93, MSVal Pby; O May 21, 95, Cal Pby; int First P Ch, Jackson, MS, 92-93; int Cub Hill Bib P Ch, Baltimore, 93-94; int Mount Cal P Ch, Roebuck, SC, 94, astp 95-97; op Hickory Grove P Ch, Mt. Juliet, TN, 97-98, p 98-00; p Concord P Ch, Gulf Breeze, FL, 00-10; p New Cov P Ch, Lewes, DE, 10-

35466 Red Tail Road, Lewes, DE 19958 – 302-396-1916　　　　　　　　　　　　　Heritage
E-mail: robertdekker@ymail.com
New Covenant Presbyterian Church – 302-644-6800

MINISTERIAL DIRECTORY

Delaplane, Clint – b Canoga Park, CA, Dec 25, 62; w Rocio; chdn Henry, John, Diego, Pedro, Pablo, Ana; HU 93, BA; RTSFL 13, MDiv; O Dec 04, Costa Rica; Recd PCA Aug 14, CentFL Pby; astp University P Ch, Orlando, FL, 14-17; astp Truth Point Church, West Palm Beach, FL, 17-

2400 Kemps Bay, West Palm Beach, FL 33411   Gulfstream
E-mail: clintdelaplane@yahoo.com
Truth Point Church

Delfils, Octavius – mis MTW, 07-

c/o MTW   Calvary
PCA Mission to the World

DeLong, Matthew Jay – O Nov 9, 14, SEAL Pby; campm RUFI, 14-18; campm RUFI, GMU, 18-

5065 Village Fountain Place, Centreville, VA 20120 – 606-375-1564   Potomac
E-mail: matthew.delong@ruf.org
PCA Reformed University Ministries International

Delvaux, William Preston – b Durham, NC, Mar 23, 57; f Thomas C; m Martha Jean McConnell; w Heidi Ann Coulter, Baltimore, MD, Mar 15, 86; DukeU 79, BA; TEDS 85, MDiv; L Jan 14, 89, TNVal Pby; O Sept 10, 89, TNVal Pby; ap Christ Comm Ch, Franklin, TN, 88-90; p Christ Flwsp Ch, Franklin, TN, 90-92; ob t Christ P Ac, Nashville, TN, 92-16; dir Landmark Journey Ministries, 12-; *Landmarks: Turning Points in your Journey Toward God*, 13; *Divided: When the Head and Heart Don't Agree*, 15

1020 Boxwood Drive, Franklin, TN 37069 – 615-574-3167   Nashville
E-mail: landmarkjourney@gmail.com

DeMass, Richard Howard – b Tawas City, MI, Jun 5, 57; f Richard J; m Paula Heis; w Lisa Mills, Minneapolis, MN, Jun 7, 86; chdn Greta Grace, Sarah Elizabeth; SUNYB 79, BA; CTS 94, MDiv; O Nov 6, 94, PacNW Pby; ascp Faith P Ch, Tacoma, WA, 94-

624 South Lawrence Street, Tacoma, WA 98405-2207 – 253-761-7860   Pacific Northwest
E-mail: rdemass@faithtacoma.org
Faith Presbyterian Church – 253-752-7601

Dempsey, William Everett – b Byhalia, MS, Oct 24, 55; f Otis Roberts; m Katherine Bailey; w Debra Rae Schulz, Waverly, TN, Jul 3, 75; chdn William David, Mary Katherine, Andrew Tyler; LambC 73-75; DSU 75-78, BA; RTS 80-85, MDiv, 80-85, MCE; L May 84, Gr Pby; O Jun 25, 85, MSVal Pby; campmRUM, BelC, 85-92; campm RUF, UMO, 92-97; p New Port P Ch, Washington, MO, 97-05; p Grace P Ch, Fort Payne, AL, 05-11; astp First P Ch, Jackson, MS, 11-

69 Napa Valley Circle, Madison, MS 39110   Mississippi Valley
E-mail: bdempsey@fpcjackson.org
First Presbyterian Church – 601-353-8316

Deneen, Scott – b Radford, VA, Aug 21, 66; f W. Fred III; m Marianne Hale; w Suzy S.; chdn Micah, Emma; ascp First P Ch, Stanley, NC, 02-15; p 15-17

103 Boyd Drive, Stanley, NC 28164 – 704-263-4275   Catawba Valley
E-mail: sdeneen@carolina.rr.com

Denholm, Todd – b Grand Rapids, MI, Dec 8, 76; f Mark; m Joan; w Sherdonna; chdn Tristan, Jackson, Andrew; WheatC 99, BA; CTS 11, MDiv; O May 7, 17, Mo pby; p Crossroads P Fell, St. Louis, MO, 17-

2640 Oakview Terrace, Maplewood, MO 63143   Missouri
E-mail: todd@crossroadspres.com
Crossroads Presbyterian Fellowship – 314-644-0030

Denk, Daniel John – b Chicago, IL, Jul 15, 44; f John; m Elfrieda Rathunde; w Sharon S. Ehresman, Omaha, NE, Jun 18, 66; chdn Ramona, Carmen, Allison, Ransom; GraceBibC 68, ThB; TEDS 70, MA; O 70, Grace Gospel Fell; Recd PCA 83, GrLks Pby; p Lakeview Bible Ch, Omaha, 70-74; Grace Bible College, 74-78; admin, Dir IVCF, Great Lakes East (regional), 78-95; coord IFES, SE Europe, 95-00; IFES, coord Leadership Dev, 01-03; ob exec dir Cedar Campus IVCF, 03-15; hr 17; *Large Group Leaders' Handbook*, IVCF; *Exec Planning Resource Kit*, IVCF; art *HIS* mag; *Apologetics for the Heart and Mind*, IVCF

2247 Glen Echo Drive SE, Grand Rapids, MI 49546 – 616-575-7211   Great Lakes
E-mail: ddenkmeister@gmail.com
HR

Dennert, Brian – b Des Moines, IA, Jun 2, 82; w Beth Schumacher, Naperville, IL, Mar 29, 08; chdn Micah, Emma, Mia; CedC 03, BA; TIU 06, MDiv, 09, ThM; Loyola 13, PhD; O Mar 07, ChiMet Pby; astp Naperville P Ch, Naperville, IL, 07-09; wc 09; astp Trinity PC, LaGrange, IL, 10-13; ascp 13-15; ob Faith Ch, Dyer, IN, 15-; art, "The Use of Isa 7:14 in Matt 1:23 Through the Interpretation of the Septuagint, *Trinity Journal*, Spr 09; contr *Big Ideas of the Bible*, 10; "Appendix: A Survey of the Interpretative History of the Parable of the Dishonest Steward (Luke 16:1-9)," *From Judaism to Christianity: Tradition and Transition: A Festschrift for Thomas H. Tobin, S.J. on the Occasion of His Sixty-fifth Birthday*, 10; "John Calvin's Movement from the Bible to Theology and Practice," *Journal of the Evangelical Theological Society*, 11; "Hanukkah and the Testimony of Jesus' Works (John 10:22-39)," *Journal of Biblical Literatur,* 13'; "'The Rejection of Wisdom's Call': Matthew's Use of Proverbs 1:20-33 in the Parable of Children in the Marketplace (Matthew 11:16-19//Luke 7:31-35)," in *Searching the Scriptures: Studies in Context and Intertextuality*, 15; *John the Baptist and the Jewish Setting of Matthew*,15

184 Beiriger Drive, Dyer, IN 46311   Chicago Metro
E-mail: brian_dennert@yahoo.com
Faith Church, Dyer, IN

Dennis, Phillip – b Columbia, MO, Oct 15, 73; f Phillip Wayne; m Cynthia Louise Forbach; w Allison Blake Woolard, Santa Cruz, CA, May 4, 02; chdn Philippa Elise, Catherine Clare; CSUN 99, BA; CTS 06, MAET; UMOSL 05; FordhamU 08, MPhil; UPre, PhD cand; O Jun 2, 12, MNY Pby; t FordhamU 08-10; sp New Hope Christian Ch, Monsey, NY, 11-12, p 12-17; lect Kg'sC, 12; assc mbmr CCCC 10-; rc MNY pby, 13-

7956 NW 19th Court, Pembroke Pines, FL 33024 – 845-426-0321   Metropolitan New York

Dentici, Joe – campm RUF, UALBirm, 08-14; campm RUF, PennSt, 14-

1974 Norwood Lane, State College, PA   Susquehanna Valley
E-mail: jdentici@ruf.org
PCA Reformed University Fellowship

Denton, Jay – O Sep 9, 12, Ecar Pby; astp Midtown Comm Ch, Raleigh, NC, 12-15; campm RUF, UNCW, 15-

6014 Shinnwood Road, Wilmington, NC 28409   Eastern Carolina
E-mail: jay.denton@ruf.org
PCA Reformed University Fellowship

Denton, Peter Tedford Jr. – b Knoxville, TN, Feb 14, 58; f Peter Tedford Sr.; m Bobbie Jewel Arnhart; w Desirée Kathleen Park, Knoxville, TN, Mar 13, 82; chdn Peter Tedford III, Jeanne Elizabeth, Charles Andrew; EmU 80, BA; TEDS 86, MDiv; DukeU 91, PhD; L Jan 88, Ecar Pby; O Aug 4, 91, Ecar Pby; int Village Ch of Lincolnshire, IL , 85-86; int Church of the Good Shepherd, Durham, NC, 90-91, ascp 91-96; ob headm Trin sch, Durham, NC, 96-

3815 Cottonwood Drive, Durham, NC 27705 – 919-408-3588   Eastern Carolina
E-mail: ptdenton@trinityschoolnc.org
Trinity School – 919-402-8262
4011 Pickett Road, Durham, NC 27705

DePace, Reed – b Wilmington, DE, Apr 11, 61; f William F.; m Dianne F. McGinley; w Adelene Mary Foster, Newark, DE, Mar 3, 90; chdn Kelhi Diane, Haeley Anne, Maeghan Adelene, Graeme William Charles, Brennan Reed; UDE 83, BA; WTS 99, MAR; L Feb 01, Hrtg Pby; O Nov 18, 01, Asc Pby; int Grace P Ch, Dover, DE, 00-01; p Reformed P Ch of Slate Lick, Kittanning, PA, 01-03, wc 03-08; p The Ch at Chantilly (form First P Ch, Montgomery, AL), 08-

9299 Vaughn Road, Pike Road, AL 36064 – 334-279-1372   Southeast Alabama
E-mail: pulchre.calvus@gmail.com
The Church at Chantilly – 334-279-1372

Der, Justin Chong – O 17, CentInd Pby; astp Midtown Ch, Indianaplis, IN, 17-

5242 North Park Avenue, Indianapolis, IN 46220   Central Indiana
Midtown Church – 317-414-0602

Deringer, Brian Keith – b Germany, Dec 27, 58; f George C; m Elizabeth I; w Lorrie Wilkes, Augusta, GA, Jan 18, 80; chdn Anna, Joshua, Amy, Sarah; AugC 82, BS; RTS 86, MDiv; L Jul 84; O Feb 87, CentFL Pby; mis MTW, France, 87-94; Dir MTW, Recruitment, 94-96; p Friendly Hills P Ch, Jamestown, NC, 96-01; staff MTW, Internat'l dir, Europe, 01-07; staff MTW, International Director Global Support Ministries 07-17; dir MTW Member Care & Development

1285 Timber Lake Trail, Cumming, GA 30041 – 678-528-4558   Piedmont Triad
E-mail: brian.deringer@mtw.org
PCA Mission to the World – 678-823-0004

Derreth, Robert Drew – b Baltimore, MD, Sept 22, 64; f Robert Hugh; m Julie Nellie Langenfelder; w Rebecca Susan Charles, Ellicott City, MD, May 24, 86; chdn Robert Tyler, Hannah Morgan, Kathryn Ruth; UMD 82-86, BA; WTS 86-89, MDiv; L Feb 11, 89, DMV Pby; O Dec 10, 89, DMV Pby; ydir Bucks Central Ch, Richboro, PA, 86-89; ascp Valley P Ch, Lutherville, MD, 89-97; op Hanover Valley P Ch, Hanover, PA, 98-03, p 03-

34 Blue Spruce Drive, Hanover, PA 17331-9121 – 717-630-8258   Susquehanna Valley
E-mail: drewderreth@gmail.com
Hanover Valley Presbyterian Church – 717-630-9510

Desch, Joshua – b Apr 15, 83; w Betsy; chdn Howie, Justice, Wren, Summer; CC 06, BA; CTS 11, MDiv; O Nov 20, 11, MNY Pby; astp Grace Redeemer Ch, Teaneck, NJ, 11-17; astp Northeast P Ch, Columbia, SC, 17-

6 Corinth Court, Elgin, SC 29045   Palmetto
Northeast Presbyterian Church – 803-788-5298

Desforge, David M. – b Somerville, MA, Jul 8, 55; f Maurice; m Lenora Jones; w Margaret McNeil, Derry, NH, Sept 25, 76; chdn Sarah Lynn, Ashley Paige; HeC 74-75, AA; CC 77-80, BA; WTS 81-83, MAR, 81-83, MDiv, 87, DMin; L 84, Phil Pby; O 84, Phil Pby; ap Calvary P Ch, Willow Grove, PA, 84-91; ev, chp Wcar Pby, 91-93; op Grace Comm Ch, Fletcher, NC, 91-93, p 93-15; ob ev PEF, 15-

1449 Mossy Rock Lane, Knoxville, TN 37922   Tennessee Valley
E-mail: daviddesforge@gmail.com
Presbyterian Evangelical Fellowship

DeSocio, Samuel – b Middletown, NY, Nov 23, 82; w Joanna; chdn Augustine Ambrose Gabriel David Michael, Delia Grace; GenC BA; RPTS 05, MDiv; O Sept 7, 08, Pitts Pby; astp City Reformed P Ch, Pittsburgh, PA, 08-10; op Grace & Peace P Ch, Pittsburgh, PA, 10-14, p 14-16; chp 16-; ss Church of the Redeemer, Cortland, NY, 16-17; op Good Shepherd P Ch, Cobleskill, NY, 18-

446 Crommie Road, Cobleskill, NY 12043   New York State
E-mail: sdesocio@protonmail.com
Good Shepherd Presbyterian Church – 518-231-4409

DeSousa, Cristiano – b Fortaleza, Brazil, Mar 21, 74; f Jose-Maria; m Maria Silva; w Aimee, May 29, 99; UT 96; CTS 00, 15, DMin; Duke 18, ThM; O Jan 06, SFL Pby; Chap USN; Chap 06-

111 SweetGum Court, Stafford, VA 22554 – 904-614-8500   South Florida
E-mail: acdesousa@msn.com
United States Navy

Deutschmann, Hans G. – b Neustadt, Germany, May 20, 46; w Gretchen Knudson, Jasper, MN, Jun 19, 71; chdn Jeremy, Maria, Krista, Selam, Lucy, Mamush; UWI 68, BS, 71, MA; LTSPA 73-74; CTS 80, MDiv; L 80, Midw Pby (RPCES); O 80, Midw Pby (RPCES); p Bible P Ch of Cono Center, 80-83; ob t ConoCS, 83-00; astp Bible P Ch of Cono Center, 99-00; mis, chp MTW, Czech Republic, 00-12; ascp Cov PC, Holland, MI, 13-

4760 Allyson Avenue SW, Wyoming, MI 49519 – 616-666-4465   Iowa
E-mail: hgdeutschman@gmail.com
Covenant Presbyterian Church

Dever, William H. Jr. – b Hattiesburg, MS, Mar 30, 47; f William H. D. Sr; m Hazel Rester; w Cynthia Tucker, Hattiesburg, MS, Jun 3, 67; chdn Emily Jane, Amy Elizabeth, William Tucker, Mary Ellen, Anna Marie, Mark Andrew, Jonathan Paul; USM 70, BS; RTS 74, MDiv; O Jun 74, MSVal Pby; p Lebanon P Ch, Learned, MS, 74-77; ss Bethesda P Ch, Edwards, MS, 74-77, campm 75-77; p Carthage P Ch, Carthage, MS, 77-83; ss Forest Grove P Ch, Carthage, MS, 77-83; p First P Ch, Troy, AL, 83-91; ascp Village Seven P Ch, Colorado Springs, CO, 91-97; ascp Chapelgate P Ch, Marriottsville, MD, 97-05; astp Arden P Ch, Arden, NC, 05-07; p Columbia P Ch, Columbia, MS, 08-17; hr 17

16 Big Ridge, Lumberton, MS 39455 – 601-582-5463   Grace
HR

DeVries, Brad – b Grand Rapids, MI, Mar 14, 80; f Kel; m Deb Hendricks; w Katie Dykhouse; chdn Nathanael, Hannah, Lydia; USAFA 03, BS; CTS 12, MDiv; O Aug 5, 12, Iowa Pby; ob 1st Cong Ch, 12-16; p Trinity Flwsp Ch, Sherwood, AR, 17-

4 Scott Cove, Jacksonville, AR 72076 – 515-538-0439   Covenant
E-mail: brad@trinityfellowshippca.org
Trinity Fellowship Church – 501-834-0907

DeWitt, Charles Millikan – b Nashville, TN, May 23, 56; f Ward Jr.; m Barbara Millikan; w Emily Carol Wade, Knoxville, TN, Aug 21, 82; chdn Peter Vance, John Charles, Marcus Bearden, Sara Jane; USo 79, BS; UT 82, MBA; TEDS 90, MDiv; L Oct 9, 90, TNVal Pby; O May 26, 91, TNVal Pby; mis SIMA, 86-89; mis MTW, Mexico, 91-99; astp Christ P Ch, Nashville, TN, 99-03; mis MTW, 05-

c/o Mission to the World   Nashville
E-mail: charlesdewitt@gmail.com
PCA Mission to the World

DeYoung, Kevin – b Chicago, IL, Jun 23, 77; f Teunis Lee; m Sheri Lynn VandenHeuvel; w Trisha Larene Bebee, Laurel, MD, Jan 5, 02; chdn Ian, Jacob, Elizabeth, Paul, Mary, Benjamin, Tabitha; HopeC 99, BA; GCTS 02, MDiv; ULeic, PhD; O Aug 02, RCA; Recd PCA May 2, 15, GrLks Pby; ascp First Ref Ch, Orange City, IA, 02-04; srp University Ref Ch, East Lansing, MI, 04-17; srp Christ Cov Ch, Matthews, NC, 17-; *Freedom and Boundaries: A Pastoral Primer of the Role of Women in the Church*, 06; *Why We're Not Emergent: By Two Guys Who Should Be*, 08; *Why We Love the Church, In Praise of Institutions and Organized Religion*, 09; *Just Do Something, A Liberating Approach to Finding God's Will*, 09; *The Good News We Almost Forgot: Rediscovering the Gospel in a 16th Century Catechism*, 10; ed, *Don't Call It a Comeback: The Old Faith for a New Day*, 11; *Why Our Church Switched to the ESV*, 11; *What Is the Mission of the Church: Making Sense of Social Justice, Shalom, and the Great Commission*, 11; *Crazy Busy: A (Mercifully) Small Book about a (Really) Big Problem*, 12; *The Hole in Our Holiness: Filling the Gap*

DeYoung, Kevin, continued
between Gospel Passion and the Pursuit of Godliness, 14; *Taking God At His Word: Why the Bible is Knowable, Necessary, and Enough, and What That Means for You and Me*, 14; *What Does the Bible Really Teach About Homosexuality*, 15; *The Biggest Story: How the Snake Crusher Brings Us Back to the Garden*, 15; "John Witherspoon and Late Reformed Orthodoxy," *CHF Bulletin,* 15; "Divine Impassibility and the Passion of Christ in the Book of Hebrews," *WTJ*, 15; *The Biggest Story ABC*, 17; *The Ten Commandments: What They Mean, Why They Matter, and Why We Should Obey Them,* 18; *Grace Defined and Defended: What a 400-Year-Old Confession Teaches Us about Sin, Salvation, and the Sovereignty of God*

800 Fullwood Lane, Matthews, NC 28105   Central Carolina
E-mail: kdeyoung@christcovenant.org
Christ Covenant Church – 704-847-3505

   Diack, Joshua Fraser – b Melbourne, Australia, Feb 28, 83; f Fraser; m Dianne Deroon; w Stacey Eileen Holliday, Alexandria, VA, Jun 27, 09; chdn Hudson, Samuel, William, Henry; Otago Tech 03; RTS 13, MDiv; O Jun 28, 15, Pot Pby; astp Alexandria P Ch, Alexandria, VA, 13-

6613 Cottonwood Drive, Alexandria, VA 22301   Potomac
E-mail: josh.diack@alexandriapres.org
Alexandria Presbyterian Church – 703-683-3348

   Diaso, David Anthony – b Frankfurt, Germany, Dec 2, 58; f Ronald John; m Virginia Garoupa; w Dawn Elizabeth Moore, Redlands, CA, Mar 5, 89; chdn David Anthony, Jr, Jonathan Daniel, Hannah Elizabeth; CSUFr 77-81, BS; IST 84-88, MDiv; NGTS 06, DMiss; L Nov 11, 88, Pac Pby; O Mar 25, 90, NoCA Pby; chp, mis MTW, Mexico City, 90-03; ob Center/Org & Min Dev, 03-06; ob Greater Europe Mission, 06-10; chp, mis MTW 10-

665 Crescent Drive, Chula Vista, CA 91911 – 619-407-7746   Rocky Mountain
E-mail: ddiaso@me.com
PCA Mission to the World

   DiBenedictis, Craig Louis – b Pittsburgh, PA, Jul 1, 47; f Louis; m Alma Cyphers; w Linda Yosko, Coatesville, PA, Mar 4, 72; chdn Seth Andrew, Whitney Danae;BreCC 73-74, AA; UWFL 75-76, BA; EBapTS 86-89, DMin; L 80, OH Pby (OPC); O 80, OH Pby (OPC); p Nashua Ch, Edinburg, PA, 80-85; p Calvary P Ch, Allenwood, NJ, 85-

546 Carroll Fox Road, Brick, NJ 08724-4915 – 732-513-4829   New Jersey
E-mail: Craig@calvarynj.org
Calvary Presbyterian Church – 732-449-8889

   Dickens, Patrick J. – b Little Rock, AR, Mar 17, 49; f Arles J; m Lucille Hankins; w Susan Thompson, Jacksonville, NC, Aug 7, 70; chdn Joshua, Jeremiah, Jessica, Josiah; FWBC 68-73, BA; UOK 82; UTXAu 86-87; CMA 77-78; Bapt sch of Nursing 89-90; FSWM 73-74; O, Free Will Bapt; Recd PCA Apr 28, 94, Cal Pby; mis Côte d'Ivoire, W Africa, 77-84; Westside FWB Ch, Midland, TX, 85-89; mis Albania, 92-

157 East Cadron Ridge Road, Greenbrier, AR 72058 – 501-679-5796   Calvary

   Dickerson, Keith – b Boynton Beach, FL, Dec 2, 74; f Jon; m Susan; w Kimberly, Matthews, NC, Sept 30, 06; CMU 96, BS; UTXAu 98, MS; RTS 06, MDiv; O Oct 12, 06, NFL Pby; Christ Cov P Ch, Matthews, NC, 01-06; astp Christ Ch Mandarin, Jacksonville, FL, 06-10; ascp 10-15; op Christ Ch East, Jacksonville, FL, 10-15, p 15-

11734 Dartmoor Court, Jacksonville, FL 32256 – 904-422-8125   North Florida
E-mail: kdickerson@christchurcheast.org
Christ Church East – 904-323-1623

Dickey, Steve – O Aug 31, 14, Cal Pby; astp Clemson P Ch, Clemson, SC, 14-15, ascp 15-

8 Oleander Drive, Anderson, SC 29621   Calvary
E-mail: stevedickey57@gmail.com
Clemson Presbyterian Church – 864-654-4772

Dicks, Nathan – O Jun 27, 15, SNE Pby; campm RUF, Boston U, 15-

58 Antwerp Street, Brighton, MA 02135   Southern New England
E-mail: nateframbes@gmail.com
PCA Reformed University Fellowship

Dickson, David – b Atlanta, GA, Jul 12, 55; f Otto Talmadge; m Nancy Hand; w Elizabeth Tabor Hollis, Dec 27, 77; chdn Kathryn Collier, Charles Searcy, Robert Tabor; UGA 77, BS; GATech 81, MS; RTSNC 01, MDiv; O Aug 14, 05, JR Pby; sp South Point P Msn, Gastonia, NC, 97-98; DCE Westminster Ref P Ch, Suffolk, VA, 01-05, astp 05-09; ascp 09-11; op Crosswater P Ch, 11-13; p 13-

1302 Mill Run Court, Suffolk, VA 23434 – 757-934-2021   Tidewater
E-mail: david@wrpca.org
Crosswater Presbyterian Church – 757-392-4566

Dickson, James – op Christ Ch PCA, Trussville, AL, 12-

106 South Chalkville Road, Trussville, AL 35173   Evangel
E-mail: jdickson@christchurchpca.net
Christ Church PCA

Diebold, Christopher Michael – O Jan 9, 18, MNY Pby; astp Covenant P Ch, Short Hills, NJ, 18-

46 West End Avenue #A, Summit, NJ 07901 – 704-999-8056   Metropolitan New York
E-mail: christopher@covenantshorthills.org
Covenant Presbyterian Church – 973-467-8454

Diedrich, Mark Daniel – b Ithaca, NY, May 28, 50; f William; m Ruth Meiers; w Karen Madderom, Dalton, IL, May 13, 72; chdn Jeremiah, Hannah, Rachel, Leah; MBI 68-71, dipl; MSMC 72-74, BA; PTS 80, MDiv, 82, ThM; L Jan 93, NoE Pby; O Dec 12, 93, NoIL Pby; p Westminster P Ch, Paxton, IL, 93-05; astp Westminster P Ch, Rock Tavern, NY, 05-

451 Cherrytown Road, Kerhonkson, NY 12446   New York State
Westminster Presbyterian Church – 845-496-7971

Diehl, Timothy P. – b Chicago, IL, Aug 16, 42; f Paul R; m Eileen J. Caster; w Gayle A. Homstad, Duluth, MN, Nov 7, 70; chdn Mark, Matthew, Daniel, Deborah, Nicholas, Katie; UMN 60-63; PasC 63-67; BethC 75-76, BA; BethlTS 79, MDiv; O Jun 80, NO Waters (UPCUSA); p First P Ch, Hinckley, MN, 80-84; p Faith P Ch, Ackley, IA, 84-04; ss Zion Evangelical and Ref Ch, Garner, IA, 05-06; hr 06

104 South Hague, PO Box 74, Hollandale, MN 56045   Iowa
E-mail: diehltim@yahoo.com
HR

Dietmeier, Daren Scott – b Freeport, IL, Nov 17, 61; f Kirk Lee (d); m Connie Lee Fuchs; w Jan Lee Hachmeister, Pecatonica, IL, Oct 9, 82; chdn Zachary Scott, MollyGrace; SIU 92, BS; TrSU 96, MS; BhamTS 99, MABS; L Jan 26, 99, SEAL Pby; O Aug 8, 99, SEAL Pby; USAF, (ret), 79-99; astp First P Ch, Prattville, AL, 99-00, ip 01; p Trinity P Ch, Aledo, IL, 01-; chap Aledo Amer Leg #121, 06-; chap Aledo Vol FD, 12-

810 South College Avenue, Aledo, IL 61231 – 309-582-1170   Northern Illinois
E-mail: trinpca@frontiernet.net
Trinity Presbyterian Church – 309-582-5324

Dietsch, Peter Martin – b Papua New Guinea, Jul 8, 70; f Norman; m Hilda Bolzner; w Stacie Lee Boggs, Liberty Corner, NJ, Oct 9, 98; chdn Stephen Chamberlain, Timothy Martin, Lydia Elizabeth, Titus Abraham; RutgU 92, BS; RTSFL 99, MDiv; O Mar 12, 00; ascp Evan Fell Chapel, 99-00; Chap USArmy, Ft. Bragg, NC, 00-03; astp North Macon P Ch, Macon, GA, 03-05, srp 05-10; ob Chap Fellowship Deaconry, NJ, 10-12; p Providence P Ch, Midland, TX, 12-; *Living Stones: Why Church Membership Matters*, 10

3608 Gulf Avenue, Midland, TX 79707   North Texas
E-mail: peter@providencemidland.org
Providence Presbyterian Church – 432-520-5255

Dillard, Jeff – b Milwaukee, WI, May 31, 63; f Don; m Elma; w Lauren; chdn Christopher James Mullinax, Bradley Caldwell Mullinax, Caleb Samuel, Hannah Elizabeth; WinC 85, BA, 89, MA; CTS 92, MDiv; ColumbusSt 09, MS; Recd PCA 99, NoE Pby; yp First P Ch, Tuscumbia, AL, 92-94; Airman Ft. Drum, NY (4 mos in Haiti), 94-98; Chap USArmy, Ft. Story, VA, 98-00; Chap USArmy, Illesheim, Germany (Iraq 7 mos), 00-03; Chap USArmy, Ft. Campbell, KY (Iraq 11 mos), 03-06; Chap USArmy, Ft. Benning, GA, 06-09; Chap USArmy, Dague, Korea

1410 Redfield Road, Bel Air, MD 21015   Central Georgia
E-mail: jeffrey.d.dillard@us.army.mil
United States Army

Dillard, Robert Dorris Jr. – b Chattanooga, TN, Feb 9, 54; f Robert D. Sr.; m Peggy J. Braziel; w Juanita Kay Metzler, Sarasota, FL, Sept 6, 75; chdn Lucas Aaron, Annie Jean, Joseph Robert, Alicia Jane; FSU 75, BA; AshTS 78, MDiv; O Jun 78, The Breth Ch; Recd PCA Sept 9, 90, LA Pby; ascp Sarasota First Brethren, 78-80; Spanish Lang Inst, San Jose, Costa Rica, 80-81; mis Colombia, 82-85; srp Brethren Ch, New Lebanon, OH, 85-90; op Southern Pines P Ch, Shreveport, LA, 90-94, p 94-96; cop Grace P Ch, Shreveport, LA, 96-98; astp Coral Ridge P Ch, Ft. Lauderdale, FL, 98-03; p Inverness P Ch, Baltimore, MD, 03-16; astp Providence Christian Ch, Cape Coral, FL, 17-18; wc

6312 Mosby Place, Sarasota, FL 34231 – 941-922-8218   Suncoast Florida
E-mail: rddillard@gmail.com

Dillon, Kyle A. – O Jun 29, 14, Cov Pby; Chap USN, 14-16; astp Riveroaks Ref P Ch, Germantown, TN, 16-

181 Picardy Street, Memphis, TN 38111 – 206-909-8807   Covenant
E-mail: kdillon@wamemphis.com
Riveroaks Reformed Presbyterian Church – 901-755-7772

DiMaggio, Joseph Paul – b Monterey, CA, Jul 27, 29; f Joseph; m Rose Bruno; w Isabel Martin Solis, San Francisco, CA, Aug 26, 61; chdn Rose Erin, Frank Eldon; RBI 61-64, cert; BarC 64-66, BA; CTS 66; TalTS 76; L Oct 26, 77; O May 26, 78, Pac Pby; op Fountain Vly, CA, 78-81; ss Hacicada Hgts, OPC, 82-85; Covenant Fellowship P Ch, 85-88; Inland Korean Ch, 86-87; ob ip Hi-Desert CRC, Hinkley, CA, 88-92, wc 92-98; hr 98; ip GOPC, Moreno Valley, CA, 98-00; ip Spring Meadows P Ch, Las Vegas, NV, 00-01

220 East Adams Street, Petersburg, IL 62675   Pacific
E-mail: jpjdm1@gmail.com
HR

DiNardo, Andrew – astp First P Ch of Coral Springs, Margate, FL, 06-07; srp 07-

11859 NW 11th Place, Coral Springs, FL 33071 – 954-752-3030   South Florida
E-mail: adinardo@fpcmargate.org
First Presbyterian Church of Margate/Coral Springs – 954-752-3030

Dionne, Andrew Paul – w Sarah; chdn Anna, Ezekiel, Thomas, Esther, Magdalene, Ruth; UNC 95, BMus; INU 99, MMus, 02, DMus; CTS 04, MDiv; L Jul 31, 04, GrLks Pby; O Nov 21, 04, GrLks Pby; astp Christ the Word Ch, Toledo, OH, 04-07, ascp 07-11; dean Ref Evan Pastor's College, 07-11; p Trinity P Ch, Spartanburg, SC, 11-

512 East Tara Lane, Duncan, SC 29334 – 864-384-8770   Calvary
E-mail: dionne.andrew@gmail.com
Trinity Presbyterian Church – 864-707-0751

Dirks, Tyler – campm RUF, Johnson&Wales, 07-13; astp Uptown Ch, PCA, Charlotte, NC, 13-14; p East Charlotte P, Charlotte, NC, 14-

1016 Timber Lake Drive, Charlotte, NC 28227 – 980-254-4588   Central Carolina
E-mail: tyler@eastcharlottepres.org
East Charlotte Presbyterian – 980-254-4588

Dishman, Peter – WLU 96, BA; CTS 03, MDiv; O Nov 04, NoTX Pby; campm, mis MTW, UNAM Mexico, 05-17; campm, mis MTW/RUF Bogota, 17-

3503 Ash Circle, Richardson, TX 75082 – 214-556-9626   North Texas
E-mail: pwdishman4@gmail.com
PCA Mission to the World

Dively, David Randall – b Pittsburgh, PA, Jul 25, 54; f Dorsey; m Shirley Leturgey; w Kathleen Kistler, Apollo, PA, Jun 30, 73; chdn Jennifer Ann, Daniel McClain, Julie Kay; GroCC 72-76, BA; UPitt 73-74; WTS 76-77; RPTS 77-79, MDiv; RTS 94, DMin; L Apr 25, 78; O Jul 1, 79, Asc Pby; op Bethel Park Area, Pittsburgh, PA, 79-80; p Westminster Ch, High Point, NC, 80-84; p First P Ch, Bad Axe, MI, 85-89; Chap Huron Cty Fireman's Assoc, 86-89; Chap Bad Axe Vol Fire Dept, 86-89; op Community P Ch, Louisville, KY, 89-92, p 92-04; Chap Louisville VAMC, 91-98; sc GrLks Pby, 92-01; Chap Lyndon Fire Dept, 93-97; sc OHVal Pby, 01-14; op Redeemer P Msn, Louisville, KY, 04-07; p 07-15; prof Edinburg Theo Sem, Edinburg, TX, 09-15; hr 15

600 Wickfield Drive, Louisville, KY 40245 – 502-647-7350   Ohio Valley
E-mail: david@dively.org
HR

Dixon, Michael Grey – p Christ Ridge P Ch, Fort Mill, SC, 08-

425 Danielle Way, Fort Mill, SC 29715 – 803-554-8324   Fellowship
E-mail: mdixon@christridge.com
Christ Ridge Presbyterian Church – 803-548-2020

Dixon, Paul S. – DTS 75, ThM; WestTS 95, DMin; p Haven Bible Ch, Portland, OR, 86-93; Ladd Hill Bible Ch, Wilsonville, OR, 94-99; EFC, Iowa Falls, IA, 99-02; p First P Ch, Camden, AL, 02-05; p Hope P Ch, Collinsville, IL, 06-16; hr 17

112 Sugarmill Road, Troy, IL 62294 – 618-667-6535   Illiana
E-mail: dixonps@juno.com
HR

Dixon, Ross – campm RUF, UMO, 05- 18; op Midtown P Ch, Columbia, MO, 18-

708 West Boulevard South, Columbia, MO 65203   Missouri
E-mail: ross@midtownpres.com
Midtown Presbyterian Church

Doan, Steven L. – b Port Huron, MI, Mar 30, 54; f Kenneth L; m Norma Bubel; w Consuelo Farach, Miami, FL, Jun 13, 87; BJU 72-75; ClrCC 76-77, BA; BibTS 77-78; RTS 78-81, MDiv, 78-81, MCE; DenTS 08, DMin; O Aug 19, 90, CentFL Pby; ascp Seminole P Ch, Tampa, FL, 90-93; t Seminole P sch, 82-93; ss Comm Ch, Palm Harbor, FL, 93; p Covenant P Ch, Ft. Lauderdale, FL, 94-96, wc 96-99; astp First Ch West, Plantation, FL, 99-10, ascp 10-14; adjprof Trinity IntU Florida Reg Cent, Davie, FL, 08-; ob Dir

MINISTERIAL DIRECTORY   163

Doan, Steven L., continued
Healing Word Couns Min of Cooper City, FL, 14-15; ob Dir Grace and Peace Christian Couns, Tamarac, FL, 15-; astp First Ch West, Tamarac, FL, 18-; *Scripture and Family Life Skills*

9421 NW 39th Place, Sunrise, FL 33351 – 954-609-1775   South Florida
E-mail: steve45doan@gmail.com
Grace and Peace Christian Counseling
First Church West

Doane, Keith – b St. Louis, MO, Jan 20, 75; f Paul; m Linda; w Susan Weaver, Jun 10, 00; chdn Schaefer, Beckett; TrumanSt 97, BA; CTS 02, MDiv; O Oct 04, GrLks Pby; astp Crossroads Comm Ch, 02-11; ascp 11- 16; op, chp Living Branch, Noblesville, IN, 16-

9568 Fairview Parkway, Noblesville, IN 46060   Central Indiana
E-mail: keith@doanes.net
Living Branch

Dockery, Claudius Hunter – b Greensboro, NC, May 4, 56; f Claudius III; m Virginia Louise Hunter; w Julie Louise, Durham, NC, Feb 3, 79; chdn Jackson, Jonathan, Spencer; ASU 74-78, BA; RTS 91-93, MA; L Apr 90; O Sept 93, CentCar Pby; Dir IVCF, Winston-Salem, NC, 79-86; mis WHM, Ireland, 86-91; WHM, fld dir, 91-99; srp Redeemer P Ch, Winston-Salem, NC, 99-11; astp Redeemer Yadkin Valley, Yadkinville, NC, 18-

2153 Hilltop Drive, Winston Salem, NC 27106 – 336-725-2408   Piedmont Triad
E-mail: chunterdockery@gmail.com
Redeemer Yadkin Valley – 336-426-8771

Doctor, Craig – astp Kirk of the Hills P Ch, St. Louis, MO, 13- 18; ip Old Orchard Ch, Webster Groves, MO, 18-

156 Bellington Lane, St. Louis, MO 63141   Missouri
E-mail: doctorfam@gmail.com
Old Orchard Church – 314-962-3795

Dodd, John R. – b Harrison, NJ, Aug 24, 29; f John R; m Nancy E Cron; w Jeanette Thomas, Malden, WV, Jun 2, 78; chdn Daniel G (d)., John R. (d), David A. (d), Lydia A, Robert R; CBC 60-62; ColC 63; CTS 63-66, dipl; L 58, Newton Pby (UPUSA); O 66, Congaree Pby; p Grace P Ch, Aiken, SC, 66-68; p First Ch, Bloomsbury, NJ, 68-71; p First Ch, Clairton, PA, 71-75; p Kanawha Salines P Ch, Malden, WV, 75-80, ev 80-83; p Hopewell P Ch, Rock Hill, SC, 83-90; p Kingstree P Ch, Kingstree, SC, 90-96; hr 96-00; p Central P Ch, Kingstree, SC, 01-04; ss Sardinia P Ch, Sardinia, SC, 04-06; p Sardinia, 06-10; ss New Harmony P Ch, Alcolu, SC, 04-05; illus *Lessons In Love*, 83; *Bucky and Friends* – Children's Ministry 07; *From the Bottom of the Glass to the Top of the Hill*, 14; *Controlling Your Emotions*, 15; *The Journey to Glory*, 16; *The Journey Continues*, 18; hr 10

1436 Fulton Avenue, Kingstree, SC 29556 – 843-355-7294   Pee Dee
HR

Dodds, Dan – w Christy; chdn Anna, Jenna, Will, Wyatt; HDC 79, BA; GPTS 03, MA; O Oct 04, Cal Pby; yp Grace Immanuel Bible Ch, Jupiter, FL, 95-00; astp Woodruff Road P Ch, Simpsonville, SC, 01-

104 Hickory Drive, Simpsonville, SC 29681 – 864-386-0714   Calvary
E-mail: dan@woodruffroad.com
Woodruff Road Presbyterian Church – 864-297-5257

Dodson, Rhett P. – b Pickens, SC, Sept 2, 66; f Clyde Franklin; m Lucille Powell; w Theresa; BJU 88, BA, 90, MA, 98, PhD; p Grace P Ch of the W Reserve, Hudson, OH, 10-; "Down From His Glory," *Let the Bible Speak Quarterly*; "Discerning Truths of Holiness: The Theology and Message of Leviticus 11-15,"

Dodson, Rhett P., continued
Biblical Viewpoint; "Interpreting Biblical Symbols and Types," *Methods of Bible Exposition*; *This Brief Journey: Loving and Living the Psalms of Ascents*, 12; *To Be a Pilgrim: Further Reflections on the Psalms of Ascents*, 12; *Unashamed Workmen: How Expositors Prepare and Preach*, 14; *Every Promise of Your Word: The Gospel According to Joshua*, 16; *Marching to Zion: Ancient Psalms for Modern Pilgrims*, 17

7543 Red Fox Trail, Hudson, OH 44236 – 234-380-5240 Ohio
E-mail: rdodson@gracechurchpca.org
Grace Presbyterian Church of the Western Reserve – 330-650-6548

Doerfler, Peter – op Stillwaters P Ch, PCA, Kennett Square, PA, 09-0; astp 10-11; ascp 11-17; chp 17; op Redemption Hill Ch PCA Msn, Pittsburgh, PA, 17-

202 East Bruceton Road, Pittsburgh, PA 15236 – 412-477-8380 Pittsburgh
E-mail: pldoerfler@gmail.com
Redemption Hill Church PCA Mission – 412-368-2223

Doherty, Mark – O Feb 05, Hrtg Pby; astp Berea P Ch, Hockessin, DE, 05-07; ascp 07-15; wc 15-16; hr 16

701 Haddon Road, Wilmington, DE 19808 – 302-239-4910 Heritage
HR

Dolby, Dwight L. – b DuBois, PA, Jul 24, 60; f Milford L.; m Dorothy Austin; w Marcia A. Jewell, Zephyrhills, FL, Dec 31, 82; chdn Austin James, Natalie Joy, Samuel Johnson, David Livingstone, Robert Douglas, Hope Bernadette (d), Cedric Jackson, Montrel Jackson, Princess Jackson; AsbC 82, BS; CTS 90, MDiv; L Apr 21, 90; O Jul 22, 90, CentFL Pby; p Auburn Road P Ch, Venice, FL, 90-

2371 Englewood Road, Englewood, FL 34223 – 941-473-2718 Suncoast Florida
E-mail: dwightdolby@gmail.com
Auburn Road Presbyterian Church – 941-485-3551

Doll, Dan – O Sp 1, 18, PD Pby; astp Kingstree P Ch, Kingstree, SC, 18-

704-910-9815 Pee Dee
E-mail: Dan.william.doll@gmail.com
Kingstree Presbyterian Church – 843-355-5336

Domin, Douglas Charles – b Evanston, IL, Apr 15, 59; f Daniel Joseph; m Annie Kalous; w Linda Marie Stanfa, Ft. Lauderdale, FL, Mar 24, 79; chdn Daniel Joseph, Andrew Wayne, Jonathan Douglas; UKY 77; BroCC 77-79, AD; FAU 79-81, BA; RTS 82-85, MDiv; L 86; O 86, MSVal Pby; int First P Ch, Yazoo City, MS, 85-86, ap 86-87; ap Old Cutler P Ch, Miami, FL, 87-88; ascp New Cov P Ch, Aiken, SC, 88-96; ascp Grace P Ch, Laconia, NH, 96-01; op First P Ch of Concord (PCA), Concord, NH, 96-01, p 01-15; ascp Peace P Ch, Cary, NC, 15-

4917 Lily Garden Drive, Apex, NC 27539 Eastern Carolina
E-mail: ddomin59@gmail.com
Peace Presbyterian Church – 919-467-5977

Donnelly, Christopher David – b North Hornell, NY, Apr 1, 66; f Michael Roy; m Rose Hollenbeck; w Kathryn Alyce Smiley, Rock Hill, SC, May 23, 92; chdn Meredith Kathryn, Zachary Michael, Olivia Grace, Emily Elizabeth; UT 91, BS; RTSNC 05, MDiv; O Nov 23, 08, Chspk Pby; int Westminster P Ch, Rock Hill, SC, 02-05; astp Valley P Ch, Lutherville, MD, 08-11; ascp 11-14; p Grace P Ch, Cookeville, TN, 14-

715 Stoneybrook Court, Cookeville, TN 38506 – 443-841-2985 Nashville
E-mail: cdd8657@gmail.com
Grace Presbyterian Church – 931-537-6400

Donohue, Patrick M. – Baltimore, MD, Nov 8, 78; w Rebecca Lynn Boice; chdn William John, Cameron Patrick, Ella Lucy; RTS 12, MAR; astp Chapelgate P Ch, Marriottsville, MD, 12-15; op City Ch P, Baltimore, MD, 14-15, p 15-

301 Broadmoor Road, Baltimore, MD 21212   Chesapeake
E-mail: patrick@citychurchbaltimore.org
City Church Presbyterian – 410-746-6346

Donovan, David – b Dayton, OH, Nov 4, 71; w Christy, May 15, 99; chdn Hannah, Lydia; SEBC 00, BA; RTSFL 08, MDiv; L, TNVal Pby; p Grace P Ch, Lookout Mountain, GA, 10-14; ascp Church Creek P Ch, Charleston, SC, 14-

2150 Pierpont Avenue, Charleston, SC 29414   Lowcountry
E-mail: pastordavid@church-creek.org
Church Creek Presbyterian Church – 843-766-1381

Dorcinvil, Gueillant – b St. Michel, Haiti, Apr 3, 66; f Celiphene; m Eliane; w Genese, Miami, FL, Jan 29, 95; chdn Jennifer, Gueshnia, Catherine; KingsRiverC 92, AS; JacksonvilleSem 96, BA; KTS 00, MDiv; L Oct 17, 00, SFL Pby; O Nov 19, 00, SFL Pby; ydir El Shaddai P Ch, Miami, FL, 93-98, DCE 98-99; astp Redeemer P Ch, Miami, FL, 99-04; op Redeemer P of North Miami, North Miami, FL, 01-05; p 05-

1580 NE 144th Street, North Miami, FL 33161 – 305-949-3403   South Florida
Redeemer Presbyterian of North Miami – 305-945-4283

Doriani, Daniel M. – b New York, NY, OcT 24, 53; f Max; m Marjorie Muldoon; w Deborah Heller, Sunbury, PA, Mar 20, 76; chdn Abigail Jean, Sarah Elizabeth, Elizabeth Anne; GenC 75, BA; WTS 79, MDiv, 86, PhD; YDS 81, STM; L Apr 79, Phil Pby (RPCES); O JaN 10, 82, Asc Pby; yp Rochester Meth Ch, 75-76; p Faith P Ch, LaVale, MD, 81-86; prof GenC, 86-91; ap Berean P Ch, Ellwood City, PA, 87-91; prof CTS, 91-, DnFac 95-03, VP 96-99; srp Central P Ch EPC, 03-13; prof, VP CTS, 13-; auth, *David the Anointed* 84; *Teach the Nations* 91; *Getting the Message: A Plan for Interpreting and Applying the Bible*, 96; *Putting the Truth to Work: The Theory and Practice of Biblical Application*, 01; *The Life of a God-Made Man*, 01; *Women and Ministry*, 03; *The Sermon on the Mount*, 06; *James*, 07; *Matthew*, 08; co-auth *Four Views of Moving Beyond the Bible to Theology*, 09; *I Peter*, 14; *A New Man*, 15

14456 Rogue River Drive, Chesterfield, MO 63017 – 636-519-9611   Missouri
E-mail: ddoriani@covenantseminary.edu
Covenant Theological Seminary – 314-434-4044

Dorsainvil, Sainvil – op El Shaddai of Gr Ch, Naples, FL, 06-16, p 16-

3670 43rd Avenue NE, Naples, FL 34120 – 239-455-1485   Suncoast Florida
E-mail: sdorsainvil@hotmail.com
El Shaddai of Grace Church

Dorsey, Jason Tobias – b Seattle, WA, May 23, 69; f Jack E.; m Ann Cory Dodgson; w Jenny Marie Wallace, Redding, CA, Jun 20, 92; chdn Jacob Steven, Julian Cory, Judah Ethan, Jacqueline Grace Marie; WBapC 87-91, BS; TEDS 91-95, MDiv, MA; O Nov 2, 97, PacNW Pby; astp Green Lake P Ch, Seattle, WA, 97-02; op Redeemer P Ch, Indianapolis, IN, 02-08; srp 08-15; p Redeemer Redmond Ch, Redmond, WA, 15-; *I Remember Fishing With Dad*, 15

15791 Bear Creek Parkway #A531, Redmond, WA 98052 – 317-209-6768   Pacific Northwest
E-mail: j.dorsey23@gmail.com
Redeemer Redmond Church – 425-296-1493

Dorst, David A. – b Pittsburgh, PA, Jan 7, 48; f Ralph A; m Mary Margaret Bitzer; w Anna Catherine Besterman, Pittsburgh, PA, Jul 5, 69; chdn David Robert, Jonathan Alan, Joshua Peter; UPitt 65-69, BA; PittsTS 69-72, MDiv; FulTS 87-89, DMin; O May 14, 72, Pitts Pby (PCUSA); Recd PCA Jan 21, 92, SFL Pby; astp First P Ch, Pittsburgh, PA, 71-72; ascp First P Ch, Bethlehem, PA, 73-78; srp

Dorst, David A., continued
Beverley Hgts UP, Pittsburgh, PA, 79-84; ascp First P Ch, Houston, TX, 85-90; ev Christ EPC, Houston, TX, 91; srp Rio Vista Comm Ch, Ft. Lauderdale, FL, 92-01; ascp Northwest P Ch, Dublin, OH, 01-04, ip 04-05, 06-07; hr 08; *The Sermon Support Group: Partners in Developing and Evaluating Preaching;* auth *A Year With the New Testament*

3258 Holley Terrace, The Villages, FL 32163 – 352-255-5225   Central Florida
E-mail: ddorst1948@gmail.com
HR

    Dorst, David Robert – b Pittsburgh, PA, Jun 27, 73; f David Alan; m Anna Besterman; w Kathryn Parks, Jupiter, FL, Nov 2, 96; BayU 95, BS; RTSDC 10, MAR; O Nov 7, 10, Pot Pby; ap Potomac Hills P Ch, Leesburg, VA, 02-10, ascp 10-

1405 Barksdale Drive NE, Leesburg, VA 20176 – 703-431-0343   Potomac
E-mail: ddorst@potomachills.org
Potomac Hills Presbyterian Church – 703-771-1534

    Dorst, Jonathan Alan – b Pittsburgh, PA, Jun 27, 73; f David Alan; m Anna Besterman; w Rachel Cotton, Waco, TX, Mar 9, 96; BayU 91-96, BS; RTSNC 96-99, MDiv; L May 23, 99, Flwsp Pby; O May 23, 99, Flwsp Pby; astp Bethel P Ch, Clover, SC, 99-01; astp Grace Flwsp Ch, Chantilly, VA, 01-03; chp, op Grace Ch Stillwater Msn, Stillwater, OK, 03-06; p 06-14; astp RiverOaks P Ch, Tulsa, OK, 14-15, ascp 15-

9945 South 72nd East Avenue, Tulsa, OK 74133 – 405-612-5299   Hills and Plains
E-mail: jdorst@riveroakstulsa.com
RiverOaks Presbyterian Church – 918-346-4850

    Dortzbach, Karl Gray – b Bellefontaine, OH, Sept 12, 49; f Elmer; m Marjorie Norton; w Debbie Mull, Sunbury, PA, Aug 27, 71; chdn Joshua Timothy, Hannah Ruth, Jesse David; WheatC 67-69; GSU 69-71, BS; WTS 71-76, MDiv; UPre 02, PhD; L 73, OPC; O 76, OPC; op Hope OPC, 76-80; mis WPM, Kenya, 80-89; mis MTW, Kenya, 89-15; mis MTW Kenya, PhD prog dir IGSL Manila 15-; *Kidnapped*, 75; *Our Communities: A Pastoral Counseling Manual for HIV/AIDS Conflict and Reconciliation*; *You, Your Church and Your Community*; Africa Resources Video Productions including: "LivingHope: The Church and HIV/AIDS," "Home But Not Alone," "Our Children are Not Alone"

2806 North Calvert Street, Baltimore, MD 21218 – 443-570-3668   Chesapeake
E-mail: kdortzbach@mac.com
PCA Mission to the World
International Graduate School of Leadership

    Dotson, Kelly – w Amy Foote, Mar 3, 06; chdn Alexander Wayne, Amelia Rose; O Nov 21, 10, SELA Pby; astp Faith P Ch, Clinton, LA, 10-14; p 14-

12525 Saint Helena Street, Clinton, LA 70722   Southern Louisiana
E-mail: kellydotson@gmail.com
Faith Presbyterian Church – 225-683-8722

    Doty, Greg – b Asheville, NC, Jan 12, 76; f Stephen; m Martha Lynn Cox; w Leanne Renee Leavell, Asheville, NC, Jul 3, 98; chdn Renee Lynn, Kaitlin Laurin; UNCA 98, BA; CTS 01, MDiv; O Aug 3, 03, NGA Pby; astp Midway P Ch, Powder Springs, GA, 02-07; astp Evangelical P Ch, Annapolis, MD, 07-11; ascp 11-

1006 Tasker Lane, Arnold, MD 21012 – 410-266-8091   Chesapeake
E-mail: gdoty@epannapolis.org
Evangelical Presbyterian Church – 410-266-8090

MINISTERIAL DIRECTORY

Doud, Shawn Timothy – b Loma Linda, CA, Sept 14, 71; f Barnie Gene; m Kathleen Mary O'Connor; w Nancy Elaine Olsson, Oakland, CA, May 25, 97; chdn Burke Everett, Tucker Davenport, Trevor Patrick, Cooper Bailey; JBU 89-93, BA; DTS 93-98, ThM; L Jan 29, 00, SoTX Pby; O May 21, 00, SoTX Pby; ydir Metrocrest P Ch, Carrollton, TX, 96-98; astp, moy, mfam Westminster P Ch, Bryan, TX, 99-02, wc 02-03; p North Ridge P Ch, Calgary, AB, 03-10; astp Hope P Ch, Lawrenceville, NJ, 14-18

768 East High Point Terrace, Peoria, IL 61614 – 609-369-1373   Metropolitan New York

Doughan, Larry – b Britt, IA, Jan 28, 56; f Dale; m Marcella Wellik; w Connie Heyer, Titonka, IA, Jun 17, 77; chdn Colin, Adam, Ryan; MaC 74-75; UIA 75-78, BBA; CTS 85-89, MDiv, 04, DMin; O Jul 1, 90, MSVal Pby; astp First P Ch, Louisville, MS, 90-93; p Bethany Evangelical & Ref Ch, Ledyard, IA, 93-04; astp Colfax Center P Ch, Holland, IA, 04, ascp 05-12; p New Life Flwshp, Elk Run Heights, IA, 12-; *Emails to Rail: Liar in Training*, 08

605 10th Street, Grundy Center, IA 50638 – 319-825-2805   Iowa
E-mail: lld.ccp@gmail.com
New Life Fellowship Church – 319-233-0458

Douglas, Brian – b Ft. Lauderdale, FL, Jul 23, 79; f Gene; m Daneen Martin; w Jordan Gough, Newark, OH, Jun 2, 01; chdn Iain, Elinor, Mila; Stetson 01, BBA; KTS 06, MDiv, 06, MA; O Oct 25, 13, PacNW Pby; adj fac BoiseStU, 11-13; ascp All Saints P Ch, Boise, ID, 13-; chap Wyakin Found, 17-

652 East Idaho Avenue, Meridian, ID 83642 – 208-863-3762   Pacific Northwest
E-mail: bdouglas@allsaintspca.org
All Saints Presbyterian Church – 208-658-0670

Douglas, Charles Wayne – b Monroe, LA, Apr 12, 50; w Dianne; chdn Charles Jr; Michael B; Rebecca Lynne; USM 72-74, BS; RTS 85-88, MDiv, 96, DMin; L Mar 87, Cov Pby; O Mar 89, Cov Pby; sp Old Lebanon P Ch, Ackerman, MS, 87-88, int 88-89, p 89-90; p Newton P Ch, Newton, MS, 90-03; ss Mount Moriah P Ch, Newton, MS, 90-01; p Wynndale P Ch, Terry, MS, 03-12; ip Newton P Ch, Newton, MS, 12-

902 South Main Street, Newton, MS 39345 – 601-990-9430   Mississippi Valley
E-mail: cw.douglas@yahoo.com
Newton Presbyterian Church – 601-683-3617

Douglas, Jerry Noel – b Birmingham, AL, Nov 7, 38; f Noel Alexander; m MayBelle Reid; w Nelle Leigeber ; chdn Reid Douglas; UAL 60, BS, 63, MA; BibTS 79, MDiv; L Jan 79, War Pby; O Jan 80, Pac Pby; prin HCS, Window Rock, AZ; TBerBC, San Diego, CA, 80-86; ob t BrChS, 86-87; ss Reform PCUSA Ch; t Central High, Tuscaloosa, AL, 87-96; hr

2025 Fox Ridge Road, Tuscaloosa, AL 35406-3056 – 205-345-1969   Warrior
HR

Douglas, William Culbert – b Lee Cty, AL, Apr 27, 53; f William C.; m Anne McMillan; w Brooke Riherd, Lake Butler, FL, May 27, 78; chdn Erin McMillan, Emmeline Phillips, Leigh Carroll; AU 75, BA; CTS 83, MDiv; O Feb 83, CentGA Pby; op St. Andrews P Ch, Midland, GA, 84-86, p 86-

6080 Canterbury Drive, Columbus, GA 31909 – 706-323-9964   Central Georgia
E-mail: wmcdouglas@bellsouth.net; bill@sapcnet.org
St. Andrews Presbyterian Church – 706-327-7750

Douglass, Philip David – b Jackson, TN; f John Elmore Douglass; m Martha McGehee; w Rebecca Love, Rochester, MN, Sept 2, 72; chdn Christopher David, Clayton Taliaferro, Stephen Burchett, Marta Randle (Willcox); WLU 66-70, BA; PTS 70-74, MDiv; StLU 92-95, PhD; O Mar 16, 75, Nat Cap Un Pby (UPCUSA & PCUS); ap Fairlington P Ch, Alexandria, VA, 74-79; op Gainesville P Ch, Gainesville, VA, 79-86; op Cornerstone P Ch, Manassas, VA, 83-86; op Heritage P Ch, Warrenton, VA, 85; prof CTS, 86-;

Douglass, Philip David, continued
op Heritage P Ch, St. Louis, MO, 86-87; op Dayspring Msn, St. Louis, MO, 87-88; op Good Shepherd P Ch, St. Louis, MO, 88-90; srp 90-92; MNA, dir chp Midwest, 89-91; ss Emmanuel P Ch, St. Louis, MO, 96-02; *What Is Your Church's Personality?: Discovering and Developing the Ministry Style of Your Church*, 08

12273 North Forty Drive, St. Louis, MO 63141-8617 – 314-576-3750   Missouri
E-mail: pdouglass@covenantseminary.edu
Covenant Theological Seminary – 314-434-4044

    Dourado, Lucas Fast – b Rio de Janeiro, Brazil, Jan 30, 84; f Carlos Gouvea; m Pamela Joy; w Margaret Carnes, McLean, VA, Mar 10, 12; chdn Margaret Viola, Asher Fast; WFU 06, BA; CTS 11, MDiv; O Oct 2, 11, SNE Pby; campm RUF, UConn, 11-

226 Lewis Hill Road, Coventry, CT 06238   Southern New England
E-mail: lucas.dourado@ruf.org
PCA Reformed University Fellowship

    Dove, Donald – ascp New Cov P Ch, Abingdon, MD, 08-10; op Living Hope PCA, Aberdeen, MD, 10-11; p 11-

200 Northway, Havre de Grace, MD 21078 – 410-939-7836   Chesapeake
E-mail: dove.don@gmail.com
Living Hope PCA – 443-502-0343

    Dowda, Clinton Barclay – b Baltimore, MD, Sept 6, 70; f Bernard Francis Goldberg; m Cristie Anita Dowda; w Jennifer Nicole Wallace, Winston-Salem, NC, Dec 16, 95; chdn Olivia Grace, Harry Clinton, Samuel Wallace; WFU 92, BA; WTS 98, MDiv; L Jun 25, 00, CentCar Pby; O Oct 17, 00, CentCar Pby; astp Redeemer P Ch, Winston-Salem, NC, 99-02, ascp 02-04; astp West End P Ch, Richmond, VA, 04-07; op Grace Comm P Ch, Mechanicsville, VA, 05-07; p 07-

10052 Rinker Drive, Mechanicsville, VA 23116 – 804-814-7433   James River
E-mail: clint@gcpres.org
Grace Community Presbyterian Church

    Dowlen, John – b Chattanooga, TN, Sept 4, 84; w Allison; chdn Walker Harris; FurU 07, BA; CTS 12, MDiv; O Jun 13, BlRdg Pby; astp Christ the King P Ch, Roanoke, VA, 13-15; astp North Shore Flwsp, Chattanooga, TN, 15-

903 Islander Way, Chattanooga, TN 37402 – 423-886-2874   Tennessee Valley
E-mail: johndowlen@nsfellowship.org
North Shore Fellowship – 423-266-3757

    Downie, Alasdair Trevor – b Edinburgh, Scotland, Mar 7, 64; f Robert; m Janet Hunter Robertson; w Rebecca Lynn Compton, Laurens, SC, Jun 3, 89; chdn Sarah Elizabeth; RhC 82-86, BS; UWI 86-87, PhD cand; UTSVA 87-91, MDiv; O Jul 28, 91, Shen pby PCUSA; Recd PCA 01, Westm Pby; p Gerrardstown P Ch, WV, 91-95; p Windsor Ave P Ch, Bristol, TN, 95-00; ob p Bellemont P Ch, Bristol, TN, 00-03; p Liberty Springs P Ch, Cross Hill, SC, 03-05; wc; astp Westminster P Ch, Clinton, SC, 17-

102 Sherwood Drive, Laurens, SC 29360   Calvary
E-mail: presbypro@aol.com
Westminster Presbyterian Church – 864-833-1275

    Downing, Richard Lynn – b French Camp, MS, Jul 2, 42; f Remer Moffett D; m Lucy Henderson; w Dianne Siegenthaler, Ft Lauderdale, FL, Aug 6, 65; chdn Philip Henderson (d), Amy Elizabeth; BelC

Downing, Richard Lynn, continued
65, BA; ColTS 65-66; RTS 69, BD; O Jul 13, 69, Evgld Pby (PCUS); Men in Action, 69-71; srp Lake Osborne Continuing P Ch, Lake Worth, FL, 71-08; astp Briarwood P Ch, Birmingham, AL, 08-17; hr 17

6140 MS Highway 413, French Camp, MS 39745   Evangel
E-mail: ldgofly2@gmail.com
HR

Downs, Jeff – O Aug 25, 15, Cal Pby; p Lebanon P Ch, Abbeville, SC, 15- 18; p Knox Ref P Ch, Mechanicsville, VA, 18-

8116 North Mayfield Lane, Mechanicsville, VA 32111   James River
E-mail: jeff.countercult@gmail.com
Knox Reformed Presbyterian Church – 804-779-7608

Downs, Richard E. Jr. – b Greenville, SC, Dec 28, 52; f Richard Elwood; m Catharine Virginia Burton; w Ricarda Berry, Aug 18, 79; chdn Arwen Rebecca, Catharine Cornelia, Richard Noah, Crystal Elizabeth, James Emerson, Cecelia Joanna; FSU 74, BS; WTS 79, MAR, 81, MDiv; GrTS 86, MA; O Sept 18, 83, CentCar Pby; campm IVCF, 81-85; ap Redeemer P Ch, Winston-Salem, NC, 85-90, srp 90-99; srp Christ The King P Ch, Cambridge, MA, 00-

27 Pemberton Street, Cambridge, MA 02140 – 857-242-4189   Southern New England
E-mail: rickdowns@gmail.com
Christ The King Presbyterian Church

Doyle, Peter Reese – b Pensacola, FL, May 13, 30; f Austin Kelvin; m Jamie Reese; w Sally Ann Jackson, Roanoke, VA, Aug 13, 55; chdn Jonathan Jackson, Susan Elisabeth; WLU 54, BA; SeaWTS 57, MDiv; UBas 61-63; TTS 80, ThD; EpTS 68, DD; L 57, Epis Dioc of SwVA; O 73, Evan Pby; p St. Peter's Epis Ch, Altavista, VA, 57-58; mis Epis Ch, Liberia, Africa; instr CCDS; p St. James Epis Ch, Leesburg, VA, 64-68; prof EpTS, 68-70; p Church of Our Saviour, Rock Hill, 70-72; ap Briarwood P Ch, Birmingham, AL, 72-77; t BhamES, 72-77; p Covenant P Ch, Auburn, AL, 77-85; p Christ P Ch, Nashville, TN, 85-87; Dir AIM, 88-91; srp Trinity P Ch, Opelika, AL, 91-00, ascp 00-08; hr 08; The Daring Adventure Series: *Ambushed In Africa, Trapped In Pharoah's Tomb, Stalked In The Catacombs,* 93; *Surrounded By The Crossfire* 94; *Hot Pursuit On The High Seas* 94; *Hunted Along The Rhine* 94; *Launched From the Castle* 95; *Escape From Black Forest* 95; *Kidnapped in Rome* 96; *Lost in the Secret Cave* 96, *Las Marcas del Discipulo* 99; *Chased by the Jewel Thieves* 97; *Independence* 97; *Bunker Hill,* 98; *A Captive in Williamsburg,* 00

3800 Flintwood Lane, Opelika, AL 36804 – 334-742-0620   Southeast Alabama
E-mail: pdoyle@integrityonline.com
HR

Doyle, Ryan – astp Christ P Ch, Nashville, TN, 11-14; ev 14-16; op Mercy Flwsp, Nashville, TN, 16-18, p 18-

1487 Sneed Road West, Franklin, TN 37069 – 615-293-3172   Nashville
E-mail: cpc.doyle@gmail.com
Mercy Fellowship

Dragicevic, Bojan – campm RUFI, UTxAu, 13-17

1703 Forest Hill Drive, Austin, TX 78745   South Texas
E-mail: bojan.wts@gmail.com

Drake, Brent S. – b Jackson, MI, Aug 18, 59; f Ronald S.; m Dorothy M. Fulford; w Patricia Lynn Williams, Ft. Lauderdale, FL, Apr 23, 83; chdn Daniel, Melanie, Christopher; MCC 82, BS; TEDS 86,

Drake, Brent S., continued
MDiv; L Jan 87, SFL Pby; O Jan 88, SFL Pby; astp Kendall P Ch, Miami, FL, 86-93; p Comm P Ch, Live Oak, FL, 93-97; op New Life Ch, Viera, FL, 97-00, p 00-

1444 Victoria Boulevard, Rockledge, FL 32955 – 321-305-5805   Central Florida
E-mail: brentdrake4@cfl.rr.com
New Life Church – 321-432-7188

    Drake, Robert Russell – b Minneapolis, MN, Jul 19, 44; f Robert Grant; m Corrine Jane Russell; w Victoria Anderson Rustand, Glenside, PA, Jun 16, 77; chdn Paul, Kjirstin, Tanja, Erin; BethC 62-66, BA; WKU 70-71, MA; REpS 66; WTS 67-70; L Sept 71, Phil Pby (OPC); O Feb 72, Phil Pby (OPC); p Calvary OPC, Glenside, PA, 72-77; campm CRC, UMN, 79-82; p Covenant Ref P Ch, Asheville, NC, 83-14; hr 14; ss Friendship P Ch, Black Mountain, NC, 15-

13 Rhododendron Place, Asheville, NC 28805 – 828-298-0133   Western Carolina
E-mail: rrusselldrake@gmail.com
Friendship Presbyterian Church
HR

    Draughon, Randall – op Midtown Flwsp Ch, Nashville, TN, 03-06; srp 06-

1607 North Observatory Drive, Nashville, TN 37215-3035   Nashville
Midtown Fellowship Church – 615-269-9015

    Drew, Charles Davis – b Long Island, NY, Aug 2, 50; f Edward A.; m Harriet B. Sage; w Jean Stewart Sinnott, Rumson, NJ, Jun 8, 72; chdn Edward Allen, Sarah White (Lanfer); HarvU 72, BA; WTS 78, MDiv; L May 10, 81, MidAtl Pby; O May 10, 81, MidAtl Pby; ap Trinity P Ch, Charlottesville, VA, 81-87; ob p Three Village Ch, East Setauket, NY, 87-99; ascp Redeemer P Ch of New York, New York, NY, 99-01; op Emmanuel P Ch, New York, NY, 01-03, p 03-17; hr 17; *A Public Faith*, 00; *The Ancient Lovesong: Finding Christ in the Old Testament*, 00; *A Journey Worth Taking: Finding Your Purpose in This World*

5900 Arlington Avenue #2U, Bronx, NY 10471 – 718-432-0581   Metropolitan New York
E-mail: emmanuelcdd@aol.com
HR

    Drexler, James Leonard – b Pensacola, FL, Apr 4, 57; f James L., Sr.; m Eula Gilmore; w Sara Belz, Walker, IA, Jun 28, 80; chdn Mary Catherine, Nate, Julie Rebecca, John; CC 79, BA; CTS 84, MDiv; UMO 89, MEd; StLU 00, PhD; L Sept 83, DMV Pby; O Nov 86, MO Pby; prin WestmCAc, 84-04; ascp New City Flwsp, University City, MO, 95-04; CC, chair, ed dept, dean MEd prog, 04-; ascp New City Flwsp, Chattanooga, TN, 08-; ed and contr *Schools as Communities: Educational Leadership, Relationships, and the Eternal Value of ChristianSchooling*, 07; "Feeding our Young: Helping New Teachers Grow Through Comprehensive Induction," *AILACTE Journal* 3, no. 1 (Fall, 06); "Checking the Temperature of Your School," *Christian School Educator* 9, no. 2 (Fall, 05); "Can Moral Education Be Measured?" *Christian Educators Journal* (Oct., 03); "Relationships: The Key to Character Education," *Christian School Teacher* (Fall, 03); "Why a Christian School" bklt for Christian Schools Assn of St. Louis 04; "Celebrating 25 Years: A History of Westminster Christian Academy," for WestmCAc, St. Louis, 01; "Character in the Schoolhouse: A Qualitative Assessment of the Moral Education at an Independent Christian Academy," diss. Saint Louis University, 00; "A Biblical Approach to Discipline in the Christian School," *Christian Educators Journal;* "Principals for Moral Communities" review of "Leadership for the Schoolhouse" by Thomas Sergiovanni, *Christian School Administrator*, Jan 96; *Nurturing the School Community*, 11

4114 St. Elmo Avenue, Chattanooga, TN 37409 – 423-777-0254   Tennessee Valley
E-mail: jdrexler@covenant.edu
Covenant College – 706-820-1560
New City Fellowship – 423-629-1421

Driggers, Jason – O Oct 25, 07, NR Pby; campm RUF, MarshU, 07-11; p Covenant Life P Ch, Saltillo, MS, 11-17

181 Scotland Drive, Saltillo, MS 38866-9120   Covenant
E-mail: driggers.jason@gmail.com

Driskill, David – astp Trinity P Ch, Tuscaloosa, AL, 10-12; astp Covenant P Ch, Birmingham, AL, 13-

65 Old Montgomery Highway, Birmingham, AL 35209   Evangel
E-mail: ddriskill@covpres.com
Covenant Presbyterian Church – 205-871-7002

Druen, Sid – campm RUF, NMState, 09-13; campm RUF, Davidson, 13-

PO Box 1568, Davidson, NC 28036   Catawba Valley
E-mail: sid.druen@ruf.org
PCA Reformed University Fellowship

Dryden, Tim – astp Pear Orchard P Ch, Ridgeland, MS, 10-13; astp New Covenant P Ch, Virginia Beach, VA, 13-18; ascp 18-

229 Sierra Drive, Chesapeake, VA 23322 – 757-550-7601   Tidewater
E-mail: mytimdryden@gmail.com
New Covenant Presbyterian Church – 757-467-5945

Duble, Eric – p Bible P Ch of Cono Center, Walker, IA, 05-10; wc 10-12; ip Colfax Center P Ch, Holland, IA, 12-13; wc 13- 14; p Red Bank P Ch, Chattanooga, TN, 14-

109 Narragansette Avenue, Red Bank, TN 37415   Tennessee Valley
E-mail: wedube@juno.com
Red Bank Presbyterian Church – 423-877-3414

Dubocq, Matthew A. – astp Old Cutler P Ch, Miami, FL, 02-03; p Hope Chapel, Miami, FL, 03-

13864 SW 122 Court, Miami, FL 33186 – 786-255-5252   South Florida
E-mail: mattdubocq@gmail.com
Hope Chapel – 305-222-8800

DuBose, Curtis W. – b Florence, SC, May 4, 58; f Ray; m Lina; w Christine Kamerschen, Aug 10, 91; chdn Andrew Curtis, Jonathan Kamerschen, Mary Iris, Melissa Laura ; FurU 80, BA; RTS 84, MEd, 93, MDiv, 99, ThM; O Nov 4, 07, Cal Pby; t Shannon Forest CS, 80-87; DCE First P Ch, Dillon, SC, 87-90; mis MTW, Malawi, South Africa, Uganda, 94-06; astp Mitchell Road P Ch, Greenville, SC, 07-

10 Bendingwood Circle, Taylors, SC 29687 – 864-704-2609   Calvary
E-mail: cdubose@mitchellroad.org
Mitchell Road Presbyterian Church – 864-268-2218

DuBose, Toby A. – b Tallahasse, FL, Dec 16, 69; f Lawrence; m Carolyn; w Deborah Perkins, Jun 29, 91; chdn Adin Christopher, Ethan Gabriel; FSU 00, BA; RTS 02, MDiv; O Mar 03, NFL Pby; p Redeemer P Ch, Jacksonville, FL, 03-09; op Trinity Ref P Msn, 13-

Brunnengasse 4, Stelzenberg 67705 GERMANY – 0114963063110134   Southeast Alabama
E-mail: tobydubose@gmail.com
Trinity Reformed Presbyterian Mission

Dugan, Eric Ansell – chdn Gage; GenC 90, BA; RTS 94, MA; O Dec 14, 14, NR Pby; astp Redeemer P Ch, Hurricane, WV, 14-; *New & Improved: Being Transformed by Grace*; *Isaiah:A Study in Grace for Youth*; *Philippians & Colossians: Letters From a Friend*; *Judges: A Cycle of Grace*; *Acts: The Gospel Advances*; *Ephesians: Growing in Faith*; *The Game Guide*; *Esther, Ezra & Nehemiah-Faithful Servants*; *Colossians & Philemon-First Things First*

2125 Mt. Vernon Road, Hurricane, WV 25526 – 304-549-5746 New River
E-mail: edugan7@yahoo.com
Redeemer Presbyterian Church – 304-757-1197

Duhs, Seth – b Jackson, MS, Dec 17, 87; DSU, BS; RTS 15, MDiv; O Jan 29, 17, Gr Pby; p New Cov P Ch, Natchez, MS, 17-

130 Homochitto Street, Natchez, MS 39120 Grace
E-mail: seth.duhs@yahoo.com
New Covenant Presbyterian Church – 601-445-5010

Duke, John W. – b North Richland Hills, TX, Apr 17, 65; f William Robert; m Carolyn Ann Holland; w Lydia Ruth Wrinkle, Denton, TX, Jun 25, 88; chdn John Christopher, Hannah Holland, David Michael (d); HSU 87, BA; RTS 96, MDiv; L Oct 94, MSVal Pby; O Feb 23, 97, NoTX Pby; astp Arlington P Ch, Arlington, TX, 95-05; astp Lakeland P Ch, Brandon, MS, 05-

206 Camelot Way, Brandon, MS 39047 – 601-566-4761 Mississippi Valley
E-mail: jduke@lakelandpres.org
Lakeland Presbyterian Church – 601-992-2448

Dunahoo, Charles Hugh – b Winder, GA, Feb 24, 40; f Charles Wynn; m Myrtle Everett; w Colleen Roberts, Atlanta, GA, Dec 27, 63; chdn John Charles, Melanie Colleen, Mark Wynn; UGA 62, BA; ColTS 65, MDiv; WTS 89, DMin; O Jun 65, Atlanta Pby; ap Westminster P Ch, Atlanta, GA, 65-67; p Oak Park P Ch, Montgomery, AL, 67-71; p Smyrna P Ch, Smyrna, GA, 71-76; dean, prof AUBS, 71-75; coord CEP, 77-12; bd trust WestTS, 81-; BdDirBethCS, Grand Rapids, MI, 94-03; *Changing Trends in Missions*; *Team Building, The Key to Success in Ministry*; *Making Kingdom Disciples*; *Foundations and Authority*; *The Gospel of Mark*; *The Mystery of the Kingdom Revealed*

1207 Berkeley Road, Avondale Estates, GA 30002-1517 – 404-284-8809 Metro Atlanta

Duncan, Andrew – O Sept 20, 14, Phil pby; ob Grace City Ch Tokyo, 14-

Grace City Church Tokyo Philadelphia

Duncan, Benjamin S. – b Ft. Leonard Wood, MO, Dec 6, 76; f Michael Scott; m Patricia Ann; w Kathrina Marie LeClere, Jan 1, 97; chdn Daniel Benjamin, Rebekah Ann-Marie, Joshua Fredrick, Josiah Jacob, Noah Michael; MBI 02, BS; SBTS 06, MDiv; O Jul 16, 06, OHVal Pby; Chap USArmy, 06-15; p Grace Cov Ch - PCA, Dallas, GA, 15-

159 Angel Oak Trail, Dallas, GA 30132 Northwest Georgia
E-mail: bduncan@gracecovenantpca.com
Grace Covenant Church - PCA – 770-443-5550

Duncan, Christopher Michael – b Atlanta, GA, Nov 14, 74; f Michael; m Lura Akin; w Kelli Johnson, Opelika, AL, Dec 19, 98; chdn Georgia Loraine, Clara Evelyn; AU 93-97, BA; BDS 97-00, MDiv; RTSFL 00-01; AU 08, PhD; O May 23, 01, SEAL Pby; astp Trinity P Ch, Opelika, AL, 01-04; ascp 04-06, srp 06-; chmn Trinity Ch School board, 04-; rvw "Autobiographical Reflections on Southern Religious History" in *Southern Historian*, (Spring 02)

503 Winterburn Avenue, Opelika, AL 36801 – 334-705-8834 Southeast Alabama
E-mail: pastor@tpcopelika.org
Trinity Presbyterian Church – 334-745-4889

Duncan, J. Gordon – w Amy; chdn Meredith, Landry, Emma; ECU 93, BA; RTSNC 05, MAR; O Jul 05, Ecar Pby; astp Redeemer P Ch, Raleigh, NC, 03-05; op Sovereign King PCA, Garner, NC, 05-13; astp New Life in Christ Ch, Fredericksburg, VA, 13-15; op Evident Gr Flwsp, Fredericksburg, VA, 14-15, p 15-; *Because I Said So*; *Who Are We*? *Who We Are*; *Sabbath Rest*; "All Hospitable Eve," "Bill Clinton Stole My Line," "Pay Your Rent," "Seven Degrees of Separation," "What Did We Do?" and "In Praise of Drinking Beer," on www.seedstories.com; "Nacho Libre and the Freedom to Serve," "What Trump Taught Me About Being Right," on www.theooze.com

6311 Prospect Street, Fredericksburg, VA 22407 – 919-329-6778   James River
E-mail: jgordonduncan@yahoo.com
Evident Grace Fellowship – 919-412-8161

Duncan, J. Ligon III – b Greenville, SC, Nov 29, 60; f J. Ligon Jr.; m Shirley Ledford; w Marjorie Anne Harley, Columbia, SC, Jan 25, 92; chdn Sarah Kennedy, Jennings L. IV; FurU 79-83, BA; CTS 83-87, MDiv, 83-87, MA; UEdin 95, PhD; L Jul 85; O Aug 19, 90, Cal Pby; int Covenant P Ch, St. Louis, MO, 86-87; ob prof RTS, 90-96; ob astp Trinity P Ch, Jackson, MS, 90-95; ob ip First P Ch, Yazoo City, MS, 93; srp First P Ch, Jackson, MS, 96-13;ob Chanc RTS, 13-; mod, Cal pby, 96; GA Theo Exam Co, chair 00-01, 02-; vice chair GA Study Co on Creation, mod MSVall pby, 00-01; GA B&O Co, chair 02; GA Strategic Planning Co, 00-; GA Study Committee on FV and AA Theologies, 06-07contr *The Westminster Assembly: A Guide to Basic Bibliography*, 93; *A Short History of the Westminster Assembly*, 93; *Matthew Henry's Method for Prayer*, 93; ed *Shared Life*, 94; ed John Girardeau's *Federal Theology*, 94; ed S.W. Carruthers' *Everyday Work of The Westminster Assembly*, 94; art for *Tabletalk, Modern Reformation, Christian Observer, Premise, Christian Research Network Journal, O Jornal Os Puritanos, Presbyterion (The Covenant Seminary Review), Madison County Journal, NLA Review, AFA Journal, Presbyterian Network, Christian Perspectives, The Presbyterian Witness*; ed B.M. Palmer's *The Broken Home*, 94; ed Herman Witsius's *The Character of a True Theologian* 95; ed S.W. Carruthers's *The Westminster Confession: The Preparation and Printing of its Seven Leading Editions and A Critical Edition*, 95; auth *Moses' Law for Modern Government?* 95; ed Derek Thomas's *A Guide to the Essential Commentaries for Preachers*, 96; intro Derek Thomas's *Taken up into Heaven, The Ascension of Christ*, 96; ed David Calhoun's *A Place for Truth*, 98; intro John Brown's *The Puritans*, 98; intro Donald Macleod's *A Faith toLive By*, 98; contr *The Genesis Debate*, 00; ed Gordon Reed's *Plain Talk on Christian Doctrine: A Pastor's Look at the Shorter Catechism*, 01; ed Wilson Benton's *Everything You Always Wanted to Know About Predestination but were Afraid to Ask*, 00; ed Terry Johnson's *Reformed Worship*; ed Howard Kelly's *A Scientific Man and the Bible*, 00; ed Terry Johnson's *The Pastor's Public Ministry*, 01; ed Philip Ryken's *The Sovereignty of God's Mercy*, 01; ed J.V. Fesko's *Diversity within the Reformed Tradition: Supra-and Infrapsaraianism in Calvin, Dort, and Westminster*, 02; ed Geoffrey Thomas' *Preaching: The Man, The Message, and The Method*, 02; ed, contr *The Westminster Confession in the 21st Century: Essays in Remembrance of the 350th Anniversary of the Publication of the Westminster Confession of Faith*, Vol I, 03; ed, contr (with Derek W.H. Thomas and Philip Ryken) *Give Praise to God: Sola Scriptura et Soli Deo Glora - A Festschrift for James Montgomery Boice*, 03; auth (with Mark Talbot) *Should We Leave Our Churches? A Biblical Response to Harold Camping*, 04; auth *Worshiping God Together*, 05; auth (with Susan Hunt) *Women's Ministry in the Local Church*, 06; ed. Richard Gaffin Jr.'s *God's Word in Servant-form: Abraham Kuyper and Herman Bavinck on the Doctrine of Scripture* (07); contr. *Preaching the Cross* (07); ed. *Reformed Thought: Selected Works of William Young* (08); auth *Fear Not!: Death and the Afterlife from a Christian Perspective* (08); contr *In My Place Condemned He Stood*, (08); art in *reformation21, The Alliance Quarterly, Tabletalk, Australian Presbyterian, Reformed Quarterly, JBMW; Does Grace Grow Best in Winter: Suffering, Sovereignty, and Sanctification;* "Traditional Evangelical Worship" in *Perspectives on Christian Worship: 5 Views,* 09; *Does Grace Grow Best in Winter,* 09; "Will the Church Stand or Fall" in *Risking the Truth: Handling Error in the Church,*09; "Recent Objections to Covenant Theology" in *The Westminster Confession of Faith into the 21st Century : Essays in Remembrance of the 350th Anniversary of the Westminster Assembly,* 09; "Betrayed, Denied, Deserted" in *Jesus, Keep Me Near the Cross: Experiencing the Passion and Power of Easter,* 09; ed. *The Westminster Confession of Faith into the 21st Century: Essays in Remembrance of the 350th Anniversary of the Westminster Assembly,* Volume III, 09; "Federal Vision? A worrying recent movement within Reformed theology," *Evangelicals Now,* Sept 09; "Ephesians: The Queen of Letters," *The Madison County Journal,* 09; *Deacon and Elder Training Manual,* 10; w/ William Barcley *Gospel Clarity*, 10; "An Unpopular Doctrine," *Ministry and Leadership*, Spr/Sum 11; w/ Guy Prentiss Waters *Children and the Lord's Supper*, 11; "Solid Joys and Lasting Treasure: A Series on

Duncan, J. Ligon III, continued
Aug 11; "With God in the Wilderness: A Series on Numbers," *The Madison County Journal,* 11; Cont, *Proclaiming a Cross-Centered Theology,* 09; Cont, *Entrusted with the Gospel,*10; Cont, *Preaching Like Calvin,* 10; Cont, *Calvin for Today,* 10; w/ Thabiti Anyabwile *Baptism and the Lord's Supper,* 11; Cont, *The Gospel as Center,* 12; A Series on James: "Pilgrim through this Barren Land" *Madison County Journal,* 12; A Series on Romans "The Righteousness of God for Salvation" *Madison County Journal* 13

2215 Heritage Hill Drive, Jackson, MS 39211 – 601-366-5710   Mississippi Valley
E-mail: lduncan@rts.edu
Reformed Theological Seminary – 601-923-1600

Dunn, Caleb – b Montemorelos, N.L., Mexico, Apr 12, 75; f Glen; m Linda; w Aimee Janelle, Jul 27, 98; chdn Abigail Grace, Andrew Caleb, Samuel Glen, Josiah Chun Ju; DTS 01, ThM; O 03; mis MTW, 03-12; susp 12-14; wc 14-15; ss Cristo Rey, Dallas, TX, 15-16, p 16-

11023 Watterson Drive, Dallas, TX 75228   North Texas
E-mail: cristorey.calebdunn@gmail.com
Cristo Rey – 214-654-0945

Dunn, Dwight – b Pittsburgh, PA, Jul 28, 63; f George J.; m Ethel M.; w Connie, Pittsburgh, PA, Aug 3, 85; chdn Hannah Elizabeth, Seth Jonathan, Nathan Philip, Rachel Joy; ClarU 84; RPTS 90, MDiv; CTS 03, DMin; L Sept 23, 89, Asc Pby; O Dec 9, 90, Hrtg Pby; srp Reformed P Ch, Boothwyn, PA, 90-17; op Loganville Project, Lawrenceville, GA, 17-; *A Study of God-Sent Revival as a Motivation for and Method of Personal Renewal*

369 Blue Creek Lane, Loganville, GA 30052 – 610-485-0902   Georgia Foothills
E-mail: dwightdunn@comcast.net
Loganville Project

Dunn, Mark J. – b Belfast, N. Ireland, Sept 29, 68; f Robert Samuel; m Arlene Maude McKeown; w Jessica Erin MacPherson, Germantown, NY, May 9, 98; chdn Joshua Mark, Timothy Samuel, Benjamin Jesse; UUJ, BS; QUB, BD; RTS 10, DMin; L Jun 13, 97, N. Ireland; O Sept 3, 99, N. Ireland; Recd PCA May 4, 04, Pitts Pby; astp 1st Ahoghill P Ch, N. Ireland, 97-99; p Carnlough & Newtowncrommelin P Ch, N. Ireland, 99-04; p First Evangelical P Ch, East Liverpool, OH, 04-14; ascp First P Ch, Schenectady, NY, 14-17, p 17-

1679 Mariaville Road, Schenectady, NY 12306   New York State
E-mail: revdrmjdunn@gmail.com
First Presbyterian Church – 518-374-4546

Dunn, Reed – w Lee Ann; chdn Jennalee, Adeline, Tarikwa; UAR, BA; WTS, MDiv; O Jul 30, 06, Cov Pby; op Christ the King Ch, Joplin, MO, 06-10, p 10-

1930 Virginia Avenue, Joplin, MO 64804 – 417-629-2571   Hills and Plains
E-mail: reed@christthekingpca.com
Christ the King Church – 417-624-4220

Dunn, Robert L. – b Gadsden, AL, Apr 18, 45; f Howard; m Wanza Eiland; w Marie Webb, Anniston, AL, Aug 1, 65; chdn Scott, David, Elizabeth; JAXSU 74, BS; RTS 79, MDiv; L Oct 16, 79; O Oct 16, 79, Evan Pby; op King City Comm Ch MO, 80-81; ap New Hope P Ch in America, Olathe, KS, 81-85; ev OK Pby, 85-86; p Christ P Ch, Kansas City, MO, 86-98; hr, mdis 98

16620 Nall Avenue, Stilwell, KS 66085-9121 – 913-685-4689   Heartland
E-mail: rdunn34@kc.rr.com
HR

Dunn, Seth – O 17, SusqV Pby; Chap USAR, 18-

PO Box 526, Mount Joy, PA 17552   Susquehanna Valley
United States Army Reserve

Dunning, Jonathan – b Neenah, WI, Nov 22, 74; f Charles E.; m Elizabeth E.; w Tricia, St. Louis, MO, Dec 18, 99; chdn Lucy Ellen, John Charles (Jack), Thaddaeus Mark; MUOH 97, BS; CTS 01, MDiv; O Jun 5, 04, Hrtl Pby; ascp Oak Hills P Ch, Overland Park, KS, 04- 13; campm RUF, KSU, 13-

1304 Wreath Avenue, Manhattan, KS 66503 – 913-908-9957   Heartland
E-mail: jonathan.dunning@ruf.org
PCA Reformed University Fellowship

Dunnington, Edward William – b Ft. Eustis, VA, Aug 20, 69; f Warren Harvey; m Elizabeth Ryan; w Stefanie Ellen Walton, McLean, VA, Jun 6, 92; chdn Patrick Edward, Hunter Madison, Adelaine Destiny, Corinne Ashley; VMI 87-91, BS; CTS 94-98, MDiv, 16, DMin; O Sept 20, 98, PacNW Pby; campm RUF, UW, 98-06; op Christ the King P Msn, Roanoke, VA, 06-07; p 07-15; admin RBI, 15-; contr *PCA Call Package Guidelines, PCA RBI Retirement Plan Review, PCA RBI Benefit Bulletin*

3264 Bakers Mill Court, Dacula, GA 30019 – 678-804-9122   Georgia Foothills
E-mail: edunnington@pcanet.org
PCA Retirement & Benefits, Inc. – 678-825-1260

Dunton, Ronald Wade – b Columbus, OH, May 26, 56; f Myron L.; m Anne S.; w Amy Cochran, Knoxville, TN, Jun 18, 77; chdn David Nathaniel, Jonathan Michael, Andrew Joel; CC 78, BA; CTS 83, MDiv; L Oct 81, SW Pby (RPCES); O May 83, TX Pby (PCA); ap Town North P Ch, Richardson, TX, 83-89; op Metrocrest P Ch, Carrollton, TX, 89-93, p 93-11; wc 11-12; p Bay Area P Ch, Webster, TX, 12-

2010 Woodland Haven Drive, Houston, TX 77062 – 281-954-6450   Houston Metro
E-mail: rdunton@bapc.org
Bay Area Presbyterian Church – 281-280-0713

Dupee, David V. – b Chicago, IL, Nov 13, 39; f Kenneth J.; m Jean Vickers; w Prue Ellen Warner, Santa Barbara, CA, Sept 7, 63; chdn Neonetta L., David Douglas, Kimberly Ann, Kenneth Bruce, Jinah Lee; USNA 58-62, BS; LPTS 66-69, MDiv; O Jul 13, 69, NCent IA Pby (UPCUSA); p East Friesland Ch, 69-81; p Faith P Ch, Ackley, IA, 81-82; ob headm ConoCS, 82-99; astp Bible P Ch of Cono Center, Walker, IA, 99-01; op Redeemer P Ch, Des Moines, IA, 99-00; t ConoCS, 99-01; ob t Zion HS, Kentwood, MI, 01-03; p Providence P Ch, Ft. Wayne, IN, 03-15; hr 15

68 Oak Creek Lane, Unit 4, Hendersonville, NC 28739 – 828-489-8365   Great Lakes
E-mail: dvdxrs@gmail.com
HR

Durant, David W. – b Bethesda, MD, Jun 3, 52; w Kathy M. Kisling, Largo, MD, Jun 21, 75; chdn David K., Christopher L., Jonathan W.; PU 74, BA; USCA 78, MS; ChTS 96, MDiv; L May 11, 93, Pot Pby; O Jun 2, 96, Pot Pby; p Mount Airy P Ch, Mount Airy, MD, 96-

2410 Duvall Road, Woodbine, MD 21797-8111 – 410-489-7401   Chesapeake
E-mail: pastor@mtairypca.org
Mount Airy Presbyterian Church – 301-829-5223

Durham, A. Glenn – b Memphis, TN, Nov 13, 62; f Larry V.; m Merrel Hutchison; w Helen Holmes, Memphis, TN, Aug 6, 88; chdn Daniel Pierce, Rebekah Patton; GATech 85, BME; RTS 94, MDiv; L Oct 93, MSVal Pby; O Jun 12, 94, Hrtl Pby; astp Trinity P Ch, Omaha, NE, 94-95; ev Hrtl Pby;

Durham, A. Glenn, continued
op Harvest Comm Ch, Omaha, NE, 94-99, p 99-02; ev, op Christ the King P Msn, Conway, AR, 02-03; op Faith Comm Ch of Lemont, Lemont, IL, 04-05; ascp Dominion Cov Ch, Omaha, NE, 05-06; srp Church of the Cov, Cincinnati, OH, 06-11; hr 15

2046 Casa Loma Drive, Fairfield, OH 45014 – 513-829-1095　　　　　　　　　　Ohio Valley
E-mail: PastorGlenn@fuse.net
HR

　　Dusenbery, Ashley – w Kathryn; chdn Waverly, Darby; astp, yp Grace P Ch, Fort Payne, AL, 10-13; ascp 13-14; astp Covenant P Ch at Cleveland, Cleveland, MS, 14-

500 South 5th Avenue, Cleveland, MS 38732 – 256-630-4876　　　　　　　　　　Covenant
E-mail: ashdusenbery@gmail.com
Covenant Presbyterian Church at Cleveland – 662-843-9598

　　Dusenbury, Julian D. – b Columbia, SC, Aug 25, 52; f Bernard D.; m Mary Etta; w Bonnie Gene Quillian, Charleston, SC, Aug 10, 74; chdn Julie, David, Timothy, Amy; Citadel 74, BA; CTS, MDiv; L Jan 20, 90, MO Pby; O Feb 24, 91, Pot Pby; astp Wallace P Ch, Hyattsville, MD, 91-92; p Christ Ref P Ch, Laurel, MD, 93-

8707 Crestmont Lane, Laurel, MD 20708-2451 – 301-497-9739　　　　　　　　　　Potomac
E-mail: jddusenbury@gmail.com
Christ Reformed Presbyterian Church – 301-498-3700

　　Duty, Bryan Hopkins – w Patricia; chdn Hannah, Emily; RTS, MDiv; O Oct 04, GrLks Pby; ob p Zion Church, Winesburg, OH, 04-05; astp Christ Cov Ref (PCA), Reynoldsburg, OH, 05-06; p 06-09; ascp 09-10; mis 10-

242 Bluff Ridge Drive, Pataskala, OH 43062-8069 – 740-927-0380　　　　　　　Columbus Metro
E-mail: bryanduty@gmail.com

　　Dye, Eric R. – b St. Joseph, MO, Feb 23, 53; f Elvis R.; m Iona Marie Larson; w Margaret Manfield, Oct 25, 86; CentBC 73-76, BA; CTS 80-84, MDiv, 94, ThM; ULon, MA; L Oct 82, Midw Pby (RPCES); O Aug 84, MO Pby; ap Providence Ref P Ch, St. Louis, MO, 84-87; Chap USArmy, 87-04; p Covenant P Ch, Columbia, SC, 04-15; Chap, Charlie Norwood VA Med Cntr, 15-16; Chap Erie VA Med Center, 17-

2939 West 31st Street, Erie, PA 16506　　　　　　　　　　　　　　　　　　　　Palmetto
E-mail: Calvin3Max@aol.com

　　Dye, Roger Merle – b Asheville, NC, Jul 22, 66; f Richard H; m Susannah Marie Solomon; w Laura Rose Park, Winnsboro, SC, Oct 17, 92; chdn Deanna Marie, Isaac Solomon, Hudson Richard, Suzannah Grace; CBC 84-88, BA; CTS 88-91, MDiv, 88-91, MA; L Jul 22, 92, Palm Pby; O Nov 13, 94, CentCar Pby; ss South Point P Msn, 92-94, p 94-96; mis, chp MTW, Chile, 96-14; FamilyLife Latin America, 14- *¿De dónde vinimos? Un estudio crítico de orígenes (*Spanish: *Where Did We Come From? A Critical Study of Origins)*, 04

7709 State Hwy 213, Winnsboro, SC 29180 – 803-530-6571　　　　　　　　　Catawba Valley
E-mail: rdye@familylife.com
FamilyLife Latin America

　　Dykes, Robert E. – O Oct 1, 17, CentCar Pby; astp Sovereign Gr P Ch, Charlotte, NC, 17-

10021 Wild Dogwood Court, Charlotte, NC 28273 – 980-406-8444　　　　　　Central Carolina
E-mail: rob.dykes@sovereigngrace.org
Sovereign Grace Presbyterian Church – 704-553-9600

MINISTERIAL DIRECTORY

Dykshoorn, Jan G. – b Netherlands, Aug 12, 58; f Ewoud; m Maria P.; w Patricia Anne Ambrus, Allen Park, MI, Nov 28, 87; chdn Elizabeth Anne (Weiss), John Mark; CalvC 81-85, BA; CalvS 85-87; RPTS 87-90,MDiv; L Oct 88, CRC; O Jul 3, 94, RCUS; Recd PCA Oct 13, 95, GrLks Pby; ss East Martin CRC, Martin, MI, 92-93; ss, p Walnut Creek P Ch, 93-94; ss First P Ch, Bad Axe, MI, 95, p 95-11; wc 11-14; sc GrLks Pby 06-15; ob Second Cong Ch, Douglas, MA, 14-

10 Depot Street, PO Box 464, Douglas, MA 01516 – 508-476-5675   Southern New England
E-mail: sub.pastor5@gmail.com
Second Congregational Church

Eades, Brad – b St. Louis, MO, Nov 4, 69; w Cindy; UMD 98, BS; CTS 04, MDiv; cert CT; Chap, Bereavement Mngr, Hospice of the Valley, Decatur, AL, 05-; p Courtland P Ch, Courtland, AL, 12-14

2007 Franklin Avenue SW, Decatur, AL 35603   Providence
E-mail: 2eades@gmail.com
Hospice of the Valley, Decatur, AL – 256-350-5585

Eades, Harold D. (Buddy) – b Greenville, SC, Jul 14, 65; f Harold Dean, Sr.; m Brenda Catherine Brown; w Victoria Anne Taylor, Atlanta, GA, Jun 7, 03; FurU 88, BMus; RTSNC 00, MDiv; O Nov 25, 01, SEAL Pby; astp Covenant P Ch, Auburn, AL, 01-06; astp Christ Ch Newnan, Newnan, GA, 07-10; wc 10-11; ob WDA 11-

2988 Stonegate Trail, Atlanta, GA 30340 – 770-354-2143   Metro Atlanta
E-mail: budeades5@mac.com

Eades, James David – b Charleston, WV, Jun 23, 66; f James William II; m Judith Sue Foutty; w Laura Dorothy Watson, Greensboro, NC, Aug 9, 86; chdn James William III, Carlton Daniel, Lynnae, Kathryn, Hope; GuilC 84-88, BS; UNC 88-91; RTS 93-96, MDiv; L Oct 18, 94; O Mar 23, 97, MSVal Pby; astp Pear Orchard P Ch, Ridgeland, MS, 94-98; op Covenant P Ch, Washington, WV, 98-02; p Trinity P Ch, New Martinsville, WV, 02-06; p Grace P Ch, Dalton, GA, 15-

2019 Southview Drive, Dalton, NC 30720   Tennessee Valley
E-mail: colossians334@gmail.com
Grace Presbyterian Church – 706-226-6344

Earman, Joshua – b Harrisonburg, VA, Aug 15, 79; w Katie; chdn Anna, Beth, Eva, Isaac; JMU 01, BS; CTS 13, MDiv; O May 18, 14, EPA Pby; astp New Life P Ch, Dresher, PA, 14-15; astp City Ch of Richmond, Richmond, VA, 15-

1202 Whitby Road, Richmond, VA 23227   James River
E-mail: joshua@citychurchrva.com
City Church of Richmond – 804-767-8038

Easterling, Joe Perry – b Greenville, MS, Jun 2, 53; f Stanley J.; m Jonnie M. Hayes; w Jane Carol Beverly, Hattiesburg, MS, Feb 1, 75; chdn Loren Rae, Beverly Hayes; USM 75, BS; RTS 79, MDiv; L Mar 77, Gr Pby; O Nov 79, GulCst Pby; p Knox Ch, Cantonment, FL, 79-81; p Grace P Ch, Pinellas Park, FL, 81-86; p First P Ch, Philadelphia, MS, 86-90; chp CentGA Pby; op Christ Comm P Ch, Thomasville, GA, 90-93, p 93-98; ascp First P Ch, Dothan, AL, 98-01; p First P Ch, Yazoo City, MS, 01-07; p Christ Comm P Ch, Thomasville, GA, 07-16; astp Perry P Ch, Perry, GA, 17-

112 Celeste Court, Thomasville, GA 31792 – 229-289-7680   Central Georgia
E-mail: pjoee1975@hotmail.com
Perry Presbyterian Church – 478-987-1403

Easton, Brent – b Murphysboro, IL; f Rev. James; m Linda; w Holly; chdn Hosanna, Justus; IBCS 93, ThB, 95, MAC; SCS 04, MDiv, 06, MMin; O Aug 97, SBC; Recd PCA Jan 06, Ill Pby; ss Reformed P Ch, Cutler, IL, 06-07, p 07-09; wc 10; chap Lourdes Hosp, Paducah, KY, 14-; brd cert Chap, 17

140 Spring View Drive, Paducah, KY 42003 – 618-924-2502   Illiana
E-mail: brenteaston@rocketmail.com

Eby, David Lincoln – b Pomona, CA, May 31, 45; f Robert L.; m M. Eleanor Robson; w Darlene D. Runnion, Denver, CO, Aug 2, 69; chdn Matthew David, Joshua Aaron, Andrew Nathaniel, Katherine Elizabeth, Peter Jason; SDSU 67, BA; FulTS 71, MDiv; WTS 82, ThM; WSCAL 90-95, DMin; O Sept 72, Lake Ave Cong Ch, Pasadena, CA; Dir Young Life, Ft. Collins, CO, 71-74; p Evergreen (Ind), Evergreen, CO, 74-78; p Sherman St (Ind), Denver, CO, 79-80; p Cent Denver F, Denver, CO, 80-85; op San Diego, CA, 85-86; op Grace P Ch, San Diego, CA, 86-89, p 89-92; p North City P Ch, Poway, CA, 92-06; *Power Preaching for Church Growth*, 96

858-484-1280 South Coast
E-mail: ebyuganda@gmail.com

Eby, Josh – astp Redeemer Ch of Knoxv, Knoxville, TN, 04-08; ascp All Saints P Ch, Austin, TX, 12-

3 7808 Rialto Boulevard, Austin, TX 78735 – 512-351-2904 South Texas
E-mail: jeby@allsaintsaustin.org
All Saints Presbyterian Church – 512-732-8383

Eck, Peter James – O Dec 7, 14, NJ Pby; astp New City Flwsp of Atlantic City, Atlantic City, NJ, 14-

1205 North Michigan Avenue, Atlantic City, NJ 08401 – 919-607-3868 New Jersey
E-mail: petereck127@gmail.com
New City Fellowship of Atlantic City – 609-442-1219

Eddy, Thomas Allen – b Bayshore, NY, Dec 21, 63; f Carl Everett; m Joan Ann Krasse; w Lorelei Ann Rouse, Weeki Wachee, FL, Jun 2, 84; chdn Andreana Christina, Jonathan Patrick, Joseph Earl, Christopher Krasse, Paul Philip, Samuel Michael; FSC 82-86, BA; RTS 91-95, MDiv; L Jan 92; O Feb 11, 96, CentFL Pby; Chap USArmy, Ft. Bragg, NC, 96-99; Chap USArmy, Madigan Med Cntr, Tacoma, 99-01; Tacoma 99-02, Chap USArmy, Fort McPherson, GA 02-05, Chap USArmy, Fort Gillem, GA 05-08, Chap USArmy Fort Bragg, NC 08-09, Chap USArmy Pentagon VA 09-13; Chap USArmy Fort Meade, MD 13-15; astp Harvester P Ch, Springfield, VA, 13-18; MTS assoc dir for State Capitols, 15-

105 Weldon Place, Fayetteville, GA 30215 – 404-694-0644 Metro Atlanta
E-mail: teddy@pcanet.org
Mission to North America/Ministry to State

Edema, George – O Dec 11, 11, Iowa Pby; astp Redeemer P Ch, Des Moines, IA, 11-15; op New Parish Msn, Ames, IA, 16

1010 36th Street, Des Moines, IA 50311 Iowa
E-mail: george.edema@gmail.com

Edenfield, Rob – O Nov 30, 14; ascp Covenant P Ch, Oviedo, FL, 14-17; p Treasure Coast P Ch, Stuart, FL, 17-

3100 SW Captiva Court, Palm City, FL 34990 Gulfstream
E-mail: rob@treasurecoastpca.org
Treasure Coast Presbyterian Church – 772-223-8718

Edgar, Justin – astp Crossroads Flwsp, Albuquerque, NM, 11-16, p 16-

2004 Valencia Drive NE, Albuquerque, NM 87110 – 214-218-7947 Southwest
E-mail: justin@crossroadsabq.com
Crossroads Fellowship – 505-296-9900

Edgar, William III – b Wilmington, NC, Oct 11, 44; f William Jr; m Mary Miller Boatwright; w Barbara Spofford Smyth, Norfolk, CT, Apr 20, 68; chdn William Keyes Hill-Edgar, Deborah Boatwright Edgar-Goeser; HarvU 66, BA; WTS 69, MDiv; ColU 77, grad wk; UGeneva 92, DTh; L Feb 77, Asc Pby;

Edgar, William III, continued
O Dec 78, Asc Pby; mis MTW, France, 78-89; prof FLTR/Aix, 78-89; ob assoc prof WTS, 89-93, ob prof 93-; *In Spirit and in Truth* 76; *Taking Note of Music* 86; *Sur le Rock* 88; *Reasons of the Heart*, 96; *La Carte Protestante*, 97; *The Face of Truth*, 01; *Truth in All Its Glory: Commending the Reformed Faith*, 04; *Les dix commandements*, 07; *Christian Apologetics Past and Present*, Vol I, 09; *Christian Apologetics Past and Present*, Vol II, 11; *Francis Schaeffer on the Christian Life: A Counter-Cultural Spirituality*, 13; *You Asked: Your Questions, God's Answers*, 13; *Does Christianity Really Work?*, 16; *Created and Creating*, 17; *The Christian Mind*, 18

501 Twickenham Road, Glenside, PA 19038-2032 – 215-884-6334   Philadelphia
E-mail: wedgar@wts.edu
Westminster Theological Seminary – 215-887-5511
PO Box 27009, Philadelphia, PA 19118

Edging, Steven – b Morristown, TN, Feb 22, 78; f Boyd Rutledge, Jr.; m Rebecca Sue Hylton; w Brooke Avarene Moody, Nashville, TN, Mar 8, 08; chdn Sarah Evelyn, Samuel Kidron, Titus Rutledge, Ezra Knox; UT 00, BS; CTS 11, MDiv; O Apr 22, 12, Nash Pby; fm MTW, Uganda, 11-

7053 Homestead Circle, Hixson, TN 37343   Nashville
E-mail: steven.edging@gmail.com
PCA Mission to the World

Edgington, Darren – O Feb 26, 17, Ohio Pby; p Veto P Ch, Vincent, OH, 17-

63 Reese Road, Fleming, OH 45729   Ohio
E-mail: darrenedgington@hotmail.com
Veto Presbyterian Church – 740-445-5013

Edmiston, Robert Edwin – b St. Louis, MO, Feb 22, 39; f Irwin; m Virginia Schacht; w Judith Lamplugh, Philadelphia, PA; chdn Karen Sue, Holly Ann; BJU 59-60; CC 60-62; WTS 65, BD; L Jan 69, Phil Pby (RPCES); O Sept 69, Phil Pby (RPCES); ap Calvary P Ch, Willow Grove, PA, 65-69; p Christ P Ch, New Castle, PA, 69-70; dir dev WilmCS, Wilmington, DE, 70-71; WPM, 70-72; CTI, 72-76, exec dir 77-82; dir trng CEP; hr

107 Rosewood Court, Peachtree City, GA 30269-2237 – 770-716-9764   Metro Atlanta
E-mail: revandjudy2@bellsouth.net
HR

Edmonds, Brandon J. – O Dec 2, 18, NoCA Pby; astp Trinity P Ch, Kailua, HI, 18-

174 Loma Bonita Drive, San Luis, CA 93401-6629   Northern California
Trinity Presbyterian Church – 808-262-8587

Edwards, Allan – O Nov 4, 12, Pitts Pby; p Kiski Valley P Ch, Leechburg, PA, 12-17; sus

157 Floral Avenue, Leechburg, PA 15656 – 724-236-0452   Pittsburgh
E-mail: allan.e.edwards@gmail.com

Edwards, C. Bradley – astp Rocky Mountain P Ch, 12-18; Chap USARNG; op The Table Ch, Lafayette, CO, 18-

644 South Bermont Drive, Lafayette, CO 80026 – 314-249-4177   Rocky Mountain
E-mail: brad@tablechurch.com
USARNG
The Table Church – 720-772-8722

Edwards, Daniel J. – b Hopewell, VA, Mar 21, 54; f James G.; m Agnes Hart; w Leslie Callen, Tampa, FL, Aug 18, 77; chdn James Daniel, Stuart Callen, Erin Hart, Jacob Stephen; BelC 78, BS; RTS 94, MDiv, 94, MA; L Jul 95, SWFL Pby; O Mar 16, 97, Palm Pby; int Seminole P Ch, Tampa, FL, 94-96; p Union Mem P Ch, Winnsboro, SC, 96-00; astp Covenant P Ch, Birmingham, AL, 00-

2307 Lime Rock Road, Vestavia, AL 35216 – 205-822-5563   Evangel
E-mail: dedwards@covpres.com
Covenant Presbyterian Church – 205-871-7002

Edwards, Jason – b Orlando, FL, Oct 17, 70; w Meg Brown, Jan 10, 98; chdn Jake, Will, Hudson; AU 94; RTS 02, MDiv; O Sept 15, 02, MSVal Pby; astp Pear Orchard P Ch, Ridgeland, MS, 02-06; p Grace P Ch at Starkville, Starkville, MS, 07-11

Address Unavailable   Covenant

Edwards, Michael Kyle – ob Holy Trinity Ch, 15-

5031 North Major Avenue, Chicago, IL 60630   Chicago Metro
E-mail: mkyleedwards@gmail.com
Holy Trinity Church

Edwards, Randall Kirk – b Columbus, OH, May 11, 65; f David Thomas; m Linda Anne Schley; w Jennifer Anne Pilkington, Boone, NC, Jun 25, 88; chdn Catherine Anne, William Cochran, Madeleine Louise; ASU 87, BS; RTSFL 94, MDiv; L Apr 22, 95; O Feb 11, 96, CentCar Pby; astp Redeemer P Ch, Winston-Salem, NC, 96-98, ascp 98-99; astp Grace P Ch, Kernersville, NC, 00; sc PTri Pby, 01-02; ascp Grace P Ch, Kernersville, NC, 01-03, p 03-; sc PTri Pby 05-10; *The Night is O'er*, 16; *Walking with Jesus*, 18

1008 Megan Cross Lane, Kernersville, NC 27284 – 336-749-1857   Piedmont Triad
E-mail: randy@gracekernersville.org
Grace Presbyterian Church – 336-993-1305

Edwards, William Robert – b Opelika, AL, Jan 30, 71; f William Stanley; m Carolyn Simpson; w Angie Joy Fasnacht, Powder Springs, GA, Jul 31, 93; chdn Emma Kathryn, Lucy Elizabeth, William Wallace; UGA 93, BA; WTS 99, MDiv; L Oct 23, 99, NGA Pby; O Apr 30, 00, NGA Pby; ydir Clemson P Ch, Clemson, SC, 93-96; campm RUF, UGA, 99-10; astp Redeemer P Ch, Lynchburg, VA, 10; op Mercy P Msn, Forest, VA, 10-13, p 13-; *Study Guide for John Owen's 'Mortification of Sin,'* 08; "John Flavel on The Priority of Union with Christ: Further Historical Perspective on the Structure of Reformed Soteriology," *WTJ* 74 (2012): 33-58; "Redirecting the Church's Drama," *JBC* 28.2 (2014): 59-69; "Participants in What We Proclaim: Recovering Paul's Narrative of Pastoral Ministry," Themelios 39.3 (2014): 455–69

1185 Kensington Parkway, Forest, VA 24551 – 434-386-7045   Blue Ridge
E-mail: rob@mercypres.org
Mercy Presbyterian Church – 434-386-7045

Edwards-Luce, Daniel – astp Mosaic Community Ch, Silver Spring, MD, 16-17; op Port Towns Ch, Bladensburg, MD, 17-

PO Box 217, Hyattsville, MD 20781 – 240-623-4695   Potomac
E-mail: danny@porttownschurch
Port Towns Church – 240-623-4695

Egbert, Thomas H. – b Philadelphia, PA, Feb 19, 42; f William C.; m Adelaide Anne Baker; w Joan Marie Gillis, Darby, PA, Sept 10, 66; chdn Laurie Michele, Rebecca Susan, Karen Marie; PhilCB 67, BS; REpS 70, BD; CTS 82, DMin; O May 70, Maranatha Tab; p Hyde Park Bap Ch, 70-71; p Camden Bib Ch, 72-73; p Westminster Ref P Ch, Ballwin, MO, 74-81; p Loudonville Comm Ch, Albany, NY, 81-87; op Brookwood P Ch, Snellville, GA, 87-90, p 90-93; PCAF, 93-95; ob t Master's Acad, Atlanta, GA, 95-96; srp Trinity P Ch, Plano, TX, 96-00, wc 01-04; hr 04

1875 Richlake Court, Suwanee, GA 30024-3296 – 770-277-6533   North Texas
HR

MINISTERIAL DIRECTORY

Eggar, Brandon – b Odessa, TX, Feb 11,75; f William Michael; m Nancy Lee; w Neecia Gayl Beckner, Springfield, MO, Mar 6,99; chdn Addisyn Gayl, William Brandon, Owen Nicholas, Corbitt Shane; DBU 95-97, BBibSt; WTS 00-06, MDiv; L July 29, 06; O Nov 19, 06, So TX Pby; astp Redeemer P Ch, San Antonio, TX, 06-08; ascp 08-12; p Trinity P Ch, Murfreesboro, TN, 12-

1506 Belle Oaks, Murfreesboro, TN 37130   Nashville
E-mail: brandon@trinitymboro.com
Trinity Presbyterian Church – 615-895-2018

Egli, Ryan – O Jan 15, Phil Pby; astp liberti- Fairmount, Philadelphia, PA, 15-17

271 Harvey Street, Philadelphia, PA 19144 – 267-912-1281   Philadelphia
E-mail: eggs00@gmail.com

Eguilez, Daniel – b Lima, Peru, Jan 17, 81; f Walter Juan; m Flor de Maria Calle Chuecas; w Abigail Damaris Bedrinana Castaneda, Lima, Peru, Jan 10, 15; chdn Nathaniel; MDCC 02, AA; FIU 06, BFA; DTS 12, ThM; CalvS, PhD cand; O May 27, 18, GrLks Pby; astp Christ Ch, Grand Rapids, MI, 18-; op Gracehill Ch, Grand Rapids, MI, 18-

2897 Englewood Avenue SE, Grand Rapids, MI 49508   Great Lakes
E-mail: d_eguilez@yahoo.com
Christ Church – 616-949-9630
Gracehill Church – 616-949-9630

Ehlers, Mark Christopher – b Wiltshire Cty, England, Jun 23, 53; f George R.; w Peggy Lynn, Nov 13, 82; chdn Jennifer Lauren, Kevin Christopher, Eric Ryan, Rachel Noel; UFL 71-73; BelC 73-75, BA; WTS 75-76; RTS 76-79, MDiv; O Nov 10, 79, CentFL Pby; op Tampa, FL, 79-81; ap Lake Osborne Continuing P Ch, Lake Worth, FL, 81-92; astp, mout Westminster P Ch, Rock Hill, SC, 92-99; srp Covenant P Ch, Cherry Hill, NJ, 00-08; astp First P Ch, Chattanooga, TN, 09-

1701 Jackson Square Drive, Hixson, TN 37343   Tennessee Valley
E-mail: cehlers@1stpresbyterian.com
First Presbyterian Church – 423-267-1206

Eickelberg, Robert Purdy – b Baltimore, MD, Mar 3, 50; f Robert H.; m Rose G. Purdy; w Anne Paige Wheeler, Timonium, MD, Aug 10, 74; chdn Carrie Elizabeth, Sarah Rebecca; MaryvC 68-72, BA; WTS 72-75, MDiv; GenC 87-91, MA; L Jan 75; O Nov 75, DMV Pby (RPCES); ap Liberty Ref P Ch, Owings Mills, MD, 75-76; p Munson Hill Ch, Falls Church, VA, 77-81; p Covenant P Ch, Pittsburgh, PA, 82-92; astp Covenant of Gr P Ch, Reisterstown, MD, 92-95; couns New Hope Pastoral Ministries, Inc., Timonium, MD, 92-, pres 93-; ascp Timonium P Ch, Timonium, MD, 95-00, srp 00-03; p Trinity P Ch, Harrisburg, PA, 03-; MTW pastoral assoc couple, Australia, 09-; RM "From the Pulpit," 89-92

6502 Liptak Drive, Harrisburg, PA 17112 – 717-657-0123   Susquehanna Valley
E-mail: beickelberg@trinityhbg.com
Trinity Presbyterian Church – 717-545-4271
New Hope Pastoral Ministries – 410-409-2415

Eide, Dennis Dean – b Adrian, MN, Jun 7, 48; f Lyle; m LaVerne Kennedy; w Bonnie Wallace, Mankato, MN, Dec 28, 68; chdn Matthew, Aaron, Careth; ManSC 66-68; AndC 70, BA; TEDS 70-72; MTS 73, MDiv; O Jul 73, Mankato Pby; p First Bap Ch, Russell, MN, 73-77; p Russell P Ch, MN, 73-79; p Calvin-Sinclair Ch, Cedar Rapids, IA, 80-81; srp Lennox Ebenezer P Ch, Lennox, SD, 81-98; op Living Hope Comm Ch, Tea, SD, 93-95; p Forreston Grove Ch, Forreston, IL, 98-02; p Christ P Ch, Mobile, AL, 02-15; hr 15

327 Casa Grande Court, Winter Springs, FL 32708 – 251-533-8417   Gulf Coast
E-mail: dennisdeide@gmail.com
HR

Eide, Jonathan A. – b Philadelphia, PA, Mar 21, 70; f Orris O'neil; m Carole Jean Kvam; w Tracy Lynn McRobbie, Philadelphia, PA, Aug 20, 93; chdn Alison Rachel, Natalie Jean, Zachary Ivan; UWI 92, BS; BibTS, MDiv; O Sept 03, Phil Pby; mis MTW, 03-

c/o MTW – 717-681-8885   Eastern Pennsylvania
E-mail: jeide@mtwukraine.org, jeide3@gmail.com
PCA Mission to the World

Eide, Matthew Paul – b Oct 1, 73; f Dennis; m Bonnie Wallace; w Sara Bunger, Lennox, SD, Aug 10, 96; chdn Emma Grace, Isaac Solomon, Beth Kathryn; DordtC 97, BA; WhTS 14, MDiv; O Mar 9, 14, GulCst Pby; astp Christ P Ch, Mobile, AL, 14-15; p Covenant Ref P Ch, Pueblo West, CO, 15-

44 East Spaulding Avenue, Bldg. 2, Pueblo West, CO 81007   Rocky Mountain
E-mail: matteide@me.com
Covenant Reformed Presbyterian Church – 719-404-1833

Eldridge, Nathan – b Jackson, MS, Nov 13, 79; f Ricky; m Sara Townsend; w Megan Eldridge; chdn Asher Thomas, Evie Karis, Rebekah Mical; WmCarey 03, BA; RTS 12, MDiv; O Dec 2, 12, Prov Pby; ascp Westminster P Ch, Huntsville, AL, 12-; srp 16-18; wc

2509 Excalibur Drive SE, Huntsville, AL 35803 – 601-503-0642   Providence
0

Elenbaum, Larry Ray – b Cass City, MI, Sept 20, 51; f Ralph Eugene; m Marion Margret Morris; w Betsy Lythgoe Davis, Blue Bell, PA, Nov 20, 82; chdn Bryan Lamson, Andrew Levering, Stephanie Lythgoe; CIU 76, BS; WTS 81, MA, 83, MDiv; TrinSchMin 13, DMin; L May 83, Phil Pby; O Nov 84, Asc Pby; p Christ P Ch, Beaver Falls, PA, 84-

262 Blackhawk Road, Beaver Falls, PA 15010-1404 – 724-843-6530   Ascension
E-mail: larryelenbaum@gmail.com
Christ Presbyterian Church – 724-843-6530

Elkin, Thomas E. – b Kosciusko, MS, Jun 11, 40; f Paul Davis; m Ada Corinne Black; w Mary Ella McDowell, Atlanta, GA, Jun 21, 63; chdn Thomas David, Elisabeth Daye (Virosstek), Mary Christina (Green); BelC 62, BA; ColTS 65, BD; FulGrad 72, PhD; O 65, EastAL Pby; Recd PCA Feb 1, 00, Cov Pby; astp Independent P Ch, Memphis, TN, 00-09; hr 09

230 Forest Lake Drive, Madison, MS 39110   Covenant
HR

Ellerbee, Jason – astp Briarwood P Ch, Birmingham, AL, 18-

2200 Briarwood Way, Birmingham, AL 35243   Evangel
E-mail: jellerbee@briarwood.org
Briarwood Presbyterian Church

Elliott, Gary H. – op Trin P Msn, Griffin, GA, 87-91; ob t CovCS, 91-94; ob headm Cov Ac, Macon, GA, 94-01; p Brookwood P Ch, Snellville, GA, 01-

3502 Harvest Moon Trace, Lilburn, GA 30047 – 678-344-0797   Metro Atlanta
Brookwood Presbyterian Church – 770-972-4827

Elliott, Jeffrey Thane – b Oak Park, IL, Apr 6, 61; f James H.; m Kay Halstead; w Margaret Hasty, Fayetteville, NC, Jul 30, 88; WFU 79-83, BA; WTS 88, MDiv; RTS 02, DMin; L Mar 90, DMV Pby; O a Feb 91, MSVal Pby; int McLean P Ch, McLean, VA, 88-89; astp, ms/sa First P Ch, Jackson, MS, 90-98; astp Pear Orchard P Ch, Ridgeland, MS, 99-00, ascp 00-09; srp New Cov P Ch, Virginia Beach, VA, 09-

333 Preservation Reach, Chesapeake, VA 23320   Tidewater
E-mail: jelliott1961@gmail.com
New Covenant Presbyterian Church – 757-467-5945

Elliott, Kenneth Ray – b Batesville, IN, Sept 12, 53; f Kenneth G.(d); m Kathryn; w Linda Colleen Malinski, Tampa, FL, Jun 15, 74; chdn Jeremy Paul, Albrey Michelle, Matthew Kennon; BelC 72-76, BA; USF 77-81, MA; RTS 81-84, MDiv; MSU 07, PhD; USWarCollege, 12; O Jun 86, MSVal Pby; lib RTS, 81-87; mgr RTS Bookstore, 87-93; Chap MSANG 172 AW Jackson, 86-13; ss Shiloh P Ch, Pickens, MS, 87-18; lib RTS, 93-13; Dean Adult Stud, BelhC, 13-18; *Anglican Church Policy, Eighteenth Century Conflict, and the American Episcopate*, 11; hr 18

506 Church Street, Clinton, MS 39056 – 601-506-5865   Mississippi Valley
E-mail: knik7777@gmail.com
HR

Elliott, Timothy – O Feb 23, 97, GrLks Pby; p Good Shepherd P Ch, Warsaw, IN, 97, wc 98; astp Christ Cov Ref (PCA), Reynoldsburg, OH, 98-00; ob New Hope CRC, Monsey, NY, 00-04; wc 04-10, ob 10-17; astp New Hope P Ch in America, Olathe, KS, 17-

716 East 70th Terrace, Kansas City, MO 64131 – 707-293-5175   New York State
E-mail: elliotts916@hotmail.com
New Hope Presbyterian Church in America – 913-782-7325

Ellis, Carl F., Jr. – b Brooklyn, NY, Nov 3, 46; f Carl F. Sr., m Mildred Ellis Protho; w Karen Angela Bishop, Baltimore, MD, Aug 20, 11; chdn Carl F. III, Nicole R.; Hampton 70, BA; WTS 79, MAR; OxfordGrad 10, PhD; ev Delmarva Pby, 84-89: ap Forest Park Comm Ch, Baltimore, MD, 85- 87, wc S9-92; ascp New City Flwsp, Chattanooga, TN. 92-95; ob Project Joseph, 96-; Ellis Perspectives, 11-; WTS, 06-09; asst prof Redeemer sem, Dallas, TX. 09-15; ascp New City Flwsp, Chattanooga, TN. 11-15; prof RTS, 16-; *Free At Last?* 96; *Going Global*, 05; *Saving Our Sons*, 07

4010 Melinda Drive, Chattanooga, TN 37416-3003 – 423-280-4183   Tennessee Valley
E-mail: carlellisjr@gmail.com
Project Joseph
Ellis Perspectives - 423-280-4183
Reformed Theological Seminary

Ellis, Frank Compton, Jr. – b Montgomery, AL, Jul 7, 53; f Frank C.; m Gertrude Eatman; w Joan Buchanan, Cullman, AL, Feb 13, 93; chdn Hannah C. Crisler, Frank Compton III; AU 75, BS, 83, BS; CTS 10, MDiv; O Jan 15, 12, SEAL Pby; p Ozark P Ch, Ozark, AL, 12-

616 Country Club Drive, Ozark, AL 36360 – 334-733-1023   Southeast Alabama
E-mail: fellisjr@gmail.com
Ozark Presbyterian Church – 334-774-5494

Ellis, J. David – b Lafayette, IN, Jan 27, 62; f John; m Shirley Hall; w Sebeyda Valle, Queens, NY, Jul 7, 90; chdn Chris Rios, Ingrid Rios, Josiah, Kendra; GrnvC, BA; AsbTS 86-89; NYTS 91-93, MDiv; CTS 14, DMin; L 86, FreeMeth; O 90, FreeMeth; Recd PCA 01, MNY Pby; chp, op Astoria Comm Ch, Astoria, NY, 01-05, srp 05-12; p Queens P Ch, Long Island City, NY, 12-13; ascp 13-17; p Astoria Comm Ch, Long Island, City, NY, 17-

PO Box 2102, Astoria, NY 11106 – 718-305-8783   Metropolitan New York
E-mail: David@astoriachurch.org
Astoria Community Church – 718-721-3440

Ellis, Robert Peter – b Plainfield, NJ, Mar 3, 47; f William; m Dorothy Kreyling; w Susan Croxton, Baltimore, MD, Aug 31, 79; chdn Daniel, Michelle, Shiloh, Samuel; JHU 69, BS, 73, MS; UB 76, JD; CTS 88, MDiv; L Jan 16, 88, MO Pby; O Mar 19, 89, Ill Pby; DCE Covenant P Ch, St. Louis, MO, 85-88; p Bethel Ref P Ch, Sparta, IL, 89-16; hr 16

113 Lions Gate Road, Savannah, GA 31419 – 912-777-4676   Illiana
E-mail: twinrpe@gmail.com
HR

Ellis, Ronald Raymond – b Havre, MT, May 14, 47; f Raymond W.; m Eva E. Maze; w Catherine L. Watts, Birmingham, AL, May 18, 74; chdn Thomas, Tabitha (Lookabill), Timothy, Titus, Talitha(Tucker); AU 83, BS; SCS 88-90, MDiv; O May 5, 96, RMtn Pby; mis MTW Kang-Won-Do, South Korea, 75-88; chp, ss Gallatin Valley P Ch, Bozeman, MT, 90-96, op 96-98; op, chp Elkhorn P Msn, Helena, MT, 98-02; mis MTW, Evangelical P Ch (GPCNZ), ChristChurch, New Zealand, 04-08; op, evan New Covenant P Msn, Sheridan, WY, 09-16; hr 16

54 Country Castle Lane, Glasgow, VA 24555 – 307-763-2593　　　　　　　　　　Rocky Mountain
E-mail: ron.cathy.ellis@gmail.com
HR

Ellis, Thomas Talbot – b Birmingham, AL, Jan 15, 41; f Talbot; m Mary Lanier; DavC 59-60; BelC 60-63, BA; ColTS 64-66, DMin; O Jul 66, EastAL pby; p First P Ch, Florala, AL, 66-69; p Eastside P Ch, Gadsden, AL, 69-74; t Minor CS, B'ham, AL, 74-75; p Capitol View P Ch, Atlanta, GA , 75-84; p Northshore P Ch, Jacksonville, FL, 84-93; p Grace OPC, Rocky Mount, VA, 93-99; p Christ P Ch, Kansas City, MO, 00-11; hr

5 Crimson Glory Way, Travelers Rest, SC 29690　　　　　　　　　　　　　　　　　Heartland
HR

Elswick, Anthony – O Jun 3, 18, SWFL Pby; fm MTW, 18-

c/o Mission to the World – 863-265-0242　　　　　　　　　　　　　　　Southwest Florida
E-mail: anthonyelswich@gmail.com
PCA Mission to the World

Ely, David Patrick – b Birmingham, AL; f Bruce; m Karen; w Mary Beth Stegall, Birmingham, AL, Jun 24, 06; chdn Caroline, Elizabeth Joy, Anna, Andrew; AU 06, BS; CTS 12, MDiv; O Aug 5, 12, SavRiv Pby; astp Westminster P Ch, Martinez, GA, 12-14; campm RUF, Furman, 14-

400 Cold Branch Way, Greenville, SC 29609　　　　　　　　　　　　　　　　　　Calvary
E-mail: david.ely@ruf.org
PCA Reformed University Fellowship

Emberger, Bob – ob ex dir, Whosoever Gospel Msn

8126 Hennig Street, Philadelphia, PA 19111 – 215-718-7691　　　　　　　　　Philadelphia
E-mail: remberger@whosoevergospel.org
Whosoever Gospel Mission

Emerick, Ederson – w Claudia; chdn Rebeca, Lucas, Gabriel; SemTeolPres, Brazil 96-99, ThB; CPAJ, Brazil 02-04, MAC; L Dec 00, PCES Brazil; p Redentor P Ch, South River, 04-09; op Emanuel P Msn Ch, Boca Raton, FL, 09-14; p 14-

21908 Paletto Circle North #2A, Boca Raton, FL 33433 – 561-577-2140　　　　Gulfstream
E-mail: eemerick_4@hotmail.com
Emanuel Presbyterian Church – 561-577-2140

Emerson, Chuck – b Pittsburgh, PA, Jan 30, 55; f Leslie F.; m Dorothy Brouwer; w Debbie Jean Barr, Pittsburgh, PA, Dec 4, 82; chdn David Emmanuel, Rachel Elizabeth; PASU 77, BS, 80, MS; WTS 91, MDiv; O , MetAtl Pby; ob Equipping Leaders Int, Inc., 10-; RUFI, GATech, 10-

4872 Sturbridge Crescent, Roswell, GA 30075 – 770-355-1528　　　　　　　　Metro Atlanta
E-mail: c_emerson55@bellsouth.net
Equipping Leaders International, Inc.
Reformed University Fellowship International

Emerson, Daniel – O Jul 11, 10, NYS Pby, mis 10-

c/o 206 Greenfield Avenue, Ballston Spa, NY 12020– 518-409-0652   New York State
E-mail: dnmjsaemerson@gmail.com

Emmanouilidis, Kostas – ob 10-

15 Bowen Street, Newton, MA 02459   Southern New England

Emmanuel, Joachim J. – b St. Lucia, Jamaica, Jan 30, 51; f Henry; m Martha Blanchard; w Fay Groves, Jamaica, Sept 16, 75; chdn Jay, Kay; JBC 71-75, ThB; NU 86-90; JBC, dipl; O, Ev Ch of West Indies; Recd PCA Jul 18, 95, SFL Pby; chp Grenada, 75-79; p St. Lucia Ch, 79-83; chp Florida, 89-96; op; hr 17; Lighthouse Gospel Comm Msn, Coral Springs, FL, 96-02, wc 02-03; ob Ministries in Action, 03-

8542 NW 25th Place, Coral Springs, FL 33065 – 954-341-7721   South Florida
E-mail: Jman1241@myacc.net
HR

England, Brent F. – ob 12-14; Chap Federal Medical Center, Ayer, MA, 14-

E-mail: brentski76@yahoo.com   Southern New England
Federal Medical Center, Ayer, MA

Engle, Paul Edward – b Buffalo, NY, Aug 19, 42; f George; m Marion; w Margaret Walker, Vineland, NJ, Dec 20, 69; chdn Christine Anne, Heather Elizabeth; HougC 60-64, BA; WheatGrS 64-67, MDiv; WTS 75-77, DMin; L 72, EFC; O 77, EFC; Recd PCA 85, GrLks Pby; ap Lownes Free Ch, Springfield, PA, 67-72; p Christ Ch, Branford, CT, 72-77; p Village Ch, Lincolnshire, IL, 77-86; instr TEDS, 80-85; p Christ Ch, Grand Rapids, MI, 86-89; vis lect/prof RTS, RTSFL, RTSNC; vis lect/prof KTS; ob Baker Book House, 91-99; ob Zondervan Publishing House, 99-09; hr 09; vis lect/prof NGTS; *Discovering the Fullness of Worship*, 78; *Worship Planbook*, 81; *The Governor Drove Us Up the Wall*, 85; co-auth, *Minister's Service Manual*, 80; auth *Guarding and Growing*, 88; ed *Baker's Wedding Handbook*, 94; ed *Baker's Funeral Handbook*, 96; *Baker's Worship Handbook*, 98; *God's Answers for Life's Needs*, 00; *The Baker Wedding Handbook*, 17; *The Baker Funeral Handbook*, 17

5233 Shannamara Drive, Matthews, NC 28104 – 616-635-1418   Great Lakes
E-mail: geomaxpaul@gmail.com
HR

Englestad, Gary Clarke – b Meadville, PA, Jun 30, 52; f Donald Martin; m Carol Mae Anderson; w Marilyn Louise Davis, Ft. Washington, PA, Jun 14, 75; chdn Rebecca Lynn, Sarah Elizabeth; DrexU 75, BS BusAdmin; BibTS 79, MDiv; O Jun 79; yp Ch of the Open Door, 75-79; ap 79-81; p Evang Ch, Chesapeake, VA, 82-85; sec TRM, 83, pres 84; Chap Haddon Township PD, 90-; p Evangelical P Ch, Mount Laurel, NJ, 85-14; ascp Grace P Ch, Mount Laurel, NJ, 14-17; hr 17; treas NJ pby, 91-

134 Penn Avenue, Westmont, NJ 08108-2035 – 856-858-3231   New Jersey
E-mail: genglestad@aol.com
HR

Entrekin, D. Rodney – b Cullman, AL, Jul 27, 55; f James E.; m Martha Paschal; w Janice Clonts (d) (2) Christy, Jun 23, 07; chdn Ellen Ruth, Catherine Elizabeth, David Rodney Jr., William Howard, William Mobley Hill, Jamalyn Hill, Elizabeth Hill, Mary Clare Hill, Lillian Hill; JAXSU, BS; CTS, MDiv; O Sept 8, 91, NGA Pby; admin, DChPl Perimeter Ministries, Atlanta, GA, 91-93; op Oakwood P Ch, San Antonio, TX, 93-96, p 97-99; coord, chp MNA, 99-01; ascp Ivy Creek Ch, Lawrenceville, GA, 01-03; ascp Big Creek Ch, Alpharetta, GA, 03-05; ob exec dir Church Multiplication Ministries, 05-09; op ChristCh Suwanee, Suwanee, GA, 09-13, p 13-

941 Moores Walk Lane, Suwanee, GA 30024 – 404-451-8122   Georgia Foothills
E-mail: rod@christchurchsuwanee.org
ChristChurch Suwanee – 404-451-8122

Entrekin, Jonathan – Chap USArmy, 07-

2604 Placid Avenue NW, Olympia, WA 98502　　　　　　　　　　Tennessee Valley
United States Army

Eom, Timothy – O Nov 16, 14, KorSE Pby; astp New Ch of Atlanta, Peachtree Corners, GA, 14-17

E-mail: cftimothy@gmail.com　　　　　　　　　　　　　　　　Korean Southeastern

Eppstein, Alex – b Hong Kong; w Amy; chdn Elias Kang, Ezra Alexander; UPA 05, BA; WSCAL 12, MDiv; O Apr 8, 17, Ill Pby; p Bethel Ref P Ch, Sparta, IL, 17-

1004 Hillcrest Drive, Sparta, IL 62286　　　　　　　　　　　　　　Illiana
E-mail: alex.eppstein@gmail.com
Bethel Reformed Presbyterian Church – 618-443-3521

Erwin, Don – b Ft. Worth, TX, Feb 3, 49; f Paul F.; m Frances Florrow; w Jacqueline Alford, Cleveland, MS, May 26, 74; chdn Andrew, Micah, Susanna; UTXA 71, BA; UTXD 72, cert; DTS 77, ThM; L May 23, 00, Cov Pby; Recd PCA May 22, 00, Cov Pby; p Ft. Worth Bible Ch, 76-77; mis SIM, 79-93; p Fellowship Ch, Russellville, AR, 93-97; ss, op Covenant P Ch, Russellville, AR, 00-01, p 01-13; ob Chap Arkansas Hospice, 13-

1714 West 17th Circle, Russellville, AR 72801 – 479-857-3019　　　　Covenant
E-mail: dperwin49@gmail.com
Arkansas Hospice – 479-498-2050

Esswein, Matt – b Long Beach, CA, Jun 8, 85; f Daniel P.; m Mary Kay Schmedake; w Sarah Christine Gothold, Chesterfield, MO, Jul 12, 14; CPStU 07, BS; CTS 12, MDiv; O Oct 27, 13, MO Pby; astp Chesterfield P Ch, Chesterfield, MO, 13-

581 Highland Ridge Drive, Ballwin, MO 63011　　　　　　　　　　Missouri
E-mail: matte@chespres.org
Chesterfield Presbyterian Church – 636-394-3337

Estock, Stephen T. – b Mobile, AL, Apr 10, 64; f Harold M; m D. Lynette Upchurch; w Susan Marie Curry, San Bernardino, CA, Sept 9, 90; chdn Brandon Michael, Nathan Thomas, Morgan Marie; RhC 82-86, BA; CTS 91-95, MDiv; Capella 08, PhD; O Aug 13, 95, SEAL Pby; astp Covenant P Ch, Montgomery, AL, 95-96, ascp 97-99, srp 99-02; ascp Kirk of the Hills P Ch, St. Louis, MO, 02-12; coord CDM, 13-

1700 North Brown Road #102, Lawrenceville, GA 30043 – 770-708-7591　　Georgia Foothills
E-mail: sestock@pcanet.org
PCA Committee on Discipleship Ministries – 678-825-1100

Etienne, Esaie – op El Shaddai Missionary Ch, Winter Haven, FL, 01-05; mis MTW, Haiti, 05-

c/o Mission to the World　　　　　　　　　　　　　　　　　Southwest Florida
E-mail: zatachie@juno.com
PCA Mission to the World

Eubanks, John Edgar Jr. – b Columbia, SC, Nov 26, 72; f John Sr.; m MaryAnn Smith; w Martha Carey Ward, Columbia, SC, Mar 7, 98; chdn John Edgar III; Molly Elizabeth; Abigail Ellis; Anna Caroline; USC 99, BA; CTS 06, MDiv; L Oct 07, Cov Pby; O Feb 17, 08, Cov Pby; ss Hickory Withe P Ch, Eads, TN, 07, srp 08-11; p Dove Mountain Ch, Oro Valley, AZ, 11-13; ob srp Trinity Ref Ch, Rossville, TN, 17-; "Leading Students in Worship," *Youthworker Journal*, 99; co-auth *Covenant Discipleship Communicant's*

MINISTERIAL DIRECTORY

Eubanks, John Edgar Jr., continued
Curriculum, 00; contr *byFaith* mag; contr *Relevant* mag (online); ed *William the Baptist*, 09; *For All the Saints: Praying for the Church*, 10; *Grafted Into the Vine: Rethinking Biblical Church Membership*, 11; *From MDiv to Rev.: Making an Effective Transition from Seminary into Pastoral Ministry*, 11

195 Mack Edwards Drive, Oakland, TN 38060 – 520-619-0927   Southwest
E-mail: ed@eubankshouse.org
Trinity Reformed Church (non-PCA)

Eudaly, Dustyn – w Julie; chdn Elizabeth Claire, Mary Ellen, William Langford, Katherine Brainerd; SMU 95, BA; WTS 02, MDiv; O Jun 04, SWFL Pby; ascp Holy Trin P Ch, Tampa, FL, 04-14; ob 14-17; ascp Holy Trin P Ch, Tampa, FL, 17-

4625 Lowell Avenue, Tampa, FL 33629 – 813-777-5208   Southwest Florida
E-mail: deudaly@holytrinitypca.org
Holy Trinity Presbyterian Church – 813-259-3500

Eun, Sang Ki – b South Korea, Jan 1, 40; f Hi-Bong Eun; m Kap Kyung Park; w June Yun, Atlanta, GA, Mar 31, 78; chdn Denny; KCC 64, BA; WashTS 97, MDiv; RegU, doct stu; O Oct 5, 98; Recd PCA Oct 5, 98, KorCap Pby; fndr Multi-cultural praising & prayer, DC; coord Nat'l Day of Prayer, DC; op Peniel P Ch, Springfield, VA, 00-10; hr 10

1805 Faversham Way, Woodbridge, VA 22192 – 703-451-4653   Korean Capital
E-mail: eun_steve@hotmail.com
HR

Eun, Sang-Kee – b Taegu, Kor, Jan 15, 39; f In-Sool; m Tae-Im; w Seung-Bok Paik, Taegu, Kor, Apr 7, 70; chdn Timothy, Daniel, John; KBNU 64; HTS 74; WTS 86-88; O Aug 30, 76, BPC, Korea; Recd PCA Jan 90; op State College Korean Ch, State College, PA, 88-09; hr

24918 Castleton Drive, Chantilly, VA 20152 – 814-234-7210   Korean Eastern
E-mail: skeun2@hotmail.com
HR

Eusey, Matthew – astp Redeemer Redmond Ch, Redmond, WA, 08-10; ip, ss Bellewood P Ch, Bellevue, WA, 10-11; ob ascp Church of the Savior, Wayne, PA, 11-14; p Trinity Ch Central Oahu, Mililani, HI, 14-

95-1013 Moaula Street, Mililani, HI 96789 – 484-318-0487   Northern California
E-mail: matt@ttcoahu.org
Trinity Church Central Oahu – 808-625-5055

Eutsey, Kevin – w Debbie; chdn William, Barbara; LibU, BS; RPTS, MDiv; O Oct 95, Hrtg Pby; astp Reformed P Ch, Boothwyn, PA, 94-03; astp Westminster P Ch, Muncie, IN, 03-05; astp Ingleside P Ch, Lawrenceville, GA, 05-13; astp Grayson Ch Mission, Lawrenceville, GA, 15-

752 Tanner's Point Drive, Lawrenceville, GA 30044 – 770-963-3842   Georgia Foothills
E-mail: keutsey@bellsouth.net
Grayson Church Mission

Evans, Brad D. – b Grove City, PA, Jun 9, 51; f Jack T.; m Joanne Carlson; w Patsy Wheatley, Covington, PA, Jul 7, 73; chdn Megan A., Brent C.; PASU 73, BA; WTS 78, MDiv; CTS 06, DMin; L 78, Phil Pby (RPCES); O 79, Phil Pby (RPCES); ap Willow Grove, PA, 79-80; p Presbyterian Ch of Coventry, Coventry, CT, 80-

35 Grant Hill Road, Coventry, CT 06238-1115 – 860-498-5017   Southern New England
E-mail: pastorbradevans@aol.com
Presbyterian Church of Coventry – 860-742-7222

Evans, Glenn – ascp Glasgow Ref P Ch, Bear, DE, 04-06; op Eastern Shore Ref P Ch, Centreville, MD, 05-06; op Glasgow Ref - Southern Kent, Dover, DE, 05-06; ss Heritage P Ch, New Castle, DE, 06-07; p 07-

18 East Shakespeare Drive, Middletown, DE 19709 – 302-449-0552   Heritage
Heritage Presbyterian Church – 302-328-3800

Evans, John Frederick – b Greensboro, NC, Dec 12, 62; f Frederick Walter Jr.; m Sarah Irene Payne; w Maxine Elizabeth Jennings, Bluefield, WV, Nov 9, 85; chdn Henry Martyn, Grace Elisabeth (Schroeder), Daniel Rowland; CalvC 81-84, BA; CBS 84-85, grad wk; CTS 86-89, MDiv, 95, ThM; UStel 06, DTh; CU, 10, 11; L Apr 21, 90, MO Pby; O Sept 29, 91, WCar Pby; int Covenant OPC, Burtonsville, MD, 90-91; p Faith P Ch, Morganton, NC, 91-96; mis SIM, Zambia, 97-08; mis Kenya 09-17; prof NEGST 09-17; p Covenant P Ch, Sun City West, AZ, 17-; Edtl Bd, *Journal for the Evangelical Study of the Old Testament*, 11-; Edtl Bd, *Sapientia Logos,* 16-18; "Death-Dealing Witchcraft in the Bible? Notes on the Condemnation of the 'Daughters' in Ezekiel 13:17-23," *Tyndale Bulletin* 65, 14; *A Guide to Biblical Commentaries & Reference Works,* 10th ed, 16; *You Shall Know that I Am Yahweh: An Inner-Biblical Interpretation of Ezekiel's Recognition Formula,* 19

13601 Aleppo Drive, Sun City West, AZ 85375 – 317-827-9444   Arizona
E-mail: pastorjohnfevans@gmail.com
Covenant Presbyterian Church – 623-584-7417

Evans, John M. – w Deborah, Aug 26, 90; chdn Casey, Mallory, Audrey; NGTS, MDiv; O Aug 14, 05, North GA; astp Intown Comm Ch, Atlanta, GA, 05-09; astp Briarwood P Ch, Birmingham, AL, 09-

3091 Thrasher Lane, Birmingham, AL 35244 – 205-776-5181   Evangel
E-mail: jevans@briarwood.org
Briarwood Presbyterian Church – 205-776-5200

Evans, Luke – b Jul 1, 80; f Dr. David L.; m Sally; w Marianne Mackenzie Moldovan, Jan 8, 05; chdn Nathaniel Luke, Ainsley Meredith, Benjamin Birch; BayU 02, BA; WTS 06, MDiv; astp Rincon Mountain P Ch, Tucson, AZ, 07-09; ascp 09-13; op Christ Ch SA, San Antonio, TX, 13-16, p 16-

221 Nandina, Cibolo, TX 78108   South Texas
E-mail: lukedevans@gmail.com
Christ Church San Antonio – 210-306-4411

Evans, Robert S. – b Chicago, IL, Feb 5, 50; f Robert David; m Helen Jean Brammer; w Debra Jean Elrod, Anderson, SC, Jun 8, 74; chdn Robert, Andrew, Kathryn; BGSU 72, BS; TSIL 79, MDiv; L 79; O Oct 3, 80, OPC; Recd PCA Aug 13, 91, GulCst Pby; p Hope P Ch, Libertyville, IL, 80-84; p Calvary P Ch, Tallahassee, FL, 84-91; astp Wildwood P Ch, Tallahassee, FL, 91-95, ascp 95-96, srp 96-17, astp 17-

7120 Heritage Ridge Road, Tallahassee, FL 32312-6706   Gulf Coast
Wildwood Presbyterian Church – 850-894-1400

Evans, Rufus Norman – b Burlington, NC, Aug 20, 50; f William Foy; m Geneva Massey; w Linda Felty, Burlington, NC, Mar 13, 71; chdn Lorraine Geneva, Rufus Daniel, Jeremy Douglas; KgC 68-73, BA; RTS 74-76, MDiv; O Jul 76, Car Pby; p Faith P Ch, Mooresville, NC, 76-78; p Faith P Ch, Charleston, WV, 78-84; p Trinity Ref P Ch, Wilmington, NC, 84-98; sc Ecar Pby, 89-95, wc 98; ss Village Chapel P Ch, New Bern, NC, 98-99, p 99-

113 Massachusetts Road, New Bern, NC 28562 – 252-638-8259   Eastern Carolina
E-mail: evans.norm50@gmail.com
Village Chapel Presbyterian Church – 252-633-2005

MINISTERIAL DIRECTORY 189

Evans, William III – w Dana; chdn Madison, Lilly, Slaton; UT, BA; CTS, MDiv; O Feb 04, Cov Pby; mis MTW, Nairn, UK, 04-08; ascp Severna Park Evan P Ch, Pasadena, MD, 08- 17; p First P Ch at Dyersburg, Dyersburg, TN, 17-

111 Gordon Street, Dyersburg, TN 38024   Covenant
E-mail: pastorbill.fpcdyersburg@gmail.com
First Presbyterian Church at Dyersburg – 731-285-6284

Evaul, Philip Dudley – b Chicago, IL, Oct 20, 54; f Philip Oscar; m Margaret Cloud; w Melinda Watterson, Crossnore, NC, Mar 25, 78; chdn Brian Jeremy, Amanda Michelle; UNC 72-76, BA; CTS 78-81, MDiv; L Sept 91, Wcar Pby; O Jan 12, 92, Wcar Pby; ss Blevins Creek Chapel, Elk Park, NC, 81-85; Chap BSA Camp, Goshen, VA, summer 80; DCE Fletcher UMC, 89-90; p Covenant P Ch, Waynesville, NC, 91-96; ob p Sale Creek Indep Pres. Ch, Sale Creek, TN, 96-

11408 North Oak Street, Soddy Daisy, TN 37379-6740 – 423-332-3907   Tennessee Valley
Sale Creek Independent Presbyterian Church (non PCA)
15017 Dayton Pike, Sale Creek, TN 37373

Everitt, Elliott – O Aug 19, 12, MSVal Pby; ascp First P Ch, Yazoo City, MS, 12-13; campm RUF, Mercer U, 13-17; campm RUF, MSU, 17-

201 Greenbriar Street, Starkville, MS 39759 – 662-705-1809   Covenant
E-mail: elliott.everitt@ruf.org
PCA Reformed University Fellowship

Ew, Andy – O Jan 18, 14, Phil Pby; astp Philadelphia Bible Ref Ch, Wynnewood, PA, 14-15; astp Trinity Park Ch, Morrisville, NC, 15-

1915 Kelly Glen Drive, Apex, NC 27502   Eastern Carolina
E-mail: andyew79@gmail.com
Trinity Park Church – 919-439-3718

Ewing, Graydon Allan – O Oct 13, 13, SW Pby; astp New Valley Ch, Phoenix, AZ, 13-16; ascp 17-

863 East Edgemont Avenue, Phoenix, AZ 85006   Southwest
E-mail: gray@newvalleychurch.org
New Valley Church – 480-940-5560

Ewing, Spencer William – O Sept 16, 17, EPA Pby; op Christ the King P Ch, Willow Grove, PA, 17-

2405 Shelimire Avenue, Philadelphia, PA 19152 – 541-778-2405   Eastern Pennsylvania
Christ the King Presbyterian Church – 215-659-0554

Eyrich, Howard A. – b Reading, PA, Feb 12, 39; f Howard Irwin; m Mary Catherine Ulrich; w Pamela Jayne Clark, Atlanta, GA, Sept 1, 62; chdn Tamela Jayne, David Kenneth; BJU 62, BA; FTS 65, BD; DTS 68, ThM; LibU 92, MA; O May 68, Colonial Hills (SBC); Recd PCA May 83, SFL Pby; dean, prof LanBC, 68-70; p Calvary Fell Ch, Downingtown, PA, 70-75; couns, lect CCEF, Philadelphia, PA, 75-81; ap Granada P Ch, Coral Gables, FL, 81-85; asst prof CTS, 86-94; ap, couns Kirk of the Hills P Ch, St. Louis, MO, 86-89; ob exec dir CBCE, St. Louis, MO, 91-94; p Knollwood P Ch, Sylacauga, AL, 94-97; astp Briarwood P Ch, Birmingham, AL, 97-98; chmn BhamTS, Dept of Biblical Couns; ascp Briarwood P Ch, Birmingham, AL, 98-00; ob prof ErskTS, 00; dean BhamTS, 01-03; ascp Briarwood P Ch, Birmingham, AL, 01-17; pres BhamTS, 03-17; dir DMin prog; couns The Owen Center, Auburn, AL; mbr The Biblical Counseling Coalition, fell Assoc Cert Biblical Couns; hr; *Three to Get Ready: A Premarital Manual*; *The Christian Handbook on Aging*; *Totally Sufficient: Why the Bible is All You Need*; co-auth *Curing the Heart;* ed *What To Do When; Grief: Learning to Live With Loss; The Art of Aging; A*

Eyrich, Howard A., continued
Call to Christian Patriotism; The Pursuit of Wisdom: Key to Success in Life from Proverbs 1-10; contr *Paul the Counselor, Paul's Model for Change* (co-auth Jeffery Young) and *A Biblical Understanding of Anxiety* (co-auth Pamela Eyrich), 14; *Scripture and Counseling, Caution: Counseling Systems Are Belief Systems,* 14; on Kindle: *Voting: An American Privilege,* 14; *Christian Decision Making and the Will of God,* 14; *Life Lessons from Ancient Prophets; After the Affair: Rebuilding Your Trust; Rebuilding Your Marriage;* co-auth *Hope for New Beginnings;* The Art of Aging: Preparing and Caring (rev and exp version of *The Art of Aging*)

3867 James Hill Circle, Hoover, AL 35226 – 205-527-3444　　　　　　　　　Evangel
E-mail: earkiel@bellsouth.net
HR

　　Faber, Dan A. – b Plymouth, IN, Jan 28, 53; f John Albert; m Carol Maxine; w Margaret Dale Compton, Montgomery, AL, May 24, 75; chdn Kristen Elizabeth, Carol Ann, Martha Eloise; BelC 71-75, BA; RTS 75-78, MDiv; O Jul 16, 78, MSVal Pby; p First P Ch, Union, MS, 78-81; p Knollwood P Ch, Sylacauga, AL, 81-86; mis MTW, Mexico, 86-92; astp Chapelgate P Ch, Marriottsville, MD, 92-93; ascp 93-03; astp Trinity P Ch, Montgomery, AL, 03-09

1619 Wentworth Drive, Montgomery, AL 36106 – 334-272-1686　　　　　Southeast Alabama

　　Fagerheim, Keith Andrew – b Atlantic City, NJ; f Rev. F. Kenneth; m Judith Soper; w Doreen Lynette Marshall, Newfane, NY, Dec 30, 95; chdn Andrew, Matthew; HougC 91-95, BA; RTSFL 96-99, MDiv; L May 01, GulCst Pby; O Oct 01, GulCst Pby; astp, ydir Covenant P Ch, Panama City, FL, 99-03; wc 03; Covenant Bible Ch, NY, 05-07; ascp Armor Bible P Ch, Orchard Park, NY, 07-09; ascp Ch of the Redeemer, Cortland, NY, 12-15; ip New Hope P Ch, Vestal, NY, 15-17

3975 Woodside Road, Cortland, NY 13045 – 607-662-4009　　　　　　　　New York State
E-mail: kfagerheim@twcny.rr.com

　　Fagerheim, Kenneth – b Pt. Pleasant, NJ, Sept 26, 38; f Olav; m Frances Phillips; w Judith Soper, Pleasantville, NJ, Dec 27, 58; chdn Cynthia (Doherty), Karen (Kupp), Kristin (Kapp), Erik, Keith; MuhC 60, BS; REpS 83, MDiv; chp Resurrection REC, Rochester, NY, 83-84; p Wagner Memorial REC, Ventnor, NJ, 85-01, hr 02

950 Willow Valley Lakes Drive H412　　　　　　　　　　　　　　Susquehanna Valley
Willow Street, PA 17584 – 717-464-0580
E-mail: FKFagerheim@Hotmail.com
HR

　　Faichney, Thomas J. – w Kristina Mary; chdn Lillian Grace, Sarah Irene, Jocelyn Hope, Rachel Alexandria; CanBC 89, BA; UWatO 91, BA; WSCAL 98, MATS; RTSFL 01, MDiv; O Jan 23, 94, C&MA; Recd PCA 00, NGA Pby; astp Guelph All Ch, Ontario, 90-91; exec dir Ligonier Min, Canada, 91-95; p Escondido All Ch, 96-97; mis MTW, 98-00; dirStSvs RTS Atlanta, 00-01; Chap USArmy, 02-

5020 Arcadia Road, Columbia, SC 29206　　　　　　　　　　　　　Northwest Georgia
United States Army

　　Fair, Earl F. – b North Washington, PA; f Frank F.; m Selma L.; w Glenda L. Sherwin, Fairview, PA, Jul 12, 57; chdn Mark Calvin, Matthew Lee; SRU 55, BS; UPitt; PittsTS 61, MDiv; O May 61, Beaver-Butler Pby; hm NV, 61-63; hm Elba, NY, 63-65; hm Wilkinsburg, PA, 66-78; p Middlesex P Ch, Butler, PA, 78-92; ob ss Grace Ref P Ch, Monroeville, PA, 93-94; p Rocky Springs P Ch, Harrisville, PA, 93-01; hr 02

139 Haysville Road, Karns City, PA 16041 – 724-445-3247　　　　　　　　　Ascension
HR

MINISTERIAL DIRECTORY

Fair, Jeremy – b Tulsa, OK, Aug 28, 76; f Steven; m Debbie; w Kimberly, Plano, TX, Dec 18, 99; chdn Caedmon Lee, Creth Thomas, Cale Haddon, Cooper Grace; DBU 99, BA; SWBTS 05, MDiv; O Feb 7, 06, GulCst Pby; astp Cottonwood Creek Bapt Ch, Allen, TX, 00-04; ascp Eastern Shore P Ch, Fairhope, AL, 04-08; srp Arlington P Ch, Arlington, TX, 08-11; srp Christ P Ch, Tulsa, OK, 12-

4913 East 88th Place, Tulsa, OK 74137 Hills and Plains
E-mail: j.fair@cpctulsa.com
Christ Presbyterian Church – 918-749-1629

Fairbrother, Mark E. – b Walnut Creek, CA, Jan 22, 55; f Forrest Jr.; m Shirley Hilton Lantz; w Marise Lynn Walker, Pleasanton, CA, Jun 12, 76; chdn Jonathan Mark, Suzanne Rochelle; UCD 74-75; BIOLA 75-79, BA; WTS 79-82, MAR, MDiv; GCTS 03, ThM; L Sept 85; O Jul 86, Pac Pby; astp Comm Bible Ch C&MA, 83-85; astp Covenant P Ch, Orange, CA, 85-87; op Peninsula P Ch, Monterey Peninsula, CA, 87-91, p 91-95; Chap (1LT) USAR, 6219th Reception Batt, 89-92; Chap (CPT) USAR, 14th Psych Oper Batt, 92-95; Chap (CPT) 101st Airborne Division (Air Assault), 101st AVN Bde, astp, Soldiers Chapel, Ft. Campbell, KY, 96-97; Chap (MAJ) USArmy, 160th Special Operations Aviation Regiment (Airborne), astp, Hope Chapel, Ft. Campbell, KY, 98-02; Chap (MAJ) USArmy, Ist Brig., 1st Armor Division, srp Friedberg Kaserne Chapel, 00-02; stu GCTS, 03; Chap USArmy, Ft. Leavenworth, KS, 03-06 astp, Adult Education, Reformed Prison Fellowship (Ft. Leavenworth Disciplinary Barracks); lect USACGS, 04-06; Chap (MAJ), US Army, Ft. Bragg, NC, XVIII Airborne Corps, 06-07; Chap (MAJ), US Army, 1st Bde Combat Team, 82d Airborne DIV, 07-08; Chap (LTC), US Army, Fort Gillem, GA, HQ First US Army, 09-10; Chap (LTC), West Point, NY, Center for the Army Profession and Ethic (CAPE), astp, Cadet Chapel, Adult Education teacher 10-13; Chap (COL), Fort Shafter, HI, Eighth Theatre Sustainment Command, 14-16, Command Chaplain, srp, Ft. DeRussy Chapel, Ft. DeRussy, Waikiki; ip Cheyenne Mountain P Ch, Colorado Springs, CO, 18; cert trainer/instr Bethel Bible Series, EE; "The Intersection of Just War Theory, Romans 13:4, and the 1967 Arab-Israeli War"

1618 Gold Hill Mesa Drive, Colorado Springs, CO 80905 Northern California
E-mail: memlfairbrother@reagan.com

Faires, William H. Jr. – b Raleigh, NC, Jul 6, 49; f Wm Howard; m Louise Kerr; w Martha Jones, Abbeville, SC, Mar 4, 78; chdn Wm Jered, Caleb Everett, Mark Robinson; MonC 67-69, AA; KgC 69-71, BA; RTS 71-74, MDiv; L 74; O 74, Second Pby (ARP); p Bethelehem Ch, Due West, SC, 74-78; ap Covenant P Ch, Winter Haven, FL, 78-81; mis MTW, Taiwan, 81-92; chp Shih Gwang Ref P Ch, Taipei; ISCF, 92-; campm RUM, CentCar Pby, Charlotte, NC, 93-11; wc 11-

12540 Rocky River Church Road, Charlotte, NC 28215 – 704-573-0795 Catawba Valley
E-mail: wmfaires@earthlink.net

Falconer, Benjamin – b Traverse City, MI, Dec 2, 74; f Bruce Campbell; m Julie Ann Haworth; w Kimberly Ruth , Glenview, IL, Oct 20, 01; chdn Joshua Thomas, Claire Elizabeth, Luke Campbell, Titus Benjamin, Cecelia Abigail, Ezra Watts; NWU 97, BMus; TEDS 08, MDiv; O Jun 09, RCA; Recd PCA May 15, PhilMetW Pby; ascp University Ref Ch, East Lansing, MI, 07-15; srp Proclamation P Ch, Bryn Mawr, PA, 15-

3402 Lewis Road, Newtown Square, PA 19073 Philadelphia Metro West
E-mail: ben@proclamation.org
Proclamation Presbyterian Church – 610-520-9500

Falls, Douglas Lee Jr. – b Itazuki AFB, Japan, Sept 8, 56; f Douglas Lee; m Dorothy Jones; w Ruth Bading, Hopewell, VA, Aug 21, 82; chdn James Douglas, Lee Anne, Virginia Nicole; VCU 79, BS; RTS 86, MDiv; ArgosyU 01, Ed.D; L Oct 86, Cov Pby; O Jun 87, Cov Pby; ap Riveroaks Ref P Ch, Germantown, TN, 87-90, wc 90-92; ob Reg RTSFL, 92-97; sc CentFL Pby, 92-97; ob prof RTS, 97-00; ob prof RTSNC, 00-02; astp StoneBridge Ch Comm, Charlotte, NC, 02-06; ascp 06-

7015 Rollingridge Drive, Charlotte, NC 28211 Catawba Valley
E-mail: doug@stonebridge.org
StoneBridge Church Community – 704-549-8272

Faria, Christopher Allen – b Richmond, CA, Jul 2, 56; f Leo P.; m Bette J. McKee; w Brenda E. Hicks, Lodi, CA, Sept 10, 78; chdn Ana Marlene; SanJoaquin 74-76, AD; WesternBC 81-84, BA; DTS 85-89, ThM; CIU 97-98, MA; O Oct 16, 88, Metro Tabernacle, Dallas; Recd PCA Oct 23, 99, CentCar Pby; Chap USArmy, Ft. Jackson, SC, 89-93; Chap USArmy, Korea, 93-95; Chap USArmy, Ft. Stewart, GA, 95-97; Chap USArmy, Columbia, SC, 97; Chap USArmy, Ft. Bragg, NC, 98-07; astp Forestgate P Ch, Colorado Springs, CO, 07-13; op Westm P Flwsp, Falcon, CO, 08-13; ss Rocky Mountain P Ch, Westminster, CO, 15-17

3405 Brompton Court, Colorado Springs, CO 80920 Rocky Mountain
E-mail: drchristopherfaria@gmail.com

Farinacci, James – Recd PCA Dec 4, 13, NYS Pby; ss Hope Ch, Ballston Spa, NY, 13-16, astp 18-

14 Collins Avenue, Troy, NY 12180 – 518-573-8247 New York State
E-mail: pastjim@me.com
Hope Church – 518-885-7442

Farmer, William Robert – b Rocky Mount, NC, May 8, 50; f William B; m Bea Batts; w Bonnie Jordan, Fremont, NC, Aug 1, 70; chdn Robert William, Jordan Ashley; CIU 90, BA; RTS 94, MDiv; L Oct 94; O May 95, Palm Pby; p Grace Cov Ch, Blythewood, SC, 95-99; astp Northeast P Ch, Columbia, SC, 99-; hr 11; Chap Combat Vets Motorcycle Assoc, CEO Project Josiah

404 Olde Springs Road, Columbia, SC 29223 Palmetto
Northeast Presbyterian Church
HR

Farnsworth, William Haliburton – b Greenville, SC, May 19, 55; f James Oliver; m Elizabeth Earle; w Mary Elizabeth Chandler, Greenville, SC, Jun 10, 78; chdn William Benjamin, Elizabeth Hamer, Robert Haliburton, Jack Chandler; FurU 73-76; GrTech 77-78, AD; USC 79-81, BS; CTS 82-85, MDiv; L 85, Cov Pby; O 86, Cov Pby; campm RUM, MSU, 86-89; campm RUM, VandU, 89-96; op Redeemer P Ch, Athens, GA, 97-00, srp 00-

143 Bent Tree Drive, Athens, GA 30606-1945 – 706-543-4960 Georgia Foothills
E-mail: hfarns@redeemathens.com
Redeemer Presbyterian Church – 706-227-3344

Farquhar, Brandon William – astp Grace Ch of Greenwich, Greenwich, CT, 13-15; ob FOCUS, 15-

250 Pemberwick Road, Greenwich, CT 06831 – 314-302-7670 Metropolitan New York
E-mail: brandonfarquhar@gmail.com

Farr, W. Thomas – b Birmingham, AL, Sept 17, 50; f William R.; m Clara Charlene Miller; w Dorothy Jean Henry, Stilwell, OK, Aug 11, 73; chdn Kristen Jean, Clara Grace; UAL 68-70; CC 70-72, BA; CTS 75, MDiv, 76, ThM; L 75, Midw Pby; O Feb 27, 77, NoE Pby (RPCES); op Covenant of Grace Ch, Binghamton, NY, 76-90; ob t BrChS, 90-

916 Ryecroft Road, Pelham, AL 35124-1524 – 205-664-4935 Evangel
E-mail: tfarr@briarwood.org
Briarwood Christian School

Farrand, Greg – astp Redeemer P Ch, Winston-Salem, NC, 02-03; op Spring Garden Comm Msn, Greensboro, NC, 02-06; p 06-11

1714 Friar Tuck Drive, Greensboro, NC 27408 Piedmont Triad
E-mail: gbfarrand@aol.com

Farrant, Bruce L. – b Daytona Bch, FL, Sept 5, 53; f Vernon; m Irene Taylor; w Linda Love, New Smyrna Bch, FL, Sept 1, 78; chdn Shelly, Jeremiah; RTS 88-91, MDiv; L Oct 16, 90; O Mar 15, 92, MSVal Pby; ss Concord P Ch, Pickens, MS, 90-92, p 92-94; p Old Madison P Ch, Canton, MS, 92-94; p Grace P Ch, Cedartown, GA, 94-98; staff MTW/Impact, 98-99; MTW/Impact, virtual staff, Cherokee, NC, 99-06; coord MNA, Native Amer/First Nations, 06-

1007 Windemere Circle, Maryville, TN 37804   Tennessee Valley
E-mail: hoplumber@aol.com
PCA Mission to North America – 678-825-1200

Farrar, Melvin Howard – b Highland Park, MI, Dec 25, 35; f Melvin Edwin; m Emma Vivian Hoskin; w Kathryn Elizabeth Fitch, Weston, CT, Aprr 4, 59; chdn Douglas Howard, Denise Elizabeth, Christine Ellen; USMA 58, BS; ISU 64, MS; CTS 84, MDiv; L 84, MO Pby; O 85, MO Pby; ap Westm Ref Ch, 85-87; p Providence P Ch, Quakertown, PA, 87-05; sc EastPA Pby, 05-; hr

37 South 10th Street, Quakertown, PA 18951-1209 – 215-529-0714   Eastern Pennsylvania
E-mail: mhfarrar37@verizon.net
HR

Farris, Delbert Lloyd – b Fresno, CA, Mar 27, 54; f Delbert Wilson; m Fern Cagle; w Hazel Becker, Little Rock, AR, Jan 2, 83; chdn Loddrick Joseph, Hannah Christine; LSU 77, BA; RTS 85, MDiv; O Jun 86, Cov Pby; ap Covenant P Ch, Little Rock, AR, 86-87; p Coulwood P Ch, Charlotte, NC, 87-91; ob Chap, DPC Arkansas Chdns Hosp, 91-; Chap Hospice Home Care, Little Rock, AR, 92-95; astp Covenant P Ch, Little Rock, AR, 00-02; op Covenant P Ch, Hot Springs, AR, 97-02; Assoc Coord for Civ Chaps, Chap Ministries, MNA, 13-

2120 Cherry Tree Lane, Peachtree City, GA 30269   Covenant
E-mail: dfarris@pcanet.org
PCA Mission to North America Chaplain Ministries

Fartro, Jeffrey – b Pittsburgh, PA, Oct 6, 65; f Thomas; m Sarah Boyce; w Lynn Louise Margenau, Greenville, SC, Jul 18, 98; chdn Leeland Thomas, James Robert, Sarabeth; CalvC 96, BA; GPTS 01, MDiv; O Oct 12, 02, OPC NJ; Recd PCA Oct 14, 07, Asc Pby; p Cherry Hill OPC, NJ, 02-05; ip Christ P Ch, Elkton, MD, 06-07; ob p Pleasant Valley P Ch, Cleveland-Parma, OH, 08-

3459 West Pleasant Valley Road, Parma, OH 44134-5909 – 440-887-1644   Ohio
E-mail: jtfgpts@aol.com
Pleasant Valley Presbyterian Church – 440-887-1644

Fary, Timothy – w Sara Elizabeth; chdn Malcom, Madeline, Patrick; BryC 95, BA; ChapOffBasicC 96-02; RTSFL 00, MDiv; O Aprr 1, 01, Wcar Pby; astp First P Ch, Weaverville, NC, 01-02; ascp 02-03, wc 03-04, Chap 04-

CMR 405, Box 1006, APO, AE 09034   Western Carolina

Faryga, Mykola – O TNVal Pby; stu RTSFL

Reformed Theological Seminary, FL – 407-366-9493   Tennessee Valley
1231 Reformation Drive, Oviedo, FL 32765

Fastenau, John Richard – b Clinton, LA, Jan 3, 53; f Emmett H; m Doris Propst; w Laura Murphey, Columbia, SC, Jul 26, 80; chdn Michelle, Paul, Stephen, Rachel, Kate, Isabella; USC 71-75, BS; RTS 90-93, MDiv; L Jul 24, 93; O Aug 1, 93, Cal Pby; astp Westminster P Ch, Rock Hill, SC, 93-97; chp, op Christ Ridge P Ch, Fort Mill, SC, 93-97, p 97-99, wc 00; p Liberty Springs P Ch, Cross Hill, SC, 00-02; ob admin Cal Home for chdn, Anderson, SC, 02-05; p Center Point P Ch, Moore, SC, 05-07; Cov P Ch, Anderson, SC, 07-08; p New Hope P Ch, Abbeville, SC, 08-17; hr 17

110 Bedford Road, Greenwood, SC 29649 – 864-369-1899   Calvary
E-mail: jfastenau@yahoo.com
HR

Faulkner, Wesley Dean – b Charlotte, NC, Jun 1, 67; f Jerry W.; m Marilyn Barrow; w Elizabeth Somers, Williamsburg, VA, Sept 21, 91; chdn Bethany Leigh, Mitchell Anderson; NCSt 85-89, BEEn; GCTS 93-97, MDiv; RTSNC DMin stu, 11-; L Apr 25, 98, CentCar Pby; O Dec 6, 98, CentCar Pby; int Redeemer P Ch, Concord, MA, 96-97; int Christ Cov P Ch, Matthews, NC, 97-98; p Goshen P Ch, Belmont, NC, 98-01; astp, chp Christ Cov P Ch, Matthews, NC, 01-03; op Church of the Redeemer, Monroe, NC, 01-03, srp 03-16; astp Uptown Church, PCA, Charlotte, NC, 16-; op South Charlotte P Ch, Charlotte, NC, 17-vis lect/prof RTSNC, 16-

11726 Cricketfield Court, Charlotte, NC 28277 – 704-619-2832   Central Carolina
E-mail: deanfaulkner0608@gmail.com
Uptown Church, PCA – 704-375-7355
South Charlotte Presbyterian Church – 704-619-2832

Fearing, Ross – b San Antonio, TX, Jun 30, 88; f Kirk; m Lisa Radford; w Emily Prouty, Loveland, CO, Dec 14, 13; chdn Olin Barnabas; TXA&M 10, BS; GPTS 14, MDiv; O Aug 25, 14, SEAL Pby; int Woodruff Road P Ch, Simpsonville, SC, 12-14; Chap USAR, 14-

7242 Rimwood, Live Oak, TX 78233   Southeast Alabama
E-mail: orfearing@gmail.com
United States Army Reserve

Feichtmann, Adam – astp Redeemer P Ch, Newport Beach, CA, 13-

2485 Irvine Avenue, Costa Mesa, CA 92627   South Coast
E-mail: adamf@redeemeroc.org
Redeemer Presbyterian Church – 949-553-2060

Felich, Anthony J. – b Buffalo, NY, Aug 24, 71; f Anthony, Sr.; m Lillian Alice O'Keefe; w Shari Lynn Busenitz, Whitewater, KS, Jul 31, 93; chdn Anthony James Jr., Nicolas Jon, Jordan Micah, Willow Grace; MBI 89-93, BA; CTS 95-98, MDiv; WhTS 12, DArts; Mar 98, Hrtl Pby; O Sept 98, Hrtl Pby; int Wilson P Ch, PA, 92; int Redeemer P Ch, Overland Park, KS, 97-98, astp, yp 98-00, ascp 00-01, p 01-

16400 Riggs Road, Stilwell, KS 66385 – 913-522-1719   Heartland
E-mail: tfelich@redeemer-pca.org
Redeemer Presbyterian Church – 913-685-2322

Felker, David – O Aug 12, 12, MSVal Pby; astp First P Ch, Jackson, MS, 12-

2004 Laurel Street, Jackson, MS 39202   Mississippi Valley
E-mail: dfelker@gmail.com
First Presbyterian Church – 601-353-8316

Fender, John D. – b Jesup, GA, Nov 28, 72; f Lamar Carlton; m Karen Loretta; w Leslie Elise Turnage, Lawrenceville, GA, Nov 4, 95; chdn Caroline Elise, Catherine Elizabeth; MerU 91-95, BBA; CTS 99-02, MDiv; L Oct 21, 01, Ill Pby; O Jun 16, 02, War Pby; ss Reformed P Ch, Cutler, IL, 01-02; p Marion P Ch, Marion, AL, 02-05; op First P Ch, Pooler, GA, 05-06; p 06-

238 Pampas Drive, Pooler, GA 31322 – 912-658-2773   Savannah River
E-mail: jlcfender@juno.com
First Presbyterian Church – 912-330-9415

Fennema, Michael Henry – w Stephanie Kirkpatrick; chdn Elliott Michael, Oliver Henry, Mattie Grace, Abigail Elisabeth, Isaac Jeffrey; O May 3, 09, SavRiv Pby; astp Redeemer P Ch, Evans, GA, 09-10; ascp 10-13; srp Trinity Flwsp Ch, Sherwood, AR, 13-16; chp 16-18; op Spring Hill P, Thompson Station, TN, 18-

538 Maury Hill Street, Spring Hill, TN 37174   Nashville
E-mail: mike@springhillpca.com
Spring Hill Presbyterian

Fennig, Richard Alan – b Decatur, IN, Nov 10, 51; f Brice; m Delora Graber; w Robin Hartenstein, Bridgeton, NJ, Dec 16, 72; chdn Zachary, Nicole, Adam, Thaddeus; BJU 73, BA; L , C&MA; O Feb 17, 91, GulCst Pby; YFC, Indianapolis, 73-84; C&MA, 77-84; exec dir YFC, Dothan, AL, 84-90; ydir Grace Flwsp P Ch, Gulf Shores, AL, 90-91, astp 91-93, p 93-

22985 County Road 12, Foley, AL 36535 – 251-747-7223   Gulf Coast
E-mail: gfpca.gulfcoast@gmail.com
Grace Fellowship Presbyterian Church – 251-968-5302

Ferguson, H. James – b Akron, OH, Jan 5, 31; f Earl L.; m Eva Pressler; w Donna Rabjohn, Akron, OH, Aug 12, 50; chdn James Earl, Allan H., Ronald L., Faith J.; AkBI, dipl; WBC, BA; BowSt, MA; O Feb 1, 60, IndBap; p Bethel Chap, Ravenna, OH, 60-68; CSB, 68-80; ap Evangelical P Ch, Annapolis, MD, 80-84, ascp 84-01; hr 01

940 Astern Way #401, Annapolis, MD 21401 – 410-757-5060   Chesapeake
HR

Ferguson, Jeffrey Daniel – b Sumter, SC, May 22, 75; f Jack E.; m Jane C. Jarvis; w Tracey Leigh Caison, Surfside Beach, SC, Jan 6, 01; chdn Wilkes Allen, Ella Jane; ClemU 97, BS, 99, MS; RTSNC 03, MDiv; O Oct 12, 03, Flwsp Pby; campm RUF, WinthU, 03-12; srp Calvary Ref P Ch, Hampton, VA, 12-

403 Whealton Road, Hampton, VA 23666   Tidewater
E-mail: jeff@calvaryrpc.org
Calvary Reformed Presbyterian Church – 757-826-5942

Ferguson, Kyle – b Atlanta, GA, Dec 15, 80; f James Earl; m Laurel Amsden; w Michelle Froelich, Green Bay, WI; chdn Elayna, Aubrey, Amaria, Ciara, Tyler, Kaleb ; TIU 03, BA; TEDS 08, MDiv; O Jun 22, 08, Wisc Pby; ydir Cornerstone Ch, Delafield, WI, 01-03; Cornerstone Ch, dir Family Min, Delafield, WI, 03-08, astp 08-13; p Westminster P Ch, Roanoke, VA, 13-

8513 Barrens Road, Roanoke, VA 24019   Blue Ridge
E-mail: kyleferguson@westpca.org
Westminster Presbyterian Church – 540-562-0924

Ferguson, LeRoy Henderson III – b Columbia, SC, Aug 6, 53; f LeRoy H. Jr.; m Audrey Marie Hopper; w Deborah Elizabeth Cranford, Rock Hill, SC, Sept 13, 75; chdn Bethany Grace, Robert Davie, Andrew Scott; ClemU 71-75, BS; RTS 77-81, MDiv; O Aug 9, 81, Cal Pby; campm USC, 81-89; p Grace Ref P Ch, Dale City, VA, 89-91; p Covenant P Ch, Columbia, SC, 91-02; srp Trinity P Ch, Murfreesboro, TN, 02-10; wc 10-; *The Enduring Community*, 2nd ed study guide, 08; cert inst Ken Sande's Relational Wisdom 360, 13-

1919 Hamptonwood Road, Rock Hill, SC 29732   Fellowship
E-mail: leeferg@me.com

Fernandez, Ernesto Manuel – b Havana, Cuba; w Kathryn Suzanne Awara Conrad, Atlanta, GA, Dec 31, 89; chdn Kathryn Ashley, Amanda Joy Margaret, Edwin Benjamin, Cristian Alberto; TFBC 92, BA; Southern Evan Sem 04, MA; op Iglesia del Redentor, Monroe, NC, 05-13; astp Church of the Redeemer, Monroe, NC, 14-16; ascp First Ch (PCA), Lansing, IL, 16-18

3361 Shorelake Drive, Tucker, GA 30084   Chicago Metro
E-mail: ernestoawara@gmail.com

Fernandez del Nogal, Enrique (Fernandez, Henry) – b Tampa, FL, Sept 18, 56; f Servando; m Mercedes; w Cindy L. Barr, May 28, 83; chdn Samuel David, Elisa Ruth, Anna Christine; ClrCC 78, BA; RTS 81, MDiv; GPTS, doct stu; O Jul 26, 81, CentFL Pby; ev Nueva Vida Mission, Tampa, FL, 81-84; ap Shenandoah P Ch, Miami, FL, 85-87; p Bryce Avenue P Ch, Los Alamos, NM, 87-

118 La Vista Drive, Los Alamos, NM 87544 – 505-672-3918   Southwest
E-mail: pastor@bapca.org
Bryce Avenue Presbyterian Church – 505-672-3364

Ferrell, George Thomas – b Murfreesboro, TN, Jun 11, 50; f Alton Don; m Martha Jean Robertson; w Julia Elizabeth Cummings, Nashville, TN, Apr 10, 76; chdn Katheryn (Titsworth), David Jackson; DTS 89, ThM; L Jul 23, 88, NoTX Pby; O Nov 19, 89, NoTX Pby; srp Arlington P Ch, Arlington, TX, 89-07; wc 08-12; hr 12

138 2nd Avenue North #400, Nashville, TN 37201 – 615-584-1580 North Texas
E-mail: ferrell@thefamilyoffice.org
HR

Ferris, William Lawrence Jr. – b Macon, MS, Mar 17, 53; f W.L. Sr.; m Bess Ellison; w Lisa Hemby, Nashville, TN, Oct 10, 81; chdn Margaret Elisabeth, Rebecca Claire, William Lawrence III; ColStCC 71-73; UT 73-76, BS; RTS 82-86, MDiv; L 84, SFL Pby; O 86, TNVal Pby; mis MTW, Paris, 86-92; chp, op Hickory Grove P Ch, Mt. Juliet, TN, 93-97; astp Covenant P Ch, Nashville, TN, 00-01; ascp 01-12; p Covenant P Ch, Easley, SC, 12-

106 Wood Creek Drive, Piedmont, SC 29673 Calvary
E-mail: larryferris01@gmail.com
Covenant Presbyterian Church – 864-859-0967

Ferry, Brian – O Nov 3, 13, OHVal Pby; astp New City P Ch, Cincinnati, OH, 13-

2716 Arbor Avenue, Cincinnati, OH 46209 – 513-289-3630 Ohio Valley
E-mail: Brian.ferry@newcitycincy.org
New City Presbyterian Church – 513-886-0676

Fidati, David John – b Scranton, PA, Oct 26, 54; f David Anthony; m Phyllis Ruth Ball; w Kathryn Ann Upson, Aldan, PA, May 17, 75; chdn Lindsay Anne, David Andrew, John William; MesC, BA; WTS, MDiv; CTS 98, DMin; O 82, DMV Pby; ap Evangelical P Ch, Newark, DE, 82-87; ap Westminster P Ch, Lancaster, PA, 87-90; op Hope Ref P Ch, Shippensburg, PA, 90-93, p 93-

4051 Campbell Circle, Orrstown, PA 17244-9507 – 717-530-8673 Susquehanna Valley
E-mail: pastor.hopepca@embarqmail.com
Hope Reformed Presbyterian Church – 717-532-8998

Field, Andrew E. – b Springfield, PA, Feb 5, 66; f Harvey E.; m Joan Lentz; w Donna Lee Rusk, New York, NY, Oct 21, 89; chdn Timothy A., Sarah J., Elizabeth G., James; UVA 84-88, BS; WTS 92-96, MDiv; L Jan 96, NoE Pby; O Jun 2, 96, NoE Pby; ascp Redeemer P Ch of New York, New York, NY, 96-00; op, ev Grace P Ch of Silicon Valley, Palo Alto, CA, 00-11; sc NoCA Pby, 03-06; astp Trinity P Ch, Charlottesville, VA, 11-14; ascp 14-16; ascp, exec p Redeemer P Ch of New York, New York, NY, 16-

25 West 81st Street 11C, New York, NY 10024 Metropolitan New York
E-mail: andrewfield@redeemer.com
Redeemer Presbyterian Church of New York – 212-808-4460

Fikes, William R. – b Augusta, GA, Nov 19, 70; f Joseph William; m Janice Elizabeth Hundley; w Pamela Lynn Gower, Augusta, GA, Jun 11, 94; chdn Caleb Joseph, William Elias; UFL 93, BA; RTSNC 01, MDiv; L Jul 28, 01, Cal Pby; O Feb 9, 02, Cal Pby; p Reidville P Ch, Reidville, SC, 01-04; astp West Hills P Ch, Knoxville, TN, 04-09; ss Smoky Mountain P Ch, Maryville, TN, 13-14, p 14-

2413 Sevierville Road, Maryville, TN 37804 – 865-441-4936 Tennessee Valley
E-mail: billfikes@att.net
Smoky Mountain Presbyterian Church – 865-983-9019

Filson, David O. – b Lebanon, TN, Sept 26, 66; f Leslie; m Elizabeth Dean Jones; w Rosalyn Diane Poland, St. Louis, MO, Dec 21, 96; chdn Luke, Lydia; OakCC 88, BA; CTS 97, MDiv; WTS, PhD; L Feb 14,

Filson, David O., continued
99, Nash Pby; O Jul 6, 99, Nash Pby; op & p Good Shepherd P Ch, Nashville, TN, 99-10; astp Christ P Ch, Nashville, TN, 10-14, ascp 14-

7804 Farmington Place, Nashville, TN 37221 – 615-673-9890　　　　　　Nashville
E-mail: davidlovesdiane@mac.com
Christ Presbyterian Church – 615-373-2311

Finch, Paul Legree Jr. – b Spartanburg, SC, Mar 24, 49; f Paul L.; m Gladys Robison; w Sue Reece, St. Louis, MO, Jul 21, 72; chdn Scott Matthew, Jennifer Sue; CBC 67-71, BA; CTS 71-74, MDiv; L Jan 74, Midw Pby; O Jun 29, 75, IL Pby (RPCES); ss Reformed P Ch, Cutler, IL, 74-75, p 75-88; ascp Westminster P Ch, Bryan, TX, 88-97; chp SoTX Pby, 97-98; p Christ P Ch, Marietta, GA, 98-14; p em Christ P Ch, Marietta, GA; ss Grace Cov Ch - PCA, Dallas, GA, 14-15; hr 15

1163 Dogwood Forest Drive NE, Marietta, GA 30068 – 678-560-9815　　　　Northwest Georgia
E-mail: pf4595@aol.com
HR

Findlay, John Brown Jr. – b Birmingham, AL, Aug 20, 46; f John B; m Merceedes Plough; w Janice Brown, Birmingham, AL, Nov 29, 68; chdn Laurie Jan (Storey), Jennifer Elise (Ferguson); SamU 64-68, BA; UAL 71, MS; RTS 74-78, MDiv; L Jun 11, 78; O Jun 11, 78, GulCst Pby; srp Pinewoods P Ch, Cantonment, FL, 78-99; ascp Pinewood P Ch, Middleburg, FL, 99-11; ob prog dir Day Resource Center, Waterfront Rescue Mission, Pensacola, 11-; ss Loxley P Ch, Loxley, AL, 12-15

6426 Sarasota Street, Pensacola, FL 32526 – 850-478-4044　　　　　　　　Gulf Coast
E-mail: jfindlay@waterfrontmission.org
Waterfront Rescue Mission, Pensacola

Finn, Bruce R. – b Upper Darby, PA, Jun 30, 52; f Joseph Raymond; m Georganna M. Bonsall; w Deborah Ann Tikkala, Springfield, VA, Jun 8, 74; chdn Brian Scott, Kelly Ann, Karrie Beth; UHou 70-71; WChSC 71-74, BA; WTS 75-78, MDiv; O Sept 80, MidAtl Pby; ap Chapelgate P Ch, Marriottsville, MD, 80-84; ap Hilton Head P Ch, Hilton Head Island, SC, 84-86; op Faith P Ch, Richboro, PA, 86-92, p 92-05; chp, coord Metro Phil ChPlant Partnership, 05-18; ascp Cov P Ch, Doylestown, PA, 12-

87 Holyoke Road, Richboro, PA 18954-1921 – 215-953-9228　　　　Eastern Pennsylvania
E-mail: bruce.finn1@gmail.com
Covenant Presbyterian Church

Fiol, Bruce Richard – b Mussoorie, India, Oct 4, 38; f Frank Louis (d); m Esther Ruth Storey (d); w Judith Ann Kesselring, Underwood, ND, Sept 29, 62; chdn Tina Laurie (Simpson), Londa Jean (Sneller), Lisa Kay (Powers), Andrew Bruce; WheatC 56-57; CC 57-60, BA; CTS 64, MDiv; RTS 95-00, DMin; L Feb 64, SE Pby (RPCES); O Feb 64, SE Pby (RPCES); p Faith RP Ch, Charlotte, NC, 64-66; mis, admin, t PTSDD, 66-83; op Marco P Ch, Marco Island, FL, 83-87, srp 87-08; hr 08; coord MTW India/Sri Lanka partnership, 11-14; adj prof RTSNC, 10-14; assoc Chap Quarryville Presbyterian Retirement Community, 14-

421 South Church Street, Quarryville, PA 17566 – 717-786-8922　　　　Susquehanna Valley
E-mail: brucefiol@gmail.com
HR

Fiscus, Joel W. – b Kittanning, PA, Mar 24, 55; f Earl W.; m Betty L. Claypoole; w Debra A Stuber, Schooley's Mountain, NJ, Jul 28, 79; chdn Shawna Beth, Sara Rose; GenC 77, BA; CTS 82, MDiv; L Sept 82; O Oct 83, GrLks Pby; p First P Ch, Bad Axe, MI, 83-85; asst, Dir Camp Susque, Trout Run, PA, 85-86; ascp Manor P Ch, Cochranville, PA, 88-08; nat'l dir field staff, US/Can Christian Serv Brigade, 09-15, VP field staff and Men's Min, 15-

54 Saddler Drive, Christiana, PA 17509– 610-365-7767　　　　　　Susquehanna Valley
E-mail: joel.fiscus@gmail.com
Christian Service Brigade

Fisher, Chris – astp Redeemer P Ch, Austin, TX, 09-11

5000 Tahoe Trail, Austin, TX 78745 – 512-804-5814   South Texas
E-mail: Chris_fish@sbcglobal.net

Fisher, Joseph – Recd PCA Apr 29, 16, SNE Pby; astp Christ Comm P Ch, West Hartford, CT, 16-; op Trinity Gr Ch, Suffield, CT, 16-

812 Halladay Avenue West, Suffield, CT 06078   Southern New England
Christ Community Presbyterian Church – 860-521-0211
Trinity Grace Church – 860-839-1157

Fisher, Matthew – ascp Village P Ch, Mount Laurel, NJ, 07- 14; ascp Grace P Ch, Mount Laurel, NJ, 14-

624 Old Orchard, Cherry Hill, NJ 08003 – 856-341-4251   New Jersey
E-mail: pastormatthew@gpml.org
Grace Presbyterian Church – 856-778-5472

Fisher, Matthew R. – O Sept 9, 18, Pitts Pby; astp New Life P Ch, Harrison City, PA, 18-

241 Grandview Avenue, Greensburg, PA 15601   Pittsburgh
New Life Presbyterian Church – 724-744-4760

Fisher, Richard E. – b Philipsburg, PA, Sept 30, 49; f Robert A.; m Dorothy Jones; w Karen Horner, Cherry Hill, NJ, Jun 1, 74; chdn Dorothy Louise, Rachel Elizabeth (d), Jessica Ruth; IUP 71, BA; WTS 74, MDiv; L May 74, OPC; O Feb 75, OPC; p Tri-County OP Ch, Lewisburg, PA, 74-76; ap Covenant P Ch, Cherry Hill, NJ, 76-79; p Calvary P Ch, Stilwell, OK, 79-84; ev Wichita, KS, 84-88; Chap Hernando-Pasco Hospice, Hudson, FL, 88-89; p Westm Ref P, Westminster, MD, 89-90; ss Forest Park Comm Ch, Baltimore, MD, 90, wc 90-94; ss Abbott Mem P Ch, Baltimore, MD, 94; ss Inverness P Ch, Baltimore, MD, 02-03; Chap HPH Hospice, Dade City, FL, 04-12; ss DaySpring Ch, Spring Hills, FL, 07; assoc evan PEF, 08-12; Chap Hearth Hospice, Chattanooga, 13-15; astp mov, First P Ch, Chattanooga, TN, 14-; staff mis International Biblical Training, 17-; "You Were Made to Last Forever," PEF's *Come... Follow*, Fall/Winter 08, Spring 09, and in *Metamorphosis*, 17

4913 Alabama Avenue, Chattanooga, TN 37409 – 423-544-7975   Tennessee Valley
E-mail: ref27@msn.com
First Presbyterian Church – 423-267-1206

Fisher, Stephen Daniel – FurU, BA; RTS, MA, MDiv; AmilU MA; O Jul 16, 00, CentFL Pby; Chap USN, 00-

119 Iyona Drive, Yona, GU 96915 – 912-467-4799   Central Florida
E-mail: revfisher@gmail.com
United States Navy

Fisk, David – O Sept 19, 10, Cal Pby; campm RUF, Wofford, 10-16; astp Intown Comm Ch, Atlanta, GA, 16-

1861 Ravenwood Way, Atlanta, GA 30329   Metro Atlanta
Intown Community Church – 404-633-8077

Fitzgerald, James – srp Covenant P Ch, Oviedo, FL, 00-08; ob VP Equipping Pastors, Internat'l, 08-

1231 Reformation Drive, Oviedo, FL 32765 – 407-359-1240   Central Florida
Equipping Pastors International, Inc. – 352-394-5180

Fitzpatrick, Joseph – b Bronx, NY, May 3, 62; f John; m Encarnacion Valentine; w Beverly Wolfgang, Glenside, PA, Jun 17, 95; chdn Joey, Anna, Justin; PhilCB 93, BS; WTS 96, MDiv, 07, DMin; O May 16, 99, Phil Pby; mis MTW, Philippines, 99-05; t Pres Theo Sem, Philippines; mis MTW, Puerto Rico, 06-

c/o MTW – 787-219-8852   Philadelphia
E-mail: joeandbev@gmail.com
PCA Mission to the World

Fix, Stephen A. – b St. Louis, MO, Sept 6, 78; f John; m Kerry Lee; w Rachel Brockman, Dec 31, 02; chdn Rock Daniel, Louisa Theo, Gillespie Grace, Macpherson Paul; GroCC 02, BS; WSCAL 07, MDiv; CathUAm 13, MA; O Dec 2, 07, Pot Pby; astp Reformed P Ch, Bowie, MD, 07-15, ascp 15-

12100 Maycheck Lane, Bowie, MD 20715 – 301-814-4770   Potomac
E-mail: pastor.fix@gmail.com
Reformed Presbyterian Church – 301-262-2280

Flatgard, Andrew – b May 1, 74; w Shelley Ross, Apr 21, 07; chdn Mary Spencer, Reagan, Samuell; UMS, BA; CTS, MAC, MDiv; O May 29, 05, MO Pby; astp Kirk of the Hills P Ch, St. Louis, MO, 05; campm RUF, UMemp, 05-08; campm RUF, Rhodes, 07- 14; astp Christ the King P Ch, Houston, TX, 14-16; astp Intown Comm Ch, Atlanta, GA, 16-

E-mail: andrewflatgard@gmail.com   Metro Atlanta
Intown Community Church – 404-633-8077

Flayhart, Robert K. – b PA, Aug 30, 59; f Robert M; m Sharon Keyser; w Laurie Kane, Tallahassee, FL, Apr 28, 84; chdn Joshua James, Hannah Legare, Michael Robert; PASU 82, BS; TEDS 88, MDiv; CTS 01, DMin; L Oct 24, 87, NoIL Pby; O Jan 29, 89, Evan Pby; ascp Briarwood P Ch, Birmingham, AL, 89-92; op Oak Mountain P Ch, Birmingham, AL, 89-92; srp 92-

2908 Oak Mountain Trail, Birmingham, AL 35242 – 205-995-9203   Evangel
E-mail: bflayhart@ompc.org
Oak Mountain Presbyterian Church – 205-995-9265

Fleeman, Lenden – fm MTW, 18-

2050 Harmony Drive, Canton, GA 30115   Providence
E-mail: 3stockton3@gmail.com
PCA Mission to the World

Fleming, Aaron – b Huntsville, AL, May 31, 50; f Walton; m Martha Crute; w Chris Parker Pursell, Apr 13, 85; UAL 68-70; CBC 70-73, BA; BhamTS 76-79, MDiv; L Aug 79; O Aug 79, Evan Pby; srp Eastwood P Ch, Montgomery, AL, 79-11; susp 11-12; hr 13

1801 Fairforest Drive, Montgomery, AL 36106-2701 – 334-279-0384   Southeast Alabama
E-mail: afpreacherman@gmail.com
HR

Fleming, Douglas G. – b Morgantown, WV, Aug 19, 50; f David G.; m Pauline Margaret Comer; w Gay Alsobrook, Miami, FL, Aug 4, 72; chdn Gary Scott, Drew Douglas, Nancy Brook, Gwen Margaret Theodore John, Todd Lawrence, Dorie Ann, Bennett Gilson; FurU 72, BA; RTS 76, MDiv, 76, MCE; O Jun 76, FL Pby (ARP); p Grace ARP Ch, Winter Springs, FL, 76-83; t Orangewood CS, 83-

220 Waverly Drive, Fern Park, FL 32730-2627 – 407-260-1214   Central Florida
Orangewood Christian School – 407-339-0223

Fleming, Gorden – astp Midtown Comm Ch, Raleigh, NC, 16-17, ascp 17-

100 Beaver Pine Way, Cary, NC 27511　　　　　　　　　　　　　　Eastern Carolina
E-mail: gorden@midtown-church.org
Midtown Community Church – 919-601-3903

Fleming, Scott L. – b Marshall, MO, May 16, 71; f Larry D.; m Peggy Sue (d); w Nalene Dawn Carpenter, Willow Street, PA, Jun 21, 97; chdn Nathanael Scott, Anna Nalene, Emma Grace, Matthew Iain, Noah Jonathan; GroCC 96, BA; RTS 99, MDiv; L Feb 1, 00, Cov Pby; O Feb 20, 00, Cov Pby; int Providence P Ch, Clinton, MS, 98-99; astp, yp First P Ch, Dyersburg, TN, 99-02; p Rocky Springs P Ch, Harrisville, PA, 02-

604 Georgetown Road, Harrisburg, PA 16038 – 724-967-2756　　　　　　　　　　　Ascension
E-mail: rscpca@gmail.com
Rocky Springs Presbyterian Church – 724-967-1226

Fletcher, Brian – b Jan 20, 67, Julie Taylor, Sept 16, 89; chdn Taylor, Tessa, Molly; VCU 89, BA; CTS 93, MDiv, 07, DMin; O Feb 28, 09, JR Pby; astp Spring Run P Ch, Midlothian, VA, 07-

612 Watch Hill Road, Midlothian, VA 23114 – 804-897-4617　　　　　　　　　　　James River
E-mail: fletch@springrunpc.org
Spring Run Presbyterian Church – 804-608-8233

Flom, James Alan – b Minneapolis, MN, Oct 4, 57; f Floyd O; m Eleanore Paffrath; w Susan Weber, Havertown, PA, Nov 29, 86; chdn Anders Jamesen, Hannah Louise, Abigail Leigh, Katherine Marie; PSC 77, AAS; UID 80, BS; WTS 90, MDiv; L Sept 89; O Dec 9, 90, Phil Pby; yp Crossroads Comm Ch, Upper Darby, PA, 87-89, ascp 90-92; ascp Springton Lake P Ch, Newtown Square, PA, 92-00, wc 00-02; ascp Meadowcroft P Ch, West Chester, 02-04; p Mountainview Comm Ch, Agassiz, BC, 04-10; wc; hr 16

PO Box 2193, Stn Sardis Main　　　　　　　　　　　　　　　　　　　　　Western Canada
Chilliwack, BC V2R 1A6 CANADA – 604-799-2779
E-mail: jamesaflom@gmail.com
HR

Florence, David Christopher – b Brownsville, TX, May 9, 69; f James David; m Tamara Shirley Webster; w Suzette Diane Whiteley, Houston, TX, Dec 16, 95; chdn Bailey Diane, Erynn Elisabeth (d); TXA&M 89-93, BS; UTXAu 94-96, MS; CTS 98-01, MDiv; L Apr 27, 01, Siouxl Pby; O Oct 28, 01, Siouxl Pby; stus Foothills Comm Ch, Sturgis, SD, 01, p 01-03; ascp Severna Park Evangelical P Ch, Pasadena, MD, 03-06; astp First P Ch, Augusta, GA, 06-07; ascp 07-11; adj prof, dean CTS, 11-14, astprof, VP Adad Admin, 14-15; ascp Westminster P Ch, Rock Hill, SC, 15-; "The History of Critical Thinking as an Educational Goal in Graduate Theological Schools," *The Journal of Christian Higher Education*, 14

566 Cotton Field Road, Rock Hill, SC 29732　　　　　　　　　　　　　　　　Fellowship
E-mail: cflorence@wpcgo.com
Westminster Presbyterian Church – 803-366-3107

Floyd, Joshua James – astp Christ P Ch, Nashville, TN, 11- 13; astp St. Pauls P Ch, Orlando, FL, 13-16; astp Trinity P Ch, Lakeland, FL, 16-18; op Grace Comm Msn, Lakeland, FL, 18-

2985 Oak Tree Lane, Lakeland, FL 33810 – 615-438-5345　　　　　　　　　Southwest Florida
E-mail: joshuajfloyd@gmail.com
Grace Community Mission – 615-438-5345

Floyd, Scott – b Spartanburg, SC; O Nov 05; ascp Harvest Comm Ch, Omaha, NE, 05-08; p Covenant P Ch, Harlingen, TX, 08-

19320 Kilbourn Road, Harlingen, TX 78550 – 956-535-3553　　　　　　　　　　　South Texas
E-mail: covenantpcasotx@gmail.com
Covenant Presbyterian Church – 956-425-3136

Floyd, Stuart – astp Grace Toronto Ch, Toronto, ON, 14-15; op Braselton Home Ch Msn, Buford, GA, 15-

2345 Thompson Mill Road #106, Buford, GA 30519 – 770-855-4235   Georgia Foothills
E-mail: stuartnfloyd@gmail.com
Braselton Home Church Mission

Fodale, Mark J. – b Red Bank, NJ, M 20, 62; f Joseph Vito; m Patricia Costello; w Shannon Tansey, Easton, PA, Aug 20, 93; chdn Kathryn Patricia, Jordan Joseph, Laura Tansey, Rebekah Noelle; LafC 84, BA; BibTS 97, MDiv; O Dec 11, 05, Phil Pby; ob campm DiscipleMakers, LaFayetteU & EastStroudsU, 92-; p Providence P Ch, Quakertown, PA, 10-

3306 Margate Road, Bethlehem, PA 18020 – 610-882-0413   Eastern Pennsylvania
E-mail: fodalem@dm.org
Providence Presbyterian Church – 215-536-2881

Forbes, Ola Jr. – b Greenville, NC; f Ola, Sr.; m Edna E. Smith; w Gloria B. Thomason, Phenix City, AL, Sept 9, 56; chdn Melisa (Gaskins), Olive (Jones), Jason; PJC 52-53; OBU 56-58, BA; ECU 60-61, BS, 60-61, MA; L Jun 16, 57; O Jun 16, 57, MSBC; Mt. Bethel, Arkadelphia, AR; Bethany, Wilson, NC; Grace, Falkland, NC; Calvary, Swan Quarter, NC; Wanoco, Washington, NC; ev Pamlico P Ch, Oriental, NC, 85-86; p Wayside P Ch, Chocowinity, NC, 75-

7093 NC 33 East, Chocowinity, NC 27817 – 252-946-4683   Eastern Carolina
E-mail: rkswolfe@yahoo.com
Wayside Presbyterian Church – 252-946-4683

Ford, Alexander – w Holly Danielle, Jun 14, 08; chdn Ivy Elanor, George Wendell; CCSC 03, BA; CTS 10, MDiv; O Aug 11, 13, Ecar Pby; int RUF, ASU 03-05; astp Westminster P Ch, Sumter, SC, 11-13; p Sovereign King PCA, Garner, NC 13-14; p Kanawha Salines P Ch, Malden, WV, 15-18; ip Winifred P Ch, Winifrede, WV, 18-

2919 Fields Creek Road, Winifrede, WV 25214 – 304-513-6573   New River
E-mail: alexander.raymond.ford@gmail.com
Winifrede Presbyterian Church

Ford, Harrison – O Feb 12, 17, JR Pby; campm RUF, VACommon, 17-

2117 Floyd Avenue, Richmond, VA 23220 – 662-790-3452   James River
E-mail: rhford1988@gmail.com
PCA Reformed University Fellowship

Ford, Michael Anderson – O Nov 8, 15, Cov Pby; campm RUF, UArk, 15-

2823 N. Stanton Avenue, Fayetteville, AR 72703   Hills and Plains
E-mail: mike.ford@ruf.org
PCA Reformed University Fellowship

Ford, Stephen B. – b Norristown, PA, Sept 26, 39; f Roscoe C.; m Anna Belle Brewer; w Ann Margaret Walters, Sarnia, Ont., Canada, May 29, 65; chdn Megan Elizabeth, Stephen Walters; BJU 63, BA; FTS 63-65; WTS 66-68, MDiv; L Apr 68, Phil Pby (RPCES); O Jul 18, 69, So Pby (RPCES); p Westminster Ch, Bowling Green, KY, 69; p Westminster P Ch, Godfrey, IL, 74-90; sc Ill Pby, 89-90; p Covenant P Ch, Harleysville, PA, 90-04; hr

2653 Bergey Road, Harleysville, PA 19438 – 610-287-5935   Philadelphia Metro West
E-mail: sbford1@comcast.net
HR

Forester, Jay – b West Palm Beach, FL, Oct 3, 80; f James F.; m Rebecca A. Harper; w Anna B. Knight, Birmingham, AL, Jun 7, 03; chdn Linley Bishop, Clare Reeder; BelC 02, BA; RTS 06, MDiv; O Oct 09, Glfstrm Pby; astp Lake Osborne P Ch, Lake Worth, FL, 09-10; astp Seacrest Boulevard P Ch, Delray Beach, FL, 11-

262 Gulfstream Boulevard, Delray Beach, FL 33444   Gulfstream
E-mail: jforester@seacrestchurch.com
Seacrest Boulevard Presbyterian Church – 561-276-5533

Forrester, Sam J. – b Macon, GA, Sept 14, 47; f G. A. Jr.; m Dorothy Merritt; w Sharon Bradford, Tifton, GA, Jul 15, 78; chdn Nathan A; Susanna; ABAC 66-69, AD; GPTS 90-93, BD; L Jul 21,90; O Aug 1, 93, Wcar Pby; stus Whiteside P Ch, Cashiers, NC, 90-93, p 93-

PO Box 2053, Cashiers, NC 28717 – 828-743-6687   Western Carolina
E-mail: Whiteside@dnet.net
Whiteside Presbyterian Church – 828-743-2122

Forsyth, James William – b Sternway, Scotland, Mar 18, 82; f Donald Campbell; m Mairi MacDonald; w Rosie Susan Gardner, Edinburgh, Scotland, Jun 9, 01; chdn Mia Rose, Caleb James, Seamus William, Isla Grace; UEdin 04, MA; RTS 07, MDiv; astp McLean P Ch, McLean, VA, 08-13; srp 13-

1310 Red Hawk Circle, Reston, VA 20194 – 703-435-2065   Potomac
E-mail: james@mcleanpres.org
McLean Presbyterian Church – 703-821-0800

Fortner, H. Timothy Jr. – b DeKalb Co, GA, Jul 9, 40; f H.T. Sr.; m Evelyn Martin; w Anna Ware, May 29, 65; chdn Daniel Ware, Matthew VanDyke; BelC 63, BA; ErskTS; RTS 68, MDiv; O Jun 68, Evgld Pby (PCUS); ap Granada P Ch, Coral Gables, FL, 68-72; p First P Ch, Hazlehurst, MS, 72-74; p Westminster P Ch, Jacksonville, FL, 74-78; p Covenant P Ch, St. Louis, MO, 78-83; op Heritage P Ch, West Columbia, SC, 83-85; srp Lawndale P Ch, Tupelo, MS, 85-06; astp College Hill P Ch, Oxford, MS, 06-13; hr 13

103 Colonial Road, Oxford, MS 38655   Covenant
E-mail: lpc@netdoor.com
HR

Foshee, Hubert Lynn – b Paris, AR, Jun 28, 41; f Jesse Abram; m Anna Mae Lile; w Sylvia M. Smith, Rockland, ME, Sept 8, 73; chdn Sara Elizabeth; APC 59-63, BS; CBS 71-75, MDiv; L Oct 79, So Dade Bible Ch; O Sept 24, 84, Ev Ch of West Indies; Recd PCA May 11, 91, Phil Pby; dean CBS, 75-78; mis, p Palmiste ECWI, 78-85; admin Bib Chr Union, Hatfield, 87-90; ob Chap Abington Mem Hosp, Abington, PA , 90-91; Chap Monroe Co Correctional Facility, Stroudsburg, PA, 91-98; ob astp Knowlton P Ch, Columbia, NJ, 93-97; ob Chap Cumberland County Prison, 98-15; ob Chap Claremont Nursing/Rehab Center, 98-10; hr 15

9755 Newham Drive #A, Afton, MO 63123 – 314-226-9153   Susquehanna Valley
E-mail: foshsmith77@yahoo.com
HR

Fossett, Robert – O Oct 6, 13, SEAL Pby; p First P Ch, Greenville, AL, 13-

264 Springwood Drive, Greenville, AL 36037445   Southeast Alabama
First Presbyterian Church – 334-382-3937

Foster, Alan – b Atlanta, GA, Jun 17, 60; f Howard Noel; m Verie Johnson; w Kim Dean, Dallas, TX, Jul 9, 88; chdn Virginia Jo (Garvin), Howard Lura (Bud); GATech 78-83, BIE; DTS 86-91, ThM; L Apr 92; O May 93, SEAL Pby; int Faith P Ch, Montgomery, AL, 92; astp, ss Oak Park P Ch, Montgomery,

Frame, John McElphatrick, continued
87; *Medical Ethics*, 88; *Perspectives on the Word of God*, 90; *Evangelical Reunion*, 91; *Apologetics to the Glory of God*, 94; *Cornelius Van Til: An Analysis of His Thought*, 95; *Worship In Spirit and Truth*, 96; *Contemporary Worship Music: A Biblical Defense*, 97; *No Other God: A Response to Open Theism*, 01; *Doctrine of God*, 02; *Salvation Belongs to the Lord*, 06; *Doctrine of the Christian Life*, 08; *Doctrine of the Word of God*, 10, *Systematic Theology*, 13; *History of Western Philosophy and Theology*, 15; *Theology of My Life: a Theological and Apologetic Memoir*, 17; *Theology in Three Dimensions: A Guide to Triperspectivalism and Its Significance*, 17; *Christianity Considered*, 18; *Nature's Case for God*, 18

909 Kingsbridge Drive, Oviedo, FL 32765 – 407-977-4489   Central Florida
E-mail: jframe@rts.edu
HR

    Francis, Michael R. – b Torrance, CA, Feb 21, 62; w Maria Svensson, Berkeley, CA, May 31, 87; chdn Madeline, Luke, Lydia; UCB 84, BA, 88, JD; RTSFL 00, MDiv; L Oct 28, 00, CentFL Pby; O Mar 25, 01, CentFL Pby; p Immanuel P Ch, DeLand, FL, 00-

1532 Covered Bridge, DeLand, FL 32751 – 386-747-3517   Central Florida
E-mail: sicnarfekim@gmail.com
Immanuel Presbyterian Church – 386-738-1811

    Francis, Nathan Bruce – O 17, Wcar Pby; astp Arden P Ch, Arden, NC, 17-

9 Springfield Way, Arden, NC 28704 – 704-561-1232   Western Carolina
E-mail: nathanbfrancis@gmail.com
Arden Presbyterian Church – 828-684-7221

    Franklin, Tom – campm RUF, BhamSC, 09-

564 Forrest Drive South, Homewood, AL 35209 – 205-585-1233   Evangel
E-mail: tfranklin@ruf.org
PCA Reformed University Fellowship

    Franks, John – w Erin; chdn Callie Elizabeth, Anna Bray, Caleb Alexander; CTS 03, MDiv; O Nov 14, 04, SavRiv Pby; First P Ch, Augusta, GA, 95-01, astp 03-07, ascp 07-

500 Scotts Way, Augusta, GA 30909   Savannah River
E-mail: jfranks@firstpresaugusta.org
First Presbyterian Church – 706-262-8900

    Franks, Joseph A., IV – b Fairmont, WV, Sep 22, 69; f Jospeh Franks III; m Martha Shaw; w Laura Evans, Greenville, SC, Nov 16, 91; chdn Joseph, Ashlyn, Andrew; BJU, BA; KTS, MDiv; WTS 10, ThM; L Jul 01, SFL Pby; O Aug 11, 02, SFL Pby; yp Christ Community Ch PCA Palm Beach, Wellington, FL, 98-01; p Cornerstone P Ch, Palm Beach Gardens, FL, 01-04; p Palmetto Hills P Ch, Simpsonville, SC, 04-17; astp Briarwood P Ch, Brimingham, AL, 17-18; astp Horizon Ch, Greenville, SC, 18-

12 Red Fern Trail, Greenville, SC 29681 – 864-434-3326   Calvary
Horizon Church – 864-286-9911

    Franks, Richard Edward – b Columbia City, IN, Feb 15, 62; f L. Edward; m P. Delores Johnson; w Robbie Jane White, Montreat, NC, May 2, 87; chdn Katherine Elise, Benjamin Edward, Nathan James, Andrew Mitchell, Elizabeth Grace, Sarah Anne, Timothy Richard; MonC 88, BA; RTS 90-93, MDiv, 90-93, MCE; L Jan 8, 94; O Oct 23, 94, Westm Pby; astp Westminster P Ch, Johnson City, TN, 93-99; p Cornerstone P Ch, Lutz, FL, 99-06; ascp Heartland Community Ch, Wichita, KS, 06-17; op Kirk of the Plains, Andover, KS, 17-

PO Box 483, Andover, KS 67002 – 316-712-4100   Heartland
E-mail: Rick@KOTP.org
Kirk of the Plains – 316-854-5200

Frantz, Kerry Anthony – b Brainerd, MN, Aug 11, 62; f Gary Leslie; m Sharon Zogas; w Nancy Jean Munger, Westchester, IL, Jun 16, 84; chdn Cassandra Leslie, Nathaniel John, Bethany Joy, Victoria Blessings, Brittany Rebecca, Andrew Mumba, Andre Mumba; NIU 80-83, BA; WheatGrS 84-85, MA; TEDS 84-86, MDiv; L Jun 87; O Jun 89, RCA; Recd PCA Sep 92, NoIL Pby; p Normandale Ref Ch, 87-92; p Hanna City P Ch, Hanna City, IL, 92-98; srp Covenant P Ch, Macomb, IL, 99-07; astp Grace P Ch, Peoria, IL, 07-

12921 North Bland Road, Dunlap, IL 61525 – 309-243-2152   Northern Illinois
E-mail: stfrantzis@frontier.com
Grace Presbyterian Church – 309-693-3641

Fray, Matthew David – b Rochester, NY, Jul 3, 92; w Erin Stortz, St. Louis, MO, Dec 21, 04; chdn Lydia, Hudson, Samuel; WSCAL 09, MDiv; O Sep 27, 09, SavRiv Pby; astp First P Ch, Pooler, GA, 09-13; int Park Cities P Ch, Dallas, TX, 14-15, astp 15-

7373 Valley View Lane #3001, Dallas, TX 75240 – 214-952-0998   North Texas
E-mail: matt.fray@pcpc.org
Park Cities Presbyterian Church – 214-224-2500

Frazier, Michael Ford – b Alexandria, LA, Jan 3, 51; f Andrew N (d); m Eldred Maye Ford; w Carolyn Sue Ford, Alexandria, LA, Aug 18, 73; chdn Kristy Michelle, Matthew Thomas; NWSU 74, BA; RTS 81, MDiv; LBTS 08, ThD; O Mar 14, 82, LA Pby; instr, Reg WhitBC, 81-82; ss, p Tabb Street P Ch, Petersburg, VA, 83-86; Chap USAR 85-87; Chap US Army Ft. Irwin, CA 87-90; Republic of Korea 90-91; Ft. Polk, LA 91-93; Redstone Asrenal, AL 94-97; Republic of Korea 97-98; Ft. Gordon, GA 98-00; Ft.Totten, NY 00-01; Chap Recruiter Grand Prairie, TX 01-06; Chap Trainer Ft. Meade, MD 06-08; Ret.USArmy 08; pulpit supply; hr 14

7 Ford Road, Boyce, LA 71409 – 817-819-5694   Nashville
E-mail: mffchagr@yahoo.com
HR

Frech, Tom – O Apr 5, 09, Chspk Pby; op Gateway Comm of Faith, White Hall, MD, 09-

16 Deer Woods Court, Glen Arm, MD 21057   Chesapeake
E-mail: tomfrech@verizon.net
Gateway Community of Faith – 410-692-6100

Freitas, Fernando – p Redentor P Ch, South River, NJ, 11-

90 Leonardine Avenue, South River, NJ 08882 – 732-257-2453   Metropolitan New York
E-mail: fernandolaf@verizon.net
Redentor Presbyterian Church – 732-257-5611

Freitas, Mario – astp Mercy Hill P Ch, Sewell, NJ, 17-18

1053 Quakenbush Road, Unit J, Snow Camp, NC 27349   New Jersey
E-mail: mario@moreusa.org

Frese, John – O Jul 8, 12, PlVall Pby; astp Zion Ch, Lincoln, NE, 15-16; p Grace Cov Ch, Bloomington, MN, 16-

12916 Highclere Drive, Burnsville, MN 55337   Siouxlands
E-mail: john.frese@gracecovmn.org
Grace Covenant Church – 952-888-4988

Frett, Calvin Franklin – b Camden, NJ, Feb 21, 33; f Harry; m Louise Friedrich; w Dorothy Gray, Newark, DE, Sept 6, 58; chdn Daniel Calvin, Jan Louise, Pamela Mary; ShelC 55, BA; CTS 58, BD; WTS

Fritz, Freddy, continued
83-86, MDiv; L Mar 3, 87; O Mar 10, 91, EFC; ascp Chippewa EFC, Beaver Falls, PA, 86-91; p Oakwood P Ch, State College, PA, 91-02; srp Tampa Bay P Ch, Tampa, FL, 02-

28750 Skyglade Place, Wesley Chapel, FL 33543 – 813-731-0456   Southwest Florida
E-mail: freddy@freddyfritz.com
Tampa Bay Presbyterian Church – 813-973-2484

Frizzell, Roger D. – b Charlottetown, PEI, Jun 17, 49; m Annie Todd; w Gloria Jean MacMillan, Charlottetown, PEI, Feb 3, 68; chdn Mark, Helen, Matthew; UPEI 72, dipl, 81, BEd; FCSC 89-92, dipl; L Jul 92; O Aug 30, 83, Free Ch of Scotland; Recd PCA May 31, 97, Ecar Pby; p PEI, Canada, 93-96; p Covenant Ref P Ch, Miramichi, NB, 97-

547 Newcastle Boulevard, Miramichi, NB E1V 2K5 CANADA – 506-622-7176   Eastern Canada
Covenant Reformed Presbyterian Church

Froehlich, Steven D. – b Abington, PA, Jun 12, 56; f Harry James (d); m Helen Yerga Sorchik (d); w Sheryl Ann Cummings, Lima, OH, Jun 10, 78; chdn Christopher Ryan, Jonathan Andrew, Timothy James; BJU 78, BA; RTS 91, MDiv; GCTS 15, DMin; L Feb 10, 90; O Mar 8, 92, MSVal Pby; int First P Ch, Jackson, MS, 89-91; Chap, dirAdm RTS, 91-95, admin, exec vp 95-98; astp Highlands P Ch, Ridgeland, MS, 94-96;srp New Life P Ch, Ithaca, NY, 98-; brd pres Chesterton House Cent for Christ Stud, CornellU, Ithaca, NY, 00-11; brd mbr PCA Found, 01-03, 06-14

611 Mitchell Street, Ithaca, NY 14850-1260 – 607-273-1733   New York State
E-mail: steve@newlifepres.com
New Life Presbyterian Church – 607-277-8398

Frost, Donald Charles Jr. – b Macon, GA, Dec 10, 46; f Donald Charles; m Margie Elizabeth Hobby; w Lou April Cable, Macon, GA, May 18, 69; chdn Christopher Charles, Cable Matthew; ClemU 69, BA; RTS 79, MDiv, 08, DMin; L Jan 14, 78, CentGA Pby; O May 27, 79, Cov Pby; p Morgan City & Itta Bena chs, MS, 79-81; op Dayspring P Ch, Forsyth, GA, 81-87; srp Pear Orchard P Ch, Ridgeland, MS, 87-93; ev, chp CentFL Pby, 93; op Redeemer P Ch, Jacksonville, FL, 94-96, srp 96-98; srp Westminster P Ch, Atlanta, GA, 99-11; ob special asst to Chancellor, RTS, 11-14; ascp Madison Heights P Ch, Madison, MS, 14-18; ip, ss Evangelical P Ch, Newark, DE, 18-

4500 Linden Hill Road, A-310, Wilmington, DE 19808 – 601-946-6838   Mississippi Valley
E-mail: chuck.frost46@gmail.com
Evangelical Presbyterian Church – 302-737-2300

Frost, Tim – b Jan 17, 78; f Richard P.; m Julayne K.; w Jonelle Sobran, Nov 15, 08; chdn Adelyn May, Declan Myers; JMU 00; CTS 07, MDiv; ascp Covenant P Ch, Harrisonburg, VA, 08-

32 Southgate Court, Suite 101, Harrisonburg, VA 22801   Blue Ridge
E-mail: tim@cov-pres.org
Covenant Presbyterian Church – 540-433-3051

Fuller, George C. – b Ft. Wayne, IN, Apr 13, 32; f Roger Alden; m Eleanor Cain; w Margaret Jane Longenecker, Havertown, PA, Sept 7, 57; chdn Catherine Ann, David Alden, Deborah Lee, Suzanne Joy; HavC 53, BS; BabsC 76, MBA; PTS 56, MDiv; WTS 62, ThM, 64, ThD; L Apr 56, Phil Pby (UPCUSA); O Jun 56, Phil Pby (UPCUSA); ap Baltimore, 56-60; prof NWC, 63-65; p Birmingham, 66-68; p Duluth, 68-71; prof RTS, 71-72; p Boston, 72-76; exec dir NPRF, 76-82; DnFac WTS, 79-82, pres 82-91, prof 91-99; srp Covenant P Ch, Cherry Hill, NJ, 92-99; hr 99; *Play It My Way;* ed *Serving and Challenging Seniors*

129 Farmington Road, Cherry Hill, NJ 08034-2513 – 856-429-3404   New Jersey
E-mail: FullerGJ@verizon.net
HR

Frett, Calvin Franklin, continued
95, DMin; O Jun 58, NJ Pby (BPC); ap First Evan Ch, Memphis, TN, 58-61; mis WPM, Japan, 61-75; p EP Ch, Trenton, NJ, 75-79; p Evangelical P Ch, Newark, DE, 79-87; ap Timonium P Ch, Timonium, MD, 87-90; p Rainbow P Ch, Rainbow City, AL, 90-93, wc 93-95; PIR Ministries, VA Beach, VA, 95-; hr 97

908 General Jackson Drive, Virginia Beach, VA 23454-2721 – 757-481-6485　　　　　Tidewater
E-mail: cdfrett@verizon.net
Pastor In Residence Ministries
HR

　　Frey, Brian Gibson – b Knoxville, TN, May 2, 81; w Gail, Nashville, TN, Jul 2, 05; chdn Maggie Grace, Owen Hailey, Ellis Gibson; UGA 04, BS; WTS 11, MDiv; O Nov 11, 11, PacNW Pby; campm RUF, Boise S, 11-

1115 North 15th Street, Boise, ID 83702　　　　　Pacific Northwest
E-mail: brian.frey@ruf.org
PCA Reformed University Fellowship

　　Frickenschmidt, Tim – astp All Saints P Ch, Austin, TX, 06-12; srp 12-

1304 Goeth Circle, Austin, TX 78746　　　　　South Texas
E-mail: tfrickenschmidt@allsaintsaustin.org
All Saints Presbyterian Church – 512-732-8383

　　Friederichsen, Donald – O Mar 25, 12, MNY Pby; p Covenant P Ch, Short Hills, NJ, 12-

106 Glen Avenue, Millburn, NJ 07041 – 973-545-6301　　　　　Metropolitan New York
E-mail: pastordonny@covenantshorthills.org
Covenant Presbyterian Church – 973-467-8454

　　Frierson, David Minor – b Summerville, SC, Oct 6, 54; f Manton R.; m Lillian Wingfield; w Suzette Jones, Greenville, SC, Jun 3, 78; chdn David Minor, Rebecca Michelle, Jonathan Edwards; USC 73-77, BA; GCTS 77-81, MDiv; NCentTheoSem 15, DMin; O Jan 31, 82, Cal Pby; p Reidville P Ch, Reidville, SC, 82-86; p Second Street P Ch, Albemarle, NC, 86-91; p Mount Carmel P Ch, Ellerbe, NC, 91-97; op Norman P Ch, Norman, NC, 93-96; sc CentCar Pby, 93-06; p Norman P Ch, Norman, NC, 96-06; p Sherwood Shores Chapel, Gordonville, TX, 06-16; chap Sherwood Shores Vol Fire Dept, 09-16; sc NoTX pby, 10-16; p Covenant P Ch at Greenville, Greenville, MS, 17-; alt PCA AC, 10-11

304 Crittenden Street, Greenville, MS 38701 – 662-702-3615　　　　　Covenant
E-mail: pastordavid@covenantgreenvillems.org
Covenant Presbyterian Church at Greenville – 662-332-6074

　　Friesen, Lynell – b Red Wing, MN, Mar 11, 56; f Erwin K.; m Janet Ann Heide; w Deborah Jane Dockendorff, Limerick, ME, Jul 19, 80; chdn Joshua David, Sarah Kathryn, Micah Benjamin; LeTC 78, BS; RTSFL 00, MDiv; L Sept 28, 00, Siouxl Pby, O Ma 25, 01, Soiouxl Pby p Alexander P Ch, Underwood, ND 01-03; p Christ The King P Ch, Surrey. BC, 04-06; asst dir TWU-B, 07-09; CH intern Peace Health, Bellingham, WA 10-11; CH resident/Staff Providence AK Med Ctr 12-13, StaffChap, 13-17; Chap St. Nicholas Hospital, Sheboygan, WI, 17-;　"Richard Baxter, Part I: Baxter's Life and Ministry," *IIIM Magazine Online*; "Richard Baxter, Part 2: Baxter's Work and Thought" *IIIM Magazine Online*

4701 A Amanda Lane, Sheboygan, WI 53081 – 360-820-2097　　　　　Pacific Northwest
E-mail: lynell.friesen@comcast.net
St. Nicholas Hospital

　　Fritz, Freddy – b Brakpan, South Africa, Nov 18, 56; f Gerhard Franz; m Emily Denise; w Eileen Marie McCloy, Deerfield, IL, Dec 14, 85; chdn Lauren Leigh, Jonathan Leighton; UCTSA 77-81, BS; TEDS

MINISTERIAL DIRECTORY 209

Fuller, J. Scott – b Rome, GA, Jul 15, 64; f Ken; m Paula Whitehead; w Renée Rogers, Bristol, TN, Jun 6, 87; chdn Hannah, Rebekah, Grace, Mary Everett, Miriam Lee; MonC 84, AA; KgC 86, BA; GCTS 91, MDiv; L Jul 92; O Jun 27, 93, Wcar Pby; Chap Crossnore Sch, Inc, Crossnore, NC, 90-92; stus Fellowship P Ch, Newland, NC, 92-93, p 93-06; op Grace Highlands Ch, Boone, NC, 06-10; p 10-14; wc 14-18; ip, ss First P ch, Summerville, GA, 18-

5 Bray Road, Rome, GA 30161 – 828-387-0752   Northwest Georgia
E-mail: jscottfuller@gmail.com
First Presbyterian Church – 706-857-4338

Fullilove, William – b Atlanta, GA, Mar 20, 73; f Thomas; m Donna; w Jill; chdn Caroline, Evelyn; PU 95, AB; RTS 06, MDiv; CathUAm 08, MA, 14, PhD; astp McLean P Ch, McLean, VA, 07-13; prof RTSA, 13- 16; astp McLean P Ch, McLean, VA, 16-; assoc prof RTSNY; "Kings" in *A Biblical Theological Introduction to the Old Testament*, 16; *Introduction to Hebrew: a Guide for Learning and Using Biblical Hebrew*, 17; *A Graded Reader of Biblical Hebrew: Mastering Different Literary Styles from Simple to Advanced*, 18

3200 North Rochester Street, Arlington, VA 22213   Potomac
E-mail: bill@mcleanpres.org
McLean Presbyterian Church – 703-821-0800

Funyak, James Daele – b Pittsburgh, PA, Jul 11, 72; f Adolph Jack; m Dayle Ruthann Stang; w Dori Ellen Doutt, Valencia, PA, May 20, 95; chdn Jakub, Isaak, Andru, Luke; GroCC 91-95, BA; RPTS 95-99, MDiv; CTS 14, DMin; L Jan 30, 99, Asc Pby; O Aug 15, 99, Asc Pby; ydir Gospel Flwsp P Ch, Valencia, PA, 95-98; astpSt. Johns United Evang. Ch (Ind), Rochester, PA, 98-99; astp Westminster P Ch, Butler, PA, 99-01; p Covenant Comm P Ch, Wexford, PA, 01-09; srp Pinewood P Ch, Middleburg, FL, 09-

905 Clay Street, Fleming Island, FL 32003   North Florida
E-mail: jd.funyak@pinewoodpca.org
Pinewood Presbyterian Church – 904-272-7177

Furey, James Michael – b Passaic, NJ, Jul 25, 58; f John F.; m Carol E. Vetri; w Carol A. Landau, Antioch, TN, Jul 26, 80; chdn Christine, Megan, Laura, Andrew; ClarU 80, BS; RTS 99, MDiv; L Oct 00, GrLks Pby; O Mar 01, GrLks Pby; astp Christ Comm Ch, Carmel, IN, 01-03; chp, op Trinity P Ch, Indianapolis, IN, 01-05, p 05-14; ev 14-15; op Christ Ch, Buffalo, NY, 15-; ss Armor Bible P Ch, Orchard Park, NY, 16-17

33 Greenhill Terrace, Buffalo, NY 14224 – 716-328-3070   New York State
E-mail: jcfurey@sbcglobal.net
Christ Church – 716-328-3070

Furman, John Riva – b Philadelphia, PA, Dec 24, 52; f Alester G.; m Alma Lawless; w Martha C. Marshall, Greenville, SC, Jul 07, 79; chdn Jennifer A., Riva M.; MonC 71-73, As; ClemU 73-75, BS; CTS 76; StLU 76-79, MA; RTS 83-86, MDiv, 06, DMin; O Aug 86, Wcar Pby; ydir Glendale P Ch, 76-78; ydir Grier Mem P Ch (ARP), 85; ascp Arden P Ch, Arden, NC, 86-94; p Westminster P Ch, Roanoke, VA, 94-12; chap Gentle Shepherd Hospice, Roanoke, 12-

2977 Golf Colony Drive, Salem, VA 24153 – 540-309-0686   Blue Ridge
Gentle Shepherd Hospice, Roanoke

Furuto, Donald K. – b Los Angeles, CA, Mar 23, 48; f Kazuto; m Sadako Domoto; w Bonnie Lu Houtz, Birmingham, AL, May 7, 83; chdn Daniel Jeremy, Luke Zachary, Matthew Kirk; UCLA 70, BA; USCA 77, PhD; BhamTS 85, MDiv; CTS 00, DMin; L Jan 28, 97; O Mar 9, 97, Evan Pby; mgr Briarwood P Ch, adult ed, Birmingham, AL, 87-96, astp 97-98, ascp 98-; t BrChS, 03-; *The Effect of Team Competency Enhancement on the Outreach of Christian Small Groups*

404 Oak Glen Lane, Birmingham, AL 35244 – 205-985-9864   Evangel
E-mail: dfuruto@bcsk12.org
Briarwood Presbyterian Church
Briarwood Christian School – 205-776-5900 ext. 694

Futato, Mark David – b Beaver Falls, PA, Dec 30, 54; f Rudolph David; m June E. Kalinoski; w Adele D. Hammerlee, Corry, PA, Jul 12, 75; chdn William D., Evan D., M. David Jr., Anne D.; GenC 76, BA; WTS 79, MDiv; CathUAm 82, MA, 84, PhD; L May 79, RPCES; O Oct 83, OPC; Recd PCA May 26, 91, SoCst Pby; p Covenant OPC, Burtonsville, MD; assoc prof WSCAL, 88-99; ascp New Life P Ch, Escondido, CA, 91-99; ob prof RTSFL, 99-

600 Lakeport Trail, Oviedo, FL 32765 – 407-971-1208   Central Florida
E-mail: mfutato@rts.edu
Reformed Theological Seminary, FL – 407-366-9493
1231 Reformation Drive, Oviedo, FL 32765

Futo, Robert E. – b St. Louis, MO, Aug 1, 66; f Albert; m Anna Reinbold; w Tunde Eva Sipos, Hungary, Jun 17, 95; chdn Tunde Hajnal, Csenge Adrienn; UMO 86-90, BA; CTS 95-99, MDiv; O Nov 14, 99, MO Pby; ob mis Budapest, Hungary, 99-

2051 Biatorbagy, Arany Janos u.8 63301 Hungary – 0113620 964 1530   Missouri
E-mail: rtfuto95@gmail.com

Futoran, Philip – b Washington, DC, Feb 5, 52; f Josef; m Helen Watson Luther Bowden; w Liisabeth Jo Mentgen, San Bernardino, CA, Aug 4, 79; chdn Benjamin Joseph, Anna Danielle; O Jul 78, GrLks Pby (BPC); Recd PCA Jul 2, 96, GrLks Pby; astp Covenant Bible Ch, 75-76; astp Grace BPC, 76-79; p Comm BPC, 79-87; Chap USArmy, 87-96; ascp Faith P Ch, Cincinnati, OH, 96-06; Chap USArmy, 06-12; p Warrington P Ch, Pensacola, FL, 12-16; hr 18

328 South 61st Avenue, Pensacola, FL 32506   Gulf Coast
HR

Gage, Warren – w Betty; chdn Leah Grace, Nathaniel; prof KTS, 02-15; astp Coral Ridge P Ch, Ft. Lauderdale, FL, 03-15; ob pres The Alexandrian Forum, 15-; astp Rio Vista Community Ch, Ft. Lauderdale, FL, 17-; *The Gospel of Genesis: The Story of Joseph & Judah; Milestones to Emmaus, Romance of Redemption, There Is No Greater Love*

PO Box 39845, Ft. Lauderdale, FL 33339 – 954-565-7358   South Florida
E-mail: wgage@alexandrianforum.org
The Alexandrian Forum
Rio Vista Community Church – 954-522-2518

Gahagen, Donald H. Jr. – b Windber, PA, Sept 29, 36; f Donald; m Bernice Abram; w Sue Sporleder, Atlanta, GA, May 28, 61; chdn Donald Craig, Timothy Carter; MHC; USC; UMiami; BelC; ColTS 59-62, MDiv; O Oct 18, 77, SFL Pby; mis Peru, 62-76; mis Bolivia, 76-79; mis MAF, 80-84; astp Coral Ridge P Ch, Ft. Lauderdale, FL, 84-86; MTW, coord, Africa & Latin Am, 86-99; MTW, Sr. Assoc Field Services, 99-06; hr 06

3570 North Longpine Point, Beverly Hills, FL 34465   South Florida
E-mail: DGahagen@compuserve.com
HR

Gaking, Mark – astp Hunt Valley Ch, Hunt Valley, MD, 02-03; wc 03-

8 Overgate Court, Cockeysville, MD 21030 – 410-667-6282   Chesapeake

Gale, Stanley D. – b Lewes, DE, Oct 23, 53; f Enoch R III; m Gale Lee; w Linda Louise Neilon, West Chester, PA, Feb 8, 75; chdn Samantha Tamar, Luke Aaron, Sarah Louise, Nathan Michael; UDE 75, BA, 78, MEd; WTS 85, MAR, 86, MDiv; CTS 97, DMin; L May 86, DMV Pby; O Oct 86, DMV Pby; ap Wallace P Ch, Hyattsville, MD, 86-88; srp Reformed P Ch, West Chester, PA, 88-16; astp Iron Works Ch, Phoenixville, PA, 16-18; hr; *Who Am I? A Primer in Career Planning From a Christian Perspective*, 81;

Gale, Stanley D., continued
The Effect of Strategic Prayer on the Evangelistic Attitude and Activity of the Local Church, 97; *Community Houses of Prayer Ministry Manual: Reaching Others for Christ through Strategic Prayer*, 02; *Warfare Witness: Contending With Spiritual Opposition in Everyday Evangelism*, 05; *God's Good News: A Summary of the Bible's Message of Life*, 05; *The Prayer of Jehoshaphat: Seeing Beyond Life's Storms*, 07; *Community Houses of Prayer Ministry Manual* rev & exp, 07; "The Battle of Our Lives," *Tabletalk*, July 07; "Praying the Imprecatory Psalms," *Worldview Church*, 08; *What is Spiritual Warfare?* (Basics of the Reformed Faith series), 08; *How Can I Know Eternal Life?* 10; *Making Sanity Out of Vanity: Christian Realism in the Book of Ecclesiastes*, 11; *What is Prayer ?* (Basics of the Faith series), 12; "God's House of Prayer: Extreme Makeover Edition," *Presbyterion*, Spring 13; *A Vine-Ripened Life: Spiritual Fruitfulness through Abiding in Christ*, 14; *Why Must We Forgive?* 15; *Finding Forgiveness: Discovering the Healing Power of the Gospel*, 16; *The Christian's Creed: Embracing the Apostolic Faith,* 18; *The Christian's Creed: A Workbook*, 18

426 Hightop Road, West Chester, PA 19380-4611 – 610-696-6491   Philadelphia Metro West
HR

Gallo, Jordan Mark – O Jan 31, 16, PD Pby; p Faith P Ch, Florence, SC, 16-

200 Bentree Lane #A12, Florence, SC 29501 – 843-496-2472   Pee Dee
E-mail: gallojm1@gmail.com
Faith Presbyterian Church – 843-665-9235

Galloway, Caleb – b Enterprise, AL, Apr 3, 80; w Whitney; chdn Annsleigh Lynn, Stella Elizabeth, Scarlett Grace, Helen Hattie; AUM 03, BS; CTS 13, MDiv; O Jun 9, 13, SEAL Pby; p Covenant P Ch, Eufaula, AL, 13-18; astp First P Ch, Dothan, AL, 18-

409 Eton Drive, Dothan, AL 36305 – 334-850-1813   Southeast Alabama
E-mail: calebcgalloway@gmail.com
First Presbyterian Church – 334-794-3128

Galloway, Gerald R. – ascp New Life P Ch, Escondido, CA, 00-04; sc SoCst Pby, 00-05; hr 04

E-mail: didocrew11@cox.net   South Coast
HR

Gamble, Larry J. – b Akron, OH, Feb 4, 55; f James W.; m Elizabeth Gilanyi; w Debra A. Smith, Atlanta, GA, Nov 18, 78; chdn Darci Kay, Zachary Nicholas; GSU 77, BBA; RolC 85, MBA; RTS 94, MDiv; L Apr 93, CentFL Pby; O Nov 6, 94, CentGA Pby; astp First P Ch, Macon, GA, 94-99; srp Westminster P Ch, Clinton, SC, 99-05; astp Christ Comm Ch, Simpsonville, SC, 05-08; wc 09-

318 Majesty Court, Greenville, SC 29615 – 864-962-8743   Calvary
E-mail: debbielarryg@yahoo.com

Gambrell, David – astp Orangewood P Ch, Maitland, FL, 15-18

844 West Shadowlawn Drive, Chattanooga, TN 37404   Central Florida

Games, Fred Edward – b Lake Milton, OH, Oct 15, 70; f William B.; m Carol Ann Marino; w Virginia Aimee, Cleveland, MS, May 29, 93; chdn Ann Lundy, Evangeline, Edward, Chloe; DSU, BA; RTS, MDiv; L May 99, Nash Pby; O Sept 99, Nash Pby; campm RUF, MTSU, 99-07; campm RUF, WestKY, 07-15; srp Redeemer P Ch, Louisville, KY, 15-

7304 Maria Avenue, Louisville, KY 40222 – 270-799-0179   Ohio Valley
E-mail: fritz@redeemer-pca.com
Redeemer Presbyterian Church – 502-456-5500

Gammage, Anthony – O Mar 22, 15, EPA Pby; astp New Life P Ch, Dresher, PA, 15-17, srp 17-

773 Cricket Avenue, Glenside, PA 19038   Eastern Pennsylvania
E-mail: anthony.gammage@newlifedresher.org
New Life Presbyterian Church – 215-641-1100

Ganas, Nicholas – w Christine; CC 90, BA; WSCAL 93, MDiv, 03, DMin; O Jul 94, OPC; srp Timonium P Ch, Timonium, MD, 05-

303 West Timonium Road, Timonium, MD 210932930 – 410-804-1654   Chesapeake
E-mail: drg@timpca.org
Timonium Presbyterian Church – 410-252-5663

Ganey, George Francis III – b Laurinburg, NC, Jan 4, 62; f G.F. Jr; m Pamela Lee Parker; w Katherine Elizabeth Tucker, Mullins, SC, Jun 23, 85; chdn Ashley Elizabeth, Lesley Susanna, Caroline Grace; BelC 82; FMarC 85, BS; RTS 85-88, MDiv; L Oct 88; O Aug 20, 89, Cal Pby; p Zion P Ch, Chester, SC, 88-92; p First P Ch, Villa Rica, GA, 92-96; astp Harvester P Ch, Douglasville, GA, 96-98; prin Harvester Chr Ac, 96-98; p Smyrna P Ch, Smyrna, GA, 98-15

1308 North Park Street Ext, Mullins, SC 29574-1616 – 770-431-0400   Northwest Georgia

Ganucheau, Michael J. – b Baton Rouge, LA, Oct 25, 48; f John J (d); m Norma B (d); w Stephanie L. Hunter, Knoxville, TN, Jun 20, 81; chdn Kristen L., Adam M., Jared H., Nathan D.; TusC 88, BS; RTS 88-91, MDiv; L Jun 91; O Mar 1, 92, MSVal Pby; stus Wesson P Ch, Wesson, MS, 90-91; stus Monticello P Ch, Monticello, MS, 90-91; ss Pickens P Ch, Pickens, MS, 91-92, p 92-97; p First P Ch, Hazlehurst, MS, 97-; ss Wesson P Ch, Wesson, MS; hr

1023 Perrett Road, Hazlehurst, MS 39083 – 601-894-4303   Grace
E-mail: mjgfamily@bellsouth.net
HR

Ganzel, Cornelius (Neal) J. Jr. – b Gainesville, FL, Jun 17, 49; f Cornelius Joseph, Sr.; m Elizabeth Hooker; w Suzanne Margaret Lutz, Jackson, MS, Aug 20, 77; ABAC 69, AA; FAU 76, BA; RTS 76; RTSFL 01, MDiv; L Apr 17, 99, NFL Pby; L Oct 28, 00, CentFL Pby; O Jun 17, 01, CentFL Pby; sp Redeemer P Ch, Jacksonville, FL, 99-00; stus Coquina P Ch, Ormond Beach, FL, 00-01, p 01-

68 Creek Bluff Way, Ormond Beach, FL 32174 – 386-677-2041   Central Florida
E-mail: ipneal@juno.com
Coquina Presbyterian Church – 386-677-2041

Garbarino, Tony – b Idaho, Nov 23, 71; f Charles Edwin; m Patricia Marie Gale; w Mica Christephany Westin, Las Vegas, NV, Apr 3, 94; chdn Vincente Marshall, Abriana Ciella; Western Int U 07, AB; WSCAL 12, MDiv; Recd PCA Sept 17, 16, GrLks Pby; p Providence P Ch, Ft. Wayne, IN, 16-

1302 West Rudisill Boulevard, Fort Wayne, IN 46807   Great Lakes
E-mail: tonygarbarino@live.com
Providence Presbyterian Church – 260-744-1022

Garber, Aaron Patrick – w Lacey; chdn Emily, Daniel, Jonathan, Claire, Levi; WheatC; GCTS; O Sept 10, 06, Pitts Pby; ascp Calvin P Ch, North Huntingdon, PA, 06, srp 06-

4273 Walurba Avenue, Trafford, PA 15642   Pittsburgh
E-mail: agarber@calvinpca.org
Calvin Presbyterian Church – 724-863-1192

Garcia, Ronnie – w Amanda; chdn Micah, Adeline, Mia, Ruthie; astp Briarwood P Ch, Birmingham, AL, 10-; op Iglesia La Travesía, Río Piedras, San Juan, PR, 10-; op Trinity Ch Dorado, San Juan, PR, 15-

Urb. Pacifica, PG-70 Via Horizonte, Trujillo Alto, PR 00976 – 787-550-6387   Evangel
E-mail: ronniegarcia@mac.com
Briarwood Presbyterian Church – 205-776-5200
Iglesia La Travesía – 787-294-6791
Trinity Church Dorado – 787-550-6387

Gardner, Bruce J. – b Crossville, TN, Jul 31, 50; f Dr. James L; m Margaret Ewing; w Christy Merville, Wurtemburg, May 29, 76; chdn Bruce Jay II, Michael Lee, Erin Elizabeth, Stephen Matthew; GenC 72, BS; RPTS 77, MDiv; L Sept 77, Asc Pby; O Feb 78, MidAtl Pby; op Grace Ch, Hancock, MD, 77-79, p 79-81; op Berean P Ch, Ellwood City, PA, 81, p 82-

383 Gardner Lane, Ellwood City, PA 16117 – 724-758-6732   Ascension
E-mail: berean@zoominternet.net
Berean Presbyterian Church – 724-758-7671

Gardner, Forrest Curt – b Nashville, TN, Jun 13, 61; f Joe C. Jr.; m Dora Aliene Shumaker; w Kimberlee Ann Duncan, Charlestown, IN, May 20, 83; chdn Dora Abigail, Eliot Duncan; WKU 79-83, BA; GCTS 83-87, MDiv; L Apr 87; O May 89, NGA Pby; ydir Round Pond Ch, 82; astp Plains P Ch, 83; stus Rock P msn, 87; int Hope P Ch, Marietta, GA, 87-89, astp 89-91; op Trinity Ch, Richmond, KY, 91-94, p 94-

406 Prospect Street, Berea, KY 40403 – 859-986-5842   Ohio Valley
E-mail: curt@trinitychurchpca.org
Trinity Church PCA – 859-624-8910

Gardner, Joe C. Jr. – p Hopewell P Ch, Mount Olive, MS, 04-; p Mount Olive P Ch, Mount Olive, MS, 04-

PO Box 148, Mount Olive, MS 39119   Grace
E-mail: mopc148@hughes.net
Hopewell Presbyterian Church – 601-797-3523
Mount Olive Presbyterian Church – 601-797-3817

Gardner, Kevin – b Dearborn, MI, Nov 8, 76; f Bruce R.; m Kathryn A. Yarwood; w Katie Gorbey, Media, PA, Dec 23, 11; PASU 98, BA; WTS 13, MDiv; O Jun 3, 18, CentFL Pby; ob LigMin, Sanford, FL

1114 South Park Avenue, Sanford, FL 32771 – 215-407-1951   Central Florida
E-mail: kgardner@ligonier.org
Ligonier Ministries – 407-333-4244
421 Ligonier Court, Sanford, FL 32771

Gardner, Paul Douglas – w Sharon; chdn Jonathan, David, Hannah; KingsC, London, BA; RTS, MDiv; UCam, PhD; astp St. Martins, Cambridge, 80-83; lect Oak Hill Theological College, London, 83-90; srp St John's Hartford, Cheshire, England, 90-02; archdeacon, Exeter, England, 02-05; srp ChristChurch P, Atlanta, GA, 05-17; hr 17; *The Gifts of God and the Authentication of a Christian: an Exegesis of 1 Corinthians 8:1-11:1*, 90; Focus on the Bible commentaries: *Revelation*, 01, and *Ephesians*, 07 and *1& 2 Peter and Jude*, 13; ed *Zondervan Encyclopaedia of Bible Characters*, latest reprint 14; "1 Corinthians," *Zondervan Exegetical Commentary Series,* 18

30 Archibald Road, Exeter, GA EX1 1SA United Kingdom – +44-1392-920020   Metro Atlanta
E-mail: paul01@cantab.net
HR

Gardner, Robert W. – b Birmingham, AL, Mar 23, 49; f John W; m Ada D. Noblitt; w Sherrill Lynne Bailey (d), (2) Kip Caroline Fichtner, Birmingham, AL, May 21, 05; chdn Gregory Matthew, Jonathan Andrew, Christy Colleen; JAXSU 71, BS; CTS 80, MDiv; L Apr 80; O Apr 80, Evan Pby; Chap USAF, Castle AFB, CA, 80-83; Chap USAF, Diyarbakir, Turkey, 83-84; Chap USAF, Eglin AFB, FL, 84-88; Chap USAF, Izmir, Turkey, 88-90; Chap USAF, Loring AFB, ME, 90-93; Chap USAF, Offutt AFB, NE, 93-96; Chap USAF, Hurlburt Field, FL, 96-00; Chap USAF, MacDill AFB, FL, 00-03; Chap USAF, Eglin AFB, 04-06; Chap USAF, Ramstein, Germany, 07-08; USAF Ret 08; hr 10

3407 Polo Downs, Hoover, AL 35226-3370   Gulf Coast
E-mail: afchapo6@yahoo.com
HR

Garland, Charles – b Asheville, NC, Mar 4, 63; f Ray Lewis; m Evelyn Naomi Rogers; w Julie Kay Payne, Chattanooga, TN, Aug 22, 87; chdn Zachary Doyle, Alexandria Payne; UGA 84, BA; CTS 93, MDiv; L Oct 92, SEAL Pby; O Jun 7, 93, Evan Pby; campm WDA, AU, 84-90; srp Decatur P Ch, Decatur, AL, 93-01; op Intown P Ch, Portland, OR, 01-04, p 04-05; p Ivy Creek Ch, Lawrenceville, GA, 05-16; srp Restoration P Ch, Hoschton, GA, 16-17; chp 17-

1324 North Norton Avenue, Tucson, AZ 85719 – 678-849-7918   Arizona
E-mail: charles@gracetucson.net

Garmany, Hutch – w Ashleigh; chdn Hutchinson, Winters, Grey, Bo, Mae; UGA 01, BS; RTSFL 08, MDiv; astp Rock Creek Flwsp, Rising Fawn, GA, 09-18; op Gr Comm Trenton, Trenton, GA, 14-18, p 18-

50 Wren Avenue, Trenton, GA 30752   Tennessee Valley
E-mail: hutch@gracetrenton.org
Grace Community Trenton – 423-313-5441

Garner, David Bruce – w Minda; chdn Daniel, Charissa, Darin, Melynda, Dawson, Cherith; UNC, BS; DTS, ThM; WTS, PhD; L 03, Phil Pby; mis MTW, Bulgaria, 02; ascprof WTS; p/teach Proclamation P Ch, Bryn Mawr, PA, 12-15

4005 Center Avenue, Lafayette Hill, PA 19444   Philadelphia Metro West
E-mail: dgarner@wts.edu
Westminster Theological Seminary

Garofalo, Santo – b Pt. Pleasant, NJ, Dec 20, 66; f Santo; m Rose Carratello (d); w Mary Ellen McClaren, Alexandria, VA, Jan 3, 89; chdn Collyn Roy, Caleb; CC 93, BA; MidARS 96; CTS 11, DMin; L Jul 95, TNVal Pby; L Sept 97, Pot Pby; O Mar 1, 98, Pot Pby; int Grace Ref P Ch, Relay, MD, 96, astp 97-98, ascp 98-99; p Reformed P Ch, Duanesburg, NY, 00-08; op New City Flwsp of Atlantic City, Atlantic City, NJ, 08-

2007 Keuhnle Avenue, Atlantic City, NJ 08401 – 609-350-3328   New Jersey
E-mail: pastorsanto@gmail.com
New City Fellowship of Atlantic City – 609-442-1219

Garretson, James Marshall – b Gettysburg, PA, Nov 11, 58; f Marshall S.; m Jane P. Small; w Susan J. White, San Diego, CA, Sept 22, 90; chdn Asha Y, Trace Laurence M., Michaela Quinn, Isaiah, Rebekah; PineJC 77; CC 81, BA; CTS; WTS, MDiv; RegC 86, STM, 87, MDiv; WSCAL 03, DMin; L May 87; O Mar 5, 88, OPC; Recd PCA 94, Pac Pby; p Trinity OPC, Chicago, IL, 88-92; p Covenant Comm P Ch, Columbia, TN, 92-94; p Calvary P Ch, Glendale, CA, 94-01; p Tulpehocken UCC, Richland, PA, 01-03; srp Providence P Ch, Quakertown, PA, 05-07; ob KTS, 07-09; wc 10-; *Princeton and Preaching: Archibald Alexander and the Christian Ministry*, 04

4117 West Palm Aire Drive #B1, Pompano Beach, FL 33069 – 954-366-6422   South Florida
E-mail: aaprinceton@yahoo.com

MINISTERIAL DIRECTORY

Garrett, Christopher Morgan – b Ponca City, OK, Oct 8, 67; f Edward Paul; m Patricia Trower; w Virginia Humphrey Wilson, Houston, TX, May 31, 97; UNC 90, BA; GCTS 99, MDiv; O May 21, 00, Ecar Pby; astp, yp Church of the Good Shepherd, Durham, NC, 98-02; mis MTW, Manila, 02-08; ob exec dir Samaritan Health Center, 08-12; astp Ch of the Good Shepherd, Durham, NC, 12-13; ascp 13-

9 Finchley Court, Hillsborough, NC 27278 – 919-794-8776   Eastern Carolina
E-mail: chrisgarrett@cgsonline.org
Church of the Good Shepherd – 919-490-1634

Garrett, Joshua – b Savannah, GA, Nov 16, 81; O Sept 22, 13, CentGA Pby; astp North Macon P Ch, Macon, GA, 13-5; ascp 15-

780 Captain Kell Drive, Macon, GA 31204 – 912-655-5491   Central Georgia
E-mail: Josh@nmpc.net
North Macon Presbyterian Church – 478-477-7777

Garriott, Charles Michael – b Baltimore, MD, Mar 29, 53; f Charles W.; m Cleo Lehmann; w Debby Cacace, Baltimore, MD, Jan 29, 74; chdn Charles Phillip, Katie Michelle, Anna Christine, Peter Michael; CatCC 74, AA; UB 76, BS; CTS 79, MDiv; L Mar 79, DMV Pby; O Jun 80, NJ Pby (RPCES); ap Covenant P Ch, Cherry Hill, NJ, 79-83; srp Heritage P Ch, Edmond, OK, 83-03; ascp 03-05; SrStaff MNA, Director of Ministry to State, 05-; *Work Excellence- a Biblical Perspective of Work*, 05; *Obama Prayer: Prayers for the 44th President*; ed/contr *Rulers: Gospel and Government*, 14; *Prayers for Trump: Petitions for the 45th President*, 2017

2908 18th Street NW, Washington, DC 20009-2954 – 202-363-1677   North Texas
E-mail: cgarriott@pcanet.org
MNA Ministry to State – 202-316-5571

Garriott, Christopher William – b Baltimore, MD, Sept 25, 64; f Charles W.; m Cleo K. Lehmann; GenC 87, BS; CTS 96, MDiv; L Jan 01, NoTX Pby; O Jun 10, 01, NoTX Pby; yp Heritage P Ch, Edmond, OK, 98-, astp 01-06; campm RUF, UMD, 06-

4207 Woodberry Street, University Park, MD 20782 – 301-448-9047   Potomac
E-mail: cgarriott@ruf.org
PCA Reformed University Fellowship – 678-825-1070

Garriott, Craig Wesley – b Baltimore, MD, Apr 22, 54; f Charles; m Cleo Lehmann; w Maria Dawkins, Baltimore, MD, May 31, 80; chdn Rebecca Kay, Melissa Joy, Caroline Amy, Calvin Michael, Juliana Maria; VPI 76, BS; CTS 78-82, MDiv; WTS 96, DMin; L Feb 81; O Mar 83, DMV Pby; p Faith Christian Flwsp Ch, Baltimore, MD, 83-18; "Leadership Development in the Multi-ethnic Church," *Urban Mission Journal*; *Growing Reconciled Communities*, 96, MNA chair, Ches pby

505 East 42nd Street, Baltimore, MD 21218 – 410-935-4830   Chesapeake

Garris, Joseph – O Apr 29, 13, Palm Pby; p Grace P Ch, Conway, SC, 13-

406 Herringbone Court, Conway, SC 29526 – 843-438-8133   Pee Dee
E-mail: jfgarris@hotmail.com
Grace Presbyterian Church – 843-347-5550

Garrott, Thomas McMurray IV – b Memphis, TN, May 3, 66; f Thomas M. III; m Allison Moore; w Elizabeth Parks, Knoxville, TN, Dec 14, 91; chdn Thomas McMurray V, Rebecca Grace; VandU 85-89, BS; RTS 91-94, MDiv; UEdin 04, PhD; O May 17, 98, Ecar Pby; astp Church of the Good Shepherd, Durham, NC, 97-98, ascp 98-09; astp Independent P Ch, Memphis, TN, 09-12; ascp 12-16

4738 Walnut Grove Road, Memphis, TN 38117   Covenant

Gastil, Thomas Gregory – w Liz; chdn Garrett, Miles, Paige; PTS, MDiv; Recd PCA Aug 22, 98, SoCst Pby; srp Aliso Creek Ch, Aliso Viejo, CA, 98-

2A Liberty, Aliso Viejo, CA 92656-3829   South Coast
E-mail: TGastil@acpc.net
Aliso Creek Church – 949-460-0080

Gaston, Jackie Dean, Jr. – b Montomery, AL, Mar 31, 68; f Jackie Dean; m Mattie Faye; w Mary Shea Buchanan, Huntsville, AL, Mar 14, 92; chdn Mary Morgan, Virginia Grey, Abigail Grace; HntC 90, BA; UAB 92, MS; UStAug; BhamTS 07, MDiv; O Mar 07, Evan Pby; srp Grace Flwsp P Ch, Albertville, AL, 06-

5634 Jackson Trail, Guntersville, AL 35976 – 256-541-4103   Providence
E-mail: jackie.gaston@comcast.net
Grace Fellowship Presbyterian Church – 256-891-0924

Gault, Brian – O Nov 18, 18, MSVal Pby; astp Redeemer Church, PCA, Jackson, MS, 18-

104 Rosalie Court, Clinton, MS 39056   Mississippi Valley
E-mail: briancgault@gmail.com
Redeemer Church, PCA – 601-362-9987

Gearhart, R. Christopher – b Wilmington, DE, Jun 28, 65; f Michael; m Sharon Darrell; w Claudette Struthers, Columbia, SC, Oct 27, 90; chdn Christopher Hathaway, Courtney Nicole; UDE 88, BS; CBS 93, MDiv; WTS 00, ThM; L Apr 22, 93, Cal Pby; O Oct 24, 93, GulCst Pby; ydir Glasgow Ref P Ch, Bear, DE, 86-88; int Westminster P Ch, Rock Hill, SC, 92-93; astp Eastern Shore P Ch, Fairhope, AL, 93-96, wc 96-00; stu TIU; p Lakeview P Ch, Vernon Hills, IL, 00-17

1381 Huntington Drive, Mundelein, IL 60060 – 847-367-1407   Chicago Metro

Geier, Brian – b Independence, MO, Sept 7, 82; w Stephanie Thies, Champaign, IL, Jul 21, 11; chdn Benjamin; O Mar 11, 18, ChiMet Pby; astp Lincoln Square P Ch, Chicago, IL, 16-

4635 North Rockwell Street, Chicago, IL 60625   Chicago Metro
E-mail: bgeier@lincolnsquarepres.org
Lincoln Square Presbyterian Church – 773-677-7782

Geiger, Joshua L. – chp 02-05; op Cristo Rey, Dallas, TX, 05-14; p 14-15; astp Pacific Crossroads Ch, Santa Monica, CA, 15-15

11475 Cromwell Court, Dallas, TX 75229   Pacific

Geiger, Timothy J. – b Aug 12, 68; w Susan; chdn Mercer; WTS 06, MDiv; O Jul 13, 08, Pitts Pby; ob mis Harvest USA, Philadelphia, PA, 08-; contr *The Homosexual Debate and The Church*, 07; *First Steps of Compassion: Helping Someone Who Struggles with Same-Sex Attraction*, 09; *Gay . . .Such Were Some Of Us*, 09

471 Plymouth Road, Glenside, PA 19038 – 412-848-0320   Philadelphia
E-mail: tim@harvestusa.org
Harvest USA
3901B Main Street 304, Philadelphia, PA 19127-2109

Gelston, Philip – b Jul 19, 74; f Albert Hugh; m Elizabeth Ann; w Nora Maria Peters; chdn Paul Conrad, Thomas Rocco, Johannes Philip, Anna Elisabeth; CC 98, BA; WTS 04, MDiv; O Feb 08, JR Pby; astp Sycamore P Ch, Midlothian, VA, 08-10, ascp 10-11; op Christ Ch of Wiesbaden, 11-

Eichenweg 40, Wiesbaden, 65207 GERMANY – 804-767-2122   Southeast Alabama
E-mail: pngelston@gmail.com
Christ Church of Wiesbaden

Genin, Robert Scott – O Jan 10, 16; astp Briarwood P Ch, Birmingham, AL, 16-

4648 Amberley Drive, Birmingham, AL 35242 – 205-497-4519   Evangel
Briarwood Presbyterian Church – 205-776-5200

Gensheer, Christopher Edward Davies – O Oct 28, 12, SW Pby; astp Christ Ch Santa Fe PCA, Santa Fe, NM, 12-13; astp Fort Worth P Ch, Fort Worth, TX, 14-; op Christ P Ch, Mansfield, TX, 14-

2709 St. Charles Drive, Mansfield, TX 76063 – 817-575-7882   North Texas
E-mail: gensheer@mac.com
Fort Worth Presbyterian Church – 817-731-3300
Christ Presbyterian Church – 682-518-7911

Gentino, David – b College Park, MD, Oct 7, 81; f Stephen C.; m Linda K.; w Julia C. McWilliams, Columbia, SC, Jan 31, 82; chdn Judah, Amelie; CIU 04, BA, 10, MDiv; O May 23, 10, Palm Pby; mis MTW, South Asia, 10-13; op Columbia P Ch, Columbia, SC, 13-

412 Cumberland Drive, Columbia, SC 29203   Palmetto
E-mail: dgentino@gmail.com
Columbia Presbyterian Church

George, Judson Wyatt – b Laurens, SC, Nov 22, 40; f John Scott, Sr.; m McDaniel; w Betsy Clark, Indianapolis, IN, May 11, 68; chdn Seth Haddon, Nathan Clark, Luke Augustin, Benjamin Rush; CC 67, BA; CTS 70, MDiv; L 70; O 70, Midw Pby (RPCES); op, p Evangelical P Ch, Carbondale, IL, 70-86, wc 86-87; ev, op First P Ch, West Frankfort, IL, 87-97, p 97-00; ip Evangelical P Ch, Carbondale, IL, 99-00, p 00-11; hr 11; exec sec TheTentMaker Project, 99-; *Church History; Way to Grow: Conversations out of Philippians*

173 Lamb's Lane, Murphysboro, IL 62966 – 618-687-3751   Illiana
E-mail: Wyatt67@juno.com
HR

George, Nathan Clark – astp Parish P Ch, Franklin, TN, 17- 18; astp Christ Cov Ch, Matthews, NC, 18-

5200 Mintridge Road, Mint Hill, NC 28227 – 615-944-8831   Central Carolina
E-mail: ngeorge@christcovenant.org
Christ Covenant Church – 704-847-3505

George, Philip – b India, Jul 29, 69; f Matthew; m Elizabeth Kuravilla; FulTS 94, MDiv; L Sept 01, Pac Pby; O Jun 23, 02, Pac Pby; ascp Calvary P Ch, Glendale, CA, 02-03, p 03-

3115 Foothill Boulevard, Suite M340, LaCrescenta, CA 91214 – 626-676-5977   Pacific
E-mail: philipgeorge@calvaryonglendale.com
Calvary Presbyterian Church – 818-244-3747

George, Seth Haddon – b Kirkwood, MO, Apr 24, 70; f J. Wyatt; m Betsy Clark; CC 92; SCS 97, MDiv; L Jan 00, RMtn Pby; O Mar 10, 02, RMtn Pby; Chap, dean, instr SCS, 98-03, Chap 03-

411 Del Norte Street, Colorado Springs, CO 80907 – 618-559-3665   Rocky Mountain
E-mail: sethgeorge68@gmail.com

Gerber, Jacob – w Allison; chdn Evelyn Christine, Zachariah Daniel, Caleb Joseph; BDS, MDiv; O Feb 11, PlVall Pby; astp Redeemer PCA, Lincoln, NE, 11-15; p Harvest Comm Ch, Omaha, NE, 15-; sc Platte Valley Pby, 18 *That You May Know: A Primer on Christian Discipleship*, 14

3119 Coffey Avenue, Bellevue, NE 68123 – 402-830-1548   Platte Valley
E-mail: jacob@harvestpca.org
Harvest Community Church – 402-558-4119

Gess, John Andrew – b Decatur, GA, Jun 2, 48; f Paul W; m Dorothy Louise McClanahan; w Brenda Thornton, Grundy, VA, Jun 8, 69; chdn Matthew Adam, Andrew Jacob, Jonathan Luke, Rachel Kristin; KgC 69, BA; VPI 80, MS; RTS 74, MDiv; VPI 86-, grad wk; O Feb 75, PCUS; p First Ch, Narrows, VA, 75-83; p Faith P Ch, Pearisburg, VA, 83-86; srp Bethel P Ch, Clover, SC, 86-15; hr 15

2289 Scenic Ridge Circle, Blacksburg, VA 24060   Fellowship
E-mail: gessj@bellsouth.net
HR

Ghormley, Keith – w Jana; chdn Bess, Sam, Kate, Anne, Joe; TEDS, MA; O Aug 02, Hrtl Pby; astp Zion Ch, Lincoln, NE, 02-03, ascp 03-; sp New Hope PCA, Olathe, KS, 03; ss Harvest Comm Ch, Omaha, NE, 15

1836 South 26th Street, Lincoln, NE 68502 – 402-477-8713   Platte Valley
E-mail: keith@zionpca.com
Zion Church – 402-476-2524

Gibbs, Thomas C. – b Pensacola, FL, Mar 18, 69; f James Allen; m Mary Ann; w Tara Anne Hart, Louisville, MS, Mar 26, 94; chdn Anna Catherine, Thomas Clyde Jr., Lucy Evelyn, Caroline Hart; AU 87-92, BChE; CTS 94-97, MDiv, 15, DMin; L Apr 12, 97; O Nov 23, 97, NoTX Pby; campm RUM, BayU, 97-02; chp, op Redeemer P Ch, San Antonio, TX, 02-04, p 04-

147 Oakhurst Place, San Antonio, TX 78209 – 210-930-4974   South Texas
E-mail: tom@redeemersa.org
Redeemer Presbyterian Church – 210-930-4480

Gibson, Cody – b Oneonta, NY, Aug 12, 85; f Leon; m Margaret Mary Gutierrez; w Melody Astin Grapes, Duanesburg, NY, Oct 1, 16; SUNYOneonta 08, BA; SUNYEmpire 15, MA; GCTS 16, MDiv; O Oct 8, 17, NYS Pby; astp Duanesburg Ref P Ch, Duanesburg, NY, 17-

9 Pearl Street, Apt 4, Oneonta, NY 13820 – 607-433-4670   New York State
E-mail: jcodygibson@hotmail.com
Duanesburg Reformed Presbyterian Church – 518-895-2448

Gibson, Dax – b Birmingham, AL, Apr 22, 77; f Earl Morrow; m Betty Blackburn; w Michelle Mullis; chdn Knox, Karis, Kase, Katy, Khloe; SamU 99, BA; BDS 08, MDiv; ascp Christ Comm Ch, Lakeland, FL, 08-

5604 Stratford Lane, Lakeland, FL 33813 – 863-255-0852   Southwest Florida
E-mail: dax@ccpclakeland.org
Christ Community Church – 863-644-7717

Gibson, Herbert Esch – b Memphis, TN, Mar 4, 50; f John William; m Dorothy Esch; w Carole Jeanne Osborn, Atlanta, GA, Sept 25, 71; chdn Justin Alan, Ryan Matthew, Emily Stowe; UGA 73, BS; RTS 90, MDiv; L Jan 90; O Jul 28, 91, CentGA Pby; mis, ev MTW, Australia, 91-95; ev, chp Crossroads P Msn, Statesville, NC, 95-96; p Crestwood P Ch, Edmonton, AB, 97-15; ev 15-

103 10421 42nd Avenue NW   Western Canada
Edmonton, AB T6J 7C8 CANADA – 780-906-3119
E-mail: bertgibson@protonmail.com

Gibson, Shane – b Clovis, NM, Sept 15, 76; f Wayne Franklin; m Carolyn Gayle; w Kim Byrd, Austin, TX, Nov 23, 02; chdn Adison Kay, Deacon Franklin, George Owen, Jude Alan; TXStU 03, BA; CTS 07, MDiv; O , SELA Pby; ydir New Start, Austin, 03-04; int Redeemer P Msn, New Orleans, LA, 07-08, astp 08-14; ascp 14-; op St. Peters P Ch, New Orleans, LA, 15-

4001 Dumaine Street, New Orleans, LA 70119   Southern Louisiana
E-mail: shngbsn@gmail.com
Redeemer Presbyterian Church – 504-894-1204
St. Peter's Presbyterian Church

Giddens, Casey – astp Cahaba Park Ch PCA, Birmingham, AL, 10-18; wc

1001 Edgewood Boulevard, Birmingham, AL 35209 – 205-757-6857 Evangel

Gienapp, Walter L. – b Ryan, IA, Jan 1, 41; f Ernest; m Wilma; w Carole DePrine, Baltimore, MD, Jun 6, 64; chdn Walter Jr., Steven Andrew, John Duvall, Shannon Marie, James Michael, Marie Donnell, Rosetta Lynn, Mitchell Allen; CC 64, BA; CTS 68, BD; L 68; O 69, Midw Pby (RPCES); p Coulterville, IL, 68-69; p Westminster Bible P Ch, Sydney, NS, 69-70; t ConoCS, 73-77; ap Bible P Ch of Cono Center, Walker, IA, 73-77; p EP Ch, Elkton, MD, 77-87, wc 87-89; p Bible P Ch of Cono Center, Walker, IA, 89-94; p Immanuel P Ch, Shrewsbury, PA, 94-00, wc 01-04; p Mountain View P Ch, Chattanooga, TN, 06-

130 Fern Avenue, Chattanooga, TN 37419 Tennessee Valley
E-mail: waltergienapp@gmail.com
Mountain View Presbyterian Church – 706-764-6221

Giesman, Matthew William – b Lima, OH, May 25, 81; f William; m Mary Jo; w Elizabeth Lauren Gibson, Atlanta, GA, Jan 2, 10; chdn Mary Annabelle, Benjamin Walter; UAL 03, BA; RTS 09, MDiv; O Jul 5, 09, NoTX Pby; astp Fort Worth P Ch, Fort Worth, TX, 09-11; astp Providence P Ch, Clinton, MS, 11-15; p Forestgate P Ch, Colorado Springs, CO, 15-

10869 Rolling Cloud Drive, Colorado Springs, CO 80908 – 817-602-7155 Rocky Mountain
E-mail: mgiesman@gmail.com
Forestgate Presbyterian Church – 719-495-5672

Giffen, Danny – b Dallas, TX, Apr 3, 72; w Emily Boling, Nov 30, 04; chdn Britton Daniel, Lia Katherine, Caroline Collins; UTXAu 94, BBA; BDS 07, MDiv; astp Covenant P Ch, Birmingham, AL, 08-17

1924 Southwood Road, Birmingham, AL 35216 – 205-994-1531 Evangel

Gilbert, David – astp Second P Ch, Yazoo City, MS, 04-05, ascp 05-07, p 07- 14; p Grace P Ch, Douglasville, GA, 14-

5000 Stewart Mill Road, Douglasville, GA 30135 Northwest Georgia
E-mail: dagilberts@gmail.com
Grace Presbyterian Church – 770-489-6758

Gilchrist, Daniel Scot – b Philadelphia, PA, Mar 28, 66; f Paul; m Barbara Hawkins; w Mako Doki, Chiba, Japan, Dec 29, 95; chdn Naoki Josiah, Tomoya Joel, Manami Grace; CC 89, BA; CTS 01, MDiv; O Nov 03, TNVal Pby; mis LIFE Ministries, 89-90; mis MTW, 91-94; p Chattanooga Valley P Ch, Flintstone, GA, 03-; sc TNVal Pby, 05-13

95 Fox Run Circle North, Flintstone, GA 30725 – 423-536-9472 Tennessee Valley
E-mail: dsgilx@gmail.com
Chattanooga Valley Presbyterian Church – 706-820-2833

Gilchrist, Daniel IV – b Decatur, AL, May 2, 41; f Daniel; m Martha Anne Fowler; w Carolyn J. Bickerstaff, Oxford, MS, Aug 29, 64; chdn Kathryn Russell, Daniel V, Lillian B.; SWUM 59-63, BA; UMS 63-64; RTS 81-84, MDiv; O Jul 84, MSVal Pby; p Carthage P Ch, Carthage, MS, 84-07; hr 07

300 Woodhaven Drive, Carthage, MS 39051-3200 – 601-267-8883 Mississippi Valley
E-mail: dangil4@bellsouth.net
HR

Gilchrist, Paul Rowland – b Santiago, Chile, Feb 4, 32; f George R.M.; m Annie Ruth Sanborne; w Barbara Mae Hawkins, Philadelphia, PA, Sept 8, 56; chdn Stephen Paul, Lois Marie, Martha Evelyn (Easterbrook), Daniel Scott; CBC 53, BA; FTS 56, BD; DrU 67, PhD; UCam; UEdin; L Oct 56; O Oct 56,

Gilchrist, Paul Rowland, continued
Phil Pby (EPC); p Meadowcroft P Ch, West Chester, 56-60; p Evangelical P Ch, Levittown, PA, 60-67; prof CC, 67-88; sc General Synod (RPCES), 71-82; assoc, sc PCAGA, 82-84; Chap IHLS, 77; vis lect/prof CTS, 79; sc PCAGA, 88-98; vis lect/prof RTS, 90-91; bd adm NAE, 91-98; adj prof KTS, 92; chmn NAPARC, 92-93; adj prof CTS, 98-00; adj prof EE/KTS Advanced Studies on the Great Commission, 09-14; adj prof MAS, 10-14; hr 99; founding bd member of Lkt. Mtn CS, (now Chattanooga CS), 69; fnd mbr, exec sec World Reformed Fellowship, 94-15; exec sec emeritus WRF: 05 to present; sec of bd, WRF: 05-; ed *Documents of Synod*, 65-82; trans & exec rev comm, *New King James Version*, 79-81; contr *Theological Word Book of the Old Testament*; "Government" in *International Standard Bible Encyclopedia, II*; "Old Testament Ethics" in *Encyclopedia of Biblical & Christian Ethics*; "Deuteronomy" in Baker's *Evangelical Commentary on the Bible*; "PCA: What Kind of Presbyterianism," "Towards a Covenantal Definition of Tora" in *Interpretation and History*; "Israel's Apostasy: Catalyst of Assyrian World Conquest" in *Israel's Apostasy and Restoration*; ed *PCA Messenger*, 87-88; adv bd ChdnBS; ed *Position Papers (PCA) 1973-93*; ed PCA *Digest, 1973-93, 94*; memb ASARB, 88-97, pres, 96-97; ed *Supplement to PCA Digest, 1994-1997*; "Toward A Global Ministry: Ezra, Nehemiah and Malachi –Patterns for a Global Ministry" commencement address at Bandung Theol Sem, Indonesia, 05; contr. *Presbyterian Church in America – A Manual for New Members*, 10; syllabi (Eng and Span) for WRF & CLIR, "How to Rule Well: Biblical Presbyterianism," "Ministerial Ethics," "Biblical Doctrine of Baptism"; bk rvw *McGowan's Divine Spiration of Scripture*, 09; *Continuing the Reformation: Historical Timeline of WRF*, 15; num art in Spanish, 02-14

3017 Express Lane, Buford, GA 30519 – 678-463-1337   Georgia Foothills
E-mail: prgil@comcast.net
HR

    Giles, Tony Blair – b Maryville, TN, May 27, 54; f Frank Darrell; m Mary Ellen Blair; w Mary Lynn Salmon, Nashville, TN, May 23, 81; chdn Rebecca Blair, Mary Grace; VandU 76, BA; RTS 84, MDiv; O Sept 85, JR Pby; ascp Trinity P Ch, Charlottesville, VA, 84-08; mout CFCS, 89-98; ascp Grace P Ch, Nashville, TN, 08-11; dir ChPlant Network, Nashv Pby, 11-12; ip Christ Comm Ch, Franklin, TN, 12-14; astp Cornerstone P Ch, Franklin, TN, 14-

6905 Southern Woods Drive, Brentwood, TN 37027 – 615-834-7120   Nashville
E-mail: tony@cstonepres.org
Cornerstone Presbyterian Church – 615-618-4707

    Gill, Dennis Joseph – b Rochester, PA, Mar 15, 53; f Louis; m Thelma Lorraine Roberson; w Susan Fouse, Aliquippa, PA, Nov 21, 75; chdn Timothy Paul; Carrie Denise; AsbC 75, BA; RTS 79, MDiv; O Nov 16, 80, PCUSA; Recd PCA 93; p Winifrede P Ch, Winifrede, WV, 79-93; p Cabin Creek Ch, WV, 79-93; p Middlesex P Ch, Butler, PA, 93-01; p New Life P Ch, Harrison City, PA, 01-

103 Slack Road, Jeannette, PA 15644-9731 – 724-744-1963   Pittsburgh
E-mail: dennis@newlifepresbyterian.org
New Life Presbyterian Church – 724-744-4760

    Gill, Jerry Dean – w Sharon; EastILU, BS; CTS, MDiv; L Jul 8, 00, JR Pby; O Nov 11, 01, JR Pby; ascp New City Flwsp, Fredericksburg, VA, 01-10; hr 10

3105 Anglican Court, Henrico, VA 23233 – 804-360-4937   James River
E-mail: jdbgygrace@gmail.com
HR

    Gillen, Richard L. – b Detroit, MI, Dec 13, 35; f John L.; m Vena E.; w (1) Janet A. Meyer (d); (2) Tracey Benjamin, Grand Rapids, MI, Oct 16, 99; chdn Scott Richard (d), Sandra Jean, Bruce William; MISU 54-55; MUOH 55-57; RTS 79, dipl; L Oct 17, 78, MSVal Pby; O Aug 72, 79, SFL Pby; ap Lake Osborne Continuing P Ch, Lake Worth, FL, 79-83; p Jupiter P Ch, Jupiter, FL, 83-90; ob exec dir Hebron

Gillen, Richard L., continued
Colony & Gr Homes, Inc, 91-96; op Faith P Msn, Okeechobee, FL, 97-00; hr 00; ip Christ Comm P Ch, Clearwater, FL, 04; ip First P Ch, Crossville, TN, 05-06; Chap Bailey Manor, Clinton, SC, 09-10; astp Westminster P Ch, Clinton, SC, 09-10; astp First P Ch, Crossville, TN, 13-

10 Lakeshore Trail #70, Fairfield Glade, TN 38558 – 931-456-3670   Tennessee Valley
E-mail: rtgillen@frontier.com
First Presbyterian Church – 931-484-4644

    Gilleran, David Paul – b Stockton, CA, Oct 9, 54; f Francis Dennis; m Margaret Frances Calvert; w Kathryn Allene Jackson, Montgomery, AL, Jun 14, 86; chdn Samuel David; GSJC 72-74, AA; AU 74-76, BS; RTS 77-81, MDiv; O Jun 28, 81, Evan Pby; p Providence P Ch, Montgomery, AL, 81-84; p Friendship P Ch, Hope Hull, AL, 81-84; p Woodland P Ch, Notasulga, AL, 84-90; p Pea River P Ch, Clio, AL, 90-95; Chap ALANG; srp Faith P Ch, Robertsdale, AL, 95-00, wc 00-01; op Covenant P Ch, Daphne, AL, 01-02, p 02-04; Chap USArmy, 04-06; p Hope P Ch, Martinsville, VA, 06-; (Chap USArmy 09-10) ; sc Blue Ridge Pby, 12-

709 Mulberry Road A, Martinsville, VA 24112 – 276-638-2050   Blue Ridge
E-mail: dgilleran@embarqmail.com; pastor@martinsvillehopepca.org
Hope Presbyterian Church – 276-638-2050

    Gilliam, Joseph William – b Columbia, SC, Jun 10, 77; f John Thomas; m Elizabeth Ann Butler; w Sabrina Ayoub, Tallahassee, FL, Jun 6, 04; chdn Noah, Georgia Ann, Titus, Silas, Asher; ClrCC 00, BS; LRTS 05, MDiv; Ligonier Academy 14, DMin; O Aug 4, 14, Tidw Pby; srp Antioch Bapt Ch, Merritt Island, FL, 03-07; srp Grace Cov Ch, Virginia Beach, VA, 07-14; Chap USNR, 14-

217 Scarlett Drive, Chesapeake, VA 23322 – 757-870-6809   Tidewater
United States Navy Reserve

    Gillikin, John Edward – b Washington, DC, Jan 5, 58; f Jack Edward; m Orletta Taylor; w Kathryn Kelly, Annapolis, MD, Aug 15, 81; chdn Matthew, Brian, Kelly; WheatC 76-80, BA; WTS 82-85, MAR, 82-85, MDiv; O Oct 85, CentGA Pby; astp Vineville P Ch, Macon, GA, 85-89; astp Tates Creek P Ch, Lexington, KY, 90-94; op Michiana Cov Ch, South Bend, IN, 94-96, p 96-97; astp Arden P Ch, Arden, NC, 98-02; sc Wcar Pby, 01-; ascp Arden P Ch, Arden, NC, 02-05; ss First P Ch, Weaverville, NC, 05-06; p 06-

PO Box 247, Weaverville, NC 28787 – 828-658-9493   Western Carolina
E-mail: bigskip@fpcweaverville.com
First Presbyterian Church – 828-645-7344

    Gilman, Joshua – astp University P Ch, Orlando, FL, 17- 18; astp Redeemer P Ch, Riverview, FL, 18-

4705 Fernstone Court, Brandon, FL 33511 – 941-224-4629   Southwest Florida
E-mail: josh@redeemerriverview.org
Redeemer Presbyterian Church – 813-741-1776

    Gilmartin, Richard John – b Fairfax, VA, Mar 16, 78; f Richard, Sr.; m Barbara Montney; w Jessica Dreiman; chdn Madison, Rebecca, Andrew, Luke; JMU 00, BA; RTSFL 04, MDiv; O Nov 06, BlRdg Pby; ascp Tabernacle P Ch, Waynesboro, VA, 06-09; op Holy Cross P Ch, Staunton, VA, 09-11, p 11-

1103 Walnut Street, Staunton, VA 24401   Blue Ridge
E-mail: rick@holycrosspca.org
Holy Cross Presbyterian Church – 540-885-5551

    Gilmour, Neil M. – b County Antrim, North Ireland; f Neil, Sr.; m Mary Law; w Nancy Evers, Ft. Lauderdale, FL; chdn Marie Suzanne; TC 69, BA; WTS 74, MDiv, 80, ThM; srp First P Ch, Montgomery,

Gilmour, Neil M., continued
AL, 76-80; srp Immanuel P Ch, Miami, 80-85; srp Grace P Ch, Ocala, FL, 85-95; prchg team Christ Ch Suwanee, GA; adj prof Metro Atl Sem, 11-; adj prof Trinity Bib Inst, East Africa, 14-

4093 Windgrove Crossing, Suwanee, GA 30024 – 770-614-8299 Georgia Foothills
E-mail: neilnancy@bellsouth.net
Metro Atlanta Seminary

Gilpin, Lawrence Anderson – b Nashville, TN, Nov 24, 59; f Lawrence; m Betty Jean Brush; w Emily Corley Hawkins, Macon, GA, Aug 22, 87; chdn Emily Katherine, Lauren Elisabeth; UT 77-78; BelmC 79-80; AugC 80-82, BA; CTS 83-86, MDiv, 06, DMin; L Jul 19, 86, Wcar Pby; O Aug 2, 87, Wcar Pby; p Fellowship P Ch, Newport, TN, 87-90; p Monroeville P Ch, Monroeville, AL, 90-00; p Westminster P Ch, Martinez, GA, 00-14; wc 14-

311 Calico Trail, Martinez, GA 30907 – 706-825-4842 Savannah River
E-mail: larryagilpin@gmail.com

Ginn, Gary – op Redeemer P Ch, Titusville, FL, 07-

5960 Coker Avenue, Cocoa, FL 32927 Central Florida
E-mail: gary@myredeemer.cc
Redeemer Presbyterian Church – 321-264-0035

Gladding, Kevin – O Feb 28, 16, NoTX Pby; astp Christ the King, DeSoto, TX, 16-

1520 North Beckley Avenue 416, Dallas, TX 75203 North Texas
E-mail: kgladding@ctktexas.com
Christ the King – 407-496-7720

Glass, Michael Anderson – b Knoxville, TN, Feb 14, 65; f Glenn M; m Rebecca Barnett; w Charlotte Coleman, Knoxville, TN, Mar 26, 88; chdn Emily Anne, Hannah Ruth, Sophie Rebecca; MTSU 83-84; CBC 84-87; RTS 92-95, MDiv; O Aug 20, 95, NGA Pby; ydir Coquina P Ch, Ormond Beach, FL, 87-92; astp Perimeter Ch, Duluth, GA, 95-00; op Christ Comm Ch, Kennesaw, GA, 00-05, p 05-14

1738 Nemours Drive, NW, Kennesaw, GA 30152 – 770-419-1222 Northwest Georgia

Glassmeyer, Philip – CTS 07, MDiv; ev, op City-Wide Redeemer P Msn, North Las Vegas, NV, 07-13; ev Las Vegas, 13-16; p Fellowship of Gr, Peoria, AZ, 17-

26856 North 84th Lane, Peoria, AZ 85383 – 702-540-0304 Southwest
E-mail: philip6@fgcpca.org
Fellowship of Grace – 623-979-3514

Gleason, Geoff – b Knoxville, TN, September 30, 71; f Ronald N; m Sally Yopp; w Lisa Gleason, Thornhill, ON Canada, Dec 4, 92; chdn Rachel, Laken, Naya, Sawyer, Noel, Marin, Emma, Charlotte, Harris, Elise, Calvin; York University 91-95, BA; RTS Jackson 05-11, MDiv; O Oct 11, SavRiv Pby; p Cliffwood P Ch, Augusta, GA, 11-; *A Family Worship Guide to Luke*, 17

4140 Elders Drive, Augusta, GA 30909 Savannah River
E-mail: geoff.gleason@cliffwoodpca.com
Cliffwood Presbyterian Church – 706-798-2691

Gleason, Ronald Nelson – b Charlotte, NC, May 1, 45; f Paul T; m Julliette Knight; w Sally Yopp, Charlotte, NC, Aug 5, 67; chdn Ronald II, Geoffrey, Janneke, Paul (d), Nicoline, Hans; Citadel 63-67, BA; GCTS 73-75, MDiv; FrUAmst 75-76; THGKN 76-80, Drs; WTS 00, PhD; O Jul 6, 81, Ref Ch Netherlands; Recd PCA Sept 16, 95, SoCst Pby; p Vrijgemaakt, Rijswijk, Netherlands, 81-85; p Bethel Canadian Ref Ch,

MINISTERIAL DIRECTORY

Gleason, Ronald Nelson, continued
Toronto, Canada, 85-94; p Covenant P Ch of Orange, CA, 94-95; chp, op Grace P Ch, Yorba Linda, CA, 95, p 96- 17, chp 17-18; *Reforming or Conforming?* 08; *The Death Penalty on Trial*, 08; *Herman Bavinck: Pastor, Churchman, Statesman, and Theologian*, 10; various art *The Reformation*; art *Westminster Theological Journal, Ref21*

1118 North Corrida Place, Orange, CA 92869 – 714-538-5144   Savannah River

Gleason, William Larkin – b Washington, DC, Dec 18, 53; f Robert Lee; m Carolyn Stiteler; w Edna Lee Covington, Kingstree, SC, Sept 25, 76; chdn Rachel Elisabeth, Jonathan Lee; PC 76, BA; RTS 86, MDiv; L Mar 85; O Jun 86, Cov Pby; ap Covenant P Ch, Little Rock, AR, 86-87; p First P Ch, Demopolis, AL, 87-92; srp Westminster P Ch, Valdosta, GA, 92-00; p First P Ch, Clarksdale, MS, 00-16

129 Post House Trail, Pooler, GA 31322 – 662-302-2453   Covenant
E-mail: firstpres@gmi.net

Glenn, Ricky M. – O Aug 14, 10, MSVal Pby; p Macon P Ch, Macon, MS, 10- 16; p Bethel P Ch, Lake Charles, LA, 16-

357 East Park Manor Drive, Lake Charles, LA 70611   Southern Louisiana
E-mail: rmglenn@gmail.com
Bethel Presbyterian Church – 337-478-5672

Glover, Jason – O Mar 5, 17, Cov Pby, Chap 17-

108040 S. 4801 Rd., Muldrow, OK 74948 – 314-809-2597   Covenant
E-mail: jason.glover.ts5a@statefarm.com

Glover, Jeff – ascp The Crossroads @ Lake Stevens, Lake Stevens, WA, 12-14

1711 Gambel Quail Drive, El Paso, TX 79936 – 3602-722-5765   Pacific Northwest
E-mail: fivesolas@juno.com

Goddard, Stephen Ira – b Denver, CO, Nov 12, 76; f Glen I.; m Joann Little; w Cally R. Duncan, Golden, CO; chdn Alexis Renee, Liena Naomi; MBI 06, BS; WTS 12, MAR; O May 18, 14, Phil Pby; Chap USAR, 14-

11 Shetland Circle, Horsham, PA 19044 – 267-315-2790   Philadelphia
E-mail: stephen.i.goddard@gmail.com
United States Army Reserve

Godwin, Charles Robert – b Greenville, MS, Jul 24, 70; f William Pollard; m Alice Hazel Black; w Pamela Frances Bundy, Greenville, MS, Jul 23, 94; chdn Alice Elizabeth, Charles Thomas, Katherine Grace, Amy Claire; MSU 88-89; DSU 89-91, BS; CTS 93-96, MDiv; O Aug 25, 96, Cov Pby; astp Grace P Ch, Starkville, MS, 96-99, ascp 99-00; MTW, dir, recruit, short term, 00-08; astp Ivy Creek Ch, Lawrenceville, GA, 08-13; p East Lanier Comm Ch, Buford, GA, 13-16; astp Restoration P Ch, Buford, GA, 16-

1709 Praters Point, Dacula, GA 30019   Georgia Foothills
E-mail: cgodwin@restpres.org
Restoration Presbyterian Church – 770-945-7800

Godwin, Clyde Lee – b New Bern, NC, Jul 11, 51; f James L.; m Elizabeth M. Rountree; w Valerie M. Bender, Charlotte, NC, Jun 28, 75; chdn James Luke, Anna Elizabeth, Claire Maurer; UNC 74, BA; WTS 79, MAR; L Jul 12, 81; O Jul 12, 81, CentCar Pby; staff IVCF; op Winston-Salem, NC, 82-84;

Godwin, Clyde Lee, continued
p Redeemer P Ch, Winston-Salem, NC, 84-90; op, p Friendly Hills P Ch, Jamestown, NC, 90-95; ascp Christ Comm Ch, Franklin, TN, 95-00; p The Village Ch, New York, NY, 00-02; ob exec dir WHM, 02-04; op Highland Gr Ch, Atlanta, GA, 05-06; p Hope P Ch, Winston-Salem, NC, 07- 18; ob Dir Barnabas Center, 18-

3010 Prytania Road, Winston-Salem, NC 27106 – 336-575-4489   Piedmont Triad
Barnabas Center

Godwin, Jeffrey Wayne – b Cocoa Beach, FL, Oct 20, 68; f Peter Hoyle; m Judith Lee Heller; w Cristina Marie Rogers, East Ridge, TN, Jun 6, 92; chdn Elizabeth Grace, Victoria Grace, Jamieson Nole; CC 87-90, BA; RTSFL 96-99, MDiv; O Feb 13, 00, RMtn Pby; astp, yp Village Seven P Ch, Colorado Springs, CO, 99-05; p Northside P Ch, Melbourne, FL, 05-

1779 Clover Circle, Melbourne, FL 32935 – 321-254-8519   Central Florida
E-mail: jeffnorthside@bellsouth.net
Northside Presbyterian Church – 321-255-0701

Godwin, Kenneth Marvin – Chap US Army, 15-

2720 Bennington Road, Fayetteville, NC 28303 – 254-213-1940   Potomac
E-mail: ken_godwin@hotmail.com
United States Army

Goebel, Paul – O May 27, 12, NoTX Pby; astp Park Cities P Ch, Dallas, TX, 12-15; ascp 15-

5907 McCommas Boulevard, Dallas, TX 75206   North Texas
E-mail: paul.goebel@pcpc.org
Park Cities Presbyterian Church – 214-224-2500

Golackson, Joshua – O Jan 31, 16, Wisc Pby; astp Emmaus Road Ch, Appleton, WI, 16-17; op Living Stone Ch, Oshkosh, WI, 17-

683 Monroe Street, Oshkosh, WI 54901   Wisconsin
E-mail: josh@livingstoneoshkosh.org
Living Stone Church – 920-903-7512

Golden, Paul – O Nov 26, 17, Evan Pby; p Southwood P Ch, Talladega, AL, 17-18

1540 Flag Pole Mountain Road, Childersburg, AL 35044   Evangel
E-mail: paulcgolden@yahoo.com

Goligher, Liam – b Glasgow, Scotland; w Christine Hughes; chdn Louise, Ruth, David, Sarah, Andrew; IrishBaptTheoC 73; RTS 04, DMin; churches in Ireland, Canada, England, Scotland; srp Duke Street Ch, West London, 00-11; srp Tenth P Ch, Philadelphia, PA, 11-; *A Window on Tomorrow*, 94; *The Fellowship of the King*, 03; *The Jesus Gospel*, 06; *Joseph - The Hidden Hand of God*, 08

1701 Delancey Street, Philadelphia, PA 19103   Philadelphia
E-mail: lgoligher@tenth.org
Tenth Presbyterian Church – 215-735-7688

Gomes, Neemias – w Deborah Marie; chdn Rebecca Marie, Porfirio Gueiros Neto, Melissa Marie; U Catolica de Pernambuco 83, BS; Sem Pres Fundamentalista do Brasil 87, BA; O Dec 89, Brazil; p Presbyterian Ch of Ipsep - Brazil, 90; Greater Recife Presbytery, 91-92, 93-97; astp First Presbyterian Ch of Recife, 98-00; astp Faith P Ch, Gainesville, FL, 04-11; wc 12-

1212 NW 22nd Street, Gainesville, FL 32641 – 352-336-9514   North Florida
E-mail: gomesnr4@gmail.com

Gomez, Angel – O Dec 2, 18, EPA Pby; ascp Calvary P Ch, Willow Grove, PA, 18-

Calvary Presbyterian Church – 215-659-0554   Eastern Pennsylvania

Goncalves, Antonio J. Moura – op Hebron P Msn, Newark, NJ, 02-

390 Long Avenue, Hillside, NJ 07205 – 908-964-4146   Metropolitan New York
E-mail: revmoura@aol.com
Hebron Presbyterian Mission – 973-504-8887

Goneau, David Paul – astp New Life P Ch, Glenside, PA, 06-08, ascp 08- 13; p CrossPointe Ch, Media, PA, 13-17

273 Aronimink Drive, Newtown Square, PA 19073 – 610-368-9517   Philadelphia Metro West

Gonzales, Ron – b San Francisco, CA, Oct 25, 55; f Albert; m Dora Raineri; w Cheryl Ruth Brizius, La Grange, IL, Nov 26, 77; chdn Jenni Elizabeth, Laura Ruth, David Andrew; UPac 77, BA; IST 84, MA; The Cole Center for Biblical Studies 87, MDiv; CTS 13, DMin; O Jun 94; Recd PCA 03, PacNW Pby; ascp Cole Comm Ch, Boise, ID, 84-94; p Christ Comm Fell, Walla Walla, WA, 94-03; op Covenant P Ch, Walla Walla, WA, 03-08; p 08-

7934 Mill Creek Road, Walla Walla, WA 99362 – 509-522-4272   Pacific Northwest
E-mail: ron@covenantwallawalla.org
Covenant Presbyterian Church – 509-522-1020

Gonzales, Stephen – b Goshen, IN, Jul 28, 62; f Jose E.; m Mabel M. Lambright; w Angela Nelson, Oct 15, 11; chdn Leah Renee, Ellen Beth, Brady Stephen; BallSU 85, BS; CTS 90, MDiv; WMU 09; L Jan 89; O Oct 7, 90, NoE Pby; astp Hope Ch, Ballston Spa, NY, 90-95; ev NoE Pby, 95; op, ev Faith P Ch, Clifton Park, NY, 95-99, p 00-03; op Covenant P Ch, Wilmington, OH, 03-05; ascp Christ Ch, Grand Rapids, MI, 06-09; ob adj inst KuyperC, 09; Chaplain Grace Hospice, Okemos, MI, 11-; *The Regulative Principle and Drama in Worship*

1747 Ashton Lane, Mason, MI 48854 – 517-604-6777   Great Lakes
E-mail: wreckdiver1@wowway.com
Grace Hospice, Okemos, MI

Good, Raymond Wayne – b Petersburg, VA; w Arleen; chdn Sharon (McMillan), Raymond, Nathan; BJU 55-59, BA, 59-62, BD; O 67, Gosyelasso; p Sandy Ridge & Bethel P chs, Prince George, VA, 65-68; p Rivers Edge Bible Ch, Hopewell, VA, 68-72; Chap USN, 77-83; p Faith P Ch, Charleston, WV, 85-87; p Rivers Edge Bible Ch, Hopewell, VA, 87-97; hr; ss Centralia P Ch, Chester, VA, 98-00; ip West End P Ch, Hopewell, VA, 01-03

3071 Lydia Lane, Hopewell, VA 23860-8165 – 804-452-0117   James River
E-mail: wagood2@juno.com
HR

Good, Richard Scott – b Cleveland, OH, Jun 7, 64; f Richard L.; m Daneen E. Schiltz; w Dawn Schmidt, May 17, 03; chdn Adrianna Dawn, Richard Evan; StanU 82-86, BA; CTS 94-97, MDiv; L Jul 12, 97, Siouxl Pby; O Feb 22, 98, Siouxl Pby; astp Trinity P Ch, Rochester, MN, 98-00; astp Grace P Ch, Peoria, IL, 00-03; astp Trinity P Ch, Norfolk, VA, 04-06; p Harvest Flwsp, Lusby, MD, 06-

11592 Winnebago Lane, Lusby, MD 20657 – 410-394-6110   Potomac
E-mail: rich@harvestfellowshippca.org
Harvest Fellowship – 410-326-0033

Goode, Keith N. – b Houston, TX; w Katherine; chdn James, Anna, Deborah, Jonathan, Benjamin, Caleb, Daniel, Sarah, Joshua, Samuel; O Feb 86; p Vanguard Ch, Houston, TX, 86-93; Chap USArmy, 93-

7124 Ardennes Loop, Fort Hood, TX 76544 – 254-213-9931   South Texas
E-mail: keith.goode@us.army.mil
United States Army

Goodlin, Michael – O Mch 18, 18, EPA Pby; campm RUF, Lehigh, 18-

620 West Union Boulevard, Bethlehem, PA 18018   Eastern Pennsylvania
PCA Reformed University Fellowship

Goodman, Matthew – O Aug 11, 15, Evan Pby; astp Cahaba Park Ch PCA, Birmingham, AL, 15-; op Trinity Gr Ch - Irondale, Irondale, AL, 16-

5222 Paramont Drive, Irondale, AL 35210 – 205-567-4924   Evangel
E-mail: goodmmd@gmail.com
Cahaba Park Church PCA – 205-870-1886
Trinity Grace Church - Irondale

Goodrich, Gary – O Dec 4, 16, Hrtl Pby; astp Heartland Comm Ch, Wichita, KS, 16-

457 South Woodlawn, Wichita, KS 67218 – 316-686-0060   Heartland
E-mail: gary@heartlandpca.org
Heartland Community Church – 316-686-0060

Goodrich, Richard Robert – O Nov 2, 09; mis

3735 CR 2208, Greenville, TX 75402   North Texas
E-mail: richeygoodrich@gmail.com

Goodsell, Alex – w Amy; chdn Annie, Hallie, Meg; UAL, BS; BDS, MDiv; O Oct 21, 02, Evan Pby; astp Briarwood P Ch, Birmingham, AL, 00-05; astp Evangel Ch PCA, Alabaster, 05-06, ascp 06-

115 Glen Abbey Way, Alabaster, AL 35007 – 205-620-6675   Evangel
E-mail: agoodsell@evangelchurchpca.org
Evangel Church PCA – 205-664-0889

Goodson, Curtis C. – b Miami, FL, Oct 30, 28; f Wm Munroe; m Elnora Rusk; w (1) Lourdes Alves, (d) (2) Elisa G. Pierre (d), May 3, 85; chdn Patricia; UMiami 46-47; GATech 47-50, BEEn; USCA 66-67, MA; ColTS 50-53, MDiv; L 53; O 53, KgsMt Pby; p Saluda Ch, Saluda, NC, 53-54; mis Brazil (PCUS), 54-74; mis Brazil (PCA), 74-88; prof Seminario Presbiteriano Do Sul, Campinas, SP, 74-87; prof Seminario Presbiteriano Jose Manuel Da Conceicao, 81-87; hr 88

11819 Pavilion Boulevard, Unit 118, Austin, TX 78759 – 512-331-9064   South Texas
E-mail: curtgood@yahoo.com
HR

Goodwin, Samuel M. – b Youngstown, OH, Jun 14, 66; f Mark; m Georgia Daniel; w Elizabeth Eremic, Columbia, SC, Dec 11, 04; chdn Sarah Katherine, Sophia Gray; FurU 88, BA; CIU 97, MDiv; mis MTW, England, 08-

1714 East Buchanan Drive, Columbia, SC 29206   Palmetto
E-mail: samgoodwin@yahoo.com
PCA Mission to the World

MINISTERIAL DIRECTORY

Gorbey, Tim – O Mch 11, 18, EPA Pby; astp New Life P Ch, Dresher, PA, 18-

3100 Terwood Road #H75, Willow Grove, PA 19090   Eastern Pennsylvania
New Life Presbyterian Church – 215-641-1100

Gordon, Bruce E. – b Nashua, NH, Nov 6, 31; f George F.; m Bernice Howarth; w Brenda Winther, Hollis, NH, Jun 13, 59; chdn Brett David, Brad Steven, Brian Paul; GordC 58, BA; WTS 63, MDiv; O Sept 63, Phil RPC; op Calvary Ch, King of Prussia, PA, 60-65; p Trinity P Ch, Kearney, NE, 65-66; p First Congr Ch, Merrimack, NH, 67-80; ev, op Jefferson P Ch, Jefferson, NH, 85-00; hr 01

PO Box 236, Jefferson, NH 03583 – 603-586-7964   Northern New England
E-mail: bnb@yahoo.com
HR

Gordon, Michael James – b Ft. Wayne, IN, Jun 15, 58; f James M.; m M. Ann Carney; w Robyn Lynn Waite, Miami, FL, May 21, 82; chdn Drew, Karley; MCC 77-81, BS; RTS 83-86, MDiv; O Feb 87, CentFL Pby; astp, moy Grace P Ch, Ocala, FL, 87-93, ascp 93-01; Centerpoint Comm Ch, Ocala FL, 01-05; susp

971 North Covenant View Way, Eagle, ID 83616 – 352-817-7333   Central Florida
E-mail: mjg549@gmail.com

Gordon, Michael Myron – b Rutherfordton, NC, Jun 25, 71; f Tim; m Betty Linda Nantz; w Kristen Lauren Neely, Rock Hill, SC, Jul 18, 98; chdn Abigail Elizabeth, Hannah Neely, Joshua; WinC 94, BA; RTS 02, MDiv; L Apr 19, 03, PTri Pby; O Feb 8, 04, PTri Pby; astp Friendly Hills P Ch, Jamestown, NC, 04-08; astp Christ P Ch, Winterville, NC, 08- 12; p Grace Covenant Ch, Hickory, NC, 13-

3420 4th Street Boulevard NW, Hickory, NC 28601 – 336-841-2574   Catawba Valley
E-mail: mikegordon3927@gmail.com
Grace Covenant Church – 828-345-0345

Gordon, Michael Roland – b Tuscaloosa, AL, Nov 19, 74; f Robert; m Diane Williamson; w Christine Burkley , Jan 1, 01; chdn Elliot Atticus, Elsa Maloy, Ezra Alton Amir; MerU 96, BA; CTS 01, MDiv; ascp Gr & Peace Flwsp, St. Louis, 06-08; campm RUF, SCAD, 08-13; srp Redeemer PCA, Lincoln, NE, 13-16; admin RUF, Mid-west Area Coord, 16-

15 Claiborne Place, Webster Groves, MO 63119   Platte Valley
PCA Reformed University Fellowship

Gordon, T. David – b Richmond, VA, Nov 13, 54; f John Chalmers; m Gertrude Elizabeth Hoyt; w Dianne Carol White, Roanoke, VA, May 27, 78; chdn Marian Ruth (d), Grace Elizabeth, Dabney Anne; RoC 77, BA; WTS 79, MAR, 80, ThM; UTSVA 84, PhD; L 84, JR Pby; O May 86, NoE Pby; asst prof, p GCTS, 84-97; srp Christ P Ch, Nashua, NH, 89-98, wc; ob prof GroCC, 99-; "The Problem at Galatia," *Interpretation*, 87; "A Note on Paidagogos in Gal. 3:24-25," *New Testament Studies*, 89; "Weeping with Those Who Weep," *Lay Leadership*, 89; "Why Israel Did Not Obtain Torah-Righteousness," *Westminster Theological Journal*, 92; *Why Johnny Can't Preach: The Media Have Shaped the Messengers*, 09; *Why Johnny Can't Sing Hymns: How Pop Culture Re-Wrote the Hymnal*, 10

213 Edgewood Avenue, Grove City, PA 16127 – 724-450-0636   Ascension
E-mail: tdgordon@gcc.edu; web: www.tdgordon.net
Grove City College

Gordy, John, III – Louisville, GA, Mar 27, 81; w Sarah Elizabeth Tatro, Augusta, GA, May 30, 09; chdn Grace Kathryn, Charlotte Anne; UGA 04, BA; CTS 14, MDiv; O Mar 8, 15, Prov Pby; astp Decatur P Ch, Decatur, AL, 14-16; astp Trinity P Ch, Rochester, MN, 16-

2577 Schaeffer Lane NE, Rochester, MN 55906   Siouxlands
E-mail: john@trinityrochester.org
Trinity Presbyterian Church – 507-282-6377

Gorski, James J. – b Detroit, MI, Oct 11, 58; f Casimir; m Christine; w Paula; chdn Paul, Shannon; Moody 01, MDiv; RTS DMin stu; int Rocky Mountain Comm Ch, Billings, MT, 07-08; p Three Rivers P Ch, Covington, LA, 08-

214 Bamboo Drive, Covington, LA 70433-5821 – 985-273-8951   Southern Louisiana
E-mail: jjpgorski@gmail.com
Three Rivers Presbyterian Church – 985-893-0101

Gorsuch, Anthony – O Feb 19, 17, RMtn Pby; astp Rocky Mountain Comm Ch, Billings, MT, 17; astp Evangelical P Ch, Newark, DE, 17-

E-mail: amgorsuch@gmail.com   Heritage
Evangelical Presbyterian Church – 302-737-2300

Gossett, G. Everett – b Chattanooga, TN, Feb 26, 36; f James Frederick; m Tressie Lee Cavin; w Shirley Ann Watts, Chattanooga, TN, Jan 4, 58; chdn Michael Timothy, George Allen; UChat 58, BA; ColTS 61, MDiv; O Jul 61, Athens Pby; Recd PCA Jul 10, 83, TNVal Pby; p Calvary Ch, Elberton, GA, 61-67; p Red Bank P Ch, Chattanooga, TN, 67-13; hr 13

100 Lavonia Avenue, Chattanooga, TN 37415 – 423-875-2348   Tennessee Valley
E-mail: rbpchurch@gmail.com
HR

Gothard, Todd – b Omaha, NE, Oct 31, 71; f F. Thomas III; m Sandra Hart; w Jaclynn Bigelow, Columbus, MS, May 20, 95; chdn Joshua Michael, Nelson Thomas, Austin James, Ruby Caroline; MSU 89-93, BS; CTS 95-99, MDiv; L Oct 28, 00, NoIL Pby; O Jan 14, 01, NoIL Pby; astp Christ Ch, Woodridge, IL, 00-03; sc NoIL Pby, 01-03; p Salem Ch, Gaffney, SC, 03-07; astp Briarwood P Ch, Birmingham, AL, 07-12

1605 Brookview Cove, Birmingham, AL 35216 – 205-824-9906   Evangel
E-mail: toddgothard@bellsouth.net

Goyzueta, Andrew – O Apr 29, 17, Cal Pby; astp Redeemer P Ch, Greenville, SC, 17-

102 Hillside Drive, Travelers Rest, SC 29690   Calvary
E-mail: angoyzueta@gmail.com
Redeemer Presbyterian Church – 864-610-9400

Graber, Benjamin – mis MTW, 14-

c/o MTW   North Texas
PCA Mission to the World

Grady, John Charles – b Morristown, NJ, Oct 6, 49; f Frederick Louis; m Elizabeth Mary Terrill; w Ruth Ann Petersen, Denville, NJ, Nov 13, 70; chdn Miriam, Jason, Karen, Benjamin, Laura; RutgU 68-69; PineJC 69-71; CC 71-73, BA; WTS 76-80; L Apr 82, OPC; O May 83, OPC; p Sarasota P Ch, Sarasota, FL, 80-86; p Faith P Ch, Sarasota, FL, 87-15, ascp 15-17; hr 17

1222 Georgetowne Court, Sarasota, FL 34232 – 941-379-8766   Southwest Florida
HR

Graff, Lyle R. – b Bancroft, NE, Oct 18, 24; f R. Chester; m Ida C. Hanson; w Shirley A. Kimball (d) (2) Camilla Vanderburg; chdn Norman, Russell, Carol (Aslesen), Linda (Lovrien), Roger, Ronda (Sawatzky), Lori (Petersen); WheatC 52-53; WesC 57, BA; DubTS 60, BD; L May 59; O Jun 60, Omaha Pby (UPCUSA); p Nelson-Edgar Parish (UPC), 60-62; p First Ch, Ord, NE, 62-66; p Hus Mem Ch, Cedar

Graff, Lyle R., continued
Rapids, IA, 67-71; p Willow Lake Ch, SD, 71-75; p Pollock Mem P Ch, Pollock, SD, 75-80; op Hope Ch (PCA), Sioux Falls, SD, 81-83; Chap VA, Sioux Falls, SD, 82-99; hr 99

108 South Oakley Street, Luverne, MN 56156 – 507-283-2003   Siouxlands
E-mail: slgraff@iw.net
HR

Graham, Andrew – b E. Stroudsburg, PA, Oct 19, 67; f Thomas Edward; m Anna Green; w Sharon Page, Rockford, IL, Nov 16, 91; chdn James Emory, Claire Sorrells, Esther Elizabeth; WheatC 85-89, BA; WTS 96-99, MDiv; L Sept 12, 03, MNY Pby; O Apr 4, 04, MNY Pby; int Tenth P Ch, Philadelphia, PA, 97-99; adj prof SBI, Russia, 01; adj prof EU, 02-04; stus Knowlton P Ch, Columbia, NJ, 03-04, p 04-14; srp Covenant Comm Ch, Scottsdale, AZ, 14-18

5008 East Le Marche Avenue, Scottsdale, AZ 85254   Southwest

Graham, Douglas Weir – b Youngstown, OH, Jun 6, 67; f George Dudley; m Margaret Weir; w Lesley Kristin McMillan, Clayton, MO, Sept 3, 94; chdn Andrew, George, Mac; NWU 89, BA; CTS 94, MDiv; RTS 10, DMin; O Feb 95; mis CCC, Argentina, 89-90; ydir Central P Ch, Clayton, MO, 91-94, ascp 95-03; p Knox P Ch, Harrison Township, MI, 03-

1452 South Renaud Road, Grosse Pointe Woods, MI 48236   Great Lakes
E-mail: DouglasGraham@KnoxPCA.org
Knox Presbyterian Church – 586-469-8500

Graham, Edwin Patrick – b Charlotte, NC, Jan 11, 37; f Clyde Moffett; m Jennie Patrick; w Gail Frances Emory, Charlotte, NC, Jul 2, 60; chdn Lisa Gail, Cindy Elaine, Todd Patrick, Mark Edwin, Kevin Ford; BelC 59, BA; ColTS 59-62, MDiv; O Aug 5, 62, Enre Pby; p Mount Cal P Ch, Roebuck, SC, 62-66; srpArden P Ch, Arden, NC, 66-01, wc 01-02; ob PRes The Cove, Billy Graham train cent, 02-14; hr 14

6 Clovelly Way, Asheville, NC 28803 – 828-274-4273   Western Carolina
HR

Graham, John Louis – b Pahokee, FL, Jan 5, 35; f Leslie Arthur; m Grace Viola Mahan; w (1) Jacqueline Jane Fowler, (d) (2) Barbara Gayle Withrow, Brandon, FL, Oct 22, 94; chdn Steven Randolph, Stanley Robert, Sean Reagan; MBC 53-54; MCU 67-71, dipl; L Jan 70; O Jun 71, Coun InCh; ap Faith Bible Ch, Hendersonville, NC, 71-73; p First P Ch, North Port, FL, 76-84; ap Covenant P Ch, Hendersonville, NC; op Whiteside P Ch, Cashiers, NC, 84-89; srp Westminster P Ch, Brandon, FL, 92-99; hr 99; ip Redeemer P Ch, McKinney, TX, 01; ip Covenant P Ch, Winter Haven, FL, 02, ip 05-06

2904 Mission Lakes Drive, Lakeland, FL 33803 – 863-816-4600   Southwest Florida
E-mail: grahamcracker@tampabay.rr.com
HR

Graham, Michael – w Vicki; chdn Mary Helen, Michael Alan Jr., Molly Wilkes, James Daniel; UAL 83-88, BS; CTS 97-01, MDiv; L Sept 11, 01, Nash Pby; O Oct 21, 01, Nash Pby; p Hickory Grove P Ch, Mt. Juliet, TN, 01-

304 Forest Bend Drive, Mt. Juliet, TN 37122 – 615-587-3339   Nashville
E-mail: mikeatwork@comcast.net
Hickory Grove Presbyterian Church – 615-754-8337

Graham, Preston Don Jr. – b Sumter, SC, Aug 12, 58; w Lisa Harris; chdn Stephen Harris, Nathan Meador, Anna Somers; UGA 82, BS; GCTS 91, MDiv; YDS 92, ThM; L Sept 14, 91; O Oct 11, 92, NoE Pby; Inner-City Min, Atlanta, GA, 82-85; Dir, campm WDA, UGA, 82-88; No Shore Bap Ch, Beverly Farms, MA, 88-90; int, ip Grace P Ch, Braintree, MA, 90-91; ev, op Christ P Ch, New Haven, CT, 93-94; p 94-

56 Roger Road, New Haven, CT 06515 – 203-315-5041   Southern New England
E-mail: cpc.preston@snet.net
Christ Presbyterian Church – 203-777-6960

Grainger, Chad – O Jun 11, 17, Evan Pby; astp Urban Hope, Fairfield, AL, 17-

Urban Hope – 205-514-3715   Evangel

Grames, Robert W. III – w Susie; chdn Will, Micah, Mary Noel; MSC 99; BDS 03; O Nov 14, 04; astp Knollwood P Ch, Sylacauga, AL, 05-07; p New Life P Ch, Clermont, FL, 07- 13; p Colfax Center P Ch, Holland, IA, 13-

18921 K Avenue, Holland, IA 50642 – 319-505-0507   Iowa
E-mail: rgrames@live.com
Colfax Center Presbyterian Church – 319-824-5231

Granberry, Chris – ev 08-12; op Hope Flwsp, White Swan, WA, 12-

4711 Branch Road, Wapato, WA 98951   Pacific Northwest
E-mail: cgranberry@msn.com
Hope Fellowship – 253-315-1833

Granberry, George S. III – b Grenada, MS, Aug 27, 55; f George S. Jr; m Patricia Ann Watts; w Vicki Gale McEndree, Wichita, KS, Aug 6, 77; chdn Stephanie Charise, George Stephen IV; KSU 73-77; DenTS 78-81, MDiv; O Mar 22, 82, Bapt; Recd PCA May 1, 93, Hrtl Pby; ascp, yp Calvary Bap Ch, Longmont, CO, 81-85; Doulos Min, Branson, MO, 85-89; moa, medu Eastminster P Ch, Wichita, KS, 89-93; ev, op Heartland Comm Ch, Wichita, KS, 93, p 94-

6409 East Elm Street, Wichita, KS 67206 – 316-512-1216   Heartland
E-mail: georev@sbcglobal.net
Heartland Community Church – 316-686-0060

Grant, George – w Karen; chdn Joel, Joanna, Jesse; UHou, BA; MWBTS, MDiv; WhTS, MA, DLitt, PhD; BelC, Dhum; KTS, DMin; astp 3rd Baptist, Houston, 75-76; p Golf Drive Bapt, Houston, 76-77; p Humble Bible Ch, Humble, TX, 77-79; astp Bethel Bapt Ch, New Caney, TX, 79-80; p Believer's Fellowship, 80-88; astp Coral Ridge P Ch, Ft. Lauderdale, FL, 88-92; Dir King's Meadow Study Center, Franklin, TN, 92-; ascp Christ Comm Ch, Franklin, TN, 04-06, ascp 06-07; op Parish P Ch, Franklin, TN, 06-07, p 07-; auth/contr over 100 titles

929 Hickory Hills Drive, Franklin, TN 37067   Nashville
E-mail: george@parishpres.org
King's Meadow Study Center, Franklin, TN
Parish Presbyterian Church – 615-574-1029

Grant, James Harold, Jr. – Recd PCA 15, Cov Pby; ob 15-

100 Sugar Hill Drive, Moscow, TN 38057 – 901-877-7638   Covenant
E-mail: jhgrantjr@gmail.com

Grauley, John Edwin – b Wilmington, DE, Feb 21, 34; f John Meads; m Amy E. Casey; w Marjorie A. Ross, Pittsburgh, PA, Aug 22, 59; chdn James Stuart, Lynn Carole, Karen Ruth; ShelC 57, BA; FTS 60, MDiv, 62, STM; WTS 80, DMin; L 63; O 63, Phil Pby (BPC); t FTS, 60-63; mis FEBibC, 64-68; BibEv, 68-82; prof BibTS, 71-82; couns MGPCC, 82-89; ss First P Ch, Macon, GA, 86; p Westminster P Ch, Butler, PA, 89-96; srp Westminster P Ch, Gainesville, GA, 96-01; ss Westminster P Ch, Elgin, IL, 02-03; p Grace Comm P Ch, Blairsville, GA, 03-09; hr 09

3968 Thomas Town Road, Young Harris, GA 30582 – 706-379-9833   Georgia Foothills
E-mail: johngrauley@windstream.net
HR

Graulich, Doug – b Rochester, NY; f Robert H. (d); m Luanne Broomhall; w Catheyrine Contheria Fisher, Atlanta, GA, Jul 17, 99; chdn Robert James, Ralphael Thomas Lee; CSU 80-84, BS; SUNY 84-89, MBA; ColTS 89-90; AUBS 90-95, MDiv; O Apr 99, NGA Pby; ob ev PEF, Reynoldstown Msn, Atlanta, 93-

1693 Mary Lou Lane, Atlanta, GA 30316 – 404-223-0567　　　　　　　　　　　　　Metro Atlanta
E-mail: rtmfdoug@yahoo.com
Presbyterian Evangelistic Fellowship
425 State Street, Bristol, VA 24201 – 276-591-5335

Graves, Thomas J. – p Leakesville P Ch, Leakesville, MS, 14-18

501 Main Street, Leakesville, MS 39451　　　　　　　　　　　　　　　　　　　　　　Grace
E-mail: thomas.graves@comcast.net

Gray, Phillip Aaron – O Jun 5, 16, CatVal Pby; astp NorthCross Ch, Cornelius, NC, 16-

164 Bluffton Road, Mooresville, NC 28115　　　　　　　　　　　　　　　　　Catawba Valley
E-mail: aaron@northcrosschurch.com
NorthCross Church – 704-237-4853

Gray, Richard MacDonald – b Philadelphia, PA, Jan 24, 48; f Richard W.; m Emily MacDonald; w Karen Smick, St. Louis, MO, May 23, 70; chdn Emily Jane, Robert MacDonald, Carrie Elizabeth; CC 70, BA; CTS 74, MDiv; L 74; O 76, FL Pby (RPCES); ap Covenant P Ch, Lakeland, FL, 74-77; p Presbyterian Ch of Manchester, Manchester, CT, 77-96; srp Knowlton P Ch, Columbia, NJ, 96-00, wc 00-03; astp Wellington P Ch, Wellington, FL, 03-14; ss First Evangelical P Ch, East Liverpool, OH, 14-15, p 15-18; hr 18

7 Arnold Drive, Bloomfield, CT 06002 – 561-651-0880　　　　　　　　　　　　　　　Pittsburgh
HR

Gray, Rick Allen – b Wilmington, DE, Dec 18, 57; f A Samuel; m Janet Barnett; w Wendy Cullen, Jun 17, 00; chdn Grant Tucker, Aidan Samuel, Chase Fletcher; UDE 80, BS; CTS 87, MDiv; L Nov 88; O Sept 89, DMV Pby; ap Olive Branch P Ch, St. Louis, MO, 84-87; yp Evangelical P Ch, 87-88; chp MTW/Impact, WHM, Uganda, 89-93; chp MTW, WHM, Uganda, 93-02; MTW, reg dir, East Africa, 03-08; MTW miss res coord, Sub Saharan Africa, 08-10; campm, RUFI, UDE 10-

228 Rhett Drive, Newark, DE 19702 – 302-365-5075　　　　　　　　　　　　　　　　Heritage
E-mail: rick.gray@ruf.org
Reformed University Fellowship International

Gray, Robert M. – O Feb 12, 12, Pitts Pby; astp First Ref P Ch, Pittsburgh, PA, 12-13; astp City Ref P Ch, Pittsburgh, PA, 13-17; p Christ Comm P Ch, West Hartford, CT, 17-

7 Arnold Drive, Bloomfield, CT 06002　　　　　　　　　　　　　　　　　　Southern New England
Christ Community Presbyterian Church – 860-521-0211

Gray, William James – b Barre, VT, Feb 5, 34; f William; m Margaret Olsen; w Janet L. Glenn, Johnstown, PA, Nov 10, 62; chdn Nancy J., William G., Cynthia A. (Carter); UPitt 56, BS; SCS 80-86; CTS 90, MDiv; L Mar 11, 89, GrLks Pby; O Jan 26, 91, MO Pby; ss Olive Branch P Ch, St. Louis, MO, 88-91, p 91-97, wc 97-00; mis MTW, Johannesburg, 00-13; hr 13

822 Windmill Drive, Ballwin, MO 63011-3566 – 636-256-6859　　　　　　　　　　　　Missouri
HR

Greco, Fredrick – b Niagara Falls, NY Oct 25, 69; f Frank R.; m Nancy Holody; w Deb Chaves, Lancaster, NY Aug 10 96; chdn Peter, Daniel, Paul, Abigail; SUNYBuff 91, BA; UChi 93, MA; UMI 96,

Greco, Fredrick, continued
JD; RTS 06, MDiv; L 00, GrLks Pby; L 03, MSVal Pby; O Oct 17, 06, HouMet Pby; stus Tchula PCA, Tchula, MS, 04-06; srp Christ Ch, Katy, TX, 06-; chmn SJC 14-16, 18-; contr *Mounce's Complete Expository Dictionary;* contr *Tabletalk Magazine*

23434 Fairbranch Drive, Katy, TX 77494 – 832-922-7060   Houston Metro
E-mail: fred.greco@cckpca.org
Christ Church – 281-392-0002

    Green, Bradford Clark – O Aug 4, 13, Cov Pby; campm RUF, UCAR-Hendrix Col, 13-

12 Summerfield Drive, Conway, AR 72034   Covenant
E-mail: bradford.green@ruf.org
PCA Reformed University Fellowship

    Green, Charles David – b Hagerstown, MD, Feb 22, 56; f Charles Walter (d); m Mary Thelma Shay (d); w Ruth Marie Feaver, Bethlehem, PA, Jun 15, 80; chdn Daniel David, Peter Andrew, Christopher Douglas, Stephen Charles, Benjamin Stuart; VPI 74-76; JHU 76-79, BA; WTS 93-98, MDiv; CTS 96-97; L May 11, 96, Phil Pby; O Mar 28, 99, Phil Pby; campm Reformed Student Fellowship, LehU, 96-99, campm 99-08; area coord RUF, 08-

631 4th Avenue, Bethlehem, PA 18018-5558 – 610-691-0988   Eastern Pennsylvania
E-mail: dgreen@ruf.org
PCA Reformed University Fellowship

    Green, James Livingston, II – b Burlington, NC, Jul 22, 62; f James Livingston (d); m Julia H.; w Barbara, Apr 21, 90; chdn James Benjamin, Lily Noele; Elon 86, AB; CTS 01, MDiv; O Feb 27, 05, Palm Pby; p Union P Ch, Salters, SC, 05-12

728 Ansley Street, Florence, SC 29505 – 843-206-8060   Palmetto
E-mail: rev.jimmygreen@gmail.com

    Green, Jon Dale – b Ft. Worth, TX, Jun 24, 52; f Rev. Thomas S.; m Anith Newell; w Carolyn A. Wilson, Clear Lake City, TX, Jun 23, 73; chdn Rachel Lynn, Benjamin Wilson; HBU 76, BS; SWBTS 80, MDiv, 94, DMin; L May 12, 76, SBap; O Nov 27, 77, SBap; Recd PCA Apr 29, 95, SoTX Pby; p First Bap, Donic, TX, 77-79; p Park Mem Bap, Houston, TX, 82-95; p Covenant P Ch, Harlingen, TX, 95-99; ascp Spring Cypress P Ch, Spring, TX, 99-00; p Oakwood P Ch, San Antonio, TX, 00-18; hr 18

5527 Peralta Mills Way, Katy, TX 77449 – 210-378-4904   South Texas
E-mail: paradox@paradox72.net
HR

    Green, Josiah – b Franklin, TN; f Steve; m Marijean; w Jamie-Lee; chdn Georgia, Skylar; MBI 08, BA; CTS 16, MDiv; astp Chesterfield P Ch, Chesterfield, MO, 18-

15019 Clayton Road, Chesterfield, MO 63143   Missouri
E-mail: josiahg@chespres.org
Chesterfield Presbyterian Church – 636-394-3337

    Green, Peter Andrew – w Megan Lynn Cook; chdn Elijah, Amelia, Isaac; LehU 06, BA; CTS 10, MDiv; WheatC 16, PhD; O Nov 26, 17, NR Pby; campm RUF, WVU, 17-

139 McCormick Hollow Road, Morgantown, WV 26508 – 610-417-8931   New River
E-mail: peter.green@ruf.org
PCA Reformed University Fellowship

Greene, Eric Alan – w Katy Ferrell, Baton Rouge, LA, Mar 19, 05; chdn Grayson, Mary Gibson, Ella Grace; L Apr 27, 97, Bapt; O Aug 9, 98, Bapt; Recd PCA Jul 28, 01, SELA Pby; astp Westminster P Ch, Baton Rouge, LA, 01-05; p Thomson Mem P Ch, Centreville, MS, 05-; art in *Bible Editions & Versions: Journal of the International Society of Bible Collectors* Vol 12, June-Sept 11

210 South Caroline Street, Centreville, MS 39631   Grace
E-mail: ericalangreene@hotmail.com
Thomson Memorial Presbyterian Church – 601-645-6245

Greene, Kevin – b Allentown, PA, Apr 22, 67; f William LeVan; m Gail Enid; w Kimberly Pike, Winston-Salem, NC, Aug 26, 90; chdn Emma Barwick, Coleman Pike; WFU 89, BA; RTS 05, MAR; L Oct 98; O Nov 05, JR Pby; astp West End P Ch, Richmond, VA, 94-06, ascp 06-

10603 Orkney Road, Richmond, VA 23238 – 804-740-7560   James River
E-mail: kevin@wepc.org
West End Presbyterian Church – 804-741-6562

Greene, Richard Robert Hinds – b Toledo, OH, Aug 31, 60; f Kenneth William, Sr.; m Virginia Irene Hinds; w Laura Ellen Goggan, St. Louis, MO, Nov 10, 90; chdn Frances Virginia (d), Kenton Augustin, Amberleigh Joy, Jackson Isaac; UTol 78-83, BA; CTS 86-89, MDiv, 94, MA; L Apr 7, 90; O Aug 5, 90, Ill Pby; int Concord P Ch, Waterloo, IL, 89-90; p Grandcote Ref P Ch, Coulterville, IL, 90-97; p Good Shepherd P Ch, Valparaiso, IN, 97-; lect CTS, 92-95; chmn Tall Oaks C Sch, 05-08

2008 North Sturdy Road, Valparaiso, IN 46383-3839 – 219-309-3208   Great Lakes
E-mail: RLEGreene@gmail.com
Good Shepherd Presbyterian Church – 219-464-8435

Greenwald, Randall R. – b Cincinnati, OH, Apr 11, 56; f Darold D.; m Martha E. Budd; w Barbara Kay Black, E. Lansing, MI, Jul 8, 78; chdn Adria Michal, Seth Andrew, Matthew Leslie, Hannah Catherine, Jerusha Kay, Colin Jerome; MISU 78, BA; CTS 85, MDiv; L Nov 85; O Nov 85, CentFL Pby; p Hope P Ch, Bradenton, FL, 85-10; p Covenant P Ch, Oviedo, FL, 10-; vis lect RTSFL, 17-

PO Box 622962, Oviedo, FL 32762 – 407-542-0813   Central Florida
E-mail: info@cpconline.net
Covenant Presbyterian Church – 407-542-0813

Greer, Joseph Autry – b Valdosta GA, Jul 3, 33; f Lloyd Barton; m Julie Winn Varnedoe; w (dv) Margaret Elizabeth Stanford; chdn David, Steven (d), Allison (White), Andrew; DavC 55, BS; ColTS 59, BD; CTS 91, ThM; L Jan 92, Ill Pby; O May 5, 96, SEAL Pby; ascp First P Ch, Bradenton, FL, 59-61; campm USM, 61-62; ev Gatlinburg, TN, 62-65; p, ascp First P Ch, Clinton, SC, 65-66; p Tattnall Square, Macon, GA, 66-67; ascp Clairmont P Ch, Atlanta, GA, 67-70; ascp First P Ch, Hendersonville, NC, 70-73; p Research Triangle, NC, 73-77; p Pea River P Ch, Clio, AL, 96-99; ss Clayton P Ch, Clayton, AL, 96-99; ss Pleasant View P Ch, Clayton, AL, 96-99; p Hayneville P Ch, Hayneville, AL, 99-03; p Lowndesboro P Ch, Lowndesboro, AL, 99-03; p Good Hope P Ch, Benton, AL, 99-03; astp Christ Comm Ch Msn, Gainesville, FL, 03-04; sc NFL Pby; astp Faith P Ch, Gainesville, FL, 05-14; hr 14

3945 NW 27th Lane, Gainesville, FL 32606 – 352-505-6775   North Florida
E-mail: josephgreer2@att.net
HR

Greete, Richard – b Oak Park, IL, Mar 28, 59; f Richard Allen; m Jean Fransis Straka; w Christine Elizabeth Caldwell, Mt. Prospect, IL, Jun 19, 82; chdn Elizabeth Eileen, Jonathan Christopher, Julia Christine; CIU 81, BA; TIU 84, MDiv; RTSFL 05, MA; O Apr 19, 97, CentFL Pby; mis MTW, Chiba, Japan, 97-01; MTW, Missionary care, 01-09; couns, 01-

4221 West Gulf to Lake Highway, Lecanto, FL 34461   Central Florida

Gregoire, Jean Yves – astp Christ Cov Ch, Southwest Ranches, FL, 01-03; op El Shalom Haitian Comm Ch, Tamarac, FL, 03-

17219 64th Place North, Loxahatchee, FL 33470 – 954-726-5456   South Florida
El Shalom Haitian Community Church

Gregory, Jason – RTS 05, MDiv; O Jul 16, 06, TNVal Pby; astp Covenant P Ch, Oak Ridge, TN, 06-07; Chap USN, 07-

3420 Granada Avenue, San Diego, CA 92104 – 865-382-5335   Tennessee Valley
E-mail: jason.a.gregory3@navy.mil
United States Navy

Gregory, Michael – O Nov 26, 17, Pac Pby; astp The Way, San Marino, CA, 17-

1621 South 6th Street, Alhambra, CA 91803   Pacific
E-mail: michaelg31@gmail.com
The Way

Gresham, Glenn H. – b Kansas City, MO, Feb 22, 61; f Neal; m Catherine Hamby; w Elena Maria Correa, Miami, FL, Jul 3, 92; chdn Katharyn, Jacob, Andrew, Ana Elisa, Ethan; AU 83, BA; RTSFL 93-96, MDiv; O Feb 23, 97, CentFL Pby; Chap USAF, MacDill AFB, Tampa, FL, 97-00; Walter Reed Army Hosp, 00-01; Chap USAF, Spangdahlem AB,GE 01-04; Chap USAF, Onizuka AFS, Sunnyvale, CA,04-07; Chap USAF, Shaw AFB, Sumter SC, 07-09; Chap USAF, Schriever AFB, CO, Co Springs, CO, 10-13; Chap USAF, Andersen AFB, Guam 13-16; Chap USAF, Peterson AFB, CO, 16-

12124 Stanley Canyon Drive, Colorado Springs, CO 80921   Central Florida
E-mail: glenn.gresham@us.af.mil
United States Air Force

Gretzinger, Andrew – b Peru, IN, Jun 27, 80; f John J.; m Shirley K.; w Jennifer M.; chdn Kathleen, William, David, Mark, Ryan; INU 04, BA; RTS 09, MDiv; O Jul 24, 10, Cal Pby; astp Trinity P Ch, Spartanburg, SC, 08-11; ascp New Cov P Ch, Abingdon, MD, 11-17; mis Northern Ireland, 17-

58 Garron Road, Carnlough Ballymena, BT44 0JP Northern Ireland – 443-619-2819   Chesapeake

Grider, Joseph C. – b Gadsden, AL, Jul 22, 54; f Daniel Y.; m Ruth L. Cox; w Louise A. McLellan, Miami, FL, Jun 12, 82; chdn Jonathan Daniel, Jennifer Lynn, Stephen James; GSJC 72-74, AA; UAL 74-76, BA; RTS 77-81, MDiv; O Apr 84, Cov Pby; p Carrollton P Ch, Carrollton, MS, 84-87; p First P Ch, Osceola, AR, 87-95; astp McIlwain Mem P Ch, Pensacola, FL, 95-97, ascp 97-04; p First P Ch, Niceville, FL, 04-

119 Raintree Boulevard, Niceville, FL 32578-8711 – 850-478-3037   Gulf Coast
E-mail: joe@fpcniceville.org
First Presbyterian Church – 850-678-2521

Griesbeck, Matthew Jordan – astp All Saints P Ch, Austin, TX, 18-

606 West Lynn #8, Austin, TX, 78703, Austin, TX 78703 – 901-268-5531   South Texas
E-mail: jgriesbeck@allsaintsaustin.org
All Saints Presbyterian Church – 512-732-8383

Griffith, Benjamin Paul – w Rebecca; chdn Margaret, Owen, Elizabeth; RTS 14, MDiv; O Oct 12, 14, Gr Pby; astp First P Ch, Hattiesburg, MS, 14-17; ascp 17-

601 Longwood Court, Hattiesburg, MS 39402   Grace
E-mail: benjaminpaulgriffith@gmail.com
First Presbyterian Church – 601-268-0303

Griffith, Bobby G., Jr. – b Midwest City, OK, May 1, 77; w Jennifer Hammond, Grove City, PA, Mar 15, 03; chdn Esteban Samuel; CTS 07, MDiv; WVU 09, MA; UOK 18, PhD; astp Greene Valley P Ch, Carmichaels, PA, 08-09; astp Christ the King P Ch, Norman, OK, 09-11; adj prof Mid-AmChU, 10-; ascp City P Ch, Oklahoma City, OK, 11-; instr UOK, 17-; contr *Rulers: Gospel and Government; Everything is Meaningless? Ecclesiastes*, 15; contr *Heal us Emmanuel: A Call for Racial Reconciliation, Representation, and Unity in the Church*, 16; *Confessions of Sin and Assurances of Pardon: A Pocket Resource*, 16; *The Birth of Joy: Philippians*, 17

2220 NW 25, Oklahoma City, OK 73107 – 405-824-8931   Hills and Plains
City Presbyterian Church

Griffith, Howard – b Washington, DC, Dec 28, 54; f Charles H.; m Gustava LaMond; w Jacqueline Gray Shelton, Baltimore, MD, Dec 15, 79; chdn Alexander Shelton, Abigail LaMond, Charles Calvin, Graham Michael, Samuel Davies; UVA 76, BA; PittsTS; GCTS 82, MDiv; WTS 04, PhD; O Jan 28, 83, JR Pby; ap Stony Point Ref P Ch, Richmond, VA, 82-84; op All Saints Ref P Ch, Richmond, VA, 84-85, p 85-07; adj prof RTS, 02-07; ob prof , acad dn, RTSDC, 07-; auth "Richard Baxter and the Godly Brotherhood," *Banner of Truth*; "Eschatology Begins with Creation," *Westminster Theological Journal* (87); "John Knox," "Nestorius" in *Evangelical Dictionary of Theology*, 84; "Adoption in Calvin's Soteriology," *Evangelical Quarterly* (01); "Introduction to the Sermons of Samuel Davies" in *The Sermons of Samuel Davies, vol. 1*, 93; "The Churchly Theology of Basil's De Spiritu Sancto," *Covenant Seminary Review* (99); trans "Pierre Marcel on Brothers and Sisters of Christ"; *In God's School*; ed *Creator, Redeemer, Consummator;* "Frame as a Reformed Theologian" in *Speaking the Truth in Love, A Festschrift for John M. Frame;* "The Signs of Jesus in Calvin's Christology," *RTS 50 Year Commemoration Volume,* 15; *Spreading the Feast, Instruction and Meditations for Ministry at the Lord's Table*

13939 Malcolm Jameson Way, Centreville, VA 20120 – 703-408-3157   Potomac
E-mail: Howard.Griffith@Alumni.Virginia.edu
Reformed Theological Seminary DC

Griffith, James Ray – b Kokomo, IN, Jul 19, 50; f Earl Newell; m Alice M. Mize; w Nancy Elaine Herndon, Red Bank, NJ, Jul 23, 77; chdn Douglas Edward, Julie Michelle; VMI 69; Purdue 70-73, BS; PittsTS 77-80, MDiv; O Dec 80, Asc Pby; ap Sovereign Grace Ch, Monroeville, PA, 80-81; op Good Shepherd P Ch, Middletown, NY, 82-83; moy Park St Congr Ch, Boston, MA, 83-85; Chap USArmy, 85-11, ret Col 11

6311 Fall River Drive, Colorado Springs, CO 80918   Rocky Mountain
E-mail: Griffithjr001@gmail.com

Griffith, Malcolm Murphy – b Pensacola, FL, Mar 14, 50; f Henry Grady Jr.; m Betty Estelle McMillan; w Christine Claire Waggoner, Hattiesburg, MS, Aug 26, 72; chdn Catherine Blake (Noah), Bethany Christine (Belue); PenJC 70, AA; FSU 72, BS; RTS 79, MDiv; L Feb 20, 79, MSVal Pby; O Jul 15, 79, MSVal Pby; p Lebanon P Ch, Learned, MS, 79-81; ap McIlwain Mem P Ch, Pensacola, FL, 81-87; Chap NCANG, 83-90; ap Westminster P Ch, Rock Hill, SC, 87-90; Chap ALANG, 91-03; srp Eastern Shore P Ch, Fairhope, AL, 90-00; min dir Ridge Haven Conference Center, 00-04; Chap USAR, 04-12; Army Chap, Ret, assoc dir PRCC, 13-

307 South Tee Drive, Fairhope, AL 63537 – 828-371-0121   Gulf Coast
E-mail: mackgriffith@gmail.com
Presbyterian and Reformed Commission on Chaplains

Griffith, Thomas (Bud) – b Columbus, OH, Oct 1, 59; f Thomas E. Feeney; m Priscilla F. Meek; w Kimberly D. Glenn, Greenville, SC, Jun 4, 83; chdn Matthew Thomas; BJU 83, BA, 90, MDiv; L Oct 93; O May 12, 96, Cal Pby; p Norris Hill P Ch, Anderson, SC, 96-02; op Blue Ridge P Msn, Taylors, SC, 02-06; p 06-

PO Box 1348, Taylors, SC 29687 – 864-292-2037   Calvary
E-mail: bud.griffith@att.net
Blue Ridge Presbyterian Church – 864-292-2037

Griffith, Warner Dennis – b Abington, PA, Aug 21, 63; f Warner Dennis; m Phyllis Graham; w Carolyn Elizabeth Sells, Knoxville, TN, Aug 12, 89; chdn Warner Andrew, Matthew Graham, Rebekah DuBose; UT 81-85; RTS 90-93; L Feb 94, Pot Pby; O Jun 19, 94, TNVal Pby; stus Cuba P Ch, Cuba, AL; chp Winchester, VA, 93-94; p Chattanooga Valley P Ch, Flintstone, GA, 94-02; srp New Hope P Ch, Monroeville, PA, 02-07; p Walnut Hill P Ch, Bristol, TN, 07-12; p Grace Cov P Ch, Williamsburg, VA, 12-

1677 Jamestown Road, Williamsburg, VA 23185   Tidewater
E-mail: dennis@gracecovpca.org
Grace Covenant Presbyterian Church – 757-220-0147

Griffith, Wayne Douglas – b Lancaster, PA, Nov 19, 56; f C. Wayne; m Jacqueline Jones; w Cynthia Stull, Ft. Lauderdale, FL, Jul 12, 80; chdn Katie, Mary, Luke; FurU 79, BA; CTS 84, MDiv, 05, DMin; L Nov 84; O Nov 84, Cal Pby; yp Concord P Ch, Waterloo, IL, 79-82; astp Second P Ch, Greenville, SC, 82-84; ap Westminster P Ch, Atlanta, GA, 86-90; op Carriage Lane P Ch, Peachtree City, GA, 90-92, p 92-

304 Welton Way, Peachtree City, GA 30269-2839 – 678-697-2238   Metro Atlanta
E-mail: wdouggriff@carriagelanepres.org
Carriage Lane Presbyterian Church – 770-631-4618

Grigg, Andrew Steven – O Jul 10, 16, NJ Pby; astp Covenant P Ch, Cherry Hill, NJ, 16-17, ascp 17-

112 North Valleybrook Road, Cherry Hill, NJ 08034 – 804-564-4471   New Jersey
E-mail: dgrigg@covenantcherryhill.com
Covenant Presbyterian Church – 856-429-1225

Grimm, Justin Charles – O May 31, 15, Ohio Pby; astp Walnut Creek P Ch, Gahanna, OH, 15-; op Story P Ch, Westerville, OH, 18-

10980 Gorsuch Road, Galena, OH 43021 – 636-980-0966   Columbus Metro
E-mail: justing73@gmail.com
Walnut Creek Presbyterian Church – 614-337-9200
Story Presbyterian Church

Grimsley, Matt – astp Redeemer Ch of Knoxville, TN, 06-16; chp 16-17; op Resurrection Madison, Madison, WI, 17-

201 Lathrop Street, Madison, WI 53726   Wisconsin
Resurrection Madison

Grindinger, Greg – b Kansas City, MO, Nov 25, 58; f Donald J.; m Alice Henzke; w Cecilia Mae Dodd, Myrtle Beach, SC, Sept 15, 84; chdn Breanna Jody, Isaac Donald, Joshua David, Rachel Nicole; UMOR 81, BSCE; WebsU 85, MAM, MAB; CTS 98, MDiv; ascp Comm Bible Ch, Swansea, IL , 98-08, mfam 09-11; astp, exec p Grace P Ch, Peoria, IL, 11-18; ascp assimilation/mobilization, 18-

10929 North Jason Drive, Dunlap, IL 61525 – 309-690-8583   Northern Illinois
E-mail: ggrindinger@gracepres.org
Grace Presbyterian Church – 309-693-3641

Grindstaff, Chad William – b Ann Arbor, MI, Jun 21, 73; f Tom; m Joanne Reed; w Erin Lynn Carney, Urbana, IL, Aug 11, 01; chdn Reed Michael, Meredith Grace, Anna Katherine, Nicholas Matthew; BallSU,95, BA; RTSNC 05, MDiv; O Jul 23, 06, NFL Pby; staff CCC, Champaign/Urbana, 95-01; astp Faith P Ch, Gainesville, FL, 06-10; astp North Cincinnati Comm Ch, Mason, OH, 11-12; op Living Hope PCA, Hamilton, OH, 12-

3065 Calusa Drive, Hamilton, OH 45011 – 513-204-9607   Ohio Valley
E-mail: chad@livinghopepca.org
Living Hope PCA

MINISTERIAL DIRECTORY 237

Grisham, Jules – b Brooklyn, NY, Mar 31, 65; f James; m Catherine; w Virginia, Bethesda, MD, Dec 24, 93; chdn Guy; NYU 90, BA; RTS 03, MDiv; O Nov 16, 03, EPC; Recd PCA Nov 12, 05, Phil Pby; astp Fourth EPC, Bethesda, MD, 03-05; p Faith P Ch, Yardley, PA, 05-; ed *The Fourth Quarterly*, 02-05

3 Snowdrop Place, Newtown, PA 18940 – 240-731-0004   Eastern Pennsylvania
E-mail: jgrisham@faithprez.org
Faith Presbyterian Church – 267-364-5538

Grooms, Greg – f Hank; m Sue; w Mary Jane, May 21, 80; chdn Fiona, Ian, Peter, Catherine, Emily; TulU 76, BS; astp All Saints P Ch, Austin, TX, 08-12; ascp 12-; "Evolution and Reductionism" in *The Journal of the Society for Classical Learning*, Volume VIII, Fall 15; numerous movie and book reviews in *Critique* and *Commentary*, 96-14;

2104 Nueces, Austin, TX 78705 – 512-542-0035   South Texas
E-mail: ggrooms@allsaintsaustin.org
All Saints Presbyterian Church – 512-732-8383

Gross, Edward N. – f Ralph; m Ruth; w Deborah, Dec 18, 76; chdn Charity, John, Faith, Hope; ShelC 75, BA; FTS 78, MDiv; TEDS 88, DMiss; O 78, BPC; p Knoxville BPC, 78-80; prin Bible College of East Africa, 81-84; t FTS, 84-88; Ft. Washington PCA, 84-88; chp, p Grace Fell OPC, Philadelphia, 89-92; t BibTS, 89-95; chp, p Gwynedd Valley OPC, 95-00; chp, cop Hope Comm Church, South Africa, 00-02; p Pilgrim Ch, Philadelphia, PA, 02-10; coord Discipleship Renewal, CityNet Ministries, 14-; *Systematic Theology of Charles Hodge, Abridged*, 88; *Demons, Miracles and Spiritual Warfare: An Urgent Call for Discernment*, 90; *Christianity Without a King: The Results of Abandoning Christ's Lordship*, 92; *Will My Children Go to Heaven? Hope and Help for Believing Parents*, 95; several articles in *Evangelical Dictionary of World Missions*, 02; *Let Love Win through YOU*, 11; *Are You a Christian or a Disciple? Rediscovering and Renewing New Testament Discipleship*, 14; *Fruitful or Unfruitful? Why it Really Matters*, 17; *Disciples Obey: How Christians Unknowingly Rebel against Jesus*, 16; *The Amazing Love of Paul's Model Church: How the Thessalonians became Disciples and Reached their Region with the Gospel*, 17; *100 Days with Jesus: A Guide to Transformation by Knowing God and Living in His Presence*, 18

58 Whistling Duck Drive, Bridgeville, DE 19933 – 215-805-2153   Philadelphia
E-mail: ed.gross@comcast.net
CityNet Ministries
PO Box 37, Glenside, PA 19038

Grossruck, Collin Stuart – UW; CTS; O Jan 18, 99, PacNW Pby; yp Seattle, WA, 92-95; astp St. Louis, 95-98; Chap USArmy, 99-

973 B McLeod Court, Columbia, SC 29206 – 910-429-6324   Pacific Northwest
E-mail: macruck12@yahoo.com
United States Army

Grudem, Elliot – Recd PCA May 10, 18, Ecar Pby; p Christ The King P Ch, Raleigh, NC, 05-10; astp Christ The King P Ch, Raleigh, NC, 18-

2720 Gordon Street, Raleigh, NC 27608 – 919-306-7648   Eastern Carolina
E-mail: egrudem@leaderscollective.com
Christ The King Presbyterian Church

Gu, Jabum – ob ev NY Kwang Yeom P Ch, Whitestone, NY, 10-

2206 Clintonville Street 1st Floor, Whitestone, NY 11357   Korean Northeastern
E-mail: jabumgu@gmail.com
New York Kwang Yeom Presbyterian Church

Guerra, Alberto – O Jul 20, 11, ChiMet Pby; op Iglesia Nueva Esperanza, Wheaton, IL, 11-

125 North Beverly Street, Wheaton, IL 60187 – 630-456-4309 Chicago Metro
E-mail: aguerra@nesperanza.org
Iglesia Nueva Esperanza

Guerrin, Robert E. – O Feb 28, 93, GulCst Pby; astp Wildwood P Ch, Tallahassee, FL, 93; astp Grace Cov P Ch, Brevard, NC, 97-99, ascp 99-02; hr 02

6822 Winners Drive, Whitsett, NC 27377 – 336-446-6525 Western Carolina
E-mail: solafide@embarqmail.com
HR

Guinan, Jeph – w Heidi, Abingdon, VA, May 29, 04; chdn Grant, Olivia, Lily, Griffin; UAZ 03, BA; BhamTS 12, MDiv; O Dec 30, 12, Evan Pby; op Cornerstone Church, PCA, Calera, AL, 12-16, p 16-18; ob Dir AL ChPlnt Net, 18-

108 Tintern Abbey, Alabaster, AL 35007 – 205-690-0488 Evangel
E-mail: jephguinan@gmail.com

Gullett, Benjamin David – b St. Augustine, FL, Apr 23, 38; f Benjamin David; m Carolyn Best Wallace; w Nancy Jo Dowlen, Ringgold, GA, Feb 16, 59; chdn Kevin David, Mark Carlton, Susan Diane (Livengood), John Manford; GATech 56-61, BE; ColTS 61-64, MDiv; O Jul 12, 64, Fayetteville Pby (PCUS); p Maxton, NC, 64-66; p Covington, GA, 66-68; p Norris Lk Ch, Lithonia, GA, 68-71; p Immanuel Ch, China Grove, NC, 71-75; p New Hope P Ch, China Grove, NC, 75-92; ss Faith P Ch, Charlotte, NC, 92-01; ss Second Street P Ch, Albemarle, NC, 01; ss Faith P Ch, Charlotte, NC, 01-07; p 07-11

192 Edgewater Drive, Concord, NC 28027 – 704-721-3592 Central Carolina
E-mail: gullettd@sndcoffee.com

Gunn, Grover Earl III – b Forrest City, AR, Jun 26, 49; w Mary Smith, Gulfport, MS, Dec 30, 72; chdn April Leanne, Jesse Scott, Lindsey Elizabeth, Grover Earl IV; MSU 67-72, BA; DTS 72-77; RTS 77-78, MDiv, 13-18, DMin; O Oct 78, Cov Pby; ev Cov Pby, 78-80; p First P Ch, Charleston, AR, 78-80; p Covenant P Ch, FortSmith, AR, 81-87; p Carrollton P Ch, Carrollton, MS, 88-00; sc Cov Pby, 95-08; p Grace P Ch, Jackson, TN, 00-09; p First P Ch at Winona, MS, 09-12; ss McDonald P Ch, Collins, MS, 13-17, p 17-

295 East Williamsburg Road, Collins, MS 39428 – 731-394-7967 Mississippi Valley
E-mail: gegunn3@att.net
McDonald Presbyterian Church

Gunter, William – p Redeemer Comm Ch, New Port Richey, FL, 03-

7866 Roundelay Drive, New Port Richey, FL 34654 – 724-849-9590 Central Florida
E-mail: pastor.billgunter@verizon.net
Redeemer Community Church – 727-842-5278

Guthrie, Fred Farrell Jr. – b Brooklyn, NY, Dec 27, 33; f Fred F.; m Effie Munyer; w Shirley Anderson, Atlanta, GA, Aug 9, 58; chdn Ruth, Ann (Sorrell), Fred F III; KgC 51-53; DEC 53-56, BA; UTSVA 56-60, MDiv, 74, DMin; O Aug 6, 60, PCUS; Recd PCA Jan 19, 91, NGA Pby; p Franklin, NC, 60-64; p St. Andr P Ch Orlando, FL, 64-70; Chap Wm S. Hall Psy Inst, Cola, SC, 70-71; p Lake Cty, SC, 71-75; Chap RGNS, 75-78; p Helen, GA, 78-84; Jackson, GA, 84-87; pres FGEA, Inc; ss Ingleside P Ch, Lawrenceville, GA, 91-92; p Westminster P Ch, Gainesville, TX, 92-96; ob ARKNET Inc., Atlanta, GA, 96-97; op Grace P Ch, Palm Coast, FL, 98-02, p 02-06; hr 06; ss Thyatira Olney P Ch, Jefferson, GA, 09-11; ip Open Door Comm Ch, Alpharetta, GA, 11-12; min cong care, Redeemer P Ch, Parker, CO, 14-17

9 Forbes Place, Apt 809, Dunedin, FL 34698 – 720-459-2439 Georgia Foothills
E-mail: drfredgu3@hotmail.com
HR

Gutierrez, Gerardo L. – b Huanta, Peru, Nov 15, 46; f Gerardo V; m Modesta R. Santillana; w Ruth Marshall Weir, Lima, Peru, Mar 26, 74; chdn Osman, Keila, Lois, Nathaniel, Benjadiah, Caleb; USanCris 76, BA, 76, MA; ColTS 82, MDiv; L Oct 15, 82; O Mar 4, 84; pres AES of Peru, 73-74; chp Chile, 84-87; ev MTW, Lat Amer, 88-16

74 South Victor Drive, Flintstone, GA 30725   Missouri
E-mail: gerardoguterrez46@gmail.com

Guyer, Edward D. – b Altoona, PA, Dec 18, 52; f Paul; m Mary Esther; w Sharon Faith, Altoona, PA, Oct 9, 76; chdn Rebekka Elisabeth (Parry), Hannah Ruth, Daniel Edward, Jonathan David, Caleb Jeremiah, Josiah Paul; WBC 74, BA; CapBS 78, ThM; TEDS 93, DMiss; O Jun 79, Frizellburg Bible Church; p Frizellburg B Ch, Westminster, MD, 76-80; mis InterAct Ministries of Canada, 81-98; p Susquehanna Bible Fell OPC, Wilkes-Barre, PA, 98-07; p Gr Christian Flwsp, Hancock, MD, 07-

5799 Pigeon Cove Road, Needmore, PA 17238 – 717-573-4744   Potomac
E-mail: eguyer06@gmail.com
Grace Christian Fellowship – 301-678-6036

Guzi, G. Matthew – astp Uptown Ch, PCA, Charlotte, NC, 04-05; ascp Hope Comm Ch, Charlotte, NC, 05-

4714 Truscott Road, Charlotte, NC 28226 – 704-759-1260   Central Carolina
E-mail: mattguzi@hopecommunity.com
Hope Community Church – 704-521-1033

Guzman, Joshua – RTS 04, MA; ascp Crossroads P Ch, Middletown, DE, 04-

627 Vance Neck Road, Middletown, DE 19709   Heritage
E-mail: jguzman@crossroadsfamily.com
Crossroads Presbyterian Church – 302-378-6235

Guzman, Pedro –b Ciudad Victoria, Mexico, Nov 26, 50; f Pedro, Sr.; m Juana Reyna; w Sara Plata, Mexico, Aug 23, 75; chdn Efrain, Eliud; STPM 72, ThB; L Jun 74, Presbitery of Tamaulipas, Mexico; O Feb 10, 90, Primera Iglesia Baptista Hispana; Recd PCA Oct 31, 92, SoTX Pby, ev 75-84; p Mexico, 84-88; p Chicago, IL, 89-92; ascp Oaklawn P Ch, Houston, TX, 92-98; chp Project Houston, 92-94; op Iglesia Presbiteriana Vida Nueva(m), 94-98, wc 98-01; ob ev PEF; p Iglesia Presbiteriana "Dios con Nosotros," Edinburg, TX, 18-; auth *Siguiendo A Una Estrella, (Following a Star), Poems and Dramas*

3602 North Tequila Drive, Pharr, TX 78577   South Texas
E-mail: pedro.guzman.reyna@gmail.com
Iglesia Presbiteriana "Dios con Nosotros"

Gwennap, Todd – b Asheville, NC, Aug 22, 83; f Jack; m Elizabeth; w Jennifer; chdn Jack, Audrey, Raney; UNC 05, BA; CTS 09, MDiv; O Aug 2, 09, Wcar Pby; astp Arden P Ch, Arden, NC, 09- 14; astp Christ P Ch, Winterville, NC, 14-16, ascp 16- 18; srp Christ the King, DeSoto, TX, 18-

903 Middle Run Place, Duncanville, TX 75137 – 828-231-5001   North Texas
E-mail: todd@ctktexas.com
Christ the King – 407-496-7720

Gwin, Charles F. Jr. – b Pensacola, FL, Jan 30, 41; f Charles F; m Muriel Lee Moses; w Anita Jean Hargis, Pensacola, FL, Jul 26, 68; chdn Rebekah Jean, Andrew Charles; USM, BS; CTS 69, MDiv; TTS 80, ThD; L May 20, 69; O Nov 9, 69, Midw Pby (RPCES); p Reformed P Ch, Cutler, IL, 69-70; p Covenant P Ch, Issaquah, WA, 70-73; p Pea River P Ch, Clio, AL, 73-78; p Clio P Ch, Clio, AL, 73-78; p Westminster P Ch, Milton, FL, 78-91, wc 91-93; ss Loxley P Ch, Loxley, AL, 93-05; hr

PO Box 171, Malakoff, TX 75148 – 210-501-5273   Gulf Coast
HR

Gwin, Timothy – astp Carriage Lane P Ch, Peachtree City, GA, 07-11, ascp 11-

256 Ebenezer Church Road, Fayetteville, GA 30215 – 770-719-2165   Metro Atlanta
E-mail: timgwin@hotmail.com
Carriage Lane Presbyterian Church – 770-631-4618

Gyger, Terry L. – b Glendale AZ, May 21, 34; f Fred L; m Blanche Young; w Dorothy Schmoker, Glendale, AZ, Jun 12, 54; chdn Daniel, Grant, Eric; UAZT 52-56, BS, 57, MEd; CBTS 58-61, MDiv; O Nov 9, 75, SFL Pby; pres MIA, 61-75; p Immanuel P Ch, Miami, FL, 75-80; VP MIA, 80-81; asst, coord MNA, 81-84; ap Perimeter Ch, Duluth, GA, 84-86; coord MNA, 86-94; chp, op NoE Pby; ev Christ The King P Ch, Cambridge, MA, 94-96, srp 96-99; ascp Redeemer P Ch of New York, New York, NY, 99-06, astp, DChPl 06-08; ob Dir Church Planting, Redeemer City to City, 08-13; ss Intown Comm Ch, Atlanta, GA, 13-15; pres LinX, 13-

3793 Northlake Creek Drive, Tucker, GA 30084 – 470-255-2631   Metropolitan New York
E-mail: terrygyger@gmail.com

Ha, David – astp Maranatha Vision Ch, Livermore, CA, 16-18

4309 Springhurst Drive, Plano, TX 75074   Korean Northwest
E-mail: dyh.mvc@gmail.com

Ha, Jin Chul – ob mis Seed Int'l, 08-

SEED Int'l, PO Box 69, Merrifield, VA 22116   Korean Capital
E-mail: email@seedusa.org

Haack, Joe – O Sept 12, 10, Ohio Pby; astp Grace Central P Ch, Columbus, OH, 10-11, ascp 12-; op Hope P Ch, Columbus, OH, 11-

888 Timberman Road, Columbus, OH 43212 – 614-447-9744   Columbus Metro
E-mail: joe@hopechurchcolumbus.org
Grace Central Presbyterian Church – 614-299-0919
Hope Presbyterian Church – 614-285-7060

Haan, Brandon – O Mar 24, 17, Siouxl Pby; campm RUF, UMN, 17-

1853 Howell Street, Falcon Heights, MN 55113 – 605-595-8669   Siouxlands
E-mail: brandonhaan@yahoo.com
PCA Reformed University Fellowship

Haan, Floyd Alan – b Sioux Falls, SD, Sept 13, 54; f Fred C.; m Clarice D. Fossum; w Janice Marie Odens, Springfield, SD, May 9, 75; chdn Matthew Alan, Mark Stephen, Luke Brian, John Robert; USD; SFC, BA; WTS 79, 80, MA, MDiv; CTS 90, DMin; O 15, 81, Siouxl Pby; p Pollock Mem P Ch, Pollock, SD, 81-

614 C Avenue, Box 97, Pollock, SD 57648 – 605-889-2820   Siouxlands
E-mail: fhaan@valleytel.net
Pollock Memorial Presbyterian Church – 605-889-2830

Haas, Guenther Horst – b Eschenlohe, Germany, Jul 31, 47; f Joseph; m Clara Mendel; w Dana Lorine Soper, Winnipeg, Manitoba, May 21, 83; chdn Joel Andrew, Evan Taylor; USask 69, BA; UReg 78, BA; CTS 74, MDiv, 77, ThM; UTor 89, ThD; L Jun 77; O Jul 80, PacNW Pby; CanBC & CanTS, 77-81; ap Grace Fell, Waterloo, Ont, 87; op, ev Willow West P Msn, 87-90; ob prof RedC, 90-18; hr 18; *The Concept of Equity in Calvin's Ethics*, 97

3 Idlewilde Lane, Mt. Hope, ON L0R 1W0 CANADA – 905-679-0990   Eastern Canada
E-mail: gene.haas2017@gmail.com
HR

Habig, Brian C. – b Jackson, MS, Oct 9, 67; f Paul M. Jr.; m Alyce M. Chesser; w Dana Gaye Freeman, Newton, MS, Jul 30, 94; chdn Henry, John, Betsy; MSU, BBA; CTS, MDiv; O Nov 5, 95, Cov Pby; campm RUF, MSU, 95-01; campm RUF, VandU, 01-05; op Downtown P Ch, Greenville, SC, 05-; co-auth *The Enduring Community*; "Hosea 6:7 Revisited" *Presbyterion*, Fall 16

6 Waccamaw Circle, Greenville, SC 29605 – 864-979-2215   Calvary
E-mail: bhabig@downtownpres.org
Downtown Presbyterian Church

Hackmann, Kyle – astp Grace Toronto Ch, Toronto, ON, 10-12; ascp 12-17; op Christ Ch Toronto, Toronto, ON, 17-

383 Jarvis Street, Toronto, ON M5B 2C7 CANADA   Eastern Canada
E-mail: kyle@christchurchtoronto.ca
Christ Church Toronto – 416-880-0506

Hager, J – BelmC 02, BFA; CTS 08, MDiv; astp Covenant P Ch, Nashville, TN, 09-14; wc 14-15; op Flatrock Comm Ch, Nashville, TN, 15-18, p 18-

117 Valeria Street, Nashville, TN 37210 – 615-480-1144   Nashville
E-mail: j@flatrockcc.org
Flatrock Community Church – 615-840-8718

Hahm, Hank – w Jean Hae Jin; chdn Elijah, Ezra, Edmund; TuftsU 92, BA; GCTS 96, MDiv; O Apr 8, 02, KorCap Pby; astp, pEng Korean Central P Ch of Wash, Vienna, VA, 98-05; ascp Christ Central P Ch of Wash, Vienna, WA, 98-08; chap USAF, 08-

11617 Cypress Barn, Schertz, TX. 78154 – 703) 638-8998   Korean Capital
E-mail: hankhahm@gmail.com
United States Air Force

Hahn, James Paul Jr. – b Lakeland, FL, Nov 12, 62; f James Paul, Sr.; m Ruby Jo Darr; w Frances Cantey Duggan, Birmingham, AL, May 10, 86; chdn MaryFran Tyson, Duggan Darr, Kathleen Bailey, James Paul; YU 80-84, BA; RTS 87-90, MDiv; L Jun 6, 89, MSVal Pby; O Nov 18, 90, SEAL Pby; ydir First P Ch, Gulfport, MS, 87-88; stus Westminster P Ch, Meridian, MS, 89-90; campm RUM, AU, 90-94; op Redeemer P Ch, Austin, TX, 94-96, p 96-03; op Redeemer Ch of Knoxville, TN, 03-08; p 08-15; p chp/renewal TNVal Pby, 15-16; coord MNA, 16-

597 Pinecrest Drive, Athens, GA 30605 – 865-237-8178   Tennessee Valley
E-mail: phahn@pcanet.org
PCA Mission to North America

Hahn, John Hong – O Feb 12, 95, SoCst Pby; ob ascp Orange County First P Ch, S. Pasadena, CA, 95-96; ob Cho Dae P Ch, Paramus, NJ, 96-

201-265-6095   South Coast
Cho Dae Presbyterian Church, Paramus, NJ (non PCA)

Hahne, Joshua – w Melissa; chdn Lara, Christian; WTS 05, MDiv; ascp Flwsp of Gr, Peoria, AZ, 05-07; op King of Kings, Goodyear, AZ, 07, p 07-

645 East Bird Lane, Litchfield Park, AZ 85340   Southwest
E-mail: josh@kkchurch.org
King of Kings – 623-385-6607

Hailey, Benjamin Michael – Beth; chdn Hannah, Nathan; DSU, BS; RTS, MDiv; O Jun 6, 04, MSVal Pby; campm RUF, HindsCC, 04-08; campm RUF, TXA&M, 08-17; astp Westminster P Ch, Bryan, TX, 17-

2803 Arroyo Court, College Station, TX 77845   South Texas
E-mail: ben@wpc-collegestation.org
Westminster Presbyterian Church – 979-776-1185

Haines, William Joseph – ob Inter-Varsity Christian Flwsp, UDE, Newark, DE, 14-15; ascp Cornerstone P Ch, Landenberg, PA, 15-16, srp 16-

735 Harvard Lane, Newark, DE 19711   Heritage
E-mail: hainesw@gmail.com
Cornerstone Presbyterian Church – 610-255-5512

Haist, Sam – O May 31, 15, MO Pby; astp South City Ch, St. Louis, MO, 15-17, ascp 17-

3002 Texas Ave, St. Louis, MO 63118   Missouri
E-mail: sam@southcitychurch.com
South City Church – 314-276-5816

Halbert, Aaron – mis MTW, Honduras, 15-

c/o MTW   Mississippi Valley
E-mail: abhalbert@gmail.com
PCA Mission to the World

Halbert, Andy – O Apr 28, 13, Palm Pby; ob mis United World Mission, 13-

9913 Tierra Verde Drive, Knoxville, TN 37922   Tennessee Valley
E-mail: ahalbert@christcov.org
United World Mission

Hale, Kevin – op Christ Ch Conway, Conway, AR, 08-11; p 11-

1926 Caldwell, Conway, AR 72034 – 501-269-6680   Covenant
E-mail: kevin@christchurchconway.org
Christ Church Conway – 501-328-5711

Hales, Bryce – p Christ Ch of Pasadena, CA, 07-09; campm RUF, UUT, 09-15; op Resurrection Orange Co, Rancho Santa Margarita, CA, 15-

29 Tarleton Lane, Ladera Ranch, CA 92694 – 801-560-5335   South Coast
E-mail: brycehales@gmail.com
Resurrection Orange County – 949-558-1418

Haley, Jay – O Jan 9, 13, Evan Pby; ascp Pleasant Grove P Ch, Pleasant Grove, AL, 13-

1203 Sequoia Circle, Alabaster, AL 35007 – 205-425-2353   Evangel
E-mail: cshaley01@peoplepc.com
Pleasant Grove Presbyterian Church – 205-744-4077

Hall, David Sasser – b Columbia, SC, May 24, 79; f Stephen G., Sr.; m Mary Leslie Shaw; w Carly Elizabeth Lester, Rock Hill, SC, Dec 28, 02; chdn Karis Elizabeth, Berit Sasser, Piper Katherine; WinC 03, BA; RTSNC 07, MDiv; O May 27, 07, Flwsp Pby; ascp Filbert P Ch, York, SC, 07-

120 Education Lane, York, SC 29745 – 803-322-7781   Fellowship
E-mail: davecarlyhall@gmail.com
Filbert Presbyterian Church – 803-684-6881

Hall, David Wayne – b Memphis, TN, Jan 1, 55; f Richard E; m Joyce M. Gwaltney; w Ann Louise Fleming, Memphis, TN, Sept 6, 80; chdn Megan Kathleen, Devon Elizabeth, Andrew David; MempSU 75, BA; CTS 80, MDiv; WhTS 02, PhD; O Aug 3, 80, Chero Pby (PCUS); ap First Ch, Rome, GA, 80-84; p Covenant P Ch, Oak Ridge, TN, 84-02; srp Midway P Ch, Powder Springs, GA, 03-; *Windows on Westminster*; *Welfare Reformed: A Compassionate Approach*; *Paradigms in Polity*; *To Glorify And Enjoy God: A Commemoration of the 350th Anniversary of the Westminster Assembly*; *Evangelical Renderings: To God And To Caesar*; *The Practice of Confessional Subscription*; *Jus Divinum: The Divine Right of Church Government*; cont *Evangelical Hermeneutics*; *Savior or Servant? Putting Government In Its Place*; *Evangelical Apologetics*; ed, *Election Day Sermons*; *The Arrogance of the Modern: Historical Theology Held in Contempt*; *The Millennium of Jesus Christ: An Exposition of the Revelation for All Ages*; co-ed *Did God Create in Six Days?* contr *The Genesis Debate*; *Holding Fast to Creation*; *The Genevan Reformation and the American Founding*; *A Manual for Officer Training*; *Lectures on Integrity*; *The Legacy of John Calvin: His Influence on the Modern World*; *Theological Guide to Calvin's Institutes: Essays and Analysis* (co-ed); *Calvin in the Public Square: Liberal Democracies, Rights, and Civil Liberties*; *Calvin and Commerce: The Transforming Power of Calvinism in Market Economies*; *Tributes to John Calvin* (ed); *Preaching Like Calvin: Sermons from the 500th Anniversary Celebration*; *Calvin and Culture: Exploring A Worldview* (co-ed); *Questioning Politics: Five Essential Questions for Believers to Answer*; *Summer Reading: Christian Classics*; *Election Sermons*; *Declaring Independence: By Whom and From Where*; *Essays on Calvin and Calvinism* (vol. 1)*: Post Tenbrae*; *Essays on Calvin and Calvinism (*vol. 2*): Lux Essays on Calvin and Calvinism* (vol. 3)*: Lux Supra Tenebrae Practicing Christian Marriage*; *Twenty Messages to Consider Before Voting*; co-auth *Theology Made Practical: New studies on John Calvin and His Legacy*; *The Divine Plan for Church Structure, Abridged: Jus Divinum*; *On Reforming Worship*

648 Goldenwood Court, Powder Springs, GA 30127   Northwest Georgia
E-mail: david.hall@midwaypca.org
Midway Presbyterian Church – 770-422-4974

Hall, Joshua M. – O Oct 17, 15, Ill Pby; astp Marissa P Ch, Marissa, IL, 15- 18; ob ip Sparta Ref P Ch, Sparta, IL, 18-

516 North Maple Street, Sparta, IL 62286 – 615-988-1231   Illiana
E-mail: michael.joshua.hall@gmail.com
Sparta Reformed Presbyterian Church

Hall, Michael Anderson – w Kirby McCarley; chdn McKenzie Reid, Carter Anderson, John Thomas McCarley; UMS 95, BA; CTS 00, MDiv; L Oct 26, 00, Cal Pby; O May 20, 01, Cal Pby; int Kirk of the Hills P Ch, St. Louis, MO, 97-99;-` astp, mfam Clemson P Ch, Clemson, SC, 00-05; astp Kirk of the Hills P Ch, St. Louis, MO, 05-12; astp Trinity P Ch, Charlottesville, VA, 12-16; ob RYM, 16-

1580 Robin Lane, Charlottesville, VA 22911 – 314-323-3374   Blue Ridge
Reformed Youth Ministry

Hall, William Michael – b Huntington, WV, Nov 3, 48; f William H; m Betty Jane Blazer; w Vicki Sue Steele, Point Pleasant, WV, Nov 20, 70; chdn Johnathan Eric, William Michael; MarU 66-70, BA; GCTS 72-73; MST 75-78, MDiv; L Jun 72; O Jun 78, WV Meth Conf; p Mt. Union, Moores Chapel, & Glenwood, 72-78; p Beale Chapel (Meth), 72-80; p Riverview P Ch, Charleston, WV, 81-94; p Wittenberg Comm P Ch, 95-97; RBI, mktg dir, 94-04; ss Faith P Ch (non PCA), Crosslands, WV, 08-09; wc 11-15; hr 15

76 Crystal Springs Drive, Winfield, WV 25213 – 304-757-8249   New River
E-mail: delegate200@hotmail.com
HR

Hallenbeck, Tyler – O Feb 11, 18, ChiMet Pby; astp Covenant P Ch, Chicago, IL, 18-

E-mail: thallenbeck@covenantchicago.org   Chicago Metro
Covenant Presbyterian Church – 773-486-9590

Halsey, Andrew – RTS 06, MDiv; O Jul 9, 06, Cov Pby; p First P Ch, Charleston, MS, 06-

210 North Waverly, Charleston, MS 38921 – 662-647-5382   Covenant
E-mail: fpccharleston@bellsouth.net
First Presbyterian Church – 662-647-5382

Ham, Isaac Kwang Hoon – b Seoul, Kor, Nov 1, 58; f Sung Han; m Soon Duk Kim; w Myung Soon Kim, Los Angeles, CA, Apr 11, 81; chdn David Sunhee, Jonathan Junhee; ChShC 77-80, BA; IBCS 85-87; ITSLA 82-85, MDiv; MWTS; L Jan 87; O Oct 13, 87, KorSW Pby; p Eternity P Ch, Panorama City, CA, 89; sc KorSW Pby, 92-96; p The Paul Msn Ch, Glendale, CA, 92-97; op Glory Christian Ch of S. CA, Gardena, CA, 97-08

Address Unavailable   Korean Southwest

Ham, Matt – astp Hope Comm Ch, Charlotte, NC, 10-

6901 Dulverton Drive, Charlotte, NC 28226 – 704-562-0451   Central Carolina
E-mail: mattham@hopecommunity.com
Hope Community Church – 704-521-1033

Ham, Steve Sung Hyun – b Seoul, KOR, Apr 25, 54; f Ki Hong; m Soon Sil Kim; w Yun Mi Ji, Seoul, Korea, May 10, 80; ChShC; CalvS; LVBCS 83, MDiv; L 85; O 86, KorSW Pby; p Torrance First P Ch, Hawthorne, CA, 83-86; ap Orange P Ch, Garden Grove, CA, 87-88; ob World Sports Missions , 89-91; p Valley Bethel Korean Presby. Ch, Van Nuys, CA, 91-92; ob p Los Angeles Peace Ch (non-PCA), 92-96; t Good News Bible College and Ch, 96-08

E-mail: saikoam@gmail.com   Korean Southwest

Hamamatsu, Kotaro – astp Briarwood P Ch, Birmingham, AL, 09-

E-mail: khamamatsu@briarwood.org   Evangel
Briarwood Presbyterian Church – 205-776-5200

Hamby, Robert – w Kendall; chdn Wells, Simeon; Citadel; CTS; O Oct 8, 00, Cal Pby; campm RUF, FurU, 00-06; campm RUF, TCU, 06-11; astp Providence P Ch, Dallas, TX, 11- 13; op Mercy P Ch, Dallas, TX, 13-

2831 6th Avenue, Ft. Worth, TX 76110   North Texas
E-mail: rob@mercydallas.com
Mercy Presbyterian Church

Hames, Ben – w Erin; UGA 02, BA; SEBTS 05, MDiv; O Jul 15, 06, NGA Pby; astp Christ P Ch, Marietta, GA, 06-08; wc 09-

657 East Paces Ferry Road NE, Atlanta, GA 30305 – 706-499-4216   Northwest Georgia

Hamilton, David Eugene – b Korea, Jan 21, 29; f Floyd E; m Ruth Bonebrake; w Marilyn Long, Jamestown, NY, Jun 17, 50; chdn Beth (Stanton), Becky (Vierling), Sarah (Goeglein), Jill (Martin); GordC, BA; GCTS 53, MDiv; ColTS 60, ThM; FTSSWM 83, ThM; O Jun 54, FL Pby (PCUS); ap McIlwain Mem P Ch, Pensacola, FL, 54-56; op, p Fairfield P Ch, Pensacola, FL, 56-60; mis Mexico, 60-72; p Northside P Ch, Burlington, NC, 72-76; mis Ecuador, 76-82; WSCAL, dir field ed, 84-85, dean 85-87; ob astp Independent P Ch, Memphis, TN, 87-96; Grace Evangelical Ch, dir evangelism, Germantown, TN, 97-04; hr 97; vol WBT, 00-04; vol Operation Mobilization, Tyrone, GA, 04-

517 Perkins Road #23, Palmetto, GA 30268 – 770-631-9307   Covenant
E-mail: davidmarilyn16@att.net
HR

MINISTERIAL DIRECTORY

Hamilton, Frank Edward – b Kearny, NJ, May 1, 33; f Frank E. Sr.; m Jennie B. Alexander; w Helen M. Sawyer, Newark, NJ, Apr 28, 55; chdn Nancy (Kimble), Richard A., Russell A., Robert A., Elizabeth J. (Derreberry); RTS 82, dipl; IntSem 87, ThB; O Jul 25, 82, Cov Pby; p First P Ch, Water Valley, MS, 82-85; exec dir Hebron Colony & Gr Homes, Inc, 85-87; exec dir GSC, 87-88; ev PEF, 88; p Andrews P Ch, Andrews, NC, 89-97; ob ev, mis PEF, Scotland, 97-02; hr 02; assoc ip Westminster P Ch, Muncie, IN, 06-07; ascp Michiana Cov P Ch, Granger, IN, 08-; op Faith Comm Ch, LaPorte, IN, 08-11; p Andrews P Ch, Andrews, NC, 11-15, hr 15; p Andrews P Ch, Andrews, NC, 16-18

652 Granny Squirrel Drive, Andrews, NC 28901 – 828-321-9176   Western Carolina
E-mail: revhamilton99@gmail.com
HR

Hamilton, Robert Matthew – w Hayley; chdn Molly, Maggie, Katherine; UNCW, BA; GCTS, MDiv; O Nov 5, 05, JR Pby; astp New Cov P Ch, Virginia Beach, VA, 05-07; astp Covenant P Ch, Naples, FL, 07-08; ascp 08-10; op Christ the King Ch, Wilmington, NC, 10-

704 Antler Drive, Wilmington, NC 28409   Eastern Carolina
E-mail: rob@ctkwilmington.org
Christ the King Church

Hamilton, Theodore (Ted) Charles – srp New Life P Ch, Escondido, CA, 01-

2439 Eucalyptus Avenue, Escondido, CA 92029 – 760-735-8775   South Coast
E-mail: ted.h@newlifepca.com
New Life Presbyterian Church – 760-489-5714

Hamling, Jeff – astp Rocky Mountain Comm Ch, Billings, MT, 06-07; astp Gallatin Valley P Ch, Bozeman, MT, 07-08; p 08-

1115 Woodland, Bozeman, MT 59718 – 406-256-9342   Rocky Mountain
E-mail: jeff@gvpchurch.org
Gallatin Valley Presbyterian Church – 406-585-2223

Hamm, George – b Birmingham, AL, Sept 5, 88; w Laura Ann Rast; chdn Marion Wells; AU 11, BA; CTS 17, MDiv; O Aug 13, 17, OHVal Pby; campm RUF, ULou, 17-

3003 Harrison Avenue, Louisville, KY 40217   Ohio Valley
E-mail: george.hamm@ruf.org
PCA Reformed University Fellowship

Hamm, Jeffrey L. – b Hochstadt, Germany, Feb 19, 68; f Jimmy L.; m Jean Register; w Kelly Elizabeth, Huntsville, AL, Jan 4, 92; chdn Joshua Victor, David Hunter, Luke Nathanel, Elisabeth Duffey; AU 90, BS; RTS 99, MDiv; UAber 17, PhD; O Jan 23, 00, Gr Pby; int Second P Ch, Yazoo City, MS, 98-99; p Thomson Mem P Ch, Centreville, MS, 00-04; p First P Ch, Greenville, AL, 04-13; astp 13-17; srp ChristChurch P, Atlanta, GA, 17-

1740 Peachtree Street, Atlanta, GA 30309 – 256-715-7083   Metro Atlanta
E-mail: jeffh@christchurchatlanta.org
ChristChurch Presbyterian – 404-605-0505

Hamm, Ted Harry – astp Cornerstone of Lakewood Ranch, Bradenton, FL, 07-13; Chap USArmy, 13-

3234 Greenway Drive, Ellicott City, MD 21042 – 941-323-7818   Suncoast Florida
E-mail: Ted.h.hamm.mil@mail.mil
United States Army

Hammack, Brandt – p Marion P Ch, Marion, AL, 11-16

502 South Washington Street, Marion, MS 36756   Warrior
E-mail: BrandtHammack@hotmail.com

Hammack, Ronald John – w Carolyn; chdn Joshua, Bethany, Cayla; BarC 82, BA; REpS, MDiv; ob Dir Whosoever Gospel Msn, Philadelphia, 05-

7408 Bingham Street, Philadelphia, PA 19111 – 215-722-7715   Philadelphia
E-mail: rjhammack@msn.com
Whosoever Gospel Mission, Philadelphia

Hammett, Vernon – O Jan 20, 13, Gr Pby; p Lagniappe P Ch, Bay St. Louis, MS, 14-

839 Chiniche Street, Bay Saint Louis, MS 39520   Grace
E-mail: pastorhammett@gmail.com
Lagniappe Presbyterian Church

Hammond, David Arthur – b Beaver Falls, PA, Jul 13, 46; f Lester McClure; m Dorothy V. Moore; w Dixie Lee Davenport, Huntsville, AL, Dec 18, 71; chdn Matthew David, Aaron Christopher, Emily Rebekah; CC 68, BA; CTS 68; RPTS 69-70; CC 94, MEd; L Apr 12, 80; O Jun 14, 81, So Pby (RPCES); astp Westminster P Ch, Huntsville, AL, 81-98; WestmCA, 70-; ascp North Hills P Ch, Meridianville, AL, 98-

166 Derwent Lane, Huntsville, AL 35810 – 256-508-6529   Providence
E-mail: David.Hammond@Comcast.net
North Hills Presbyterian Church – 256-829-0333

Hammond, Dee – astp Chestnut Mountain P Ch, Chestnut Mountain, GA, 12-

1308 Overland Park Drive, Braselton, GA 30517 – 770-967-0766   Georgia Foothills
E-mail: dee_hammond@hotmail.com
Chestnut Mountain Presbyterian Church – 770-967-3440

Hammond, Seth – b Knoxville, TN, Apr 13, 82; f Michael; m Vivica Pippenger; w Stephanie; UTC, BS; RTSFL, MDiv; astp University P Ch, Orlando, FL, 09-13; astp Christ Cov P Ch, Knoxville, TN, 13-

1355 Yarnell Station Boulevard, Knoxville, TN 37932   Tennessee Valley
E-mail: seth.hammond@gmail.com
Christ Covenant Presbyterian Church – 865-671-1885

Han, Changhun – p Milwaukee Gospel Ch, Whitefish Bay, WI

819 East Silver Spring Drive, Whitefish Bay, WI 53217   Korean Central
Milwaukee Gospel Church – 847-693-9720

Han, Charles – astp Renewal P Ch of West Philly, Philadelphia, PA, 09-

4616 Sansom Street, Unit 2, Philadelphia, PA 19139   Philadelphia
E-mail: charleshan@renewalchurch.org
Renewal Presbyterian Church – 215-727-7200

Han, James Junghun – b Pomona, CA, Jun 15, 71; f Sam Eun; m Chung; UCI 89-93, BA; WSCAL 93-97, MDiv; L Oct 14, 97, KorSW Pby; O Apr 13, 99, KorSW Pby; LA Immanuel Mission Ch, Los Angeles, 93-99; ob ascp First PC of Or Co, Midway City, CA, 99-02; p Redeemer P Ch, Los Angeles, CA, 02-

1924 Middlebrook Road, Torrance, CA 90501 – 562-634-7737   Korean Southwest
E-mail: JamesHan@msn.com
Redeemer Presbyterian Church – 562-602-2474

Han, Jim – ob

E-mail: jimhan@cfchome.org   Korean Central

MINISTERIAL DIRECTORY

Han, Jonathan Kyung – op Korean P Ch of Salinas Msn, Salinas, CA, 91-; sc KorNW Pby, 92-96

998 Snug Harbor Street, Salinas, CA 93906 – 408-757-8531   Korean Northwest
E-mail: jonathankhan2001@yahoo.com
Salinas Korean Presbyterian Church – 831-422-4588

Han, Kenneth – w Yoori; chdn Calvin, Sophia, Seth; UCLA, BA; WSCAL, MDiv; O Sept 14, 04, SoCst Pby; p Grace P Ch, Fallbrook, Fallbrook, CA, 04-

31644 Seastar Place, Temecula, CA 92592-4801 – 760-481-4097   South Coast
E-mail: ken.han@gracefallbrook.church
Grace Presbyterian Church, Fallbrook – 760-689-2213

Han, Samuel – srp Segaero P Ch, Los Angeles, CA, 07-09; ob

121 Chaffee Circle, Norwood, NJ 07648   Korean Southwest
E-mail: kyusamhan@hotmail.com

Han, Sang Woo – astp McLean Korean P Ch, McLean, VA, 10-12; op Light of the World Ch, Centreville, VA, 12- 16; op Grace Comm, Centreville, VA, 17-

5413 Middlebourne Lane, Centreville, VA 20120 – 703-349-1625   Korean Capital
E-mail: pastorhan@0409@gmail.com
Grace Community – 703-818-2393

Han, Seunghoon – p Korean-American PC of Arizona Msn, Phoenix, AZ, 08-

7656 West Spur Drive, Peoria, AZ 85383   Korean Southwest
E-mail: thdhan@hanmail.net
Korean-American Presbyterian Church of Arizona Mission – 602-788-5112

Han, Sung Yun – ascp Korean Westm P Ch, Orange, CA, 99-00; p Lamp P Ch of LA, Gardena, CA, 00-

24001 Neece Avenue #1, Torrance, CA 90505   Korean Southwest
E-mail: sungyhan@hotmail.com
Lamp Presbyterian Church of Los Angeles – 310-327-8778

Han, Young Hwan – p Hamonah P Ch, 10-14; hr 14

E-mail: pyhhan@yahoo.com   Korean Northwest
HR

Hand, Brian – astp Lansdale P Ch, Hatfield, PA, 16-

2305 Davis Circle, Hatfield, PA 19440 – 215-696-3417   Eastern Pennsylvania
E-mail: brian@lansdalepres.org
Lansdale Presbyterian Church – 215-368-1119

Hand, Kelley – astp Covenant P Ch, Little Rock, AR, 02-05, ascp 05-06; p Desert Palms Ch, Chandler, AZ, 06-

2188 East Glacier Place, Chandler, AZ 85249-3494 – 480-699-0278   Southwest
E-mail: Kelley.hand@dpc-pca.org
Desert Palms Church – 480-422-2499

Hane, Andrew Davis – O Aug 26, 18, Cal Pby; fm MTW, 18-

c/o MTW   Calvary
PCA Mission to the World

Hanley, Tim – b 54; w Debbie; chdn Joshua, Daniel; O Jan 24, 04, Palm Pby; astp Chapin P Ch, Chapin, SC, 04-13; ev PEF, 13-

100 Stonemaker Court, Chapin, SC 29036 – 803-345-0982   Palmetto
E-mail: timhanley.pef@gmail.com
Presbyterian Evangelistic Fellowship

Hanna, John – astp All Souls Comm Ch, Nanuet, NY, 11-17; ascp 17-

125 Momar Drive, Ramsey, NJ 07446 – 201-783-8287   Metropolitan New York
E-mail: john@allsoulscommunity.com
All Souls Community Church – 845-598-5582

Hansen, Brad – O May 1, 16, Hrtl Pby; ascp Heartland Comm Ch, Wichita, KS, 16-

6932 East Winterberry Circle, Wichita, KS 67226 – 316-744-1600   Heartland
E-mail: bkhansen71@gmail.com
Heartland Community Church – 316-686-0060

Hansen, Bryant – w Karen Bratcher; chdn Kiersten, Wesley, John Peter, Samuel, Hayleigh; MempSU, BA; CTS, MDiv; O Nov 04, Cov Pby; astp Independent P Ch, Memphis, TN, 04-10; p First P Ch, Prattville, AL, 10-; Meth Healthcare Sys, CPE

502 Fiveash Oaks, Prattville, AL 36066 – 334-380-3040   Southeast Alabama
E-mail: bryant@fpcministries.org
First Presbyterian Church – 334-365-6387

Hansen, Steven – astp Redeemer P Ch, Riverview, FL, 10-16, ascp 16-

15417 Peach Stone Place, Ruskin, FL 33573 – 813-383-4376   Southwest Florida
E-mail: steven@redeemerriverview.org
Redeemer Presbyterian Church – 813-741-1776

Haralson, John – w Linnea Kaiser; chdn Julia Margaret, Rebekah Lee, John Kenneth III, Katherine Joan; USAFA 89, BS; CTS 99, MDiv; O Jun 17, 00, NoCA Pby; int Old Orchard Ch, Webster Groves, MO, 97-98; int Redeemer P Ch of New York, New York, NY, 99-00; ev, astp City Ch of San Francisco, San Francisco, CA, 00-01, ascp 01-03; p Grace Ch Seattle, Seattle, WA, 03-

2414 East Aloha Street, Seattle, WA 98112   Pacific Northwest
E-mail: john@graceseattle.org
Grace Church Seattle – 206-512-0842

Harbison, John Henry Jr. – b Fort Campbell, KY, Jul 2, 54; f John Henry; m Mary Catherine McLaverty; w Roberta Jean Ewing, Bristol, PA, Oct 10, 81; chdn Andrew James, Mark David; VilU 73; PASU 74-78, BS; WTS 81-85, MAR, 81-85, MDiv; CTS 01, DMin; L Jan 84; O Jan 85, OPC; Recd PCA Dec 14, 91, RMtn Pby; p Covenant P Ch (OPC), Mechanicsville, PA, 85-91; astp Grace P Ch, Colorado Springs, CO, 93, ascp 93-99; ob ARDM, 99-03; ob Comm Christian College, Redlands, CA, 03-; astp Calvary P Ch, Glendale, CA, 13-14; ob VP TRACS, 14-

303 Cambridge Drive, Lynchburg, VA 24502-5809 – 434-944-1459   Blue Ridge
E-mail: john.h.harbison@gmail.com
Transnational Association of Christian Colleges and Schools

Harbman, Graham – Recd PCA 15, NoCA Pby, Chap 15-18; hr 18

330 Sposito Circle, San Jose, CA 95136   Northern California
E-mail: gharbman@sbcglobal.net
HR

Hard, Ian G. – w Rebecca Spencer; chdn Gideon; CC 05, BA; CTS 11, MDiv; O Nov 26, 11, Iowa Pby; astp One Ancient Hope Msn Ch, Iowa City, IA, 11-13; ascp 13-16; p Christ Ch PCA, Pembroke, NH, 16-

11 Pine Street, Pembroke, NH 03275 – 319-855-2748   Northern New England
E-mail: iangehard@gmail.com
Christ Church PCA – 603-225-7377

Hardeman, Leslie Michael – b Greenville, SC, Nov 16, 48; f George W. Jr.; m Annie R. Mann; w Suzanne Marlow, Greenville, SC, May 20, 72; chdn Michele S., George W. IV; FurU 66-69; CBC 73-76, BA; CTS 76-79, MDiv; KSU 90, MS; BosU 85, MEd; O Jun 80, Midw Pby; Chap USArmy, 80-; Fam Life Chap, 90-93; Sr. Protestant Comm & Fam Life Chap, 93; Dir Fam Life Min, 100th Area Support Grp, 94-96; Dir Chap Resources USAARMC, Ft. Knox, KY, 96-98; 1st Armour Trng Bdg, Ft. Jackson, SC, 98-99; 4th Inf Trng Bdg, Ft. Jackson, SC, 99-02; 22nd Signal Brgd, Darmstadt, Germany, 02-05; 1st Trng Bgd, Ft. Jackson, SC, 05-08; USArmy ret 08; hr

205 Placid Drive, Irmo, SC 29063   Missouri
E-mail: mikexsuzanne@yahoo.com
HR

Harding, David Lewis – b Augusta, GA, May 19, 62; f Major B; m Jane Lewis; w Lynn Siegmann, Atlanta, GA, Aug 17, 91; chdn Lindsey, Sarah; CatC 85, BA; RTS 95, MDiv; CTS 13, DMin; O Aug 27, 95, CentGA Pby; astp First P Ch, Augusta, GA, 95-98; srp Young Meadows P Ch, Montgomery, AL, 98-01; op St. Petersburg P Ch, St. Petersburg, FL, 02-05, p 05-

1541 Eden Isle Boulevard NE, St. Petersburg, FL 33704 – 727-823-9048   Southwest Florida
E-mail: d.harding@stpetepca.org
St. Petersburg Presbyterian Church – 727-329-6346

Hardman, Marlin Conrad – b Charleston, WV, Nov 5, 34; f Conrad Eugene; m Esther Victoria Fulks; w Sylvia Carole Holden, Charlotte, Aug 2, 58 (d) (2) Peggy Fern Watts Allison, McLean, VA, Feb 3, 91 (d); chdn David Marlin, Charles Kevin; WVU 52-53; PBC 53-56, BRE; CBS&SM 56-58, MA; CathUAm 71-74, 81-82; VTS 76-77; WTS 76-81, DMin; L Aug 4, 54; O Jun 10, 58, Bap; Recd PCA May 14, 91, Pot Pby; YFC, Wash DC, 58-64; p Barcroft Bib Ch, Arlington, VA, 65-75; Dir Wayside Chr Min, Falls Church, VA, 76-81; cop Covenant Comm Ch, Falls Church, VA, 82-89; astp McLean P Ch, McLean, VA, 91-94, ascp 94-12; hr 12; art *Youth for Christ, Moody Monthly, Christianity Today, Brigade Leader*

15 Teasdale Court, Potomac Falls, VA 20165-6242 – 703-430-7403   Potomac
E-mail: bphardman951@verizon.net
HR

Hardy, Alton – op Urban Hope, Fairfield, AL, 15-

PO Box 53, Fairfield, AL 35064   Evangel
E-mail: ahardy@urbanhopecc.com
Urban Hope – 205-514-3715

Hardy, Jeffrey Lincoln – O Aug 29, 10, CentCar Pby; op Cross Park Ch, Charlotte, NC, 10-12; p 12-

6109 Hickory Forest Drive, Charlotte, NC 28277-2425 – 919-698-9288   Central Carolina
E-mail: jeff@crossparkchurch.org
Cross Park Church – 980-285-7020

Hare, Kenneth Todd – w Nancy; chdn Paul, Mark; MesC 82, BA; BibTS 93, MDiv; O Jun 5, 05, Chspk Pby; ascp Hunt Valley Ch, Hunt Valley, MD, 05-07; op Cornerstone Ch PCA, Hampstead, MD, 06-

17830 Foreston Road, Parkton, MD 21120 – 410-374-5108   Chesapeake
E-mail: thare@cstone.org
Cornerstone Church PCA

Hargis, Kenneth R., Jr. – b Cleveland, OH, Aug 4, 49; f Kenneth R.; m Marie H. Knight; w Janet Kay Piebenga, Rogers, AR, May 17, 86; chdn Matthew, Ian, James, Jenny, Martin; UMO 75, BS; WhTS 13, MACS; O Jul 21, 13, Cov Pby; astp Covenant Ch, Fayetteville, AR, 13-16; ob chap Wash Reg Med Cent, Fayetteville, AR, 16-

3168 Ozark Acres, Bentonville, AR 72712 – 479-366-4229   Hills and Plains
E-mail: ken.hargis@gmail.com

Haring, Brian – O Oct 30, 16, Glfstrm Pby; astp Spanish River Ch, Boca Raton, FL, 16-

2400 Yamato Road, Boca Raton, FL 33431   Gulfstream
E-mail: bharing@spanishriver.com
Spanish River Church – 561-994-5000

Harlow, John Porter – b Alexandria, VA, Aug 3, 71; f John Curtis; m Coleen Edwards Moore; w Catherine Elizabeth Armstrong, Dillon, SC, Aug 27, 94; chdn Andrew Porter MacQueen, Grace Solveig, Calvin Armstrong; The Citadel, BA; USC JD; Army JASchool, LLM; RTSDC MAR; O Jun 11, 17, Pot pby; astp Shady Grove P Ch, Derwood, MD, 17-18; op Christ P Ch Burke, Burke, VA, 18-; *How Should We Treat Detainees? An Examination of 'Enhanced Interrogation Techniques' under the Light of Scripture and the Just War Tradition,* 16

5124 Swift Court, Fairfax, VA 22032   Potomac
E-mail: porter@cpcburke.org
Christ Presbyterian Church Burke – 571-354-0623

Harper, Christopher – b Richmond, IN, Dec 28, 70; f David F.; m Rebecca J. Harris; w Stephanie K. Brown, Richmond, IN, Aug 1, 92; Purdue 89-91; ButU 91-93, BA; CTS 93-96, MDiv; L Jan 96; O Nov 96, GrLks Pby; campm RUF, OHSU, 96-99; staff MTW, 99-02; astp Grace P Ch, Indianapolis, IN, 02-03; ascp 03-08; p Trinity P Ch, Rochester, MN, 08-

2577 Schaeffer Lane NE, Rochester, MN 55906 – 507-226-1524   Siouxlands
E-mail: chris@trinityrochester.org
Trinity Presbyterian Church – 507-282-6377

Harper, Deren – astp Immanuel P Ch, DeLand, FL, 15-

811 Orange Camp Road, Deland, FL 328724   Central Florida
E-mail: derenharper@gmail.com
Immanuel Presbyterian Church – 386-738-1811

Harper, Richard T. – b Atlanta, GA, Sept 7, 69; f Jackson Thomas Harper Jr.; m Cheryl Jan Caylor; w Anne Arlene Heinemann, Atlanta, Jul 10, 93; GSU 88-91, BS; RTS 93-96, MDiv; L Oct 25, 97; O Nov 2, 97, CentCar Pby; astp Stone Bridge Ch Comm, Charlotte, NC, 97-00, ascp 00-05, srp 05-

19822 River Falls Drive, Davidson, NC 28036 – 704-895-4360   Catawba Valley
E-mail: rharper@stonebridgecharlotte.com
Stone Bridge Church Community – 704-549-8272

Harper, Russell Cline – b Macon, GA, May 20, 55; f Oliver Cline; m Lowery; w Jan Drew, Macon, GA, Jun 2, 79; chdn Jennifer Kathleen, Joshua Russell, Elizabeth Janice; WGAC 78, BA; RTS 81, MDiv; O Apr 82, Wcar Pby; astp First P Ch, Weaverville, NC, 82-84, ascp 84-89; astp Christ P Ch, Richmond, IN, 89-95; p Fairview Christian Flwsp, Fairview, NC, 95-

29 Vehorn Road, Fairview, NC 28730-9534   Western Carolina
Fairview Christian Fellowship – 828-628-1044

MINISTERIAL DIRECTORY

Harr, Thomas Michael – b Nov 14, 73; f Thomas; m Linda; w Stacey, Newark, DE, May 4, 02; chdn Austin, Davis, Esther, John, Anastasia; UDE 96, BS; RTS 14, MAR; O Jul 15, 12, Hrtg Pby; ascp Faith P Ch, Wilmington, DE, 12- 18; srp Calvary P Ch, Allenwood, NJ, 18-

1216 Mohegan Road, Manasquan, NJ 08736 – 302-427-8329   New Jersey
E-mail: tom@calvarynj.org
Calvary Presbyterian Church – 732-449-8889

Harrell, David Robert – b Chattanooga, TN, Sept 2, 52; f Robert Denton; m Betty Jo Henry; w Sarah Jane Hayes, Chattanooga, TN, Jul 7, 79; chdn Jonathan David, Joseph Daniel; CC 77-81, BA; RTS 81-84, MDiv; O Jun 84, Cov Pby; p Faith P Ch, Aberdeen, MS, 84-

219 Glendale Circle, Aberdeen, MS 39730-2903 – 662-369-4123   Covenant
E-mail: davidrharrell@bellsouth.net
Faith Presbyterian Church – 662-369-7737

Harrell, Joseph Robin – b Chattanooga, TN, Apr 12, 54; f Robert Denton; m Betty Jo Henry; w Rebekah Ruth Gumm, Bristol, TN, Aug 18, 79; chdn Susan Elizabeth, Rachel Rebekah; CC 72-76, BA; RTS 76-79, MDiv; O Jul 15, 79, Evan Pby; moy Trinity P Ch, 79-80; p Friendship P Ch, 80-86; mis MTW, Mexico, 86-06; mis MTW, Colombia, 07-

c/o MTW – 615-261-8650   Southeast Alabama
E-mail: joerharrell@gmail.com
PCA Mission to the World

Harrell, William Wesley Jr. – b Norfolk, VA, Apr 21, 51; f William Wesley; m Marion Arlene Conway; w Debra Anne Miller, Virginia Beach, VA, Aug 14, 70; chdn Rachel Dawn, Melodi Anne, Gabrielle Esther; ODU 77, BA; AberU 81, BD; O Sept 27, 81, MidAtl Pby; p Immanuel P Ch, Norfolk, VA, 81-; *Let's Study 1 Peter*

1915 Claremont Avenue, Norfolk, VA 23507-1121 – 757-717-4265   Tidewater
E-mail: williamharrell@cox.net
Immanuel Presbyterian Church – 757-440-1100

Harriman, Brent – campm RUF, area coord, 04- 18; op Resurrection P Ch, Knoxvillle, TN, 18-

1100 Burton Road, Knoxville, TN 37919 – 865-525-4026   Tennessee Valley
E-mail: brent@resurrection.com
Resurrection Presbyterian Church

Harrington, Marc – ascp Kirk O the Isles P Ch, Savannah, GA, 04-05; ascp Golden Isles P Ch, St. Simons Island, GA, 06-08; astp Midway P Ch, Powder Springs, GA, 08-

4635 Dallas Highway, Powder Springs, GA 30127   Northwest Georgia
E-mail: meh8171@yahoo.com
Midway Presbyterian Church – 770-422-4974

Harris, Ben – O Apr 11, 13, NFL Pby; astp Pinewood P Ch, Middleburg, FL, 13- 15; astp Covenant P Ch, Palm Bay, FL, 15-

202 Certosa Avenue NE, Palm Bay, FL 32907   Central Florida
E-mail: benjaminandrewharris@gmail.com
Covenant Presbyterian Church – 321-727-2661

Harris, Derrick Jeffreys – astp McLean P Ch, McLean, VA, 11-13; astp Christ P Ch, Nashville, TN, 13-17; astp Southwood P Ch, Huntsville, AL, 17-

Southwood Presbyterian Church – 256-882-3085   Providence

Harris, Glen Edward, Jr. – b Pensacola, FL, Jan 2, 80; f Glen; m Gail; w Abby Lea Christian, Oskaloosa, IA, Jul 29, 06; SamU 02, BA; BDS 05, MDiv; CTS 18, DMin; O Dec 3, 06, Iowa Pby; campm RUF, UIA, 06-07; Chap USAF, 07-; ascp Redeemer Comm Ch, O'Fallon, IL, 09-10; "Revelation in Christian Theology," *The Churchman* Spr 06 120/1; "When Prophets Speak to Kings: Air Force Chaplains and the Praxis of Leadership Advisement," CTS diss, 18

127 Coral Court, Minot AFB, ND 58704   Pacific
E-mail: chaplainharris@gmail.com
United States Air Force

Harris, Jordan – O Sep 24, 17, EPA Pby; ob p Faith ARP, Dickson, PA, 17-

222 Nichols Street, Clarks Summit, PA 18411 – 507-261-5613   Eastern Pennsylvania
E-mail: jharris@student.wts.edu
Faith ARP, Dickson, PA

Harris, Max R. – b Rotherham, Yorkshire, England, Mar 26, 49; f Ernest Jack; m Betty Wragg; w Ann Pierce Wysor, Petersfield, Hampshire, England, May 25, 74; chdn John Joel Orlando, Matthew Henry Owen; UCam 70, BA; UCSB 72, MA; CTS 78, MDiv; UVA 89, PhD; L Jun 78, Midw Pby (RPCES); O Oct 10, 78, Eng Pby (IPC); p Intnat'l P Ch, Ealing, London, 78-79; p Grace Cov P Ch, Blacksburg, VA, 79-83; p Liberty Ch, PCA, Owings Mills, MD, 83-85; ss Covenant P Ch, Harrisonburg, VA, 86; op Peace P Ch, Waynesboro, VA, 86-88, p 88-92; ob prof UVA, 92-94; ob exec dir WI Humanities Council, Madison, WI, 94-04; cop Lake Trails P Ch, Madison, 95-03, astp 14-; auth *Theatre and Incarnation*; *The Dialogical Theatre*; *Aztecs, Moors, and Christians*; *Carnival and Other Christian Festivals*; *Sacred Folly*

14 North Harwood Circle, Madison, WI 53717-1314 – 608-833-4506   Wisconsin
E-mail: max.harris@wisc.edu
Lake Trails Presbyterian Church – 608-833-4497

Harris, Ronald T. – b Toronto, Ont, Canada, Mar 17, 52; f Thomas Huffman; m Shirley Ethyl Drysdale; w Linda Diane Toogood, London, Ont, Canada, Oct 11, 75; chdn Angela Marie, Dawna Laurie, Noel Adam; UWO 75, BMus; UPA 77, MA; WTS 80, MAR, 81, MDiv, 86, DMin; L Aug 83; O Aug 84, Ecan Pby; ev, ss Good Shepherd P Ch, Timmins, Ont, 84-86, ss 86-87; ap Coral Ridge P Ch, Ft. Lauderdale, FL, 87-91; ob couns Wellspring of Life Biblical Counseling Service, 91-; ob AcadDn Ukraine Family Inst, Kiev, 02-07; dir/fndr Storehouse of the King, Kiev, 07-18; hr 18

2091 2nd Line East, RR #5, Campbellford, ON K0L 1L0 CANADA – 705-653-1748   Eastern Canada
E-mail: Ron.Harris@worldteam.org
HR

Harris, Todd – b DeKalb, IL, Jul 1, 67; f Dewey Lynn; m Eugenia Scott; w Elisabeth Anne Ohlen, Corvallis, OR, Aug 17, 91; chdn Laurie Elisabeth, Ashley Jeanne, Jessica Marie; INU 90, BA; WTS 95, MDiv; O Nov 19, 95, Phil Pby; ev, chp Frontiers, Mesa, AZ, 95-99; p Amman Int Ch, Amman, Jordan, 97-99, wc 99-00; ascp Lansdale P Ch, Lansdale, PA, 00-02, wc 02-07; ascp Colleyville P Ch, Colleyville, TX, 07-09

2216 Thorne Street, Newberg, OR 97132   North Texas
E-mail: toddharris9@comcast.net

Harritt, William L. III – O Nov 22, 14, Ecar Pby; astp Church of the Good Shepherd, Durham, NC, 14-17; astp Eastbridge P Ch, Mount Pleasant, SC, 17-

Eastbridge Presbyterian Church – 843-849-6111   Lowcountry

Hart, Malcom Douglas – astp Westminster P Ch, Roanoke, VA, 02-05; op Hope P Ch, Martinsville, VA, 02-05; ascp Christ the King P Ch, Roanoke, VA, 08-12; wc 13-15; ss Christ the King P Ch, Roanoke, VA, 15-16; hr 18

3801 Highwood Road NW, Roanoke, VA 24012-3307 – 540-366-6136   Blue Ridge
E-mail: m.douglashart@gmail.com
HR

Hart, Marvin Thomas – O Sept 13, 14, Ecar Pby; campm RUF, ECarU, 14-

107 Queen Anne's Road, Greenville, NC 27858-6214 – 229-869-3704   Eastern Carolina
E-mail: tom.hart@ruf.org
PCA Reformed University Fellowship

Hart, Michael – astp Covenant P Ch at Cleveland, Cleveland, MS, 07-13; astp University P Ch, Orlando, FL, 13-17, ascp 17-

1013 Marisol Court, Orlando, FL 32828   Central Florida
E-mail: mhart@upc-orlando.com
University Presbyterian Church – 407-384-3300

Hart, Zane – b Hanford, CA, May 7, 82; f Joseph Edward; m Mahala Watkins; w Elizabeth Anne Sloan, Richmond, VA, May 13, 82; chdn Miranda Joy, Isaac Sloan; JMU 04, BA; CTS 09, MDiv; O Apr 20, 10, MO Pby; astp Grace P Ch of St. Charles Co, St. Charles, MO, 10-12; astp Covenant Life P Ch, Sarasota, FL, 12-17

1652 Summer Breeze Way, Sarasota, FL 34232 – 941-587-4131   Southwest Florida

Hartman, Brett S. – b Kansas City, KS, Jul 6, 69; f Dr. Charles R.; m Carolyn Ann Hogan; w Tara Lee Whitworth, Iola, KS, Dec 28, 91; chdn Caleb Stephen, Nathan Andrew, Seth Daniel, Anna Sharon; UKS 88-91, BS; RTSFL 96-97; CTS 97-01, MDiv; L Feb 15, 02, SusqV Pby; O Apr 28, 02, SusqV Pby; staff CCC, IndU, 91-95; ascp New Cov Flwsp, Mechanicsburg, PA, 02-, ip 05-06; srp 06-

809 Anthony Drive, Mechanicsburg, PA 17050 – 717-732-3950   Susquehanna Valley
E-mail: bretth@newcovfel.org
New Covenant Fellowship – 717-732-8500

Hartman, Edward A. – b Sighsoria, Romania, May 31, 61; f George; m Elisabeth Schieb; w (1) Amy B. Hogan (d) (2) Emily M. Potts, Kosciusko, MS, May 17, 97; chdn Michael William, Kathryn Elisabeth, Abigail Kelsey, Daniel Lee; CBC 86, BS; WTS 87-90; RTS 90-91, MDiv; WSCAL 93-94, 98, DMin; L Oct 15, 91; O Feb 23, 92, MSVal Pby; ascp Ch of the Savior, Philadelphia, PA, 86-88; p Edwards P Ch, 92-95; p First P Ch, 95-04; mis MTW, Romania, 04-13; astp First P Ch, Jackson, MS, 14-; *Homeward Bound: An Eternal Perspective on the Godly Home*

1004 Euclid Avenue, Jackson, MS 39202   Mississippi Valley
E-mail: ehartman@fpcjackson.org
First Presbyterian Church – 601-353-8316

Hartman, L. Stanley – b Memphis, TN, Feb 25, 24; f Royal Lauren; m Martha Stanley; w Maribeth Williams, Pulaski, TN, Jan 31, 53; chdn Martha Gail (Moore), Patricia Sue (Page), Lauren Beth (Ward), David Stanley; MBI; VandU; CBC; SETS; O Oct 52, RPCES; p Calvary BPC, Nashville, TN, 50-59; Westminster Ch, Bowling Green, KY, 59-66; Parkwood Mem Bib Ch, Harlingen, TX, 66-71; p First ARP Ch, Burlington, NC, 71-74; p The P Ch, Columbus, MS, 74-78; p Meadow Creek P Ch, Greeneville, TN, 78-81; p First P Ch, Union, MS, 81-83; p First P Ch, Picayune, MS, 83-88; p First P Ch, Sandersville,

Hartman, L. Stanley, continued
GA, 88-91; ip St. Andrews P Ch, Americus, GA, 91; hr 91; ip Westminster P Ch, Valdosta, GA, 93; ob ss McCutchen Mem P Ch, Union, SC, 95-97; ip Millbrook P Ch, Millbrook, AL, 98; ob astp Trinity P Ch, Montgomery, AL, 98-05

Emeritus at Riverstone, 125 Riverstone Terrace # 107, Canton, GA 30114   Northwest Georgia
678-880-3625
HR

Hartzell, Mark W. – b Carlisle, PA, Aug 24, 60; f William M.; m Helen Mae Minnick; w Linda Mary Jennings, Gettysburg, PA, Jun 11, 83; chdn Lauren, Kevin, Jonathan; GetC 82, BA; WTS 86, MDiv; L May 97, Phil Pby; O Feb 20, 99, Phil Pby; ob Dir Harvest USA, Philadelphia, PA, 99-01; ob Dir Harvest USA Mid-South Region, Chattanooga, TN, 01-08; astp New City Flwsp, Chattanooga, TN, 08-18; wc

304 Vista Drive, Chattanooga, TN 37411 – 423-364-0284   Tennessee Valley
E-mail: markwhartzell@gmail.com

Harvey, James L. III – w Melody; chdn Tabitha, Jacob, Mary Faith, Susanna; PU 95, AB; RTS 02, MDiv; L Mar 01, MSVal Pby; O Jun 02, MNY Pby; astp Princeton P Ch, Princeton, NJ, 02-03; ob Christian Union, 03-05; srp Evangelical P Ch, Newark, DE, 05-18; ob RTS NYC, 18-

E-mail: pastorharvey@gmail.com   Heritage
Reformed Theological Seminary NYC

Harvey, John D. – b Johnstown, PA, Mar 11, 51; f John A.; m M. Joyce Dyer; w Anita D. Burns, Greenville, IL, May 25, 74; SyU 74, BA, 74, BArch; CBS&SM 86, MDiv; WCUTor 97, ThD; O Apr 6, 97, Palm Pby; ob prof CIUSSM, 97-; *Listening to the Text: Oral Patterning in Paul's Letters*, 98; *Greek is Good Grief*, 07; *Anointed With the Spirit and Power*, 08; *Interpreting the Pauline Letters*, 12; *Romans (EGGNT)*, 17

133 Wynfield Court, Columbia, SC 29210 – 803-731-0603   Palmetto
E-mail: jharvey@ciu.edu
Columbia International University Seminary and School of Ministry

Harvey, Scott – w Judith Ann (d), (2) Mary; chdn Kenny, Jeff, Stephanie; astp Lehigh Valley P Ch, Allentown, PA, 08-16

15315 82nd Avenue East, Puyallup, WA 98375 – 484-284-1823   Pacific Northwest
E-mail: scottharvey2807@gmail.com

Harwell, Andrew – O 18, MetAtl Pby; astp Perimeter Ch, Johns Creek, GA, 18-

11765 Carriage Park Lane, Johns Creek, GA 30097   Metro Atlanta
E-mail: andrew.harwell@gmail.com
Perimeter Church – 678-405-2000

Harwood, Gerald Ott – b TN, Sept 11, 74; f Franklin D.; m Effie Miranda Ott; w Heather Adelle Fowler, Chattanooga, TN, Aug 13, 94; chdn Ruslan Franklin, Snizzana Morgan, Hayley Mia, Scott Bruce IV; UTC 92-96, BA; BDS 96-99, MDiv; L Jul 11, 00, TNVal Pby; O Jan 7, 01, TNVal Pby; astp, yp Hixson P Ch, Hixson, TN, 00-06; astp Christ P Ch, Nashville, TN, 06-07; astp First P Ch, Chattanooga, TN, 07-13; wc 13-

729 Lancaster Drive, Signal Mountain, TN 37377   Tennessee Valley

Haslett, Reggie H. – w Gail A; L Jan 21, 89; O Nov 1, 92, CentGA Pby; p Sparta P Ch, Eatonton, GA, 92-08; p Bethany P Ch, Greensboro, GA, 92-08; p Penfield P Ch, Penfield, GA, 92-08; p Crawfordville

Haslett, Reggie H., continued
P Ch, Crawfordville, GA, 92-03; p Bethany P Ch, Greensboro, GA, 10-; p Penfield P Ch, Penfield, GA, 10-; p Sparta P Ch, Eatonton, GA, 10-

147 South Springs Road, Eatonton, GA 31024 – 706-485-9750   Central Georgia
Bethany Presbyterian Church – 706-486-2682
Penfield Presbyterian Church – 706-453-7872
Sparta Presbyterian Church – 706-485-9750

Hass, Kevin M. – O Oct 6, 16, Tidw Pby; p By Gr Comm Ch, Yorktown, VA, 16-

103 Edgewood Court, Yorktown, VA 23692 – 757-594-0852   Tidewater
E-mail: pastor@bygrace.cc
By Grace Community Church – 757-234-1222

Hatch, James Donald – b Kosciusko, MS, Sept 22, 42; f James M, Jr; m Mittie Lee Orr; w Janet Mae Heiser, Gibson City, IL, Jun 12, 65; chdn James Christopher, Courtney Eileen (Sensenig), Caren Orr (Henning); CBC 64, BA; CTS 68, BD, 68, MA; TrSU, MS; O May 68, MSVal Pby (ARP); p Elsberry Ch, 68-69; ap ARP, Bartow, FL, 69-70; p Edwards Mem Ch ARP, 70-73; NADir MiA, 73-75; p Oak Park P Ch, Montgomery, AL, 75-82; p Faith P Ch, Montgomery, AL, 82-85; ap Perimeter Ch, Duluth, GA, 85-87; asst, coord MNA, 87-94, coord 94-95; admin, DnStu CTS, 95-99, DAlRel 99-01, dir Ch rel 01-03; ascp New City Flwsp, University City, MO, 02-; admin MNA, 03-

5719 DeGiverville Avenue, St. Louis, MO 63112 – 314-361-6871   Missouri
E-mail: jhatch@pcanet.org
New City Fellowship – 314-726-2302
PCA Mission to North America – 314-308-4226

Hatcher, Herschel – O Feb 26, 14, MetAtl Pby; astp Perimeter Ch, Johns Creek, GA, 14-

E-mail: herschelh@perimeter.org   Metro Atlanta
Perimeter Church – 678-405-2000

Hatcher, Joseph – p Comm P Ch, Live Oak, FL, 16-17; Chap USArmy, 18-

PO Box 206, Live Oak, FL 32064   North Florida
E-mail: joseph_r_hatcher@hotmail.com
United States Army

Hatfield, Harrison – astp Rainbow P Ch, Rainbow City, AL, 13-15

956 Buck Hill Road, Prescott, AZ 86303   Evangel
E-mail: hatfield.harrison@gmail.com

Hatfield, Shane – campm RUF, OKSt, 14-

1302 South Mansfield Drive, Stillwater, OK 74074   Hills and Plains
PCA Reformed University Fellowship

Hathaway, Nicholas – w Catherine Ann; chdn Aiden Cole, Sophia Childress, Daniel Clipston, Martin Seth, Cosette Capelle, Annelise Margaret, Haddon Nicholas; St.MarysMD 00, BA; CTS 07, MDiv; astp Liberty Ch, PCA, Owings Mills, MD, 08- 17; ascp New Covenant P Ch, Abingdon, MD, 17-

1630 Brimfield Circle, Sykesville, MD 21784 – 443-609-4360   Chesapeake
E-mail: thehathawayhome@gmail.com
New Covenant Presbyterian Church – 410-569-0289

Hatton, Jeffrey Christian – b Peoria, IL, Oct 15, 64; f Christian; m Jean Marie Elverum; w Nancy Elizabeth Bell, Dallas, TX, Aug 21, 92; chdn Calvin, Bryn, Knox, Belle, Ty Phillip; UMA 87, BA; DTS 94-98, ThM; TrTS 16, DMin; L Jul 98, NoTX Pby; O Jul 98, NoTX Pby; chp Waco, TX, 98-00; p Redeemer P Ch, Waco, TX, 00-

2501 Ritchie Road, Waco, TX 76712 – 254-655-4125   North Texas
E-mail: mail@redeemerwaco.org
Redeemer Presbyterian Church – 254-776-7292

Hatton, Pete Phillip – b Dallas, TX, Dec 28, 67; f Christian P.; m Jean Marie Elverum; w Kristen Elizabeth Bech, Houston, TX, Jan 27, 96; chdn Rebecca, David, Jonathan; PASU 87-91, BA; DTS 92-00, MABS; L Apr 01, NoTX Pby; O Jul 8, 01, NoTX Pby; astp Redeemer P Ch, Waco, TX, 01-02; campm RUM, BayU, 02-08; op Redeemer P Ch, Edmond, OK, 09-

4625 Briar Meade Road, Edmond, OK 73025 – 405-550-1464   Hills and Plains
E-mail: pph167@gmail.com
Redeemer Presbyterian Church – 254-723-4287

Haubert, Mitchell Lee – b Nov 3, 78; w Amy; chdn Mitchell III, Mary-Grace, Jedidiah; TrSU 06, BS; RPTS 11, MDiv; O May 11, Pitts Pby; astp Providence P Ch, Robinson Township, PA, 11- 15; p Brent P Ch, Brent, AL, 15-

199 Tabernacle Road, Brent, AL 35034   Warrior
E-mail: mhaubert@brentpc.org
Brent Presbyterian Church – 205-926-4722

Havener, Jared – w Kelsey; chdn Charis, Emma; GenC 10; RPTS 13, MDiv; O Aug 17, 14, Pitts Pby; ascp Trinity P Ch, Johnstown, PA, 14-15, srp 15-

939 Drexel Avenue, Johnstown, PA 15905 – 841-341-9726   Pittsburgh
E-mail: jared.havener@gmail.com
Trinity Presbyterian Church – 814-269-3947

Haverhals, Ross F., Jr. – b Anaheim, CA, Apr 2, 78; w Leah Kuipers, Platte, SD, May 25, 01; chdn Grant, Anna, Elena, Gerrit; NWC 00, BA; TEDS 11, MDiv; O Jan 19, 12, ChiMet Pby, Chap 12-13; ascp Redeemer Comm Ch, O'Fallon, IL, 13-14, ob Chap 14-

1041 9th Street SW, Pine City, MN 55063 – 719-331-7084   Illiana
E-mail: rossfh@gmail.com

Hawk, William B. – b Brewton, AL, Jun 3, 46; f R.B.; w Joyce Lovik, Daytona Beach, FL, Aug 16, 69; chdn Benjamin Jon, Darren Joel, Jina Joyce, Dana Anne; BelC 68, BA; RTS 69-70; TEDS 71, MDiv; O Jun 76, UPCUSA; p First Ch, Canoga Park, CA, 76-78; op Cov Ch (PCA), Atascadero, CA, 78-86; op Covenant P Ch, Paso Robles, CA, 86-87, p 87-94, wc 94-95; ev NoCA Pby, 95; op Trinity P Ch, San Luis Obispo, CA, 96-01; astp Covenant P Ch, Paso Robles, CA, 01-07; ascp 07-

PO Box 722, Templeton, CA 93465-0722 – 805-434-2363   Northern California
E-mail: wbuford@yahoo.com
Covenant Presbyterian Church – 805-238-6927

Hawkes, Thomas D. – b Jacksonville, FL, Dec 23, 55; f Townsend D.; m Virginia Abernethy; w Ann Carpenter, Rye, NH, Oct 7, 79; chdn Collin T., Taylor D., Brandon A., Preston C.; GordC 78, BA; GCTS 85, MATS; FrUAmst 06, MTS; LondSchTheo 14, PhD; L Oct 25, 94; O Nov 19, 95, CentCar Pby; Dir Ch grwth svcs, Evan Assn, New England, 80-84; MNA, dir Ch grwth, 86-90; Billy Graham Evan Assoc,

Hawkes, Thomas D., continued
Amsterdam, 86; Leighton Ford Min, 91-97; op Uptown Ch, Charlotte, NC, 94-96, p 96-; dir The Church Planting Center, RTSNC; co-editor *Laying Firm Foundation; Pious Pastors, Calvin's Theology of Sanctification and the Genevan Academy,*16

1407 Burtonwood Circle, Charlotte, NC 28212 – 704-537-7845   Central Carolina
E-mail: tomhawkes@uptownchurch.org
Uptown Church – 704-375-7355

   Hawkins, Addison – b Columbia, MO, Nov 1, 86; f Jim; m Mary Jane Wozniak; w Lynnette Kay Yarger, Columbia, MO, Jun 3, 11; chdn Theodore James, Louisa Jane; UMO 09, BA; CTS 16, MDiv; O Oct 7, 18, GrLks Pby; astp Christ Ch, Grand Rapids, MI, 18-

642 Winchell Street SE, Grand Rapids, MI 49507   Great Lakes
E-mail: addison@christchurchgr.org
Christ Church – 616-949-9630

   Hawkins, Richard – ascp Christ P Ch at Olive Branch, Olive Branch, MS, 18-

4021 Los Padres Dr, Nesbit, MS 38651   Covenant
E-mail: richawk@hotmail.com
Christ Presbyterian Church at Olive Branch – 662-895-7035

   Hawley, Martin Lee – b Springdale, AR, Nov 15, 62; w Shari, May 20, 89; CTS 04, MDiv, 05, MA, 14, ThM; UAberdeen PhD cand; srp Hope P Ch, Marietta, GA, 05-; exec dir Reformation Hope, Inc., 11-; *Hope for Haiti: An Account of Pastor Jean Jacob Paul and Reformation Hope, Inc.*, 13; *The God-centered Statesman: God's Sovereignty, Faith, and Civil Service from Daniel for Today*, 14; *Gospel Feasting: 104 Lord's Supper Devotions from the Old and New Testaments*, 15; *The Gospel Feast: Proclaiming the Gospel Through the Lord's Supper*, 15

5008 Cross Ridge Court, Woodstock, GA 30188-4380 – 404-771-9180   Northwest Georgia
E-mail: rev.hawley@gmail.com
Hope Presbyterian Church – 770-971-4673

   Hay, William Gifford – b Duluth, MN, May 1, 40; f William Walter; m Dorothy Gifford; w Cynthia Hagman, Duluth, MN, Aug 21, 65; chdn John, Philip, Rebekah; UMD 59-63, BA; SamU, MA; ColTS 63-66, BD; TEDS 99, DMin; O Sept 66, Duluth Pby (UPCUSA); p Edgewood United P Ch, B'ham, AL, 66-78; srp Covenant P Ch, Birmingham, AL, 78-11; p em 11-; hr 12

230 Crest Drive, Birmingham, AL 35209-5326 – 205-871-4366   Evangel
E-mail: bhay@covpres.com
HR

   Hayes, Mark – USNA 76-80; NPGS 86-87; CTS 90-00; astp Harvester P Ch, Springfield, VA, 02-08; ascp 08-15, srp 15-

4102 Adrienne Drive, Alexandria, VA 22309 – 703-619-0942   Potomac
E-mail: mark@harvesterpca.org
Harvester Presbyterian Church – 703-455-7800

   Hayes, Robert Spence – b Panama City, FL, Apr 9, 47; f James E H; m Laura S; w Elizabeth Hildreth, Panama City, FL, Jun 25, 71; chdn Jonathan Hildreth, Carrie Ellen, Dabney Elizabeth, James Henry, Jessica Michelle; UWFL 71, BA; RTS 74, MDiv; L Jul 4, 74; O Aug 3, 74, Cov Pby; p Carrollton P Ch, Carrollton, MS, 74-82; sc Cov Pby, 80-81; op Faith Chapel, Panama City Beach, FL, 82-84; p Covenant P Ch, Panama City, FL, 84-07; ascp 07-11; US Dir, Africa Christian Training Inst; short-term missions, Uganda; ss Chattahoochee P Ch, Chattahoochee, FL, 15-

1401 Calhoun Avenue, Panama City, FL 32401-1543 – 850-814-6322   Gulf Coast
E-mail: bob@ugandamission.net; bhayes409@aol.com
Chattahoochee Presbyterian Church – 850-663-2195

Haygood, Emory Langston – b Montgomery, AL, Jun 5, 42; f Laurie C; m Lillian Compton; w Mary Emily Cooper, Jackson, MS, Jun 11, 66; chdn Elizabeth Lovelace, Mary Margaret, Alice Compton; BelC 62-65, BA; ColTS 65-68, BD; EmU 68-69, grad wk; ColTS 69-70, ThM; UEdin 75-76, grad wk; WTS 77-79, DMin; UAL 95, PhD; O Aug 11, 68, Atl Pby (PCUS); Barnett Pres Ch, Atlanta, GA, 68-70; p First Ch, Winder, GA, 70-75; p Altadena Valley P Ch, Birmingham, AL, 77-80; p First P Ch, Gadsden, AL, 80-92; t BhamTS, 77-; fac GSJC; ob adj prof BDS, 92-; astp Covenant P Ch, Birmingham, AL, 95-14; Dir Cov Couns & Ed Ctr, Birmingham, AL, 95-14; fndr/chrmn Odessa Spr Family Couns Ctr, Odessa, Ukraine; President, Pathway Ministries, Inc.; hr 14

288 Huntington Parc Road, Birmingham, AL 35243 – 205-942-5010   Evangel
E-mail: lank@haygood@msn.com
HR

Haynes, Matthew – w Sarah; chdn Elena, Andrew, Ethan, Russell; BJU 95, AS; CIU 97, BS; CTS 10, MDiv; NWU 15, ThM; O Oct 19, 10, MO Pby; mis Flying Mission, Botswana, 98-01; mis MTW, Cape Town, South Africa, 10-

c/o MTW – 919-342-5173   Missouri
E-mail: reformedpilot@gmail.com
PCA Mission to the World

Hays, Nathan – O Oct 12, 14, SNE Pby; campm RUF, BostonU, 14-15; Chap 15-

12 Westwood Terrace, Westwood, MA 02090 – 781-752-7382   Southern New England

Hays, Robert Evermont – b El Dorado, AR, Nov 17, 44; f Benjamin Franklin; m Martha Waive Gladstone; w Martha Louise Emmons, Madison, MS, Jun 15, 68; chdn Benjamin Paul, Susan Louise; BelC 67, BA; RTS 77, MDiv, 84, DMin; L Jun 76, MSVal Pby; O Jun 12, 77, Cov Pby; p First P Ch, Clarendon, AR, 77-81; p Beal Heights P Ch, Lawton, OK, 81-88; sc MidA Pby, 85-88; p Pearl P Ch, Pearl, MS, 88-02, wc 02-03; p Forest Presbyterian Church, 03-05; ss First P Ch, Philadelphia, MS, 07; ss Bay Springs P Ch, Bay Springs, MS, 07-10; hr 10; staff Cov EPC, Jackson, MS, 10-12; ss First P Ch, Philadelphia, MS, 15; mission trips to Czech Rep, 95, 96, 97, 99, Honduras, 10, 12; guest lect Donetsk Reg Bible Coll, Ukraine, 00; ss Pearl P Ch, Pearl, MS, 16

740 Sweetwater Drive, Pearl, MS 39208 – 601-939-9268   Mississippi Valley
E-mail: robertehays@bellsouth.net
HR

Hayse, Tim – astp North Shore Flwsp, Chattanooga, TN, 10-15; p Christ Comm Ch, Gainesville, FL, 15-

9910 NW 17th Road, Gainesville, FL 32606   North Florida
E-mail: timhayse@gmail.com
Christ Community Church – 352-379-4949

Heard, Jerrard Case – b Jackson, MS, Nov 10, 68; f Louie Peaster; m Nan Brantley (d); MSU 86-90, BA; SIU 90-91, MA; RTS 92-95, MDiv; UWales 04-09, PhD; L Feb 21, 95, MSVal Pby; O Jan 14, 96, Pac Pby; int Brandon P Ch, Brandon, MS, 94-95; p Redeemer P Ch, Torrance, CA, 96-06; wc 06-12; mod Pac Pby, 97-98, 12-13; ob adj fac Comm Christ Coll, 12-17; sc Pac Pby, 16-; ob instr CGST, 17-; Dn Stu Serv, 18-; Dir of M.A./M.Div. programstheol contr *Tusitala,* a Samoan publication

916 Esplanade, #107, Redondo Beach, CA 90277 – 310-529-2037   Pacific
E-mail: revjheard@netzero.net
California Graduate School of Theology - 714 636-1722
11277 Garden Grove Boulevard, Garden Grove, CA 92843

Heard, William Curry – b Macon, GA, Feb 3, 63; f Charles F.; m Betty Morgan Finn; w Sydney Foreman, Newport, CA, Jun 26, 88; chdn Ann Fant, Cecilia Sydney, Sarah Tyson; DavC 85, BA; WTS 90, MDiv; O Oct 20, 91, CentGA Pby; astp First P Ch, Macon, GA, 91-95; chp, op Harbor Ch PCA, Mooresville, NC, 95-00, p 00-10; p Grace P Ch at Starkville, Starkville, MS, 12-

603 Shadowood Lane, Starkville, MS 39759   Covenant
E-mail: wcheard@outlook.com
Grace Presbyterian Church at Starkville – 662-324-0180

Hearon, Mike – w Sandra Blair, Aug 6, 83; UNAL 83, BA; BhamTS 99, MA; FulTS, DMin cand; O Jul 11, SavRiv Pby; ascp First P Ch, Augusta, GA, 11-18; srp 18-

817 Windsor Ct, Augusta, GA 30909   Savannah River
First Presbyterian Church – 706-262-8900

Hebert, Joel – wc

1553 Trenton Lane, Cape Girardeau, MO 63701 – 573-335-7169   Illiana
E-mail: jabear043@gmail.com

Heck, Sebastian – b Baden-Baden, Germany, Aug 7, 75; w Isabel; chdn Sophia, Tabea, David; TheolSemEwersbach 03; WTS 06; TheolUApeldoorn; O Oct 29, 10, NWGA Pby; astp Grace P Ch, Douglasville, GA; Reformation2Germany, 10-; chp Heidelberg, Germany, 10-

Bergheimer Strasse 147, Heidelberg 69115 GERMANY   Northwest Georgia
E-mail: sebheck@mac.com
Reformation2Germany

Hedman, Martin – b Jan 26, 63; f Gerald; m Ruth; w Kathleen, Dec 3, 94; chdn Ashleigh, Alysia, Andrew, Rachel; UW 87, BS; ClGS 91, MBA; WSCAL 07, MA; O May 08, SoCst Pby; op Mission P Ch, La Habra, CA, 08-17; astp Hope P Ch, Bellevue, WA, 18-; *Augustine on Justification: Made Righteous or Declared Righteous?*

811 152nd Place SW, Lynnwood, WA 98087   South Coast
E-mail: mwhedman@yahoo.com
Hope Presbyterian Church – 425-454-1247

Hegtvedt, Kenneth L – b Bremerton, WA, Feb 14, 51; f Arthur Kenneth; m Peggy Deloris Curtis; w Janet Louise Walsworth, Olympia, WA, Jul 18, 74; chdn Benjamin, Aaron, Allison (McKay), Joseph; WWSU 74, BA; CGST 88, DMin; NavWC 04, MA; ArmWC 09, MA, 14, ThM; O Dec 7, 80, Bible Ch; ascp Lincoln Ave Bible Ch, 80-86; srp Peninsula Bible Ch, 86-89; Chap USArmy, 89-; srp Lincoln Ave Bible Ch, 98-08; op Grace Comm P Ch, Bremerton, WA, 13-

PO Box 2511, Bremertown, WA 98310 – 360-981-0171   Pacific Northwest
E-mail: hegtvedt@comcast.net
United States Army
Grace Community Presbyterian Church – 360-981-0171

Heibel, Luke G. – b Leonardtown, MD, Sept 9, 75; w Anne Holloway Kesler, Signal Mountain, TN, Jul 9, 03; chdn Conrad Gerard, Judah Grant; UNCA, BA; WTS, MDiv; O Oct 24, 10, TNVal Pby; astp New City Flwsp, Chattanooga, TN, 10-13, Chap 10-13; Chap USArmy, 13-

260 Dominica Circle West, Niceville, FL 32578   Tennessee Valley
E-mail: lgheibel@gmail.com
United States Army

Heiberg, Christo Frederik – Recd PCA 17, Ecan Pby; astp Providence Comm Ch, St. Catharines, ON, 17-

22 Southdale Drive, St. Catherines, ON L2M 3N4 CANADA - 905-577-7572   Eastern Canada
E-mail: cfheib@gmail.com
Providence Community Church – 289-273-2477

Heidt, Philip – Recd PCA Oct 4, 16, Pac Pby; chp 16; ob p Journey Cov Ch, 17-

2751 Onrado Street, Torrance, CA 90503 – 310-561-9792   Pacific
E-mail: pandakruon@gmail.com
Journey Covenant Church

Hein, Benjamin – O Apr 22, 18, Pot Pby; astp Shady Grove P Ch, Derwood, MD, 18-

14804 Edman Circle, Centreville, VA 21021   Potomac
E-mail: ben@shadygrovepca.org
Shady Grove Presbyterian Church – 301-330-4326

Heinbaugh, Steve Allen – b Harrisburg, PA, Sept 22, 54; f Lee E.; m Corrine J. Wert; w Shelley Ann Peifer, Millersburg, PA, Jun 1, 85; chdn Benjamin Joseph, Rachel Elizabeth; ShSU 79, BS; BibTS 86, MAR, 86, MDiv; L Jan 87, SusqV Pby; O Oct 87, SusqV Pby; ap Trinity P Ch, Harrisburg, PA, 86-88, p 89-91; ev, Chap New Cumberland Depot, 92-97, wc 92-97; op The Citys Gate PCA Ch, Harrisburg, PA, 97-07; astp Trinity P Ch, Harrisburg, PA, 08-09; ob p Trinity UCC, Millersburg, PA, 09-13; hr 15

2607 Hoffer Street, Harrisburg, PA 17103-2047 – 717-991-8552   Susquehanna Valley
E-mail: ssbr@msn.com
HR

Heinrich, James Weston – b Indianapolis, IN, Mar 26, 75; f Dr. James; m Carol; w Angela Lloyd Packard, Nashville, TN, May 16, 98; chdn Cody Bradfield, Houston James; WheatC, BA; DTS, ThM; O Aug 17, 03, Ecar Pby; astp Church of the Good Shepherd, Durham, NC, 03-04; wc 04-

4001 Branchwood Drive, Durham, NC 27705 – 919-479-7384   Eastern Carolina
E-mail: jheinrich@fmrealty.com

Heiple, Ray E. Jr. – f Ray; m Marcia; w Robin; chdn Calvin Ray, Daniel Ray, Jacob Ray, Sarah Rae; PASU, BA; RPTS, MDiv; RPTS 13, DMin; O Nov 23, 03, Pitts Pby; astp Providence P Ch, Robinson Township, PA, 03-06; ascp 06-10; srp 10-; host *Origins*, Cornerstone Network; t Robinson Township CS, 14-; *Preaching with Biblical Motivation,* 17; *Pocket History of the PCA,* 17

832 Neely Heights Avenue, Coraopolis, PA 15108 – 724-926-8544   Pittsburgh
E-mail: rheiple@providence-pca.net
Providence Presbyterian Church – 412-788-6100

Heisten, Ernest Lad III – b Carthage, MO, Dec 26, 50; f Ernest L Jr.; m Bettie Deitz; w Gaellan McIlmoyle, St. Louis, MO, Jun 30, 79; chdn Ernest Lad IV, Jackson Albert; FWBC 73, BA; TEDS 76, MDiv; StLU 86, MA; L 81; O 81, Cov Pby; ap Memorial P Ch, St. Louis, MO, 81-83, wc 84-; sc MidA Pby, 01

1328 South Chestnut Avenue, Broken Arrow, OK 74012-4715 – 918-251-0480   Hills and Plains

Hellings, Raymond A. Sr. – b Philadelphia, PA, Oct 20, 44; f Roy A.; m Meier; w Patricia Fulton, Ft. Lauderdale, FL, Mar 17, 72; chdn Cheryl Ann, Christine R., Raymond A. Jr.; WhitBC 78-82, BA; RTS 82-85, MDiv; L 84; O 85, Gr Pby; p First P Ch, Taylorsville, MS, 85-87; YFC, Greenville, SC, 87-88; ss Trinity P Ch, Spartanburg, SC, 87-88, p 88-11; hr 11; p Center Point P Ch, Moore, SC, 12-

249 Dartmoor Drive, Spartanburg, SC 29301-5368 – 864-574-0307   Calvary
E-mail: pastorray@bellsouth.net
Center Point Presbyterian Church

Helm, David Richard – b St. Charles, IL, Apr 7, 61; f Richard L.; m Andrea A. Morken; w Lisa A. Schmid, Wheaton, IL , Aug 11, 84; chdn Noah David, Joanna Catherine, Stephen Baxter, Silas James, Mariah Elise; WheatC 79-83, BA; GCTS 84-88, MDiv; O Jun 5, 88; Recd PCA Apr 26, 91, NoIL Pby; ob astp, mout/evan College Ch, Wheaton, IL, 88-98; ob p Holy Trin Ch (Ind), Chicago, IL, 98-

5624 South Dorchester Avenue #1, Chicago, IL 60637 – 773-493-3272   Chicago Metro
Holy Trinity Church (Independent) – 773-288-5870
5757 South University Avenue, Chicago, IL 60637

Helopoulos, Jason M. – b Urbana, IL, May 12, 77; w Leah; chdn Gracen Journey, Ethan Taylor; EastIll 99, BA; DTS 03, ThM; O Jun 5, 05, PTri Pby; astp Meadowview Ref P Ch, Lexington, NC, 05-07; astp Christ Ch, Grand Rapids, MI, 07-12; op Providence PCA Msn, Lansing, MI, 07-12; ob astp University Ref Ch, East Lansing, MI, 12-15, ascp 15-; *A Neglected Grace: Family Worship in the Christian Home*, 13; *The New Pastor's Handbook: Help and Encouragement for the First Years of Ministry*, 15; *Let the Children Worship*, 16; *These Truths Alone: Why the Reformation Solas Are Essential for Our Faith Today*, 17

5060 Patrick Circle, Holt, MI 48842 – 517-599-8956   Great Lakes
E-mail: pastorjason55@gmail.com
University Reformed Church – 517-599-8956

Hembree, K. Robie – b Carrollton, GA, May 28, 63; f Oscar Virgil; m Dolores; w Talena Faye Foster; chdn Chris, Leslie, Cameron, Rachel, Caleb, Cole; NBBC 93, BA; RTSA; O Feb 06; p Grace Ch, Canton, GA, 99-

217 Diamond Valley Pass, Canton, GA 30114 – 770-265-5811   Northwest Georgia
E-mail: robie@gracecanton.org
Grace Church – 770-265-5811

Henderson, Daniel – b Pittsburgh, PA, Oct 18, 73; w Sarah; chdn Micah, Luke, Lydia, oshua; CTS 09, MDiv; O 13, GAFH Pby; astp Grace P Ch, Blairsville, GA, 13- 18; srp Manor P Ch, Cochranville, PA, 18-

300 Faggs Manor Road, Cochranville, PA 19330   Susquehanna Valley
E-mail: daniel.manorpca@gmail.com
Manor Presbyterian Church – 610-869-2402

Henderson, Geoffrey C. – w Amy; FurU 99, MA; RTS 05, MDiv; O Feb 06, SWFL Pby; ydir Westminster P Ch, Clinton, SC, 99-02; int University P Ch, Orlando, FL, 03-05; ascp Hope P Ch, Bradenton, FL, 05-09; astp Redeemer P Ch, Hurricane, WV, 10-13, chp 13-14; op Harbor Comm Msn, Bradenton, FL, 14-18, p 18-

4107 24th Avenue West, Bradenton, FL 34205 – 941-932-6154   Southwest Florida
E-mail: geoffsnook@gmail.com
Harbor Community Mission – 941-932-6154

Henderson, Rodney – b Westerly, RI, June 22, 77; f Reg Henderson; m Pamela Henderson; w Brooke Elizabeth Brigdens, North Stonington, CT, Jan 4, 03; chdn Annie Elizabeth; GordonC 95-99, BS; GCTS 99-05; MDiv; GCTS 05-06; ThM; astp Trinity P Ch, Johnstown, PA, 06-08; ascp 08-13; p Covenant P Ch, Ledyard, CT, 13-

8 Tanglewood Drive, Preston, CT 06365   Southern New England
E-mail: pastor.rodney@yahoo.com
Covenant Presbyterian Church – 860-464-8476

Henderson, S. Phillip – b Charlotte, NC, Sept 15, 46; f John Washington; m Ola Mae Hogue; w Merilyn Savage Graves, Stanley, NC, Feb 15, 75; chdn Nathan Phillip, Joanna Grace; KgC 68-71, BA; UNCC 72; UTSVA 71-72; RTS 75-78, MDiv; O Aug 6, 78, Car Pby, mis 78-88, wc 88; MNA, MM, 89-

Henderson, S. Phillip, continued
92, wc 92; ss Coulwood P Ch, Charlotte, NC, 92-93, p 93-95, wc 95-99; astp Southlake P Ch, Huntersville, NC, 99-05; mis MTW, 05-07; wc 07-; t Cov Class S, 09-12; hr 12

5427 Gristmill Lane, Mint Hill, NC 28227 – 704-650-0560   Central Carolina
E-mail: phsouthlake@yahoo.com
HR

Henderson, Sean Michael – w Samantha; chdn Patience, Charles, William, George; DTS 99, MA; WTS 05, MDiv; astp Sierra View P Ch, Fresno, CA, 06-09, ascp 09-16, srp 16-

1562 East Quincy Avenue, Fresno, CA 93720 – 559-301-0125   Northern California
E-mail: sierraview_sean@yahoo.com
Sierra View Presbyterian Church – 559-248-9136

Hendley, Andrew – O Jul 21, 12, NWGA Pby; p Kings Chapel P Ch, Carrollton, GA, 12-

372 Lakeview Way, Carrollton, GA 30117   Northwest Georgia
E-mail: andrew.hendley@gmail.com
King's Chapel Presbyterian Church – 770-834-0729

Hendrick, Robbie L. – b Jul 12, 66; f Bob; m Grace; w Tamela Jayne Eyrich, Atlanta, GA, Dec 18, 88; chdn Trey, Hayden, Megan, Myles, Preston; AU 84-89, BS; CTS 91-95, MDiv; L, SWFL Pby; O Jun 21, 98, Nash Pby; ydir Emmanuel EPC, St. Louis, 91-95; ydir Seminole P Ch, Tampa, FL, 95-97; astp Christ P Ch, Nashville, TN, 95-02, ascp 02-09; srp Rainbow P Ch, Rainbow City, AL, 10-17; srp Christ P Ch, Evans, GA, 17-

4201 Southern Pines Drive, Evans, GA 30809 – 706-210-9090   Savannah River
E-mail: robbiehendrick66@gmail.com
Christ Church, Presbyterian – 706-210-9090

Hendrikse, Thomas John – b Oak Park, IL, Aug 29, 65; f Nelson; m Patricia Lynn; w Mary Elizabeth, Jacksonville, FL, Aug 8, 92; chdn Morgan Elizabeth, Haley Anne, Thomas John Jr.; FSU 88, BS; MerU 92, JD; KTS 08, MDiv; srp Rio Vista Comm Ch, Ft. Lauderdale, FL, 01-

1808 Bayview Drive, Ft. Lauderdale, FL 33305 – 954-567-2246   South Florida
E-mail: tom@riovistachurch.com
Rio Vista Community Church – 954-522-2518

Hendrix, F. Leonard Jr. – b Durham, NC, Jul 22, 51; f Frank L, Sr.; m Shirley Lois Frazier; w Patricia Louise Nevins, Lookout Mtn, TN, Jun 10, 78; chdn Amelia Louise, Laura Conwell, Leigh Frazier, Thomas Winfield; UT 74, BS; GCTS 80, MDiv; RTS 87, DMin cand; O 80, PCUS; p Columbia P Ch, Columbia, MS, 80-88; rc Gr Pby, 85-88; op Trinity P Ch, Murfreesboro, TN, 88, p 89-95; sc Nash Pby, 94-02; p Covenant P Ch, Tullahoma, TN, 95-

305 Lannom Circle, Tullahoma, TN 37388-2463 – 931-455-3193   Nashville
E-mail: lenhendrix@gmail.com
Covenant Presbyterian Church – 931-455-5446

Henegar, Walter H. – b Chattanooga, TN, Dec 4, 71; f Henry A. Jr.; m Jane Humphrey; w Anne Sexton, Knoxville, TN, Aug 19, 95; chdn Abigail Sexton, Emily Jane; NWU 94, BA; WTS 02, MDiv; O Nov 3, 02, NGA Pby; astp ChristChurch P, Atlanta, GA, 02-04, ascp 04-07; op Atlanta Westside P, Atlanta, GA, 07-11, srp 11-; co-auth *Heal Us, Emmanuel*

1255 Collier Rd NW, Atlanta, GA 30318 – 404-567-5428   Metro Atlanta
E-mail: walter@atlantawestside.org
Atlanta Westside Presbyterian – 404-567-5428

MINISTERIAL DIRECTORY

Henning, Barry – b Dearborn, MI, Jan 8, 54; f Harold; m Freda Miller; w Ann Filer, Taylor, MI, Aug 25, 72; chdn Aaron, Jeremiah, Joshua, Sarah; WmTynC 77, BBE; WTS 80, MAR, 81, MDiv; L Mar 81; O Oct 82, OPC; Recd PCA Oct 10, 89, TNVal Pby; p Covenant OPC, Hixon, TN, 81-87; ascp NewCity Flwsp, Chattanooga, TN, 89-92; op New City Flwsp, University City, MO, 92-95; srp 95-

5948 Maple Avenue, St. Louis, MO 63112 – 314-725-2170   Missouri
E-mail: barry@ncfstl.org
New City Fellowship – 314-726-2302

Henninger, Mark J. – b Davenport, IA, Oct 4, 55; f Elmer Albert, Jr; m Geraldine Wilhelmina Sinclair; w Lesley Gay Little, Northbrook, IL, Sept 6, 86; chdn Christyn Leigh; PJC 74-75; UNIA 75-78, BA; TEDS 79-84, MDiv; L Jan 28, 89; O May 21, 89, NoIL Pby; p Redeemer P Ch, Peoria, IL, 89-

217 North Kickapoo Terrace, Peoria, IL 61604 – 309-674-8002   Northern Illinois
E-mail: markjhenninger@gmail.com
Redeemer Presbyterian Church – 309-676-8658

Henry, Daniel Edwin Hayes – O Jan 19, 17, SW Pby; ev 17-

PO Box 9090, Window Rock, AZ 86515 – 602-663-3970   Southwest
E-mail: dhandemilyhenry@gmail.com

Henry, David Michael – b Ephrata, PA, Oct 26, 70; f Spencer; m Doris Kurtz; w Lisa Landis, Feb 24, 01; chdn Joshua, Jeremy, James; GroCC 93, BS; WTS 99, MDiv; L Sept 99, SusqV Pby; O Apr 01, SusqV Pby; ob p Johnsville Ref Ch, 00-11; ob ev Child Evangelism Fellowship, Lehigh Valley, PA, 11-; astp Bridge Comm Ch, Easton, PA, 13-

791 Chestnut Lane, Easton, PA 18045 – 717-201-5696   Eastern Pennsylvania
E-mail: dmlmhenry@aol.com
Bridge Community Church – 215-264-7532

Henry, Paul Whitford – Crystal; chdn PJ, Calvin, Adele, Elizabeth; O Aug 21, 16, NFL Pby, mis 16-

1788 Emerald Lane, Middleburg, FL 32068 – 904-662-8716   North Florida
E-mail: paulwhitfordhenry@gmail.com

Henry, Phillip Edward – b Pasadena, CA, May 25, 70; f Robert Edwin; m Sally Eileen Hoyt; w Polly Robb Burdick, Bloomington, IN, Jul 10, 93; chdn Lydia, Fitch, Maggie, Noah, Grace, Stasi; INU 88-92, BS; WSCAL 96-99, MDiv; ThM stu WTS, 16-; L Jan 99, SoCst Pby; O Sept 17, 00, NoIL Pby; p Hanna City P Ch, Hanna City, IL, 00-03; astp, yp Rincon Mountain P Ch, Tucson, AZ, 03-07; op Mercy Hill P Ch, Sewell, NJ, 08-16, p 16-

162 Chancellor Drive, Woodbury, NJ 08096 – 856-693-4800   New Jersey
E-mail: philliphenry1@gmail.com
Mercy Hill Presbyterian Church – 856-556- 0427

Henry, Thomas F. – w Toni Thompson; chdn Ashley, Thomas, Trevor, Cord; CTS 89, ThM; O Oct 82; ap Grace P Ch, Ocala, FL, 82-85; ascp Christ Cov P Ch, Matthews, NC, 85-00, srp 00-04; ob WorldView Mission, 04-11; pres ReEntry, 11-; *Covenant and Kingdom: A Right Relationship*, 89

6608 Rothchild Drive, Charlotte, NC 28270 – 704-839-1355   Central Carolina
E-mail: tomh.reentry@gmail.com
ReEntry

Heo, Kyeon – UIL 07, BFA; GCTS 16, MDiv; O May 13, 18, KorNE Pby; astp New England Gr P Ch, West Hartford, CT, 18-

265 Slater Street #336, Manchester, CT 06042   Korean Northeastern
New England Grace Presbyterian Church – 860-461-1272

Herberich, John C. – b Akron, OH, Mar 6, 48; f Walter William; m Mildred Housel; w Eva Edvinsson, Sweden, Jul 18, 81; chdn Heidi Anna, Emily Maria, Adam William, Jonathan David, David Thomas; UAkr 74, BA; TEDS 85, MDiv; CTS 94, ThM; L 85; O 92, EFC; Recd PCA Nov 29, 94, NoIL Pby; astp Peoples Ch EFC, Pinckney, MI, 84-88; srp Oak Hill EFC, Evansville, IN, 88-93; p Trinity P Ch, Aledo, IL, 95-01; ob Harvest USA Mid-South Region, Chattanooga, TN 01-06; wc; adj CC Quest, 05-10; adj prof BelhU, 10–

8819 Hurricane Ridge, Chattanooga, TN 37421 – 423-894-6013   Tennessee Valley

Herche, Luther Dietrich (Luke) – b Jul 21, 78; w Debra Joy; chdn Thomas Obadiah, Nathaniel John, Andrew Adam, Jeremiah James; UArts, Phil 00, BFA; WTS 07, MDiv; PRTS 17, ThM; O Aug 28, 09, SiouxI Pby; p Faith P Ch, Grand Forks, ND, 09-12; p All Souls P Ch, Champaign, IL, 14–

603 East Colorado Avenue, Urbana, IL 61801 – 701-213-6099   Northern Illinois
E-mail: lukeherche@gmail.com
All Souls Presbyterian Church – allsoulspca@gmail.com

Hermerding, Dennis – b Selma, AL, Jan 4, 66; f Dennis C.; m Elizabeth James King; w Jane Keeton, Memphis, TN, Jun 4, 88; chdn Olivia, Jeshua, Lydia May; UMemp 90, BA; TEDS 98, MA; RTS 01, MDiv; L Jun 00, SW Pby; O Jun 01, SW Pby; campm RUF, UAZ, 01-05; p Desert Springs P Ch, Tucson, AZ, 05-08; astp Spring Cypress P Ch, Spring, TX, 09-15; op Kings Cross Cypress, Cypress, TX, 15–

10519 Desert Springs Circle, Houston, TX 77095 – 832-247-0423   Houston Metro
E-mail: dennis@kingscrosscypress.org
King's Cross Cypress – 832-247-0423

Hernandez, Jacinto – ascp Hisp min, Covenant P Ch, Harrisonburg, VA, 06–

5061 Scholars Road, Mt. Crawford, VA 22841-2209   Blue Ridge
E-mail: jacinto@cov-pres.org
Covenant Presbyterian Church – 540-433-3051

Hernandez, Michael – astp Pinelands P Ch, Cutler Bay, FL, 18–

10739 SW 52 Terrace, Miami, FL 33165   South Florida
E-mail: m.hernandez@pinelandspca.org
Pinelands Presbyterian Church – 305-235-1142

Herr, Jonathon – O May 20, 18, GrLks Pby; astp Knox P Ch, Harrison Township, MI, 18–

39411 Baroque Boulevard, Clinton Township, MI 48038   Great Lakes
E-mail: herrjr@gmail.com
Knox Presbyterian Church – 586-469-8500

Herrera, Timothy – w Judy; chdn Rebekah, Lindsay, Danny, Angie, Andres; UMKC 88, BS; CTS 02, MDiv; O Dec 03, MO Pby; astp New Port P Ch, Washington, MO, 02-03, ascp 04-09; op Redeeming Gr Flwsp, Owensville, MO, 04-09; p 09–

118 Highway T, Rosebud, MO 63091 – 573-764-8890   Missouri
E-mail: tim@redeeminggracepca.org
Redeeming Grace Fellowship – 573-437-4630

Herring, Wayne C. – b Quitman, MS, Jun 13, 46; f Jefferson Clement H; m Nancy Christine Wilder; w Joyce Horton, Clinton, MS, Jun 8, 69 (d), (2) Dena Gibson Culpepper, May 25, 16; chdn Jennifer Kate, Dabney Elizabeth, Amanda Collins, Susannah Joyce, Emily Christine; BelC 64-65; MSU 65-68, BS; RTS 68–

MINISTERIAL DIRECTORY   265

Herring, Wayne C., continued
71, MDiv; O Aug 1, 71, Beth Pby PCUS; ap First Ch, Rock Hill, SC, 71-72; p Forest-Covenant P Ch, Forest, MS, 72-74; p Faith P Ch, Birmingham, AL, 74-78; t RTS, 78-82; p Woodland P Ch, Hattiesburg, MS, 82-85; p Faith P Ch, Brookhaven, MS, 85-88; ascp Independent P Ch, Memphis, TN, 88-98; op St. Andrews P Ch, Cordova, TN, 96-08; astp Covenant P Ch, Nashville, TN, 08-16; ch rel officer, PCAAC, 08-

1695 Moses Road, Raymond, MS 39154 – 615-319-8252   Mississippi Valley
E-mail: wayneand6@gmail.com
PCA Administrative Committee – 678-825-1000

Herrington, John Allen – b New Albany, MS, Sept 23, 47; f John A; m Nannie Little; w Joan May Morris, Columbia, SC, May 31, 71; chdn Joy Ann, Mark Allen, John Andrew; NEMSJC 66-67; CBC 67-71, BBE; BhamES 72; RTS 75, MCE, 77, MDiv; WestTS 86, DMin; AUBS 97, ThD; L Jan 20, 76; O Jun 26, 77, MSVal Pby; p Willowood Ch, Jackson, MS, 76-83; p New Cov P Ch, Raleigh, NC, 83-84; ob ev PEF, 84-95; ydir Calvary P Ch, Raleigh, NC, 88-95; ob exec dir PEF, 95-99; ob ev PEF, Bibles and Bees Min, 99-; p Antioch P Ch, Goldsboro, NC, 01-06; chap PRJC Hosp, 02-

691 Highway 15 North, New Albany, MS 38652 – 662-534-1967   Eastern Carolina
E-mail: Jalherrington@aol.com
Presbyterian Evangelistic Fellowship – 423-573-5308

Herron, Daniel Ferrell – b Harriman, TN, Oct 13, 49; f Fred D.; m Leda Esther Barnett; w Elizabeth (d); (2) Gini, Chattanooga, TN, May 5, 01; chdn Esther Elizabeth, Daniel Musa, Peter Sanders, Luke David, Lydia Grace, Matthew Davis, Johnny Anthony, Timothy Emmanuel; CC 68-72, BA; WTS 72-76, MDiv; TJU 78-80, BS; UT 82-83, MS; O Sept 84, TNVal Pby; mis MTW, 84-04; mis WHM, Ft Portal, Uganda, 84-00; mis WHM, UK, 00-04; mis Serge, Granada, Spain, 05-; Field Director E Africa 89-95; Overseas Director 95-04; Field Dir S. Europe & N. Africa 04-; listed in *Who's Who in American Colleges and Universities*

Calle Tudela, 38, 18007 Granada, ESPANA – +34 673-411-177   Tennessee Valley
E-mail: herrondan@mac.com
Serge
101 West Avenue #305, Jenkintown, PA 19046-2039

Herron, Daniel Todd – b Urbana, IL, May 26, 76; f Ron; m Kathie; w Erica Lynn Dupuis, Champaign, IL, May 20, 00; chdn Alexander, Gabriel, Isabel; ILSU 00, BS; CTS 11, MDiv; O Feb 26, 12, CentInd Pby; ev Hope P Msn, Bloomington, IN, 12-13; op 13-

3690 South Sowder Square, Bloomington, IN 47401 – 812-679-7453   Central Indiana
E-mail: dan@hopebtown.org
Hope Presbyterian Mission

Herron, Rob – astp Redeemer P Ch, Athens, GA, 16-17; ascp 17-

165 Pulaski Street, Athens, GA 30601 – 706-247-3154   Georgia Foothills
E-mail: rherron@redeemerathens.com
Redeemer Presbyterian Church – 706-227-3344

Herron, Scott – O Feb 22, 15, RMtn Pby; astp Trinity Ch PCA, Bozeman, MT, 15-17, ascp 17-

99 East Hyalite Peak Drive, Bozeman, MT 59718 – 479-372-1718   Rocky Mountain
E-mail: scott@trinitybozeman.org
Trinity Church PCA – 406-585-2223

Hershberger, Mike – w Susan; chdn Cameron, Zachary, Ellen, Mary; RTS; O Jun 13, 04, Hrtl Pby; mis MTW, Sofia, Bulgaria, 05-11

E-mail: hersheybar6@aol.com   Heartland

Hershberger, Monty Hans – b Sarasota, FL, Sept 25, 73; m Mary Lou; w Karyn; chdn Tessa; RTS 16, MDiv; O Apr 15, 18, Nash Pby; astp Trinity P Ch, Murfreesboro, TN, 18-

1506 North Highland Avenue, Murfreesboro, TN 37130   Nashville
E-mail: monty@trinitymboro.com
Trinity Presbyterian Church – 615-895-2018

Hertenstein, Mark – astp New City Flwsp, Fredericksburg, VA, 17-

4706 Retreat Lane Apt 285, Fredericksburg, VA 22408 – 334-782-3452   James River
E-mail: mhertenstein@newcityfellowship.org
New City Fellowship – 540-899-5349

Herzer, Mark A. – b Seoul, Kor, May 7, 63; w Martha Louise Huckins, Richmond, IN, Nov 21, 87; chdn Grace Elisabeth, Karis Faith, Calvin Augustine; EC 86, BA; WTS 93, MAR, 03, PhD; O Nov 27, 94, Phil Pby; astp Korean United Ch of Phil, Philadelphia, PA, 94-96, wc 96-98; op Christ Cov P Ch, Hatboro, PA, 99-00, p 00-; "Arminianism Exposed" in *Christian Research Network*

320 Ridge Road, Telford, PA 18969 – 267-450-5902   Eastern Pennsylvania
E-mail: markherzer@comcast.net
Christ Covenant Presbyterian Church – 215-481-9561

Hess, Douglas O. – w Amber; chdn Eliza Rose, Jude Douglas, Hope Elizabeth; op Grace Ref Ch, Elizabethtown, KY, 06-07; Chap USAF, Davis-Monthan AFB, Tucson AZ, 07-11; chap USAF, McGuire-Dix-Lakehurst, NJ, 11-15

627 Kilcullen Drive, Niceville, FL 32578 – 609-694-7922   Ohio Valley
E-mail: douglas.hess.2@us.af.mil
United States Air Force

Hesterberg, L. William – b Red Bud, IL, Feb 7, 51; f William Charles; m Frieda Rose Fauss; w Lorinda Ruth Purcell, Columbia, IL, Aug 13, 77; chdn Anna Abigail, William Barton Andreas; SIU 72, BA; CTS 76, MDiv, 96, ThM; WKU, pgs; L 76; O 76, Ill Pby (RPCES); ap Evangelical P Ch, Carbondale, IL, 76-78; op Christ P Ch, Owensboro, KY, 79-82, p 82-93, wc 93; p Concord P Ch, Waterloo, IL, 94-07; srp 07-13; hr, 13; vis lect/prof Eastern Ukranian Theo Sem; Ref Theo Inst, Romania; vis prof at Maranatha Bible College, Romania; CEP Com, 10-; vis lect/prof Reformed Bible Institute, Churachandpur, Manipur, India; DirDev, International Theological Education Ministries; *Let Grace Begin*

5536 Wildwood Drive, Covered Bridge Estates, Waterloo, IL 62298-3159 – 618-939-5069   Illiana
E-mail: lwhesterberg@gmail.com
HR
International Theological Education Ministries

Hettinger, Samuel William – astp Good Hope P Ch, Fulton, MD, 10-

8483 Kings Meade Way, Columbia, MD 21046   Potomac
E-mail: samhettinger7@yahoo.com
Good Hope Presbyterian Church – 301-317-1398

Heuss, Anton – b Des Moines, IA, Sept 24, 77; f Carl; m Susan Barnes; w Leah T. Schiebout, Pella, IA, May 26, 07; UTXD 01, BA; WSCAL 05, MDiv; L Aug 25, 07, NoTX Pby; astp Bethel Ch PCA, Dallas, TX, 07-10; ascp 10-16, srp 16-

3100 Bonniebrook Drive, Plano, TX 75075   North Texas
E-mail: bethelch.aheuss@sbcglobal.net
Bethel Church PCA – 972-248-4401

Hiatt, Giorgio W.K. – b Frankfort, Germany, Oct 7, 72; f Ralph Joseph W.K.; m Maria Morandini; w Amanda Beth Carver, Columbus, GA, Aug 10, 96; DavC 91-95, BA; CTS 97-00, MDiv; L Oct 28, 00, CentCar Pby; O Jan 14, 01, CentCar Pby; astp, modis Uptown Christ Cov Ch, Charlotte, NC, 00-08; ascp Christ Central Ch, Charlotte, NC, 03-12; p Redeemer P Ch, Winston-Salem, NC, 12-

570 Westover Avenue, Winston Salem, NC 27104 – 704-609-5492   Central Carolina
E-mail: ghiatt@redeemerws.org
Redeemer Presbyterian Church – 336-724-2217

Hickey, Charles – astp Church of the Cov, Cincinnati, OH, 06-08; op Trinity P Ch of N. KY, Burlington, KY, 07-08; p 08-

9419 Daly Road, Cincinnati, OH 45231   Ohio Valley
E-mail: chuckhickey@trinitynky.org
Trinity Presbyterian Church of Northern Kentucky – 859-486-3923

Hickman, Pat – w Stephanie; chdn Hogan, Patton, Libby; FurU; CTS; L Mar 5, 06, MNY Pby; campm RUF, St. Johns, 06-08; astp Denver P Ch, Denver, CO, 08-12; astp Redeemer P Ch, Indianapolis, IN, 13-

1330 Fletcher Avenue, Indianapolis, IN 46203 – 303-408-9720   Central Indiana
E-mail: pat.hickman@gmail.com
Redeemer Presbyterian Church – 317-238-5487

Higginbottom, Robert – O Jan 15, NoTX Pby; astp Park Cities P Ch, Dallas, TX, 14-

6714 Belford Drive, Dallas, TX 75214   North Texas
E-mail: robby.higginbottom@pcpc.org
Park Cities Presbyterian Church – 214-224-2500

Higgins, Craig Royce – b Demorest, GA, Apr 25, 61; f Royce; m Dorothy; w Ann Owens, Macon, GA, Jul 21, 84; chdn Caroline Noelle, Andrew Craig, Laura Abigail; MerU 79-83, BA; WTS 86-89, MDiv; Trinity Epis Sch/Ministry 05, DMin; L Apr 85; O Aug 6, 89, CentGA Pby; First P Ch, dir student min, Macon, GA, 83-86; ydir Korean United Ch of Phil, Philadelphia, PA, 86-89; campm RUM, GASoU, 89-94; chp Trinity P Ch, Rye, NY, 94-97; srp 97-; sc MNY Pby, 97-99; mod MNY pby, 01-03; "Christian: An Evangelical and Catholic Definition," *Reformation and Revival Journal* 14/2 (05); "Spiritual Formation and the Lord's Supper," *Journal of Biblical Counseling* 24/3 (06); "Word and Deed in Missional Worship and Ministry," in *Reformed Means Missional* (ebook), 13

1 Wards Park West, Rye, NY 10580 – 914-967-0884   Metropolitan New York
E-mail: craighiggins@trinitychurch.cc
Trinity Presbyterian Church – 914-967-6247

Higgins, J. Michael – b St. Louis, MO, Jul 25, 56; f John Benjamin; m Yvonne Kennedy; w Renee Brownlee, St. Louis, MO, Aug 10, 79; chdn Mary Yvonne, Michelle Joanna; UMOSL 82, BA; CTS 96, MDiv; O Jun 3, 85, COGIC; Recd PCA Apr 19, 97, TNVal Pby; cop Ft. Riley, KS; chp Germany; srp St. Louis, MO; ascp New City Flwsp, Chattanooga, TN, 97-01; ip Redemption Flwsp P Ch, Fayetteville, GA, 00-01, srp 01-11; Chap USAR; DnStu CTS, 11-; p South City Ch, St. Louis, MO, 12-

2109 South Spring Avenue, St. Louis, MO 63110 – 314-802-8241   Missouri
E-mail: armychapmike@gmail.com
Covenant Theological Seminary – 314-434-4044
South City Church – 314-276-5816

Hightower, Daniel – b Montgomery, AL, Jul 18, 87; f William Hightower; m Judi Hightower; w Courtney Mixon Hightower, Dothan, AL, Aug 15, 09; chdn Naomi Grace, Rebekah Jane, Cole Mixon; TrSU

Hightower, Daniel, continued
09 BA; BDS 14 MDiv; O Dec 13, 15, Providence Pby; astp, yp Grace P Ch, Fort Payne, AL, 14-17; Recd May 15, 17, Evan Pby; campm RUF, JAXSU 17 -

707 12th Avenue NE, Jacksonville, AL 36265   Providence
E-mail: dnlhightower@gmail.com
PCA Reformed University Fellowship

Hightower, Russell – b Greenville, SC, May 9, 75; f Harry; m Cynthia Diane Durham; w Amanda, Nov 23, 02; WFU 93-97, BA; PTS 97-00, MDiv; L May 01, MNY Pby; O Dec 01, MNY Pby; ydir Princeton P Ch, Princeton, NJ, 00-01, astp 01-03; astp First P Ch, Chattanooga, TN, 03-10; p Faith P Ch, Brookhaven, MS, 10-18; astp Pacific Crossroads Ch, Santa Monica, CA, 18-

20538 Vaccaro Avenue, Torrance, CA 90503   Pacific
E-mail: russchightower@gmail.com
Pacific Crossroads Church – 310-551-0081

Hill, Charles E. – b Syracuse, NE, May 15, 56; f Raymond Merlin; m Iris Elaine Todd; w Marcy Ann McPheeters, Gothenburg, NE, May 26, 84; chdn Sean Christopher, Charity Rose, James Lloyd Burton; UNE 74-78, BFA; WSCAL 82-85, MAR, 82-85, MDiv; UCam 85-88, PhD; L, RCUS, Eureka Classis; O Oct 3, 92, RCA, East Sioux classis; Recd PCA Oct 17, 98, CentFL Pby; asst prof NWC, 89-94; assoc prof RTSFL, 94-03, prof 03-

963 Stonewood Lane, Maitland, FL 32751 – 407-339-9147   Central Florida
E-mail: chill@rts.edu
Reformed Theological Seminary, FL – 407-366-9493
1231 Reformation Drive, Oviedo, FL 32765

Hill, Jason Eric – b Nov 25, 73; w Christy, Nov 19, 00; chdn Carleigh, Matthew; PhilBibU 06, BS; LBTS 09, MDiv; WTS, doct stu; chp Galloway, NJ, 02-04; ascp Medford, NJ, 04-06; Chap USArmy, Ft. Riley, KS, 09-11; Chap USArmy, Operation Iraqi Freedom, 09-10; Chap USArmy, Langley/Eustis, VA, 11-14; Chap USArmy, Europe, 14-

CMR 415 Box 3506, APO, AE 09114 – 972-333-4291   James River
E-mail: Jason.hill@hotmail.com
United States Army

Hill, Louis Alphonso – b Columbus, GA, Dec 18, 39; f Louis A. Jr.; m Helen Pate; w Barbara Kay Culpepper, Columbus, GA, Jun 11, 61; chdn Michael Del, Kimberly Lynn (DeGraaf); SamU 63, BS; AU 68, MEd; RTSFL 93, MATS, 95, DMin; O Sept 12, 97, RMtn Pby; staff Navs; ob fndr, pres Ref Discipleship Ministries, Colorado Springs, CO, 95-

2627 Flintridge Drive, Colorado Springs, CO 80918 – 719-598-8026   Rocky Mountain
E-mail: louishill@rdm.org
Reformed Discipleship Ministries – 719-473-5102
PO Box 7168, Colorado Springs, CO 80933-7168

Hill, Michael – p Covenant Ch, Millers Falls, MA, 18-

53 Pleasant Street, Unit 1B, Greenfield, MA 01301   Southern New England
E-mail: mshill9917@gmail.com
Covenant Church – 413-659-3430

Hill, Omari – campm RUF, UNCChar, 09-12; astp Redeemer P Ch of New York, New York, NY, 12-15; astp Christ Central Ch, Charlotte, NC, 17-

3646 Central Avenue, Charlotte, NC 28205 – 704-756-4781   Central Carolina
E-mail: ohill@christcentralchurch.com
Christ Central Church – 704-608-9146

Hill, Quinn – b Sept 3, 77; f Richard; m Linda; w Kimberly Hill; chdn Corin, Silas, Felix, Lida; RTS 12, MDiv; O May 12, Evan Pby; astp Comm P Ch, Moody, AL, 11-16; p Grace P Ch, Shreveport, LA, 17-

821 Wilkinson Street, Shreveport, LA 71104 – 205-790-5896   North Texas
E-mail: quinnhill@gmail.com
Grace Presbyterian Church – 318-219-5556

Hill, Robert Steven – b Webster, TX, Dec 10, 78; f Peter Campbell; m Carol Ann McGarvey; w Megan Evans; chdn Brad McGarvey, Caleb Campbell, Nathan Amanue, Evelyn Wheatley; GroCC 01, BA; RTS 04, MDiv; L Dec 00, Asc Pby; O Aug 29, 04, MSVal Pby; p Pinehaven P Ch (form St. Paul P Ch), Jackson, MS, 04-15; p West Springfield Cov Comm Ch, West Springfield, MA, 15-;"Walter Lowrie (1784-1868): Champion of Presbyterian Missions," *Puritan Reformed Journal,* January 14

32 Ely Avenue, West Springfield, MA 01089 – 413-310-5808   Southern New England
E-mail: robhill1978@gmail.com
West Springfield Covenant Community Church – 413-733-2828

Hill, Scott Eugene – b Muncy, PA, Aug 12, 62; f William R. Sr; m Carolyn Ann Klinefelter; w Ruth Juanita Gaskey, Surfside Bch, SC, Dec 17, 88; chdn Bethany Ann, Scott Eugene Jr., Johnathan William, Katie Lynn; USC 80-85, BS; CBS 89-92, MDiv; L Jan 25, 92; O Aug 9, 92, Cal Pby; p Salem P Ch,Gaffney, SC, 92-02; p Smyrna P Ch, Newberry, SC, 02-13; MTW mis 13-

PO Box 2375, Cherokee, NC 28719 – 828-508-7836   Western Carolina
E-mail: revscotthill@yahoo.com
PCA Mission to the World

Hill, Steven Clark – b Ripley, MS, Feb 10, 57; f Jimmy L.; m Elizabeth Clark; w L. Dianne Bruce, Oct 2, 93; NEMSJC; MSU, BS; RTS 88, MDiv; L Jun 6, 88, Wcar Pby; O Jul 22, 90, MSVal Pby; int, ydir Dillingham P Ch, Barnardsville, NC, 88-89; astp, ydir Brandon P Ch, Brandon, MS, 90-94; p Thomson Mem P Ch, Centreville, MS, 94-99; astp Sandhills P Ch, Southern Pines, NC, 99-04; astp Lawndale P Ch, Tupelo, MS, 04-06; ss ARP Ch, Cotton Plant, MS, 06-10

14610 Highway 15 North, Ripley, MS 38553-8055   Covenant
E-mail: stevdianhill@utinet.net

Hill, William F. – b Mar. 3, 66; f William F Hill, Sr; m Sandra Campman Hill; w Gwendolyn L. Hill, GPTS 88, BDiv; O May 28, 16, WCar pby; p Landis P Ch, Marion, TN, 16-17; p Fellowship P Ch, Newport, TN, 17-

2747 Cosby Highway, Cosby TN, 37722 – 864-363-9055   Western Carolina
E-mail: wfhill@fellowship-pca.org
Fellowship Presbyterian Church – 423-623-8652

Hilliard, Justin – b Sulphur, OK, Jun 12, 79; f Fred; m Rita; w Valerie, May 31, 03; chdn Zayne Thomas, Abrielle Josephine, Titus Gregory; UOK 01, BA; RTSNC 12, MATS; O Nov 26, 13, NoTX Pby; p Faith P Ch, Paris, TX, 13-

935 Brandyn Place, Paris, TX 75462 – 903-517-6315   North Texas
E-mail: justinjhilliard@gmail.com
Faith Presbyterian Church – 903-784-4806

Hills, Greg – b New York, Aug 14, 63; f Richard; m Rose Miner; w Gretchen (d); (2) Heather Schappert, MD, Sept 16, 05; chdn Andrew, Collin, Jonathan, Benjamin, Mackenzie, Paige; NCStU 86, BSIE; GCTS 93, MATS; O Apr 95, OPC; Recd PCA Jan 21, 17, SNE Pby; ev Istanbul, Turkey, 96-00; srp First P Ch North Shore, Ipswich, MA, 02-

475 Newburyport Turnpike, Rowley, MA 01969   Southern New England
First Presbyterian Church North Shore – 978-356-7690

Hina, David – b Brevard, NC, Apr 7, 65; f Edward B.; m Peggy L. Jones; w Amy E. Logan, Columbus OH, Feb 18, 67; chdn Kalista Jean, Jocelyn Fu Mei, Caleb Min Wong; DePU 83-87, BA; USNPGS, MS; DTS 09-14, ThM; L Nov 8, 14, NoTX Pby; O Nov 4, 15, Wcar Pby; p Providence P Ch, Murphy, NC, 15-

10 Bunker Place, Murphy, NC 28906 — 858-395-3051   Western Carolina
E-mail: dhina@mac.com
Providence Presbyterian Church – 828-837-9412

Hinchliff, Anthony S. – b England, Oct 3, 61; f Peter Micheal; m Jean Crockett; Sussex U 89-93, BA; PTS 93-97, MDiv; L Sept 12, 98, MNY Pby; O Sept 12, 98, MNY Pby; astp Redeemer P Ch of New York, New York, NY, 97-03; op Redeemer Hoboken, Hoboken, NJ, 03-05; p 05-

1035 Bloomfield Street, Basement Apt   Metropolitan New York
Hoboken, NJ 07030 – 917-554-7181
E-mail: hinchliff@gmail.com
Redeemer Hoboken – 201-939-2577

Hines, Patrick – b Cincinnati, OH, Mar 4, 75; f Howard; m Peggy; w Amy, Cincinnati, OH, Mar 22, 97; chdn Abigail, Seth, Paul, Maria, Lily, Hannah, Malachi; OU, BBA; RTS, MDiv; O Apr 09; astp Grace Bible P Ch, Sharonville, OH; p Bridwell Heights P Ch, Kingsport, TN, 12-

432 Dunwoody Court, Blountville, TN 37617   Westminster
E-mail: pwhines@gmail.com
Bridwell Heights Presbyterian Church – 423-288-3664

Hinson, Joshua – O May 28, 17, NFL Pby, p Ortega P Ch, Jacksonville, FL, 17-

2734 Algonquin Avenue, Jacksonville, FL 32210 – 912-242-7893   North Florida
Ortega Presbyterian Church – 904-389-4043

Hinton, N. Robbie – b Baton Rouge, LA, Jul 25, 71; f Travis; m Deborah Collins; w Ann-Maura Conley, Madisonville, TN, Aug 20, 94; UT, BS; RTS, MDiv; L Oct 97; O Jan 18, 98, Cov Pby; campm RUM, UTMartin, 97-00; op Covenant P Ch, Jackson, TN, 00-01, p 01-05; ob headm Regents School of Oxford, MS, 05-; ss First P Ch at Water Valley, Water Valley, MS, 07-09; headm Westminster School (formerly Oak Mtn Psby S), 10- 17; ob Fixed Point Foundation, 17-

3152 Sunny Meadows Lane, Birmingham, AL 35242   Evangel
Fixed Point Foundation

Hirko, Andrew Michael – b Nashua, NH, Jan 10, 80; f Michael; m Patricia Russell; w Kristina, St. Augustine, FL, Jun 14, 02; chdn Lilyann Grace; Flagler, BA; LAMP TheoS, MDiv; O May 15, 11, NFL Pby; chp, op Good News World Golf Village Msn, St. Augustine, FL, 11-

907 Alicanete Road, St. Augustine, FL 32086 – 904-819-0064   North Florida
Good News World Golf Village Mission – 904-819-0064

Hitchcock, Albert Clement – b Enid, OK, Apr 29, 44; f Howard Addison; m Mildred Annette Mansfield; w Jane Louise Sutton, Birmingham, AL, Jul 30, 65; chdn Tricia Pique, Nathan Andrew; SEBC 62-66, BA; WTS 74-78, MDiv; L Jan 20, 79; O Apr 17, 79, Evan Pby; p Village P Ch, Mount Laurel, NJ, 79-92; ob p Wiser Lake Chapel (Ind), Lynden, WA, 92-

549 H Street Road, Lynden, WA 98374 – 360-354-7957   Pacific Northwest
E-mail: bert@pogozone.net
Wiser Lake Chapel (Independent) – 360-354-2378
PO Box 591, 7121 Guide Meridian, Lynden, WA 98264

MINISTERIAL DIRECTORY

Hitchcock, Nathan – b Tacoma, WA, May 15, 74; f Albert; m Jane Sutton; w Anna Kate Hatcher, Augusta, GA, Aug 5, 95; chdn Elisabeth, Andrew, Abigail, Tobias, Whitney; CC 96, BA; WSCAL 03, MDiv; O Oct 5, 03, SoCst Pby; ascp North City P Ch, Poway, CA, 03-10; astp Green Lake P Ch, Seattle, WA, 10-14; op Ascension P Ch, Edmonds, WA, 10-14, p 14-

5110 159th Place SW, Edmonds, WA 98026 – 425-420-5249   Pacific Northwest
E-mail: nate@ascension-pca.org
Ascension Presbyterian Church

Hitchings, Frank Albert III – b Memphis, TN, Jul 26, 60; f Frank A Jr.; m Mary Catherine Lynn; w Mary Vassar Ballard, Tupelo, MS, Nov 18, 89; chdn Hannah Catherine, Mary Manning, Frank Albert IV; UT 82, BA; MempSU 84, MBA; RTS 91, MDiv; O Mar 8, 92, TNVal Pby; astp Lookout Mountain P Ch, Lookout Mountain, TN, 92-96, ascp 96-02; sr ascp 02-

316 Marvin Lane, Lookout Mountain, GA 30750 – 706-820-9288   Tennessee Valley
E-mail: frank@lmpc.org
Lookout Mountain Presbyterian Church – 423-821-4528

Hivner, Richard Leroy Jr. – b Harrisburg, PA, Apr 20, 55; f Richard L.; m Esther Marie Engle; w Clare Elizabeth Shelley, Epsom, England, Aug 4, 84; chdn Sarah Elizabeth, Matthew Paul; GroCC 73-76; RegC; SUNY, BA; USAf 04, MA; USAf 11, DLitt et Phil; L Feb 83, Phil Pby; O May 20, 90, SusqV Pby; MTW, OM, India, 83-01; US Center for World Mission, 01-

1605 East Elizabeth Street, Pasadena, CA 91104 – 626-296-6689   Pacific
E-mail: rick@uscihs.com
US Center for World Mission

Ho, Wei – O Jun 4, 17, MetAtl Pby; astp Westminster P Ch, Atlanta, GA, 17-

1244 Club Walk Drive, Atlanta, GA 30319   Metro Atlanta
E-mail: weifho913@gmail.com
Westminster Presbyterian Church – 404-636-1496

Hoadley, Phil – op Mision Vida Nueva, Escondido, CA, 11-17; hr 17

E-mail: pmhjr@msn.com   South Coast
HR

Hobaugh, Greg – b Harrisburg, PA, Sept 24, 68; f Maurice; m Irene; w Kathy Granberg, Elverson, PA, Aug 23, 97; chdn Jacob Gregory, Zane Zacharias, Trinity Jewel Ardis; CedC 90, BA; WTS 99, MDiv, 00, ThM; O Sept 28, 03, Phil Pby; ob ascp Chinese Christian Ch and Center, Philadelphia, PA, 98-08; ob DnStu WTS, 08-12; ob 12-

4846 Pulaski Avenue, Philadelphia, PA 19144 – 215-438-2305   Philadelphia
E-mail: statedclerk@phillypca.com

Hobson, Robert Eugene Jr. – b Washington, DC, Dec 22, 47; f Robert E.; m Virginia Branan; w Pamela Anne Revolinsky, Virginia Beach, VA, Jun 12, 71; chdn James Edward, Thomas James, Adam Matthew; CWM 71, BA, 75, MA; RTS 82, MDiv; O Nov 14, 82, MSVal Pby; p Rolling Fork P Ch, Rolling Fork, MS, 82-89; ob Chap EStHosp, Williamsburg, VA, 89-91; ob Chap St. Elizabeths Hosp, Wash, DC, 91-92; ob Chap Union Mission Min, Norfolk, VA , 93-95; p Eastminster P Ch, Virginia Beach, VA, 94-05; wc 05-15; hr 15

9500 South Ocean Drive, Apt. 1201, Jensen Beach, FL 34957-2331 – 757-466-7053   Tidewater
E-mail: bob-pam1971@cox.net
HR

Hoburg, Glenn Jeffrey – b Pittsburgh, PA, Jul 19, 65; f Clair J.; m Patricia Ann Bannister; w Margaret Henry, Nashville, TN, Oct 19, 91; chdn Madeline Taylor, Isabelle Katherine; BerkleeCoMus 84-88, BMusEd; CTS 93-97, MDiv; L Sept 20, 97, NoE Pby; O Aug 9, 98, NoE Pby; astp Christ the King P Ch, Cambridge, MA, 98-03; campm RUF, HarU, 98-03; astp McLean P Ch, McLean, VA, 03-05; op Grace P Ch of Wash, D.C., Washington, DC, 03-05, srp 05-

208 10th Street NE, Washington, DC 20002 – 202-547-1935　　　　　　　　　　　Potomac
E-mail: pastor@gracedc.net
Grace Presbyterian Church of Washington, D.C. – 202-577-3191

Hock, Evan Conrad – b Cedar Falls, IA, Nov 26, 56; f Leland Thane; m Olga L Lacina; w Janet C. Hoglund, Greeley, CO, Dec 27, 80; chdn Elizabeth Katherine, Hannah Christine; UNCO 75-80, BME; DenTS 80-83; AberU 83-86, MDiv; TEDS 90-91, ThM, 91-99, PhD; L Jun 86; O Jun 25, 89, SW Pby; int Mannofield Parish CoS, 86-87; int Village Seven P Ch, Colorado Springs, CO, 88, ap 89-90; wc; adj prof TEDS, 95-00; p Covenant P Ch, Wheat Ridge, CO, 00-08; wc 08-; book revws *Trinity Journal*, *Reformation and Revival Journal*, *Modern Reformation*; "Theology and Ethics," *Reformation and Revival Journal*; "Covenantal Ethics: A Study in Contrast," diss

555 Dudley Street, Lakewood, CO 80226 – 303-205-8591　　　　　　　　　　　Rocky Mountain

Hodge, Darren Christopher – b Nashville, TN, Jul 19, 67; f Jack; m Janice Moss; w Karen Adams, Charleston, SC, Jun 30, 90; chdn Anna Grace, Haddon Martin; CCSC 90, BA; RTS 90-91; BDS 92, MDiv; L Jan 28, 95; O May 21, 95, CentCar Pby; int Briarwood P Ch, Birmingham, AL, 91-92; astp Christ Cov P Ch, Matthews, NC, 93-96; op Treasure Coast P Ch, Stuart, FL, 96-00, p 00-06; srp Naperville P Ch, Naperville, IL, 06-

943 Sanctuary Lane, Naperville, IL 60540　　　　　　　　　　　Chicago Metro
E-mail: chris@npchurch.org
Naperville Presbyterian Church – 630-961-0579

Hodge, Marty – O May 1, 11, Palm Pby; astp New Cov P Ch, Manning, SC, 11-12; p Union P Ch, Salters, SC, 12-

216 Glad Street, Salters, SC 29590 – 803-387-6967　　　　　　　　　　　Pee Dee
E-mail: martydhodge@gmail.com
Union Presbyterian Church – 843-387-5355

Hodges, Dudley R. – w Christine; FAU, BA; RTS, MDiv; O Aug 27, 95, SFL Pby; op Boynton Beach Comm Ch, Lake Worth, FL, 95-99, p 99-

228 Gregory Road, West Palm Beach, FL 33405 – 561-302-9627　　　　　　　　　　　Gulfstream
E-mail: bbcc@bbcconline.com
Boynton Beach Community Church – 561-733-9400

Hodges, Louis Igou – b Dayton, TN, Dec 24, 46; f Louis Igou; m Gladys Louise Walker; w Linda S. Leinenweber, Dec 14, 85; chdn Daniel Fleming, Jonathan Lee, Elizabeth Jane; CBC 64-67, BA; TEDS 67-70, MDiv; PTS 70-71, ThM; UEdin 71-75, PhD; O Sept 6, 81, Cal Pby; prof TFBC, 75-78; ob prof CBS, 78-; ss New Cov P Ch, Aiken, SC, 87; ss Church Creek Ref P Ch, Charleston, SC, 87-88; ss Union Mem P Ch, Winnsboro, SC, 89-91; ss Calvary P Ch, Columbia, SC, 91-93; ss Union Mem P Ch, Winnsboro, SC, 95-96; ss St. Matthews P Ch, St. Matthews, SC, 98; ss Union Mem P Ch, Winnsboro, SC, 18-; contr *The Dictionary of Scottish Church History and Theology*, *Reformed Theology Today*, 95, *New Dimensions in Evangelical Theology*, 98

1114 Blakely Court, West Columbia, SC 29170-3511 – 803-739-0051　　　　　　　　　　　Palmetto
E-mail: igouhodges@earthlink.net
Columbia Biblical Seminary
Union Memorial Presbyterian Church – 803-712-2220

MINISTERIAL DIRECTORY

Hodges, Richard Byron – b Miami, FL, Feb 22, 50; f Charles G. Jr.; m Nell Jones; w Judy Lee Fain, Miami, FL, Aug 11, 72; chdn Mary Lee, Charles David, John Daniel, Joseph Samuel; Citadel 72, BA; CBS 84, MDiv; L Jan 26, 84; O Nov 18, 84, Palm Pby; p Salem P Ch, Blair, SC, 84-; adj prof CBS, 94-; USAF 70-10; Ret, USAFR, 10

276 State Highway 215 North, Blair, SC 29015-9470 – 803-635-6097; 803-718-2807   Palmetto
E-mail: rhodges50@gmail.com
Salem Presbyterian Church – 803-635-6097
Columbia Biblical Seminary

Hodges, Ross – O Nov 16, 14, Palm Pby; astp Christ Ch P, Mount Pleasant, SC, 14-

1990 Armory Drive, Mt. Pleasant, SC 29466   Lowcountry
E-mail: ross@christchurchcharleston.org
Christ Church Presbyterian – 843-606-0572

Hoff, Jack J. – b New Orleans, LA, Oct 16, 30; f James T. Sr.; m Ethel T. Luce; LeTC 55; TFBC 56-59, BA; FTS 60-62, MDiv; O Sept 5, 62, BPC; p BPC, Grand Junct, CO, 64-67; p BPC, Minerva, OH, 67-71; p Trinity P Ch, Dothan, AL, 86-89; p Clayton P Ch, Clayton, AL, 89-94; p Pleasant View P Ch, Clayton, AL, 89-94; ss Bethel P Ch, Union Springs, AL, 94-95; hr 95

PO Box 165, Andalusia, AL 36420-0165 – 334-343-0267   Southeast Alabama
HR

Hoffman, Greg – b Indianapolis, IN, Jul 31, 63; f David Henry; m Sandra Lee Elliott; w Karin Lynne Beton, Coral Springs, FL, Dec 17, 84; chdn Josiah David; RTS 95; TIU 96; L Oct 95, SFL Pby; O Feb 16, 97, Cov Pby; int First P Ch of Coral Springs, Margate, FL, 95-96; p First P Ch, Clarendon, AR, 97-98, wc 98-14; astp Spanish River P Ch, Boca Raton, FL, 14-; *The Forest From the Trees*

4770 NE 22nd Avenue, Lighthouse Point, FL 33064 – 954-757-7847   Gulfstream
E-mail: gregandkarin@gmail.com
Spanish River Presbyterian Church – 561-994-5000

Hofius, Aaron David – b St. Louis, MO, Jan 22, 77; f David Stephen; m Margaret Ruth; w Andrea Marie Arnold, St. Louis, MO, May 6, 00; chdn Aurora Eve, Amaris Noel, Aria Bella; MOBC 03, BA; CTS 07, MDiv; O Jul 27, 08, BlRdg Pby; ascp Christ the King P Ch, Roanoke, VA, 08-10; p Cornerstone P Ch, St. Louis, MO, 10-17

5174 Olde Silver Place, St Louis, MO 63128 – 314-849-0363   Missouri

Hogan, Sam – O 16, Hrtg Pby; astp Crossroads P Ch, Middletown, DE, 16-18; astp Carriage Lane P Ch, Peachtree City, GA, 18-

Carriage Lane Presbyterian Church – 770-631-4618   Metro Atlanta

Hogan, William LeGrange – b Little Rock, AR, Mar 31, 34; f M L; m Elizabeth; w Jane Kee, Memphis, TN, Jun 13, 59; chdn Marion Elizabeth (Larson), Amy Barton (Hartman) (d); RU 55, BA; DTS 59, ThM; ColTS 61, ThM; WTS 81, DMin; ECol 84, DD; L 59; O 60, EAL Pby (PCUS); ap Trinity P Ch, Montgomery, AL, 59-61; ap Tenth P Ch, Philadelphia, PA, 61-64; CCC, 64-71; p Church of the Saviour, Wayne, PA, 72-88; Dir Proclamation, Wayne, PA; ev Proclamation P Ch, Bryn Mawr, PA, 89-90; ob assoc prof RTS, 90-93, ob prof 93-99; hr 99; adj prof Bethel Sem, St. Paul, MN, 99-; ascp Calvary CRC, Edina, MN, 99-05; ip Independent P Ch, Memphis, TN, 06; ss First P Ch, Schenectady, NY, 08-09; astp, ms Independent P Ch, Memphis, TN, 10-14, p em 14-

4738 Walnut Grove Road, Memphis, TN 38117 – 901-685-8206   Covenant
HR

Hohenberger, Steve G. – b Baltimore, MD, Aug 12, 49; f Wallace I.; m Marie W. Auer; w Josephine Ann Knox, Voorhees, NJ, Sept 4, 71; chdn Kathryn, Ann, Amy, Jennifer, Christine; DrexU 67-71, BS; WTS 71-75, MDiv; L Apr 76; O Oct 29, 76, NJ Pby (OPC); Recd PCA Mar 16, 97, Pot Pby; p Stratford OPC, NJ, 76-79; chp, op NJ Pby (OPC), 79-86; p Grace OPC, Vienna, VA, 86-90; McLean P Ch, chdn min, McLean, VA, 90-93; p Heritage P Ch, Warrenton, VA, 97-11; hr 11

107 Pine Court, Gordonsville, VA 22942 – 540-272-2029   Potomac
HR

Hoke, Timothy Keisler – b Houston, TX, Oct 23, 47; f William Keisler; m Vera Birdwell; w Cheri May, Lubbock, TX, Aug 6, 77; chdn Andrea, James; SFAU 71, BBA, 73, MBA; DTS 79, ThM; UMOKC 84-87; WTS 87, DMin cand; O 78, Lubbock Bib Ch; op, p Lawton, OK, 79-81; p Kearney, MO, 81-89; p Faith P Ch, San Antonio, TX, 90-09; ob 10-

PO Box 94510, Lubbock, TX 79493   South Texas
E-mail: timhoke@earthlink.net

Holbert, Rick – b Amarillo, TX, Dec 19, 69; f Bruce; m Janice Hughes; w Jennifer Elaine Scrugham, Jackson, MS, Mar 15, 03; chdn Stephen, Ansley, Sadie, Emma; UTXAu 92, BBA; RTS 03, MDiv; O Nov 16, 03, MSVal Pby; p First P Ch, Philadelphia, MS, 03-05; ss Lebanon P Ch, Learned, MS, 07-08; p 08- 12; ss Magee P Ch, Magee, MS, 12-14; lob CMDA, 15-

5364 Suffolk Drive, Jackson, MS 39211 – 601-382-8871   Mississippi Valley
E-mail: rickwholbert@gmail.com
Christian Medical & Dental Associations – 888-230-2637

Holbrook, Andrew S. – O Aug 29, 10, CentCar Pby; astp Christ Cov Ch, Matthews, NC, 10-15; astp Christ P Ch, New Haven, CT, 15-; op Christ P Msn, Fairfield, CT, 16-

37 Blueberry Lane, Fairfield, CT 06825   Southern New England
E-mail: alholbrook8203@gmail.com
Christ Presbyterian Church – 203-777-6960
Christ Presbyterian Mission

Holdridge, Chris – O May 15, 16, NYS Pby; op New City Flwsp Beechwood, Rochester, NY, 16-

497 Grand Avenue, Rochester, NY 14609 – 585-451-2498   New York State
E-mail: chris@ncfbeechwood.org
New City Fellowship Beechwood – 585-451-2498

Holladay, Steve – O May 20, 09, GrLks Pby; ascp Christ Ch, Grand Rapids, MI, 09-18

2539 Orchard View Drive, Grand Rapids, MI 49506 – 616-581-0970   Great Lakes
E-mail: swholladay@gmail.com

Holland, Joseph Jett Jr. – b Norfolk, VA, Aug 1, 78; f Joseph J.; m Elizabeth Accord Taylor; w Hallie Elizabeth Simms, Lynchburg, VA, Jun 24, 00; chdn Joseph Jett III, William Canaday, David Latane, Charles Edward; UVA, BS; RTSNC, MDiv; O Jul 13, 03, MSVal Pby; astp First P Ch, Jackson, MS, 03-06; astp First P Ch, Kosciusko, MS, 06-08; ascp 08-09; op Christ Cov P Ch, Culpeper, VA, 09-15, p 15-

PO Box 880, Culpeper, VA 22701   Blue Ridge
E-mail: joe@christcov.com
Christ Covenant Presbyterian Church – 540-445-1245

Holland, Peter Clay – b Jackson, MS, Jun 3, 71; f J.D.; m Jane Elizabeth Stallings; w Shannon Elizabeth Silman, Hattiesburg, MS, Jun 21, 97; chdn Jackson David II, Emma Campbell, Andrew Silman; MillsC 89-93, BA; UMS 94-96, MA; CTS 96-00, MDiv; L Jul 29, 00, SoTX Pby; O Nov 19, 00, SoTX Pby; astp Christ the King P Ch, Houston, TX, 00-02, ascp 02-11; srp 11-

1201 Silber Road, Houston, TX 77055 – 713-464-1179　　　　　　　　　　　Houston Metro
E-mail: pcholland@me.com
Christ the King Presbyterian Church – 713-892-5464

Holland, William Wesley – b East Point, GA, Aug 18, 67; f William Wesley Sr.; m Barbara Jane Gordon; w Amanda Marie Young, Savannah, GA, Feb 29, 92; chdn Rachel Marie, Molly Kathryn, Sarah Abigail, William Blair; GASoC 85-87; CC 88-90, BA; KTS 90-91; WTS 92-95, MDiv; L Oct 95, GulCst Pby; O May 12, 96, GulCst Pby; int Covenant P Ch, Panama City, FL, 95-96, astp 96-98; astp New Cov P Ch, Aiken, SC, 98-06; p Westminster P Ch, Brandon, FL, 06-

2205 Colewood Lane, Dover, FL 33527 – 813-383-4724　　　　　　　　　　Southwest Florida
E-mail: wes@wpcbrandon.org
Westminster Presbyterian Church – 813-689-6541

Hollenbach, Michael S. – b Perkasie, PA, Feb 3, 67; f Thomas; m Joan Hendicks; w Judith Ann Jaczun, Perkasie, PA, Jul 30, 94; chdn John, Rachyeed, Kaira, Talia; TempU 90, BA; WTS 98, MDiv; L Mar 00, Phil Pby; O Apr 02, Phil Pby; ascp New Life P Ch, Dresher, PA, 02-10; astp Cornerstone P Ch, Center Valley, PA, 10-11; op Bridge Comm Ch, Easton, PA, 10-

326 North 9th Street, Easton, PA 19050 – 215-264-7532　　　　　　　　　Eastern Pennsylvania
E-mail: mhollenbach.bridge@gmail.com
Bridge Community Church – 215-264-7532

Hollenbeck, Dale – b Baltimore, MD, Jul 29, 71; f Everett; m Joan Marie Grambo; w Kathleen Louise Lemker, Marshalltown, IA, Oct 21, 94; chdn Micah Everett, Benjamin Henry, Zachary Dale; SanJChC 94, BA; RTS 99, MDiv; O Mar 4, 01, MSVal Pby; mis MTW, Uganda, 01-12; wc 12 Chap Friendship Village of West Co, Chesterfield, MO, 15-

15201 Olive Boulevard, Chesterfield, MO 63017　　　　　　　　　　　　　　　Missouri
E-mail: dkhollenbeck@aimint.net
Friendship Village of West County

Holler, Mark William – b Terre Haute, IN, May 16, 53; f William Edward; m Louise Vina Miller; w Virginia Ann Ellis Garner, Chattanooga, TN, Feb 26, 05; chdn Brook Edward, Esther, Kate, Travis Mark, Jacob Lyle, Alec Stephen; CC 80, BA; WTS 83, MDiv, 83, MAR; O May 18, 85, OPC; chp Trinity OPC, Phoenixville, PA, 83-85, p 85-00; p Bethany OPC, Oxford, PA, 04-09; ob Pastor-in-Residence, SE Dir, 13-

1915 Hickory Valley Road, Chattanooga, TN 37421 – 423-991-8801　　　　Susquehanna Valley
E-mail: revmarkholler@gmail.com
Pastor-in-Residence

Holliday, Charles B. III – b Rochester, PA, Dec 3, 50; f Charles B. Jr.; m Katherine Armes; w Debra Barres, Ft. Lauderdale, FL, May 31, 74; chdn Jewell Katherine, Christine Faye, Erica Jean, Charles B. IV; CC 72, BA; CTS 75, MDiv; ColCU 93, MA; L Jul 74; O Jun 75, Pitts Pby (RPCES); p Westminster P Ch, Elgin, IL, 75-94; op River of Life P Ch, Orlando, FL, 94-98, p 98-14

8323 Sand Lake Road, Orlando, FL 32819 – 407-905-9553　　　　　　　　　　Central Florida

Holliday, Thomas G. – b Pittsburgh, PA, Oct 23, 54; f Charles B.; m Katherine Armes; w Sharon Ann Canfield, Wilmington, DE, Jun 5, 76; chdn Thomas Galbreath Jr., Stacey Eileen, Caitlin Grace; CC

Holliday, Thomas G., continued
72-76; CTS 77-81, MDiv; L Mar 30, 80, Pitts Pby (RPCES); O Aug 23, 81, Westm Pby; p Abingdon P Ch, Abingdon, VA, 81-90; p Alexandria P Ch, Alexandria, VA, 90-

2505 Crest Street, Alexandria, VA 22302 – 571-334-3686   Potomac
E-mail: tom.holliday@alexandriapres.org
Alexandria Presbyterian Church – 703-683-3348

Hollis, James – O May 15, 16, Prov Pby; astp Valley P Ch, Madison, AL, 16-

719 Hughes Road, Madison, AL 35758   Providence
E-mail: jhollis@valleymadison.com
Valley Presbyterian Church – 256-508-9020

Holm, Joel D. – b Hammond, IN; f Lynn Holm; m Marcie Andersen; MBI 83, dipl; NWC 85, BA; WTS 95-99, MDiv; L Sept 13, 97, Phil Pby; O Sept 19, 99, Phil Pby; stus Church of the Redeemer, Philadelphia, PA, 98-99, srp 99-04; ob

4346 Jersey Avenue North, Crystal, MN 55428 – 218-845-0008   Philadelphia
E-mail: jdholm@juno.com

Holmes, Wesley Ernest – astp Church of the Resurrection, Flagstaff, AZ, 17; astp Rocky Mountain Comm Ch, Billings, MT, 17-

2901 Custer Avenue, Billings, MT 59102 – 760-715-3896   Rocky Mountain
E-mail: wesley@rmccmontana.org
Rocky Mountain Community Church – 406-259-7811

Holowell, Joshua – op City Hope Fellowship, Muncie, IN, 18-

219 North Pershing Drive, Muncie, IN 47305   Central Indiana
E-mail: josh@hopeformuncie.org
City Hope Fellowship

Holroyd, Kristofer – ob mis, p Internat'l Theo Ed Ministries, 06-07; astp Westminster P Ch, Muncie, IN, 07-09; ascp 09-15, srp 15-

3401 West Godman Avenue, Muncie, IN 47304-4427 – 765-716-0295   Central Indiana
E-mail: kdholroyd@gmail.com
Westminster Presbyterian Church – 765-288-3455

Holst, Matt – b St. Charles, MO, Nov 7, 71; f Frank; m Mary Beth McCain; w Shaunna Osborne, Blythe, CA, Aug 10, 95; chdn Nathan, Samuel, Zachariah, Emily; WBC 95, BS; WSC 00; NGTS 10, MDiv; O 13, RMtn Pby; t Evangelical Christian Acad, 00-; astp High Plains Flwsp, Falcon, CO, 13-

2880 Warrenton Way, Colorado Springs, CO 80922 – 719-661-7310   Rocky Mountain
E-mail: holstworld@yahoo.com
Evangelical Christian Academy
High Plains Fellowship – 719-683-8746

Holt, Robby – astp North Shore Flwsp, Chattanooga, TN, 06-10; ascp 10-14; srp 14-

1603 Mitchell Avenue, Chattanooga, TN 37408 – 423-504-6973   Tennessee Valley
E-mail: robby@nsfellowship.org
North Shore Fellowship – 423-266-3757

MINISTERIAL DIRECTORY

Holt, Toby B. – op Harvest Ref P Ch, Gillette, WY, 12-15; p Christ P Ch, Marietta, GA, 15-

2627 Hampton Park Drive, Marietta, GA 30062 – 470-214-4810   Northwest Georgia
E-mail: tbholt@christpca.org
Christ Presbyterian Church – 770-956-7572

Honeycutt, Michael W. – b Raleigh, NC, Feb 16, 67; f Charlie; m Gail; w Judy; chdn Wade, Wesley, Mary Katherine; ClemU 79, BS, 81, MS; CTS 93, MDiv; UEdin 02, PhD; O Aug 16, 98, TNVal Pby; astp Cedar Springs P Ch, Knoxville, TN, 98-99; srp Southwood P Ch, Huntsville, AL, 00-09; p Westminster P Ch, Rock Hill, SC, 13-

2958 Sancreek Drive, Rock Hill, SC 29732   Fellowship
E-mail: mhoneycutt@wpcgo.com
Westminster Presbyterian Church – 803-366-3107

Hong, Abraham – astp Highland Korean P Ch, Vernon Hills, IL, 11-16

1400 Chicago Avenue, Apt 807, Evanston, IL 60201 – 630-828-3394   Korean Central
E-mail: arhong327@gmail.com

Hong, Chang Sok – op Seattle Lamp P Ch, Bellvue, WA, 08-10; p Light of the Gospel Ch, Glen Burnie, MD, 12-14; ob 14-

3776 Bonnybridge Place, Ellicott City, MD 21043 – 443-924-4045   Korean Capital
E-mail: redlongstone@hotmail.com

Hong, Eui Man – b Korea, Jan 19, 43; f Dr. Boong Hee; m Chun Bock; w Hyekyung Yoon, New York City, NY, Aug 23, 69; chdn Sharon Miyoung; YonU 67, BA; WTS 87, MDiv; L Jul 30, 85; O Jul 30, 85, KorSE Pby; p Emmanuel P Ch, Timonium, MD, 90-97; ob Open Door Mission Group

212-12 73rd Avenue #3F, Bayside, NY 11364 – 347-426-4558   Korean Northeastern

Hong, Eui Seon – b Korea, Feb 13, 54; f Yong Do; m Byong Sun Jang; w Ok Hee , Korea, Jun 22, 79; chdn Eun Il, Eun Se; PGATCS 84, MDiv; O Apr 15, 85; medu Sung Duck Ch, 81-83; p Dan Saem Ch, 84-87; op Wheat Grain Korean P Msn, Columbus, GA, 91-93; ev, op East Gate Korean P Msn, Marietta, GA, 93-96, wc 96-97; op, ev Vision Comm Ch, Marietta, GA, 97-08

Address Unavailable   Korean Southeastern

Hong, Jason – b Seoul, Mar 16, 62; f Kyeung-Soo Hong; m Jung-Ae Ahn; w Myeongsook Yoo, Seoul, Oct 28, 89; chdn Daniel, Rebecca; SSCU, BA; ChShTS, MDiv; O Oct 15, 90, South Seoul Pby; sc KorNW Pby, 97-03; p Stockton Bansuk P Ch, Stockton, CA, 94-

4949 Timepiece Circle, Stockton, CA 95219 – 209-474-2334   Korean Northwest
E-mail: hijason62@hotmail.com
Stockton Bansuk Presbyterian Church – 209-957-9191

Hong, Jong-Su – b Seoul, Sept 9, 71; f Jae-Yoon Hong; m Soon-Young Kim; w So-Jeong Kim; chdn Ye-Bhit, Ye-Bon, Ye-On; CalvC, BA; NPTS, MATS; TEDS, MDiv; p New Life Comm Ch, Fayetteville, NC, 06-

1774 Katonah Drive, Fayetteville, NC 28314 – 910-987-3923   Korean Southeastern
E-mail: hongjs3@hotmail.com
New Life Community Church – 910-988-9771

Hong, Joohyung – ob 18-

6110 Temple Street, Bethesda, MD 20817   Korean Capital
E-mail: jhong@dc2dcchurch.org

Hong, Kenny Kyungha – b Seoul, M 4, 64; f Joon Chul Hong; m Dong Hee Lee; w Ann Jung Ahe Hwangbo, Los Angeles, CA, Aug 26, 89; chdn Julianne, Andrew; CSUN 90, BA; FulTS 93, MDiv; L Apr 25, 95, KorSW Pby; O Apr 26, 96, KorSW Pby; ob astp LA Immanuel Mission Church, 96-98; ob ascp Jubilee P Ch, 98-00; op New Jersey New Life P Msn, Green Brook, NJ, 00-03; op San Diego New Life Msn Ch, San Diego, CA, 05-07; astp New Life Msn Ch of Colorado, Englewood, CO, 07-

18052 East Lake Avenue, Aurora, CO 80016 – 303-693-8134   Korean Southwest
E-mail: pastorkenny@gmail.com
New Life Mission Church of Colorado – 303-617-1005

Hong, Richard – astp New Life Msn Ch of Fremont, Newark, CA, 13-

37282 Spruce Terrace, Fremont, CA 94536   Northern California
E-mail: richardjhong@gmail.com
New Life Mission Church of Fremont – 510-761-6562

Hong, Wonki – b Korea, Dec 29, 58; f Song Son; m Chi Sun Ku; w Myonghui Jon, Honolulu, HI, Mar 20, 82; chdn Peter, Anne; UHI 83, BS; TalTS 87, MDiv; DTS 90, STM; O May 5, 90, Kor PC, Irving; astp Korean Central P Ch of Wash, Vienna, VA, 90-97; p McLean Korean P Ch, McLean, VA, 98-05; ob p The Church for All Nations, 05-

2214 Stefan Drive, Dunn Loring, VA 22027 – 703-893-2602   Korean Capital
E-mail: wonkimyonghui@hotmail.com
The Church for All Nations – 703-573-3767

Hong, Young Chul – b Seoul, Korea, Feb 26, 42; f Chong Se; m Chung Soon Han; w Hong Yeon Ra, New York, NY, Mar 15, 72; chdn Clara, Philip, John; YonU 64, BE; KSU 70, BA; PTS 87, MDiv; L Mar 14, 87; O Jul 10, 88, NJ Pby; op Somang Korean Ch of Princeton Msn, Princeton Junction, NJ, 90-93, p 93-94; p Agape Korean P Ch, Floral Park, NY, 94-08; hr 08

1702 Mier Street, Laredo, TX 78013 – 718-224-5524   Korean Northeastern
HR

Hong, Zadok – O Apr 9, 13, KorSE Pby; p Panama City Korean Ch, Panama City, FL, 13-

3422 Picadilly Lane, Panama City, FL 32405   Korean Southeastern
Panama City Korean Church – 850-769-8836

Honomichl, Paul Oliver – b Hackett, AR, Oct 3, 36; f Emanuel O.; m Mildred Elnora; w LaNora Ann Tuggle, Cavanaugh, OK, Nov 23, 53; chdn Alicia Ann, Bradley Keith; PeabC 60, BA; RTS 79, MDiv; IntSem 86, ThD, 86, DD; O Mar 29, 81, Cov Pby; p Houston P Ch, Houston, MS, 81-87; sc Cov Pby; p Bay Street P Ch, Hattiesburg, MS, 87-02; fndr General European Ministries Inc., 96-; ip Bailey P Ch, Bailey, MS, 02-12; wc; rm WHLV, Hattiesburg, MS, "A View From the Bay" 90-96

805 West 5th Street, Hattiesburg, MS 39401 – 601-582-3510   Grace
General European Ministries Inc.

Hood, Jonathan Ernest – b Portland, OR, Sept 11, 81; w Erica Paige Hall; chdn Aeryn, Claire, Emma; RTS 13, MDiv; O Nov 24, 13, NYS Pby, ev 13-15; op Christ Ch, Syracuse, NY, 15-

514 Fayette Boulevard, Syracuse, NY 13224-1306 – 315-726-3579   New York State
E-mail: jonathan@christchurchsyr.org
Christ Church – 315-726-3847

Hoogstrate, John Philip – b Passaic, NJ, Jul 30, 24; f Marinus; m Clara Sisco; w Shirley Lockwood, Trenton (d), NJ, Sept 3, 49; chdn Barbara Jean (Turner), Ruth Ellen; UPA 41-43; MISU 43-44; RutgU 48,

Hoogstrate, John Philip, continued
BA; FTS 51, BD; L 51; O 51, NJ Pby (RPCES); p BP Ch, Wilton, Dodge, Underwood, ND, 51-57; p BP Ch, Bowling Green, KY, 57-60; p Trinity P Ch, Kearney, NE, 60-65; op Carbondale, IL, 65-68; p Westminster P Ch, Everett, WA, 68-91; hr 91; p em Westminster P Ch, Everett, WA, 00-

3915 Colby Avenue, Room 301, Everett, WA 98201 – 425-290-7718   Pacific Northwest
E-mail: johnhoogstrate@gmail.com
HR

Hooker, John F. III – w Nancy; chdn John IV, Lucas, Mary Liles; ClemU, BS; RTSNC, MDiv; L Jan 26, 02, Cal Pby; O Apr 28, 02, Cal Pby; astp Woodruff Road P Ch, Simpsonville, SC, 01-04; astp Christ P Ch, Oxford, MS, 04- 13; ascp Decatur P Ch, Decatur, AL, 13-; op Grace Cov Ch, Athens, AL, 14-

18800 Wentworth Drive, Athens, AL 35613 – 662-281-1870   Providence
E-mail: jeff@gracecovenantathens.org
Decatur Presbyterian Church – 256-351-6010
Grace Covenant Church

Hooks, Stephen – O Feb 12, 13, Prov Pby; astp Westminster P Ch, Huntsville, AL, 13-

7713 North Catawba Circle NW, Madison, AL 35757   Providence
E-mail: stephen.hooks@wca-hsv.org
Westminster Presbyterian Church – 256-830-5754

Hoop, Larry Charles – b Bellefontaine, OH, May 23, 50; f Charles Cluxton; m Elizabeth Berniece Brown; w Deborah Dee Wolfe, New Vienna, OH, Jun 8, 73; chdn Charles Bernard, Andrew James; MUOH 72, BA; TEDS 84, MDiv; CTS 04, DMin; L Jul 83; O Apr 85, NoIL Pby; ap Westminster P Ch, Elgin, IL, 85-88; sc NoIL Pby, 87-88; p Colfax Center P Ch, Holland, IA, 88-12;p em, 12-; hr 12; sc OhVl pby, 15-; ch/pby relations rep, PCAAC, 15-; ss Russellville EPC, 14-17; ss Wheat Ridge EPC, 14-

422 Tater Ridge Road, West Union, OH 45693 – 937-544-0532   Ohio Valley
E-mail: larry.c.hoop@gmail.com
HR

Hooper, Charles N. Jr. – b Atlanta, GA, Apr 12, 63; f Charles N. Sr.; m Belle Corey; w Jill Daniel, Atlanta, GA, Mar 11, 89; chdn Daniel, Benjamin, Graham, Andrew, Joshua, Cole; SamU 26, BA; BDS 98, MDiv; L Sept 97, Evan Pby; O Nov 8, 98, NGA Pby; astp, ms/sa Intown Comm Ch, Atlanta, GA, 99-02; astp, modis 02-06; astp Perimeter Ch, Johns Creek, GA, 06-17; admin Life on Life; *Ignition Guide, Life on Life Guide*

3730 Longlake Drive, Duluth, GA 30097 – 678-366-8131   Metro Atlanta

Hoover, David J. – b Abington, PA, Oct 10, 46; f A. Jackson; m M. Jane Brockmeier; w Barbara Johnson, Lookout Mtn, GA, Oct 13, 90; chdn Allegra Noel, Jonathan Paul, Laura Marie; CC 68, BA; WTS 71, MDiv, 77, grad wk; VPI 87, PhD; L Oct 73; O May 5, 74, DMV Pby (RPCES); ap First Bap Ch, 71-72; ap Grace Ch, Roanoke, VA, 72-74; p RP Ch, King of Prussia, PA, 74-77; ap Christ Ref P Ch, Roanoke, VA, 78-82; ap Grace Cov P Ch, Blacksburg, VA, 83-85; assoc prof CC, 88-09; dir trg Chalmers Cent for Econ Dev, Chattanooga, 00; hr 09; prof TroyU, 09-

909 Lookout Crest Lane, Lookout Mountain, GA 30750 – 423-902-1868   Tennessee Valley
E-mail: djhoover46@gmail.com
HR

Hoover, Douglas C. – b. Newtown, PA, Mar, 61; f Richard; m Louise; w Katherine, Newtown, 92; chdn Erin, David, Robyn, Adam, Kelly, Richard; GuilC 85, BS; CBS 96, MDiv; ColStU 09, MS; ErskS 11, DMin;

Hoover, Douglas C., continued
L GrLks Pby; O Oct 4, 98, GrLks Pby; Chap USArmy, Ft. Bliss, TX, 99-01; Chap USArmy, Germany (Iraq 03-04), 01-04; Chap USArmy, Ft. Leonard Wood, MO, 05-08; Chap USArmy, Ft. Benning, GA, 08-12; Chap USArmy, Ft. Bragg, NC, 12-

1165 Pineywood Church Road, Cameron, NC 28326 – 573-586-9379 Ohio Valley
E-mail: douglas.c.hoover2.mil@mail.com
United States Army

Hope, Henry Melville Jr. – b Atlanta, GA, Oct 19, 31; f Henry Melville; m Sylvia Shepard; w Betty Ann McFadden, Spartanburg, SC, Jun 17, 55; chdn Sharon Rebekah (Hansard), Henry Melville III; UGA 52, BFA; ColTS 56, MDiv; LRTS 03, DMin; L 56; O 56, CentMS Pby (PCUS); p Pearl P Ch, Pearl, MS, 56-60; astp First P Ch, Jackson, MS, 60-65; p First Ch, Brookhaven, MS, 65-71; p Vineville P Ch, Macon, GA, 71-82; p Mitchell Road P Ch, Greenville, SC, 82-86; ob Dir Msn India, SE area, 86-05; hr 05; guest lect Paraguay, Argentina 78; Mission trips to Mexico, 79, India, 85, Singapore, 92; arch tour Jordan, 84; tour leader India 92, 99; preached in Austria 81, Ireland 86; cartoons pub *Presbyterian Journal*, 60-63; "Let's Uphold the Law!" *Presbyterian Journal*, 74; sermon in *The Historical Birth of the Presbyterian Church in America*, 87; *A Model for Modern Missions*, 03; *The Poor Houses – A Story of Atlanta's Almshouses*, 08; *Westminster!*, 14; *The Changing Winds, A story of Adventure, Romance, and Spiritual Victory*, 15

1010 Stonegate Court, Roswell, GA 30075 Calvary
HR

Hope, James Michael – b York, SC, Aug 13, 45; f Thomas M. Sr; m Lucy Maurice Howell; w Rachel James Brackett, York, SC, Dec 27, 69; chdn Jamie Michelle, James Patrick, Frederick Howell; WFU 68, BA; RTS 76, MDiv; L Jul 15, 76; O Aug 1, 76, Cal Pby; p Andrews P Ch, Andrews, SC, 76-80; p Union Mem P Ch, Winnsboro, SC, 80-89; adj prof CBC, 88-92; p Grace P Ch, Aiken, SC, 89-98, wc 98; ss Liberty P Ch, Sylvania, GA, 98, p 98-13

1334 Evans Road, Aiken, SC 29803 – 803-443-2944 Savannah River
E-mail: jimjimhope1@netscape.net
HR

Hopkins, David Rhodes – b Chester, PA, Dec 9, 42; f Samuel Hopkins; m Lucretia Rhodes; w Carolyn Spencer, Chester, PA, Jun 4, 66; chdn Brenda, David, Amy Joy; BJU 64, BA; FTS 68, MDiv; WTS 93, DMin; O 71, RPCES; p Christ P Ch, New Castle, PA, 71-76; ob mis InterAct Min, 76-89, ob mis 90-95; ob CHIEF (Native American Org), 96-00; ascp Evergreen P Ch, Beaverton, OR, 00-

14808 South Plum Drive, Oregon City, OR 97045-8854 – 503-657-7388 Pacific Northwest
E-mail: davcarhop@juno.com
Evergreen Presbyterian Church – 503-626-1520

Hoppe, Vincent – O 16, RMtn Pby; astp Village Seven P Ch, Colorado Springs, CO, 16-

1319 East Platte Avenue, Colorado Springs, CO 80909 Rocky Mountain
E-mail: vhoppe@v7pc.org
Village Seven Presbyterian Church – 719-574-6500

Hopwood, John M. – b Long Island, NY, Jun 25, 52; f John L.; m Beatriz Molina; w Grace, Chattanooga, TN, Jul 1, 78; chdn Elizabeth; FIU 75, BA; RTS 83, MCE; ErskTS 90, MDiv; L Mar 16, 93; O Nov 21, 93, GulCst Pby; DCE Bartow ARP, 87-89; p Chattahoochee P Ch, Chattahoochee, FL, 93-99; p GraceComm Ch, Palm Harbor, FL, 99-05; p Grace P Ch, Madison, FL, 05-13; astp Grace P Ch, Peoria, IL, 16-

12300 North Brentfield Drive, Apt. 114, Dunlap, IL 61525 Northern Illinois
E-mail: jhopwood@gracepres.org
Grace Presbyterian Church – 309-693-3641

MINISTERIAL DIRECTORY

Horan, Brent – O Dec 15, 13, NoTX Pby; astp Providence P Ch, Dallas, TX, 13- 16; srp First Ref P Ch, Pittsburgh, PA, 16-

2238 Woodmont Drive, Export, PA 15632 – 214-680-9212   Pittsburgh
E-mail: bhoran@frpc.org
First Reformed Presbyterian Church – 412-793-7117

Horn, Dwight – b Bartlesville, OK, Jun 25, 62; f John Arthur; m Betty Jo Reid; w Cynthia (Cyndee) Ann Hankins, Nashville, TN, May 16, 87; chdn (twins) Charles Parker, John Turner, William Connor, Catherine McKenzie; DLipsC 84, BA; VandU 90, ThM; TEDS 90, MDiv; WTS 00, DMin; L Mar 15, 91, TNVal Pby; O Feb 2, 92, Phil Pby; int Christ Comm Ch, Franklin, TN, 91; ascp New Life P Ch, Dresher, PA, 92-95; Chap USN, 95-

2535 Vendimia Court, Vista, CA 92084-5849 – 760-842-8049   Philadelphia Metro West
E-mail: dwighthorn@cox.net
United States Navy

Horn, Mark Edwin – b Huntsville, AL, Feb 20, 71; f James William; m Linda Rose Alderman; w Stephanie Michelle Vanover, Jackson, MS; MSC 89-93, BS; CTS 94-97, MDiv; O Nov 23, 97, SEAL Pby; astp, yp Trinity P Ch, Montgomery, AL, 97-99; astp, yp Shannon Forest P Ch, Greenville, SC, 99-01; srp Maryville Evangelical Ch, Maryville, TN, 01- 13; p Gr P Chelsea, Chelsea, AL, 13-

2102 Colonial Circle, Maryville, TN 37803 – 865-414-2145   Evangel
Grace Presbyterian Chelsea – 205-678-2663

Horn, Timothy R. – b Pascagoula, MS, Jun 27, 67; f Sanford C; m Linda J. Baylis; w Sarah W. Barnes, Clarksdale, MS, Aug 18, 90; chdn Katherine Grace, Robert Winston, Timothy Harrison, Virginia Anne; AU 86-89, BA; RTS 90-92, MDiv, 90-92, MCE; L May 18, 93; O Mar 13, 94, Cov Pby; astp Covenant P Ch, Little Rock, AR, 93-94, ascp 94-96; astp First P Ch, Jackson, MS, 96-00; ss First P Ch, Clarksdale, MS, 00; chp, mis MTW, England, 00-09; ascp First P Ch at Clarksdale, Clarksdale, MS, 09-12; p First P Ch, Biloxi, MS, 12-

1337 Father Ryan Avenue, Biloxi, MS 39530 – 662-313-8445   Grace
E-mail: tim.horn@firstbiloxi.org
First Presbyterian Church – 228-374-6880

Horne, Chris – w Sara Jane; chdn Georgia, Bonnie, Rosemary; O Apr 7, 13, Wcar Pby; campm RUF, Appalachian State, 13-

584 Oak Street, Boone, NC 28607   Western Carolina
E-mail: chris.horne@ruf.org
PCA Reformed University Fellowship

Horne, Mark – b Melbourne, FL, Dec 3, 67; f John Franklin; m Ruth; w Jennifer Ellen Burkett, Ft. Lauderdale, FL, Dec 20, 91; chdn Calvin Andrew, Mark "Nevin," Evangeline Jael; HougC 85-89, BA; CTS 95-98; O Jun 30, 99, PacNW Pby; ob p Christ the Sovereign Covenant Ch (ind), 98-00; p First Ref P Ch, Minco, OK, 01-05; astp Providence Ref P Ch, St. Louis, MO, 05-10; wc 11-; *Legislating Immorality* (with Geo. Grant); *Unnatural Affections* (with Geo. Grant); *The Victory According to Mark: An Exposition of the Second Gospel*

E-mail: mark@hornes.org   Missouri

Horne, Mark A. – b Greenwood, SC, Aug 25, 74; f Gary A.; m Vivian Dalton (d); step Clare P.; w Lisa Bosler, Abbeville, SC, May 20, 95; chdn Tanner, Jonathan, Katherine Grace; ErskC 96, BA; ErskTS 02,

Horne, Mark A., continued
MDiv; O Nov 3, 02, Cal Pby; RE Lebanon P Ch, Abbeville, SC, 01-02; p Norris Hill P Ch, Anderson, SC, 02-13; p Smyrna P Ch, Newberry, SC, 13-15; chmn bd dir, Calvary Home for Child, 04-06; op Carolina Forest, Myrtle Beach, SC, 16-

4011 Manor Wood Drive, Myrtle Beach, SC 29588 – 864-391-1780, 843-903-7365   Pee Dee
E-mail: purifyandelevate@gmail.com
Carolina Forest – 843-391-7379

Horne, Scott Vernon – b Huntsville, AL, Apr 20, 63; f Charles V.; m Elizabeth Harwell; w Marian Lewis, Augusta, GA, Dec 17, 88; chdn Anna Katharine, Charles Scott, Fielding Lewis, Elizabeth Lansdell; AU 82-86, BS; WCBS 86-87, dipl; CBS; CIU 89-92, MDiv; L Oct 9, 92; O Oct 24, 93, Mid-America; astp Christ P Ch, Tulsa, OK, 92-95; p West Hills P Ch, Knoxville, TN, 95-12; op Redeemer Valdosta, Valdosta, GA, 12-14; p 14-

10 Ashton Place, Valdosta, GA 31602 – 865-789-9009   Central Georgia
E-mail: scottvhorne@gmail.com
Redeemer Valdosta – 865-789-9009

Horne, Wesley N. – b Greensboro, NC, Jun 17, 54; f Wesley Newton; m Joan Heath; w Renee Prosch, Nashville, TN; chdn Jonathan Wesley, Victoria Renee, Josiah Wesley; CC 77, BA; RTS 83, MDiv; L Feb 81, MSVal Pby; O Nov 83, Wcar Pby; ap Trinity P Ch, Asheville, NC, 83; Chap ARNG, 84-; p First P Ch, Centreville, AL, 84-85; ap Trinity P Ch, Asheville, NC, 85-88; p Fellowship P Ch, Greer, SC, 88-92; chp Perimeter Ministries, Atlanta, GA, 92-96; op Town Hills Comm Ch, Kennesaw, GA, 92-99, p 99-02; wc 02-03; astp East Cobb P Ch, Marietta, GA, 03-09; ob; hr 16

512 Summer Terrace, Woodstock, GA 30188 – 770-928-7318   Metro Atlanta
E-mail: tarheel1954@gmail.com
HR

Horner, Richard V. – b Wilmington, DE, Jan 20, 52; f Kenneth A.; m Dorothy Raymond; w April Cutri, Charlottesville, VA, May 12, 84; chdn Rachel Noel, Kenneth Austin, Jenna Grace; HougC 74, BS; CTS 77, MDiv; UVA 92, PhD; L Oct 78; O Jun 79, Phil Pby; ap Reformed P Ch, Boothwyn, PA, 79-80, ob 83-89; srp Berea P Ch, Hockessin, DE, 89-95, wc 95-98; astp Trinity P Ch, Charlottesville, VA, 98-01; ob 02-

2137 SW 95th Terrace, Gainesville, FL 32607 – 352-379-7375   North Florida
E-mail: richardvhorner@aol.com

Hornick, Robert Saylor – b Johnstown, PA, Oct 3, 43; f Robert W.; m Margaret Saylor; w Jane Eppley, Johnstown, PA, Aug 14, 65; chdn Amy Lynne, Karin Leigh, Eric Paul, Beth Erin; INU 65, BS; PASU 71, MEd; RTS 77, MDiv; O Jun 5, 77, Evan Pby; ap First P Ch, Gadsden, AL, 77-80; p Warrington P Ch, Pensacola, FL, 80-10; sc GulCst Pby, 85-18; PCAAC 10-; ss Westminster PC, Milton, FL 11-18, p 18-

3124 Abel Avenue, Pace, FL 32571 – 850-910-4352   Gulf Coast
E-mail: gcpstatedclerk@gmail.com; bhornick@pcanet.org
PCA Administrative Committee
Westminster Presbyterian Church

Horning, Stevan M. – b West Bend, WI, Oct 17, 48; f Donald Mitchel; m Libby Marshalek; w Jeanne Ruth Barnard, Kathmandu, Nepal, Jul 1, 73; chdn Hannah Ruth, Sarah Elizabeth, John Christian, Mary Beth; MaryvC 70, BA; PhUG; GWU; WTS 79, MDiv; L Apr 79, Phil Pby (RPCES); O Jan 81, Pitts Pby (RPCES); op Westminster P Ch, Broadview Heights, OH, 80-83, srp 83-07; Chap USAR, 87-10; staff NIH, Bethesda, MD, 10-; Pause For Prayer rad min, 86-; hr 10; contr GCP, Swatantra Vishwa, Asian Forum; WTS Bulletin, *World; Connections* USAG-Hessen

CMR 427 Box 3809, APO, AE 09630   Ohio
E-mail: stevanmhorning@yahoo.com
HR

MINISTERIAL DIRECTORY

Horrigan, Michael P. – b Annapolis, MD, Mar 27, 53; f Edward R.; m Sarah D'Alfonzo; w Kathleen Mary White, Glen Burnie, MD, Oct 25, 80; chdn Jaime, Kevin, Stephen, Benjamin; UMD 71-73; ChTS 00, MDiv; O Oct 14, 01, Pot Pby; ascp Timonium P Ch, Timonium, MD, 01-03; op DaySpring P Msn, Linthicum, MD, 04-08; p 08-

219 St. James Drive, Glen Burnie, MD 21061 – 410-582-9326   Chesapeake
E-mail: mp.horrigan@gmail.com
DaySpring Presbyterian Church – 410-582-9159

Hough, Brian – astp Redeemer P Ch, Overland Park, KS, 08-13; op Manhattan P Ch, Manhattan, KS, 13-

2300 Chris Drive, Manhattan, KS 66502   Heartland
E-mail: brian@manhattanpres.com
Manhattan Presbyterian Church – 913-439-9319

Houmes, John – b Miami, FL; w Virginia Massey; chdn Sofia Nan, Lola Rosalie, Evelyn Virginia; AU, BA; CTS, MDiv; O Oct 19, 10, MO Pby; ascp New City Flwsp, St. Louis, MO, 10-14; astp St. Andrews P Ch, Hollywood, FL, 14-; op New City Flwsp Hollywood, FL, 14-

2230 Rodman Street, Hollywood, FL 33020 – 954-609-6922   South Florida
E-mail: jhoumes@gmail.com
St. Andrews Presbyterian Church – 954-989-2655
New City Fellowship Church – 954-609-6922

House, Mark Aaron – b Sioux City, IA, Sept 22, 53; f Richard Vernon; m Jeannine Green; w Sharon Grey, LaMirada, CA, Jul 19, 75; chdn Jessica Erin, John Daniel, David Richard, Andrew Joshua; BIOLA 71-76, BA; WTS 76-80, MDiv; TalTS 92-94, ThM; FulTS 94-02, PhD; L Jun 20, 81; O Feb 21, 82, Pby of SoCA (OPC); int Cerritos Valley OPC, Artesia, CA, 80-81, ap 81-83; srp Redeemer P Ch, Torrance, CA, 83-91; ascp Cornerstone Comm Ch, Artesia, CA, 92-94, srp 94-05; ed Hendrickson Publishers, MA, 05-09; prof NGTS 09-

8948 Picabo Lane, Cascade, CO 80809 – 719-434-7411   Rocky Mountain
E-mail: mhouse@newgeneva.org
New Geneva Theological Seminary – 719-573-5395

Housewright, Jason – p Tchula P Ch, Tchula, MS, 11-15; p First P Ch, Aliceville, AL, 15-

416 Carrollton Road, Aliceville, AL 35442 – 205-399-3127   Warrior
E-mail: jhousewright@psalm68.com
First Presbyterian Church – 205-373-2133

Houstoun, Ogden King III – b Atlanta, GA, Dec 5, 47; f O.K. Jr.; m Brown; w Kuhns, Gainesville, FL, Jun 20, 75; chdn Charles Benjamin, David Andrew, Stephen Phillip; WLU 65-66; UMiami 66-69, BA; RTS 73-77, MCE, 73-77, MDiv; O Nov 78, NGA Pby; t Mt. Vernon CAc, Atlanta, GA, 77-79; ap Smyrna P Ch, Smyrna, GA, 78-80; t CCAc, Atlanta, GA, 79-80; t WestmCS, Miami, FL, 80-82; ob t MCS, 88-97; ob t FCS, 97-06; hr

20700 Marlin Road, Miami, FL 33189-2428 – 305-255-5253   South Florida
HR

Howard, Anthony – b St. Louis, MO, Apr 6, 82; w Caroline Gamache; chdn Carter Howard; CTS 12, MDiv; astp Chesterfield P Ch, Chesterfield, MO, 13-

215 Clear Meadows Dr, Ballwin, MO 63011 – 314-600-0607   Missouri
E-mail: tonyh@chespres.org
Chesterfield Presbyterian Church – 636-394-3337

Howard, Mark – O Nov 9, 14, MNY Pby; astp Grace Ch of Greenwich, Greenwich, CT, 14- 15; srp West Valley P Ch, Emmaus, PA, 15-

5251 Town Square Drive, Macungie, PA 18062 – 610-730-5013   Eastern Pennsylvania
E-mail: mark.james.howard@gmail.com
West Valley Presbyterian Church – 610-421-8066

Howard, Michael Middleton – b Memphis, TN, Nov 24, 64; m Frances Vollmer Howard; w Shannon Campbell Roper, Cape Girardeau, MO, Mar 28, 92; chdn Walker Leigh, Michael M. Jr.; MillsC 82-86, BA; CTS 90-93, MDiv; O May 22, 94, JR Pby; astp Sycamore P Ch, Midlothian, VA, 93-96; chp NoCA Pby, 96-97; op Grace Ch of Utah, Layton, UT, 96-00; Chap USAFR, 98-00; p Grace Ch of Utah, Layton, UT, 00-02; campm RUM, UUtah, 02-04; Chap USAF, 04-

PSC 9 Box 3451, APO AE 09123 – 509-385-7434   Northern California
E-mail: mikehowardsr@gmail.com
United States Air Force

Howard, Robert Brian – w Missy; chdn Caleb, Connor, Joe, Jadyn; L Aug 8, 99, Nash Pby; O Aug 8, 99, Nash Pby; ascp Trinity P Ch, Murfreesboro, TN, 99-07; chp Bowling Green, KY, 06-08; op Grace & Peace Ch, Bowling Green, KY, 08-

1930 Cedar Ridge Drive, Bowling Green, KY 42101 – 270-796-5522   Nashville
E-mail: brian@gracepeacebg.com
Grace & Peace Church – 270-799-0176

Howard, W. Keith – b Dallas, TX, Jan 15, 58; f C.H., Jr.; m Lucille B.; w Dana Swanson; chdn Timothy Allen (KIA Iraq 2007), Carrie Beth, Charles D.; Baylor 80, BA; St. Marys Sch/Law 85, JD; astp Faith P Ch, San Antonio, TX, 09-11; srp 11-

13330 Syracuse, San Antonio, TX 78249   South Texas
E-mail: khoward@satx.rr.com
Faith Presbyterian Church – 210-492-8038

Howarth, Alexander – w. Bethany; chdn Elias, Autumn, Caedmon; O Sep 16, 12, Wcar Pby; astp Covenant Ref P Ch, Asheville, NC, 12-15; p New Hope P Ch, Vestal, NY, 17-

1480 Hawleyton Road, Bimghamton, NY 13903 – 607-725-5246   New York State
E-mail: alexjhowarth@gmail.com
New Hope Presbyterian Church – 607-757-2777

Howe, David G. K. – b Newark NJ, Aug 23, 47; f John S; m Pauline P Wilson; w Leslie E Smith, N. Olmsted, OH, Jun 26, 71; chdn Elisabeth Irene; RutgU 65-69, BA; GCTS 69-72, MDiv; HDS 72-73; L Jun 26, 72; O Jul 1, 73, ConnVall Pby (UPCUSA); ap Bethel Ch, Sydney, NScotia, Can, 73-75; p Ebenezer P Ch, Knoxville, TN, 75-; "The Membership Covenant"; "Another Christmas Carol: a Sequel to Charles Dickens' Tale"

1821 Hart Road, Knoxville, TN 37922-5623 – 865-690-3614   Tennessee Valley
E-mail: davidgkhowe@comcast.net
Ebenezer Presbyterian Church – 865-690-4821

Howell, Carl Curtis Jr. – b York, SC, Sept 14, 52; f Carl Curtis; m Sarah Emma Bratton; w Sandra Anne White, Blacksburg, SC, Jun 21, 75; chdn Clara Lee (Soundara), Carrie Louise (Cornett), Chrisa Lynn (Johnson), Emma Anne (Sinclair); GWC 79, BA; WTS 82, MAR, 82, MDiv; L Mar 83, Midw Pby (OPC); O Sept 83, Westm Pby; p Pulaski PCh, Pulaski, VA, 83-86; p Covenant P Ch, Cedar Bluff, VA, 86-

223 Mall Church Road, Cedar Bluff, VA 24609 – 276-964-5630   Westminster
E-mail: cchowell@gmail.com
Covenant Presbyterian Church – 276-963-0028

Howell, L. Jackson – b Richmond, VA, Apr 18, 71; f William James; m Cecelia Joy Stump; w Rebecca Frances Tatum, Savannah, GA, Jun 12, 93; chdn Leland Jackson Jr., Ann Frances, Marshall Tatum, Kathryn Wood; VandU 89-93, BA; CTS 95-98, MDiv; L Sept 13, 98, JR Pby; O Sept 13, 98, JR Pby; astp Calvary P Ch, Norfolk, VA, 98-99; op Trinity P Ch, Norfolk, VA, 99-03, p 03-

6200 Monroe Place, Norfolk, VA 23508 – 757-446-9214   Tidewater
E-mail: jack@trinitynorfolk.com
Trinity Presbyterian Church – 757-466-0989

Howell, Matthew – O Aug 30, 09, Wcar Pby; campm RUF, AppSt, 09-13; campm RUF, UT, 13-

6819 Sheffield Drive, Knoxville, TN 37909 – 704-438-8025   Tennessee Valley
E-mail: matt.howell@ruf.org
PCA Reformed University Fellowship

Howell, Stephen Michael – b Decatur, AL, Mar 3, 53; w Frosty, Jackson, MS, Feb 24, 78; JAXSU 75, BA; RTS 78, MCE, 82, MDiv; O 82, MSVal Pby; ss Eastside P Ch, Gadsden, AL, 00-03; astp Trinity P Ch, Montgomery, AL, 04-

5419 Kenyon Road, Montgomery, AL 36109   Southeast Alabama
E-mail: mhowell@trinitypca.org
Trinity Presbyterian Church – 334-262-3892

Hsieh, Mark Ting-Wang – b Taiwan, ROC, Oct 12, 36; f Chao Chuan; m Chen Hsieh; w Shu-Hui Lai, North Hollywood, CA, Aug 8, 69; chdn Stephen Ming-Che, Timothy Ming-Der; HighC 71, BA; RTS 62, ThB; FTS 76, ThM; O 66, China P Ch of Christ; lect Tao-Sheng ChrC, Taipei, 66-68; p China P Ch of Christ, Taipei, 66-68; ob p Formosan Gr Ch (Ind), Philadelphia, PA, 81-

1001 Valley Glen Road, Elkins Park, PA 19027 – 215-635-1904   Philadelphia
Formosan Grace Church (Independent) – 215-635-1904

Hsu, Jason – astp City Ch, Philadelphia, PA, 08-11; p City Line Ch, Bala Cynwyd, PA, 11-

220 Wickford Road, Havertown, PA 19083   Philadelphia
E-mail: jason@citylinechurch.net
City Line Church – 267-259-8387

Hsu, Michael N. – b Chicago, IL, May 22, 71; f Cheng; m Yao Lin; w Tanya Lyn Novak, Lawrence, KS, Apr 8, 95; chdn Mia, Issac, Calvin; UKS 93, BA; RTS 98, MDiv; L Nov 14, 98, Hrtl Pby; O Aug 15, 99, Hrtl Pby; astp Zion Ch, Lincoln, NE, 99-00; op Gr Chapel, Lincoln, NE, 00-04, p 04- 13; srp Gr Vancouver, Vancouver, BC, 13-

6658 Ross Street, Vancouver, BC V5X 4B2 CANADA – 785-845-0738   Western Canada
E-mail: mike@gracevancouver.com
Grace Vancouver – 604-738-3537

Hu, Yuanqi – p Philadelphia Bible Ref Ch, Wynnewood, PA, 14-

5406 Gainor Road, Philadelphia, PA 19131   Philadelphia
Philadelphia Bible Reformed Church – 610-296-1262

Hubbard, Beryl Theodore – b New Berlin, NY, Dec 4, 39; f Theodore Irving; m Edna Carmel Crispel; w Carolyn Roberta Strain, Franklin, NJ, Aug 18, 62; chdn Deborah Lynn, Sharon Lee; BJU 62, BA; PhilTS 65, MDiv; ACSC 80-81; FulTS 82, DMin; O Dec 1, 68, Phil Pby (RPCES); ap Faith P Ch, Wilmington, DE, 68-69; Chap USAF, 69-79; Chap USAF, Montgomery, AL, 80-84; Chap USAF, Howard

Hubbard, Beryl Theodore, continued
AFB, Rep of Panama, 84-86; Chap USAF, HQ SAC, Offutt AFB, NE, 86-89; Dir Comm Cntr Chapel, Chap USAFA, 89-91; Command Chap, USAFA, 91-93; Sr Staff Chap, Kadena AB, Japan, 93-95; hr 95; dir sm grp Westminster P Ch, Ft. Walton Beach, FL, 95-97; ip Key Biscayne P Ch, Key Biscayne, FL, 97-98; assoc, Dir PRJC, 98-09; dir disc/out Westminster P Ch, Ft. Walton Beach, FL, 10-12

5601 Sirius Court, Atlantic Beach, FL 32233 – 904-241-3252   Heritage
E-mail: btcrhub@aol.com
HR

Hubbard, Claude – astp Redeemer Hoboken, Hoboken, NJ, 00-03; astp Grace Redeemer Ch, Teaneck, NJ, 00-03; wc 04-

250 Marietta Street, Englewood Cliffs, NJ 07632-1642 – 201-224-8571   Metropolitan New York

Hubbard, Roy – campm RUF, AL A&M, 10-16; ascp New City South, St. Louis, MO, 16-

3940 Nebraska Avenue, St. Louis, MO 63118 – 256-858-8566   Missouri
E-mail: rhubbard@ncfstl.org
New City South – 314-762-9915

Huber, Eric C. – b MD, Jul 13, 65; f Louis Ferdinand; m Jean Francis Eigenbrodt; w Lauren Marie Pfeifer, Timonium, MD, Sept 12, 87; chdn Timothy Conrad, Danielle Marie, Nathan Robert; UMD 83-87, BA; ChTS 89-97, MDiv; L Feb 96; O Nov 30, 97, Pot Pby; astp Wallace P Ch, Hyattsville, MD, 89-92; mis MTW, Ukraine, 97-10; srp Christ The King P Ch, Conshohocken, PA, 10-

44 Lincoln Lane, Conshohocken, PA 19428 – 410-869-2964   Philadelphia Metro West
E-mail: eric.c.huber@gmail.com
Christ The King Presbyterian Church – 610-828-2415

Huber, Scott R. – Germany, Dec 11, 58; f Lowell H.; m Sandra Sue Robinson; w Megann Gilmore, Omaha, NE, Mar 31, 84; chdn Katheryn, Alexander, Andrew; UNE, BS; WTS, MDiv; L Apr 91, SoCst Pby; O Jan 26, 92, RMtn Pby; Chap USArmy, Ft. Riley, KS, 92-94; Chap USArmy, Chap sch, Ft. Monmouth, NJ, 94-95; Chap USArmy, Korea, 95-96; Chap USArmy, Germany, 96-98; Chap USArmy, Ft. Carson, CO, 98-99; Chap USArmy, Ft. Gillem, GA, 99-08; instr ROTC ; p First P Ch, Lexington, MS, 14-17; hr18

7019 Eastwick Lane, Indianapolis, IN 49256   Mississippi Valley
E-mail: scott.r.huber@gmail.com
HR

Huber, Steven J. – b New Brighton, PA, Oct 8, 69; f J. Wallace Jr.; m Virginia Ann Krebill; w Christine Ann Richner, Southampton, PA, Aug 7, 93; chdn Hannah, Lukas; WheatC 92, BA; WTS 93-97, MDiv; L May 98, Phil Pby; O Jul 25, 99, Phil Pby; ascp New Life P Ch, Glenside, PA, 97-02; chp, op liberti Ch, Philadelphia, PA, 02-09; p Liberti Ch of the River Wards, Philadelphia, PA, 09-

2424 East York Street, Suite 122, Philadelphia, PA 19125 – 267-767-8945   Philadelphia
E-mail: steve@liberti.org
Liberti Church of the River Wards – 215-291-4248

Hudson, Franklin Douglas – b Charlotte, NC, Feb 8, 48; f James L (d); m Ethel Arrants (d); w Gertie Ziemer, York, SC, Jan 28, 71; chdn Jennifer Nicole, Amber Noele; BelC 80, BA; RTS 83, MDiv; O Oct 83, DMV Pby; ap Loch Raven P Ch, Baltimore, MD, 83-89; Chap Maryland ANG; op Christ P Ch, Farmington, MN, 90, p 90-93; Chap USAR, 90-; ob ev, chp Trin Ref P Msn, 93-08

8921 Green Chase Drive,Montgomery, AL 36117 – 731-756-3962   Southeast Alabama

Hudson, Mark – astp Tyrone Cov P Ch, Fenton, MI, 07-14; astp 16-

1000 Shiawassee Avenue, Fenton, MI 48430 – 810-750-2656   Great Lakes
E-mail: Mark.Hudson94@gmail.com
Tyrone Covenant Presbyterian Church – 810-629-1261

Hudson, Samuel Berry – b Spartanburg, SC, Nov 12, 70; f Claude P.; m Elaine Chapman Berry; w Rachel Eleanor Todd, Oct 9, 99; WheatC 89-92, BA; CTS 93-97, MDiv; L Apr 23, 98; O Aug 16, 98, Palm Pby; campm RUF, Citadel, C of Charleston, 98-07; astp Two Rivers P Ch, Charleston, SC, 07-09; ob couns Hindsight Bib Couns, 09-

354 Barnsley Drive, Evans, GA 30809   Palmetto
E-mail: bhudson@insight-ministries.com
Hindsight Biblical Counseling

Hudson, Thomas D. – b Portsmouth, VA, Nov 16, 50; f Leo V.; m Mary A. Culotta; w Carol A. Roseke, Boca Raton, FL, Mar 17, 73; chdn Daniel Vincent, Abigail Rose (Bishop), William Spencer, John Rafael, Ana Cristina; FAU 74, BA; WTS 77, MDiv; L Aug 23, 77, SFL Pby; O Feb 19, 78, MidAtl Pby; ascp Immanuel Ch, West Chester, PA, 78-80; mis MTW, Portugal, 81-05; wc 05-; FLET U, Miami, 05-13; op Christ the King P Ch in Quincy, Quincy, MA, 13-

184 Thacher Street, Milton, MA 02186   Southern New England
E-mail: tomhudson.mtw@gmail.com
Christ the King Presbyterian Church in Quincy – 617-472-0523

Huensch, Justin – astp Chesterfield P Ch, Chesterfield, MO, 17-

2 Chesterton Lane, Chesterfield, MO 63017   Missouri
E-mail: justinh@chespres.org
Chesterfield Presbyterian Church – 636-394-3337

Huey, Harry Cummings Jr. – b Greenwood, MS, Jan 24, 62; f Harry Cummings H. Sr.; m Peggy Bishop; w Kristin White, Dec 26, 98; USM 80-85, BS; RTS 87-91, MDiv; O Jan 31, 93, Gr Pby; ydir First Bap Ch, Hattiesburg, MS, 85-86; ydir Westm P Ch (EPC), Laurel, MS, 88; ydir Woodland P Ch, Hattiesburg, MS, 89-90; campm UMS, 91-92; campm USM, 92-93; Chap USArmy, Ft. Benning, GA, 94-97; Chap USArmy, 97-

PO Box 10413, Columbia, SC 29207   Grace
United States Army

Huffman, Jared – b Cincinnati, OH, Jul 8, 82; f Greg; m Chris; w Erin Huffman, May 13, 06; chdn Knox, Cormac, Carsen, Conor, Cohen; CTS 08, MDiv, 09, MAC; astp Christ the King P Ch, Houston, TX, 09-13; astp Lookout Mtn P Ch, Lookout Mountain, TN, 13-15; ascp 15-18; chp 18-

316 North Bragg Avenue, Lookout Mountain, TN 37350   Tennessee Valley

Hughes, Owen – astp Oakwood P Ch, State College, PA, 17-18, ascp 18-

110 Cherry Ridge Road, State College, PA 16803 – 321-693-9198   Susquehanna Valley
E-mail: owen.d.hughes@gmail.com
Oakwood Presbyterian Church – 814-238-5442

Hughes, Ronald – b Edinburg, TX, Jul 17, 56; f W. Frank; m Patsy; w Leslie C. Galliano, Slidell, LA, Jul 31, 82; chdn David, Jeffrey, Austin; UTXAu, BA; LSU, BS; RTSNC, MDiv; O Nov 07, Cal Pby; astp Clemson P Ch, Clemson, SC, 07-08; p Keowee P Ch, Central, SC, 08-

119 Roslyn Drive, Clemson, SC 29631 – 864-654-8255   Calvary
E-mail: navron@bellsouth.net
Keowee Presbyterian Church – 864-650-3362

Hughes, William C. – b Louisville, KY, Jan 11, 39; f Philip J H; m Mary Cooke; w Mary Fain, Jackson, MS, Dec 26, 62; chdn William Fain, Amy Ayers; BelC 62, BA; ColTS 65, MDiv; O Jun 20, 65, StAnd Pby; p Weir Gp, Weir, MS, 65-67; p First P Ch, Indianola, MS, 67-71; ap Trinity Ch, 71-74; p First P Ch, Yazoo City, MS, 74-86; astp First P Ch, Jackson, MS, 86-08; hr 09

7 Enclave Circle, Ridgeland, MS 39157 – 601-853-3030   Mississippi Valley
E-mail: wmahughes@comcast.net
HR

Hughs, Ryan – campm RUF, UWA, 06-12; campm RUF, COSt, 12-18; ascp Grace Ch P, Ft. Collins, CO, 18-

3118 Cumberland Court, Ft. Collins, CO 80526   Rocky Mountain
E-mail: ryan@gracefortcollins.org
Grace Church Presbyterian – 970-412-8551

Hui, Phillip – astp Covenant Ch, Whitestone, NY, 08-

36 Broadway, Garden City Park, NY 11040 – 516-777-0484   Metropolitan New York
E-mail: pastorhui@gmail.com
Covenant Church – 718-352-8646

Hulsey, Donald Richard Jr. – b Evansville, IN, Oct 16, 61; f Donald R. Sr.; m Phyllis Lee Koenig; w Genie Mae Scherer, Evansville, IN, Sept 21, 85; chdn Josiah Donald, Abigail Mae, Grace Ellynne, Isaac Donald; USIN 80-84, BS; CTS 95-98, MDiv; L Sept 3, 98, Ill Pby; O Nov 7, 99, SWFL Pby; int Concord P Ch, Waterloo, IL, 96-98; astp Marco P Ch, Marco Island, FL, 99-01; p Westminster P Ch, Vincennes, IN, 01-04; astp Center Grove P Ch, Edwardsville, IL, 05-06; ascp 06-12; p Grace P Ch, Baton Rouge, LA, 12-

9556 Joor Road, Baton Rouge, LS 70818 – 225-757-6525   Southern Louisiana
E-mail: donhulsey@juno.com
Grace Presbyterian Church – 225-261-0890

Hunt, Jason Bennett – O Mar 13, 16, Palm Pby; astp St. Andrews P Ch, Columbia, SC, 16-

129 Lost Lure Lane, Chapin, SC 29036   Palmetto
E-mail: jason@sapc.net
St. Andrews Presbyterian Church – 803-732-2273

Hunt, John K. – b Dixon, IL, Nov 3, 24; f Harold V.; m Gertrude H. Kilburn; w E. Inez Simpson, Greenville, SC, May 27, 55; chdn John Stephen, Collyn Louise (Gomez); UMI, BS; FTS 54, BD; CTS 82, ThM; L Oct 55; O Feb 17, 56, Phil Pby (BPC); ap Faith Ref P Ch, Quarryville, PA, 54-57; mis Korea, 58-80; p RP mis Ch, Carbondale, IL, 65; p RP mis Ch, Knoxville, TN, 82; t CC, 81-82; mis MTW, Australia, 82-89; fndr, prin WTC, Perth, Australia; lect Ko Shin Missionary School, 91; ob prof AUBS, 94-00; hr 96; lect PTSDD, 98

1240 Ashford Center Parkway #347, Atlanta, GA 30338 – 404-274-1443   Philadelphia Metro West
E-mail: jandihunt@aol.com
HR

Hunt, Jonathan Wittman – b Montgomery, AL, Nov 26, 80; f Harold; m Margaret Ann Wittman; w Heather Ann Huhta, Dunbar, WI, Sept 15, 07; NorthlandIU 03, BA; RTS 17, MDiv; O 03; Recd May 13, 17, NYS Pby; p Armor Bible P Ch, Orchard Park, NY, 17-

4615L Brompton Drive, Blasdell, NY 14219 – 716-648-4559   New York State
E-mail: jonathan.hunt@armorpca.org
Armor Bible Presbyterian Church – 716-648-4559

Hunt, Richard Eugene – b Columbus, GA, Mar 9, 39; f Samuel Ross H; m Nell Poston; w Susan McLaurin, Myrtle Beach, SC, Dec 28, 63; chdn Kathryn Elaine, Richard Eugene Jr; Susan McLaurin; UGA 62, BA; ColTS 65, MDiv; L Jun 65; O Jun 65, Hmny Pby; p McDowell Ch, Greeleyville, SC, 65-68; p First P Ch, Greenville, AL, 68-72; p Emmanuel P Ch, Jonesboro, GA, 72-76; op, p Covenant P Ch, Fayetteville, GA, 76-87, ms 88-89; astp Midway P Ch, Powder Springs, GA, 89-08; hr 08

11 Trail Road NW, Marietta, GA 30064 – 770-425-7781   Northwest Georgia
HR

Hunter, Bradford Lee – b Hollywood, FL, Mar 15, 73; f Fredrick Benjamin II; m Caryl Lyn Ramberg; w Stacey Renne Porter, Bloomington, IL, Aug 16, 97; chdn Bradford Luke, Abigail Marylyn, Levi Fredrick; UNotD 95, BA; KTS 00, MDiv; O Jul 19, 00, SFL Pby; astp, mout St. Andrews P Ch, Hollywood, FL, 00-04; ascp St. Andrews P Ch, Hollywood, FL, 04-07; WHM, chp team ldr, 07-15; op New City Wien, Vienna, 09-

Wiedner Hauptstrasse 108/11, A-1050 Vienna, AUSTRIA, EU – 954-380-3838   South Florida
E-mail: viennahunters@gmail.com
New City Wien, Vienna

Hunter, Fredrick Benjamin III – b Hollywood, FL, Oct 3, 70; f Frederick B. II; m Caryl Lyn Ramberg; w Frederika Thompson, Ft. Lauderdale, Aug 13, 94; chdn Elisabeth, Ben, Michael; MDCC 92, AS; TIU 96, BA; KTS 00, MDiv; L Jul 00, SFL Pby; O Jul 02, SFL Pby; astp Rio Vista Comm Ch, Ft. Lauderdale, FL, 02-03, ascp 03-05; op CityChurch, Ft. Lauderdale, FL, 05-

1353 Middle River Drive, Ft. Lauderdale, FL 33304 – 954-695-1832   South Florida
CityChurch – 954-634-2489

Hunter, Mark – b Connersville, IN, Jan 26, 59; f Marvin; m Alta Ruth Allen; w Jennifer Leigh Albert, Birmingham, AL, May 30, 92; chdn Julia, Mary Beth; WKU 81, BA; ETSU 91, MA; BDS 95, MDiv; L Jan 98, Evan Pby; O May 17, 98, Evan Pby; astp Oak Mountain P Ch, Birmingham, AL, 98, ascp 99-12; ob 12-

19 Jennifer Court, Madison, MS 39110 – 205-967-4145   Evangel

Hunter, Phil – O Jan 19, 17, SW Pby; astp Grace P Ch, Scottsdale, AZ, 17-18

15478 Blackbird Drive, Fountain Hills, AZ 85268 – 480-585-5063   Southwest

Hurley, Edward Lee – b Charlotte, NC, May 21, 53; f Charles Lee; m Jewel Burlene Hodge; w Vivian Turner, Jackson, MS, Aug 25, 79; chdn Meredith Alyn, Evan Patrick; BelC 77-80, BA; RTS 80-85, MDiv, 80-85, MAR; L Oct 84; O Jun 85, MSVal Pby; p Scooba P Ch, Scooba, MS, 85-89; p Shuqualak P Ch, Shuqualak, MS, 85-04; NAS, Family Service Cntr, 89-12; lic Marr/Fam Ther; ss Pamlico P Ch, Oriental, NC, 12, wc 12-

832 Stonegate Court, Fort Walton Beach, FL 32547   Eastern Carolina
E-mail: edhlmft@gmail.com

Hurley, James B. – w Phyllis Black; chdn James Bassett Jr., Andrew Laird, Timothy Phillip; CC 73-78; WTS 79-83; CU, PhD; FSU 93, PhD; L 75; O 75, SO Pby (RPCES); ob prof RTS, 85-; *Man and Woman in Biblical Perspective*; *When Christians Disagree*

310 Linda Drive, Clinton, MS 39056-3152 – 601-924-3190   Gulfstream
E-mail: jameshurley@bellsouth.net
Reformed Theological Seminary – 601-923-1600
5422 Clinton Boulevard, Jackson, MS 39209

Hurrie, Shaun – b Johannesburg, South Africa, Nov 30, 77; f Leslie Clifford (d); m Susan Margaret Price; w Rebecca Ann Propst, Lincolnton, NC, Nov 23, 02; chdn Isaac, Anywn, Elise, Karis; UCTSA 00, BA; RTSNC 16, MDiv; O Jun 25, 17, CatVal Pby; fm MTW, 17-

12423 Cumberland Crest Drive, Huntersville, NC 28078 – 828-638-0296   Catawba Valley
E-mail: hurrie_sm@hotmail.com
PCA Mission to the World

Hurst, Kerry Wassum – b Grundy, VA, Jan 12, 46; f Claude W H; m Mabel Sutherland; w Brenda Hoover, Hopewell, VA, Sept 4, 71; chdn Rebekah Whitefield (Hughes),Kerry Joshua, Matthew Caleb, Katherine Elizabeth (Parker); KgC 68, BA; ColTS 68; RTS 72, MDiv; O Jul 9, 72, PCUS; p Coeburn P Ch, Coeburn, VA, 72-74; p Mary Martin Mem, Mt Olivet chs, Coeburn, VA, 72-74; p Westminster P Ch, Kingsport, TN, 74-78; p Faith P Ch, Birmingham, AL, 78-82; adj prof St. Leo U, 83-05; srp Calvary Ref P Ch, Hampton, VA, 85-12; ascp 13-15; hr 15; contr *Worship in the Presence of God*

16 Eagle Point Road, Hampton, VA 23669 – 757-788-8911   Tidewater
E-mail: pete@calvaryrpc.org
HR

Hurst, Paul C. – b Hamilton, ON, Aug 25, 55; f Malcom Clacher; m Jane Young Orr; w Lesley Ann Richards, Virginia Beach, VA, Aug 6, 83; chdn Kyle David, Joel Grant; OntarioBC 80, BRE, 81, ThB; KTS 98, MDiv; L Oct 20, 98, SFL Pby; O Feb 7, 99, SFL Pby; DCE St. Andrews PC, Belle River, ON, 83-87; astp, ms/sa Coral Ridge P Ch, Ft. Lauderdale, FL, 99-17; astp South Dayton P Ch, Centerville, OH, 18-

9540 Windwood Point, Dayton, OH 45458   Ohio Valley
E-mail: paul@sdpc.org
South Dayton Presbyterian Church – 937-433-1022

Husband, Samuel – b Memphis, TN, Jun 30, 80; f Paul; m Dixie; w Sara Tyson McDaniel; chdn Samuel Christopher, Jr.; BelC 03; RTS 08, MDiv; campm RUF, UMemp, 08-11; astp Independent P Ch, Memphis, TN, 11-18; chp 18-

4861 Mendenhall Place, Memphis, TN 38117 – 601-573-5931   Covenant
E-mail: shusband@indpres.org

Huster, Jim – w Sally; chdn Faith, Isaac, Evan, Lauren, Caleb; ascp Harbor Ocean Beach P Ch, San Diego, CA, 09-13; wc 13-15; astp Ponte Vedra P Ch, Ponte Vedra, FL, 15-16, ascp 16-

1160 Eddystone Lane, Ponte Vedra, FL 32081 – 904-654-3021   North Florida
E-mail: jimrhuster@gmail.com
Ponte Vedra Presbyterian Church – 904-285-8225

Huston, Justin – ob

5472 Danville Road, Huntsville, AL 35640 – 256-683-7145   Providence
E-mail: justin.huston@wca-hsv.org

Hutchens, James Milton – b Indianapolis, IN, Jul 18, 34; f Ora Milton; m Helen K.; w Patricia Mercer, Kenilworth, IL, Jun 9, 59; chdn Mather B., Sarah M., Rachel C.; WheatC 60, BA; DTS 64, ThM; FulTS 74, DMiss; LBU 79, PhD; L Jun 62, GBC; O Jun 64, GBC; O Jul 31, 82, DMV Pby (RPCES); Chap USArmy, 55-92; mis Israel, 69-70; Chap WheatC, 70-72, mis 74-76; op, p Potomac Chapel, McLean, VA, 80-82; op Christ Ch of Arlington, Arlington, VA, 82, p 82-04; ob Christians for Israel, 04, The Jerusalem Connection, 05; hr 05; Chap (BrigGen) USA; hr from military, 94; *Beyond Combat; Guilty, Keeping God's Covenant of Love with Israel*

1851 Stratford Park Place # 407, Reston, VA 20190 – 703-217-7577   Potomac
E-mail: hutchensjm@aol.com
HR

Hutchings, Christopher Lee – b Akron, OH, Jun 23, 84; f Doug; m Lynn; w Diane, Hudson, OH, Jul 27, 07; ConcU 07, BA; RTS 12, MDiv; O Aug 12, 12, MSVal Pby; astp Highlands P Ch, Ridgeland, MS, 12-18; adj prof BelhU, 14-18; astp Grace PCch of the W Reserve, Hudson, OH, 18-; chp North Canton, OH, 18-

1750 Kingsley Avenue, Akron, OH 44313   Ohio
E-mail: cleehutchings@gmail.com
Grace Presbyterian Church of the Western Reserve – 330-650-6548

Hutchinson, Christopher A. – b Charleston, SC, Jan 24, 67; f Joseph Dwight; m Lydia Somers Coleman; w Kirstan Grace Reinhardt, Leesburg, VA, Jun 29, 90; chdn Taylor Grace, Geneva Lark; DukeU 89, BA; GCTS 95, MDiv; O Feb 22, 98, CentGA Pby; cop Third Protestant Mem Ch, Cincinnati, 95-96; int Trinity P Ch, Statesboro, GA, 97-98, ascp 98-04; srp Grace Cov P Ch, Blacksburg, VA, 04-; contr *The Auburn Avenue Theology, Pros and Cons: Debating the Federal Vision; Rediscovering Humility: Why the Way Up is Down,* 18

2113 Chestnut Drive, Blacksburg, VA 24060   Blue Ridge
E-mail: chris@gracecovenantpca.org
Grace Covenant Presbyterian Church – 540-552-3364

Hutchinson, David A. – b Norfolk, NE, Sept 6, 62; f Larry Arthur; m Luanne Kay Sorenson; w Paula Ann Ritchey, New Grenada, PA, Jun 27, 87; chdn Sarah Elizabeth, Abigail Christiana, David A. Jr., Lily Noelle; PenCC; RTS, MDiv; L Mar 21, 99, GulCst Pby; O Mar 21, 99, GulCst Pby; astp Pinewoods P Ch, Cantonment, FL, 98-00; ascp Glasgow Ref P Ch, Bear, DE, 01-04; astp Christ P Ch, New Haven, CT, 05-15; op Christ the Shepherd Ch, Danbury, CT, 06-15, p 15-

42 Hine Hill Road, New Milford, CT 06776 – 860-210-0736   Southern New England
E-mail: pastorhutch@sbcglobal.net
Christ the Shepherd Church – 203-743-3506

Hutchinson, Jeffrey Dwight – b Cambridge, MA, Sept 19, 64; f Joseph Dwight; m Lydia Somers Coleman; w Troy Lorraine Brickhouse, Durham, NC, Jul 10, 88; chdn Hunter Anne, Claire Lorraine, Joseph Dallas; DukeU 86, BA; RTSFL 93, MDiv; WTS 07, DMin; L Sept 25, 94; O Sept 25, 94, Ecar Pby; int Ch of the Good Shepherd, Durham, NC, 93-94; astp 94-96, wc 96-97; ascp Calvary P Ch, Willow Grove, PA, 97-00; srp Trinity P Ch, Asheville, NC, 00-10; srp Christ Comm P Ch, West Hartford, CT, 12-16; astp Christ P Ch, New Haven, CT, 16 -; Coord. Mission Anabaino, 16-

420 Yale Avenue, New Haven, CT 06515 – 860-817-8149   Southern New England
Christ Presbyterian Church
Mission Anabaino

Hutchinson, Rick – O Mar 10, 13, Evan Pby; astp Comm P Ch, Moody, AL, 13-17; op Christ Comm Ch, Springville, AL, 13-17, p 17-

75 Pickford Place, Springville, AL 35146   Evangel
Christ Community Church – 205-202-0742

Hutchinson, Travis David – Austin, TX, Mar 30, 67; f John Douglas; m Norma Jean Lisso; w Kimberly Jean Pfranger, Corpus Christi, TX, Nov 21, 92; chdn George Edward Haverland, Paul Balian Mather ; CC 98, BA; BDS 00, MDiv; USo, STM; L 99, TNVal Pby; O Apr 00, TNVal Pby; ip Highlands P Ch, LaFayette, GA, 00-01, p 01-13; adj fac CC, QUEST Prog, 00-; CC, adj inst Bib/Theo Studies, 01-; co-auth *Spirituality in the Workplace – A Course for Students of Organizational Management* (QUEST)

One Fair Oak Place, Chattanooga, TN 37409 – 423-821-1861   Tennessee Valley
E-mail: revtrav@gmail.com
Covenant College – 706-820-1560

Hux, Billy Cletis – b Brookhaven, MS, Aug 20, 50; f Berkley Conway Jr.; m Mary Geneva Jordan; w Karen Michele Stemple, Birmingham, AL, Jul 31, 82; chdn Michael Nathan, Aaron Elliot; MSC 74, BS; BhamTS 84, MDiv; O 84, War Pby; p First P Ch, Eutaw, AL, 84-86; p Roebuck P Ch, Roebuck, SC, 86-90; ob Watchman Flwsp, Inc., Birmingham, AL, 90-01; t BhamTS, 92-; t RTS, 92; vis lect/prof WTC; vis lect/prof Emanuel College, Australia, 96; t YWAM School of Evan, Nashville, 97; t Wesley C, Florence, MS, 97; ob Apologetics Resource Center, Birmingham, AL, 01-; dir 12-; dir Partners in Asian Missions; art *Watchman Expositor*; art and book rev *Radix and Areopagus Journal*

5066 Shelby Drive, Birmingham, AL 35242-3056 – 205-980-9355   Evangel
E-mail: clete@arcapologetics.org
Birmingham Theological Seminary
Apologetics Resource Center
Partners in Asian Missions

Hwang, David – b Korea, Mar 3, 51; f Chul; m Soo; w Grace S., Los Angeles, CA, Jan 16, 84; chdn Jennifer Y., Christine S.; YonU 71-75; CalSt 86-88, MA; ChShCS 90-93, MDiv; WSCAL 94-97, DMin; L Oct 12, 93, SoCA pby, KPC; O Oct 18, 94, West pby, KPC; Recd PCA 98, SFL Pby; p Valley Calvary P Ch, 90-93; prof ChShCS, 93-97; ap Antioch P Ch, 93-97; srp Bansuk P Ch, Miami, FL, 98-00, wc 00-02; Chap Bapt Hosp of Miami, 02-

6720 SW 159 Place, Miami, FL 33193 – 305-386-7312   South Florida
E-mail: dhwangbethel@msn.com
Baptist Hospital of Miami

Hwang, Ilha – astp Sae Han P Ch of Atlanta, Alpharetta, GA, 04-07; ob; p Korean Cov P Msn, Marietta, GA, 11-

Address Unknown   Korean Southeastern
Korean Covenant Presbyterian Mission – 770-565-4777

Hwang, Jae Joong – srp Korean P Ch Cf Ann Arbor, Ann Arbor, MI, 17-

3073 Signature Boulevard #F, Ann Arbor, MI 48103   Korean Central
E-mail: charis42714@gmail.com
Korean Presbyterian Church of Ann Arbor – 734-761-3407

Hwang, John – astp Antioch Korean Christian Comm Ch, Los Angeles, CA, 04-

24326 Sylvan Glen Road #G, Diamond Bar, CA 91765 – 909-355-6697   Korean Southwest
Antioch Korean Christian Community Church – 323-930-0678

Hwang, Kee Timothy – b Korea, Nov 15, 60; f yun Sook; m Pal Hee Chung; w Mi Suk Cho, Chicago, IL, Aug 29, 98; chdn Sharon Kim, Youngeun Hwang, Jessica Kim, Sinneun Hwang, Jonathan Kim, Rebekah Hwang; PhilCB 91, BS; WTS 97, MDiv; L Apr 00, KorE Pby; O Apr 01, KorSW Pby; ascp Sa Rang Comm Ch, Anaheim, CA, 00-10

2812 Park Vist Court, Fullerton, CA 86004 – 714-523-9562   Korean Southwest Orange County

Hwang, Moses – w Eunice Sugene Kim, Jun 4, 05; chdn Abigail Yireh, Sophia Rohi; Biola 06, BA; TalTS 13, MDiv; GCTS 15, ThM; astp Sa Rang Comm Ch, Anaheim, CA, 14-

880 East Chisholm Court, Brea, CA 92821   Korean Southwest Orange County
E-mail: mose.hwang@sarang.com
Sa Rang Community Church – 714-772-7777

Hwang, Sunwoo – ob Edinburgh Korean Church; ob Korea

Address Unavailable   Korean Northeastern

Hwang, Won Seon – b Pusan, S Kor, Jan 4, 57; f Chang Joo; m Kie Oak Lim; w Hye W., Pusan, Kor; chdn David Woohyun, Deborah Seiwon; SogangU 81, BA; BIOLA 87, MA; Talbot 89, MDiv; TEDS 94, DMiss; L Oct 90; O Oct 8, 91, KorCent Pby; ob p non-PCA Ch, Madison, WI, 91-92, campm 92-; op Korean P Ch of Milwaukee, Whitefish Bay, WI, 94-95; p Madison Sah-lang Msn Ch, Madison, WI, 95-08

Address Unavailable   Korean Central

Icard, Matthew – O May 5, 13, Cal Pby; astp Clemson P Ch, Clemson, SC, 13-

115 Shadowood Road, Clemson, SC 29631   Calvary
E-mail: matthew.icard@gmail.com
Clemson Presbyterian Church – 864-654-4772

Ilderton, Clenton Arthur – b Summerville, SC, Jan 2, 54; f Robert William; m Pattie Belle Clarkson; w Betsy Mason, Aiken, SC, Jun 11, 77; chdn Nathan Arthur, Robert Rudolph, Martin Lee; BelC 76, BA; RTS 79, MDiv; L Jul 78; O Jul 79, Cal Pby; p Rock P Ch, Greenwood, SC, 79-91; srp Hilton Head P Ch, Hilton Head Island, SC, 91-11; p Eagle Heights P Ch, Winchester, VA, 11-

1941 Kathy Court, Winchester, VA 22601 – 540-662-6873   Blue Ridge
E-mail: pastorclent@yahoo.com
Eagle Heights Presbyterian Church – 540-722-5650

Ilderton, Rob – w Jennifer, Dec 16, 06; chdn Miriam; ClemU; RTSNC 07, MDiv; campm RUF, Millersville, 07-13; mis MTW, 13-

1941 Kathy Court, Winchester, VA 22601   Susquehanna Valley
E-mail: rob.ilderton@gmail.com
PCA Mission to the World

Illman, Robert S. – b Champaign, IL, Sept 19, 47; f Robert L.; m June T.; w Sara Lively, Dayton, OH, Jun 13, 69; chdn Tracy (Jarvis), Robert, David, Sara; USCGA 65-69, BA; UMiami 73-75, JD; WTS 84-85, MDiv; L 83; O 85, Pac Pby; ob admin Contra Costa CS, 96-00; p Crafton Hills Ch, Yucaipa, CA, 84-87; op Christ P Ch, Los Osos, CA, 87-91, p 91-96; astp Westminster P Ch, Huntsville, AL, 00-02, astp 02-07; wc 08-

897 Capshaw Road NW, Madison, AL 35757 – 256-489-0574   Evangel

Im, Chandler H. – w Debbie; chdn Sabrina, Isaiah; BosU 87, BA; WSCAL 99, MDiv; FulTS 01, ThM, 09, PhD; ob Dir Ethnic Min, Billy Graham Center, 08-16, Wheaton; ob Dir Ethnic America Network, 08-16; mis Japan, 16-; co-ed *Global Diasporas & Mission,* 14

4-41-1 Takadanobaba, Shinjuku-ku, Tokyo 169-0075 Japan   Korean Southwest
E-mail: chandlerim@hotmail.com

Im, Seongmin – astp Briarwood P Ch, Birmingham, AL, 18-

Briarwood Presbyterian Church – 205-776-5200   Evangel

Inawashiro, Diogo – Recd PCA 16, EPA Pby; op Christ the King P Ch, Willow Grove, PA, 16-

40 Mount Carmel Avenue #B1, Glenside, PA 19038 – 267-471-9926   Eastern Pennsylvania
Christ the King Presbyterian Church – 215-659-0554

Ince, Irwyn L. Jr. – b Brooklyn, NY, Sept 2, 68; f Irwyn L. Sr.; m Margaret Louise Foy; w Kimberley Diane Shepard-El, Brooklyn, NY, May 24, 92; chdn Jelani Irwyn, Nabil Joseph, Zakiya Margaret Elizabeth, Jeremiah Lawrence; CUNY 95, BEEn; RTS 06, MAR; CTS 16, DMin; O Feb 07, Chspk Pby; srp City of Hope P Ch, Columbia, MD, 07-17; astp Grace P Ch of Washington, DC, Washington, DC, 18-

732 Whittier Street NW, Washington, DC 20012 – 202-808-5685   Potomac
E-mail: Irwyn@gracedc.institute
Grace Presbyterian Church of Washington, DC – 202-386-7637

Ingle, Aaron Banks – O Nov 19, 17, CentCar Pby; astp Hope Comm Ch, Charlotte, NC, 17-

744 Merriman Avenue, Charlotte, NC 28203 – 828-776-1489   Central Carolina
E-mail: aaron.ingle.43@gmail.com
Hope Community Church – 704-521-1033

Ingram, Robert Forrest – b Pittsburgh, PA, May 19, 51; f Robert Martin Jr. (d); m Marjorie Ann McGregor; w Marjean Wilson Wallover, Pittsburgh, PA, Jan 10, 75; chdn Katherine Boyce (Deatherage), Sara Ann (Cain); CWoos 73, BS; PittsTS 76, MDiv, 79, ThM; GenC 11, MHED; O Aug 6, 78, ARP; Recd PCA Oct 16, 95, CentFL Pby; ascp First P Ch, Lake Wales, FL, 78-86; VP LigMin, Orlando, FL, 86-95; ascp St. Paul's P Ch, Orlando, FL, 95-03; ob headm The Geneva School, Orlando, 03-

506 Burnt Tree Lane, Apopka, FL 32712 – 407-342-4966   Central Florida
The Geneva School, Orlando

Inman, Benjamin T. – b Raleigh, NC, Sept 9, 66; f Thomas P.; m Lucy Cathcart Daniels; w Sara Kathryn Bell, Chapel Hill, NC, Jul 8, 89; chdn Kathryn Noble, Benjamin Jesse, Anna Ruth, Sara-Elizabeth Daniels; UNC, BA; WTS, MDiv, PhD; L May 95, Phil Pby; O Sept 16, 00, Ecar Pby; campm RUF, NCStU, 00-04; campm RUF, UNC-CH, 04-12; astp Grace P Ch, Fuquay-Varina, NC, 18-

216 Woods Ream Drive, Raleigh, NC 27415 – 919-851-9264   Eastern Carolina
E-mail: pavementturnstosand@gmail.com
Grace Presbyterian Church – 919-557-5690

Inman, Jonathan D. – b Durham, NC, Jul 20, 63; f Thomas Patrick Inman; m Lucy Daniels; w Sonja Jeanne, Hillsborough, NC, May 20, 95; chdn Isabel Evangeline, Ezra Stelling; UNC, BA; WTS, MDiv; O Feb 18, 96, Phil Pby; ob Harvest USA, Stu Serv, Philadelphia, PA, 95-98; op Grace & Peace P Ch, Asheville, NC, 98-99, p 99-

20 Duke Street, Asheville, NC 28803 – 828-250-9559   Western Carolina
E-mail: jonathaninman@gmail.com
Grace & Peace Presbyterian Church – 828-243-3488

Inman, Timothy – O Mch 18, 18, Ecar Pby, chp 18-

809 East Church Street, Orlando, FL 32801   Eastern Carolina
E-mail: inmantimr@gmail.com

Irby, Elton Stephen – b Jonesboro, AR, Jan 15, 42; f Elton Turner; m Moore; w Royce, Little Rock, AR, Jun 17, 67; chdn Boyd Christopher, Scott Andrew; UCAR 60-62; UAR 62-65, BS; RTS 72, MDiv, 95, DMin; L Jun 72; O Jun 72, ARP; p Richland ARP Ch, Rosemark, TN, 71-77; p Southwest ARP Ch, Little Rock, AR, 77-86; msn dev Jonesboro, AR, 86-89; ap Westminster P Ch, Brandon, FL, 89-91; ob ss Covenant P Ch (Ind), Jacksonville, NC, 92-93, ob p 93-99; p Trinity Flwsp Ch, Sherwood, AR, 99-09; hr 09

33 South Pego Way, Hot Springs Village, AR 71909   Covenant
HR

Ireta, Carlos – b Mexico, Sept 14, 50; f Francisco; m Emma Lopez Diaz de Ireta; w Adela Gonzales, San Benito, TX, Sept 2, 88; chdn Adela Denise, Karla Alexandra, Emma Carolina; UMex 75; Sem Theo Pres, Mexico 92, dipl; Recd PCA Sept 26, 97, SoTX Pby; p Tampico, Mexico, 91-92; p Pres Ch, Manie, 92-94; p Pres Ch, Rio Bravo, Mex, 94-97; chp SoTX Pby, Laredo, TX, 97-99; op Divine Providence Ch, Harlingen, TX, 99-06; astp Grace P Ch, Dalton, GA, 06-12; wc 12-13; astp Faith P Ch, San Antonio, TX, 13-15; ob Children's Hunger Fund, 15-

8555 Laurens Lane #2309, San Antonio, TX 78218   South Texas
E-mail: cireta@chfus.org
Children's Hunger Fund

MINISTERIAL DIRECTORY

Irvin, Joel – b Elkhart, Jun 16, 75; f Jerry; m Maureen Ruth Humpley; w Jamie Lynn Baxter, Goshen, IN, Jul 21, 07; INU 13; MidARS 18; O May 25, 18, GrLks Pby; ascp Michiana Cov Ch, Granger, IN, 18-

21150 State Line Road, Bristol, IN 46507 – 574-215-9879   Great Lakes
E-mail: joel.irvin@michianacovenant.org
Michiana Covenant Church – 574-273-5906

Irvine, Keith – b Pittsburgh, PA, Dec 24, 44; w Rebecca, Northwood, NH, Aug 7, 71; chdn Matthew, Joshua, Charity; ShelC 66, BA; FTS 70, MDiv; O 75, Faith Bible Ch, PA; Recd PCA 07, SusqV Pby; p Faith Bible Ch, Norristown, PA , 70-76; p Bible Baptist Ch (Ref), Akron, PA, 76-87; ascp Westminster P Ch, Lancaster, PA, 07-08, ascp 08-

404 East Main Street, Ephrata, PA 17522 – 717-733-0024   Susquehanna Valley
E-mail: knrirvine@gmail.com
Westminster Presbyterian Church – 717-569-2151

Irving, David T. – O May 28, 15, MSVal Pby; p Raymond P Ch, Raymond, MS, 15-

220 Lakeview Place, Raymond, MS 39154   Mississippi Valley
E-mail: dtirving@gmail.com
Raymond Presbyterian Church – 601-857-8115

Irwin, Eric – b Oakland, CA, Jun 30, 58; f Grant L.; m Barbara Jean Andruss; w Lisa Diana Slocum, Eugene, OR, Jul 14, 84; chdn Luke, Hannah, Abby; UCB 81, BA; CTS 96, MDiv; L May 96; O Jan 26, 97, PacNW Pby; moy Korean P Ch of St. Louis, St. Louis, MO, 92-96; p Covenant P Ch, Issaquah, WA, 97-

4517 186th Avenue SE, Issaquah, WA 98027 – 425-458-8116   Pacific Northwest
E-mail: erici@cpcissaquah.org
Covenant Presbyterian Church – 425-392-5532

Irwin, John Mark – b Waterloo, NY, Feb 4, 72; f John Walter; m Patricia Jane Conroy; w Jennifer Strickland, Jul 20, 02; chdn Elena, Micah, Xander; SterC 94, BA; CTS 99, MDiv; L Oct 9, 99, Westm Pby; O Aug 27, 00, Westm Pby; ss Arcadia P Ch, Kingsport, TN, 99-00, p 00-12; p Reformed P Ch, Lemmon, SD, 12- 17; p Faith P Ch, Myrtle Beach, SC, 17-

960 Silvercrest Drive, Myrtle Beach, FL 29579 – 423-863-0366   Pee Dee
E-mail: theirwin5@yahoo.com
Faith Presbyterian Church – 843-449-7972

Isaac, Charles – w Marivi; chdn Justin, Daniel; RTSFL 00, MDiv; O Apr 20, 01, ARP; p Pleasant Hill ARP, Kissimmee, FL, 00-03; p Christ the King P Ch, El Paso, TX, 03-

3938 Flamingo, El Paso, TX 79902 – 915-276-2058   Southwest
E-mail: chuckisaac@gmail.com
Christ the King Presbyterian Church – 915-585-2264

Ivancic, Mike – RegC; ascp Gr Toronto Msn, Toronto, ON, 03-05; astp New City Ch, Calgary, AB, 10-15, ascp 15-

3608 Benton Drive NW, Calgary, AB T2L 1W8 CANADA – 403-282-3454   Western Canada
E-mail: mike@newcitychurch.ca
New City Church – 403.354.0525

Iverson, Daniel III – b Atlanta, GA, Jul 29, 52; f William T.; m Ann Oliver; w Carol Jean Chase, Knoxville, TN, Aug 28, 76; chdn Daniel IV, Jonathan, Joel, Sara-Beth, Martha, Mark, Hannah, Micah,

Iverson, Daniel III, continued
David; WCU 74, BA; RTS 81-84, MDiv; L Jan 84, MSVal Pby; O Jan 86, DMV Pby; mis, p MTW, Oyumino P Ch, Japan, 86-

c/o Mission to the World   Chesapeake
E-mail: danivermtw@gmail.com
PCA Mission to the World

Iverson, Daniel, IV – O May 19, 14, MetAtl Pby; astp Perimeter Ch, Johns Creek, GA, 14-; op Shalom City, Atlanta, GA, 16-

1974 Maywood Place, Atlanta, GA 30318   Metro Atlanta
E-mail: dannyi@shalomcity.org
Perimeter Church – 678-405-2000
Shalom City

Iverson, William Thorpe – b Miami, FL, Feb 20, 28; f Rev. Daniel; m Vivian Thorpe; w Ann Oliver (d) , Miami, FL, Jun 18, 51; chdn Daniel III, William Thorpe Jr., Jennifer Lee; DavC 45-49; ColTS 49-52; NYU 76, PhD; O 52, Ath Pby; p Calvary Ch, Elberton, GA, 52-53; p First Ch, Port St. Joe, FL, 53-57; RCA, 57-75; p South Orange, NJ, 75; op Cov Fell Ch, 75-81; p Fell Ch, Irvington, NJ, 81; dean, prof Reg Sem NE; vis lect/prof WTS; adj prof RTS; dean IST; op Cov Fell Ch, San Bernadino, CA, 84-87; admin Inst WCV of ICGU, 86-; pres IICS; ss Shenandoah P Ch, Miami, FL, 88-90; ob Dir DICCS, 90-98; ob ev PEF; ip First Ch West, Plantation, FL, 96-98; astp Princeton P Ch, Princeton, NJ; pres Jonathan Edwards Inst, 99-, hr 99; "Essays on the Obvious," "The Idea of a Study Center"

8 Gaywood Avenue, Colonia, NJ 07067 – 732-381-7781   Metropolitan New York
E-mail: soniver@juno.com
HR

Ivey, Myron Lee – b Augusta, GA, Aug 19, 58; f John A.; m Alice J. Burns; AugC 85, BBA; WTS 94, MDiv; O May 7, 95, CentGA Pby; ob CMI, 95-02; p Crawfordville P Ch, Crawfordville, GA, 04-07; wc 08-

1305 Grand Prairie Chase, Peachtree City, GA 30269 – 706-651-0235   Savannah River

Jabbour, Nabeel T. – b Syria, Jul 13, 41; f Toufic; m Julie; w Barbara June Stair, England, Aug 8, 70; chdn Farid, Nader; AmUB, BA; NEST 68, MA, 91, ThD; O Mar 15, 92, RMtn Pby; Navs, Beirut, Lebanon, 72-75; Dir Navs, Egypt, 75-90; ob Navs, Colorado Spgs, CO, 91-; missions cons, Muslim countries; adj prof on Islam, several US seminaries; PCA Study Co on Insider Movement, 11-13; auth two books in Arabic; *The Rumbling Volcano*, (on Islamic Fundamentalism); *The Unseen Reality, A Panoramic View of Spiritual Warfare; Unshackled and Growing; The Crescent Through the Eyes of the Cross*

545 Mesa Vista Court, Colorado Springs, CO 80904 – 719-578-8973   Rocky Mountain
E-mail: nabeel@nabeeljabbour.com; www.nabeeljabbour.com
en.wikipedia.org/wiki/nabeel_jabbour
The Navigators

Jackman, Marcus – p Chapin P Ch, Chapin, SC, 17-

304 Eagle Claw Drive, Chapin, SC 29036   Palmetto
E-mail: marcjackman@gmail.com
Chapin Presbyterian Church – 803-345-0500

Jackson, Corey – b Aug 13, 76; AU 98, BA; RTS 08, MDiv; O Mar 22, 09, Ecar Pby; astp Peace P Ch, Cary, NC, 09-10; op Trinity Park Ch, Morrisville, NC, 10-13; p 13-

536 Sandy Whispers Place, Cary, NC 27519 – 919-518-3535   Eastern Carolina
E-mail: corey@trinityparkchurch.org
Trinity Park Church – 919-439-3718

MINISTERIAL DIRECTORY

Jackson, Daniel – b St. Louis, MO, Feb 1, 78; f Jay; m Jaqucline Ann Paulin; w Tricia Lynn Gunderson, Eau Claire, WI, Feb 10, 01; chdn Corban, Caleb, Carissa, Cooper; UMOC 00; CTS 07, MDiv; O Mar 20, 10, Wisc Pby; op Jacobs Well P Ch, Green Bay, WI, 10-12; p 12-

3340 Lineville Road, Green Bay, WI 54313 – 920-469-3421   Wisconsin
E-mail: danjackson@jacobswellgb.org
Jacob's Well Presbyterian Church – 920-362-6825

Jackson, John (Kelly) Dunwody – b Statesboro, GA, Aug 22, 88; f Oscar; m Vicki Madalyn Kelly; w Caroline Leah Wicker, Athens, GA, Jul 2, 11; chdn nora, Johnny; UGA 11, BA; RTS 17, MDiv; O Jan 11, 17, GulCst Pby; campm RUF, FSU, 17-

1122 Waverly Road, Tallahassee, FL 32303 – 850-661-3137   Gulf Coast
E-mail: kelly.jackson@ruf.org
PCA Reformed University Fellowship

Jackson, Peter Edward – b Gainesville, FL, Mar 26, 64; w Paulette, Anderson, IN, May 28, 88; chdn Emma Katherine, Anna Grace; AndC 86, BA; RTS 95, MDiv; L Oct 95; O May 12, 96, SWFL Pby; moy Westminster P Ch, Ft. Myers, FL, 91-95, astp 96-97; astp Willow Creek Ch, Winter Springs, FL, 97-00, wc 00; ascp ChristChurch P, Atlanta, GA, 01-

5785 Garber Drive, Atlanta, GA 30328 – 404-257-9535   Metro Atlanta
E-mail: petej@ccpnet.org
ChristChurch Presbyterian – 404-605-0505

Jackson, Randolph – O Jun 8, 14, TNVal Pby; astp Grace P Ch, Dalton, GA, 14-

4004 Stillwater Drive, Rossville, GA 30741   Tennessee Valley
E-mail: steelshepherd@comast.net
Grace Presbyterian Church – 706-226-6344

Jackson, Robert Allen – b Atlanta, GA, May 27, 53; f Thomas A.; m Cletis French; w Deborah Lowery Thompson, Laurel, MS, Nov 17, 79; chdn Robert Jeremiah, Corrie Anne, Benjamin David; UGA 75, BA; RTS 81, MDiv; O Aug 2, 81, Cov Pby; ap Independent P Ch, Memphis, TN, 81-83; p Faith P Ch, Brandon, MS, 83-89; p Covenant P Ch, Louisville, MS, 89-93; p Grace P Ch, Stone Mountain, GA, 93-13; Cornerstone Church, PCA, Calera, AL, 16-

185 Oaklyn Hills Drive, Chelsea, AL 35043 – 205-477-6187   Evangel
E-mail: rev1jack@yahoo.com
Cornerstone Church, PCA – 205-690-0388

Jackson, Rush – O Aug 14, 18, Evan Pby; p Salem P Ch, Alpine, AL, 18-

5011 Bridlewood Parc Lane, Helena, AL 35080 – 205-745-5154   Evangel
E-mail: rushjackson@gmail.com
Salem Presbyterian Church

Jackson, Stephen Edward – b Washington, DC, Feb 10, 50; f Frank S.; m Bernice Snider; w Laura Candice Weaver, Savannah, GA, Sept 12, 70; chdn Heather, Stephen, David; ArmSC 73-75, BBA; CTS 84-88, MDiv; L Mar 88; O Mar 88, ARP; stus, p Elsberry Ch (ARP), 85-88; ap Evangelical P Ch, Cape Coral, FL, 88-90; p Christ P Ch, Marietta, GA, 90-91; ss Eastern Heights P Ch, Savannah, GA, 91-93; astp East Cobb P Ch, Marietta, GA, 93-94, ascp 94-97; op Sovereign Gr P Ch, Charlotte, NC, 97-99, p 99-07; hr 11

5 Fat Friars Retreat, Savannah, GA 31411-1705 – 912-704-7647   Central Carolina
E-mail: s.jackson853@comcast.net
HR

Jackson, Tim – O 15, MO Pby; astp Chesterfield P Ch, Chesterfield, MO, 15-

709 Ginger Wood Court, Ballwin, MO 63021   Missouri
Chesterfield Presbyterian Church – 636-394-3337

Jackson, Trey – O May 13, 18, CentGA Pby; p Christ Comm P Ch, Thomasville, GA, 18-

1040 Glenwood Drive, Thomasville, GA 31792   Central Georgia
E-mail: spiderdawg258@gmail.com
Christ Community Presbyterian Church – 229-226-6848

Jackson, William Allen – b Tacoma, WA, Apr 19, 57; m Carmadean Fleming; w Jean M Laudadio, Tacoma, WA, Mar 21, 81; chdn Aaron, Adam, Asa, Asher, Abel, Amos, Abram, Annika; EWU 79, BA; RTS 88, MDiv; L Jan 15, 89; O Feb 11, 90, PacNW Pby; mis MTW, Japan, 90-08; wc 09-

1314 11th Street Place SW, Puyallup, WA 98371 – 253-459-0067   Pacific Northwest
E-mail: wajackson@comcast.net

Jacob, Chuck – b Palo Alto, CA, Nov 12, 62; f Charles; m Lidabelle MacFadon; w Diane Thuen; chdn Hannah Grace, Noah, Abigail; StanU 85, BA; RTSFL 98, MDiv; L Jul 1, 15, Ecar Pby; O Nov 14, 99, EPC; astp Second P Ch, Memphis, TN, 99-03; p Knox EPC, Ann Arbor, MI, 04-15; srp Church of the Good Shepherd, Durham, NC, 15-

3607 Stonegate Drive, Durham, NC 27705 – 984-219-1147   Eastern Carolina
E-mail: chuckjacob@cgsonline.org
Church of the Good Shepherd – 919-490-1634

Jacobs, Jon – p Grace P Ch, Blairsville, GA, 09-

242 Cabin Drive, Hayesville, NC 28904 – 828-557-6789   Georgia Foothills
E-mail: chatuge@yahoo.com
Grace Presbyterian Church – 706-745-3653

Jacobson, Andrew L. – O May 8, 15, Glfstrm Pby; p Sand Harbor P Ch, Jupiter, FL, 15-

17609 Carver Avenue, Jupiter, FL 33458   Gulfstream
E-mail: andrewljacobson@gmail.com
Sand Harbor Presbyterian Church – 561-316-3862

Jakes, Glenn M. – b Atlanta, GA, Jul 4, 64; f M.A.; m Jean Botdorf; w Norma Cook, Oxford, GA, Jun 14, 86; chdn Micah, Ana, David; DeKCC 83-86, AD; GSU 86-90,BBA; CTS 94-97, MDiv; L Feb 8, 98; O Feb 8, 98, SEAL Pby; astp First P Ch, Dothan, AL, 98-00; p First P Ch, Crossville, TN, 00-04; astp Perry P Ch, Perry, GA, 04-

526 Ansley Avenue, Perry, GA 31069 – 478-224-2931   Central Georgia
E-mail: gmj.ppc@gmail.com
Perry Presbyterian Church – 478-987-1403

Jakes, Jeffrey – srp Orangewood P Ch, Maitland, FL, 02-18

978 Stonewood Lane, Maitland, FL 32751 – 407-740-7814   Central Florida

James, Edward Lester – b Washington, DC, Nov 10, 43; f Edward B.; m Pauline Ella Manning; w Joan Elarbee, Hancock, MD, Feb 5, 66; chdn Traci Lyn, Rob Lee, Rebekah; BryC 76, BA; RTS 79, MDiv;

James, Edward Lester, continued
O Sept 2, 79, GulCst Pby; p Chattahoochee P Ch, Chattahoochee, FL, 79-88; Chap USAR, 83-04; Chap Desert Shield & Desert Storm, 400 MP Bn (EPW/CI), 90-91; p Gr Christian Flwsp, Hancock, MD, 88-05; Chap Arlington Nat'l Cemetery, 99-04; hr

202 West High Street, Hancock, MD 21750 – 850-663-4906   Potomac
E-mail: e.l.james43@gmail.com
HR

James, Frank – ob

Address Unavailable   Central Florida

James, Michael Wesley – O Sept 6, 09, Prov Pby; p Courtland P Ch, Courtland, AL, 09-10; srp Harbor Ch PCA, Mooresville, NC, 10-15; srp Center Grove P Ch, Edwardsville, IL, 15-

6279 Center Grove Road, Edwardsville, IL 62025   Illiana
E-mail: pastorwes@centergrove.org
Center Grove Presbyterian Church – 618-656-9485

James, Parker – O Oct 25, 08, GAFH Pby; p The University Church, Athens, GA, 08-16; op Lord of Glory Flwsp Msn Ch, Athens, GA, 15-

140 Fortson Drive, Athens, GA 30606 – 706-207-3144   Georgia Foothills
E-mail: parkerscottjames1@gmail.com
Lord of Glory Fellowship Mission Church – 706-207-3144

James, William Allen – b Tulsa, OK, Dec 20, 63; f Basil R.; m Barbara P.; w Kelly Mattocks, Pollocksville, NC, Jun 3, 89; chdn Philip, Andrew, Victoria, Kathryn; UOK, BBA; TEDS, MDiv; L Apr 29, 00, NoIL Pby; O Apr 29, 00, NoIL Pby; astp Naperville P Ch, Naperville, IL, 99-01; op Grace P Ch of the North Shore, Winnetka, IL, 01-06; wc; astp Ch of the Good Shepherd, Durham, NC, 09-10; ascp 10-17; wc 17-18; ob Corporate Chaplains of America, 18-

4107 Indigo Drive, Durham, NC 27705 – 919-475-8381   Eastern Carolina
E-mail: billjames6@gmail.com
Corporate Chaplains of America

Jameson, Steven Alan – b Ft. Smith, AR, Dec 30, 49; f Miles W.; m Evelyn Ann Brady; w Karen B. Long, Springfield, MO, Jan 16, 76; chdn Colleen Cristeen, Erin Ann; UARFay 71, BA; UMOCol 80, MAJ; CTS 94, MDiv; L Jan 94, MO Pby; O Feb 18, 96, MO Pby; mis Nigeria, CRC, 83-90; int New City Flwsp, St. Louis, 94-96, ascp 96-98; op Olive Branch Ch (New City South), St. Louis, MO, 97-01, srp 01-06; ob mis CCC, Jesus Film Project, 06; ob mis One Door Min, 07-; *Beyond Yet Still With You*, 10; *God Knows You By Name (Bondye Konnen Ou Pa Non Ou)*, 10; *Byen Lwen, Poutan Toujou Avèk Ou*, 11

41 Camille Street, Sardis, MS 38666 – 662-487-1487   Covenant
E-mail: steve@hushharbor.org
One Door Ministries

Jamison, Wayne Fredrick – b Dansville, NY, Apr 1, 40; f Charles Pierce; m Phoebe Janet; w Mariela Rojas, Jan 30, 92; chdn Jennifer Louise, Stephen Wayne, Elliott Charles; NyC 65, BS; TEDS 68, MDiv; O Jun 4, 76, Asc Pby; Chap USArmy, 68-71; ap Calvary Bap Ch, NYC, 71-72; t Flushing Chr Sch, 73; p Glenmore Ch, Brooklyn, NY, 73; ap Wheaton Free Ch, Wheaton, IL, 74-76; op NYC, 76-84; USAR, 68-88; Ft Trotten, NY, 88-90, wc 91-97; Chap Florida Hospital, Orlando, 97-02; Chap TROA of Cent FL, 00-02; Bronze Star for Valor, VietNam, 69; vp The Retired Officer's Assoc of Cent FL, 99; hr

Address Unavailable   Central Florida
E-mail: waynfred@aol.com
HR

Jang, Daniel – ascp Grace Ch of Greenwich, Greenwich, CT, 08-12; op Grace Ch Stamford, 09-

572 Roxbury Road, Stamford, CT 06903 – 203-314-4989   Metropolitan New York
Grace Church Stamford – 203-314-4898

Jang, Jae Deok – O Dec 12, 71; Recd PCA Feb 9, 83, KorSW Pby; p Servant Ch, San Jose, CA, 84-07; hr

Address Unavailable   Korean Northwest
HR

Jang, Joon Yung – p Smyrna Korean P Ch, Enterprise, AL

3341 Tansey Court, Tallahassee, FL 32308 – 817-793-7297   Korean Southeastern
E-mail: joonyungjang@gmail.com
Smyrna Korean Presbyterian Church

Jang, Ki Won – astp Korean Ch in Jackson Msn, Jackson, MS, 07-10

601-922-8459   Korean Southeastern

Jang, Suyoung – Recd PCA 16, KorS Pby; p Tree of Life Ch, Cypress, TX, 16-

17807 Lakecrest View Drive #6302, Cypress, TX 77433 – 832-993-8829   Korean Southern
E-mail: jasonjang74@gmail.com
Tree of Life Church – 832-993-8829

Jang, Woonjee – O May 6, 18, KorCent Pby

224-209-7403   Korean Central
E-mail: ilikewj@gmail.com

Jang, Yo Han – b Korea, Jan 9, 63; f Han Ku Jang; m Kyung Ok Kim; w Bokyoung Park, Seoul, Jun 7, 94; chdn Angela, Edward; AUTC, BA; PThS, Tonghap, MDiv; O Apr 13, 99, KorSW Pby; ascp Sa Rang Comm Ch, Anaheim, CA, 99-08; ob p Han Sammul Ch

8141 Firth Grn, Buena Park, CA 90621 – 626-403-5671   Korean Southwest
E-mail: wayntrue@hotmail.com

Janicek, Cody Mitchell – O Sept 8, 13, CentCar Pby; astp Faith Comm Ch, Prague, 13-17; mis 17-

Jana Zajice 216/29, Praha 7 17000 CZECH REPUBLIC – 704-224-5380   Central Carolina
E-mail: codyjanicek@gmail.com

Janssen, Brian – b Forreston, IL, May 13, 59; f Vernon Christopher; m Marian Esther Kampen; w Susanne Jean DeWall; chdn David Brian, Kristin Marie, Jonathan Michael; WheatC 81, BA; TEDS 86, MDiv; CTS 07, DMin; O Aug 25, 86, PCUSA; p Hospers P Ch, Hospers, IA, 06-

PO Box 112, 205 3rd Avenue South, Hospers, IA 51238 – 712-752-8716   Iowa
E-mail: jannssenb@nethtc.net
Hospers Presbyterian Church – 712-752-8648

Jardin, James – O Jun 4, 17, GAFH Pby; astp Restoration P Ch, Hoschton, GA, 17-

770-688-0143   Georgia Foothills
E-mail: jjardin@restpres.org
Restoration Presbyterian Church – 770-945-7800

MINISTERIAL DIRECTORY

Jarrett, Robert Lee – b Charleston, WV, Nov 27, 43; f Garland Sylvester; m Kathleen Margaret Webb; w Beverly Ann Lukemire; chdn Rachel Elizabeth, Kathryn Ashley, Nathan Edward Lee; NorC 61-63, AA; GASoC 63-65, 68-69, BS; CBS 74-75, cert, 75-77, MDiv; L Jul 9, 77, CentGA Pby; O Feb 12, 78, CentGA Pby; p First P Ch, Waynesboro, GA, 78-79; srp Covenant P Ch, Warner Robins, GA, 79-; Chap USAFR, 81-04 (ret); Chap Houston Med Ctr, 85-; actv dty, Desert Storm, 91; Air Command and Staff College, 92; active duty, Operation Enduring Freedom, 01-02; actv duty Operation Iraqui Freedom, 03-04

428 Lake Front Drive, Warner Robins, GA 31088-4080 – 478-923-5850   Central Georgia
E-mail: rjarrett43@cox.net
Covenant Presbyterian Church – 478-929-4770

Jarstfer, Daniel J. – b Lansing, MI, May 9, 59; f Gary Jaynes; m Marjorie Ellen Catey; w Donna Kay Manning, Leesburg, FL, Jun 1, 79; chdn Derek, Danelle, Dorothy, Deborah; Three Riv Tech 92-94, AS; ECTSU 94-96, BS; GPTS 97-03, MDiv; L Jul 98, Cal Pby; L Jul 00, CentCar Pby; O May 26, 02, CentCar Pby; p BPC, Concord, NC, 02-04; p Dickenson First P Ch, Haysi, VA, 06-15; p Big Ridge P Ch, Haysi, VA, 06-11; srp Christ Our Hope P Ch, Wakefield, RI, 15-

11 Clearview Drive, Richmond, RI 02892 – 401-601-0076   Southern New England
E-mail: rhode.island.preacher@gmail.com
Christ Our Hope Presbyterian Church – 401-789-8007

Jasin, Jacob – O Nov 23, 14, Evan Pby; astp Briarwood P Ch, Birmingham, AL, 14-18; campm RUF, 18-

Jasso, Trey – w Alaina; ascp New Life P Ch, La Mesa, CA, 13-

5333 Lake Murray Boulevard, LaMesa, CA 91942   South Coast
E-mail: treyjasso@newlifelamesa.org
New Life Presbyterian Church – 619-667-5999

Jea, Joshua Suk Ho – b Kyung Buk, Korea, Jul 6, 51; f Sung Gi; m Ma Thew Lee; w Sarah HyunSim Choi, Seoul, Feb 26, 76; chdn David; LibBC 83, ThB; STS 73-74; RTS 83-85, MCE, 86, MDiv; O Dec 1, 85; op FWB Int Comm Ch Msn, Ft. Walton Beach, FL, 86-; op, ev Panama City Korean Ch, Panama City, FL, 90-93

705 Overbrook Drive, Fort Walton Beach, FL 32548 – 850-244-5770   Korean Southeastern
E-mail: JoshuaJea@Yahoo.com
FWB International Community Church Mission – 850-244-0691

Jeantet, Steve – w Kim; chdn Jeremiah, Charis, Rachel, Micah; RTSFL 07, MDiv; ECol 18, PhD; Recd PCA Nov 9, 10, SWFL Pby; astp Covenant Life P Ch, Sarasota, FL, 10-; diss "Considering a Relationship Between Moral Disengagement, Faith Maturity and Organizational Commitment: An Empirical Study of PCA Churches in Florida"

4099 Green Tree Avenue, Sarasota, FL 34233 – 302-824-6496   Suncoast Florida
E-mail: steve@covenantlifepca.com
Covenant Life Presbyterian Church – 941-926-4777

Jeffares, Russell – b Marietta, GA, Jun 26, 74; f Larry; m Janice Terri Touchberry; w Amanda Karyn Chandler, Aug 8, 02; chdn Ashton, Knox, Watts; TFBC 98, BA; CBS 08; O Jul 25, 10, NFL Pby; astp Pinewood P Ch, Middleburg, FL, 10- 15; op Vintage Gr Ch, Orange Park, FL, 15-

3312 Village Oaks Lane, Orange Park, FL 32065 – 901-326-2448   North Florida
E-mail: russell@vintagegrace.church
Vintage Grace Church

Jefferson, Donald Lee – b Omaha, NE, Feb 22, 47; f Don; m Rose Kovarik; w Mary Kay Svanda, Omaha, NE, Dec 28, 73; chdn Jenelle Nicole, Marc Thomas; UNE 65-69, BA; UCO; CTS 82-85, MDiv; L Sept 84, Siouxl Pby; O Nov 85, St. Louis pby; op Redeemer P Ch, Columbia, MO, 85-91, p 91-08; hr 10

1900 Shearer Road, Kansas City, KS 66106 – 417-986-0131   Missouri
E-mail: don70jefferson@gmail.com
HR

Jeffes, Ryan Stewart – b Flint, MI, Sept 26, 72; w Jennifer Nightingale, Lecanto, FL, Jun 16, 95; chdn Madeline, Jane, Eleanor Anne; ClrCC, BA; RTSFL 99, MDiv; O May 26, 02, CentFLPby; astp Seven Rivers P Ch, Lecanto, FL, 99-03; op Redeemer P Msn, Inverness, FL, 04-

919 West Massachusetts Street, Hernando, FL 34442 – 352-527-1686   Central Florida
Redeemer Presbyterian Mission – 352-726-0077

Jelgerhuis, Ross – O Jan 12, 17, NFL Pby; astp Christ Comm Ch, Gainesville, FL, 17-

5731 NW 29th Street, Gainesville, FL 32653 – 616-510-9449   North Florida
E-mail: rjelgerhuis@christcommunitychurch.com
Christ Community Church – 352-379-4949

Jenkins, Jeffrey Dale – b Sweetwater, TN, Apr 24, 70; f Wilburn D. (Butch); m Linda Kay Fisher; w Lisa Michelle Dunn, Sweetwater, TN, Jun 26, 93; chdn Wesley, Grant, Abby, Brook; KgC 92, BA; UT 94, MA; RTS 00, MDiv; O Jan 01, TNVal Pby; p West Hills P Ch, Harriman, TN, 01-

115 Circle Drive, Harriman, TN 37748 – 865-590-0007   Tennessee Valley
E-mail: harrimanpc@juno.com
West Hills Presbyterian Church – 865-882-6640

Jennings, Christopher Stephen – b Lima, OH, Sept 14, 76; f Richard James; m Martha Coleman; w Nicole Christine, St. Louis, MO, May 30, 03; chdn Samuel David, Thomas Elijah, Caroline Wicker, Claire Alethea, Matthew James, John Christopher, Amelia Jane; GrinC 98, BA; CTS 02, MDiv, 04, MAC; O Oct 23, 05, CentGA Pby; astp St. Andrews P Ch, Midland, GA, 05-11; Chap UK Good Samaritan Hospital, Lexington, KY, 12-15; Chap NEGA Med Center, Braselton, GA, 15-16; Chap NEGA Med Center, Gainesville, GA, 16-

7039 Tree House Way, Flowery Branch, GA 30542 – 859-327-0147   Georgia Foothills
E-mail: Christopher.s.jennings@gmail.com

Jennings, John Nelson – b Murfreesboro, TN, Nov 30, 57; f John Elber; m Marjorie Nelson; w Kathy Teachout, Nashville, TN, May 16, 81; chdn Elizabeth Mae, Anna Louise, Wendy Kathryn; VandU 80, BA; CTS 85, MDiv; UEdin 95, PhD; L Sept 84; O Oct 85, TNVal Pby; mis MTW, Japan, 85-99; asst prof TokCU, 96-99; assoc prof CTS, 99-07; prof CTS, 08-11; President, Presbyterian Mission International, 02-11; assoc dir Overseas Ministries Study Center, 11-13; exec dir OMSC, 13-15; mission pastor-consultant, international liaison, Onnuri Comm Ch, Seoul, 15-; Editor, *Global Missiology*, 18-; *God the Real Superpower: Rethinking Our Role in Missions*, 07; *Theology in Japan: Takakura Tokutaro, 1885-1934*, 05; co-auth *Philosophical Theology in East-West Dialogue*, 00; art "Christianity and Other Non-western Religions," 01; "Suburban Evangelical Individualism: Syncretism, (Harvie) Conn-textualization, or Something Else," 06; "Iranian–Shi'a–Muslim and U.S.–Reformed–Christian Interreligious Dialogue," 05; "The Tapestry of Contextualization," 03; "Missions in Asia," 08; "Christ-Centered Missions," 06; "God's Zeal for His World," 08; "Is America a Mission Field?" 08; "Paul in Japan: a Fresh Reading of Romans and Galatians," 08; "A Missional Theology of the Glory of God," 10; trans. Presbyterian Church in Japan "Official Statement Concerning War," 02; Editor, *Missiology: An International Review*, 08-11; assoc ed *International Bulletin of Missionary Research (IBMR)*, 11-13; editor IBMR, 13-15; "The Diety of Christ for Missions, World Religions, and Pluralism," 11; "Who Did They Say That He Is? Four Hopeful and Suffering Generations of Japanese-Reformed Christologies," 11

185 Wintergreen Avenue, Hamden, CT 06514 – 203-931-5757   Southern New England
E-mail: jnelsonjennings@gmail.com
Onnuri Community Church, Seoul

Jennings, Richard Lewis – b Pulaski, VA, Sept 4, 45; f William G.; m Roberta Baker; w Jane Chumbley, Belspring, VA, Dec 27, 69; chdn David Benjamin, Joseph Matthew, Stephen Titus, Jonathan Seth, Thomas Nathanael, Dorothy Ann; KgC 71, BA; RTS 77, MDiv; O Sept 4, 77, SFL Pby; moy Lake Osborne Continuing P Ch, Lake Worth, FL, 77-80; p First Ch, Louisville, KY, 80-84; ascp Christ P Ch, Nashville, TN, 85-92; p Faith P Ch, Goodlettsville, TN, 92-11; astp Hickory Grove P Ch, Mt. Juliet, TN, 11-

8020 Hooten Hows Road, Nashville, TN 37221-1010 – 615-275-8608 Nashville
E-mail: rljennings@bellsouth.net
Hickory Grove Presbyterian Church – 615-754-8337

Jennings, Stephen Craig – b Centralia, IL, Aug 30, 49; f Fred A.; m Evelyn A. Volkmar; w Mary E. Nelson, Port Hope, MI, Jun 13, 71; chdn Joel, Ruth, Timothy; USNA 71, BS; USNPGS 80, MS; CTS 86, MDiv; RTS 97, DMin; O Jun 11, 86, EPC; Recd PCA Oct 12, 96, GulCst Pby; p New Cov Ch, Tuscon, AZ, 86-90; p First P Ch, Atmore, AL, 90-98, wc 98-99; p Westminster P Ch, Jacksonville, FL, 99-16; p Grace Covenant Mission, Hillard, FL, 12-16; ascp Grace Community Ch, Palm Harbor, FL, 17-18; ss Cornerstone P Ch, Lutz, FL, 18-

3840 Sunrise Lane, Tarpon Springs, FL 34688 – 904-327-7599 Southwest Florida
E-mail: jsmjenn@gmail.com
Cornerstone Presbyterian Church – 813-962-3584

Jensen, Ben – O Aug 24, 14, Hrtl Pby; mis MTW, 14-

c/o MTW Heartland
PCA Mission to the World

Jensen, Peter Cochran – b Urbana, IL, May 24, 40; f Vernon P.(d); m Marjorie C. (d); w Karen Susanna Larson, Glendale, CA, Nov 26, 66; chdn Heidi Elizabeth, Hans Peter, Vernon Lars; PepU 63, BA; FTS 71, MDiv; SRegU 93, MA; L Apr 72, Phil Pby (BPC); O Jun 10, 73, Cov Pby (Ind); p Faith Bible Ch, Villanova, PA, 74-82; Chap USN, 82-94; hr

4301 West Avenue 42, Los Angeles, CA 90065-4707 – 323-982-9918 South Coast
HR

Jeon, Chul Won – Chap 17-

13938 Saddleview Drive, North Potomac, MD 20878 Potomac
E-mail: pxwmke@hotmail.com

Jeon, Jeong Koo – ob ChTS, 08-

10874 Olde Woods Way, Columbia, MD 21044 – 410-997-1276 Korean Capital
E-mail: covenantjeon@yahoo.com
Chesapeake Theological Seminary – 410-789-5242

Jeon, Paul – astp Christ Central P Ch of Washington, DC, 08-11; op NewCity Ch, Falls Church, VA, 11-18, p 18-

3903 Bradwater Street, Fairfax, VA 22031-3708 – 703-309-2523 Potomac
E-mail: psj200@gmail.com
NewCity Church – 571-213-6736

Jeon, Yohan – ob 18-

7 Gerard Avenue, Lutherville-Timonium, MD 21093 Korean Capital
E-mail: kihojeon@hanmail.net

Jeong, Jeongsu – O Oct 27, 13, KorS Pby; astp The True Light Ch of Dallas, Irving, TX, 13-

1907 Douglas Circle, Irving, TX 75062   Korean Southern
The True Light Church of Dallas – 469-522-4655

Jeong, Yongho – astp New Ch of Atlanta, Peachtree Corners, GA, 14-17

E-mail: papajoy77@gmail.com   Korean Southeastern

Jeong, Youngsu – O Apr 9, 13, KorSE Pby; p Korean Cornerstone P Ch of Jacksonville, Jacksonville, FL, 13-

109 North Torwood Drive, Saint Johns, FL 32259 – 347-387-4749   Korean Southeastern
Korean Cornerstone Presbyterian Church of Jacksonville – 347-387-4749

Jessen, Stephen Charles – Recd PCA Jan 26, 16, CatVal Pby; astp First P Ch, Stanley, NC, 16-18, p 18-

1522 Kellys Landing Drive, Mt. Holly, NC 28120   Catawba Valley
E-mail: steve@fpcstanley.org
First Presbyterian Church – 704-263-4275

Jessup, James – astp Friendly Hills P Ch, Jamestown, NC, 08-16; astp Lakeside P Ch, Southlake, TX, 16- 18, ascp 18-

4541 Dragonfly Way, Fort Worth, TX 76244 – 336-887-3011   North Texas
E-mail: Jamesjessup@gmail.com
Lakeside Presbyterian Church – 817-431-0151

Jessup, Mark William – O 18, SEAL Pby; astp First P Ch, Brewton, AL, 18-

107 Pine Street, Brewton, AL 36426   Southeast Alabama
First Presbyterian Church – 251-867-5395

Jett, Calvin Churchill – b Batesville, AK, Feb 1, 49; f William Baker; m Billie Frances Churchill; w Susan Perry Sartelle, Bristol, VA, Nov 26, 70; chdn Anna Saxon, Samuel Pendleton, Grace Munson, Mary Prentis; KgC 67-71, BA; RTS 71-74, MDiv; HBI 93, DD; L Jul 7, 74; O Jul 7, 74, Catawba Pby (ARP); p Bethany Ch (ARP), Clover, SC, 74-77; p Calvin Ch, Marion, NC, 77-82; srp Story Mem P Ch, Marion, NC, 82-03; mis MTW, 03-14; p Memorial P Ch, Elizabethton, TN, 14-18; hr 18

12 Taylor Ridge Court, Johnson City, TN 37601 – 828-527-8016   Western Carolina
E-mail: calvinjett79@gmail.com
HR

Jewell, Elwin E. – b Woodland, MI, Jul 8, 39; f David W.; m Laurie Murphy; w Carol J. Pennington, West Grove, PA, Jun 11, 66; chdn Tiffany, Elwin E. Jr.; UDE 73-75; LincU 78, BA; PhilTS 73, MDiv; L 79; O 80, RPCES; p Faith P Ch, Northfield, NJ, 80-

320 North Cambridge Avenue, Ventnor City, NJ 08406-1727 – 609-822-5098   New Jersey
E-mail: ejewell@verizon.net
Faith Presbyterian Church – 609-822-8179

Jhu, Christopher – O Mar 6, 16, NYS Pby; op Christ Central Buffalo, Buffalo, NY, 16-17, p 17-

351 Charlesgate Circle, East Amherst, NY 14051 – 716-255-5408   New York State
E-mail: Chris@christcentralbuffalo.com
Christ Central Buffalo – 716-255-5408

MINISTERIAL DIRECTORY

Jimenez, Jaime – astp Christ the King P Ch, Houston, TX, 17-

Christ the King Presbyterian Church – 713-892-5464   Houston Metro

Jimenez, Jamid – b Manizales, Colombia, Jan 4, 63; f Pedro Pablo; m Laura Ariztizabal; w Pilar Robledo, Cali, Colombia; chdn Sebastian, Samuel; MINTS 06, BATS, 10, MATS; astp Granada P Ch, Coral Gables, FL, 08-

950 University Drive, Coral Gables, FL 33134 – 305-661-2103   South Florida
E-mail: jamid@granadapca.org
Granada Presbyterian Church – 305-444-8435

Jin, Hansoo – O Jun 2, 13, KorCap Pby; astp Calvary P Ch, Towson, MD, 13- 14; astp Abbott Mem P Ch, Baltimore, MD, 14-17; astp Harvest P Ch, Clarksville, MD, 17- 18; op Harris Creek Comm Ch, Baltimore, MD, 18-

3418 E Pratt Street, Baltimore, MD 21224   Korean Capital
E-mail: hansoo@harriscreekchurch.com
Harris Creek Community Church

Jin, William Yong T. – O NGA Pby; op Open Door Comm Ch, Suwanee, GA, 95, p 95-98, wc 98-03; sc KorE Pby, 04-08; ob Bethel Ch

2059 Crescent Moon Court, Woodstock, MD 21163   Korean Capital
E-mail: williamyongjin@gmail.com

Jo, Sungho – ob admin Briarwood P Ch, Asian ministries, Birmingham, AL, 98-

2200 Briarwood Way, Birmingham, AL 35243 – 205-985-9643   Korean Southeastern
Briarwood Presbyterian Church – 205-776-5200

Johnson, Alan Henington – w Barbara Ann Bingham, Hattiesburg, MS, Oct 15, 88; chdn Caleb Henington, Rebekah Bingham; USM 86, BA; RTS 91, MDiv; L Jan 25, 92; O Aug 9, 92, Cal Pby; astp Westminster P Ch, Clinton, SC, 91-95; p Old Peachtree P Ch, Duluth, GA, 95-

4730 Glen Level Drive, Sugar Hill, GA 30518 – 678-315-3696   Georgia Foothills
E-mail: alan@oldpeachtree.org
Old Peachtree Presbyterian Church – 770-476-7945

Johnson, Ande – campm RUF, UCFL, 10-14; RUF, LSU, 14-

232 Kenwood Avenue, Baton Rouge, LA 70806   Southern Louisiana
E-mail: ajohnson@ruf.org
PCA Reformed University Fellowship

Johnson, Arnold Carson – b Scottsboro, AL, Feb 25, 44; f Arnold W.; m Esther Mae; w Barbara Elaine Brooks, Chestnut Mtn, GA, Dec 27, 75; chdn Nathan Arnold, Stephen Brooks; MarI 64, AS; UAL 70, BS; RTS 82, MDiv; O Jan 82, NGA Pby; Chap USN, Norfolk, VA, 82; Chap USS South Carolina, 82-84; Chap NDRC, NAS, Miramar, San Diego, CA, 84-87; Chap Okinawa, Japan, 87-89, wc 89; Chap NAVRESCTR, Atlanta, GA, 90-92; p Bullock Creek P Ch, Sharon, SC, 91-96; Chap 4th MAINT BN, Charlotte, NC, 92-95; p Harvest P Ch, Jacksonville, NC, 96-98; Chap VTU 0711, Wilmington, NC, 96; Chap Onslow Hospice, 98-02; p Lebanon P Ch, Abbeville, SC, 02-12; Chap NR VTU 0702G, Augusta, GA, 02-12; hr 12

1008 Walini Way, Sevierville, TN 37876 – 865-453-2948   Calvary
E-mail: ajohnson24@wctel.net
HR

Johnson, C. Todd – b Columbus, OH, Sept 25, 68; f Owen; m Joyce; w Laura Lee Downer, Fairfax, VA, Mar 23, 91; chdn Maddie, Kate, Anna; UVA 90, BS; RTSFL 01, MDiv; O May 15, 11, BlRdg Pby; staff CCC, 90-10; int Trinity P Ch, Charlottesville, VA, 10-11, astp 11-; op Hope P Ch, Crozet, VA, 12-

5524 Summerdean Road, Crozet, VA 22932 – 434-823-4148　　　　　　　　　　Blue Ridge
E-mail: todd.johnson@hopecrozet.org
Trinity Presbyterian Church – 434-977-3700
Hope Presbyterian Church – 434-409-4634

Johnson, Carter Allred – b St. Louis, MO, Oct 28, 56; f Joe Breese Sr.; m Elizabeth Allred; w Gale Christine Stahl, Knoxville, TN, Aug 18, 84; chdn Benjamin Allred, Evan Breese, Nathan Carter; SArC 74-76; UT 78-81, BS; CBS 84, MDiv, 85, MEd; ColGS 86, MA; L Sept 82, TNVal Pby; O Dec 85, CentGA Pby; ap Westminster P Ch, Martinez, GA, 85-89; ap St. Andrews P Ch, Columbia, SC, 89-91; op Westminster P Ch, Dayton, TN, 91-95, p 95-

672 Pine Hill Drive, Dayton, TN 37321 – 423-775-3385　　　　　　　　　　Tennessee Valley
Westminster Presbyterian Church – 423-775-0879

Johnson, Charles – O 14, MO Pby; astp Covenant P Ch, St. Louis, MO, 14-15; astp Christ Comm Ch, Franklin, TN, 15-17, ascp 17-

3208 Dark Woods Drive, Franklin, TN 37064　　　　　　　　　　　　　　Nashville
E-mail: charles.johnson@christcommunity.org
Christ Community Church – 615-468-2200

Johnson, Dennis Edward – b Los Angeles, CA, Mar 19, 48; f Ralph E.; m Barbara K.; w Jane Doreen McChesney, Santa Barbara, CA, Jun 14, 70; chdn Eric, Christina (Jones), Peter, Laurie (Gates); WestC 70, BA; WTS 73, MDiv, 77, ThM; FulTS 84, PhD; O Oct 12, 73, OPC; Recd PCA Sept 19, 92, SoCst Pby; p Grace OPC, Fair Lawn, NJ, 73-76; p Beverly OPC, Los Angeles, CA, 76-81; asst prof WSCAL, 82-84, assoc prof 84-00, AcadDn 83-87, AcadDn 91-97; ascp New Life P Ch, Escondido, CA, 92-18; prof WSCAL, 00-18; AcadDn 03-09; *The Message of Acts in the History of Redemption*, 97; *Triumph of the Lamb*, 01; *Let's Study Acts*, 03; *Him We Proclaim: Preaching Christ from All the Scriptures*, 07; *Heralds of the King: Christ-Centered Sermons in the Tradition of Edmund P. Clowney*, 09; *Counsel from the Cross: Connecting Broken People to the Love of Christ* (coauth w/ Elyse M. Fitzpatrick), 09; *Philippians (Reformed Expository Commentary)*, 13; *Walking with Jesus through His Word: Discovering Christ in All the Scriptures*, 15

163 Grey Ridge Dr, Dayton, TN 37321 – 760-480-9591　　　　　　　　　　South Coast
E-mail: dennisejohnson48@gmail.com

Johnson, Donald Paul – w Jenny; chdn Ellie, Daphne, Delaney; MUOH 84, BS; INU 88, MBA; RTSNC 04, MDiv; CTS 17, DMin; O Jun 06, SoTX Pby; astp Christ P Ch, New Braunfels, TX, 04-08; p Hanna City P Ch, Hanna City, IL, 08-12; p Spring Valley P Ch, Roselle, IL, 12-15; wc 15-16; ss Lakeview P Ch, Vernon Hills, IL, 17-18; ob

900 High Ridge Drive, West Chicago, IL 60185 – 847-857-0345　　　　　　　Chicago Metro
E-mail: dpj1johnson@gmail.com

Johnson, Edward – b Quincy, MA, Jan 8, 31; f Hector J.; m Elsie Graham; w Lucy Lacy (d); (2) Elizabeth Thomas, Montgomery, AL, Nov 9, 85; chdn Lucy Elizabeth, Martha Frances (Caron); BelC 60, BA; WTS 60-63; REpS 64, MDiv; O Aug 2, 64, CMS Pby; p Wynndale P Ch, Terry, MS, 64-66; p Mount Salus P Ch, Clinton, MS, 66-69; ap Coral Ridge P Ch, Ft. Lauderdale, FL, 69-70; p First P Ch, Hattiesburg, MS, 70-81; p First P Ch, Montgomery, AL, 81-91; p Wynndale P Ch, Terry, MS, 92-97; hr 98

219 North Azalea Circle, Madison, MS 39110 – 334-361-9061　　　　　　　Mississippi Valley
E-mail: bibbaoj56@aol.com
HR

Johnson, Gary – b Hazelhurst, MS, Mar 29, 63; f Glen; m Nancy Craith Burton; w Linda Sofia-Margareta Wallmyr, Alingsas, Sweden, Oct 3, 92; chdn Daniel Glen-Erik, Joel Gary, Rebekah Maria, Jan Mikael; BelC, BA; RTS, MDiv; L Feb 17, 98; O Feb 17, 98, MSVal Pby; staff CCC, Athletes inAction, 84-92; mis MTW, 88-92; mis Sweden, 88-92; ydir Westminster P Ch, 96-99; tm ldr MTW-Sweden, 00-12

239 Daleshire Place, Montgomery, AL 36117   Mississippi Valley
E-mail: garyglen@bigfoot.com

Johnson, Greg – UVa 94, BS; CTS 97, MDiv; SLU 07 PhD; astp Memorial P Ch, St. Louis, MO, 03-06, ascp 06-16, srp 16-; *The World According to God: A Biblical View of Culture, Work, Science, Sex & Everything Else*, 02; Portuguese ed, 06

5539 Waterman 3S, St. Louis, MO 63112 – 314-580-1665   Missouri
E-mail: gjohnson@memorialpca.org
Memorial Presbyterian Church – 314-721-0943

Johnson, James A.C. – b Nassau, Bahamas, Jan 27, 70; f Hesketh Allen Cuthbert J.; m Dawn Elythe Noziglia; WheatC 91, BA; KTS 92-95; RTS 97, MDiv; L Oct 97; O Oct 97, SFL Pby; mov Coral Ridge P Ch, Ft. Lauderdale, FL; wc

304 SE 7th Avenue, Deerfield, FL 33441 – 954-421-2089   South Florida

Johnson, Jeremy – w Rachel Adele Rowan, Bryn Mawr, PA, May 12, 12; chdn Lydia Rose, Micah Rebble; BayU 07, BA; TEDS 10, MDiv; O Jan 31, 16, PhilMetW Pby; astp Proclamation P Ch, Bryn Mawr, PA, 16-

8 Creshire Circle, Broomall, PA 19008 – 254-717-7466   Philadelphia Metro West
E-mail: jeremy@proclamation.org
Proclamation Presbyterian Church – 610-520-9500

Johnson, John Joseph – b Brooklyn, NY, Mar 9, 50; f Jay V; m Margaret J Shaw; w Barbara J. Stanton, S. Westerlo, Jun 8, 74; chdn Gabriel Jay, Jessica Sarah, Benjamin John, Timothy Micah; URoch 72, BS; WTS 77, MDiv; HowardU 02, MD; L May 77, Phil Pby (OPC); O Nov 82, Pby of NY/N Eng (OPC); ss Ocean City (OPC), NJ, 77-79; op Cov OPC Chap, Amsterdam, NY, 79-85; op New Life P Ch, Ithaca, NY, 88-91, p 91-98; Abington Mem Hosp, 02-03; Bryn Mawr Hosp, 03-06; Indian Health Services: Navajo Nation, 06-14; hr 17

216 Aspen Lane, Lititz, PA 17543 – 505-786-4043   Southern New England
E-mail: jjj8878jjj@yahoo.com
HR

Johnson, Joseph – O Aug 14, 18, Evan Pby; campm RUF, BhamSou, 18-

705 56th Street South, Birmingham, AL 35212 – 601-573-5602   Evangel
E-mail: joe.johnson@ruf.org
PCA Reformed University Fellowship

Johnson, Josh – O Nov 13, 18, Evan Pby; astp Covenant P Ch, Birmingham, AL, 18-

Covenant Presbyterian Church – 205-871-7002   Evangel

Johnson, R. Parker – b Oct 1, 84; f Paul; m Katherine; w Kristy Kirkpatrick; chdn Thomas Scott, Elizabeth Ann; UAL 07, BA; BDS 10, MDiv; O Nov 6, 11, SEAL Pby; astp 2Cities Ch, Montgomery, AL, 11-13; p First P Ch, Brewton, AL, 13-

114 Virginia Drive, Brewton, AL 36426   Southeast Alabama
E-mail: parker@fpcbrewton.org
First Presbyterian Church – 251-867-5395

Johnson, Robert J. – b Bethesda, MD, Oct 13, 64; f Erling G.; m Susan E. Gilkey; w Lynne M. Koller, Morristown, NJ, Jun 11, 88; chdn Bethany L., Daniel M.; JMU 87, BA; RegC 98, MA, 98, ThM; L Jan 9, 99, TNVal Pby; O Jan 24, 99, TNVal Pby; astp, mout Hixson P Ch, Hixson, TN, 98-99, ascp 00-04, srp 04-

8141 Richland Drive, Hixson, TN 37343 – 423-847-1479   Tennessee Valley
E-mail: robertj@hixsonpres.org
Hixson Presbyterian Church – 423-875-0616

Johnson, Ryan – astp Perimeter Ch, Johns Creek, GA, 14-17; op New City Ch, Lawrenceville, GA, 15-17, p 17-

E-mail: ryan@newcitychurchatl.org   Metro Atlanta
New City Church – 770-765-5285

Johnson, Ryan Andrew – astp Calvary P Ch, Towson, MD, 12-16; astp Cornerstone P Ch, Lexington Park, MD, 16-

45241 Coledorall Court, California, MD 20619   Potomac
E-mail: ryanandrewjohnson@gmail.com
Cornerstone Presbyterian Church – 301-862-5016

Johnson, Stephen William – b Evanston, IL, Sept 2, 54; f Edward William; m Betty Jane Bayer; w Renae Marie DeMott, Andalusia, IL, Dec 21, 82- chdn Travis Liam; UWI 72-78; RTS 92-95, MDiv; O Jul 17, 96, CentFL Pby; chp, ev MTW, Manila, Philippines, 96-03; sus

Address Unavailable   Central Florida

Johnson, Steve – b Miami, FL, Dec 18, 62; f Bruce; m Sarah Baird Johnson; w Heather Harrington; chdn Erin, Hannah, Lauren, Hunter; WKU 85, BS; O Nov 08; staff CCC, MSSU, SoMS, UAL, 86-03; astp Trinity P Ch, Tuscaloosa, AL, 03-13; srp CrossPointe Ch, Austin, TX, 13-

5703 McNeil Drive, Austin, TX 78729   South Texas
E-mail: steve@crosspointeaustin.org
CrossPointe Church – 512-249-1006

Johnson, Terry Lee – b Pasadena, CA, Apr 5, 55; f Gerald S.; m Eleanor Lewis; w Emily Evans Billings, Coral Gables, FL, May 23, 86; chdn Andrew Billings, Samuel Lewis, Sally Johnson (Girgis), Abigail Bennett, Benjamin Bancker; USCA 73-77, BA; TCE 77-79; GCTS 79-81, MDiv; ErskTS 08, DMin; O Feb 83, SFL Pby, ap 83-86; ob srp Independent P Ch, Savannah, GA, 87-; bd mbr WSCAL; ed/compiler *Trinity Psalter*; *Leading in Worship*; *The Family Worship Book*; *Reformed Worship*; *When Grace Comes Home*; *The Pastor's Public Ministry*; *When Grace Transforms*; *When Grace Comes Alive*; *The Case for Traditional Protestantism*; *The Parables of Jesus: Entering, Growing, Living & Finishing in God's Kingdom*; *Galatians: A Mentor Expository Commentary*; *Catechizing Our Children: The Whys and Hows of Teaching the Shorter Catechism Today*; *Leading in Worship*; *Adoracã Reformada: Adoracao Segundo as Escrituas* (Portuguese translation of *Reformed Worship: Worship that is According to Scripture*); *The Family Worship Book* (Chinese version); *Contemporary Worship: Thinking about Its Implication for the Church*; *Worshipping with Calvin*; *Serving with Calvin*; *The Epistles of John: A Mentor Expository Commentary*; *The Identity and Attributes of God*

110 Lee Boulevard, Savannah, GA 31405-5611 – 912-355-7668   Savannah River
E-mail: tjohnson@ipcsav.org
Independent Presbyterian Church – 912-236-3346
207 Bull Street, Savannah, GA 31401

Johnson, Thomas Kurt – b Holland, MI, Oct 11, 54; f Justin; m Leola Keene; w Leslie Pett, Holland, MI, Aug 13, 77; chdn Justin T., Heather N., Aimee L.; HopeC 77, BA; CTS 81, MDiv; UIA 87, PhD; L Jan 87; O Oct 25, 87, Siouxl Pby; op Hope Evangelical Ch, North Liberty, IA, 87-90, p 90-94; ob Global

Johnson, Thomas Kurt, continued
Seminars, 94-; Dir Comenius Institute, Prague, 04-13; VPres Research Martin Bucer European Seminary and Research Institutes, 07-; counc International Institute for Religious Freedom, 07-; vis lect/prof European Humanitarian Univ, Minsk, Belarus; t AngloAmerican U/Charles U, Prague; adv Theological Commission, World Evangelical Alliance, 12-; brd pres The Comenius Institute, Prague, 13-; Religious Freedom Ambassador to the Vatican, World Evangelical Alliance, 16-; *Natural Law Ethics: An Evangelical Proposal*, 05; *Human Rights: A Christian Primer*, 08, 2nd ed, 16; *What Difference Does the Trinity Make? A Complete Faith, Life, and Worldview*, 09; *The First Step in Missions Training: How our Neighbors are Wrestling with God's General Revelation*, 14; *Christian Ethics in Secular Cultures*, 14; co-auth *Creation Care and Loving our Neighbors*, 16

IICS, Box 12147, Overland Park, KS 66282-2147 – 011-422-3600   Heartland
E-mail: johnson.thomas.k@gmail.com
Global Seminars

Johnson, William David – b Palo Alto, CA, Jun 28, 52; f Ralph R Jr.; m Anita Louise Silfies; w Gale Ilene Mottram, Shippensburg, PA, Sept 25, 82; chdn Rachael Anna, Nathanael Redington, Kyria Lindsey, William Luke; NyC 80, BA; WTS 84, MAR, 85, MDiv; CTS 11, DMin; L 85; O 85, Phil Pby; mis MTW, France, 85-97; ss Christ's Comm Ch, Williamsport, PA, 97, op 97-99, p 99-07; ob Chap Geisinger Med Cent, Danville, PA, 08-09; ob Chap LIFE-Pittsburgh, Pittsburgh, PA, 09- 15; astp City Ref P Ch, Pittsburgh, PA, 14-16; ob mis PEF, France, 16-

2I de Couserans-Perisse, Lorp-Sentaraille 09109 FRANCE   Pittsburgh
E-mail: famillejohnson@yahoo.com
Presbyterian Evangelistic Fellowship

Johnston, Benjamin Charles – b Dallas, TX, Dec 16, 57; f Wendell; m Martha Lamb; w Sheri Snipes, Clovis, NM, Dec 27, 81; chdn Taylor, Katherine, Christine; WmTynC, BBE; DTS, MA, ThM, DMin; Recd PCA Jul 24, 93, NoIL Pby; p Galveston Bible Evang Free Ch, 86-93; astp Grace P Ch, Peoria, IL, 93-00, srp 00-12

4032 Lawngate Drive, Dallas, TX 75287   Northern Illinois

Johnston, E. Scott – b New Castle, PA, Oct 16, 56; f Warren C.; m Dorothy M.; w Sandra Akin, Erie, PA, Jun 25, 83; chdn Annie Elise, Seth Andrew; GroCC 74-78, BA; GCTS 78-81; RPTS 84-86, MDiv; CTS 02-09, (ABD) DMin; L Jun 86; O Jun 87, Asc Pby; campm CCO, Pitts and Indiana, PA, 81-84; op Kiski Valley P Ch, Leechburg, PA, 87-89, p 89-91; op New Life P Ch, Harrison City, PA, 91-95, p 95-00; ascp Westminster P Ch, Lancaster, PA, 00-05; op Living Hope P Msn, Lititz, PA, 05-07; srp 07-11; ip Meadowcroft P Ch, West Chester, PA, 12-13; ip, North Country Bible Fell, Speculator, NY, 14; ob Chap, Willow Valley Comm, Willow Street, PA, 15-

522 Magnolia Drive, Lititz, PA 17543 – 717-481-7790   Susquehanna Valley
E-mail: johnston5683@gmail.com
Willow Valley Communities

Johnston, John Edward – b Ft. Leavenworth, KS, Jun 6, 53; f Wm Franklin; m Elizabeth Ann Walker (d); w Mary Ellen Perkins, Jul 4, 87; chdn Christina Marie, Sarah Elizabeth; UVA 75, BA; GSU 78, MEd; CTS 82, MDiv; KSU 96, PhD; O Oct 24, 82, DMV Pby, ap 82-83; ap Inverness P Ch, Baltimore, MD, 83-84; Chap USAR, (active duty) 84-87, 83-95, ob couns 95-; Chap USAR, Ft. Lewis, WA, 98-; "Predictive Factors Regarding Extra-Marital Relationships in Ministers," PhD diss

906 Tacoma Avenue North, Tacoma, WA 98403-2927 – 253-272-3131   Pacific Northwest
E-mail: johnsje@dshs.wa.gov
United States Army Reserve – 253-582-1502

Johnston, P. Quentin – w Pam; WhTS, MDiv, DMin, PhD; ascp Edinburgh City Fellowship, Scotland, 77-91; ascp Tampa Cov Ch, Tampa, FL, 92-95; ascp, cop Church of Christian Liberty, Arlington

Johnston, P. Quentin, continued
Heights, IL, 95-00; AcadDn Whitefield College, Lakeland, 00-08; astp Tampa Bay P Ch, Tampa, FL, 04-08; princ Chamberlain-Hunt Mil Acad, Port Gibson, MS, 08-13; headm Whitefield Academy, Kansas City, MO, 13-

10748 West Bridlespur Terrace, Kansas City, MO 64114 – 601-529-8411 Southwest Florida
E-mail: quentin.johnston@gmail.com
Whitefield Academy, Kansas City, MO

Johnston, Ralph – w Lisa; chdn Elizabeth, Matthew, Andrew; ascp East Lanier Comm Ch, Buford, GA, 06-07; astp Perimeter Ch, Johns Creek, GA, 07-11; op GracePointe Ch of Forsyth, Cumming, GA, 08-11, p 11-

8712 Timber Walk Cove, Gainesville, GA 30506 Metro Atlanta
E-mail: ralph@gracepointeforsyth.org
GracePointe Church of Forsyth – 770-530-2714

Joiner, Paul – b Royal Oak, MI, Mar 5, 72; f Donald W.; m Catherine Ann Stevens; w Jill Paige Elliott, Columbia, TN, Sept 10, 94; chdn Samuel Owen, Sarah Grace, Karalynn Hope; RTSFL 96-99, MDiv; L Aug 99, SWFL Pby; O Aug 99, SWFL Pby; campm RUM, FLSoC, 99-08; cop Zion P Ch, Columbia, TN, 08-09 srp 09-

2322 Zion Road, Columbia, TN 38401 – 931-381-1272 Nashville
E-mail: psjoiner@gmail.com
Zion Presbyterian Church – 931-381-1272

Joines, Greg – O Oct 5, 12, PacNW Pby, chp 12-14; op Christ Central P Ch, Corvallis, OR, 14-

6700 NE Pettibone Drive, Corvallis, OR 97330-9678 – 503-358-2164 Pacific Northwest
E-mail: greg.joines@gmail.com
Christ Central Presbyterian Church

Jolliffe, Ben – O Mar 30, 14, Ecan Pby; op Resurrection Ch, Ottawa, 14-

126 Sherbrooke Avenue, Ottawa, ON K1Y 1R9 CANADA – 613-402-0079 Eastern Canada
E-mail: ben@resurrectionchurch.ca
Resurrection Church – 613-402-0079

Jolly, Robert – O Aug 12, 12, Palm Pby; p Sardinia P Ch, Sardinia, SC, 12-

1446 Garland Road, Gable, SC 29051 Pee Dee
E-mail: robertjolly_1999@yahoo.com
Sardinia Presbyterian Church – 803-473-4329

Jon, Stephen – astp First Korean P Ch, Glenview, IL, 17-

1350 Longacre Lane, Wheeling, IL 60090 Korean Central
E-mail: stephenjon@gmail.com
First Korean Presbyterian Church – 847-299-1776

Jones, Adam Andrew – b Dallas, TX, Nov 28, 62; f Lloyd A.; m Dee Shelton; w Anne Elisabeth Clark, Dallas, TX, Jun 18, 88; chdn Sarah Elisabeth, Samuel Adam, Sashika Grace; TXA&M 87; DTS; RTS 99, MDiv; O Aug 27, 00, CentFL Pby; astp, yp Seven Rivers P Ch, Lecanto, FL, 99-

2630 West Antioch, Lecanto, FL 34461 – 352-746-3615 Central Florida
E-mail: adam@sevenrivers.org
Seven Rivers Presbyterian Church – 352-746-6200

Jones, Bradley – mis Serge, North Africa, 10-

c/o 399 Hunters Blind Drive, Columbia, SC 29212   Palmetto
E-mail: bradandapril@psmail.net
Serge
101 West Avenue #305, Jenkintown, PA 19046-2039

Jones, Bradley – ascp Westm Chapel, Lethbridge, AB, 10-13; p Woodgreen P Ch, Calgary, AB, 14-

97 Somerset Circle SW, Calgary, AB T2Y 3P7 – 403-970-5052   Western Canada
E-mail: Brad.Jones@woodgreenpca.org
Woodgreen Presbyterian Church – 403-251-4855

Jones, Charles Andrew III – b Nov 20, 81; w Janel, Aug 7, 04; chdn Timothy, Evangeline, Lainey, Hannah Gayle; AU 04, BA; SEBTS 07, MDiv; O Jul 17, 09, Ecar Pby; Chap USN, 09- 14; astp First P Ch, Gulfport, MS, 14-16; p Forreston Grove Ch, Forreston, IL, 16-

7250 North Freeport Road, Freeport, IL 61030 – 815-291-2123   Northern Illinois
E-mail: candrewjones@gmail.com
Forreston Grove Church – 815-938-3605

Jones, Darrell Eli – O Aug 19, 18, Nash Pby; astp Southpointe Comm Ch, Nolensville, TN, 18-

192 Mountainhigh Drive, Cane Ridge, TN 37013   Nashville
E-mail: darrell.eli.jones@gmail.com
Southpointe Community Church – 615-746-7722

Jones, David Andrew – b Birmingham, AL, Oct 11, 76; f Lawrence Walter; m Gay Nell Benson; w Leah Heleena Honea, Aug 10, 96; chdn Emma L'abri, Eliot Benson, Daniel McCheyne; The Master's 98, BA; RTS 04, MDiv; O Jul 04, Ecar Pby; ydir Valley P Ch, North Hills, CA, 97-98; DCE Smyrna P Ch, Smyrna, GA, 99-01; int First P Ch, Crystal Springs, MS, 01-04; astp Peace P Ch, Cary, NC, 04-05, ascp 05-07; srp 07-12; sc ECar Pby 09-12; wc 12; ob 13-15, wc 15-

115 Roundtree Court, Flintstone, GA 30724 – 919-601-1439   Eastern Carolina
E-mail: toandyjones@gmail.com

Jones, David H. – campm RUF, Stanford, 03-13; op Grace P Ch of Silicon Valley, Palo Alto, CA, 13-15, p 16-

221 Leland Avenue, Menlo Park, CA 94025 – 650-324-3352   Northern California
E-mail: dhjones74@gmail.com
Grace Presbyterian Church of Silicon Valley – 650-326-7737

Jones, Donald C. – b Huntsville, AL, Nov 12, 59; f J. D. Jr. Carter; w Kelly; chdn Anna, Piper; UAL 82, BA; GCTS 85, MDiv; L Jul 86; O May 87, NGA Pby; int Briarwood P Ch, Birmingham, AL, 84; ob YL, CCC, 79-82; p Kings Chapel P Ch, Carrollton, GA, 86-11

209 Lakewood Drive, Carrollton, GA 30117 – 770-846-6598   Northwest Georgia
E-mail: donaldcarterjones@yahoo.com

Jones, James Abbott Jr. – b Bristol, VA, Aug 15, 50; f James Abbott; m Nancy Jane Hodge; w Deborah Karen Conner (d), Lakeland, FL, Mar 1, 73; chdn Sarah Elizabeth, Lydia Ruth; KgC 68-72, BA; RTS 72-75, MDiv; GPTS 93-94, ThM, 94-98, ThD; L Apr 19, 75; O Jul 19, 75, Westm Pby; mis France, 75-80; p Asbury P Ch, Johnson City, TN, 81-86; p Oakland Rd P Ch, Lawrenceville, GA, 86-88; p Dickenson First P Ch, Haysi, VA, 88-97; Chap BSA, 91-97; Chap Sons of Conf Vets Camp 1573, 92-95;

Jones, James Abbott Jr., continued
Chap Sons of Conf Vets Camp 1863, 95-97; p Bethel P Ch, Lake Charles, LA, 97-05; sc LA Pby, 99-03; 08-11; ss DeRidder P Ch, DeRidder, LA, 05-06; p 06-; chp/ev First Ref P Ch, Moss Bluff, LA, 05-; contr *The Presbyterian Advocate, The Presbyterian Witness, The Concerned Presbyterian Magazine*

518 O'Neal Street, DeRidder, LA 70634 – 337-460-9480   Southern Louisiana
E-mail: pastor@deridderpresbyterian.org
DeRidder Presbyterian Church – 337-462-3911
First Reformed Presbyterian Church

Jones, James Josiah – O Jun 3, 12, SavRiv Pby; p Christ Ch P, Evans, GA, 12- 17; srp Christ Comm Ch, Carmel, IN, 17-

E-mail: jjosiah78@gmail.com   Central Indiana
Christ Community Church – 317-580-9020

Jones, John F. IV – b Oklahoma City, OK, Mar 15, 69; f John F. III; m Dianna Sue Couch; w Karen Joy Carlson, Richvale, CA, Jan 9, 93; chdn John F. V, Erik Carlson, Linnea Grace; UTXSanAn 95, BA; WheatGrS 97, MA; CTS 02, MDiv; O Oct 5, 03, SW Pby; astp University P Ch, Las Cruces, NM, 03-06; srp Intown P Ch, Portland, OR, 06-08; p Faith P Ch, Anchorage, AK, 09-18; srp Covenant P Ch, Chattanooga, TN, 18-

2936 Fernleaf Lane, Chattanooga, TN 37421 – 907-250-2087   Tennessee Valley
E-mail: jjones@covenantchattanooga.org
Covenant Presbyterian Church – 423-899-5537

Jones, Jonathan Craig – b Reddish, England, Apr 11, 62; f Norman; m Sheila Jane Draper; w Tracey Anne Thomas, Camden, SC, Sept 22, 90; CBC 94, BA; RTS 97, MDiv; L Jan 20, 98, CentFL Pby; O Apr 18, 98, CentFL Pby; p Northshore P Ch, Jacksonville, FL, 98-05; ob

1420 Silver Street, Jacksonville, FL 32206 – 904-768-1551   North Florida
E-mail: yehonathan@juno.com

Jones, Justin – ascp First P Ch, Madison, MS, 10-14; astp Independent P Ch, Memphis, TN, 14-18; astp Grace Comm Ch PCA, Cordova, TN, 18-

4738 Walnut Grove Road, Memphis, TN 38117   Covenant
Grace Community Church PCA – 901-309-7848

Jones, Ken – astp Oak Mountain P Ch, Birmingham, AL, 12-

1016 Wicklow Lane, Birmingham, AL 35242   Evangel
E-mail: kjones@ompc.org
Oak Mountain Church – 205-995-9265

Jones, Larry Stephen – b Raleigh, NC, Oct 15, 60; f Charles T.; m Peggy Ruth Stephens; w Bonnie Jean Penny, Garner, NC, Mar 11, 84; chdn Carla Celeste, Hannah Brooke, Blake Stephen; TBC 90-94, ThB; GPTS 11, MDiv; L Mar 16, 96, Wcar Pby; O May 2, 99, Wcar Pby; ss Fellowship P Ch, Newport, TN, 96; ss Covenant P Ch, Waynesville, NC, 97-99, p 99-

72 Sanctuary Road, Maggie Valley, NC 28751 – 828-926-5209   Western Carolina
E-mail: pastorlsjones@att.net
Covenant Presbyterian Church – 828-456-4381

Jones, Laurie Voltz Jr. – b Lake Charles, LA, Oct 15, 43; f Laurie Voltz J. Sr.; m Margaret Black; w Jacquelyn Bell, Atlanta, GA, May 4, 68; chdn Laurie V III, Katherine Elizabeth, Julianne Kaitlin; BelC 65, BA; WTS 66; RTS 69, MDiv; CTS 87, DMin; O Feb 70, Congaree Pby; ap Covenant P Ch, Columbia

Jones, Laurie Voltz Jr., continued
SC, 69-71; p Oak Park P Ch, Montgomery, AL, 71-75; p Covenant P Ch, Houston, TX, 75-78; p Marks P Ch, Marks, MS, 78-; Dir Delta Christ Couns Cntr, 96-

3000 Highway 35 North, Enid, MS 38927 – 662-563-9179   Covenant
E-mail: laurie@markspres.org
Marks Presbyterian Church – 662-326-7227

Jones, Mark – p Faith Ref P Ch, Vancouver, BC, 07-

6457 Summit Crescent, Delta, BC V4E 2C3 CANADA – 604-598-1075   Western Canada
E-mail: mark.jones.leiden@gmail.com
Faith Reformed Presbyterian Church – 604-438-8755

Jones, Michael L. – b San Francisco, CA, Mar 4, 62; f Sterling T.; m Elizabeth C. Grimes; w Kimberly Ann Cater, Chicago, IL, Jun 22, 85; chdn Candace, Temperance, Christina, Tiara; Morehouse 80-84, BA; BhamTS 92-00, MRE; L Jul 84, Pleasant View Bapt Ch, CA; O Apr 89, Sardis Bapt Ch, B'ham, AL; Recd PCA Aug 1, 95, Evan Pby; ascp Sardis Bapt Ch, B'ham, AL, 85-95; op Harvest Comm Ch, Birmingham, AL, 95-05, p 05-

1308 Highpoint Terrace, Birmingham, AL 35235 – 205-815-3020   Evangel
E-mail: harvestcpc@aol.com
Harvest Community Church – 205-853-5033

Jones, Peter Ronald – b Liverpool, England, Nov 13, 40; f Thomas Ronald; m Ellen Shackleton; w Rebecca Clowney, Willow Grove, PA, Jan 30, 71; chdn Eowyn, Stasie, Julien, Myriam, Tessa, Zoe, Toby; UWales 63, BA; GCTS 67, MDiv; HDS 68, ThM; PTS 72, PhD; O Oct 25, 92, SoCst Pby; mis MTW, 73-91; profFLTR/Aix, 74-91; ascp North City P Ch, Poway, CA, 92-95; ob prof WSCAL, 91-; scholar-at-large, 03-; scholar-in-res; exec dir truthXchange, 03-; aascp New Life P Ch, Escondido, CA, 14-; *The Gnostic Empire Strikes Back: An Old Heresy for the New Age*, 92; *Deuxième Epitre de Paul aux Corinthiens*, 92; *Spirit Wars: Pagan Revival in Christian America*, 97; *Gospel Truth/Pagan Lies: Can You Tell the Difference?* 99; *Pagans in the Pews*, 01; *Capturing the Pagan Mind*, 03; *Cracking DaVinci's Code*, 04; *The God of Sex*, 06; *Stolen Identity*, 06; ed *On Global Wizardry: Techniques of Pagan Spirituality and a Christian Response*, 10; *One or Two: Seeing a World of Difference*, 10; *The Other Worldview: Exposing Christianity's Greatest Threat*, 15

1057 Chestnut Drive, Escondido, CA 92025 – 760-741-3750   South Coast
E-mail: prjonestx@att.net; www.truthxchange.com
truthXchange
333 South Juniper Street #214, Escondido, CA 92025 – 760-746-1346
New Life Presbyterian Church – 760-489-5714

Jones, Reid – w Kelli Myers; chdn Lucy Olive, Jordan Ivey; TrSU, BS; RTS, MDiv; O Feb 27, 11, NoCA Pby; astp Jordan P Ch, West Jordan, UT, 11-12; campm RUF, UALHunts, 12-17; campm RUF, ClemU, 17-

8 Poplar Drive, Clemson, SC 29631-1828   Calvary
E-mail: reid.jones@ruf.org
PCA Reformed University Fellowship

Jones, Richard L. – b Pasadena, TX, Aug 20, 52; f Edgar W.; m Velma Rex; w Dayna Lynn Darr, Aug 23, 76; chdn Anna E., Aaron C., Ian A.; SWTU, BS; UHou, MA; SWBTS; L Apr 91; O Apr 29, 96, SoTX Pby; p Christ P Ch, New Braunfels, TX, 91-

425 Edgewater Terrace, New Braunfels, TX 78130-6634 – 830-629-2538   South Texas
E-mail: tulips5@satx.rr.com
Christ Presbyterian Church – 830-629-0405

Jones, Ricky Dean – b Dresden, TN, May 28, 69; f Kenneth; m Bonnie Brundige; w Bianca Huth, Houston, TX, Jun 6, 92; chdn Thomas Brundige, Harold Mark, William Richard, James Isaac; VandU 91, BS; RTS 95, MDiv; L Sept 3, 95; O Feb 18, 96, Cov Pby; campm RUF, DSU, Cleveland, MS, 96-01; campm RUF, MSSU, 01-05; op, chp RiverOaks P Ch, (form Redeemer P Ch), Tulsa, OK, 05-

5150 East 101st Street, Tulsa, OK 74137　　　　　　　　　　　　　　　　　　　Hills and Plains
E-mail: rjones@riveroakstulsa.com
RiverOaks Presbyterian Church – 918-346-4850

Jones, Stephen C. – w Charity Irvine, Ephrata, PA; chdn August King, Eden Shalom, Boaz Crawford; ClemU 04, BA; CTS 09, MAC, 09, MDiv; O Oct 09, MO Pby; chp, mis WHM/Serge, Spain, 10-15; chp, mis Serge, London, 15-

c/o 404 East Main Street, Ephrata, PA 17522　　　　　　　　　　　　　　　　　　　Missouri
E-mail: stephenchristopherjones@gmail.com
Serge
101 West Avenue #305, Jenkintown, PA 19046-2039

Jones, Steve – p Westminster P Ch, Paxton, IL, 06-

318 East Center Street, Paxton, IL 60957 – 217-379-0719　　　　　　　　　　　Northern Illinois
E-mail: sjones1256@yahoo.com
Westminster Presbyterian Church – 217-379-2017

Jones, Steven E. – b Norfolk, VA, Jun 19, 52; f Robert C.; m Ruth Alice Scoblic; w Barbara Lynn Pfitzer, Virginia Beach, VA, Jun 15, 73; chdn Matthew Steven, Christopher Michael, Rebekah Lynn, Anna Katherine; CBC 73-76, BA; RTS 81-84, MDiv; L Oct 82, Gr Pby; O Oct 84, MSVal Pby; p Bailey P Ch, Bailey, MS, 84-88; p Providence P Ch, Royal Palm Beach, FL, 88-90; astp Lake Osborne Continuing P Ch, Lake Worth, FL, 90-00, ascp 00-01; srp Westminster P Ch, Valdosta, GA, 01-06; ss Providence P Ch, Murphy, NC, 06-07; p Carthage P Ch, Carthage, MS, 09-11; op Shore P Msn, Painter, VA, 13-

PO Box 91, Wachapreague, VA 23480-0091 – 757-787-4238　　　　　　　　　　　　　Heritage
E-mail: parson_sej@yahoo.com
Shore Presbyterian Mission – 757-787-3306

Jones, Thomas F. – b Jerseyville, IL, Apr 26, 36; f Frederick T.; m Mary A. Holder; w (1) Jeannette L. Walker, (dv), (2) Reidun M. Knaust, Waterloo, IL, Aug 24, 85; chdn Bradley T, Kristina R, Jon A; SIU 61, BA; CTS 65, BD; UGA 73, MA; L 65, Midw Pby (RPCES); O 65, So Pby (RPCES); p Reformed P Ch, Lookout Mountain, GA, 65-72; p Concord P Ch, Waterloo, IL, 73-76; ev Ill Pby, 77-80; op Immanuel Ref P Ch, Belleville, IL, 82-86, p 86-89; ob VP Fresh Start Seminars, Paoli, PA, 90-96; ob Dir Fresh Start Midwest, Manchester, MO, 96-09; staff Twin Oaks P Ch, p couns, Ballwin, MO, 00-11; hr 09; *Sex & Love When You're Single Again*; *The Single-Again Handbook*, 93

405 Palmer Road, Columbia, IL 62236 – 618-281-6779　　　　　　　　　　　　　　　Illiana
HR

Jones, Victor Allan Jr. – b Bethesda, MD, Jan 25, 48; f Victor Allan Sr.; m Dorothy Simpson Wedding; w Patricia Rogers (dv); chdn Brian Timothy, Bradley Allan, Stephen Christopher, Traci Rebecca; MJC 66-68; UMD 68-70, BA; FulTS 70-74, MDiv; O May 28, 78, CentGA Pby; mis Italy Gem, 74-77; ap First P Ch, Augusta, GA, 77-79; p Fifth Street P Ch, Tyler, TX, 79-83; p Calvary P Ch, Greenville, SC, 83-89, wc 90-95; ob admin Perimeter Ministries, Atlanta, GA, 95-; Ivy Creek Ch, coord small grp min, Lawrenceville, GA; p Reedy River P Ch, Conestee, SC

12 Boyce Avenue #1315, Greenville, SC 29601　　　　　　　　　　　　　　　　　　Calvary
Perimeter Ministries

MINISTERIAL DIRECTORY

Jones, W. Jeremy – b Jackson, MS, Jan 21, 71; f Walter R.; m Gerry Wilson; w Mary Maylon Jackson, Hattiesburg, MS, Jun 19, 93; chdn Isaac Walker, Lucy Hollis, Nathaniel Jackson, Irene Fairley; UMS 89-93, BA; CTS 93-96, MDiv; L May 97; O Oct 27, 96, Gr Pby; campm RUF, USM, 96-00; campm RUF, Emory, 00-05; ev, op Redeemer P Msn, Memphis, TN, 06-12; astp Independent P Ch, Memphis, TN, 12-

1274 Sledge Avenue, Memphis, TN 38104-4715 – 901-289-9801   Covenant
E-mail: jjones@indepres.org
Independent Presbyterian Church – 901-685-8206

Jones, William – b Colver, PA, Dec 18, 32; f Lloyd G J; m Elizabeth Hood; w Nancy Wittenberg, Washington, DC, Aug 4, 56; chdn David Lloyd, Julia Ann; DCC 60, BS; UTSVA 63, BD; LRTS 84, DMin; O Jun 23, 63, Pot Pby; p Brentsville Ch, Bristow, VA, 63-66; p Inverness P Ch, Baltimore, MD, 67-75; op High Point, NC, 76-77; p Oaklawn P Ch, Houston, TX, 77-78; p Inverness P Ch, Baltimore, MD, 78-00; hr 00

4878 Brightleaf Court, Baltimore, MD 21237 – 410-931-4514   Chesapeake
E-mail: williamjones32@comcast.net
HR

Joo, Gene – Recd PCA Sept 8, 15, KorNE Pby, astp Exilic Ch, New York, NY, 15-

448 Washington Avenue Fl 2, Cliffside Park, NJ 07010   Korean Northeastern
E-mail: gene@exilicchurch.com
Exilic Church – 917-705-0048

Joo, Kyung Ro – O Oct 5, 98, KorCap Pby; astp Korean Central P Ch of Wash, Vienna, VA, 98-04; p Harrisonburg Korean P Ch, 04-; *365 Daily Devotions* (Korean); *Holy War* (Korean)

5082 Swartz Road, Maurertown, VA 22644 – 540-436-8654   Korean Capital
Harrisonburg Korean Presbyterian Church

Joo, Young Ho – b Seoul, Feb 10, 48; Maua Inst of Tech, Brazil 78, BS; CapBS 96, MDiv, 97, ThM; O Apr 7, 97, KorCap Pby; astp Korean Central P Ch of Wash, Vienna, VA, 97-05; p Washington Bible Ch, Gaithersburg, MD, 05-10; wc 10-

Address Unavailable   Korean Capital

Jordan, David Barrett – b Rock Hill, SC, Mar 2, 69; f David; m Carol McWhorter; w Judith Marjorie Bovee, Lake Wylie, SC, Oct 12, 96; chdn Alley Frances, Jeremiah David, Caroline Grace; SamU 91, BA; RTS 98, MDiv; O Jun 28, 98, Flwsp Pby; yp Scherer Mem P Ch, Lake Wylie, SC, 96-98, astp 98-01; op Redeemer P Ch, Hurricane, WV, 01-06; p 06-

3965 Teays Valley Road, Hurricane, WV 25526   New River
E-mail: jordanclover@juno.com
Redeemer Presbyterian Church – 304-757-1197

Jordan, David C. – b Rock Hill, SC, Jun 13, 43; f Curtis D.; m Frances B. Smith; w Carol D. McWhorter, Lexington, NC, Aug 21, 65; chdn David Barrett, Timothy Noel; PfeifferC 63-67, BA; RTS 95-98, MDiv; L Sept 17, 98, Flwsp Pby; O May 16, 99, NGA Pby; p Grace P Ch, Cedartown, GA, 99-01; p Vineville P Ch, Macon, GA, 01-08; hr 14

509 Blue Crush Court, Rock Hill, SC 29732 – 478-737-4440   Central Georgia
E-mail: cmjdcj@gmail.com
HR

Jordan, Jeff – campm RUF, MSC, 08-

9 Pond Side, Jackson, MS 39211   North Texas
E-mail: jjordan@ruf.org
PCA Reformed University Fellowship

Jordan, Lewis Darwin – b Birmingham, AL, Oct 2, 51; f Charles Darwin; m Marilyn Lunell Lewis; w Wanda Kaye Calvert, Louisville, MS, Feb 25, 78; chdn Charles Calvert (Chase), Anna Kate, John Darwin; UAL 75, BMus; RTS 82, MDiv; L Oct 80, Gr Pby; O May 82, LA Pby; ss Auburn Avenue P Ch, Monroe, LA, 81-82, p 82-88; srp Main Street P Ch, Columbus, MS, 88-96; ascp Park Cities P Ch, Dallas, TX, 96-98; p Highlands P Ch, Ridgeland, MS, 98-04; p Fort Worth P Ch, Fort Worth, TX, 04-

3215 Cockrell Avenue, Ft. Worth, TX 76109　　　　　　　　　　　　　　　　　　　　North Texas
E-mail: darwin@fortworthpca.org
Fort Worth Presbyterian Church – 817-731-3300

Joseph, Thomas Taylor – b Montgomery, AL, May 30, 56; f William F. Jr.; m Florence Hall; w Peggy McDavid, Birmingham, AL, Aug 26, 78; chdn Thomas Taylor Jr., Edmund William; AU 78, BS; BhamSoC 87, MPPM; BDS 96, MDiv; L Jan 96; O Feb 2, 97, Evan Pby; ss Lake Crest P Ch, Birmingham, AL, 95-97, p 97-; sc Evan Pby, 03-15

3378 North Broken Bow Drive, Birmingham, AL 35242 – 205-991-7579　　　　　　　Evangel
E-mail: ttjoseph@charter.net; newcovenanter01@gmail.com
Lake Crest Presbyterian Church – 205-982-2807

Joseph, William (Billy) Francis III – b Montgomery, AL, Feb 6, 53; f William F. Jr.; m Peggy; w Marian Camille Smith, Jackson, MS, May 10, 75; chdn Camille (Carroll), William Francis IV; BelC 75, BA; RTS 80, MDiv; O Sept 80, War Pby; campm RUF, UAL, 80-02; ascp Riverwood P Ch, Tuscaloosa, AL, 80-94; astp First P Ch, Jackson, MS, 02-14; ss Eastwood P Ch, Montgomery, AL, 14-15, ascp 15-

3207 Jasmine Road, Montgomery, AL 36111 – 334-318-3025　　　　　　　Southeast Alabama
E-mail: jillyboseph@gmail.com
Eastwood Presbyterian Church – 334-272-3103

Jost, Lyndon Micah – b Canada, Dec 3, 86; w Lami Obaro, Apr 20, 13; chdn Naomi Olamide, Knox Ayomide; CarltonU 12, BA; UTor 15, MDiv, PhD cand; O Apr 12, 16, Ecan Pby; astp Grace Toronto Ch, Toronto, ON, 16-

211-30 Sunrise Avenue, Toronto, ON M4A 2R3 – 416-805-0311　　　　　　　　Eastern Canada
E-mail: lyndon@gracetoronto.ca
Grace Toronto Church – 416-860-0895

Joung, Sang Chul – op Yebon Ch of New York, Flushing, NY, 10-16, p 16-

197-50 C Peck Avenue #C, Fresh Meadows, NY 11365 – 917-392-7063　　　　Korean Northeastern
E-mail: scj322@yahoo.com
Yebon Church of New York – 917-392-7063

Joye, Brian Jay – astp Young Meadows P Ch, Montgomery, AL, 10-

8701 Wible Court, Montgomery, AL 36116-6618 – 334-260-9150　　　　　　Southeast Alabama
Young Meadows Presbyterian Church – 334-244-1385

Joyner, Samuel Balfour Jr. – b Anniston, AL, Oct 21, 57; f Samuel B.; m Diane Baylor Lee; w Druid Meriwether Hamrick, Charleston, SC, Jul 4, 81; chdn Samuel Balfour III, Thomas Fitzhugh, Meriwether Hammond, Melanie Hamrick; FurU 80, BA; CTS 86, MDiv; L Apr 24, 86; O Jun 28, 87, Cal Pby; campm RUM, WinC, 87-97; p Eastbridge P Ch, Mount Pleasant, SC, 97-10; astp Redeemer P Ch, Charleston, SC, 11-12; p Grace Coastal P Ch, Bluffton, SC, 12-

12 Minuteman Drive, Bluffton, SC 29910 – 843-901-3275　　　　　　　　　　　Lowcountry
E-mail: sam@gracecoastalchurch.com
Grace Coastal Presbyterian Church – 843-379-5520

MINISTERIAL DIRECTORY

Ju, Myung Shik – O Apr 10, 12, KorSE Pby; op Tampa Bay Open Ch, Tampa, FL, 12-

10647 Great Falls Lane, Tampa, FL 33647   Korean Southeastern
Tampa Bay Open Church – 813-362-4516

Jue, Jeffrey – ob prof WTS, 10-

2960 Church Road, Glenside, PA 19038 – 267-909-8387   Philadelphia
E-mail: jjue@wts.edu
Westminster Theological Seminary – 215-887-5511
P.O. Box 27009, Philadelphia, PA 19118

Juelfs, David – b San Diego, CA, Jul 14, 78; w Heather Joy Paino, Temecula, CA, Jul 1, 00; chdn Wyatt, Adelaide, Lila, Hadleigh, Finley; WheatC 00, BA; CTS 08, MDiv; O Oct 12, 08, SoCst Pby; astp Redeemer P Ch, Newport Beach, CA, 08-09, ascp 09-12; srp 12-

965 Magellan Street, Costa Mesa, CA 92626   South Coast
E-mail: davidj@redeemeroc.org
Redeemer Presbyterian Church – 949-553-2060

Juliani, Angelo J. – p New Life P Ch, Glenside, PA, 03-07; op Bridge Comm Ch, Philadelphia, PA, 07-

415 Walnut Street, Jenkintown, PA 19046-2032   Philadelphia
E-mail: ajuliani@bridgephilly.org
Bridge Community Church – 215-886-4780

Julien, John Charles – b San Francisco, CA, Aug 18, 52; f Jack Henry; m Delsie Louisa Kanen; w Michelle Lu Young, CA, Jun 29, 74; chdn Timothy, Jeffrey, Jeremy, Christopher; StanU 74, BA; WTS 78, MDiv; L Jan 15, 79; O Jun 7, 81, Pby of Phil (OPC); Recd PCA Sept 10, 88; cop New Life Ch (OPC), Jenkintown, PA, 81-84; srp New Life Ch of Phil, Philadelphia, PA, 84-18; hr 18

6208 North 6th Street, Philadelphia, PA 19126-3801 – 215-927-4552   Philadelphia
E-mail: john-julien@comcast.net
HR

Jung, Andrew Eun Yong – astp iVision Comm Ch, Pomona, CA, 08-09; p The Light of Life Ch, Los Alamitos, CA, 09-10; p Living Hope Ch, Pasadena, CA, 10-

20804 Starshine Road, Walnut, CA 91789 – 562-328-9780   Korean Southwest
E-mail: itzgd@yahoo.com
Living Hope Church – 562-328-9780

Jung, Darrell – p Swiss Evangelical Ref Ch, Hermann, MO, 12-astp New Port P Ch, Washington, MO, 14-

235 West 3rd Street, Hermann, MO 65041   Missouri
New Port Presbyterian Church – 636-239-3371

Jung, Gyuho – w Jungeun; chdn Lydia, Keren; RTSFL, MDiv; CTS, ThM; O May 11, 03, KorCent Pby; int First Korean P Ch of St. Louis, St. Ann, MO, 00-03; ob medu Living Stone Korean Presbyterian Church, 04-06; ob srp Maryland Christian Ch, 06-17; chp 17-18; wc

5155 Bordeaux Avenue, Irvine, CA 92604   Korean Capital
E-mail: pastorbible@gmail.com

Jung, Hyun Jin –

1730 Starboard Pt., Schaumburg, IL 60194   Korean Central
E-mail: denver7@naver.com

Jung, Jaewoo – p 15-

E-mail: n435jjw@nate.com   Korean Northeastern

Jung, Jaymes – mis

2300 James M Wood Boulevard #201, Los Angeles, CA 90006   Korean Southwest
E-mail: jaymesjung@gmail.com

Jung, Jin Eun – p Korean Sarang P Ch of Knoxville, TN, 15-

1540 Robinson Rd, Knoxville, TN 37923   Korean Southeastern
E-mail: jesusl0v2@gmail.com
Korean Sarang Presbyterian Church of Knoxville

Jung, Joo Hwoan –

E-mail: jubbong58@gmail.com   Korean Central

Jung, Joshua Inwon – srp Korean Saints P Ch, Warminster, PA, 15-

804 Long Meadow Drive, Chalfont, PA 18914 – 267-467-5965   Korean Eastern
E-mail: joshij3927@gmail.com
Korean Saints Presbyterian Church – 215-674-1133

Jung, Yohan – p Savior P Ch, Great Neck, NY, 17-

Savior Presbyterian Church – 718-673-6448   Korean Northeastern

Jung, Yun Hyo –

E-mail: jyhjung@msn.com   Korean Central

Jussely, David Hatten – b Hattiesburg, MS, Mar 8, 49; f Rev Edward A.; m Winnie Hatten; w Andrea Herring, Hattiesburg, MS, Aug 13, 72; chdn Joshua David, Daniel Herring, Jonathan Newton, Carrie Jeanne; USM 71, BS; RTS 74, MDiv; USM 97, PhD; O Jul 21, 74, Gr Pby; p Bethany, Hoyte Mem & Thomson Chs, 74-77; p Second P Ch, Yazoo City, MS, 77-85; p Woodland P Ch, Hattiesburg, MS, 85-95; Chap Forrest Gen Hosp, 95-96; ob prof RTS, 99-; ascp First P Ch, Hattiesburg, MS, 14-

109 Greenwood Place, Hattiesburg, MS 39402   Grace
E-mail: jusselys@netdoor.com
Reformed Theological Seminary – 601-923-1600
5422 Clinton Boulevard, Jackson, MS 39209
First Presbyterian Church – 601-268-0303

Jussely, James Stephen – b Decatur, GA, Apr 29, 52; f Edward Armstrong (d); m Winnie Hatten; w Mary Carol Smith, Hattiesburg, MS, May 28, 83; chdn Thomas Aaron, Adam Armstrong (d), Catherine Ellen, Mary Claire; USM 74, BS; RTS 82, MDiv, 97, DMin; L Oct 82; O Jan 83, Gr Pby; ap First P Ch, Hattiesburg, MS, 82-85; p Rainbow P Ch, Rainbow City, AL, 85-89; p Alta Woods P Ch, Jackson, MS, 89-96; p Lakeland P Ch, Brandon, MS, 96-

29 Crossgates Drive, Brandon, MS 39042-2604 – 601-212-0534   Mississippi Valley
E-mail: drswonder@gmail.com
Lakeland Presbyterian Church – 601-992-2448

Kadiri, Bolawole O. – b Nigeria, Oct 1, 60; f Kadiri; m Esther Reuben; w Janet Joseph Abiodun, Kaduna, Nigeria, Jul 27, 87; chdn Folasade, Bola-B, Tosin; VictoryC 81, dipl; ImoU 89; DynamicSem 92; L Mar 10, 01, Phil Pby; L Mar 10, 01, Phil Pby; Nigeria, 89-94; Germany, 94-97; CMA, 99-00; chp Philadelphia, PA, 01-02, ev 03-; *Ultimate Appointment* (booklets)

7609 Brentwood Avenue, Philadelphia, PA 19101 – 215-871-0179   Philadelphia

Kady, Joel – astp Redeemer P Ch East Side, New York, NY, 18-

660 Fort Washington Avenue, Apt. 6F, New York, NY 10040   Metropolitan New York
E-mail: joel.kady@redeemer.com
Redeemer Presbyterian Church East Side

Kahan, Devin – O May 15, 16, MSVal Pby; astp Highlands P Ch, Ridgeland, MS, 16-

116 Cypress Drive, Madison, MS 39110   Mississippi Valley
E-mail: devin@highlandspca.org
Highlands Presbyterian Church – 601-853-0646

Kalberkamp, Carl H. Jr. – b Pittsburgh, PA, Mar 15, 57; f Carl H; m Constance Atwell; w Jeanette Kay Santschi, Pittsburgh, PA, Jun 28, 80; chdn Allyson Rebecca, Ryan Christian, Amy Katherine; AllC, BS; WTS, MDiv; L Oct 84; O May 1, 88, Palm Pby; DCE Lexington P Ch, Lexington, SC, 90-94, astp 88-90, ascp 90-94; srp Pear Orchard P Ch, Ridgeland, MS, 94-

627 Wendover Way, Ridgeland, MS 39157 – 601-605-9419   Mississippi Valley
E-mail: carl@pearorchard.org
Pear Orchard Presbyterian Church – 601-956-3283

Kalehoff, Richard – w Barbara; chdn Richard II, Aubrey, Jonathan, Allison; astp, mfam Coral Ridge P Ch, Ft. Lauderdale, FL, 04-17; hr 17

5891 NE 22 Avenue, Ft. Lauderdale, FL 33308 – 954-491-5891   South Florida
HR

Kalfa, Paul – b Cold Spring, NY, Apr 28, 67; f Emanoil; m Efseviya Psaridi; w Lisa Michelle Cropenbaker, Brooksville, FL, Sept 28, 91; USF 91, BA; RTS 97, MDiv; O Nov 18, 01, CentFL Pby; astp Seven Rivers P Ch, Lecanto, FL, 01-08; t Seven Rivers CS, 99-08; p New Hope Christian Ch, Monsey, NY, 08-09; p Cross Creek P Ch, Jacksonville, FL, 11-17

505 Royal Stewart Court, St. John's, FL 32259   North Florida

Kalinovsky, Vitaly – b Bishkek, Kyrgyzstan, Sept 5, 78; f Peter; m Galena; w Marina; chdn Anna, Peter; ImmTheoInst, Kyrg 00, BA, 05, MA; Recd PCA 11, Phil Pby; Immanuel Theo Inst, Kyrgyzstan, 05-08; ascp Immanuel P Ch, Kyrgyzstan, 05-10; ev, op Rock of Israel Messianic Congregation, Glenside, PA, 11-

1998 Ambassador Street, Philadelphia, PA 19115 – 267-239-1086   Philadelphia
E-mail: roipca@gmail.com
Rock of Israel Messianic Congregation – 215-576-7425

Kallioinen, Dylan – wc

340 SE 8th Street, Pompano Beach, FL 33060   South Florida

Kang, Bo Hyung – b Seoul, Sept 18, 57; f Young Sun; m Cha Su Kim; w Sook Cha Jong, Seoul, Aug 15, 78; chdn Na Hee, Yee Hee; ChShC 81, BA, 83, MA; ChShTS 87, MDiv; L 87, PCKorea; O 88, Nam Seoul pby; srp Eden Korean P Ch, Castro Valley, CA, 98-13; *Labor, Blessing or Curse?* 98

Address Unavailable   Korean Northwest

Kang, Dae Sung – astp Inland Korean P Ch, Pomona, CA, 09-15

No 40, Taoyuan Road Zhenxing Gi, Dandong City, Liaoning Province, CHINA Korean Southwest
E-mail: daesungkang001592@gmail.com

Kang, Daniel – w Ruth; chdn Joy, Danny; FulTS, MDiv; O Apr 17, 01, mis 02-

Address Unavailable Korean Southwest

Kang, Daniel Dukhee – Chap 03-

95-696 Makaiolani Street, Mililani, HI 96789 – 704-572-9740 Central Carolina
E-mail: daniel.d.kang.mil@mail.mil
United States Army

Kang, Daniel M. – astp Koinos Flwsp Ch, Burke, VA, 08-11; ob astp Koinos Young Saeng P Ch, Centreville, VA, 11-

25029 Riding Center Drive, South Riding, VA 22015 – 571-435-0706 Korean Capital
E-mail: danieljdsn@gmail.com
Koinos Young Saeng Presbyterian Church, Centreville, VA

Kang, David –

104 East Tomaras Avenue, Savoy, IL 61874 Korean Central
E-mail: davidkang@cfchome.org

Kang, David Seidae – b Korea, Jun 4, 43; f Duck Song; m Bong Whan Choi; w Helen Heenyoung Lee, Seoul, Korea, Apr 28, 73; chdn Stephen Kyung Jin, Timothy Sejin, Joseph Daejin; SNU 63-67, BS; GATS 69-71; ErskTS 73-75, MDiv; PTS 75-77, ThM; L Oct 75; O May 76, MidAtl Pby; p Kor Central Ch of NJ, 76-81; p Immanuel Kor Ch, Queens, NY, 81-84; p Agape Kor Ch, Berkeley Heights, NJ, 84-90; p Phila Soh Mang P Ch, Ambler, PA, 90-97; p Gospel P Ch, Parsippany, NJ, 97-13; hr 13

51 Audrey Place, Dover, NJ 07081 – 973-442-8242 Korean Northeastern
HR

Kang, Dennis – op City Light Ch, Los Angeles, CA, 10-

City Light Church Pacific

Kang, In-Duk – b Wonsan, Korea, Dec 18, 28; f Pilsung; m Ji Sung Kim; w Su Hae Lee, Seoul, Kor, Jun 7, 56; chdn James W; Ruth J (Kwak); Chung-Ang Univ, Seoul, Korea 48-52, BA, 52-54, MA; MTS 69, MDiv; O Oct 22, 72; srp First Korean P Ch, Chicago, IL, 94-95, p em 95-; hr 95

13720 Saint Andrews Drive, M-1 #46 F, Seal Beach, CA 90740 – 562-794-9089 Korean Central
HR

Kang, James J. – astp Evergreen Comm Ch, Mt. Prospect, IL, 99-02

5420 South East View Park #3, Chicago, IL 60615 – 773-955-3728 Korean Central

Kang, Joo Young – b Ulsan, South Korea, Feb 3, 78; f Dong Suk; m Cha Yeon Kim; w Yu Yeon Choi, Buena Park, CA, Jul 28, 07; chdn Isaac, Noah, Elizabeth; KosU 00, BA; WSCAL 10, MDiv; TEDS 15, ThM; O Sept 20, 11, KAPC; Recd PCA 16, KorNW Pby; int New Life Msn Ch of Buena Park, Buena Park, CA, 06-08; CollD Cerritos P Ch, 09-13; astp Vineyard P Ch, Elmhurst, IL, 13-16; srp New Morning Korean Ch, Pullman, WA, 16-

1955 NW Canyon View Drive, Pullman, WA 99163 Korean Northwest
E-mail: kang@newmorningkc.org
New Morning Korean Church – 509-592-9660

Kang, Joon Won – b Korea, Oct 24, 40; f Tae Sun; m Dae Ya Lee; w Young Bae Cheng, Seoul, Korea, Apr 24, 64; chdn Dong Hee, Duk Hee; DKU 63-72, DMin; KorPTS 80-84; L Sept 17, 86; O Sept 27, 89, Kor Pby (Seoul); Recd PCA Oct 92, KorSE Pby; ev, op Korean Bethel P Ch, Fayetteville, NC, 89-95, p 95-99; op, ev Columbia P Msn, Columbia, SC, 99- 14; p All Nations P Msn Ch, Rock Hill, SC, 15-

701 Scaleybark Road, Charlotte, NC 28209   Korean Southeastern
E-mail: cpmckang@gmail.com
All Nations Presbyterian Mission Church – 704-340-6611

Kang, Kenneth – p Hawaii Korean Central P Ch, Honolulu, HI, 13-

3516 Pilikino Street, Honolulu, HI 96822 – 808-988-9206   Korean Northwest
E-mail: kensarahk@yahoo.com
Hawaii Korean Central Presbyterian Church

Kang, Nam Hyun – astp Myung Sung P Msn, Norcross, GA, 07-

2790 Northcliff Drive, Suwanee, GA 30024   Korean Southeastern
Myung Sung Presbyterian Mission

Kang, Sam Dong Suk – b Seoul, Korea, Sept 19, 80; f Jong Kang; m Hyo Sook Lee; w Peggy Ahn, Silver Spring, MD, Apr 15, 09; chdn Elijah Hyun, micah Min; GMCUVA, BA; RTS, MDiv; O May 22, 16, KorCap Pby; ob Rothem Risen Sun P Ch, Springfield, VA, 16-

25549 Feltre Terrace, Chantilly, VA 20152   Korean Capital
Rothem Risen Sun Presbyterian Church, Springfield, VA

Kang, Sam Yongho – b Korea, Nov 27, 34; f Koum Kyu; m Yun Ji Kim; w Youg Soon Ko, Korea, Mar 23, 45; chdn Sung Wun, In Kyung, Sung Min; PGATCS 61-62, 67-69; L Sept 24, 71, KPC; O Oct 15, 72, RPC Kor; Recd PCA Apr 13, 93, KorSE Pby; astp Ku-Am P Ch, 60-66; astp Pyng Ne P Ch, 67-70; Soon Chun Ka Kock P Ch, 71-74; Seoul Sadang First P Ch, 75-82; Han Sung P Ch, Los Angeles, 83-91; op, ev First Korean P Msn, Biloxi, MS, 93-96; hr

11916 Centralia Road #102, Hawaiian Gardens, CA 90716 – 562-924-1340   Korean Southeastern
HR

Kang, Seok Joo – O May 15, 16, KorSE Pby; astp Sae Han P Ch of Atlanta, Alpharetta, GA, 16-

5440 Donehoo Court, Alpharetta, GA 30005   Korean Southeastern
E-mail: holysj@gmail.com
Sae Han Presbyterian Church of Atlanta – 770-619-5340

Kang, Shin Sok – mis 10-

2340 Nash Circle, Anchorage, AK 99508 – 201-788-3763   Korean Southern

Kang, Steve Meenho – b Seoul, May 15, 59; f Hong Kee Kang; m Nochung Kang; w Elizabeth Chu, Chicago, IL, Apr 26, 88; chdn Stephanie Eunhae; UIL 80-84, BS; TEDS 84-87, MDiv; L, KAPC; O Oct 23, 90, KAPC; Recd PCA Apr 13, 99, KorCent Pby; pEng Hebron P Ch, Chicago, IL, 88-97; srp Evergreen Comm Ch, Mt. Prospect, IL, 98-11

2811 North Windsor Drive, Arlington Heights, IL 60004 – 847-632-1672   Korean Central
E-mail: steve.kang@onebox.com

Kang, Won Shik – op Dong San P Msn, Dublin, CA, 92-05; hr

11478 Silvergate Drive, Dublin, CA 94568 – 510-833-0546   Korean Northwest
HR

Kang, Young Hoon – w Sinae Kang; chdn Kenny, Stacy; Hankook 78-81, BA; London Polytech 83-85, dipl; FulTS 92-95, MDiv; L Apr 16, 96, KorSW Pby; O Oct 12, 99, KorSW Pby; yp Valley First P Ch, 92-95; The Paul Msn Ch, Glendale, CA, 95-96; ascp Glory Christian Ch of S. California, Gardena, CA, 96-02

3239 Heather Field Drive, Hacienda Heights, CA 91745 – 626-333-0262   Korean Southwest
E-mail: kennynstacy@psmail.net

Kappers, Ben – p First Church (PCA), Lansing, IL, 14-

18533 Walter Street, Lansing, IL 60438 – 920-918-3793   Chicago Metro
E-mail: kappers.ben@gmail.com
First Church (PCA) – 708-474-9610

Kapur, Eric – astp Harbor P Ch, San Diego, CA, 11-13; ascp Redeemer P Ch of San Diego, Encinitas, CA, 13-16; p Trinity P Ch of Or Co, Orange, CA, 16-

505 N Tustin Ave 222, Santa Ana, CA 92705   South Coast
E-mail: eric@trinitypresoc.org
Trinity Presbyterian Church of Orange County – 714-515-4686

Kapusinski, Russell Edward II – b Akron, OH, Jan 27, 66; f Russell Sr. (d); m Geraldine Patsy Hale (d); w Diane Michelle Shirley, San Diego, CA, Jun 12, 93; chdn Joshua Aiden, Caleb Russell, Katherine Elizabeth; North Park C 89, BA; FulTS 89-91; WSCAL 92-94; RTSFL 97, MDiv; O Sept 6, 98, CentFL Pby; Dir YL, Canton, OH, 89-91; ydir North City P Ch, Poway, CA, 91-94; ydir Tampa Bay P Ch, Tampa, FL, 94-95; ydir St. Pauls P Ch, Orlando, FL, 95-98, astp 98-03; ascp Harbor P Ch - Chula Vista, Chula Vista, CA, 03-14; ob admin The Cambridge School, San Diego, CA

9472 Maler Road, San Diego, CA 92129   South Coast
E-mail: russ12@mac.com

Karlberg, David Lee – b Philadelphia, PA, Apr 8, 47; f Louis; m Dorothy May; w Patricia Louise Criswell, Sept 27, 75; chdn Benjamin David, Jill Elizabeth; GordC 64-67, BA; CTS 67-70, MDiv; PittsTS 70-71, grad wk; CTS 84, DMin; O Sept 72, Pitts Pby (UPCUSA); ap Homestead Ch, Homestead, PA, 72-75; op Trinity P Ch, Johnstown, PA, 75-78, srp 78-15, astp 15-

837 Coon Ridge Road, Johnstown, PA 15905-5207 – 814-288-5124   Pittsburgh
E-mail: pastordlkarlberg@msn.com
Trinity Presbyterian Church – 814-269-3947

Karlberg, Paul L. – b Philadelphia, PA, Nov 17, 49; f Leo; m Florence Newkirk; w Patricia A. Redmond, Mt. Laurel, NJ, May 25, 85; chdn Drew Paul, Rachel Aletta; TempU 71, BA; WTS 75, MDiv; L Dec 6, 75; O Jun 11, 76, CentGA Pby; p Providence P Ch, Savannah, GA, 76-78; p Ref P Ch, King of Prussia, PA, 78-81; p Beechwood Comm Ref P Ch, Havertown, PA, 83-98; astp Proclamation P Ch, Bryn Mawr, PA, 98-00, ascp 00-11; ob City Lights, 12-16; hr 16; *A Christian Vision and The Power of the Word*

124 Tee Drive, Maidsville, WV 26541   Philadelphia Metro West
E-mail: pkarl2006@icloud.com
HR

Kastensmidt, Sam – O Aug 23, 15, SFL Pby; astp Rio Vista Comm Ch, Ft. Lauderdale, FL, 15-

Rio Vista Community Church – 954-522-2518   South Florida

Katches, Daniel Peter – b San Francisco, CA, May 29, 64; f Ernest Pete; m Julie Marie Stanasich; w Bonnie Jean Bruce, Long Beach, CA, Sept 9, 88; chdn Rebekah, Caleb, Daniel, Jonathan, Hannah,

Katches, Daniel Peter, continued
Gabriel; SJSU 87, BS; ChTS 00, MATS; L Oct 2, 99, NoCA Pby; O Mar 9, 01, NoCA Pby; p Covenant P Ch, Paso Robles, CA, 01-

2115 Kit Fox Lane, Paso Robles, CA 93446 – 805-237-1207   Northern California
E-mail: dan@covenantpaso.com
Covenant Presbyterian Church – 805-238-6927

Katumu, Josiah – O Feb 13, 14, Glfstrm Pby; astp Treasure Coast P Ch, Stuart, FL, 14; ascp Grace Ref P Ch, Relay, MD, 14-17, p 17-

135 Winters Lane, Coatesville, MD 21228   Chesapeake
E-mail: jkatumu@gmail.com
Grace Reformed Presbyterian Church – 410-247-4088

Kaufmann, Richard Paul – b Atlantic City, NJ, Mar 14, 46; f Joseph L.; m Marie Von Bosse; w Elizabeth Elmer, Egg Harbor City, NJ, Jun 24, 67; chdn Kristi, Kim, Michael; BucknU 68, BS; HarvU 72, MBA; WTS 76-82, MDiv; FulTS 94, DMin; L Mar 80, Phil Pby; O Dec 14, 80, Pby So CA (OPC); Recd PCA Feb 3, 89, SoCst Pby; srp New Life P Ch, Escondido, CA, 80-94; ascp Redeemer P Ch of New York, New York, NY, 94-99; op Harbor P Ch Downtown, San Diego, CA, 99-03, ascp 03-09; ascp Harbor P Ch Uptown, San Diego, CA, 04-09; srp Harbor P Ch, San Diego, CA, 09-14; astp Redeemer P Ch of San Diego, Encinitas, CA, 14-17; hr 17; contr articles *New Horizons*; contr *The Pastor-Evangelist*

500 West Harbor Drive #720, San Diego, CA 92101-7717 – 619-238-0372   South Coast
HR

Kavanaugh, Joel – w Corine; chdn Esther, Luke, Ruth; O 04, MSVal Pby; astp First P Ch, Belzoni, MS, 04; p Brent P Ch, Brent, AL, 04-09; astp Westminster P Ch, Johnson City, TN, 09-10; ascp 10-14

1505 East 11th Avenue, Johnson City, TN 37601 – 423-557-6885   Westminster
E-mail: joelkavanaugh@gmail.com

Kay, Arthur L. – b Upland, PA, Dec 10, 27; f John McMillan; m A. Elizabeth Huston; w Barbara Joyce Fries (d), Franklinville, NJ, Mar 22, 52; chdn Linda Joyce (Eklund), George A.; David J.; Barbara J. (LeFrancois), Stephen M.; RutgU 53, BA; FTS 54; L 60; O Jun 61, NJ Pby (RPCES); p Ventnor City, NJ, 61-64; ydir nat'l RPCES, 64-65; Dir CTI (RPCES), 65-76; CovHse, Inc., Coventry, CT, 67-82; hr 85

3 Sullivan Drive, Newark, DE 19713 – 302-366-1931   Southern New England
E-mail: artkay3@gmail.com
HR

Kay, Thomas George Jr. – b Richmond, VA, Feb 23, 41; f Thomas George; m Jane Simpson Ramsey; w Connie Gibson, Fairfield, FL, Jun 20, 63; chdn Thomas George III, Timothy Gibson, Andrew Allen; PerkJC 59; BelC 62, BA; ColTS 65, MDiv; ChrBC 04, ThD; O Jul 18, 65, CMS Pby; p Rolling Fork & Friendship Chs, MS, 65-68; p St. Paul P Ch, Jackson, MS, 68-71; p First Ch, Albany, GA, 71-79; srp First P Ch, Clarksdale, MS, 79-93; p First P Ch, Aliceville, AL, 94-14; p Pleasant Ridge P Ch, Eutaw, AL, 94-; hr 15; pem First P Ch, Aliceville, AL, 16; p Central P Ch, Emelle, AL, 18-; *In the Fire*

266 Club House Drive, Aliceville, AL 35442 – 205-373-8700   Warrior
E-mail: pepsiparson@gmail.com
Pleasant Ridge Presbyterian Church
Central Presbyterian Church

Kay, Timothy Gibson – b Greenville, MS, Mar 1, 67; f Thomas G. Jr; m Connie Gibson; w Andrea Lassiter, Clarksdale, MS, Dec 18, 93; chdn Hannah Allen, Rachel Brooks, Margaret Ramsey; BelC 89,

Kay, Timothy Gibson, continued
BA; RTS 94, MDiv; O Aug 14, 94, War Pby; astp, moy Trinity P Ch, Tuscaloosa, AL, 94-99; astp Westminster P Ch, Atlanta, GA, 99-01, ascp 01-13; op Harvest P Msn, Comer, GA, 13-14; ob 17-

180 Dunwoody Drive, Athens, GA 30605 – 706-248-8385   Georgia Foothills
E-mail: tgkay24@gmail.com

Kayser, Ian – O Nov 6, 16, Cov Pby; astp Westminster P Ch, Greenwood, MS, 06-18; p Providence P Ch, Clinton, MS, 18-

407 Lindale Drive, Apt. D, Clinton, MS 39056   Mississippi Valley
E-mail: iankayser@gmail.com
Providence Presbyterian Church – 601-924-4747

Keane, Thomas Gerard Jr. – b Oceanside, NY, Sept 30, 53; f Thomas; m Dorothy Wolf; w Cathleen Ehatt, Oreland, PA, Oct 30, 76; chdn Chelsea Marie, Thomas Gerard III; SusqU 71-75; WTS 75-78, MDiv, 78-81, ThM; L Jan 89; O Jul 89, Phil Pby; astp Lansdale P Ch, Lansdale, PA, 86-89, ascp 89-99, srp 99-

429 Turnberry Way, Souderton, PA 18964 – 215-721-0170   Eastern Pennsylvania
E-mail: tom@lansdalepres.org
Lansdale Presbyterian Church – 215-368-1119

Keck, Logan – astp Christ The King P Ch, Cambridge, MA, 10-; p Christ the King JP/Roxbury, Cambridge, MA, 13-

20 Notre Dame Street, Boston, MA 02119 – 617-997-6004   Southern New England
E-mail: logan@ctkdorchester.org
Christ The King Presbyterian Church – 617-354-8341
Christ the King JP/Roxbury – 617-506-9345

Keel, Joshua – b Savannah, GA, Apr 8, 83; w Erin Griffin; chdn Jackson, Molly, Caroline; GASoC, BS; BDS 09, MDiv; astp Covenant P Ch at Little Rock, Little Rock, AR, 11-17; campm RUF, GASou, 17-

265 Surrey Lane, Statesboro, GA 30458   Savannah River
E-mail: joshua.keel@ruf.org
PCA Reformed University Fellowship

Keel, Ralph Hardy Jr. – b Huntsville, AL, Dec 6, 48; f Ralph Hardy Sr.; m Lillian Fowler; w Alice Singley, Tuscaloosa, AL, Sept 23, 72; chdn Michelle Elizabeth; UAL 72, BA; FulTS; BhamTS 98, MABS, 98, MRE; L May 11, 99; O May 23, 99, Evan Pby; astp Southwood P Ch, Huntsville, AL, 99, ascp 99-09; ob; hr 18

2728 Deford Mill Road, Hampton Cove, AL 35763 – 256-536-0670, 256-653-5494   Providence
E-mail: ralphkeel@integrity.com
HR

Keem, Henry P. H. – p Korean P Ch of Wash, 03-05; sus

Address Unavailable   Korean Capital

Keen, John Kirkland – b Miami, FL, Jul 4, 61; f Lloyd Wiggins; m Patricia Merle Hutchinson; w Diane Marie Derheimer, Orlando, FL, Jun 2, 84; chdn Katherine Marie, Jonathan Garrett, Carolyn Joy, Jacquelyn Grace; UCF 84, BA; RTS 90, MDiv; L Sept 11, 88; O May 20, 90, LA Pby; op Orleans P Ch, New Orleans, LA, 90-93, p 93-95; p Immanuel P Ch, DeLand, FL, 95-99; astp Chapelgate P Ch, Marriottsville, MD, 99-01; p First P Ch, Gadsden, AL, 01-04; p Christ Cent P Ch, Tampa, FL, 04-

11412 Paldao Road, Tampa, FL 33618 – 813-449-0376   Southwest Florida
E-mail: jkeen@christcentralpca.org
Christ Central Presbyterian Church – 813-774-3881

MINISTERIAL DIRECTORY

Keenan, Johnathan – campm RUF, UMemp, 11-16; campm RUF, UCSB, 16-

761 Dos Hermanos Road, Santa Barbara, CA 93111 Pacific
E-mail: johnathan.keenan@ruf.org
PCA Reformed University Fellowship

Keene, Tommy – b TX, Mar 8, 80; f James; m Gail Frye; w Sarah Terris Gehrmann, Greenville, SC, Mar 16, 02; chdn Emma Lee, Katherine Terris; FurU 98-02 BS; WTS 02-05 MDiv, 05-10 PhD; O Sept 25, 11, PhilMetW Pby; astp Christ the King P Ch, Conshohocken, PA, 11-15, ascp 15-18; adj prof WTS 09-18; lect RTSDC 10-18, assoc prof 18-

1833 Hilltop Road, Jenkintown, PA 19046 Philadelphia Metro West
E-mail: keenetommy@gmail.com
Reformed Theological Seminary DC

Keidel, Christian Lewis – b Baltimore, MD, Jan 15, 47; f Albert K Jr.; m Justine Lewis; w Frances Keyes, Chestnut Hill, MA, Sept 6, 69; chdn Kimberly Anne, Sarah Frances, Christian Lewis Jr; UPA 69, BA; WTS 73, MDiv; O Jul 22, 74, MidAtl Pby; p Stamford, CT, 74-76; ip Congr Chs, Haverhill, NH & Newbury, VT, 76; Dir FOCUS (Philadelphia), 76-82; ob area dir Greek Coord IVCF (Mid-Atlantic), 82-14, hr 14; p Proclamation P Ch, Bryn Mawr, PA, 14-15, astp 15-18

455 Timber Lane, Devon, PA 19333-1232 – 610-254-9222 Philadelphia Metro West
E-mail: keidel1@cs.com
HR

Keisel, Nathaniel – O Nov 2, 14, Pitts Pby; astp Murrysville Comm Ch, 14-17, chp 17; op Jeanette Ch Plant, Jeanette, PA, 17-

130 South 11th Street, Jeannette, PA 15644 – 412-215-4748 Pittsburgh
E-mail: nate@jeannettechurch.com
Jeanette Church Plant

Keith, Bryan Edward – b Roanoke, VA, Mar 4, 63; f Edward; m Virginia Seibel; w Tracey Webb, Callaway, VA, Oct 9, 93; chdn Nancy "Kelly", Virginia "Grace"; CC, BA; RTSFL, MDiv; L Nov 12, 95; O Nov 12, 95, TNVal Pby; ydir First P Ch, Ft. Oglethorpe, GA, 86-88; ydir Clairmont P Ch (PCUSA), Decatur, GA, 88-91; ydir Kissimmee Alliance (CMA), Kissimmee, FL, 92-94; ascp, yp Christ Cov P Ch, Knoxville, TN, 95-00, wc 00-01; astp Westminster P Ch, Roanoke, VA, 01-05; ss Hope P Ch, Martinsville, VA, 05-06; ascp 06-

543 Custers Ridge Road, Boones Mill, VA 24065 – 540-314-3463 Blue Ridge
E-mail: bryankeith5@gmail.com
Hope Presbyterian Church – 276-638-2050

Keithley, David – w Jennifer; chdn Peterson, Wesley, Abigail, Kathryn; WestIl, BA; CTS, MDiv; O Jul 22, 03, NoIL Pby; ascp Christ Ch, Normal, IL, 03-04; p Hanna City P Ch, Hanna City, IL, 13-; sc NoIL Pby, 03-04

324 North Lakeshore Drive, Hanna City, IL 61536 – 309-310-6302 Northern Illinois
E-mail: david@hannacitypres.org
Hanna City Presbyterian Church – 309-565-4465

Kellahan, Richard H. Jr. – b Kingstree, SC, Jul 29, 49; f Richard H Sr.; m Helen Reid Barker; w Nancy Louise Geisz, Frontenac, MO, Dec 29, 79; chdn Reid Louise, Kathleen Rose, Richard Haddon; Citadel 71, BS; FMC 74-75; RTS 80, MDiv; L Oct 81, Cal Pby; O Jun 82, Evan Pby; p First P Ch, Jasper, AL, 82-04; hr

2517 Sandy Bay Road, Kingstree, SC 29556 Evangel
E-mail: rkellahan1@sc.rr.com
HR

Keller, Josh – O May 18, 14, SoTX Pby; astp All Saints P Ch, Austin, TX, 14-

4508 Kalama Drive, Austin, TX 78749 South Texas
E-mail: jkeller@allsaintsaustin.org
All Saints Presbyterian Church – 512-732-8383

Keller, Kent L. – b Kansas City, MO, May 23, 57; f George; m Marthelle Snodgrass; w Heidi Elisabeth Ringuette, Miami, FL , Nov 16, 85; chdn Christine Hope, Andrew Joseph, Allison Savannah, Charissa Michelle; UMonte 76-78, BA, 78-79, MEd; RTSFL 89-93, MDiv; L Jan 92; O Jan 23, 94, SFL Pby; ob World Sports, Inc, Key Biscayne, FL, 94; chp, op Redeemer P Ch, Miami, FL, 94-96, p 96-02; astp Kendall P Ch, Miami, FL, 02-04, p 04-; *The Mayan Mystery*; contr *Life Application Bible for Students*; *Parents' Resource Bible*; *Life Application Bible,* commentary on Ephesians; *Youth Worker*; *Campus Life Magazine*; *The Odyssey Bible*; contr *Life Application Bible,* commentary on Luke

5840 SW 51st Terrace, Miami, FL 33155 – 305-665-2459 South Florida
E-mail: kent57@bellsouth.net
Kendall Presbyterian Church – 305-271-5262

Keller, Michael – astp Citylife P Ch of Boston, Boston, MA, 08; campm RUF, City Campus Ministry, 08-17; ascp Redeemer P Ch of New York East Side, New York, NY, 17; astp Redeemer P Ch Westside, New York, NY, 17-

160 West 87th Street Apt 1C, New York, NY 10024 Metropolitan New York
E-mail: michael.keller@redeemer.com
Redeemer Presbyterian Church Westside – 212-808-4460

Keller, Timothy James – b Allentown, PA, Sept 23, 50; f William B; m Louise A Clemente; w Kathy Louise Kristy, Monroeville, PA, Jan 4, 75; chdn David Andrew, Michael Stephen, Jonathan Daniel; BucknU 72, BA; GCTS 75, MDiv; WTS 82, DMin; O Aug 75, MidAtl Pby; p West Hopewell P Ch, Hopewell, VA, 75-84; prof WTS, 84-; Dir mercy MNA, 84-89; op Redeemer P Ch of New York, New York, NY, 89-91, srp 91-18; *Resources for Deacons* 85; *Ministries of Mercy* 89

30 River Road #5N, New York, NY 10044-1116 – 212-754-2857 Metropolitan New York
HR

Kelley, Harold O. – b Uniontown, PA, Dec 28, 36; f Eugene L.; m Verna Calhoun; w Norma L. Mackenzie, Uniontown, PA, Aug 13, 60; chdn Michael, Lisa, Scott, Sean; MaryvC 58, BA; PittsTS 61, MDiv; O Jun 15, 61, Redstone Pby (UPCUSA); Dir Klondike Larger Parish (6 chs), Uniontown, PA, 61-64; p First Ch, Carmichaels, PA, 64-67; p Greene Valley P Ch, Carmichaels, PA, 67-83; op, ev, p Trinity P Ch, New Martinsville, WV, 83-90; op Faith Ref P Ch, Wheeling, WV, 88-90; op Faith Ref P Ch, Fairmont, WV, 89-90; chmn chaplaincy advisory bd, WV penit, Moundsville, WV, 84-90; op, ev Immanuel P Ch, Shrewsbury, PA, 90-92, p 92-94; p Greene Valley P Ch, Carmichaels, PA, 94-08, hr 08; ip Trinity P Ch, New Martinsville, WV, 08-12; ip Christ Comm Church, Fairmont, WV, 12-17

180 Harts Road, Carmichaels, PA 15320 – 724-883-2160 New River
E-mail: gvpc@helicon.net
HR

Kelley, John Michael – b Minneapolis, MN, Dec 23, 50; f Francis James K.; m Helen Louise Olsen; w Mary Dana Ried, Sp30, 06; chdn Ryan Francis, Brynna Kathleen; StOlC 68-69; UMN 69-71; NCBC 73-74, BA; UniTS 74-77, MDiv; ColTS 84-89, DMin; O Dec 26, 76, UPCUSA; Recd PCA Mar 21, 92, Wcar Pby; p Reems Crk Parish, Buncombe Co, NC, 77-84; Chap Biltmore Manor Nursing Home, Asheville, NC, 84-86; Etowah P Ch, 86-89; p Sweetwater P Ch, 89-92; ob chmn Hickory Crisis Pregnancy Ctr, 90-92; p New Cov P Ch, Hickory, NC, 92-94, wc 94; p Faith P Ch, Paris, TX, 95-13; hr 13

15594 North Naegel Drive, Surprise, AZ 85374 Suncoast Florida
E-mail: jk2350@gmail.com
HR

Kelley, Ralph – b Normal, IL, Jun 4, 65; f Thomas; m Nancy; w Wendy, Columbia, SC, Jul 1, 89; chdn Scott Edward, Jonathan Andrew; CC 89, BA; RTSA 04, MAR; O Jan 15, 05, NGA Pby; dir ch rel GCP, Suwanee, GA, 00-07; astp, exp St. Andrews P Ch, Columbia, SC, 07-12; astp, execp First P Ch, Jackson, MS, 12-; *MightyToSave: A Devotional Guide for Mission Conferences*, 04

4418 East Ridge Drive, Jackson, MS 39211   Mississippi Valley
E-mail: ralphk@fpcjackson.org
First Presbyterian Church – 601-353-8316

Kelly, David R. – O 17, CentFL Pby; ascp New Hope P Ch, Eustis, FL, 17-

2756 Monte Carlo Drive, Eustis, FL 32726 – 352-250-9419   Central Florida
E-mail: dkelly@newhopepca.com
New Hope Presbyterian Church – 352-483-3833

Kelly, Douglas Floyd – b Lumberton, NC, Sept 23, 43; f Floyd Ferguson; m Lucy Martha Pate; w Caroline Anne Frances Switzer, Lumberton, NC, Sept 1, 73; chdn Douglas F. II, Martha McCrummen Fraser, Angus Robertson III, Daniel IV, Patrick Blue McMillan Campbell; UNC 61-64, BA; UFL 64-65; UTSVA 65-68, BD; UEdin 68-69, 70-73, PhD; TueU 71; O Jul 68; ap First Ch, Raeford, NC, 68-70; p First P Ch, Dillon, SC, 73-81; prof RTSNC, 83-; ss Second P Ch, Yazoo City, MS, 93-94; *If God Already Knows, Why Pray?* 89; *The Sermons of John Calvin on II Samuel - A Translation*, 92; *Preachers with Power: Four Stalwarts of the South*, 92; *Emergence of Liberty in the Modern World*, 92; *Creation and Change*, 97; *Carolina Scots*, 98; *Systematic Theology, Volume I*, 08

3313 Kelly Plantation Road, Carthage, NC 28327 – 910-947-2626   Central Carolina
E-mail: dkelly@rts.edu
Reformed Theological Seminary, NC – 704-366-5066

Kelly, Michael Francis – b St. Louis, MO, Dec 14, 61; f Joseph P; m Mary Ann DeGrandpre; w Sandra S. Klaeger, St. Louis, MO, Aug 19, 89; chdn Erin Marie, Luke Michael, Ian Farrell; StLU 86; CTS 91; L Apr 12, 92; O Apr 12, 92, GrLks Pby; astp Westminster P Ch, Muncie, IN, 92; op New Life P Ch, Yorktown, IN, 92-95, p 95; srp CrossPoint Churches, Seattle, WA, 95-14; ascp Green Lake P Ch, Seattle, WA, 14-

9011 Latona Avenue NE, Seattle, WA 98115 – 206-523-2473   Pacific Northwest
E-mail: michael@greenlakepc.org
Green Lake Presbyterian Church – 206-789-7320

Kelso, Brian Lee – b Washington, IN, Jan 10, 58; f Marlin; m Sarah; w Barbara East, Dade Cnty, FL; chdn Timothy, Robert, Caleb, Joshua; SEC 80, BA; KTS 94, MDiv; L Oct 17, 89; O May 22, 94, SFL Pby; asst St. Andrews P Ch, Hollywood, FL; p Christ Cov Ch, Southwest Ranches, FL, 94-

18274 NW 21st Street, Pembroke Pines, FL 33029 – 954-816-5813   South Florida
E-mail: brian@christcovenant.cc
Christ Covenant Church – 954-434-4500

Kemp, Jeremy – O Sept 28, 14, SWFL Pby; ascp Christ Comm P Ch, Lakeland, FL, 14-18; op Good Shepherd Msn, Bartow, FL, 18-

3170 Valley Vista Circle, Lakeland, FL 33812 – 404-422-0983   Southwest Florida
E-mail: jeremy@ccpclakeland.org
Good Shepherd Mission – 863-899-9363

Kendagor, Solomon Kiptoo – b Kenya, Sept 16, 50; f George; m Suter; w Haynes, Montreal, Canada & Kenya, Dec 5, 95; chdn Joshua, Joy, Joseph, Joanna; Kenya Highlands BC 72-74, BRE; CIU 77-81, MDiv; CTS 82-84, ThM; UMO 89-96, MEd; Recd PCA Jul 18, 95, MO Pby; ob staff ISI, 95-

2297 Fairoyal Drive, Des Peres, MO 63131 – 314-965-8696   Missouri
International Students, Inc.
2864 South Circle, Suite 600, Colorado Springs, CO 80906

Kendrick, John Justin – b Ozark, AL, Mar 21, 71; f Roy C.; m Donna Sue Harmon; w Susan Lee Bryant, Birmingham, AL, May 20, 95; chdn Emma Grace, John William, Thomas Jackson; AU 93, BS; RTSNC 98, MDiv; O Sept 19, 99, Wcar Pby; campm RUF, AppSU, 99-07; astp Mount Cal P Ch, Roebuck, SC, 07-17; op Grace P Spartanburg, Spartanburg, SC, 10-17, p 17-

235 Hillbrook Drive, Spartanburg, SC 29307 – 864-582-3567　　　　　　　　　　　　　Calvary
E-mail: justinkendrick@gmail.com
Grace Presbyterian Spartanburg – 864-576-6156

Kennedy, Ewan Peter – b Glasgow, Scotland, Aug 22, 70; f Donald; m Susanne Cameron; w Heather Leigh Padgett, Nashville, TN, Jul 31, 93; chdn Calvin, Cooper, Canon; GlasgBibC, dipl; CU, dipl; DLipsC 93-96, BA; CTS 96-00, MDiv, 96-00, MAC; L Nov 5, 00, JR Pby; O Nov 5, 00, JR Pby; CollD Christ P Ch, Nashville, TN, 94-96; campm RUF, WashU, MO, 96-98; int Old Orchard Ch, Webster Groves, MO, 98-00; astp Trinity P Ch, Norfolk, VA, 00-03; p Westminster P Ch, Elgin, IL, 03-07; p Park City P Ch, Park City, UT, 07-08; p Ch of the Redeemer, Atlanta, GA, 08-; "Anorexia Nerovsa: The Struggle for Control and the Control of the Struggle," *Career and Counselor*, 99; "Sexual Abuse, Sanctification, and the Psalms," *Christian Counselor*, 00

5185 Peachtree Dunwoody Road, Atlanta, GA 30342　　　　　　　　　　　　　　　　Metro Atlanta
E-mail: ewan@redeemeratlanta.org
Church of the Redeemer – 678-298-1150

Kennedy, Jason – b Nov 9, 72; SPU 95, BA; CTS 05, MDiv; O Feb 07, Evan Pby; astp Westminster P Ch, Huntsville, AL, 07-15; Chap Westm ChAcad, Huntsville, AL, 10-15; ob t Fellowship CS, 15-

1395 Chatley Way, Woodstock, GA 30188　　　　　　　　　　　　　　　　　　Northwest Georgia
E-mail: jasonkennedy1109@gmail.com
Fellowship Christian School

Kennison, Michael Paul – b Pittsburgh, PA, Feb 28, 54; f William J; m Beverly A. McElroy; w Kelly Jean Thompson, Feb 27, 88; chdn Michael Paul Jr., Katherine Elizabeth; GenC 76, BA; WTS 79, MAR; WTSFL 81, MDiv; CTS 12, DMin; L Oct 80; O Nov 81, SFL Pby; mis Jamaica, MiA, 82-84; mis Miami MiA, 84-88; p Redlands Comm Ch, Homestead, FL, 88-98, 98-99; astp Kirk of the Hills P Ch, St. Louis, MO, 99-03, ascp 04-

1329 Palm Ridge Court, St. Louis, MO 63146　　　　　　　　　　　　　　　　　　　Missouri
E-mail: mkennison@thekirk.og
Kirk of the Hills Presbyterian Church – 314-434-0753

Kenyon, David Russell – b Pittsburgh, PA, Aug 1, 55; f Walter Russell; m Mary Lillian Gethin; w Sheila Coddington, Margate, FL, Dec 29, 84; chdn Joshua, Daniel, Sarah, Hannah, Benjamin, Jacob; MariC 77, BS; PittsTS 78-81; RTS 81-82, MDiv; O Mar 25, 90, Asc Pby; moy Gospel Flwsp P Ch, Valencia, PA, 82-90, ascp 90-93; p Pioneer P Ch, Ligonier, PA, 93-

213 West Vincent Street, Ligonier, PA 15658 – 724-238-7146　　　　　　　　　　　　Pittsburgh
E-mail: drkenyon@verizon.net
Pioneer Presbyterian Church – 724-238-4777

Kenyon, John Paul – b Pittsburgh, PA, May 19, 60; f Walter R.; m Gethin; w Isabella Schwarz, Concord, CA, Sept 5, 92; chdn W. Ian, Anni M., Katrina J., Lindsay N., Lillian G.; CCK 82-84, BS; RPTS 94-98, MDiv; BostonU, 07-08, MST; L Oct 18, 97, Asc Pby; O Feb 14, 99, Asc Pby; astp Reformed P Ch of Slate Lick, Kittanning, PA, 99; Chap USAF, 99-16; hr 16

501 Hillside Avenue, Ligonier, PA 15658 – 575-495-3091　　　　　　　　　　　　　Pittsburgh
E-mail: flyingkenyon1s@gmail.com
HR

Kenyon, Tyler – b Rogers, AR, May 10, 85; f Allen Timothy; m Elizabeth June Burge; w Jessica Lee Mattingly, Rogers, AR, May 26, 07; chdn Joel Joshua, Luke Landon, Calvin Louis; JBU 10, BA; CTS 17, MDiv; O Jun 4, 17, Cov Pby; astp Christ P Ch of Fayette Co, Somerville, TN, 17-

270 Seawood Drive, Oakland, TN 38060 – 479-426-5206   Covenant
E-mail: tylerkenyon@gmail.com
Christ Presbyterian Church of Fayette County – 901-235-0848

Kerens, Scott – b Dec 16, 76; w Elizabeth; chdn Kate, Benjamin, Emily, William; COz 01, BA; CTS 07, MDiv; O Jan 19, 10, MO Pby; astp Twin Oaks P Ch, 10-11, wc 11-12; astp Twin Oaks P Ch, 12-15, ascp 15-18; ascp Marco P Ch, Marco Island, FL, 18-

1996 Sheffield Avenue, Marco Island, FL 34145 – 314-965-0662   Suncoast Florida
Marco Presbyterian Church – 239-394-8186

Kerhoulas, Andrew – O Oct 30, 16, SNE Pby; astp Citylife P Ch of Boston, Boston, MA, 16-

128 Garden Street #2, Cambridge, MA 02178   Southern New England
E-mail: akerhoulas@gmail.com
Citylife Presbyterian Church of Boston – 617-292-0990

Kerhoulas, Jonathan – astp Citylife P Ch of Boston, Boston, MA, 10-14; astp Redeemer P Ch of San Diego, Encinitas, CA, 14-

11230 Berryknoll Street, San Diego, CA 92126   South Coast
E-mail: highlands31@yahoo.com
Redeemer Presbyterian Church of San Diego – 760-753-2535

Kerley, Dan P. – b St. Mary's, OH, Dec 20, 63; f Horace A.; m Sidney Etta Earp; w Lesa Anne Bowersox, Leesburg, FL, Jun 7, 87; chdn Joshua Braden, Reid Aaron; USC 86, BS; RTSFL 95, MDiv; WTS 09, DMin; L Feb 25, 96; O Feb 25, 96, Asc Pby; astp Westminster P Ch, Butler, PA, 96-97; srp New Hope P Ch, Eustis, FL, 97-05; astp Westminster Ref P Ch, Suffolk, VA, 05-09; ascp 09-11; op Crosswater P Ch (Mission), Suffolk, VA, 11-13, p 13-

4804 Phoenix Drive, Chesapeake, VA 23321 – 757-923-1150   Tidewater
E-mail: dan@crosswaterpc.org
Crosswater Presbyterian Church – 757-934-2021

Kerns, Stuart Lee – b Lincoln, NE, Jun 1, 62; f Guy W.; m Valerie E. Papke; w Kelli R. Livengood, Lincoln, NE, Aug 13, 83; chdn Lindsay Kaye, Bryson William, Schyler Stuart; UNE 84, BS; CTS 91, MDiv, 09, DMin; L Jan 88, Siouxl Pby; O Aug 91, Hrtl Pby; astp Zion Ch, Lincoln, NE, 87-88, ascp 90-93, srp 93-

12670 South 25th Street, Roca, NE 68430   Platte Valley
E-mail: stu@zionpca.com
Zion Church – 402-476-2524

Kerr, Jeffrey – b Halifax, Nova Scotia, Mar 21, 84; w Katrina Joanne Starshuk, May 6, 06; chdn Elsie Colleen, Hudson Alexander, Brighton Jeffrey; BrockU 06, BA; CTS 10, MDiv; O Nov 7, 10, Wcan Pby; astp Crestwood P Ch, Edmonton, AB, 10-12; ascp 12-16, p 16-

8419 189 Street NW, Edmonton, AB T5T 4Z2 CANADA   Western Canada
E-mail: jeff@crestwoodpca.ca
Crestwood Presbyterian Church – 780-452-3020

Kerr, Matthew – O May 6, 12, SNE Pby; astp Redeemer P Ch, Concord, MA, 12-14; ascp 14-16, p 16-

16A Rivermeadow Drive, Chelmsford, MA 01824 – 978-810-5028   Southern New England
E-mail: kerrmatth@gmail.com
Redeemer Presbyterian Church – 978-254-7353

Kertland, David – b Carlisle, PA, Jun 19, 62; f Owen A. Jr.; m Lois Ann Buttorff; w Bonnie Lynne Clayton, Dresher, PA, Apr 19, 86; chdn Timothy, Hannah, Jonathan, Michael; KutzU 84, BFA; WTS 91, MDiv, 14, DMin; L May 16, 92, SusqV Pby; O Apr 11, 99, SusqV Pby; astp Trinity P Ch, Harrisburg, PA, 99-00, ascp 00-; op Hershey P Ch, Hummelstown, PA, 15-

1521 Sand Hill Road, Hummelstown, PA 17036 – 717-489-1535   Susquehanna Valley
E-mail: dkertland@trinityhbg.com; dkertland@hersheypca.com
Trinity Presbyterian Church – 717-545-4271
Hershey Presbyterian Church

Kessler, James – b Columbus, OH, Mar 25, 79; w Laura S. Childs, Anniston, AL, Aug 14, 99; USouthAL 02, BA; CTS 05, MDiv; O Jan 06, Great Lakes Pby; astp Northwest P Ch, Dublin, OH, 06-07; ascp Northwest P Ch, Dublin, OH, 07-; op New City P Ch, Hilliard, OH, 15-

3591 Lagoon Lane, Hilliard, OH 43026 – 614-850-6171   Columbus Metro
E-mail: JKessler@NPC-Dublin.org
Northwest Presbyterian Church – 614-799-2300
New City Presbyterian Church – 614-742-7885

Ketchum, Danton Boyce – b Hattiesburg, MS, Apr 4, 49; f Danton Toone K; m Mary Adams; w Alexa Runnels, Louisville, MS, Jan 24, 71; chdn James Boyce, John Dallis; UMS 71, BA; RTS 74, MDiv; Kg'sC, ThM; AberU 77-78; RTS 87, DMin; L Jan 74; O Jun 14, 74, MSVal Pby; p Shuqualak P Ch, Shuqualak, MS, 74-77; p Scooba P Ch, Scooba, MS, 76-77; p First P Ch, Indianola, MS, 78-85; op, p Christ P Ch, Denton, TX, 85-88; pres SALT Min, Denton, TX, 88; p Westminster P Ch, Gainesville, TX, 89-92; ob PalmHC, 92; DCE Transformed Life Chr Treatment Ctr, Memphis, TN, 92-95; ob couns Mem Park Funeral Home & Cemeteries, Memphis, TN, 95-16; prof BelC, Memphis ext, 97-00; Chap Memphis Funeral Homes, 99-16; prof Union U, Memphis, 02-16; *A Spiritual Warfare; A Christian Survey of Philosophy and Humanities*

229 Eastbrooke Street, Jackson, MS 39216-4716 – 615-646-9292   Covenant

Keys, Joseph Ty – b Salinas, CA, Apr 26, 63; f Joseph Harvey; m Elizabeth Lynn Crooks; w Cindy Lee, Wauchula, FL, Jul 22, 89; chdn Nicole Elizabeth, Hannah Leigh; UFL 91, BA; RTS 97, MDiv; L Apr 19, 97, CentFL Pby; O Apr 5, 98, CentFL Pby; astp Faith P Ch, Gainesville, FL, 98-09 op Grace Comm Ch, Newberry, FL, 04-09

530 SW 255th Street, Newberry, FL 32669-4910 – 352-472-9787   North Florida

Khandjian, Michael Lee – b Coral Gables, FL, Oct 2, 57; f Leo; m Marie Philibosian; w Katherine M. Snider, Nashville, TN, Jun 5, 82; chdn Kevin Lee, Emily Joyous, Erin Elizabeth; BelC 80, BA; RTS 83, MDiv; O Sept 83, SFL Pby; ap Old Cutler P Ch, Miami, FL, 83-86; srp Wildwood P Ch, Tallahassee, FL, 86-96; srp Old Cutler P Ch, Miami, FL, 96-06; srp Chapelgate P Ch, Marriottsville, MD, 06-

6040 Logans Way, Ellicott City, MD 21043   Chesapeake
E-mail: mikek@chapelgate.org
Chapelgate Presbyterian Church

Kidd, John – O Dec 3, 17, BlRdg Pby; astp Covenant P Ch, Harrisonburg, VA, 17-18, ascp 18-

Covenant Presbyterian Church – 540-433-3051   Blue Ridge

MINISTERIAL DIRECTORY

Kidd, Reggie – astp Orangewood P Ch, Maitland, FL, 04-08

Address Unavailable   Central Florida

Kiedis, Tommy – srp Spanish River P Ch, Boca Raton, FL, 10-

2400 Yamato Road, Boca Raton, FL 33431   Gulfstream
E-mail: tkiedis@spanishriver.com
Spanish River Presbyterian Church – 561-994-5000

Kieffer, David – Baltimore, MD, Apr 15, 74; w Marty; chdn Jack, Kelly, Liam, Margo, Michael; BucknU 96, BS; BibTS 03, MDiv; O Apr 10, 05, SusqV Pby; BloomsburgU lead staff, 97-01; GettysburgC lead staff, 01-15; ob tm ldr, DiscipleMakers, Mason-Dixon Region, 01-17; astp Westminster P Ch, Lancaster, PA, 17-18, ascp 18-

2634 Beechwood Rd, Lancaster, PA 17601 – 717-357-1185   Susquehanna Valley
E-mail: kieffer@westpca.com
Westminster Presbyterian Church – 717-569-2151

Kiehl, Daniel Scott – b Brookville, PA, Jun 8, 61; f George Lewis; m Verda Sarilda Cook; w Suzanne Elaine Spear, Walton, NY, May 28, 83; chdn Seth Andrew, Josiah Daniel, Leah Marie, Bethany Grace, Brandon Christopher; GenC 79-83, BS; RPTS 88, MDiv; L May 30, 87; O Apr 15, 88, RPCNA; Recd PCA Nov 14, 92, Hrtg Pby; p Rimersburg RPC, Rimersburg, PA (RPCNA), 88-90; p RPC, Shawnee, KS, 90-92; srp Meadowcroft P Ch, West Chester, 92-12; srp Oakwood P Ch, State College, PA, 12-

659 Berkshire Road, State College, PA 16803 – 814-360-4638   Susquehanna Valley
E-mail: danielskiehl@gmail.com
Oakwood Presbyterian Church – 814-238-5442

Kiewiet, David Richard – b Kalamazoo, MI, Sept 23, 48; f Isaac (d); m Nellie Goldschmeding (d); w Jan Cox, Kansas City, MO, Jul 25, 70; chdn Rachel (Lowe), Nathan, Amy (Barrow), Rebecca (Brouwer); BJU 70, BA; CTS 73, MDiv; L 72, Midw Pby; O 73, Dmv Pby (RPCES); p Calvary Ref P Ch, Hampton, VA, 73-84; ss New Life P Ch, Virginia Beach, VA, 85; ss Evang RPC, Chesapeake, VA, 85-86; mis MTW, Australia, 86-; prin West Theo C, Brisbane, Australia, 86-08; CH prof West Theo C, 08-10; chp Toowoomba, Queensland, 08-12; HMA 13-15; hr 15

31 Doranne Court SE, Smyrna, GA 30080 – 814-753-0775   Tidewater
E-mail: djkiewiet@bigpond.com.au
HR

Killeen, Edward – w Margaret; chdn Ben, Sophie, Emmett; UTulsa 87, BBA; UKS 93, BFA; CTS 00, MDiv, MAC; O 03, SNE Pby; astp Christ The King P Ch, Cambridge, MA, 01-03; p Lake Trails P Ch, Madison, WI, 04-09; ob

144 Slocum Avenue, St. Louis, MO 63119   Missouri

Killy, Scott Paul, II – Lynnette; chdn Anthony, Phoebe; O Sept 5, 10, Ohio Pby; ascp Christ the Word Ch, Toledo, OH, 10-14; op Amazing Grace, Watseka, IL, 14-

709 South 2nd Street, Watseka, IL 60970 – 815-216-8842   Northern Illinois
E-mail: skilly@amazinggracewatseka.com
Amazing Grace – 815-216-8842

Kilman, Brent R. – O Nov 27, 11, NJ Pby; astp Covenant P Ch, Cherry Hill, NJ, 11-14; astp, chp Mercy Hill P Ch, Sewell, NJ, 14-17; campm RUF, RowanU, 17-

301 Overbrook Avenue, Glassboro, NJ 08028 – 856-426-5222   New Jersey
E-mail: brent.kilman@gmail.com
PCA Reformed University Fellowship

Kilpatrick, Ronald Thomas – b Germantown, PA, Dec 22, 43; f James Nelson; m Elisabeth Rhodes Shaw; w Nancy Laverne Blewitt, Penn Hills, PA, Jun 21, 69; chdn Amy Elisabeth, Peter John, Michelle Jeannette, Jennifer Elise; WestmC 66, BA; GCTS 69, MDiv; KTS 99, DMin; L Oct 3, 69, Wheeling Pby (UPCUSA); O Sept 21, 69, Pitts Pby; p Roneys Point UP Ch, Wheeling, WV, 69-72; ap First Ch, Rome, GA, 72-80; astp Coral Ridge P Ch, Ft. Lauderdale, FL, 80-14; t WestAcad, 91-94; mgr CRM resrch, 94-14; lib KTS, 95-14; hr 14

4517 Dalmahoy Court #103, Ft. Myers, FL 33916   South Florida
E-mail: Rkilpat@aol.com
HR

   Kim, Andrew – p Cornerstone P Ch, Chalfont, PA, 16-

639 South Broad Street #R8, Lansdale, PA 19446   Korean Eastern
E-mail: akim37@gmail.com
Cornerstone Presbyterian Church – 215-412-3622

   Kim, Benson – op New Life Msn Ch of Colorado, 06-

6373 South Jackson Gap Court, Aurora, CO 80016 – 303-841-0393   Korean Southwest
E-mail: pastorbenkim@yahoo.com
New Life Mission Church of Colorado – 303-617-1005

   Kim, Byungeun Benjamin – b Chonnam, Korea, Mar 3, 61; f Mun-Bin; m Si-Sun Song; w Sin-Myung, Kwangju, Korea, Jun 18, 88; chdn Mokyang Paul, Mogin Bliss, Mokhyun Moses, Mok-Sun John, Mokyoung Gloria, Joey Mokeun, Rebekah Mokwon; CAU 87, BA; FIU 90, MHSA, 92, MPH; KTS 90-94, MDiv, 94-, DMin cand; UCEBOL 08, Hon EdD; L Apr 18, 94; O Aug 13, 95, SFL Pby; chp Han Sarang Korean Msn, Hollywood, FL, 94-01; op Han-Sarang Evangelical P Ch, Millersville, MD, 02-

496 Brampton Court, Millersville, MD 21108 – 410-987-3150   Chesapeake
E-mail: bekim111@yahoo.com
Han-Sarang Evangelical Presbyterian Church – 410-852-0999

   Kim, Chang Seh – O Jan 3, 73; Recd PCA Oct 16, 84; p Victory P Ch, Los Angeles, CA, 84-97 srp 97-04; hr

24725 Senator Avenue, Harbor City, CA 90710-2021 – 310-534-3707   Korean Southwest
E-mail: changsehkim@yahoo.com
HR

   Kim, Charles – O Apr 18, 17, KorE Pby; om KorPC of Minnesota, 17-

Korean Presbyterian Church of Minnesota   Korean Eastern

   Kim, Chong Hyup – op Chosen P Ch, 05-

9304 Nester Road, Fairfax, VA 22032 – 703-866-0965   Korean Capital
E-mail: solafida@cox.net
Chosen Presbyterian Church – 703-589-5136

   Kim, Choong Pae – p Columbia P Msn, Columbia, SC, 15-

108 Cart Way, Blythewood, SC 29016 – 704-604-3650   Korean Southeastern
E-mail: ythird@hotmail.com
Columbia Presbyterian Mission – 803-788-3043

Kim, Christian – p Petra P Ch, Northbrook, IL

989 Enfield Drive, Northbrook, IL 60062 – 847-542-2245   Korean Central
E-mail: pjinhokim@gmail.com
Petra Presbyterian Church

Kim, Cliff – astp, yp Church for All Nations, Vienna, VA, 12-

14812 Edman Road, Centreville, VA 20120   Korean Capital
E-mail: seekhim012@gmail.com
Church for All Nations – 703-573-3767

Kim, DaeGyu – O Dec 16, 18, Pot Pby; astp Cornerstone P Ch, Lexington Park, MD, 18-

114 August Lane, Lansdale, PA 19446   Potomac
E-mail: Daegyuk@gmail.com
Cornerstone Presbyterian Church – 301-862-5016

Kim, Daijoong – p Washington Zion City Ch, Vienna, VA, 11-

5819 Strem Pond Court, Centreville, VA 20120   Korean Capital
E-mail: him4him@gmail.com
Washington Zion City Church – 703-300-2067

Kim, Dan Dae Gee – b Korea, Dec 20, 45; f Byung Wan; m Kwak, Bun Y; w Lee, Young Seel, Chon-ju, Korea, Jul 18, 73; chdn John Joong-Eun, Paul Sung-Eun; TPC 68; CTS 76, ThM; FTSSWM 85, MA, DMiss; L May 79; O Mar 20, 80, RPCES; p Los Angeles Hanmi Ch, Glendale, CA, coord 84-95; p Sung Yahk P Ch, 90-91; op Sung Kwang P Msn, Doraville, GA, 95-12; hr 12; *Major Factors Conditioning the Acculturation of Korean-Americans With Respect to the PCA and Its Missionary Obedience*

1410 Charing Cross Way, Lawrenceville, GA 30045 – 678-377-9094   Metro Atlanta
E-mail: daykeykim@gmail.com
HR

Kim, Daniel – srp Ark Msn Ch, Carmichael, CA, 15-

3344 Oak Stream Court, Carmichael, CA 95608 – 916-913-1061   Korean Northwest
E-mail: solomonyk@hotmail.com
Ark Mission Church – 916-482-8800

Kim, Daniel – O May 21, 17, KorSE Pby; astp Korean Cov P Ch, Marietta, GA, 17-

2620 North Berkeley Lake Road NW, Duluth, GA 30096   Korean Southeastern
E-mail: myongjin81@gmail.com
Korean Covenant Presbyterian Church – 770-565-4777

Kim, Daniel Bunshik – b Inchon, Kor, May 3, 48; f Kyu Haing; m Young Hee Kim; w Grace Hae Sook Jung, Seoul, Dec 8, 79; chdn Esther K, Timothy C; KKU 70, BA; CCM 87-90; BibTS 94, MDiv; L Apr 5, 94, KorE Pby; O Apr 11, 95, KorE Pby; astp Korean Saints P Ch, Warminster, PA, 88-95; wc 95; srp Korean Open Door Ch, Lansdale, PA, 96-15

254 Hampshire Drive, Sellersville, PA 18960 – 215-258-1237   Korean Eastern

Kim, Daniel Daesoon – b Korea, Nov 20, 64; f Sun Jung; m Dong Ok Chun; w Song Suk Kim, Los Angeles, CA, Jun 29, 91; chdn Joshua, Hannah; UCLA 87, BS; TalTS 93, MDiv, 94, ThM; L Apr 25, 95; O May 19, 96, KorSW Pby; astp Sa Rang Comm Ch, Anaheim, CA, 88-08; mis, OMF Intnatl

729 South Hobart Boulevard #4, Los Angeles, CA 90005   Korean Southwest Orange County
E-mail: daniel2song@yahoo.com
OMF International

Kim, Daniel Jeesung – Recd PCA Oct 15, 94, KorSW Pby; ob p Global Mission Ch, 97-

13506 Francesca Court, Chino, CA 91710 – 909-628-3564　　　　　　Korean Southwest
E-mail: pastordanielkim@yahoo.com
Global Mission Church – 909-396-4441

Kim, Daniel Lee – b Korea, Jan 8, 71; f Jung W. Kim; m Soon Kyo Lee; w Tammy Jhun, Wayne, NJ, Jul 26, 97; chdn Joseph, Noelle, Jonathan; WesleyanU 88-91, BA; CIT 91-93, BS; TEDS 93-96, MDiv, 04, ThM, 06, PhD; L Apr 6, 98, KorCap Pby; O Apr 5, 99, KorCap Pby; yp McLean Korean P Ch, McLean, VA, 97-99, astp 99; mis Thailand, 99-05; prof CTS, 06-14; prof ITC 14-16; prof, Dean ITC 16-

Jl. Jimbaran Golf no 38, Taman Mediteranean Golf　　　　　　Korean Central
Lippo Karawaci Tangerang 15811 INDONESIA

Kim, Daniel Penn – O Jul 11, 10, KorE Pby; ob Korean United Ch of Phil, Philadelphia, PA, 10-16; ob Korean Central Ch of Pittsburgh, PA, 16-

1135 Foxhill Drive #210, Monroeville, PA 15416 – 412-687-7775　　　　　　Korean Eastern
E-mail: dpk777@gmail.com
Korean Central Church of Pittsburgh

Kim, Daniel S. – b Seoul, Korea, Dec 16, 64; f Kisung Kim; m Kyesoon Shin; w Jongsun Lee, Flushing, NY, Jun 9, 90; chdn Christian, Charissa, Caleb; Vassar 87, BA; BibTS 90, MDiv, 92, STM; O Oct 92, KAPC; Recd PCA May 99, Phil Pby; yp KAPC, Queens, NY, 87-92; srp Davis Korean Ch, 92-99; srp Korean United Ch of Phil, Philadelphia, PA, 99-04; srp Sa Rang Comm Ch, Anaheim, CA, 04-11

2137 Northam Drive, Fullerton, CA 92833 – 714-674-0191　　　　　　Korean Southwest

Kim, Daniel Soung Gu – ob 15-

90 Byron Avenue, Yonkers, NY 10704 – 646-763-4411　　　　　　Korean Eastern
E-mail: stars9@gmail.com

Kim, Daniel Yun Jin – b Seoul, Korea, Jan 16, 61; f Tae-dong; m Yang-Soon L; w Ju Yun D, Seoul, Kor, Jan 28, 84; chdn Su-Won, Hye Won; THTS 78-83, ThB; UGST 87-89; CBS 89-92, MDiv; RTS 95, DMiss; L Sept 20, 85; O Oct 16, 86, Kung-In Pby, PCKor; op First Korean P Ch (msn), Columbia, SC, 90-93; ob prof THTS, 96-98; Chap USAR, 98-00; Chap USArmy, 00-; trans into Korean *The Baptism with Holy Spirit*, by R. A. Torrey, 83; *Introduction to Missiology*, 95; *Biblical Mission*, 96

Address Unavailable　　　　　　Korean Southeastern
E-mail: yjshkkim@aol.com
United States Army

Kim, David H. – UPA, BA; WTS, MDiv; PTS, ThM; O Jan 25, 03, MNY Pby; ob campm, Chap Manna Christian Fellowship, 04-

175 West 87th Street, Apt. 17A, New York, NY 10024 – 609-731-3511　　　　　　Metropolitan New York
E-mail: dhkim@princeton.edu
Manna Christian Fellowship

Kim, David Jikwang – O Jul 25, 10, KorE Pby; astp Emmanuel Ch in Phil, 10-18; astp Grace Ch PCA, Dover, DE, 18-

167 Jacks Way, Camden, DE 19934 – 215-939-6050　　　　　　Heritage
E-mail: davidjkkim@hotmail.com
Grace Church PCA – 302-734-8150

MINISTERIAL DIRECTORY

Kim, David Kwang – b Seoul, Korea, Aug 27, 62; f Eun Soo Kim; m Ock Soon Moon; w Hye Kyung Kim, Seoul, Jan 27, 87; chdn Jonathan, Daniel; SNU 89, BFA; TEDS 98, MDiv; L Apr 12, 98, KorCent Pby; O Oct 13, 98, KorCent Pby; tentmaker, China, 91-94; yp Sung Min P Ch, Chicago, IL, 96-98; mp Christlike Ch, Korea, 98-03; op His Loving Ch, Arlington Heights, IL, 03-05; Gloria Msn Ch of Chicago, Deerfield, IL, 05-10; Chap Elizabeth Hospice, Escondido, CA, 12-14; Chap New York Presbyterian Hospital, 14-18; DPC Siloam Hospital System, Indonesia, 18-

UPH Tower Fakultas Kedokteran, 12LT, #123, JL. Jend Sudirman 1688   Korean Northeastern
Lippo Karawaci, Tangerang, 15810 INDONESIA
E-mail: david.kim@siloamhospitals.com
Siloam Hospital System, Indonesia

Kim, David Young – b Korea, Jul 14, 42; f Herung Mann; m Yurun Eun; w Kang Ja, Korea, Nov 18, 69; chdn Jae Eun (Hong), Jae Ho, Sung Eun; ChShC 63-64, MDiv; ChShTS 65-67; AUTC 80, MA; YonU; L Apr 69, Kung Jung Pby, Kor; O Oct 12, 70, Cap Pby, Seoul; ev Kyung Buk, Uiseong-Eup Ch, 68; Chap Kor Army, 71-74; cop SinHyon Ch, Seoul, 76-79; p Kwang Hyon Ch, 79-89; p Central P Ch of Sacramento, Fair Oaks, CA, 95-13; sc KorNW Pby, 96; hr

15325 Magnolia Boulevard #168, Sherman Oaks, CA 91403 – 916-965-6206   Korean Northwest
E-mail: davidyoungkim@hotmail.com
HR

Kim, Dennis Sungsoo – srp Cheltenham P Ch, Cheltenham, PA, 18-

214 Carson Terrace, Hungtingdon Valley, PA 19006   Korean Eastern
E-mail: revdenniskim@gmail.com
Cheltenham Presbyterian Church – 215-635-6543

Kim, Deuk Young – ob astp First PC of Or Co, Midway City, CA, 00-09; hr

13250 Highway 138, Hesperia, CA 92345 – 760-389-2268   Korean Southwest
HR

Kim, Dong Kwon – mis Kazakhstan, 10-

1905 SW 318th Place #B, Federal Way, WA 98023 – 215-667-1108   Korean Eastern
E-mail: dkkim427@gmail.com

Kim, Dong Kyung – b Korea, Oct 5, 63; f Hwayong Kim; m Yongsook Lee; w HeJu Kim, Korea, May 5, 90; chdn Sanghyuk, Jisoo; ChonnamU 89, BS; HPTS 96, MDiv; LibU 98, MRE; ErskTS, DMin cand; L Oct 6, 95, Dong Seoul Pby; O Oct 6, 96, Dong Seoul Pby; Recd PCA Nov 8, 99, KorSE Pby; astp Songpa First P Ch, Seoul; ascp Kor P Ch of Jacksonville, PCUSA; op Christ Comm Ch of Jacksonville, Jacksonville, FL, 99-01; astp Korean First P Ch, Tucker, GA, 01-03; wc 04-

Address Unavailable   Korean Southeastern

Kim, Dong Woo – b Seoul, Korea; w Se Young Lee; chdn Hana, Yena; CornU 97, BS, 99, ME; WTS 03, MDiv; O Apr 13, 04, KorE Pby; astp Cornerstone P Ch, Lansdale, PA, 04-09; ob astp Bethel Kor P Ch, Ellicott City, MD, 09-

1607 Cantwell Road #D, Windsor Mill, MD 21244   Korean Capital
E-mail: dongwoo17@gmail.com
Bethel Korean Presbyterian Church

Kim, Dongsu – b Jeongju, Kor, Mar 23, 60; f Young Hwa Kim; m Soonyeol Han; w You Me Kim, Seoul, Kor, Dec 24, 87; chdn Elliot Christian, Luke Christian, Andrew; SNU 79-83, BA, MA; UPA, grad

Kim, Dongsu, continued
wk; WTS 90-93, MDiv, 99, PhD; L May 95, SusqV Pby; O Feb 21, 96, Phil Pby; moy First P Ch, 93-95; ob Korean Msn P Ch, (KAPC), Lansdale, PA, 95-96; yp Holy Grace P Ch, 97-98; adj prof NyC, 98-99, asst prof 99-06; prof 06-; astp Central P Ch, NY, 99-; NyC, Bible dept chair, 01-02; acad dean Torch Trinity Institute For Lay Education, 06-; John's *Anti-apostasy Polemic and its Effect on the Narratives of Peter and Judas*; trans *Let the Reader Understand: A Guide to Interpreting and Applying the Bible*, 00

11 Ford Court, Monroe, NY 10950 – 845-782-6154　　　　　　　　　　　　　Metropolitan New York
E-mail: ttidean@gmail.com

　　Kim, Dukjin – srp New England Grace P Ch, West Hartford, CT, 14-15; ob 15-

33 Henry Place, Apt. B1, Hackensack, NJ 07601-6600　　　　　　　　　　　　Korean Northeastern
E-mail: pastordjkim@gmail.com

　　Kim, Edward Sung-Chul – b Seoul, Korea, Dec 28, 55; w Christine Eun-Kyung Lee, Seoul, Kor, Aug 13, 80; chdn Susanna Sun-Young, Gloria Eun-Young; HanoverC 76-80, BA; LPTS 80-81; RefPSem 84-87, MDiv; WesleyTS 00, MDiv; O Jul 21, 87, Kor-Am P Ch; DCE Louisville Kor P Ch, L'ville, KY, 80-81; DCE Kor-Amer P Ch, L A, CA, 83-85; DCE Peniel P Ch, Rowland Heights, CA, 86-88; astp Washington Sae Han P Ch, Annandale, VA, 88-90; p Wash Shin Il P Ch, Annandale, VA, 90-91; ob p Yenasung P Ch (Indep), Fairfax Station, VA, 91-95; p Korean Central P Ch of Baltimore, Baltimore, MD, 96-00; sc KorCap Pby, 98-00; ob astp New Cov Fell Ch, Germantown, MD, 00-05; mod KorCap pby 08-09, 10-11; p Baltimore Central Comm Ch, Baltimore, MD, 05-12; wc 12-13; ob 13-

13513 Prairie Mallow Lane, Centreville, VA 20120　　　　　　　　　　　　　Korean Capital
E-mail: esckim@gmail.com

　　Kim, Edward Sungman – b Korea, Mar 9, 30; f Heung Soon; m Soon Dan; w Seung Hie Choi, Korea, Oct 30, 55; chdn David C.; WonK, BA; KorPTS 56, BD; TCU 77, ThM; L 57, GA; O Jan 59, Choen Nam Pby; p Soe Suk Ch, 59; Chap Soong-il High, 61; p Soe-kwang Ch, 62; p Sung-nack Ch, 64-71; Chap Trinity hosp, 74; srp Korean P Ch, Houston, TX, 77-97; hr 97

11600 Wavner, Apt. 639, Fountain Valley, CA 92708 – 714-424-9135　　　　　South Texas
HR

　　Kim, El H. – b Seoul, Sept 23, 65; f Dong Y.; m Mun Ja Ahn; w Nancy Jungin, Hoffman Estates, IL, Sept 7, 66; SanJChristC, BS; TEDS 93-97, MDiv; L Oct 12, 99, KorSW Pby; O Apr 17, 01, KorSW Pby; ascp New Life Msn Ch of Northern California, San Jose, CA, 01-05; op New Life Msn Ch of Bay Area, Morgan Hill, CA, 05-10

2185 Cimarron Drive, Morgan Hill, CA 95037 – 408-778-1071　　　　　　　　Korean Southwest
E-mail: elvive23@hotmail.com

　　Kim, Elliot Y.K – op New Life Msn Ch of Silicon Valley, Campbell, CA, 08-09; ob

3948 Multonmah Boulevard, Portland, OR 97219　　　　　　　　　　　　　　Korean Southwest
E-mail: elliotkim@hotmail.com

　　Kim, Ernest – b Chicago, IL, May 31, 69; f Sun Ha; m Kui Nam Rhee; w Lillian Hyun, Oakland, CA, May 18, 02; chdn Dawna, Timothy; UCB 92, BA; GGBTS 97, MDiv; CalvS 99; O Sept 12, 06, KAPC; Recd PCA Feb 22, 13, NoCA Pby; ascp Kor CRC, El Cerrito, CA, 95-00; ascp Berkeley Kor Ch, 00-08; p Berkeley Gr P Ch, Berkeley, CA, 08-

720 Stannage Avenue #B, Albany, CA 94706　　　　　　　　　　　　　　　　Northern California
E-mail: ernest@jps.net
Berkeley Grace Presbyterian Church – 510-527-9191

MINISTERIAL DIRECTORY

Kim, Eun Soo – b Jeonju-City, Korea, Nov 5, 58; f Jontai; m Malrye Choi; w Hyunyoung Cho, Seoul, Korea, Dec 28, 88; chdn Joseph Youngeun, John Youngha, Joshua Youngkang, Susie Rebekah, Yesie Anna; ChShC 85, BA; KRTS 89, MDiv; BhamTS 96, MA; RTS, PhD; O Apr 8, 91, The Biblical Church, Tokyo, Japan; Recd PCA Oct 4, 94, KorSE Pby; ascp The Biblical Ch, Takata Toshima-Ku, Tokyo, Japan; ob Dir Briarwood P Ch, Asian Ministry (Jap & Kor), Birmingham, AL, 93-07; admin RTS Kor program

3850 Cabalzar Lane, Cumming, GA 30040-6052   Korean Southeastern
E-mail: esookim@hotmail.com
Reformed Theological Seminary – 601-923-1600
5422 Clinton Boulevard, Jackson, MS 39209

Kim, EunChul – ob; astp Oregon Eden P Ch, Aloha, OR, 13-

2461 NW Schmidt Way #310, Beaverton, OR 97006   Korean Southwest
E-mail: Eunchulkim7@gmail.com
Oregon Eden Presbyterian Church – 503-848-8168

Kim, Eunseob – astp Korean P Ch of St. Louis, St. Louis, MO, 17-

614 Broadmoor Drive, Apt. A, Chesterfield, MO 63017   Korean Central
E-mail: happyeunseob@gmail.com
Korean Presbyterian Church of St. Louis – 314-984-9466

Kim, Evan – ob 13-

E-mail: evan.kim@my.densem.edu   Rocky Mountain

Kim, Goong Hun – p Maranatha Vision Ch, Livermore, CA, 13-

5435 Rainflower Drive, Livermore, CA 94551 – 925-648-3588   Korean Northwest
E-mail: goongkim@gmail.com
Maranatha Vision Church – 925-449-2241

Kim, Han Hae – mis

Address Unavailable   Korean Southwest

Kim, Hyoungik – srp Cornerstone P Ch, Germantown, MD, 11-

18009 Cottage Garden Drive, Apt. 303   Korean Capital
Germantown, MD 20874-5811 – 301-424-8148
E-mail: haggaikim@hotmail.com
Cornerstone Presbyterian Church

Kim, Hyucksoo -

E-mail: hyucksookim@gmail.com   Korean Central

Kim, Hyun Jin – p Walnut Creek Heavenly Ch, Walnut Creek, CA

3170 Oak Road #115, Walnut Creek, CA 94597   Korean Northwest
Walnut Creek Heavenly Church – 925-988-9136

Kim, Hyun-seok – p Korean Central P Ch of Cincinnati, 09-16

8366 Waterbury Court #101, West Chester, OH 45069 – 513-860-1223   Korean Central
E-mail: kcoic@hotmail.com

Kim, Hyunkeun – b Seoul, Jun 10, 60; f Sung Tae Kim; m Youngsook Lee; w Haekyung Yim, Seoul, Dec 22, 86; chdn Jihoon; SoORU 89, BA, 92, MBA; EmU 97, MDiv; O Oct 18, 98, KorSE Pby; astp, medu Korean First P Ch, Tucker, GA, 94-01; op Icthus P Msn, Duluth, GA, 01-

2181 Sugar Valley Lane, Lawrenceville, GA 30043 – 678-376-0774   Korean Southeastern
Icthus Presbyterian Mission

Kim, In Whan – b Kyungsang-book Doh, Korea, May 10, 46; f Byung Chae; m Yong Hee Chin; w Chung Sook Joo, NY, Dec 27, 76; chdn H. Jashin, Youmie Janice, Jayoung Ezra; PGATCS 70-74, BA, 74-75; WTS 76-80, MDiv, 95, ThM; UWales 95-00, PhD; O Jul 81, Phil Pby; ap Korean Saints P Ch, Warminster, PA, 81; prof Chongshin U/Sem, 82-, VPres, 97-00, 02-04, Pres Chongshin U/Sem, 04-08; ss New Man P Msn, Phila, PA, 87-89; President, Society of Reformed Theology, 06-10; brdmbr World Reformed Fellowship, 06-; art "A Role of the Divine Curse in the Redemptive History Reflected in Deuteronomy 32:19-25," *Korean Theological Review 50*, 83; "Oracles Against the Nations in the History of Research," *Faculty's Articles 8,* 89; "An Exegesis on the Tithe Law in the Pentateuch," in *Korean Theological Review 56,* 89; "How Many Tithes in the Old Testament," in *Korean Theological Review 57* 90; "An Exposition on the Book of Exodus," *Christian Times,* 90; "A Study of the Message of Amos," *Faculty's art*, 92; "God of Amos," *Faculty's art*, 93; "A Study of the Legitimacy of Yahweh in Judging the Nations in the Oracles of Amos," *Chongshin Review 1,* 96; auth *Theology of Tithe*(in Korean), 01

Chong Shin University, 31-3 Sadang Dong, Dongjak Gu, Seoul, KOREA   Philadelphia
E-mail: inwkim@gmail.com
Chongshin University and Seminary, Seoul, Korea

Kim, Iron D. – b Seoul, Dec 13, 69; f Kook Rip; m Chung Ja Chung; w Grace Park, New York, Nov 11, 00; chdn Charlotte; SUNYStonyBr 90, BA; WTS 94, MDiv; NCEd 97, ThM; L Apr 94, KorE Pby; O Jun 25, 00, MNY Pby; astp Redeemer P Ch of New York, New York, NY, 98-02; ascp City Ch of San Francisco, San Francisco, CA, 02-06; op Trin P Msn, Orange, CA, 06-14; p Grace P Ch of Silicon Valley, Palo Alto, CA, 14-; sc NoCal Pby, 16-

411 Kipling Street, Palo Alto, CA 94301   Northern California
E-mail: iron.kim@gmail.com
Grace Presbyterian Church of Silicon Valley – 650-326-7737

Kim, Jacob Ethan – b Toronto, ON, Jul 18, 79; WTS 06, MDiv; O Nov 07; ob Antioch Church of Philadelphia, 10-15; astp liberti- Fairmount, Philadelphia, PA, 15-17; op liberti Montgomery Co, Philadelphia, PA, 17-

1601 Kellog Drive, Lower Gwynedd, PA 19002 – 267-738-4415   Eastern Pennsylvania
E-mail: jacob.kim@liberti.org
liberti Montgomery County

Kim, Jae Son Paul – astp Koinos Flwsp Ch, Burke, VA, 08-11; ob Loving Hill Ch, 11-

41784 Purpose Way, Aldie, VA 20105 – 703-722-2273   Korean Capital
E-mail: psalm145@gmail.com
Loving Hill Church

Kim, James Gunyong – b Daegu, Korea Dec 09, 59; f Hee Soo; m Bok Sil Sa; URoch 82, BSEE; GCTS 94, MDiv; L Sep 95 KorE pby; O Jun 10, 00, KorE pby; ob mis Mexico 96-; member WEC 96-10; fraternal member INP-HPEM 01-p; socio A.C. Amigos Sin Frontera

157 Arbour Court, North Wales, PA 19454   Korean Eastern
E-mail: kimjmexico@gmail.com

Kim, James Jeewoun – b Seoul, Oct 6, 67; f Chang Seh Kim; m Chang Sil Jang; w Jane H. Oh, Los Angeles, CA, Apr 26, 97; chdn Dillon Seungkwan, Yeri Sophie, Karis Yeun; UCI 86-91; WSCAL 91-

MINISTERIAL DIRECTORY

Kim, James Jeewoun, continued
95, MDiv; FulTS 96-99, ThM; L Oct 96, KorSW Pby; O Oct 14, 97, KorSW Pby; medu Victory P Ch, Los Angeles, CA, 97-00, astp 00-01; medu Seohyun Church, Seoul, 01-03; srp Victory P Ch, Los Angeles, CA, 03-

3340 Los Olivos Lane, LaCrescenta, CA 91294 – 818-541-9675   Korean Southwest
E-mail: chmonk106@yahoo.co.kr
Victory Presbyterian Church – 323-664-1824

Kim, James Jungbae – b Seoul, Korea, Apr 8, 68; f Kook Hwan; m Cathy Chaekil; CSPUP 93, BS; WSCAL 97, MDiv; CTS 13, DMin; O Jun 22, 98, KAPC; Recd PCA Apr 16, 02, KorSW Pby; ydir Korean UMC, San Diego, CA, 94-95; ydir First P Ch of Orange Co, Westminster, CA, 95-98; astp New Life Korean P Ch, Lake Forest, CA, 98-01; chp Redeeming Grace Ch, Anaheim, CA, 02-07; astp The Lord's Comm Ch, Hacienda, CA, 07; cons Redeemer P Ch, Torrance, CA, 08-10; astp Jubilee P Ch, Irvine, CA, 10-11; astp Cornerstone Chapels, 11-14; cons reChurch Consultants, 14-; prof Int Ref U and Sem, 18-

24 Richemont Way, Aliso Viejo, CA 92656 – 949-292-4042   Korean Southwest Orange County
E-mail: pastorjameskim@cox.net
International Reformed University and Seminary

Kim, Jang K. – ob; p Redeemer P Ch South Bay, Torrance, CA, 15-18

E-mail: jangkkim@gmail.com   Pacific

Kim, Jeeil – O Nov 6, 16, KorSE Pby; astp New Ch of Atlanta, Peachtree Corners, GA, 16-

E-mail: kjicool@hotmail.com   Korean Southeastern
New Church of Atlanta – 770-447-6663

Kim, Jeffrey –

9200Williamette Place, Apt. 402, Frederick, MD 21704   Korean Central
E-mail: jeffekim@gmail.com

Kim, Jeong Ho – p Korean P Ch of Houston, Houston, TX, 18-

10800 Clay Road#8302, Houston, TX 77041   Korean Southern
Korean Presbyterian Church of Houston – 713-973-1123

Kim, Jeong In – p Eastern Long Island P Ch, Greenlawn, NY; wc

668 Wheeler Road, Hauppaugeon, NY 111788 – 631-656-0057   Korean Northeastern

Kim, Jimmy Joowoun – b Seoul, Dec 10, 65; f Chang Seh Kim; m Chang Sil Chang; w Jessica Chiyun Jung, Los Angeles, CA, Jul 12, 97; chdn Lois Yeajin; UCLA 93, BS; WSCAL 97, MDiv; ascp Choong Hyun Msn Ch, Los Angeles, CA, 99-08; ob

18725 Gledhill Street, Northridge, CA 91324 – 818-701-1517   Korean Southwest
E-mail: jlk9498@yahoo.com

Kim, Jisup – b Seoul, Jun 20, 57; f Daniel; m Jung-Ja Cho; w Kyungae Im, Seoul, Nov 10, 83; chdn Esther, Janice, James; SUNY, BA; WTS, MDiv; O Oct 12, 93, KAPC; astp Jaong-Bu P Ch KAPC, Little Neck, NY, 93-96; ascp Bethel P Ch, MD, 96-99; p Faith Ch of Westchester, White Plains, NY, 99-

19 Sunset Drive, White Plains, NY 10605 – 914-421-9034   Korean Northeastern
Faith Church of Westchester – 914-949-9441

Kim, Joel Eunil – p Segaero P Ch, Los Angeles, CA, 03-06; prof 07-

1869 Cathedral Glen, Escondido, CA 92029   Korean Southwest Orange County
E-mail: joelekim@yahoo.com

Kim, John – O Apr 29, 18, KorSE Pby; astp New Ch of Atlanta, Peachtree Corners, GA, 18-

3292 Willow Oak Drive, Peachtree Corners, GA 30092   Korean Southeastern
E-mail: writepastorjohn@gmail.com
New Church of Atlanta – 770-447-6663

Kim, John H. – ob Korean Evangelical Church of Guam, 10-18; Asian Prison Min

275 Glen Riddle Road #G11, Media, PA 19063   Korean Eastern
Asian Prison Ministry

Kim, John Isaac – astp The Way Ch, Los Angeles, CA, 07- 12; mis MTW, China, 12-15; campm RUF, UHawaii, 16-

38 S. Judd Street #3B, Honolulu, HI 96817 – 808-990-2775   Northern California
E-mail: jk81906@gmail.com
PCA Reformed University Fellowship

Kim, John S. – op Se Um Ch, Auburn, AL, 15-

2749 Sophia Way, Auburn, AL 36830   Korean Southeastern
E-mail: johnskim00@gmail.com
Se Um Church

Kim, Jonathan – srp State College Korean Ch, State College, PA, 09-

766 Glenn Road, State College, PA 16803 – 814-689-9865   Korean Eastern
E-mail: gkim@sckc.org
State College Korean Church – 814-380-9191

Kim, Jonathan J. – O Apr 3, 13, Evan Pby; astp Briarwood P Ch, Birmingham, AL, 14-15

201 Providence Lane, Lansdale, PA 19446 – 215-205-7278   Korean Eastern
E-mail: jbkelmission@gmail.com

Kim, Jong Kyu – astp Sae Han P Ch of Atlanta, Alpharetta, GA, 14-

710 Pine Circle, Alpharetta, GA 30022   Korean Southeastern
E-mail: mydearkim@gmail.com
Sae Han Presbyterian Church of Atlanta – 770-619-5340

Kim, Joo Young – astp The Ch for All Nations, Vienna, VA, 17-

14518 North Barros Court, Centreville, VA 20120   Korean Capital
E-mail: jyk110011@gmail.com
The Church for All Nations – 703-573-3767

Kim, Joseph C. J. – b Seoul, Korea, Feb 14, 37; f Soon Nam; m Kum Soon Yoon; w Hwa Ja Lee, New York, Oct 7, 67; chdn Paul, Susan, John; WashU 75; WTS 81, MDiv; O Oct 81, Phil Pby; p New Life Ch of Phil, Philadelphia, PA, 81-82; p Korean Bethel P Ch, Chicago, IL, 82-84; sc KorCent Pby; srp Sung Min P Ch, Chicago, IL, 84-01; hr 01; p Korean Comm Church, Cape Coral, FL, 01-08

3400 Balsam Hollow Court, Catharpin, VA 20143-2410 – 703-753-8234   Korean Capital
E-mail: changjaekim@netzero.net
HR

Kim, Joseph Sun Yang – astp Inland Korean P Ch, Pomona, CA, 99-09; p Hana P Ch, Glendale, CA, 09-

2851 Altura Avenue, La Crescenta, CA 91214 – 818-548-2451   Korean Southwest
E-mail: josephkim1@gmail.com
Hana Presbyterian Church – 818-241-0000

Kim, Joshua S.B. – ob

Address Unavailable   Korean Southwest

Kim, Julius – b Los Angeles, CA, Jul 6, 68; f Gwan H.; m Sook Ja Bang; w JiHee Shin, Mission Viejo, CA, Sept 4, 93; chdn Emma Grace, Phoebe Elise; VangU 93, BA; WSCAL 97, MDiv; TEDS 03, PhD; L Jan 00, NoIL Pby; O Aug 6, 00, NoIL Pby; assoc prof, DnStu WSCAL, 00-; ascp New Life P Ch, Escondido, CA, 04-

1183 Rocky Point Way, Escondido, CA 92026 – 760-735-9306   South Coast
E-mail: jjkim@wscal.edu
Westminster Seminary California – 760-480-8474
1725 Bear Valley Parkway, Escondido, CA 92027
New Life Presbyterian Church – 760-489-5714

Kim, Jung An – b Seoul, Jan 1, 67; f Sung Sang; m Duck Im Lee; w Hanna Lee, Seoul, Jun 5, 92; chdn Anna; YonU 85-88, BA; TEDS 97, MDiv; L Apr 12, 99, KorCent Pby; O Apr 11, 00, KorCent Pby; ob campm IVCF, 98-

1377 Boundary Road, Middleton, WI 53562   Korean Central
E-mail: kivfgs@gmail.com
Inter-Varsity Christian Fellowship – 608-274-4823

Kim, Jung Bok – b Korea, Jan 6, 47; f Myung-Chun; m Sun-Yee Park; w Young-Sook Hong, Korea, Apr 28, 79; chdn Hope S, Faith S; KorBC; SungkulTS; EMenC, BA; EMenS, MDiv; L Aug 1, 74; O May 13, 79, Kor Bible Msn; ap Suweon Central Bible Ch, Korea, 74-79; ev, op Eden Korean P Ch, Norfolk, VA, 87-92, p 92-05; hr 12

4948 Admiration Drive, Virginia Beach, VA 23464-3002 – 757-467-2654   Tidewater
E-mail: jungbkim@verizon.net
HR

Kim, Justin – b Korea, Apr 21, 77; w Virginia; chdn Tabitha, Barnabas; RTS 06, MDiv; O 08, KorCap Pby; astp Korean P Ch of Wash, Fairfax, VA, 08-09; ob Comm Ch of Seattle, 09-16

24485 Chamalea, Mission Viejo, CA 92691 – 425-949-9437   Korean Capital
E-mail: jungstin@gmail.com

Kim, Ka Hyung – srp Calvary P Ch, Baltimore, MD; wc

4322 Archway, Irvine, CA 92618   Korean Capital
E-mail: stone1115@gmail.com

Kim, Keedai – astp Open Door Comm Ch, Alpharetta, GA, 15-18, ascp 18-

2566 Staunton Lane, Duluth, GA 30096 – 908-922-3701   Georgia Foothills
E-mail: kimkeedai@gmail.com
Open Door Community Church – 678-812-4578

Kim, Keun Tai – b Najoo, Korea, Nov 19, 45; f Hee Suk; m Yang Soon; w Choon Ja Choi, Pusan, Korea, Mar 27, 71; chdn Sung Min, Samuel; O Dec 27, 83, Kor P, Seoul; Recd PCA Jan 15, 94, NGA Pby; p Emmanuel Korean P Ch, Buffalo, NY, 84-91; srp Faith Korean P Ch, Atlanta, GA, 91-94; op Faith Korean P Msn, Alpharetta, GA, 94-

5131 Charmant Place, Dunwoody, GA 30360 – 770-396-0340   Metro Atlanta
Faith Korean Presbyterian Mission – 770-667-0969

Kim, Kevin J. –

402 Buttercup Drive, Savoy, IL 61874   Korean Central
E-mail: kevinjkim@gmail.com

Kim, Key Young – p Hanmaeum P Ch, San Jose, CA, 99-02; astp San Jose Servants P Ch, San Jose, CA, 02-13; hr 13

230 South Jackson Street # 107, Glendale, CA 91205-1196   Korean Northwest
HR

Kim, Kihyung – srp Hanmaum P Ch, Duluth, GA, 14-

3109 Duluth Highway, Duluth, GA 30096   Korean Southeastern
E-mail: kkh2441@gmail.com
Hanmaum Presbyterian Church – 770-442-9809

Kim, Kisup – b Seoul, Korea, Jan 27, 65; f Young-Hwal; m Jung-Ji Kim; w Yoonsung Suh, Seoul, Jun 26, 93; chdn Christine Hyewon, Joshua Jangwon, Augustine Seokwono; SMBC 90-91, dipl; MTC 92-94, ThB; CalvS ThM; L Oct 95; O Oct 15, 96, KorCent Pby; ob astp Hanh-In CRC, Grand Rapids, MI, 96-97; astp, exec p Sa Rang Comm Ch, Anaheim, CA, 97-06; p LA Sa-Rang Comm Ch, Los Angeles, CA, 07-

2732 Piedmont Avenue #9, Montrose, CA 91020 – 818-248-2123   Korean Southwest
E-mail: kisupkim@gmail.com
LA Sa Rang Community Church – 213-975-1111

Kim, Kwang Kun – b Seoul, Korea, Sept 20, 56; f Eun Su; m Ok Soon Moon; w Yeo Kyung Na, Seoul, May 31, 86; chdn John, Katherine; SNU 83, BS; GWU 92, MS; TEDS 96, MDiv, 02, PhD; L Oct 95; O Oct 14, 96, KorCent Pby; ascp Petra P Ch, Northbrook, IL, 96-97; srp Northfield P Ch, Northfield, IL, 97-99, wc; ob prof Korea, 04-

E-mail: ggg21c@hotmail.com   Korean Central

Kim, Kyoo Hun – astp Lamp P Ch of Los Angeles, Gardena, CA, 09-

E-mail: enheaven@hotmail.com   Korean Southwest
Lamp Presbyterian Church of Los Angeles – 310-327-8778

Kim, Kyoung Sik – b Tajeon, KOR, May 7, 57; f Hong-Suk; m Te-Keun Oh; w Myung-Jin Hahm, Chicago, Oct 13, 84; chdn Rebecca, John, Joseph; ChShCS 80, BA; NBTS 92, MDiv; L Apr 7, 92; O Nov 8, 92, KorCent Pby; p Pilgrim Korean P Ch, Prospect Heights, IL, 92-00; sc KorCent Pby, 94-00; srp First Korean P Ch of St. Louis, St. Ann, MO, 00-17; ob 17-

1116 Pierpoint Lane, St. Charles, MO 63303 – 314-495-4267   Korean Central
E-mail: amensalom@hotmail.com

Kim, Kyunghwa – wc

14623 Indian Summer Court, Centreville, VA 20120 – 703-644-3314   Korean Capital
E-mail: 1009vision@gmail.com

MINISTERIAL DIRECTORY

Kim, Leo – ev City Fellowship Comm Church, 10-

41-42 42nd Street #3K, Sunnyside, NY 11104   Korean Northeastern
E-mail: ljkim@cityfellowship.com
City Fellowship Community Church

Kim, Lloyd – b Turlock, CA, Apr 10, 72; f Kwang Young; m Ann Jong Ok Tak; w Eda Moonhi Kwak, Orange County, CA, May 31, 97; chdn Kaelyn Sunhee, Christian Hong Won, Katy Sunyoung; UCB 90-94, BS; WSCAL 95-99, MDiv; FulTS, PhD; L Sept 98, SoCst Pby; O Oct 99, SoCst Pby; ascp Anaheim New Life Msn Ch, Buena Park, CA, 99-04; mis MTW, 04-14; prov coord MTW, 14; coord MTW, 15-; *Polemic in the Book of Hebrews,* Princeton Theological Monograph Series 64, 06

1600 North Brown Road, Lawrenceville, GA 30043   South Coast
E-mail: lloyd.kim@mtw.org
PCA Mission to the World

Kim, Luke Kyungmoon – b Seoul, Korea, Jan 8, 76; f Young Ryul; m Yeon Choi; w Hye Young Ryu, Seoul, Korea, Dec 24, 05; chdn Sean Benjamin, Rachel Teree, Nathaniel; CSULB 00, BS; WSCAL 07, MDiv; TEDS 14, ThM; L Mar 07, KorSW Pby; O Mar 08, KorSW Pby; yp Joy of Jesus CRC, La Puente, CA, 01-04; yp, astp Inland Korean P Ch, Pomona, CA, 04-09; srp Highland Korean P Ch, Vernon Hills, IL, 09-15; srp Korean P Ch of St. Louis, St. Louis, MO, 15-

11032 Manchester Road, Kirkwood, MO 63017   Korean Central
E-mail: pastor@lukekim.com
Korean Presbyterian Church of St. Louis – 314-984-9466

Kim, Manny – ob

16852 Citronia Street, Northridge, CA 91343   Korean Southwest
E-mail: mansun328@yahoo.com

Kim, Matae – ob 13-

Address Unavailable   Korean Northeastern

Kim, Michael – astp Disciple Comm Ch, Irvine, CA, 16-

Disciple Community Church – 949-502-4923   Korean Southwest Orange County

Kim, Min – astp First Korean P Ch, Glenview, IL, 17-

1310 Devonshire Road, Buffalo Grove, IL 60089   Korean Central
E-mail: minkim17@gmail.com
First Korean Presbyterian Church – 847-299-1776

Kim, Moon Hyung – b Suwon, Korean, Jul 22, 60; f Sang-Min; m Kyung-Ja Lee; w Min-Jung Chung, Seoul, Jan 20, 87; chdn Sung-Eun Nathan, Sung-Hee Steven; KHU 80-84, BA; RTS 93-96, MDiv; L Apr 9, 96; O Dec 12, 96, KorSE Pby; astp Korean Ch in Jackson Msn, Raymond, MS, 96-98; Chap USArmy, Ft. Jackson, SC, 99-

United States Army   Korean Southeastern

Kim, Myung Il – ob Korea, 09-

Address Unavailable   Korean Southern

Kim, Myung Kook – b Seoul, Korea, Jul 17, 36; f Byung Whan; m Sun Do Hu; w Sung Wha Choi; chdn Hye Kyung (Choi), Jun Woong, Eun Kyung; DKU 68, BA, 74, BD; TempU 75, PhD; WashTS 89, MDiv; L Jan 1, 75; O Feb 18, 75; op Korean PC of South Wash, Woodbridge, VA, 87-93, p 93-95; prof WashTS, 88-95; sc KorCap Pby, 92-93; p Korean Zion P Ch of Baltimore, Baltimore, MD, 96-98, wc 98-99; p New Life Ref P Ch, Burtonsville, MD, 99-05; hr; mod KorCap 94, 00

15051 Medinah Court, Haymarket, VA 20169 – 540-507-8421   Korean Capital
E-mail: myungkim1936@gmail.com
HR

Kim, Nam Jin – p Jesus Family P Ch, Santa Clarita, CA, 08-

4 Montelegro, Irvine, CA 92614 – 661-263-2372   Korean Southwest
E-mail: njeykim@hanmail.net
Jesus Family Presbyterian Church – 661-317-5372

Kim, Oh Peter – ob SEED Int'l, 08-

SEED International, PO Box 69, Merrifield, VA 22116   Korean Capital

Kim, Paul – mis; op Gracepoint North Church, Dresher, PA, 18-

3406 South Carriage Court, North Wales, PA 19454   Eastern Pennsylvania
E-mail: paulkim@gmail.com
Gracepoint North Church

Kim, Paul – ev 02-03; ascp Harbor Carmel Valley P Ch, San Diego, CA, 03-09; ascp Harbor Carlsbad P Ch, Carlsbad, CA, 09-10; ascp Harbor North County, 10-13; Redeemer PC of San Diego, Encinitas, CA, 13-

13872 Kerry Lane, San Diego, CA 92130-5608 – 858-481-4893   South Coast
Redeemer Presbyterian Church of San Diego – 760-753-2535

Kim, Paul David – b St. Louis, MO, Mar 4, 69; f Joseph C.J.; m Patty H.J. Lee; UIL 91, BS; BibS 94, MDiv, MA; WTS 01, ThM; BibTS 07, DMin; L Nov 22, 94, KorE Pby; O Nov 25, 97, KorE Pby; astp Emmanuel Ch in Phil, Philadelphia, PA; op Renewal P Ch, Philadelphia, PA, 06-08, p 08-11; astp Pacific Crossroads Ch, Santa Monica, CA, 12-

15213 Hartsook Street, Sherman Oaks, CA 91403   Pacific
E-mail: paul@pacificcrossroads.org
Pacific Crossroads Church – 310-551-0081

Kim, Paul Hyunkook – b Korea, Nov 27, 43; f Park Jae Yeon; m Kuk Soo; w Chung Tae Sook, Korea, May 17, 82; chdn Timothy; YUE 67-72, BE; HPTS 78-80, BD; L Oct 82, Inchon Pby; O Mar 83, Kangnam Pby; ap Eungok P Ch, 82-83; p First Korean Ch, Dillsburg, PA, 84-13; hr 13

350 Coffeetown Road, Dillsburg, PA 17019 – 717-502-7258   Susquehanna Valley
E-mail: paulkim1127@yahoo.com
HR

Kim, Paul Sungeun – b Wijoo, Korea, Sept 28, 35; f Chul Yoon; m Kap Wha Lee; w Grace Pahng, Seoul, Kor, Apr 15, 74; chdn Stephen, Joseph; KCC 66, BA; HntC 67-68; StFrC 68-71, MEd; EBapTS 89, MDiv; L Dec 2, 91; O Apr 20, 92, KorE Pby; astp Korean United Ch of Phil, Philadelphia, PA, 80-92, ob astp 92-10; hr 10

765 Limekiln Pike #5, Glenside, PA 19038 – 215-887-0575   Korean Eastern
HR

MINISTERIAL DIRECTORY

Kim, Paul Taek-Yong – b Korea, Apr 29, 34; f Chang Woon; m Yoo Soon; w Kyung Soon, Seoul, Feb 13, 67; chdn David Sunmin; PGATCS 65, BD; KorU 61-63, MA; CBTS 68-69, ThM; HowU 71-73, DMin; CGST 80-84, ThD; L 66, Korean PGA; O 67, Kyung-gi Pby; srp Korean P Ch of Wash, Fairfax, VA, 70-00; pres WashTS, 83-00; chmn Korean World Mission Council, 96-00; adj prof RegU, 97-; hr 00; mod KorSE Pby 88-89; sc KorSE Pby 86-88, 90-92; Mod, KorCap Pby, 92-93, 96-97; *History of the Korean Church in America, 1903-1978*, 79; *Korean Church Growth in America*, 85; *Heavenly Gates of Blessings*, 90

10153 Wavell Road, Fairfax, VA 22032-2337 – 703-323-7221   Korean Capital
E-mail: typaulkim@hotmail.com
HR

Kim, Robert – w Wonmin; chdn Elijah, Sophia, Clay; UCI, BA; GCTS, MDiv; FulTS, ThM; RTS DMin; O Nov 7, 04, KorNW Pby; astp Ark Msn Ch, Carmichael, CA, 04-06; ob p Gracepoint Ch, Philadelphia, 06-11; p 11-18; chp coord Metro Phil, 18-

1519 Isaacs Court, Ambler, PA 19002-3176 – 215-767-5336   Eastern Pennsylvania
E-mail: robxkim@gmail.com
Metro Philadelphia Church Planting Partnership - 215-326-9150

Kim, Roger – ob p 12-14; ob p By Grace Church, 14-17; mis MTW, 17-

3120 Chisolm Way #157, Fullerton, CA 92833   Pacific
E-mail: is613@yahoo.com
PCA Mission to the World

Kim, Sam – b Korea, Mar 30, 67; f Yonwon Kim; m Baekja Park; w MiJeong Kim, Korea, Jan 1, 96; chdn John(Dahun), Esther(Daey), Hannah; KTC 92, ThB; ChU&TS 96, MDiv; LibU 99, ThM, RTS 06, MATS; L Oct 15, 96, Kwang-ju P; O Oct 17, 97, Kwang-ju P; Recd PCA Aug 12, 99, KorSE Pby; p Kwang-ju Bansuk P Ch, Korea, 92-94; mis Philippines, 93-94; p Shinsung P Ch, Korea, 96-97; p Ocala Korean P Ch, Ocala, FL 99-

3110 NE 24th Place, Ocala, FL 34470 – 352-867-0191   Korean Southeastern
E-mail: kimsamuel32@gmail.com
Ocala Korean Presbyterian Church – 352-867-0191

Kim, Samuel – mis 14-

807 Lori Ln, Opelika, AL 36804   Korean Southeastern
E-mail: holysamuel@hotmail.com

Kim, Samuel C. – b Tea-Jun, Korea, Feb 11, 45; f Chang-Jea; m Oak-S-Kho; w (1) (dv); (2) Alicia Livingston, Denver, CO; chdn David, Daniel, Jennifer, Andrea; KorPTS 74-75; MBI 76-77; DBC 83; SEBC 87-88; CBS 91-94, MDiv; L Jan 81; O Oct 18, 81, Bapt; Recd PCA Oct 5, 93, KorSE Pby; chp Cheyenne, WY, 81-83; chp Temple, TX, 84-86; chp Killeen, TX, 84-85; chp Austin, TX, 86-91; op, ev Bethel Korean P Msn, Evans, GA, 92-96, wc 96-

E-mail: aliciakim23@yahoo.com   Korean Southeastern

Kim, Samuel Jon – p iVision Comm Ch, Pomona, CA, 03-10

4941 Angeles Crest Highway, La Canada, CA 91011 – 714-671-5924   Korean Southwest

Kim, Samuel Moon – op Korean Open Door P Ch, Houston, TX, 03-17; hr 17

8603 Braes River, Houston, TX 77074 – 713-776-0037   Korean Southern

Kim, Samuel Sang Won – p Myung Sung P Msn, Norcross, GA, 06-

Myung Sung Presbyterian Mission   Korean Southeastern

Kim, Samuel Sung Hoon – b Seoul, Korea, Sept 30, 63; f Tae Wung; m Chun Ja Hwang; w Young soon Choi, Seoul, Kor, Aug 12, 89; chdn Ji Hye, Ji Yun; PC 82-86, ThB; KorPTS 86-89, MDiv; O Mar 6, 89, Seoul SE Pby, (PCK); Recd PCA Oct 4, 94, KorSE Pby; p Choongil P Ch, Choongjoo City, Choongbook-Do; op, ev First Korean P Msn, Columbia, SC, 94-95; op Columbia P Msn, Columbia, SC, 95-99; op Columbia Agape P Ch, Columbia, SC, 09-

251 Rabon Road, Columbia, SC 29223 – 803-260-2090   Korean Southeastern
Columbia Agape Presbyterian Church – 803-445-7877

Kim, Sang Mook – b Kyung Ki, Korea, Jul 17, 36; f Kyu Hee; m Sung Nyu Kang; w Suk Bun, Kyung Ki, Korea, Mar 6, 55; chdn Hak Je, Ki Je, Mi Sook, Sun Sook; KorU 66, BA; DHTS 64, ThM; FTS 82, DMin; O Apr 67, Seoul Pby; p McLean Korean P Ch, McLean, VA, 77-98, wc 98-99; Chap Chonan College/U, 99-10; hr 10; *The Way of Love and Desire*; *By the Grace of God I am What I am*; *Defending Inspiration of the Bible*

6810 Old Chesterbrook Road, McLean, VA 22101   Korean Capital
HR

Kim, Sang Seon – b Seoul, Kor, Jun 17, 60; f Jae Chul; m Young Wom Jung; w Chris Kim Kyoung, Los Angeles, CA, Apr 14, 90; chdn Ye Joo, Ye Ha; AtManU, BA; FulTS, MDiv; L Oct 15, 94; O Oct 15, 94, KorSW Pby; p Gateway P Ch, San Fernando, CA, 94-

17736 Superior Street #2, Northridge, CA 91325 – 818-462-5153   Korean Southwest
E-mail: dulosforhim@gmail.com
Gateway Presbyterian Church – 818-361-1884

Kim, Sanghun – w Jong Sook Won; chdn Woihwan, Sunghwan, Bueniel; CAU 84; SBTS 02; campm ULV; srp Korea SaeHan Ch of Louisv, Louisville, KY, 04-

10909 Symington Circle, Louisville, KY 40241   Korean Central
E-mail: sanghunkim30@gmail.com
Korea SaeHan Church of Louisville – 502-267-1416

Kim, Se Min – b Jangheung, Korea, Jul 20, 67; f Jinsil; m Jina; w Hyun Sook Lee; CalvTheoSem, Korea 98, ThB; GeoTruettSem 04, MDiv; UMaryHardin 08, MA; O May 15, 05; ob Heavenville P Ch, Korea, 08-

82-31-261-44760   Korean Southern
Heavenville P Ch, Korea

Kim, Sebastian – ob p 14-16; p Hope Chapel, Lutherville, MD, 17-

16 Evans Avenue, Lutherville Timo, MD 21093   Chesapeake
E-mail: pastorsebastiankim@gmail.com
Hope Chapel

Kim, Sebastian – O 18, SNE Pby; Chap USArmy, 18-

119 Laurelwood Drive, Hopedale, MA 01747   Southern New England
United States Army

Kim, Seung H. – b Korea, Nov 20, 66; f Tae Hwa; m Sun Wal Shin; w Sook Hee Kim, Korea, Aug 15, 92; chdn Peter; IBCS, MRE; DTS, MACE; srp The True Light Ch of Dallas, Irving, TX, 01-

2316 Northlake Court, Irving, TX 75038 – 214-228-2206　　　　　　　　　Korean Southern
E-mail: bridgebuilding@hotmail.com
The True Light Church of Dallas – 972-438-5956

Kim, Seung Hun – b Seoul, Korea, Feb 23, 51; f Hee Won; m Chun Keum Choi; w Kyung Sook Cho, Seoul, Korea, Oct 10, 74; chdn Jin Ho, Naeri; SNU 69-73, BA; WTS 90-93, MDiv; L Sept 93; O Nov 23, 93, KorE Pby; srp Petra P Ch, Northbrook, IL, 93-

1419 North Park Drive #C1, Mt. Prospect, IL 60056 – 847-759-9941　　　　Korean Central
Petra Presbyterian Church – 847-498-5880

Kim, Shungho – O Feb 22, 09, KorE Pby; astp Emmanuel Ch in Philadelphia, 09-15; ob 15-

110 Aspen Court, Marlton, NJ 08053　　　　　　　　　　　　　　　　　Korean Eastern
E-mail: ksh8462@gmail.com

Kim, Solomon – p The Lords Ch, Los Angeles, CA, 02-

1129 South Mariposa Avenue #2, Los Angeles, CA 90006 – 323-938-0261　　　Pacific
The Lord's Church

Kim, Solomon – O Oct 19, 14, SNE Pby; campm RUF, MIT, 14-

10 Hackensack Circle, Chestnut Hill, MA 02467 – 857-500-0557　　　Southern New England
PCA Reformed University Fellowship

Kim, Soo Dong – Recd PCA 16, KorS Pby; p Houston Ch for the Lord, Webster, TX, 16-

15718 Wandering Trail, Friends Wood, TX 77546 – 281-512-7108　　　　Korean Southern
E-mail: harang1112@gmail.com
Houston Church for the Lord – 281-512-7108

Kim, Stephen T. – p The Lords Comm Ch, Flushing, NY, 09-

168-07 43rd #2 Floor, Flushing, NY 11358 – 718-460-0577　　　　　Korean Northeastern
The Lord's Community Church – 646-642-3533

Kim, Steve – astp Emmanuel Ch in Phil, Philadelphia, PA, 03-05; op CityLine Ch, Wynnewood, PA, 05-08; p 08-11

5019 Prince Caspian Lane, Burke, VA 22015　　　　　　　　　　　　　　Philadelphia

Kim, Steve S. – mis Kazakhstan

Address Unavailable　　　　　　　　　　　　　　　　　　　　　　　Korean Southern

Kim, Sung Soo – b Korea, Jun 17, 48; f Chong Rok Kim; m Il Soon Cho; w Woon Sook Ahn, Seoul, Korea, Aug 14, 78; chdn Suzanne, Shirley; HanU 76, BS; MTTech 81, MS; DTS 99, ThM; L Apr 10, 00, KorS Pby; O Oct 15, 01, KorS Pby; medu Korean Ch of A & M, College Station, TX, 01; op New Somang P Ch, Bryan, TX, 05-

4809 Treadgold Lane, Bryan, TX 77802 – 979-731-0569　　　　　　　　Korean Southern
E-mail: sawkim@msn.com
New Somang Presbyterian Church – 979-229-6307

Kim, Sung Woon – O Aug 24, 14, SoTX Pby; astp Christ P Ch, Georgetown, TX, 14-

2503 Armstrong Drive, Leander, TX 78641 – 215-740-1178 South Texas
E-mail: wkim@cpcgeorgetown.org
Christ Presbyterian Church – 512-966-9644

Kim, Sungho – Recd PCA 15, KorS Pby; srp Korean P Ch of Houston, 15-18; op Joyful Comm Ch of Texas, Katy, TX, 18-

20230 Prince Creek Drive, Katy, TX 77450 Korean Southern
E-mail: daehan718@gmail.com
Joyful Community Church of Texas – 443-857-0129

Kim, Sungjun Sean – astp Korean P Ch of Southern New York, Woodside, NY, 10-

52-57 39th Avenue, Sunnyside, NY 11104 – 347-255-5245 Korean Northeastern
E-mail: therefore12@yahoo.com
Korean Presbyterian Church of Southern New York – 718-639-8383

Kim, Tae Kwon – b South Korea, Jan 10, 54; f Duk-Yong; m Chong-Suk; w Kyong-Suk, South Korea, Oct 3, 78; chdn Stacy, Amy, David; HUFS 72-80, BA; TEDS 85-87, MDiv; L Apr 5, 88; O Apr 3, 89, KorSE Pby; Phila Soh Mang P Ch, Ambler, PA, 89; p Kor Orth P Ch, Arlington (McLean), VA, 89-91; Korea; p Korean P Ch of Wash, Fairfax, VA, 05-08; srp Emmanuel Ch, Philadelphia, PA, 08-

184 Mansion Road, Newton Square, PA 19073 – 610-680-6349 Korean Eastern
E-mail: taekwontaekwon@gmail.com
Emmanuel Church in Philadelphia – 215-476-0330

Kim, Taehun – Recd PCA Sept 9, 14, KorNE Pby; op Greater Springfield Korean Ch, 14-

Greater Springfield Korean Church – 413-789-4522 Korean Northeastern

Kim, Taipyung Paul – b Korea, Dec 15, 52; f Hyun Kim; m Boo Rae Chung; w Myung Sook Ryu, Jul 10, 82; chdn Chung Mi, Sung Mi; SNU, BS; CWRU, MS, PhD; CTS, MDiv; astp Chapelgate P Ch, Marriottsville, MD, 13-

10745 Red Dahlia Drive, Woodstock, MD 21163 – 410-461-5111 Chesapeake
E-mail: taipkim@gmail.com
Chapelgate Presbyterian Church – 410-442-5800

Kim, Tony – ob 12-

2051 Crescent Moon Court, Woodstock, MD 21163 – 410-461-2880 Chesapeake
E-mail: tonykim64@hotmail.com

Kim, Walter – Recd PCA Nov 14, 17, BlRdg Pby; srp Trinity P Ch, Charlottesville, VA, 17-

Trinity Presbyterian Church – 434-977-3700 Blue Ridge

Kim, Won Joo – b Kimhae, Korea, Jul 15, 53; f Young Moo; m Jae Sung Moon; w Kum Yea Park, Pusan, Korea, Jun 10, 80; chdn Joo Ane, Joo yeal; KosU 81, ThB; KorTS 84, MDiv; L Mar 6, 81; O Oct 10, 86, East Pusan Synod, Korea; Recd PCA Apr 12, 94, KorSE Pby; p SaSang Ch, Pusan, Kor, 86-88; p Somang Ch, Pusan, Kor, 88-90; p Boeun Ch, Ulsan, Kor, 90-93; astp Daleville P Ch (Msn), Daleville, AL, 94-96; ev, op First Korean P Msn, Biloxi, MS, 96-

12427 Airport Road, Biloxi, MS 39532 – 228-388-3523 Korean Southeastern
First Korean Presbyterian Mission – 228-432-8573

Kim, Woody – mis Thailand, 98-

PO Box 79, Rajburana, Bangkok, 10140 THAILAND — Korean Northwest

Kim, Woosup – astp Eunhye Korean P Ch of Indianapolis, Indianapolis, IN, 17-

8851 Broadwell Place, Fishers, IN 46037 — Korean Central
E-mail: livetogod@gmail.com
Eunhye Korean Presbyterian Church of Indianapolis – 317-722-0372

Kim, Yoon Whan – b Kochang, Kor, Feb 28, 53; f Kwon Jin; m Soon Deuk Ryou; w Soon Ae Park, Nov 8, 78; chdn Abraham, Paul, Lois, Justin; ChShCS, BA; WTS 93, MDiv; O Nov 23, 93, KorE Pby; astp Korean United Ch of Phil, Philadelphia, PA, 94-00; p Arumdawn P Ch, Village of Palmetto Bay, FL, 00-14

Address Unavailable — South Florida

Kim, Young Ho – ob mis Germany, 92-; astp Segaero P Ch, Los Angeles, CA, 03-06; ob

Address Unavailable — Korean Capital

Kim, Young Hwan – b Korea, Sept 25, 47; f Eun-Suk Kim; m Kum Rae So; w Hee-Sook Oh, Korea, Mar 25, 72; chdn Daniel, Sarah; ChosunU 66-70, BE; EBapTS 87, 90, DMin; O Dec 9, 84, SBC; Recd PCA May 10, 99, KorSE Pby; Seamen's Church Inst, Philadelphia, 87-90; Korean Hallelujah Ch, Philadelphia, 90-94; Kwang-Shin U, 94-98, ob 99-14; srp Eternal Life P Ch, Suwanee, GA, 14-; *Men of Whom the World Was Not Worthy* (Korean), 97

200 Leaf Lake Drive, Suwanee, GA 30024 – 770-682-6332 — Korean Southeastern
E-mail: yhkim30024@yahoo.com
Eternal Life Presbyterian Church

Kim, Young Hwan – b Seoul, Korea, Sept 14, 55; f In Jin; m Chun Sub Choi; w Woo, Seoul, Kor; chdn Christian Iris; ChShC 82, BA; WashTS 91, MDiv; O 92, KorSE Pby; ev, op The Korean Antioch Ch of Wash Msn, Silver Spring, MD, 92-96; wc 96-

Address Unavailable — Korean Capital

Kim, Young Jun – b Seoul, Mar 28, 58; f Doo Pyo Kim; m Ae Sook Park; w Mee Sook Kim, Seoul, Sept 10, 88; chdn Lee Lye, Ee Sl, Isaac, Isaiah; DKU 79-86, BE; ErskTS 92-94, MDiv, 94-95, MCE, 95-98, DMin, 98-00, MATS; L Oct 15, 90, NSeoul Pby; O Apr 5, 91, NSeoul Pby; Recd PCA Aug 12, 99, KorSE Pby; op Atlanta Saints P Ch, Dacula, GA, 99-; *Holistic Ministry in Immigrant Churches*

4040 Mars Hill Road, Cumming, GA 30040 – 678-860-0480 — Korean Southeastern
E-mail: kimyoungjun@msn.com
Atlanta Saints Presbyterian Church – 678-407-1332

Kim, Young Kuk – astp Korean First P Ch, Tucker, GA, 07-

2353 Chancery Mill Lane, Buford, GA 30519 – 770-882-9106 — Korean Southeastern
E-mail: youngkimezra@gmail.com
Korean First Presbyterian Church – 770-934-8282

Kim, Young Man – p Raleigh Bethel P Ch, 07-15

111A Corporate Park East Drive, LaGrange, GA 30241 — Korean Southeastern
E-mail: a6131201@hanmail.net

Kim, Younghoon – O KorCent Pby

864-784-5449   Korean Central
E-mail: blazinghoon@gmail.com

Kim, Youngjoon – ob

531 Kirkland Drive, Coppell, TX 75019   Korean Southwest
E-mail: hiservant@gmail.com

Kim, Youngmok Joseph – Recd PCA Oct 10, 17, KorCap Pby; p Cornerstone Ch, Grayslake, IL, 17-

Cornerstone Church – 224-541-4359   Korean Central

Kimbrough, Randy H. – b Phenix City, AL, Oct 23, 53; f Horace O.; m Joyce Ann Rogers; w Ruth McKinney, Biloxi, MS, May 26, 79; chdn Caroline Rogers, Wendell Scott; UAL 72-76, BA; RTS 78-82, MDiv; O Jun 3, 83, Evan Pby; p Pea River P Ch, Clio, AL, 83-89; sc SEAL Pby, 87-89; p Mount Olive P Ch, Mount Olive, MS, 89-02; p Hopewell P Ch, Mount Olive, MS, 89-02; p Moss Point P Ch, Moss Point, MS, 02-

3701 Dantzler Street, Moss Point, MS 39563 – 228-475-7505   Grace
E-mail: rkim23@cableone.net
Moss Point Presbyterian Church – 228-475-2146

Kines, Joshua – astp Madison Heights P Ch, Madison, MS, 08-14; mis MTW, 14-15; op Parish Ch, Lafayette, LA, 16-

412 East Peck Boulevard, Lafayette, LA 70508   Southern Louisiana
E-mail: josh@ourparishchurch.com
Parish Church

King, Gregory A. – w Patricia(d); chdn Mary Catherine (Buckland), Michael; CNC 74, BS; VPI 78, MS; RTSNC 06, MDiv; O Oct 22, 06, NWGA Pby; p First P Ch, Summerville, GA, 06-18

659 South Brow Drive, Menlo, GA 30731 – 706-331-6324   Northwest Georgia
E-mail: gkpkinjc@gmail.com

King, Larry Joe – b Birmingham, AL, Jul 23, 53; f Herman Larry; m Doris Ann Whitley; w Nancy Charlyce Hughes, Thomson, GA, Jul 30, 83; chdn Meredith Ann; SEBC 76, BA; RTS 83, MDiv, 99, DMin; L 83; O 83, Gr Pby; p Heidelberg P Ch, Heidelberg, MS, 83-85; op Decatur P Ch, Decatur, AL, 85-87, p 87-92; astp Christ Ch, Jacksonville, FL, 92-95; p Swannanoa Valley P Ch, Swannanoa, NC, 95-00; srp Lake Oconee P Ch, Eatonton, GA, 00-12; srp Ingleside P Ch, Lawrenceville, GA, 12-15

1075 Greensboro Road, Eatonton, GA 31024 – 706-473-6522   Georgia Foothills
E-mail: joekingfamily3@yahoo.com

King, Robert Daniel – b Donalsonville, GA, Mar 7, 49; f Robert Wayne; m Mabel Daniels; w Carol Stanway, Jackson, MS, Apr 28, 73; chdn Thea Susan, Robin Elizabeth; FSU; RTS 86-89, MDiv; L Feb 89, MSVal Pby; O Aug 13, 89, CentCar Pby; srp First P Ch, Stanley, NC, 89-15; hr 15

PO Box 514, Stanley, NC 28164 – 704-263-2949   Catawba Valley
E-mail: dking77@carolina.rr.com
HR

Kinneer, Jack – astp Pioneer P Ch, Ligonier, PA, 04-09; ascp 09-

652 Pritts Road, Normalville, PA 15469 – 724-455-7802   Pittsburgh
E-mail: jkinneer@lhtot.net
Pioneer Presbyterian Church – 724-238-4777

Kinney, David George – b Birmingham, AL, Sept 19, 55; f Harold; m Grace Modenia Cost; w Teresa Rebecca Hardy, Lexington, SC, Aug 10, 91; chdn Diana, David McVicker, Kevin McVicker, Megan; CIU 98, BS; RTS 02, MDiv; L Apr 02, Palm Pby; O Dec 15, 03, Evan Pby; p First P Ch, Russellville, AL, 02-07; p Countryside P Ch, Cameron, NC 07-

127 Ponderosa Road, Cameron, NC 28326 – 919-499-9710 Eastern Carolina
E-mail: yennikad@gmail.com
Countryside Presbyterian Church – 919-499-2362

Kinser, John Charles – b West Palm Beach, FL, Dec 31, 48; f Ralph Edgar; m Florence Palmer; w Patricia Jean Kline, West Palm Beach, FL, Jul 5, 74; chdn John Knox, John Calvin, Dabney Catherine; FAU 74-76, BEd; ColGS 76-77; RTS 77-81, MDiv; O Jun 2, 81, MSVal Pby; campm BelC, 81-84; p First P Ch, Florala, AL, 84-88; srp Covenant P Ch, Milledgeville, GA, 88-96; op Lake Oconee P Ch, Eatonton, GA, 97-99, ss 99-00; chp Putnam Co, GA, 00-02; ob ss Young Meadows P Ch, Montgomery, AL, 02; MTW, church resourcer, 03-; ip First P Ch, Gulfport, MS, 04; exec p, ip St. Andrews P Ch, Columbia, SC, 05-06; astp First P Ch, Macon, GA, 07-

629 Old Lundy Road, Macon, GA 31210 – 478-954-4344 Central Georgia
E-mail: jckinser@bellsouth.net
First Presbyterian Church – 478-746-3223

Kinyon, John Donald Jr. – b Brockport, NY, Jul 1, 62; f John D. Sr.; m Jean Bassett; w Martha Claire Armistead, Atlanta, GA, Aug 8, 87; chdn John Donald III, James Armistead, Eric Andrew Pool, Paul Bassett, William Thaddaeus; CornU 80-84, BS; VandU 85-88, JD; RTS 91-94, MDiv, 98-, DMin cand; L Jun 25, 94; O Oct 15, 94, NoCA Pby; int University P Ch, Orlando, FL, 91-94; chp, ev Second City Fell, Kapolei, HI, 94-97, p 97-00; prof/Dean Int Coll & Grad Sch, Honolulu, 98-00; chp, op Cornerstone P Ch, Center Valley, PA, 00-05, srp 05-16; op Redeemer Ch, Southern Pines, NC, 16-; adj prof Sem in China, 11-

105 Grampian Way, Southern Pines, NC 28387 – 910-528-7349 Central Carolina
E-mail: john@redeemerchurchpca.org
Redeemer Church – 610-554-1425

Kiple, Mason – O Aug 21, 16, MSVall pby; astp Northpointe P Ch, Meridian, MS, 16-18, p 18-

4413 22nd Avenue, Meridian, MS 39305 Mississippi Valley
E-mail: mason@northpointepca.org
Northpointe Presbyterian Church – 601-482-7744

Kirk, Bee – ob Chap 16-

3008 Lake Ellen Lane, Tampa, FL 33618 – 407-494-9054 Southwest Florida
E-mail: beeshepardkirk@hotmail.com

Kirk, Jim – ascp Trinity P Ch, Rye, NY, 15-

618 Warbuton Avenue, Hastings-on-Hudson, NY 10706 Metropolitan New York
E-mail: jimkirk@trinitychurch.cc
Trinity Presbyterian Church – 914-967-6247

Kirk, Montgomery Blair III – b Mobile, AL, Apr 1, 56; f Montgomery Blair, Jr; m Virginia A. Parrott; w Catherine McDuffie, Jackson, MS, Aug 11, 84; chdn Montgomery Blair IV, Justin Thomas, Nancy Catherine; USM 78-83, BA; CTS 83-87, MDiv; L Oct 13, 87, Gr Pby; O Sept 11, 88, GrLks Pby; p Great Lakes P Ch, Wyoming MI, 88-89; ascp Grace P Ch, Moreno Valley, CA, 90-92, wc 92-94; p Leakesville P Ch, Leakesville, MS, 94-98; Chap USAF, 98-07; chap USAFR 07-11; ascp Cross Creek P Ch, Fayetteville, NC, 10-17; wc; hr 18

6520 Brookrun Drive, Fayetteville, NC 28306 – 910-835-2233 Central Carolina
E-mail: carisalone@yahoo.com
HR

Kirk, Timothy Douglas – b Pittsburg, PA, May 1, 61; f Jerry Ross; m Patricia Snyder; w Sally Ann Orr, Grove City, PA, May 12, 84; chdn Andrew Douglas, Philip James, Joel Timothy, Stephen Ross; GroCC 79-83, BA; GCTS 84-87, MDiv; RTSFL 02, DMin; L May 28, 88; O Mar 2, 89, NoIL Pby; ap Naperville P Ch, Naperville, IL, 87-90; op Christ Comm Ch, Carmel, IN, 90-93, srp 93-16; dir chp, CentIn Pby, 16-

12907 Brookshire Parkway, Carmel, IN 46033   Central Indiana

Kirker, P. Cameron – b St. Johns, MI, Sept 6, 50; f John Gilmore; m Anne Margarethe Johannessen; w Carol Sue Thompson, Boca Raton, FL, Sept 24, 77; chdn Kristin Leigh & Kelley Lynne (twins); StCCCC 68-70; LCAAT 70-71; PBJC 75-76; BroCC 80; FAU 82-83, BS; CBS 83-86, MDiv; L Jul 24, 86; O Jun 7, 87, Palm Pby; op Oakbrook Comm Ch, Summerville, SC, 86-88, p 88-02; op StillWaters, Salisbury, NC, 03-08; ob HIS Intnatl exec dir Inst of Intnatl Student Ministry, 08-11; ob Dir HIS Int, Inc., Columbia, SC, 11-12; astp Lexington P Ch, Lexington, SC, 12-18; hr 18

129 Leaning Pine Trail, Lexington, SC 29072   Palmetto
E-mail: cameronkirker@gmail.com
HR

Kitchen, Joshua Moores – b Philadelphia, PA, Nov 10, 74; f Gilbert; m Deborah Moores; w Sarah Christiansen, May 13, 00; chdn Makenna, Connor, Reagan; WmPatU 00, BA; SetonHall 03, MPAdm; RTSNC 12, MDiv; O Dec 2, 12, CentCar Pby; mis The Seed Comp, Papua, New Guinea, 12-

393 Hill Street, Whitinsville, MA 01588 – 682-888-3853   Central Carolina
E-mail: joshuakitchen@gmail.com
The Seed Company, Papua, New Guinea

Kittredge, Douglas Warren – b Boston, MA, Jul 26, 46; f Warren Lamont; m Margaret Nevada MacDonald; w Mary Jane Geoffrion, Lanesborough, MA, Dec 20, 69; chdn Douglas Charles, Naomi Elizabeth, Rachel Marie, Andrew Mark; ConcCI 66, AA; WheatC 68, BA; WTS 71, BD; GCTS 89, DMin; L Oct 70; O Oct 71, NJ Pby (OPC); p Grace OP Ch, Trenton, NJ, 71-75; p New Life in Christ Ch, Fredericksburg, VA, 75-98, srp 98-

1600 Washington Avenue, Fredericksburg, VA 22401 – 540-371-9254   James River
E-mail: dkittredge3@cox.net
New Life in Christ Church – 540-786-4848

Klein, David – b Encino, CA, Mar 18, 70; f George Barry; m Barbara Sharon; w Jill Christian Beck, Mar 11, 95; chdn Nathan Benjamin, Emily Grace, Zachary Adam; CMU 92, BS; WSCAL 99, MDiv; RegC 13, ThM; O May 12, 00, OPC; Recd PCA Jan 24, 14, PacNW Pby; p Grace OPC, Mt. Vernon, WA, 00-14; p Grace P Ch, Mt. Vernon, WA, 14-

3906 Apache Drive, Mount Vernon, WA 98273   Pacific Northwest
E-mail: dave@gracemountvernon.org
Grace Presbyterian Church – 360-399-6060

Klein, Robert Louis – b Baltimore, MD, Jun 16, 53; f Edward Arnold; m Harriett Ortel Sarraf; w Karen Esther Oerter, Worcester, PA, Mar 20, 93; chdn Kelsie Hanna, Jed Timothy, Brietta Ruth; HopeC 75, BA; FTS 94, MDiv; L Apr 94, SoCst Pby; O Jun 11, 95, Hrtg Pby; Dir YL, Columbus, OH, 84-88; ascp Berea P Ch, Hockessin, DE, 94-00; op Harbor P LaJolla-UTC, LaJolla, CA, 00-03, ascp 03-10; ascp Harbor Presbyterian Mira Mesa, San Diego, CA, 05- 15; srp Redemption Ch, San Diego, CA, 14-

6633 Maycrest Lane, San Diego, CA 92121 – 858-442-4459   South Coast
E-mail: bob@redemptionsd.org
Redemption Church

MINISTERIAL DIRECTORY

Klemm, Jerry – w Katherine; chdn Jerry III, Jakob; TNTC 90, BA; Sem in LA 04, MABS; O Mar 05, NFL Pby; p Old Stone Bapt Ch, Rome, GA, 87-89; ascp Temple Bapt Ch, Gulfport, MS, 90-95; srp Bostwick Bapt Ch, Bostwick, FL, 95-98; p Gr Comm Msn, Fernandina Beach, FL, 05-08; p Covenant P Ch, Palm Bay, FL, 08-

717 Nevada Drive NE, Palm Bay, FL 32907 – 904-215-1845   Central Florida
E-mail: jerryklemm@yahoo.com
Covenant Presbyterian Church – 321-727-2661

Klett, Fredrick Emil III – b La Rochelle, France, May 17, 53; f Frederick Emil Jr.; m Florence Adele Fish; w Jean Harvey, Darlington, MD, Nov 4, 78; chdn Nathan, Natalie, Nicole; JHU 71-75; TowU 75-77, BA; WTS 78-82, MAR, 83, grad wk; L Feb 89; O Jul 8, 90, Phil Pby; Jewish Evang spec, IVCF & Jews for Jesus, 84-88; mal Messianic Jewish Cntr, Philadelphia, PA, 88-89; fndr CHAIM, Glenside, PA, 89; ob ev to Jews, Philadelphia Pby, 90-; ob coord Lausanne Consultation on Jewish Ev (N. Amer), 95-99; ob lect WTS, 92-; vis lect/prof WSCAL, 99; vis lect/prof RTSFL, 00; p Rock of Israel Messianic Cong, 06-; art pub *New Horizons* (OPC); *Issues* (Jews for Jesus), *LCJE Intl Bulletin*, *Messianic Times*, *Christian Observer*; *Mishkan*, *CWI Herald;* contr *On Global Wizadry*

1457 Holcomb Road, Huntingdon Valley, PA 19006 – 215-576-6828   Philadelphia
E-mail: chaim@chaim.org
Rock of Israel Messianic Congregation – 215-576-7325

Klett, Kenneth Eric – b Plainfield, NJ, Aug 24, 60; f F. E., Jr; m Florence A. Fish; w Laurie A. Polderman, Kalamazoo, MI, Jun 25, 88; chdn Faith Christiana, Leah Marieann, Susannah Adele, Abigail Laurie, Kenneth Eric Jr., Jonathan Frederick, Nathaniel Elijah; MonSC, BA; WTS, MDiv; L Nov 5, 89; O Dec 10, 89, NJ Pby; int Calvary P Ch, Willow Grove, PA, 88-89; astp Calvary P Ch, Allenwood, NJ, 89-91, ascp 91-95, wc 95; p New Life P Ch, Middletown, NJ, 95-06; p Covenant P Ch, Holland, MI, 06-

4876 Green Ridge Trail, Hamilton, MI 49419   Great Lakes
E-mail: keklett60@gmail.com
Covenant Presbyterian Church – 616-355-2036

Kline, Nathan Eugene – b King City, CA, Feb 5, 62; f Daniel K.; m Charlotte Earline Stone; w Suzanne Kay Hopma, Muskegon, MI, Aug 11, 84; chdn Evan Michael, Anna Elizabeth, Allison Nicole, Alexander Morgan; JBU, BA; TEDS, MDiv; L Nov 2, 91; O Apr 26, 92, NoIL Pby; astp First P Ch & Rosedale P Ch, Pardeeville, WI, 90-91; astp Grace P Ch, Pardeeville, WI, 91-92, p 92-08; astp Friendly Hills P Ch, Jamestown, NC, 08-09; p 09-

2371 Alderbrook Drive, High Point, NC 27265 – 336-662-6999   Piedmont Triad
E-mail: nathan@friendlyhillschurch.org
Friendly Hills Presbyterian Church – 336-292-8992

Knaak, Patric – b Stoughton, WI, Jan 24, 71; f James Arnold; m Jill Birdie; w Jennifer White, East Moline, IL, Dec 19, 92; chdn Parker Thomas Graeme; MBI 93, BA; WheatGrS 95, MA; O Jun 11, 06, ChiMet Pby; astp Naperville P Ch, Naperville, IL, 99-07; ob Serge, 07-

601 Lindley Road, Glenside, PA 19038 – 215-758-2286   Eastern Pennsylvania
E-mail: pknaak@serge.org
Serge, 101 West Avenue #305, Jenkintown, PA 19046-2039

Knaebel, Christopher – O Jul 14, 12, SusqV Pby; astp Providence P Ch, York, PA, 12-14; wc; p Faith P Ch, Sarasota, FL, 15-17; astp Covenant Life P Ch, Sarasota, FL, 17-

8490 McIntosh Rd, Sarasota, FL 34238 – 941-404-7972   Suncoast Florida
E-mail: christopher.knaebel@gmail.com
Covenant Life Presbyterian Church – 941-926-4777

Knaebel, Garry Lee – b Detroit, MI, Oct 25, 52; f Carl; m Betty Jane Commerson; w Carole Ann Pribble, Hazel Park, MI, May 27, 78; chdn Christopher Daniel, Bethany Elizabeth, Kimberly Ruth; WmTynC 76, BCE; WTS 80, MDiv; L May 16, 81, Phil Pby; O Jun 27, 82, MidAtl Pby; p Gr Christian Flwsp, Hancock, MD, 82-88; astp Pilgrim P Ch, Martinsburg, WV, 91-92; op Gr Ref Flwsp, Williamsport, MD, 88-92, p 92-

651 Highland Way, Hagerstown, MD 21740-6237 – 301-739-0645   Potomac
E-mail: glk1025@aol.com
Grace Reformed Fellowship – 301-797-6784

Knapp, Gary Francis – b Toledo, OH, Dec 5, 65; f Gary Edward; m Germaine Julia Hendricks; w Alise Marcile Reilly, Toledo, OH, Sept 30, 95; chdn Josiah, Thea, Elijah, Joshua, Abigail, Anna; Circleville, BA; MITheoSem, MDiv; L May 92; L Dec 01; ascp Christ the Word Ch, Toledo, OH, 01-04; p Eastgate P Ch, Millsboro, DE, 04-

20243 Bridgewater Road, Millsboro, DE 19966 – 302-858-9706   Heritage
E-mail: pilgrimgary@verizon.net
Eastgate Presbyterian Church – 302-945-5498

Knauf, Keith Harlan – b Minneapolis, MN, Nov 28, 52; f Harlan; m Dolores; w Ida Garrison, Gridley, CA, Jan 16, 83; chdn LaWonna, Matthew; BethlC, BA; BethlTS, MDiv; L Apr 13, 83, Bapt; O Jan 3, 88, PCUSA; Recd PCA Mar 1, 96, NoCA Pby; srp Pioneer P Ch, Winters, CA, 88-95; Chap, DPC California Department of Corrections, Med Facility, Vacaville, 95-

237 Montville Court, Vacaville, CA 95688 – 707-446-4270   Northern California
California Department of Corrections – 707-448-6841

Knecht, Glen C. – hr 17

327 Carroll Avenue, Laurel, MD 20707   Potomac
E-mail: glenknecht@gmail.com
HR

Kneeshaw, Keith – b Kingston, NY, Nov 9, 74; f Preston; m Judith; w Linda Ruth Molbach, St. Louis, MO, Dec 11, 99; USF 95, BA; CTS 00, MDiv; O Apr 02, SWFL Pby; ascp Redeemer P Ch, Riverview, FL, 01-10; p Grace Point P Ch, Irmo, SC, 10-

205 Hearthwood Circle, Irmo, SC 29063   Palmetto
E-mail: kmkneeshaw@hotmail.com
Grace Point Presbyterian Church

Knight, Gerald J. – b Erie, PA, Oct 11, 57; f John K.; m Ann M. Wilson; w Karen E. Cope, Buffalo, NY; chdn Lindsay, Lee, Drew, Derek, Amy; SUNYM 80, AA; BSC 86, BS; GCTS 91, MDiv; O Feb 16, 95, Asc Pby; ascp Faith Ref Ch, Erie, PA, 95-99; op West Erie Bible PCA, Erie, PA, 96-99, p 99-10; mis AfrBibC, Uganda, 09-

132 Paige Avenue, Buffalo, NY 14223 – 716-725-9729   Ascension
E-mail: geraldjknight@gmail.com
African Bible University, Kampala, Uganda

Knight, James Parker – b Atlanta, GA, May 5, 48; f Cecil Parker; m Vesta Green; w Helen Honea, Jonesboro, GA, Mar 21, 70; chdn James Nathan, Joel Andrew; GATech 66-70, BS; GCTS 70-73, MDiv; O Oct 7, 73, Meckl Pby (PCUS); ap Thomasboro Ch, 73-74; p Cooleemee Ch, 74-76; p Westview Ch, 76-78; ap Westminster P Ch, Atlanta, GA, 78-80; p First P Ch, Waynesboro, GA, 80-00; p Faith Ref P Ch, Frederick, MD, 00-04; p First P Ch, Waynesboro, GA, 04-13; hr 13

2922 Kipling Drive, Augusta, GA 30909 – 706-364-1901   Savannah River
E-mail: write2knight@yahoo.com
HR

Knott, Joshua – b Tampa, FL, Nov 7, 79; f Michael; m Marlyn; w Erin Anita Keltonic, Richmond, VA, Jun 30, 01; chdn Sophia Frances, Zoe Evangeline, Shiloh Anastasia; GroCC, BA; RTS, MDiv; O Jan 14, 07, Hrtg Pby; astp Evangelical P Ch, Newark, DE, 06-13; ascp 14-18; p Cornerstone P Ch, Columbia, SC, 18-

27 Glenhawk Loop, Irmo, SC 29343   Palmetto
E-mail: joshua627@gmail.com
Cornerstone Presbyterian Church

Knowles, Tommie Ray – b Ridgeland, SC, Jun 25, 41; f Karl Ray; m Alice Saxon; w (1) Gloria Langford (dv) (2) JoAnn Morrell (d) (3) Linda Morrell (d); chdn Tommie R. Jr., Tammy Fay, Grady, Michael Allison, Jeffery Allison; GBibC 80, BBE; CTS 84, MDiv; L 82; O 84, CentGA Pby; p Liberty P Ch, Sylvania, GA, 84-97; ob exec dir Hebron Colony & Gr Homes, Inc, 97-06; hr 08

129 Lecka Lane, Banner Elk, NC 28604 – 828-898-4005   Western Carolina
E-mail: tknowles3@hotmail.com
HR

Knox, Jason – O Jan 17, 15, Ill Pby; ob yp Presbyterian Ch of Boatswain Bay, 15-16

709 Twining Way, Collegeville, PA 19426   Illiana
E-mail: knox.r.jason@gmail.com

Knox, Mic – O Oct 1, 17, NWGA Pby; astp Midway P Ch, Powder Springs, GA, 17-

Midway Presbyterian Church   Northwest Georgia

Knutson, William James – b Illinois, Oct 20, 41; f Orvin; m Pearle Woodhouse; w Willa Blood, Illinois; chdn Kevin, Daniel; UIL 67, BS; RTSFL 93, MDiv; L Jan 94; O Apr 17, 94, SWFL Pby; headm Seminole P sch, 94-96; ascp Seminole P Ch, Tampa, FL, 94-96, wc 96-01; astp Surfside P Ch, Surfside Beach, SC, 01-08, hr 08

7A Westlake Drive, Orange City, FL 32763 – 843-283-5223   Palmetto
E-mail: wknutson1@gmail.com
HR

Ko, Edward Keon – w Michelle; chdn Elizabeth, Abraham; L Apr 15, 97, KorSW Pby; O Oct 14, 97, KorSW Pby; p Holy Hill Comm Ch, Los Angeles, CA, 97-99; p Holy City Ch, Cerritos, CA, 99-

13906 Rose Street, Cerritos, CA 90703 – 562-809-0017   Korean Southwest
E-mail: holycitychurch@hotmail.com
Holy City Church

Ko, Hyunkwon – srp McLean Korean P Ch, McLean, VA, 18-

2002 Highboro Way, Falls Church, VA 22043   Korean Capital
E-mail: hyunkwonko@gmail.com
McLean Korean Presbyterian Church – 703-893-8651

Ko, Jaeseok – b Seoul, Korea, Aug 8, 79; f Kevin Kwangmin; m Songhee; w Hye Won Hwang, California, Oct 13, 12; chdn Abigail, Jayden; NamSeoul 05, BS; GGBTS, DMin; TalTS, MDiv; Recd PCA Sept 13, 16, KorSW Pby; ascp Inland Ch PCA, Pomona, CA, 16-

14578 Manchester Avenue, Chino, CA 91710   Korean Southwest
E-mail: jaeko@inlandchurch.org
Inland Church PCA – 909-622-2324

Ko, Joseph – Chap USArmy, 16-

716 Southwick Avenue, Grovetown, GA 30813 – 443-977-9910   Potomac
E-mail: chapjko@gmail.com
United States Army

Ko, Kwang Ryong –

E-mail: abeko0112@gmail.com   Korean Central

Ko, Paul H.J. – srp Disciple Comm Ch, Irvine, CA, 16-

17502 Daimler Street, Irvine, CA 92614 – 949-333-3836   Korean Southwest Orange County
E-mail: pastorko@disciplecc.org
Disciple Community Church – 949-502-4923

Kobb, James Arley – b Akron, OH, Mar 7, 53; f Arley Raymond; m Bertha Elizabeth Davidson; w Janet; chdn Daniel Lance, Nathaniel James, Jonathan David; UAkr 71-75, BA; RTS 76-79, MDiv; O Jun 10, 79, Asc Pby; mis MTW, Korea, 79-97; ob astp Cleveland Korean Ch, 97-04; astp Faith P Ch, Akron, OH, 04-14, ascp 14-

1150 Stanwood Avenue, Akron, OH 44314-1242 – 234-788-9451   Ohio
E-mail: jimkobb@yahoo.com
Faith Presbyterian Church – 330-644-9654

Kockler, Kyle Patrick – b Annapolis, MD, Sept 8, 74; f Frank; m Madeline Teresa Alloway; w Virginia Hope, Aug 04, 07; chdn Drew; JMU 92-96, BS; RTSNC 99-02, MDiv; L Jul 20, 03, BlRdg Pby; O Jul 20, 03, BlRdg Pby; ascp Grace Cov P Ch, Blacksburg, VA, 02-08; Castp Faith P Ch, Gainesville, FL, 09-13; ip Christ Comm Ch, Gainesville, FL, 14-15; astp Tabernacle P Ch, Waynesboro, VA, 16-

530 Winding Way, Waynesboro, VA 22980 – 352-275-1303   Blue Ridge
E-mail: kyle@tab-pres.org
Tabernacle Presbyterian Church – 540-932-1778

Koerber, Matthew – b Washington, DC, Jun 11, 74; w Chrissie; chdn Isaac Dwight, Theodore Robert, Norah Grace; PASU 98, BS; GCTS, MDiv; astp Citylife P Ch of Boston, Boston, MA, 05; op City Ref P Ch, Pittsburgh, PA, 05-08, p 08-

4021 Lydia Street, Pittsburgh, PA 15207 – 412-421-1803   Pittsburgh
E-mail: pastor@cityreformed.org
City Reformed Presbyterian Church – 412-720-7014

Koh, Edward S. – w Jennifer; chdn Phoebe Abigail Eunkyung, Ezra James Sungwook; UIL, BS; TEDS, MDiv; O Nov 04, PacNW Pby; ascp Hillcrest P Ch, Seattle, WA, 03-11; chp, op New City Church, Seattle, 13-

3007 SW Hinds Street, Seattle, WA 98126 – 206-658-1120   Pacific Northwest
E-mail: edward.s.koh@gmail.com
New City Church, Seattle

Koh, I. Henry – b Chinnampo, KOR, Dec 24, 35; f Yei Shik Koh; m Hak Sun Kim; w Myung Sun Chung, Seoul, KOR, Nov 22, 71; chdn Grace Eunhey, Joyce Eunjoo; SEMOStC 54-56; UIA 56-60, BS; PTS 69, BD, 70, ThM; O Jun 28, 70, UPCUSA; ap Riverview UPC, Drexel Hill, PA, 70-72; p Korean United Ch of Phil, Philadelphia, PA, 72-81; srp Emmanuel Ch in Phil, Philadelphia, PA, 81-98; admin MNA, coord of Korean min, 98-16; hr 16

15 Barbara Lane, Havertown, PA 19083   Korean Eastern
E-mail: ihenrykoh@gmail.com
HR

MINISTERIAL DIRECTORY

Koh, Robert K.M. – mis The Way Ch

36503 China Place, Palmdale, CA 93551   Korean Southwest
E-mail: robertkoh@gmail.com
The Way Church – 323-735-0200

Koh, Sanghyun – astp Korean Ch of the Lord, Carrollton, TX, 09-10; p Bright Castle P Ch, Killeen, TX, 10-

516 Arapaho Dr, Harker Heights, TX 76548   Korean Southern
E-mail: pospe@juno.com
Bright Castle Presbyterian Church – 254-554-3332

Kona, Albert – b May 7, 71; w Jennifer; chdn Annabella Natalie, Miriam Catherine, Johannes Calvin; GPTS 05, BD; astp Woodruff Road P Ch, for chp in Albania, Simpsonville, SC, 07-

2519 Woodruff Road, Simpsonville, SC 29681   Calvary
E-mail: bertikona@gmail.com
Woodruff Road Presbyterian Church – 864-297-5257

Konopa, Benedict Walter Jr. – b Portsmouth, VA, Aug 21, 50; f Benedict W. Sr.; m Leola Wilson; w Barbara Mell Bessenger, Columbia, SC, Nov 6, 71; chdn Jessica Wilson, Matthew Benedict; USC, BS; RTS, MDiv; O Aug 22, 76, GulCst Pby; ap Fairfield P Ch, Pensacola, FL, 76-78; p Westminster P Ch, Valdosta, GA, 78-91; p Westminster P Ch, Johnson City, TN, 91-02; p Grace P Ch, Fort Payne, AL, 02-04; hr 04

1012 Bennington Drive, Charleston, SC 29492 – 843-446-1280   Evangel
E-mail: BBKONOPA@gmail.com
HR

Kooistra, Paul David – b Duluth, MN, Oct 11, 42; f David; m Laura Bowman; w Janet M. Carlson (d); (2) Sandra Tucker, Aug 29, 09; chdn Paul Jr., Shary, Jennifer; UMN 60-64, BA; ColTS 64-67, MDiv; UAL 75-80, PhD; O Jun 19, 67, Duluth Pby (UPCUSA); ap Pinelands P Ch, Miami, FL, 67-69; ap Seminole P Ch, Tampa, FL, 69-73; asst prof BelC, 73-75; assoc prof RTS, 75-84; prof 84-85; pres CTS, 85-94; coord MTW, 94-14; pres Erskine, 14-16; hr 17; *Thirty-one Days of Grace*; *Supper's Ready*; *Faith Promise*; *Following God*; *Pursuit of Joy*

PO Box 415, Suwanee, GA, 30024   Warrior
E-mail: duluth42@gmail.com
HR

Kook, Kenneth Youn-Kwon – astp Sae Han P Ch of Atlanta, Alpharetta, GA, 07-

Address Unavailable   Korean Southeastern
Sae Han Presbyterian Church of Atlanta – 770-619-5340

Kooy, Albert – op New City Ch, Newmarket, ON, 12-

242 Plymount Trail, Newmarket, ON L3Y 6G7   Eastern Canada
E-mail: albertkooy@gmail.com
New City Church – 289-264-3866

Korljan, Robert R. – b Phoenix, AZ, Jun 19, 52; f Robert J (d); m Jeanne Gale (d); w Jayne Jernberg (d) (2) Ginger Madi, Nov 12, 05; chdn Scott, Lisa (Harding), Dawn (Beyer), Kristine (Jorgensen), Jim Madi, Melody Madi (Stiles), Christy Madi (Rivera); AZSU 74, BS; CTS 84, MDiv; L Aug 87; O Feb 14, 88, NoE

Korljan, Robert R., continued
Pby; p Berea P Ch, E. Providence, RI, 87-92; astp South Valley P Ch, Chandler, AZ, 92-93; chp SW Pby, 93-; ob p Roosevelt Comm Ch, 04-

1524 West Winter Drive, Phoenix, AZ 85021 – 602-717-9129   Southwest
E-mail: bob@eatoncambridge.com
Roosevelt Community Church

Korljan, Scott – w Lindsay; chdn Tenley, Cade; WSCAL 11, MDiv; astp North City P Ch, Poway, CA, 12-13; p Redeemer P Ch, Traverse City, MI, 13-; "In the Presence of a Common Foe: Billy Sunday and Conservative Presbyterians in the Fight Against Liberalism," *Confessional Presbyterian*, vol 9, 13

402 West 9th Street, Traverse City, MI 49684 – 773-971-4055   Great Lakes
E-mail: scott.korljan@gmail.com
Redeemer Presbyterian Church – 231-946-1700

Korn, Robert H. – w Sheri; chdn Margaret, Isabel; CIU, MDiv; O Nov 03, Palm Pby; p Union Mem P Ch, Winnsboro, SC, 02-09; astp Cornerstone P Ch, Columbia, SC, 09-12; ascp 12-14; srp 14-17

532 Glencove Court, Lexington, SC 29072   Palmetto

Kornreich, Andrew – O Nov 16, 97, Palm Pby; astp Northeast P Ch, Columbia, SC, 97-99; p Rose Hill P Ch, Columbia, SC, 06-12; p New Cov P Ch, Aiken, SC, 13-18; hr 18

3045 Verbena Drive, Aiken, SC 29083 – 803-348-8543   Palmetto
HR

Korzep, Daniel Louis – Martinsburg, WVA, Jun 9, 50; f Louis; m Analee Ingram; w Sheila Jean Elder, Annapolis, MD, Jan 13, 79; p Harvest P Ch, Lincolnton, NC, 18-

6 Overlook Avenue, Haverhill, MA 01832-4656   Catawba Valley
Harvest Presbyterian Church – 704-732-9978

Koslowsky, Kevin – b Woodbury, NJ, Feb 21, 78; f John Michael Jr.; m Jeanne Marie Gelsinger; w Laura Beth Ingalls, Shamong, NJ, Aug 14, 99; chdn David, Leah, Samuel; MesC 00, BA; CTS 01-02; WTS 07, MDiv; L Sept 9, 05, Hrtg Pby; O Mar 5, 06, Hrtg Pby; astp Faith P Ch, Wilmington, DE, 06-07, ascp 07-12; srp 12-

214 Rowland Park Boulevard, Wilmington, DE 19803 – 609-923-9096   Heritage
E-mail: Kevin@faithwilmington.com
Faith Presbyterian Church – 302-764-8615

Kothe, Doug – O May 20, 12, PacNW Pby; p Crossroads @ Lake Stevens, Lake Stevens, WA, 13-17

1226 84th Avenue SE, Lake Stevens, WA 98258 – 425-212-9440   Pacific Northwest
E-mail: doug.kothe@gmail.com

Kountze, Tower – O May 22, 16, PlVall Pby; astp Harvest Comm Ch, Omaha, NE, 16-17; op The Midtown Project, Omaha, NE, 18-

5208 Cuming Street, Omaha, NE 68132 – 402-203-5180   Platte Valley
E-mail: tkountze@gmail.com
The Midtown Project

Kozak, Mark – p Providence Ref P Ch, Barboursville, WV, 13-

6282 Aracoma Road, Huntington, WV 25705   New River
E-mail: markoza@netzero.net
Providence Reformed Presbyterian Church – 304-736-0487

Krasowski, Andrew Thomas – b Baltimore, MD, Nov 4, 51; f Walter S.; m Sophie A. Antkeiwicz; w Nancy Carol Sandusky, Baltimore, MD, Jul 13, 74; chdn Cindy Michele, Brian Gabriel, Paula Lynette, Matthew Thomas; Kg'sC 69-72; TowU 74, BA; CTS 78, MDiv; L Apr 78, Ill Pby; O Apr 79, DMV Pby (RPCES); ap Evangelical P Ch, Newark, DE, 79-82; p Rocky Springs P Ch, Harrisville, PA, 83-86; p Liberty Bay P Ch, Poulsbo, WA, 86-

18568 10th Avenue NE, Poulsbo, WA 98370-8721 – 360-697-2447   Pacific Northwest
E-mail: atkraskowski@comcast.net
Liberty Bay Presbyterian Church – 360-779-7545

Krause, Jeff – O Feb 28, 16, SucstFL Pby; astp Auburn Road P Ch, Venice, FL, 16-

2551 Dawn Road, Venice, FL 34293   Suncoast Florida
E-mail: jskrause2@liberty.edu
Auburn Road Presbyterian Church – 941-485-3551

Kreisel, Jeffrey – O Oc 17, 17, RMtn Pby

5350 Sevenoaks Drive, Colorado Springs, CO 80919   Rocky Mountain
E-mail: jeffkreisel@gmail.com

Kreitzer, Mark R. – b Denver, CO; f Robert Edward; m Lois Eleanor McCullough; w Nancy Carol Edwards, Jackson, MS, May 21, 94; chdn Mark, Caroline, Sarah Anne; BIOLA 71-75, BA; TalTS 79-83, MDiv; RTS 93-97, DMiss, 01, PhD; L 94, MSVal Pby; O 98, Cov Pby; op Covenant P Ch, Russellville, AR, 98-99, wc 99-00; p Bailey P Ch, Bailey, MS, 00-02, wc 02-04; prof Montreat, 05-08; ob mis 10-; co-auth *A Christian Manifesto for Southern Africa: Study Edition; God's Plan for Christian South Africa: Dominion or Missions; A Missiological Evaluation of the Nederdirtse Gereformeerde Kerk's New Social Theology, Church and Society*, 90; *Good News for All Peoples: A Covenantal Understanding of Ethnicity and People Movements*

E-mail: markkreitzer@juno.com   Western Carolina

Krispin, William C. – ob admin 03-07; hr 07

100 Breyer Drive, Apt. 1F, Elkins Park, PA 19027 – 267-259-6768   Philadelphia
HR

Kristoffersen, Tom – w Debbie; BucknU 95, BS; BibTS 06, MDiv; O Oct 22, 06, NYS Pby; p Presbyterian Ch of Wellsville, Wellsville, NY, 06-

55 Oak Street, Wellsville, NY 14895 – 585-593-6890   New York State
E-mail: pastortompcw@yahoo.com
Presbyterian Church of Wellsville – 585-593-5069

Krueger, David – p Forreston Grove Ch, Forreston, IL, 04-07; ob Pittsville EFC, 07-14; op Wausau Ch Plant, Weston, WI, 14-16; ob srp Gibbsville Ref Ch, 17-

W2615 Riverview Terrace, Sheboygan Falls, WI 53085 – 715-650-1100   Wisconsin
E-mail: limpingon@yahoo.com
Gibbsville Reformed Church

Kruger, Kurt – p Peace Comm Ch, Frankfort, IL, 14-

21300 South LaGrange Road, Frankfort, IL 60423   Chicago Metro
E-mail: kurtkruger@peaceinfrankfort.org
Peace Community Church – 815-469-2868

Kruger, Michael – ob assoc prof RTSNC, 04-; ascp Uptown Ch, Charlotte, NC, 04-

7332 St. Clair Drive, Charlotte, NC 28270 – 704-564-8182   Central Carolina
E-mail: mkruger@rts.edu
Reformed Theological Seminary, NC – 704-366-5066
2101 Carmel Road, Charlotte, NC 28226
Uptown Church, PCA – 704-375-7355

Kruis, Philip Scott – b Rehoboth, NM, Oct 12, 62; f Richard Kruis; m Mae Van Zwol; w Shelley Cox, Las Cruces, NM, Jul 22, 89; chdn Johnathan Philip, Melissa Grace, Caleb Scott; DordtC 84, BA; RTS 93, MA, 95, MDiv; L Jan 20, 95; O May 19, 96, SW Pby; astp Catalina Foothills Ch, Tucson, AZ, 96-02; op Rincon Mountain P Ch, Tucson, AZ, 00-02, p 02-

3444 North Camino Esplanade, Tucson, AZ 85750 – 520-733-5679   Southwest
E-mail: pkruis@gmail.com
Rincon Mountain Presbyterian Church – 520-327-2390

Krulish, Jerid – O Feb 14, 10, PacNW Pby; astp Faith P Ch, Tacoma, WA, 10-13; p Westminster P Ch, Vancouver, WA, 13-

814 NE 109th Court, Vancouver, WA 98664 – 360-601-9208   Pacific Northwest
E-mail: pastor@solochristo.org
Westminster Presbyterian Church – 360-602-1501

Kruntorad, Raymond E. – b Chicago, IL, Apr 10, 42; f Raymond; m Josephine Horvatic; w Sharon Wolf, Hollywood, FL, Jul 23, 61; chdn Mark, Lori; RTS 84, dipl; O 84, SFL Pby; ap First P Ch of Coral Springs, Margate, FL, 84-87; op Spruce Creek P Ch, Port Orange, FL, 87-91, p 91-95; op Grace Cov Ch, Hickory, NC, 95-97, p 97-12; hr 12; p Christ Ch at River's Edge, Belmont, NC, 12-

408 Planters Way, Mt. Holly, NC 28120 – 828-256-7590   Catawba Valley
E-mail: raykruntorad@gmail.com
Christ Church at River's Edge

Ku, Dong Rip – astp Global Msn Ch, Diamond Bar, CA

12468 North Park Avenue, Chino, CA 91710 – 909-988-7324   Korean Southwest
E-mail: dongripku@hotmail.com
Global Mission Church – 909-396-4441

Ku, Joshua Jung – UIL 95, BA; TEDS 98, MDiv; ob astp Life Creek Church, WI, 05-07; astp Kor Ch of Chicago, IL, (Chicago Grace Ch), 10-17

1589 South Kembley Avenue, Palatine, IL 60067   Korean Central
E-mail: joshuaku@gmail.com

Ku, Silas – astp Church for All Nations, Vienna, VA, 12-

20390 Charter Oak Drive, Ashburn, VA 20147   Korean Capital
E-mail: silasku@gmail.com
Church for All Nations – 703-573-3767

Kublik, Connan A.V. – b Edmonton, Alberta, Sept 16, 71; f Ray; m Carol; w Brenda, Nov 4, 00; chdn Kira, Brysan, Evan, Rylan; UCalg 95, BA; RegC 05, MDiv; op New City Ch, Hamilton, ON, 06-

138 Stanley Avenue, Hamilton, ON L8P 2L4 CANADA – 905-906-7613   Eastern Canada
E-mail: conankublik@yahoo.ca
New City Church – 888-908-6293

MINISTERIAL DIRECTORY   361

Kuebler, John Francis – b Lackwanna, NY, May 2, 48; f Francis P.; m Doris J. Culligan; w Mary Elizabeth Shreenan, Buffalo, NY, Aug 13, 71; chdn Lawrence, Scott; BroCC 71, AA; NU 84, BS; RTS 87, MA, 88, MDiv; L Jun 14, 90; O Nov 7, 90; couns Alta Woods P Ch, Pearl, MS, 87-90; Chap Police, Jackson, MS , 85-88; ob Chap Police, Charlottesville, VA, 92-95; ascp Trinity P Ch, Charlottesville, VA, 90-02; couns First Stone Ministries, 97-02; ascp Covenant P Ch, Harrisonburg, VA, 02-13; ob Dir Journey Counseling Ministries, 13-

5812 Hounds Chase Lane, Harrisonburg, VA 22801-6604 – 540-574-2495   Blue Ridge
E-mail: johnkjcm@gmail.com
Journey Counseling Ministries

Kuiper, A. Bernhard – b Arnhem, Holland, May 3, 35; f August Bernhard K; m Annie Moesker; w Noelene Wiseman, Sydney, Australia, Mar 15, 58; chdn Berenice Nicolene (Rarig), Elizabeth Anne (Harvey), Paul Bernhard, Mark David, Jonathan Edwards; SABibC 61; RTS 74, MDiv; St Albans TC 76, ThB; ColCU 92, DD; EvTS 94, ThD; O May 74, MSVal Pby, ev 67-71; p Mount Salus P Ch, Clinton, MS, 74-75; ap First P Ch, Chattanooga, TN, 75-77; p North Atlanta Ch, Atlanta, GA, 77-79; srp Village Seven P Ch, Colorado Springs, CO, 79-97, mal; ip Trinity P Ch, Asheville, NC, 98-99; ob p Little River Ch, Alpharetta, GA, 99-01; p North Hills P Ch, Meridianville, AL, 01-04; p Thomson Mem P Ch, Centreville, MS, 04-05; ss Christ Cov P Ch, Matthews, NC, 05-06; astp Lawndale P Ch, Tupelo, MS, 07-09; ip Main Street P Ch, Columbus, MS, 07-08; ob ip Covenant EPC, Jackson, MS, 08; p Covenant Life P Ch, Saltillo, MS, 09-10; hr 10; *When Bad Things Happen to Good Prophecies*

5961 Vermelle Drive, Tupelo, MS 38801 – 662-205-4358   Covenant
HR

Kuiper, Mark D. – b Wauchope, Australia, Nov 16, 64; f A. Bernhard; m Noelene Fay Wiseman; w Tammy Lynda Porter, Colorado Springs, Nov 30, 85; chdn Jordan, Luke, Anna; MSC 83; UCO 84-87; ColCU 90-92, BS; CTS, MDiv; L Nov 10, 96; O Nov 10, 96, JR Pby; astp Trinity P Ch, Charlottesville, VA, 96-01; op Christ Ch of Pasadena, Pasadena, CA, 01-05, p 05-06; p Lawndale P Ch, Tupelo, MS, 06-09; srp Kirk of the Hills P Ch, St. Louis, MO, 09-15; op Three Rivers Ch (PCA), Grove, OK, 16-

4982 Lighthouse Springs Drive, Grove, OK 74344-7931   North Texas
E-mail: mdkuiper@msn.com
Three Rivers Church (PCA) – 314-960-1598

Kulp, Dale – b Harrisburg, PA, Mar 25, 63; f Donald; m Doris Elizabeth Roberts; w Shelly Lynn Kautz, Sherman Station, ME, Apr 13, 87; chdn Emily Jane, Selah Lynn, Samuel Warren, Isabel Anna, Grace Elizabeth, Kathy Irene, Daniel Warren; Harrisburg CC 85, AA; CTS 03, MDiv; O Nov 9, 03, OHVal Pby; ascp Christ P Ch, Richmond, IN, 03-07; p Shore Harvest P Ch, Easton, MD, 07-16; wc 16-

202 Tubman Drive, Easton, MD 21601   Heritage

Kulp, Dave – astp Uptown Ch, PCA, Charlotte, NC, 09-11; ascp 11-

9432 Sardis Glen Drive, Matthews, NC 28105 – 704-564-8184   Central Carolina
E-mail: davekulp@uptownchurch.org
Uptown Church, PCA – 704-375-7355

Kuo, Mike – astp Redeemer Sugar Land, Sugar Land, TX, 15-

1810 Ravenel Lane, Sugar Land, TX 77479   Houston Metro
E-mail: michaelkuo@yahoo.com
Redeemer Sugar Land – 832-576-2216

Kutai, Yakubu – Recd PCA Apr 18, 17, EPA Pby; Chap Abington Mem Hosp, 17-

3 Douglas Street, Ambler, PA 19002   Eastern Pennsylvania
Abington Memorial Hospital

Kwalk, Joseph – O Nov 4, 12, KorSE Pby; astp New Ch of Atlanta, Peachtree Corners, GA, 12-15; astp Sae Han P Ch of Atlanta, Alpharetta, GA, 15-18; astp Emmanuel Ch in Phil, Philadelphia, PA, 18-

166 E Kennilworth Circle, Newtown Square, PA 19073 – 908-552-8829   Korean Eastern
E-mail: joek527@gmail.com
Emmanuel Church in Philadelphia – 215-476-0330

Kwasny, Josh – ascp Redeemer P Ch, Winston-Salem, NC, 12- 15; p Grace Foothills, Tryon, NC, 15-16; p Redeemer Yadkin Valley, Yadkinville, NC, 18-

6417 Hampton Knoll Road, Clemmons, NC 27012 – 336-782-8457   Piedmont Triad
E-mail: jckwas@gmail.com
Redeemer Yadkin Valley – 336-426-8771

Kwon, Daniel J. – w Mi Kyung Choi; chdn Yong Kweon, Christian Kweon, Minha Kweon; O 02, KorE Pby; ob astp Korean United Ch of Phil, Philadelphia, PA, 00-05; Dir A Cup of Water International, 05-

PO Box 9809, Kansas City, MO 64134   Korean Eastern
A Cup of Water International

Kwon, Danny – ob Young Sang Presbyterian Church, Horsham, PA, 10-

460 Barrington Street, Horsham, PA 19044 – 215-957-5638   Korean Eastern
E-mail: drdkwon@gmail.com
Young Sang Presbyterian Church, Horsham, PA

Kwon, Duke – GCTS, MDiv, ThM; O Jul 31, 05, Pot Pby; astp Grace P Ch of Wash, D.C., Washington, DC, 05-07; ascp 07-

3619 11th Street NW, Washington, DC 20010 – 202-491-9114   Potomac
E-mail: duke@gracemeridianhill.org
Grace Presbyterian Church of Washington, D.C. – 202-386-7637

Kwon, Hukmin – O Jun 25, 09, KorE Pby; ob astp Korean United Ch of Philadelphia, 09-10; ob admin WTS

8 Knox Court, Chesterbrook, PA 19087 – 267-403-0179   Korean Eastern
E-mail: hukmin@gmail.com
Westminster Theological Seminary – 215-887-5511
P.O. Box 27009, Philadelphia, PA 19118

Kwon, Peter Oh – mis SEED Int

PO Box 69, Merrifield, VA 22116   Korean Capital
E-mail: acdkwon@gmail.com
SEED International

Kwon, Seongryong – p Jesus Family P Ch, Valencia, CA, 16-

28466 Constellation Road, Valencia, CA 91355   Korean Southwest
E-mail: jfpckwon@gmail.com
Jesus Family Presbyterian Church

Kwon, Seungwon – astp Emmanuel Ch in Phil, Philadelphia, PA, 18-

1403 Dogwood Cir, Blue Bell, PA 19422   Korean Eastern
E-mail: iworshiplord@naver.com
Emmanuel Church in Philadelphia – 215-476-0330

Kwon, Sherwin – O Feb 14, 16, Phil Pby; astp Grace and Peace Comm Ch, Philadelphia, PA, 16-

Grace and Peace Community Church   Philadelphia

Kwun, Shingu – astp Sa Rang Comm Ch, Anaheim, CA, 14-

2260 West Lincoln Avenue #N5, Anaheim, CA 92801   Korean Southwest Orange County
E-mail: jere94@gmail.com
Sa Rang Community Church – 714-772-7777

Kyle, Jayson Duane – b Salem, OR, Apr 27, 51; f John E. Jr.; m Lois E. Rowland; w Maureen Diane Lyman, Jackson, MS, May 24, 74; chdn Jennifer Lynn, Amy Elizabeth, Jeffrey David; BelC 73, BA; RTS 76, MDiv; BelC 07, Hon DMin; O Aug 8, 76, MSVal Pby; mis WBT, PNG, 76-78; mis MTW, 78-86, staff 78-86; mis MTW, Mexico, 86-01; mis MTW, NYC, 01-08; ob staff Redeemer City to City, New York, NY, 08-

240 Karnes Drive, Franklin, TN 10025 – 347-645-1510   Metropolitan New York
E-mail: jayk@redeemercitytocity.com
Redeemer City to City – 917-206-1457

Kyle, John Emery – b San Diego, CA, Jul 7, 26; f John E; m Agnes McDaniel; w Lois Rowland, Salem, OR, Jun 8, 47; chdn Arlette (McGrigg), Jayson D, Marcus J, Darlene P (Navis); ORSU 50, BS; ColTS 58-61, MDiv; BelC 99, DMin; O Sept 61, Guerrant Pby PCUS; USNavy 44-46; p Hull Mem Ch, Hazard, KY, 61-64; admin WBT, 65-73; coord MTW, 74-77; coord WBT, 77-78; fndr TIIR, 78; Dir SFMF, USA & Canada, 78-88; VP IVCF, 86-88; US chmn bd, Int'l bd for AD 2000 and Beyond mvmnt, 90-00; Dir Urbana 81, 84, 87, stu msns conv; coord MTW, 88-94; VP EFMA, 94-05; hr 05; pres Senior Leadership Exchange, 06-; listed *Who's Who in Religion*, 92-; CBS & GSM Board, 81-85; listed *Who's Who in America*, 96-; OverSeas Missionary Fell Brd, 82-85; chmn Concerts of Prayer Int Bd, 88-98; Exec Com of the Co-Mission, 92-97; CoMission II Leadership Council, 97-99; World Relief Corporation Board, 96-2005; Middle East Media Bd, 98-99; OM Logos II Ship Chair, 88-91; Crista Bd, 84-88; mem WBT, 64-05; Culture Insights Bd, 98-01; Christs College, Taiwan bd, 90-98; mbr Mission Americal Coalition, 98-; Pres Senior Leadership Exchange, 06-; ed *The Unfinished Task*, 84; ed *Finishing the Task*, 87; ed Urbana 87 Songbook, 87; ed *Urban Mission*, 88; co-auth *Missions Now: This Generation*, 90; "Gifts from God: God's Mercy, Spare to Serve," *Decision Magazine* (Dec 94); contr *Looking Forward–Voices From Church Leaders On Our Global Mission*, 04; contr *The CoMission*, 04; contr *Thy Kingdom Come*, 05; recd Presidential Merit Medal, Philippines, 73

918 Fitzgerald Street, Monroe, NC 28112 – 704-291-7157   Mississippi Valley
E-mail: john-lois_kyle@wbt.org
Senior Leadership Exchange
HR

Kytka, Michael – w Roseann; chdn Michael, Alexandra; CTS 04, MDiv; op Ascension Ch, Forest Hills, NY, 05-

8930 70th Road, Forest Hills, NY 11375 – 718-607-5938   Metropolitan New York
E-mail: kytkamichael@gmail.com
Ascension Church – 718-575-0024

Labby, Kevin – w Molly; chdn Elijah, Micah, Andrew, Nina; GroCC, BA; RPTS, MDiv; GenC, MSOL; O May 03, Pitts Pby; ydir Calvin P Ch, North Huntingdon, PA, 97-03, ascp 03-04; srp Murrysville Comm Ch, Murrysville, PA, 04-12; srp Willow Creek Ch, Winter Springs, FL, 12-

4725 East Lake Drive, Winter Springs, FL 32708   Central Florida
E-mail: klabby@willowcreekchurch.org
Willow Creek Church – 407-699-8211

Labrada, Victor Manuel – O Nov 16, 14, Ecar Pby; astp Grace Comm Ch, Carrboro, NC, 14-15; astp Kendall P Ch, Miami, FL, 15-

9281 SW 88th Street, Miami, FL 33176 – 305-804-7199   South Florida
E-mail: victorlabrada@gmail.com
Kendall Presbyterian Church – 305-271-5262

Lacock, Robert D. – b Philadelphia, PA, Jun 15, 50; f Ira J.; m Doris Mengel; w Carol Snook, Elkins Park, PA, Jun 22, 74; chdn Gregory James, Steven Bradley; BIStC 72, BS; CTS 76, MDiv; L 77, NoE Pby; O Feb 78, DMV Pby (RPCES); ap Liberty Ref P Ch, Owings Mills, MD, 77-80; op, p Providence P Ch, Quakertown, PA, 80-86, wc 86-00; ascp Providence P Ch, Quakertown, PA, 00-10; p 10-17; hr 18

12 Live Oak Drive, Quakertown, PA 18951-1065 – 215-536-8869   Eastern Pennsylvania
E-mail: bclacock@verizon.net
HR

LaCour, Joseph Alcide III – b Meridian, MS, Mar 9, 48; f Joseph Alcide Jr.; m Sarah Lincoln Tew; w Elaine Madeline Barnes, Richmond, VA, Jun 15, 74; chdn Rachel Elizabeth, Jonathan Alcide; GATech 66-71, BIE; UniTS 72; WTS 75-78, MDiv; L Apr 8, 78, Delmarva Pby (RPCES); O Aug 27, 78, Cal Pby; p Filbert P Ch, York, SC, 78-80; p Westminster P Ch, Bryan, TX, 80-86; srp Immanuel P Ch, Miami, FL, 86-95; p ChristChurch P, Atlanta, GA, 95-04; campm RUFInt, GATech, 04-10; coord PCA RUF International, 10-18; hr 18

435 Franklin Road NE, Atlanta, GA 30342 – 404-964-1760   Metro Atlanta
E-mail: jal@thelacours.org
HR

Lacy, George – O Feb 10, 13, SoTX Pby; p Providence P Ch, Beeville, TX, 13-17

1011 East Hefferman Street, Beeville, TX 78102   South Texas
E-mail: gelacy@hotmail.com

Lafferty, Patrick – b Sept 17, 71; w Christy; chdn Seamus, Savannah, Jedidiah; astp Park Cities P Ch, Dallas, TX, 08-12; op Christ the King Msn, DeSoto, TX, 12-13; p Christ the King Ch, DeSoto, TX, 13-17; adj prof Redeemer sem, Dallas, TX, 15-17; p Grace Comm Ch, Mills River, NC, 17-

9 Maple Road, Arden, NC 28704   Western Carolina
E-mail: pclafferty@gmail.com
Grace Mills River – 828-891-2006

LaGuardia, Rafael (Ralph) P. De – b Washington, DC, Jul 17, 62; w Robin Neely; chdn Kristen, Kari, John; TBC 86, BA; BJU 93, MA; GPTS 99, MDiv; O May 20, 00, 2nd pby, ARP; Muscle Shoals ARP, AL, 00-03; chp ARP, 03-04; p Covenant P Ch, Daphne, AL, 05-08; ip Fairfield P Ch, Pensacola, FL, 09-11, p 11-

11602 Lisa Court, Fairhope, AL 36532 – 251-605-5001   Gulf Coast
E-mail: rplaguardia@gmail.com
Fairfield Presbyterian Church – 850-455-7245

Laird, Joseph W. – b Atlanta, GA, Jun 11, 53; f Deane; w Stuart, Athens, GA, May 2, 92; chdn Jonah Blue, Aston Raiford; RTSNC 94-98, MDiv; L Aug 26, 01, NGA Pby; O Aug 26, 01, NGA Pby; astp Intown Comm Ch, Atlanta, GA, 02-09; hr 13

2934 Pine Orchard Drive, Tucker, GA 30084 – 770-908-8765   Metro Atlanta
E-mail: jw11953@gmail.com
HR

Lajara, Cecilio Nicolas – b Lares, PR, Apr 22, 42; m Camelia; w Carmen Sanchez Lugo, PR, Aug 10, 63; chdn Iris del Carmen, Mariselle, Juan Cecilio; UPR 66, BA; ColTS 69, MDiv, 73, ThM; LRTS, DMiss; O Jul 6, 69, Atl Pby (PCUS); mis, prof Mexico, 74-76; mis, prof Guatemala, 76-79; Evangelism Explosion III Int., Fort Lauderdale, FL, 80-89; mis Latin Am; ob SOLA FIDE, Int. (PEF), 89-94; Evangelism Explosion III Int., Fort Lauderdale, FL, 95-; *Palabras DesDe LaCruz*, 74; *Un Pueblo con Mentalidad TeLogica*, 78

815 Martin Field Drive, Lawrenceville, GA 30045 – 678-407-9396   Georgia Foothills
E-mail: titolajara@aol.com
Evangelism Explosion III International – 954-491-6100
5554 North Federal Highway, Fort Lauderdale, FL 33308

Lam, Kin – w Kathleen; chdn Emmett Michael, Alethea Zoay, Theodore Lukas; MIT 93, BS; WTS 98, MAR, 02, ThM; O Jan 05, Phil Pby; Chinese Christian Ch and Center, Philadelphia, PA, 98-00; op New City Ch (Mission), Philadelphia, PA, 04-13; wc 14; ob Chap China Grad School of Theology, Hong Kong, 15-16; ob p China Congregational Church, Hong Kong, 16-

China Congregational Church, 119 Leighton Road,– 215-755-1091   Philadelphia
Causeway Bay Hong Kong
E-mail: kin@alum.mit.edu
China Congregational Church, Hong Kong

Lamb, Andrew Stewart – b Nov 21, 61; w Anne Cardwell, Lakeland, FL, Ag 8, 87; chdn Drew, Daniel, Michael, Richard; CBC 84, BS; RTS 89, MDiv; L Ap 90, CentFL Pby; O Mch 5, 95, SWFL Pby, ydir 84-86; chp MTW, Mexico City, 90-00; MTW, church partnering facilitator, 00-14, ob VP Third Millennium Ministries, Inc., Casselberry, FL, 14-

2793 Admiral's Walk Drive North, Orange Park, FL 32073 – 904-278-6877   Southwest Florida
E-mail: PCAMissionsGuy@gmail.com
Third Millennium Ministries, Inc. – 404-278-8841
316 Live Oaks Blvd, Casselberry, FL 32707

Lambert, Jamie – w Bethany, Nov 18, 06; UT 00; MetAtlSem 10, MDiv; O Feb 11, MetAtl Pby; ascp Covenant P Ch, Fayetteville, GA, 11-12, srp 12-

35 Barnsley Court, Fayetteville, GA 30215   Metro Atlanta
E-mail: jamie@covenantpres.net
Covenant Presbyterian Church – 770-460-9450

Lambert, Roger Lee – b Kansas City, KS, Aug 24, 38; f Roy Lee; m Pearl Beatrice Ely; w Sarah Elizabeth Stigers, St. Louis, MO, Sept 4, 65; chdn Rachel Elizabeth, Andrew Mark; UHeid 60, cert; CTS 65, BD, 76, ThM; FulTS 82, PhD; L 65; O 66, So Pby (RPCES); mis WPM, Chile, 66-79; prof CC, 82-17; mod Gen Synod, 80; area cons for MTW, 83-85; hr 17

4916 Beulah Avenue, Chattanooga, TN 37409-1813 – 423-821-2932   Tennessee Valley
HR

Lamberth, William Joseph Jr. – b Dallas, TX, Apr 3, 52; f William J Sr.; m East; w Jones, Shreveport, LA, Mar 3, 79; chdn Caroline, John, Lindsay; SMU 74, BBA; GCTS 91, MDiv; L Apr 25, 93; O Apr 25, 93, NoTX Pby; astp Park Cities P Ch, Dallas, TX, 93-97; op Redeemer P Ch, McKinney, TX, 96-98, p 99-00; astp Park Cities P Ch, Dallas, TX, 05-

4819 Bellerive Drive, Dallas, TX 75287 – 972-732-6120   North Texas
E-mail: bill.lamberth@pcpc.org
Park Cities Presbyterian Church – 214-224-2500

Lamerson, Samuel P. – b West Palm Beach, FL, Nov 15, 59; f Luzene; m Ruth Gunter; w Cynthia Hope Dayhoff, West Palm Beach, FL, Jun 14, 82; chdn Charity, Josiah; BJU, BA; KTS, MDiv; TEDS 01, PhD; Recd PCA Oct 97, SFL Pby; p Westside Baptist, 83-95; astp Coral Ridge P Ch, Ft. Lauderdale, FL, 97, wc 97; prof KTS, 98-; astp Coral Ridge P Ch, Ft. Lauderdale, FL, 98-; Pres KTS, 14-; art *Erdman's Dictionary of the Bible*; *English Grammar to Ace New Testament Greek*; *Currents in Biblical Research*; *Bible Study Magazine*; *Lexham Bible Dictionary*

648 SW 4th Avenue, Boynton Beach, FL 33426 – 561-364-9419 South Florida
E-mail: slamerson@knoxseminary.edu
Knox Theological Seminary – 954-771-0376
5554 North Federal Highway, Ft. Lauderdale, FL 33308
Coral Ridge Presbyterian Church – 954-771-8840

Lamkin, William Curry – b Montgomery, AL, Jul 31, 70; f John Carl; m Kathryn Marie Norred; w Margaret McQueen Carroll, Montgomery, AL, Aug 9, 97; TrSU 91, BS; RTS 95, MDiv; L Feb 21, 95, MSVal Pby; O Aug 11, 96, SEAL Pby; int, moy Young Meadows P Ch, Montgomery, AL, 95-96, astp, moy 96-97; p Linden P Ch, Linden, AL, 97-00; p Redeemer P Ch, Jacksonville, FL, 00-02; astp Northshore Comm Ch, Jacksonville, FL, 03-05; astp First P Ch, Panama City, FL, 07-09; t Parkway Acad, Miramar, FL, 09-10; t Hollywood CAcad, 10-11; ob astp New P Ch (ind), Pompano Beach, FL, 11-14; Chap FLARNG, 12-14; Chap ALARNG, 14-; ob t Eastwood CS, 14-;15; Chap Res Central AL VA, 15-16; Chap Baptist Health Systems, Montgomery, AL, 16-; brd cert chap, Assoc Cert Christian Chap, 17-

1826 Vaughn Lane, Montgomery, AL 36106 – 850-866-6706 Southeast Alabama
E-mail: wclamkin@yahoo.com

Lammers, Steve Robert – b Minneapolis, MN, Mar 18, 72; f Richard Roy; m Carolyn Barbara Miller; w Jenna Linn Ellwanger, Charleston, SC, Jun 8, 96; chdn Zoe Karis, Ali Karis; ClemU 95, BS; CTS 03, MDiv; O Oct 26, 03, NFL Pby; campm RUF, UFL, 03-13; srp Faith P Ch, Gainesville, FL, 13-

3200 NW 16th Avenue, Gainesville, FL 32605 – 352-281-0973 North Florida
E-mail: steverlammers@gmail.com
Faith Presbyterian Church – 352-377-5482

Landrum, James Mark – b Jackson, MS, Feb 20, 48; f Dr. John W.; m Barbara Fern Harrington; w LaVerne Gray, Fordyce, AR, Jun 1, 70; chdn Jonathan Mark, LaVerne Renee; MSC 66-70, BA; SWBTS 72-75, MDiv; L May 12, 92, Gr Pby; O Aug 70, SBC; O Feb 27, 94, MSVal Pby; Chap Riverside, CA, 70-72; p Calvary Bap, Macon, MS, 75-76; ascp First Bap, Newton, MS, 76-78; p Goodwater Bap, Magee, MS, 78-79; p Covenant P Ch, Louisville, MS, 94-05; p First P Ch, Ft. Oglethorpe, GA, 05-09; wc 09-11; hr 11

30 Boseman Lane, Chicamauga, GA 30707 – 423-227-9085 Tennessee Valley
E-mail: jameslandrum@bellsouth.net
HR

Landry, Eric – w Sarah, Jul 28, 01; chdn Andrew David; Allison Beth; NAZU 98, BA; WSCAL 03, MDiv; O Feb 20, 05, SoCst Pby; op Christ P Ch, Murietta, CA, 04-09; p 09-16; srp Redeemer P Ch, Austin, TX, 16-

2111 Alexander Avenue, Austin, TX 78722 South Texas
E-mail: elandry@redeemerpres.org
Redeemer Presbyterian Church – 512-708-1232

Lane, Robert Clinton – b Savannah, GA, Nov 9, 51; f Carlton Clinton; m Helen Louise Peters; w Jewell Kay Mock, Savannah, GA, Jul 13, 73; chdn Douglas Clinton; ArmSC 69-73; RTS 83-86, MDiv; L Oct 8, 85, Gr Pby; O Jul 13, 86, Pby of the Cent So. (EPC); p Calvin P Ch (EPC), Houston, TX, 86-87;

Lane, Robert Clinton, continued
ap Trin P Ch (Ind), Savannah, GA, 87-88; p Faith P Ch, Charleston, WV, 88-91; p Grace P Ch, Baton Rouge, LA, 91-01; p First P Ch, Madison, MS, 01-

116 Woodland Drive, Madison, MS 39110 – 601-605-6236 Mississippi Valley
E-mail: rclaneccpd@att.net
First Presbyterian Church – 601-856-6625

Lane, Timothy Stanley – b Sylvania, GA, Oct 12, 61; f Clyde E.; m Jo Ann Reddick; w Barbara S. Casey, Jonesboro, GA, Aug 12, 89; chdn Hannah Rebekah, Timothy Josiah, Esther Kathryn, Benjamin Tryals; AlbJC 80-82; UGA 82-84; WTS 87-91, MDiv, 06, DMin; L Jul 13, 91; O Sept 6, 92, Cal Pby; campm WDA, UGA, 84-87; astp Clemson P Ch, Clemson, SC, 91-94, srp 94-01; ob fac CCEF, 01-07; lect WTS, 01-; ob exec dir CCEF, 07-13; pres Institute for Pastoral Care, 14-; Tim Lane and Assoc, 14-; "Normal Sunday Mornings and 24/7;" *Journal of Biblical Counseling* 21, no. 2 (03); "Walking the Razor's Edge of Truth and Love in Personal Ministry," *Journal of Biblical Counseling* 22, no. 1 (03); *Practicing Forgiveness: Joining Wisdom and Love*; *Conflict*; co-auth *How People Change*; co-auth "How Christ Changes Us By His Grace," and "Pursuing and Granting Forgiveness," *Journal of Biblical Counseling* 23, no. 2 (05); *Relationships: A Mess Worth Making*; "One Couple's Story," *Journal of Biblical Counseling* 24, no. 2 (06); "One Church's Story" and "More Than Counseling: A Vision for the Entire Church," *Journal of Biblical Counseling* 24, no. 3 (06); *Freedom From Guilt: Finding Release From Your Burdens*, 08; *Family Feuds: How to Respond*, 08; *Sex Before Marriage: How Far is Too Far*, 09; *Change and Your Relationships: A Mess Worth Making* (curric); *How People Change* (curric); *PTSD: Healing for Bad Memories*, 12; "Godly Intoxication: The Church Can Minister to Addicts," *Journal of Biblical Counseling, 26:2*, 12; *Living Without Worry: How to Replace Anxiety with Peace*, 15; *Unstuck: A Nine-Step Journey to Change that Lasts*

320 Sidney Lane, Fayetteville, GA 30215 – 267-625-3224 Metro Atlanta
E-mail: tlane@instituteforpastoralcare.co
Institute for Pastoral Care

Lang, Richard H. – b Pittsburgh, PA, Jul 15, 51; f Howard W.; m Harriet M. Cobler; w Cherie Ann Elias, Pittsburgh, PA, Sept 29, 79; chdn Sara Elizabeth, Joshua David, Hannah Elizabeth; PASU 73, BS; GCTS 76, MDiv; O Jul 76, UPCUSA; p Neville Island Ch, PA, 76-81; p Christian Fellowship Chapel, Coraopolis, PA, 81-83; p St. Paul's Ref Ch, (non-PCA), Bedford, PA, 84-95, wc 95-98; p Grace Ref P Ch, Monroeville, PA, 98-

181 Kelvington Drive, Monroeville, PA 15146 – 412-380-9096 Pittsburgh
E-mail: grpca@yahoo.com
Grace Reformed Presbyterian Church – 724-327-8370

Langer, Michael John – b Iowa City, Apr 24, 67; w Tess White, May 19, 90; chdn Josie, Libby, Owen, Phoebe; CTS 07, MDiv; O Sept 07, Mo pby; astp Grace P Ch of St. Charles Co, St. Charles, MO, 07-08; op One Ancient Hope Msn Ch, Iowa City, IA, 08-13; srp 13-15; astp Trinity P Ch, Hinsdale, IL, 15-18; MNA, Ministry to State, 18-

1828 Park Road NW, Washington, DC 20010 Potomac
E-mail: mlanger@ministrytostate.org
PCA Mission to North America – 678-825-1200

Langford, John Harris – b Paris, TX, Oct 7, 41; f Ralph M; m Mary Elizabeth Keller; w Kay Carol Smith, Vero Beach, FL, Jul 11, 64; chdn Sharon Kay; UGA 60-64, BA, 65, grad wk; RTS 66-68, MDiv; UGA 81, MEd; L Oct 15, 68; O Nov 30, 68, Midw Pby (RPCES); Combat Chap USArmy, 69-72; p Town North P Ch, Richardson, TX, 72-75; assoc, coord CEP, 75-78; First P Day sch, Macon, GA, 78-82; asst, prin TrPS, Montgomery AL, 82-86; prin TrPS, Opelika, AL, 86-88; ss Calebee P Ch, Shorter, AL, 85-87, ap 87-88; ap First P Ch of Coral Springs, Margate, FL, 88-90; CSCS, Coral Spgs, FL, 88-90; prin Seacrest CS, 90-93; astp Seacrest Blvd P Ch, Delray Beach, FL, 90-93, wc 93-96; hr 97; Pastor in Residence Service

Langford, John Harris, continued
Minstries, Inc, writer; staff writer, Pastor-In-Residence Service; *Traps: A Probe of those Strange New Cults*, 77; *The Barley Field Incident*, 78, repub, *Hope in Hard Times*, 99; *Strength for Dangerous Times: A Study of the Book of Esther*, 09

869 Holbrook Drive, Newport News, VA 23602-8998 – 757-874-4855   Evangel
E-mail: lightningstrike308@reagan.com
HR

    Langley, McKendree Gordon – b Southbridge, MA, Oct 8, 76; f McKendree; m Sandra; w Amy Elizabeth Fowler, Richmond, VA, Jul 31, 04; chdn Daniel McKendree, Olivia Lewis; CC 02, BA; CTS 11, MDiv; O Mar 26, 17, Ecar Pby; astp Peace P Ch, Cary, NC, 17-

127 Loch Bend Lane, Cary, NC 27518   Eastern Carolina
E-mail: kenl@peacepca.org
Peace Presbyterian Church – 919-467-5977

    Langston, Rob – b Austell, GA, Dec 11, 73; f Perry; m Elizabeth; w Dana DeLoach, Dalton, GA, Mar 15, 97; chdn Abigail Grace, Rachel Anne, Ryan Baxter; SamU 96, BA, 96, BS; EmU 98, MS; RTS 10, MDiv; O Feb 13, 11, NWGA Pby; int Christ Comm Ch, Kennesaw, GA, 08-10; astp Grace Cov Ch - PCA, Dallas, GA, 11-14; wc 14-

6281 Woodlore Drive NW, Acworth, GA 30101   Northwest Georgia
E-mail: rdlangston@yahoo.com

    Lanier, Greg Ryan – ascp River Oaks P Ch, Lake Mary, FL, 17-

843 Royalwood Lane, Oviedo, FL 32765 – 619-538-5842   Central Florida
E-mail: glanier@rts.edu
River Oaks Presbyterian Church – 407-330-9103

    Lantz, Steven Michael – b Lafayette, IN, Mar 29, 72; f David Lennis; m Rebecca Jo Garman; RU; LAMPTS 07, BD; O Aug 17, 08, SFL Pby; astp Christ Cov Ch, Southwest Ranches, FL, 08-09; ob Respect Ministries; op New City Flwsp Ch Miami, Miami, FL, 18-

11767 South Dixie Highway #343, Miami, FL 33156 – 786-306-6185   South Florida
New City Fellowship Church Miami

    LaPointe, Peter B. – b Groton, CT, Mar 27, 54; f John A.; m Meral P.; w Melissa Ann Wyatt, Jackson, MS, Jun 30, 84; chdn Leah Anna, Lara Elizabeth; BelC 79-82; RTS 82-86; L Jul 86; O Jul 26, 87, Wcar Pby; op, p New Cov P Ch, Hickory, NC, 86-92; p Cornerstone P Ch, Lutz, FL, 92-99; op Christ the King PCA Ch, Seminole, FL, 99-02, p 02-

14118 Passage Way, Seminole, FL 33776 – 727-593-5619   Southwest Florida
E-mail: Hisrock@juno.com
Christ the King PCA Church – 727-394-0787

    LaRose, Willard G. – b St. Louis, MO, Aug 27, 42; f Willard George, Sr.; m Ola Ethel Frazee; w Geraldine Turner, St. Louis, MO, Sept 7, 62; chdn Timothy, Stacie Lynne (Tucker), Tracie Anne (Tyler); UMD 74, BBA; Marymount U 84, MBA; RTSNC; O Apr 21, 98, NGA Pby; ydir Evangelical P Ch, Annapolis, MD, 85-95; ydir, admin CEP, 95-99; astp Grace Evangelical P Ch, Davidsonville, MD, 99-04, ascp 04; astp Safe Harbor P Ch, Stevensville, MD, 04-07; hr 07

706 Harmony Way, Centreville, MD 21617   Chesapeake
E-mail: willard@atlanticbb.net
HR

Larrison, Brook Thomas – b Toledo, OH, Sept 19, 59; f Dale; m Jean Biltz; w Sandra Thorpe, Sandra Thorpe, Dec 8, 78; chdn Daniel Thomas, Andrew William; BGSU 77-78; NyC 79-82, BA; TEDS 82-85, MDiv; L Feb 1, 86; O Sept 21, 88, C&MA; Recd PCA Apr 11, 95, SWFL Pby; p Yellowstone Comm Ch, Savage, MT, 86-90; p Sylvania Alliance Ch, Sylvania, OH, 90-93; p Faith P Ch, Wauchula, FL, 95-15, ss 15-

PO Box 1986, Wauchula, FL 33873 – 863-832-0565   Southwest Florida
E-mail: brook.larrison@earthlink.net
Faith Presbyterian Church – 863-773-2105

Larsen, Erik Ludvig – b Springfield, MA, Dec 11, 75; f James Magnus; m Beverly Ann Lohne; w Amanda Avery Wheeler, Xenia, OH, Jun 24, 00; chdn Madda Rose, Olive Margaret; CedC 98, BA; HarvU 04, MA; GCTS 05, MDiv; Mar 2, 08, Phil Pby; astp New Life P Ch, Glenside, PA, 06-09; p Pilgrim Ch, Philadelphia, PA, 09-; "God, Man, or Animal?" *Proceedings of Harvard Celtic Colloquium*, 03

110 West Salaignac Street, Philadelphia, PA 19127   Philadelphia
E-mail: erikludviglarsen@gmail.com
Pilgrim Church – 215-483-8878

Larsen, Samuel Eric – b Annapolis, MD, Jul 5, 71; f Samuel Harry; m Natalie Louise Mahlow; w Rebecca Susan Egbert, Atlanta, GA, Apr 10, 93; chdn Abigail Nicole, Meghan Marie, Natalie Keren, Emma Hope; CC 95, BA; CTS 00, MDiv; FulTS 08, DMin; O May 20, 01, MO Pby; Our Saviors Ch, 90-93; ydir/Jr. Hig min, Evangelical P Ch, Annapolis, MD, 93-95, moy 95-96; dir stud min Chesterfield P Ch, Chesterfield, MO, 97-99, astp 01-07; exec dir of Global Youth and Family Min, MTW, 07-

630 Oak Path Drive, Ballwin, MO 63011   Missouri
E-mail: eric.larsen@gyfm.org
PCA Mission to the World – 678-823-0004

Larson, P. Keith – p Greene Valley P Ch, Carmichaels, PA, 08-

200 East Greene Street, Carmichaels, PA 15320 – 724-966-5588   Pittsburgh
E-mail: parsonlarson@outlook.com
Greene Valley Presbyterian Church – 724-966-5291

Larson, Wayne – b Central City, NE, Oct 21, 64; f Donald C.; m Dorothy M. Rodekohr; w Janelle A. Westerbuhr, Geneva, NE, Sept 8, 90; chdn Eric D., Michael L., Greta E.; UNLincoln 83-88, BA; OHSU 88-90, MA; CTS 94-97, MDiv; L Oct 11, 97, GrLks Pby; O Feb 15, 98, GrLks Pby; ascp Grace P Ch, Indianapolis, IN, 97-00; op Redeemer P Ch, Des Moines, IA, 00-02, p 02-

4118 Lynner Drive, Des Moines, IA 50310 – 515-274-5004   Iowa
E-mail: walarson@juno.com
Redeemer Presbyterian Church – 515-440-3407

LaRue, Caleb Maui – b Yokosuka, Japan, Nov 2, 57; f Howard A.; m Catherine Mae Rae Barnes; w Mary Elizabeth Doar, Greenwood, VA, Jun 7, 81; chdn Katie, Shannon, Abigail, LauraBeth, Isaac; UVA 80, BA; WTS 93, MDiv; L May 8, 93; O Sept 24, 94, NoE Pby; int Redeemer Ref P Ch, Queensbury, NY, 93-94, p 94-96, wc 96-

744 Burgoyne Avenue, Ballston Spa, NY 12020 – 518-378-5111   New York State

Lash, John Edward – b Middletown, CT, Sept 26, 54; f Michael; m Janet McCutcheon; w Mary Ann Weaver, Bethesda, MD, Jun 5, 76; chdn Timothy James, Michelle Elizabeth, Deborah Ann, Rebekah Marie, Josiah Michael, Jacob David, Nathanael John, Abigail Grace, Marianna Joy, Elijah John, Ezra Nasir; UMD 76, BS; GCTS 83, MDiv; O Mar 83, DMV Pby; ap Gainesville P Ch, Gainesville, VA, 83-86, p 86-

6124 Saints Hill Lane, Broad Run, VA 20137-2318 – 540-347-3848   Potomac
E-mail: jacklash11@gmail.com
Gainesville Presbyterian Church – 703-754-8791

Latham, Dave – w Rebecca; chdn Stokes, Ellie Grace; PC 03; RTSNC 10; O Nov 7, 10; campm RUF, ChrisNewpU, 10-15; ob admin RTSNC, 15-; astp Uptown Church, PCA, Charlotte, NC, 17

13709 Portpatrick Lane, Matthews, NC 28105 – 828-275-8991   Tidewater
E-mail: davelatham2003@gmail.com
Reformed Theological Seminary, NC – 704-366-5066
Uptown Church, PCA – 704-375-7355

Lauber, John R. – b Port Jefferson, NY, Apr 25, 70; f John Walter; m Barbara Joan Hokanson; w Phyllis Chew, Rye, NY, May 18, 02; chdn Matthew Wan, Samantha Chew, Eli Kwan; NyC 92, BA; RTSFL 96, MATS; O Oct 19, 03, MNY Pby; ascp Trinity P Ch, Rye, NY, 03-04; ascp City P Ch, Denver, CO, 04-05; couns Hindsight Bib Couns, Vienna, VA; couns Heart Song Couns, Vienna, VA

1720 Paisley Blue Court, Vienna, VA 22182 – 703-272-8231   Potomac
E-mail: john@heartsongcounseling.org
Heart Song Counseling

Lauder, Brent Stuart – w Jennifer; chdn Job, Miriam, Ethan, Lydia; BallSU, BS; CTS, MDiv; O Sept 05, NoTX Pby; p First Ref P Ch, Minco, OK, 05-8; astp Covenant P Ch, Hammond, IN, 08-09; op Christ Our Hope Comm Ch, Dyer, IN, 09-11; p Providence Christian Ch, Cape Coral, FL, 11-

424 SE 31st Street, Cape Coral, FL 33904 – 219-844-2512   Suncoast Florida
E-mail: brent@providencecapecoral.com
Providence Christian Church – 239-549-5556

Laug, Steven Alan – b Denison, IA, Dec 7, 54; f Matthew T.; m Mary A. Anderson; w Irene Leal, Idaho Falls, ID, Jul 10, 76; chdn Naphtali Marie, Abigail Johanna, Jessica Irene, Sarah Elizabeth; MuSB 73-77, BS; PSU 76-78; WCBS 78-79; WTS 80-83, MAR, 80-83, MDiv, 01, DMin; L Sept 81, CRC; O May 83, CCCC; Recd PCA Apr 27, 90; ap Union Gosp Msn Bib Ch, 73-77; ap Comm Ch of Vista, 83-90; fndr, Dir Faith & Love Ministries, Vista, CA, 88-90; op Fraser Valley P Msn, 90-93; ev, op Mountainview Comm Ch, Agassiz, BC, 92-95, p 95-03; chp Vancouver, 03-07; op Grace Vancouver Ch Eastside, Vancouver, BC, 07-08; Dir. of Mentorship ServAnon Foundation, 09-; *Stepping Stones: Toward an Understanding of the Bible*

1156 East 21st Avenue, Vancouver, BC V5V 1S8 CANADA – 604-708-8910   Western Canada
E-mail: slaug@uniserve.com; steve@safoundation.org
Servants Anonymous Foundation

Laughlin, Fredric Ryan – w Heather; chdn Nathan, Luke, Zachary; USMA, BS; CTS, MDiv; O Nov 21, 04, Pot Pby; astp McLean P Ch, McLean, VA, 04-06; srp Covenant P Ch, St. Louis, MO, 06-

1578 Mason Knoll Road, St. Louis, MO 63131 – 314-394-1995   Missouri
E-mail: rlaughlin@cpcstl.org
Covenant Presbyterian Church – 314-432-8700

Laun, William Henry – b Sheboygan, WI, Aug 28, 54; f John H.; m Ruth Eckhart; w Kathryn E. Hill, Mundelein, IL, May 30, 81; chdn Samuel B., Caitlin A., Benjamin John, Charlotte Grace; UWI 72-76, BA; TEDS 77-80, MDiv; L Sept 16, 86; O Mar 7, 87, OPC; Recd PCA Mar 90, Phil Pby; p Grace P Ch (OPC), 86-88; ascp New Life P Ch, Glenside, PA, 88-94; op Valley Springs P Msn, Sherwood, WI, 94-96, wc 96-03; ob Calvin CRC, Sheboygan, WI, 03-06; p Prosperity P Ch, Charlotte, NC, 06-08; wc 08; ss West Hopewell P Ch, Hopewell, VA, 09-11; p 11-18; mdis 18

3119 Quail Hill Drive, Midlothian, VA 23112 – 804-405-2656   James River
E-mail: bill.laun@gmail.com

Lauranzon, Brandon – b Richmond, VA, Oct 11, 83; f Robert Manuel; m Denise Castillo; w Robyn Lynn, St. Louis, MO, Aug 25, 07; chdn Karis May, Noelle Hope, Fischer Gabriel; JMU 06, BA; CTS 09, MDiv; O Mar 18, 12, CentFL Pby; astp Seven Rivers P Ch, Lecanto, FL, 12-

191 West Liberty Street, Hernando, FL 34442 – 314-258-6011   Central Florida
E-mail: blauranzon@sevenrivers.org
Seven Rivers Presbyterian Church – 352-746-6200

Lauterbach, Mark – b Pittsburgh, PA; w Rondi, Dec 9, 78; chdn Rachel (Ellis), David Perez-Lauterbach, Rebecca Jane (Elmore); PU 76, BA; WestBaptSem 79, MDiv, 81, ThM; TEDS 98, DMin; O Jul 82; Recd PCA 15, SoCst Pby astp Hinson Bapt, Portland, OR, 81-85 astp Parkside Ch, Cleveland, OH, 85-87; srp El Camino Bapt, Tucson AZ, 87-97; srp First Bapt Ch of Los Altos, CA, 98-03; srp Grace Ch, San Diego, 04-14; astp North City P Ch, Poway, CA, 16; astp Rincon Mtn P Ch, Tucson, AZ, 16-

8445 E Tanque Verde Road, Tucson, AZ 85749 – 858-761-5120   Arizona
E-mail: mlauterbach@rinconpres.org
Rincon Mountain Presbyterian Church – 520-327-2390

LaValley, Alfred E. – b Norwood, MA, Nov 9, 43; f Alfred E Sr.; m Dorothy York; w Nancy June Mitchell, N Attleboro, MA; chdn Lisa Virginia, Lynne Nancy, Stephen Mark, Kristen Jeanne; BerkCC 69-73, BA; RTS 74-77, MDiv; O Feb 26, 77, MSVal Pby; p Flatbrook Bapt Ch, 71-74; ap Alta Woods P Ch, Pearl, MS, 78-79; p West Springfield Cov Comm Ch, West Springfield, MA, 78-14; hr; Chap, bd mbr Pioneer Vly Chr Sch, 83-85; headm Cov Comm CS, 89-98; *A Life Outpoured*, 82; *Ministry in the Fast Lane*, unpub mss, 90

44 Mercury Court #R1, West Springfield, MA 01089 – 413-733-9031   Southern New England
E-mail: alnan3@juno.com
HR

LaValley, Stephen – b Foxboro, MA, Mar 7, 68; f Alfred E.; m Nancy June Mitchell; w Kristine N. Johnson; chdn Matthew, Jessica, Alanna, Victoria, John William, Susanna; GenC; BelC 97, BBE; RTS 99, MDiv; O Sept 24, 99, NoE Pby; astp West Springfield Cov Community Ch, West Springfield, MA, 99-04; op Springfield P Ch, Springfield, MA (now Grace P Ch, Enfield, CT), 01-05; p Grace P Ch, Enfield, CT, 05-; sc SNE Pby, 10-12

18 Spencer Street, Springfield, MA 01118 – 413-214-2406   Southern New England
E-mail: pastorlavalley@gmail.com
Grace Presbyterian Church – 860-749-4199

Lawler, John – O May 7, 17, NFL Pby; astp Christ Ch Mandarin, Jacksonville, FL, 17-

4228 Birchwood Avenue, Jacksonville, FL 32207   North Florida
Christ Church Mandarin – 904-262-5588

Lawrence, Bernard A. – b Richmond, VA, Mar 31, 50; f Earl Ashby; m Ellen Marie Venning; w Patricia Ann Kohnle, Charlotte, NC, Oct 13, 79; chdn Jessica Ann, Jonathan Daniel, Ian Ashby, Graham Mast, Hayden Kohnle; Okaloosa Watton JC 75, AA; UWFL 77, BS; RTSNC 10, MATS; O Aug 22, 10, CentCar Pby; USAF, 68-75; ascp Christ Cov P Ch, Matthews, NC, 10-

7310 Pine Lake Lane, Mint Hill, NC 28227 – 704-573-8484   Central Carolina
E-mail: blawrence@christcovenant.org
Christ Covenant Presbyterian Church – 704-847-3505

Lawrence, Greg – CTS; astp Trinity P Ch, Rochester, MN, 03-07; op Christ Ch Msn, Mankato, MN, 03-07; p 07-14; Chap USAF, 14- 18; p Community P Ch, Louisville, KY, 18-; Chap USAFR, 18-

6009 Laurel Lane, Prospect, KY 40059   Ohio Valley
E-mail: gdlawrence2000@gmail.com
Community Presbyterian Church – 507-469-0091
United States Air Force Reserve

Lawrence, Jefferson L. – b Louisville, KY, May 18, 61; f Randolph; m Catherine; w Bette Jean Penton, Montgomery, AL, Apr 17, 93; chdn Brandon, Erin, Wayne; VandU 83, BE; VPI 88, ME; BhamTS 97, MABS, 00, MRE, 03, MDiv; SBTS 08, DMin; L Jul 18, 95 & Oct 23, 01, SEAL Pby; O Nov 21, 04, SEAL Pby; int, ss Providence P Ch, Legrand, AL, 95-00; past res Briarwood P Ch, Birmingham, AL, 02, min assim, 03-04; admin, astp Young Meadows P Ch, Montgomery, AL, 04-05, exec min, ascp 05-09; op Westside P Msn, Jacksonville, FL, 09-10; wc 10-12; ob p Beatrice Comm Ch, Beatrice, AL, 13-; Aiken Taylor Award, PCA Hist Cent, for *The Role and Influence of Francis A. Schaeffer in the Founding and Shaping of the Presbyterian Church in America*

PO Box 228, Beatrice, AL 35425 – 251-369-0811　　　　　　　　　　　　　　Southeast Alabama
E-mail: PastorJeff.Lawrence@gmail.com
Beatrice Community Church, Beatrice, AL

Laws, Bryan David – O Nov 4, 17, NoCA Pby; astp Ridge P Ch, Paradise, CA, 17-

1857 Lillian Avenue, Paradise, CA 95969 – 916-899-0790　　　　　　　　　　　Northern California
E-mail: bdavidlaws@gmail.com
Ridge Presbyterian Church – 530-872-8270

Laxton, William Perry – b Lenoir, NC, Dec 21, 46; f Perry Lee; m Doris Earp; w Dianne Teeter, Lenoir, NC, Dec 9, 66; chdn Barry Lee, Melissa Anne, Carrie Elizabeth; BerkCC 72-75; BelC 75-76, BA; RTS 76-79, MDiv, 95, DMin; O Jun 79, CentCar Pby; p Faith P Ch, Mooresville, NC, 79-82; p Trinity P Ch, Asheville, NC, 82-97; sc Wcar Pby, 87-92; srp Covenant P Ch, Easley, SC, 97-06; hr

3 Korbel Court, Mauldin, SC 29662　　　　　　　　　　　　　　　　　　　　　　Calvary
E-mail: clive@att.net
HR

Layman, Dan – Recd PCA Sept 4, 18, ColMet Pby; p The Granville Chapel, Granville, OH, 18-

E-mail: pastorlayman@gmail.com　　　　　　　　　　　　　　　　　　　Columbus Metro
The Granville Chapel – 740-503-3941

Layton, Stanley Eugene – b Montgomery, AL, May 8, 62; f Eugene; m Myra June Reynolds; w Virginia Lee, Feb 4, 05; chdn James Dylan Kennett, William Knox, Benjamin Reynolds; AU 84, BS; RTS 01, MDiv; O Sept 21, 01, Gr Pby; p First P Ch, Picayune, MS, 01-12; p First P Ch, Ellerbe, NC, 12-

PO Box 151, Ellerbe, NC 28338 – 910-652-5231　　　　　　　　　　　　　　　Central Carolina
E-mail: stanelayton@gmail.com
First Presbyterian Church – 910-652-5231

Le Duc, Luke – O Sept 20, 09, SusqV Pby; astp Wheatland P Ch, Lancaster, PA, 09-10; ascp 10-16; srp 16-

429 College Avenue, Lancaster, PA 17603 – 717-917-8519　　　　　　　　　　Susquehanna Valley
E-mail: lukeleduc@gmail.com
Wheatland Presbyterian Church – 717-392-5909

Le, Vinh Paul – astp Westminster P Ch, Everett, WA, 15-

425-252-3757　　　　　　　　　　　　　　　　　　　　　　　　　　　　　Pacific Northwest
E-mail: wpcae@frontier.com
Westminster Presbyterian Church – 425-252-3757

Leach, William B. – b Macon, GA, Nov 14, 64; f Dan; m Genevieve McCullers; w Sarah Ann McMillan, Tampa, FL, Jul 2, 88; chdn Corban Burnes, Madeline Ann, Mikaela Joy, Declan William, Josiah

MINISTERIAL DIRECTORY

Leach, William B., continued
Ransom; WFU 87, BS; RTSFL 93, MDiv; L Jan 96; O Jan 12, 97, JR Pby; Covenant P Ch, dir of min, Harrisonburg, VA, 95-96, ascp 97-10; op Christ P Ch Harrisonburg, VA, 10, p 10-

1046 Chestnut Drive, Harrisonburg, VA 22801-1608 – 540-433-1723   Blue Ridge
E-mail: bill@christ-presbyterian.org
Christ Presbyterian Church – 540-383-5014

Leachman, Taylor – b Houston, TX, Aug 6, 83; f D. Richard; m Marcia Jean Kelley; w Julianna Teresa Lee, Nashville, TN, Jul 29, 06; chdn Emilia Grace, Gillian Sonia, Mary Margaret Taylor; VandU 06, BS, RedTS, TX, 15, MDiv; O Feb 7, 16, HouMet Pby; astp Christ the King P Ch, Houston, TX, 16-17, ascp 17-

6206 Locke Lane, Houston, TX 77057 – 704-941-7107   Houston Metro
E-mail: taylor.leachman@christtheking.com
Christ the King Presbyterian Church – 713-892-5464

Leadbetter, Lee – b Knoxville, TN, Aug 30, 73; w Jennifer Leigh Campbell; chdn Daniel Courtney, Phillip Campbell; UT 95, BA; WTS 96; CTS 03, MDiv; O Feb 08, TNVal Pby; ydir Redeemer P Ch, McKinney, TX, 97-00; int Redeemer Ch of Knoxv, Knoxville, TN, 06-07; campm RUFI, UT, 08-

1717 Cliftgate Road, Knoxville, TN 37909 – 865-292-3439   Tennessee Valley
E-mail: lleadbetter@ruf.org
PCA Reformed University Ministries International

Leal, Diocelio – b Presidente Soares, MG, Brazil, Dec 16, 56; w Mirian Pires Santos; chdn Priscila Leal Neto, Paulo Henrique Santos Leal, Mateus Santos Leal; SouthPresSem, Campinas, 82, ThB; Inst Psychoanalysis, Brazil, 98; Maui AdvLeadership, 96; doct stu, Sao Paulo; O Jan 9, 83, Brazil; Hagaii Inst, 86; liaison Latino Comm, Essex College, 08-09; srp Ebenezer P Ch, Newark, NJ, 11-

91 Oliver Street # 2nd Floor, Newark, NJ 07105 – 973-582-8534   Metropolitan New York
E-mail: revdiocelio@hotmail.com
Ebenezer Presbyterian Church – 973-732-2164

Leal, Enrique – b Jan 24, 80; w Lisandra Diaz; FletU, ThB; USimonBolivar, BIE; BibS, MDiv, DMin cand; Recd PCA Sept 21, 13, Phil Pby; astp Tenth P Ch, Philadelphia, PA 13-

E-mail: eleal@tenth.org   Philadelphia
Tenth Presbyterian Church – 215-735-7688

Leary, Mick – ev Homer, NY, 06-08; op Church on the Green, Homer, NY, 08-; p Church of the Redeemer, Cortland, NY, 10-16; chp 16-

2038 Three Notch Road, Kents Store, VA 23084 – 607-299-4017   Blue Ridge
E-mail: micleary@gmail.com

Leary, Paul – ascp New Life P Ch, Dresher, PA, 03-13; mis Serge 13-

101 West Avenue #305, Jenkintown, PA 19046   Eastern Pennsylvania
E-mail: pleary@serge.org
Serge

Leavengood, Daniel – p Lakewood P Ch, Pell City, AL, 14-

1801 3rd Avenue North, Pell City, AL 35125   Evangel
E-mail: Crumbsnatcher@gmail.com
Lakewood Presbyterian Church – 205-884-2631

LeCroy, Timothy – b Anderson, SC, Jul 23, 78; f Roger Anthony; m Carolyn Sue Kelley; w Rachel Flowe, Raleigh, NC; chdn Ruby Mae, Lucy Belle; NCSt 01, BS; CTS 06, MDiv; StLU 12, PhD; O Aug 23, 09, MO Pby; MTW, Trnava, Slovakia , 01-02; astp Providence Ref P Ch, St. Louis, MO, 09-12; p Christ Our King P Ch, Columbia, MO, 12-; vis instr CTS, 13-; mbr PCAAC, 15-; "Correcting Leon: An Analysis of the conjecture of προεξομολογησάμενοι for προσεξομολογησάμενοι in Didache 14:1" in *The Use of Textual Criticism for the Interpretation of Patristic Texts*, 13; "A New Lens for Race, Media, and the Gospel," in *Heal Us Emmanuel: a Call for Racial Reconciliation, Representation, and Unity in the Church*, 16; *Commentary on the Sentences: Sacraments. Bonaventure Texts in Translation*, Volume XVII, Franciscan Institute, 16

2103 Iris Drive, Columbia, MO 65202-12 – 314-604-2088   Missouri
E-mail: pastor.tim.lecroy@christourkingcolumbia.org
Christ Our King Presbyterian Church – 573-723-1323

Ledden, John Augustus Sr. – b Paulsboro, NJ, Mar 25, 23; f George Elmer; m Edna F. Griffith; w Lorrane Christine, Pensacola, FL, Dec 13, 44; chdn John A. Jr., Susan C. (Crumrine), Daniel R., Elizabeth A. (Colville); ShelC 51, BA; FTS 57, MDiv; ColU 62, MA; WTS 62-63; FrSC 83; GroCC 83-84; WVU 87; O 54; Bible Prot Ch, Millville, NJ, 54-58; dean ShelC, 58-62; p Skylands Bible Ch, Ringwood, NJ, 58-62; dean John Knoc JrC, Wilmington, DE; op Faith P mis, Oakland, MD, 78-81; hr; ss Faith Ref P Ch, Fairmont, WV, 99-00, p 00-05; *Monday Morning*, 10; *Treasury of Biblical Moments*, 12; ed "Biblical Truth Concerning Wine"

1108 Old Stage Road, Amherst, VA 24521 – 434-381-6014   New River
E-mail: jhnlrn44@gmail.com
HR

Ledford, Daniel – b Detroit, MI, Dec 16, 69; f R. Kenneth; m Carolyn Sykes; w Jennifer Ratcliffe, Jul 24, 93; chdn Abigail L., Rachel L., Noelle L.; GVSU 97, BS; RTSFL 07, MDiv; srp Westminster P Ch, Butler, PA, 08-

283 Holyoke Road, Butler, PA 16001 – 724-256-3001   Ascension
E-mail: DanL@westminsterpca.com
Westminster Presbyterian Church – 724-283-4204

Ledford, Keith C. – b. Memphis, TN, Aug 15, 77; f Dennis Keith; m Jennifer Shelton; w Kathryn Pope, Tampa, FL Jun 30, 01; chdn Madelyn Lee, Andrew Timothy, Isaiah John, Grant Charles; UNC 99, BA; CTS 05, MDiv; O Dec 2, 07, ECar; astp Christ P Ch, Winterville, NC 50-08; astp Grace P Ch, Ocala, FL 08-10; ascp 10-

3029 NE 27th Street, Ocala, FL 34470 – 352-629-3237   Central Florida
E-mail: Ledford7@yahoo.com
Grace Presbyterian Church – 352-629-1537

Lee, Alan William – b Pittsburgh, PA, Jul 28, 54; f Frederick William; m Elise Wolf; w Sally Jean Millington, Philadelphia, PA, Aug 25, 78; chdn Nathaniel David, Benjamin Baruch (d), Hannah Ruth, Tamarah Millington; DuqU 72-75, BS; WTS 77-81, MAR, 77-81, MDiv; ColCC 90-91, MA; O Feb 18, 84, OPC; Recd PCA Sept 14, 91, Phil Pby; ev Uganda, EAfr, 84-91; op Peace Valley Ch, Warminster, PA, 91-93, p 93-95, wc 95; p Peace Valley Ch, Warminster, PA, 96-01, wc 01-03; ob chp SIM, Ghana, 03-10; astp Stony Point Ref P Ch, Richmond, VA, 11-

749 Worsham Road, Richmond, VA 23235   James River
E-mail: alanlee@stonypointchurch.org
Stony Point Reformed Presbyterian Church – 804-272-8111

Lee, Andrew Sik Wai – w Melinda; chdn Matthias; WTS 02, MDiv; O Aug 14, 04, MNY Pby; astp Covenant Ch, Whitestone, NY, 04-

15 Erie Court, Jericho, NY 11753 – 917-434-5042   Metropolitan New York
E-mail: andrew.soluschristus@gmail.com
Covenant Church – 718-352-8646

Lee, Andy Chul Soon – b Seoul, Korea, Jul 19, 36; f Bong Hyui; m Moon Ah; w Becky J., Seoul, Korea, Dec 3, 65; SNU 62, BA; TempU 76, MA; WTS 71, BD; PTS 73, ThM; L Jun 19, 73; O Feb 23, 75, PCUSA; Recd PCA Nov 14, 89, DMV Pby; ap Mkt Sq Ch, Harrisburg, PA, 75-81; p Kor Centr Ch, Houston, TX, 81-82; p Pitts United Kor Ch, Pitts, PA, 83-85; p United Kor P Ch, Bethesda, MD, 85-89; p Bethesda Korean P Ch, Rockville, MD, 89-01; hr 01

13 Apple Seed Lane, Gaithersburg, MD 20878-2801 – 301-963-4788   Potomac
E-mail: andylee12365@verizon.net
HR

    Lee, Anson – p Bethel P Ch of Chicago, Palatine, IL, 17-

423 Park Avenue, Wheeling, IL 60090   Korean Central
E-mail: ansonlee626@gmail.com
Bethel Presbyterian Church of Chicago – 773-545-2222

    Lee, Anthony – b Chicago, IL, Nov 16, 80; NCSt 04, BS; RTSNC 12, MDiv; astp, yp Sae Han P Ch of Atlanta, Alpharetta, GA, 14-15; astp, yp Siloam Korean Ch of Atlanta, Norcross, GA, 16-

2043 Fosco Drive NW, Duluth, GA 30097   Korean Southeastern
E-mail: chungjinlee@gmail.com
Siloam Korean Church of Atlanta – 770-638-1600

    Lee, Brendon – O Dec 14, 10; astp Sae Han P Ch of Atlanta, Alpharetta, GA, 13-

620 Madison Creek Court, Suwanee, GA 30024 – 678-580-5716   Korean Southeastern
E-mail: brendon4him@hotmail.com
Sae Han Presbyterian Church of Atlanta – 770-619-5340

    Lee, Bryan – O Oct 19, 14, NoCA Pby; astp JordanValley Ch, West Jordan, UT, 14-

4923 West Calton Lane, South Jordan, UT 84009   Northern California
E-mail: bryan@jordanvalleychurch.org
Jordan Valley Church PCA – 801-280-6778

    Lee, Caleb – ob astp Global Mission Ch, Korea, 08-

E-mail: calebkyulee@gmail.com   Korean Capital

    Lee, Chang Kyu – ob p Medford Kor P Ch, Medford, OR, 98-

2677 Paloma Avenue #4, Medford,   Korean Northwest
E-mail: abclee7221@gmail.com
Medford Korean Presbyterian Church

    Lee, Choong Hee – wc

6533 Patti Drive #1708, Corpus Christi, TX 78414 – 361-688-3459   Korean Southern

    Lee, Choonghyun – srp Korean Central P Ch of Cincinnati, Cincinnati, OH, 16-18

E-mail: davidlee405@hotmail.com   Korean Central

    Lee, Christopher Jong – ascp Lamp P Ch, Los Angeles, CA, 16-

401 East Bay State Street #86, Alhambra, CA 91801   Korean Southwest
E-mail: christianitus@gmail.com
Lamp Presbyterian Church

Lee, Chul – astp Church for All Nations, Vienna, VA, 12-

8506 Amanda Place, Vienna, VA 22180 – 703-865-7686 Korean Capital
E-mail: maestro0719@hotmail.com
Church for All Nations – 703-573-3767

Lee, Dae Kyung – astp Emmanuel Ch in Phil, Philadelphia, PA, 17-18; ob 18-

2011 Moreland Boulevard #202, Champaign, IL 61822 Korean Eastern
E-mail: studybible00@gmail.com

Lee, Dan Dongkyo – b Kyungbook-Do, Korea, Jan 5, 47; f Eui Seung; m Keun Hee Lee; w Susan Sang Soon Kwon, Seoul, Korea, Oct 25, 71; chdn Esther, Hannah; PGATCS 74, BA, 79, BD; ColTS 81-83, 86; L Oct 29, 79, Kyunggy Pby; O Oct 28, 80, Kyunggy Pby; ap Dong Won P Ch, Seoul, 79-81; op Kor Ch (PCUSA), Asheville, NC, 83-86; op Kor Riverside P Ch, Atlanta, GA, 87-89; op Gwinnett Korean P Msn, Norcross, GA, 90-97; sc KorSE Pby, 92-00, wc 97-01, ev 01-

PO Box 921128, Norcross, GA 30010 – 770-645-0778 Korean Southeastern

Lee, Daniel S. – ob p Korea, 02-

Address Unavailable, KOREA Korean Central

Lee, Daniel Soonho – b So Korea, Feb 28, 65; f Doo-Il; m Tae Hee Park; w Mi Hyang Lee, Chicago, IL, May 5, 90; chdn Christopher S., Benjamin W., Danielle S.; UIL 87, BS; TEDS 91, MDiv, 94, ThM; L Apr 92; O May 93, KorCent Pby; astp Highland Korean P Ch, Vernon Hills, IL, 91-94; ob ascp Kansas Ch (non-PCA msn), Roeland Park, KS, 94-95, ob srp 95; srp The Covenant Ch, Northbrook, IL, 96-01; ob ascp Los Angeles Christian P Ch, 01-06; ob ascp Hanaro Comm Ch, La Puente, CA, 06-10; ob srp Evergreen Christan Ch, Fullerton, CA, 10-17

704 South Stoneman Avenue, Apt. B, Alhambra, CA 91801-5824 – 323-255-2102 Korean Central

Lee, David – astp Siloam Korean Ch of Atlanta, Norcross, GA, 07-17

11235 Blackstone Way, Suwanee, GA 30024 Korean Southeastern

Lee, David – O Mch 13, 18, MNY Pby; ascp Covenant Flwsp Ch, West Orange, NJ, 18-

60 Sherwood Road, Colonia, NJ 07067 – 908-463-9647 Metropolitan New York
E-mail: david@covenantnj.com
Covenant Fellowship Church

Lee, David Byunghee – O Feb 15, 09, KorE Pby; astp Cheltenham P Ch, 09-12; Open Door Ch, 12-

22586 Scattersville Gap Terrace, Ashburn, VA 20148 Korean Capital
E-mail: odpcdavid@gmail.com
Open Door Church

Lee, David Dukhee – w Sonia; chdn Sophia, Derek; UTXAu 96, BA; CTS 01, MDiv; ob astp New Church of Atlanta, 01-02; astp Sae Han P Ch of Atlanta, Alpharetta, GA, 02-04; ip New Ch of Atlanta, Atlanta, GA, 02-05, ascp 05-10; ev, op Mustard Seed Flwsp, Peachtree Corners, GA, 12-

5268 Fox Hill Court, Norcross, GA 30092 – 404-428-8242 Korean Southeastern
E-mail: daviddlee@hotmail.com
Mustard Seed Fellowship – 404-428-8242

Lee, David Heung D. – srp Peniel P Ch, Los Angeles, CA

225 North Vermont Avenue #423, Los Angeles, CA 90004 – 213-384-7379   Korean Southwest
E-mail: heungdo_lee@hotmail.com
Peniel Presbyterian Church – 310-951-6963

Lee, David J. – astp New Life Msn Ch of Northern California, San Jose, CA, 06-09; op New Life Msn Ch of Fremont, Fremont, CA, 09-

47000 Warm Springs Boulevard #417, Fremont, CA 94539 – 510-761-6562   Northern California
E-mail: rev.dave.lee@gmail.com
New Life Mission Church of Fremont

Lee, Deck Soo – astp The Way Ch, Los Angeles, CA, 08-

16922 Virginia Avenue, Bell Flower, CA 90706 – 562-867-7847   Korean Southwest
E-mail: leeds52@hotmail.com
The Way Church – 323-735-0200

Lee, Dong Gu – ob ascp 99-03; mis MTW, Japan, 03-07; p SEED, 07-12; p 13-

3055 Peyton Road, LaVerne, CA 91750 – 909-592-4072   Korean Southwest
E-mail: ddlee1520@gmail.com

Lee, Dong Yeob – astp Lamp P Ch of Los Angeles, Gardena, CA, 18-

3138 Montrose Avenue #106, La Crescenta, CA 91214   Korean Southwest
E-mail: dongyeob68@gmail.com
Lamp Presbyterian Church of Los Angeles – 310-327-8778

Lee, Douglas Emery – b Minneapolis, MN, May 16, 47; f Emery W.; m May C. Magnuson; w Nancy E. Fredericks, Minneapolis, MN, Jun 14, 69; chdn Wendy, Amanda, Nathaniel, Darren; UMN 70, BA; CTS 73, MDiv; L Apr 19, 73; O Apr 19, 73, FL Pby (RPCES); ap Faith P Ch, Sarasota, FL, 73-75; p Highline Ref P Ch, Seattle, WA, 75-85; Chap USArmy, ARNG, 77-89 ; op Christ P Ch, Farmington, MN, 85-89; sc Siouxl Pby, 88-89; Chap USArmy, Ft. Gillem, GA, 89-92; Chap USArmy, Ft. McPherson, GA, 92-97; Chap USArmy, War College, Carlisle, PA, 97-98; Chap USArmy, Ft. McPherson, GA, 98-04; Chap US Army, Pentagon, Arlington, VA, 03-08; Ret USArmy 08; Exec Dir PRCC 08-17

2644 Emma Stone Drive, Marriottsville, MD 21104-1493 – 678-701-5151   Potomac
E-mail: dougelee@gmail.com

Lee, Edward Eun Jai – srp Choong Hyun P Ch, Houston, TX, 91-09; hr 09

2004 Apple Drive, Little Elm, TX 75068   Korean Southern
HR

Lee, Eunsub – astp Korean Central P Ch of Wash, Vienna, VA, 08-10; ob srp First Kor P Ch of Washington, Rockville, MD, 10-12; op Great Love Msn Ch, Kensington, MD, 12-

217 Hemingway Drive, Gaithersburg, MD 20878   Korean Capital
E-mail: pastoreslee@gmail.com
Great Love Mission Church – 703-470-5879

Lee, Gi Hwan – astp Calvary P Ch, Baltimore, MD, 10-14

7002 Willow Place #3, Yakima, WA 98908 – 410-825-6025   Korean Capital
E-mail: ricky.hwan@gmail.com

Lee, Gu Kwang – op Hope P Ch of Dallas Msn, Carrollton, TX, 08-

1142 Holly Drive, Carrollton, TX 75010 – 972-395-0191   Korean Southern
E-mail: L290kk@hotmail.com
Hope Presbyterian Church of Dallas – 972-446-3477

Lee, Hae Chun – astp Korean Central P Ch of Wash, Vienna, VA, 02-05; p Korean Canaan Comm Ch, Annandale, VA, 05-08; wc 08-

5020 Marshall Crown Road, Centreville, VA 20120-5431 – 703-642-3872   Korean Capital
E-mail: abraham9863@hotmail.com

Lee, Haengjin – astp McLean Korean P Ch, McLean, VA, 18-

8112 Anna Court, Falls Church, VA 22042   Korean Capital
E-mail: wwlhj0324@gmail.com
McLean Korean Presbyterian Church – 703-893-8651

Lee, Henry Hyunsoo – O May 23, 93, KorSW Pby; astp Sa Rang Comm Ch, Anaheim, CA, 95-97, mis 97-

Address Unavailable   Korean Southwest Orange County

Lee, Hong Bae – astp Kor Cent P Ch of Washington, DC, 03-07; ob srp Hong Kong Central Ch, 08-

Hong Kong Central Church, 2302, 23/F Vertical Square 28 Heung Yip Road,   Korean Capital
Wong Chuck Hang, HONG KONG
E-mail: leehkcc@gmail.com
Hong Kong Central Church

Lee, Hoochan Paul – w Jin Sun Kwon; chdn Ariel Chanjoo, Eliana Yejoo; astp Korean United Ch of Phil, Philadelphia, PA; ob Galilee Ch; p Glory Comm Ch, Cliffside Park, NJ, 14- 16

PO Box 9195, Paramus, NJ 07653 – 267-210-8957   Korean Northeastern
E-mail: pastorpaullee@gmail.com

Lee, Hoyoung – b Seoul, Korea, Mar 21, 37; w Myungja Choi, Annapolis, MD; chdn Jean, Sally; SNU 59, BA; UMD 65, MA, 70, PhD; CRDS 85, MDiv, 86, DMin; WTS, PhD cand; L 85, Emmanuel Jesus Christ Ch; srp Rochester Korean Central Ch, 91-94; srp Bethel Korean P Ch, 95-97; ob prof RIT; hr

4000 Clagett Road, Hyattsville, MD 20782 – 301-927-1956   Korean Capital
HR

Lee, Huey – O Apr 17, 16, KorCap Pby; astp Christ Central P Ch, Centreville, VA, 16-

11862 Aberdeen Landing Lane, Midlothian, VA 23113   Korean Capital
E-mail: hueyhlee@gmail.com
Christ Central Presbyterian Church – 703-815-1300

Lee, Hyun Suk – astp Rothem Risen Sun P Ch, Springfield, VA, 18-

14906 Greymont Drive, Centreville, VA 20120 – 703-946-8299   Korean Capital
E-mail: leehun36@yahoo.com
Rothem Risen Sun Presbyterian Church – 703-321-0101

Lee, Il Gon – op Lord's P Ch, San Diego, CA, 08-15; op All Generations P Ch, Corona, CA, 15-

14139 Bay Circle, Eastvale, CA 92880   Korean Southwest Orange County
E-mail: lig102@hotmail.com
All Generations Presbyterian Church – 714-864-9998

MINISTERIAL DIRECTORY

Lee, In Seung – b Junbook, Korea, Dec 4, 54; f Sang Wook; m Hee Sup Jin; w Won Ja Choi, Seoul, Oct 30, 82; chdn Jung Jin, Jung Hyun; ChShC 73-77, BA; ChShTS 77-80, MDiv; HGST 90-91, MDiv, grad wk; SRTCS 13, DD; L Feb 25, 80; O Feb 25, 80, Ham-Nam of Korea; Chap Kor Army, 80-83; astp Dong-am P Ch, Seoul, 83-84; srp Dong-Eun P Ch, Seoul, 84-95; astp Choong Hyun P Ch, Houston, TX, 96-99; op Choong Hyun P Ch of Austin, Austin, TX, 99-00; op Korean Faith P Msn, Houston, TX, 00-; sc KorS Pby

20810 Mossy Hill Lane, Katy, TX 77449   Korean Southern
E-mail: lee1954us@yahoo.com; inseunglee1954@gmail.com
Korean Faith Presbyterian Mission – 832-264-9566

Lee, Jacob – astp New Life P Ch, Dresher, PA, 17-

1868 Willow Avenue, Willow Grove, PA 19090 – 347-226-0880   Eastern Pennsylvania
New Life Presbyterian Church – 215-641-1100

Lee, Jae Ryong – w Sung Hee Lee; chdn Sara, John; SogangU, BS,, MS; UDet, MS; CTS, MDiv; L Apr 98, KorCent Pby; O Apr 99, KorCent Pby; op Open P Ch Msn, Schaumburg, IL, 98-07; p Orlando Korean P Ch in America, Apopka, FL, 07-

219 Sterling Springs, Altamonte Springs, FL 32714 – 407-682-1789   Korean Southeastern
E-mail: jaelee4christ@hotmail.com
Orlando Korean Presbyterian Church in America – 321-251-5252

Lee, James – wc

Address Unavailable   Korean Southwest

Lee, James – O Mch 13, 18, MNY Pby; srp Covenant Flwsp Ch, West Orange, NJ, 18-

416 Elizabeth Street, Fort Lee, NJ 07024 – 201.648.5417   Metropolitan New York
E-mail: james@covenantnj.com
Covenant Fellowship Church

Lee, James Andrew – b South Korea, Aug 6, 63; f Stephan Youngtei ; m Sarah; w Soo Jin Kim ; chdn Timothy James, Candice Kim; UCLA 87, BA; WTS 91, MDiv; PTS 99, DMin; O Apr 25, 93, Phil Pby; astp Korean United Ch of Phil, Philadelphia, PA, 89-94; em p Presbyterian Church of the Palisades NJ, 94-96; em p Korean Central P Ch of Wash, Centreville, VA, 96-01; fndr/dir Strategic Leadership Alliance, 01-; mis China, 01-11; fndr, p My Father's House/Newsong, Pasadena, CA, 11-15; vp, rpvost Southern Ref Sem, 15-16, pres 16-

4740 Dacoma Street #H, Houston, TX 77092 – 713-467-4501   Korean Southwest
E-mail: srtcshouston@gmail.com
Strategic Leadership Alliance
Southern Reformed College and Seminary

Lee, James Jeong Woo – b Seoul, Korea, Aug 6, 64; f Pyung Jae; m Kwi Im; w Cassie; chdn Audrey, Connor, Averey; UCB 87, BA; WSCAL 91, MDiv; L Sept 94; O Oct 8, 95, SoCst Pby; ev, chp New Life Msn Ch, San Diego, CA, 94-08; p 08-

10914 Ivy Hill Drive #7, San Diego, CA 92131 – 858-566-2447   South Coast
E-mail: nljames4x@sbcglobal.net
New Life Mission Church – 858-566-2447

Lee, James Jinsuk – ev New Hope Comm Ch, Marlton, NJ, 10-

20 Old Cedarbrook Road, Wyncote, PA 19095 – 215-887-9777   Korean Eastern
E-mail: mox4mox@gmail.com
New Hope Community Church, Marlton, NJ

Lee, Jean Young – srp Light of the Gospel Ch, Columbia, MD, 18-

5913 Rowanberry Drive, Elkridge, MD 21075 　　　　　　　　　　　Korean Capital
E-mail: theophilo1435@gmail.com
Light of the Gospel Church

Lee, Jeff – O Sept 12, 09, SWFL Pby; campm RUF, USFL, 09- 16; campm RUF, FLAtlU, 16-

400 NE 47th Street, Boca Raton, FL 33431 – 813-767-9063 　　　　Southwest Florida
E-mail: jeff.lee@ruf.org
PCA Reformed University Fellowship

Lee, Jeffrey David – O Jan 20, 13, Pot Pby; astp Potomac Hills P Ch, Leesburg, VA, 12-15; campm RUF, NewportU, 15-

206 Parkway Dr., Newport News, VA 23606 　　　　　　　　　　　　　Tidewater
PCA Reformed University Fellowship

Lee, Jin Hyoung – p Light of the Gospel Ch, MD, 15-

4113 River Forth Drive, Fairfax, VA 22030 　　　　　　　　　　　Korean Capital
E-mail: jlee3927@gmail.com
Light of the Gospel Church

Lee, John – op Good News Ch, Edison, NJ, 04, p 04-09; wc 10-

286 County Road #B, Tenafly, NJ 07670 – 201-941-5427 　　　Metropolitan New York

Lee, John Hyung Ro – b Jechon, So Korea, Feb 8, 41; f Keun Taek; m Okchool Cho; w Sharon Kyuyung Lee, Seoul, Korea, Apr 5, 69; chdn Ahree Lee; ChungCE 62-64; KookC 66-68, BA; WTS 84-87, MAR; L Mar 3, 88; O Mar 26, 89, KorE Pby; ascp Emmanuel Ch in Phil, Philadelphia, PA, 89-93; ob srp Mil-al P Ch (non-PCA), Chamblee, GA, 93-95, wc 95; srp Main Line Korean P Msn, Bryn Mawr, PA, 96-10; ob astp Bethel Korean P Ch, Ellicot City, MD, 09-11; hr

3165 St. Johns Lane, Ellicott City, MD 21042 – 610-645-6533 　　　Korean Eastern
E-mail: rev.johnlee@gmail.com
HR

Lee, John Taehoon – w Keun Ah Cho; chdn Joseph Youngkwon, Grace Youngeun; SNU 94, BA; TEDS 00, MDiv; ob Fountain of Joy Ch, Los Angeles, 11-

4920 Via Fresco, Camarillo, CA 93012 　　　　　　　　　　　　　Korean Capital
E-mail: ztlee@hotmail.com
Fountain of Joy Church, Los Angeles

Lee, John Thomas Jr. – b Starkville, MS, Nov 26, 69; f John Thomas; m Waanda Pearle Barnhill; w Barbara Elizabeth Brownlee, Memphis, TN; chdn Jonathan Alexander, Callicott Marie, Jaden Thomas, Joseph William, Caitlin Elizabeth; MSU 91, BA; CTS 98, MDiv; L Apr 21, 98, MO Pby; O Aug 9, 98, MO Pby; astp Providence Ref P Ch, St. Louis, MO, 98-00, ascp 00-03; op Cornerstone P Ch, St. Louis, MO, 03-04, p 04-09; p Decatur P Ch, Decatur, AL, 09-

2422 Jarvis Street, SW, Decatur, AL 35603 　　　　　　　　　　　　　　Providence
E-mail: tommy@decaturpca.org
Decatur Presbyterian Church – 256-351-6010

Lee, Jong Yun – b Chon-An, Choong-nam, So Korea, Aug 23, 40; w Soon Bok; chdn Miriam, Gloria, Paula; O Nov 28, 76, Phil Pby (RPCES); p First Kor P Ch, Phila, PA, 76-78; prof ACTS, Seoul, Kor, 76-83; p Hallelujah Chr Ch, Seoul, 81-83; pres Jeon Ju Univ, Chonju, Korea, 84-88; ob p Choong Hyun P Ch

Lee, Jong Yun, continued
(non PCA), Seoul, Korea, 88-91; ob srp Seoul P Ch, Seoul (non PCA), Kor, 91-; *The Problem of Paul's Understanding of the Historical Jesus in Critical Study, Sermon on the Mount, Invitation to the New and Old Testament, Biblical Greek Inductive Study Method; Parables Jesus; NT Introduction;* 88; *The Challenge of Marxism and the Christian Response; Lectures on the Gospel of John* vols. 1-5; *Lectures on Philippians; New Testament Greek: An Inductive Study of the Complete Text of the Gospel of John; Pilgrim*: compiled religion columns; *The Chart of Christian Faith; The Ten Commandments; Lectures on the Minor Prophets; The Miracles of Jesus; Lectures on Ephesians; Lectures on Genesis; Church Growth Theory*; ed *South-North Unification and North Korea Missions; Church and Nation; Lectures on Romans 1-4; Christian Leadership: Joshua & Nehemiah; An Expositional Commentary on Biblical Difficulties,* Pilgrim Publ, 2004; *The Path of Discipleship in a Mindless Age,* Pilgrim Publ, 2005; *Psalms I-III,* Pilgrim Publ, 2007

701 Nobility Village, 1017-1 Daechi-dong, Kangnam-gu, Seoul, KOREA – 02-557-0691   Philadelphia
E-mail: jylee@seoulchurch.or.kr
Seoul Presbyterian Church, Seoul (non PCA)

    Lee, Joon Ho – mis Russia

3732 Southport Drive, Plano, TX 75025-3851 – 562-926-9149   Korean Southwest Orange County
E-mail: junhodao@hanmail.net

    Lee, Joonha – astp First Korean P Ch, Glenview, IL, 04-07; p Sungmin Cov P Ch, Arlington Heights, IL, 07-17; astp First Korean P Ch, Glenview, IL, 17-

3513 Lake Avenue #206, Wilmette, IL 60091   Korean Central
E-mail: joonhalee31@gmail.com
First Korean Presbyterian Church – 847-299-1776

    Lee, Joseph –

4435 Fortran Drive, San Jose, CA 95134   Korean Southeastern
E-mail: josephlee@kepc.org

    Lee, Joseph –

Address Unavailable   Korean Central

    Lee, Joseph K. – b Korea, Mar 2, 54; f Kwang-il; m Juhee Lee; w Haju Yu, Chicago, IL, Dec 8, 85; chdn Mary, Francis; KorU 73-80, LLB; TEDS 93-96, MDiv; O Oct 14, 97, KAPC; Recd PCA Apr 13, 99, KorCent Pby; medu Hebron Church, IL, 96-97; ascp Evergreen Comm Ch, Mt. Prospect, IL, 97-00; ip Pilgrim Korean P Ch, Prospect Heights, IL, 00-01; p Sungmin-Pilgrim P Ch, Prospect Heights, IL, 01-07

7232 North Tripp Avenue, Lincolnwood, IL 60712   Korean Central
E-mail: kfranmaryh@gmail.com

    Lee, Joseph Kyung Chun – srp Eden Korean P Ch, Castro Valley, CA, 92-98; hr

14727 NW Benny Drive, Portland, OR 97229   Korean Northwest
HR

    Lee, Joseph S.C. – b Seoul, Korea, Nov 21, 65; f Jong Keum; m Ran Sook Park; w Seo Kyeong Na, Glenview, IL, Jan 1, 94; chdn Shinah, Noah, Grace; UIL, BArch; TEDS, MDiv; O Oct 7, 97, KorCent Pby; Korean Bethel P Ch, Chicago, IL, 94-96; ob medu Wonchon Ch (non-PCA), 96-99; ob p Antioch Korean Covenant Ch, 99-01; p Emmanuel Ch in Phil, Philadelphia, PA, 01-03; ob p Hana Church, Buena Park, CA, 05-

76 Chula Vista, Irvine, CA 92602 – 714-669-5490   Korean Central
E-mail: josephsclee@yahoo.com
Hana Church, Buena Park, CA (non PCA)

Lee, Josh – O Nov 21, 10, NoCA Pby; astp Ridge P Ch, 10-12; ascp 12-17, p 17-

1230 Elliott Road #18, Paradise, CA 95969　　　　　　　　　　　Northern California
E-mail: jlee150@gmail.com
Ridge Presbyterian Church – 530-872-8270

Lee, Joshua SJ – b Seoul, Jan 28, 61; f Myung Kwan Lee; m Ae Sin Im; w Nadia Young, Los Angeles, CA, Jul 1, 89; UCSB 84, BA; NPTS 89, MDiv; L Apr 13, 93, KorSW Pby; O Sept 12, 94, KorSW Pby; New Life Msn of Anaheim, 93-96; op New Life Msn Ch of Northern California, San Jose, CA, 97-10

1818 Moore Boulevard #124, Davis, CA 95618　　　　　　Korean Southwest Orange County
E-mail: joshuanlmc@yahoo.com

Lee, Jung Yeop –ob Cov Life Ch, MN

3454 Chatsworth Street North, Shoreview, MN 55126　　　　　　　　　　Korean Central
E-mail: junglee@covlifecities.com
Covenant Life Church (non-PCA)

Lee, Junhee – O Feb 15, 09, KorE Pby; ob Toronto Korean Presbyterian Church, stu

35 Slender Fern Way, North York, ON M2J 4P4 CANADA – 416-792-8791　　　Korean Eastern
E-mail: biblicaljhlee@hotmail.com

Lee, Kang Hoon –

E-mail: ohpeace@gmail.com　　　　　　　　　　　　　　　　　　　　　　Korean Central

Lee, Kangtaek – astp Cheltenham P Ch, Cheltenham, PA, 09-15; ob 15-17; srp New England Gr P Ch, West Hartford, CT, 17-

305 Amy Court, North Wales, PA 19454　　　　　　　　　　　　　Korean Northeastern
E-mail: petroslee@hotmail.com
New England Grace Presbyterian Church – 860-461-1272

Lee, Kisup – O Mar 12, 00; astp Proclamation P Ch, Bryn Mawr, PA, 15-

219 2nd Avenue, Broomall, PA 19008 – 610-331-7732　　　　　　　　　Korean Eastern
E-mail: kisup@proclamation.org
Proclamation Presbyterian Church – 610-520-9500

Lee, Kwang Jae – op Ye Darm P Ch of Houston, Houston, TX, 12-

874 Yorkchester Drive #236, Houston, TX 77097 – 714-328-5851　　　　　Korean Southern
Ye Darm Presbyterian Church of Houston – 713-461-0709

Lee, Kwangeun Paul – p The Lord P Ch, Fairfax, VA, 17-

9722 Ashbourn Drive, Burke, VA 22015　　　　　　　　　　　　　　　Korean Capital
E-mail: gospel323@gmail.com
The Lord Presbyterian Church

Lee, Kyu Hyun – Kook MinU, BA; ChShTS, MDiv; FaithEvSem, MA, DMin; O Oct 29, 91, Korea; ob prof, vp, dean Faith Int U, Tacoma, WA, 06-

35412 4th Avenue SW, Federal Way, WA 98023 – 253-881-3311　　　　　Korean Northwest
E-mail: klee@faithseminary.edu
Faith International University, Tacoma, WA

Lee, Macky – astp Covenant Ch, Whitestone, NY, 07-09; op Covenant of Faith, Flushing, NY, 09-12; p 12-

137-44 Northern Boulevard, Flushing, NY 11354   Metropolitan New York
Covenant of Faith Church

Lee, Matthew Wonjoon – astp Sa Rang Comm Ch, Anaheim, CA, 10- 14; p Seoul Sa Rang P Ch (non PCA)

526 South Melrose Street, Anaheim, CA 92805 – 714-533-1024   Korean Southwest Orange County
E-mail: mattspace@gmail.com
Seoul Sa Rang Presbyterian Church (non PCA)

Lee, Michael D. – w Tricia; St.LeoC, BA; RTSNC, MDiv; O Apr 24, 05, Flwsp Pby; int Bethel P Ch, Clover, SC, 01-05, ascp 05-09; mis MTW Mexico, 07-13; prof ITEM, 11-13; reg coord member care MTW LatAm, 13-; mis MTW Panama, 15-16; reg coord MTW CentAm, 16-; reg rep GTD MTW LatAm 16-

c/o MTW – 803-222-5733   Fellowship
E-mail: re4merz@gmail.com
PCA Mission to the World

Lee, Min Young – Recd PCA Sept 9, 14, KorNE Pby, ob 14-

399 Bedford Road, Apt G, Pleasantville, NY 10570 – 914-874-3606   Korean Northeastern
E-mail: mylee4x@gmail.com

Lee, Moses – b Seoul, Sept 22, 87; f Jun; m Choi; w Lee, Lakewood, WA, Jun 27, 15; UMD, BA; WTS 13, MDiv; O Jun 14, KorCap Pby; astp Bethel Korean P Ch, Ellicot City, MD, 11-15; ob p Redeemer P Ch, Arlington, VA, 16-

4100 Massachusetts Avenue NW Apt. 1001, Washington, DC 20016 – 443-538-3383   Korean Capital
E-mail: mlee922@gmail.com
Redeemer Presbyterian Church, Arlington, VA (non PCA)

Lee, Moses Dong Seung – astp New City Ch, Hamilton, ON, 12-16, ascp 16-

75 London Street North, Hamilton, ON L8H 4B4 CANADA – 289-684-4182   Eastern Canada
E-mail: mosesdslee@gmail.com
New City Church – 888-908-6293

Lee, Murray W. – f Mark; m Emily Corr; w Kimberly Baugh, Alex City, AL; chdn Ella Suzanne, Miller Wesley, Sara Wells; SamU 02, BA; CTS 05, MDiv; UAL 17, PhD; ascp Covenant P Ch, Birmingham, AL, 06-08; op Cahaba Park Ch PCA, Birmingham, AL, 07-08, p 08-

4465 Old Overton Road, Birmingham, AL 35201 – 205-266-9653   Evangel
E-mail: mlee@cahabapark.org
Cahaba Park Church PCA – 205-870-1886

Lee, Nam Jong – p San Jose Servants P Ch, San Jose, CA, 07-13; mis 13-

Address Unavailable   Korean Northwest

Lee, Nathan – O Apr 12, 15, Siouxl Pby; p Grace P Ch, Duluth, MN, 15-

123 East 9th Street #2, Duluth, MN 55805 – 805-405-5774   Siouxlands
E-mail: nlee.gracepresduluth@gmail.com
Grace Presbyterian Church – 218-349-3535

Lee, Oh Yeon – op The Word Ch of Southern California, Gardena, CA, 96-97, p 97-06; sc KorSW Pby, 98-99; ob

16204 Perrin Circle, Riverside, CA 92503 – 310-516-1678   Korean Southwest
E-mail: leeohyeon@gmail.com

Lee, Owen Young – b Glendale, CA, Oct 13, 71; f Samuel; m Mary Park; w Margaret Uhm, Torrance, CA, Jun 29, 99; chdn Abigail Hope, Caleb Nathaniel, Elizabeth Grace; UCB, BA; WSCAL, MDiv; L Apr 11, 00, KorSW Pby; O Apr 17, 01, KorSW Pby; ascp Anaheim New Life Msn Ch, Buena Park, CA, 00-02; op New Life Msn Ch of Burbank, Burbank, CA, 02-12; srp Christ Central P Ch of Wash, Centreville, VA, 12-

5221 Rushbrook Drive, Centreville, VA 20120   Korean Capital
E-mail: owenylee@gmail.com
Christ Central Presbyterian Church – 703-815-1300

Lee, Paul Woan Jae – b Korea, Jun 25, 50; f Man-Chul; m Boon-Dong Choe; w Chong Suk Kim, Los Angeles, CA; chdn Juli Lee, Sarah Minjung; WooSU 72, BS; QUCC 75-76; IntSem 83, MDiv; RegC 85, MS; WTS 85; TalTS 87; FulTS 88; RTS 95, DMin; L Oct 6, 84; O Sept 28, 85, KorSW Pby; op LA Amen Msn, 85-94; AcadDn ICUS, 95-; t, p Western Ch of Los Angeles, 95-99; ob fndr, admin Puritan Spirituality & Ref Studies Conf, 99-; fndr/admin Biblical Puritan U, 08-; "A Study of Pastoral Burnout and the Quality of Pastoral Leadership: Learning Through the Ministry of Richard Baxter as a Reformed Puritan Pastor," RTS DMin diss 95; *A Quest for Spirituality: A Guide to Godliness-Disciplines*, 99; *A Quest for Spiritual Theology: The Root of Puritanism*, 01; *The Essence of Christian Life: Mystic Experience, Holiness, Godliness, and Growing Strong*, 01

1311 North San Fernando Road #107, Los Angeles, CA 90065 – 323-276-3997   Korean Southwest
E-mail: p.parsc@gmail.com; www.parsc.net
Puritan and Reformed Studies Center

Lee, Peter – ob

3015 Eden Street, Camp Lejeune, NC 28547   Korean Southeastern
E-mail: songpeter@gmail.com

Lee, Peter – ob

5 Grant, Irvine, CA 92620 – 949-654-9669   Korean Southwest
E-mail: bahnseok@cornerstoneusa.org

Lee, Pyung Duk – b Seoul, Korea, Aug 27, 47; f Chun Jong Lee; m Ki Sun Jung; w Bok Nam Lee, Seoul, Kor, Jul 7, 79; chdn Won Pyo, Kwang Pyo; DHTS 78-82, dipl, 84-88, ThB; DTS 91-93, MA; HGST 96, MDiv; FulTS 98, DMin; L Apr 5, 84; O Apr 5, 84, Kor Pusan Pby, Kor; Recd PCA Oct 10, 91; p Sam-Wha P Ch, 81-84; p Hadong-Kyung Nam, Kor, 81-83; p Dong-Am P Ch, In-Chon, Kor, 84-86; op, p P Ch Seoul, Kor , 86-89, wc 91-92; astp Korean Young Nak Ch of Dallas, Dallas, TX, 92-93, wc 94; astp Choong Hyun P Ch, Houston, TX, 94-96; astp Hope P Ch of Dallas Msn, Carrollton, TX, 96-97; admin SBTS, 96-97; astp Choong Hyun P Ch, Houston, TX, 97-02; op Peace P Ch, Houston, TX, 06-13; hr 13

10440 Valley Forge Drive, Apt. 1, Houston, TX 77042 – 832-252-6136   Korean Southern
HR

Lee, Robin – O Jan 28, 12, Pac Pby; astp King's Ch, Long Beach, CA, 12-18; astp, exec p New Life P Ch, Escondido, CA, 18-

PO Box 50048, Long Beach, CA 90815   South Coast
E-mail: robin.l@newlifepca.com
New Life Presbyterian Church – 760-489-5714

MINISTERIAL DIRECTORY

Lee, Samuel August – O Oct 29, 17, KorCap Pby; astp Korean P Ch of Wash, Fairfax, VA, 17-

6601 Westbury Oaks Court, Springfield, VA 22152 – 703-470-9702   Korean Capital
E-mail: samaugustlee@gmail.com
Korean Presbyterian Church of Washington – 703-321-8090

Lee, Samuel Hwapyung – astp Korean Central P Ch, Centreville, VA, 18-

6637 Green Ash Drive, Springfield, VA 22152 – 703-913-8401   Korean Capital
E-mail: samuel.lee@kcpc.org
Korean Central Presbyterian Church – 703-815-1200

Lee, Sang Chul – astp Sa Rang Comm Ch, Anaheim, CA, 08-

5300 Trabuco Road #111, Irvine, CA 92620   Korean Southwest
E-mail: sangcleem@hotmail.com
Sa Rang Community Church – 714-772-7777

Lee, Sang Do – ascp Korean Faith P Ch of Houston, Houston, TX, 10-

11900 Wickchester Lane, Apt. 315, Houston, TX 77043 – 281-558-5504   Korean Southern
Korean Faith Presbyterian Church of Houston – 832-264-9566

Lee, Sang Rok – p Gloria Korean P Ch, Glen Burnie, MD, 06-; srp The Joy Msn Ch, Bethesda, MD, 10-11

89 Richard Avenue, Severn, MD 21144 – 410-551-5955   Korean Capital
E-mail: srlee309@yahoo.com
Gloria Korean Presbyterian Church – 410-766-1784

Lee, Sean Wang –

2408 Windward Boulevard, Champain, IL 61821   Korean Central
E-mail: seanlee@cfchome.org

Lee, Seung – Chap VA Natl Guard, 12-

5484 Oxbow Drive, Crozet, VA 22932 – 434-205-4644   Blue Ridge
Virginia National Guard

Lee, Shinkwon – staff First Korean P Ch of St. Louis, St. Ann, MO, 17-

10966 Ridgecrest Drive, St. Ann, MO 63074   Korean Central
E-mail: shinkwonlee@gmail.com
First Korean Presbyterian Church of St. Louis – 314-395-3719

Lee, Stephen – srp On-Bit P Ch, Suwanee, GA, 14-

155 Ruby Forest Parkway, Suwanee, GA 30024   Korean Southeastern
E-mail: stephenlee4066@hotmail.com
On-Bit Presbyterian Church

Lee, Sung Eun Scott – astp Living Faith Comm Ch, Flushing, NY, 06-07; astp Calvary P Ch, Towson, MD, 08- 14; astp Beloved P, Rutherford, NJ, 14-16

224-11 57th Avenue, Fl.2, Bayside, NY 11364 – 646-522-6166   Korean Northeastern
E-mail: s.scottlee@gmail.com

Lee, Sung S. – ascp New Life in Christ Ch, Fredericksburg, VA, 03-06; op Agape Korean P Msn, Fredericksburg, VA, 06-

4 Eugene Court, Fredericksburg, VA 22407 – 540-548-4949   James River
E-mail: nlicspotsy@aol.com
Agape Korean Presbyterian Mission – 540-548-4949

Lee, Sungho – op Good News Ch, New Brunswick, NJ, 09-

E-mail: yisunghois@gmail.com   Metropolitan New York
Good News Church – 908-227-8543

Lee, Sunkyu – astp The Ch for All Nations, Vienna, VA, 17-

13840 Ashington Ct., Centreville, VA 20120   Korean Capital
E-mail: singlogos@gmail.com
The Church for All Nations – 703-573-3767

Lee, Walter Chong Won – b Seoul, Aug 26, 71; f Chun Jae Lee; m Myung Ja; w Susan S. Reed, Chicago, IL, Jul 1, 95; chdn Kristen, Sean, Iain; MBI 95, BA; TEDS 98, MDiv; L Oct 13, 98, KorCent Pby; O Oct 12, 99, KorCent Pby; yp Korean Unitd P Ch, Chicago, 92-95; yp Lakeview P Ch, Vernon Hills, IL, 96-97; pEng Anticoh Cov Ch, 97-98; astp, pEng Bethel Christian Ch, Chicago, IL, 98-05; astp, pEng Bethel Korean P Ch, Ellicot City, MD, 05-10; chp, op Harvest P Ch, Columbia, MD, 10-

10126 Century Drive, Ellicott City, MD 21942 – 410-900-5557   Korean Capital
E-mail: pwalterlee@gmail.com
Harvest Presbyterian Church

Lee, Wondae Abraham – b Chullanam-Do, KOR, Feb 20, 42; f Sang Hyuk Lee; m Soo Yo Yun; w Sung Ja Lee, Seoul, KOR, Jan 5, 74; chdn Paul Joon, Daniel Joon-Sung; Kwang Ju JrTc 63, cert; GATS 74, BD; FTS 94, ThM; L Oct 74, Chun-Nam Pby; O Jun 79, Kor GA; Recd PCA Jan 80, Cal Pby; p Greenville Kor Ch, SC, 79-80; p Korean Saints P Ch, Warminster, PA, 80-85; op Inland Korean P Ch, Pomona, CA, 85-92; p Holy Mountain Korean P, Aurora, CO, 92-96; ob p New Life Korean P Ch, Denver, CO, 96-00; p Korean P Galilee Ch, Albuquerque, NM, 00-08; ob Hudson Korean P Ch; ob astp Palm Springs Kor Ch, 14-

70200 Dillon Road #149, Desert Hot Springs, CA 92241   Korean Southwest
E-mail: wonalee777@hotmail.com
Palm Springs Korean Church

Lee, Woo Jin – Recd PCA 16, KorCap Pby; astp McLean Korean P Ch, McLean, VA, 17-

2029 Gallows Road Vienna, VA 22101 – 571-339-9630   Korean Capital
E-mail: forhisglory@gmail.com
McLean Korean Presbyterian Church – 703-893-8651

Lee, Woo Shin – Recd PCA 14, KorNE Pby; op Lighthouse Korean P Ch, Palisades Park, NJ, 14-

241 Hillside Avenue, Leonia, NJ 07605   Korean Northeastern
E-mail: wslee4@liberty.edu
Lighthouse Korean Presbyterian Church – 201-560-6688

Lee, Yong S. – p The Good Ch, Tacoma, WA, 02-

2112 South 90th Street #146, Tacoma, WA 98444 – 253-539-1809   Korean Northwest
E-mail: ezra4511@hanmail.net
The Good Church

Lee, Young Chan – p Open Door Ch of Orange Co, Fullerton, CA, 14-

8210 Gorden Green, Buena Park, CA 90621   Korean Southwest Orange County
E-mail: yclee100@gmail.com
Open Door Church of Orange County – 714-904-0691

Lee, Young Dai – p Calvary P Ch, Waynesville, MO, 02-

PO Box 477, Waynesville, MO 65583   Korean Central
E-mail: paulyounglee71@ymail.com
Calvary Presbyterian Church – 573-336-2293

Lee, Young Hwan –

E-mail: yhdaniellee@gmail.com   Korean Central

Lee, Young Kyun – astp Emmanuel Ch in Phil, Philadelphia, PA, 04-08; ascp Renewal P Ch, Philadelphia, PA, 08-09; astp Emmanuel P Ch, Arlington, VA, 09-13, ascp 13-

1408 North Fillmore Street, Suite 16, Arlington, VA 22201 – 267-253-3267   Potomac
E-mail: ylee@emmanuelarlington.org
Emmanuel Presbyterian Church – 703-525-5605

Leetch, Eric William – b Danbury, CT, Dec 29, 72; f John; m Janice; w Karen, West Point, NY, Oct 20, 01; chdn Grace, Christian, Mary, David; USMA 95, BS; KTS 08, MDiv; MWBTS 15, DMin; O Jul 15, 08, SFL Pby; Chap USArmy, 08-

3105 Sheaser Way, DuPont, WA 98327   South Florida
E-mail: leetche@outlook.com
United States Army

Leggett, Kenneth G. – b Charleston, SC, Jul 5, 71; w Jeanette Wolf, Columbia, SC, Aug 21, 99; chdn Ayers, Addie Grace, Keller; CIU 94; RTS 01, MDiv; O Evan Pby; yp First ARP, Columbia, SC, 92-97; astp, yp Southwood P Ch, Huntsville, AL, 01-02, ascp 03-09, ip 09-10, ascp 10-12; astp Christ P Ch, Nashville, TN, 12-13; ascp 13-15; astp Christ Comm Ch, Franklin, TN, 16-17, ascp 17-

1215 Hillsboro Road, Franklin, TN 37069 – 256-683-2235   Nashville
E-mail: Ken.Leggett@Christcommunity.org
Christ Community Church – 615-468-2200

Leibovich, Gary – ascp New City Flwsp, St. Louis, 11-15; srp Strong Tower Flwsp Msn, Macon, GA, 15-17

E-mail: garyleibo@gmail.com   Central Georgia

Leist, Jason – O May 31, 15, Pitts Pby; astp Murrysville Comm Ch, Murrysville, PA, 15-17, ascp 17-

310 McJunkin Road, Pittsburgh, PA 15239   Pittsburgh
E-mail: jason@murrysvillechurch.com
Murrysville Community Church – 724-327-8411

Lemenager, Scott – w Polly S. Kistler, Jun 4, 78; chdn Patrice Renee, Susan Marie, Katherine Irene, Benjamin John, Elizabeth Anne, Mark Robert, Joseph Scott, Aimee Louise, Andrew Kistler, Kares Abigail; MBI 79, BA; TEDS 80, MA; TIU 88, MDiv; 14, DD; O Jan 27, 04, NoIL Pby; First EFC, Chicago, IL, 80-84; p Portage Park Covenant Church, 84-87; Bethel Free Church, 89-96; Chap Riverside Med Cntr, Kankakee, IL; astp Faith Ref Ch, Kankakee, IL, 98-00; p Christ Covenant Church, Bourbonnais, IL , 01-05; ob Evangelical Church Alliance, 12-17; hr 17

842 South Main Avenue, Kankakee, IL 60901-4539   Chicago Metro
HR

Lennon, Joseph Bertram – b Nova Scotia, Canada, Feb 18, 17; f John Patrick; m Marcella McDougall; w Gloria Bossman, Buffalo, NY, Jun 28, 38; chdn David Lance, Jonathan Brian (d), Jeffrey Lynn, NaMark; BJU 51-55, BA; GrTS 55-58, MDiv; CBTS 61-63, ThM; O Oct 58, First Bapt Ch, Aspen, CO; p First Bapt Ch, Aspen, 58-60; p Community Ch, Armes, CA, 60-63; p Comm Bapt Ch, Wash Falls, NY, 64-67; Milwaukee Resc Msn, 70-78; p Grace Ch (ARP), Spartanburg, 78-80; p Beech Street P Ch, Gaffney, SC, 84-90; hr 90

132 Brookdale Drive, Buffalo, NY 14221   Calvary
HR

Leonard, John S. – b Miami, FL, Jul 28, 55; f Talbert Armlon; m Lucy Louise Setzler; w Christy Snyder, Miami, FL, Apr 27, 85; chdn Kimberly Louise, Katherine Elise, Elizabeth Patricia; BelC 73-77, BA; RTS 80-83, MDiv; TEDS 04, PhD cand; L Jan 83; O Aug 14, 83; ss Lebanon P Ch, Learned, MS, 82-83; ap Redlands Comm Ch, Homestead, FL, 83-87; mis MTW, 88-98; ob asst prof WTS, 98-; op Cresheim Valley Ch, Chestnut Hill, PA, 06-; *Beyond Brazil, An Introduction to Missions*; *Great Faith*; "Jesus' Words to the Canaanite Woman" in *The Urban Face of Mission,* 02; "The Church Between Cultures," *Evangelical Missionary Quarterly* (Jan 04); *Oasis: An Ethnography of a Muslim Convert Group in France*. Ann Arbor: UMI; "Reaching the Muslims Around Us," *Reformed Presbyterian Witness*, 07; *Get Real: Sharing Your Everyday Faith Every Day*, 13; "Sharing the Gospel in Light of Common Grace," *The Problem of Good*, 14:

37 Summit Street, Philadelphia, PA 19118 – 267-763-0971   Philadelphia
E-mail: jleonard@wts.edu
Westminster Theological Seminary – 215-887-5511
P.O. Box 27009, Philadelphia, PA 19118
Cresheim Valley Church

Leonard, Stephen Woodworth – b Sacramento, CA, Feb 8, 46; f William B. Jr.; m Helen Stephens; w Bronwyn Rayburn (d); (2) Glenda Anderson; chdn Linnea (Kickasola), Joshua, Dagney (Olson), Samantha (d), Caleb, Paula (Schaefer); WheatC 68, BA; CTS 74, MDiv; UEdin 75, ThM; L Jun 73; O Jun 74, RMt Pby (RPCES); p Green Lake P Ch, Seattle, WA, 76-85; fndr, Dir PYA, Horn Creek, CO, and Cov College, GA, 77-97; Chap USAR, 75-85; Chap USArmy, 85-02; bd trust CC, 80-91; PRJC, 85-; NAE Chap bd, 92-02; exec dir NAE Chap comm, Int Assoc of Evan Chap, 01-06; brd Int Assoc of Evan Chap 06-; Chap Paul Anderson Youth Home, 06-

PO Box 525, Vidalia, GA 30475 – 912-537-2389   Rocky Mountain
E-mail: sleonard@payh.org
Presbyterian Youth in America, Horn Creek, CO
Presbyterian & Reformed Joint Commission on Chaplains & Military Personnel
Paul Anderson Youth Home

Leslein, Justin – O Sept 27, 15, CentGA Pby; astp First P Ch, Macon, GA, 15-

163 Weatherby Drive, Macon, GA 31210 – 478-737-8066   Central Georgia
E-mail: jleslein@fpcmacon.org
First Presbyterian Church – 478-746-3223

Lesondak, John Edward – b Clearfield, UT, May 12, 51; f Thomas Robert; m Barbara Luke; w Katherine Galbreath Armes, St. Elmo, TN, May 19, 79; chdn Reuben Jonathan, Benjamin Edward, Aaron Thomas, Ethan Byram, Laurel Elizabeth, Alanna Armes; CC 71-80, BA; O Nov 86, TNVal Pby; mis Rep of Seychelles, AIM, 81-87; mis MTW, Kenya, 87-91; mis MTW, Czech Republic, 92-97; mis MTW, Slovak Republic, 97-

c/o Mission to the World   Tennessee Valley
E-mail: lesondak@mac.com
PCA Mission to the World

Lester, Barton Todd – b Huntsville, AL, Oct 3, 69; f Leon R.; m Sandra K. Whaley; w Allison Maria Bowman, Savannah, GA, Jun 18, 94; chdn Caroline Camden, Barton Todd Jr., Madison Oliver, Thomas Scott, John Bennett; AU 88-92, BS; RTS 92-93; RTSNC 94-96, MDiv; L Feb 2, 97; O Feb 2, 97, SEAL Pby; astp Eastwood P Ch, Montgomery, AL, 97-98, ascp 98-15, p 15-

1712 Radcliffe Road, Montgomery, AL 36106 Southeast Alabama
E-mail: btluther@mac.com
Eastwood Presbyterian Church – 334-272-3103

Lester, James Theodore Jr. – b Miami, FL, Nov 13, 48; f James T.; m Martha J. Singleton; w Judith Ann Bivins, Atlanta, GA, Jun 3, 78; chdn Rachel Elise (Staven), Kristin Faith (Hughes), Sarah Jessica(Chrzan), James Theodore III; UAL 70, BS, 72, MA; RTS 79, MDiv; L 82; O 82, NGA Pby; srp Cherokee P Ch, Woodstock, GA, 82-01, ascp 01-02; admin CC, Quest, 02-05; astp Hope P Ch, (p/t), Marietta, GA, 03-; t Cherokee CS, Woodstock, GA, 07-13; p Christ Cov Ch, Woodstock, GA, 13-

1061 Hendon Road, Woodstock, GA 30188-3070 Northwest Georgia
E-mail: jtedlester@gmail.com
Christ Covenant – 770-337-1591

Lester, Robert – b Miami, FL, Oct 8, 53; f James T.; m Martha J. Singleton; w Debra Ann Cagle, Roswell, GA, Dec 31, 74; chdn Robert Thomas, Jr., Benjamin David, Bethany Ann (Baker), James Bryan, Bonnie Grace; BryC 75, BA; UGA 02, MEd; O 97, RPCUS; headm Chalcedon CS, Cumming, GA, 82-02; prin Cherokee CS, 03-15; astp Christ Cov, Woodstock, GA, 16-

313 Devon Court, Woodstock, GA 30188 Northwest Georgia
E-mail: Robert.lester1@gmail.com
Christ Covenant – 770-337-1591

Letizia, Phil – O Jan 27, 17, Glfstrm Pby; astp Boynton Beach Comm Ch, Boynton Beach, FL, 17-

E-mail: jphil.letizia@gmail.com Gulfstream
Boynton Beach Community Church – 561-733-9400

Leung, Stephen K. – b St. Louis, MO, Mar 12, 64; f Samuel S.; m Esther K. Wong; w Vicki H. Woo; chdn Benjamin, Matthias, Isaiah, Timothy; MIT 86, BS; GMU 96, MBA; CTS 08, MDiv; O Nov 08, MO Pby; astp Gr & Peace Flwsp, St. Louis, MO, 08-10; astp Ascension Ch, Forest Hills, NY, 10-

6944 Nansen Street, Forest Hills, NY 11375 – 718-350-6125 Metropolitan New York
E-mail: stephen@ascensionforesthills.org
Ascension Church – 718-575-0024

Leverett, Robert Glen Jr. – b Macon, GA, Oct 23, 60; f Robert Glen Sr.; m Margaret Francis Shirah; w Sheetal Rajah, New Delhi, INDIA, Dec 19, 03; chdn Ronia Rajah, Riana Rajah; MerU 86, BA; WTS; O Mar 24, 96, Cal Pby; ydir Dayspring P Ch, Forsyth, GA, 84-85; int Clemson P Ch, Clemson, SC, 94; mis, chp WHM, London, 97-05; t Desire St Acad, 06-08; ip Grace P Ch, Baton Rouge, LA, 06-07; t Riverdale C Acad, Baton Rouge, LA, 08; chap Hospice, Baton Rouge, LA, 08-; wc

2080 Lobdell Boulevard #3603, Baton Rouge, LA 70806 – 225-614-8405 Southern Louisiana
E-mail: leverettrob@yahoo.com

Levi, Daniel – w Carolyn; chdn Bennett, Owen; O Mar 8, 15, SFL Pby; astp Old Cutler P Ch, Palmetto Bay, FL, 15-16; astp Christ Comm Ch, Titusville, FL, 16-

E-mail: pastordaniellevi@gmail.com Central Florida
Christ Community Church – 321-269-2478

Levi, Danny Clarence – b Hendersonville, NC, Sept 17, 48; f Clarence Burgeon (d); m Lillian Justus (d); w Martha Suzanne Fain, Hendersonville, NC, May 31, 69; chdn Amanda Joy, Janna Suzanne (Mawhinney), Daniel Joseph, Micah David, Samuel Fain; ASU 70, BA; CBC; TEDS 74, MDiv; WTS 92, DMin; O Jan 78, SFL Pby; ap Granada P Ch, Coral Gables, FL, 78-87; p First P Ch, Gulfport, MS, 87-91; NANC, 88; astp Old Cutler P Ch, Miami, FL, 91-92, ascp 93-98; ss Granada P Ch, Coral Gables, FL, 97-99, ascp 98-00, wc 00; ob Latin American Msn, Miami, FL, 01-; ss Redlands Comm Ch, Homestead, FL, 08-09

14200 SW 78th Avenue, Miami, FL 33158 – 305-254-8679   South Florida
Latin American Mission – 305-884-8400
PO Box 52-7900, Miami, FL 33152-7900

Levine, Mark R. – b Chicago, IL, Jul 7, 61; f Marvin S.; m Marlene Lesnick; w Cameron Carey, Syracuse, NY, Mar 7, 87; chdn David W., Lucinda J.; SyU 84, BA, 87, MA; RTS 95-98, MDiv; GCTS 08, ThM; L Jan 14, 97, Gr Pby; O Jan 24, 99, GrLks Pby; p Michiana Cov Ch, South Bend, IN, 98-01; Chap USArmy, 01-

141 Bloxome Drive, Hopkins, SC 29061-8225   Missouri
E-mail: marklevine28@gmail.com
United States Army

Lewis, Andre – b Spokane, WA; UW 92, BA; CTS 04, MDiv; astp CrossPoint Green Lake, Seattle, WA; op Redeemer Redmond Ch, Redmond, WA, 04-10, srp 10-15; ob YFC Spokane, 15-

421 West Riverside Avenue, Suite 335, Spokane, WA 99201 – 509-327-7721   Pacific Northwest
E-mail: info@spokaneyfc.org
YFC Spokane

Lewis, Andy – w Elizabeth; chdn Kate, Maggie, Daniel; ErskC, BA; ErskTS, MDiv; O 02, Cal Pby; yp Mitchell Road P Ch, Greenville, SC, 00-02, astp 02-07; srp 07-

111 Middle Brook Road, Greer, SC 29650-3406 – 864-322-8529   Calvary
E-mail: alewis@mrpca.org
Mitchell Road Presbyterian Church – 864-268-2218

Lewis, Chad – b Scranton, PA, Mar 17, 75; f Jerry; m Quenlin Young; w Jodee Collins, St.Louis, MO, Jun 5, 99; chdn Grace Olivia, Lila Merle, Owen Douglas, WashU 97, BA; TEDS 01, MDiv; O Feb 24, 02, NoIL Pby; astp Covenant P Ch, Chicago, IL, 01-06; ascp 06-09; op Lincoln Square P Ch, Chicago, IL, 09-

4957 North Claremont, Chicago, IL 60625 – 773-425-1574   Chicago Metro
E-mail: clewis@lincolnsquarepres.org
Lincoln Square Presbyterian Church – 773-677-7782

Lewis, Dane Edward – b Concord, MA, Jun 14, 56; f Edward; m Nancy E. Ohs; w Jo E. May, W. Palm Bch, FL, Nov 23, 78; chdn Daniel Edward; Matthew Keil; MCC 78, BS; TEDS 86, MDiv, 90, MA; L Feb 13, 93; O Feb 13, 93, Pot Pby; astp Chapelgate P Ch, Marriottsville, MD, 91-96; chp Ecan Pby, 96-99; op Thames Valley P Msn, London, ON, 99-02; op Rivers Edge Comm Ch, Oella, MD, 03-07, p 07-

500 Durango Road, Catonsville, MD 21228 – 410-747-0399   Chesapeake
E-mail: daneandjo@verizon.net
River's Edge Community Church – 410-747-0399

Lewis, Lance E. – w Sharon; chdn Sarah, Charles; TempU, BA; ChTS, MA; L Jan 97, JR Pby; O Feb 02, Phil Pby; int New City Flwsp, Fredericksburg, VA, 95-99; int Redemption Flwsp P Ch,

Lewis, Lance E., continued
Fayetteville, GA, 99-00; int Tenth P Ch, Philadelphia, PA; op Christ Liberation Flwsp, Philadelphia, PA, 02-09, p 09-12; op Christ Redemption Flwsp, Inc., Havertown, PA, 12-13; p Soaring Oaks Ch, Elk Grove, CA, 14-

10270 East Taron Drive, Apt 363, Elk Grove, CA 95757 – 916-509-1592   Northern California
E-mail: lance.lewis818@gmail.com
Soaring Oaks Church – 916-714-4111

Lewis, Nathan Edward – b Oregon, Dec 9, 61; f Philip E.; m Lloyd; w Glenda Joy Portukalian, California, Aug 19, 89; chdn Hannah Serene, Everett James, Benjamin Philip, Sophia Joy, Jackson Edward; BIOLA 84, BA; WTS 91, MDiv; L Apr 27, 91; O Oct 13, 91, SoCst Pby; astp New Life P Ch, Escondido, CA, 89, ascp 91-92; chp MNA, Portland, OR, 92-97; ev, op Evergreen P Ch, Beaverton, OR, 92-97, p 97-

1765 NW 138th Avenue, Portland, OR 97229 – 503-502-3026   Pacific Northwest
E-mail: rev.nathan.lewis@gmail.com
Evergreen Presbyterian Church – 503-626-1520

Lewis, Stephen Philip – b Fullerton, CA, Nov 18, 67; f Philip E.; w Amanda, Ukiah, CA, Dec 18, 93; chdn Nadine, Ariadne, Kyrie, Peter, Calvin, Zachary, Xavier; BIOLA 85-89, BA; WSCAL 95-98, MDiv; WTS 18, PhD; L Jan 24, 98, SoCst Pby; O Jun 18, 00, PacNW Pby; int New Life P Ch, Escondido, CA, 95-98; chp, int Evergreen P Ch, Beaverton, OR, 98-00, ascp 00-02; op Evergreen P Ch, Salem, OR, 00-06; p 06-11; srp Knowlton P Ch, Columbia, NJ, 15-; diss *Narrative Analogy and the Theological Message of Esther: Israel's Conflicted Relationship with an Angry Sovereign*

205 Hardwick Street, Belvidere, NJ 07823 – 908-750-3107   Metropolitan New York
E-mail: revsplewis@gmail.com
Knowlton Presbyterian Church – 908-459-5170

Li, Mingming – O Sept 24, 17, SoCst Pby; p Chinese Ref Ch of San Diego, Poway, CA, 17-

Chinese Reformed Church of San Diego – 760-213-9978   South Coast

Libby, Nate – astp Providence P Ch, Dallas, TX, 17-

E-mail: nate.libby@providencedallas.com   North Texas
Providence Presbyterian Church – 214-270-1220

Lien, Timothy John – w Melissa; chdn Laurian, Anderson, Lainey, Jameson; BryC, BA; CTS, MDiv; O Jun 04, War Pby; astp Riverwood P Ch, Tuscaloosa, AL, 04-06; srp 06 14; astp Pacific Crossroads Ch, Los Angeles, CA, 14-18; op The Way, San Marino, CA, 17-18, p 18-; *This Is For You: Forty Reflections on the Sacrament of Communion*

1120 Meridian Avenue, South Pasadena, CA 91030   Pacific
E-mail: tim.lien@gmail.com
The Way

Light, John Steven – b State College, PA, May 25, 53; f John Henry; m Mary; w Patricia Louise Maloney, Carlisle, PA, Jun 21, 75; chdn Jennifer Anne, John Steven Jr., Mariwyn Grace; DicC 71-75, BS; TEDS 77-81, MDiv, MA; WTS 02, DMin; L Jun 81; O Oct 85, EFC; p Hanover EFC, Hanover, PA, 81-87; p New Life P Ch, Middletown, NJ, 87-95; ascp Westminster P Ch, Lancaster, PA, 95-

2882 Weaver Road, Lancaster, PA 17601 – 717-569-0929   Susquehanna Valley
E-mail: light@westpca.com
Westminster Presbyterian Church – 717-569-2151

Light, John Steven, Jr. – b Hanover, PA, Mar 24, 82; f John S.; m Patricia Louise; w Loren Blair; GroCC, BS; WTS 09, MDiv; L Feb 21, 09, SusqV Pby; O Jun 26, 11, SWFL Pby; astp Holy Trin P Ch, Tampa, FL, 11-13; ascp 13-; op Sojourner P Msn, Tampa, FL, 14-

9901 North Olawaha Avenue, Tampa, FL 33617 – 813-362-3573　　　　　　　　Southwest Florida
E-mail: steven.light@gmail.com
Holy Trinity Presbyterian Church – 813-259-3500
Sojourner Presbyterian Mission – 813-362-3573

Light, Joshua – GBibC 09, BBE; BhamTS 16, MDiv, DMin cand; O Aug 14, 16, Westm Pby; PEF, COO, 04-; astp Westminster P Ch, Johnson City, TN, 16-, adj prof Graham Bible College, 17-

100 5th Street, Suite 330, Bristol, TN 37420　　　　　　　　　　　　　　　　Westminster
E-mail: btsmdiv2015@outlook.com
Presbyterian Evangelistic Fellowship – 423-573-5308
Westminster Presbyterian Church – 423-283-4643
Graham Bible College

Light, Rick Jay – b Kingsport, TN, Oct 13, 58; f Junior E.; m Ona V. Medlin; w Evangeline Patricia Wilkinson, Stone Mountain, GA, Oct 17, 81; chdn Joshua Loyd, Victoria Renee, Nathan Andrew; GBibC 77-80, BCE; AUBS 81-85, MA; L Oct 82, NGA Pby; O Feb 86, Westm Pby; ev PEF, 85-99; p Eastern Heights P Ch, Bristol, TN, 86-; ob exec dir PEF, 99-

29 Kingsbridge, Bristol, TN 37620 – 423-538-5774　　　　　　　　　　　　　Westminster
E-mail: ehpc@chartertn.net
Eastern Heights Presbyterian Church – 423-968-7134
Presbyterian Evangelistic Fellowship – 276-591-5335
100 5th Street, Suite 330, Bristol, VA 37620

Lightner, Andrew – astp Harvest Comm Ch, Omaha, NE, 18-

2614 Dow Drive, Bellevue, NE 68123 – 717-683-6089　　　　　　　　　　　　Platte Valley
E-mail: andrew@harvestpca.org
Harvest Community Church – 402-558-4119

Lillback, Peter Alan – b Painesville, OH, Jun 9, 52; f Eugene R; m Elaine C. Tikka; w Debra Kay Harris, Painesville, OH, Jun 16, 73; chdn Cara-Beth, Priscilla Anne; CedC 71-74, BA; DTS 74-78, ThM; WTS 78-85, PhD; L May 81; O Feb 12, 82, OPC; p Bethany OPC, Oxford, PA, 83-88; ap Evangelical P Ch, Newark, DE, 88-91; srp Proclamation P Ch, Bryn Mawr, PA, 91-10; pres WTS, 05-

328 Sentry Lane, Wayne, PA 19087 – 610-975-9586　　　　　　　　　　Philadelphia Metro West
E-mail: plillback@wts.edu
Westminster Theological Seminary – 215-887-5511
PO Box 27009, Philadelphia, PA 19118

Lim, Abraham Moogwang – b Korea, Oct 2, 42; f Jong You; m Oak Jin Lee; w Sara E. Park, Korea, Dec 16, 80; chdn Isaac, Lois; PiersC 76-78, DMiss; PGATCS 78-81, DMiss; RiC 83-86, DMiss; L Apr 81; O Jun 83, PCKor; p Korean P Ch of Denton, Denton, TX, 83-86; p Korean Dallas P Ch, Carrollton, TX, 86-90; p Ft. Worth First Korean P Ch, Richardson, TX, 92-17; hr 17

2107 Mistletoe Drive, Richardson, TX 75081-3940 – 972-235-8356　　　　　　Korean Southern
HR

Lim, Bok Jae – p New Orleans Onnuri P Ch, Metairie, LA, 09-

1505 North Atlanta Street, Metairie, LA 70003 – 504-472-0117　　　　　　　Korean Southern
New Orleans Onnuri Presbyterian Church – 504-300-3400

Lim, Chae Young – p Korean Gr P Ch of Corpus Christi, Corpus Christi, TX, 13-18; wc

5929 Woodbridge Road #1905, Corpus Christi, TX 78414 – 361-425-9384 Korean Southern

Lim, Charles –

420 South Hanley Road #1W, Clayton, MO 63105 Korean Central
E-mail: charlesjsg@gmail.com

Lim, Dong Ha – b Korea, Jul 7, 38; f Young Woo Lim; m So Hae Kown; w Kyong Ae Yi, Korea, Sept 16, 69; chdn Timothy, Luke, Bo Hyon; KBNU; O Apr 9, 76, KAPC; astp Ark Msn Ch, Carmichael, CA, 98-02; op Hamonah P Ch, Concord, CA, 02-09

E-mail: donghalim@hotmail.com Korean Northwest

Lim, Edward – astp Grace Comm P Ch, Suwanee, GA, 13-

142 Avonlea Park Place, Suwanee, GA 30024 – 770-344-7996 Korean Southeastern
E-mail: edlim315@gmail.com
Grace Community Presbyterian Church – 678-622-9856

Lim, Hyong Kon – op Korean P Ch of Salinas Msn, Salinas, CA, 91-92; hr 92

Address Unavailable Korean Northwest
HR

Lim, Joseph Hong Il – p Madison Sah-lang Ch, Madison, WI, 08-15; ob p Vision Mission, College Station, TX

4107 Halifax Drive, College Station, TX 77845 – 979-690-9944 Korean Central
E-mail: pastor.hong.lim@gmail.com
Vision Mission, College Station, TX

Lim, Kil Soo – w Sook Young Park, Apr 20, 62; chdn Sun Min; ChShC, BMus; GATS, MDiv; O Oct 12, 98, KorS Pby; astp Bright Castle P Ch, Killeen, TX, 98-00; ob mmus Saemoon Dongsan Ch, 00-02; p Bright Castle P Ch, Killeen, TX, 02-10

E-mail: cymaker@hanmail.com Korean Southern

Lim, Paul C. – O Oct 5, 92, KorCent Pby; astp Korean P Ch of Wash, Fairfax, VA, 92-95; ascp Korean P Ch of St. Louis, St. Louis, MO, 95-

c/o 11032 Manchester Road, St. Louis, MO 63122 Korean Central
Korean Presbyterian Church of St. Louis – 314-984-9466

Lim, Sanghoon – p First Korean Ch, Dillsburg, PA, 13-

81 North US Highway 15, Dillsburg, PA 17019 – 213-290-8129 Korean Eastern
E-mail: hish2004@naver.com
First Korean Church – 717-432-8637

Lim, Seung Jae (SJ) – w Susie; chdn Devin, Justin; campm RUF, WashU, St.Louis, 14-

32 Pricewoods Lane, Olivette, MO 63132 Missouri
E-mail: sjlim723@yahoo.com
PCA Reformed University Fellowship

Lim, Sung Chol – p Hamonah P Ch, Pleasant Hill, CA, 14-

53 Camelback Court, Pleasant Hill, CA 94523 – 925-222-9938 Korean Northwest
E-mail: limsc113@gmail.com
Hamonah Presbyterian Church

Lim, Taek Kwon – b Eun-Yul, KOR, Aug 11, 34; f Jong Bock; m Chong Shin; w Hyun Sook Cho, Seoul, Oct 26, 63; chdn Elizabeth Meehyun, Christina Meesun; DKU 60, BA; KorPTS 62, BD, 64, ThM; CTS 68; ChJC 75, DMin; L Mar 64, Seoul Pby; O Nov 65, Seoul Pby; p Kor Ch, Chicago, IL, 69-73; p Korean Bethel P Ch, Chicago, IL, 73-80; p Kor Emmanuel Ch, San Jose, CA, 80-82; srp Korean United Ch of Phil, Philadelphia, PA, 82-98; lect WTS, 84-98; hr 98; pres Ashin U (ACTS), Seoul, 98-; *Critics on 1967 Confession*, 67; *A Second Chance*, 93

E-mail: tedlim@chol.com Philadelphia
HR

Lim, Timothy – mis

E-mail: timshlim@yahoo.com Korean Northwest

Lim, Yaung Hwan – srp El Centro Korean P Ch, El Centro, CA, 10-14

E-mail: suplim@gmail.com Korean Southwest

Lima, Renan Rodrigues – b Sao Paulo, Brazil, Jun 11, 48; f Ismar; m Orlanda Costa; w Elizabeth Amaral, Sao Paulo, Dec 10, 80; chdn Raquel, Rodolfo; McKenzie, Brazil 72, BCEng; IndPSem 78; BibSem of SPaulo 80; L Jan 9, 82, SaoPaulo; O Jun 13, 82, SaoPaulo; Recd PCA 02, MNY Pby; Igreja Pres de Perus e Franco da Rocha, S. Paulo, 80-83; Igreja Pres de Francisco Morato, S. Paulo , 84; Igreja Pres Vila Pompeia, S. Paulo, 85-86; Igreja Presb Jardim Regina, S. Paulo, 87-88; Igreja Presb Parque Esplanada, S. Paulo, 89-97; Igreja Pres Emaus, S. Paulo, 98-00; Igreja Pres Betania, S. Paulo, 01-02; p Comunidade Crista Presbiteriana, Mineola, NY, 02-; *Kingdom of God - Present Reality*

315 Pennsylvania Avenue, Mineola, NY 11501 – 516-640-4212 Metropolitan New York
E-mail: presbychristian@aol.com
Comunidade Crista Presbiteriana – 516-877-8090

Lin, John – b Boston, MA, Oct 16, 71; f Chan Kie Lin; m Sandra; w Kyoko; BrU 93, BS; GCTS 98, MDiv, 05, ThM; O Mar 22, 99, KAPC; Recd PCA 01, MNYPby; ascp First Kor P Ch, Hartford, CT, 98-01; astp Redeemer P Ch of New York, New York, NY, 02-11; ascp 11- 17; srp Redeemer P Ch Downtown, New York, NY, 17-

146 West 57th Street #48E, New York, NY 10019 Metropolitan New York
E-mail: johnlin@redeemer.com
Redeemer Presbyterian Church Downtown

Lindberg, David – w Julie; chdn Hadden, Tennyson, Roan, Graham, Naomi; O Feb 17, 13, MetAtl Pby; astp ChristChurch P, Atlanta, GA, 13-

257 Rope Mill Road, Woodstock, GA 30188 – 404-790-2781 Metro Atlanta
E-mail: davidl@christchurchatlanta.org
ChristChurch Presbyterian – 404-605-0505

Lindell, Jerald Carl – b Chicago, IL, Dec 16, 43; f Arthur W.; m Gladys E. Gray; w Janet Louise Aichele, Chatham, NJ, Jun 22, 68; chdn Amy Joy, Steffany Anne; TayU 67, BS; DenvU 72-73; DenTS 76, MDiv; CTS 96, DMin; O Jun 14, 68, Faith Bap Ch, Littleton, CO; First Bap Ch of West LA, CA, 76-80; p First Bap Ch of Ashland, OR, 80-89; p Davenport Rd. P Ch, Simpsonville, SC, 90-99; p Christ Comm Ch, Simpsonville, SC, 99-11; hr 11

247 Reddington Drive, Greer, SC 29650 – 864-238-8624 Calvary
HR

Linden, David Hiram – b Moncton, NB, Aug 41; w Shirley Ann Baker (d), (2) Jenette Chavez Camporedondo, Las Cruces, NM, Nov 17, 17; chdn Joseph Paul (d), Julie Ann, John Edwin; astp University P Ch, Las Cruces, NM, 10-17; hr 17

905 Conway, Unit 43, Las Cruces, NM 88005 – 575-523-0815   Southwest
E-mail: imputed@gmail.com
HR

Lindley, Lanty Ross – b Maryville, TN, Sept 20, 49; f James Marvin; m Margaret Vestine; w Lillie Roe, Abingdon, VA, Jun 5, 71; chdn Laura Joan, Benjamin Ross, Jacob Seth; BJU 71, BA, 73, MA; WTS 76, MDiv; L May 73; O Apr 13, 77, SE Pby (RPCES); mis Barcelona, Spain, 76-79; p Dickenson First P Ch, Haysi, VA, 81-88; p Midway P Ch, Jonesborough, TN, 88-

111 Woodland Drive, Jonesborough, TN 37659-5723 – 423-753-5295   Westminster
E-mail: midwaypca@earthlink.net
Midway Presbyterian Church – 423-753-6941

Lindsay, John Preston – b Fayetteville, NC, Dec 19, 70; f William Marvin Jr.; m Patricia Jane Batten; w Amy Beth Whittington, Winston-Salem, NC, Jan 2, 93; chdn John Preston Jr., Sarah Elizabeth, Caleb William, Nathan Wesley; UNC 88-92, BA; GCTS 95-99, MDiv; L Nov 13, 99, JR Pby; O Sept 10, 00, JR Pby; int, ss West Hopewell P Ch, Hopewell, VA, 99-00, p 00-08; p New Hope P Ch, Clemmons, NC, 08-

3722 Tanglebrook Trail, Clemmons, NC 27012 – 336-283-1121   Piedmont Triad
E-mail: john@newhopepca.org
New Hope Presbyterian Church – 336-778-1556

Ling, Samuel Dz-Sing – b Hong Kong, May 29, 51; f John C.; m Mary Shen; w Mildred Yick-ka Chen, Philadelphia, PA, Dec 23, 72; chdn Philip Calvin Ch'eng-tao, Ingrid Marie Tao-chen; UPA 68-71, BA; WTS 75, MDiv, 78, ThM; TempU 81, PhD; L Feb 80; O Oct 11, 80, MidAtl Pby; op, p Covenant Ch, Whitestone, NY, 80-85; adj prof FTSSWM, 84-00; coord Chinese Min MNA, Flushing, NY, 86-89; adj prof ATS, 89-95; astp Covenant Ch, Whitestone, NY, 91; ob srp Chinese Christian Union Ch of Chicago, 92-95; adj prof WheatGrS, 92-97; ob Dir Inst for Chinese Stu, Billy Graham Ctr, 93-97; ob adj prof RTS, 93-97; Chinese Bible Ch, Los Angeles, CA (consultant), 97-; adj prof CTS, 97-; chmn China Service Coordinating Office, 95-97; lect Yanjing Theo Seminary, Beijing, 95; vis lect/prof WSCAL, 97-; scholar in res, Logos Evan Sem, CA, 98-; ob pres China Horizon, Redondo Beach, CA, 89-; lect Singapore Bible College, 99-; lect Ontario Theo Sem, 86, 88; coord Christian Ref Chinese Lit Comm, 85-88; adv China Outreach Min, 97-; adv The MacLaurin Institute, 97-; prof Hist & System Theo, International Sem, El Monte, CA, 01-09; pres 10-; internet/TV theology lect, Chinese Christianity Network Television, 08-; auth *The Other May Fourth Movement: The Chinese "Christian Renaissance," 1919-1937*, 81; contr *Chinese Around the World*, 82-; *China Graduate School of Theology Journal*, 86, 94, 95; *Evangelical Review of Theology*, 86; *Crux*; contr *A Winning Combination: ABC/OBC; Faith & Freedom*, 91; *Chinese Theological Journal*; contr *Mainland Chinese in North America: An Emerging Kinship*, 91; ed *China Horizon*, 89-93; ed *Horizon Letter*, 95-97; *Great Commission Quarterly*, 94; contr *Twentieth-Century Dictionary of Christian Biography*, Baker, 95; auth *The Holy Spirit and Salvation*, 96; ed *Together for China*, 96; ed *Soul Searching: Chinese Intellectuals on Faith and Society*, 97; auth *Xian Qu Yu Guo Ke*, 96; contr *World Evangelization*, 90, 97; adv *Ambassadors* mag, 97-; auth *The Chinese Way of Doing Things*, 00; co-ed *Chinese Intellectuals and the Gospel*, 00; trans *What is Apologetics?*; contr *The Evangelical Dictionary of World Missions*, 00; auth *An Evening Conversation Concerning Christianity*, 99; auth *Assurance of Salvation*, 00; ed *The Christian Life: A Doctrinal Introduction*; trans *Introduction to Biblical Counseling: Course Syllabus*; auth *Christianity and Western Culture: A Piano Lecture*, 00; ed *Competent to Counsel*, 01

2214 Nelson Avenue #A, Redondo Beach, CA 90278 – 310-793-1275   Pacific
E-mail: laoshi1031@gmail.com
China Horizon

Lino, Pedro – Recd PCA Jan 16, SNE Pby; astp Christ The King P Ch, Cambridge, MA, 16-

26 Westwood Road, Medford, MA 02155   Southern New England
Christ The King Presbyterian Church – 617-354-8341

Linton, Joel Hugh – b Kwangju, Korea, Oct 24, 73; f David; m Phyllis; w Judy Huan-Chun Lin; chdn Faith, Charis, Ashlyn, Saorsa, Seren; ColU 95, BA, 96, BS; NYU 99, MS; BhamTS 16, DMin; O Nov 19, 04, NoCA Pby; ob chp ChMI, 02-04; chp, mis MTW, Taiwan, 06-10; ob chp, mis, VP MSS Taiwan, 10-; BdDir TCEF, 07- VP MSS, 10-;

610 County Road 33, Killen, AL 35645   Providence
E-mail: taiwanlintons@gmail.com
Mission Sending Service

Linton, Kenneth Dale – b Brookhaven, MS, Nov 27, 30; f Ernest; m Hazel Tillotson; w Ann Cameron, Brookhaven, MS, Oct 15, 66; chdn Angela (Lutz), Julie Anna (Smith), Karen (Strowd), Laura (Johnson), Julie (Wilcox), Janie (Clarke); UTamp 61, BS; CBC 73-74; RTS 82, MDiv; L Oct 9, 81, Gr Pby; O Jun 6, 82, Cov Pby; Bolivia, SA, 75-79; p Sardis P Ch, Sardis, MS, 82-86; ap Coral Ridge P Ch, Ft. Lauderdale, FL, 86-88; ap Immanuel P Ch, Miami, FL, 88-92; p Sharon P Ch, Magee, MS, 92-97; hr 97-00; p Magee P Ch, Magee, MS, 00-06; p Meadville P Ch, Meadville, MS, 06- 12; astp Faith P Ch, Brookhaven, MS, 12-

154 Jaci Drive, Brookhaven, MS 39601   Grace
E-mail: dalelinton@bellsouth.net
Faith Presbyterian Church

Lints, Drew T. – PASU 02, BA; CTS 04, MDiv; O Jan 18, 05, SFL Pby; astp Old Cutler P Ch, Miami, FL, 05-10; astp Village Seven P Ch, Colorado Springs, CO, 10-

3635 Saddle Rock Road, Colorado Springs, CO 80918 – 719-646-9931   Rocky Mountain
Village Seven Presbyterian Church – 719-574-6700

Lints, Richard – b Pittsburgh, PA, Feb 5, 56; f Douglas; m Helene Jahnke; w Ann Elizabeth Quinn, Miami, FL, Mar 26, 83; chdn Catherine Helene, Sarah Elizabeth, Richard Lucas; WCPA 74-78, BA; UNotD 78-83, MA, PhD; UCDS, MA; L Sept 86, NoIL Pby; O May 88, NoE Pby; assoc prof GCTS, 86-95; op Redeemer P Ch, Concord, MA, 95-96, p 96-01; ob prof GCTS, 01-; *The Fabric of Theology*, Erdmans, 93

34 Old Planters Road, Beverly, MA 01915   Southern New England
E-mail: rlints@gcts.edu
Gordon Conwell Theological Seminary – 704-527-9909

Lipe, Jesse Paul – b China Grove, NC, Dec 31, 35; f A P L; m Julie Hobbs; w Linda Hastings, Davidson, NC, Aug 4, 62; chdn Mary Linda, Jonathan Paul; DavC 58, BA; ColTS 61, MDiv; O Jul 11, 61, Red Riv Pby; p Delhi P Ch, Delhi, LA, 61-68; p Chestnut Mountain P Ch, Chestnut Mountain, GA, 68-69; p Delhi P Ch, Delhi, LA, 69-15; hr 15

133 Comanche Trail, Delhi, LA 71232 – 318-878-5276   Mississippi Valley
HR

Lipford, William Daniel – b Cheylan, WV, Mar 9, 50; f William Richard; m Anna Jean Filbin; w Glendine Elizabeth DeJarnatt, Ft Worth, TX, Dec 5, 81; chdn Liesl Anne, Ian David; SWBTS 79, 88, MDiv; chp Redeemer P Msn, Denton, TX, 93-95, srp 95-03; p Centralia P Ch, Chester, VA, 05-

126 South Adams Street, Petersburg, VA 23803 – 804-768-4385   James River
E-mail: dan.l@verizon.net
Centralia Presbyterian Church – 804-706-9200

Lipscomb, Eric – b Richmond, VA, Jan 11, 87; w Brittany Noel Newell, Richmond, VA, Jul 25, 09; UVA 09, BA; CTS 14, MDiv; O Feb 8, 15, MNY Pby; campm RUF, ColumbiaU, 14-

255 West 108th Street, Apt. 2A, New York, NY 10025 – 804-363-4333   Metropolitan New York
E-mail: eric.lipscomb@ruf.org
PCA Reformed University Fellowship

Litchfield, Gary Allen – b Baltimore, MD, Aug 30, 53; f Harry Sr; m Madeline Geiger; w Patricia Beard, Jonesville, NC, Jun 4, 77; chdn Paul Timothy, Joshua Samuel, Stephen James; GBibC 79, BCE; RTS 88, MDiv, MCE; L Oct 21, 86, MSVal Pby; O Feb 19, 89, SEAL Pby; ydir Westminster P Ch, Roanoke, VA, 80-82; moy, mout/evan New Cov P Ch, Virginia Beach, VA, 82-84; ydir Edwards P Ch, Edwards, MS, 88; stus Utica P Ch, Utica, MS, 86-88; ap First P Ch, Dothan, AL, 88-92, wc 92; ss Covenant P Ch, Eufaula, AL, 93-96, wc 97; p Andrews P Ch, Andrews, NC, 97-10; wc 10-14; hr 14

2049 Highway 67, Jonesville, NC 28642 – 336-835-1025   Western Carolina
E-mail: chappy710@gmail.com
HR

Littell, Michael – O Nov 16, 14, OHVal Pby; astp South Dayton P Ch, Centerville, OH, 14-17, ascp 17-18, srp 18-

455 Clareridge Lane, Centerville, OH 45458   Ohio Valley
E-mail: mikelittell@southdaytonpca.com
South Dayton Presbyterian Church – 937-433-1022

Little, Jason Christopher – b Manhattan, KS, Nov 11, 71; f Terry J.; m Cathy L. Howell; w Caroline Stohl Bicksler, Tabernash, CO, Oct 14, 00; chdn Cathryn Louise, Eleanor Thompson; SMU 94, BFA; WTS 00, MDiv; L Jul 00, SoTX Pby; O Nov 00, SoTX Pby; ascp Southwest P Ch, Bellaire, TX, 00-02; campm RUF, UTChatt, 02-07; chp, op Hope P Ch, Portland, OR, 07-10; ascp Grace P Ch of the North Shore, Winnetka, IL, 10-

445 Cove Lane, Wilmette, IL 60091 – 847-784-4021   Chicago Metro
E-mail: jason@gracenorthshore.org
Grace Presbyterian Church of the North Shore – 847-920-9517

Little, Joseph Jarrell Jr. – b Philadelphia, PA, Jul 18, 41; f Joseph J.; m Gladys Estella Ditzler; w Margaret Ann MacKenzie, Levittown, PA, Jun 30, 62; chdn Scott, Lauri, Joseph III, Rebecca; REpS 67, MDiv; StJosC 70, BS; L Dec 70; O Dec 71, Phil Pby (RPCES); mis WPM, Peru, SA, 72-76; fndr, Dir, ev Phila Spanish Outreach (BHM), 77-81, wc 81-85; mis HCJB, Quito, Ecuador, 85-86, wc; hr 07

11 Alexander Way, Newtown, PA 18940 – 215-860-1626   Eastern Pennsylvania
E-mail: jjlittlejr@verizon.net
HR

Littlepage, Joel – b Montgomery, AL, Feb 17, 89; f Thomas McGuire, Jr.; m Barbara Williams; w Melissa Ann Hill, Nashville, TN, May 21, 11; chdn Oscar Ambrose, Thelonius Walter, Wynton King; BelmC 11, BMus; CTS, MDiv; O Aug 14, 16, PTri Pby; astp Redeemer P Ch, Winston-Salem, NC, 16-18; astp Grace P Ch of Washington, DC, Washington, DC, 18-

3008 20th Street NE, Washington, DC 20018   Potomac
E-mail: joel@gracemosaic.org
Grace Presbyterian Church of Washington, DC – 202-386-7637

Liu, Daniel – b Staten Island, NY, Sept 16, 85; f Siu Yau; m Kwan Ying Lam; w Jennifer Jen, Princeton, NJ, May 26, 13; chdn Evangeline; RutgU 07, BS; WTS 15, MDiv; O May 17, 16, MNY Pby; astp Crossroads Comm Ch, Hillsborough, NJ, 16-

11 Stevens Road, Kendall Park, NJ 08824   Metropolitan New York
E-mail: danielhliu@gmail.com
Crossroads Community Church – 908-431-4373

Liu, Leonard – b Sao Paulo, Brazil, Feb 7, 58; f Luke; m Julie; w Anne Macowski (Nancy), Jun 13, 92; chdn Gabriel, Taylor, Alexandra; PepU 79, BS; USCA 84, MS; BibTS 95, MA, 95, MDiv; O Oct 10,

Liu, Leonard, continued
04, JR Pby; ascp Sycamore P Ch, Midlothian, VA, 04-11; op Evergreen Comm Ch, Powhatan, VA, 09-11, p 11-18; wc

3519 Fairfield Road, Powhatan, VA 23139 – 804-543-3852   James River
E-mail: deo.volente@gmail.com

Lloyd, Thomas P. – b Pueblo, CO, Jul 20, 53; f William; m Anne Morrison Young; w Sally; chdn Jessica (Blanner), Patrick, Andrew; CTS 04, MDiv; O Jul 25, 04, MO Pby; ascp Heritage Ref P Ch, Eureka, MO, 04-06; p Comm P Ch, McIntosh, FL, 06-08; p St. James Evan Ref Ch, New Haven, MO, 08-

4310 Highway East, New Haven, MO 63068-2319 – 573-237-5837   Missouri
E-mail: tplloyd53@yahoo.com
St. James Evangelical Reformed Church (non PCA)

Loaney, Jeff – astp Chesterfield P Ch, Chesterfield, MO, 09-

15037 Clayton Road, Chesterfield, MO 63017   Missouri
E-mail: JeffL@chespres.org
Chesterfield Presbyterian Church – 636-394-3337

Locke, Donald Wiggins – b Memphis, TN, May 7, 42; f Harold Lee; m Julia Wiggins; w Ruth Ann Gean, Oxford, MS, Dec 17, 67; chdn Joy Elaine, Bradley Harold, Rachel Lynn; UMS 64, BA; MSU 68, MEd; RTS 88, MDiv; L Jan 13, 87, Gr Pby; O Feb 19, 89, LA Pby; stus Geneva P Ch, Matherville, MS, 86-88; p John Knox P Ch, Ruston, LA, 88-97; sc LA Pby, 96-97; ob American Family Radio, network dev, Tupelo, MS, 97-13; p Houston P Ch, Houston, MS, 99-

11 County Road 417, Oxford, MS 38655 – 662-234-1897   Covenant
E-mail: donlocke2012@gmail.com
Houston Presbyterian Church – 662-456-6392

Locke, Jeffrey – b West Covina, CA, Jan 25, 82; f John; m Cynthia; w Katherine Cho, Ventura, CA, Jul 8, 06; chdn Jonas, Penelope, Emmanuelle, Margaret; CWM 04, BA; PaceU 06, MS; WSCAL 09, MA; Recd PCA May 16, NoCA Pby; ascp Christ Ch, San Francisco, 09-12; ob p Grace Alameda, 12-

412 Mitchell Avenue, Alameda, CA 94501   Northern California
E-mail: jeff@gracealameda.org
Grace Alameda (non PCA)

Locke, Nick – O Feb 12, 17, SoCst Pby; astp Aliso Creek P Ch, Aliso Viejo, CA, 17-

22681 Oakgrove #612, Aliso Viejo, CA 92656   South Coast
E-mail: nick@alisocreekchurch.org
Aliso Creek Presbyterian Church – 949-460-0080

Locke, Timothy R. – b Lansing, MI; w Deborah; chdn David Anthony, Rebecca Noel, Matthew Robert, Jonathan Carroll; BJU, BA, MA, MDiv; O Oct 05, GulCst Pby; Faith Bapt Ch, Taylors, SC, 94-99; Grace Bible Ch, Tecumseh, MI, 99-02; Faith Bapt Ch, Taylors, SC, 02-04; astp Pinewoods P Ch, Cantonment, FL, 04-07; p Grace Comm Ch, Bridgewater, NJ, 07-14; srp East Cobb P Ch, Marietta, GA, 14-

4616 Roswell Road NE, Marietta, GA 30062   Metro Atlanta
E-mail: tim@ecpca.org
East Cobb Presbyterian Church – 770-973-4114

Lockwood, Ross – w Anne Todd; chdn Boswell (Bo) Gaines, Ira Conner; MSU 12, BA; CTS 15, MDiv; O 16, Nash Pby; campm RUF, WKYU, 16-

525 Ashmoor Avenue, Bowling Green, KY 42101   Nashville
E-mail: ross.lockwood@ruf.org
PCA Reformed University Fellowship

Loftis, Jim – b Abbeville, SC, Oct 14, 47; f James Herman; m Mary Elizabeth Mundy; w Martha Frances Brown, Abbeville, SC, May 13, 70; chdn Tracy (Hayes), James Carl; LanderU 65-69, BA; GPTS 91-98, MDiv; L Jul 10, 93, Westm Pby; O Sept 6, 98, Wcar Pby; stus King Mem P Ch, Bristol, VA, 92-94; stus Fellowship P Ch, Newport, TN, 97-98, p 98-17; hr 17

603 Chestnut Street, Abbeville, SC 29620 – 864 366 9674   Western Carolina
E-mail: jloftis8256@charter.net
HR

Logan, Steven Edward – b Moses Lake, WA, Apr 29, 55; f William J.; m Marie Rotter; w Althea Ruth Horton, Pensacola, FL, Dec 22, 79; chdn Joshua, Jeremy, Seth, Heather; PenCC 78, BA; ErskTS 90, MDiv; L Oct 86; O Oct 25, 90, Cal Pby; int Bethel ARP Ch, 89; Chap USArmy, Redstone Arsenal, AL, 91-92; Chap USArmy, Camp Casey, Korea, 93-94; Chap USArmy, Carlisle Barracks, PA, 95-96; Chap USArmy, 96-11

101 Scenic Circle, Winchester, VA 22602 – 540-665-1898   Calvary
E-mail: stevenlogan@loudoun.gov

Lombardo, Anthony Joseph – b Ames, IA, Sept 16, 77; w Heather; IAStU 01, BA; DenTS 08, MDiv; O Aug 5, 12, Anglican Mission; Recd PCA Jun 7, 15, Chspk Pby; astp Safe Harbor P Ch, Stevensville, MD, 15-

PO Box 564, Stevensville, MD 21666   Chesapeake
E-mail: tony@safeharborpca.org
Safe Harbor Presbyterian Church – 410-604-1700

Lomenick, Matthew C. – b St. Louis, MO, Sept 20, 68; f Robert E.; m Dorothy Lee Windsor; w Delina A. Osborn, New Port Richey, FL, Apr 1, 95; chdn Delaney, Reina, Rachel; SMU, BFA; RTSFL, MDiv; L Oct 95, CentFL Pby; O Oct 98, CentFL Pby; ip, moya Highland Park PC, 90-91; astp, yp River Ridge P Ch, New Port Richey, FL, 92-99, ascp 99; ap, yp Old Cutler P Ch, Miami, FL, 99-02, wc 02-05; astp Rio Vista Comm Ch, Ft. Lauderdale, FL, 05-14; ascp 14-

3627 NE 19th Avenue, Ft. Lauderdale, FL 33308 – 954-612-9994   South Florida
Rio Vista Community Church – 954-522-2518

Loney, Bryan – O Nov 13, 11, SNE Pby; astp Christ The King P Ch, 11-; p Christ the King Roslindale, MA, 13-

98 Fletcher Street #1, Boston, MA 02131   Southern New England
Christ the King Presbyterian Church – 617-354-8341
Christ the King Roslindale – 617-942-0880

Long, Caleb – O Aug 12, 18, HlsPlns Pby; op New City Fellowship, Inc., Tulsa, OK, 18-

235 West Zion Street, Tulsa 74106 – 9125852262   Hills and Plains
E-mail: caleb@crossoverbible.org
New City Fellowship, Inc.

Long, Harry D. – b Chattanooga, TN, Jul 2, 54; f George W; m Katherine Philips; w Mary Yadon; chdn H. Davison, Margaret L. (Ward), James W.; WheatC 76, BA; GCTS 82, MDiv Summa Cum Laude; O Jun 82, TNVal Pby; op Sycamore P Ch, Midlothian, VA, 82-84, p 84-93, srp 93-; GA Intern Cert committee; GA Nom Co, 98-00, 04-06, 07-09, 10-12; JRP Chair for 2011 GA Worship, 07-08

14032 Elmstead Road, Midlothian, VA 23113 – 804-794-0337   James River
E-mail: hlong@sycamorepres.com
Sycamore Presbyterian Church – 804-794-0238

Long, John Wade Jr. – b Tampa, FL, Sept 23, 42; f Dr John W.; m Mary Elizabeth Leonard; w Rebecca Ann Morse, Brent, AL, Jun 25, 65; chdn John Wade III, Rebecca Elizabeth, Mary Elizabeth; UMS; BelC 65, BA; RTS 68, MDiv; GCTS 98, DMin; O 70, Evgld Pby; ap First Ch, Miami Spgs, FL, 70; ap First Ch, Plantation, FL, 70-71; mis WPM, Kenya, 72-77; p Tchula P Ch, Tchula, MS, 77-80; p Altadena Valley P Ch, Birmingham, AL, 81-92; mis MTW, WHM, Nairobi, Kenya, 93-04; mis Serge, London, 05–

E-mail: johnwadelong@gmail.com; www.grace4life.org   Evangel
Serge, 101 West Avenue #305, Jenkintown, PA 19046-2039

Long, Mark Edward – b Jellico, TN, May 2, 60; f Robert E; m Fonzie Marie Green; w Frances Dubose Walker, Anniston, AL, Jun 1, 85; chdn Katherine, Morgan, Walker, Hayden, Elijah; UAL 86, BS; CTS 93, MDiv; L Dec 17, 95; O Dec 17, 95, Palm Pby; ydir Riverwood P Ch, Tuscaloosa, AL, 86-89; ydir Chesterfield P Ch, Chesterfield, MO, 89-93; astp, yp Lexington P Ch, Lexington, SC, 95-00; astp Independent P Ch, Memphis, TN, 00-03; astp Oak Mountain P Ch, Birmingham, AL, 03-09; ascp 09–

3136 Woodbridge Drive, Birmingham, AL 35242 – 205-980-6408   Evangel
E-mail: mlong@ompc.org
Oak Mountain Presbyterian Church – 205-995-9265

Long, Paul Brown Jr. – b Elmhurst, IL, Mar 27, 50; f Paul; m Merry Dalton; w Mary Jo Miller, Kalona, Iowa, Apr 26, 80; chdn Aaron, Amanda, Caleb, Joanna; BelC 68-70; WheatC 70-72, BA; RTS 76, MDiv, 86, DMin, 03, PhD; L Apr 21, 76; O Jul 11, 76, Evan Pby; p Providence P Ch, 76-77; p Friendship P Ch, 76-77; mis MTW, Portugal, 78-92; mis MTW, Poland, 93-97; mis MTW, Portugal, 98-01; adjprof RTS & Belhaven, 02-17; ip First P Ch, Charleston, MS, 05-06; astp Trinity P Ch, Jackson, MS, 08-16; ss 16-17

405 Hathaway Drive, Clinton, MS 39056 – 601-924-2439   Mississippi Valley
E-mail: longbrownpaul@gmail.com

Long, Stanley J. – b Washington, DC, Jan 11, 54; f James B.; m Valeria Spencer; w Terri L. Martin, Reisterstown, MD, Jan 3, 81; chdn Joshua Stephen, Timothy Joseph, Daniel Josiah, Grace Joanna Nicole, James Michael; FrSC 76, BS; TEDS 89, MDiv; L Nov 89, DMV Pby; O Mar 3, 91, Pot Pby; campm IVCF, Baltimore, 76-87; p Forest Park Comm Ch, Baltimore, MD, 91-00; ascp Faith Christian Flwsp Ch, Baltimore, MD, 00–

505 East 42nd Street, Baltimore, MD 21218 – 410-653-3241   Chesapeake
E-mail: stanlong23@verizon.net
Faith Christian Fellowship Church – 410-323-0202

Long, V. Philips – b Atlanta, GA, Mar 15, 51; w Polly; chdn Philip, Taylor, Andrea, Duncan; CU, PhD; O Jan 11, 86, TNVal Pby; GEM, FrTA, 77-81; prof CTS, 85-00; ob prof RegC, 00-; *The Reign and Rejection of King Saul: A Case for Literary and Theological Coherence*, 89; *The Art Of Biblical History, Foundations of Contemporary Interpretation* vol. 5, 94; ed *Israel's Past in Present Research*, 99; ed *Windows Into Old Testament History*, 02; co-auth *A Biblical History of Israel*, 03; *First and Second Samuel, Zondervan Illustrated Bible Background Commentary*, 09

462 Felton Road, North Vancouver, BC V7G 127 CANADA – 604-924-4621   Tennessee Valley
Regent College – 604-221-3337

Longenecker, Byron – O Jun 2, 13, RMtn Pby; astp Rocky Mountain Comm Ch, Billings, MT, 13-17

PO Box 21585, Billings, MT 59104-1585 – 406-890-3906   Rocky Mountain
E-mail: byron.longenecker@gmail.com

Longfellow, Richard Charles – b Port Gamble, WA, Dec 12, 34; f Jacob Harris; m Mamie Marie Hoover; w Sally Jane Ross, Seattle, WA, Sept 19, 53; chdn Constance Ann (Shetler), Kenneth Alan, Diane Christine (Beard); L 75; O 82, PacNW Pby (RPCES); hm AMF, SW Washington area, 65-86; ob p Msn Ch Fell (non-PCA), 86-96; hr 96

2811 Nilan Road, Port Marion, PA 15474   Pacific Northwest
E-mail: dickandsally@verizon.net
HR

Looper, Robert B. – b Smyrna, TN, Dec 18, 63; f Marcus Pat; m Barbara L. Baumgarner; w Lisa A. Duck, Twin Oaks, MO, Jul 11, 92; chdn Hannah Michelle, Robert Bennett, Laura Elizabeth; USC 88, BA; CTS 93, MDiv; L Jan 18, 94, MO Pby; O Jun 26, 94, MO Pby; astp Twin Oaks P Ch, Ballwin, MO, 93-98; srp Trinity P Ch, Tuscaloosa, AL, 98-01, wc 01-02; srp McIlwain Mem P Ch, Pensacola, FL, 02-

4655 Avenida Marina, Pensacola, FL 32504 – 850-475-2170   Gulf Coast
E-mail: rob@mcilwain.org
McIlwain Memorial Presbyterian Church – 850-438-5449

Loos, Benjamin – astp Grace Chapel, Lincoln, NE, 10-12; ascp 12-15, p 15-

4345 Prescott Avenue, Lincoln, NE 68506 – 402-617-6147   Platte Valley
E-mail: ben@gracepca.com
Grace Chapel – 402-484-8555

Lopez, Joshua – astp Christ Cov Ch, Southwest Ranches, FL, 04-17; op Miami River Msn Ch, Miami, FL, 04-17

13261 SW 209th Street, Miami, FL 33177 – 305-541-8345   South Florida

LoPiccolo, Brian – b Brooklyn, NY, Apr 18, 76; f Joseph James; m Lynnette Marie; w Rebecca Lorraine, Hilton, NY, Aug 8, 98; chdn Sara Grace, Micah Joseph, Joshua Benjamin, Kate Elizabeth, Mia Jane, Celia Joy; SUNY 98, BMus; GCTS 02, MDiv; O Jan 8, 06, Chspk Pby; int Koinonia Church, Potsdam, NY, 98-99; The Cong Church, Wilmington, MA, 99-02; int Severna Park Evangelical P Ch, Pasadena, MD, 02-05, astp 06-07; ascp 07-14; op Deep Run Ch, Westminster, MD, 14-

223 Morning Star Way, Westminster, MD 21157 – 443-289-8044   Chesapeake
E-mail: brianlopiccolo@gmail.com, brianlopiccolo@deeprunchurch.org
Deep Run Church – 410-353-6764

Lorenz, Walter – w Mynda; chdn Rachel, David, Abigail, Jonathan, James; O 78, MO Pby; p Trinity P Ch, Union, MO, 77-89; Chap Franklin Co Detention Ctr, 85-91; Chap Friendship Village, St. Louis, MO, 90-91; p Christ Ch, Grand Rapids, MI, 91-14; ascp 14-16, mal GrLks Pby 16-

7677 West State Road, Middleville, MI 49333 – 269-795-7583   Great Lakes
E-mail: wmlorenz@gmail.com

Lorick, Carl Keith – b Columbia, SC, Jul 13, 56; f Carl Prevoste; m Sarah Jacqueline Sturkie; w Elizabeth Glenn Willson, Hughes, AR, Jun 30, 84; chdn Sarah Elizabeth, Daniel Keith, Anna Joy, John Carl; USC 78, BA; CTS 87, MDiv; L Apr 11, 87, Ill Pby; O Oct 11, 87, Evan Pby; ap Third P Ch, Birmingham, AL, 87-89; p Chattahoochee P Ch, Chattahoochee, FL, 89-92; p Comm P Ch, Madison, AL, 92-94; astp Westminster P Ch, Huntsville, AL, 94; Chap Madison PD, 93-94; mis MTW/Impact, Lima, Peru, 95-00; mis MTW, Lima, Peru, 00-05; ob

Address Unavailable   Providence

Lorish, Matt – astp Grace Comm P Ch, Mechanicsville, VA, 10-13; op Northside Ch of Richmond, Richmond, VA, 11-18, p 18-

3033 Moss Side Avenue, Richmond, VA 23222 – 804-516-3322   James River
E-mail: matt@northsidechurchrva.org
Northside Church of Richmond – 804-516-3322

Lorow, Nat – O Nov 10, 15, SFL Pby; astp Christ Cov Ch, Southwest Ranches, FL, 15-

1134 Laguna Springs Drive, Weston, FL 33326 – 954-389-1405   South Florida
Christ Covenant Church – 954-434-4500

Lort, R. David Jr. – b Salisbury, MD, Sept 18, 55; f Richard David; m Cecile Marie Bunting; w Jeanette C. Correll, Red Lion, DE, Jan 28, 78; chdn Melanie K., Johanna F., Kathryn J., Richard D. III; Maria H., Gretchen C., Gregory O., Jeffrey C., Anthony K.; UDE 76, BCEng; WTS 81, MAR, 82, MDiv; O Jun 20, 82, Red Lion Evan Ch; astp Red Lion Evan Ch, 82-86; p Trinity Bible Ch, 87-94; astp Christ P Ch, Elkton, MD, 96-05; wc 05-

38 Cole Road, Townsend, DE 19734 – 302-378-0306   Heritage
E-mail: troldr@aol.com

Louis, Dennis – O Jun 29, 14, GulCst Pby; astp McIlwain Mem P Ch, Pensacola, FL, 14-17, ascp 17-

1220 East Blount Street, Pensacola, FL   Gulf Coast
E-mail: solodeogloria10@gmail.com
McIlwain Memorial Presbyterian Church – 850-438-5449

Love, Robert Grady – b Charlotte, NC, Jun 9, 40; f Robert Price L; m Nancy Sigmon; w Virginia (Gini) Williams, Chester, CT, Aug 17, 63; chdn Lynn Elizabeth (Erickson), Robert William, Kelly Leigh (Perkins); ErskC 62, BA; ColTS 65, BD; O Jul 20, 65, EAL Pby; p First Ch, Wetumpka, AL, 65-67; ap Brainerd P Ch, Chattanooga, TN, 67-69; ap Northside P Ch, Burlington, NC, 69-71; p Midway Ch, Anderson, SC, 71-72; p Lebanon P Ch, Abbeville, SC, 72-77; op, p Providence P Ch, Spartanburg, SC, 77-87; srp Smyrna P Ch, Smyrna, GA, 87-97; p Cornerstone P Ch, Brevard, NC, 97-06; hr 06; p Story Mem P Ch, Marion, NC, 11-14

37 Brock Drive, Suite 201, Lookout Mountain, GA 30750 – 706-841-2685   Western Carolina
E-mail: lovesrus@epbfi.com
HR

Loveall, Matthew – O Sept 26, 10; chp; op Oak River P Msn, Bonita Springs, FL, 13-14; p 14-

26911 South Bay Drive, Bonita Springs, FL 34134 – 239-293-2045   Suncoast Florida
E-mail: mjloveall@gmail.com
Oak River Presbyterian Church – 239-293-2045

Lovelady, James – O Mar 25, 12, EPA Pby; astp Cornerstone P Ch, Center Valley, PA, 12-15; wc 15-

421 Manor Road, Hatboro, PA 19040 – 915-274-3545   Eastern Pennsylvania
E-mail: senorlovelady@gmail.com

Lovell, William Terry – b Tupelo, MS, Sep 26, 58; f Jimmy Dwayne Pearson; m Jeanne Pendergest Lovell; w Leslie Grace Smith, Alexandria, VA, Dec 31, 88; chdn Grace A.E., William D.S., John O.S., Mary C.M., James R.L.; UMS 82, BA; ProtEpisTheoSem, VA 89, MDiv; O Feb 24, 90, EpiscCh; Recd PCA Nov 5, 11, NoTX Pby; astp Christ Ch Hamilton Episc, Hamilton, MA, 89-93; astp St. John's Shaughnessy Angl Ch, Vancouver, BC, 93-97; p Trinity Episc Ch, Dallas, TX, 97-10; p Christ Ch Carrollton Angl, Carrollton, TX, 10-11; op Christ Ch Carrollton, Carrollton, TX, 11-14; p 14-

14527 Meandering Way, Dallas, TX 75254 – 972-720-8755   North Texas
E-mail: wlovell@sbcglobal.net
Christ Church Carrollton – 972-672-1388

Lovett, Leon Day III – b Atlanta, GA, Oct 6, 52; f Leon Day Jr.; m Sue Ann Morgan; w Julia L. Robinson, Chattanooga, TN, Aug 24, 74; chdn Kristin Lee, Adam Robinson, Stephen Day; UGA 74, BA; RTS 81, MDiv; L Jan 81; O May 24, 81, Gr Pby; p Thomson Mem P Ch, Centreville, MS, 81-85; ap Westminster P Ch, Gainesville, GA, 85-86; srp 87-95; ascp Golden Isles P Ch, St. Simons Island, GA, 95-04; p Northside P Ch, Winder, GA, 04-17; *Have You Dealt with the Truth?*

130 Holly Lane, Athens, GA 30606 – 770-842-4630   Georgia Foothills
E-mail: prov3560@gmail.com

Lovett, Lewis – O Jun 7, 15, BlRdg Pby; campm RUF, W&LU, 15-

622 Stonewall Street, Lexington, VA 24450   Blue Ridge
E-mail: lewis.lovett@ruf.org
PCA Reformed University Fellowship

Lowe, Brian Scott – w Amy; chdn Davis, Ella; UMemp 98, BA; RTS 04, MDiv; O May 1, 05, RMtn Pby; yp St. Patrick p Ch, Memphis, 98-01; Pear Orchard P Ch, dir of college, Ridgeland, MS, 03-04; op Grace Ch P, Ft. Collins, CO, 04-

2237 Iroquois Drive, Ft. Collins, CO 80525   Rocky Mountain
E-mail: scott@gracefortcollins.org
Grace Church Presbyterian – 970-412-8551

Lowe, Christopher Brian – b Charleston, SC, May 7, 72; f Clyde Eugene; m Barbara Johnson; w Dell Robinson, Rock Hill, SC, Jun 24, 95; chdn Christopher Brian Jr., Sarah Tomlinson, Agatha Katherine; CCSC 95, BA; RTSNC 97-00, MDiv; O Sept 24, 00, Flwsp Pby; p Zion P Ch, Chester, SC, 00-03, wc 03-

129 Access Road, Deep Gap, NC 28618 – 828-264-3074   Fellowship
E-mail: brian_lowe@bellsouth.net

Lowe, F. Matthew – b Ocala, FL, Nov 2, 69; f Frank Lowe; m JoAnn Byers; w Cindy; chdn Joshua, Caleb, Anna; CC 92, BA; CTS 96, MDiv; L Oct 17, 95; O May 5, 96, MO Pby; astp Covenant P Ch, St. Louis, MO, 96-98, wc 98-00; astp Grace P Ch, Ocala, FL, 00-01; astp Centerpoint Comm Ch, Ocala, FL, 01-04; astp Conway Comm P Ch, Orlando, FL, 04-05; op Waypointe Flwsp, Wildwood, FL, 06-07

6854 SE 11th Place, Ocala, FL 34472 – 352-748-4659   Central Florida

Lowe, Grant – w Sandi; chdn Henri, Flannery; O Oct 10, Pac Pby; astp Grace Pasadena Ch, Pasadena, CA, 10-13; Chap CC 13-

1302 Aladdin Road, Lookout Mountain, GA 30750   Tennessee Valley
E-mail: grant.lowe@covenant.edu
Covenant College – 706-820-1560

Lowery, Todd – w Josie; chdn Gray, Mary Catherine, Nathan; p St. Andrews P Ch, Americus, GA, 09-11; astp Plains P Ch, Zachary, LA, 11-16; astp Redeemer P Ch, Athens, GA, 16-

165 Pulaski Street, Athens, GA 30601   Georgia Foothills
E-mail: tlowery@redeemerathens.com
Redeemer Presbyterian Church – 706-227-3344

Lowman, Jeffrey E. – b Montgomery, AL, Dec 13, 57; f S. L.; m Jean S.; w Sallie Park Hughes, Jackson, MS, Sept 21, 82; chdn Jeffery Jr. (d), Sarah Sansom, Graham Hughes; BelC 75-79, BA; RTS 80-

Lowman, Jeffrey E., continued
83, MDiv; HighC 05, DMin; O Jul 84, MSVal Pby; ap Pear Orchard P Ch, Ridgeland, MS, 84-86; p Macon P Ch, Macon, MS, 86-90; srp Evangel P Ch, Helena, AL, 90-; prof BhamTS, 94-

111 Oxford Way, Pelham, AL 35124-2851 – 205-664-0602   Evangel
E-mail: covenanter@aol.com
Evangel Presbyterian Church – 205-664-0889
Birmingham Theological Seminary

Lowrey, Mark Leonard Jr. – b Jackson, MS, Sept 27, 45; f Mark Leonard; m Emelie R. Olson; w Priscilla R. Miller, Jackson, MS, Jul 15, 72; chdn Mark Leonard III, Emelie Elizabeth (Laube); USM 63-67, BS; RTS 70-71, 74-77, MDiv, MCE; O Feb 21, 78, MSVal Pby; coord RUM, MS, 77-83; coord RUM, 83-96; GCP, dir pub, Suwanee, GA, 96-

3076 Sumac Drive, Atlanta, GA 30360-1552 – 770-393-0421   Mississippi Valley
E-mail: mark.lowrey@gcp.org
Great Commission Publications – 770-831-9084 ext: 108

Lowry, Wiley P. III – astp First P Ch, Jackson, MS, 13-; adj prof Belhaven, 14-

4144 Oakridge Drive, Jackson, MS 39216 – 601-982-5033   Mississippi Valley
E-mail: wileyl@fpcjackson.org
First Presbyterian Church – 601-353-8316
Belhaven University

Lucas, Sean Michael – b Stratford, NJ, Dec 19, 70; f Stephen Hunter; m Susan Buchanan Copenhaver; w Sara Elizabeth Young, Connersville, IN, Jan 1, 94; chdn Samuel Nathan, Elizabeth Anne, Andrew Thomas, Benjamin Michael; BJU 93, BA, 94, MA; WTS 02, PhD; O Jan 26, 03, OHVal Pby; astp Comm P Ch, Louisville, KY, 02-04; adj prof, admin CTS, 04-05, asst prof 05-08; astp Covenant P Ch, St. Louis, MO, 05-06; VPres Academics, CTS, 07-09; assoc prof, 08-09; srp First P Ch, Hattiesburg, MS, 09-16; assoc prof RTS, 14-; srp Independent P Ch, Memphis, TN, 16-; co-ed *The Legacy of Jonathan Edwards: American Religion and the Evangelical Tradition*; *Robert Lewis Dabney: A Southern Presbyterian Life*; *On Being Presbyterian: Our Beliefs, Practices, and Stories*; *What is Church Government?*; *What Is Grace?*; *God's Grand Design: The Theological Vision of Jonathan Edwards*; *Daniel: Trusting the True Hero*; *J. Gresham Machen*; *For a Continuing Church: The Roots of the PCA*

4738 Walnut Grove Road, Memphis, TN 38117   Covenant
E-mail: slucas@ipcmemphis.org
Independent Presbyterian Church – 901-685-8206

Luchenbill, Matthew S. – b Wyandotte, MI, Apr 14, 76; w Michelle C., Jun 29, 06; chdn Andrew Thomas, Ashley Marie, Sarah Michelle, Emily Elizabeth; CC 98, BA; MetAtlSem 14, MDiv; O Mar 5, 14, MetAtl Pby; ydir St. Elmo P Ch, Chattanooga, TN, 95-97; ydir West End P Ch, Hopewell, VA, 98-99; ydir East Cobb P Ch, Marietta, GA, 99-08; ydir Westminster Ref P Ch, Suffolk, VA, 08-11; astp Perimeter Ch, Johns Creek, GA, 12-18

235 Ascalon Court, Johns Creek, GA 30005   Metro Atlanta
E-mail: Msluche@gmail.com

Luchenbill, Thomas G. – b Flint, MI, Jun 9, 52; f Albert LaVerne; m Donna Mae Harkness; w Sandra Kay Abbott, Durand, MI, Dec 8, 73; chdn Matthew Scott, Tamara Kay (Hall); MISU 74, BS; CTS 99, MDiv; L Jul 24, 99, Ill Pby; O Aug 1, 99, Ill Pby; ydir Tyrone Cov P Ch, Fenton, MI, 93-96; ydir Marissa P Ch, Marissa, IL, 96-98, int 98-99, srp 99-00; op New Hope Flwsp, PCA, Fenton, MI, 00-02; astp Christ Comm Ch, Carmel, IN, 02-12; astp Cypress Ridge P Ch, Winter Haven, FL, 12-14; srp 15-

232 Santa Rosa Drive, Winter Haven, FL 33884 – 863-325-0317   Southwest Florida
E-mail: tgluke@gmail.com
Cypress Ridge Presbyterian Church – 863-325-9864

Lucht, Brad – astp Christ Ch, Normal, IL, 15-

2015 East Taylor Street, Bloomington, IL 61701 — Northern Illinois
E-mail: brad@christchurchpca.org
Christ Church – 309-452-7927

Ludt, Edward W. – Recd PCA Jan 21, 17, Gr Pby; p United P Ch, Sandersville, MS, 17-

38 Erata Road, Laurel, MS 39443 — Grace
United Presbyterian Church – 817-716-4067

Luekens, Craig – astp Christ P Ch, New Haven, CT, 13-

199 Race Hill Road, Madison, CT 06443 — Southern New England
E-mail: craig.luekens@gmail.com
Christ Presbyterian Church – 203-777-6960

Lupton, Andrew – O Mar 18, 12, Wcar Pby; mis MTW, 12-

907 NW Maynard Road, Cary, NC 27513 — Western Carolina
E-mail: luptonandrew@gmail.com
PCA Mission to the World

Lusk, Morgan – b Jacksonville, FL, Aug 30, 80; f Larry Bryan; m Janet Lynn Morgan; w Jennifer Lynn Eaton, Jun 28, 08; chdn Nathaniel Aron, Elijah Dan, Isaac Jonathan; FlaglerC 02, BA; RTSFL 08, MDiv; astp Hixson P Ch, Hixson, TN, 10-11; ascp 11-18; astp Westtown Ch, Tampa, FL, 18-

12808 Killarney Court, Odessa, FL 33556 – 863-860-7592 — Southwest Florida
E-mail: morgan@westtownchurch.org
Westtown Church – 813-855-2747

Luther, James Phillip, Jr. – O Feb 12, 17, Palm Pby; mis MTW, Greece, 17-

1401 Hampton Street #207, Columbia, SC 29201 — Palmetto
PCA Mission to the World

Lutjens, Kurt Herman – b Hackensack, NJ, Apr 29, 53; f Herman; m Amy Elizabeth Luecke; w Susan Spahn (d), Steubenville, OH, Dec 18, 76; chdn Heidi Jeanne, Jeffrey Kurt, Carrie Johanna; BGSU 75, BA; CTS 82, MDiv; L Jan 82, Pitts Pby (RPCES); O Oct 82, Asc Pby; op Redeemer Ch, Pittsburgh, PA, 88, p 89-92, wc 92-95; p Gr & Peace Flwsp, St. Louis, MO, 95-17; hr 18

6044 McPherson, St. Louis, MO 63112 — Missouri
E-mail: klutjens@sbcglobal.net
HR

Lutjens, Ronald George – b Hackensack, NJ, Feb 12, 51; f Herman; m Amy Elizabeth Luecke; w Katherine Anne Omlie, Ollon, Switzerland, Jun 21, 74; chdn Jonathan Mark Harris, Anne Elizabeth (Kuhn), Susannah Katherine (Newman); RutgU 69-70; BGSU 74, BA; TEDS 81, MA; CTS 81, MDiv; L Jun 81; O Jan 82, Midw Pby (RPCES); p Old Orchard Ch, Webster Groves, MO, 81-18; hr 18

416 Fairlawn Avenue, Webster Groves, MO 63119 – 314-518-0212 — Missouri
E-mail: ronlutjens@yahoo.com
HR

Lutz, Brandon – O Nov 17, 13, Palm Pby; astp Kingstree P Ch, Kingstree, SC, 13-14; astp Church of the Redeemer, Winter Haven, FL, 15-

3072 Buckeye Point Drive, Winter Haven, FL 33881-5916 – 407-247-4264 — Southwest Florida
E-mail: brandon@redeemerwinterhaven.org
Church of the Redeemer – 863-298-9849

Lutz, C. Al – b Keystone, IA, Apr 13, 34; f Ed; m Mary Vogler; w Julie Belz, Walker, IA, Jun 19, 59; chdn Stephen, Mary (Smallman); ISU 55, BS; CTS 60, MDiv, 86, DMin; L 60; O 60, EPC; yp Augusta Street P Ch, 60-62; op, p Shannon Forest P Ch, 62-83; op Tates Creek P Ch, 83-84, p 84-98; op Okatie P Ch, 98-01, p 01-04; chp, mis MTW, England, 05-07; hr 07

620 Frontier Bluff Road, Lookout Mountain, GA 30750 – 706-820-2876   Tennessee Valley
E-mail: ajlutz@bellsouth.net
HR

Lutz, Ronald Edward – b Scranton, PA, Jul 2, 48; f Robert E; m Janet R Winkler; w Susan L. Tonnessen, N. Plainfield, NJ, Jun 16, 73; chdn Stephen, David, Benjamin; PASU 70, BA; WTS 74, MDiv, 87, DMin; L Jan 75; O Oct 76, Phil Pby (OPC); cop New Life OPC, Jenkintown, PA, 76-87; srp New Life P Ch, Dresher, PA, 87-17; Serge 17-

355 Roslyn Avenue, Glenside, PA 19038-3517 – 215-884-6009   Eastern Pennsylvania
E-mail: ronlutz0702@gmail.com
Serge Global, Inc. – 215-885-1811
101 West Avenue, #305, Jenkintown, PA 19046

Lymberopoulos, Gavin – O Sept 10, 16, Phil Pby; astp Tenth P Ch, Philadelphia, PA, 16-

Tenth Presbyterian Church – 215-735-7688   Philadelphia

Lyon, Benjamin Cameron – b Philadelphia, PA, Aug 20, 82; w Breann, Jan 3, 09; UVA 05, BA; WTS 09, MDiv; O Jan 22, 11, JR Pby; astp Trinity P Ch, Norfolk, VA, 11-13; ascp 13-

1133 Graydon Avenue, Norfolk, VA 23507– 757-374-2020   Tidewater
E-mail: ben@trinitynorfolk.com
Trinity Presbyterian Church – 757-466-0989

Lyons, Joshua – astp Atlanta Westside P Ch, Atlanta, GA, 15; wc 15-

1002 Curran Street, Atlanta, GA 30318   Metro Atlanta
E-mail: jnlyons83@gmail.com

Lyu, Ju-Heon – w Jeong-Ae Kim; chdn Se-Jeong John, Daniel Sejoon; Kyungpook 86, BA, 88, MA; WAState 96, MA; WSCAL 00, MDiv; CTS 02, ThM; O Oct 03, KorCent Pby; astp Korean P Ch of St. Louis, St. Louis, MO, 02-05; p First Korean P Ch of Springfield, Nixa, MO, 06-

2912 North Fremont Road, Ozark, MO 65721 – 417-581-3966   Korean Central
E-mail: juheonlyu@hotmail.com
First Korean Presbyterian Church of Springfield – 417-725-2300

Lyu, Sun Myung – w Eun Jung; chdn Janet, Jennifer, Jonathan; astp Korean Ch of Chicago, Hoffman Estates, IL, 03-08; srp Korean P Ch of Ann Arbor, Ann Arbor, MI, 08-14

E-mail: smlyu2000@yahoo.com   Korean Central

Maas, Jon Kermit – b Shawano, WI, Mar 16, 53; f Duane H.; m Sonja Johannsen; w Martha Lasoski, St. Louis, MO, Aug 8, 81; chdn William Harris, Jon David, Benjamin Timothy; WheatC 75-76; UWI 80, BA; CTS 80-84, MDiv; TrSU 94, MS; L Apr 84; O 85, MO Pby; Chap USArmy, Ft. Campbell, KY, 85-88; Chap USArmy, CampCasey, Korea, 88-89; Chap USArmy, Ft. Monmouth, NJ, 89; Chap USArmy, San Antonio, TX, 90-91; Chap USArmy, Desert Storm, 91; Chap USArmy, Ft. Benning, GA, 91-94; Civilian Hosp Chap Stu, 94-95; Clinical Pastoral trng, 94-95; hr 17

16031 Waterleaf Lane, Ft. Myers, FL 33908 – 419-688-2483   Missouri
E-mail: chcolmaas@gmail.com
HR

MINISTERIAL DIRECTORY

Mabbott, Eric – O Nov 11, 12, MSVal Pby; p Bailey P Ch, Bailey, MS, 12-

1214 62nd Court, Meridian, MS 39305   Mississippi Valley
E-mail: eamabblott@gmail.com
Bailey Presbyterian Church – 601-737-2188

MacCaughelty, Michael Cameron – b Bealle AFB, CA, Jan 16, 72; f T. Cameron; m Bennie Jo Riley; w Amy Leigh Carden, Birmingham, AL, Jul 12, 97; chdn Mason Cameron, Caroline Bailey, Molly Ferguson, Ethan Moore; FurU 90-94, BA; BDS 95-98, MDiv; L May 99, Evan Pby; O Oct 10, 99, Evan Pby; astp Altadena Valley P Ch, Birmingham, AL, 99-03; astp Christ Cov P Ch, Cullman, AL, 03-05; p Monroeville P Ch, Monroeville, AL, 06-16; astp Altadena Valley P Ch, Birmingham, AL, 16-

E-mail: michael@avpc.org   Evangel
Altadena Valley Presbyterian Church – 205-967-0680

MacDonald, Brian DeWitt – O Feb 7, 10, SEAL Pby; astp Young Meadows P Ch, Montgomery, AL, 10-11; op 2Cities Ch, Montgomery, AL, 11; p 11-17; astp Redeemer P Ch, Lakeland, FL, 18-

705 East Church Street, Bartow, FL 33830 – 334-294-1226   Southwest Florida
E-mail: brian@redeemerlakeland.org
Redeemer Presbyterian Church – 863-660-5448

MacDonald, Dan – w Sunija Abraham, Jun 8, 96; McGU, BA; UWO, LLB; RTSFL, MDiv; O Jun 27, 06, Ecan Pby; ev, op Gr Toronto Msn, Toronto, ON, 05-09; p 09-

248 Glebeholme Boulevard, Toronto, ON M4J 1T2 CANADA – 416-841-8171   Eastern Canada
E-mail: dan@gracetoronto.ca
Grace Toronto Church – 416-860-0895

MacDougall, Dan – b Guelph, Ontario, Apr 27, 55; f Daniel; m Phyllis Correne Laishley; w Barbara Jean Moolenaar, Midland, MI, May 27, 78; chdn Daniel Robert, John Gregor, Christine Heather; UMI 72-76, BS; WTS 76-79, MDiv; CalvS 88, ThM; UAber 88-93, PhD; O Sept 80, PCCanada; Recd PCA 00, TNVal Pby; astp Bethel P Ch, Syndey, Nova Scotia, 79-82; p St. John's P Ch, Dahousie, New Brunswick, 83-88; prof CC, 93-

210 Wendy Trail, Lookout Mountain, GA 30750 – 706-820-0377   Tennessee Valley
Covenant College – 706-820-1560

MacDougall, Gregg Ian – b Philadelphia, PA, Jan 20, 65; f John; m Nancy Roberts; w Lynn Bossenbroek, Willow Grove, PA, Feb 11, 89; chdn Micaela Kaye; CalvC, BA; WTS, MDiv; L Nov 95, Phil Pby; O Sept 01, Phil Pby; ascp Calvary P Ch, Willow Grove, PA, 01-10; ev 10-13; mis MTW 13-14

404 Holly Drive, Annapolis, MD 21403 – 443-994-7752   Eastern Pennsylvania
E-mail: greggmacdougall@gmail.com

MacGregor, James Matthew – b Elgin, IL, Jun 7, 68; f Samuel; m Karen Hatlestad; w Deborah Mansfield, California, MD, Sept 4, 93; chdn Lydia, Hannah, Luke, Daniel, Emma; UMiami 90, BS; UMD 94, MS; CTS 98, MDiv; L Feb 14, 98, Pot Pby; O Oct 4, 98, Pot Pby; astp Cornerstone P Ch, California, MD, 98, ascp 98-06; op La Plata Comm Ch, La Plata, MD, 01-06; p 06-12; ascp Redeemer P Ch, Indianapolis, IN, 13-18; ob ip, ss Cornerstone Ch, Delafield, WI, 18-

N6 W31449 Alberta Drive, Delafield, WI 53018   Central Indiana
E-mail: jamiemacgregor@cornerstone-pca.com
Cornerstone Church – 262-646-6445

MacGregor, Thomas Alexander – b Lockport, NY, Jul 23, 51; f John Murdo; m Jane Elizabeth Pettit; w Bonnie Mae Baldwin, Wilmington, DE, Oct 15, 77; chdn Ian Baldwin, Andrew Scott, Paul Alexander,

MacGregor, Thomas Alexander, continued
Catherine Anne, Melvin Thomas, Elizabeth Jane, Robert Stewart, Jonathan Knox; CC 73, BA; BerryC 79, MEd; CTS 83, MDiv; L Apr 83; O Jan 84, NGA Pby; ap Midway P Ch, Powder Springs, GA, 84; Chap USArmy, Ft. Bragg, NC, 84-87; Chap USArmy, Elefsis, Greece, 87-90, stu, Chap 90; Chap USArmy, Ft. Riley, KS, 90-94; Chap USArmy, Uijongbu, Korea, 94-95; Chap USArmy, Ft Stewart, GA, 95-98; Chap USArmy, Ft. Bragg, NC, 98-06; Chap USArmy, Ft. Gillem, GA, 06-07; Chap USArmy, Kaiserslautern, Germany, 07-10; Chap USArmy, Ft. Benning, GA, 10-13; USArmyRet

6517 Mink Drive, Midland, GA 31820 – 706-325-8435 　　　　　　　　　　Northwest Georgia
E-mail: chaplainmacgregor@yahoo.com
HR

MacLeod, Donald E. – b Avondale, NS, Canada, Dec 25, 33; f Freeman; m Edna Louise Cameron; w Merelyn Ruth MacLellan, Sydney Mines, NS, Jul 14, 59; chdn Wayne, Donna (Burrell), Darlene (MacLennan), Wanda (Wolstenholme); GordC 70-71; McGU 71-75, ThB; L 75, Pby of Quebec; O Jun 10, 75, PCC; Recd PCA 01, Ecan Pby; hr 01; p North Shore, North River, Englishtown, 75-78; p Tatamagouche, 78-84; p River Denys, Orangedale, Malagawatch, 84-98; hr

75 Leblanc Road, Millville, NS B1Y 2J4 CANADA – 902-674-2422 　　　　　　　　　Eastern Canada
HR

MacNaughton, Scott – b Lancaster, PA, Jul 31, 58; f William E. McNutt; m Beulah Mae Penrod; w Gail Janet Thomas, Perth, W. Australia, Jan 7, 84; chdn James, Andrew, Megan, Robert; CC 81, BA; CTS 92, MA; BhamTS 01, MDiv; L Aug 97, Westm P Ch, Aus; O Jun 14, 98, Westm P Ch, Aus; Recd PCA 01, RMtn Pby; p Covenant P Ch, Lander, WY, 01-08; ob cofndr, Vpres Fathers in the Field, 08-13; p Covenant P Ch, Lander, WY, 13-

545 South 4th Street, Lander, WY 82520 – 307-349-0091 　　　　　　　　　　Rocky Mountain
E-mail: smacnaughton@wyoming.com
Covenant Presbyterian Church – 307-332-3834

MacRae, John Phillip – b Wilmington, DE, Nov 13, 48; f Allan A; m Grace Elizabeth Sanderson; w Signe Lynne Mentgen, San Bernardino, CA, Jun 23, 73; chdn Elizabeth Joanne, Douglas Andrew; ShelC 70, BA; FTS 70-71; BibTS 73, MDiv, 89, STM; CTS 98, DMin; L 73; O 73, Cov Pby; p Dunnings Crk Ind Bible Charge, Bedford, PA, 73-84; srp Faith Ref P Ch, Quarryville, PA, 84-12, hr 12; ip Carlisle Ref P Ch, Carlisle, PA, 12; astp Westminster P Ch, Maida Vale, Australia, 13-

4 Old Maida Vale Road, Maida Vale, WA 6057 AUSTRALIA 　　　　　　　　　Susquehanna Valley
E-mail: jpmacrae@aol.com
Westminster Presbyterian Church, Maida Vale, Australia

Madden, James – b Dallas, TX, Jan 30, 86; f James David; m Margaret Yeates; w "Happy" Georganna Carlock; O Jun 1, 14, NoTX Pby; campm RUF, SMU, 14-

3416 Potomac Avenue #B, Dallas, TX 75205 　　　　　　　　　　　　　　　　North Texas
E-mail: james.madden@ruf.org
PCA Reformed University Fellowship

Maddox, Winston – b Wickenburg, AZ, Feb 12, 49; f Frank Robert; m Berneice Hord; w Delores Snyder, Parker, AZ, Jul 23, 77; chdn Shelbie Dianne, Winston Ashley, Hayley Eliza; UAZ 72, BS; PhoeSem 06, MDiv; O Oct 15, 06, SW Pby; RE Catalina Foothills Ch, Tucson, AZ, 95-06; dir min Catalina Foothills Ch, Tucson, AZ, 01-05, astp 06-08; ascp 08-

6631 North Swan, Tucson, AZ 85718 – 520-615-8500 　　　　　　　　　　　　　Southwest
E-mail: winston@cfcpca.org
Catalina Foothills Church – 520-615-8400

Maeder, Robert – chdn Leo Daniel, Zoe Rosalynn, Lux Elizabeth; O Aug 31, 14, MNY Pby; astp Crossroads Comm Ch, Hillsborough, NJ, 14-

120 Fucillo Street, Manville, NJ 08835 – 301-204-9303   Metropolitan New York
E-mail: rmaeder@gmail.com
Crossroads Community Church – 908-431-4373

Magee, Stephen Christopher – b Teaneck, NJ, Sept 23, 57; f William Preston; m Grace Spencer; w Candyce DuPont, Williamstown, MA, Sept 6, 80; chdn Katherine DuPont, Jeffrey David, Samuel Stephen (d), Kristin Nicole; WmsC 79, BA; UCB 81, MBA; GCTS 93, MDiv; L Jun 93; O Jun 4, 95, NoE Pby; ascp Christ P Ch, Nashua, NH, 95-97; chp, op Exeter P Ch, Exeter, NH, 96-97, p 97-

1 Butterfield Lane #3, Stratham, NH 03885 – 603-772-9442   Northern New England
E-mail: pastor@exeterpca.org
Exeter Presbyterian Church – 603-772-7479

Maginas, Stephen – b Miami, FL; w Lesley; ColCU 02, BS; RTSA 10, MDiv; campm, mis MTW, RUF, Athens, Greece, 11-13; campm RUF, Emory, 13-

1296 Merry Lane NE, Atlanta, GA 30329 – 678-770-9806   Metro Atlanta
E-mail: stephen.maginas@ruf.org
PCA Reformed University Fellowship

Maginnis, David – b Winder, GA, Feb 1, 72; f Coulter; m Shirley Seagraves; w Hester Tippett, Savannah, GA; chdn Mary Lavens, Miles, Anne Coulter; UGA, BA; BDS, MDiv; moy Calvary Bapt Temple, Savannah, 95-99; ydir Evangel Ch PCA, Alabaster, 99-07, ascp 07-

503 Fieldstone Drive, Helena, AL 35080 – 205-835-0890   Evangel
E-mail: dmaginnis@evangelchurchpca.org
Evangel Church PCA – 205-664-0889

Magneson, Steven – O Nov 5, 16, MNY Pby; astp Trinity P Ch, Rye Brook, NY, 16-

526 Anderson Hill Road, Purchase, NY 10577 – 914-428-8214   Metropolitan New York
E-mail: stevemagneson@trinitychurch.cc
Trinity Presbyterian Church – 914-967-6247

Magri, Joseph Andrew – b Cleveland, OH, Jul 21, 56; f Joseph E.; m Virginia Lee; w Karen Louise; chdn Andrea Kean, Alana Chaffee; LibU, BA; RTS 10, MDiv; O Nov 20, 14, BlRdg Pby; astp Trinity P Ch, Charlottesville, VA, 14-

1732 Concord Drive, Charlottesville, VA 22901   Blue Ridge
Trinity Presbyterian Church – 434-977-3700

Maguire, Jerry Ivan – b Harrisburg, PA, Jan 6, 51; w Margaret Anne Frain, Baltimore, MD, Sept 15, 73; chdn Kathleen Dawn; PASU 73, BS; RPTS 82, MDiv; L Feb 82; O Oct 82, Asc Pby; staff YL, 73-77; p Hillcrest P Ch, Volant, PA, 82-92; p Providence Ref P Ch, Barboursville, WV, 92-01; p Covenant P Ch, Harlingen, TX, 01-06; p Redeemer P Ch, Concord, MA, 07-16; astp Christ Ref P Ch, Laurel, MD, 16-

1171 Sean Circle, Woodbine, MD 21793 – 978-201-2758   Potomac
E-mail: jmaguire1776@gmail.com
Christ Reformed Presbyterian Church – 301-498-3700

Mahaffey, Ted Vincent – b Laurens, SC, Dec 18, 34; f R. V.; m Ethel Wilson; w Shirley Bruns, Sarasota, FL, Jun 19, 70; chdn Todd; StrC 57; TCIN 81-86, ThB; SEBTS 67-69; TTS 81-86, MMin; L Apr 91; O Dec 69, SBapt; O Apr 92, Wcar Pby; ev United Ch of Jamaica (PCUS), 66-67; p Mulberry B

Mahaffey, Ted Vincent, continued
Ch, Napanee, VA, 69-70; GC Ministerial Fell, Bradenton, FL, 70-90; mis Jamaica, Belize, CAm, Mex Border; p Tabernacle Ch, Charleston, SC; tv/rm; ed publ; Int Chr Embassy, Jerusalem; p Landis P Ch, Marion, NC, 92-02; hr 02; ss Frank P Ch, Crossnore, NC, 04-06; ss Story Mem P Ch, Marion, NC, 10-

235 South Garden Street, Apt. C, Marion, NC 28752 – 828-559-2249   Western Carolina
E-mail: ted.mahaffey@frontier.com
HR

Mailloux, Marc – b Woonsocket, RI, Oct 19, 53; f Herman A.; m Paulette Belhumeur; w Aline Maurin, Aix-en-Provence, France, Mar 4, 78; chdn Calix, Justin, Anais; GtwnU 71-72; GordC 74-75; UParis 75-76, MA; FLTR/Aix 76-81, ThM; L Oct 23, 86; O Apr 23, 92, Cal Pby; CCC, France, 83-86; chp, ev, mis MTW, Marseille, FRANCE, 87-98; mis MTW, French speaking nations, 98-; *Discovery on the Katmandu Trail; God Still Loves the French*, 06

c/o MTW – 954-283-8131   Calvary
PCA Mission to the World

Mak, Thomas – astp Covenant of Gr Ch, Elmhurst, NY, 08-09; ascp 09-

29-26 167th Street, Flushing, NY 11358   Metropolitan New York
E-mail: yetomak@juno.com
Covenant of Grace Church – 718-352-8646

Maker, Steven – b Philadelphia, PA, May 11, 54; f Irwin W.; m Elizabeth M. Ramsay; w Nancy Ann Hickman, Winfield, MD, Jun 2, 79; chdn Julie Kathleen, Lila Elizabeth, Joanna Lynn; WMDC 76, BA; WTS 79, MDiv; L Sept 80, Rky Mtn Pby (RPCES); O Oct 84, TNVal Pby; op Grace Ch, Centerville, TN, 84-85; p Chapel P Ch, Beaver, PA, 85-

1300 Struby Avenue, Beaver, PA 15010 – 724-384-0670   Ascension
Chapel Presbyterian Church – 724-495-0297

Makhalira, Confex – Malawi, Apr 3, 82; f G.D.; m Naomi Nagama; w Mwai Kamwendo, Malawi, Oct 2, 10; chdn Evangeline, Eliana; AfBC Malawi, BA; PurRefTS, MDiv; O May 20, 18, GrLks Pby; fm, ev MTW, Malawi, 18-

1731 Holly Way, Lansing, MI 48910   Great Lakes
E-mail: conmakhalira@yahoo.com
PCA Mission to the World

Maliepaard, Mark – wc; astp Bridge Ch, San Diego, CA, 14-17

4346 54th Street, San Diego, CA 92115 – 619-271-7610   South Coast

Malin, Donald Richard – b Pittsburgh, PA, Oct 17, 53; f Donald R.; m Betty Beno; w Bess Sutherland, Birmingham, AL, Dec 31, 85; chdn Tara; NMSU 76-80, BA; BhamTS 82-86; RTS 87-88, MDiv; L Oct 87, Evan Pby; O Oct 21, 91, MSVal Pby; Chap Sch, 88; staff Watchman Flwsp, Inc., Birmingham, AL; ydir Covenant P Ch, York, AL; stus Ebenezer P Ch, Huntsville, AL, 85; Chap MS ANG, 91-13; Dir Watchman Flwsp, Inc., MS, Birmingham, AL; ss Westminster P Ch, Meridian, MS, 98-03; chap Iraq 03-04; Bible t Mt. Salus CS, 05-06; CPE 06-07; chap Afghanistan, 08-09; DeptVA, 07-13; state chap 12-13; p/t t BelhC, 14-

307 Trailwood Drive, Clinton, MS 39056-5846 – 601-506-2497   Mississippi Valley
E-mail: richardmalin898@gmail.com

Mallow, Duane Douglas – b Battle Creek, MI, Oct 21, 47; f Duane C; m Elizabeth Sparling; w Margaret Lynn Loos, Tampa, FL, Aug 15, 74; chdn Jason Douglas, Stefanie Lynn, Stephen Joseph; USF

Mallow, Duane Douglas, continued
69-73, BA; RTS 73-78, MDiv, MCE; L Apr 76, SFL Pby; O Jul 30, 78, Gr Pby; ap First P Ch, Hattiesburg, MS, 78-81; Chap ARNG, 79-81; Chap USN, 81-94; ob ss Harvest P Ch, Jacksonville, NC, 95; admin MTW, Short term, 95-09; wc 09-14; hr 14

944 Bexhill Drive, Lawrenceville, GA 30043-6692 – 770-601-6864　　　　　　　　　　　Grace
E-mail: ddmallow@yahoo.com
HR

    Malloy, Gabriel – astp Arden P Ch, Arden, NC, 17-

78 Braddock Way, Asheville, NC 28803　　　　　　　　　　　　　　　　　　　Western Carolina
E-mail: gabrielfmalloy@gmail.com
Arden Presbyterian Church – 828-684-7221

    Malone, Michael Norris – b South Bend, IN, Apr 17, 51; f Richard B.; m Jacqueline Ann Norris; w Barbara Lee Moore, Pittsburgh, PA, Jun 3, 78; chdn Kathryn Asher, Leslie Allen, Anna Elizabeth; UMI 75, BA; GCTS 78, MDiv; O Nov 23, 79, MidAtl Pby; ap Harvester P Ch, Springfield, VA, 78-81; ap Ind P Ch, Brandon, FL, 82-85; op, p Christ P Ch, Richmond, IN, 85-91; op St. Pauls P Ch, Orlando, FL, 91-92; srp 92-06; p Christ the King P Ch, Vero Beach, FL, 06-14; astp Independent P Ch, Memphis, TN, 14-

268 Woodmont Drive, Memphis, TN 38117 – 901-443-5699　　　　　　　　　　　　　　Covenant
Independent Presbyterian Church – 901-685-8206

    Maney, Sean William – b Aug 21, 74; w Sarah; chdn Matthew, Lillian; astp Malvern Hills P Ch, Asheville, NC, 07-10

1001 Danworth Court, Kirkwood, MO 63122 – 314-426-7516　　　　　　　　　　　　　Missouri
E-mail: seanmny@netzero.com

    Mang, Michael Edward – b Indianapolis, IN, May 20, 56; f Eugene H; m Marygene Young; w Laurie L Smith, Wellsboro, PA, Sept 27, 86; chdn Courtney R., Samantha J., Josef M.; INU 74-77; AurU 81, BA; BJU 85, MDiv; L Jan 24, 87; O Aug 9, 87, Cal Pby; int Beech Street P Ch, Gaffney, SC, 86-87; p Powell P Ch, Spartanburg, SC, 87-89; op Immanuel P Chapel (Msn), Greer, SC, 89-93; p Fellowship P Ch, Greer, SC, 93-97; p Cornerstone P Ch, Manassas, 97-07; p Spriggs Road P Ch, Manassas, VA, 07-

3729 Katie Place, Triangle, VA 22172　　　　　　　　　　　　　　　　　　　　　Potomac
E-mail: memang44@comcast.net
Spriggs Road Presbyterian Church – 703-791-5555

    Manickavasagam, Melvin – O Aug 5, 18, Cov Pby; astp Christ P Ch at Oxford, Oxford, MS, 18-

108 Victory Hill Lane, Oxford, MS 38655　　　　　　　　　　　　　　　　　　　　Covenant
E-mail: mmanica@email.com
Christ Presbyterian Church at Oxford – 662-234-3399

    Manley, Chris – astp New City Ch, Indianapolis, IN, 16-18

4819 Lake Haven Drive, Chattanooga, TN 37416 – 706-614-3288　　　　　　　　　Tennessee Valley
E-mail: csmanly@gmail.com

    Manning, William Joseph – b New Orleans, LA, Apr 8, 55; f Eugene Marinus; m Joan Stanier; w Petra Manuella Manning, Leesville, LA, Jun 19, 98; chdn Jonathan Abraham, Michelle Elizabeth, Tracy Diane, Aaron Luke, Samuel Marc, Rachel Leilani, Hannah Kate; BA, Univ of SW Louisiana, 73-77; M.Div., RTS-Jackson, 77-80; O Apr 17, 83, Jackson Bible Ch (MS); USA Chap USAR, 87-89; asstp, Covenant P Ch, Lafayette, LA, 89-91; ob t WestmChrAc, Opelousas, LA, 91-92; USA Chap LAARNG, 89-98(Desert Storm

Manning, William Joseph, continued
90-91); wc 92-96; p First P Ch, Oakdale, LA, 96-98; USA Chap 1st Reg 25th Avn Bn, WAAF, HI, 98-00; USA Chap, HQ, 65th Eng, Sch Brks, HI, 00-01; USA Chap, HHT, 3rd Sqdn, 4th US Cav, 01-03; USA Chap, HQ, 2-11 FA Bn, Sch Brks, HI, 03-05 (OIF, 04); USA Chap, HQ, USA Recruiting Cmd, Ft Knox, KY, 05-08; USA Chap, HQ, USA Res Cmd, Ft McPherson, GA, 08-11; Dep Cmd Chap, HQ, 80th Trng Comm (TASS), 11-15; ret USArmy, 15; hr 15

2213 Holliwell Valley Court, Winterset, IA 50273   Ohio Valley
E-mail: williamjmanning@gmail.com
HR

Manuel, Paul Kenneth – b Springfield, MO, Aug 6, 67; f Donald Leeds; m Alice Louise Edmonson; w Heather Diane Strom, Pompano Beach, FL, Dec 18, 93; chdn Emily Grace, Elijah Thomas, Elisabeth Cora; PenCC 89, BA, 91, MA; RTS 98, MDiv; L Oct 20, 98, SFL Pby; O Jan 18, 00, SFL Pby; mmus River Oaks P Ch, Lake Mary, FL, 96-98; int First P Ch of Coral Springs, Margate, FL, 98-99; astp Key Biscayne P Ch, Key Biscayne, FL, 99-01; astp Evangelical P Ch, Cape Coral FL, 01-05; p New City EPC, Coconut Creek, FL, 05-09; p Redlands Comm Ch, Homestead, FL, 09-13; p Seven Rivers PCA, Lecanto, FL, 13-

5630 West Nobis Circle, Homosassa, FL 34448 – 305-246-4016   Central Florida
E-mail: pmanuel@sevenrivers.org
Seven Rivers Presbyterian Church – 352-746-6200

Maples, Jim – b Knoxville, TN, Jan 7, 48; f James; m Evelyn Marie Clem; w Robyn Hillary Dean, Birmingham, AL, Jan 20, 83; chdn Lee Brooks, Hillary Frosberg, James III; CalCoastU 03, BS; RTS 07, MA; USAf 15, DTh; p Pleasant Grove P Ch, Pleasant Grove, AL, 06-; prof BhamTS, 07-

405 CR 1502, Cullman, AL 35058   Evangel
E-mail: jimmaples@charter.net
Pleasant Grove Presbyterian Church – 205-744-4077
Birmingham Theological Seminary

March, Brian Cummings – O Oct 13, 13, SWFL Pby; ascp Trinity P Ch, Lakeland, FL, 13-14; ascp Broadneck Evangelical P Ch, Arnold, MD, 14-16; srp 16-

1235 Stonewood Court, Arnold, MD 21012 – 863-430-3113   Chesapeake
E-mail: brian@broadneckep.org
Broadneck Evangelical Presbyterian Church – 410-626-8122

Marcott, John – O Oct 1, 11, EPA Pby; ascp Covenant P Ch, Doylestown, PA, 11-

518 Waltham Lane, Perkasie, PA 18944 – 215-257-7699   Eastern Pennsylvania
Covenant Presbyterian Church – 267-880-3713

Mardy, Hector R. – Haiti, Nov 18, 68; f Clebert; m Merita LaDouceur; chdn Ansheila, Hector Jr., Isaac; Kings River 92, AS; MiamiDade 93-94; JxnvilleTSem 98, BA; KTS 01, MDiv; O Oct 16, 01, SFL Pby; astp St. Andrews P Ch, Hollywood, FL, 01; chp Hope Hatian Comm Ch, Chicago, 01-14; mis MTW, 14-

c/o MTW – 773-410-7368   Chicago Metro
E-mail: newhopehaitian@yahoo.com
PCA Mission to the World

Mark, Alexander Dorn – b Beaufort, SC, Sept 15, 81; f Larry; m Robyn; w Stefany Stidham, Greenwood, SC, Mar 10, 82; chdn Joshua David, Charles James, Samuel Alexander; PC 03, BA; RTSNC 13, MDiv; O Aug 24, 14, Palm Pby; op First Scots P Ch of Beaufort, Beaufort, SC, 14-

2105 River Rock Way, Beaufort, SC 29902 – 843-845-0242   Lowcountry
E-mail: admark915@gmail.com
First Scots Presbyterian Church of Beaufort – 843-593-0176

MINISTERIAL DIRECTORY 413

Markert, Richard Woodson – b Indianapolis, IN, Sept 16, 41; f Frank Richard; m Edna Lorett Larsen; w Linda Nell Pike, Slidell, LA, Mar 9, 63; chdn Richard Woodson, Jeffrey Pike, John Samuel, Elizabeth Nell; PRJC 59-61; TulU 61-63; BelC 74-75, BS; RTS 75-79, MDiv; L Apr 8, 77, Gr Pby; O Mar 79, TNVal Pby; p Westm Ch, Louisville, KY, 79-84; p Mount Olive P Ch, Mount Olive, MS, 84-88; p Hopewell P Ch, Mount Olive, MS, 84-88; p First P Ch, Tuscumbia, AL, 88-95; p Plains P Ch, Zachary, LA, 95-08; astp South Baton Rouge Ch, Baton Rouge, LA, 08-

10228 Springtree Avenue, Baton Rouge, LA 70810 – 225-368-5429   Southern Louisiana
E-mail: rwmarkert@gmail.com
South Baton Rouge Church – 225-768-9999

Marlowe, Jeffrey David – b Hammond, IN, Nov 8, 51; f William Rex; m Eleanore Marie Korem; w Mischa Ann Gross, Fairhope, AL, May 1, 82; chdn Jeffrey Alexander, Eric William, Magali Elisabeth, Michael Edward, Andrew Brock; PASU 69-73, BA; RTS 84-85; FLTR/Aix 85-87, LicTh; TempU 97-98, MEd; O Sept 17, 88, NoE Pby; p, chp Eglise Chretienne reformee de la Rive-Sud, Quebec, 87-92; chp, p MTW, Dakar, Senegal, West Africa, 92-01; Dir MTW, Enterprise/Global Training, 01-04; MTW, Enterprise - Area Director, 04-

691 Glenns Farm Way, Grayson, GA 30017 – 770-236-8927   Southern New England
PCA Mission to the World – 678-823-0004

Marseglia, Tony – b Long Beach, CA, Apr 27, 64; BIOLA 87, BA; RTS 98, MDiv; p Hope EPC, 01-11; astp Redeemer P Ch, Santa Rosa, CA, 14-17

109 Creek Way, Santa Rosa, CA 95403   Northern California
E-mail: tonymarseglia@gmail.com

Marsh, Frederick Thomas – b Tanzania, E. Africa, Jul 10, 49; f Allan G. (d); m Mary Elizabeth; w Janet Ward; chdn Nathaniel Benson, David Graham, Stephen Wallis; CC 70, BA; CTS 74, MDiv; VandU 85, DMin; USM 88, MSW; O Oct 5, 75, TNVal Pby; Proj Coord MiA, Miami, FL, 75; p St. Elmo P Ch, Chattanooga, TN, 75-81; ap First P Ch, Jackson, MS, 82-86; ob BethCS, Jackson, MS, 86-93; MNA, coord of Church Relations, 93-00; MNA, Asst Coord, 00-04; MNA, Assoc Coord, 04-

209 Eastwood Avenue, Swannanoa, NC 28778 – 404-307-8266   Mississippi Valley
E-mail: fmarsh@pcanet.org
PCA Mission to North America – 678-825-1200

Marsh, Robert C. – b Norwich, England, Jun 24, 45; w Sally J, Mar 29, 70; chdn Robert C, John H; L Dec 2, 85; O Dec 2, 85, Phil Pby; Recd PCA May 16, 95, Ill Pby; Chap Phil Police Dept, Philadelphia, PA, 84-85; chp Williamsport, PA, (OPC), 86-89; Chap USArmy, 89-95; chp Springfield P Ch, Springfield, IL, 95-98; ss 98-99; Chap USArmy, 99-05; hr 05

1320 SE Palm Beach Road, Port St. Lucy, FL 34952 – 772-777-4270   Illiana
E-mail: robertmarsh0705@comcast.net
HR

Marsh, Travis John – astp Canyon Creek P Ch, San Ramon, CA, 07-

9015 South Gale Ridge Road, San Ramon, CA 94582 – 925-786-8456   Northern California
E-mail: tmarsh@canyoncreekchurch.com
Canyon Creek Presbyterian Church – 925-244-1200

Marshall, Craig G. – b Wilmington, DE, Aug 30, 64; f Richard G.; m Kay Denise Cooney; w Kimberly Sue Sisson, Newak, DE, Sept 17, 88; chdn Nathan James, Abigail Leigh, Samuel Grant; TempU 82; UDE 87, BA; RTSNC 03, MDiv; O Jun 1, 03, Flwsp Pby; mis MTW, Belize, 03-13; p Bullock Creek P Ch, Sharon, SC, 13-

7381 Lockhart Road, Sharon, SC 29742   Fellowship
E-mail: craiggmarshall@aol.com
Bullock Creek Presbyterian Church – 803-927-0475

Marshall, Greg – astp Lexington P Ch, Lexington, SC, 03-10; astp First P Ch, Macon, GA, 12-15; astp Bethel P Ch, Clover, SC, 16-

2431 Highway 557, Clover, SC 29710   Fellowship
E-mail: gmarshall1970@gmail.com
Bethel Presbyterian Church – 803-222-7166

Marshall, Harry G. – b Ilion, NY, Jan 11, 18; f Floyd; m Ruth Goodale; w Florence Weir, Columbia, SC, Apr 26, 42; chdn Ruth (Gutierrez), Lois (Clark), Colin, Verne, Nathan; CBC 47, BA, 48, MA; FTS 51, MDiv; O May 25, 52; mis Peru, SA (InBPFM & WPM), MTW, 53-85; hr; ss Manor Ref P Ch, New Castle, DE, 03-16

2505 Ferris Road, Wilmington, DE 19805-1124 – 302-994-9285   Heritage
E-mail: weirmarshalls@aol.com
HR

Marshall, Martin Sr. – b Jackson, MS, Jun 10, 35; f John Bush M; m LaVelle Pauline Warren; chdn Martin Jr., Renee (Smith), Rose Marie, Carmen Therese, Michael; UMS 62, BS; RTS 92, MDiv; O Jul 7, 93, MSVal Pby; p Scooba P Ch, Scooba, MS, 93-94; wc 94-97; ss Carolina P Ch, Philadelphia, MS, 97-99, wc 99-04; hr 04

171 County Road 103, Oxford, MS 38655 – 662-234-9798   Mississippi Valley
HR

Marshall, Rick – p Springton Lake P Ch, 09-

3522 Tyson Road, Newtown Square, PA 19073 – 610-325-0693   Philadelphia Metro West
E-mail: rickm3birches@verizon.net
Springton Lake Presbyterian Church – 610-356-4550

Marshall, Robert – op Christ Ch P, Irvine, CA, 09-12; hr 12

10492 Barbara Anne Street, Cypress, CA 90630 – 714-343-7148   South Coast
E-mail: calvin4all@sbcglobal.net
HR

Marshall, Verne G. – b Huanta, Peru, May 21, 55; f Harry G; m Florence Weir; w Alina Zuniga, Birmingham, AL, Jun 28, 80; chdn Naphtali Alan, Larissa Florence, Christopher Manuel, Stefan Harry, Anelise Nuris; CC; CBC, BS; CTS, MDiv; IHLS; L Apr 82, So Pby (RPCES); O Nov 82, Evan Pby; ap First P Ch, 82; mis MTW, Chile, 84-

c/o MTW   Evangel
E-mail: familiamarshall@gmail.com
PCA Mission to the World

Marshall, Wallace Williams Jr. – b Richmond, VA, Sept 1, 36; f Wallace W.; m Katherine Foster Lumsden; w Gabriele Annabella Rosenau, Glenside, PA, May 13, 67; chdn Michal L., Wallace W. III, Ann R., Calvin S., Katherine F., Jonathan A., Sarah S.; USNA 58, BS; UTSNY 64-65; WTS 65-68, BD; L May 68, Phila Pby (OPC); O Nov 68, NY & Neng Pby (OPC); p Grace OPC Ch, Fall River, MA, 68-70; p St. Andrews Ch, Montgomery, AL (PCUS), 70-71; p Puritan OPC, Rockville, MD, 75-79; p Pres Ref Ch, Gaithersburg, MD, 79-82, wc 83-87; ss Lednum Street P Ch, Durham, NC, 87-90; ev, op Gr Cov Pres. Flwsp (m), Raleigh, NC, 91-02; hr 02

102 Jasmine Court, Morehead City, NC 28557 – 252-773-0273   Eastern Carolina
E-mail: wwmarshall@ec.rr.com
HR

MINISTERIAL DIRECTORY 415

Martin, Andrew Joseph – b Oceanside, CA, Jul 26, 80; f Alton Larry; m Joanna Marie; w Margaret Snowden Howes, Chapel Hill, NC, Sept 7, 02; chdn Charlotte Grace, Samuel Howes, Benjamin Mayne, Rosalyn Lorae, Andrew Snowden; UNC 02, BA; GCTS 06, MA, 07, MDiv; VandU 14, MA, 16, PhD; O Jan 13, 08, CentCar Pby; astp Sandhills P Ch, Southern Pines, NC, 08-11; astp City Ch of East Nash, Nashville, TN, 14-16; astp Christ Central Ch, Charlotte, NC, 16-17; ascp West Charlotte Ch, Charlotte, NC, 17-

720 Walnut Avenue, Charlotte, NC 28208 – 980-277-0304   Central Carolina
E-mail: drewmartin@westcharlottechurch.com
West Charlotte Church – 704-609-5492

Martin, David – O Feb 23, 14, CentGA Pby; astp First P Ch, Macon, GA, 14-15; ob Covenant Acad, Macon, GA, 15-17; p Dayspring P Ch, Forsyth, GA, 17-

201 Alexandria Drive, Macon, GA 31210 – 478-284-2487   Central Georgia
E-mail: dave-martin@juno.com
Dayspring Presbyterian Church – 478-994-4503

Martin, David – op Redeemer P Msn, Lakeland, FL, 08-11; p 11-

4632 Lathloa Loop, Lakeland, FL 33811 – 081-300-7160   Southwest Florida
E-mail: redeemerlakeland@yahoo.com
Redeemer Presbyterian Church – 863-660-5448

Martin, John – O Feb 7, 16, Tidw Pby; astp Westminster Ref P Ch, Suffolk, VA, 16-

347 Spring Hill Place, Smithfield, VA 23430 – 757-784-1755   Tidewater
E-mail: johnmartin04@gmail.com
Westminster Reformed Presbyterian Church – 757-539-0540

Martin, Joshua Alan – b Greenville, SC, Jul 21, 75; f Kenneth James; m Judith Adeline Lippert; w Sara Parks Stewart, Starkville, MS, Nov 20, 99; chdn Benjamin Stewart, Sara Margaret; USCSpart 93-97, BS; GPTS 97-01, MDiv; O Oct 28, 01, Cov Pby; campm RUM, DltSU, 01-08; campm RUF, LSU, 08-14; astp South Baton Rouge P Ch, Baton Rouge, LA, 14-18; p Palmetto Hills P Ch, Simpsonville, SC, 18-

4 Lake Valley Court, Simpsonville, SC 29681   Calvary
E-mail: joshuaalanmartin@yahoo.com
Palmetto Hills Presbyterian Church – 864-963-9600

Martin, Martin Huskey – b Raleigh, NC, Jun 5, 65; f Martin Sweezey; m Margaret Cosette Huskey; w Celanie Adaire Smith, Greenville, SC, Mar 20, 93; chdn Madeline Adaire, Oliver Hamilton, Grayson Southerlin, Eliza Aetheling; ClemU 87, BS; CTS 95, MDiv; L Oct 26, 95; O May 5, 96, Cal Pby; ss Liberty Springs P Ch, Cross Hill, SC, 95, p 96-00; p Fellowship P Ch, Greer, SC, 00-

10 Birnam Court, Greenville, SC 29615 – 864-281-0850   Calvary
E-mail: office@fellowshippres.org; martyandcelanie@earthlink.net
Fellowship Presbyterian Church – 864-877-3267

Martin, Randy – b Tehachapi, CA, May 26, 52; w Julie Lynn Short, St. Louis, MO, Dec 3, 02; UCLA 74, BA; CTS 78, MDiv; O Jul 22, 06, Pac Pby; p Providence Ref P Ch, Bakersfield, CA, 06-

5817 Cypress Point Drive, Bakersfield, CA 93309 – 661-472-5501   Pacific
E-mail: rmartin@pcabakersfield.com
Providence Reformed Church of Bakersfield – 661-431-5487

Martin, Shane – O Nov 25, 18, Palm Pby; p Lebanon P Ch, Winnsboro, SC, 18-

6394 Newberry Road, Winnsboro, SC 29180   Palmetto
E-mail: t.shane.martin@gmail.com
Lebanon Presbyterian Church – 803-635-9202

Martin, Wesley – O Jul 15, NoCA Pby; campm RUF, UUT, 15-16, wc; p Westminster Bible P Ch, Sydney, NS, 16

2848 NW 17th Street. Oklahoma City, OK 73107   Eastern Canada
E-mail: wes.martin918@gmail.com

Martinez, Alejandro – O May 7, 17, Pitts Pby; astp Covenant Comm P Ch, Wexford, PA, 17-

591 Jane Street, Cranberry Township, PA 16066 – 240-351-6354   Pittsburgh
Covenant Community Presbyterian Church – 724-934-1234

Martinez, Juan Carlos – O Apr 19, 13, HouMet Pby; astp Christ the King P Ch, Houston, TX, 13-; campm RUF, RiceU, 15-

3719 Turnberry Circle, Houston, TX 77025   Houston Metro
E-mail: jjuancarlos.xr@gmail.com
Christ the King Presbyterian Church – 713-892-5464
PCA Reformed University Fellowship

Martinez, Jules – astp Briarwood P Ch, Birmingham, AL, 15-18; astp Trinity Church Dorado, PR, 15-18; astp Iglesia la Travesia, PR, 15-18; wc

1267 Bradwell Lane, Apt A, Mundelein, IL 60060   Evangel
E-mail: jmartinezolivieri@gmail.com

Martinez, Victor – astp Redeemer P Ch, San Antonio, TX, 08-12; ascp 12-

601 West Mulberry Avenue, San Antonio, TX 78212 – 210-268-6110   South Texas
E-mail: victor@redeemersa.org
Redeemer Presbyterian Church – 210-930-4480

Marusich, Steven Patrick – b Montgomery, AL, Jun 9, 71; f Paul; m Sandra Jean Stevens; w Kelly Suzanne Wooden, Indianapolis, IN, Aug 2, 97; chdn Jackson Stevens, Eli Fields, Savannah Grace; AU 95, BA; CTS 00, MDiv; O Nov 11, 01, Pot Pby; campm RUF, UMD, 01-06; mis MTW, England, 06-07; ip Wallace P Ch, College Park; p Trinity P Ch, Brownsburg, IN, 14-

558 Heartland Lane, Brownsburg, IN 46112 – 317-319-6984   Central Indiana
E-mail: steve.marusich@gmail.com
Trinity Church of Brownsburg – 317-852-5554

Marvel, Judson – Recd PCA Jun 25, 15, Siouxl Pby; p Good Shepherd P Ch, Minnetonka, MN, 15-

4267 Drew Avenue North, Robbinsdale, MN 55422   Siouxlands
E-mail: judsonmarvel@gmail.com
Good Shepherd Presbyterian Church – 952-473-2828

Mascara, Tim – b Pittsburgh, PA, Apr 2, 81; f William; m Victoria Marsh; w Amanda Hansen, Charlotte, NC, Dec 17, 05; NCBC 04, BA; RTSNC 08, MDiv; O May 3, 09, CentCar Pby; astp StoneBridge Ch Comm, Charlotte, NC, 07-16, ascp 17-

2203 Prestigious Lane #G, Charlotte, NC 28269 – 704-562-7402   Catawba Valley
E-mail: tim@mascarafamily.com
StoneBridge Church Community – 704-549-8272

Mascow, James – Recd PCA Jul 16, 97, GrLks Pby; srp Tyrone Cov P Ch, Fenton, MI, 97-17; astp Knox P Ch, Harrison Township, MI, 17-

25700 Crocker Boulevard, Harrison Township, MI 48045 – 586-868-3637   Great Lakes
E-mail: jamesmascow@knoxpca.org
Knox Presbyterian Church – 586-469-8500

Mashburn, William Lee – b Miami, FL, Nov 1, 55; f William C.; m Barbara E. Boyle; w Laurie Jane Nyborg, Miami, FL, Nov 24, 84; chdn Robert Lee, Lindsay Ann; WheatC 78, BA; WTS 84, MAR, MDiv; CTS 94, DMin; L May 87; O May 87, SFL Pby; ap Granada P Ch, Coral Gables, FL, 87-88; p West Friesland P Ch, Ackley, IA, 88-93; srp Shannon Forest P Ch, Greenville, SC, 93-00; ev, op Hidden Valley P Ch, Draper, UT, 00-03, p 03-15; p Redlands Comm Ch, Homestead, FL, 15-

2145 NE 38 Road, Homestead, FL 33033 – 786-377-3266   South Florida
E-mail: hiddenvalleypc@mac.com
Redlands Community Church – 305-258-1132

Maskevich, Jeff – wc; ss West Friesland P Ch, Ackley, IA, 10-14; Chap Hospice DelValle; ss New Life Flwsp Ch, Elk Run Heights, IA, 16-

32696 Highway 57, Aplington, IA 60604 – 719-298-7825   Iowa
E-mail: godsmercytohaiti@gmail.com
New Life Fellowship Church – 319-234-1985

Mason, Daniel – op Christ Central Durham, Durham, NC, 13-17, p 17-

309 North Elizabeth Street, Durham, NC 27701 – 919-259-3145   Eastern Carolina
E-mail: daniel@christcentraldurham.com
Christ Central Durham – 919-884-6323

Mason, John Shattuck – b Caracas, Venezuela, Jan 13, 45; f John F.; m Margaret Arms; w Sandra Campbell, Glenside, PA, Sept 22, 79; chdn Irene, Isaac; PU 66, AB; WTS 73, MDiv, 77, ThM; VandU 01, PhD; L 73, Phil Pby (OPC); O Aug 4, 74, Phil Pby; mis Eritrea, 74-76; mis Lebanon, 78-79; p Centreville, TN, 79-81; prof GBibC, 81-82; mis MTW, Daystar, Nairobi, Kenya, 82-86, wc; mis MTW, Lyon, France, 99-02, wc 03-; ed *Tigrinya Grammar*, 94; contr *New Geneva Study Bible*, 95; contr *Life & Times Historical Study Bible*, 97

4 4967 Karen Ray Drive, Antioch, TN 37013 – 323-229-3149   Nashville
E-mail: nefasit@gmail.com

Massey, William Dwight – b Ft Walton Bch, FL, Mar 18, 57; f John W.; m Ruth Kuckherman; w Valerie Burroughs, Newbury, VT, Jun 13, 87; chdn William J., Ruth A.; UWY 80, BA; CTS 94, MDiv; L Jul 94; O Mar 5, 95, Pitts Pby; CCC, 80-87; astp First Ref P Ch, Pittsburgh, PA, 94-96, ascp 96-01, chp 01-02; op Harvest P Ch, Lancaster, PA, 02-04, p 04-

10 Thomas Road, Lancaster, PA 17602 – 717-464-1547   Susquehanna Valley
E-mail: massey.wd@gmail.com
Harvest Presbyterian Church – 717-464-8755

Masterson, Adam – O 14, SFL Pby; astp Coral Ridge P Ch, Ft. Lauderdale, FL, 15-18; srp Lake Osborne P Ch, Lake Worth, FL, 18-

Lake Osborne Presbyterian Church – 561-582-5686   Gulfstream

Mateer, Samuel Andrew – b Evanston, IL, Mar 21, 40; f Bruce DeLoss; m Ann Timson; w Lois Marion Peyton, Port Huron, MI, Sept 1, 62; chdn Kathryn Ann, Stephen Andrew, Yvonne Elizabeth, Dawn Marie; NWU 62, BA; FulTS 65, BD; PTS 66, ThM; WTS 89, DMin; O Aug 10, 66, Chicago Pby (UPCUSA); Recd PCA Jul 5, 76, Asc Pby; ap Sixth Ave Ch, B'ham, AL, 66-67; p Altadena Valley P Ch, 67-73; p Ohio Ch, Aliquippa, PA, 73-76; p Ch of the Master, Aliquippa, PA, 76-79; mis, chp MTW, Ecuador, 79-88; tm ldr Quito 82-83, 84-87; mis, chp MTW, 88-, tm ldr, Santiago, Chile, 88-99, country dir, Chile, 01-10; San Marcos International Church Santiago Chile, 04-15; hr 15

c/o MTW – 011-562-220-2228   Ascension
E-mail: smateer@mtwsa.org
HR

Mateo, Jose – op Emmanuel P Msn, Powder Springs, GA, 08-10; wc 10-11; astp Crosspoint P Ch, Smyrna, GA, 11-13; wc 13-16; ob 16-

212 Williamsburg Drive, Dallas, GA 30153 – 770-505-7427   Metro Atlanta
E-mail: Jose@mateonet.net

Mather, Jason – op King's Church, Long Beach, CA, 05-

5276 East Abbeyfield Street, Long Beach, CA 90815 – 714-595-5641   Pacific
E-mail: matherjk@gmail.com
King's Church – 562-388-5557

Mathews, Mark D. – p Bethany P Ch, Oxford, PA, 15-; *Riches, Poverty, and the Faithful: Perspectives on Wealth in the Second Temple Period and the Apocalypse of John,* 13; "The Apocalypse of John, 1 Enoch, and the Question of Influence," in *The Myth of Rebellious Angels: Studies in Second Temple Judaism and New Testament Texts,* 14; "The Function of Imputed Speech in the Apocalypse of John" *Catholic Biblical Quarterly* 74, 12; "The Apocalypse of John, 1 Enoch, and the Question of Influence," *In Die Johannesapokalypse: Kontexte - Konzepte – Rezeption,* 12; "Community Rule and Romans 5:1-11: The Relationship Between Justification and Suffering," in *Reading Romans in Context: Paul and Second Temple Judaism,* 15; "The Genre of 2 Peter: A Comparison with Jewish and Early Christian Testaments" *Bulletin for Biblical Research* 21, 15; "The Literary Relationship of 2 Peter and Jude: Does the Synoptic Tradition Solve this Synoptic Problem?" *Neotestamentica* 44.1, 16

2483 Baltimore Pike, Oxford, PA 19363   Susquehanna Valley
E-mail: Pastor@bethanypca.org
Bethany Presbyterian Church – 610-932-3962

Mathews, Michael – ascp St. Patrick P Msn, Greeley, CO, 08-12; p 12-

2012 18th Avenue, Greeley, CO 80631 – 970-371-3120   Rocky Mountain
E-mail: michael@saintpatrickpc.org
St. Patrick Presbyterian Mission – 970-346-8812

Mathews, Roland – astp Draper's Valley P Ch, Draper, VA, 10-12; ascp 12-

2663 Old Baltimore Road, Draper, VA 24324 – 540-440-1497   Blue Ridge
E-mail: roland.mathews@dvpca.org
Draper's Valley Presbyterian Church

Mathieu, John Pierre Jr. – b Memphis, TN, Jan 28, 47; f John P.; m Faye Smith; w Kathy Kenney, Winston-Salem, NC, May 2, 87; chdn David M., John William; UVA 65-69, BA; O Jan 94, Central South EPC; Recd PCA 00, GulCst Pby; p Trinity EPC of Mobile, 93-99; p Redeemer Comm Ch, Mobile, AL, 00-02, wc 02-03; p First P Ch, Brewton, AL, 03-13; ip Grace P Ch, Fort Payne, AL, 13-14; p 14-

PO Box 680422, Ft. Payne, AL 35968 – 251-363-1538   Providence
E-mail: mathieu.john@gmail.com
Grace Presbyterian Church – 256-845-4756

Matlack, Kenneth Alan – b Westheim, Germany, Sept 22, 57; f John S.; m Marie L. Hassett; w Tammie L. Kaser, Jackson, MS, Feb 23, 80; chdn Jane Caitlin, Evangeline Victoria; ClrCC 79, BA; RTS 84, MDiv, MCE; L May 82, Phil Pby (RPCES); O Nov 25, 84, CentFL Pby; op Comm P Ch, Palm Harbor, FL, 84-86, p 86-91; mis MTW, Berlin, 91-

6527 Arbor Point, Flowery Branch, GA 30542   Southwest Florida
E-mail: ken.matlack@mtw.org
PCA Mission to the World

Matocha, Todd – Recd PCA May 27, 14, Cov Pby; srp Main Street P Ch, Columbus, MS, 14-

402 Jolly Road, Columbus, MS 39705　　　　　　　　　　　　　　　　　　　Covenant
E-mail: tdmatocha@yahoo.com
Main Street Presbyterian Church – 662-328-2523

Matsinger, James R. – b Lansdowne, PA, Oct 28, 50; f John Dunbar; m Garaldine Ann Basler; w Nancy Marie Adrian, Clemson, SC, May 11, 74; chdn James Ralph, Joseph Richard; ClemU 69-74, BA; ColGS 77-82, MDiv; O Jul 28, 96, CentGA Pby; mis MTW, 88-

c/o MTW　　　　　　　　　　　　　　　　　　　　　　　　　　　　　Savannah River
E-mail: jmatsinger@gmail.com
PCA Mission to the World

Matter, Drew – astp City Ch, Philadelphia, PA, 10-13

7 North Park Street, Hanvoer, NH 03755 – 603-277-9327　　　　　　　　　Philadelphia
E-mail: drewmatter@gmail.com

Matthews, Andrew Walter George – w Eleanor Ferguson, Spring, TX, Aug 3, 02; chdn Gaius; TXA&M 92, BA; RTS 01, MDiv; astp Spring Cypress P Ch, Spring, TX, 03-05; p Westminster P Ch, Webster, TX, 10-11; ip Bay Area P Ch, Webster, TX, 11-12; ip Galveston Bapt Ch, 13-14; chp military families in Korea, 14-; *Christian CoreStrength*, 13; *Christian JumpStart*, 13

10430 Sanibel Falls Court, Houston, TX 77095　　　　　　　　　　　　Southeast Alabama
E-mail: andrewwg.matthews@gmail.com

Matthews, Brad – prof CTS, 10-

12330 Conway Road, St. Louis, MO 63141　　　　　　　　　　　　　　　　Missouri
Covenant Theological Seminary – 314-434-4044

Matthews, Dave Walker – b Dallas, TX, Jul 20, 45; w Elizabeth French, Memphis, TN, Dec 28, 72; chdn Betsy, Carrie; SFAU 67, BS; DTS 75, ThM; CTS 06, DMin; O Aug 84, TX Pby; Recd PCA Oct 23, 93, NoTX Pby; astp Fifth Street P Ch, Tyler, TX, 75-78; astp Casa Linda P Ch, Dallas, TX, 83-86; p Matt Comm ARP, 86-93; astp Trinity P Ch, Plano, TX, 93-96; astp Briarwood P Ch, Birmingham, AL, 96-98, ascp 98-

2840 Cahawba Trail, Birmingham, AL 35243 – 205-972-8797　　　　　　　　　Evangel
E-mail: dmatthews@briarwood.org
Briarwood Presbyterian Church – 205-776-5211

Matthews, Frank Lockhart – b Toccoa, GA, Jan 11, 70; f Robert; m Dorothy Lockhart; w Suzanne Lynette Bunch, Due West, SC, Dec 14, 96; chdn Joshua, Micah, Aaron, Elisabeth; ErskC 93, BA; CTS 02, MDiv; O Nov 02, Cal Pby; ydir Covenant P Ch, Easley, SC, 95-98; mis MTW, Peru, 03-06; ascp Christ Comm Ch Msn, Gainesville, FL, 06-12; astp Sycamore P Ch, Midlothian, VA, 12-15, ascp 15-

300 Hinson Drive, North Chesterfield, VA 23236　　　　　　　　　　　　　James River
E-mail: fmatthews@sycamorepres.com
Sycamore Presbyterian Church – 804-794-0238

Mattis, Ted – b Greenwich, CT, Jul 12, 65; f Louis P.; m Patricia Diane Brown; w Sally Ann Thompson, Memphis, TN, Jun 22, 91; chdn Tripp, Meg, John Price, William; GSU, BS; RTS 97, MA, 99, MDiv; O Oct 14, 01, CentFL Pby; astp Orangewood P Ch, Maitland, FL, 00-02; astp Highlands P Ch, Ridgeland, MS, 03-04; astp Independent P Ch, Memphis, TN, 04-15

6337 Common Oaks Court #106, Memphis, TN 38120 – 901-761-5192　　　　　Covenant
E-mail: tmattis@mac.com

Matu, Aung Lai – op Open Arms in Christ Comm Ch, 08-10; op Atlanta Matu Comm Ch, Stone Mt., GA, 10-

942 Belle Glad Drive, Stone Mountain, GA 30083 – 404-228-4019   Metro Atlanta
E-mail: aunglaimatu@gmail.com
Atlanta Matu Community Church

Mau, George Fredric – b Atlanta, GA, Jun 12, 61; f George; m Joyce Juanita Edgar; w Sandra Diane Fye, Ocean Spgs, MS, Jun 16, 84; chdn Amelia Joyce, Carolyn Sarah, George Alexander; MerU 79-80; CC 80-84, BA; WSCAL 84-87, MDiv; RTS 90-92, DMin; L Oct 18, 88; O May 14, 89, War Pby; p Woodland Heights P Ch, Selma, AL, 88-93; ascp Crescent Hill P Ch, Selma, AL, 94; srp First P Ch, Dyersburg, TN, 94-98; srp Faith P Ch, Irmo, SC, 99-01, wc 01-03; ob exec dir Christ Central Min, Columbia, SC, 03, wc 04-10; ob couns Watermark Counseling LLC, 10-; brd cert Nat'l Cert Couns; *Emotion: the Power of Change*, 13; *A Different Reality*, 14; *The Relaxation-Based Pain Relief Certification Manual*, 18

139 Hunters Blind Drive, Columbia, SC 29212 – 803-407-8828   Palmetto
E-mail: fredric5@gmail.com

Maureira, Carlos Roberto – p Paraguay, 14-

Independencia. Nacional 494, Barrio Centro. Villa Elisa, Asunción, PARAGUAY   Potomac
E-mail: roberto5ve@gmail.com

Maves, Samuel Cooper – b Atlanta, GA, Dec 30, 62; f Arnie; m Barbara Boyd; w Amy Elizabeth Lowrey, May 25, 96; chdn Martha Cameron, Mallory Elizabeth; BelC 81-85, BS; RTS 86-89, MDiv; L Feb 17, 90, MSVal Pby; O Feb 16, 92, CentGA Pby; int First P Ch, Philadelphia, MS, 89-91, ip 91; astp Covenant P Ch, Milledgeville, GA, 91-95; p St. Andrews P Ch, Americus, GA, 95-09; p New Life P Ch, Tifton, GA, 09-

713 East 48th Street, Tifton, GA 31794   Central Georgia
E-mail: smaves@friendlycity.net
New Life Presbyterian Church – 229-382-7238

Mawhinney, Allen – b Philadelphia, PA, Apr 30, 46; f Nevin; m Laura; w Carole, St. Petersburg, FL, Aug 31, 67; chdn Nevin Allen, Scott Allen, Erin Liesle; WJBC 68, BA; WTS 71, BD, 73, ThM; BayU 82, PhD; O Jun 1, 80, So Pby (RPCES); prof CC, 72-80; prof WTS, 80-90; prof RTSFL, 90-18

2715 Dudley Court, Bensalem, PA 19020   Central Florida

Mawhinney, Bruce C. – b Washington, PA, Jun 1, 49; f William Bradford; m Ethel Mary Hunt; w Carol Ann Chudik, Johnstown, PA, Apr 2, 71; chdn Paul Andrew, Susan Elisabeth; GenC 71, BA; PittsTS 76, MDiv; WTS 91, DMin; O Jul 76, Wash Pby (UPCUSA); ap Canonsburg UP Ch, PA, 76-78; p Hillcrest UP Ch, Monroeville, PA, 78-81; p New Hope P Ch, Monroeville, PA, 81-92; srp New Cov Flwsp, Mechanicsburg, PA, 92-05; srp Wheatland P Ch, Lancaster, PA, 05-16, ascp 16-18; hr 18; *Preaching with Freshness*, 91

634 Oakwood Lane, Lancaster, PA 17603 – 717-975-3425   Susquehanna Valley
HR

Mawhinney, Scott – w Janna Levi; chdn Michael Allen, Matthew Levi, Grace Suzanne, Carolelynn Hope, John Luke; DordtC 94, BA; RTS 04, MDiv; astp Covenant Life P Ch, Sarasota, FL, 06-

8490 McIntosh Road, Sarasota, FL 34238 – 941-587-9579   Southwest Florida
E-mail: scott@covenantlifepc.com
Covenant Life Presbyterian Church – 941-926-4777

MINISTERIAL DIRECTORY 421

Maxwell, Phillip – w Christina; astp Fort Worth P Ch, Fort Worth, TX, 16-

4237 Whitfield Avenue, Ft Worth, TX 76109 – 720-256-1728   North Texas
E-mail: phillip@fortworthpca.org
Fort Worth Presbyterian Church – 817-731-3300

May, Matt – O Mar 12, 17, OHVal Pby; astp North Cincinnati Comm Ch, Mason, OH, 17-

5060 Barnwood Court, Mason, OH 45040 – 706-799-6534   Ohio Valley
E-mail: matt@northcincy.org
North Cincinnati Community Church – 513-229-0190

May, Paul – b Lawrence, KS, Apr 28, 80; w Meaghan Ann; chdn Austen Amelia, Claire Abigail, Evan Martin, Lydia Corinne, Nathan William; UKS 02, BA; RTSFL 07, MDiv, 07, MAC; astp Redeemer P Ch, Riverview, FL, 08-09; astp Marco P Ch, Marco Island, FL, 09-11C; op Grace P Ch, Sioux Falls, SD, 11-15; astp McLean P Ch, McLean, VA, 15-; op King's Cross Ch, Ashburn, VA, 16-

42972 Chesterton Street, Ashburn, VA 20147   Potomac
E-mail: paul@mcleanpres.org
McLean Presbyterian Church – 703-821-0800
King's Cross Church – 571-293-0590

May, Ron – op Ethos P Msn, Chicago, IL, 08-

738 West Melrose Street, Chicago, IL 60657 – 773-935-9758   Chicago Metro
Ethos Presbyterian Mission – 773-935-9758

May, Thomas M. – b Opelika, AL, Apr 5, 56; f Jack T.; m Martha L. Love; w Linda Jo Lee, Snellville, GA, Jun 2, 79; chdn Zachary, Jessica, Katherine, Andrew Thomas, Rebekah, Joel Philip; UGA 77, BS; RTS 86, MDiv; L Feb 85, MSVal Pby; O Nov 86, NGA Pby; mis MTW, 86-97; astp Comm P Ch, Moody, AL, 97-00; p Westminster P Ch, Columbus, GA, 00-05; astp Westminster P Ch, Gainesville, GA, 05-06; ascp 06-14; p Highlands P Ch, LaFayette, GA, 14-

1211 West North Main Street, Lafayette, GA 30728   Tennessee Valley
E-mail: tommhpc@comcast.net
Highlands Presbyterian Church – 706-638-8940

Mayes, Steve – b Newton, MS, Feb 29, 64; f Pete (d); m Pat Weaver; w Mary Ann McGee, Newton, MS, Jun 10, 89; chdn Beth, Ben (d), Timothy; ECJC 84, AA; WmCareyU 93, BS; BDS 97, MDiv; O May 91, SBC; Recd PCA Nov 08, Evan Pby; p Pinckney Bap Ch, Union, MS, 91-93; West Point Bap Ch, Jacksonville, AL, 94-98; p Pelahatchie Bap Ch, Pelahatchie, MS, 01-07; astp, chp Faith P Ch, Anniston, AL, 08-13; op Hope Comm Ch, Jacksonville, AL, 08-13, p 13-

226 Jones Street, Jacksonville, AL 36265 – 256-343-3365   Evangel
E-mail: stevemayes@cableone.net
Hope Community Church – 256-435-5005

Mayfield, Daniel Morgan – O Feb 3, 13, Pot Pby; astp Cornerstone P Ch, Lexington Park, MD, 13; campm RUF, TXTechL, 16-

3512 58th Street, Lubbock, TX 79413 – 806-224-3148   North Texas
E-mail: dmayfield7081@gmail.com
PCA Reformed University Fellowship

Mayk, William G. – w Renee; chdn Daniel, Michelle; EasternU, BA; BibTS 01, MDiv; O May 04, Phil Pby; mis Mexico, 88-89; mis Jordan, 90-91; op Grace & Peace P Ch, Pottstown, PA, 04-06; p 06-

972 West Cedarville Road, Pottstown, PA 19465 – 610-970-5909   Philadelphia Metro West
E-mail: bill_mayk@graceandpeacePC.org
Grace & Peace Presbyterian Church – 610-323-2021

Maynor, William W. – b Montgomery, AL, Jul 2, 42; f William Thomas(d); m Fannie Alice Carroll (d); w Mary Helen Wood, Moss Pt, MS, Oct 10, 64; chdn Brian Wood (d), Andrew William, Allen Gregory (d), Peter Thomas; BelC 60-64, BA; RTS 67-70, MDiv; DSU 76, MEd; UAL 82, PhD; O Aug 2, 70, CMC Pby (PCUS); p Bailey P Ch, Bailey, MS, 70-73; p Mount Carmel P Ch, Bailey, MS, 70-73; ap First Ch, Cleveland, MS, 73-78; prin Day School; p First Ch, Rosedale, Shelby & Shaw, MS, 73-74; p First P Ch, Eutaw, AL, 78-84; t Chatt Chr sch, Chattanooga, TN, 84-85; prof CC, 85-87; Collinsville P Ch, Collinsville, AL, 87-89; ss Salem P Ch, Alpine, AL, 89-17; prof SEBC, 90-17; hr 17

702 Thunderbird Avenue, Birmingham, AL 35212-4012 – 205-908-5242   Evangel
E-mail: bmaynor316@gmail.com
HR

Mays, Clarence R. – w Bettie O'Haver; chdn Catherine Denise, Laura Dianne; FWBC 64, BA; CTS 70, MDiv; ConcS 75, ThM; p Bethel Bapt Ch, Ashland City, TN, 63-64; p Cordova Bapt Ch, Cordova, AL, 64-66; Wurdack P Ch, UPCUSA, St. Louis, MO, 72-76; p Town North P Ch, Richardson, TX, 76-79; Crown & Cov P Ch (OPC), Richardson, TX, 79-82; ascp Colleyville P Ch, Colleyville, TX, 87-04; hr 07

4609 Faulkner Drive, Plano, TX 75024-7397 – 972-377-7556   North Texas
E-mail: clarencemays76@gmail.com
HR

Mays, Rod S. – b Logan, WV, Sept 22, 50; f Robert R; m Mary Frances Bell; w Debra McMahon, Dalton, GA, Dec 28, 75; chdn Morgan Elisabeth; CC 72, BA; WGAC 75, MEd; NOBTS 73; LRTS 78, DMin; WTS 86; L Jun 72, SBap; O Oct 74, SBap; ap Kinsey Dr Bap Ch, Dalton, GA, 74-76; p Starcher B Ch, Charleston, WVA, 76-77; p Covenant P Ch, Nitro, WV, 77-87; ap McLean P Ch, McLean, VA, 87; p St. Paul P Ch, Jackson, MS, 87-90; srp Woodruff Road Ch, Simpsonville, SC, 90-99; coord RUM, 99-13; vis lect CTS, RTS, WSCAL; ascp Mitchell Road P Ch, Greenville, SC, 14-17; admin RUF 17- ; co-auth *Things That Cannot Be Shaken*, 08; contr *Tabletalk, Modern Reformation*

54 Latour Way, Greer, SC 29650 – 864-676-9474   Calvary
E-mail: rmays@ruf.org
PCA Reformed University Fellowship

McAndrew, Robert F. Jr. – b N. Chelmsford, MA, Jun 24, 47; f Robert F.; m Jeanne L. Swallow; w Phyllis J. Goodrum, Scottdale, GA, Mar 21, 75; chdn Christopher, Scott, Mark; CBC 72, BBE; ColTS 78, MDiv; ErskTS 92, DMin; L Oct 82; O Nov 82, ARP; Recd PCA Apr 16, 91, NGA Pby; ap Doraville ARP, Doraville, GA, 82-91; ascp Faith P Ch, Watkinsville, GA, 91-94, srp 94-

1310 North Woods Road, Watkinsville, GA 30677 – 706-769-5022   Georgia Foothills
E-mail: bob@faithpcachurch.org
Faith Presbyterian Church – 706-769-8315

McArthur, Charles Webster – b Meridian, MS, Mar 23, 59; f John M, Sr; m Margaret L Williams; w Sheree L Dubois, Ft. Lauderdale, FL, Sept 5, 81; chdn Christopher Daniel, Timothy Alan, Joshua Charles; HJC 77-78; BelC 78-81, BA; RTS 85-88, MDiv; L Jan 13, 87, Gr Pby; O Jan 8, 89, CentFL Pby; stus Bay Street P Ch, Hattiesburg, MS, 87; stus Bethesda P Ch, Edwards, MS, 87-88; op New Hope P Ch, Eustis, FL, 88-90, p 90-96; op Cross Creek P Ch, Jacksonville, FL, 96-99, p 99-11; ob Equipping Leaders Int, Inc., Clermont, FL, 11-

384 Village Drive, St. Augustine, FL 32084   North Florida
E-mail: chuck929@gmail.com
Equipping Leaders International, Inc

McArthur, John Marvin Jr. – b Meridian, MS, May 24, 56; f John M. Sr.; m Margaret L. Williams; w Donna C. Branning, Jackson, MS, Jun 2, 79; chdn John Webster, Sarah Catherine; HJC 74-75; BelC 78,

McArthur, John Marvin Jr., continued
BA; RTS 83, MDiv; O Jan 84, Evan Pby; p Clayton P Ch, Clayton, AL, 84-88; p Pleasant View P Ch, Clayton, AL, 84-88; p Magee P Ch, Magee, MS, 89-92; p Olivet P Ch, McConnells, SC, 92-

161 Church Street, McConnells, SC 29726 – 803-684-5205　　　　　　　　　　Fellowship
E-mail: chipmca@bellsouth.net
Olivet Presbyterian Church – 803-684-3719

　　　McAulay, Chip – O Nov 8, 09, CentCar Pby; op Lake Tillery P Msn, Mount Gilead, NC, 09-15, p 15-

PO Box 1202, Mount Gilead, NC 27306 – 910-439-2075　　　　　　　　　Central Carolina
E-mail: chipmcaulay@nc.rr.com
Lake Tillery Church – 910-639-0324

　　　McBride, Michael A – b Jun 21, 73; f George; m Patricia; w Mandy Brown; chdn Olivia, Joseph, Margaret; Purdue 96, BS; CTS 09, MDiv; O Oct 29, 10, SoCst Pby; astp Harbor Downtown P Ch, San Diego, CA, 11- 13; ascp Harbor P Ch Golden Hill, San Diego, CA, 13-14, op Parkside P Ch, San Diego, CA, 14-

1350 29th Street, San Diego, CA 92102　　　　　　　　　　　　　　　　　South Coast
E-mail: mike@parksidesd.org
Parkside Presbyterian Church – 619-208-1638

　　　McCafferty, Andrew S. – PittsTS 80, MDiv; UPitt 87, PhD; O Jul 03, SELA Pby; prof Taosheng Theo Sem, 92-96; ob dean China Reformed Theological Seminary, 97-08; ex dir RTF Press, 07-; op Hong En Ref Ch, Taipei, Taiwan, 08-; "Calvin and Insignifying Grounds," *Faith and Philosophy*; *Dichotomy: The Orthodox View*; *China and the Gospel*

China Reformed Theological Seminary　　　　　　　　　　　　　　Southern Louisiana
#30, Lane 75, Nan King East Road
Taipei 105, TAIWAN ROC – 888-2-2173-1228
E-mail: andy.crts@gmail.com
Hong En Reformed Church, Taipei, Taiwan

　　　McCall, Alan Ray – b Effingham, IL, Sept 9, 51; f Virgil; m Louise Leffler; w Linda Milliman, West Liberty, IL, Aug 16, 70; chdn Jason Alan, Amy Rebecca, Ruth Ann; TNTC 73, BA; GrTS 73-75; RTS 75-77, MDiv; O Jun 77, Evan Pby; p Friendship P Ch, Eufaula, AL, 77-79; p Providence P Ch, Sugar Land, TX, 79-

2523 Sage Brush Lane, Sugar Land, TX 77479-1614 – 281-980-0250　　　　　Houston Metro
E-mail: arm1951@alltel.net
Providence Presbyterian Church – 281-980-2522

　　　McCall, Nathan William – astp Cov P Ch, Nashville, TN, 11-16, ob 16-18; ascp All Saints P Ch, Brentwood, TN, 18-

399 Coventry Drive, Nashville, TN 37211 – 615-542-5174　　　　　　　　　　　Nashville
E-mail: nmccall@allsaintspres.net
All Saints Presbyterian Church – 615-886-0795

　　　McCall, Perry – p Carolina P Ch, Madden, MS, 11-16; p Carthage P Ch, Carthage, MS, 16-

10121 Road 404, Philadelphia, MS 39350 – 601-656-4127　　　　　　　　Mississippi Valley
E-mail: pmccall6@gmail.com
Carthage Presbyterian Church – 601-267-5700

McCall, William Joel – St. Petersburg, FL, Aug 18, 50; f William C.; m Edith Mills; w Sarah N. Watkins, Nashville, TN, Jul 15, 72; chdn Rebecca Noelle, Nathan William, Zachary Cabell; CBC 68-72, BBE; WTS 74-77, MAR; IHLS 77-78, grad wk; WTS 87, grad wk; RTS 99, DMin; L 80; O Sept 8, 85, EFC; Recd PCA Apr 27, 91, CentCar Pby; p Comm EFC, Elverson, PA, 80-86; p Faith EFC, Rock Hill, SC, 87-90; instr MABCS, 88-90; bd mbr stmCAc, Rock Hill, SC, 88-90; fac CBCC, 89-; p Lakeshore Ch, Denver, NC, 91-08; ob Equipping Pastors Int, Inc., NC, Winter Springs, FL, 08-; astp Christ Cov P Ch, Knoxville, TN, 13-; *The Development and Implementation of a New Vision for Ministry in a Plateaued and Declining Church - A Case Study in Revitalization at Lakeshore Presbyterian Church Denver, NC*

150 Portland Drive, Lenoir City, TN 3777182　　　　　　　　　　　　　　　　　Tennessee Valley
E-mail: joelmccall2@gmail.com
Columbia Bible College (Charlotte)
Christ Covenant Presbyterian Church – 865-671-1885

McCallister, Karl Francis – b Vineland, NJ, Aug 6, 60; f Edward Albert; m Della Amy; w Cynthia Diane Cottrell, El Dorado, AR, Jul 27, 85; chdn Sarah Ashley, Jesse Luke, Ian Karl; CBC 81, AA, BA; CBS 85, MDiv; CIU 99, DMin; L Jan 86, SEAL Pby; O Sept 86, Palm Pby; p Aimwell P Ch, Ridgeway, SC, 86-97; p First P Ch, Brewton, AL, 97-02; p Faith P Ch, Irmo, SC, 02-

1811 Dutch Fork Road, Irmo, SC 29063 – 803-732-9546　　　　　　　　　　　　　　　Palmetto
E-mail: karl@growingthroughfaith.com
Faith Presbyterian Church – 803-732-1234

McCann, Sean Monroe – b Durham, NC, Jun 24, 82; w Lindsey Anne Wall; chdn Lucy, Ellie, Anna, Mary Neal; RTS 07, MDiv; O Jan 8, 12, CentCar Pby; astp Sovereign Gr P Ch, Charlotte, NC, 11-13, ascp 13-16; p Covenant Ref P Ch, Asheville, NC, 16-

631 Woodland Knolls Drive, Asheville, NC 28804 – 704-577-5910　　　　　　　Western Carolina
E-mail: smccann24@gmail.com
Covenant Reformed Presbyterian Church – 828-253-6578

McCarthy, James – b May 20, 85; w Jordan; chdn Elizabeth, Julia, Locke; EckC 08, BA; GPTS 15, MDiv; O Jul 11, 15, NFL Pby; ascp Westminster P Ch, Jacksonville, FL, 15-16, srp 16-18; p First P Ch, Hattiesburg, MS, 18-

100 Heatherwood Drive, Hattiesburg, MS 39402　　　　　　　　　　　　　　　　　　　Grace
E-mail: Mccarthy.jordan.e@gmail.com
First Presbyterian Church – 601-268-0303

McCartney, Dan Gale – b Clarksburg, WV, Jan 27, 50; f James Matthew; m Janet Summerville; w Helen Kathleen Capcara, Pittsburgh, PA, Jun 5, 71; chdn Christopher John, Cara Elisabeth; CMU 71, BFA; GCTS 74, MDiv; WTS 77, ThM, 89, PhD; L Jan 10, 81, RPCES; O May 5, 87, Phil Pby; ob prof WTS, 86-09; ob prof RedTS, Dallas, TX, 09-15; hr 15; *Let the Reader Understand*, Baker, 94; *Why Does it Have to Hurt: The Meaning of Suffering*, P&R, 98; *Machen's New Testament Greek for Beginners* (revised), Prentice-Hall, 03; *James*, BECNT, 09

6245 Tollgate Road, Zionsville, PA 18092　　　　　　　　　　　　　　　　　　　　North Texas
E-mail: dan.g.mccartney@gmail.com
HR

McCarty, Kevin – b Lubbock, TX; f Tim McKeown; m Rebecca, Jennifer; chdn Darby, James, Hezekiah, Colton; CC 99, BA; RTSFL 04, MDiv; O MetAtl Pby; Chap USArmy, 11-

111 Hollywood Boulevard, Yorktown, VA 23692　　　　　　　　　　　　　　　　Metro Atlanta
E-mail: chmccarty@gmail.com
United States Army

McCay, J. Roger, Jr. – Chap USArmy, 14-17; p Monroeville P Ch, Monroeville, AL, 17-

114 Floyd Street, Monroeville, AL 36460 – 803-528-9453   Southeast Alabama
E-mail: roger_mccay@yahoo.com
Monroeville Presbyterian Church – 251-743-3482

McClellan, Kyle – b Iowa City, IA, Mar 18, 70; f David; m Judith Carlson; w Amy Deacon, Louisville, KY, May 27, 95; chdn Gabrielle, Nathaniel; TayU 93, BA; SBTS 98, MDiv; BDS 16, DMin; O Nov 96, SBC; Recd PCA May 10, OHVal Pby; op Gr P Ch, Fremont, NE, 10-13, p 13-

424 West 11th Street, Fremont, NE 68025 – 402-619-5706   Platte Valley
E-mail: kyle.mcclellan51@gmail.com
Grace Presbyterian Church – 402-517-0099

McClimon, Philip Arthur – b Baltimore, MD, Dec 16, 67; f Philip Price; m Tekla Tittle; w Sherry Renae Mann, Clinton, SC, Dec 11, 93; PC 86-90, BA; ErskTS 90-95, MDiv; O Jan 97, Mid Atl Pby, EPC; astp Westminster P Ch, Clinton, SC, 98-99; Chap USN, 99-

2532 Country Creek Lane, Fort Worth, TX 76123   Calvary
United States Navy

McCloud, David – astp Granada P Ch, Coral Gables, FL, 12-

950 University Drive, Coral Gables, FL 33134   South Florida
E-mail: davemccloud@bellsouth.net
Granada Presbyterian Church – 305-444-8435

McClung, Glen A. – b Charleston, WV, Nov 16, 37; f Luddy W; m Eula Gladys Lively; w Melinda Ann Webster (d); chdn Karma Lynn (Howard), John Watson; O Jul 64, PeeDee Pby (PCUS); p Kentyre Ch, Hamer, SC, 64-68; p Wildwood & Cape Carteret chs, NC, 68-72; p McClure Memorial Ch, Castle Hayne, NC, 72-79; p Malvern Hills P Ch, Asheville, NC, 79-90; p Friendship P Ch, Laurens, SC, 90-97, mdis 97; hr 02; *What Did I Say? A Study of Church Vows* (English & Russian)

816 Starnes Cove Road, Asheville, NC 28806 – 828-876-3905   Calvary
E-mail: godscouple@aol.com
HR

McClure, Allen David – w Melissa; chdn Anna, Ian, Alastair, Cailin, Kelly, Beric; Whitefield College, Ireland, ThB; TTS, MABS; O Sept 22, 96, BPC; astp Bible P Ch, Collingswood, NJ, 96-98, ip 98-01, p 01-04; p Faith P Ch, Ackley, IA, 05-10; p Covenant Ch, Millers Falls, MA, 10-17; hr 18; contr *Ackley World Journal;* "Loving God through Obedience," Greenfield *Recorder*, 15

23 Wildwood Avenue, Greenfield, MA 01301 – 413-475-3767   Southern New England
E-mail: mcclure_allen@yahoo.com
HR

McClurken, Edwin Winfield III – b Montgomery County, PA, Mar 13, 56; f Edwin W. Jr.; m Flora Irene Peever; w Barbara Ann Dillard, Greenville, SC, Jun 7, 86; chdn Cailey Michelle, Sarah Anne, Rosemarie Elaine; PASU, BS; WTS, MAR, MDiv; L Oct 84; O Aug 4, 85, Cal Pby; ap Calvary P Ch, Greenville, SC, 84-88; mis MTW/Impact, Peru, 88-92; wc 92; ob Faith Comm Ch, children, y & fam min, Pearland, TX, 94; wc 94; op Red Cedar P Msn, Chetek, WI, 95-04; wc 04-08; hr mdis 08

306 Schofield Street, Chetek, WI 54728 – 715-924-3804   Wisconsin
E-mail: ednbarb@citizens-tel.net
HR

McCollum, Derek Hampton – O Apr 1, 10, SoTX Pby; campm RUF, UTX, chp 16-17; op Hope P Ch, New Braunfels, TX, 17-

66 Mission Drive, New Braunfels, TX 78130 – 512-814-9298   South Texas
E-mail: derekmccollum@mac.com
Hope Presbyterian Church – 225-588-5300

McCombe, Burress – b Pewaukee, WI, Jun 8, 76; w Kristin Elaine Jack, Oct 6, 01; chdn Cora Grace, Shay Elaine; SprC 98, BS; CTS 08, MDiv; ascp Covenant P Ch, Harrisonburg, VA, 08-

32 Southgate Court, Harrisonburg, VA 22801   Blue Ridge
E-mail: burress@cov-pres.org
Covenant Presbyterian Church – 540-433-3051

McCombs, John – O Mar 4, 18, Pitts Pby; astp City Ref P Ch, Pittsburgh, PA, 18-

27 Barton Drive, Pittsburgh, PA 15221   Pittsburgh
E-mail: john@cityreformed.org
City Reformed Presbyterian Church – 412-720-7014

McCord, Jeff – ascp Christ Ch, Normal, IL, 05-15; astp Southpointe Comm Ch, Nolensville, TN, 18-

106 Founders Pointe Boulevard, Franklin, TN 37064 – 615-538-5257   Nashville
E-mail: jbmccord@gmail.com
Southpointe Community Church – 615-746-7722

McCormick, Joseph – O 15, RMtn Pby; astp Deer Creek Comm Ch, Littleton, CO, 15-

E-mail: josephmccormick56@gmail.com   Rocky Mountain
Deer Creek Community Church – 303-933-9300

McCort, Thomas James – b Youngstown, OH, Nov 4, 65; f C. Glenn; w Rachel Elaine Wheeles, Coulterville, IL, Apr 27, 96; chdn Christopher Ryan, Haley Nicole, Brennan James; FurU 88, BA; CTS 93, MDiv, 94, ThM; PTS 10, ThM; L Sept 94, Evan Pby; O Aug 99, Ill Pby; p Hope P Ch, Collinsville, IL, 99-01; Chap USArmy, 01-

PSC 704 Box 2741, APO, AP 96338 – 360-539-9046   Illiana
E-mail: thomas.j.mccort@us.army.mil
United States Army

McCracken, Timothy – b West Palm Beach, FL, Oct 7, 65; f James Arnold; m Naomi Ruth Hudson; w Robin Marie Gibbs, Jupiter, FL, Jan 26, 85; chdn Hudson, Hope; CBC 88-92, BA; CBS 93-97; L May 01, Evan Pby; O Jun 10, 01, Evan Pby; DCE Trinity EPC, 97-00; astp Oak Mountain P Ch, Birmingham, AL, 00-05, ascp 05-

6533 Quail Run Drive, Pelham, AL 35124 – 205-403-2943   Evangel
E-mail: tmccracken@ompc.org
Oak Mountain Presbyterian Church – 205-995-9265

McCrocklin, William Michael – b Vincennes, IN, Nov 19, 42; f Claude Thompson McC; m Marjorie Bell Peyton; w Jean Anne Mitchell, Dallas, TX, Aug 28, 65; chdn ElizabethAnn (Shry), Michelle Lee (Mulder), Melissa Jean (Roberts); BayU 67, BA; SWBTS 73, MDiv; KTS 98, DMin; L Jan 86; O Jul 17, 66, Bapt; Recd PCA Jul 25, 92, SoTX Pby; BSU dir, Athens, TX, 73-75; Dir NoPlns B Conv, Rapid Cty, SD, 73-75; dir dev IA Sou B Fell, Des Moines, IA, 77-82; p Como B Ch, Sterling, IL, 82-85; p Calvary B

McCrocklin, William Michael, continued
Ch, Rockford, IL, 85-87; medu Castle Rock B Ch, Castle Rock, CO, 88-89; p Hesperus B Ch, Hesperus, CO, 89-91; astp, DCE Heritage P Ch, Corpus Christi, TX, 92; ascp Spring Cypress P Ch, Spring, TX, 93-98; op Christ the Redeemer P Ch, Cypress, TX, 98-02, p 02-04; ob 4:11 Ministries Bible Studies, 05-09; hr 09

5318 Stonemill Circle, Corpus Christi, TX 78413   Rocky Mountain
E-mail: drmccrocklin@usa.com
HR

    McCullough, Douglas B. – b Pontotoc, MS, May 18, 47; f Dr. J. B.; m Mary Ruth Cook; w Elizabeth Upchurch, Jackson, MS, Feb 23, 73; chdn Elizabeth Ann, Amy Ruth, Jonathan Douglas; MillsC 65-69, BA; RTS 72-75, MDiv; L Jan 75; O Jun 75, MSVal Pby; Chap USArmy, Ft. Bragg, NC, 75-78; Chap USAR, Ft. Bragg, NC, 78-90; Chap US Army, Ft. McCoy, WI, 91-92; Chap USAR, Ft. Bragg, NC, 93-97; Chap USAR, Pentagon, Arlington, VA, 98-01; Chap USAR, Ft. Jackson, SC, 02-07; hr 07

100 Church Street, Clinton, MS 39056-5214 – 601-924-0575   Mississippi Valley
E-mail: dbmretired@gmail.com
HR

    McCune, Christopher David – f Bill; m Marlene Hager; w Elizabeth, Oxford, OH, Sept 7, 97; chdn Annabel Hope, Samuel Connor, Isaac Lanman, Molly Ceit ; USMA 94, BS; RTS 02, MDiv; O Aug 17, 03, MSVal Pby; mis MTW, Dunfermline, Scotland, 03-08; op Grace Denver, Denver, CO, 08-12; p St. Patrick P Ch - Denver, Denver, CO, 12-13

7395 West 32nd Avenue, Wheat Ridge, CO 80033 – 303-330-9237   Rocky Mountain
E-mail: bigchiefmccune@gmail.com

    McCune, James H. – b Chicago, IL, Aug 19, 54; f Charles; m Marilyn; w Kathy, Orland Park, IL, Jun 30, 79; chdn Samuel Aaron, Abigail Ruth (Schaaf), Timothy Isaac; TCIL 77, BA; CalvS 96, MDiv; t Valley CS, Cerritos, CA, 82-94; Wayland CRC, Wayland, MI; Cottage Grove CRC, South Holland, IL; p Christ Cov Ch, La Crosse, WI, 08-

1605 Franklin Street, Onalaska, WI 54650 – 708-955-8399   Wisconsin
E-mail: jim.mccune@gmail.com
Christ Covenant Church – 608-782-7833

    McCutchen, William – astp Westminster P Ch, Rock Hill, SC, 05-12; srp Hilton Head P Ch, Hilton Head Island, SC, 12-

235 William Hilton Parkway, Hilton Head, SC 29926 – 843-422-4885   Lowcountry
E-mail: bill.mccutchen@hiltonheadpca.com
Hilton Head Presbyterian Church – 843-689-6362

    McDaniel, Erik – astp Faith P Ch, Anniston, AL, 10-16; p Grace P Ch, Jasper, TN, 16-

1102 Russell Street, Jasper, TN 37347   Tennessee Valley
E-mail: erik.gracejasper@gmail.com
Grace Presbyterian Church – 423-718-0653

    McDaniel, H. Curtis Jr. – b Richmond, VA, May 12, 59; f Henry Curtis, Sr.; m Velma Leona; w Karen Jane Preston (d), St. Louis, MO, Jul 2, 83; chdn Henry Curtis III, Megan Elizabeth, Heather Preston; CBC 77-81, BA; CTS 81-84, MDiv; FulTS 89, DMin; DuqU 09, PhD; L Oct 84, OK Pby; O Feb 22, 86, SEAL Pby; astp Trinity P Ch, Montgomery, AL, 85-97; ss Providence P Ch, Montgomery, AL, 91-95; ip, srp Trinity P Ch, Montgomery, AL, 96-97; chp, op Clarksville P Ch, Clarksville, TN, 97-01; p Christ P Ch of Clarksville, Clarksville, TN, 01-02; astp, exec p Coral Ridge P Ch, Ft. Lauderdale, FL, 02-03; srp

McDaniel, H. Curtis Jr., continued
Westminster P Ch, Butler, PA, 03-08; wc 08-; ip New Hope EPC, Ft. Myers, FL, 12-13; ss Chapin P Ch, Chapin, SC, 16-17; ip, ss Murrysville Comm Ch, Murrysville, PA, 18-; *When I Need God the Most*, 01; *Life Brighteners* series

105 Spring Ridge Drive, Butler, PA 16001 – 724-282-4684   Palmetto
E-mail: curtmcdaniel@centurylink.net
Murrysville Community Church – 724-327-8411

    McDaniel III, Henry Curtis – b St. Louis, MO, Apr 18, 84; f Henry Curtis, Jr.; m Karen Preston (d); w Margaret Ruth Curtis, Middleburg, FL, Jun 7, 08; chdn Anna Hope, Katherine Grace, Andrew Curtis; UFL 05, BA; CTS 09, MDiv; O Nov 22, 09, SavRiv Pby; astp Grace Ch of the Islands, Savannah, GA, 09-11; ascp 11-13; campm RUF, Purdue, 13-

1713 Ashbury Court, West Lafayette, IN 47906 – 314-691-8672   Central Indiana
E-mail: curtis.mcdaniel@ruf.org
PCA Reformed University Fellowship

    McDaniel, Roy – astp First P Ch, Louisville, MS, 13-17

2065 Half Day Road, T-1762, Deerfield, IL 60015 – 662-803-7069   Mississippi Valley
E-mail: roy.e.mcdaniel@gmail.com

    McDonald, Jeff Scott – b Corvallis, OR, Mar 27, 71; f Don; m Laura Jeneal Bodkin; w Robyn Lynn Hughes, Albuquerque, NM, May 15, 93; chdn Zachary Robert, Joshua Peter; UNM 94, BBA; WSCAL 98, MDiv; O May 14, 00, SWFL Pby; ascp Covenant P Ch, Lakeland, FL, 00-

3325 Shore Drive, Lakeland, FL 33812 – 863-648-2281   Southwest Florida
E-mail: jeff@covenantlakeland.org
Covenant Presbyterian Church – 863-646-9631

    McDonald, Sam – b Wiggins, MS, Feb 21, 70; w Carol LeAnne Boutwell, Dec 16, 95; chdn Amber, Molly, Sarah; USM, BA, MA; RTS 06, MDiv; O 06, Gr Pby; mis Malawi, Africa, 06-11; p Trinity P Ch, Corinth, MS, 12-18; p Faith P Ch, Brookhaven, MS, 18-

404 McNair Avenue, Brookhaven, MS 39601 – 662-415-8765   Grace
E-mail: samdmcdonald@gmail.com
Faith Presbyterian Church – 601-833-0081

    McDowell, Bruce Allen – b Asuncion, Paraguay, Oct 3, 56; f Donald E; m May C Vanderpoel; w Susan A Benthal (d), (2) Anne Budd; chdn Brooke Ann, Abby Grace; AldBC 78, BA; GCTS 81, MATS; TempU 83-84; WTS 91, DMin; AmUBibStud 99, PhD; L Mar 87; O Apr 10, 88, Phil Pby; Minister of Global Outreach, 82-; astp Tenth P Ch, Philadelphia, PA, 88-92, ascp 92-17; ob ev PEF, 17- co MTW; co-auth, *Muslims and Christians at the Table: Promoting Biblical Understanding Among North American Muslims*, 99; co-auth *Muslim and Christian Beliefs: A Comparison*, 00; *The Message of the Holy Book of God Concerning the True Path to Life*, 03; *Noah: A Righteous Man in a Wicked Age*, 04; *Liberation by God* (Chinese); *Christian Baptism: The Sign and Seal of God's Covenant Promise* (Turkish), 15; *Christian Baptism: The Sign and Seal of God's Covenant Promise* (English), 17; *Faith in the Mosaic: Finding a Biblical Focus in a Pluralistic World*, 17

418 South 47th Street, Philadelphia, PA 19143 – 267-441-0734   Philadelphia
E-mail: bruceamcdowell@gmail.com
Presbyterian Evangelistic Fellowship

    McDowell, Glenn Norris – b Asuncion, Paraguay, Mar 28, 52; f Donald E.; m May C. Vanderpoel; w Constance Kraftson, Philadelphia, PA, Sept 12, 75; chdn Alastair, Anya, Shelby, Andrei; UPA 74, BA; WTS 80, MDiv; L 81; O 82, Phil Pby (RPCES); ascp, ms/sa Tenth P Ch, Philadelphia, PA, 82-92; op Peace

McDowell, Glenn Norris, continued
Valley Ch, Chalfont, PA, 92-93, ascp 93-95, wc 95; ascp New Life P Ch, Dresher, PA, 97-03; p liberti Ch, Philadelphia, PA, 06-09; PCA-GA MNA co, 07-10; coach for church planters in 3 presbyteries, 06-; ascp liberti Fairmount, Philadelphia, PA, 09-; mod Phila Pby, 12, 13, 14; "Single Adults Impacting the City" in *Urban Mission*

359 Righter Street, Conshohocken, PA 19428-2340 – 610-828-4350　　　　　　Philadelphia
E-mail: gmcdowell@liberti.org
liberti Fairmount – 610-850-4200

McDowell, Scott – O Jun 12, 11, Wcan Pby; astp Providence Comm Ch, Victoria, BC, 11-15; op Lighthouse P Msn Ch, Victoria, BC, 15-

444 Burnside Road West, Victoria, BC V8Z 1M2 CANADA – 250-818-9252　　　Western Canada
E-mail: scottmcdowell@shaw.ca
Lighthouse Presbyterian Mission Church – 250-818-9252

McFarland, Frederick Sanford – b Schenectady, NY, Oct 14, 49; f C. Robert; m Ruth Lynch; w Celeste Sanchez, Atlanta, GA, Jun 13, 70; chdn Alicia Sill, Austina Burton, Sarah Genevieve; CC 71, BA; CTS 74, MDiv; L Oct 73, Midw Pby; O Oct 76, DMV Pby (RPCES); int Christian Training Inc., 74-75; p Grace P Ch, Lexington, VA, 76-83; p Hope P Ch, Gilbert, AZ, 84-89; Chap USAFR, 83-89; Chap USAF, Plattsburg AFB, NY, 89-92; Chap USAF, Geilenkirchen NATO, Germany, 92-95; Chap USAF, Charleston AFB, SC, 95-98; Chap USAF, Davis-Monthan AFB, AZ, 98-01; Chap USAF, Ramstein AFB, Germany, 01-04; Chap USAF, Wright-Patterson AFB Ohio, 04-10; astp South Dayton P Ch, Centerville, OH, 11, ascp 11-13; ob Pastor Coaching Ministry, 15-17

92 Royston Bypass, Royston, GA 30662　　　　　　　　　　　　　　　　　　Ohio Valley

McFarland, Jerry – b Camden, NJ, Aug 30, 49; f Charles Edward; m Lillian Rosewall; w Beverly Brown, Camden, NJ, Jun 9, 73; chdn Megan L, Matthew S, Erin E; HougC 69-72, BA; WTS 82-86, MRA, MDiv, 03, DMin; L Nov 86; O Oct 4, 87, DMV Pby; ascp Severna Park Evangelical P Ch, Pasadena, MD, 87-95; ob DnStu WTS, 95-08; ascp Peace P Ch, Cary, NC, 08-14; ascp Tenth P Ch, Philadelphia, PA, 14-

671 Lindley Road, Glenside, PA 19038　　　　　　　　　　　　　　　　　　　Philadelphia
E-mail: jmcfarland@tenth.org
Tenth Presbyterian Church – 215-735-7688

McGarity, Billy L. – srp Grace P Ch, Troy, TN, 10-

1269 Forrester Road, Union City, TN 38261 – 731-446-5157　　　　　　　　　Covenant
E-mail: gmcgarity@live.com
Grace Presbyterian Church – 731-446-5157

McGee, Bryant C. – b Dallas, TX, Aug 5, 61; f Dan; m Carla Creighton; w Jennifer Golden, Carrollton, TX, Jul 17, 82; chdn Melissa Suzanne, Allison Riley; DBU 84, BS; CTS 97, MDiv, 06, DMin; L Jul 96, NoTX Pby; O May 4, 97, MO Pby; ascp Covenant P Ch, St. Louis, MO, 97-01; p Redeemer P Ch, McKinney, TX, 01-17; op Gr & Peace P Msn, Anna, TX, 10-17; *Care for the Caregiver: Stress and Burnout in Ministry*, CTS diss, 06

58 Whooping Crane Drive, Laguna Vista, TX 78578　　　　　　　　　　　　　North Texas

McGinn, Samuel Baxter III – b Charlotte, NC, Dec 8, 50; f S B, Jr; m Margaret Bizzell; w Linda Ruth Hollingsworth (dv); chdn Ruth Elizabeth, John Samuel, Sarah Linda; MonC 69-71, AA; KgC 71-73, BA; GCTS 74-77, MDiv; L May 20, 78, Wcar Pby; O Nov 5, 78, CentCar Pby; p South Point P Msn, Gastonia, NC, 78-81; sc CentCar Pby, 80; p Westminster P Ch, Greenville, TX, 81-88; srp First P Ch,

McGinn, Samuel Baxter III, continued
Weaverville, NC, 88-96, wc 96; Chap Buncombe Cnty Sheriff's Dept, 91-96; ss Westminster P Ch, Boone, NC, 96-97; instr Caldwell CC, Boone, NC, 96-; ob Samaritan's Purse, 99-; bklt "The Questions of Origin, Purpose & Destiny," 85

PO Box 2230, Blowing Rock, NC 28605-2230 – 828-295-0171   Western Carolina
E-mail: smcginn@samaritan.org
Samaritan's Purse

   McGinnis, Mitchell A. – b LaGrange, GA, Jan 8, 71; f James Anthony; m Cheryl Lynn Gladney; w Ralana Jawan Sons, Thomasville, GA, Oct 16, 99; chdn Andrew Jameson, Luke Brasher, Abigail Rayne, Heavenly Michelle; TrSU 89-93, BS; BDS 96-99, MDiv; L May 14, 02, Evan Pby; O Jun 2, 02, Evan Pby; astp Comm P Ch, Moody, AL, 02-03; p Westminster P Ch, Columbus, GA, 05-

3826 Gray Fox Drive, Columbus, GA 31909 – 706-566-8941   Central Georgia
E-mail: mitch@wpcpca.com
Westminster Presbyterian Church – 706-323-4441

   McGoldrick, James E. – b Philadelphia, PA, Jan 5, 36; f James Edward, Sr.; m Bernardine Estelle Glenn; w Elizabeth Mary McManus, MD; chdn Gloria, James Edward III, Barbara; TempU 61, BS, 64, MA; WVU 74, PhD; O Jan 62, Pitts Bapt Ch; Recd PCA 01, GrLks Pby; Pittsgrove Bapt Ch, Elmer, NJ, 59-65; Calvary Bapt Ch, Pittman, NJ, 65-66; ss, ip various churches; prof GPTS, 01-; *Luther's English Connection*, 79; *Luther's Scottish Connection*, 89; *Baptist Successionism*, 94; *God's Renaissance Man*, 00; *Christianity and its Competitors: New Faces of Old Heresy*, 06; *Presbyterian and Reformed Churches: A Global History*, 12

Box 690, Taylors, SC 29687   Calvary
E-mail: jemcgoldrick@att.net
Greenville Presbyterian Theological Seminary – 864-322-2717

   McGowan, Charles E. – b Greenville, NC, Sept 17, 36; f Lonnie; m Eva Williams; w Alice Flye (d), Greenville, NC, Mar 29, 59; chdn Charles Jonathan, Martha Ann, Stephen Paul, Philip Ross; DavC 58, BA; ColTS 66, BD; KgC 92, DD; O Jun 26, 66, Atl Pby (PCUS); p Chapel Woods P Ch, Decatur, GA, 66-78; p First P Ch, Dothan, AL, 78-88; srp Christ P Ch, Nashville, TN, 88-03; mod GenAs, 96; ob pres The Operation Andrew Grp, Nashville, TN, 03-08; ob pres McGowan Search, 08-

5302 Meadow Lake Road, Brentwood, TN 37027-5150 – 615-330-0347   Nashville
E-mail: cmcgowan@mcgowansearch.com
McGowan Search – 615-330-0347

   McGowan, Elbert Jr. – campm RUF, JSU, 08-16; srp Redeemer Church, PCA, Jackson, MS, 16-

116 Dendron Drive, Jackson, MS 39211   Mississippi Valley
E-mail: elbertmcgowan@gmail.com
Redeemer Church, PCA – 601-362-9987

   McGraw, Eamon – astp North Macon P Ch, Macon, GA, 09-11; Chap USN, 11-

912 Handsboro Place, Gulfport, MS 39507   Central Georgia
E-mail: eamon@nmpc.net
United States Navy

   McGuire, Jonathan – O Feb 28, 16, MSVal Pby; astp First P Ch, Belzoni, MS, 16-

603 Rutherford Street, Belzoni, MS 39038   Mississippi Valley
E-mail: belzonitrek@gmail.com
First Presbyterian Church – 662-247-3326

MINISTERIAL DIRECTORY

McGuire, Justin – w Melissa Atkinson; chdn Peyton, Asher, Colin, Ransom, Bennett; USC, BS; CTS, MDiv; O Oct 24, 10, Hrtg Pby; astp Providence P Ch, Salisbury, MD, 10-12, ascp 12- 13; srp College Hill P Ch, Oxford, MS, 13-

1019 Scarlett Drive, Oxford, MS 38655   Covenant
E-mail: jmcguiregc@hotmail.com
College Hill Presbyterian Church – 662-234-5020

McHeard, Kenneth – w Lisa; chdn T.J., Charis; SUNY, BS; MidABTS, MDiv; DRS cand; O Jun 11, 06, NYS Pby; astp First P Ch, Schenectady, NY, 06-10; p Reformed P Ch, Duanesburg, NY, 10-

110 Elmer Avenue, Schenectady, NY 12308 – 518-275-7528   New York State
E-mail: kmcheard@gmail.com
Reformed Presbyterian Church – 518-895-2448

McIntosh, David L. Jr. – b Florence, SC, Aug 31, 73; f D. Lawrence; m Frances Bloodworth; w Amie Elizabeth Augustine, Columbia, SC, Dec 28, 96; chdn Rachael, Benjamin, Jonathan, David; ClemU 95, BA; CTS 99, MDiv; L Jul 99, Cal Pby; O Feb 24, 02, Cal Pby; int Twin Oaks P Ch, Ballwin, MO, 97-00; int Woodruff Road P Ch, Simpsonville, SC, 00-01, astp 02-05; op Hartsville P Msn, Hartsville, SC, 05-07; p 07-

961 Russell Road, Hartsville, SC 29550 – 843-383-8968   Pee Dee
E-mail: HartsvillePCA@roadrunner.com
Hartsville Presbyterian Church – 843-260-3208

McIntyre, Darrell Glenn – b Waxahathie, TX, Dec 13, 57; f Glenn; m Irma Remundo; w Patricia Henson, Savannah, GA, Mar 21, 96; chdn Duncan Glenn, Bethan Nicole; CBC 76-80, BA; RTS 81-85, MDiv, MCE; O Feb 86, Cal Pby; medu Westminster P Ch, Rock Hill, SC, 86-87; ap Grace Community Ch, Palm Harbor, FL, 87-89, wc 89-96; yp Christ Comm P Ch, Clearwater, FL, 96-99; p Westminster P Ch, Gainesville, TX, 99-

305 East Scott Street, Gainesville, TX 76240 – 940-612-3509   North Texas
Westminster Presbyterian Church – 940-665-5164

McKay, David Glenn – b Grove City, PA; w Margaret Ann Mechenbier; chdn Beth Ann, Katherine Grace, Daniel Walter, Timothy David; ThielC 71-73, BA; GCTS 74-77, MDiv; O Aug 14, 77, Asc Pby; p First Chr Ch, Newton, NH, 75-77; op Greensburg Ch, PA, 77-80; p Cov Ch, Greensburg, PA, 80-82; srp Grace P Ch, Indianapolis, IN, 82-

7159 Wynter Way, Indianapolis, IN 46250-2745   Central Indiana
E-mail: dave@gracepca.org
Grace Presbyterian Church – 317-849-1565

McKee, George H. – p Faunsdale P Ch, Faunsdale, AL, 05-; p First P Ch, Uniontown, AL, 06-

PO Box 5, Faunsdale, AL 36738 – 334-628-6103   Warrior
Faunsdale Presbyterian Church – 334-628-4219
First Presbyterian Church – 334-628-3731

McKee, James Rogers – b Beaver Falls, PA, Oct 6, 53; f Rogers James; m Dorthy Margret Hughes; w Pamela Christine Ault, Tampa, FL, Jul 28, 74; chdn Somer Christine, Amber Dawn; BelC 71-75, BA; WTS 75-76; RTS 76-79, MDiv, MCE; O Nov 79, CentFL Pby; ev Carrollwood Msn, Tampa, FL, 79-82; ap Westminster P Ch, Jacksonville, FL, 82-84; medu Briarwood P Ch, Birmingham, AL, 84-87; ap Kirk of the Hills P Ch, St. Louis, MO, 87-90; ascp Chapelgate P Ch, Marriottsville, MD, 90-96; asst MTW, 96-98; ob WHM, 98-04; astp Hunt Valley Ch, Hunt Valley, MD, 04-09; ascp, exec p Chapelgate P Ch, Marriottsville, MD, 09-; co-auth *Discipling by Grace*; auth *Stories of Grace*

4002 Chariots Flight Way, Ellicott City, MD 21042 – 410-302-3550   Chesapeake
E-mail: jmckee@chapelgate.org
Chapelgate Presbyterian Church – 410-442-5800

McKeen, Jeremy – O Sept 20, 09, Glfstrm Pby; op Truth Point Ch, West Palm Beach, FL, 10-13, p 13-

6473 Paradise Cove, West Palm Beach, FL 33411   Gulfstream
E-mail: pastor@truthpoint.org
Truth Point Church

McKellan, Mark – Chap USArmy, 11-

2503 East Arnold Avenue, Joint Base MDL, NJ 08641 – 609-723-6849   South Texas
E-mail: mark.mckellen@us.af.mil
United States Army

McKelvey, Michael – ob prof RTS, 15-

535 Florence Drive, Madison, MS 39110   Mississippi Valley
E-mail: mmckelvey@rts.edu
Reformed Theological Seminary – 601-923-1600
5422 Clinton Boulevard, Jackson, MS 39209

McKenzie, John – p First P Ch, Lexington, MS, 06- 13; p West Hills P Ch, Knoxville, TN, 13-

6501 Silver Fox Lane, Knoxville, TN 37090 – 865-924-7744   Tennessee Valley
E-mail: johnemckenzie@me.com
West Hills Presbyterian Church – 865-693-2031

McKeon, Thomas Vincent Jr. – b Quincy, MA, Jun 28, 57; f Thomas V. Sr; m Joan Frances Freeth; w Sandra Ruth Grasse, Ft. Collins, CO, Jan 3, 87; chdn Scott Thomas, Emily Michelle, Matthew John, Elizabeth Hannah; CSU 86, BS; RTS 91, MDiv; L Jan 31, 92; O Mar 7, 93, SoTX Pby; astp Covenant P Ch, Harlingen, TX, 91-94; p Grace P Ch, McAllen, TX, 94-

800 West Jonquil Avenue, McAllen, TX 78501 – 956-618-4909   South Texas
E-mail: mckeons@awesomenet.org
Grace Presbyterian Church – 956-631-2375

McKeown, Timothy Allen – b Orangeburg, SC, Feb 3, 47; f Thomas Oneal; m Barbara Jeanne Brouillard; w Rebecca Sue Jackson, El Paso, TX, Jan 12, 74; chdn Kevin Dale, Shannon Elizabeth, Catherine Jeanne, Elizabeth Joy; USC 69, BS; RTS 77, MDiv; O Jul 3, 77, SFL Pby; ev SFL Pby, 77-78; mis MTW, Ecuador, 78-89; mis MTW, Colombia, 89-94; Dir MTW, Andean Region, 94-99; coord MNA, multi-cultural church planting, 99-05; coord MNA, Hispanic American Min, 05-10; ob exec dir RTS Houston, 10-18; hr 12; "Peace If Not Safety," *World Magazine*, 4/11/98

8110 Brighton Place Court, Houston, TX 77095 – 832-593-4055   South Florida
E-mail: tamrsm@gmail.com
HR

McKie, David A. – b Christchurch, NZ, Jun 16, 53; f William John; m Mary Naomi Burgess; w Beverley Nance King, Christchurch, New Zealand, Jan 25, 75; chdn Sarah Catherine, Hannah Joy; LincU 72-75, BS, 76-77, MS; WTS 88-91, MDiv; O Oct 13, 91, SoCst Pby; ob chp, ev New Zealand for SoCst Pby, 92-

14 Delta Way, Brookhaven, Christchurch 8006, NEW ZEALAND   South Coast
E-mail: davemckie@soiltech.co.nz

MINISTERIAL DIRECTORY

McKillop, William – b Kingston, Jamaica, Aug 5, 60; f John; m Doris; w Sherry; chdn Caleb, Zachary, Gabrielle; TNTC 86, BS; CBS 99, MDiv; O Oct 04, SFL Pby; astp Pinelands P Ch, Miami, FL, 00-07; ob mis Ministries in Action, Miami, 07-13; astp New City Flwsp, Chattanooga, TN, 13-

2400 Ivy Street, Chattanooga, TN 37404 – 423-629-1421   Tennessee Valley
E-mail: billymckillop@gmail.com
New City Fellowship – 423-629-1421

McKinney, Daniel – ascp Jordan P Ch, UT, 06-08; op West Side P Ch, Salt Lake City, UT, 08-14; astp North Shore Flwsp, Chattanooga, TN, 14-17

35 McClelland Street, Salt Lake City, UT 84105   Northern California

McKnight, Charles Alexander III – O Oct 11, 15, CentCar Pby; astp Christ Central Ch, Charlotte, NC, 15-; op West Charlotte Ch, Charlotte, NC, 17-

2215 Dundeen Street, Charlotte, NC 28216 – 704-609-5492   Central Carolina
E-mail: charles@christcentralchurch.com
Christ Central Church – 704-608-9146
West Charlotte Church – 980-277-0304

McLaughen, Jeremy Heath – b Chattanooga, TN, Jun 2, 83; f James Hunter; m Jerry Ann Hufstetler; w Jane Fishburne Haddow, Litchfield, SC, Jun 11, 05; chdn Mary Ladson; FurU 05, BA; RTSNC 13, MDiv; O Oct 6, 13, CentCar Pby; campm RUF, UNCChar, 13-

5403 McChesney Drive, Charlotte, NC 28269 – 864-525-2536   Central Carolina
E-mail: heathmclaughen@gmail.com
PCA Reformed University Fellowship

McLaughlin, Cole – w Teressa Gutwein; chdn Micah, Eli, Emory, Adeline; UNC 97, BS; RTSNC 07, MDiv; campm CCC, 98-13; srp Peace P Ch, Cary, NC, 13-

102 Cochet Court, Cary, NC 27511 – 919-564-6689   Eastern Carolina
E-mail: cole@peacepca.org
Peace Presbyterian Church – 919-467-5977

McLaughlin, Michael G. – w Charlotte Collison, Jan 3, 98; chdn Connor Michael, Kelly Christine, Aiden James; CTS, MDiv; O Nov 17, 02, NoTX Pby; astp Redeemer P Ch, McKinney, TX, 02-03; op Crossroads Flwsp (PCA), Albuquerque, NM, 03-10; p 10-13; srp Grace P Ch of St. Charles Co, St. Charles, MO, 13-

45 Ashlawn Court, St. Charles, MO 63304 – 636-399-5059   Missouri
E-mail: mikemclaughlin100@gmail.com
Grace Presbyterian Church of St. Charles County – 636-926-2955

McLaughlin, Seth – astp All Souls Flwsp, Decatur, GA, 11-14; mis MTW, 15-

PCA Mission to the World   Metro Atlanta

McLeod, Joseph F. – p Calvary P Ch, Mize, MS, 14-

908 SCR 59, Mize, MS 39116   Grace
E-mail: joeymcleod25@yahoo.com
Calvary Presbyterian Church – 601-938-7934

McMahan, Stanley Keith, Jr. – O Jun 8, 14, SWFL Pby; ascp Trinity P Ch, Lakeland, FL, 14-; op Greater Hope Ch, Mulberrry, FL, 17-

1201 Carolina Avenue, Mulberry, FL 33860 – 863-430-5435   Southwest Florida
E-mail: stan@greaterhopemulberry.org
Trinity Presbyterian Church – 863-603-7777
Greater Hope Church – 863-430-5435

McManigal, Daniel Wayne – b Fullerton, CA, Jan 30, 71; Biola 98, BA; WSCAL 01, MA; ChristC, Sydney 16, PhD; p Covenant Grace OPC, Roseburg, OR, 05-09; p Grace United Ref Ch, Portland, OR, 09-12; p Hope P Ch, Bellevue, WA, 13-

23720 77th Avenue West, Edmonds, WA 98026   Pacific Northwest
E-mail: dwmcmanigal@gmail.com
Hope Presbyterian Church – 425-454-1247

McMillan, Gary D. – b Las Cruces, NM, Jul 15, 55; f Arnold D; m Joy Ann Drum; w Michele S. Mobley, Gardena, CA, Dec 21, 76; chdn Jonathon, Matthew, Christopher, Michael; NMSU 73-77, BS; SCS 91-93, MDiv; L Jan 93, SW Pby; L Oct 93, Cov Pby; O Mar 6, 94, Cov Pby; ascp Bible Bapt Ch, Astoria, OR, 89-91; int El Paso, TX; int University P Ch, Las Cruces, NM, 93; p Trinity Flwsp Ch, Sherwood, AR, 94-99; astp Providence P Ch, Albuquerque, NM, 99-05; op Providence P Ch-Farmington, Farmington, NM, 99-05, p 05-; p Providence P Church-Durango, Durango, CO, 05-

1305 Amsden Drive, Farmington, NM 87401-3587 – 505-326-2283   Southwest
E-mail: garyfarmington@aol.com
Providence Presbyterian Church-Farmington, NM – 505-326-4878
Providence Presbyterian Church-Durango, CO

McMullen, Jeff – ob mis Serge, 07-

750 Maple Avenue, Glenside, PA 19038 – 443-223-1304   Susquehanna Valley
E-mail: jeff.mcmullen@gmail.com
Serge

McNeal, Adam Thomas – b Cincinnati, OH, Jan 1, 88, Jul 7, 12; chdn Anne Catharine; Boyce 10, BA; WTS 15, MDiv; O Oct 7, 18, SWFL Pby; ascp Covenant P Ch, Lakeland, FL, 18-

4515 Hallamview Lane, Lakeland, FL 33813 – 513-312-3463   Southwest Florida
E-mail: adam@covenantlakeland.org
Covenant Presbyterian Church – 863-646-9631

McNeely, David – b Aug 28, 70; f Hal Eugene; m Betty Armfield; w Judith Smyth, Rome, GA, Oct 14, 95; chdn Samuel Dawson, Smyth Marcum, Davis Armfield, Emerson King, Sawyer Scott Begidu, Wyatt Elvington Mussie; CC 10, BA; MetAtlSem 10, MDiv; O Oct 20, 11, MetAtl Pby; astp Perimeter Ch, Johns Creek, GA, 11-16; srp Wildwood P Ch, Tallahassee, FL, 16-

5960 Ox Bottom Manor Drive, Tallahassee, FL 32312   Gulf Coast
E-mail: dmcneely@wildwoodtlh.com
Wildwood Presbyterian Church – 850-894-1400

McNeely, Hal Eugene – b Mooresville, NC, Feb 11, 42; f George Berry M; m Winnie Clodfelter; w Elizabeth Armfield, Black Mt, NC, Oct 24, 65; chdn Hal Eugene Jr, David Andrew, Paul Berry; MitC 63, dipl; BelC 65, BA; RTS 70, MDiv; O Jul 26, 70, CMS Pby; p First P Ch, Union, MS, 70-73; moy Granada P Ch, Coral Gables, FL, 73-77; ap Westminster P Ch, Rock Hill, SC, 77-78; astp Trinity P Ch, Montgomery, AL, 78-95; astp First P Ch, Macon, GA, 95-06; p Frank P Ch, Crossnore, NC, 06-

PO Box 39, Jonas Ridge, NC 28641 – 828-733-8777   Western Carolina
E-mail: bettyandhal@icloud.com
Frank Presbyterian Church

McNerney, Christopher – O Oct 13, 18, EPA Pby; astp Gracepoint Ch, Erdenheim, PA, 18-

2617 Miriam Avenue, Roslyn, PA 19001 – 201-388-3425　　　　　　　　Eastern Pennsylvania
Gracepoint Church – 215-326-9155

McNicoll, John S. – b Buffalo, NY, Oct 8, 40; f Alfred M; m Gladys Kehrer; w Diana Andrews, Ft Lauderdale, FL, Aug 1, 64; chdn Andrea (Beaver), Pamela, John, Daniel, Matthew; UBuf 58-59; BroCJC 60-64; FAU 65, BS; RTS 70, MDiv; WTS 86, DMin; O Aug 16, 70, Enre Pby; p McCarter Ch, Greenville, SC, 70-73; p Westm Ch, Seabrook, TX, 73-82; ap Kendall P Ch, Miami, FL, 83-88; p Hazelwood P Ch, Hazelwood, NC, 88-91; chp, op Crossroads P Ch, Middletown, DE, 91-94, p 94-99; op Amelia PCA Msn, Fernandina Beach, FL, 99-04; astp Crossgate Ch, Seneca, SC, 05-07; ss Dacusville PC, Dacusville, SC, 07-09; chp, ev St. George, UT, 09-12; hr 12

13916 SE 94 Avenue, Summerfield, FL 34491 – 864-985-9037　　　　　　　　Calvary
HR

McNutt, John Douglas – O Oct 31, 10, NoCA Pby; astp Hidden Valley P Ch, Draper, UT, 10-11; op Gospel P Ch, Riverton, UT, 11-16, p 16-

10624 South Harvest Pointe Drive, South Jordan, UT 84009 – 801-899-5454　　　Northern California
E-mail: jdm98_99@yahoo.com
Gospel Presbyterian Church – 801-899-5454

McQuitty, Timothy James – b Eden, NC, Aug 24, 61; f Eric; m Dorothy Dreher; w Dana Ellis, Troy, AL, Jun 4, 88; chdn Eric, Susannah, Samuel, Hattie, Calvin; CC 83, BA; RTS 89, MDiv, 91, MA; L May 91, Pot Pby; O Mar 22, 92, Pot Pby; moy First P Ch, Yazoo City, MS, 86-87; int, moy First P Ch, Troy, AL, 87-88; moy Grenada P Ch, Grenada, MS, 89-90, ss Pine Ridge P Ch, Natchez, MS, 90; moy Aisquith P Ch, Baltimore, MD, 91, astp 92-94; p Brent P Ch, Brent, AL, 94-96; astp, moy Eastwood P Ch, Montgomery, AL, 97-99, ascp 99; p First P Ch, Troy, AL, 99-03; p Trinity P Ch, Cleveland, TN, 03-08; p Emmanuel P Ch, Franklin, NC, 08-

233 Arrow Wood Lane, Franklin, NC 28734 – 828-371-3152　　　　　　　　Western Carolina
E-mail: mcquittyc@aol.com
Emmanuel Presbyterian Church – www.emmanuelpresbyterian.org

McRae, Bruce Harold – b Levitown, PA, Sept 23, 61; f D. Harold; m Grace Tough; w Katherine Robertson, Ft Wayne, IN, Jun 1, 85; chdn Calli, Colin, Bonnie; CC 79-82; WashU 82-83, BA; WTS 84-86, MDiv; FulTS 95, DMin; GSU 02, MBA; L May 9, 86, Phil Pby; O Oct 16, 86, Pby of the South (OPC); ap Redeemer OPC, Atlanta, GA, 86-88; p Cornerstone Comm Ch, Artesia, CA, 88-93; p Brookwood P Ch, Snellville, GA, 94-00; admin ASMT, 00-02; ascp East Lanier Comm Ch, Buford, GA, 03; ascp, exec p Ch of the Redeemer, Atlanta, GA, 04-06; adj prof RTSA, 03-; admin GCP, Suwanee, GA, 08-13; dir dev PCARBI, 13-15; ip Parkview Ch, Lilburn, GA, 16; p Ingleside P Ch, Lawrenceville, GA, 17-

483 Cricket Ridge Court, Lawrenceville, GA 30044 – 770-985-9913　　　　　　Metro Atlanta
E-mail: bruce@inglesidepca.org
Ingleside Presbyterian Church – 770-978-3555

McRae, Philip Edward – b Waynesboro, MS, Jun 3, 50; f Samuel Vidmer; m Mary Alabama Bagby; w Carolyn Beatrice Jerome, Greenville, MS, May 11, 73; chdn Philip Christopher, Patrick Carey, Jason Ryan, Samuel Jedidiah, David Jeremiah; JCJC 70, AA; MSU 73, BS; TrSU; RTS 81, MDiv; L 78, GulCst Pby; O Jul 19, 81, Cov Pby; p Shongalo P Ch, Vaiden, MS, 81-83; p Blackmonton P Ch, Vaiden, MS, 81-83; p Bay Springs P Ch, Bay Springs, MS, 84-98, wc 98-99; ss Calvary P Ch, Mize, MS, 99-00; p Waynesboro P Ch, Waynesboro, MS, 01-10; p Blackmonton P Ch, Vaiden, MS, 10-; p Shongalo P Ch, Vaiden, MS, 10-

PO Box 13, McCarley, MS 38943　　　　　　　　　　　　　　　　　Mississippi Valley
E-mail: nanamac@bellsouth.net
Blackmonton Presbyterian Church – 662-464-9311
Shongalo Presbyterian Church – 662-464-9311

McRoberts, Claude E. III – b Jackson, MS, May 31, 64; f C. Eugene, Jr; m Nan Dunklin (d); w Betsy Berry, Tunica, MS, Jul 6, 91; chdn Claude Eugene IV, Nan Neely, Abigail Berry; UMS 86, BA; RTS 90, MDiv; L Oct 87; O Oct 91, Cov Pby; astp Main Street P Ch, Columbus, MS, 91-92, ascp 92-94; srp First P Ch, Clarksdale, MS, 94-99; headm P Day Sch, 94-99; srp Trinity P Ch, Montgomery, AL, 99-

2113 Bowen Drive, Montgomery, AL 36106   Southeast Alabama
E-mail: cmcroberts@knology.net; cmcroberts@trinitypca.org
Trinity Presbyterian Church – 334-262-3892

McSevney, Ian S. – b Trinidad, BWI, Feb 14, 43; f Walter Gebhardt; m Mary Constance Lake; w Joy Alicia Delfosse, Kingston, Jamaica; UCam; JamaicaTS 74-76, ThB; WTS 77-79; KTS 92-94, MDiv, 96-99, DMin; O Oct 11, 73, Missionary Ch, Jamaica; Recd PCA Oct 22, 98, SFL Pby; p Missionary Chs in West Indies, PA, FL; p Presbyterian Ch of Boatswain Bay, 98-03; astp Coral Ridge P Ch, Ft. Lauderdale, FL, 06-14; hr 14

1470 NW 17th Street, Homestead, FL 33030-2842 – 954-253-0880   South Florida
HR

McVicar, Ryan – ascp Knox P Ch, Harrison Township, MI, 10-12; op New City P Ch, Royal Oak, MI, 12-15, p 15-

1232 Woodsboro Drive, Royal Oak, MI 48067   Great Lakes
E-mail: ryan.mcvicar@newcitypc.org
New City Presbyterian Church – 248-808-2523

McWilliams, Barry – w Marianne; chdn Paul, Sarah, David (d); CC 72, BA; CTS 75, MDiv; L Feb 75; O Sept 75, RPCES; p Dodge Ref P Ch, Dodge, ND, 75-77; p Concord P Ch, Waterloo, IL, 77-79; astp Chapel Hill P Ch, Lake Stevens, WA, 80-95, wc 96-98; astp Chapel Hill P Ch, Lake Stevens, WA, 98-03; hr 06

1609 Lombard Avenue, Everett, WA 98201-2047 – 425-252-2687   Pacific Northwest
E-mail: eldrbarry@eldrbarry.net
HR

McWilliams, David Brian – b Macon, GA, Jan 14, 56; f Ernest E.; m Betty Jean Russell; w Vicky Flesher, Macon, GA, Dec 13, 74; chdn Patrick Evan; MerU 81, BA; WTS 83, MAR, 84, MDiv; UWales 00, PhD; L Jan 81, CentGA Pby; O Jul 84, CentGA Pby; p Trinity P Ch, Elberton, GA, 84-87; ap Covenant P Ch, Lakeland, FL, 87-91, srp 91-01; adj prof KTS; ob assoc prof WTSTX, 01-03; srp Covenant P Ch, Lakeland, FL, 03-; adj prof WTS, 06-; adj prof RedTS, 09-15; brd mbr, GPTS, 17-; "The Covenant Theology of the Westminster Confession of Faith and Recent Criticism," 91; "Something New Under The Sun?" *Westminster Theological Journal*, 92; "Christ Alone," *Modern Reformation*, Sept/Oct, 99; rev art "The Nonviolent Atonement," *Westminster Theological Journal*, 02; art "When Curse Turns to Blessing," (electronic); "Calvin's Theology of Certainty" in *Resurrection and Eschatology: Essays in Honor of Richard B. Gaffin Jr.; Galatians: A Mentor Commentary*, 09; art "The Accused: J. Gresham Machen," *Mandate*, Nov/Dec 09; *Hebrews: The Lectio Continua Expository Commentary Series;* "The Free Offer of the Gospel" *Puritan Reformed Journal, 10,1* (18) pp. 57-90

2668 Highlands Vue Parkway, Lakeland, FL 33812 – 863-619-5606   Southwest Florida
Covenant Presbyterian Church – 863-646-9631
Westminster Theological Seminary

Mead, Jerry C. – b Salem, OH, Dec 13, 52; f Dewey C.; m Parthenia M. Weaver; w Linda Louise Patchen, Youngstown, OH, Jul 19, 75; chdn Rebecca Ann, Geoffrey Robert, Gregory Peter; YSU 70-79; Purdue 80-84, BA; CTS 85-89, MDiv; RPTS 15, DMin; L Jul 8, 89; O Sept 30, 90, Asc Pby; int Cornerstone P Ch, Youngstown, OH, 88-89; ob p Martinsburg P Ch (Indep), Bruin, PA, 90-98; p Pilgrim P Ch, Martinsburg, WV, 98-18; hr 18

9953 Back Creek Valley Road, Hedgesville, WV 25427 – 304-582-9344   Potomac
HR

Means, Matthew – w Kelli; chdn Emma-Kate, Adyson, Judson; VSC, BA; RTS, MA; O Nov 14, 04, NGA Pby; First P Ch, Augusta, GA, 95-98; Mitchell Road P Ch, Greenville, SC, 98-01; wrshp ldr Christ Comm Ch, Kennesaw, GA, 01-04; p South Point Ch, McDonough, GA, 05-11; ob 11-

Address Unavailable   Metro Atlanta
E-mail: matt_means@juno.com

Medlock, Jonathan B. – w Laurabeth; chdn Andrew, Jack, Chloe, Molly, Sam, Xander; OgleU 92, BA; SamU 95, JD; CTS 05, MDiv; O Sept 11, 05, MO Pby; astp Covenant P Ch, St. Louis, MO, 05-10; p Trinity P Ch, San Luis Obispo, CA, 10-

1358 Kentwood Drive, San Luis Obispo, CA 93401 – 805-234-8001   Northern California
E-mail: jon@trinityslo.org
Trinity Presbyterian Church – 805-545-8472

Meek, James Allison – b Birmingham, AL, Jul 27, 50; f J.R.S. Jr.; m Hazel E. Suter; chdn Allison Starr (Plato), Anastasia Elizabeth (Smith), Stephanie Judith (Sipes); RU 72, BA; WTS 76, MDiv, 81, ThM; ConcS 05, PhD; L Jan 76, Phil Pby (RPCES); O Oct 81, LA Pby, ev 81-82; p Covenant P Ch, Lafayette, LA, 83-90; sc LA Pby, 89-90; CTS assoc DnAc 90-95, dn acad admin 95-98, asst prof 95-03, dean admin 99-00, assoc DnAc 00-03; wc 03-06; asst to pres, Lock Haven U, 06-11; Dean ErskineTS, 12-14; hr 17; *Discover Life* (small group study guides); co-auth *Study Guide for Licensure and Ordination Exams;* "The Riches of His Inheritance," *Presbyterion* 28 (02): 34–46; "The New Perspective on Paul: An Introduction for the Uninitiated," *Concordia Journal* 27 (01): 208–33; "Connecting Faith and Vocational Discipleship at Covenant Theological Seminary" (with Donald C. Guthrie), *Theological Education* 38 (01): 73–81; "Evaluation: Context, Lessons, Methods," *Theological Education* 35 (98): 13–28; *The Gentile Mission in Old Testament Citations in Acts,* 09

612 Laurens Drive, Anderson, SC 29621 – 864-353-0782   Susquehanna Valley
E-mail: jmeek@onegreatstory.com
HR

Meeks, Brandon L. – O Jun 3, 12, CatVal Pby; ascp Shearer P Ch, Mooresville, NC, 12-14; wc 14-15; astp Christ P Ch, Clarkesville, GA, 15-; ascp 16-18; wc

372 Abbington Way, Clarkesville, GA 30523 – 704-662-2737   Georgia Foothills
E-mail: blmeeks@hotmail.com

Meenan, William – O Dec 3, 17, MSVal Pby; astp Highlands P Ch, Ridgeland, MS, 17-

507 Post Oak Place, Madison, MS 39110   Mississippi Valley
E-mail: billy@highlandspca.org
Highlands Presbyterian Church – 601-853-0636

Meinen, John William Peter – b Ontario, Canada, Jan 12, 82; w Megan, Hilton Head Island, SC, Aug 28, 10; UCO 04, BA; GCTS 12, MDiv; O Aug 4, 12, NNE Pby; campm RUF, UVT, 12-

63 Greene Street, Burlington, VT 05401 – 802-922-4202   Northern New England
E-mail: john.meinen@ruf.org
PCA Reformed University Fellowship

Meiners, Paul Richard – b Philadelphia, PA, Dec 29, 49; f Harry H. Jr.; m Betty Jean Fuller; w Elizabeth Ann Mahlow, Annapolis, MD, Jun 10, 72; chdn Lourinda Ann (Hersman), William Harry, Sarah Jean (Ward), Margaret Louise, Anna Elizabeth; CC 72, BA; WTS 76, MDiv; L 75, DMV Pby; O Oct 76, GrPl Pby (RPCES); p RP Ch, Underwood, ND, 76-79; mis MTW, (WPM), Kenya, Africa, 79-03; asc dir Africa, 87-95; MTW, Africa & Middle East, reg dir, 95-05; mis MTW, England, 03-; ldr Mbr Care, Europe, 05-; "Pursuing Sustainable Ministry" *Looking Forward* (MTW)

c/o Mission to the World – 44 (0) 79 1030 1949   Siouxlands
E-mail: paul@paulandliz.net
PCA Mission to the World

Meintjes, Rolf – ascp Redeemer P Ch, McKinney, TX, 06-15; ascp Rocky Mountain Comm Ch, Billings, MT, 15-17, p 17-

E-mail: rolf@rmccmontana.org Rocky Mountain
Rocky Mountain Community Church – 406-259-7811

Melton, Tim – astp Surfside P Ch, Myrtle Beach, SC, 11-14; ascp 14-

5041 Capulet Circle, Myrtle Beach, SC 29588 – 843-997-8862 Pee Dee
Surfside Presbyterian Church – 843-650-2020

Mendis, Douglas D. – b New York City, NY, Dec 22, 47; f Leopold A. Sr.; m Ida Mae Walker; w Rebecca J. Peters, St. Louis, MO, Aug 10, 85; chdn Michael C; NYU 69, BE; CTS 87, MDiv; L Aug 21, 88; O Aug 21, 88, MO Pby; astp Memorial P Ch, St. Louis, MO, 90-; Chap USAR; "The Sixth Commandment and the Church's Response to Acquired Immune Deficiency (AIDS)," *Presbyterion: Covenant Seminary Review*, Spring (87)

1818 O'Connell Avenue, Overland, MO 63114 – 314-426-5253 Missouri
E-mail: dougmendis@gmail.com
Memorial Presbyterian Church – 314-721-0943

Mercer, Bradford – astp Fifth Street P Ch, Tyler, TX, 98-99; astp First P Ch, Jackson, MS, 99-08; p Westminster P Ch, Greenwood, MS, 08-11; astp Highlands P Ch, Ridgeland, MS, 11-13; ascp 13-

39 Moss Woods Place, Madison, MS 39110 Mississippi Valley
E-mail: bradfordmercer@gmail.com
Highlands Presbyterian Church – 601-853-0636

Mercer Sr., Trell James – b Kolin, LA, Jul 27, 39; f Frank C (d); m Sybil White; w Janet Marie Vincent, Pomona, CA, Jan 30, 60 (2) Joyce Aree Cook, San Diego, CA, Nov 13, 09; chdn TJ Jr., Traci, Jessie, Glenda; LATU 67-70, BA; RTS 70-74, MDiv; L Jun 3, 75; O Jul 27, 75, MSVal Pby (ARP); p Sharon, Brighton, TN, (ARP), 75-76; supt Dunlap Home for Children, 75-76; ev Cov Pby, 77-79; ap Rancho Comm. Ch, 83-90; wc 90-91; Chap Riverside Cnty Sheriff's Dept, Riverside, CA, 92-04; astp Coastal P Ch, Vista, CA, 91-92, ascp 92-99; p Tenaja Comm Chapel, 99-04; hr

28636 Middlebury Way, Sun City, CA 92586 – 563-370-9454 South Coast
E-mail: tjmercersr@yahoo.com
HR

Merkey, Douglas – b Salisbury, MD, Jul 21, 67; f Dale W.; m Rosalie Knight; PASU 89, BS; CTS 00, MDiv; L Aug 11, 03, MO Pby; O Aug 11, 03, MO Pby; int Christ P Ch, Marietta, GA, 97-98; astp Twin Oaks P Ch, Ballwin, MO, 00-04; ob Chap Pregnancy Resource Center; ob pres/CEO Churches for Life, 08-; staff Twin Oaks P Ch, St. Louis, MO

PO Box 411752, St. Louis, MO 63141 – 314-267-4238 Missouri
E-mail: doug@getintolife.org
Churches for Life
Twin Oaks Presbyterian Church – 636-861-1870

Messer, Merle A. – b Skowhegan, ME, Aug 30, 44; f Ralph Waldo; m Clytie Ruby Batcher; w Donna Mary Sargent, Skowhegan, ME, Sept 21, 67; chdn Stephen James, Aaron Joel; ThC 67, BS; RTS 87, MDiv, 92, DMin; L Feb 87, Gr Pby; O Oct 87, Gr Pby; p Trinity P Ch, Slidell, LA, 87-96; srp Alta Woods P Ch, Pearl, MS, 96-05; ascp Pearl P Ch, Pearl, MS, 05-06; srp 07-15; pres RITE; hr 15

125 East Water Drive, Brunswick, GA 31525 – 601-573-8973 Southwest
E-mail: merle.messer@yahoo.com
HR

Messner, Aaron David – w Nancy Jo Carlson, Wheaton, IL; chdn Nathan David, Micah Andrew, Ilsa Rebekah, Titus Alexander, Soren Elias; WheatC 96, BA; WheatGrS 99; PTS 02, MDiv; L Sep 02; O Feb 23, 03, Phil Pby; astp Tenth P Ch, Philadelphia, PA, 02-04, ascp 04-07; prof CC, 07-13; srp Westminster P Ch, Atlanta, GA, 13-

5356 Vinings Lake View SW, Mableton, GA 30126   Metro Atlanta
E-mail: a.messner@wmpca.org
Westminster Presbyterian Church – 404-636-1496

Metallides, John S. – b Greece, Aug 15, 30; f Socrates; m Sideropoulos; w Pestekides, Bedford Hills, NY, May 28, 83; chdn Kenneth John, David Theodore; BarC; NPU 61, BA; PTS 64, ThM; O Jul 64, Newark Pby; p Hillside Ch, Orange, NJ, 64-68; p Monticello Ch, NY, 68-78, wc; Mntl Hab Spec, Letchworth Vlg, 87-96; hr 96

257 Washington Street, Weymouth, MA 02188 – 781-331-1766   Metropolitan New York
HR

Metzger, William F. – b Baltimore, MD, Jan 28, 40; f Albert; m Margaret Tucker; w Suzanne Stevens, Montclair, (d); chdn Scott, Todd; DicC 61, BA; WTS 65, MDiv; L 79, RPCES; O Dec 93, Hrtg Pby; campm IVCF, UDE, 65-, IVCF SrStaff, 14-; op Friendship Ch (Msn), Newark, DE, 93-97; campm Christian InterAction, UDE, 97-; *Tell The Truth*, IVP, 81, 3rd ed, rev & exp, 02, 4th ed, 12; art "Making The Bible Your Prayer Book," *His* (79); "The Kind of Student God Uses," IV *Student Leadership Journal*, Winter (93); contr "J. I. Packer" in *More Than Conquerers*, 92; "Cliffe Knechtle," in *Ambassadors for Christ*, 94; "Evangelism: Naturally Speaking Good News", *Tabletalk Magazine*, 12

396 Briar Lane, Newark, DE 19711 – 302-368-7070   Heritage
222 South College Avenue, Newark, DE 19711
Inter-Varsity Christian Fellowship, University of Delaware
Christian InterAction, University of Delaware

Meyer, Ross – w Aislinn; chdn Nora, Silas, Baird; CC 10, BA; RTSFL 16, MDiv; ob mis Serge, England, 16-

20 Carron Close, Poplar, London E14 6NN United Kingdom   Central Florida
E-mail: rmeyer@serge.org
Serge Global, Inc.
101 West Avenue, #305, Jenkintown, PA 19046

Meyer, Timothy Charlton – b Bethesda, MD, Mar 13, 61; f Charlton G.; m Shirley Steinquest; w Julianne Befus, Grand Rapids, MI, Aug 4, 90; UMD 84, BA; ChrTS; WTS; RTS 94, MDiv; L Feb 21, 95; O Jun 18, 95, MSVal Pby; astp Alta Woods P Ch, Pearl, MS, 95-96; astp Westminster Ref P Ch, Suffolk, VA, 97-02; wc; hr 09

Address Unavailable   James River
HR

Meyerhoff, Donald Steven – b St. Louis, MO, Apr 9, 53; f Don W.; m Grace E. Bramstedt; w Gayle Kruenegel, St. Louis, MO, Mar 22, 75; chdn Kurt, Erich, Johanna, Katrina; GrinC 75, BA; CTS 78, MDiv, 90, DMin; L Oct 77, Midw Pby (RPCES); O Nov 5, 78, RkyMtn Pby (RPCES); sc RkyMtn Pby (RPCES), 79-82; p Trinity P Ch, Kearney, NE, 78-88; sc Siouxl Pby, 83-88; p Memorial P Ch, Elizabethton, TN, 88-02; sc Westm Pby, 99-02; srp Grace Evangelical P Ch, Davidsonville, MD, 02-18; hr 18

4 Strachan Place, Edgewater, MD 21037 – 410-798-5440   Chesapeake
E-mail: Dmeyer1073@aol.com
HR

Meyers, Brent – w Ellie Gospodinova; WSCAL 14, MDiv; O Mar 29, 15, SoCst Pby; ob mis MTW, Ciutat Nova, Barcelona, Spain, 15-

Carrer Santa Maria 3, 2-1, 08340 Vilassar de Mar, Barcelona Spain South Coast
E-mail: brent.meyers7@gmail.com
PCA Mission to the World

Meyers, Jeffrey J. – b St. Louis, MO, Jun 1, 57; f Jack; m Beverly Givens; w Mary Christine Moore, St. Louis, MO, Aug 4, 79; chdn Rebekah Grace, Lauren Elizabeth, Julia Bryson, Jeffrey John Jr.; UMO 75-79, BS; CTS 83-88, MDiv; ConcS 98, STM; L Jan 88, MO Pby; O Oct 9, 88, Evan Pby; ap Westminster P Ch, Huntsville, AL, 89-91; srp Covenant P Ch, Houston, TX, 91-94; srp Providence Ref P Ch, St. Louis, MO, 94-; *The Lord's Service: The Grace of Covenant Renewal Worship*, 03; *A Table in the Mist: Ecclesiastes Through New Eyes*, 06

9229 Lawndale Drive, Crestwood, MO 63126 – 314-374-5258 Missouri
E-mail: jeffmeyers@earthlink.net
Providence Reformed Presbyterian Church – 314-843-7994

Midberry, James Hugh – b Grove City, PA, Nov 4, 48; f F. Hugh; m Jane V. Patterson; w Lavonne Kathy Siebert, St. Louis, MO, Jan 19, 74; chdn Jennifer Elizabeth, Rebekah Michelle, Benjamin James; GenC 70, BA; CTS 76, MDiv; L Mar 77; O Oct 77, DMV Pby (RPCES); ap Timonium P Ch, Timonium, MD, 76-80; srp Hope Ch, Lawrenceville, NJ, 80-05; p Locktown P Ch, Flemington, NJ, 07-09 chap Life Choice Hospice, 07-16; chap ACTS Retirement Life Communities, 16-

224 Clover Hill Court, Yardley, PA 19067-5736 – 215-595-3323 New Jersey
E-mail: jimmidberry@comcast.net
ACTS Retirement Life Communities

Middlebrooks, Chad – ascp Zion P Ch, Columbia, TN, 10-18; astp Lookout Mountain P Ch, Lookout Mountain, TN, 18-

1206 Cinderella Road, Lookout Mountain, GA 30750 Tennessee Valley
E-mail: chad@lmpc.org
Lookout Mountain Presbyterian Church – 423-821-4528

Middlekauff, Mark – b Houston, TX, Mar 19, 66; f Charles; m Marilyn; w Lesley, St. Louis, MO, Oct 2, 99; chdn Grace, Lily, Ella; INU 89, BA; CTS 05, MDiv; O Sept 17, 06, MNY Pby; op Grace P Ch, Water Mill, NY, 06-14, p 14-

14 Ocean View Parkway, Southampton, NY 11968 – 631-283-0309 Metropolitan New York
E-mail: markm@gracehamptons.org
Grace Presbyterian Church – 631-726-6100

Miedema, Luke – campm RUF, NwesternU, 14-

1008 Dewey Avenue 1, Evanston, IL 60202 Chicago Metro
E-mail: luke.miedema@ruf.org
PCA Reformed University Fellowship

Mietling, Werner George – b Wilkes Barre, PA, Jan 18, 28; f George; m Lucy Luft; w Jean Miller, Chester, PA, Aug 25, 56; chdn Samuel, Susan, Margie; DetIMA 48; LawrIT 49-51; CBC 56, BBE; FTS 56-57; CTS 57-59, BD, 72, MDiv; L Apr 59; O May 60, Phil Pby (RPCES); op RP Ch, Youngstown, OH, 60; mis WPM, Chile, SA, 60-72; p Meadowview Ref P Ch, Lexington, NC, 72-80; assoc, exec dir WPM, 80-83; p Trin P Ch, Miami, FL, 83-87; p First P Ch, Dyersburg, TN, 87-94; hr 94

3690 Hickory Ridge Court, Marietta, GA 30066-2942 – 770-977-4886 Covenant
E-mail: wjmiet@aol.com
HR

MINISTERIAL DIRECTORY

Miladin, George – p New Life P Ch, La Mesa, CA, 04-05; op Grace Flwsp, Alpine, CA, 06-11; hr 11

9141 Brier Road, La Mesa, CA 91942 – 619-464-3312   South Coast
HR

Miles, Roderick – w Gwendolyn; chdn Reid, Kevin, Rick; UGA 86, BBA; RTS 04, MDiv; O Nov 04, NoCA Pby; astp CityCch of San Francisco, San Francisco, CA, 04-06; op Grace Ch of Marin, Kentfield, CA, 06-

270 Redwood Road, San Anselmo, CA 94960 – 415-730-9337   Northern California
E-mail: rod@gracemarin.org
Grace Church of Marin – 415-295-7554

Miley, Lynn – astp Westwood P Ch, Dothan, AL, 10-

410 Madison Avenue, Dothan, AL 36301 – 334-687-6357   Southeast Alabama
Westwood Presbyterian Church – 334-794-4080

Milgate, BJ – astp University P Ch, Orlando, FL, 15-17; op University Presbyterian Church of Lake Nona, FL, Orlando, FL, 15-16; ascp University P Ch, Orlando, FL, 17-

1118 California Avenue, St Cloud, FL 34769 – 941-228-1254   Central Florida
E-mail: bj@upc-lakenona.com
University Presbyterian Church – 407-384-3300

Miller, Bryan – p Spout Springs P Ch, Ripley, MS, 09-12

Address Unavailable   Covenant

Miller, Christopher Arnold – b Little Rock, AR, Jul 17, 70; f Charles H.; m Carol Elaine Skelton; w Jenny Elizabeth Payne, Houston, TX, Dec 19, 92; chdn Elliott, Madison, Garrett, Luke, Charles; RU 89-93, BA; RTS 00-02, MDiv; LigAcad 15, DMin; L Jun 23, 02, Cov Pby; O Jun 23, 02, Cov Pby; Young Life, Springdale, AR, 93-99; astp Covenant P Ch, Little Rock, AR, 99-00; chp, op Trinity Gr Ch, Bentonville, AR, 02-03, p 03-

103 NE 7th Street, Bentonville, AR 72712   Hills and Plains
E-mail: chris@trinitygrace.org
Trinity Grace Church – 479-636-9977

Miller, Craig H. – b Ocala, FL, Dec 31, 71; f Glen; m Elieen Sue Britain; w Paige Elizabeth Burns, Jackson, MS, Dec 19, 92; chdn Abby, Hunter; BelC 93, BA; RTS 97, MDiv, 97, MA; L Jan 19, 00, GrLks Pby; O May 01, GrLks Pby; ydir New Hope P Ch, Eustis, FL, 94-96; astp, yp Faith P Ch, Cincinnati, OH, 98-04; astp Centerpoint Comm Ch, Ocala, FL, 04-06; ob

158 West Santa Clara Street, Ventura, CA 93001 – 805-207-9727   Central Florida
E-mail: craigm970@yahoo.com

Miller, David Jay – b Philadelphia, PA, Sept 9, 45; f Jay W.; m Eleanor Schulze; w Judith Ann Whitted, Willow Grove, PA, Oct 23, 71; chdn Deborah, Joanna, Kristin; TempU 67, BA; WTS 70, MDiv, 87, ThM; AUBS 07, PhD; L 70; O Feb 6, 71, OPC; Recd PCA Nov 9, 92, Phil Pby; p Westm OPC, Bend, OR, 70-74, wc 92; astp Promise P Ch, Philadelphia, PA, 96-00, t Beulah Heights Bible College, Atlanta, 01-09; astp Holy Cross Ang Ch, Loganville, GA 04-09; Recd Epis Ch Bolivia, 06; Recd Anglican Orth Ch Sept 09; p Redeemer AOC, Loganville, GA, 09-12; Recd PCA Jan 14; ob Chap Hospice, Athens, GA, 09-; auth *Pentecost and the Images of the Spirit*

725 Club Drive, Athens, GA 30607 – 678-779-7490   Georgia Foothills
E-mail: djmpost45@gmail.com

Miller, Derek William – b Newton, NJ, Mar 24, 71; f David R.; m Marjorie; w Kelly Lynn Margo, Pittsburgh, PA; chdn Rachel, Rebekah, Nathanael; WCPA 95, BA; RPTSW 98, MDiv; O Mar 24, 00, RPCNA; Recd PCA Apr 15, 08, MetAtl Pby; ascp Sterling RPCNA, Sterling, KS, 00-02, p 02-07; astp St. Pauls P Ch, Atlanta, GA, 08-09; ascp Grace Ref P Ch, DuBois, PA, 10-12; p 12-

124 West Scribner Avenue, DuBois, PA 15801 – 814-603-3660   Ascension
E-mail: revdwmiller@comcast.net
Grace Reformed Presbyterian Church – 814-661-2033

Miller, Douglas Howard – b Atlanta, GA, May 23, 41; f James Howard M; m June Swagerty; w Anna Miller, Mobile, AL, Sept 7, 63; chdn Michele Hope (Sigg), Matthew Elliott; BhamSoC 59-60; HntC 63, BA; ColTS 65-66; RTS 68, MDiv; O Jun 23, 68, EAL Pby; ap First P Ch, Pike Road, AL, 68-70; p Calvary Ch, Montgomery, AL, 70-71; p Inner-City Augusta, GA, 71-75; mis MTW, France, 75-94; ob ev PEF, 94-06; hr 06

1231 10th Street Lane, NW, Hickory, NC 28601 – 828-322-3509   Gulf Coast
E-mail: dhm1968@aol.com
HR

Miller, George W. Jr. – b Gadsden, AL, Sept 9, 55; f Wayne; m Jeanette Burke; w Barbara Hauser, Decatur, AL, Aug 26, 78; chdn John-David, Julie, Sarah, Rebecca, Stephen; UAL 77, BA; RTS 82, MDiv; O Sept 82, Cov Pby; campm UMS, 82-83; campm UAR, 83-87; astp First P Ch, Macon, GA, 87-93, ss, 93-94; srp 94-

122 Arlington Row, Macon, GA 31210-2102 – 478-757-8809   Central Georgia
E-mail: chipmiller2000@yahoo.com
First Presbyterian Church – 478-746-3223

Miller, J. Dawson – b Akron, OH, Dec 20, 62; f Wallace; m Clarann; w Dayna, Akron, OH, May 26, 84; chdn Caleb, Ethan, Abigail; WheatC 81, BA; CTS 06, MDiv; ascp Concord P Ch, Columbia, IL, 08-11; ip Westminster P Ch, Vincennes, IN, 14-15; ob 16- 17; op First P Ch of Jasper, Jasper, IN, 17-

3042 Bittersweet Drive, Jasper, IN 47546   Illiana
E-mail: illianaclerk10@yahoo.com; pastordawson06@yahoo.com
First Presbyterian Church of Jasper – 812-482-4475

Miller, J. Wade – w Jill; UGA 81, BBA; GCSU 88, BBA; CTS 10, MDiv; O Oct 14, 12, MetAtl Pby; op Comm Ch Griffin, GA, 14-

PO Box 907, Griffin, GA 30224   Metro Atlanta
E-mail: miller444@sbcglobal.net
Community Church Griffin

Miller, Jay – b Florence, SC, May 17, 78; f Jeffrey Kyle; m Elizabeth Trent Felton; w Amy Marie Loushine, Augusta, GA, May 31, 03; chdn Jeffrey Grant, Lily Reese, Lyla Rose; FSU 00, BS; ErskTS 13, MDiv; O Oct 15, 13, SavRiv Pby; ydir First P Ch, Augusta, GA, 04-10; ascp Redeemer P Ch, Evans, GA, 13-

2540 Williams Few Parkway, Evans, GA 30809 – 706-513-3776   Savannah River
E-mail: jay@redeemerevans.org
Redeemer Presbyterian Church – 706-854-9707

Miller, Jeffrey David – b Needham, MA, May 15, 66; f Dr. Donald S.; m Sandra Lee Beck; w Hope Baldwin Lanier, Wilmington, NC, Sept 18, 93; chdn Jackson David, Lainey Hope, Benjamin Andrew,

Miller, Jeffrey David, continued
Jeremiah Daniel; UNC 89, BA; RTSNC 00, MDiv; L Oct 00, CentCar Pby; O Apr 01, CentCar Pby; mfam Friendly Hills P Ch, Jamestown, NC, 00-01, astp 01-03, ascp 03-; op Christ Ch Greensboro, Greensboro, NC, 11-13; p 13-

414 North Church Street, Greensboro, NC 27401 – 336-209-5659　　　　　　　　　Piedmont Triad
E-mail: jeff@ChristChurchGreensboro.org
Christ Church Greensboro – 336-209-5659

　　　Miller, Joel – op Providence Ch, Birmingham, AL, 03-09; chp McKinney, TX, 10-11; op The Summit Ch, McKinney, TX, 11-13

2256 Morning Dew Court, Allen, TX 75013　　　　　　　　　　　　　　　　　　　North Texas
E-mail: pastorjoelthesummit@gmail.com

　　　Miller, M. David – b Pensacola, FL, Jan 16, 55; f Robert W.; m Betty Lou Nixdorf; w Esther Jean Dubs, Hanover, PA, Jul 8, 77; chdn Sarah Jean (Hinch), Michelle Joy (Griffith), Sharon Naomi (Canavan), Benjamin David; LanBC 81, BS; WTS 87, MAR; L Sept 90; O Jun 8, 97, Phil Pby; int Promise P Ch, Philadelphia, PA, 89-90; op, p New Life Northeast P Ch, Philadelphia, PA, 95-01, wc 01-05; mis Serge (form WHM), Chile, 05-16; mis seeJesus, Inc., Latin America, 16-

360 Fillmore Street, Jenkintown, PA 19046 – 267-630-2697　　　　　　　　　　　Philadelphia
E-mail: davemiller@seejesus.net
seeJesus, Inc. – 215-721-3113

　　　Miller, Marc D. – O Jan 30, 11, Asc Pby; p West Erie P Ch, Erie, PA, 11-

3301 Cindy Lane, Erie, PA 16506 – 616-893-0018　　　　　　　　　　　　　　　Ascension
E-mail: westeriepca@gmail.com
West Erie Presbyterian Church – 814-504-6513

　　　Miller, Matt – O Nov 26, 17, MSVal Pby; astp First P Ch, Louisville, MS, 17-

295 East Park Street, Louisville, MS 39339　　　　　　　　　　　　　　　　Mississippi Valley
E-mail: mattm4444@gmail.com
First Presbyterian Church – 662-773-3146

　　　Miller, Mike – op Sand Harbor P Msn, Jupiter, FL, 05-08; p 08-10; astp Christ Cov P Ch, Matthews, NC, 10-13; ascp 13-

6715 Newhall Road, Charlotte, NC 28270 – 704-234-2685　　　　　　　　　　Central Carolina
E-mail: mmiller@christcovenant.org
Christ Covenant Presbyterian Church – 704-847-3505

　　　Miller, Patrick – astp New Cov P Ch, Anderson, SC, 04-05; astp Covenant P Ch PCA, Honea Path, SC, 05-07; op Redeemer P Ch, Anderson, SC, 07-10, p 10-11

103 Pinehurst Drive, Anderson, SC 29625　　　　　　　　　　　　　　　　　　　　Calvary
E-mail: patrickpca@gmail.com

　　　Miller, Paul – astp Southside Comm Ch, Corpus Christi, TX, 09-11; campm RUF, TXA&MCC, 11-15; ascp Redeemer P Ch, McKinney, TX, 15-17

6900 Red Bluff Drive, McKinney, TX 75070　　　　　　　　　　　　　　　　　　South Texas

Miller, S. Beau – b Aug 4, 64; w Tara Springfield, Sept 8, 01; chdn Cole, Phoebe; UAL 86; RTS 94, MDiv; CIU 18, DMin; O Nov 03, Evan Pby; staff CCC, OK, Europe, 87-91; astp Briarwood P Ch, Birmingham, AL, 01-14; ExecDir ACMI, 14-

6215 Haddon Avenue, Baltimore, MD 21212 – 205-908-9062   Chesapeake
E-mail: bmiller@acmi-ism.org
Association of Christians Ministering Among Internationals (ACMI) – 205-908-9062

Miller, Scott Eugene – b Shelby, MT, Aug 16, 63; f Andrew Franklin; m Barbara Helen Haven; w Christine Lugo, Orlando, FL, Mar 19, 94; UFL 89, BA; HarvU; RTS 96, MDiv; L Feb 16, 97; O Feb 16, 97, CentFL Pby; astp Covenant P Ch, Palm Bay, FL, 97, ascp 98; ss Christ P Ch, Vero Beach, FL, 97-98; chp, op West Lakes Ch-PCA, Windermere, FL, 98-03

270 East Kings Way, Winter Park, FL 32789-5711 – 407-435-5887   Central Florida
E-mail: pcashepherd@gmail.com

Milligan, William David – b Mt. Holly, NJ, Jan 18, 70; f William D.; m Edith Maude; w Sue Ellen Baker, Cleveland, OH, Jun 26, 93; chdn Walter Benjamin, Lesley Nicole, Laura Elizabeth, Kathryn, Ethan; GroCC 92, BA; GCTS 97, MDiv; L Apr 24, 99, Pitts Pby; O Mar 5, 00, Pitts Pby; p Kiski Valley P Ch, Leechburg, PA, 00-12; p Loch Raven P Ch, Baltimore, MD, 12-

9500 Hickory Falls Way, Nottingham, MD 21236 – 410-870-3837   Chesapeake
E-mail: david.milligan@comcast.net
Loch Raven Presbyterian Church – 410-661-5777

Milliken, Troy – b Waynesburg, PA, Jul 31, 67; PSU 89, BS; UMass 94, MS, 94, PhD; KTS 01, MA; RTS 03, MDiv; Chap USAR, 08-

107 Shadow Lake Drive, Clinton, MS 39206 – 724-466-6616   Mississippi Valley
E-mail: troymilliken@hotmail.com
United States Army Reserve

Mills, Brad – astp Sierra View P Ch, Fresno, CA, 12-16; op Grace Clovis P Ch, Clovis, CA, 16-

2982 Saginaw Avenue, Clovis, CA 93611   Northern California
E-mail: Braddmills@gmail.com
Grace Clovis Presbyterian Church – 559-997-5721

Mills, Larry Crawford – b Concord, NC, Aug 3, 38; f Harry Smith M; m Bertie Aldridge; w Sally Poole, Jackson, MS, Jun 6, 59; chdn Larry C Jr, Sarah Catherine, Stephen Smith, Elizabeth; BelC 61, BA; WTS 61-64; REpS 64, BD; UTSVA 64-65; O Nov 7, 65, SMS Pby; p Thomson Mem P Ch, Centreville, MS, 65-73; p Hoyte Mem Ch, Gloster, MS, 65-73; p Bethany P Ch, Centreville, MS, 65-73; coord MUS comm-PCA, 73-78; ev Honolulu, HI, 78-86; p Hilton Head P Ch, Hilton Head Island, SC, 86-89; ob admin FEBC, 89-93; exec dir Liebenzell Msn USA, Schooley's Mtn, NJ, 93-00, pal 01-03; VP LDI, Scottsdale, AZ, 00-03; ob BelC, asst to Pres, 03-14; hr 15

E-mail: mills1331@bellsouth.net   Grace
HR

Mills, Robert H. – O Mar 15, 15, SNE Pby; astp Christ The King P Ch, Cambridge, MA, 15-16; chp 16-17; op New City Flwsp, Plano, TX, 17-

2700 Polo Lane, Plano, TX 75093 – 336-409-9463   North Texas
E-mail: robbie.mills@gmail.com
New City Fellowship

MINISTERIAL DIRECTORY   445

Mills, Stuart M – b Baton Rouge, LA; w Megumi Fujioka, Zachary, LA; chdn Satomi Ruth, Samuel Takashi, Ezra Mizuki; RTS 06, MDiv; O Feb 17, 13, SELA Pby; ob mis MissionPeru, 13-

PO Box 25912, Greenville, SC 29616 – 225-330-2649   Southern Louisiana
E-mail: stuartmills@perumission.org
MissionPeru

Millward, Dan – w Laura; RTS, MA; O Apr 24, 05, GrLks Pby; p Northland Church, 01-04; p Redeemer P Ch, Traverse City, MI, 04- 13; op New City P Ch, Royal Oak, MI, 13-14; op Redemer P Ch of Detroit (form New City Midtown)

3100 Woodward Avenue, Apt 213, Detroit, MI 48201 – 313-656-4423   Great Lakes
E-mail: dan@newcitydetroit.com
Redeemer Presbyterian Church of Detroit – 313-871-8700

Milner, Benjamin – w Margie; chdn Rosabelle, Cooper; PTS 02; O Jun 04, PTri Pby; astp Redeemer P Ch, Winston-Salem, NC, 02-06, ascp 06-13; op Salem P Ch, Winston-Salem, NC, 10-13, p 13-

636 South Sunset Drive, Winston-Salem, NC 27103 – 336-724-0498   Piedmont Triad
E-mail: benjaminmilner@gmail.com
Salem Presbyterian Church – 336-724-4421

Milton, James Reid – p Grace Flwsp P Ch, Clanton, AL, 05-10; srp First P Ch, Dothan, AL, 17-

1112 Hillbrook Drive, Dothan, AL 36303   Southeast Alabama
First Presbyterian Church – 334-794-3128

Milton, Michael Anthony – b New Orleans, LA, Feb 26, 58; f Jessie Ellis (d); m Willene Dillon (d) aunt Eva Turner - lgl guard (d); w Mae Slow, Sevierville, TN, Jun 8, 85; chdn John Michael Ellis; DLI 77, dipl; MidANU 89, BA; KTS 93, MDiv; UWales 98, PhD; UNC 16, MPA; L Aug 20, 90; O Jul 16, 93, Hrtl Pby; int NewHope P Ch in America, Olathe, KS, 89-90; int Coral Ridge Ministries, Fort Lauderdale, FL, 92-93; Chap (Colonel), Command Chaplain, U.S. Military Intelligence USAR, 92-18; op, ev Redeemer P Ch, Overland Park, KS, 93-94, srp 94-97; ob admin KTS, 97-98, adj prof 97-; op Kirk O the Isles P Ch, Savannah, GA, 98-99, srp 99-02; adj prof ErskTS, 00-08; srp First P Ch, Chattanooga, TN, 02-08; pres/Chanc RTS, 08-15; ob Teaching Pastor, Truth in Action Ministries; President and CEO, Faith for Living; fnd p Trinity Chapel, Charlotte, 17-; hr 17; 1989 Award for Excellence in Leadership at Mid-America NazU; 1993 Preaching Award, KTS; 1993 Systematic Theology Award, KTS; listed *Who's Who in America*, 08-; listed Who's Who in the World, 09-; Who's Who in Religion, 09-; fndr Westm Ac, Overland Park, KS, 93; fndr/speak "The Redeeming Factor" rm, 93-95; speak "Knox Radio Bible Hour," "The Jerusalem Chamber" rm, 97-98; fndr/spkr "The Living Word" rm, 99-05; memb GA AC; memb, Bd of Dir PCA, 98-04, 07-11, vice-chair 08-11; mentor, MNA Chp Apprenticeship prog, 99-; memb Bd Dir KTS, 05-08; Founder, CEO, Faith for Living, Inc.: 01-; Teaching Pastor, Truth that Transforms with Dr. Michael Milton, 13-; founder, President and Senior Fellow, President and Senior Fellow. D. James Kennedy Institute for Reformed Leadership, 13-; Member Evangelical Theological Society, 92-; contr *Minister's Manual*; contr *Preaching: A Professional Journal*; contr *The Christian Observer;* contr *World*; contr *The Culture Project*; brd memb Twin Lakes Fellowship 03-08; memb Bd of Contr Eds, Preaching Journal, 05-; brd memb Truth in Action Ministries 13; auth journal art *"The Pastoral Predicament of Vavasor Powell (1617-1670): Eschatological fervor and its relationship to the pastoral ministry," The Journal of the Evangelical Theological Society* (00), *"'So What Are You Doing here?' The Role of the Minister of the Gospel in Hospital Visitation and, or a Theological Cure for the Crisis in Evangelical Pastoral Care," The Journal of the Evangelical Theological Society* (03); "Preaching from the Footnotes: Expository Preaching and the Challenge of Textual Criticism," *monergism.com (electronic);* member Rotary Internat'l; singer/songwriter/ perf on "He Shall Restore," 05; "Follow Your Call," 08; "Through the Open Door," 09, "Christmastime Again," 12; "The Wind and Waves," 13" auth *The Application of the Theology of the Westminster Assembly in the Ministry of the Welsh Puritan, Vavasor Powell*; *Leaving A Career to Follow a Call: A Vocational Guide to the Ordained Ministry*, 99; contr *Preaching Journal*; *Authentic Christianity and the Life of Freedom:*

Milton, Michael Anthony,continued
Expository Messages from Galatians, 05; *The Demands of Discipleship: Expository Messages from Danie,* 05;*Giving as an Act of Worship,* 06; *Following Ben; Expository Preaching for Frail Followers of Pulpit Giants; Cooperation without Compromise: Faithful Gospel Witness in a Pluralistic Age,* 07; *Hit by Friendly Fire: What to Do When Christians Hurt You;* "Engrafted, notReplaced," *Reformed Perspective Magazine,* 08; art on Christianity.com, Crosswalk.com, monergism.com, Preaching.com ; auth "Confession Out of Crisis: Historiography and Hope in the Westminster Assembly of Divines, 1643-52," in *The Hope Fulfilled: Essays in Honor of O. Palmer Robertson,* 08; *Giving as an Act of Grace; O the Deep, Deep Love of Jesus: Expositions from John 17; What God Starts, God Completes: Help and Hope for Hurting People,* 07, 2nd ed., 09; *What is the Perseverance of the Saints?* 09; *Discerning God's Call on Your Life,* 09; *Small Things, Big Things: Inspiring Stories of God's Grace,* 09; songs "I Glory in the Cross," "When Heaven Came Down," 11; auth *Songs in the Night: How God Transforms our Pain into Praise,* 11; *Hit by Friendly Fire,* 2nd ed, 11; *Silent No More: A Biblical Call for the Church to Speak to State and Culture,* 13; *Journey of a Lifetime: The New Believer's Guide to Following Jesus Christ,* 13; *Sounding the Depths: A Study on John 17;* "In Jesus' Name I Pray: Exclusivity in Public Prayer and the Restrictive Contours of Modern Civic Discourse" a paper presented to the 63rd Annual Meeting of the Evangelical Theological Society, Nov 11; contr, *ByFaith; The Secret Life of a Pastor,* 15; contr, Center for Vision and Values, Grove City College; contr, *The Gospel Coalition;* faculty member and speaker, Intercollegiate Studies Institute, 11-; member, National Religious Broadcasters, 11-present; The James Ragsdale Chair of Missions and Evangelism, Erskine Theological Seminary; Director of Strategical Leadership Initiatives, Erskine Theological Seminary, 15-; Found Dir, Senior Teaching Fellow, C.S. Lewis Institute of Charlotte and the Carolinas, 15-; auth *Lord I Want to Follow Your Call,* 17;

4006 Ainsdale Drive, Matthews, NC 28104 – 704-246-6297   Tennessee Valley
E-mail: michaelmilton@faithforliving.org
Faith for Living – 1-800-983-2051
D. James Kennedy Institute for Reformed Leadership
HR

   Min, Kyung yob – op Nachimban Ch, Buena Park, CA, 08-

1200 West Lambert Road, Brea, CA 92821 – 714-828-4750   Korean Southwest Orange County
E-mail: danielkmin@yahoo.com
Nachimban Church – 714-826-6245

   Miner, David Hugh – b Jun 20, 44; f Jack M; m Mina L. Taylor; w Eleanor Kipps Reynolds, Wheaton, IL, May 23, 70; chdn Elizabeth Grace, David William, Mary Eleanor, Ruth Hope, Katherine Ann, Carol Joanna; WheatC 66, BA; TEDS 70, MA; SIU 78, PhD; L Jan 81, RPCES; O Jul 19, 92, NJ Pby; p Covenant P Ch, Short Hills, NJ, 92-12; sc MNY Pby, 99-; hr 12; astp Wallace P Ch, College Park, MD, 14-

5811 Goucher Drive, Berwyn Heights, MD 07040 – 301-982-0463   Potomac
E-mail: davidandeleanorminer@gmail.com
Wallace Presbyterian Church
HR

   Mirabella, Thomas L. – b Washington, DC, Oct 19, 74; f John V.; m Rose Marie Merritt; w Karen Wu, Vienna, VA, Jan 3, 98; chdn Kylie Grace, Josiah Thomas, Ashley Joy, Matthias Timothy, Leighton Ann; JMU 96, BS; CTS 05, MDiv; O 07, SWFL Pby; astp Faith P Ch, Wauchula, FL, 07-08, ascp 08-09; p Trinity Flwsp Ch, Sherwood, AR, 09-13; mis MTW 13-

PCA Mission to the World   Covenant

   Mirich, Stephen, Jr. – O Dec 9, 12, CentCar Pby; astp Carolina P Ch, Locust, NC, 12-14; p Covenant P Ch, Hendersonville, NC, 14-

Covenant Presbyterian Church – 828-693-8651   Western Carolina

Mirtolooi, Bijan – O Nov 24, 13, MNY Pby; astp Redeemer P Ch of New York, New York, NY, 13-17; astp Redeemer P Ch Westside, New York, NY, 17-

120 West 86th Street, Apt. 12C, New York, NY 10024 – 908-967-9994   Metropolitan New York
E-mail: bijan.mirtolooi@redeemer.com
Redeemer Presbyterian Church Westside – 212-808-4460

Misner, James Willard – b Panama Canal Zone, Jul 29, 47; f Willard B.; m Harriet Jean Hoffman; w Sharon E Plummer, Anniston, AL, Sept 10, 71; chdn Sarah Elizabeth, Jonathan David, Joshua Benjamin; TNTU 70, BS; RTS 76, MDiv, MCE, 83; L Jul 74, War Pby; O Jul 11, 76, MSVal Pby; t First P Ch Jackson (MS) School, 76-79; t Trin P Sch, Montgomery, AL, 79-81; Cov P Ch, 81-82; Peninsula CS, 82-84; ap Covenant P Ch, Columbia, SC, 84-90; p Emmanuel Ref P Ch, McAllen, TX, 89-93; p Westminster P Ch, Greenwood, MS, 93-94, wc 94; ob admin First P Ch Chr Sch, Dyersburg, TN, 95-00, wc 00-; admin Fellowship Christian Acad, Roswell, GA, 01-; astp Cherokee P Ch, Canton, GA, 03-04, ascp 04-08; op First P Ch, Jasper, GA, 08-11; ob Chamberlain-Hunt Ac, Port Gibson, MS, 11-13; Pres CS, Hattiesburg, 13-15; hr 15

800 Sioux Lane, Hattiesburg, MS 39402   Grace
HR

Mitchell, Daniel – b Ft. Knox, KY, May 8, 69; f Carl B.; m Carolyn C.; w Mary Patricia Robinson, Chattanooga, TN, May 23, 92; chdn Claire Elisabeth, Benjamin Campbell; CC 92, BS; CTS 07, MDiv; O 09, MetAtl Pby; CEP, 07-09; astp New City Flwsp, Chattanooga, TN, 09-11, ascp 11-14; MTW, Global Youth and Family Min, 13-

113 Asbury Drive, Chattanooga, TN 37411   Tennessee Valley
E-mail: dannynmarypat@hotmail.com
PCA Mission to the World

Mitchell, H. Petrie Jr. – b Venice, FL, Jun 17, 62; f H. Petrie, Sr.; m MaryBelle Maddin; w Ruth Roslyn Green, Dallas, TX, Jun 8, 85; chdn Roger John, Charles Thomas, James Alexander, Mary-Ellen Love; MonC 80-81; KgC 81-84, BA; GCTS 84-87, MDiv; L 87; O Aug 28, 88, TNVal Pby; yp First Bapt Ch, Manchester, MA, 85-87; int, ap Christ Comm Ch, Franklin, TN, 87-91; mis MTW, Marseille, France, 90-14; mis MTW, Toulouse, France, 14-

c/o MTW   Nashville
E-mail: pierreroselyne@gmail.com
PCA Mission to the World

Mitchell, James – b Durham, NC, Apr 16, 57; f Robert P; m Vivian Magedanz; w Carla Robison, Durham, NC, Feb 9, 80; chdn Kristy Lynn, Benjamin Grant, Kate Grace; BJU 79, BA; RTS 94, MDiv; L 94; O May 7, 95, SWFL Pby; srp Open Door Bible Ch, Goldsboro, NC; int Christ Comm P Ch, Clearwater, FL, 92-94, ascp 95-96, srp 96-04; p Northside P Ch, Burlington, NC, 04-

4048 Mebane Oaks Court, Mebane, NC 27302 – 336-329-7157   Piedmont Triad
E-mail: northsidepca@juno.com
Northside Presbyterian Church – 336-226-9451

Mitchell, Scott – O Aug 9, 09, EPA Pby; campm RUF, Lehigh, 09-17; astp Trinity P Ch, Owasso, OK, 17-

Trinity Presbyterian Church – 918-516-2772   Hills and Plains

Mixon, George – b Dec 28, 62; w Martha; chdn Beth, Carrie, Jim, Nathan, Laura; FurU 85, BS; UGA 89; RTSNC 04, MDiv; vet, Griffin, GA, 89-94; Christian Vet Mission, Kenya, 94-00; mis Serge, Kenya, 04-

755 Falls Road, Rock Hill, SC 29730   Calvary
E-mail: georgetmixon@gmail.com
Serge
101 West Avenue #305, Jenkintown, PA 19046-2039

Mizelle, Stuart – ascp Clayton Comm Ch, Clayton, NC, 06-07; astp Westminster P Ch, Sumter, SC, 07-09; ascp 09-12; p 12-

2708 Powhatan Drive, Sumter, SC 29150   Pee Dee
E-mail: stuart@westminsterpca.net
Westminster Presbyterian Church – 803-773-7235

Mock, Michael David – b AZ, Aug 9, 83; f Michael Robert; m Bonnie Lorraine Piazza; w Elizabeth LaPierre, AZ, Aug 7, 04; chdn Timothy, Alethea, Charis, Joshua, Caleb; GrCC 04, BA; PhoenixSem 13, MDiv; O Jun 10, 18, CentCar Pby; ascp Cross Creek P Ch, Fayetteville, NC, 18-

3625 Sugar Cane Circle, Fayetteville, NC 28303 – 602-418-0371   Central Carolina
E-mail: pastormock@crosscreekpca.org
Cross Creek Presbyterian Church – 910-864-4031

Moehn, J. Andrew – b Aug 20, 71; w Kacey; chdn Justin, Noah, Sarah, Jennifer; TayU 93, BA; CTS 03, MDiv; O Nov 16, 03, MO Pby; astp Grace P Ch of St. Charles Co, St. Charles, MO, 03-05; p Stonebridge EPC, Perrysburg, OH, 05-07; astp Christ Comm Ch, Johnson City, TN, 07-08; p Walnut Hill P Ch, Bristol, TN, 13-

366 Carr Drive, Blountville, TN 37617 – 865-696-0802   Westminster
E-mail: andy@walnuthillchurch.org
Walnut Hill Presbyterian Church – 423-764-8729

Molicki, Eric R. – b Baltimore, MD, Mar 3, 68; f Gleb; m Barbara Ann Floyd; w Alice Wysong, Wilmington, DE, Jun 29, 91; chdn Nathan Robert, Nicholas Alexander; BucknU, BSBA; ChTS, MDiv; CTS 11, DMin; O Dec 6, 98, Pot Pby; campm RUF, TowU, 95-01, wc 01; ascp Trinity P Ch, Providence, RI, 01-06; campm RUF, BrownU, RISD, 01-06; p Wellington P Ch, Wellington, FL, 06-13; srp Murrysville Comm Ch, Murrysville, PA, 13-17; wc

3991 Murry Higlands Circle, Murrysville, PA 15668   Pittsburgh
E-mail: emolicki@gmail.com

Montgomery, Alexander Warren – O Jul 17, 01, SEAL Pby; astp Young Meadows P Ch, Montgomery, AL, 01-02; yp Mitchell Road P Ch, Greenville, SC, 02-05; wc 06-

1520 Alma Road, Columbia, SC 29209-2202   Calvary
E-mail: alexmontgomery51@hotmail.com

Montgomery, Chad S. – WheatC 97, BA; WTS 05, MDiv; SAfrTS 17, PhD; O 08, SoTX Pby; Chap USAF, 08-

6430 Rico Road, Wichita, KS 67204 – 910-987-7052   South Texas
E-mail: chadm74@hotmail.com
United States Air Force

Montgomery, John M. Jr. – b Coral Gables, FL, Apr 12, 41; f John Sr.; m Cathrine Hibben; w Linda Marion, Coral Gables, FL, Jun 29, 63; chdn John Fletcher, Linda Ann; FSU 63, BS; GCTS 75, MDiv; BethlTS 87, DMin; O May 75, UPCUSA; p Knox Ch, Minneapolis, 75-79; p Westminster P Ch, Atlanta, GA, 79-91; chp, op River Oaks P Ch, Lake Mary, FL, 91-93, p 93-10; hr; p/t astp Orangewood P Ch, Maitland, FL, 10-12; hr 12

101 Quail Run Court, Lake Mary, FL 32746-3922 – 407-323-2785   Central Florida
HR

Moon, David – ob 18-

681 Fenley Avenue, San Jose, CA 95117   Korean Capital
E-mail: davidm1983@gmail.com

MINISTERIAL DIRECTORY

Moon, James R. Jr. – b Knoxville, TN, Oct 7, 64; f James R.; m Barbara Ford; w Elizabeth Regina Kreiner, Atlanta, GA, Jun 27, 87; chdn Jake, Erica, Elysia; BerryC 86, BA; RTSFL 01, MDiv; O Dec 19, 94, Flwsp Bib Ch; yp Flwsp Bib Ch, Roswell, GA, 88-99; p Winter Park Ch of the Brethren, 00; op Crosspoint P Msn, Smyrna, GA, 01-07; p 07-14, ascp 14-15; ob Church Multiplication Ministries, Alpharetta, GA, 15-

1681 North Milford Creek Lane SW, Marietta, GA 30008 – 404-423-5466   Metro Atlanta
E-mail: jimmoonjr@gmail.com
Church Multiplication Ministries
P. O. Box 3284, Alpharetta, GA 30023

Moon, Joshua – CTS 04, MDiv; UStAnd 07, PhD; p Good Shepherd P Ch, Minnetonka, MN, 08-13; sus 13-15; wc

2805 Louisiana Avenue South, St. Louis Park, MN 55426 – 952-303-5987   Siouxlands
E-mail: moon.josh@gmail.com

Moon, Kyung Soo – astp Korean Central P Ch, Centreville, VA, 17-

10828 Clover Court, Manassas, VA 20109   Korean Capital
Korean Central Presbyterian Church – 703-815-1200

Moon, Paul Hongkuk – Recd PCA Apr 23, 92; p Korean-American PC of Arizona Msn, Glendale, AZ, 92-08; op

1429 Edgewood Avenue, Roslyn, PA 19001 – 267-331-1770   Korean Eastern
E-mail: paulhkmoon42@gmail.com

Moon, Shelby Zahnd – O Feb 12, 12, SW Pby; p Westminster P Ch, Alamogordo, NM, 12-

3002 Los Robles, Alamogordo, NM 88310   Southwest
E-mail: wpcpca88310@gmail.com
Westminster Presbyterian Church – 575-434-1851

Moon, Soonsang – astp Cheltenham P Ch, Cheltenham, PA, 17-18, ob 18-

317 West Marple Street, Ambler, PA 19012   Korean Eastern
E-mail: holymoonss@gmail.com

Mooney, Will – astp Covenant P Ch, Nashville, TN, 15-18, wc

504 Baxter Lane, Nashville, TN 37220   Nashville

Moore, Brian – O 16, GAFH Pby; astp Chestnut Mountain P Ch, Flowery Branch, GA, 16-

6339 Flat Rock Drive, Flowery Branch, GA 30542 – 770-540-9469   Georgia Foothills
E-mail: brian.moore@cmpca.org
Chestnut Mountain Presbyterian Church – 770-967-3440

Moore, Curtis – b Orlando, FL, Oct 13, 61; f Edward O.; m Judith Balzli; FSU 85, BS; RTS 98, MDiv; O, Gr Pby; astp First P Ch, Biloxi, MS, 98-03; MNA, disaster response Gulf Coast, 06-; ascp Lagniappe P Ch, Bay St. Louis, MS, 06-11; astp Willow Creek Ch, Winter Springs, FL, 13-16; ss First P Ch, Gulfport, MS, 17

950 Torrey Pine Drive, Winter Springs, FL 32708 – 407-977-7903   Grace
PCA Mission to North America – 678-825-1200

Moore, James Archie Jr. – b Mullins, SC, Oct 31, 49; f James Archie; m Clara Mae Edwards; w Glenda K Weatherly, Augusta, GA, Nov 22, 75; chdn James Archie III, Julie Claire, Barry Edwards, John Calvin McCheyne, Stephen Andrew; SECC 68-69; BapCC 71-72; CBC 72-74, BBE; RTS 75-77; O Feb 21, 78, MSVal Pby; mis Korea, 78-79; p Westminster P Ch, Martinez, GA, 79-95; p Concord P Ch, Gulf Breeze, FL, 95-99; p Greenwood P Ch, Greenwood, SC, 99-

145 Kensington Drive, Greenwood, SC 29649 – 864-344-0483   Calvary
E-mail: mail@gpc-pca.org
Greenwood Presbyterian Church – 864-942-0950

Moore, Jason – op New Creation P Ch, Wentzville, MO, 10-

312 Pleasant Meadows Drive, Wentzville, MO 63385 – 314-363-1921   Missouri
New Creation Presbyterian Church – 636-791-0201

Moore, Jay Garrett – O 18, MetAtl Pby; astp Perimeter Ch, Johns Creek, GA, 18-

5205 Craftsman Street, Johns Creek, GA 30097 – 678-457-5128   Metro Atlanta
E-mail: garrettm@perimeter.org
Perimeter Church – 678-405-2000

Moore, Joe Thomas – b Salisbury, NC, Oct 23, 52; f John Mercer; m Virginia Chadwick; w Joli, Nov 18, 78; chdn Joshua, Joanna, Joseph, John, Jason; CC 78, BA; RTS 82, MDiv, 85, MCE; O Jun 88, RCA; ascp First Ref Ch, Cedar Grove, WI, 86-89; instr Chattanooga CS, Chattanooga, TN, 99-; astp Chattanooga Valley P Ch, Flintstone, GA, 07-17

22 Bankston Avenue, Flintstone, GA 30725 – 706-820-7983   Tennessee Valley
E-mail: joemoore@ccsk12.com
Chattanooga Christian School – 423-265-6411 ext. 522
3354 Charger Drive, Chattanooga, TN 37409

Moore, John – astp First P Ch of Coral Springs, FL, 13-

First Presbyterian Church of Coral Springs – 954-752-3030   South Florida

Moore, Mark – b Harrisonburg, VA, Dec 9, 76; f Paul; m Shelby Blosser; w Jennifer Lynn Herron, Wesley Chapel, FL, Dec 7, 02; chdn Natalie, Mark, Hannah, Micah; USAFA 99, BS; KTS 08, MDiv; O Jan 20, 09, SFL Pby; Chap USAFR, 09-; chp Okinawa Covenant Msn, Japan, 09-

PSC 80 Box 21585, APO, AP 96367 – 540-414-7930   Southeast Alabama
United States Air Force Reserve
Okinawa Covenant Mission, Japan

Moore, Ryan – campm RUF, UAL, 11-15; astp Fort Worth P Ch, Fort Worth, TX, 15-17, ascp 17-

4305 Bilglade Road, Fort Worth, TX 76109   North Texas
E-mail: ryan@fortworthpca.org
Fort Worth Presbyterian Church – 817-731-3300

Moore, Scott – w Katie; chdn Emma, Jude, Camille, Luke; RTS 10, MDiv; O May 23, 10, GulCst Pby; astp Grace Comm Ch, Mobile, AL, 10-13; op Trin Family Msn, Mobile, AL, 13-

2602 Warsaw Avenue, Mobile, AL 36617 – 251-423-8238   Gulf Coast
E-mail: scott@trinityfam.org
Trinity Family Mission

Morales, Michael – ob; ascp Grace P Ch, Stuart, FL, 14-

E-mail: me3morales@yahoo.com   Gulfstream
Grace Presbyterian Church – 772-692-1995

Moran, David Leslie – b Concord, NC, Nov 15, 51; f Alfred Leslie; m Miriam Alice Coone; w Ann Lorraine Zwemer, Vero Beach, FL, Sept 4, 76; chdn Michael David, Leah Lorraine, Nathan Richard, Andrew James, Miriam Suzanne; BelC 69-74, BA; TEDS 74-78, MDiv; RTS 95, DMin; L Jan 26, 79; O May 6, 79, TX Pby; srp Oaklawn P Ch, Houston, TX, 79-98; p Key Biscayne P Ch, Key Biscayne, FL, 98-

799 Curtiswood Drive, Key Biscayne, FL 33149 – 305-361-0860   South Florida
E-mail: office@kbpc.org
Key Biscayne Presbyterian Church – 305-361-2058

Moreau, Michael Arthur – b Forest, MS, Aug 11, 59; f Henry Barton; m Sara Ruth; w Georgia Hail, Dec 27, 85; chdn Michael Arthur II, Peter Barton, Rachel Caren; ORU 77, BA; RTS 02, MDiv; O Jan 24, 04, CentCar Pby; p Goshen P Ch, Belmont, NC, 04- 13; p Providence P Ch, Murphy, NC, 13-15; p Covenant P Ch, Rockingham, NC, 16-

146 Barrett Street, Rockingham, NC 28379 – 910-434-8893   Central Carolina
E-mail: mmtulip5@bellsouth.net
Covenant Presbyterian Church – 910-817-9556

Moreland, Scott P. – O Jan 16, 16, Ill Pby; p Westminster P Ch, Vincennes, IN, 16-

1802 North 13th Street, Vincennes, IN 47591   Illiana
E-mail: sbmoreland105@gmail.com
Westminster Presbyterian Church – 812-882-2735

Moretto, Nathan – chdn Evalena; USIN, BA; UMI, MA; GCTS, MDiv; UMI, PhD cand; O Oct 1, 17, GrLks Pby; astp New City P Ch, Royal Oak, MI, 17-18, ascp 18; p Liberty Church, PCA, Owings Mills, MD, 18-

E-mail: nmoretto@libertychurchpca.org   Chesapeake
Liberty Church, PCA – 410-655-5366

Morgan, Aaron Matthew – b May 15, 78; w Rachel Marie Caruso, Jun 28, 03; chdn Elijah Matthew, Joshua Luke, Caleb Jonathan, Levi Nathaniel, Rebekah Kate; AUBS, MATS; RTSNC, MDiv; L Jan 07, Flwsp Pby; astp Redeeming Grace P Ch, Lake Wylie, SC, 08-13; ascp 13-15, srp 15-

4800 Charlotte Highway, Lake Wylie, SC 29710   Fellowship
E-mail: reformedmorgan@gmail.com
Redeeming Grace Presbyterian Church – 803-831-7533

Morgan, Davis – O Sep 14, 16, Westm Pby; campm RUF, ETNStU, 16-

2923 Newbern Drive, Johnson City, TN 37604   Westminster
E-mail: davis.morgan@ruf.org
PCA Reformed University Fellowship

Morgan, Davis – O Feb 9, 14, NoTX Pby; astp Grace Comm P Ch, Fort Worth, TX, 14-16, ascp 16-

5960 Tuleys Creek Drive, Ft. Worth, TX 76137 – 817-944-9115   North Texas
E-mail: dtmorg1607@gmail.com
Grace Community Presbyterian Church – 817-847-7766

Morgan, Gerald Goodwin – b Jackson, MS, Oct 2, 35; f Charles Fred M; m L'Marie Goodwin; w Bette Mallory, Vicksburg, MS, Jun 13, 59; chdn Deborah Jeanne, Fred Keith, Davis Kevin, Gerald Jonathon, Mallory Elisabeth; UMS 59, BBA; RTS 71, MDiv; O Apr 30, 72, CMS Pby; p St. Paul P Ch, Jackson, MS, 71-74; ap First P Ch, Gadsden, AL, 74-75; op Hattiesburg, MS, 76; p Woodland P Ch, Hattiesburg, MS, 76-82; ap Village Seven P Ch, Colorado Springs, CO, 82-87; MNA, 83-87; DnStu RTS, 87-91; MNA, 88-92; ss West P Ch, West, MS, 88-91; ascp Cedar Springs P Ch, Knoxville, TN, 91-93; dir ch rel MTW, 93-

2012 Anemone Drive, Flower Mound, TX 75028 – 662-234-9181   Tennessee Valley
E-mail: gerald.morgan@mtw.org
PCA Mission to the World – 678-935-1440

Morgan, Jeff – astp Chapel Woods P Ch, Snellville, GA, 08-10; op Monroe P Msn, Monroe, GA, 08-10; p 10-

2565 Cedar Way, Loganville, GA 30052 – 770-554-9590   Georgia Foothills
E-mail: jmorgan@monroepca.org
Monroe Presbyterian Church

Morgan, Steve – astp Comm P Ch, Moody, AL; p Grace Foothills, Tryon, NC, 17-

E-mail: morgan.steveng@gmail.com   Western Carolina
Grace Foothills – 828-338-8887

Morginsky, Matt – O Nov 4, 12, RMtn Pby; astp St. Patrick P Ch - Denver, 12-13; astp Denver P Ch, Denver, CO, 13-16; op Grace and Peace Denver, Denver, CO, 16-

3122 Merion, Denver, CO 80205 – 615-969-3372   Rocky Mountain
E-mail: matt@graceandpeacedenver.org
Grace and Peace Denver – 615-969-3372

Morris, Aaron – ascp New St. Peters P Ch, Dallas, TX, 11-14; p Hope P Ch, Portland, OR, 14-

E-mail: aaronchristianmorris@gmail.com   Pacific Northwest
Hope Presbyterian Church – 971-303-9722

Morris, Chas – O Aug 23, 09, Wcar Pby; astp Grace Comm Ch, Mills River, NC, 09-12; op Gr Blue Ridge, Hendersonville, NC, 11-12; p 12-

78 Indian Bluff Trail, Hendersonville, NC 28739 – 404-290-4555   Western Carolina
E-mail: chasmorris1@gmail.com
Grace Blue Ridge – 828-891-2006

Morris, Edward – astp Grace P Ch of the W Reserve, Hudson, OH, 13-17; ob 17-

11400 Tinkers Creek Road, Valley View, OH 44125   Ohio
E-mail: edwardmmorrisjr@gmail.com

Morris, Henry H. – b Chicago, IL, May 5, 63; f Walter F.; m Frances McNeil Newman; w Elizabeth Ann Wheat, Birmingham, AL, Aug 17, 91; chdn John Hardin, Henry Haynes, Carolyn Elizabeth; AU 81-85, BS; RTS 87-91, MDiv; O Sept 8, 91, CentGA Pby; campm RUM, MerU, 91-96; campm RUM, FSU, 96-99; op Redeemer P Ch, Florence, AL, 99-01, p 01-02; astp First P Ch, Dothan, AL, 03-09; ascp 09-

202 Montezuma Avenue, Dothan, AL 36303 – 334-791-7686   Southeast Alabama
E-mail: hmorris@firstpresdothan.com
First Presbyterian Church – 334-794-3128

MINISTERIAL DIRECTORY 453

Morris, Scott – O Aug 7, 16, NoTX Pby; campm RUF, UOK, 16-

314 South Pickard Avenue, Norman, OK 73069　　　　　　　　　　　Hills and Plains
E-mail: scott.morris@ruf.org
PCA Reformed University Fellowship

Morris, Sean – b Conneaut, OH, Mar 9, 89; f Gregory Allen; m Jo Anne Schor; w Sarah Marie Parris, Grove City, PA, Jan 8, 11; chdn Benjamin Elijah, Gabriel Martin; GroCC 10, BA; RTS 14, MDiv; O May 24, 15, BlRdg Pby; int First P Ch, Jackson, MS, 13-14; ascp Westminster P Ch, Roanoke, VA, 15-; brd trust, acad dean Blue Ridge Inst for Theo Ed, 17-; "How Do You Solve a Problem Like Maria?: John Knox and the Lady Regents" (Part 1), *Ad Fontes* Journal, 16; "How Do You Solve a Problem Like Maria?: John Knox and the Lady Regents" (Part 2), *Ad Fontes* Journal, 17; "Review: *Scottish Theology from John Knox to John McLeod Campbell* by Thomas F. Torrance," 17, *Ad Fontes* Journal; "Theological Education and the Local Church," *Reformation21*, May 18; "Benefits of Theological Education in the Local Church," *Reformation21*, May 18; *Earnest Prayer: The Joyous Cry of the Redeemed*, 18; *A Feast of Life-Giving Joy: The Necessity of Expository Preaching*, 18

2216 Peters Creek Road, Roanoke, VA 24017 – 440-645-1078　　　　　Blue Ridge
E-mail: seanmorris@westpca.org
Westminster Presbyterian Church – 540-562-0924
Blue Ridge Institute for Theological Education

Morrison, Charles Henry III – b Bremerton, WA, Oct 21, 42; f Charles Henry Jr.; m Barbara Kaull Wentworth; w Susan Carol Swartz, Annapolis, MD, Aug 21, 65; chdn Matthew Macdonald, Melinda Main; USNA 65, BS; CTS 78, MARC, 81, MDiv; L Jun 81; O Nov 81, Midw Pby (RPCES); Chap hospital, St. Louis, MO, 77-79; Chap USArmy, 82-99; astp Evangelical P Ch, Annapolis, MD, 00; ascp Severn Run Evangelical P Ch, Millersville, MD, 01-04; hr 05

1454 Wilderness Ridge Trail, Crownsville, MD 21032-2123 – 410-923-6321　　　Chesapeake
E-mail: morrisonch@aol.com
HR

Morrison, Chris – campm RUF, SMU, 14-

4421 Southwestern Boulevard, Dallas, TX 75225 – 214-693-7662　　　　　North Texas
E-mail: chris.morrison@ruf.org
PCA Reformed University Fellowship

Morrison, Matthew Dean – O Nov 6, 16, NFL Pby; astp Faith P Ch, Gainesville, FL, 16-17, ascp 17-

10557 NW 29th Lane, Gainesville, FL 32606　　　　　　　　　　　North Florida
Faith Presbyterian Church – 352-377-5482

Morrison, Thomas Jacob – O Apr 27, 14, Cal Pby; astp Palmetto Hills P Ch, Simpsonville, SC, 14-

217 Oakwood Court, Greenville, SC 29607　　　　　　　　　　　　　Calvary
E-mail: tomjmorrison1@gmail.com
Palmetto Hills Presbyterian Church – 864-963-9600

Morrow, Jeff – b Stockton, CA, May 26, 59; f Raleigh Douglas, Jr.; m Jeanne Marie Wilson (d); w Gayla Marie Searcy, Jun 19, 84; chdn Jake, Kyle; TXTU 83, BBA; WTSTX 12, MDiv; astp Trinity P Ch, Plano, TX, 17-

E-mail: jeff.morrow@trinityplano.org　　　　　　　　　　　　　　　North Texas
Trinity Presbyterian Church – 972-335-3844

Morton, Clifford Stanley – b Akron, OH, Nov 1, 52; f Clifford Smith; m Dorothy Mae; w Terry L. Griggs, Jan 3, 76; chdn Clifford Simeon, Joy Christina (Turner), David Emmanuel; UPitt, BS; WTS 07, MDiv; astp Westminster P Ch, Lancaster, PA, 07-08; op New City Flwsp, Lancaster, PA, 08-15; ascp Second City Ch, Harrisburg, PA, 15-18; op Crown and Joy, Richmond, VA, 18-

511 Langhorne Avenue, Richmond, VA 23222 – 717-393-6399   James River
E-mail: csmorton2@gmail.com
Crown and Joy – 804-298-5241

Morton, Luke – b Mar 20, 79; w Karen; chdn Harper Grace Justina, Eloise Delaney Mae, Geneva Blaise Evangeline; UW 03, BA; CTS 09, MDiv; O Jan 10, 10, PacNW Pby; astp Covenant P Ch, Issaquah, WA, 10-14; ascp Green Lake P Ch, Seattle, WA, 14-

6715 3rd Avenue NW, Seattle, WA 98117 – 425-478-2771   Pacific Northwest
E-mail: luke@greenlakepc.org
Green Lake Presbyterian Church – 206-789-7320

Mosal, William Louis Jr. – b Canton, MS, Sept 5, 37; f William Louis; m Margaret James; w Betty Bergland, Alexandria, LA, Jul 21, 59; chdn Rebecca Margaret (Nielsen), Melinda Anne, William Louis III; BelC 59, BA; ColTS 63, BD; O Jan 26, 64, St And Pby (PCUS); p First P Ch, Water Valley, MS, 64-68; ev PEF, 68-72; ev CNEC, 73-77; p First P Ch, Biloxi, MS, 77-89; mis, admin AfrBC, USA off, 89-; ob ss Raymond P Ch, Raymond, MS, 91-03

411 Wayne Street, Clinton, MS 39056-4415 – 601-924-2034   Grace
African Bible Colleges, Inc.
PO Box 103, Clinton, MS 39060

Moseman, Bart Steven – b St. Paul, MN, Oct 23, 70; f Steven Lee; m Judith Ann Van Wambeke; w Carrie Jean Lovette, Birmingham, AL, Dec 30, 93; chdn Abigail Ruth, Amelia Joanne, Andrew Steven, Elijah Emmett; WheatC 89-93, BA; CTS 95-00, MDiv; O Aug 20, 00, Hrtl Pby; campm RUF, UNELincoln, 00-08; chp Twin Cities, MN, 08-09; op CityLife Ch, St. Paul, MN, 09-

1507 Simpson Street, St. Paul, MN 55108-2342 – 651-645-0637   Siouxlands
E-mail: bartmoseman@gmail.com
CityLife Church – 612-559-4505

Moser, Frank David – b Pittsburgh, PA, Jun 26, 40; f Walter L; m Ilse K Poehlmann; w Rosemary C Krebill, Bethesda, MD, Sept 15, 61; chdn Jonathan R, Katherine M (Potter); GroCC 58-63, BMus; PittsTS 63-66, MDiv; L May 12, 66; O Jun 19, 66, Pitts Pby (UPCUSA); p First UP Ch, Caldwell OH, 66-70; p Bethel UP Ch, Monroeville, PA, 70-75; p Grace Ref P Ch, Monroeville, PA, 75-90; sc Asc Pby, 75-88; p Third Ref P Ch, Philadelphia, PA, 90-05; sc Phil Pby, 91-07; hr 05; DirMus Providence P Ch, Robinson Township, PA, 11-

1027 Slippery Rock Road, Grove City, PA 16127 – 724-458-0439   Pittsburgh
E-mail: moserfd11@gmail.com
HR

Moser, Mark – O Sept 15, Phil Pby; astp New Life P Ch, Glenside, PA, 15-

127 Berkeley Road, Glenside, PA 19038   Philadelphia
E-mail: mmoser@newlifeglenside.com
New Life Presbyterian Church – 215-576-0892

Moulson, Steven – O Nov 27, 16, JR Pby; astp All Saints Ref P Ch, Richmond, VA, 16-18, ascp 18-

9338 Saddle Court, Mechanicsville, VA 23116   James River
E-mail: steve@allsaintspres.org
All Saints Reformed Presbyterian Church – 804-353-7321

Mountan, Donald Lee – w Merril L. Knoble, Oct 3, 64; chdn Paula K., Mark D.; ECC, AA; ECol 75-76, BA; WTS 76-79; RTS 80-81, MDiv, 00-; O Aug 9, 81, NGA Pby; ap Midway P Ch, Powder Springs, GA, 81-82; op, p Chapel Hill P Ch, Douglasville, GA, 82-93; admin Harvester Christian Ac, 87-90; astp New Hope P Ch, Eustis, FL, 94-97; chp, op New Life P Ch, Clermont, FL, 97-00; sc CentFL Pby, 97-01; p New Life P Ch, Clermont, FL, 00-01; ob Equipping Pastors, Intnl, 01-08; ob exec dir Equipping Leaders Intnat'l, 08-15, exec dir em, project ldr, 15-

9039 Village Green Boulevard, Clermont, FL 34711-8524 – 352-394-5180   Central Florida
E-mail: dmountan@gmail.com
Equipping Leaders International

Mountfort, Timothy Joseph – ob campm China Outreach Min, UMD, 08-09; mis MTW, East Asia, 09-

c/o MTW – 301-825-5612   Potomac
E-mail: tjm406@gmail.com
PCA Mission to the World

Moynihan, Matthew R. – Robert Francis; m Sandralee King; w Allison Rae, Charlotte, NC, Jul 13, 13; UOK 05, BA; RTS 12, MDiv; O Jun 22, 14, CentCar Pby; Chap PA NatlGuard, 14-18; Chap USN, NSA Hampton Roads, Norfolk, VA, 18-

3636 Amherst Street, Norfolk, VA 23513 – 757-524-1775   Central Carolina
E-mail: chaplain.moynihan@gmail.com
United States Navy

Mueller, Steffen – astp Christ Cov P Ch, Matthews, NC, 10-11; mis, p Gospel Church, Muenchen, Germany 11-

Untere Leiten 8A, Baierbrunn 82065 GERMANY – 89-7908-6688   Central Carolina
E-mail: steffen@gospelchurchmuenchen.de
Gospel Church Munich – 0151-4662-8536

Muhlfeld, John P. – b Elmsford, NY, Sept 5, 73; f John P., Sr.; m Marion P. Hashim; w Sharon Marie Sauder, Lewisburg, PA, Jun 23, 01; chdn Amy Samantha, Jasmine Christine; BucknU 95, BS; BibTS 00, MDiv; L Mar 11, 00, Phil Pby; O Jun 11, 00, Phil Pby; ascp Covenant P Ch, Harleysville, PA, 00-04, srp 05-

923 Mount Airy Road, Collegeville, PA 19426 – 215-412-4128   Philadelphia Metro West
E-mail: muhlfeld@aol.com
Covenant Presbyterian Church – 215-256-1007

Muhlig, John Robert Jr. – b Goodlettsville, TN, Sept 12, 30; f John Robert; m Evelyn Morris; w Mary Anne Ross, Madison, TN, Jun 15, 53; chdn Patricia M. (Burton), Elizabeth M. (Henderson); USNA 49-53, BS; VPI 48-49; CTS 73-77, MRE, MDiv; L Mar 79, Midw Pby (RPCES); O Aug 80, Evan Pby; ev Evan Pby, 80-84; ascp Altadena Valley P Ch, Birmingham, AL, 85-91, wc 92; hr 97; USMC 20 yrs; Lt.Col; Bronze Star, Merit Serv, Navy Commend

3850 Galleria Woods Drive #134, Hoover, AL 35244 – 205-988-0246   Evangel
HR

Mulholland, David B. – b Lebanon, PA, Aug 8, 64; f Kenneth Bruce M.; m Ann Christensen; w Maren Ann Fisk, Columbia, SC, Jun 22, 91; chdn Anna Grace, Heather Maren, Stephen David Bruce; USC 82-86, BS; CBS 88-91, MDiv; RTSNC 99, DMin; O May 31, 92, Palm Pby; admin Cornerstone P Ch, Columbia, SC, 91-92, astp 92-09; wc 09-

2113 Mary Hill Drive, Columbia, SC 29210   Palmetto
E-mail: dmulholland5@gmail.com

Mull, Andy – O Mar 12, 17, Palm Pby; ob prof Nairobi Evan Sch of Theology, 17-

162 Hunters Ridge Drive, Lexington, SC 29072   Palmetto
Nairobi Evangelical School of Theology

Mullen, James – O May 13, 18, SWFL Pby; op College Hill Ch Plant, Tampa, FL, 18-

316 E. Lumsden Road, Brandon, FL 33511 – 612-229-5042   Southwest Florida
E-mail: jamforChrist@msn.com
College Hill Church Plant – 612-229-5042

Mullen, Jeremy – b Norfolk, VA, Oct 4, 79; f Joseph A. III; m Brenda Knott; w Adrienne Klock, Nashville, TN, Dec 20, 03; chdn Lila, Oliver; VandU 02, BA; GCTS 06-09, MDiv; O Nov 7, 09, SNE Pby; campm RUF, HarvU, 09-

19 Spencer Avenue #1, Somerville, MA 02144 – 978-473-1383   Southern New England
E-mail: jeremy.mullen@ruf.org
PCA Reformed University Fellowship

Mullen, Joseph Aloysius III – b Passaic, NJ, Nov 18, 49; f Joseph A.; m Margaret Sogorka; w Brenda Knott, Virginia Beach, VA, Dec 21, 74; chdn Jonathan, Jeremy; ODU 72-76, BS; BibTS 80-84, MA, MDiv; WTS 06, DMin; L Sept 84; O Sept 84, JR Pby; p New Cov P Ch, Virginia Beach, VA, 84-09; ascp Trinity P Ch, Asheville, NC, 09-

35 Forest Lake Drive, Asheville, NC 28803 – 828-505-3099   Western Carolina
E-mail: joe@trinityasheville.com
Trinity Presbyterian Church – 828-299-3433

Mullens, David B. Jr. – b Clarksdale, MS, Jul 22, 59; f D.B. Sr; m Donna Anderson; w Judith Louise Wyatt, Wayne, PA, Aug 1, 86; chdn David William Bobo III, Caroline Keith, Charles Emerson; UVA 81, BS; WTS 87, MDiv; L Feb 13, 88; O Dec 9, 88, Pac Pby; op Peninsula Hills P Ch, Mountain View, CA, 88-93, wc 93; ob Tampico, Mexico, 93-99; ev SoTX Pby, 99-

3225 Turtle Creek Boulevard, Unit 1447, Dallas, TX 75219 – 972-975-2350   South Texas
E-mail: bobomullens@gmail.com

Mullinax, Eric Carroll – b Spartanburg, SC, Aug 10, 51; f Horace W.; m Virginia I. Smith; w Roberta Allen Stephens, Havertown, PA, Aug 23, 75; chdn Leigh Carre, Kyle Gregory, Heath William; NewbC 73, BA; FBC 75, BA; CTS 87, MDiv; L 87, Ill Pby; O Jan 19, 88, SFL Pby; op Grace P Ch, Arcadia, FL, 89-90; astp Evangelical P Ch, Cape Coral, FL, 88-90, ascp 90-96, srp 96-99; ascp Covenant P Ch, Chattanooga, TN, 00-

8903 Hurricane Ridge Road, Chattanooga, TN 37421 – 423-313-7956   Tennessee Valley
E-mail: emullinax@covenantchattanooga.org
Covenant Presbyterian Church – 423-899-5377

Mumpower, Adam – b Bristol, TN, Mar 18, 77; w Deirdre; chdn Brock, Macie Catherine, Jack; KgC 99, BA; RTS 04, MDiv; O Aug 22, 04, CentCar Pby; yp Back Creek P Ch, Mount Ulla, NC, 99-01; yp Southlake P Ch, Huntersville, NC, 01-04, ascp 04- 17; p Church of the Redeemer, Monroe, NC, 17-

3800 Waters Reach Lane, Indian Trail, NC 28079 – 704-608-0108   Central Carolina
E-mail: amumpower@redeemerweb.com
Church of the Redeemer – 704-225-0161

Mun, Isaac K.S. – astp Inland Korean P Ch, Pomona, CA

15125 South Normandie Avenue, Unit B, Gardena, CA 90247   Korean Southwest
E-mail: ksmun@yahoo.com

MINISTERIAL DIRECTORY

Mundy, T. Camper Jr. – w Heather; chdn Hope, Ty, Mercy; WFU 94, BA; RegC 05, MDiv; O Apr 16, 06, Wcan Pby; astp Gr Vancouver, Vancouver, BC, 06-; astp Grace Cov P Ch, Williamsburg, VA, 07-08; ascp 08-

106 Loxley Lane, Williamsburg, VA 23185 – 757-565-4543   Tidewater
E-mail: camper@gracecovpca.org
Grace Covenant Presbyterian Church – 757-220-0147

Muntsinger, David W. – b Pittsburgh, PA, Jun 1, 65; f J. Mack Muntsinger (d); s/f Earnie Walker; m Virgina Helen Schwarz (d); w Jana Alison Ford, Washington, DC, Oct 12, 91; chdn John Dixon, William Ford, Kathryn Virginia; PSU 87, BS; DTS 97, ThM; L Feb 14, 98; O May 6, 98, Nash Pby; astp, ms/sa Christ Comm Ch, Franklin, TN, 97-01; astp West End P Ch, Richmond, VA, 02-06; p Spring Cypress P Ch, Spring, TX, 06-18

5307 Valleyviewcreek Court, Spring, TX 77379   Houston Metro
E-mail: Dmuntsinger@gmail.com

Munz, Steven C. – b Philadelphia, PA, Feb 25, 75; f James E.; m Nancy A.; w Heather Walsh; chdn Thomas Caleb, James Joshua; DrexU 98, BS; WTS 06, MAR; O Jun 21, 09, Phil Pby; ascp City Line Ch, Wynnewood, PA, 09-11; wc 11-

218 Kings Road, Plymouth Meeting, PA 19462   Philadelphia

Murai, Masato – b Fukushima, Japan, Mar 25, 51; f Asakichi Murai; m Fuchi Sato; w Harumi Ogura, Tokyo, Apr 24, 77; chdn Toru, Shizuka, Jun, Shoko, Aiji; TokUFS 70-75, BA; JCTS 77-80, MDiv; GCTS 84, MATS; L 81, P Ch in Japan; O Nov 17, 96, Ecan Pby; ev Yokosuka, Japan, 80-81; ascp Toronto, 85-92; astp Gr Toronto Msn, Toronto, ON, 96-00; op Grace Toronto Japanese Ch, Toronto, ON, 00-

304-1640 Lawrence Avenue West   Eastern Canada
North York, ON M6L 1C6 CANADA – 416-789-1902
E-mail: masmurai@yahoo.co.jp
Grace Toronto Japanese Church

Murchison, James Neil – b Charlottetown, PEI, CAN, Apr 14, 48; f James A.; m Margaret Grace MacKenzie; w Margaret Gertrude Roloson, Belfast, PEI, CAN, May 11, 74; chdn Paul James, Marsha Grace, Christine Margaret; UPEI 73, BS; WTS 90, MDiv; L Feb 26, 93; O Nov 1, 94, Ecan Pby; p Westminster Bible P Ch, Sydney, NS, 94-10; wc 10-14; hr 14

31 Johnson Drive, Stratford, PE C1B 1K9 CANADA – 902-892-4043   Eastern Canada
E-mail: jnmurchison@ballaliant.ca
HR

Muresan, Ben – b Timisoara, Romania; Vanguard 06, BA; FulTS 10, MDiv; astp Grace P Ch, Yorba Linda, CA, 11-16; srp 17-

23101 La Palma Avenue, Yorba Linda, CA 92887   South Coast
E-mail: benmuresan@gmail.com
Grace Presbyterian Church – 714-692-2390

Murphree, Daniel – astp New City Flwsp, St. Louis, MO, 12-

3502 Grace Avenue, St. Louis, MO 63116   Missouri
E-mail: dpmurp@gmail.com
New City Fellowship – 314-726-2302

Murphree, Ted – p Grace Comm P Ch, McDonough, GA, 03-08; astp Grace Flwsp P Ch, Albertville, AL, 08-

904 Park Avenue, Albertville, AL 35121 – 770-898-9722　　　　　　　　　　　　Providence
E-mail: tedmurphree@aol.com
Grace Fellowship Presbyterian Church – 256-891-0924

Muse, Timothy Gray – b Winston-Salem, NC, Apr 28, 63; f Thomas Gordon; m Martha Jean Brown; w Sharon Paige White, Pensacola, FL, Jan 2, 88; chdn Morgan Paige, Mark Timothy, Michael Gray, Matthew Thomas; NCSt 85, BS; RTS 97, MDiv; O Jun 15, 97, MSVal Pby; int Raymond P Ch, Raymond, MS, 96-97; astp First P Ch, Kosciusko, MS, 97-98, ascp 98-00; p Brandon P Ch, Brandon, MS, 00-13

3911 Talcott Avenue, Winston-Salem, NC 27106　　　　　　　　　　　　Mississippi Valley
E-mail: timothymuse@gmail.com

Musgrave, John A. – b Rochester, NY, Jan 8, 67; f Karl Smith; m Kay Elizabeth Cameron; w Betsy Kristin Lee, Dayton, OH, Aug 19, 89; chdn Larissa Kay, Alison Marie, Monica Lee, Tessa Renee, Mallory Quinn; WittU 85-89, BA; RTSFL 95-98, MDiv; L Jul 21, 98, CentFL Pby; O Jan 22, 99, Ecar Pby; ev, chp Clayton, NC, 99; op Clayton Comm Ch, Clayton, NC, 99-02, p 02-17; p Christ Ch, Clayton, NC, 17-

108 Gehrig Lane, Clayton, NC 27527 – 919-553-4791　　　　　　　　　　　　Eastern Carolina
E-mail: christchurch2017@icloud.com
Christ Church – 919-333-9514

Musselman, John Lawrence – b Griffin, GA, Mar 12, 50; f Wallace John (d); m Anne Louise Camp; w Colleen; chdn Kimberly, Deena, Ryan, Kelli, Lindsay, Wesley, Amelia; UAL, BS; RTS, MDiv; FulTS, DMin; O Jul 76, Evgld Pby (PCUS); moy Coral Ridge P Ch, Ft. Lauderdale, FL, 76-86; p Northwest Perim Ch, 87-91; ob The Jackson Institute, Atlanta, GA, 91-; *Classic Discipleship; The Holy Spirit and His Gifts*; Ed., *The Training of the Twelve* by A.B. Bruce; Ed., *Man's Chief End: God's Glory* by Thomas Watson; Ed., *Pilgrim's Progress* by John Bunyan

12155 Wildwood Springs Drive, Roswell, GA 30075 – 404-376-3127　　　　　　　　Metro Atlanta
E-mail: jmusselman@mindspring.com
The Jackson Institute – 770-518-7994
PO Box 500071, Atlanta, GA 31150

Musselman, Ronald Edward – b Griffin, GA, Feb 17, 48; f Wallace John (d); m Anne Louise Camp; w Connie, Jun 26, 76; chdn Jennifer Anne, Jordan Andrew, Carrie Jean (Parker), Amy Catherine; UAL 70, BS; RTS 73, MDiv, 77, MCE; O Nov 4, 73, MSVal Pby; moy First P Ch, Jackson, MS, 73-80, wc 80-83; moy Trinity P Ch, Montgomery, AL, 83-87, wc 87; p Trinity P Ch, Covington, GA, 88-98, wc 98-01; admin MTW, 01-03; hr 09

3 Deerfield Road, Covington, GA 30014 – 770-784-9508　　　　　　　　　　　　Metro Atlanta
HR

Musselman, Thomas Floyd – b Griffin, GA, Jun 23, 53; f Wallace John (d); m Anne Louise Camp; w Jennifer Joye McDonald, Decatur, AL, Jul 17, 76; chdn Kristen Joye, Katie Marie, Kimberly Lynn, Kevin Thomas; UAL 75, BS; RTS 81, MDiv; O Jul 82, CentGA Pby; op, p Camden Comm. Ch, St. Mary's, GA, 82-91; chp Eastbridge P Ch, Mount Pleasant, SC, 92-95, p 95-97; chp Cal Pby, Seneca, SC, 97-99; op Crossgate Ch, Seneca, SC, 99-02, p 02-

805 Ploma Drive, Seneca, SC 29678 – 864-886-0687　　　　　　　　　　　　Calvary
E-mail: tom@crossgatepca.orgmirab
Crossgate Church – 864-886-8005

Muutuki, Joseph Mwasi – b Mwingi, Kenya, Feb 19, 55; f David; m Lydia Kasyoka; w Elfi Marie, Nairobi, Jun 6, 81; chdn Timothy, Matthias; Anne-Ruth; DaystarU 82, dipl; FrTA 86, MDiv; StLU 94, MA; CTS 89, ThM; LaelU 94, DEd; PhD; L Oct 18, 94; O Oct 18, 94, MO Pby; lect DaystarU, 95-; srp New City Fell, Nairobi, 97-

Daystar University, Nairobi, KENYA   Missouri
New City Fellowship, Nairobi

Muzio, Steven Lee – b Berkeley, CA, Feb 16, 62; f David L.; m Raenell Kirkes; w Melanie L. Allman, Montgomery, AL, May 21, 83; chdn David Coleman, Cody McNeill, Abbey Elizabeth; MSC 80; BelC 81-84, BA; RTS, MDiv; CTS 05, DMin; L 87, NGA Pby; O Sept 13, 92, TNVal Pby; ydir Alta Woods P Ch, Jackson, MS, 84-87; ydir Grace P Ch, Stone Mountain, GA, 87-89; ydir Alta Woods P Ch, Jackson, MS, 89-92; astp Grace P Ch, Dalton, GA, 92-94; p Millbrook P Ch, Millbrook, AL, 94-98; p Church in the Canyon, Calabasas, CA, 98-06; p Millbrook P Ch, Millbrook, AL, 06-16; p Hope Evangelical Ch, North Liberty, IA, 16-

420 North Front Street, North Liberty, IA 52317   Iowa
E-mail: hopeevpastor@gmail.com
Hope Evangelical Church – 319-665-2800

Myers, Aaron – w Danielle Elise; chdn Xander Gregory, Ashlyn Jane, Ansley Joy, Sabrina Rose, Evan LeGare; AsbC 00, BA; CTS 05, MDiv; L Apr 30, 06, Ill Pby; ydir Center Grove P Ch, Edwardsville, IL, 00-04, astp 05-08; ascp 08-10; p Providence P Ch, Edwardsville, IL, 10-

10 Edwardsville Professional Park, Edwardsville, IL 62025   Illiana
E-mail: myers.aaron@gmail.com
Providence Presbyterian Church – 618-307-6590

Myers, Bill – w Wendy; chdn Amy, Stephanie, Katie, Julia, Jimmy; astp Twin Oaks P Ch, Ballwin, MO, 06-11, ascp 11-

1230 Big Bend Road, Ballwin, MO 63021 – 636-579-1173   Missouri
E-mail: bmyers@twinoakschurch.org
Twin Oaks Presbyterian Church – 636-861-1870

Myers, Dan – ascp Spanish River P Ch, Boca Raton, FL, 08-

115 S Seacrest Boulevard, Boynton Beach, FL 33484 – 561-638-3618   Gulfstream
E-mail: dmyers@spanishriver.com
Spanish River Presbyterian Church – 561-994-5000

Myers, Daniel – op New Creation Ch, Valley Village, CA, 16-

E-mail: eeboymusic@gmail.com   Pacific
New Creation Church

Myers, David Thomas – b Lemmon, SD, Oct 7, 40; f David Kearns; m Johanna Brinsin Sneddon; w Carolyn Jane Baxter, Lakewood, OH, Jun 25, 66; chdn Ann Margaret (Stegall); HighC 59-63, BA; ChrWrInst 72, dipl; FTS 63-66, MDiv; CTS 89, DMin; L Oct 66; O Oct 66, Northwest Pby (BPC); p Edmonton, Alb, Can, 66-68; rep FTS, 69, lib 69-71; p, t First Bible Ch, Lincoln, NE, 71-79; p, t Cov Ch (PCA), Lincoln, NE, 79-80; op Trinity P Ch, Omaha, NE, 80-81, p 81-86; p Presbyterian Ch of Pitcairn, Pitcairn, PA, 86-90; srp Carlisle Ref P Ch, Carlisle, PA, 90-04; hr 04; *Stonewall Jackson: The Spiritual Side*; *Joseph White Latimer: The Boy Major of the Confederacy*; *Helps to Biblical Worship*; *This Day in Presbyterian History*, PCA History Center website, 12

14 Dandelion Drive, Boiling Springs, PA 17007 – 717-258-0534   Susquehanna Valley
HR

Myers, Robert L. – b Rushville, IN, Jun 13, 64; f Robert; m Carolyn; w Elizabeth, Brooklyn, NY, May 28, 88; chdn Robert Lee, Ruthanne Lucille, Hannah Faith, Naomi Carolyn, Nathanael Christian; INU 85, BA; WTS 88, MDiv; L Sept 23, 88, OPC; TEAM, Zimbabwe, 84; srp Covenant OPC, Burtonsville, MD, 88-02; srp Covenant P Ch, Doylestown, PA, 02-

56 John Dyer Way, Doylestown, PA 18901 – 215-340-7609   Eastern Pennsylvania
E-mail: BobM@covenantchurch.org
Covenant Presbyterian Church – 215-794-7909

Myers, Thomas L. – b Arlington, VA, Nov 21, 56; w Elizabeth Anne Knecht, Aug 16, 80; chdn Katie, Janet, Emily, Margaret; HopeC 78, BS; RTS 83, MDiv; O Jan 5, 86, CentFL Pby; p Orangewood P Ch, Maitland, FL, 84-86; Pisgah ARP, Gastonia, NC, 86-88; ascp Westminster P Ch, Lancaster, PA, 88-92; srp Trinity P Ch, Harrisburg, PA, 92-02; srp St. Andrews P Ch, Columbia, SC, 02-04; p Covenant P Ch, Fayetteville, GA, 07-11; wc 11-12; ss Cherokee P Ch, Canton, GA, 12; p Chapel Hill P Ch, Douglasville, GA, 12-

9399 Cresent Court, Douglasville, GA 30135 – 678-489-7472   Northwest Georgia
E-mail: revthomaslmyers@comcast.net
Chapel Hill Presbyterian Church – 770-942-0360

Myles, Anthony – op United Faith Comm Ch, Knoxville, TN, 07-09; ascp New City Flwsp, St. Louis, MO, 09-

1142 Hodiamont Avenue, Saint Louis, MO 63112 – 865-789-7933   Missouri
E-mail: tmyles@ncfstl.org
New City Fellowship – 314-726-2302

Mylin, Mark D. – b Havre de Grace, MD, Aug 16, 59; w Mary Martha Huber, Lancaster, PA, Jun 8, 85; WMDC 77-81, BA; CTS 88-92, MDiv; L May 12, 92; O Feb 28, 93, Pot Pby; staff IVCF, 82-88; mis MTW, France, 94-04; ob chp, mis Greater Europe Mission, 04-

PO Box 232, Willow Street, PA 17584 – 717-371-8560   Chesapeake
E-mail: mdm955i@gmail.com
Greater Europe Mission

Myung, Joseph Chi-Sung – b Seoul, May 30, 71; f Thorn Wee; m Esther Ok Ryun Chang; w Yoon Seon Ahn, Seoul, Jun 7, 96; chdn David Dae-Hyun; JHU 90-94, BA; WTS 95-98, MDiv; DBU 15, PhD; L Oct 14, 99, KorCap Pby; O Feb 25, 01, SoTX Pby; yp Korean United Ch of Phil, Philadelphia, PA, 97-00; astp Korean P Ch, Houston, TX, 00-06; ob astp Korean Hope KAPC, San Diego, 06-

11239 Linares Street, San Diego, CA 92129 – 858-672-1630   Korean Southwest Orange County
E-mail: josephmyung@aol.com
Korean Hope KAPC, San Diego

Na, Stephen – RTS, MDiv; O Jan 31, 99, North GA; ascp Open Door Comm Ch, Alpharetta, GA, 99-00, wc 00-03; p Cornerstone P Ch, Lansdale, PA, 03-10; astp Living Faith Comm Ch, Flushing, NY, 10; ob Comm Church of Greatneck, 12-

2 Stoner Avenue, Great Neck, NY 11021 – 516-305-4378   Korean Northeastern
Community Church of Greatneck

Na, Sung Kyun – w Hea Ok; chdn Jonathan, Gloria, Grace; L 77; O Oct 11, 77; Chap ROKAF, 77-80; ap, p Dae Sun P Ch, Seoul, Korea, 80-82; p Hebron P Ch, Kunsan, 82-85; op Korean Saints P Ch, Warminster, PA, 85-88, p 85-88; p Korea, 96-, wc; astp Charlotte P Ch, Charlotte, NC, 09-14, p 15 -

8740 Green Ivy Lane, Charlotte, NC 28217   Korean Southeastern
E-mail: revskna@gmail.com
Charlotte Presbyterian Church

MINISTERIAL DIRECTORY

Nabors, A. Randy – w Joan McRae; chdn Michael, Garrett, Gyven, Keren; CC 68-72, BA; CTS 76, MDiv; L 75; O 76, SO Pby (RPCES); p New City Flwsp, Chattanooga, TN, 76-82; mis Comm P Ch, Nairobi, Kenya, 83-84; p New City Flwsp, Chattanooga, 85-07; Chap USAR, 377th Combat Supp Hosp; Chap USAR, FORSCOM Aug Unit, 75-07; USA Ret (Col), 07; hr; p em New City Flwsp, Chattanooga, TN, 12-; sr staff MNA, coor Urban/Mercy Min, coor New City Network, 12-; *Merciful*, 15

100 Old Birds Mill Road, Chattanooga, TN 37421 – 770-905-6976   Tennessee Valley
E-mail: rnabors@pcanet.org
PCA Mission to North America – 678-825-1200

Naille, Todd Alan – OHSU, BS; AshTS, MDiv; O Jan 25, 04, GrLks Pby; astp Walnut Creek P Ch, Gahanna, OH, 03-04; op Granville Chapel, Granville, OH, 05-10, p 10-18

475 West Broadway, Granville, OH 43023 – 740-587-2507   Columbus Metro

Nam, Sungwoo – p Church of the Nations, Chicago, IL, 07-

4550 Lilac Avenue, Glenview, IL 60025-1453 – 847-832-0035   Korean Central
E-mail: sungwoonam@hotmail.com
Church of the Nations – 773-706-2080

Nantt, Gary Alvin – b Lodi, CA, Jan 14, 46; f Alvin Emil; m Lorina Katherina Landenberger; w Carol Ann Tune, Fairfield, CA, Sept 7, 68; chdn Aimee Elizabeth, Bradley Scott; DelC 63-66, AA; SacSt 66-68, BA; RTS 75-78, MDiv; GSSTh 08, ThD; O Oct 12, 78, Pac Pby; mis MTW, Korea, 78-92; chp MTW, Ciudad Juarez, Chihuahua, Mex, 92-98; chp MTW, Tijuana, BC, Mexico, 99-12; MTW, Africa, 12-13; hr 14; sc Prov pby 15-

1004 East 4th Street, Tuscumbia, AL 35674 – 256-814-1195   Providence
E-mail: ganantt@juno.com
HR

Napier, Nicholas – b Charlotte, NC, Dec 15, 80; f Jack Kendall II; m Beverly Crowe; w Jennifer Lefler, Rock Hills, SC, Oct 25, 08; chdn Averie Claire, Ella Grace; WingU; RTS; GPTS BDiv; ip Westminster Bible P Ch, Nova Scotia, 10; ip OPC, Sunnyvale, CA, 12; p Boyce Mem ARP, Kings Mountain, NC, 12-17; p Reformed P Ch, Beaumont, TX, 17-

3895 Champions Drive, Beaumont, TX 77707   Houston Metro
E-mail: nicholas.s.napier@gmail.com
Reformed Presbyterian Church – 409-898-3558

Nasekos, Paul Leo – b Goldsboro, NC, Sept 14, 46; w Jeannette Marie Bush, Jacksonville, NC, Dec 1, 68; chdn John Stephen, Matthew Paul, Juliana Rebekah; WheatC 64-65; CBC 71-74, BA; RTS 76-79, MDiv; O Jun 24, 79, MSVal Pby; USCG, 66-70; Chap Tamassee DAR School, 81-82; p Philadelphia P Ch, Landrum, SC, 82-87; ob FCAc, French Camp, MS, 87-98; astp Gainesville P Ch, Gainesville, VA, 98-00; admin First P Ch, school administrator, Kosciusko, MS, 00-02; p Covenant P Ch, Winter Haven, FL, 03-05; dir Child Evang Fell, Jackson, MS, 06-

118 Spanish Moss Drive, Clinton, MS 39056   Mississippi Valley
E-mail: pnasekos@bellsouth.net
Child Evangelism Fellowship

Nash, Jonathan – O Dec 9, 17, Nash Pby; astp Midtown Flwsp Ch, Nashville, TN, 17-

21 Perkins Street, Nashville, TN 37210 – 615-513-9883   Nashville
Midtown Fellowship Church – 615-269-9015

Nash, Thomas Lawrence II – b Birmingham, AL, Jan 26, 59; f James George "Jake"; m Celia Garrett; w Connie Shedd, Birmingham, AL, Jun 8, 85; SamU 81, BA; WTS 85, MAR, 86, MDiv, 88, DMin; BethTS 99, PhD; L Jun 83, Evan Pby; O Aug 86, SAL; ap First P Ch, Dothan, AL, 86; op Westwood P Ch, Dothan, AL, 86-91, p 91-99, wc 00-01; ss Pleasant Grove PC, Pleasant Grove, AL, 01-07; wc; hr 14; *The Church Planter's Telephone Outreach Manual*

HR   Evangel

Nash, William E. – b Wurtzburg, Germany, Sept 25, 63; w Sherrie Crane, Huntsville, AL, Sept 12, 87; chdn William Edward, Alec Matthew, Kelly Grace; AU 86, BArch; RTS 00, MDiv; O Jun 00, ARP; chp Hope ARP, Dacula, GA, 00-05; ascp Southwood P Ch, Huntsville, AL, 05-13; wc 13-

4802 Cove Valley Drive, Huntsville, AL 35763   Providence

Nay, Robert – b Camden, NJ, May 12, 63; f Robert O.; m Dolores J. Richey; w Judy A. Gilbert, Andrews, NC, May 29, 93; chdn Ruth Hannah, Joshua Nathan, Rachel Leah; CamU 90, BA; WTS 94, MDiv; USAWC 16, MMAS; L Mar 12, 94; O Oct 20, 94, Phil Pby; Chap USArmy, Ft. Lewis, WA, 94-97; Schweinfurt, Germany, 98-01; Ft. Stewart, GA, 01-02; Ft. Gillem, GA, 02-04; Ft. Wainwright, AK, 04-07; Ft. Leavenworth, KS, 07-08; Ft. Irwin, CA, 08-10; Ft. Lee, VA, 10-12; Camp Zama, Japan, 12-16; Redstone Arsenal, AL, 16-; *The Operational, Social, and Religious Influences Upon the Army Chaplain Field Manual, 1926-1952; The Transformation of the Army Chaplaincy during WWII*

4402 Martin Road, Redstone Arsenal, Huntsville, AL 35898   Philadelphia
E-mail: Robert.nay@us.army.mil
United States Army

Neal, John W. – EMenC, BA; WTS, MDiv, DMin; O May 17, 98, JR Pby; p Covenant P Ch, Midlothian, VA, 98-

11521 Old Carrolton Court, Richmond, VA 23236 – 804-897-6138   James River
E-mail: johnwneal916@hotmail.com
Covenant Presbyterian Church – 804-378-7606

Neale, Ted – b Santa Monica, CA, Jul 27, 49; f Arthur T.; m Arlene Garfield; w Cynthia Anne Kowalski, San Diego, CA, Jul 6, 75; chdn Sarah Michal, Laura Michal, Anna Michal; SCBC 80-85, BA; TTS 98, MA; O Dec 2, 84, Peninsula Ch Fell; Recd PCA May 18, 96, Pac Pby; ss Church in the Canyon, Calabasas, CA, 96-98; astp, mfam Valley P Ch, North Hills, CA, 98-00, wc; ob chap Baseball Chapel, LA; astp Church in the Canyon, Calabasas, CA, 13-16; hr 16

1137 Del Robles Place, Santa Susana, CA 93063 – 805-582-2603   Pacific
HR

Nealon, Daniel – O Jan 22, 17, Nash Pby; astp West End Community Ch, Nashville, TN, 17-18; astp Deer Creek Comm Ch, Littleton, CO, 18-

8131 South Pierce Street, Littleton, CO 80128   Rocky Mountain
E-mail: danieljnealon@gmail.com
Deer Creek Community Church – 303-933-9900

Nearpass, Andy – ob p Grace Ref Ch, Lansing, IL; ob p Faith Ref Ch, Dyer, IN, 14-

18445 Willow Lane, Lansing, IL 60438 – 7084742636   Chicago Metro
E-mail: anearpass@wearefaith.org
Faith Reformed Church

Nease, James Sylvester – astp Trinity P Ch, Montgomery, AL, 05-08; ascp Exile P Msn, Woodinville, WA, 08-13. p 13-18

135 Haley Farm Drive, Canton, GA 30115 – 425-440-8898　　　　　　　　Pacific Northwest
E-mail: synease@yahoo.com

Neel, Wes – astp Redeemer Sugar Land, Sugar Land, TX, 11-13; astp Grace P Ch of the North Shore, Winnetka, IL, 13-15

440 Ridge, Winetka, IL 60093　　　　　　　　　　　　　　　　　　　　Chicago Metro
E-mail: wn1517@gmail.com

Neely, Stewart – O Sept 13, 15, CentCar Pby; astp Christ Cov Ch, Matthews, NC, 15-

3100 Willowbrae Road, Charlotte, NC 28226 – 704-718-0534　　　　　　Central Carolina
E-mail: neelysm@gmail.com
Christ Covenant Church – 704-847-3505

Neikirk, Jeffrey – p Meadow Creek P Ch, Greeneville, TN, 08-18; p Foothills Comm Ch, Sturgis, SD, 18-

2650 Meadows Drive, Sturgis, SD 57785 – 423-638-4990　　　　　　　　　　Siouxlands
E-mail: neikirkjeffrey@gmail.com
Foothills Community Church – 605-347-8356

Nelson, Ben – O Jul 14, 14, GulCst Pby; astp Grace Comm Ch, Mobile, AL, 14-; op Christ Redeemer Ch, Mobile, AL, 18-

2763 South Barksdale Drive, Mobile, AL 36606 – 251-533-5711　　　　　　　　Gulf Coast
E-mail: ben@gracemobile.org
Grace Community Church – 251-345-3303
Christ Redeemer Church

Nelson, Brady – O Feb 10, 13, GAFH Pby; astp Westminster P Ch, Gainesville, GA, 13-16; mis 16-

339 William Clark Drive, O'Fallon, MO 63368 – 314-406-7261　　　　　　Georgia Foothills

Nelson, Caleb T – b Greeley, CO, Jun 21, 90; f Nels; m Annie Manthei; w Alexandria Grace Myers, York, PA, May 28, 15; chdn Kenneth Elliott, Marilee Jane, Saskia Rose; PatHenC 12, BA; GPTS 15, MDiv; O Feb 6, 16, RMtn Pby; p Harvest Ref P Ch, Gillette, WY, 16-

415 North Miller Avenue, Gillette, WY 82716 – 970-381-3549　　　　　　　Rocky Mountain
E-mail: meadolarksong@gmail.com
Harvest Reformed Presbyterian Church – 307-696-3424

Nelson, D. Kurt – b Raleigh, NC, Mar 21, 55; f Donald H; m Alice Turnage; w Patricia Ann McMillan, Dallas, TX, Sept 12, 87; chdn Tiffany, Brandon, Virginia, Christina, Alyssa, Lauren, Anton, Steve, Olivia; UNC 77, BA; CBS 80, cert; DTS 84, ThM; CIU 08, DMin; O Aug 10, 86, CentGA Pby; ob mis, chp GMF, Dallas, TX, 91-97; VP GMF, Russia, Ukraine, Cuba, Haiti; mis East West Ministries Int, Addison, TX, 97-99; Dir, exec vp East West Ministries Int, Russia, Cuba, Central Asia, 99-10; pres East West Ministries; CEO, 14-

5114 Del Roy Drive, Dallas, TX 75229 – 214-532-5032　　　　　　　　　　Savannah River
E-mail: dkn@eastwest.org
East West Ministries International – 972-941-4500
2001 West Plano Parkway, Suite 3000, Plano, TX 75075

Nelson, David Scott – b Akron, OH, Oct 17, 62; f Richard H.; m Joyce Mae Lemmert; w Laureen Harriet Maki, Cuyahoga Falls, OH, Jun 14, 86; chdn Isaiah, Micah, Gideon, Lydia; UAkr 81-82; UMI 82-85, BS; NavWC 91-94, dipl; RTS 97-00, MDiv; CPCC 13, dipl; L Oct 3, 00, Cov Pby; O May 27, 01, CentCar Pby; int Second P Ch, Memphis, TN, 99-01; astp First P Ch, Stanley, NC, 01-06; ascp 06-10; wc 10-11; ascp Harvest P Ch, Lincolnton, NC, 11-14; hr 14; mod CentCar Pby, 06-08; ed *Naval Leadership 202 – Developing Subordinates Student Guide,* 94

8430 Streamview Drive, Apt. B, Huntersvile, NC 28078 – 704-648-8179   Catawba Valley
E-mail: ncnelsonnotes@earthlink.net
HR

Nelson, Jared – astp Providence P Ch, Edwardsville, IL, 11-13; p New Life P Ch of Hopewell Twnshp, Aliquippa, PA, 14-

2861 Patterson Drive, Aliquippa, PA 15001   Ascension
E-mail: pastorjared@newlifehopewell.com
New Life Presbyterian Church of Hopewell Township – 724-378-4389

Nelson, Kevin – campm RUF, Yale, 10-13; ascp Christ P Ch, New Haven, CT, 13-

18 Dadio Road, Hamden, CT 06517 – 203-645-2065   Southern New England
E-mail: kevin.nelson@cpcnewhaven.org
Christ Presbyterian Church – 203-777-6960

Nelson, Phillip Scott – b Detroit, MI, Dec 5, 46; f David J.; m Essie May Boyd; w Gladys Anderson, Charlotte, NC, Aug 16, 80; chdn Joshua Daniel, Christina Michelle, Charisma Joy, Deborah Jade, Shannon Jasmine; Highland Park CC 65-67, AA; WaySU 67-68, BA; GETS 69-72, MDiv; L 66, ChMethEpis; O 68, ChMethEpis; Recd PCA Jan 23, 99, CentCar Pby; p Metropolitan CMEC, East Chicago, IN, 70-72; rep, t/tr CCC, 73-75; p Faith CMEC, Charlotte, NC, 75-77; p Metropolitan CMEC, Cincinnati, OH, 77-79; dirAdm, instr Miles College, Birmingham, AL, 79-80; p St. James CMEC, Flint, MI, 80-83; exec p Loveland Ch, Fontana, CA, 83-85; p Allen Temple CMEC, Portland, OR, 85-93; p Faith CMEC, Charlotte, NC, 93-96; p Langford Chapel CMEC, Monroe, NC, 96-98; chp North Charlotte Msn, 98-99, wc 00-04; ob SIM, 04-

3441 Linden Berry Lane, Charlotte, NC 28269 – 704-597-9284   Central Carolina
E-mail: phillip.nelson@sim.org
Serving in Mission, Charlotte, NC

Nelson, Seth – w Heather; chdn Lucia, Alethia; MBI 04, BA; WTS 09, MDiv; O Nov 7, 09, JR Pby; astp Trinity P Ch, Norfolk, VA, 09-11; ascp 11-17; wc

19 Glencove Court, Greenville, SC 29681 – 757-560-0040   Tidewater

Nestor, Joseph – w Aileen; chdn Kyle, Stephen; FAU 81, BS, 84, MS; AUBS 04, MDiv; O Jan 05, SFL Pby; astp Christ Cov Ch, Southwest Ranches, FL, 05-

5740 West Wakeford Drive, Davie, FL 33331 – 954-680-3033   South Florida
E-mail: JNestor@ChristCovChurch.com
Christ Covenant Church – 954-434-4500

Netzorg, David C. – w Patti; chdn Dayna, Corey, Rebekah; FAU 86, BBA; RTSFL 03, MABS; O 03, CentFL Pby; ydir Pine Ridge P Ch, Orlando, FL, 93-98, astp 98-03, ascp 03-06; op Avalon P Ch, Winter Garden, FL, 06-10; wc 10-

17525 Seidner Road, Winter Garden, FL 34787-9717 – 407-905-5678   Central Florida
E-mail: DCNetzorg@aol.com

Newbrander, Timothy Gaius – b Cleveland, OH, Oct 19, 55; f Virgil R; m Ella Jeanette Rae; w Jacqueline Torrey Renich, Montrose, PA, Oct 16, 82; chdn Timothy Frederick, David Renich, Rebecca Jeanette; WheatC 77, BA; UIL 80, MSW; WTS 89, MDiv; L Mar 10, 90; O Aug 12, 90, Phil Pby; DCE Christ Ch, 83-85; mis MTW, Amsterdam, 89-95; mis MTW, Berlin, 95-16

435 South 45th Street, Philadelphia, PA 19104   Philadelphia
E-mail: tgnewbrander@gmail.com

Newell, R. Andrew – b Louisville, KY, Jan 29, 71; f Roger C.; m Joyce Rebecca Gribble; w Kimberley Ann Murray, Summerville, SC, Aug 12, 95; chdn Murray Andrew, Caleb Rogerson, Anna Grace; Citadel 93, BA; RTSNC 00, MDiv; L May 9, 00, GulCst Pby; O Oct 22, 00, GulCst Pby; ydir Westminster P Ch, Sumter, SC, 94-96; ydir Trinity P Ch, Lancaster, SC, 97-00; p New Phil P Ch, Quincy, FL, 00-07; astp Trinity P Ch, Orangeburg, SC, 07-10; srp Covenant Comm Ch, Lexington, SC, 10-

1505 Knotts Haven Trail, Lexington, SC 29073 – 803-429-7524   Palmetto
E-mail: andy@growingnewlives.org
Covenant Community Church – 803-359-7117

Newman, Andrew – O 17, SWFL Pby; campm RUF, 17-

5005 East 110th Avenue, Tampa, FL 33617 – 336-317-4433   Southwest Florida
E-mail: Andrew.Newman@RUF.org
PCA Reformed University Fellowship

Newman, Nathan – b Huntsville, AL, Feb 2, 88; f Jeffrey Wayne; m Susan Michelle Gaylen; w Jessica Marie Jelgerhuis, Holland, MI, Aug 22, 14; CC 10, BA; RTSDC 17, MDiv; O Jul 2, 17, Pot Pby; astp McLean P Ch, McLean, VA, 17-; Chap USAF, 17-

1825 Independence Avenue, SE, Washington, DC 20003   Potomac
E-mail: nathan@mcleanpres.org
McLean Presbyterian Church – 703-821-0800
United States Air Force

Newsom, William Les – b Memphis, TN, Dec 1, 67; f Bill (d); m Ginger Sanders; w Ginger; chdn Anna Grace, Caroline, Luke; MempSU 91, BA; RTS 94, MDiv; L May 24, 94; O Mar 7, 95, Cov Pby; campm RUM, UMemp, 94-99; campm RUM, UMS, 99-11; area coord RUF AL/Mid-South, 11-18; srp Christ P Ch at Oxford, Oxford, MS, 18-; *The Enduring Community*

126 Mulberry Lane, Oxford, MS 38655 – 662-801-1267   Covenant
E-mail: lesnewsom@gmail.com
Christ Presbyterian Church at Oxford – 662-234-3399

Newsome, Charles Wayne – b Knoxville, TN, Mar 26, 59; f Robert W. (d); m Donna Zeiser; w Amy Jo Samuels, Enterprise, AL, Jun 11, 88; chdn Katelyn Jane, Samuel Zeiser, Mary Grace, Sarah Claire, Joshua Charles; UTC 77-81, BS; RTS 85-88, MDiv; L Jan 24, 89; O Apr 9, 89, Evan Pby; mis SIMA, 82-85; int Briarwood P Ch, 86-87; ap Rainbow P Ch, 88-89; mis MTW, Japan, 89-

c/o MTW   Evangel
E-mail: mtwwayne@gmail.com
PCA Mission to the World

Newsome, Shaynor – campm RUM, 03-14; p City Ch, Eugene, OR, 14-

800 Brookside Drive, Eugene, OR 97405 – 575-522-1135   Pacific Northwest
E-mail: shaynor@citychurcheugene.org
City Church – 541-343-5538

Nicholas, Thomas Everett – b Birmingham, AL, May 13, 57; f Thomas Alvin; m Emily Martin; w Linda Lee Wilson, Willow Grove, PA, Jan 2, 82; chdn Thomas Richard, Katherine Joy, Amy Elizabeth; WheatC 79, BA; WTS 81, MAR, 83, MDiv; L Nov 83, Phil Pby; O Oct 84, DMV Pby; p Evangelical P Ch, Baltimore, MD, 84-93; srp Reformed P Ch, Ephrata, PA, 93-

210 Tuckson Drive, Ephrata, PA 17522 – 717-733-4678   Susquehanna Valley
E-mail: rpcten@ephratarpc.com
Reformed Presbyterian Church – 717-733-0462

Nichols, James Peter – b Iowa City, IA, Apr 27, 80; f James Alan; m Katherine Elizabeth; w Melissa Dell, Tullahoma, TN, Jul 12, 03; chdn Isaac James, Elijah John, Abram Paul; TNTU, BS; CTS, MDiv; O Jun 9, 13, SWFL Pby; ascp Tampa Bay P Ch, Tampa, FL, 13-16; astp Westminster P Ch, Muncie, IN, 16-

2209 West Woodmont Drive, Muncie, IN 47304 – 615-598-6394   Central Indiana
E-mail: jnichols@westminpca.com
Westminster Presbyterian Church – 765-288-3355

Nickell, Cole – O Feb 20, 16, MetAtl Pby; astp The Vine Comm Ch, Cumming, GA, 16-18

Address Unavailable   Metro Atlanta

Nicoletti, Steven – astp Faith P Ch, Tacoma, WA, 14-

1802 South Winnifred Street, Tacoma, WA 98465 – 253-752-7601   Pacific Northwest
E-mail: snicoletti@faithtacoma.org
Faith Presbyterian Church – 253-752-7601

Nielson, Jon – ob astp College Ch, college pastor, Wheaton, IL; ob 16-17; p Spring Valley P Ch, Roselle, IL, 17-

E-mail: jon.nielson@gmail.com   Chicago Metro
Spring Valley Presbyterian Church – 630-980-4450

Nikides, Bill – b Astoria, NY, Dec 16, 54; f Diomides; m Athanasia Grafas; w Cheryl Ocilla Meredith, Charleston, SC, May 21, 77; chdn Meredith Irene, Mary Elizabeth, Martha Leigh; Citadel 77, BA; WebsU 86, MA; BDS 98, MDiv; FSU, PhD cand; L 79, Parkview Bapt, Alexandria, LA; O Aug 12, 94, South Bapt; Recd PCA Jul 14, 98, Evan Pby; p Providence Bapt Ch, Rockford, AL, 95-98; mis MTW, 98-10; mis i2 Ministries, 10-12; dir Church to Church: Connecting Reformed and Covenantal Churches in Global Mission," a ministry of Advancing Native Missions; "The Fountain of Wisdom: The Theology of John of Damascus" (Autumn 01), "Four Offerings From Gospel and Culture" (Spring 02), "Incarnational Ministry: The Church" (Spring 06), *Foundations: A Journal of Evangelical Theology*; "Insider Translation: Keeping Faithful to the Word of God?" *Table Talk* (British publication); "Contemporary Trends in Evangelical Missions" (Feb 06), "Evaluating Insider Movements (C5)" (Mar 06), "Evaluation of Scriptural Support for Insider Movements" (Mar 07), "The Church at the Crossroads" (Mar 07), *St. Francis Magazine* (Interserve); dir *Half Devil Half Child*, documentary film on insider movements in Bangladesh; mbr, PCA Com on Insider Movements, 11-13

1302 24th Street West #284, Billings, MT 59102 – 406-534-6542   Rocky Mountain
E-mail: bnikides@gmail.com
Church to Church

Nilsson, J. Walter H. – w Holly; chdn Julia, Adam, Susanna, Nathan; St.Mary's MD, BA; CTS, MDiv; O Jan 8, 06, Pot Pby; astp Cornerstone P Ch, California, MD, 06-07; ascp 07-09; srp 09-

20719 Colby Drive, Lexington Park, MD 20653 – 240-431-9468   Potomac
E-mail: wnilsson@cornerstonepca.org
Cornerstone Presbyterian Church – 301-862-5016

Noch, Andrew John – b Cleveland, OH, Nov 11, 54; f Arthur J.; m Helen; KSU 77, BS; WTS 83, MAR, 84, MDiv; FTS 95, DMin; L 84; O 85, Pac Pby; ap Calabasas Ch, Agoura, CA, 85; p New Hope P Ch, San Diego, CA, 86-97; mis MTW, Ethiopia, 97-00; ob ascp Rolling Hills Cov Ch, Rolling Hills, CA, 00-18; ob srp New Life Christian Alliance Ch, Whittier, CA, 18-

2021 Van Karajan Drive, Rancho Palos Verdes, CA 90275 – 310-241-1464   South Coast
E-mail: anoch316@gmail.com
New Life Christian Alliance Church

Nolan, Shaun Michael – b Lakewood, CA, Sept 16, 70; f Walter J. Jr.; m Jo Ann King; w Jennifer Irene Vassar, Artesia, CA, Jun 11, 94; chdn Hannah Jo Ann, Clare Irene, Lydia Caroline, Emma Ruth; BIOLA 93, BA; WSCAL 99, MDiv; L Sept 19, 98, SoCst Pby; O Dec 16, 01, Pitts Pby; astp Grace P Ch, Fallbrook, Fallbrook, CA, 00-01; p View Crest P Ch, Eighty Four, PA, 01-

883 Linden Road, Eighty Four, PA 15330 – 724-942-3232   Pittsburgh
E-mail: pastor@viewcrestchurch.org
View Crest Presbyterian Church – 724-941-9772

Nolen, Ralph Dennis Jr. – b Lakeland, FL, Aug 7, 48; f Ralph Dennis; m Dorothy Ann Strand; w Martha Jane Platt, Wauchula, FL, Dec 17, 71; chdn David Scott, Jonathan Edward; PolkJC 66-68, AA; UFL 72, BS; RTS 76, MDiv; L Jul 6, 76; O Dec 14, 76, Cov Pby; p Williston Ch, Williston, FL, 71-73; p Sardis P Ch, Sardis, MS, 73-81; p First P Ch, Camden, AL, 81-93; sc War Pby, 87-93; srp First P Ch, Gadsden, AL, 93-99, wc 00; p Kingstree P Ch, Kingstree, SC, 00-18; hr 18

507 Witherspoon Drive, Kingstree, SC 29556 – 843-355-2346   Pee Dee
E-mail: rdnolenjr@yahoo.com
HR

Noll, Barry – astp Christ P Ch, Tulsa, OK, 02-10; ascp 10-13; chp 13-16; op liberti Ch Bucks Co, Warrington, PA, 16-18

2241 Moss Avenue, Warrington, PA 18976 – 215-469-7149   Eastern Pennsylvania

Norfleet, H. Gregory – b Chapel Hill, NC, May 16, 63; w Cynthia L., Lincolnton, NC, Aug 15, 87; chdn Evan, Nathanael; UNC 85, BA; RTSFL 94, MDiv; O Aug 24, 97, Ecar Pby; astp Church of the Good Shepherd, Durham, NC, 97-98, ascp 98-07; cop Christ Comm Ch, Chapel Hill, NC, 07-

4616 Oak Hill Road, Chapel Hill, NC 27514 – 919-824-6644   Eastern Carolina
E-mail: greg@cccpca.org
Christ Community Church – 919-636-5258

Norgauer, Milan – w Heather; chdn Noah, Elijah, Eliana; UCLA, BA; TalTS, MDiv; CalvS, PhD; O Apr 25, 03, RMtn Pby; p Cornerstone P Ch, Castle Rock, CO, 03-09; p Northwoods P Ch, Cheyenne, WY, 09-

7151 Legacy Parkway, Cheyenne, WY 82009 – 307-287-3637   Rocky Mountain
E-mail: mnorgauer@gmail.com
Northwoods Presbyterian Church – 307-637-4817

Norris, George Van – b Palestine, TX, Jan 16, 32; f John Benjamin, Sr.; m Dorothy Marian Welsh; w Nancy Jane Stockwell, High Point, NC, Jun 6, 59; chdn Mark Andrew, Kimberlee Dawn, Jennifer Leigh; UNC 54, BS; WheatGrS 61; GCTS 62, MDiv; L Nov 82; O Feb 83, Wcar Pby; op, p Westminster P Ch, Boone, NC, 83-87, srp 87-96, astp 96-00; chp Ashe P Ch, Jefferson, NC, 99-00, p 00-07; astp Westminster P Ch, Boone, NC, 07-09; hr 09

4016 Tutbury Drive, Jamestown, NC 27282 – 336-500-0446   Western Carolina
HR

Norris, James – b Montgomery, AL, Jan 27, 85; w Elizabeth A, Jan 18, 14; O Aug 13, 17, Cal Pby; p New Hope P Ch, Abbeville, SC, 17-

2368 Hwy 72 West, Abbeville, SC 29620   Calvary
E-mail: jim.norris07@gmail.com
New Hope Presbyterian Church – 864-366-5684

Norris, Jeff – O Oct 12, 17, MetAtl Pby; astp Perimeter Ch, Johns Creek, GA, 17-

4054 Suwanee Trail Drive, Buford, GA 30518   Metro Atlanta
E-mail: jeffn@perimeter.org
Perimeter Church – 678-405-2000

Norris, Kirk Charles – b Clare, MI, Apr 22, 88; w Anna Cushman; chdn Lucy Elizabeth, Jeremiah Finn; CampU, BA; CTS, MDiv; O Oct 28, 12, MO Pby; mis MTW, Ukraine, 12-; campm RUF, Ukraine, 16-

737 Mill Springs Lane, Birmingham, AL 35244   Missouri
E-mail: kirkcharlesnorris@gmail.com
PCA Mission to the World
PCA Reformed University Fellowship

Norton, James Edward – b Winston-Salem, NC, Dec 30, 51; f Evan; m Dorothy Wright; w Sally Dahlberg, Jackson, MS, Jan 30, 82; chdn Halley Carleton, Evan Davidson, Hugh Edward Clarke; MSU 76, BS; RTS 79, MCE, 87, MDiv; L Oct 84; O Nov 22, 87, MSVal Pby; astp First P Ch, Jackson, MS, 87-90, mout/evan 91-93; chp, op Highlands P Ch, Ridgeland, MS, 93-94, p 94-97; astp Independent P Ch, Memphis, TN, 97-12; ascp 12-

4735 Normandy Avenue, Memphis, TN 38117   Covenant
E-mail: enorton@ipcmemphis.org
Independent Presbyterian Church – 901-685-8206

Norton, Robert – op Ch of the Resurrection, Flagstaff, AZ, 07-10; p 10-

2819 North Freemont Boulevard, Flagstaff, AZ 86001 – 928-699-7592   Southwest
E-mail: robertcnorton@yahoo.com
Church of the Resurrection – 928-699-7592

Nottingham, Jeff – O Nov 8, 13, CentInd Pby; astp Redeemer P Ch, Indianapolis, IN, 13-

2224 North Park Avenue, Indianapolis, IN 46205 – 765-969-2655   Central Indiana
E-mail: jeff@mats.org
Redeemer Presbyterian Church – 317-238-5487

Novak, Michael – b Memphis, TN, Aug 9, 84; w Rachel Elisabeth Camp, Memphis, TN, May 19, 06; chdn Caleb Michael, Abigail Grace, Katherine Jane; UT 06, BA; CTS 10, MDiv; L Aug 14, 10; O Nov 14, 10, SoTX Pby; campm RUF, TrinU, 10-17; op Trinity Gr Ch, San Antonio, TX, 17-

6391 DeZavala Road, 223D, San Antonio, TX 78249 – 865-773-9260   South Texas
E-mail: michael@trinitygracesa.org
Trinity Grace Church

Novak, Robert – O Oct 27, 13, SoCst Pby; astp New Life P Ch, Escondido, CA, 13-17; op Resurrection P Ch of San Diego, San Diego, CA, 17-

6109 Amaya Drive, La Mesa, CA 91942 – 619-886-4474   South Coast
E-mail: rovertnovak@resurrectionsd.com
Resurrection Presbyterian Church of San Diego – 619-387-7735

Novenson, Joseph Vincent – b Upper Darby, PA, Oct 3, 52; f Joseph John; m Louise; w Barbara Ann Boes, Trenton, NJ, May 31, 75; chdn Matthew Vincent, Andrew James, Elizabeth Marie; RidC 70-74, BA; WhitC 75-76, grad wk; WTS 74-78, MDiv; L Jul 8, 78; O Aug 20, 78, CentGA Pby; ap First P Ch, Augusta, GA, 78-81; bd mbr BLCHRSC, 88-91; t CBC, 89, lect; srp Lexington P Ch, Lexington, SC, 81-96; srp Lookout Mountain P Ch, Lookout Mountain, TN, 96-; bd trust CTS, 96-99, bd trust 04-17

116 Fleetwood Drive, Lookout Mountain, TN 37350 – 423-825-5461   Tennessee Valley
E-mail: joe@lmpc.org
Lookout Mountain Presbyterian Church – 423-821-4528

Noyes, Jeffrey C. – O Apr 2, 89; p Darlington Ref P Ch, Darlington, PA, 89-

3110 5th Avenue, Beaver Falls, PA 15010 – 724-847-2640   Ascension
Darlington Reformed Presbyterian Church – 724-827-2517

Nutting, David E. – w Priscilla; chdn Emily, Kaitlin, Caleb; NIU, BMus; ULasVegas, MMus; WSCAL, MDiv; O Nov 28, 04, NoTX Pby; mfam, ydir Spring Meadows P Ch, Las Vegas, NV, 97-00; North City P Ch, Dir Assim/Music, Poway, CA, 00-03; srp Bethel Ch PCA, Dallas, TX, 04-06; srp North City P Ch, Poway, CA, 06-

14561 Hillndale Way, Poway, CA 92064 – 858-679-0520   South Coast
E-mail: david@northcitychurch.com
North City Presbyterian Church – 858-748-4642

Nystrom, Doug – b Palos Park, IL, Apr 23, 64; f Wilford O.; m Helen D. MacDougall; w Rosemary Anne Deeley, Savannah, GA, Jun 29, 91; chdn D. Arthur Jr., Charles M., John C., Isabelle R., David G.; BayU 86, BBA; UGA 89, JD; WTS 95, MDiv; L Sept 28, 97, Palm Pby; O Sept 28, 97, Palm Pby; DCE, ydir Proclamation P Ch, Bryn Mawr, PA, 94-97; astp Lexington P Ch, Lexington, SC, 97-98; chp Westminster OPC, Wichita Falls, TX, 98-01; astp Covenant Ch, Fayetteville, AR, 03-

1920 Levi Lane, Rogers, AR 72756 – 479-381-1178   Hills and Plains
Covenant Church – 479-442-5267

O'Bannon, Robert Paul – w Mary; O Sept 19, 04, OHVal Pby; p New Life P Ch, Yorktown, IN, 04-

317 South Willow Drive, Muncie, IN 47304   Central Indiana
E-mail: obannon@newlifepca.org
New Life Presbyterian Church – 765-759-9189

O'Brien, Christopher M. – b Montgomery, AL, May 3, 62; f Stephen H.; m Barbara Broome; w Sarah Branscome, Hattiesburg, MS, Jul 20, 84; chdn Rachel Elissabeth, Kelly Kristine, Rebecca Kathryn; USM 85, BA; CTS 88, MDiv; O Sept 23, 90; astp Wallace P Ch, Hyattsville, MD, 88-92; ascp Westminster P Ch, Huntsville, AL, 92-95; p Grace P Ch, Jackson, TN, 95-99; astp Golden Isles P Ch, St. Simons Island, GA, 99-01; op Redeemer P Msn, Brunswick, GA, 99-01; ob t Hattiesburg, MS, 01-02; srp Third Ref P Ch, Philadelphia, PA, 05-11; wc 11-12; ob Chap Gulfport, MS, 12-14; p First P Ch, Picayune, MS, 14-; pamphlet "Social Security: Should Ministers Participate?"

1525 East Pass Road #1013, Gulfport, MS 39507   Grace
E-mail: chrisobrien1517@yahoo.com
First Presbyterian Church – 601-798-6189

O'Brien, Gregory – b Austin, TX, Oct 1, 81; w Ginger; chdn Jude, Crosby, Audrey, Matthew; UTXAu, BA; GCTS, MDiv, O May 8, 11, SNE Pby; astp Citylife P Ch of Boston, Boston, MA; mis sensitive area; astp First P Ch, Tuscumbia, AL, 16-18

201 Park Boulevard, Sheffield, AL 35660   Providence
E-mail: gregory.obrien@gmail.com

O'Connell, David – ascp Cross Sound Ch, Bainbridge Island, WA, 15-

206-842-6898   Pacific Northwest
E-mail: daveoc@crossound.org
Cross Sound Church – 206-842-6898

O'Donnell, Douglas S. – w Emily; chdn Sean, Lily, Evelyn, Simeon, Charlotte; ob srp New Covenant Ch, Naperville, IL, 08- 17; srp Westminster P Ch, Elgin, IL, 17-

615 Robin Ridge, Elgin, IL 60123 – 630-779-4274   Chicago Metro
Westminster Presbyterian Church – 847-695-0311

O'Dowd, Brendon Michael – b Santa Fe, NM, Sept 3, 69; f Gary; m Claire Marek; w Joan Sullo, Albuquerque, NM, Jun 8, 91; chdn Joshua, Kevin, Jason, Katherine, Kyle; USAFA 87-91, BS; RTS 96-98, MDiv; L Mar 98, MSVal Pby; O Jan 99, RMtn Pby; astp Edwards P Ch, Edwards, MS, 96-98; astp Forestgate P Ch, Colorado Springs, CO, 99-01; Chap USAF, 01-16

10619 Haskell Avenue, Granada Hills, CA 91344   Pacific
E-mail: odowdcrowd@msn.com

O'Dowd, David Martin – b Hamilton, OH, Apr 12, 47; f Raymond Michael; m Thelma Orveda Grau; w Mary Nell Quarles, Miami, FL, Jan 12, 80; chdn Michael Julian, Daniel Joseph, Erin Elizabeth Joy; NWU 69, BS; WCBS 79, MDiv; O Apr 27, 80, SFL Pby; CCC, 69-76; Key Biscayne P Ch, Key Biscayne, FL, 80-81, ascp 82-85; asst prof RTS, 85-90; adj prof RTSFL, 91-99; srp Seminole P Ch, Tampa, FL, 90-99; srp Christ P Ch, Tulsa, OK, 99-12; ss Covenant P Ch, Harrisonburg, VA, 12-14; ss Covenant P Ch, Nashville, TN, 18; lect WTS, 06-12; adj prof Redeemer Sem, 09-; fndr, Dir GAP International

2303 Sterling Road, Nashville, TN 37215   North Texas

O'Gorek, Paul – Recd PCA 17, BlRdg Pby, hr 17

Address Unavailable   Blue Ridge
HR

O'Leary, David – O Aug 23, 15, Asc Pby; astp Gospel Flwsp P Ch, Valencia, PA, 15-

4145 Grandview Drive, Gibsonia, PA 15044   Ascension
E-mail: davidtoleary@gmail.com
Gospel Fellowship Presbyterian Church – 724-898-3322

O'Neil, E. Bruce – b Los Angeles, CA, Apr 5, 61; f Edward B.; m Kathleen Fitzgerald; w Kathryn Shuman, Nashville, TN, Dec 15, 84; chdn Sarah Kathryn, Michael Paul, Matthew Coulter; AU 83, BA, 84, BS; RTS 93, MDiv; NGTS 05, DMin; L Jan 92, Gr Pby; O Jul 25, 93, TNVal Pby; astp Cedar Springs P Ch, Knoxville, TN, 93-96; p Trinity P Ch, Murfreesboro, TN, 96-01; srp Eastern Shore P Ch, Fairhope, AL, 01-06; srp Evangelical P Ch, Annapolis, MD, 06-; "Reclaiming the Office of Elder as Shepherd," diss

710 Ridgely Avenue, Annapolis, MD 21401 – 410-544-5530   Chesapeake
E-mail: boneil@epannapolis.org
Evangelical Presbyterian Church – 410-266-8090

O'Neill, E. Wesley III – b Abington, PA, Dec 31, 49; f E. Wesley Jr.; m Amanda; w Kathryn L. Knight, Scarborough, ME, Jun 20, 70; chdn Kerry (Singleton), Nathaniel; UME 67-71, BA; CTS 84-88, MDiv; L Nov 23, 87; O Jan 18, 89, CCCC; Recd PCA May 18, 96, NoE Pby; p Maplewood Cong Ch, St. Louis, MO, 86-91; p Trinity Christ Ch, 91-95; ascp First P Ch, Schenectady, NY, 96-07; ss Arlington P Ch, Arlington, TX, 07-08; ss Heritage P Ch, Edmond, OK, 08-11; ss Arlington P Ch, Arlington, TX, 12-14; srp 14- 16, p em 16-17, hr 17

6564 Mineral Belt Drive, Colorado Springs, CO 80927 – 518-505-8159   North Texas
E-mail: ewoneill3@gmail.com
HR

O'Neill, Mark Alpheus – b Lockport NY, May 2, 62; f Paul; m Kari; w Natalie Rich, Apr 28, 01; CornU 84, BS; WSCAL 96, MDiv; L Sept 16, 95, SoCst Pby; O Aug 18, 96, SoTX Pby; p Covenant P Ch, Lufkin, TX, 96-

108 Jasmine Court, Lufkin, TX 75901 – 936-632-0799   Houston Metro
E-mail: pcalufkin@consoslidated.com
Covenant Presbyterian Church – 936-637-6043

O, Gyu Myeong – p New York Se Kwang Presbyterian Church, 09-

Address Unavailable   Korean Northeastern
New York Se Kwang Presbyterian Church

O, John – UPA 94, BA; WSCAL 02, MDiv; astp Korean-American PC of Arizona Msn, Peoria, AZ, 08; astp First Kor P Ch, Philadelphia, PA, 09-10; p Grace Cov P Ch PCA, Philadelphia, PA, 10-15; Chap USArmy, 16-

3001 Limekiln Pike, Glenside, PA 19038 – 215-982-0144   Korean Eastern
E-mail: johnojundo@yahoo.com
United States Army

Oaks, Brian – astp Eastwood P Ch, Montgomery, AL, 13-15; ev 15-17; op Christ Flwsp, Roswell, GA, 17-

11840 Highland Colony Drive, Roswell, GA 30075 – 334-272-3103   Metro Atlanta
E-mail: oaksbw@gmail.com
Christ Fellowship

Oates, Robert Coit – b Sweetwater, TN, Aug 24, 52; f Jack Cotten Jr.; m Mildred Woods Coit; w Rosalie Ethel Renich, Farmington, MI, Nov 8, 74; chdn Robert Jr., Helen-Clare, Reuben, Elizabeth-Anne; CBC 70-74, BA; RTS 76-80, MDiv, MCE; O Jul 21, 81, Knoxv Pby (PCUS); Recd PCA Feb 28, 91, SEAL Pby; ap First P Ch (PCUS), Knoxville, TN, 81-85; p First P Ch, Brewton, AL, 85-95; srp Faith P Ch, Brookhaven, MS, 95-09; srp First P Ch, Dothan, AL, 09-17, astp 17-

1100 Amherst Drive, Dothan, AL 36305 – 334-792-4656   Southeast Alabama
E-mail: roates@firstpresdothan.com
First Presbyterian Church – 334-794-3128

Oates, Thomas N. – b Aug 2, 48; w Suzette de Marigny Howard, Far Hills, NJ, Jun 21, 75; chdn Charles Dewey, Suzette de Marigny, Nicholas Claiborne, Louisa Alger Howard; HarvU 71, AB; UOxf 73, BA, 73, MA; VTS 74, cert; O Sept 29, 77, St. Paul's Cath, London; Recd PCA Feb 13, 98, MNY Pby; assoc, Dir FOCUS, 74-76; Curate, St. Helens Ch, London, 76-78; Curate, St. John's Episc Ch, Huntingdon Valley, PA, 78-80; Rector, Ch of Good Shepherd, Richmond, VA, 80-89; Rector, Christ Church, South Hamilton, MA, 89-93; p Grace Ch of Greenwich, Greenwich, CT, 94-

9 Mavis Lane, Greenwich, CT 06830 – 203-622-0908   Metropolitan New York
E-mail: gracecog@aol.com
Grace Church of Greenwich – 203-861-7555

Odell, Adam Troy – b Nurenburg, Germany, Jun 7, 68; f Stewart Ira; m Vivian Elizabeth Polz; w Katherine Anne Howlett, Wheaton, IL, Dec 21, 91; chdn Caleb, Isaac, Micah, Jacob; TayU 90, BS; CTS 95; L Jan 17, 98; O Jan 17, 98, NGA Pby; astp, yp Intown Comm Ch, Atlanta, GA, 96-03; ascp Zion Ch, Lincoln, NE, 03-08; op Redeemer Ch PCA, Lincoln, NE, 08-12; p 12-13; ascp 13-

3520 Poplar Place, Lincoln, NE 68506 – 402-488-4377   Platte Valley
E-mail: adam@welcometoredeemer.com
Redeemer Church PCA

Odum, Matthew – O Sept 30, 12, NoTX Pby; astp Denton P Ch, Denton, TX, 12-14; campm RUF, UNTX, 14-17; p Redeemer PCA, Lincoln, NE, 17-

3825 South 44th Street, Lincoln, NE 68506　　　　　　　　　　　　　　　　Platte Valley
Redeemer PCA – 402-937-8904

Ogley, Edward Martin, III – b Coldspring, NY, Jul 29, 68; f Edward Martin Jr.; m Janet Marsha Ware; w Lisa Rayleen Gray, Manhattan Beach, CA, Aug 14, 93; chdn Jessica, Christina, Michelle, Elizabeth, Charis; NGTS, MDiv; O Nov 13, 11, NNE Pby; astp First P Ch of Concord (PCA), Concord, NH, 11-14; astp Christ Ch, Pembroke, NH, 14-; op Hooksett Christian Flwsp, Hooksett, NH, 16-

138 Merrimack Street, Hooksett, NH 03106 – 603-290-3050　　　　　Northern New England
E-mail: tednachi@earthlink.net
Christ Church – 603-225-7377
Hooksett Christian Fellowship – 603-290-3050

Ogrosky, Gary L. – O Nov 14, 10, JR Pby; astp Sycamore P Ch, Midlothian, VA, 10-11; admin MNA, 14-

14611 Ashlake Manor Drive, Chesterfield, VA 23832 – 804-379-1306　　　　　James River
E-mail: ogrosky@aol.com
PCA Mission to North America – 678-825-1200

Oh, Bumjoon – b South Korea, Apr 11, 72; f Kinam Oh; m Hwaja; w Sungsook, Korea, Oct 5, 96; chdn Judy, Michelle; STS 96, BA; TalTS 08, MDiv; O Jun 08, Korean PC; srp One Life Comm Ch, Paramus, NJ, 09-13; srp Ark P Ch, Fairlawn, NJ, 13-

202 Bogert Road #1, River Edge, NJ 07661 – 201-965-9876　　　　　Korean Northeastern
Ark Presbyterian Church – 201-398-9100

Oh, Chun Ho – p Central P Ch of Sacramento, Fair Oaks, CA

6124 Westport Lane, Sacramento, CA 95621　　　　　　　　　　　　Korean Northwest
E-mail: chunho217@hanmail.net
Central Presbyterian Church of Sacramento – 916-961-6631

Oh, Daniel S. – b Korea, Feb 3, 61; w Grace; chdn Gloria, Joyce; UCB 85, BS; WSCAL 95, MDiv; GCTS 06, ThM; ErskTS 11, DMin; O Apr 95, KorSW Pby; Open Door P Ch (non-PCA), Escondido, CA, 92-95; Chap US Army, 95-; astp, Chap 82nd Div Mem Chapel, Ft. Bragg, NC, 96-98; astp, Chap JFK Mem Chap, Ft. Bragg, NC, 98-00; Chap USArmy, Zoeckler Chapel, Korea, 00-03; Chap USArmy, Ft. Lewis, WA, 03-04; USArmy, Camp Arifjan, Kuwait, 04-05; art "The Relevance of Virtue Ethics and Application to the Formation of Character Development in Warriors," International Society of Military Ethics, 07, and Summer Army Chaplaincy Magazine, 08

7729 Rachael Whitney Lane, Alexandria, VA 22315　　　　　　　　Korean Southeastern
E-mail: daniel.s.oh@us.army.mil
United States Army

Oh, Gunmook – astp Sae Han P Ch of Atlanta, Alpharetta, GA, 14-

10880 Brunson Drive, Duluth, GA 30097　　　　　　　　　　　　　　Korean Southeastern
E-mail: ogm5555@gmail.com
Sae Han Presbyterian Church of Atlanta – 770-619-5340

Oh, Jonathan – O Nov 13, 16, KorSE Pby; mis 16-

2320 Ohashi, 401 Guransoa Ohashi, Meguroku, Tokyo 1530044 JAPAN　　　Korean Southeastern
E-mail: jonathan.a.oh@gmail.com

Oh, Joo Young – b Korea, Feb 6, 59; f Chang Ki; m Chul Sae Kim; w Youngmee Lee, Korea, Jan 11, 86; chdn Judy, Grace, Sarah, Christine; PhilCB 83, BA; ChShTS 88, MDiv; O , KPCA; mis Korea, 85-92; srp Open Door Ch of Or Co, Garden Grove, CA, 92-14; ob mis Cambodia, 14-

2010 North Derek Drive #219   Korean Southwest Orange County
Fullerton, CA 92831 – 714-526-5117
E-mail: opendoorch@hotmail.com

Oh, Joon – ascp Korean Central P Ch, Centreville, VA, 16-17

6611 Parville Loop, Gainesville, VA 20155   Korean Capital

Oh, Mark – w Michelle; chdn Justin, Josiah, Deborah; UVA 90, BS; BibTS 96, BA; mis CCC (now CRU), 91-; EPIC Regional Coordinator, 96-03; Campus Miss, Osaka, Japan; 03-07; Miss Receiving Coord, 07-09; East Asia Region Office (Singapore), 10; XChange (missionary cross-cultural training); assoc dir Christian Embassy DC

4640 Holly Avenue, Fairfax, VA 22030   Korean Capital
E-mail: mark.oh@cru.org
Christian Embassy DC

Oh, Michael Young-Suk – b Philadelphia, PA, Apr 19, 71; f Sung Kyu Henry; m Young Ie Lee; w Pearl Kyung Park, Philadelphia, PA, Jun 18, 94; chdn Hannah Kippum, Mikaela Sarahng; UPA 92, BS, 93, MS; TEDS 97, MDiv; HarvU 00, MA; UPA 04, PhD; L Jan 98, Phil Pby; O Apr 98, Phil Pby; mis MTW, Nagoya, Japan, 98-00, wc 00-01; astp Korean United Ch of Phil, Philadelphia, PA, 01-04; pres Lausanne Movement (via MTW), Japan, 13-

2-5-11 Midori, Miyoshigaoka, Miyoshi Shi, Aichi Ken 470-0205, JAPAN   Philadelphia
011-81-561-31-0276
E-mail: moh@lausanne.org
Lausanne Movement, Nagoya, Japan

Oh, Peter –

Address Unavailable   Korean Central

Oh, Samuel – ob

4832 Eisenhower Court, Yorba Linda, CA 92886   Korean Southwest
E-mail: samyoh@crossway-church.com

Oh, Sung Bok – p Macon Korean P Ch, Macon, GA, 07-

152 Princeton Drive, Macon, GA 31220 – 478-501-0449   Korean Southeastern
Macon Korean Presbyterian Church – 478-781-0008

Oh, Tae Hwan – ev Eun Chong Presbyterian Church of NY, 09-16

209-23 46th Avenue 2nd Fl, Bayside, NY 11361   Korean Northeastern

Oh, Thomas Sukdeuk – b Okcheon, South Korea; w Yung Sun Yoon, Seoul; chdn Jonathan, Richard; CIU 95, BA, 99, MDiv; O Jan 00; Recd PCA Oct 03, KorSE Pby; chp Immanuel Korean Ch, Columbia, SC, 99-04; p Sandol P Ch, Columbia, SC, 04-

109 Eagle Park Drive, Columbia, SC 29206   Korean Southeastern
E-mail: ohinchrist@gmail.com
Sandol Presbyterian Church – 803-665-6762

Ohl, William Lloyd – b Natrona Hghts, PA, May 6, 52; f Lloyd Herbert; m Jane Margaret Christy; w Pamela Lynn Stokes, Butler, PA, Dec 18, 82; chdn Peter W., Zachary W., Ellice M.; GroCC 74, BA; GCTS 74-75, 81-86; RPTS 92, MDiv; L Jul 13, 91; O May 2, 93, Asc Pby; ob Coalition Christian Outreach, Butler Co CC, 81-86, Dir 86-92; ob p Cochranton Comm Ch, 92-96; Chap State Reg Corr Facility, Mercer, PA, 96-16; hr 16

152 South Franklin Street, Cochranton, PA 16314 – 814-425-1540   Ascension
HR

Ok, Se Joon – p New Creation Msn, Centreville, VA, 08-12; wc 12-

5479 Ormond Stone Circle, Centreville, 20120 – 571-522-1202   Korean Capital
E-mail: okmoksa@yahoo.com

Ok, Seung Ryong – b Korea, Jan 31, 62; f Kwang Soo; m Hyeon Sook Kim; w Hyeon Jeong Lee, Korea, Jun 20, 87; chdn Unheh, Unsung, Unbyul; KHU 87, BS; UMN 89, MS; UCD 94, PhD; BibTS 99, MDiv; L Oct 2, 00, KorCap Pby; O Apr 8, 02, KorCap Pby; yp Gloria Korean P Ch, Glen Burnie, MD, 00-01; p Bethesda Korean P Ch, Rockville, MD, 01-10

11021 Outpost Drive, North Potomac, MD 20878 – 301-279-6855   Korean Capital
E-mail: pastorok7@gamil.com

Oldham, Eugene – b Jan 25, 73; f Dr. Larry E.; m Libby M.; w Laura Sue Streflling, Jul 10, 99; chdn Ethan Grant, Meredith Claudia, Jonathan Haddon, Caleb Michael, Patrick William, Thomas Knox, Benjamin Clayton, Audrey Elizabeth; RTSNC 12, MDiv; O Jun 8, 14, CatVal Pby; ascp Grace Ch, Harrisburg, NC, 14-

2007 Stallings Road, Harrisburg, NC 28075 – 704-618-6538   Catawba Valley
E-mail: leojr@me.com
Grace Church – 704-455-9312

Oliphant, David Ross – b Oak Ridge, TN, Jan 10, 54; f George W.; m Christine Sparkman; w Jeanette Marks, Lowell, MI, Dec 17, 83; chdn Aaron George, Jonathan Mark; UTC 76, BS; ClemU 77, MS; CIU 83, MDiv; L Jan 85; O Jan 85, Cal Pby; ap Second P Ch, Greenville, SC, 85-87, wc 87-95; ss Philadelphia P Ch, Landrum, SC, 95-01, p 01-

308 Elaine Avenue, Taylors, SC 29687-3226 – 864-244-6380   Calvary
E-mail: djoliphant@aol.com
Philadelphia Presbyterian Church – 864-457-2150

Oliphint, Kyle – b Amarillo, TX, Oct 1, 62; f Bud (d); m Pat Kelly (d); w Elizabeth Ann Young, Tampa, FL, Dec 10, 94; chdn Katie, Caroline, Kelly; WTXA&M 89, BA; WTS 99, MDiv; L & O Apr 10, 01, SWFL Pby; ascp Holy Trin P Ch, Tampa, FL, 01-04; op Grace Comm P Ch, Ft. Worth, TX, 05-06; p 06-

7101 North Riverside Drive, Ft. Worth, TX 76137 – 817-847-7766   North Texas
E-mail: gcpcfw@gmail.com
Grace Community Presbyterian Church – 817-637-8597

Olivares, Oscar – w Nancy; chdn Eugenia, Wendy; MTS 92, MDiv; p First P Ch, Douglas, AZ, 92-00; Chap Hospice, San Antonio, 02-09 mgr Hospice Bereavement, 09-; ascp Oakwood P Ch, San Antonio, TX, 05-13; Hope Hospice, New Braunfels, TX, 13-18

25619 Stormy Creek, San Antonio, TX 78255 – 210-602-9170   South Texas
E-mail: onolivares@hotmail.com

MINISTERIAL DIRECTORY

Oliveira, Manoel – b Jatai, Brasil, Dec 16, 65; f Manoel; m Wanda Maria Costa; w Ana Celia Fonseca, Piracanjuba, Brasil, Jul 26, 86; chdn Sarah, Pedro; Inst Biblico Boas Novas 90, dipl; Centro Formacao Teologica 94, ThB; GCTS 01, MA, 05, DMin; O Jan 4, 94, PGNA, Brasil; Recd PCA 99, NoE Pby; p, mis Presbiterio de Goiania, 91-97; astp Christ The King P Ch, Cambridge, MA, 99-04; op New Life P Comm Ch, Framingham, MA, 00-

94 Woodridge Road, Marlboro, MA 01752 – 508-229-2822   Southern New England
E-mail: revmanoel@cpnv.org
New Life Presbyterian Community Church – 508-989-2158

Oliver, John W. P. – b Vincennes, IN, Apr 9, 35; f Dwight Lorenzo O; m Elizabeth Posegate; w Cristina Shepard Hope, Atlanta, GA, Oct 19, 68; chdn John William Posegate Jr, Sloan Christian Shepard; DenU 52-55; WheatC 56, BA; FulTS 59, BD; SBTS 63, ThM; WCBS 96, DD; CIU 08, DD, 09, DD; O Aug 19, 62, Ind; ap Covenant Ch, Hammond, IN, 64-66; ap Trinity P Ch, Montgomery, AL, 66-69; srp First P Ch, Augusta, GA, 69-97; srp Trinity P Ch, Montgomery, AL, 97-99; ob prof RTSNC, 99-; hr 01

731 Stanhope Lane, Matthews, NC 28105 – 704-846-8240   Southeast Alabama
E-mail: joliver@rts.edu
HR

Oliver, Matthew – MastersC 97, BA; OKCityU 04, MBA; WTS 11, MDiv; Chap USAR, 11-13; Chap USArmy, 13

7709 Dominion Avenue NE, Lacey, WA 98516 – 405-203-6921   North Texas
E-mail: mach815@gmail.com
United States Army

Oliver, W. Michael – chapUSArmy; *What I Believe: A Combat Chaplain's Guide to God*

112 Gordon B. Hinckley Avenue, Rincon, GA 31326 – 615-956-1546   Nashville
E-mail: chaplainmichaeloliver@yahoo.com
United States Army

Olivo, John – chp, ev Metro NY, 98-99; op I'm Forgiven Bronx Comm Msn, Bronx, NY, 99-12; wc 12-

426 Calhoun Avenue, Bronx, NY 10465 – 718-239-2990   Metropolitan New York

Olsen, Jonathan – astp Tenth P Ch, Philadelphia, PA, 07-10; op Grace and Peace Comm Ch, Philadelphia, PA, 09-15, p 15-

1813 Christian Street, Philadelphia, PA 19146 – 215-520-7883   Philadelphia
E-mail: pastorjonathanolsen@gmail.com
Grace and Peace Community Church – 484-483-5837

Olshefski, Jordan Farrell – b Harrisburg, PA, Oct 6, 80; f Joseph; m Patricia Ann Farrell; w Evyn Frances Fuller-Smith, Nashville, TN, Sep 13, 03; chdn Walker, Eleanor, Knox, Evelyn; Elon 03, BS; RTS 11, MDiv; O Jul 15, 12, CentCar Pby; astp Cross Park Ch, Charlotte, NC, 11-13; ascp 13-

1379 Bellemeade Lane, Charlotte, NC 28270 – 717-433-0652   Central Carolina
E-mail: jordanolsh@yahoo.com
Cross Park Church – 980-285-7020

Olson, Edwin Harold Jr. – b Uniontown, PA, Mar 3, 47; f Edwin H. Sr.; m Wilma Ann Chadwell; w Connie Jean Brown, Ft. Lauderdale, FL, Dec 17, 77; chdn Mark Andrew, Derek Edwin, Karin Elizabeth;

Olson, Edwin Harold Jr., continued
USF 65-69; AU 70-72, BA; RTS 81-84, MDiv; O Oct 84, DMV Pby; astp Timonium P Ch, Timonium, MD, 84-92, ascp 92-95, wc 95-; moy Central P Ch (USA), 96-97, wc 98; ip Loch Raven P Ch, Baltimore, MD, 99; p Swannanoa Valley P Ch, Swannanoa, NC, 02-

292 Patton Hill Road, Swannanoa, NC 28778 – 828-686-4800   Western Carolina
E-mail: swannanoavalleypc@msn.com
Swannanoa Valley Presbyterian Church – 828-686-5716

Olson, Eric Daniel – b Valparaiso, IN, Aug 16, 67; f Dan; m Pat Johnson; w Elaine Rae Steffen, Bluffton, IN, Jul 23, 89; chdn Rachel Marlene, Tabitha Ann, Nathan Eric, Samuel Kenneth, Josiah Daniel, Jacob Fritzen, Isaac Eric, Karis Elaine; INU 90, BS; RTSFL 99, MDiv; L Jul 20, 99, CentFL Pby; O Nov 14, 99, CentFL Pby; astp Covenant P Ch, Palm Bay, FL, 99-00; p Grace Central Ch (form Grace Ref Ch), Omaha, NE, 00-

4345 North 81st Street, Omaha, NE 68134   Platte Valley
E-mail: eric@graceomaha.com
Grace Central Church – 402-573-1663

Olson, John – b Washington, DC, Jul 18, 54; f John Richard; m Marie Keenan; w Libby Marie Ridge, Charleston, SC, Oct 14, 72; chdn Genia Marie, Jennifer Renee, Erika Lyn, Amanda Jin Ah; RTS 98, MDiv; L Oct 96; O Nov 2, 97, Palm Pby; p Church Creek Ref P Ch, Charleston, SC, 97-

6 Tynte Street, Charleston, SC 29407-7324 – 803-571-5481   Lowcountry
E-mail: hasvedt@aol.com
Church Creek Reformed Presbyterian Church – 843-766-1381

Omerly, George Geiger III – b Philadelphia, PA, Feb 23, 30; f George G. Jr.; m Catherine Riggs; w Audrey Miriam Palmer, Camden, NJ, Dec 27, 58; chdn Margaret Ellen, George Calvin; StLawU 52, BA; FTS 54-56; CTS 58, BD; WTS 70, ThM, 96, PhD; L Apr 56; O May 58, Midw Pby (BPC); USArmy 53-54; ip BP chs Underwood-Dodge-Wilton circuit, ND, 58; hm NJ Pby (BPC), 59; mis WPM, Peru, 59-73; mis MTW, Peru, 73-96; Evangelical Sem of Lima, 75-95; hr 96; Bible Inst of South Africka, Kalk Bay, SA, 97; PTSDD, 97; Presbyterian Church in Belize, 99; Seminario Teol Pres, Mexico City, 00; Seminario Teol Pres, Monterey, 01; Seminario Pres San Pablo, Merida, 00-01; Pres Theo Sem, Kiev, Ukraine, 02; Pres Theo Sem, Moscow, Russia, 02-03; Seminario Evangelico de Lima, 02; Pacific Islands Bible College, 04; Hapdong Presbyterian Seminary, Suwon Korea, 04; Semin Pres San Pablo, Ciudad Victoria, Mx., 05; Seminario Evangelico de Lima, 05; Westminster Theo Sem, Brisbane, 06; Presbyterian Theo Sem, Philippines, 06-07; Westminster Bible College, Kampala, Uganda, 07; China Reformed Theological Semnary, Taipei, Taiwan, 07; Presbyterian Sem, Victoria, Mexico, 08; Presbyterian Seminary of N. India, Dehra Dun, India, 09; Theo Coll of Central Africa, Ndola, Zambia, 10

533 Park Avenue, Quarryville, PA 17566   Gulf Coast
E-mail: ggoamo@netzero.net
HR

Oommen, Shibu – b Kerala, India, 67; 92, MA; 07, MDiv; w Mary; fndr India Village Mission; O Jun 3, 12, Phil Pby; ob ev PEF, 12-; astp Crossroads Comm Ch, Upper Darby, PA, 13-

109 Barrington Road, Upper Darby, PA 19082 – 484-478-3419   Philadelphia Metro West
E-mail: shibuoommen@hotmail.com
Presbyterian Evangelistic Fellowship – 423-573-5308
Crossroads Community Church – 610-352-3130

Orlando, John – O May 17, 14, PhilMetW Pby; astp Iron Works Ch, Phoenixville, PA, 14-16; ss Redemption P Ch, Malvern, PA, 16-17; op New Life Ch of Vicenza, Italy, 17-

Unit 31408, Box 8011R, APO, AE 09639 – 484-924-9772   Philadelphia Metro West
E-mail: john@newlifevicenza.org
New Life Church of Vicenza – 011 39 349 613 5266

Orner, Robert Hugh – b Bloomington, IL, Sept 20, 62; f James R.; m Gloria J. Zehr; w Barbara Christine Stiles, Carlock, IL, Jun 7, 86; chdn Taylor Cameron; LeTC 81-82; CBC 82-85; RTS 92-94, MDiv, 05, DMin; L Jul 94; O Oct 94, CentFL Pby; int Hixson P Ch, Hixson, TN, 86-91; int Willow Creek Ch, Winter Springs, FL, 91-93; p Coquina P Ch, Ormond Beach, FL, 94-98; op, p Christ Ch Newnan, Newnan, GA, 98-09; ob RTSFL, 10-14; srp Covenant P Ch, Cherry Hill, NJ, 14-; *Why Baptizing Your Child Matters: Understanding the Benefits of Covenant Baptism*, 14; "Sacrificial Living," *Ministry and Leadership* Spr/Sum 13: 7-8; "Une Vie De Sacrifice," *Église Chrétienne Réformée De Beauce* Mar 23, 13 (elec); "Pray up a Child in the Way He Should Go," *Disciple Magazine* May 13 (elec); "Can the Church Adapt to Demographic Reality," *ByFaith Magazine* Aug 09

167 Pearl Croft Road, Cherry Hill, NJ 08034 – 678-517-5260　　　　　　　　　　　New Jersey
E-mail: bob@ornernet.com
Covenant Presbyterian Church – 856-429-1225

Orr, Kenneth William – BJU 73, BA; BibTS 76, MDiv; p EPC, Paramount, CA, 77-80; p Calvary P Ch, Glendale, CA, 80-92; t Pasadena CS, 92-96; p RPCNA, Los Angeles, CA, 96-08; prin Pasadena CS, 08-17; hr 17

1515 North Los Robles Avenue, Pasadena, CA 91104　　　　　　　　　　　　　　Pacific
E-mail: kenorr7@gmail.com
HR

Orren, Steven Todd – b San Bernadino CA, Apr 24, 64; f Bennett Hugh; m Kathryn Louise Lake; w Margaret Elizabeth Sargent, Cantonment, FL, Nov 24, 90; chdn Robert James, Josiah Daniel, Hannah Ruth; CC 87, BA; WSCAL 87-90, MDiv; L Oct 14, 95; O Aug 17, 96, NoCA Pby; Chap USN, 96-

9937 Eleral Drive, Pensacola, FL 32526　　　　　　　　　　　　　　Northern California
E-mail: p.orren@juno.com
United States Navy

Orteza, Luis – p Providence Comm Ch, Birmingham, AL; wc 15-

Address Unavailable　　　　　　　　　　　　　　　　　　　　　　　　　　　Evangel

Ortiz, Victor Omar – b San Juan, PR, Apr 18, 77; f Victor; m Susana; w Kathryn; chdn Victor Elisha, Asher Lee, Lenna Kathryn, Asa Joel; TIU 99, BA; RTSFL 04, MDiv; O Oct 04, SFL Pby; astp Old Cutler P Ch, Miami, FL, 04-09; sc SFL Pby, 06-09; p Lake Osborne Continuing P Ch, Lake Worth, FL, 09-16; astp Christ The King P Ch, Cambridge, MA, 17-

60 Roslin Drive, Apt. 1, Dorchester, MA 02124　　　　　　　　　　Southern New England
E-mail: omar@ctkboston.org
Christ The King Presbyterian Church – 617-354-8341

Osborne, David – w Jennifer Bragdon; chdn Owen Gresham, Dabney Caroline, Bergan Mae; KgC 97, BA; GPTS 02, MDiv; O Aug 16, 03, Wcar Pby; int Second P Ch, Greenville, SC, 99-01; p Emmanuel P Ch, Franklin, NC, 01-07; campm RUF, WestCarU, 07-13; srp Christ P Ch, Winterville, NC, 13-

302 Pinewood Road, Greenville, NC 27858 – 828-421-1213　　　　　　　　Eastern Carolina
E-mail: dosbornecpc@icloud.com
Christ Presbyterian Church – 252-355-9632

Osborne, Michael Edward – b Union, SC, Jan 23, 54; f Edward L.B.; m Dorothy Ellen Slaughter; w Suzanne Cook, Orlando, FL, Jul 24, 76; chdn Rebecca (Castleman), David Randel, Jennifer (Page), James Michael; FurU 76, BA; CTS 86, MDiv; L 86; O 86, MO Pby; ascp Covenant P Ch, St. Louis, MO, 86-89;

Osborne, Michael Edward, continued
srp Covenant P Ch, Easley, SC, 89-96; srp Grace P Ch, Ocala, FL, 96-01; astp University P Ch, Orlando, FL, 01-02, ascp 02-08; srp 08-13; ascp 13-; *Surviving Ministry: How to Weather the Storms of Church Leadership.*

13847 Guildhall Circle, Orlando, FL 32828 – 407-970-8847   Central Florida
E-mail: mike@upcorlando.org
University Presbyterian Church – 407-384-3300

Osterhaus, William Thompson – b Washington, DC, Dec 22, 44; f William H.; m Frances Thompson; w Judith Ann King, Arlington, VA, Dec 21, 65; chdn Daniel Steven, Timothy David, Jonathan Mark, Rachel Faith (Gregory); MBI 65, dipl; TCIL 67, BA; WheatGrS 72, MA; O Jun 68, Cherrydale Bap Ch; Recd PCA Jan 85, CentCar Pby; t TFBC, 72-75; t Westm Chr, Miami, 75-84; mis Peru, 68-70; op New Hope Ch, Charlotte, NC, 84-88; instr KgC, 89-95; srp Edgemont P Ch, Bristol, TN, 88-95; srp Valley P Ch, Lutherville, MD, 95-11; hr; adj prof Charlotte Christian Coll and Sem, 14-15

29 Panther Ridge Road, Brevard, NC 28712 – 828-393-9013   Chesapeake
E-mail: revtomost@yahoo.com
HR

Ottinger, John Thomas Jr. – b Ridley Park, PA, Jul 26, 54; f John T.; m Nancy K. McKim; w Julie Jean Vergalla, Oakland, NJ, Jun 17, 78; chdn John T. III, Stephen Paul, Christopher Daniel, Matthew David; UDE 76, BA; WTS 79, MDiv; O Aug 9, 81, SFL Pby; op New Cov P Ch, Hickory, NC, 83-86; assoc, coord PCA Investor's Fund, 86-94; coord MNA FMF, 89-91; ob P Investors Fund, 94-; ascp Brookwood P Ch, Snellville, GA, 96-98; ob; hr 12

413 Surf Road, Melbourne Beach, FL 32951 – 770-889-7766   Metro Atlanta
E-mail: jack.ottinger@gmail.com
HR

Otto, Duane – b Bloomington, IL, Jan 1, 69; f Arnold August Jr.; m Norma Jean Hooley; w Julie Elizabeth Winslow, St. Louis, MO, Jul 29, 95; chdn Calvin August, Sophia Elizabeth, Mary Elizabeth Stuart, Amelia McClean, Rose Alexandra, Jonathan Landon; UIL 91, BS; CTS 98, MDiv, 98, MAC; L Aug 2, 98, LA Pby; O Aug 2, 98, LA Pby; astp Delhi P Ch, Delhi, LA, 98-01; astp Lakemont P Ch, Augusta, GA, 01-02, ascp 02-07; ob fndr/admin Ithaka Fellowship, 07-; astp Christ Ch, Normal, IL, 08-

5821 East 1000 North Road, Gridley, IL 61744 – 309-846-0948   Northern Illinois
E-mail: duane_otto@yahoo.com
Ithaka Fellowship
Christ Church – 309-452-7927

Ottolini, Steven J. – ob ev Covenant Leadership Training Inst., 09-

1850 Williamstown Drive, St. Peters, MO 63376 – 636-236-7282   Missouri
E-mail: s_ottolini@yahoo.com
Covenant Leadership Training Institute

Ouimette, Jerry Edward – b Albany, GA, Dec 31, 47; f Armand Edward; m Bernice Mobley; w Margaret Elizabeth Ward, Albany, GA, Sept 1, 68; chdn Elizabeth Kay, Emily Kathryn; GSU, BA; RTS, MDiv; O Sept 79, SWGA Pby (PCUS); p First Ch, Cordele, GA, 79-83; ap Christ Cov P Ch, Matthews, NC, 83-84; p Second Street P Ch, Albemarle, NC, 84-85; op Thomasville Msn, Thomasville, GA, 85-89; ascp First P Ch, Dothan, AL, 89-92; p Covenant P Ch, Winter Haven, FL, 92-98; p Union P Ch, Salters, SC, 98-03; ss Mouzon P Ch, Kingstree, SC, 03-17; hr 17; bookmark "Trust God's Word"; brochure "In Answer to Your Question"; tract "Good News for Life"

1002 Terracerock Circle, Ballwin, MO 63011 – 843-356-2391   Pee Dee
E-mail: ouimette.papa@gmail.com
HR

MINISTERIAL DIRECTORY

Outen, Jay – b Lancaster, SC, Aug 30, 68; f Harold Thomas; m Gloria Jean Hicks; w Donna Elizabeth Reeves, St. Louis, MO, Jun 7, 97; chdn Sydney Rose, Reeves Scot, Sadie Lynn, Ross Thomas; WinC 91, BMusEd; CTS 97, MDiv; O Oct 19, 97, Cov Pby; astp Covenant P Ch, Cleveland, MS, 97-02; MTW, 02-03; Chap USArmy, 03-

813 Brooke Valley Trace, Clarksville, TN 37043　　　　　　　　　　　　　　　　　Covenant
E-mail: jaysouten@yahoo.com
United States Army

Overton, Thomas – astp Park Cities P Ch, Dallas, TX, 11-

3523 McFarlin Boulevard, Dallas, TX 75205　　　　　　　　　　　　　　　　　North Texas
E-mail: Tommy.overton@pcpc.org
Park Cities Presbyterian Church – 214-224-2500

Owen, Calvin Douglas – b Memphis, TN, Feb 9, 56; f Raymond William; w Lauren Kimberly Reeves, Jackson, MS, Jan 8, 83; chdn Hunter Reeves, Tyson Causey, Meredith Jameson, Reagan Alise; MempSU 76-79, BS; RTS 90-93, MDiv; L 91, MSVal Pby; O Jan 24, 98, Evan Pby; staff CCC, 81-91; astp Briarwood P Ch, Birmingham, AL, 98-02; ob CMDS, Jackson, MS, 02-16

107 Blackberry Creek Road, Flora, MS 39071-9387　　　　　　　　　　　　　　　　　Evangel

Owen, Charles Robert III – w Janet; chdn Mary, Anna, Micah, Seth, AmyLaura, John, Luke, Robert; AU, BA; UKS, MA; RTS, MDiv; O Dec 16, 95, SEAL Pby; Chap USArmy, 95-

1171 Rays Bridge Rd, Whispering Pines, NC 28327 – 910-366-5391　　　　Southeast Alabama
E-mail: charles.owen@us.army.mil
United States Army

Owen, Joshua D. – b Baltimore, MD, Jan 30, 74; f Ronald Gene; m Beverly Ann Vaughn; w Laura Renae Warren; chdn Caleb Jonathan, Abigail Grace, Benjamin David; SEBTS 98, BA, 01, MDiv; SBTS 08, PhD; O Jan 01, Bapt; Recd PCA Nov 11, CentCar Pby; p Oak Grove Bapt Ch, Roper, NC, 00-01; p Richland Bapt Ch, Owenton, KY, 03-05; p Trinity Bapt Ch, Fayetteville, NC, 06-11; p Cross Creek P Ch, Fayetteville, NC, 11-

2502 Elmhurst Drive, Fayetteville, NC 28304 – 910-366-1917　　　　　　　Central Carolina
E-mail: pastorowen@crosscreekpca.org
Cross Creek Presbyterian Church – 910-864-4031

Owens, Brad – O Aug 19, 18, Palm Pby; astp Blythewood P Ch, Blythewood, SC, 18-

244 North High Duck Trail, Blythewood, SC 29016　　　　　　　　　　　　　　　Palmetto
Blythewood Presbyterian Church – 803-786-2399

Owens, Bruce – b Toledo, OH, Aug 25, 47; f Louis E.; m Mary C. Kelly; w Willette Jane Rawlins, Ruidoso, NM, Jun 28, 86; chdn Kelly M., Megan Joy, Sarah Jane; UHou 70, BBA; CTS 95, MDiv; O Nov 10, 98, NGA Pby; admin, staff MTW, dir partner rel, 95-

1877 De Winton Place, Lawrenceville, GA 30043 – 770-513-7050　　　　　　Metro Atlanta
E-mail: bruce.owens@mtw.org
PCA Mission to the World – 678-823-0004

Owens, Jack M. III (Trey) – astp Christ P Ch, New Braunfels, TX, 10-12; astp First P Ch, Kosciusko, MS, 13-

213 Oakland Street, Kosciusko, MS 39090　　　　　　　　　　　　　　　　Mississippi Valley
E-mail: treyowens@fpckosciusko.org
First Presbyterian Church – 662-289-2435

Owens, Matthew – b Normal, IL, Apr 12, 83; w Naomi Taylor, Jul 24, 15; BDS 13, MDiv; O Oct 16, 14, SNE Pby; astp Christ the King Somerville, Somerville, MA, 14-18; astp Christ The King P Ch, Cambridge, MA, 18-, chp 18-

70 Dale Avenue, Quincy, MA 02169 – 617-302-7264   Southern New England
Christ The King Presbyterian Church – 617-354-8341

Owens, Nick – O Jun 15, Hrtg Pby; campm RUF, UDE, 15-

102 Meriden Drive, Newark, DE 19711   Heritage
PCA Reformed University Fellowship

Owens, Richard – b Pleasant Ridge, AL, Aug 6, 81; f Richard Edward; m Delbra Lindsey; w Anne Marie Sivert, Jackson, MS, Nov 1, 08; chdn Sophia Anne, Judah Richard; USAL 03, BS; RTS 10, MDiv; O Jul 11, 10, Cov Pby; astp Westminster P Ch, Greenwood, MS, 10-12; srp 12-

304 East Adams, Greenwood, MS 38930   Covenant
E-mail: owensr8@gmail.com
Westminster Presbyterian Church – 662-453-7608

Owens, Robert Paul – b Collins, GA, Jun 13, 52; f Mitchell B.; m Sallie Neil Johannessen; w Rhoda Ellen Morris, Atlanta, GA, Jul 19, 75; chdn Daniel, Anne; VSC 70-74, BS; RTS 82-87, MDiv; O Nov 8, 87, Gr Pby; stus Shiloh P Ch, Pickens, MS, 85-87; int, p McDonald P Ch, Collins, MS, 87-91; astp, chp Chapel Woods P Ch, Snellville, GA, 91-95; op Willow Woods P Ch, Snellville, GA, 92-95, p 95-97, ob mis 97-99, wc 00-02; ss Grace P Ch, Cedartown, GA, 02; p Pamlico P Ch, Oriental, NC, 03-11; wc 11-14; astp East Cobb P Ch, Marietta, GA, 14-

626 Lorell Terrace, Sandy Springs, GA 30328-4118 – 770-375-0426   Metro Atlanta
E-mail: paul.owens0@gmail.com
East Cobb Presbyterian Church – 770-973-4114

Owsley, Donald T. – w Lois; chdn Kendra, Danielle; BayU, AS; NWSU, BA; WSCAL, MDiv; NGTS, DMin; O Jan 97, OPC; p Cornerstone Comm Ch, Artesia, CA, 06-08; p Cornerstone P Ch, Ft. Collins, CO, 08-13; wc 13-

1500 South Bryan Avenue, Ft. Collins, CA 80521 – 970-493-3382   Rocky Mountain
E-mail: dto4deo@yahoo.com

Pacheco, Raul – wc; ob Campus Outreach

708 University Avenue, Troy, AL 36081 – 205-383-1640   Evangel
E-mail: raulevivi@uol.com.br

Pacienza, Robert – astp Coral Ridge P Ch, Ft. Lauderdale, FL, 14-16, srp 16-

Coral Ridge Presbyterian Church – 954-771-8840   South Florida

Padgett, Elmer Marvin Jr. – b Nashville, TN, Sept 4, 44; f Elmer Marvin; m Ruth Naomi Groom; w Jean Ralphelle Nichols, Chandler, AZ, Jul 29, 67; chdn Steven Patrick, Heather Leigh (Kennedy), Timothy David; UAL, BS; L Jul 19, 95; O Jan 26, 97, Nash Pby; coord RUM, 96-97; ob VP/editorial Crossway Books, 97-05; ob VP/editorial P&R Publ, 08-12; trans admin, GCP, 12-13; int Exec Dir GCP, 13; Exec Dir GCP, 13-; ed *Calvin and Culture*, 10

2442 North Berrys Chapel Road, Franklin, TN 37069 – 630-418-1995   Nashville
E-mail: marvpadgett@aol.com
Great Commission Publications – 770-831-9084

Padilla-Morales, Manuel – b San Antonio, TX, May 22, 58; f Manuel Padilla-Montesinos; m Norma J. Morales; w Kimberly Ann Lally, Hingham, MA, Sept 28, 85; chdn Joshua Santiago, Rebecca Grace, Elizabeth Raquel; AACC 76-80, AA; UMD 82-84, BS; RTS 87-90, MDiv; O Jun 7, 92, Pot Pby; chp, mis MTW, Madrid, Spain, 92-00; chp MTW, Malaga, Spain, 00-05; chp MTW, Border Ministry, El Paso, 05-07; p Las Tierras Comm Ch, El Paso, TX, 07-

3664 Tierra Calida Drive, El Paso, TX 79938 – 915-740-9207 Southwest
E-mail: manuelpadillaltcc@gmail.com
Las Tierras Community Church

Pae, John Hwan – astp Jesus Hope Ch of Georgia, Suwanee, GA, 16-

3671 Smithtown Road, Suwanee, GA 30024 Korean Southeastern
Jesus Hope Church of Georgia

Paek, Cuseong – astp Global Msn Ch, Diamond Bar, CA, 10-14; srp First Korean P Ch of Orlando, Orlando, FL, 14-

7258 Regina Way, Orlando, FL 32819 Korean Southeastern
E-mail: jspaek3@gmail.com
First Korean Presbyterian Church of Orlando – 407-295-1199

Paik, Daniel – Mar 22, 88; f Jin; m Jung Lee; w Jennifer Kim, Boston, MA, May 20, 17; USC 10, BS; GCTS 15, MDiv; O Oct 21, 18, SNE Pby; astp Citylife P Ch of Boston, Boston, MA, 18-

156-160 Chelsea Street #202, Boston, MA 02128 – 857-210-7040 Southern New England
E-mail: daniel@citylifeboston.org
Citylife Presbyterian Church of Boston – 617-292-0990

Paik, Kyung Whan – astp Holy Hill Comm Ch, Los Angeles, CA, 00-10

5411 Lake Crest Drive, Agoura Hills, CA 91301 – 626-964-0496 Korean Southwest
E-mail: eunicepaik@yahoo.com

Pak, Yong Dok – p Anchorage New Life P Ch, Anchorage, AK

2906 Arctic Boulevard, Anchorage, AK 99503 – 907-277-2202 Korean Northwest
E-mail: pakyongd@gmail.com
Anchorage New Life Presbyterian Church – 907-947-9059

Pak, Young Ki – b Seoul, Mar 14, 60; f San Il Pak; m Hyun Sook; w Chi Hwa Pak, Pusan, Korea, Oct 3, 92; chdn Timothy Eunchong, Grace Eunhye; UCO 86, BS; DenTS 93, MCE; WSCAL 96, MDiv; FulTS 98, ThM; L Apr 14, 98, KorSW Pby; O Apr 13, 99, KorSW Pby; ob ascp Peniel P Ch, Montclair, CA, 99; instr, mis KorPTS, 99-08; p Disciple Msn Ch, Denver, CO, 08-

6349 South Worchester, Centennial, CO 80111 – 720-200-4382 Korean Southwest
E-mail: sdgloria2@yahoo.com
Disciple Mission Church – 303-300-9517

Pakala, James Cotton – b Pittsburgh, PA, Mar 6, 44; f William Elmer; m Edythe Leona Cotton; w Marie Denise Marchand, Willow Grove, PA, Jun 13, 75; chdn Kent Marchand; ShelC 66, BA; SDSU 68; TempU 69-72; DrexU 79, MS; FTS 70, MDiv; BibTS 77, STM; L Jul 20, 74; O Jan 18, 75, Westm Pby; ap Bible Ch, Chester, PA, 70-71; lib BibTS, 74-91; Chap ARNG, 75-97; PRJC/PRCC, 78-, sec 81-94, chair 96-09; ss Locktown P Ch, Flemington, NJ, 89-91; lib CTS, 91-; MO Library Assoc. Board 96-98; Chap police,

Pakala, James Cotton, continued
Creve Coeur, MO, 98-; ATLA Board, 04-10; MO Library Network Corp. Board 06-12; Beta Phi Mu, 80-; SE PA Reg Lib Assoc, pres 85-87; St. Louis Reg Lib Network Counc, 00-03, 08-12; *Directory and Profile;* "A Librarian's Comments on Commentaries," *Presbyterion* (95-)

1303 Mautenne Drive, Ballwin, MO 63021-5627 – 636-527-4044   Philadelphia
E-mail: jim.pakala@covenantseminary.edu
Presbyterian & Reformed Commission on Chaplains
Covenant Theological Seminary – 314-434-4044

    Palmer, Damon – b Wichita, KS, Apr 9, 64; f Mark E.; m Heather S. Lindwall; w Sally Ann, Vineland, NJ, Jul 28, 84; KTS 11, MDiv; TorBibSem 13, ThM; O Aug 12, 12, SFL Pby; astp First P Ch of Coral Springs/Margate, Margate, FL, 12-15; astp First Ch West, Tamarac, FL, 15-16, ascp 16-17, srp 17-

8380 SW 39 Court, Davie, FL 33328 – 954-778-3737   South Florida
E-mail: dpalmer9@att.net
First Church West – 954-726-2304

    Palmer, Paul Robert – b Boston, MA, Jan 28, 33; f Kenneth; m Effie Cummins; w Gloria Madelyn Eggers, River Forest, IL, Sept 10, 55; chdn Kimberly (Swedlund), Michelle (Beltz), Janice (Rood); WheatC 55, BS; CTS 62, BD, 72, MDiv; FulTS 78, DMin; L 62, Midw Pby (RPCES); O 62, Midw Pby (RPCES); p Bethany Ch, New Castle, DE, 62-70; p Covenant P Ch, Naples, FL, 70-73; VP CTS, 73-79, prof 79-85; mod GenSyn, 79; p Valley P Ch, North Hills, CA, 85-89; adj prof AzPU, 86-88; ip New Cov P Ch, Dallas, TX, 90-91, srp 91-95; admin CEP, 96-07; vis prof RTSFL, 04-07; hr 13; *Improving Theological Education*; *Understanding Baptism*; "The Church In The 80's," *Theology News and Notes*; "Called To The Ministry," *Presbyterion*; "All One Body We," "Impacting the Darkness," and "Fulfilling our Covenantal Vows," *Equip; God's Heart, Our Hope*

1710 Triangle Palm Terrace, Naples, FL 34119 – 239-596-5774   Metro Atlanta
E-mail: bpalmer33@embarqmail.com
HR

    Palmertree, Phillip James – b Jackson, MS, Oct 10, 68; f James Z.; m Ida Ruth Brister; w Judith Davis, Jackson, MS, Jun 29, 91; chdn James Nelson, Ruth Anne, John Campbell, Rachel Margaret; MSU 90, BA; RTS 94, MDiv; L Jul 19, 94; O Nov 13, 94, SEAL Pby; astp Covenant P Ch, Auburn, AL, 94-97, ascp 97-99; p Macon P Ch, Macon, MS, 99-05; p First P Ch, Kosciusko, MS, 05-; contr *A Complete Index to the Southern Presbyterian Review*

603 Smythe Street, Kosciusko, MS 39090 – 662-289-6181   Mississippi Valley
E-mail: palmertree@fpckosciusko.org
First Presbyterian Church – 662-289-2435

    Pannkuk, Leon Dean – b Buffalo Center, IA, Sept 10, 50; f John Anton; m Grace Beenken; w Marlene Van Aalsburg, Des Moines, IA, Feb 16, 80; chdn Rebekah Lee, Matthew Evan, Jonathan Dean; NWC 68-69; ISU 69-72, BS, 72-74, grad wk; CTS 89, MDiv; L Jan 91; O May 24, 92, MO Pby; ob Chap Friendship Village, St. Louis, MO, 92-04; obreg coord EEInt, 04-09; ob admin Rodney D. Stortz Center for Outreach/Evanglism, 09-11; ob VP For His Glory Evangelistic Ministries, 11-14; ss Swiss Evangelical Ref Ch, Hermann, MO, 14-15, p 15-

1117 Dauphine Lane, Manchester, MO 63011-4117 – 636-675-9400   Missouri
E-mail: leonpannkuk@gmail.com
Swiss Evangelical Reformed Church – 636-675-9400

    Pardigon, Flavien –w Inyange; chdn Timothée, Nastasja, Agapée, Eden, Hosanna; FLTR/Aix, MDiv, ThM; WTS 08, PhD; O Apr 3, 05, Phil Pby; mis MTW, Eastern Europe, Sofia, Bulgaria; mis MTW, West Africa, 08-13; ob AWM, 13-;"Cornelius Van Til," *Encyclopedia of Christian Literature*, 10; "Areopagus

Pardigon, Flavien, continued
Speech" and "Theology of Religions," *Encyclopedia of Christian Civilization*, 12; *Paul Against the Idols: A Contextual Reading of the Areopagus Speech*, 19

146 Charland Forest Road, Milton, Asheville, NC 28803   Philadelphia Metro West
Arab World Ministries

Parham, Patrick J. – b Indianapolis, IN, Jul 27, 53; f Grady E.; m Kernodle; w Dyer, East Point, GA, Mar 6, 76; chdn Rhea Ann, Tammy René; GBibC, BBE; GPTS, MDiv; L Nov 91; O Aug 14, 94, Westm Pby; int Frank P Ch, Crossnore, NC, 91-93; ss King Mem P Ch, Bristol, VA, 94; p Sandlick P Ch, Birchleaf, VA, 94-98; p Asbury P Ch, Johnson City, TN, 98-00, wc 00-01; p Evangelical P Ch, Baltimore, MD, 01-06; wc 06-

1236 Carolina Avenue, Bristol, TN 37620   Chesapeake
E-mail: patrickparham@yahoo.com

Park, Andrew S. – w Laura; chdn Anderson, Liberty, Nathaniel; UCLA 98, BA; WSCAL 04, MDiv; astp The Way Ch, Los Angeles, CA, 04-12; op Living Faith P Ch, Los Angeles, CA, 12-15, p 15-

13238 Lorca Avenue, La Mirada, CA 90638   Korean Southwest
E-mail: andrewpark916@gmail.com
Living Faith Presbyterian Church – 562-716-3132

Park, Billy – w Gloria; chdn Jonathan, Elise, Sarah, David; WesleyanU 86, BA; PTS 89, MDiv; GCTS 93, ThM; pEng Orange Kor Ch, Fullerton, CA, 92-94; srp Grace Cov Campus Ch, Providence, RI, 94-00; pEng Bethel Korean P Ch, Ellicot City, MD, 01-03; chp New Comm P Ch, Clarksville, MD, 03-04; p Open Door Comm Ch, Norcross, GA, 05-08; ascp Siloam Korean Ch of Atlanta, Norcross, GA, 09-13; op Grace Comm P Ch, Suwanee, GA, 13-; Kor relations rep, PCA-AC, 13-

320 Gaines Oak Way, Suwanee, GA 30024   Korean Southeastern
E-mail: pastorbilly@gmail.com; bpark@pcanet.org
Grace Community Presbyterian Church – 678-622-9856
PCA Administrative Committee

Park, Brian – w Jane; chdn Timothy, Titus, Leah; TEDS 04, MDiv, 10, ThM; astp Korean Ch of Chicago, Hoffman Estates, IL, 04-07; ob ascp Calvary English Chapel, 06-10; p Restoration Comm Ch of Naperville, Naperville, IL, 10-17

2162 Countryside Circle, Naperville, IL 60565 – 630-421-1214   Korean Central
E-mail: bkpark@gmail.com

Park, Chan Shin – O Apr 12, 11, KorSE Pby; op Korean American Ch of Jackson, MS, 11-

Korean American Church of Jackson – 601-922-8459   Korean Southeastern

Park, Choon Sik – p Olympia First P Msn, Olympia, WA, 13-

3324 Sadie Street NE, Lacey, WA 98516   Korean Northwest
E-mail: cpark15@hanmail.net
Olympia First Presbyterian Mission

Park, Dae Woong – srp Jesus Hope Ch of Georgia, Suwanee, GA, 16-

1400 Ox Bridge Way, Lawrenceville, GA 30043 – 770-375-0900   Korean Southeastern
Jesus Hope Church of Georgia

Park, Daniel – b Nov 30, 83; CalvC 06; WSCAL 10; O Mar 12, 13, KorSW Pby; astp California Christ Comm Ch, Stanton, CA, 13-

2035 Seaview Drive, Fullerton, CA 92833　　　　　　　　　Korean Southwest Orange County
California Christ Community Church

Park, Daniel Jinkyu – astp State College Korean Ch, State College, PA, 09-

121 Clemson Court, State College, PA 16803　　　　　　　　　　　　　　Korean Eastern
E-mail: djkpark@gmail.com
State College Korean Church – 814-380-9191

Park, David – astp First Korean P Ch of St. Louis, St. Ann, MO, 17-

E-mail: jy.d.park@gmail.com　　　　　　　　　　　　　　　　　　　　　Korean Central
First Korean Presbyterian Church of St. Louis – 314-395-3719

Park, David – astp Korean Ch of Chicago, Hoffman Estates, IL, 17-

166 Rosehall Drive, Lake Zurich, IL 60047　　　　　　　　　　　　　　　Korean Central
E-mail: david2433@gmail.com
Korean Church of Chicago – 847-359-1522

Park, David Joonho – O May 6, 12, KorCap Pby; ob Open Door P Ch, VA, 12-17; astp Emmanuel Ch in Phil, Philadelphia, PA, 17-

113 Juniper Road, Havertown, PA 19083　　　　　　　　　　　　　　　　Korean Eastern
E-mail: david21c@gmail.com
Emmanuel Church in Philadelphia – 215-476-0330

Park, David Kyung – O Oct 26, 14, MNY Pby; p 14-

405 Knollwood Road, Ridgewood, NJ 07450 – 201-895-6138　　　　　　Metropolitan New York
E-mail: davepark93@gmail.com

Park, Dennis – O May 28, 17, KorCap Pby; astp Korean Central P Ch, Centreville, VA, 17-

2620 Kirklyn Street, Falls Church, VA 22043 – 703-657-7583　　　　　　　　Korean Capital
E-mail: parkdby@gmail.com
Korean Central Presbyterian Church – 703-815-1200

Park, Dong Won – astp First Korean P Ch of St. Louis, St. Ann, MO, 17-18

16223 48th Avenue West #4, Edmonds, WA 98026　　　　　　　　　　　Korean Central
E-mail: covenantdwp@gmail.com

Park, Dook Joon – O Oct 1, 90, KorSE Pby; p Alexandria Korean P Ch., Alexandria, VA; op Presbyterian Ch of Gardens Msn, Fairfax, VA, 91-05; hr

9811 Limoges Drive, Fairfax, VA 22032 – 703-425-9075　　　　　　　　　　Korean Capital
E-mail: dokjpak@gmail.com
HR

Park, Edward – O Nov 11, 07, SNE Pby; astp Trinity P Ch, Providence, RI, 07-11; campm RUF, BrownU, RISD, 07-

51 Mount Hope Avenue, Providence, RI 02906　　　　　　　　　　　　Southern New England
PCA Reformed University Fellowship

MINISTERIAL DIRECTORY 485

Park, Geel Boum – O Oct 15, KorSE Pby; mis China, 15-

E-mail: pjfan7@gmail.com   Korean Southeastern

Park, Han Joo – astp Korean P Ch of St. Louis, St. Louis, MO, 07-10; srp Korean First P Ch, Columbia, MO, 10-

3511 Berkshire Court, Columbia, MO 65203 – 573-777-3410   Korean Central
E-mail: phanjoo@gmail.com
Korean First Presbyterian Church – 573-777-3410

Park, Hoon Jong – b Seoul, Korea, Oct 15, 27; w Hei Ok Lee, Seoul, Kor, Apr 27, 51; chdn Joon Sik, Joon Kwun, Joon Soo, Joon Sung; YonU 66, MBA; DHTS 60; L Jul 5, 80; O Jul 5, 80, Kor Ref; Recd PCA Jun 21, 94, KorSE Pby; ev, op Wheat Grain Korean P Msn, Columbus, GA, 94-95, wc 95-98; hr 98

Address Unavailable   Korean Southeastern
HR

Park, Hyun-Soo – w Sung; chdn Tim, Priscilla; ChShC, BA; RTS, MDiv; TIU, MRE, ThM, PhD; ob Dir Immanuel Christian Ed Cent, Buffalo Grove, IL, 00-10; srp Bethel P Ch of Chicago, Chicago, IL, 10-16

413 Covington Terr, Buffalo Grove, IL 60089   Korean Central
E-mail: ithank4@gmail.com

Park, Hyung Yong – b Korea, Jan 20, 42; f Ji Sun P (d); m Ok Keum Oh (d); w Soonja, Philadelphia, PA, Dec 19, 70; chdn Irene Janet, Sarah Ann, Paul Joseph; KookjeC 65, BA; GATS 69, BD; WTS 72, ThM; EmU 75, STD; L 70, SoonChun Pby; O Sept 29, 73, NGA Pby; ap Grace P Ch, Atlanta, GA, 73-75; Chap, om PEF, 75-76; mis MTW, Korea, 76-13; prof AUBS, 73-76; prof KPGACTS, 77-80; prof HPTS, 80-08; pres, 01-05; hon prof 08; pres Seoul Bible Grad School Theo, 08-12; sec gen KETS, 90-94, VP 94-98, pres 01-05; sec gen Assoc of Evan Theol Schools (AETS), 99-02, VP 02-03, pres 03-05; pres Asia Graduate School of Theology, Korea, 12-13-; pres Westminster Grad Sch Theo, 13-15; prof em Hapdong Theo Sem; Theologian of the Year, Kookmin Daily Newspaper and Sebokhyub, 04; trans *The Reformed Pastor* by Richard Baxter, 70; auth *An Exposition of the Acts of the Apostles: the Expanding Church* (Kor), 81; trans *The Greatest Thing in the World by Henry Drummond*, 83; trans *How Should We Then Live?* by Francis Schaeffer, 84; auth *An Exposition of the Sermon on the Mount* (Kor), 84; ed *Agape's Exhaustive Concordance of the Bible* (7 Vols.); auth *A History of Criticism on the Gospels* (Kor), 85; trans *Revelation Unfolded* by Jack B. Scott, 85; auth *New Testament Survey*, (Kor), 86; trans *Can You Run Away from God?* by James Boice, 87; auth *An Exposition on the Epistle to the Ephesians* (Kor), 90; *Principles of Bible Interpretation* (Kor), 91; co-trans *New Testament, New Korean Standard Version*; auth *An Exposition of the Four Gospels* (I) (Kor), 94; *An Exposition of the Four Gospels* (II) (Kor), 94; *30 Essential Topics of the New Testament* (Kor), 96; *The Church and the Holy Spirit* (Kor), 97; *An Exposition of the Letter to the Philippians* (Kor), 97; *Redemption and Newness of Life* (Eng), 01; auth *The Victorious Lives of Faith* (Kor), 01; co-trans *Agape Easy Bible*, 01; auth *The New Testament Canon* (Kor), 02; *An Exposition of Hebrews* (Kor), 03; *And God said, "No"* (Kor and Eng) 03; *And God said, "Nevertheless"* (Kor and Eng) 03; *And God said, "Yes, That's it"* (Kor and Eng) 03; *And God said, "Rejoice without Reason"* (Kor and Eng) 05; *New Testament Biblical Theology* (Kor), 05; *Pauline Theology* (Kor), 05; *And God said, "Cheer Up, Son"* (Kor and Eng) 08; *An Exposition of the Letters to the Thessalonians* (Kor), 08; *Lasting Influence of Jung Am's Life* (Kor), 08; *An Exposition of the Four Gospels* (combined Kor), 09; *The Holy Spirit and the Church*, (Eng) 11; auth *And God Said, "Rest is not a Waste*," (Kor and Eng), 12; *From Incarnation to Exaltation* (Eng), 12; *Theological Books, This is How I Read Them* (Kor), 15; *Trek Through God's Word* (Kor), 18; Top 100 Professionals-2018 in Theological Education by the International Biographycal Centre

Hyundai Apt. 113-1104, Gwanak-Gu, Gwanak-Ro 304, Seoul 08730 KOREA   Metro Atlanta
E-mail: hyoungpark@hotmail.com
Hapdong Theological Seminary

Park, Ik Joon – b Pusan, Korea, Aug 2, 61; chdn Eun Woo, Woo Jin, Ha Young; CalvC 89, BA; ChShTS 92, MDiv; op Chang Dae P Ch, Lawrenceville, GA, 01-09; op Saebit Korean P Ch, Newnan, GA, 10-

2675 East 34 Highway, Newnan, GA 30264 – 770-614-0136   Korean Southeastern
E-mail: cdapc@hotmail.com
Saebit Korean Presbyterian Church – 404-200-6378

Park, James – w Sindy; chdn Hannah, Calvin, Timothy; UCI 94, BA; WTS 98, MDiv, DMin cand; Inland Korean P Ch, Pomona, CA, 96-01; srp Grace P Ch of St. Louis, St. Louis, MO, 01-08; op GracePoint Ch, Stevenson Ranch, CA, 09-16

23837 Robindale Place, Valencia, CA 91354 – 314-469-9067   Pacific

Park, James Sangmok – b Busan, Korea, Mar 10, 55; f Tae Ki; m Bok Soon Kim (d); w Sarah Myunghee Chung, Philadelphia, PA, Jan 1, 83; chdn Daniel Heejoon, Rebekah Heeryung, Esther Heejung (d), Eunice Heesun; WVUTech 81, BS; RTS 85, MDiv, 86, MA, 93, ThM, 95, DMiss; TTS PhD Cand; NTS ThD cand; L Jun 18, 86, MSVal Pby; O Nov 10, 86, KorSE Pby; yp Atlanta First P Ch, 81-85; DCE Jackson P Ch, 85-86; medu Nairobi CPC Ch, 88; mis, ev PEF, Nakuru, Kenya, 87-97; Vice Mod, KorSW Pby, 11-12; Mod KorSW Pby, 12-13; sc KorSWOC Pby, 17-; instr Nakuru Grace Bible Coll, 88-92; ob p Imani Ch of AEPC Nakuru, Kenya & Tumaini Ch, 89-97; prof EvangeliaUniv, 97-99; prof CGST, 06-09; prof CalBC&TS, 08-; prof WycliffTS, 11-15; prof MathestesTS, 12-; acadean/prof YALA Missionary Training School, 13-16; prof Tyndale International University, 14-16; prof KAPC Ref Theo College & Sem, 17-; prof Nairobi Common Ground Theo Ins, 95-97; vis lect/prof Kosin U, Kor, 96; AEPC CE dir, Nairobi, 95-98; p Dagoretti Ch of AEPC, Dagoretti, Kenya, 96-97; ob srp California Martus Ch, Fullerton, CA, 97-99; ob srp CA Christ Comm Ch, Stanton, CA, 99-; *A Mission Strategy for the Korean Immigrant Churches*; art "Evangelism Through Church Planting"; "Matthew 28: 18-20: Making Disciples"; *A Proposal to Train the Korean-American Missionary Candidates for Cross-Cultural Ministry*; *A Theological-Historical Study of the Relationship between Evangelism and Social Responsibility*; ed *East Africa Missionary Symposium*, 96; "Cross-Cultural Missionary," "The Motives of Missions," *Kenya Missionary Society Journal*, 1996; *Biblical Theology of Mission*, 08; *Understanding the Muslim with a Reformed Perspective*, 12

2279 Crestview Circle, Brea, CA 92821   Korean Southwest Orange County
714-529-5839, 714-609-6691
E-mail: jspark4c55@yahoo.com; www.joonim.com
California Christ Community Church
KAPC Reformed Theological College and Seminary

Park, Jason – astp Sovereign Gr Ch, Los Angeles, CA, 16-17; op Foothills Neighborhood Ch, Sierra Madre, CA, 17-

2716 Honolulu Avenue #108, Montrose, CA 91020   Pacific
E-mail: jasonpark716@gmail.com
Foothills Neighborhood Church – 626-243-4720

Park, Jason Hyunsoo – p Highland Korean P Ch, Vernon Hills, IL, 16-

E-mail: parkhyunsoo@hotmail.com   Korean Central
Highland Korean Presbyterian Church – 847-634-6033

Park, Jong – p The Redemption Ch, Naperville, IL, 10-

PO Box 83, Naperville, IL 60566   Korean Central
The Redemption Church – 847-984-0872

MINISTERIAL DIRECTORY

Park, Jun Shik – b Seoul, Korea, Mar 30, 74; w Kyung Hwa Kim, Seoul, Korea, Jun 22, 02; chdn Peter, Andrew; SNU 99; ChShTS 03, MDiv; WSCAL 06, MA; O Oct 08, KorCent Pby; ob Bethel Ch

21 Oxford, Irvine, CA 92612 – 714-618-7635 Korean Southwest Orange County
E-mail: jun330@yahoo.com
Bethel Church (non PCA)

Park, Jung Il – mis SEED Int

SEED International, PO Box 69, Merrifield, VA 22116 – 703-996-0717 Korean Capital
E-mail: hhglory1@gmail.com
SEED International

Park, Kisoo – p Hanmaum P Ch, Norcross, GA, 03-14

Address Unavailable Korean Southeastern

Park, Kwon Sub – p Cherry Hill Associated P Ch, Mount Laurel, NJ, 98-

2203 Stokes Road, Mt. Laurel, NJ 08054 Korean Eastern
Cherry Hill Associated Presbyterian Church

Park, Mike Samuel – astp Grace P Ch, Washington, DC, 13-15; ascp 15-

3826 Garfield Street NW, Washington, DC 20007 Potomac
E-mail: mike@gracedc.net
Grace Presbyterian Church of Washington, D.C. – 202-386-7637

Park, Moses – O 15, SNE Pby; astp Christ The King P Ch, Cambridge, MA, 15-

107 Adams Street, Dorcester, MA 02122 Southern New England
Christ The King Presbyterian Church – 617-354-8341

Park, Noh Moon – b Korea, Apr 10, 61; f Soon Jib; m Jong Suk Lee; w Kyum Eun Choi, Korea, Oct 9, 86; chdn Min Kyu, Min Ji; p Korean Comm Ch of Ft. Myers, North Ft. Myers, FL, 14-17

1275 Gerling Street Bldg 6C, Schenectady, NY 12308 Korean Southeastern
E-mail: nmp0618@gmail.com

Park, Peter Soo – b Korea, Oct 26, 64; f Young Suk; m Cheiu Sook Kim; w Jung Sook Moon, Grand Rapids, MI, May 10, 87; chdn Luke K, Faith S; WheatC 82-83; GrBC 83-86, BRE; DTS 86-92, ThM; L Oct 92; O Apr 14, 92, KorS Pby; astp Korean P Ch, Houston, TX, 92-94; astp Ark Msn Ch, Carmichael, CA, 94-00, wc 00-06; op Living Stone Comm Ch, Carmichael, CA, 07-

3459 Grant Park Drive, Carmichael, CA 95608 – 916-489-8101 Korean Northwest
E-mail: peter_park@sbcglobal.net
Living Stone Community Church – 916-213-1499

Park, Raehyeok – O May 21, 17, KorCap Pby; astp Cornerstone P Ch, Vienna, VA, 17-

900 Maple Ave East, Vienna, VA 22180 Korean Capital
E-mail: heartofphinehas@gmail.com
Cornerstone Presbyterian Church

Park, Saeyong – O Mar 13, 18, KorE Pby; ob TTS, 18-

155 Canterbury Lane, Blue Bell, PA 19422 Korean Eastern
Trinity Theological Seminary, Newberg, IN

Park, Samuel Sang Il – b Korea, Jul 6, 56; f Chi Soon; m Mong Hi; w Hea Kyoung Lee, Seoul, Korea, Jun 12, 82; chdn Sarah E., Daniel J., Peter; CCCU 76-80, BA; WTS 82, MAR, 83, MDiv, 88, ThM; NYU 94, PhD; L 84; O Jun 84, KorE Pby; astp Korean P Ch of Southern New York, Woodside, NY, 84-92, srp 92-

43-12 54th Street, Woodside, NY 11377 – 718-639-8309   Korean Northeastern
Korean Presbyterian Church of Southern New York – 718-639-8383

Park, Samuel Young Bae – b Korea, Aug 31, 62; f Heun Man; m Nam Zoo Kim; w Sanghee Kim, Los Angeles, CA, Jun 20, 92; chdn Ezekiel, Sharon, Jonathan; SJSU, BA; WSCAL 90, MDiv; O Apr 12, 94, KorSW Pby; op Anaheim New Life Msn Ch, Buena Park, CA, 94-05; srp New Life Msn Ch of Fullerton, Fullerton, CA, 05-

12400 Ashworth Place, Cerritos, CA 90703 – 562-926-8228   Korean Southwest Orange County
E-mail: nlmc@msn.com
New Life Mission Church of Fullerton – 714-526-6562

Park, Sang Yong – b Kyung-Buk, Korea, Apr 29, 53; f Hakbong; m Jum Soo Kim; w Kwangeun Lee, Kyungbuk, Korea, Nov 16, 79; chdn Tae Young, Hannah; HanU 73-80, BS; RPI 82-84; WTS 87, MDiv; KorTS 02, ThM; BibTS 12, DMin; L Apr 88; O Apr 3, 89, KorSE Pby; ap Kor Shinjung P Ch, 87-89; ob p New Life P Ch (Non-PCA), Cherry Hill, NJ, 89-92; ob p Korean Comm Ch Charlottesville, VA (non-PCA), 92-94; p Expo Korean Ch, Korea, 94-05; srp Korean Saints P Ch, Warminster, PA, 05-15; mis 15-; thesis "Missiological Perspectives on Korean Diaspora Church"; dissert *The Effectiveness of The Evangelism Explosion Program in Korean American Churches*

1419 Edgewood Avenue, Abington, PA 19001 – 267-546-6688   Korean Eastern
E-mail: diaspora2001@hotmail.com

Park, Se-Woo – b Tae-Jun, Nov 30, 61; f Hak Yong; m Jum Young Lee; w In Hye Kim, Seoul, Oct 1, 87; chdn Eun Young, Jinny Young; Hankuk U 84, BS, 86, MS; KyeYak TS 91, MDiv; O Oct 7, 96; Recd PCA Apr 23, 97, KorCent Pby; Chap USArmy, Ft. Leonardwood, MO, 97-

Address Unavailable   Korean Central
United States Army

Park, Seong IL – astp Emmanuel Ch in Phil, 08-09; p Korean P Ch of Wash, Fairfax, VA, 09-

9535 Ashbridge Court, Burke, VA 22015 – 703-485-7568   Korean Capital
E-mail: revseongilpark@gmail.com
Korean Presbyterian Church of Washington – 703-321-8090

Park, Seung Gyu – srp East Sarang Comm Ch, Chino, CA, 16-

1311 Solera Lane #4, Diamond Bar, CA 91765 – 909-590-3722   Korean Southwest
E-mail: sgpark01@gmail.com
East Sarang Community Church – 909-590-3722

Park, Shin (Hun) Wook – b Korea, May 29, 54; f Kyung Nam P.; m Soon Hee Kim; w Heisook Yoo, Seoul, Nov 30, 85; chdn Moses, Sarah; YonU 81, BS; TalTS 85, MDiv; DTS 89, STM; O May 89, KorCap Pby; mis Argentina, administration and pastor, 92-96; mis Korean Central P Ch of Wash, Vienna, VA, 90-; execdir SEED International 97-; Gospel Broadcasting Co, 13-14; exec dir Imitating Christ Ministries, 15-; pres Gospel Broadcasting Chapel of Hawaii, 15-

1769 Avenida Selva, Fullerton, CA 92811 – 703-624-7112   Korean Capital
E-mail: pastorjuan@gmail.com
Imitating Christ Ministries
Gospel Broadcasting Chapel of Hawaii

MINISTERIAL DIRECTORY 489

Park, Shinchul – srp Inland Korean P Ch, 13-

1101 North Glen Avenue, Pomona, CA 91768   Korean Southwest
E-mail: shinpark153@gmail.com
Inland Church PCA – 909-622-2324

Park, Sin Yong – astp Korean Ch of Chicago, Hoffman Estates, IL, 17-

1730 Birch Place #206, Schaumburg, IL 60173   Korean Central
E-mail: reindeermoon@hotmail.com
Korean Church of Chicago – 847-359-1522

Park, Soo Sang – ob San Jose New Hope CRC; op Revive P Ch of Silicon Valley, Santa Clara, CA, 18-

18740 Hanna Drive, Cypertino, CA 95014   Northern California
E-mail: soosang@gmail.com
Revive Presbyterian Church of Silicon Valley

Park, Soo Yeol – p Immanuel P Ch, Flushing, NY, 16-

Immanuel Presbyterian Church – 718-353-7500   Korean Northeastern

Park, Sun Sik – w Hyekyung; chdn Jieun, Jiwon, Jisu ; CalvS; ChShTS 90, MDiv; NPTS 01, MACE; Dagil Presbyterian Church(Youth pastor), 85-89; dir/ed Jesus Disciple Movement, 90-91; p/ed Happy Presbyterian Ch, 91-97; astp Christ Presbyterian Church, 98-99; p/ed Dasom Ch, 00-04; srp Hanwoory Comm Ch, 04- 06; srp Open P Ch, 06-08; StCl KorCent Pby, 08-13; p Open P Ch Msn, Schaumburg, IL, 08-10; p Vineyard P Ch, Elmhurst, IL, 13-

300 East Belden Avenue, Elmhurst, IL 60126 – 847-883-8644   Korean Central
E-mail: sunsikpark@yahoo.com
Vineyard Presbyterian Church – 630-279-1199

Park, Sung Min – ob t East Asia School of Theology, 94-

Address Unavailable   Korean Central
E-mail: sgmnpark@hotmail.com
East Asia School of Theology

Park, Thomas – op Ark Msn Ch, Carmichael, CA, 02-13; sc KorNW Pby, 03-06; ob 13-

7926 Mansel Way, Elk Grove, CA 95758 – 916-944-8099   Korean Northwest
E-mail: rev_dspark@yahoo.co.kr

Park, Thomas John Jr. – Pensacola, FL, Mar 21, 77; f Thomas John Sr.; m Nancy; w Nicoletta, Cape Coral, FL, Jul 16, 05; chdn Naphtili Grace, Asher Thomas, Isabella Rose; TCIL 02, BA; RTSFL 07, MDiv; O Aug 24, 08, NFL Pby; campm RUF, UNFL, 08-

5206 Tulane Avenue, Jacksonville, FL 32207 – 904-305-9294   North Florida
E-mail: tpark@ruf.org
PCA Reformed University Fellowship

Park, Thomas Yong Bin – ascp Valley Bethel P Ch, Chatsworth, CA; ob Yuong Sang Presbyterian Church, PA; srp New Life Msn Ch of Northern California, San Jose, CA, 10-

E-mail: thomas.park@nlmc.org   Korean Southwest
New Life Mission Church of Northern California – 408-409-6562

Park, Young – srp Christ Central P Ch of Wash, Centreville, VA, 10-11; wc 11-

2210 Woodford Rd., Vienna, VA 22182 – 703-560-1071 Korean Capital
E-mail: youngsp7@gmail.com

Park, Young Hee – b Kyung Puk, Korea, Aug 5, 37; f Won Kap; m Tae Soon Lee; w Jong Hwa, St Louis, MO, Oct 21, 67; chdn Grace, David; GAPTS 61, BDiv; KHU 63, BA; CTS 67, BD, 68, ThM; StLU 73, MA; CGST 78, PhD; L 70; O 70, Midw Pby (RPCES); p Kor Ch, St Louis, MO, 70-73; p First Korean P Ch of St. Louis, St. Ann, MO, 73-84; vis lect/prof HPTS, 81-; prof PGATCS, 84-86; pres ChShCS, 86-92; pres Kor Evan Th Soc, 89-90; ascp Choonghyun P Ch, 88-92; dean MWCC, & MWTS, 92-94; ob pres Taeshin Christ U, Korea, 94-02; ob dean MWTS, 02-06; Pres, World Vision Sem, Guatemala, 07-; *A Brief History of New Testament Times*; *The Gospel History*, 85; *The Quest of Historical Jesus* 87; contr *Christian Encyclopaedia*, vol. 2, 83; *The New Testament Exegetical Principles and Its Application in Pauline Epistles*, 88; *A Study of Christological Titles in the New Testament*, 89; trans, *Paul, An Outline of His Theology* by Ridderbos, 85; trans *Philo, An Alexandrian Jew*, by Samuel Sandmel, 89; Listed in Marquis *Who's Who in America*, 06, 07; "The Lord's Prayer" in *The World of the Bible (10 vols)* Dong A Publ, 89; auth *Introduction to New Testament Studies* (Kor), Taeshin Chr Univ Press, 00; "Fiftieth Anniversary Celebration of the Korea Mission and Liberal Theological Trends," "Theological Trends of Korean Church in 1930," "A Responsibility of Orthodox Theology in Presbyterian Church of Korea," chaps 15-17 in *One Hundred Years: A History of Presbyterian Church of Korea (2 vols)*, ed. General Assembly Publ, 06; *1907 Pyungyang Revival Movement and Its Impact in Korean Church History*, CKC Symposium 2007 (Kor & Eng); vis lect/prof ChShTS, 08; vis lect/prof SemPresParaguay, 09, 10; Lect/Prof, Cualificacion del pastor para la Predicacion Biblica, Semnario Presbiteriano del Paraguagy, Asuncion, 16; Lect/Prof, Teologia Paulina, World Vision Seminary in Bolivia, Cochabamba, 16; Lect/Prof, Spiritual Leadership in 1 Corinthians, World Vision Seminary 10th Anniversary of Guatemala City, Gautama, 16; ip, First Korean P Ch of St. Louis, MO, 16-17; Lect/Prof, Imagen del Pastor en la Biblia, World Vision Seminary in Mexico City, 17

1322 Creve Coeur Mill Road, Saint Louis, MO 63146 – 314-434-4688 Korean Central
E-mail: Younghpark7@sbcglobal.net

Parker, Adam – O Nov 6, 16, MSVal Pby; p Pearl P Ch, Pearl, MS, 16-

580 Oak Park Circle, Pearl, MS 39208 Mississippi Valley
E-mail: adamc.parker@gmail.com
Pearl Presbyterian Church – 601-939-1064

Parker, Charles Howard – b Monroe, NC, Feb 11, 59; f Vann H; m Martha B Hinson; w Michele Guillard, Charlotte, NC, Sept 5, 81; chdn Wesley, Kaitlin, Benjamin, Anna; UNCC 77-81, BS; WTS 82-87, MDiv; L Jan 17, 87; O Feb 21, 88, Phil Pby (OPC); ascp New Life P Ch, Glenside, PA, 88-92, wc 92-98; ascp New Life Ch of Phil, Philadelphia, PA, 98-00; astp Covenant Comm Ch, Lexington, SC, 07-11; ob mis Pioneers, Sudan, 11-15; p Lexington P Ch, Lexington, SC, 15-

246 Barr Road, Lexington, SC 29072 Palmetto
Lexington Presbyterian Church – 803-359-9501

Parker, J. Kyle – b Denver, CO, Mar 28, 70; w Gretchen Denise Little, Dallas, TX, Jun 28, 97; chdn Jackson Miles, Molly Clark; CSU 93, BS; CTS 03, MDiv; O Jun 22, 03, RMtn Pby; campm RUM, CSU, 03-06; p Cascade P Ch, Eugene, OR, 06-13; op Coram Deo P Ch, Spokane, WA, 13-

3906 South Manito Boulevard, Spokane, WA 99203 – 509-789-0508 Pacific Northwest
E-mail: parker@livecoramdeo.org
Coram Deo Presbyterian Church – 541-513-8000

Parker, Michael Nay – b Okmulgee, OK, Apr 24, 46; f Clyde C.; m Crystal Nay; w Joanne Todd, West Danby, NY, Aug 30, 69; chdn Todd, Heather; KgC 68, BA; CTS 72, MDiv; L 74; O 74, NJ Pby (RPCES); moy Covenant P Ch, Cherry Hill, NJ, 73-75; p Gr & Peace Flwsp, St. Louis, MO, 75-78;

MINISTERIAL DIRECTORY   491

Parker, Michael Nay, continued
p Christ Ch, Univ Cty, MO, 78-86; ob couns StLU, 86-87; t WestmCAc, 87-01, wc; astp New City Flwsp, University City, MO, 97-01, ascp 01-

5946 Maple Avenue, St. Louis, MO 63112 – 314-725-6281   Missouri
E-mail: mike@ncfstl.org
New City Fellowship – 314-726-2302

    Parker, Nathan T. – p Pinelands P Ch, Miami, FL, 14-

10201 Bahia Drive, Miami, FL 33189   South Florida
Pinelands Presbyterian Church – 305-235-1142

    Parkinson, Glenn Ross – b Annapolis, MD, Nov 7, 50; f James Robert; m Faye Whitmore; w Micki Allen, Peabody, MA, Sept 7, 74; chdn Renee; UMD 72, BS; GCTS 75,MDiv; WTS 84, DMin; L 74; O 75, DMV Pby (RPCES); p Covenant P Ch, Cherry Hill, NJ, 75-81; ap Severna Park Evangelical P Ch, Pasadena, MD, 81-86, srp 86-; *Like the Stars—Leading Many to Righteousness; Share Your Master's Happiness; Living Faith; Tapestry - the Book of Revelation*

204 Balsam Tree Court, Severna Park, MD 21146-2852 – 410-793-7116   Chesapeake
E-mail: gparkinson@spepchurch.org
Severna Park Evangelical Presbyterian Church – 410-544-5013

    Parks, Benny W. – b Birmingham, AL, Aug 20, 60; f Robert N. (d); m Ann Green; w Brenda Bennett, Birmingham, AL, Apr 11, 87; chdn Lauren, Benjamin, Abby; UMonte 84, BBA; BhamTS 93, MDiv; L Feb 6, 94; O Feb 6, 94, Evan Pby; astp Briarwood P Ch, Birmingham, AL, 94-95, ascp 95-

128 Summer Circle, Birmingham, AL 35242 – 205-980-8612   Evangel
E-mail: bparks@briarwood.org
Briarwood Presbyterian Church – 205-776-5265

    Parks, Robert – b Wetumpka, AL, Oct 4, 52; f Robert N. (d); m Ann Green; w Jan Bugg, SD, Jul 29, 78; chdn Beth Ann, Nicki; MSU 75, BA; BhamTS 07, MDiv; O Nov 18, 07, Evan Pby; CCC, 75-02; astp Briarwood P Ch, Birmingham, AL, 09-

821 Mountain Branch Drive, Birmingham, AL 35226 – 205-612-9969   Evangel
E-mail: bjparks@briarwood.org
Briarwood Presbyterian Church – 205-776-5470

    Parrish, Archie Brenton – b Bethany, OK, Jul 2, 32; f Jessie David; m Mettie Mae Steele; w Martha Jean Stancil, Huntsville, AL, Jul 10, 54; chdn John Charles, Elizabeth Anne, Martha Jane; SEBC 57, BA; GCTS 61, MDiv; FulTS 85, DMin; O 61, UPCUSA; p Limestone Larger Parish, Athens, AL, 61-67; mout/evan Wallace P Ch, Hyattsville, MD, 67-69; ascp, mout/evan Coral Ridge P Ch, Ft. Lauderdale, FL, 69-82; VP Evangelism Explosion III Int., Fort Lauderdale, FL, 73-81; ob pres Serve Int, 82-; admin MNA, coord church vitality, 94-; trng in Russia, 93-; co-auth *Learning Kit*; *Friendly Witness Training*, *Friendly Witness Training Memory Aids*, co-auth *Best Friends, Best Friends Course, Best News; Spirit of Revival; Improve Your Prayer Life; Intercede For and With Your Family; Invigorate Your Church; Impact Your World; Ignite Your Leadership*

1056 Woodruff Plantation Parkway SE, Marietta, GA 30067 – 770-998-4673   Metro Atlanta
E-mail: parrish7@aol.com
Serve International – 770-642-2449; www.kingdomprayer.org

    Parrish, John Charles – b Birmingham, AL, Nov 14, 55; f Archie B.; m Martha Jean Stancil; w Phyllis Arlene Brennan, Atlanta, GA, Nov 3, 84; chdn Jesse Brennan, Amanda Joy; CC 74-78, BA; GCTS 78-82, MDiv, 07, DMin; L Apr 82, SFL Pby; O Feb 86, NGA Pby; ob admin Serve Int; Atlanta Small Grps

Parrish, John Charles, continued
Pastors' Forum; ob Billy Graham Training Center, Asheville, NC, 94-05; ob Billy Graham Training Center, dir Prog, Asheville, NC, 05-12; Arrow Leadership Graduate, 01; brd memb On Eagles Wings Ministries/ Hope House Project, 10-15; p in Res Billy Graham Training Center, Asheville, NC, 12-; p/t exec p Missio Dei Ch, 13-; co-auth w/Archie Parrish *Best Friends: Developing an Intimate Relationship with God*, Thomas Nelson, 86

101 Castlerock Drive, Asheville, NC 28806-9517 – 828-655-1449   Western Carolina
E-mail: JCParrish55@bellsouth.net

Parrish, Ronald Harold – b Montezuma, GA, Jun 13, 51; f Marcus Harold; m Mary Ann Carr; w Donna Evans, Hamilton, Ont, Canada, Oct 26, 79; chdn Matthew Steven, Leighann Elizabeth, Andrew Jordan, David Evans; BelC 70-73, BA; RTS 73-77, MDiv; L Oct 18, 77; O Nov 5, 78, Evan Pby; ap First P Ch, Montgomery, AL, 78-80; op Trinity Msn Ch, Martinsville, VA, 80-81; p Chestnut Mountain P Ch, Chestnut Mountain, GA, 82-86; p Hull Mem P Ch, Savannah, GA, 87-90; ob ap Independent P Ch, Savannah, GA, 91; astp McIlwain Mem P Ch, Pensacola, FL, 91-94, ascp 94; ob astp Independent P Ch, Savannah, GA, 94-97, ob ascp 97-

33 East Stillwood Circle, Savannah, GA 31419-2441 – 912-927-7817   Savannah River
E-mail: rparrish@ipcsav.org
Independent Presbyterian Church – 912-236-3346
PO Box 9266, Savannah, GA 31412

Parsons, Burk – ob cop Saint Andrew's, Sanford, FL, 04-18; srp 18-

5525 Wayside Drive, Sanford, FL 32771   Central Florida
E-mail: pa@sachapel.com
Saint Andrew's (non-PCA) – 407-328-1139

Parsons, C. Wesley – O 16, TNVal Pby; astp Grace P Ch, Dalton, GA, 16-

3019 East Brookhaven Circle, Dalton, GA 30720   Tennessee Valley
E-mail: wesparsons1@gmail.com
Grace Presbyterian Church – 706-226-6344

Parsons, Joseph – w Fran; chdn Jordan, Hannah, Abigail, Katie; astp St. Vrain P Msn, Longmont, CO, 04; chp, ev Loveland, CO, 04-07; op Fields of Gr P Ch, Loveland, CO, 08-15

3860 Cheetah Drive, Loveland, CO 80537 – 970-461-8691   Rocky Mountain

Partain, Gerald Keith – b Thomas, OK, Jul 30, 29; f Cecil Marvin; m Cleo Clark; w Charlotte Trottier, La Mesa, CA, Jun 6, 53; chdn Cheri M., Elysa G. (Lochstampfor); SDSU 51; UMO 75-76; CTS, MDiv; L 77; O 78, PNW Pby (RPCES); p Liberty Bay P Ch, Poulsbo, WA, 78-85, wc; ip Lk Meridian P Ch, 87; ap Valley P Ch, North Hills, CA, 87-90; p Forestgate P Ch, Colorado Springs, CO, 90-95; p Covenant P Ch, Sun City West, AZ, 96-98; instr CC, Quest program, 99-01; hr

300 Durand Drive #19, Lookout Mountain, GA 30750 – 423-544-5291   Tennessee Valley
E-mail: gkpartain@comcast.net
HR

Passerelli, Daniel L. – astp Chapelgate P Ch, Marriottsville, MD, 13-

4002 Chariots Flight Way, Ellicott City, MD 21042 – 443-799-2736   Chesapeake
E-mail: dpasserelli@chapelgate.org
Chapelgate Presbyterian Church – 410-442-5800

MINISTERIAL DIRECTORY

Passmore, Joel – O Oct 24, 15, JR Pby; astp Northside Ch of Richmond (Mission), Richmond, VA, 15-

2426 Essex Road, Richmond, VA 23228 – 804-301-8188   James River
E-mail: joel@northsidechurchrva.org
Northside Church of Richmond (Mission) – 804-516-3322

Pate, Jeffrey Glenn – b Enterprise, AL, Apr 24, 71; f Glenn M.; m Bobbie Sue; w Lorrie Steed, Bowdon, GA, Dec 19, 93; chdn Tindol, Wilson, Sumlin, Parker, Daven, Warren; AU 94, BEd; SCS 08, MDiv; O Aug 2, 09, War Pby; p Brent P Ch, Brent, AL, 09-14; p Riverwood P Ch, Tuscaloosa, AL, 14-

2030 Idlewood Drive, Tuscaloosa, AL 35405 – 205-928-2555   Warrior
E-mail: jpate@riverwoodchurch.org
Riverwood Presbyterian Church – 205-758-8706

Patrick, John Mark – b Birmingham, AL, Oct 22, 74; f Gary Edwin; m Emily Withers; w Shea Carroll, Apr 5, 03; chdn Judah Griffin, Harper Nell, Alexandra Jean, Raybon Withers; TrSU 97, BS; BDS 07, MDiv; O Jul 23, 09, Palm Pby; p St. Matthews P Ch, St. Matthews, SC, 09- 13; astp Trinity P Ch, Orangeburg, SC, 13-14; ascp 14-17, p 17-

1170 Moss Street, Orangeburg, SC 29115 – 803-387-6225   Lowcountry
Trinity Presbyterian Church – 803-531-1274

Patrick, Matthew – O Aug 13, 17, Cal Pby; campm RUF, Woff, 17-

PCA Reformed University Fellowship   Calvary

Patterson, Randolph H. – b Miami, FL, Jun 17, 56; f Forrest F.; m Frances W. Hale; w Margaret J. DaCosta, Miami, FL, Jun 19, 76; chdn Jennifer, Christine, Daniel, Amber; FBC 76, BA; WTS 81, MAR; WTSFL 83, MDiv; L 83, SFL Pby; O May 84, Pby of NY & NE, OPC; Recd PCA Oct 20, 98, SFL Pby; p Lakeview OPC, Rockport, ME, 83-98; srp Seacrest Boulevard P Ch, Delray Beach, FL, 98-

620 Mission Hill Road, Boynton Beach, FL 33435 – 561-737-7090   Gulfstream
E-mail: randolphpatterson@juno.com
Seacrest Boulevard Presbyterian Church – 561-276-5533

Patteson, Harold Reed – b Jewell Ridge, VA, Nov 8, 27; f Harry Thomas P; m Margaret Williams; w Patricia Clayton, LaFayette, GA, Jan 23, 57; chdn Harold Reed P Jr, David Clayton, Cynthia Madge, Margaret Ann; UVA; KgC 51, BA; ColTS 54, BD; O Sept 54, PCUS; p First Ch, Appalachia, VA, 54-55; ap Signal Mt Ch, Signal Mt, TN, 56-60; p First Ch, Albertville, AL, 60-66; p Trin Ch, Travelers Rest, SC, 66-71; p Eau Claire P Ch, Columbia, SC, 71-93; hr 93; ss Grace Cov Ch, Blythewood, SC, 93-94; ss Central P Ch, Kingstree, SC, 94-95; astp, mpc Northeast P Ch, Columbia, SC, 96-02; ss Aimwell P Ch, Ridgeway, SC, 02-03; mpc Northeast P Ch, Columbia, SC, 06-11

209 Spring Tyme Court, Lexington, SC 29073 – 803-951-1659   Palmetto
E-mail: hrpattsr@juno.com
HR

Patton, Henry Thomas III – b Macon, GA, Jul 24, 60; f Henry Thomas Jr; m Frances Anne; w Diana Lynn Crouch, Macon, GA, Jun 19, 82; chdn Nathan Henry Thomas, Natalie Grace, Constance Noelle, Rebecca Neely; GASoC 78-82, BS; RTS 82-87, MDiv; L Apr 85; O Apr 87, NGA Pby; yp Perimeter Ch NW, 84-86; chp MTW, 87-98; astp St. Pauls P Ch, Orlando, FL, 98-08; ascp 08-10; ascp Oak Mountain P Ch, Birmingham, AL, 11-

2801 Lakewood Trace, Birmingham, AL 35242 – 205-531-2283   Evangel
E-mail: tpatton@oakmountainchurch.org
Oak Mountain Presbyterian Church – 205-995-9265

Patton, Jake — w Paige; chdn Laci, Luke, Aubrey, Brooke; CC 00, BA; CTS 07, MDiv; astp Southwood P Ch, Huntsville, AL, 08-09, ascp 09-11; astp Downtown P, Greenville, SC, 11-18; chp 18-

2181 Kallee Cove, Celina, TX 75009   North Texas
E-mail: jake.patton@gmail.com

Patton, John — w Donna; chdn Kelsie, Colson, Anna, Jack; VandU 83, BS; TNSU, MEd/Admin; CTS, M Gen Theo; astp Christ Comm Ch, Franklin, TN, 03-06; ascp, modis 06-11; t Christ P Acad, Nashville, TN

303 Heather Court, Franklin, TN 37069 – 615-642-7056   Nashville
E-mail: john.patton@cpalions.org

Paugh, Jason — O Dec 6, 15, SFL Pby; astp First P Ch of Coral Springs, FL, 15-

PO Box 8826, Coral Springs, FL 33075   South Florida
E-mail: jason@fpcstaff.com
First Presbyterian Church of Coral Springs – 954-461-7283

Paul, Jean — chp 08-

E-mail: soulswinningministires@yahoo.com   Northwest Georgia

Paul, John Andrew — p Rivers Edge Bible Ch, Hopewell, VA, 02-15

316 Creps Street, Lexington, SC 29072 – 804-943-8062   James River
E-mail: andyuvonne1@juno.com

Paulling, John — ascp Columbia P Ch, Columbia, SC, 14-18

4109 Monticello Road, Columbia, SC 29203   Palmetto
E-mail: john.paulling@gmail.com

Paulsen, John C. — w Judy; chdn Rebekah, Reidun; L May 76, IL Pby; O Oct 77, FL Pby; ap Covenant P Ch, Naples, FL, 77-78; t Naples CAc, 78-79; op First P Ch, West Frankfort, IL, 79-82; t Franklin ChrS, W. Frankfort, IL, 82-84; staff CC, 84-86; t Chattanooga Christian sch, 86-03; astp Reformed P Ch, Lookout Mountain, GA, 89-98; sp Kelly's Chapel, 97-; op Grace P Ch, Jasper, TN, 03-16; hr 16

137 Wayside Lane, Lookout Mountain, GA 30750-9600 – 706-820-0022   Tennessee Valley
HR

Paulson, Dieter — b Bryn Mawr, PA, Nov 29, 74; f George; m Linda Brown; w Marty Carol Lipscomb, Macon, MS, Mar 6, 99; chdn Grace Elizabeth, Tanner Jacob, Mary Claire, Georgia Carol; ECU 97, BA; RTS 02, MDiv, 02, MAMFT; O Oct 27, 02, GulCst Pby; astp Eastern Shore P Ch, Fairhope, AL, 02-03, wc 03-04; ss Covenant Ref P Ch, Daphne, 04-05; Chap Mobile Hospice, 05-10, p Trinity P Ch, Lancaster, SC, 10-17; chp Scottsboro, AL, 17-

701 Kennedy Circle, Scottsboro, AL 35768 – 803-287-0270   Providence
E-mail: dtrpaulson@gmail.com

Pavlic, James — b Mesopotamia, OH, Oct 16, 76; f Joseph James; m Treadeen Kay Charles; w Amanda Jo Branch, Hudson, OH, Feb 15, 03; chdn Shannon Rebecca, Ryan Joseph, Cornelius Treadway, Zadok Isaac; KStU 00, BS; RTSNC 16, MDiv; O Aug 21, 16, NR Pby; astp Mercy P Ch, Morgantown, WV, 16-17

5561 Kinsman Road, Middlefield, OH 44062 – 440-635-7700   New River
E-mail: james.pavlic@gmail.com

Payne, James M. – astp Crosspoint P Ch, Smyrna, GA, 08-14; ob 15-

4911 Lantern Lane, Mableton, GA 30126   Metro Atlanta

Payne, Jon D. – b Santa Clara, CA, Mar 6, 71; f David Charles; m Jeannie Kay Otis; w Marla Bruce Odom, Hartsville, SC, Sept 19, 98; chdn Mary Hannah, Hans Martin; ClemU, BA; RTS, MA; UEdin, ThM; RTS, doct stu; O 01, NGA Pby; mfam, moy Carriage Lane P Ch, Peachtree City, GA, 98-02; p Grace Ch, Douglasville, GA, 03-13; ev 13-14; op Christ Ch P, Mount Pleasant, SC, 14-; *John Owen and The Lord's Supper*, 04

1381 Scotts Creek Circle, Mount Pleasant, SC 29464 – 678-207-9572   Lowcountry
E-mail: jdpchristchurch@icloud.com
Christ Church Presbyterian – 843-606-0572

Peach, Mark – astp New Song P Ch, Salt Lake City, UT, 10-18; op City P, Salt Lake City, UT, 12-18, p 18-

180 East Coatsville Avenue, Salt Lake City, UT 84115   Northern California
E-mail: markpeach70@gmail.com
City Presbyterian – 801-910-6072

Pearson, Carl J. – b Bradley, AR, May 7, 34; f Carl C; m Edith Spruell; w Dorothy Mae Barrington, Bradley, AR, May 13, 56; chdn Gary C., Vaunda Ruth (Doty); OBU 62, BA; SWBTS 66, ThM; EBapTS 75, DMin; L Apr 59; O Aug 9, 59, Immanuel Bap Ch, Magnolia, AR; Recd PCA Oct 12, 96, GulCst Pby; p First Bap Ch, Danville, AR, 66-69; Chap USN, 69-95; p Westminster P Ch, Milton, FL, 96-04; hr 04

3441 Argyle Drive, Pace, FL 32571 – 850-994-6715   Gulf Coast
HR

Pearson, John – astp Cahaba Park Ch PCA, Birmingham, AL, 17-

1838 Brookview Lane, Hoover, AL 35216   Evangel
Cahaba Park Church PCA

Pearson, John – b Jackson, MS, Apr 19, 71; f H.H. Jr.; m Paula Jean Leigh; w Laura Marion Benton, St. Louis, MO, Mar 22, 97; chdn Marion McClain, John Maxwell, Elizabeth Paige; UMS 93, BBA; CTS 01, MDiv; O Sept 2, 01, JR Pby; campm RUF, W&LU, 01-07; RUF, area coord. VA, NC, WV, 07-

607 Ross Road, Lexington, VA 24450 – 540-463-6730   Blue Ridge
E-mail: jpearson@ruf.org
PCA Reformed University Fellowship

Pearson, Mark – w Donna; RTS 87, MA; RTSNC 05, MDiv; RTSFL 17, DMin; O 05; p Grace P Ch, Palm Coast, FL, 07-

24 Wendy Lane, Palm Coast, FL 32164 – 386-246-3952   North Florida
E-mail: mpearson26@cfl.rr.com
Grace Presbyterian Church – 386-437-8363

Peck, Keith Allen – b Corpus Christi, TX, Nov 30, 51; f Robert Oren; m Betty Herman; w Cathleen Gale Martin, Annapolis, MD, Aug 4, 73; chdn Robert Nathaniel, Heather Jerusha, Lauren Elise, Joshua Caleb, Cassandra Gale; UMD 73, BS; WTS 78, MDiv; L Feb 78, Phil Pby; O Nov 79, DMV Pby (RPCES); op RP Ch, Dover, DE, 78-80; t/tr AAChSc, 80-83; ap Westminster P Ch, Lancaster, PA, 83-87; ap Evangelical P Ch, Annapolis, MD, 87-90; p Broadneck Evangelical P Ch, Arnold, MD, 90-15; hr 15; astp Mercy P Ch, Forest, VA, 17-18, ascp 18-

225 Wayne Drive, Lynchburg, VA 24502 – 410-349-1918   Blue Ridge
HR
Mercy Presbyterian Church

Pegler, Donald – b San Diego, CA, Jul 11, 35; f John G.; m L. Ruth Grant; w Geraldine Y. Crawford; chdn Stephen, Eric, Bryce (d); UCO 61, BS; UNCO67, MA; RTS 93, MDiv; NGTS 96-; O Oct 1, 00, RMtn Pby; WDA, writer, 93-; Village Seven P Ch, dir Adult min, Colorado Springs, CO, 97-00, astp, ms 00-02, astp, mpc 03-07; wc 09-12; hr 13

185 Hillendale Lane, Gray, TN 37615 – 719-963-4320   Rocky Mountain
E-mail: dongeri@earthlink.net
HR

Pelander, Andrew – astp Grace Ch of Marin, Kentfield, CA, 06-09; astp Grace Ch Seattle, Seattle, WA, 09-16; op All Souls Ch of Seattle, Seattle, WA, 09-

3009 38th Avenue SW, Seattle, WA 98126   Pacific Northwest
E-mail: andy@allsoulsseattle.org
All Souls Church of Seattle – 206-829-8349

Pelsue, Joel Allen – b Denver, CO, Jul 2, 70; f Bradley Allen; m Georgia; w Michell Marie-Reid Klukow, Sarasota, FL, Dec 20, 91; chdn Reid Allen, Sophia Elisabeth, Alexandria Grace; WestC, BA; RTSFL 95-98, MDiv; O Mar 25, 00, MNY Pby; astp, wrshp ldr North Shore Comm Ch, Oyster Bay, NY, 00-02, ascp 02-03; astp, exec p Pacific Crossroads Ch, Los Angeles, CA, 03-06; ob pres AEM, 04-

2361 Glendon Avenue, Los Angeles, CA 90064 – 310-474-7671   Pacific
E-mail: joel@A-E-M.org
Arts & Entertainment Ministries
2361 Glendon Avenue, Los Angeles, CA 90064

Pelton, Corey – b Athens, GA, Dec 25, 67; f Michael Ramsey; m Mary Margaret Smith; w Holly Michelle Campbell, Sweetwater, TN, Aug 15, 92; chdn Miller Matthew, Mary Margaret; UT 86-90, BS; RTS 94-97, MDiv; O Nov 9, 97, MSVal Pby; campm RUF, BelC, 97-02; op Covenant P Ch, Hot Springs, AR, 02-03, p 03-10; p Redeemer P Ch, Greenville, SC, 10-

6150 Old Buncombe Road, Greenville, SC 29609   Calvary
E-mail: pelton67@gmail.com
Redeemer Presbyterian Church – 864-610-9400

Pemberton, Randy K. – b Forrest City, AR, May 22, 53; f Dennis Virgil; m Marian Frances McKenzie; w Cathy Denise Holkestad, San Gabriel, CA, Aug 16, 80; chdn Michelle Renee, Laura Beth, David Charles; EvC 75, BA; FulTS 79, MDiv; NPTS 83; L Apr 27, 01, Siouxl Pby; Recd PCA Jan 02, NoTX Pby; p Wichita, KS, 83-88; p Kerman, CA, 88-93; p New Richland, MN, 94-00; p Sherwood Shores Chapel, Gordonville, TX, 02-04; p Good Shepherd P Ch, Minnetonka, MN, 04-06; p Christ Ch, Mankato, MN, 14-

214 Dolph Road, Mankato, MN 56001 – 612-309-3695   Siouxlands
E-mail: rkpemberton@hickorytech.net
Christ Church

Pendley, William Robert – b Starkville, MS, Mar 17, 67; f James Doyle; m Julia Sue Terry; w Kimberly Bell Cotten, Starkville, MS, Feb 15, 92; chdn Andrew Hansford, Olivia Paige, John Reid; MSU 89, BS; CTS 94, MDiv; L Jul 22, 95; O Nov 19, 95, NoCA Pby; yp Seven Rivers P Ch, Lecanto, FL, 89-92; astp Valley Springs P Ch, Roseville, CA, 95-96; op, ev Christ Comm Ch Msn, Gainesville, FL, 97-07; srp 07-14; astp Trinity P Ch, Montgomery, AL, 14-

1728 South Hull Street, Montgomery, AL 36104 – 334-328-6767   Southeast Alabama
E-mail: robpendley@gmail.com
Trinity Presbyterian Church – 334-262-3892

MINISTERIAL DIRECTORY

Pennington, Jeffrey M. – b Joliet, IL, Sep 5, 58; w Sandra Jean, Jun 7, 80; chdn Nathan Caleb, Amber Nicole, Daniel Elijah, Samuel Isaiah, Ezra John, Hannah Grace, Heidi Kathryn; DBBC 80, BA; DBTS 82, MABS; Recd PCA Oct 24, 98, NoIL Pby; p Ref Evan Ch, Helena, MT, 92-98; p Trinity P Ch, Waukesha, WI, 98-

220 South Wales Road, Wales, WI 53183-9737 – 262-968-6769   Wisconsin
E-mail: jeff@trinitypresbyterianwi.org
Trinity Presbyterian Church – 262-894-8768

Penny, Robert Lee – b Baton Rouge, LA, Jan 21, 45; f Chester A.; m Mary Lindsly; w Adrianne Lillian DeYoung, Hazlehurst, MS, Jun 23, 67; chdn Victoria Joy, Elizabeth Heather, Edward Jamison; BelC 66, BA; LSU; UMS; RTS 70, MDiv; HU 80, DMin; O Sept 27, 70, StAnd Pby (PCUS); p Sardis P Ch, Sardis, MS, 70-73; op Graceview Hghts (ARP), 73-77; ss Sharon Ch, Brighton, TN, & Covington Ch, TN, 73-74; Chap Dunlap Home (ARP), Brighton, TN, 73-74; ev LA Pby (PCA), Lake Charles, LA, 78; ip Lawndale P Ch, Tupelo, MS, 78-79; p Main Street P Ch, Columbus, MS, 79-87; t Heritage Ac, Columbus, MS, 88-90; instr MSU, 90-92; ss Houston P Ch, Houston, MS, 89-97; sc Cov Pby, 93-95; headm Hebron CS, Pheba, MS, 93-97; p Houston P Ch, Houston, MS, 98; prin P Christian sch, Hattiesburg, MS, 98-01; astp First P Ch, Hattiesburg, MS, 02-07; mod Grace pby, 06; ob VP RTS, 07-13; hr 13; vis prof/dev rep African Bible College, Uganda; ed, *Interpreting and Teaching the Word of Hope: Essays in Honor of Jack Brown Scott on His Seventy-Seventh Birthday*, 05; ed *The Hope Fulfilled: Essays in Honor of O. Palmer Robertson*, 08

300 Red Eagle Circle, Ridgeland, MS 39157-9717 – 601-559-5227, 601-898-0414   Grace
E-mail: rlpenny300@gmail.com
HR

Pennylegion, John – b Burlington, ON, Oct 21, 78; f John; m Patricia; w Katherine Ann Fitch, Greenville, SC, Sept 6, 03; chdn Laine Michelle, Mead Elise, Cole Atticus; LanderU 01, BS; CTS 09, MDiv, 17, ThM; O Sept 2, 10, MO Pby; astp Covenant P Ch, St. Louis, MO, 09-14; ascp 14-16; p Christ the King P Ch, Roanoke, VA, 16-

5720 Penguin Drive, Roanoke, VA 24018 – 540-725-5835   Blue Ridge
E-mail: jpennylegion@ctkroanoke.org
Christ the King Presbyterian Church – 540-725-5835

Pensak, Joey – campm RUM, 04-11; op Redeemer Burlington, S. Burlington, VT, 11-

37 Hadley Road, South Burlington, VT 05403   Northern New England
E-mail: joseph@thevermontproject.org
Redeemer Burlington – 802-355-3440

Peoples, John F. Jr. – b Indianapolis, IN, Dec 16, 57; f J. Frederick; m Janet; w Mary Alice, Aug 29, 87; chdn Megan, John; ButU 76-80, BMusEd; CTS 81-85, MDiv; L 85; O 85, GrLks Pby; yp Chinese Gospel Ch (Ind), St. Louis, 85-88; p Grace Cov P Ch, Bloomington, IN, 88-99; p West Boca P Ch, Boca Raton, FL, 00-08; astp Grace P Ch, Indianapolis, IN, 08-09; ascp 09-

7863 Vics Court, Noblesville, IN 46062 – 561-470-4893   Central Indiana
E-mail: jpeoples@gracepca.org
Grace Presbyterian Church – 317-849-1565

Percifield, Steve – b Tyler, TX, Nov 2, 72; w Kelly, May 25, 96; chdn Lilly, Connor, Holt, Ella, Lucy; TCU 96, BS; WTS 08, MDiv; campm RUF, TXTech, 10-16; astp Trinity P, Fort Worth, TX, 16-

3800 Arroyo Road, Ft. Worth, TX 76109 – 806-789-5937   North Texas
E-mail: steve@trinitypresfw.org
Trinity Presbyterian

Perkins, Douglas Lloyd – w Pamela Lind, Richmond, VA, Nov 26, 88; chdn Luke Davidson, Caleb Lloyd, Joel Lind, Phoebe Meien, Priscilla Lien; BosU 77, BA; GCTS 80, MDiv; AmU/Wesley 88, DMin; Recd PCA Sept 90, Hrtg Pby; ascp Glasgow Ref P Ch, Bear, DE, 90-02; All Nations Flwsp, Wilmington, DE, 02-11; ev Hrtg Pby, 02-; ob ss CrossPointe PCA, Media, PA, 11-13; astp City Ch Wilmington, Wilmington, DE, 14-; ss Manor Ref/Gospel COAN, New Castle, DE, 15-; *Reformed Parishes and Responsiveness to the Poor*, 88; contr *World, Urban Mission, Sports Spectrum, Men of Integrity, Christianity Today*; writ, ed, *NIV Serendipity Bible for Groups*

15 Winterbury Drive, Wilmington, DE 19808-1429 – 302-388-1147   Heritage
E-mail: DOUGLPERKINS@gmail.com
City Church Wilmington – 302-409-0229
Manor Reformed/Gospel Church of all Nations – 302-328-1398

Perkins, Harrison – O Nov 9, 17, Evan Pby; ob Saintfield Pres Ch, Ireland, 17-

Saintfield Presbyterian Church (non PCA), IRELAND   Evangel

Perkins, Stephen L. – b Albuquerque, NM, Apr 4, 51; f Kenneth Eugene; m Carlotte Jean; w Cynthia, Olathe, KS, Aug 3, 73; chdn Kristopher Stephen, Kendra Leanne, Katelyn Drew; BJU 75, BA; CTS 02, MDiv; O Jan 22, 05, Cal Pby; astp Covenant P Ch, Easley, SC, 04-07, srp 07-10; p Christ Comm Ch, Johnson City, TN, 11-

1502 Chickamauga Trail, Lookout Mountain, GA 30750   Westminster
E-mail: slperk_is@bigfoot.com
Christ Community Church – 423-946-0357

Perret, Kyle – w Davinia; chdn J.T., Camille; BelC 00; CTS 05; O Feb 20, 06, CentGA Pby; astp St. Andrews Ch, Midland, GA, 05-08; astp Cascade P Ch, Eugene, OR, 08-11; ascp 11-12

E-mail: knperret@gmail.com   Pacific Northwest

Perrie, Andrew – srp Grace P Ch, Grenada, MS, 10-15; p Rock Bridge P Ch, Clinton, SC, 15-

Rock Bridge Presbyterian Church   Covenant

Perrin, Daniel Hurlbut – b Erie, PA, May 13, 50; f Stuart H (d); m Romaine Erickson (d); w Ruthann Van Pelt, Carteret, NJ, Jan 22, 77; chdn Rebecca Ann (Woods), Andrew Peter, Benjamin Daniel; WCPA 68-72, BA; GCTS 74-77, MDiv; O Jul 10, 77, Asc Pby; ap Westminster P Ch, Butler, PA, 77-82; op op Hudson, MA, 82; ss Rocky Springs P Ch, Harrisville, PA, 83; Cov Ch, Greensburg, PA, 83-87; srp Faith P Ch, Cincinnati, OH, 87-04; p Grace P Ch of St. Charles Co, St. Charles, MO, 05-11; prof Alexandria Sch of Theo, Cairo, Egypt, 07-10; ip Valley P Ch, Lutherville, MD, 12; Chap Quarryville P Retirement Comm, Quarryville, PA, 12-14; ip Manor P Ch, Cochranville, PA, 15-18; ss, ip Faith Ref P Ch, Quarryville, PA, 18-

10 West 5th Street, Quarryville, PA 17566 – 717-517-2884   Susquehanna Valley
E-mail: dhperrin@aol.com
Faith Reformed Presbyterian Church – 717-786-7559

Perrin, Nicholas – b Boston, MA, Sept 5, 64; f Dr. Mark; m Ursula Gutmann; w Camie B. Brown, Twin Oaks, MO, Dec 19, 92; chdn Nathaniel Gage, Luke Nicholas; JHU 86, BA; ULon; CTS 94; MarqU 01, PhD; L Nov 13, 94; O Nov 13, 94, NoIL Pby; astp Naperville P Ch, Naperville, IL, 94-97, wc 97-09; stu MarqU; ob prof WheatCol, 09-; ip Faith Comm Ch, West Chicago, IL, 18-

Wheaton College   Chicago Metro
Faith Community Church – 630-231-8230

Perry, Christopher – O Jan 21, 14, Glfstrm Pby; astp Treasure Coast P Ch, Stuart, FL, 14-15

E-mail: c.hoye.perry@gmail.com   Gulfstream

Perry, Gregory Rolan – b McAllen, TX, May 28, 62; f Robert Ray; m Dixie Deal; w Darlene Joan Walters, Augusta, GA, May 31, 14; chdn Stephen, Allie, Jonathan; LSU 80-84, BS; PTS 83; RTS 85-88, MDiv; ColTS 88-89, ThM; UTSVA 08, PhD; O Jul 27, 91, NGA Pby; astp Intown Comm Ch, Atlanta, GA, 91-94; MTW, 95-00; ob Birthmother Ministries, Inc., Arlington, VA, 00-02; adj prof CTS, 03-04, asst prof 05-09, assoc prof 09-17; Third Mill Ministries 17-; rvws in *Presbyterion* and *Catholic Biblical Quarterly*; art in *Reformed Theological Review*, 00; *Luke's Narrative Shaping of Early Christian Identity*, 08; art in *Horizons of Biblical Theology*, 09; rvws: *Interpretation*, 09, 10; *Review of Biblical Literature*, 11; *International Bulletin of Missionary Research*, 12, 14; contr *For the World: Essays in Honor of Richard L. Pratt, Jr*, 14

105 Hillcrest Drive, Longwood, FL 32779 – 636-675-9067   Missouri
E-mail: gperry@thirdmill.org
Third Millennium Ministries, Inc. – 404-278-8841
316 Live Oaks Boulevard, Casselberry, FL 32707

Perry, James – b Mar 18, 34; w Peggy Ann Fry, Chattanooga, TN, Jun 9, 56; CBC 54-57; CC 60, BA; CTS 64, BD, 72, MDiv; L Jun 62, MidSo Pby; O Mar 18, 65, NJ Pby (RPCES); p Seaside Bible Ch, Seaside Hgts, NJ, 64-67; p Trinity P Ch, Kearney, NE, 67-73; p Grace Ref Ch, Hastings, NE, 73-74; p First Conservative P Ch, Indianapolis, IN, 74-75; ap Evang Ch, Colorado Spgs, CO, 75-78; p Pres Ch, York, AL, (Ind), 78-89; p Grenada P Ch, Grenada, MS, 89-93; op Covenant P Ch, Russellville, AR, 93-97; p Brent P Ch, Brent, AL, 97-04, ev 04-18; hr

318 2nd Street North, Centreville, AL 35042 – 205-926-9937   Warrior
E-mail: pacafour@bellsouth.net
HR

Perry, John Andrew – astp Bible P Ch, Merrill, WI, 14-

1700 East 3rd Street, Merrill, WI 54452 – 701-340-5081   Wisconsin
E-mail: jandyperry@gmail.com
Bible Presbyterian Church – 715-536-4748

Perry, Ronnie – O Nov 6, 11, TNVal Pby; astp New City Flwsp, Chattanooga, TN, 11-13; astp Christ Central Durham, Durham, NC, 13-15; astp Truth Point Ch, West Palm Beach, FL, 15-17; op New Song, West Palm Beach, FL, 17-

2535 Sandy Cay, West Palm Beach, FL 33411   Gulfstream
New Song

Pesnell, Darin – O Dec 18, 11, PhilMetW Pby; op Iron Works Ch, Phoenixville, PA, 11-16, p 16-

323 Gay Street, Phoenixville, PA 19460 – 610-427-9192   Philadelphia Metro West
E-mail: darin@peznet.net
Iron Works Church – 484-928-0560

Peters, Byron Jay – b Owensboro, KY, Apr 26, 61; f Gerald Walter; m Betty Sue McEuen; w Ruby Beatrice Beckham, Heath Springs, SC, Jun 6, 87; chdn Walter Beckham, Byron Jay Jr., John Martin, Layson Carol; UKY 79-83, BA; IST 95, MABS; WTS 99, MDiv; L May 98, Phil Pby; O Nov 21, 99, ECar Pby; CCC, 84-96; astp Church of the Good Shepherd, Durham, NC, 99-00, ascp 00-05; op Christ Comm Ch, Chapel Hill, NC, 05-06, cop 06-

304 Old Piedmont Circle, Chapel Hill, NC 27516 – 919-357-1441   Eastern Carolina
E-mail: byron@cccpca.org
Christ Community Church – 919-636-5258

Peters, Christopher Morgan – b Hinsdale, IL, Oct 18, 74; f Steven; m Letty Moore; w Patience Deskins, Sipsey, AL, Jul 29, 95; chdn Cotton, Chalmers, Cannon, Clement; WashU 96, BA; CTS 00, MDiv; UAB 07, MA; UAL 14, PhD; O Oct 02, Evan Pby; camp dir, Nat'l Leadership Found, St. Louis, 96-99; college dir, Central EPC, St. Louis, 00-02; astp Covenant P Ch, Birmingham, AL, 02-09; op Cross Creek Ch, Birmingham, AL, 09-

2150 Ross Avenue, Hoover, AL 35226 – 205-822-3322   Evangel
E-mail: cpeters@crosscreekchurch.net
Cross Creek Church – 205-453-9190

Peters, Colin Reid – b Dallas, TX, Apr 9, 68; f Charles Ray, Sr.; m Kay Weaver; w Mary Elster, Winston-Salem, NC, Feb 22, 97; chdn Carson Douglas, William Elster, Ansley Katherine; VandU 91, BS; CTS 99, MDiv; cert Bib Couns, CCEF, 13; L Jan 15, 00, CentGA Pby; O Feb 27, 00, CentGA Pby; int Covenant P Ch, St. Louis, MO, 97-99; campm RUM, MercU, 99-07; ascp New St. Peters P Ch, Dallas, TX, 07-12; srp 13-

9302 Canter Drive, Dallas TX 75231 – 214-242-9172   North Texas
E-mail: colinreidpeters@gmail.com
New St. Peter's Presbyterian Church – 214-438-0120

Peters, David – O Mar 8, 15, CentInd Pby; astp Crossroads Comm Ch, Fishers, IN, 15-

10291 Cotton Blossom Drive, Fishers, IN 46038   Central Indiana
E-mail: dpeters@crossroadspca.org
Crossroads Community Church – 317-485-2175

Peterson, Brian Joseph – b Orange, CA, Aug 13, 73; f Donald; m Louise Mettler; w Anna Gregoire, New Orleans, LA, Nov 14, 99; chdn Samuel Mettler, Kiah Elizabeth, Katherine Louise, Timothy Joseph, Nathan Laine, Meghan Eilene, Micah William; CSUChico 96, BA; RTS 03, MDiv; O Nov 2, 03, NoCA Pby; p Sierra View P Ch, Fresno, CA, 03-15; astp Christ Cov Ch, Matthews, NC, 15-; "Answering Those Who Try to Live by the Golden Rule" *Christian Research Journal*, Issue 39, 16

4025 Hay Meadow Drive, Mint Hill, NC 28227 – 980-253-1954   Central Carolina
E-mail: bpeterson@christcovenant.org
Christ Covenant Church – 704-847-3505

Peterson, David Paul – b Lemmon, SD, Jan 4, 41; f Robert; m Winifred Larson; w Sandra Kay Dorcas, Albuquerque, NM, Jun 9, 64; chdn Jeffrey, J'Lane, Julie; CC 62, BA; CTS 64, MDiv; LIU 73, MA; L Jul 65; O Jul 65, GrPl Pby (RPCES); Chap USArmy, 65-95; coord MNA, Chap min, 95-08; exec dir PRJC, 95-08; hr

21115 Brimstone Place, Sturgis, SD 57785 – 605-347-5812   Siouxlands
E-mail: chappeterson@gmail.com
HR

Peterson, James Corbin, Sr. – b Ft. Oglethorpe, GA, Jul 24, 72; f William James; m Janice Marie Davis; w Anne Michelle Brandon, Memphis, TN, May 18, 02; chdn James Corbin Jr., William Davis, Anne Mae, John Brandon; SamU 95, BS; BhamTS 02, MDiv; CTS 04, ThM; O Feb 24, 02, Evan Pby; yp Briarwood P Ch, Birmingham, AL, 95-97; yp Christ Cov P Ch, Cullman, AL, 98-02; ascp 02-04; astp Faith P Ch, Birmingham, AL, 04-08; op Christ Comm Ch, Frisco, TX, 08-12; p 12-14; ascp Christ P Ch at Oxford, Oxford, MS, 14-16; astp Cahaba Park Ch PCA, Birmingham, AL, 16-

4465 Old Overton Road, Birmingham, AL 35210   Evangel
E-mail: jpeterson@cahabapark.org
Cahaba Park Church PCA – 205-870-1886

MINISTERIAL DIRECTORY

Peterson, Robert Arthur – b Newark, NJ, Nov 15, 48; f Arthur F.; m Marjorie Petrie; w Mary Pat Derx, Olean, NY, Jun 13, 73; chdn Robert Jr., Matthew, Curtis, David; PhilCB 73, BS; BibTS 76, MDiv; DrewU 79, MPhil, 80, PhD; L 80; O 81, RPCES; asst prof BibTS, 81-85, assoc prof 85-90; p Peace Chapel, Warminster, PA, 86-88; p Faith Bible Ch, Gladwyne, PA, 88-90; prof CTS, 90-; *Calvin's Doctrine of the Atonement*, 83; *Getting to Know John's Gospel: A Fresh Look at Its Main Ideas*, 89; *Hell on Trial: The Case for Eternal Punishment*, 95; *Calvin and the Atonement*, 99; *Two Views on Hell, A Biblical and Theological Dialogue*, 2000; *Adopted by God: From Wayward Sinners to Cherished Children*, 01; *Why I Am Not an Arminian*, 04; *Election and Free Will: God's Gracious Choice and Our Responsibility*, 07; *Our Secure Salvation: Preservation and Apostasy*, 09; *What is Hell?* 10; ed: *Hell Under Fire: Modern Scholarship Reinvents Eternal Punishment*, 04; *All for Jesus: A Celebration of the 50th Anniversary of Covenant Theological Seminary*, 06; *Anointed With the Spirit and Power*, 08; *Faith Comes by Hearing: A Response to Inclusivism*, 08; *Suffering and the Goodness of God*, 08; *The Nearness of God*, 09; *The Elder*, 09; *The Glory of God*, 10; "Idol Factory," *Tabletalk*, November 03; "Consequences," *Modern Reformation*, May/June 06; "The Bible's Story of Election," *Presbyterion*, Spring 07; "Apostasy in the Hebrews Warning Passages," *Presbyterion*, Spring 08

823 Wind Mill Drive, Ballwin, MO 63011 – 636-394-1981   Missouri
Covenant Theological Seminary – 314-434-4044

Peterson, Shawn Jason – astp University P Ch, Orlando, FL, 01-06

Address Unavailable   Central Florida

Petterson, Jason – astp Valley P Ch, North Hills, CA, 11-

Valley Presbyterian Church – 818-894-9200   Pacific

Petterson, Robert A. – srp Covenant P Ch, Naples, FL, 02-16; wc 16-

4200 Kensington High Street, Naples, FL 34105   Suncoast Florida
E-mail: robertpetterson@msn.com

Petty, James Chalmers Jr. – b Chicago, IL, Nov 14, 44; f James C.; m Katherine A. Johnston; w Marsha M. Hunt, Philadelphia, PA, Jul 27, 68; chdn James Hunt, Stephen MacVean, Laura Johnston; WheatC 62-66, BS; WTS 66-70, MDiv, 97, DMin; L Sept 69; O Oct 70, OPC; op Church of the Redeemer, Philadelphia, PA, 70-87, ap 87-90; ob couns, Dir CCEF, 82-03;exec dir Children's Jubilee Fund, 03-12; dir emer, 13-16; hr 16; *Step by Step: Divine Guidance for Ordinary Christians*, 99

5300 Southwind Drive, Wilmington, NC 28409 – 910-833-5108   Eastern Pennsylvania
E-mail: jpetty@navpoint.com
HR

Pfeiffer, Austin David – b Cincinnati, OH, Nov 28, 82; w Erin; chdn Silas, Lucy, Marco, Blaise; UCO 07, BA; GCTS 12, MA; DukeU 14, ThM; O Apr 26, 14, PTri Pby; ascp Salem P Ch, Winston-Salem, NC, 13-; The Secret Sacrament: The Essentiality of Biblical Community for Christians of the Twenty-First Century (thesis, GCTS); Embodied Communal Life in the Book of Hebrews (thesis, DukeU)

904 West Academy Street, Winston-Salem, NC 27101   Piedmont Triad
E-mail: austin@salempresws.org
Salem Presbyterian Church – 336-724-4421

Phee, Sean Sewon – astp Sa Rang Comm Ch, Anaheim, CA, 14-

40 Copper Leaf, Irvine, CA 90602   Korean Southwest Orange County
Sa Rang Community Church – 714-772-7777

Phelan, Stephen – ascp Harbor Mid-City P Ch, San Diego, CA, 09-14; p Bridge Ch, San Diego, CA., 14-

4346 54th Street, San Diego, CA 92115　　　　　　　　　　　　　　　　　　　South Coast
E-mail: stephen@bridgesd.org
Bridge Church – 619-955-6718

Philio, Shannon Kelly – b Saratoga Spgs, NY, Aug 4, 67; f Schuyler E; m Hoffman; MSU 85-89, BA; RTS 90-93, MDiv, MCE; L Jan 94; O May 22, 94, Gr Pby; astp First P Ch, Biloxi, MS, 94-95, ascp 95-96; Chap USAF, Pope AFB, NC, 96-00; Chap USAF, Istres AB, Istres, France, 99; Chap USAF, Osan AB, ROK, 00-01; Chap USAF, Robins AFB, GA, 01-03; Chap USAF, Clear AFS, AK, 03-04; Chap USAF, Brooke Army Med Cntr, 04-05; Chap USAF, RAF Croughton UK, 05-06; Chap USArmy, Fort Stewart, GA, 07; Chap USArmy FOB Kalsu, Iraq, 08; Chap USArmy Ft. Drum, NY, 09-11; Chap USArmy Ft. Hood, TX, 12-14

1607 Kincaid Street, DuPont, WA 98327　　　　　　　　　　　　　　　　　　　Grace
E-mail: shannon.philio@juno.com

Philips, William Ingram III – b Miami, FL, Sept 16, 39; f William I P Jr; m Frances Swygert; w Mary Powell, Texarkana, TX, Jul 2, 88; chdn Leigh Anne, Susan Elizabeth; UFL 61, BS; RTS 75, MDiv; CamU 78, BA; DrewTS 81, DMin; L Feb 25, 74; O Jan 14, 75, Evan Pby; Chap USArmy, 75-97; ob Mustang Creek Enterprises, 97-05; hr 98; Volunteer America-1776, 06; pres Care Cap Connections 501(c)(3), 06-; ACM, 6MSM, AFRM, 2NDSM, ASR, 5OSR, BSM, SWA2CS, KLM Col; fel Col Chap; Legion of Merit; const Indian Rock Township, 09-; Fairfield Bay, AR police, 15-; *War Riders*, 98; *Beyond Sundown*, 99

103 Tanglewood Circle, Fairfield Bay, AR 72088 – 501-884-3046　　　　　　　Evangel
E-mail: wiphilips@artelco.com
HR

Philliber, Michael – b Tulsa, OK, Apr 28, 61; f C. Wayne; m Patricia Sweet; w Anna Marie Reichert, Moore, OK, Oct 6, 79; chdn Audrey Lynn, Beth Anne, Caleb Michael, Derek Evan; CommCAF 79-89, AAS; GraceU; RTS 96-00, MDiv; TrinEpis 07, DMin; L Oct 20, 97, MSVal Pby; O Feb 11, 01, MSVal Pby; p Key Largo CofC, Key Largo, FL, 84-89; stus Pickens P Ch, Pickens, MS, 98-01, p 01-02; p Providence P Ch, Midland, TX, 02- 12; astp Heritage P Ch, Edmond, OK, 12-13, ascp 13-16; srp 16-; *Gnostic Trends in the Local Church: The Bull in Christ's China Shop*, 11

9724 Berkley Circle, Oklahoma City, OK 73162 – 432-570-5395　　　　　Hlls and Plains
E-mail: michaelphilliber@sbcglobal.net
Heritage Presbyterian Church – 405-752-2270

Phillips, Alton Monroe – b New Orleans, LA, Mar 23, 45; f Al N; m Annie Helen Newman; w Carol Ann Chatham, Hattiesburg, MS, May 22, 66; chdn Alton Monroe Jr, Stephanie Carol (Hill), James Jackson II, Stephen Guy; USM 74, BS; RTS 74-77, MDiv; O Sept 4, 77, MSVal Pby; p DeKalb P Ch, DeKalb, MS, 77-83; p Bloomfield Ch, DeKalb, MS, 77-83; p Pleasant Springs P Ch, DeKalb, MS, 77-83; p Grace P Ch, Madison, FL, 83-89; p Bailey P Ch, Bailey, MS, 89-96; p Columbia P Ch, Columbia, MS, 96-02; p First P Ch, Greensboro, AL, 02-11; p Newbern P Ch, Newbern, AL, 02-11; hr 11

155 Seagrass Way, Panama City Beach, FL 32407 – 256-975-5299　　　　　　　Warrior
E-mail: altonmrev@gmail.com
HR

Phillips, Andrew C. – b Bryn Mawr, PA, Dec 7, 56; f David M.; m Gretchen Ackerman; w Linda Kirsopp, Pittsburgh, PA, Aug 18, 79; chdn Christie Lee, Laura Ann, Kelli Lynn; SRU 75-79, BS; WTS 83, MAR, 84, MDiv; O Nov 84, CentFL Pby; ap Covenant Life P Ch, Sarasota, FL, 84-89; astp Westminster P Ch, Rock Hill, SC, 89-95; srp Providence P Ch, York, PA, 95-12; wc 13-

2545 Coldspring Road, York, PA 17404-6406 – 717-968-1893　　　　　　Susquehanna Valley
E-mail: acphillips1@comcast.net

MINISTERIAL DIRECTORY

Phillips, Ben – w Rebecca; chdn Joshua, Andrew, Hannah Kate; USCSpart 88, BA; RTSNC 04, MDiv; Emory 17, ThM; O Jan 30, 05, NGA Pby; astp Chestnut Mountain P Ch, Chestnut Mountain, GA, 05-07; ascp 07-

805 New Liberty Way, Braselton, GA 30517 – 706-654-5415   Georgia Foothills
E-mail: ben.phillips@cmpca.org
Chestnut Mountain Presbyterian Church – 770-967-3440 ext. 115

Phillips, David – Recd PCA 18, Hrtg Pby; ascp Cornerstone P Ch, Landenberg, PA, 17-

5 Poppy Lane, West Grove, PA 19390   Heritage
E-mail: pastordavid.cpc@gmail.com
Cornerstone Presbyterian Church – 610-255-5512

Phillips, Eric – p City-Wide Redeemer P Aliante, North Las Vegas, NV, 12-14, p 14-

7133 Bluebird Wing Street, North Las Vegas, NV 89084   Pacific
E-mail: eaphil2@gmail.com
City-Wide Redeemer Presbyterian Aliante – 702-540-2932

Phillips, Gerald – astp Oaklawn P Ch, 05-07, op Hosanna Comm Ch, Tomball, TX, 05-07; p 08-

1857 Pembrook Circle, Conroe, TX 77301 – 832-928-5805   Houston Metro
E-mail: philfinserv@yahoo.com
Hosanna Community Church

Phillips, James Gaynor – b Baton Rouge, LA, May 17, 39; f Ira R P; m Lorena Holden; w Mary Olson, Charlotte, NC, Aug 26, 61; chdn Mary Elizabeth, David Gaynor; BelC 61, BA; ColTS 64, BD; L Sept 27, 64; O Sept 27, 64, SC Pby; p Lydia Ch, Clinton, SC, 64-66; p Rock Bridge P Ch, Clinton, SC, 64-66; p First Ch, Loris, SC, 67-72; p Reedy River P Ch, Conestee, SC, 72-80, wc 80-84; p Smyrna P Ch, Newberry, SC, 84-93; ob staff Bailey Manor, Clinton, SC, 93-95; hr 95

108 Doverdale Road, Greenville, SC 29615-3938 – 864-281-7629   Calvary
HR

Phillips, John Scott – w Karin, Jun 28, 97; chdn Evelyn, Maggie, Jacob, Noah; TNTU 96, BS; CTS 02, MDiv; O Oct 27, 02, Nash Pby; campm RUF, TNTech, 02-06; p First P Ch, Louisville, MS, 06-

108 Meadowview Drive, Louisville, MS 39339-3013 – 662-736-0191   Mississippi Valley
E-mail: pastorphillips@gmail.com
First Presbyterian Church – 662-773-3146

Phillips, Michael – O Feb 23, 14, MetAtl Pby; campm RUF, GATech, 14-

415 Altoona Place SW, Atlanta, GA 30310   Metro Atlanta
E-mail: michael.phillips@ruf.org
PCA Reformed University Fellowship

Phillips, Michael V. – w Julie; chdn Val, Matt, John; TrinEpis, PA 91, MDiv; CTS 16, DMin; O Nov 00, NR Pby; astp Westminster P Ch, Roanoke, VA, 00-; astp St. Christophers Epis Ch, Spartanburg, SC, 91-93; St. James Epis Ch, Riverton, WY, 93-98; astp Westminster P Ch, Roanoke, VA, 99-03; p New Cov P Ch, Aiken, SC, 03-12; astp First P Ch, Augusta, GA, 14-;pres City View Seminary, 18-

406 Dorcester Drive, Augusta, GA 30909 – 803-640-4525   Savannah River
E-mail: mphillips@firstpresaugusta.org
First Presbyterian Church – 706-262-8900
City View Seminary

Phillips, Richard Davis – b Ft. Monroe, VA, Sept 9, 60; f Charles Davis; m Margaret Sapp; w Sharon Lynn Wilkey, Fairview Village, PA, Jun 5, 93; chdn Hannah Catherine, Matthew Holden, Jonathan Stephen, Helen Elisabeth, Lydia Margaret; UMI 82, BA; UPA 92, MBA; WTS 98, MDiv; GPTS 12, DD; L Nov 98, Phil Pby; O Jan 24, 99, Phil Pby; ascp Tenth P Ch, Philadelphia, PA, 98-02; Alliance of Confessing Evangelicals, Inc., CEO, Philadelphia, PA, 98-02; srp First P Ch of Coral Springs, Margate, FL, 02-07; srp Second P Ch, Greenville, SC, 07-; *The Heart of an Executive: Lessons on Leadership from the Life of King David*, 99; *Mighty to Save: Discovering God's Grace in the Miracles of Jesus*, 01; *Encounters with Jesus: When Ordinary People Met the Savior*, 02; *Turning Back the Darkness: The Biblical Pattern Reformation*, 02; *Faith Victorious: Finding Courage and Strength from Hebrews 11*, 02; *Turning Your World Upside Down: Kingdom Priorities in the Parables of Jesus*, 03; "The Lord's Supper: An Overview," in *Give Praise to God*, 03; *The Church: One, Holy, Catholic, and Apostolic*, 04; *Chosen in Christ: The Glory of Grace in Ephesians 1*, 04; *What Is the Lord's Supper*, 05; *Walking with God: Learning Discipleship in the Psalms*, 05; "Jeremiah 31 and the New Covenant," in *The Covenant*, 05; "Covenant Confusion," in *The Covenant*, 05; *Hebrews: Reformed Expository Commentary*, 06; *Holding Hands, Holding Hearts: Recovering a Biblical View of Christian Dating*, 06; *What Are Election and Predestination*, 06; *Only One Way: Reaffirming the Exclusive Truths of Christianity*, 06; "Assured in Christ," in *Assured by God*, 06; "A Justification of Imputed Righteousness," in *By Faith Alone*, 06; *Zechariah: Reformed Expository Commentary*, 07; *Jesus the Evangelist: Learning to Share the Gospel from the Gospel of John*, 07; *What's So Great about the Doctrines of Grace*, 08; *Saved by Grace*, 09; *Precious Blood: The Atoning Work of Christ*, 09; *Jonah & Micah: Reformed Expository Commentary*, 10; *What Is the Atonement*, 10; *The Masculine Mandate: God's Calling to Men*, 10; *These Last Days*, 11; *Can We Know the Truth?* 11;*These Last Days*, 11; *The Death of the Savior*, 12; *I Samuel*, 12; *What Happens After Death*, 13; brd dir, Alliance on Confessing Evangelicals, 00-; brd dir, KTS, 05-07; chrmn, Philadelphia Conference on Reformed Theology, 01-; cncl mbr The Gospel Coalition, 09; brd dir WTS, 11-

11 Bridgeton Drive, Greenville, SC 29615 – 864-236 7113   Calvary
E-mail: rick@secondpca.org
Second Presbyterian Church – 864-232-7621

Phillips, William G. – b Philadelphia, PA, Sept 11, 45; f A. Gordon; m Gertrude Grace Hall; w Carol Sheldon, New Providence, NJ, Jun 22, 68; chdn Cynthia, Mark; UDE 67, BA; WTS 70, BD; L 69, Phil Pby (RPCES); O Sept 70, DMV Pby (RPCES); ap Faith P Ch, Wilmington, DE, 70-73; p Reformed P Ch, West Chester, PA, 73-78; p First RP Ch, Indianapolis, IN, 78-82; op Flwsp of Gr, Peoria, AZ, 83-87, p 87-16; hr 16; astp King of Kings, Goodyear, AZ, 17-

8234 West Melinda Lane, Peoria, AZ 85382 – 623-977-7301   Southwest
E-mail: bill@kkchurch.org
King of Kings

Phillis, James William – b Peoria, IL, Mar 18, 57; f William Gerald; m Anne Elizabeth; w Susan Jean Vroman, Peoria, IL, May 31, 80; chdn Bradley James, Bethany Jean, Benjamin John; AndC 78-81, BA; TEDS 81-84, MDiv; CTS 04, DMin; L 84; O 85, NoIL Pby; op Christ msn, Schaumburg, IL, 85-87, wc 87-88; p Meadowcroft P Ch, West Chester, 88-92; ascp Evangelical P Ch, Newark, DE, 92-97; p Covenant P Ch, Hendersonville, NC, 97-04; ob New Life Ministries, 04-06; ob Front Row Life Coaching, 16-

611 Pineland Road, Hendersonville, NC 28792 – 828-243-9295   Western Carolina
E-mail: jim.phillis@frontrowlc.net
Front Row Life Coaching

Phipps, Kevin – b New Orleans, LA, Feb 24, 83; f Clayton Young; m Karen Helwick; w Emily Baumgartner, Hammond, LA, Sept 5, 09; chdn Claire, Lucas; GlobMinC 03, AA; RTS 15, MDiv; O Sept 15, EPC; Recd PCA Nov 4, 18, GrLks Pby; astp New Cov EPC, Mandeville, LA, 15-18; astp University Ref Ch, East Lansing, MI, 18-

1811 Bramble Drive, East Lansing, MI 48823   Great Lakes
E-mail: kevinclaytonphipps@gmail.com
University Reformed Church – 517-351-6810

MINISTERIAL DIRECTORY

Pickard, Robert Jason – O May 1, 12, SoTX Pby; astp Westminster P Ch, Bryan, TX, 12-13; campm RUFI, TXA&M, 13-18

3720 Springfield Drive, College Station, TX 77845 – 979-220-3210   South Texas

Pickens, Jonathan S. – b Frederick, MD, May 31, 87; f Robert Andrew; m Kathy; w Amy Hudson, Sharpsburg, MD, Sept 24, 16; GenC 09, BS; RTS 13, MDiv; O Mar 23, 14, EPA Pby; astp Faith P Ch, Richboro, PA, 14-16; astp Broadneck EP Ch, Arnold, MD, 16-

235 Bay Dale Drive, Arnold, MD 21012 – 301-787-1950   Chesapeake
E-mail: pickens.jon@gmail.com
Broadneck Evangelical Presbyterian Church – 410-626-8122

Pickens, R. Andrew Jr. – b. Baltimore, MD, May 13, 58; f Robert Andrew; m Hilda Fisher; w Kathy Gotsch, Perry Hall, MD, July 21, 79; chdn Matthew Wyatt, Robert Alexander, Jonathan Samuel, Valerie Christiana; VaTech 75-79, BS; CTS 91-96, MTS; L 97; O 06, Pot Pby; astp Shady Grove P Ch, Derwood, MD, 06-08; mis MTW, 08-12; ss LaPlata Comm Ch, LaPlata, MD, 13- 14; wc 14-15; astp Centerpoint Christ Comm Ch, Troy, OH, 15-16; astp Faith Ref P Ch, Quarryville, PA, 16-

286 Greystone Lane, Quarryville, PA 17566   Susquehanna Valley
E-mail: andyandkathypickens@gmail.com
Faith Reformed Presbyterian Church – 717-786-7559

Pickett, James Michael – b Las Cruces, NM, Mar 11, 52; f Cecil James; m Helen Lenora Peek; w Michele Albury; chdn Noah Michele, Elena Damaris; UOK 70-75, BA; CTS 81, MDiv; L 81; O 81, Midw Pby (RPCES); p Manhattan P Ch, NY, 85-91; astp Covenant P Ch, Flushing, NY, 92-94; astp New City Flwsp, Chattanooga, TN, 94-95; ascp 95-08; op New Cit Flwsp East Lake, 08-16, srp 16-18

509 Kilmer Street, Chattanooga, TN 37404-1636 – 423-774-3886   Tennessee Valley

Pickett, Jesse – O Apr 10, 14, NFL Pby; p Grace Cov Ch, Hilliard, FL, 14-

37575 Kings Ferry Road, Hilliard, FL 32046 – 904-625-6725   North Florida
E-mail: jessehpickett@yahoo.com
Grace Covenant Church – 904-845-7863

Pickett, John Charles – b Las Cruces, NM, Apr 11, 47; f Cecil J.; m Helen Peek; w Susan Mary Harris, Las Cruces, NM, Dec 23, 66; chdn Marcela, Evangeline, Micah, Tassie, Ariel; NMSU 70, BS; CTS 73, MDiv; SPU 79, cert; L 73; O 73, RMtn Pby (RPCES); op, p Emmanuel Fell, Tucson, AZ, 73-78; op Chapel Hill P Ch, Lake Stevens, WA, 79-82, p 82-92; srp University P Ch, Las Cruces, NM, 92-13; astp, mout, 13-14; bd mbr emer PYA; ExecComm mbr SWCPLN; ChPlant Coach SWCPLN; exec dir Crosstown Ministries, Las Cruces, NM, 12-; ev, 17-

4905 Tobosa Road, Las Cruces, NM 88011 – 575 650-5412   Southwest
E-mail: johnpick@gmail.com; john@crosstownlc.com

Piedt, Lawrence – w Nancy; chdn David, Joel, Philip; KTS 10, MEd; vp EE, 01-05; astp Coral Ridge P Ch, Ft. Lauderdale, FL, 05-10; hr; *Seniors Evangelism Explosion, A Forgotten Generation*; *Kid's EE World Manual*

2731 Inglewood Drive, Gainesville, GA 30504 – 954-857-3389   Georgia Foothills
E-mail: lpiedt@charter.net
HR

Pierce, Bryan Lee – b San Diego, CA, Dec 23, 71; f Richard Bryce Jr.; m Dorothy Elizabeth Harrison; w Krista Joy Kiehl, Lookout Mtn, GA, Jun 24, 95; chdn Samuel Anderson, Mae McFadden, Levi Harrison;

Pierce, Bryan Lee, continued
CC 90-94, BA; CTS 94-97, MDiv; O Feb 21, 99, NGA Pby; astp Westminster P Ch, Gainesville, GA, 98-00; dirAdm CC, 00-04; astp Perimeter Ch, Johns Creek, GA, 04-11; op Seven Hills Flwsp, Rome, GA, 08-

14 Quail Hollow, Rome, GA 30161 – 706-530-1630   Metro Atlanta
E-mail: bryanp@sevenhillsfellowship.com
Seven Hills Fellowship

    Pierce, Oliver – campm RUF, InUPA, 18-

456 Elm Street, Indiana, PA 15701   Pittsburgh
PCA Reformed University Fellowship

    Pierce, Raymond Scott – b Jacksonville, NC, Jan 6, 61; f Jerry S.; m Barbara Farris Johnston; w Janet Lee Davis, Monroeville, AL, May 12, 90; chdn Davis Scott, Nathan Luke, Joel Wade, Michelle Lee; SEBC, BA; RTS, MDiv; O Mar 21, 99, MSVal Pby; astp Trinity P Ch, Jackson, MS, 99-04; p First P Ch, Jasper, AL, 05-

1510 4th Avenue, Jasper, AL 35501 – 205-471-5843   Evangel
E-mail: firstpres_jasper@bellsouth.net
First Presbyterian Church – 205-384-3994

    Pierson, Lloyd – UNE 94, BA; CTS 98, MDiv; StLU 04, PhD; O Dec 15, 02; p KPC, St. Louis, 99-04; p Faith Covenant OPC, Kalispell, MT, 04-06; p Faith Cov P Ch, Kalispell, MT, 06-

611 3rd Avenue East, Kalispell, MT 59901 – 406-756-6465   Rocky Mountain
E-mail: LloydPierson@faithcov.com
Faith Covenant Presbyterian Church – 406-752-2400

    Pike, Melvin Ray – b Hillsboro, KS, Jul 8, 55; f Ralph Emerson Jr; m Melba Ruth Prieb; w Cindie Ralene Davis (d), Glennallen, AK, Jun 26, 76, (2) Martha McClure, Dec 5, 15; chdn Kara Joy, Peter Wayne, Andrew Ralph; AKBC 73-75; ColCC 83-86, BA; SCS 90-92, MDiv; L Feb 84; O Dec 86; Recd PCA Apr 93, RMtn Pby; astp Berean Fundamental Ch, Colorado Spgs, CO, 84, astp 84; srp Peyton Comm Ch, Peyton, CO, 84-90; srp Cody Pk Comm Ch, Texas Crk, CO, 91-96; mis MTW, 96-15; ss Trinity Ref P Ch, Montrose, CO, 15-16

PO Box 1294, Montrose, CA 81402 – 719-231-0332   Rocky Mountain
E-mail: rmrpike@gmail.com

    Pillsbury, Justin – O May 15, 16; astp Cahaba Park Ch PCA, Birmingham, AL, 16-

E-mail: jpillsbury@cahabapark.org   Evangel
Cahaba Park Church PCA – 205-870-1886

    Pilson, Eric – b Washington, DC, May 19, 81; w Annie, Jan 17, 09; chdn Evelyn Grace, Madelyn Hope; LafC 03, BA; WSCAL 09, MDiv; O Oct 21, 12, SoCst Pby; chp MSS, 13-

11325 Fawn Lake Parkway, Spotsylvania, VA 22551   South Coast
E-mail: eric@taiwanchurchplanters.com
Mission Sending Service

    Pinegar, Elliott Samuel Wantz – b Muncie, IN, Nov 8, 85; f Phillip Allen; m Beth Joyanne Wantz; w Rebecca E. Hargrave, Muncie, IN, Jan 5, 08; chdn Evalena Joy, Hope Orabel; TayU 08, BA; CTS 12, MDiv; O Oct 21, 12, GrLks Pby; p First P Ch, Bad Axe, MI, 12-15; ob ed Crossway Books & Bibles, Wheaton, IL, 15-

1011 Pershing Avenue, Wheaton, IL 60189 – 630-868-6084   Great Lakes
E-mail: epinegar@esv.org
Crossway Books & Bibles
1300 Crescent Street, Wheaton, IL 60187

Pinheiro, Leandro – Recd PCA Jan 18, 14, SNE Pby; ascp Igreja Presiteriana Cristo Rei, Cambridge, MA, 14-16, p 16-

11 Washington Street, Apt. 2, North Reading, MA 01864 – 781-290-9064   Southern New England
Igreja Presiteriana Cristo Rei – 617-864-5464

Pipa, Joseph Anthony Jr. – b Memphis, TN, Jan 12, 47; f Joseph Anthony P Sr.; m Veta Vinson; w Carolyn Floyd, Jackson, MS, Aug 7, 71; chdn Sara Elizabeth, Joseph Anthony III; BelC 68, BA; RTS 71, MDiv; WTS 85, PhD; O Jun 20, 71, CMS Pby; p Tchula P Ch, Tchula, MS, 70-77; staff GCP, Suwanee, GA, 77-79; p Covenant P Ch, Houston, TX, 79-90; lect WTS; assoc prof WSCAL, 90-98; op Trinity P Ch, Escondido, CA, 91-93, p 93-97; ob pres, prof GPTS, 98-; *Root & Branch; William Perkins and the Development of Puritan Preaching; The Lord's Day; The Westminster Confession of Faith Study Book: A Study Guide for Churches*; contr "Whatever Happened to the Reformation?" and "Onward Christian Soldiers;" *Table Talk*; Sunday School materials for GCP; ed and contr: *Did God Create in Six Days?; Written for our Instruction: The Sufficiency of Scripture for All of Life; Sanctification: Growing in Grace; Reformed Spirituality; The Worship of God*; contr *The Auburn Avenue Theology, Pros & Cons: Debating the Federal Vision*; contr *Theological Guide to Calvin's Institues*; contr *The Hope Fulfilled: Essays in Honor of O. Palmer Robertson*; contr *Interpreting and Teaching Word: Jack Scott Festschrift*; contr*Reformed Theological Journal*; contr *The Puritanical Calvinist: An Introduction to the Presbyterian and Reformed Heritage, in Honor of D. Clair Davis*, "Puritan Preaching"; auth God's Proclamation of Liberty; ed *Confessing Our Hope: Essays in Honor of Morton Howison Smith on His Eightieth Birthday; The Covenant: God's Voluntary Condescension*; contr *Interpreting and Teaching the Word of Hope: Essays in Honor of Jack Brown Scott on His Seventy Seventh Birthday*; art "From Chaos to Cosmos: A Critique of the Framework Hypothesis", presented at the West Coast meeting/Evangelical Theological Society, Apr 26, 96; "Seminary Education" *Confessional Presbyterian* 3, (Jan 1, 07); "Calvin on the Holy Spirit." *Calvin for Today*, 09; *Galatians: God's Proclamation of Liberty*, 10; contr "The Christian Sabbath" in *Perspectives on the Sabbath: 4 views*, 11; ed *The Beauty and Glory of the Holy Spirit*, 12; contr "The Holy Spirit and the Unique Power of Preaching" in *The Beauty and Glory of the Holy Spirit*, 12; "Dealing with Lust" in *Tabletalk*, Feb 13; art on Reformation 21 website: "The Lost Work of Pastoral Visitation" Aug 13; "Pastoral Visitation: The God-given Responsibility to Shepherd" Aug 13; The Mystery of the Incarnation" Dec 13; *Is The Lord's Day For You? 16; How Can I Do All Things For God's Glory?*, 17; "Let The Church Confess Her Theology By The Use Of Creeds And Confessions" in *95 Theses for a New Reformation: For the Church on the 500th Anniversary of the Reformation*, 17; "Calvin the Preacher and the Puritans" in *Puritan Piety: Writings in Honor of Joel R. Beeke*, 18; "The Holy Spirit and the Unique Power of Preaching" in Expositor Magazine No. 21, 18; "The Confessing Church" in *Celebrating the Legacy of the Reformation*, 19

116 Bridgeton Drive, Greenville, SC 29615   Calvary
Greenville Presbyterian Theological Seminary – 864-322-2717
PO Box 690, Taylors, SC 29687

Pipkin, Michael Craig – b Durham, NC, Dec 11, 51; f Preston Dawson; m Catherine Jones; w Sandra Ganey, Mullins, SC, Aug 18, 78; chdn Michael Craig Jr.; MonC 72-74, AA; BelC 75-76, BA; RTS 77-81, MDiv; L Jun 27, 81; O Jul 12, 81, Westm Pby; p Fellowship P Ch, Newland, NC, 81-83; p Frank P Ch, Crossnore, NC, 81-83; p Reedy Creek P Ch, Minturn, SC, 83-86; ob ss Fuller Mem P Ch, Durham, NC, 87; Chap USArmy, Ft Hood, TX, 87-90; Chap USArmy, Camp Casey, Korea, 90-91; Chap USArmy, Ft Monmouth, NJ, 91; Chap USArmy, Ft Huachuca, AZ, 92-93; ob Potters House, Jefferson, GA, 93-96; Chap NatGd, Dobbins AFB, Marietta, GA, 93-96; Chap USAR, 96-; adj prof TMcC, 96-98; Chap 310th TAACOM, Bosnia & Croatia, 97; p St. Matthews P Ch, St. Matthews, SC, 98-07; adj prof SoMethC, 01-; p Central P Ch, Kingstree, SC, 07-17; hr 17; contr Chapel Newsletters; art "Family In Focus"

1111 Sandy Bluff Road, Mullins, SC 29574   Pee Dee
E-mail: cspipkin@ftc-i.net
HR

Piteo, Jason Daniel – O Sept 29, 13, CentCar Pby; astp Uptown Ch, PCA, Charlotte, NC, 13-14; astp East Charlotte P, Charlotte, NC, 14-15, ascp 15-

6308 Trotters Ridge Road, Charlotte, NC 28227 – 704-323-8389   Central Carolina
E-mail: jason@piteo.net
East Charlotte Presbyterian – 980-254-4588

Pitre, Brannin – b Houston, TX, Jun 12, 71; w Tanya, Mar 30, 96; chdn Lawson Creede, Hadley Grace, Terry Judson; UHou, BS; GCTS, MDiv; O Oct 02, NoTX Pby; ascp Christ P Ch, Flower Mound, TX, 02-03; Park Cities P Ch, Dallas, TX, 04-05; op Gr Pasadena, Pasadena, CA, 05-

181 Sierra View Road, Pasadena, CA 91105 – 626-683-3860   Pacific
E-mail: brannin@gracepasadena.org
Grace Pasadena – 626-407-2557

Pittman, Carson – b Atlanta, GA, Jun 11, 81; WTS 10, MDiv; O Apr 3, 11, MetAtl Pby; ascp Atlanta Westside P Ch, Atlanta, GA, 11-14; ss Crosspoint P Ch, Smyrna, GA, 14-

1972 Main Street, Atlanta, GA 30318   Metro Atlanta
E-mail: curatecarson@gmail.com
Crosspoint Presbyterian Church – 770-333-1775

Pittman, Jason – O May 20, 18, Palm Pby; astp Northeast P Ch, Columbia, SC, 18-

16 Deerpath Court, Columbia, SC 29229   Palmetto
Northeast Presbyterian Church – 803-788-5298

Pitzer, Timothy Matthew – O Feb 15, 15, Palm Pby; astp Hilton Head P Ch, Hilton Head Island, SC, 15-

30 Arrow Wood Road, Hilton Head, SC 29926 – 843-816-0750   Lowcountry
E-mail: tim.pitzer@hiltonheadpca.com
Hilton Head Presbyterian Church – 843-689-6362

Plant, David – astp Redeemer P Ch of New York, New York, NY, 12-17; astp Redeemer P Ch Downtown, New York, NY, 17-

360 West 21st Street #2H, New York, NY 10011   Metropolitan New York
E-mail: david.plant@redeemer.com
Redeemer Presbyterian Church Downtown

Plemmons, Robby – astp Altadena Valley P Ch, Birmingham, AL, 05-09; op CrossPoint P Ch, Park City, UT, 09-

PO Box 981745, Park City, UT 84098   Northern California
E-mail: robby@crosspointpca.org
CrossPoint Presbyterian Church – 435-729-0718

Plott, William – astp North Cincinnati Comm Ch, Mason, OH, 05-08; chp Madison, AL, 08-09; op Valley P Ch, Madison, AL, 09-10, p 10-

719 Hughes Road, Madison, AL 35758 – 256-698-1319   Providence
E-mail: william.plott@gmail.com
Valley Presbyterian Church – 256-508-9020

Plummer, Wynonie – b New York City, NY, Feb 4, 47; f Isaiah; m Mabel Harris; w Shirley A. Johnson, Columbia, MD, Aug 2, 69; HowC 70, BE; JHU 78, MS; ChTS 95, MDiv; L Feb 94; O Apr 23, 95, Pot Pby; ascp New Song Community Ch, Baltimore, MD, 95-01; astp Faith Christian Flwsp Ch, Baltimore, MD, 02-05; MNA Birmingham, AL, 05-07; MNA Chattanooga, TN, 08-

313 Morning Side Drive, Rossville, GA 30741   Chesapeake
E-mail: wplummer@pcanet.org
PCA Mission to North America

MINISTERIAL DIRECTORY 509

Plunk, Jim – p New Cov P Ch, Summit, MS, 16-

1047 Clabber Creek Road, Summit, MS 39666   Grace
E-mail: jim@newcovenantpres.org
New Covenant Presbyterian Church – 601-276-7340

Poehlman, Thomas Scott – b Baltimore, MD, Apr 4, 48; f Irvin Scott; m Ruth Margaret Doggett; w Julie Ann Heggie, Ellicott City, MD, Oct 15, 83; TowU 70, BA; GCTS 73, MDiv; L May 74; O May 75, Balt Pby (UPCUSA); ap Chapel Hill UP Ch, Ellicott City, MD, 75-77; p Tollgate RP Ch, Owings Mills, MD, 78-84, wc 84-99; t AAChSc, 84-02; ascp Safe Harbor P Ch, Stevensville, 99-02, astp 02-04; chp, op Shore Harvest P Ch, Easton, MD, 02-05, p 05-06; t Stevensville MS, Stevensville, MD, 06-11; t Anchor Points Acad, 11-16; astp Shore Harvest P Ch, Easton, MD, 13-

24699 Pealiquor Road, Denton, MD 21629 – 410-479-5380   Heritage
Shore Harvest Presbyterian Church – 410-763-7070

Pohl, Craig Lyle – b Hamilton, ON, Jul 15, 70; f Ronald Lyle; m Janet Kay Deimund; w Stacy Dianne Baxter, Germantown, TN, Apr 15, 00; chdn Karis Dianne, Aimee Grace; CWM 92, BA; CTS 00, MDiv; O Nov 01, MO Pby; mis MTW, Ecuador, 94-96, 01-

c/o MTW – 901-414-2354   Missouri
E-mail: cpohl@mtwsa.org
PCA Mission to the World

Poirier, Alfred J. – b Nashua, NH, Dec 9, 52; f Gerard France; m Eleanor Elizabeth (d); w Trudy Ellen Hudgins, Sebastopol, CA, Jul 31, 76; chdn Sarah Simone (Clark), Sonja Justine (Stordahl), Anya Jeannette (Valeriano); CSUChico 82, BA; WSCAL 83, MAR, 84, MDiv; WTS 04, DMin; L Sept 24, 83, Pac Pby; O May 17, 85, OPC; Recd PCA Jan 26, 02, RMtn Pby; DelMar Comm Ch, San Diego, CA, 80-84; Oak Hill P Ch, Eugene, OR, 84-92; p Rocky Mountain Comm Ch, Billings, MT, 92-17; ascp 17-18; ob vis prof, WTS, 18-; *The Peacemaking Pastor: A Biblical Guide to Resolving Church Conflict*, 06; *El pastor pacificador*, 09, Korean ed, 10; *o pastor pacificador*, Portugese ed, 11

515 Lindley Road, Glenside, PA 19038   Rocky Mountain
E-mail: apoirier@wts.edu
Westminster Theological Seminary – 215-435-5645

Policow, Nicholas – astp New City Flwsp, Lancaster, PA, 13-15, srp 15-17; p Redemption P Ch, Palos Heights, IL, 18-

5829 Lynwood Drive, Oak Lawn, IL 60453 – 717-553-0952   Chicago Metro
E-mail: nick.policow@gmail.com
Redemption Presbyterian Church – 708-762-9303

Polk, Jason – b Knoxville, TN, Aug 3, 78; w Elizabeth Joy, Jun 3, 06; chdn Nathan Hesed, Isaiah Emmanuel, Anna Ruth; WheatC 00, BS; CTS 07, MDiv; O Nov 4, 07, MO Pby; worshipdir Grace P Ch of St. Charles Co, St. Charles, MO, 03-07, astp 07-11; mis MTW, Ethiopia, 11-

c/o SIM-ACT Project, PO Box 127, Addis Ababa, ETHIOPIA   Missouri
E-mail: jasonandlizpolk@gmail.com
PCA Mission to the World

Pollard, Michael Scott – b Memphis, TN, Oct 13, 63; f Jerry Jr.; m Barbara Hanson; w Rhoda Kathleen Ekberg, Wray, CO, Jul 28, 90; chdn Anna YuXia, Elizabeth DeHuai; WheatC 85, BA; TEDS 93, MDiv; L Nov 16, 96, SusqV Pby; O Sept 19, 98, SusqV Pby; ob modis, mout/evan Community EFC, Elverson, PA, 94-99; ob mis AWM, 99-10; ob mis Pioneers, 10-; *Cultivating a Missions Active Church*

2129 Loudenslager Drive, Thompson Station, TN 37179 – 615-428-8419   Nashville
E-mail: mikespollard@icloud.com
Pioneers

Polski, Christopher Alan – w Kathleen Lydia; chdn Ella Grace, Jonathan Rodney, Lillian Joy; CC 90, BA; CTS 00, MDiv; L Sept 16, 01, MO Pby; O Sept 16, 01, MO Pby; ydir Covenant P Ch, St. Louis, MO, 90-92; yp Twin Oaks P Ch, Ballwin, MO, 92-01, astp 01-04; srp Golden Isles P Ch, St. Simons Island, GA, 04-07; op Trin P Ch, St. Louis, MO, 07-08; srp 08-; Small Group Study Guides: *The Psalms*, 02; *The Parables*, 03

2127 Avalon Ridge Circle, Fenton, MO 63026   Missouri
E-mail: tbeza@aol.com
Trinity Presbyterian Church – 314-485-1470

Poole, Gregory J. – b Atlanta, GA, Sept 3, 60; f Joe L.; m Carolyn Meredith; w Alisa Berry, Birmingham, AL, Aug 20, 88; chdn Zachary Joseph, Hamilton Parker; SamU 82, BS; CTS 92, MDiv; L Apr 22, 92; O Jul 26, 92, MO Pby; ascp Kirk of the Hills P Ch, St. Louis, MO, 92-94; ascp Oak Mountain P Ch, Birmingham, AL, 94-01; p Decatur P Ch, Decatur, AL, 01-08; astp Oak Mountain P Ch, Birmingham, AL, 08-09, ascp 09-

2353 Woodland Circle, Birmingham, AL 35242-3163 – 205-637-0988   Evangel
E-mail: gjpoole@gmail.com
Oak Mountain Presbyterian Church – 205-995-9265

Pope, Randall Paige – b Birmingham, AL, Aug 26, 51; f Dr. Sherold; m Aylene Jennings; w Carol Hearn, Birmingham, AL, Nov 22, 75; chdn Matthew James, Rachael Jennings, Dena Elizabeth, David Randall; UAL 69-73, BS; RTS 73-77, MDiv; O Sept 11, 77, NGA Pby; srp Perimeter Ch, Johns Creek, GA, 77-; *The Prevailing Church*, 02, re-publ as *The Intentional Church, 06*; *Finding Your Million Dollar Mate*, 04; *The Answer*, 05, *Insourcing*, 13

5790 Medlock Bridge Parkway, Johns Creek, GA 30022   Metro Atlanta
E-mail: jackiel@perimeter.org
Perimeter Church – 678-405-2000

Porter, Benjamin Hurst – astp Kirk of the Hills P Ch, St. Louis, MO, 08-12; ascp 12-

1242 Momarte Lane, St Louis, MO 63146   Missouri
E-mail: bporter@thekirk.org
Kirk of the Hills Presbyterian Church – 314-434-0753

Porter, Mark E. – b Mt. Pleasant, PA, Oct 10, 53; f James S.; m Myrna Espey; w Christine Ann Farabaugh, Grove City, PA, May 11, 75; chdn Julie, Jeffrey, Jennifer; GroCC 75, BA; WTS 79, MDiv; L Apr 79, Phil Pby; O Dec 16, 79, Pitts Pby (RPCES); p Reformed P Ch of Slate Lick, Kittanning, PA, 79-86, wc 86-91; instr GenC, 89-02; ob reg Ch dir Pittsburgh ISI, 91-95; assoc prof GenC, 02-18; hr 18

736 Claypoole Road, Worthington, PA 16262-9746 – 724-297-5152   Pittsburgh
E-mail: mporterdcp@comcast.net
HR

Portillo, Jose William – O HouMet Pby; ascp Hosanna Comm Ch, Tomball, TX, 18-

8310 Amurwood Drive, Tomball, TX 77375 – 281-844-8082   Houston Metro
E-mail: williamportillotomball@gmail.com
Hosanna Community Church – 832-928-5805

Posey, William Timothy – b Munford, TN, Oct 21, 53; f Ivo; m Eloise Millican; w Pamela Kay O'Bryant, Covington, TN, Dec 28, 79; chdn Mary Elaine, Megan Elizabeth, Molly Erin; DBU, BCE; RTS, MDiv; L Feb 14, 76; O May 4, 78, SBC; p Mt. Lebanon B, Covington, TN; ip Grand Prairie Bible Ch, TX; p Bethel Bap, MS; op Spring Meadows P Ch, Las Vegas, NV, 89-91, p 91-94; chp, op Three Rivers P Ch, Covington, LA, 94-98, p 98-04; p Spring Meadows P Ch, Las Vegas, NV, 04-

10228 Donald Weese Ct., Las Vegas, NV 89129   Pacific
Spring Meadows Presbyterian Church – 702-384-3437

Post, Donald Hite Jr. – b Clarksburg, WV, Nov 4, 47; f Donald H., Sr. (d); m Patricia Robinson (d); w (1) (dv) (2) Barbara Brooks; chdn Nathan Andrew, Seth Benjamin (d), Jacqueline DuVall, David DuVall, Katherine DuVall (Young); VPI 65-69, BS; RTS 76-79, MDiv; MarU 92-93, MAT; L Jun 7, 78, MSValPby; O Mar 9, 80, Cal Pby; p Philadelphia P Ch, Landrum, SC, 80-82; ap Covenant P Ch, Nitro, WV; op Huntington, WV, 82-83; p Providence Ref P Ch, Barboursville, WV, 83-91; Chap USAR, 82-00, wc 91; ss Pliny P Ch, Pliny, WV, 92-96; ob headm Cov sch, Huntington, WV, 95-01; ob headm Tall Oaks Classical School, New Castle, DE, 01-14; astp Christ P Ch, Elkton, MD, 01-03; ob mis Rafiki Found, Ghana, 14-17; astp Evangelical P Ch, Newark, DE, 17-

5 Woodbine Circle, Elkton, MD 21921   Heritage
E-mail: don_post@comcast.net
Evangelical Presbyterian Church – 302-737-2300

Postma, Philip – O Oct 18, 15, Siouxl Pby; astp Lennox Ebenezer P Ch, Lennox, SD, 15-17; astp Hope Ref P Ch, Shippensburg, PA, 17-

125 Cumberland Avenue, Shippensburg, PA 17527   Susquehanna Valley
E-mail: phpostma@gmail.com
Hope Reformed Presbyterian Church – 717-532-8998

Poteet, Patrick N. – RTSNC; astp Trinity P Ch, Plano, TX, 03-06, ascp 06-15; p Christ Comm Ch in Frisco, Frisco, TX, 15-

1430 Cedar Lake Drive, Prosper, TX 75078-8387 – 972-540-1738   North Texas
E-mail: patrick@cccfrisco.org
Christ Community Church in Frisco – 214-471-8843

Powell, Charles R. – b Salt Lake City, UT, Oct 13, 43; f Earl Edwin; m Sarah Elizabeth Wheeler; w Esther Grace Boomstra, Grand Rapids, MI, Jul 1, 72; chdn Tamara Alexis; UCB 61-66, BA; WCBS 74-79, MDiv, ThM; GCTS, 03, DMin; O Dec 16, 91, ECA; Recd PCA Nov 20, 94, Pot Pby; mout, mp The Falls Ch, 90-94; astp McLean P Ch, McLean, VA, 94-03; ob board of Asian Access, 04-

20931 Trinity Square, Potomac Falls, VA 20165 – 703-444-1721   Potomac
E-mail: charlie@psmail.net

Powell, Christopher – astp North Shore Flwsp, Chattanooga, TN, 15-

118 Woodland Avenue, Chattanooga, TN 37405   Tennessee Valley
E-mail: chris@nsfellowship.org
North Shore Fellowship – 423-266-3757

Powell, James E. III – b Wilmington, DE, Feb 7, 43; w Sharon, New Castle, DE, Apr 7, 79; chdn Adam, Chris, Amanda, James; UDE 64, BA; UMA 67, MS; CTS 78, MDiv; O Sept 98, Hrtg Pby; astp Heritage P Ch, New Castle, DE, 77-79, ascp 98-04; ob Dir Happy Life Children's Home, Kenya, 07-14; hr 14

PO Box 11544, Wilmington, DE 19850-1544 – 302-322-9734   Heritage
E-mail: revpowell@juno.com
HR

Powell, James H. – b Chattanooga, TN, Apr 7, 55; f B. Worth; m Elizabeth Hudson; w Lisa McGarity, Greenville, SC, Apr 22, 78; chdn Amy Diane Brauer, Brian Carter; FurU 73-77, BA; CTS 78-82, MDiv; StLU 86, MA; O Jun 27, 82, TNVal Pby; p St. Elmo P Ch, Chattanooga, TN, 82-85; p Hope P Ch, Marietta, GA, 85-95; astp First P Ch, Stanley, NC, 95-98; op Harvest P Ch, Lincolnton, NC, 95-98, p 98-07; ss Skybrook Fellowship Ch ARP, Huntersville, NC, 07-08; astp Hixson P Ch, Hixson, TN 09-14; ob ss Hope Evangelical Ch, North Liberty, IA, 15-16; "Miscarriage: A Real Life, a Real Loss," *The Presbyterian Journal* (May 1, 85)

7008 Genoa Drive, Chattanooga, TN 37421 – 423-994-3329   Tennessee Valley
E-mail: jimpowell55@gmail.com

Powell, James M. – w Kori, Apr 8, 00; chdn Lina, Meggie, Nate, Oria, Pete, Quade; CNC 00, BA; TEDS 03, MDiv; O 03, Westm Pby; p Harmony P Ch, Kingsport, TN, 03-06; astp Cornerstone P Ch, Center Valley, PA, 06-08; op West Valley P Ch, Emmaus, PA, 08-11; p 11-13; ascp Blythewood P Ch, Blythewood, SC, 13- 17; p Christ Comm Ch, Johnson City, TN, 17-

205 Joe Hale Drive, Johnson City, TN 37615 Westminster
E-mail: 7jamespowell@gmail.com
Christ Community Church – 423-946-0357

Powell, Thomas – O Oct 12, 13, NNE Pby; ob p Cong Ch Cranberry Island, Isleford Cong Ch, 13-

PO Box 59, Cranberry Isles, ME 04625 Northern New England
E-mail: mailtompowell@gmail.com
Congregational Church Cranberry Island
Isleford Congregational Church

Powers, Edward Winship – b Patuxent, MD, Dec 22, 52; f William Joseph; m Evelyn Winship Weber; w Ann Marie Hutcheson, Niles, MI, Dec 22, 78; chdn Elizabeth; UAZ 71-73; UMI 73-75, BA; GCTS 75-78, MDiv; CTS 00, DMin; O Mar 80, MidAtl Pby; ap West Hopewell P Ch, Hopewell, VA, 80-85; Naperville P Ch, Naperville, IL, 85-86; op Christ Ch, Woodridge, IL, 86-91, p 91-02; chp, coord MNA, 02-

2636 Luzern Court, Woodridge, IL 60517-4522 – 630-985-0578 Chicago Metro
E-mail: tpowers@pcanet.org
PCA Mission to North America – 678-825-1200

Powis, William John II – b Akron, OH, Nov 12, 52; f Willaim John, Sr.; m Olga Irene Wagner; w Patricia Vanchoff, Akron, OH, Oct 1, 77; chdn Jennifer Nicole, Andrea Joy; CBC 81, BA; GrTS 85, MDiv; O Sept 15, 85; The Chapel of Youngstown, Poland, OH, 85-90; p Faith P Ch, Irmo, SC, 90-97; chp Pac Pby, Santa Monica, CA, 98-99; op Pacific Crossroads Ch, Santa Monica, CA, 99-04, p 04-05; op Gr North Atlanta, Alpharetta, GA, 06-08; astp Intown Comm Ch, Atlanta, GA, 11-15; chp Cleveland, OH, 15-16; op Turning Point Ch, Cleveland, OH, 16-

13174 Olympus Way, Strongsville, OH 44149 – 770-595-8107 Ohio
E-mail: powis.bill@gmail.com
Turning Point Church

Powlison, Keith Philip – b Inglewood, CA, May 16, 56; f Hugh Stanley; m Berenice Gladys Johnson; w Ruth Ann Kupferschmid, Paxton, IL, Jul 1, 78; chdn Holly Kim, Brian David, Elena Michel, Emma Louise; CBC 78, BA; O Oct 9, 89, Quito Provisional Pby; Recd PCA Jul 25, 96, Palm Pby; mis MTW, Quito, Ecuador, 87-98; mis MTW, Cusco, Peru, 98-

c/o MTW – 706-364-6456 Palmetto
PCA Mission to the World

Poynor, James Paul III – b Nashville, TN, Jun 30, 41; w Alice Burnett, Aug 16, 68; chdn Daniel James, David Vincent, Dean Houston; VandU 59-63, BE; CBC 63-66, BD; RTS 72-74, MDiv; O May 26, 74, MSVal Pby; mis, p Laos, (OMF), 67-71; ip Hueytown Ch, AL, 71-72; ip Brentwood-Parkcrest Ch, Burnaby, BC, 74-75; staff Comm MtW, 75-76; mis Indonesia (OMF & MTW), 76-80; p Edwards P Ch, Edwards, MS, 80-85; ob Dir OMF, Midw, 86-90; ob Dir OMF, SE, 90-95; astp Trinity P Ch, Montgomery, AL, 95-98; p Eau Claire P Ch, Columbia, SC, 98-06; astp St. Andrews P Ch, Columbia, SC, 06-15; hr 15

169 Stone Column Way, Columbia, SC 29212 – 803-960-4756 Palmetto
E-mail: jppoynor@gmail.com
HR

Poythress, Justin – O Apr 17, 16, CentInd Pby; astp Christ Comm Ch, Carmel, IN, 16-

Christ Community Church – 317-580-9020 Central Indiana

Poythress, Vern Sheridan – b Madera, CA, Mar 29, 46; f Ransom Huron; m Carola Eirene Nasmyth; w Diane Marie Weisenborn, Philadelphia, PA, Aug 6, 83; chdn Ransom, Justin; CIT 63-66, BS; HarvU 66-70, PhD; WTS 71-74, MDiv, ThM; CU 77, MLitt; UStel 81, ThD; O Oct 81, Phil Pby (RPCES); ob prof WTS, 76-; hr 11; *Philosophy, Science and the Sovereignty of God*; *Symphonic Theology: The Validity of Multiple Perspectives in Theology*; *Understanding Dispensationalists*; *Science and Hermeneutics: Implications of Scientific Method for Biblical Interpretation*; *The Shadow of Christ in the Law of Moses*; *God-Centered Biblical Interpretation*; *The Gender-Neutral Bible Controversy: Muting the Masculinity of God's Words* (w/ Wayne Grudem); *The Returning King: A Guide to the Book of Revelation*; *The TNIV and the Gender-Neutral Bible Controversy* (w/ Wayne Grudem); *Redeeming Science: A God-Centered Approach*; *In the Beginning Was the Word: Language–A God-Centered Approach*; *What Are Spiritual Gifts? Redeeming Sociology: A God-Centered Approach*; *Inerrancy and Worldview: Answering Modern Challenges to the Bible*; *Inerrancy and the Gospels: A God-centered Approach to the Challenges of Harmonization*; *Logic: A God-Centered Approach to the Foundation of Western Thought*; *Christian Interpretations of Genesis 1*; *Did Adam Exist?*; *Chance and the Sovereignty of God: A God-Centered Approach to Probability and Random Events*; *Redeeming Mathematics: A God-Centered Approach*; *Redeeming Philosophy: A God-Centered Approach to the Big Questions*; *The Miracles of Jesus: How the Savior's Mighty Acts Serve as Signs of Redemption*; *The Lordship of Christ: Serving Our Savior All of the Time, in All of Life, with All Our Heart*; *Reading the Word of God in the Presence of God: A Handbook for Biblical Interpretation*; *The Lordship of Christ: Serving Our Savior All of the Time, in All of Life, with All of Our Heart*; *Theophany: A Biblical Theology of God's Appearing*; *Knowing and the Trinity: How Perspectives in Human Knowledge Imitate the Trinity*

510 Twickenham Road, Glenside, PA 19038 – 215-885-7785 Eastern Pennsylvania
E-mail: vpoythress1@netscape.net
Westminster Theological Seminary
HR

Pozos, Elias Gamaliel – astp Covenant P Ch, Harlingen, TX, 15-

16708 Barnes Court, Harlingen, TX 78552 South Texas
E-mail: elias.g.pozos@gmail.com
Covenant Presbyterian Church – 956-425-3136

Prabhakar, John Rakshith – b Hubli, India, Feb 21, 91; f Prabhakar; m JeejaBai; w Kelley Beth; BBM, BangaloreU; RTS, MDiv; GlasgowU, ThM; O Aug 5, 17, MSVal Pby, ob 17-

5422 Clinton Boulevard, Jackson, MS 39209 Mississippi Valley
E-mail: john.rakshith@gmail.com

Prager, Jeffrey W. – w Kendall; chdn Riley, Garrett; CC 98, BA; CTS 06, MDiv; TEDS 17, ThM; astp Chapel Hill P Ch, Douglasville, GA, 13-14; stud TEDS, 14-17; stu SWBTS 17-

6556 Highview Terrace, Watauga, TX 76148 Northwest Georgia

Prather, Mell Thomas – w Patricia Joyce Bruns, Mountain Home AFB, ID, Apr 2, 61; FulTS 76-78, MDiv; L Jan 13, 89; O Sept 24, 78, PCUS/UPCUSA; O Feb 11, 90, TNVal Pby; p Westm P Ch, (PCUSA), 78-81; p First P Ch, Russellville, AL, 81-84; coord NACOLG Area Agency on Aging, Russellville, AL, 86-89; p Covenant P Ch, Tullahoma, TN, 90-93, wc 93-99; hr 99; pem Covenant P Ch, Tullahoma, TN, 05

22 Shady Cove Court, Estill Springs, TN 37330-3498 – 931-649-3299 Nashville
HR

Pratt, Richard L. Jr. – w Georgia O.; chdn Anna Rebecca; HDS 87, ThD; O Dec 76, DMV Pby; p Christ RPC, Roanoke, VA, 74-78; DCE Stony Point Ref P Ch, Richmond, VA, 80-81; DCE Hope CRC, Framingham, MA, 82-84; ob prof RTS, 85-90; ob prof RTSFL, 90-06; ss Independent P Ch, Memphis, TN,

Pratt, Richard L. Jr., continued
08; Third Mill Min; *Every Thought Captive* (79); *Pray with Your Eyes Open*; *He Gave Us Stories*, 91; art for *Journal of Bib Lit, WTS Journal, NISBE, Eerdmans Bible Dictionary; Designed for Dignity*, 94; trans *Living Bible* rev; art *Literary Guide to the Bible; Commentary on I and II Chronicles*

951 Moonluster Drive, Casselberry, FL 32707 – 407-788-2131   Central Florida
Third Millennium Ministries – 407-830-0222
PO Box 300769, Fern Park, FL 32730

    Preciado, Michael – ascp Christ Ch Irvine, CA, 11-13; p 13-

16 Caraway, Irvine, CA 92604 – 626-252-3878   South Coast
E-mail: pablum25@hotmail.com
Christ Church Irvine

    Preg, Stephen Michael Jr. – b Buffalo, NY, Jan 11, 41; f Stephen M Sr.; m Kathryn E Krehbiel; w Martha A Eiss, Clarence, NY, Jul 14, 62; chdn David Michael, Jeffrey Karl, Nathan John, Katy Elizabeth (Hall); CornU 63, BCE; CMU 67, MS; UPitt 71, MBA; WTS 77, MDiv; WSCAL, 90, DMin; L Dec 29, 76; O Jun 19, 77, Asc Pby; ap Granada P Ch, Coral Gables, FL, 77-83; p Westm Ref Pres Ch, Ballwin, MO, 83-90; ob VP CV, Ballwin, MO, 90-91; ascp Kirk of the Hills P Ch, St. Louis, MO, 92-01, wc 01; ip Arden P Ch, Arden, NC, 01-03; ascp Trinity P Ch, Charlottesville, VA, 03-05; wc 05-06; ip Grace Ch, Rochester, NY, 06-07; hr 07; ip First P Ch, Chattanooga, TN, 08-10; ascp Plains P Ch, Auburn, AL, 11-14; ascp Cov P Ch, Auburn, AL, 14-15; *Steps to a Sermon*

2801 Lone Eagle Lane, Opelika, AL 36801 – 334-759-8646   Southeast Alabama
E-mail: mikepreg@gmail.com
HR

    Prescott, David Demarest – b New York, NY, Oct 16, 54; f Francis J.; m Catherine Demarest; w Miriam Iona McMillan, Schenectady, NY, Apr 30, 83; chdn Esther Catherine (Graham), Joshua David, Eric Joseph, Miranda Erin; SUNY 76, BS; GCTS 80, MDiv; WTS, DMin; O Jan 81, Phil Pby; astp First P Ch, Schenectady, NY, 80-84; chp MNA, 85-86; couns Bucks County ChrCns Ctr, 86-90; op Covenant P Ch, Groton, CT, 91-93, p 93-00; p New Life P Ch, Tifton, GA, 00-02; ascp Cornerstone P Ch, Center Valley, PA, 09-14; hr 14; working with Third Mill Ministries

4415 SE 4th Place, Ocala, FL 34471 – 267-374-8240   Central Florida
E-mail: ddprescott@live.com
HR

    Presley, Curtis E. III – b Clarksdale, MS, Aug 28, 58; f Curtis Edward Jr.; m Mary Eva Crumpton; w Katherine Walne Toler, Jackson, MS, Jul 5, 86; chdn Mary Virginia, Curtis Edward IV, Daniel Toler, Kenneth Crumpton; VandU 76-78; UMS 78-82, BA, 83-86, JD; RTS 92-95, MDiv; O Mar 9, 97, MSVal Pby; astp Pear Orchard P Ch, Ridgeland, MS, 95-98; p Sharon P Ch, Magee, MS, 98-01; p Christ P Ch, Oxford, MS, 01-

811 Maplewood Drive, Oxford, MS 38655 – 662-236-1330   Covenant
E-mail: curt@christpresoxford.org
Christ Presbyterian Church – 662-234-3399

    Preston, David – O Jun 4, 17, Cal Pby; astp Covenant P Ch, Easley, SC, 17-

121 Kensett Drive, Williamston, SC 29697   Calvary
Covenant Presbyterian Church – 864-859-0967

    Previtera, Michael – O May 25, 16, OHVal Pby; astp New City P Ch, Cincinnati, OH, 16-

1835 Weyer Avenue, Cincinnati, OH 45212   Ohio Valley
E-mail: mmprevitera@gmail.com
New City Presbyterian Church – 513-512-5759

MINISTERIAL DIRECTORY

Price, Britton – Chap USArmy, 10-

4011 Gorgas Circle, Joint Base San Antonio, Fort Sam Houston, TX 78234   Southern New England
United States Army

Price, Jonathan – b Pittsburgh, PA, Dec 5, 75; f Thomas Jr.; m Alice Montini; w Megan Arnold, Lancaster, PA, Sept 4, 99; chdn Ella Shawn, Joshua Andrew, Samuel John; GenC 98, BS; CTS 06, MDiv; O Feb 11, 07, Pitts Pby; ydir Murrysville Comm Ch, Murrysville, PA, 06-07; astp 07-11; p Covenant Comm P Ch, Wexford, PA, 11-; chair, MNA Co, Pitts pby, 12-; contr *Heal Us Emmanuel: A Call for Racial Reconciliation, Representation, and Unity in the Church*, 12

124 Blue Ridge Drive, Cranberry Township, PA 16066 – 724-591-8283   Pittsburgh
E-mail: jon@covcommunity.org
Covenant Community Presbyterian Church – 724-934-1234

Price, Timothy Hunter – O May 25, 13, Ecar Pby; astp Christ Central Durham, Durham, NC, 13-17, ascp 17-

309 Canal Street, Durham, NC 27701 – 919-884-6323   Eastern Carolina
E-mail: timothy@christcentraldurham.com
Christ Central Durham – 919-884-6323

Priest, Eric Richard – b Webster, TX, Nov 29, 78; f Marshall; m Jean Ann Burkhead; w Joanne Foster, Altamonte Springs, FL, Aug 18, 07; chdn Charles, Violet; UHou, BMus; RTSFL 07, MDiv; astp Christ the King P Ch, Houston, TX, 08-15; music pub, *Psalms and Hymns: From First to Last*, 05

10402 Cutting Horse Lane, Houston, TX 77064 – 713-306-2887   Houston Metro

Privatera, Mike – O May 25, 16, OHVal Pby; astp New City P Ch, Cincinnati, OH, 16-

New City Presbyterian Church – 513-512-5759   Ohio Valley

Prost, Steve – Chap USArmy, 08-

404 Hidden Springs Court, Ft. Irwin, CA 92310   Heartland
United States Army

Protos, Nick Emanuel – b Sharon, PA, Aug 15, 49; f Emanuel; m Anna Skoloudis; w Linda Wellendorf, Sinclairville, NY, Aug 30, 70; chdn Nikki Lynn (Hagen), Timothy John; YSU 71, BS; TBTS 74, MDiv; RPTS 87-88; CTS 08, DMin; L Nov 30, 79; O Mar 29, 80, Pitts Pby (RPCES); Dir CEF, Pittsburgh, PA, 75-78; p View Crest P Ch, Eighty Four, PA, 78-89; srp Greene Valley P Ch, Carmichaels, PA, 89-93; srp Gospel Flwsp P Ch, Valencia, PA, 93-

35 Sunset Court, Cranberry Township, PA 16066 – 724-816-8609   Ascension
E-mail: nprotos@consolidated.net
Gospel Fellowship Presbyterian Church – 724-898-3322

Pruitt, Daniel Vaughn – b Anderson, SC, Jul 9, 49; f Orion Vaughn; m Mattie Lee Craft; w Linda Louise Wiest, Anderson, SC, May 2, 71; chdn Joseph Daniel, James Philip, Jason Michael; AndJC 67-69, AA; ErskC 69-70; CC 70-71, BA; CTS 76-79, MDiv; L Jul 79; O May 80, SE Pby (RPCES); p Trinity Ref P Ch, Wilmington, NC, 80-83; ap Westminster P Ch, Gainesville, TX, 83-85; ap Sherwood Shores Chapel, Gordonville, TX, 83-85; astp Norris Hill P Ch, Anderson, SC, 88-94, wc 94-95; astp Norris Hill P Ch, Anderson, SC, 95-96, wc 96-

711 McClain Road, Belton, SC 29627 – 864-296-5510   Calvary
E-mail: dvp65@hotmail.com

Pruitt, Terry L. – O Nov 13, 18, Chspk Pby; astp DaySpring P Ch, Linthicum, MD, 18-

932 Tally Court, Glen Burnie, MD 21061-3837 – 410-766-4820   Chesapeake
E-mail: terrypruitt@me.com
DaySpring Presbyterian Church – 410-582-9

Pruitt, Todd – p Covenant P Ch, Harrisonburg, VA, 14-

3025 Lynwood Lane, Rockingham, VA 22801   Blue Ridge
E-mail: office@cov-pres.org
Covenant Presbyterian Church – 540-433-3051

Puckett, Jacob Nathaniel – Recd PCA 17, PhilMetW Pby; p Reformed P Ch, Boothwyn, PA, 17-

2211 Inwood Road, Wilmington, DE 19810   Philadelphia Metro West
Reformed Presbyterian Church – 610-485-2644

Puckett, Michael Scott – b Norfolk, VA, Jun 3, 68; f H. Kent (d); m Patricia Anne Barrow (d); w Laura Reese Battle, Decatur, GA, Mar 23, 91; chdn Michael, Rileigh, Connor, Reese, Gracie, Davis; AU 86-90, BA; RTSFL 93-96, MDiv; O Dec 1, 96, CentFL Pby; ascp University P Ch, Orlando, FL, 96-16; op Christ Kingdom Ch, Orlando, FL, 05-16; ob 16-; Worship Recording Projects with University Presbyterian Church: "Waiting in the Whisper," 00; "All," 03

29 Thornbriar Court, Travelers Rest, SC 29690 – 407-381-8213   Central Florida
E-mail: scottpuckett@msn.com

Puglia, Joseph – p Covenant P Ch, Wheat Ridge, CO, 13-

6100 West 44th Avenue, Wheat Ridge, CO 80033 – 303-424-8889   Rocky Mountain
E-mail: joepuglia@earthlink.net
Covenant Presbyterian Church – 303-424-8889

Pulizzi, Jim – O May 14, 17; astp City Ch of Richmond, Richmond, VA, 17-;

5014 Sylvan Road, Richmond, VA 23225   James River
E-mail: jimpulizzi@gmail.com
City Church of Richmond – 804-767-8038

Pullen, Barksdale M. III – b Memphis, TN, Nov 17, 63; f Barksdale McPherson Jr.; m Toni McAfee; w Matissa June Sizemore, Amory, MS, Dec 21, 84; chdn Barksdale "Bob" M. IV, Kaitlin Malikah, Madeline Grace; UMS 81-85, BS; WTS 85-91, MDiv; TEDS 12, PhD; L Nov 24, 91; O Nov 24, 91, TNVal Pby; DCE Mandarin P Ch, (PCUSA), 87-88; astp Christ P Ch, Nashville, TN, 91-95, ascp 95-96; astp Kirk of the Hills P Ch, St. Louis, MO, 96-00, ascp 01-05; astp Wildwood P Ch, Tallahassee, FL, 05-07; ascp 07-; contr *Rising to the Challenge and Children's Ministry 101*

4833 Heathe Drive, Tallahassee, FL 32309 – 850-894-4358   Gulf Coast
E-mail: barksdale.pullen@wildwoodchurchonline.org
Wildwood Presbyterian Church – 850-894-1400

Pummill, Zach – O Feb 15, 15, NoTX Pby; astp Trinity Harbor Ch, Rockwall, TX, 15-

E-mail: zpummill@gmail.com   North Texas
Trinity Harbor Church – 972-772-8208

Purcell, Blake Elliott – b Wichita Falls, TX, Aug 8, 58; f Graham Boynton, Jr. Smith; w Catherine Coffey, Louisville, MS, Jan 1, 83; chdn Emily, Graham, John Mark, Lewis, Zachary, Laura; TXA&M 77-81, BA; O Oct 25, 98, MSVal Pby; ob Slavic Ref Soc; ascp Arlington P Ch, Arlington, TX, 17-

6929 Andress Drive, Fort Worth, TX 76132 – 682-333-2854   North Texas
E-mail: purcell.russia@gmail.com
Arlington Presbyterian Church – 817-261-8938

Purcell, Graham – O Jun 27, 18, NoTX Pby; fm MTW, 18-

6929 Andress Drive, Fort Worth, TX 76302 – 662-803-2660   North Texas
E-mail: gbpurcell@gmail.com
PCA Mission to the World

Purdy, Gary – w Marilyn; chdn Davis gardner, lara, Lane Elizabeth; DTS, ThM; RTS, DMin; O Jul 12, 05, TNVal Pby; p North Shore Flwsp, Chattanooga, TN, 05-13; wc 13-14; astp Oak Mountain Ch, Birmingham, AL, 14-17; op City Church Midtown, Birmingham, AL, 17-; diss: "Christ-centered Preaching to a Postmodern Audience"

120 19th Street North Suite 223, Birmingham, AL 35203 – 423-902-4332   Evangel
E-mail: gpurdy@ompc.org
City Church Midtown

Purdy, Matt T. – astp West End P Ch, Richmond, VA, 07-12; p Carlisle Ref P Ch, Carlisle, PA, 12-

215 Berkshire Drive, Carlisle, PA 17015 – 717-462-3486   Susquehanna Valley
E-mail: pastormattpurdy@earthlink.net
Carlisle Reformed Presbyterian Church – 717-249-5675

Putnam, Frederic Clarke – b Peterborough, NH, Nov 7, 52; f Stanley; m Elizabeth Sprague; w Emilie B. Harris, Philadelphia, PA, Jul 16, 76; chdn Kiersten, Lydia, Abigail; PhilCB 75, BS; BibTS 78, MDiv, 80, STM; DrU 85, MA; ARI 91, PhD; L 85; O 85, Phil Pby; ob assoc prof BibTS, 84-06; ob vis prof WTS, 06-; ob prof PhilBibS, 06-12; chair, comm on ordination, Phil pby 86-05; vice mod Phil pby, 97, 99; mod Phil pby, 00; astp parl Phil pby, 01; parl Phil pby, 02-05; assoc prof The Templeton Honors College, EasternU; PMWP leadership development co, 03-; chr, 07-14, interim chr, 18; auth commentary on Proverbs; co-auth bibliography on Proverbs; auth Hebrew grammar; auth Hebrew syntax; auth *Discourse Analysis Hebrew Poetry*; contrib *Baker Expository of Biblical Words*

2737 Beech Street, Hatfield, PA 19440 – 215-393-9683   Philadelphia Metro West
E-mail: fred.putnam@gmail.com

Quadrizius, James – astp Cornerstone P Ch, St. Louis, MO, 09-11; p Providence Comm Church, St. Catherine's, ON, 11-

327 Scott Street, Street, Catherines, ON L2N 1J7   Eastern Canada
E-mail: james.quadrizius@gmail.com
Providence Community Church – 289-273-2477

Quakkelaar, Dan – O Nov 9, 14, Wisc Pby; op Friend of Sinners Ch, Milwaukee, WI, 14-

1724 Erin Lane, Milwaukee, WI 53188   Wisconsin
E-mail: Dan@FriendofSinners.org
Friend of Sinner's Church – 414-502-9899

Quarterman, Clayton Eric – b New Orleans, LA, May 17, 52; f Palmer Louis; m Norma Wandamae Carlson; w Darlene Rene Hoover, Jackson, MS, Dec 22, 73; chdn Matthew Eric, Nathan Thomas, Tyler

Quarterman, Clayton Eric, continued
Eugene, Alex Spencer; BelC 74, BA; RTS 77, MDiv, 86, DMin; FTSSWM 78-83; UWales 05, PhD; L Jun 21, 77; O Feb 21, 78, MSVal Pby; ss First P Ch, Prattville, AL, 77; mis MTW, Portugal, 78-93; assoc prof GEM Portuguese Bible Inst, 80-93; cop Igreja Crista Evangelica de Lisboa, 81-85; op Igreja Crista Evangelica da Portela, 85-89; Igreja Presbiteriana de Telheiras, 89-93; mis MTW, Ukraine, 93-; prof Odessa P Sem, 97-00; op EPC of Odessa, 95-99; pres Evan Ref Sem of Ukraine, 99-15; prof Evan Ref Sem of Ukraine, 00-; Christian Ed, Ukraine, 15-; brd dir TULIP Publishing, 05-12; brd dir Odessa Counseling Center, 06-12; contr *O Presbiteriano*, 02-05; auth *Retooling the Church;* "Christian Ministry in Time of War," *Reformed View Journal, №1:1*, 15; rvw *Calvin in the Public Square, Reformed View Journal*, No.1:1, 15; "Submission, Collaboration, and the End of War," *Reformed View Journal*, No.2:1, 16; "Teaching All Things on the Mission Field," *Reliance*, June 15; "The Practical Influence of the Reformed System" in *Theology of the Reformation*, 17; rvw *Quest for the Historical Adam, Reformed View Journal*, No. 3:2, 17; auth *Preparing for Leadership*, 17; auth *Breath of God in the Borderlands*, 18

5125 Old Canton Road, #214, Jackson, MS 39211 – 601-291-8301   Mississippi Valley
E-mail: cqmission@yahoo.com; www.clayq.com
PCA Mission to the World
Evangelical Reformed Seminary of Ukraine

Quillen, Michael – w Julia Lynn; chdn Micah, Ellie, Jonah, Daniel, John Peter, Stephanie, Nate; UDE 92, BME, 96, MBA; CTS 06, MDiv; O Jul 30, 06, TNVal Pby; p First P Ch, Crossville, TN, 06-15; srp Crossroads Comm Ch, Upper Darby, PA, 15-; cert Relational Wisdom Inst

464 Turner Avenue, Drexel Avenue, PA 19026 – 931-210-9900   Philadelphia Metro West
E-mail: mquillen@outlook.com
Crossroads Community Church – 610-352-3130

Quinn, Neil – astp Spring Valley P Ch, Roselle, IL, 14-, ss 15- 17; astp University Ref Ch, East Lansing, MI, 17-; op Good Shepherd P Msn, Kalamazoo, MI, 17-

3043 Trapper's Cove Trail #1B, Lansing, MI 48910   Great Lakes
E-mail: revneilquinn@gmail.com
University Reformed Church – 517-351-6810
Good Shepherd Presbyterian Mission – 517-896-2668

Quinn, Paul L. – hr 91

4470 Crumpet Court, Titusville, FL 32796-1473 – 321-383-7634   Southern New England
HR

Rabe, Matthew – O Jun 18, 17, NWGA Pby; ascp Grace P Ch, Cedartown, GA, 17-18, p 18-

104 Forrest Lane, Cedartown, GA 30125   Northwest Georgia
E-mail: matthew.rabe@yahoo.com
Grace Presbyterian Church – 770-749-1142

Rabe, William Curtis – b Red Bud, IL, Dec 22, 53; f William E.; m Yvonne Mueller; w Mary Cobb, Steeleville, IL, Aug 8, 76; chdn William David, Matthew Curtis, Aaron Mark, Rachel Jane, Ruth Elisabeth; SIU 76, BS; CTS 90, MDiv; L Jan 20, 90, Ill Pby; O Oct 14, 90, TNVal Pby; astp Grace P Ch, Dalton, GA, 90-92; Rock P Ch, Greenwood, SC, 92-93; p Greenwood P Ch, Greenwood, SC, 93-99; astp, chp New Cov P Ch, Anderson, SC, 99-03; p Memorial P Ch, Elizabethton, TN, 03-04; t Westm Christian Acad, St. Louis, 05-06; astp Concord P Ch, Waterloo, IL, 05-06; ip Harmony P Ch, Kingsport, TN, 06; min dir Ridge Haven Conference Center, 06-07; wc 07-09; ss Reformed P Ch, Cutler, IL 09-10, p 10-

11975 State Route 154, Sparta, IL 62286   Illiana
E-mail: curtrabe@yahoo.com
Reformed Presbyterian Church – 618-497-2489

MINISTERIAL DIRECTORY

Rackley, D. Timothy – b Danville, IL, Aug 18, 69; f Don; m Jaclyn Rae Edwards; w Jennifer Ann Brown, Jackson, MS, May 29, 93; chdn Timothy Taylor; MBI 92, BA; CTS 96, MDiv; L Mar 99, Hrtl Pby; O Oct 99, Hrtl Pby; astp Evangel P Ch, Wichita, KS, 99-01, ascp 01-

1260 West Birch Street, Wichita, KS 67235 – 316-734-1732   Heartland
E-mail: pastortim@evangelpca.org
Evangel Presbyterian Church – 316-942-5882; 316-942-9942

Rackley, Donald W. – b Gracemont, OK, Aug 11, 42; f Al; m Esther M. Hamm; w Jaclyn Edwards, Oklahoma City, OK, Feb 14, 62; chdn Robin, Cyndee, Tim, Dan; GarC, BA; ILSU, BA; TEDS; MBI 89, MMin; L 62, Bapt; O May 22, 66, Bapt; p Bible Bap Ch, Cloverdale, IN, 67; p Calvary Bible Ch, Milford, IL, 68-71; p Westminster P Ch, Paxton, IL, 72-93; p Evangel P Ch, Wichita, KS, 93-

1335 Stony Point, Wichita, KS 67209-1140 – 316-729-7575   Heartland
E-mail: church@evangelpca.org
Evangel Presbyterian Church – 316-942-5882; 316-942-9942

Radcliff, Adam – b Clarksburg, WV, Jun 20, 82; f Carl Edward; m Terri Lynn Greathouse; w Natalie Anna Zeman, Wheaton, IL, Apr 17, 09; chdn Vivian Grace, Charles Adam; MBI 07, BA; TEDS 10, MDiv; O May 7, 17, Cal Pby; int Lincoln Square P Ch, Chicago, IL, 09-11; astp Downtown P Ch, Greenville, SC, 17-

107 Wedgewood Drive, Greenville, SC 29609   Calvary
E-mail: aradcliff@downtownpres.org
Downtown Presbyterian Church – 864-326-0624

Radford, William D – p Bedford P Ch, Bedford, NS, 13-

50 Stockton Ridge, Bedford, NS B4A 0E3 CANADA – 902-835-2505   Eastern Canada
E-mail: billradford2@gmail.com
Bedford Presbyterian Church – 902-835-0840

Radke, Sean – astp Ch of the Good Shepherd, Durham, NC, 08-13; mis MTW, Japan, 13-

1017 Kibutake, Nagakute, Aichi Ken 480-1117 JAPAN   Eastern Carolina
E-mail: sean.radke@gmail.com
PCA Mission to the World

Radney, Derek – O Dec 4, 16, PTri Pby; p Trinity Ch, Winston-Salem, NC, 16-

3151 Prytania Road, Winston-Salem, NC 27106   Piedmont Triad
E-mail: dradney@trinitychurchws.com
Trinity Church

Ragland, John Stanley – b Jacksonville, FL, Apr 6, 47; f Reuben; m Pearl Genovar; w Cherry Mulcay, Wauchula, FL, Jun 19, 70; chdn Elizabeth, Jeannie, John S. Jr., Francie; BelC 65-69, BA; RTS 69-73, MDiv; O Sept 73, EAL Pby (PCUS); p Trinity P Ch, Dothan, AL, 73-80; p Bay Street P Ch, Hattiesburg, MS, 80-86; srp Westminster P Ch, Bryan, TX, 86-96; srp Hope P Ch, Marietta, GA, 96-04; hr 04; ss Grace P Ch, Cedartown, GA, 08-09; p 09-17

101 Turning Leaf Court, Carrollton, GA 30116 – 470-955-5850   Northwest Georgia
E-mail: jraglandsr@gmail.com
HR

Ragsdale, William Ted – b Columbia, SC, Jan 15, 51; f William M.; m Zoe Churchill; w Beth Pifer, Columbia, SC, Jun 15, 74; chdn Julie Marie, Jessica Renee, Kathryn Elizabeth, John Christopher; CBC 73,

Ragsdale, William Ted, continued
BA; CTS 76, MDiv, 77, ThM; L 76; O 79, SE Pby (RPCES); p Faith P Ch, Florence, SC, 79-84; ob Lakewood Campground Min, Myrtle Beach, SC, 84-02; p Faith P Ch, Myrtle Beach, SC, 02-17; hr 17

5705 Longleaf Drive, Myrtle Beach, SC 29577 – 843-251-3708   Pee Dee
E-mail: tragsdale@yahoo.com
HR

Rahm, Jerry R. – b Dallas, TX, Apr 30, 52; f Herbert Edmund; m Irene E. Paschke; w Linda K. Boosahda, Dallas, TX, Apr 19, 86; CHerC 78, BS; DTS 84, ThM; O Nov 22, 88, BPC; Recd PCA Nov 8, 94, SoTX Pby; int Presbyterian Ch of the Hills, Austin, TX, 93-94; p Cross Pointe Ch, Austin, TX, 94-13; wc 13-14; ss Christ the King P Ch, Austin, TX, 14-16, astp 17-

7804 Brodie Lane #B, Austin, TX 78745 – 512-704-7777   South Texas
E-mail: rahmster@sbcglobal.net
Christ the King Presbyterian Church – 512-924-9760

Raines, Richard Lee – b New Brighton, PA, Nov 25, 45; f Raymond; m Edna Young; w Dolores Bradley, St. Louis, MO, Aug 20, 72; chdn 4 adult chdn and 10 grandchdn; MBI 68, BA; GenC 66-68; CTS 72, MDiv; L Oct 21, 72; O Apr 15, 73, RPCES; p Fairview Ref P Ch, Industry, PA, 73-16, p em 16-; hr 16

220 Hickory Drive, Beaver Falls, PA 15010 – 724-462-1713   Ascension
E-mail: pastorric@fairviewpca.org
HR

Rainwater, Dennis – b Bay City, MI, Jun 26, 55; f Walter C.; m Mary Lou Lehman; w Kathleen Hill; chdn Krystal (Porter), Melissa (Muylaert), David; RochC 78, BA; KTS 02, MDiv; L Apr 16, 02, SFL Pby; O Jul 16, 02, SFL Pby; p Chattahoochee P Ch, Chattahoochee, FL, 02-06; Chap Hospice of Palm Beach County, 07-09; hr 09

7300 20th Street Lot 64, Vero Beach, FL 32966 – 989-387-9989   Gulfstream
E-mail: Dennis_rainwater@hotmail.com
HR

Rakes, Jeffrey Alan – w Celeste C. Wingard, Columbia, SC, Aug 5, 78; chdn Rebekah Dawn, Joel Andrew, Daniel James; FurU 77, BS; CTS 81, MDiv; L Sept 81; O Oct 82, Ill Pby; ev Edwardsville, IL, 81-82; op Cov Ref mis, Edwardsville, IL, 82-87; astp Trinity P Ch, Plano, TX, 87-93; astp Grace Ch PCA, Dover, DE, 93-13; ascp 13-; prod worship CD "In Your House," 04; auth, prod worship CD "Lord, Receive My Praise," 10

25 Liberty Drive, Dover, DE 19904 – 302-423-7233   Heritage
E-mail: jrakes@gracedover.com
Grace Church PCA – 302-734-8150 ext. 701

Ramos, Alfredo – astp Grace P Ch, Dalton, GA, 08-11; astp Queens P Ch, Long Island City, NY, 11-13; wc 13-17, sus

E-mail: artraslosheros@aol.com   Metropolitan New York

Ramsay, Richard Beard – b Dodge City, KS, Dec 6, 48; f Bruce Alexander; m Irene Elizabeth Beard; w Maria-Angelica Perez, Dec 1, 84; chdn Nicolas David, Melany Grace; UKS 70, BA; WTS 74, MDiv; CTS 81, ThM; WTS 92, DMin; L 74, MidAt Pby (OPC); O 76, DMV Pby (RPCES); p Knox OP Ch, Silver Spring, MD, 76; mis MTW, Chile, SA, 77-99; mis MTW, on loan to Universidad FLET, 99-09; Miami Int Sem, Miami, FL, 04-09; Third Mill Min, 09-; *Am I Good Enough?; Cuan Bueno Debo Ser?*; *A*

Ramsay, Richard Beard, continued
Su Imagen; coauth *Exploremos Genesis*; *Catolicos y Protestantes – Cual es la Diferencia?*; *Integridad Intelectual*; *Certeza de la Fe*; *Griego y Exegesis*; *Basic Greek and Exegesis*; *The Certainty of the Faith*

22200 SW 93rd Place, Miami, FL 33190 – 305-505-8159   Chesapeake
E-mail: rbramsay@bellsouth.net
Third Millennium Ministries, Inc. – 407-830-0222
316 Live Oaks Boulevard, Casselberry, FL 32707

   Ramsay, Thomas Eugene – b Malta, MT, Jun 17, 38; f Thomas F; m Mavonne Kelstrup; w Jerrie Madray, El Segundo, CA, May 6, 60; chdn Jennifer, Constance (Pfefferle), Thomas M; AmUB 57-58; USC 58-61, BA; CTS 73-77, MDiv; O Nov 6, 77, Pby TX; p Westminster P Ch, Greenville, TX, 77-81; p Hillcrest P Ch, Seattle, WA, 81-90, wc 90-93; ob ss First EPC, Renton, WA, 93-54; ss Green Lake P Ch, Seattle, WA, 95; ob Union Gospel Msn, Seattle, WA, 95-98; ob astp First EPC, Renton, WA, 98-06; ob p/t astp First EPC, Kent, WA, 07-16; hr 16

22407 127th Avenue SE, Kent, WA 98031-3961 – 253-639-0443   Pacific Northwest
E-mail: tomjerrier@comcast.net
HR

   Ramsey, Russell Brown – b Atlanta, GA, May 17, 73; f Richard Floyd; m Susan Jane Aspinwall; w Lisa Marie Wold, Chesterton, IN, Jun 17, 95; chdn Christopher Richard, Margaret Noel, Kate Isabel, Jane Claire; TayU 95, BA; CTS 00, MDiv, 02, ThM; O May 17, 03, Hrtl Pby; p Oak Hills P Ch, Overland Park, KS, 03-10; astp Midtown Flwsp Ch, Nashville, TN, 10-16; astp Christ P Ch, Nashville, TN, 16-; *Behold the Lamb of God: An Advent Narrative*, 11; *Struck, One Christian's Reflections on Encountering Death*, 17; *The Advent of the Lamb of God: The Retelling the Story Series,* 18; *The Passion of the King of Glory:The Retelling the Story Series,* 18; *The Mission of the Body of Christ: The Retelling the Story Series,* 18

706 Wilson Pike, Brentwood, TN 37027   Nashville
E-mail: russramsey@me.com
Christ Presbyterian Church – 615-373-2311

   Randle, Mark – astp Tates Creek P Ch, Lexington, KY, 09-12; ascp 12-

2105 Broadhead Place, Lexington, KY 40515   Ohio Valley
E-mail: mrandle@tcpca.org
Tates Creek Presbyterian Church – 859-272-4399

   Ranheim, Paul – w Lizzy, Los Olivos, CA, Apr 16; WhitC 05, BA; CTS 11, MDiv; O Jun 30, 13, Pac Pby; astp Christ P Ch, Santa Barbara, CA, 13-16; wc 16-17; astp West End Comm Ch, Nashville, TN, 17-

4025 A Nebraska Avenue, Nashville, TN 37209   Nashville
E-mail: paul@westendcc.org
West End Community Church – 615-463-8497

   Rankin, Clifton – ascp Reformed P Ch, Beaumont, TX, 06-15; hr 15

13517 FM 421, Kountze, TX 77625 – 409-504-5904   Houston Metro
E-mail: cearlrankin@gmail.com
HR

   Rantal, John S. – b Newport News, VA, Nov 9, 49; f Col. A.J.; m Billie Ruth Holleman; w Cynthia Jo Johnson, Houston, TX, Jun 1, 74; chdn Corrie (McClure), Heather (Greene), John Mark; FSU 67-69; UHou 69-72, BA; NGTS 95-00, MDiv; O Feb 3, 02, RMtn Pby; ISI, Colorado Springs, CO, 78-96;

Rantal, John S., continued
Cheyenne Mountain P Ch, dir outreach, Colorado Springs, CO, 96-98; int Village Seven P Ch, Colorado Springs, CO, 00-01, astp 02-05; srp Redeemer P Ch, Torrance, CA, 06-08; ss Town North P Ch, Richardson, TX, 09-10; srp Bellewood P Ch, Bellevue, WA, 11-14, hr 16

90 Saint Pauls Road North, Hempstead, NY 11550 – 206-696-9792   Pacific Northwest
E-mail: revrantal@gmail.com
HR

Rapp, David – b Denver, CO, Jan 17, 77; f Gary Eugene; m Linda MacLeod Fiske; w Jennifer Erin Costello, Houston, TX, Jan 8, 00; chdn Wyatt William, Darby MacLeod, Stella Grace; BayU 99, BBA; CTS 03, MDiv; O Sept 7, 03, PacNW Pby; campm RUF, UOR, 03-08; astp Redeemer P Ch, Waco, TX, 08-10; chp Temple, TX, 08-10; op Redeemer P Msn, Temple, TX, 10-15, srp 15-

4307 Vista Court, Temple, TX 76502 – 254-760-4246   North Texas
E-mail: david@redeemerprestemple.org
Redeemer Presbyterian Church – 254-760-4246

Rapp, Robert S. – b New Kensington, PA, Aug 19, 32; f Stanley B; m Marian E. Williams; w Clara Ramsey, Bristol, TN; chdn Stephen Horton, David Williams, Susan Harnish (Hall); PASU 54, BS; FTS 59, MDiv, 60, STM; GrTS 66, ThD; O Jun 60, NJ Pby (BPC); mis Braz & Kor IBPFM, 60-71; mis WBM Pakistan & Kor, 71-74; mis Korea, 74-92; pres WST, 69-92; ss Faith Ch, Villanova, PA, 84-86; ob mis Korea; mis Hungary, 90-18; Dir KGITM, 90-18; hr 07; *Sound Theology*, 75; *Trends in the Modern Ecumenical Movement*, 80

23 Calvary Drive, Lancaster, PA 17601 – 717-672-0501   Susquehanna Valley
E-mail: rsrapp32@verizon.net
HR

Rarig, Stephen – b Bloomsburg, PA, Aug 4, 55; f Charles M.; m Dolores Miller; w Berenice Kuiper, Lookout Mtn, GA, May 7, 78; chdn Nicolene, Damion, Adam, Hanneka; CC 79, BA; RTS 84, MDiv, 86, ThM; ACT 09, ThD; O Jan 27, 85, SFL Pby; astp Calvary Ch, Ft Laud, FL, 84-85; p Collins P Ch, 86-89; mis MTW, Australia, 89-; prin WTC, 89-97; DnAc, prof Trin Theol Coll, Aust, 97-07; Trin Theol Coll, Aust, vice-princ, 97-07; Trin Theol Coll, Aust, grad stud coord, 02-05; MTW, chpl team lead, Western Australia, 03-; *Sabbath as Redemptive-Eschatological Crux in the Lordship of Yahweh: A Study in the Pentateuch*, 09

c/o MTW – 0011-618-9456-4862   Grace
E-mail: rariginoz@gmail.com
PCA Mission to the World

Rasmussen, Michael – b Portland, OR, Feb 20, 58; f Duane O.; m Donna C. Spencer; w Renatta L. Ponder, Atlanta, GA; chdn Andrew, Benjamin; UMN 76-77; UGA 78-80, BS; RTS 83-87, MDiv; AberU 11, PhD; L 84, MSVal Pby; O 87, SFL Pby; ap Bethany P Ch, Ft Lauderdale, FL, 87-88; op, p Christ P Ch, Winterville, NC, 88-91; astp Perimeter Ch, Duluth, GA, 91-94; op Ivy Creek Ch, Lawrenceville, GA, 94-95, p 95-05; vis lect/prof HighC, 05; asst prof, DnStu Redeemer Sem, Dallas, TX, 07-11; asst prof 11-14; srp Trinity P Ch, Plano, TX, 14-

8851 Kingsley Road, Dallas, TX 75231-4800 – 214-341-9378   North Texas
E-mail: mike.rasmussen@trinityplano.org
Trinity Presbyterian Church – 972-335-3844

Ratchford, Dan – w Vicky; chdn Marcie, Julie, Sandie; CIU, MDiv; O Jun 02, Palm Pby; astp St. Andrews P Ch, Columbia, SC, 97-02; op Chapin P Ch, Chapin, SC, p 03-15; p Smyrna P Ch, Newberry, SC, 15-

8 Smyrna Road, Newberry, SC 29108 – 803-960-6716   Calvary
E-mail: dannylynnratchford@gmail.com
Smyrna Presbyterian Church – 803-276-3943

Ratliff, Benjamin David – b Ft. Worth, TX, Jul 13, 87; f James Gregory; m Laura White; w Caitlin Marguerite Wolfe, Jackson, MS, May 30, 09; chdn Eliza Joy; BelC 09, BA; RTS 13, MDiv; O Feb 21, 16, Hrtg Pby; astp Providence P Ch, Salisbury, MD, 16; p First P Ch, Hazlehurst, MS, 16-

125 Westover Drive, Hazlehurst, MS 39083 – 601-454-1470   Grace
E-mail: Benjaminratliff@me.com
First Presbyterian Church – 601-894-1409

Ratliff, John – b Haskell, TX, Nov 18, 50; f David; m Priscilla Gladish; w Niki Nislar, Lubbock, TX, Dec 28, 74; chdn Benjamin August, Peter Nathaniel; TXTU 74, BA; DTS 82, ThM; O Apr 20, 85, Bapt.; Recd PCA Jul 7, 00, SoTX Pby; astp Redeemer P Ch, Austin, TX, 00-03; op Christ the King P Ch, Austin, TX, 00-03, p 03-14

10804 Greymere Court, Austin, TX 78739 – 512-288-6969   South Texas

Rauls, Michael – ascp Good Shepherd P Ch, Ocala, FL, 13-

Good Shepherd Presbyterian Church – 352-291-9199   Central Florida

Ravenhill, Colin – w Stefanie, Aug 14, 99; chdn Jacob, Jane, Kate; UMO 98, BS; CTS 05, MDiv; O Aug 06, NGA Pby; ydir Memorial P Ch, St. Louis, MO, 01-05; ydir Faith P Ch, Watkinsville, GA, 05-06, ascp 06-08; astp Memorial P Ch, St. Louis, MO, 08-13; wc 13-

463 Toft Lane, St. Louis, MO 63119   Missouri
E-mail: ravenhill@gmail.com

Rayburn, Robert G., II – b Tacoma, WA, Dec 12, 84; f Robert Stout; m Florence Ann; w Jordan Bean; chdn Robert Stout II, Abigail Kay; CC 07, BA; CTS 11, MDiv; O 11, MO Pby; Chap USAR/stu; Chap USArmy; contr *Lexham Bible Dictionary*

11199B Ashcraft Loop, Fort Campbell, KY 42223 – 253-579-7546   Missouri
E-mail: robertgrayburn@gmail.com
United States Army

Rayburn, Robert Stout – b St. Charles, IL, Aug 8, 50; f Robert Gibson; m LaVerne Swanson; w Florence Roskamp, Cedar Falls, IA, Aug 23, 75; chdn Bryonie Alice, Evangeline Sarah, Courtney Elizabeth, Robert Gibson II, James Oliver Hamilton; CC 72, BA; CTS 75, MDiv; AberU 78, PhD; L 75, Midw Pby; O 78, PacNW Pby (RPCES); srp Faith P Ch, Tacoma, WA, 78-; sc PacNW Pby, 90-12; contr *Evangelical Dictionary of Theology*; contr "Hebrews," *ECB*, 89

818 South M Street, Tacoma, WA 98405-3649 – 253-273-3393   Pacific Northwest
E-mail: rrayburn@faithtacoma.org
Faith Presbyterian Church – 253-752-7601

Rayl, Brett – mis MTW, 14-

c/o MTW   North Texas
PCA Mission to the World

Raynor, William Andrew – p Wilson P Ch, Wilson, NC, 07-

703 Trinity Drive West, Wilson, NC 27893-2128 – 252-281-4074   Eastern Carolina
E-mail: andyraynor@wilsonpca.com
Wilson Presbyterian Church – 252-399-9501

Rea, David Colyer – b Charlotte, NC, Apr 1, 71; f James Green; m Helena Colyer; w Stefani Marshall, Dallas, TX, Mar 23, 96; chdn Virginia, Cole, Jack; ASU, BS; RTSNC, MDiv; L Nov 28, 99, NoTX Pby; O Nov 28, 99, NoTX Pby; astp Park Cities P Ch, Dallas, TX, 99-04; campm RUF, SMU, 99-06; op Providence P Church, Dallas, TX, 06-07; p 07-

4310 Reaumur Drive, Dallas, TX 75229 – 214-827-6961　　　　　　　　　　　　North Texas
E-mail: david.rea@providencedallas.com
Providence Presbyterian Church – 214-270-1220

Reap, James J. Jr. – w Jennifer; chdn Jaydon; UDE, BA; WTS, MDiv; L Feb 01, Hrtg Pby; O May 01, Hrtg Pby; astp Berea P Ch, Hockessin, DE, 01-02, srp 02-

351 Mitchell Drive, Wilmington, DE 19808 – 302-996-0916　　　　　　　　　　　Heritage
E-mail: jrreap@bereapca.org
Berea Presbyterian Church – 302-239-7631

Reber, Frederick G. – b Philadelphia, PA, Jun 11, 49; f Frederick G.; m Joan M. Faber; w Celina Fuentes, Vineland, NJ, May 13, 94; chdn Samuel Esteban, Lydia Abigaile, Jonathan Frederick; ShelC 75, BA; WTS 79, MDiv; L Sept 24, 94, OPC; O Mar 26, 95, OPC; Recd PCA 01, NJ Pby; mis MTW, Mexico, 81-88; medu Covenant OPC, Vineland, NJ, 94-97; ob Chap Southwoods State Prison, NJ, 97-13; wc 13-17; hr 17

488 Irving Avenue, Bridgeton, NJ 08302 – 856-459-9392　　　　　　　　　　　New Jersey
E-mail: freber3703@aol.com
HR

Recio, Robert – ascp Christ P Ch, Murietta, CA, 11-18, p 18-

38179 Talavera Court, Murrieta, CA 92563　　　　　　　　　　　　　　　South Coast
E-mail: rrecio@christpca.net
Christ Presbyterian Church – 951-699-3484

Rector, Charles Mitchell – b Newberry, SC, Mar 16, 38; f Clifford C.; m Hallie A.; w Patricia Leonard Brickhouse, Raleigh, NC, Nov 14, 70; chdn William Howard Brickhouse, Charles Mitchell Jr. (d), Steven Allen Brickhouse, Deborah Ann Brickhouse (Donahue); NCWC 77, BA; SEBTS 80, MDiv; L Jun 1, 60, UMC; O May 23, 81, Ecar Pby; ev PEF, 81-; ip Northside P Ch, Burlington, NC, 81; Chap USArmy, 82-98 (ret 98); ip Hull Mem P Ch, Savannah, GA, 82; ip Beal Heights P Ch, Lawton, OK, 88; p Cliffwood P Ch, Augusta, GA, 98-05; chap NC Dept of Corrections, 05-07; chap Charlie Norwood VA Med Ctr, 07-; chmn shepherding com Sav Pby, 99-

2702 Oakbluff Court, Augusta, GA 30909 – 706-736-4567　　　　　　　　　Savannah River
E-mail: crector917@aol.com
Presbyterian Evangelistic Fellowship

Reddick, Phillip Alton – b Atlanta, GA, Apr 5, 52; f Alton Irwin; m Mary June Gatlin; w Anne McIntosh Floyd, Monticello, FL, Sept 3, 77; chdn Virginia Gatlin, Catherine Anne; VPI 70-71; DeKCC 71-72; UGA 72-74, BBA; BhamTS, MDiv, MRE; L Sept 25, 90; O Sept 25, 90, Evan Pby; CCC, 74-84; Dir Young Bus Ldrs, Briarwood P Ch, 84-; ascp Briarwood P Ch, Birmingham, AL, 90-

2620 Altadena Road, Birmingham, AL 35243 – 205-967-9237　　　　　　　　　Evangel
E-mail: preddick@briarwood.org
Briarwood Presbyterian Church – 205-776-5200

Ree, Jung Chul – b Korea, Mar 12, 53; f Young Ki; m Yeh Sook Kim; w Soo Bok, Korea, Apr 12, 75; chdn Darren, Ashli; SFBC 90, BA; SFTS 93, MDiv; O Oct 11, 94, KorNW Pby; p Korean Saints P Ch, Warminster, PA, 97-02; p Disciple Comm Ch in Phil, Blue Bell, PA, 02-

80 Cedar Grove Road, Conshohocken, PA 19428 – 610-397-0297　　　　　　Korean Eastern
E-mail: pjcree@hotmail.com
Disciple Community Church in Philadelphia

Reebals, Eric – O Nov 13, 18, Evan Pby; astp Briarwood P Ch, Birmingham, AL, 18-

Briarwood Presbyterian Church – 205-776-5200 — Evangel

Reed, Ben – astp Redeemer P Ch, Indianapolis, IN, 17-

Redeemer Presbyterian Church — Central Indiana
1505 North Delaware Street, Indianapolis, IN 46202
E-mail: ben@redeemindy.org
Redeemer Presbyterian Church – 317-238-5487

Reed, Chip – O Oct 23, 16, PD Pby; astp Westminster P Ch, Sumter, SC, 16-18

639 Mattison Avenue, Sumter, SC 29150 — Pee Dee
E-mail: chip.reed@yahoo.com

Reed, Edward L. Jr. – b Spartanburg, SC, Jun 4, 56; f Edward Lang; m Mary Anne Fair (d); w Martha Evelyn Earwood, Ponte Vedra Bch, FL, Jan 25, 97; chdn Margeaux Carson, Carlton Sidney; CCSC 78, BA; RTS 95, MDiv; L Jul 15, 97; O Dec 7, 97, SFL Pby; int Granada P Ch, Coral Gables, FL, 92-93; ms/sa Ponte Vedra P Ch, Ponte Vedra Beach, FL, 94-96; astp Redeemer P Ch, Miami, FL, 96-99; astp Boynton Beach Community Ch, Lake Worth, FL, 99-00; astp Grace Comm Ch, Bridgewater, NJ, 00-02; astp West End P Ch, Hopewell, VA, 04-06; ascp 06-11, srp 12-

406 Spruance Street, Hopewell, VA 23860 – 804-452-0920 — James River
E-mail: eddiereed1997@gmail.com
West End Presbyterian Church – 804-458-6765

Reed, Gordon Kenworthy – b Bristol, TN, Oct 3, 30; f Roy T; m Elizabeth Tuft; w Miriam Clark, Signal Mt, TN, May 26, 54; chdn Elizabeth (McNutt), Robert, John, Nancy (Zoeller), Virginia (Akin); MHC 49-50; KgC 51-52, BA; ColTS 56, BD; L Jul 1, 56; O Jul 1, 56, Knox Pby; p Signal Mt, TN, 56-59; p Wee Kirk P Ch, Lithonia, GA, 59-64; p Second P Ch, Greenville, SC, 64-75; p Kendall P Ch, Miami, FL, 75-78; ac dir Ridge Haven Conference Center, 78-80; p First P Ch, Macon, GA, 80-85; t, ev Word Min; prof RTS, 86-92; ss Raymond P Ch, Raymond, MS, 87-88; ob ss Trinity P Ch, Jackson, MS, 90-92; ob admin, prof RTSNC, 92-93; p Sardinia P Ch, Sardinia, SC, 93-04; p New Hrmny Ch, Alcolu, SC, 93-04; ob p Christ Ch P, Augusta, GA (ind), 04-08; ss Longtown P Ch, Ridgeway, SC, 08-09; hr 09; sr ed *Christian Observer*, 87-; *Christmas: Triumph Over Tragedy*; *Lord Teach Us to Pray*; *Study in Sermon on the Mount*; *Living Life by God's Law*

PO Box 26, Gable, SC 29051 – 803-403-2699 — Pee Dee
HR

Reed, Mark – w Kristi, Jun 26, 99; chdn Walker, Marshall, Janie; CTS 03, MDiv; L Oct 04, SNE Pby; campm RUM, 04-08; astp Christ Comm P Ch, West Hartford, CT, 04-08; astp Mitchell Road P Ch, Greenville, SC, 08-

14 Chatelaine Drive, Greenville, SC 29615 – 864-288-9119 — Calvary
E-mail: mreed@mitchellroad.org
Mitchell Road Presbyterian Church – 864-268-2218

Reed, Tim Joseph – b Kinston, NC, Nov 5, 57; f Alfred Joseph; m Helen Ann Fussel; w Renee Lynn Kinney, Evansville, IN, Dec 18, 82; chdn Jessica Kinney, Zachary George, Meghan Anne; ASU 76-80, BS; UT 80-83, MS; GCTS 84-88, MDiv; CTS 13, DMin; O Nov 5, 89, Cov Pby; ip Cedar Springs P Ch, Knoxville, TN, 88-89; ap Covenant P Ch, Little Rock, AR, 89-91, srp 91-

3 Golden Oak Cove, Little Rock, AR 72212-2132 – 501-804-5831 — Covenant
E-mail: tjreed@covenantpca.com
Covenant Presbyterian Church – 501-228-5903

Reed, Wayne William – b Maryland, Dec 24, 63; f Clyde; m Ann Millington; w Debbie Mattinen, Duluth, MN, Dec 27, 86; chdn Dale Allen, Daniel James Ryan Andrew, Robert Morrison, Callia Anne; NAZU, BS; ErskTS 89-92, MDiv; L Oct 15, 91; O Feb 23, 92, ARP; Recd PCA Sept 24, 93, Siouxl Pby; p Providence ARP, Clinton, SC, 92-93; ss Christ P Ch, Farmington, MN, 93-94; ev, chp Woodbury/Cottage Grove, Twin Cities, MN, 94; astp Lennox Ebenezer P Ch, Lennox, SD, 95-99; op Living Hope Comm Ch, Tea, SD, 95-98, p 98-

27038 469th Avenue, Tea, SD 57064-0134 – 605-368-2515   Siouxlands
E-mail: waynoreedo@yahoo.com
Living Hope Community Church – 605-498-5876

Reeder, Harry Lloyd III – b Charlotte, NC, Feb 16, 48; f Harry Lloyd Jr.; m Evelyn Sheehan Reeder; w Cynthia Lou Miller, Charlotte, NC, Jan 26, 69; chdn Jennifer Elizabeth, Harry Lloyd IV, Abigail Lois; ECU 66-68; CC 73, BA; TNTC 74-79; WTS 82, MDiv; RTS 02, DMin; L Jan 81; O Jun 82, SFL Pby; p Pinelands P Ch, Miami, FL, 82-83; srp Christ Cov P Ch, Matthews, NC, 83-99; srp Briarwood P Ch, Birmingham, AL, 99-; contr *Pastor/Evangelist; Embers to a Flame; The Leadership Dynamic; 3D Leadership*

2037 Brae Trail, Birmingham, AL 35242 – 205-437-0289   Evangel
E-mail: hreeder@briarwood.org
Briarwood Presbyterian Church – 205-776-5200

Reese, Steven McNamara – b St. Louis, MO, Nov 15, 55; f Eugene K.; m Dorthy Hornal; w Julie Muir, Sept 7, 91; chdn Elizabeth Renee, Katherine Renee, Christopher McNamara; FBC 78, BA; UMO 79; CTS 81, MA, 84, MDiv, 14, DMin; O Oct 86, Mid-America; moy Shannon Forest P Ch, Greenville, SC, 84-86; ap New Hope P Ch in America, Olathe, KS, 86-89; ascp Pinewood P Ch, Middleburg, FL, 89-95; ev, op Redeemer P Ch, Parker, CO, 95-00, p 00-

21914 East Stroll Avenue, Parker, CO 80138 – 303-902-2306   Rocky Mountain
E-mail: stevenreese@mac.com
Redeemer Presbyterian Church – 303-841-6211

Reeves, John Kenyan – b Pensacola, FL, Apr 21, 47; f David Chester R; m Goldie Jerauld; w Emily Kees, Brookhaven, MS, Jul 10, 70; chdn Meredith Aimee, Melanie Elizabeth, David Geoffrey; PenJC 66-67; BelC 69, BA; WTS 69-70; RTS 72, MDiv; O Aug 6, 72, SMS Pby; p Moss Point P Ch, Moss Point, MS, 72-81; p Westm Ch, Jackson, MS, 81-90; p Providence P Ch, Clinton, MS, 90-13; hr 13; ss Magee P Ch, Magee, MS, 14-; adj fac BelhU, 14-

1203 Huntcliff Way, Clinton, MS 39056-3425 – 601-924-4057   Mississippi Valley
E-mail: john_k_reeves@juno.com
Magee Presbyterian Church
HR

Rehrmann, Peter – op Holy Cross P Ch, Tucson, AZ, 11-14; p 14-

11432 West Harvester Drive, Marana, AZ 85653 – 520-401-9105   Southwest
E-mail: pete@holycrosstucson.com
Holy Cross Presbyterian Church – 520-401-9105

Reiber, Scott Louis – b Hastings, NE, Aug 9, 55; f Roy L.; m Carol L. Frisbie; w Mary Gwendolyn Probst, Ellisville, MS, Jun 10, 78; chdn Nicholas Ethan, AnnaElizabeth, Derrick Louis; USM 77, BS; RTS 82, MDiv; O Jul 11, 82, Gr Pby; p Calvary P Ch, Mize, MS, 82-85; p Providence P Ch, Savannah, GA, 85-99; t Providence CS, 86-99; p Westminster P Ch, Vicksburg, MS, 99-

700 Newit Vick Drive, Vicksburg, MS 39183 – 601-638-4141   Mississippi Valley
E-mail: wpcvicksburg@gmail.com
Westminster Presbyterian Church – 601-636-4292

Reichart, William George – w Lauren Ann, Aug 6, 89; chdn Emmy, Brenna; TowU, BS; RTSFL, MDiv; O Feb 12, 06, NGA Pby; campm CCC, URI, UVA, Towson, 88-05; astp The Vine Comm Ch, Alpharetta, GA, 05-09; ob Christian Medical & Dental Assoc, Atlanta, 09-

1415 Mountclaire Drive, Cumming, GA 30041 – 678-513-2361   Metro Atlanta
E-mail: billreichart@cmdaatlanta.org
Christian Medical & Dental Association, Atlanta

Reilly, Leo W. – b Philadelphia, PA, Dec 14, 57; f James Austin; m Mary C. Schad; w Barbara Eileen Remely, Warrington, PA, Aug 16, 80; chdn Sean Michael, Jonathan Leo, Ryan Matthew; WChSC 80, BS; BibTS 85, MA, MDiv; O Oct 25, 87, SFL Pby; ap Spanish River P Ch, Boca Raton, FL, 87-91; astp Orangewood P Ch, Maitland, FL, 91-92; ob WestAc, Ft. Lauderdale, FL, 93-

6861 NW 32nd Avenue, Ft. Lauderdale, FL 33309-1222   Central Florida
Westminster Academy
5620 NE 22nd Avenue, Ft. Lauderdale, FL 33308

Reinmuth, William – b Brooklyn, NY, Jun 7, 77; f Daniel; m Jayne; w Christin, Aug 6, 99; chdn Eva, Liam, Noah; WTS 06, MDiv; astp Grace Redeemer Ch, Teaneck, NJ, 07-09; op All Souls Comm Ch, Nanuet, NY, 09-

81 Washington Avenue, Suffern, NY 10954 – 845-598-5582   Metropolitan New York
E-mail: will@allsoulscommunity.com
All Souls Community Church – 845-357-0435

Reitano, Josh – b Columbus, OH, Aug 19, 76; f James Anthony; m Nancy Louise; w Paige Hobson; MUOH 98, BS, 01, MA; PTS 03, MDiv; dir stud min North Cincinnati Comm Ch, Mason, OH, 03-06, astp 06-11; op New City P Ch, Cincinnati, OH, 09-11; p 11-; *Rooted: The Apostles' Creed*, 13

4400 Floral Ave, Cincinnati 45212   Ohio Valley
E-mail: joshua.reitano@gmail.com
New City Presbyterian Church – 513-886-0676

Remillard, Donald Keith – b Hancock, MI, Dec 5, 38; f Raymond Joseph; m Lorelda Willmes; w Beverly Raynard, Mission, KS, Jan 24, 59; chdn Andrew Neil, Mark Alan, Stephen Keith, Lynn Ann; SterC 63, BA; DubTS 66, BD, 72, STM; O May 14, 67, Detroit Pby (UPCUSA); ap Drayton Plains, MI, 67-68; p Immanuel Ch, Detroit, MI, 68-70; p Bad Axe Ch, MI, 70-82; hm Traverse City, MI, 82-84; p Pioneer P Ch, Ligonier, PA, 85-89, wc 89-91; ob Dir Christian Conciliation Svc, Detroit, MI, 91-04; hr 04; *The Westminster Confession of Faith: A Contemporary Version*; *What Does it Mean to be Human?*; *The Westminster Shorter Catechism, A Contemporary Edition*

2050 South Washington Road, Holt, MI 48842 – 330-871-8359   Great Lakes
E-mail: presbypres@aol.com
HR

Rendell, Jeffrey M. – O Dec 20, 15, PhilMetW Pby; ascp Meadowcroft P Ch, West Chester, PA, 15-

811 Halvorsen Drive, West Chester, PA 19382 – 540-818-6125   Philadelphia Metro West
E-mail: jeff@meadowcroftchurch.org
Meadowcroft Presbyterian Church – 610-455-045

Render, Peter – astp Southwood P Ch, Huntsville, AL, 17-

7807 Double Tree Drive, Huntsville, AL 35802   Providence
E-mail: peter.render@southwood.org
Southwood Presbyterian Church – 256-882-3085

Renick, John Alfred – b Hagerstown, MD, Apr 15, 41; f Job R.; m Louise; w Linda Cook, Danville, VA, Sept 5, 64; chdn John Randolph, Joshua James, Jay Paul; CWM 63, BA; GrTS 67, BD; TEDS 72, ThM; O Aug 82, SFL Pby; ap Coral Ridge P Ch, Ft. Lauderdale, FL, 82-87, wc 87-99; ob t The First Acad CS, Orlando, 98-01; Solid Rock CS, Mt. Dora, FL,-04; bulBlue Lake Acad CS, Eustis, FL 06-09

12424 Draw Drive, Grand Island, FL 32735 – 407-483-1151   Central Florida

Resch, Stephen J. – b New Orleans, LA, Oct 1, 63; f Stephen J.; m Lucia V. Rowzie; w Tami L. Fichtner, W. Lafayette, IN, Jul 18, 87; chdn Stephen J. III, Emily Grace, Katherine Renee; TayU 85, BA; RTSFL 93, MDiv; O Oct 22, 95, GrLks Pby; Covenant PCUSA, W. Lafayette, IN, 85-90; astp Northwest P Ch, Dublin, OH, 93-96; p Walnut Creek P Ch, Gahanna, OH, 96-

600 West Johnstown Road, Gahanna, OH 43230-2881 – 614-337-8250   Columbus Metro
E-mail: sresch@wcpc.org
Walnut Creek Presbyterian Church – 614-337-9200

Revlett, Charles Brett – ob p Evan Fell Chapel, NJ, 05-10; ob srp Brigham City Bible Church, UT, 11-

935 US 950 South, Brigham City, UT 84302 – 435-553-5661   Northern California
E-mail: revlett@optonline.net
Brigham City Bible Church, UT

Reynolds, Mark – CTS, MDiv; AberU, ThM; StLU, PhD; O Jun 13, 04, MNY Pby; astp Redeemer P Ch of New York, New York, NY, 04-08; ob Redeemer ChPlant Cent, 08; ob Redeemer City to City, 09-

304 West 105th Street #2A, New York, NY 10025 – 917-837-2875   Metropolitan New York
Redeemer City to City

Reynolds, Paul –ascp New Hope PCA, Olathe, KS, 15-18

2311 East Cedar Street, Olathe, KS 66062   Heartland
E-mail: paulreynolds00@gmail.com

Rhea, Randy – astp Lawndale P Ch, Tupelo, MS, 08-10; op Trin P Msn, Corinth, MS, 08-10, srp 10-12; astp Madison Heights P Ch, Madison, MS, 12-14, p 14-

120 Northlake Drive, Madison, MS 39110   Mississippi Valley
E-mail: randy@madisonheightschurch.com
Madison Heights Presbyterian Church – 601-605-9929

Rhee, Dong Soo – b Korea, Oct 12, 54; f Kang Moo Rhee; m Young Ja Park; w Mi Seob Yoon, Seoul, Apr 7, 82; chdn Janet J., Marc J., Carolyn J.; GATech; NOBTS 95-99; O Feb 13, 00, NGA Pby; op Unity Korean P Ch, Atlanta, GA, 00-

11130 Morton's Crossing, Alpharetta, GA 30022 – 770-619-1839   Metro Atlanta
E-mail: dsrhee1@yahoo.com
Unity Korean Presbyterian Church – 770-448-4664

Rhodes, Samuel McBride II – campm RUF, GASou, 06-11; campm RUF, USoCar, 11-

1536 Forest Trace Drive, Columbia, SC 29204   Palmetto
E-mail: srhodes@ruf.org
PCA Reformed University Fellowship

Rhyu, Ike S. – b Seoul, Nov 13, 60; f Han M.; m Chung J. Kim; w Helen Moon, Vienna, VA, Jan 4, 86; chdn Jenny, Hannah; WBC 92, BA; CapBS 94, MDiv; L Apr 94, KorCap Pby; O Dec 94, KorCap Pby; ob mis Seed Int, Juarez, Mexico, 95-11; Seed Int/US, Southern CA, 11-16; ob mis Seed Int, Saville, Spain, 16-

14545 Valley View Avenue #A, Santa Fe Springs, CA 90670 – 626-609-9231   Korean Capital
E-mail: ikerhyu@gmail.com
SEED USA

Ribelin, Kenneth Edd – b Albemarle, NC, Sept 25, 49; f Robert Edd; m Daisy Anne Blalock; w (1) Paula Beth Crump; (2) Nancy Shirley, Petal, MS, Jun 9, 00; chdn Nathan Edd, Timothy Paul; WCU 67-71, BA; CTS 74-78, MDiv, MA; L Feb 14, 78, SE Pby (RPCES); O Aug 6, 78, Gr Pby; ss Trinity P Ch, Union, MO, 75-78; Chap J.C.A. Ret. Ctr, Chesterfield, MO, 76-78; ap Bay Street P Ch, Hattiesburg, MS, 78-80; Chap MSANG, 80-; p Petal P Ch, Petal, MS, 80-; ss New Aug P Ch, New Augusta, MS, 89-; *Pastoral Insights, Petal Presbyterian Church's Ninety Years*

127 Cherry Oak Trail, Petal, MS 39465 – 601-544-7606   Grace
E-mail: ribelin@netdoor.com
Petal Presbyterian Church – 601-582-4772
New Augusta Presbyterian Church

Rice, Timothy W. – b Atlanta, GA, May 2, 62; f Calvin; m Betty Richey; w Julie Kay Borders, Tallahassee, FL, Aug 30, 86; chdn Tyler Andrew, Molly Katherine, Abigail Julianne, George Campbell; ASU 80-84, BA; RTSFL 90-93, MDiv; L Jan 12, 93; O Aug 22, 93, SWFL Pby; staff Athletes In Action, FSU, 84-86; ydir First P Ch, Lakeland, FL, 86-90; First P Ch, Lakeland, FL College dir, 90-92; int Covenant P Ch, Lakeland, FL, 92-93, ascp 93-96; op Trinity P Ch, Lakeland, FL, 97-00, p 00-

2716 Fairmount Avenue, Lakeland, FL 33803 – 863-680-3255   Southwest Florida
E-mail: tim@trinitylakeland.org
Trinity Presbyterian Church – 863-603-7777

Rice, W. Frederick – b Warsaw, IN, Dec 18, 44; f William; m Leontine; w Nancy Tyler Jarvis; chdn William Jarvis, Elizabeth Tyler; BJU 66, BS; GTS 69, MDiv; WTS 74, ThM; TTS 03, ThD; Juanita Comm Ch, Kirkland, WA, 70-72; Inter-City Bapt Ch, Allen Park, MI, 72-74; Ch of the Cov OPC, Hackettstown, NJ, 01-05; Westm Christ Acad, Huntsville, AL, 05-09; astp Westminster P Ch, Huntsville, AL 06-12; hr 13

1219 South Blue Ridge Avenue, Culpeper, VA 22701   Providence
E-mail: frice01@gmail.com
HR

Rich, James – LibertyU 84; BibTS 88, MA, 88, MDiv; WTS 03, ThM, 15, PhD; O 09, PhilMetW Pby; astp Covenant P Ch, Harleysville, PA, 09-

3303 Carriage Court, North Wales, PA 19454 – 215-361-2074   Philadelphia Metro West
E-mail: jrich@covpreschurch.org
Covenant Presbyterian Church – 215-256-1007

Rich, Philip Walton – b Miami, FL, Aug 30, 55; f Robert S.; m Sarah Walton; w Debra Ann Daniel, Miami, FL, Aug 18, 76; chdn William, Jennifer, James, Andrew, Jonathan; VandU 77, BE, 79, MS; KTS 93, cert, 97, MDiv; L Mar 97, SFL Pby; O Nov 9, 97, Evan Pby; p Mount Cal P Ch, Pinson, AL, 97-

7942 McIntyre Road, Trussville, AL 35173   Evangel
E-mail: ikthos@mac.com
Mount Calvary Presbyterian Church – 205-681-4119

Richard, Guy M. – b May 11, 68; w Jennifer Susan Buck, Nov 21, 92; chdn Schyler Wilson, Jane Barton, Elizabeth Rutherford; AU 91, BIE; RTS 02, MDiv; UEdin 06, PhD; O Oct 2, 05, Gr Pby; int First P Ch, Jackson, MS, 98-02; p First P Ch, Gulfport, MS, 05-17; ob admin RTSA, 17-; "Samuel Rutherford's Supralapsarianism Revealed," *Scottish Journal of Theology*, 06, and *The Confessional Presbyterian*, 08; with J.V. Fesko, "Natural Theology in the Westminster Confession of Faith," *The Westminster Confession into the 21st Century 3*, 09; *The Supremacy of God in the Theology of Samuel Rutherford*, 09; "Samuel Rutherford: Of the Civil Magistrate," *The Confessional Presbyterian*, 08; "Samuel Rutherford for the 21st Century, Parts 1 and 2," *Reformation 21*, online magazine, 09; "Preaching the Loveliness of Christ," *Korean Institute for Reformed Preaching*, 07; "Our Blessed Struggle," in *Tabletalk*, 09; "Introduction" to *Sermons Preached Before the English Houses of Parliament by the Scottish Commissioners to the Westminster Assembly of Divines 1643-1645*, 11; "Glory, Glory Dwelleth in Immanuel's Land," in *The People's Theologian: Writings in Honour of Donald Macleod*, 11; *What Is Faith?* 12; "The Two shall become One Flesh: Samuel Rutherford's 'Affectionate' Theology of Union with Christ in the Song of Songs," in *Samuel Rutherford: An Introduction to his Theology,* 12; "What Faith Is and Is Not," *Tabletalk* 37:6 (Jun 13); "A Picture of Saving Faith," *ByFaith* 38 (Oct12); "What Is Faith?" *Tabletalk* 39:1 (Jan 15); "*Clavis Cantici*: A 'Key' to the Reformation in Early Modern Scotland?," in *Reformed Orthodoxy in Scotland: Essays on Scottish Theology 1560-1775*, 15; weekend contr *Tabletalk,* 15; "Should Not Perish," *Tabletalk 40:5*, 16; "The Frozen Chosen," *Tabletalk 40:8,* 16; "Ministry is Discouragement," www.reformation21.org, 16; "How Jesus Trains Husbands," *Tabletalk* 41:9, 17; "Pastor, You Need Other Pastors," *Gospel Reformation Network,* 17; "Was Jesus Really Born of a Virgin?," *Tabletalk* Dec 17; "Love that Spares no Expense," *Tabletalk* Feb 18; "The Importance of Prayer," *Gospel Reformation Network* Apr 18; "Does Heaven Have Suburbs?," *Tabletalk* Apr 18; "The Visible Body of Christ," *Tabletalk* Aug 18; "God's Control and Our Responsibility," *Tabletalk* Oct 18; "The Road to Restoration," *Ministry & Leadership* Fall 18

410 Oak Brook Court SE, Smyrna, GA 30082   Metro Atlanta
E-mail: grichard@rts.edu
Reformed Theological Seminary Atlanta – 770-952-8884

Richardson, David – p Treasure Coast P Ch, Stuart, FL, 12-15; wc 15-17; astp Coral Ridge P Ch, Ft. Lauderdale, FL, 17-18

4450 NE 18th Avenue, Oakland Park, FL 33334-5518   South Florida

Richardson, Guy Lipscomb – b Selma, AL, Aug 15, 50; f Thomas W.; m Adelyn L.; w Eva Denise White, Birmingham, AL, Dec 11, 82; chdn Eva Katharine, Joy Fleming; AU 68-72, BS; RTS 75-77, MCE; GSU 78-80, MEd; AU 81-83, DEd; O Jan 87, CentGA Pby; ap First P Ch, Augusta, GA, 87-89; astp Trinity P Ch, Montgomery, AL, 89-96; ss Evangelical P Ch, Newark, DE, 96-99; ob pres RTS, 99-

3 Avery Circle, Jackson, MS 39211 – 601-991-0337   Mississippi Valley
E-mail: grichardson@rts.edu
Reformed Theological Seminary – 601-923-1600
5422 Clinton Boulevard, Jackson, MS 39209

Richardson, Seth A. – astp Broadneck Evangelical P Ch, Arnold, MD, 07-09; ascp 09-11; astp Briarwood P Ch, Birmingham, AL, 11-

2705 Al Lin Circle, Birmingham, AL 35244   Evangel
Briarwood Presbyterian Church – 205-776-5200

Richmon, David – astp Green Lake P Ch, Seattle, WA, 09-14; srp 14-

7520 Linden Avenue North, Seattle, WA 98103   Pacific Northwest
Green Lake Presbyterian Church – 206-789-7320

MINISTERIAL DIRECTORY

Richter, David – ascp Trinity P Ch, Rochester, MN, 09-13; astp Christ The King P Ch, Cambridge, MA, 13-; p Christ the King Somerville, Cambridge, MA, 13-

5 Bond Street #2, Somerville, MA 02145 – 617-755-6050   Southern New England
E-mail: ctksomerville@gmail.com
Christ The King Presbyterian Church – 617-354-8341
Christ the King Somerville – 507-226-2939

Richter, James E. – b Cullman, AL, Oct 27, 49; f Franklin K.; m Jane South; w Linda Leary, Morehead City, NC, Dec 15, 73; chdn David, Karen; AU 72, BCE, 74, MS; RTS 82, MDiv, 03, DMin; L Sept 80, TNVal Pby; O Jan 82, Westm Pby; p Meadow Creek P Ch, Greeneville, TN, 82-89; srp First P Ch, Biloxi, MS, 89-02; srp Westminster P Ch, Johnson City, TN, 03-

302 Hillside Road, Johnson City, TN 37601 – 423-926-1419   Westminster
E-mail: jerichter@gmail.com
Westminster Presbyterian Church – 423-283-4643

Richwine, James Boyd – b Carlisle, PA, Sept 19, 48; f Marlin; m Kathleen Keim; w Brooke Kelly, Grantham, PA, May 16, 70; chdn Jamie, Timothy; GATech 66-67; MesC 70, BA; WTS 76, MDiv; O May 82, Asc Pby; exec dir Renewed Life Chr Couns Svcs, Inc, 77-83; ap Coral Ridge P Ch, Ft. Lauderdale, FL, 83-91; couns BPC&E Gp, 88-89; ob Chap Holy Cross Hosp, 87-91; p Cov Evangelical P, Calgary, AB, 91-98; srp Grace Cov P Ch, Brevard, NC, 99-01, wc 01-07; ob Miami Int Sem, Miami, FL, 07-12; fac BhamTS, 12-; p First P Ch, Eutaw, AL, 14-; p Boligee P Ch, Boligee, AL, 14-

PO Box 553, Eutaw AL 35462   Warrior
E-mail: jbr10@mail.com
Birmingham Theological Seminary
First Presbyterian Church – 205-372-3367
Boligee Presbyterian Church – 205-372-3367

Rickett, Jeffrey Scott – b Hagerstown, MD, Oct 28, 63; f Raymond E.; m Mary F. Booth; w Valerie Ann Wieder, Catonsville, MD, Dec 14, 91; chdn Samuel Jeffrey, Amanda Grace; WMDC 81-85, BA; ChTS 89-93; CTS 94-97, MDiv; O Mar 1, 98, Pot Pby; int Chapelgate P Ch, Marriottsville, MD, 95-96, astp 97-01, ascp 01; ascp Broadneck Evangelical P Ch, Arnold, MD, 01-05; op NewTown P Ch, Columbia, MD, 05-07; ascp City of Hope P Ch, Columbia, MD, 07-10; instr ChTS, 10; ascp Grace Christian Ch, Herndon, VA, 10-12; ob Dir, co-fndr Heart Song Counseling, 13-; Bible Studies for small groups: *I John, Colossians*

5293 Columbia Road, Columbia, MD 21044 – 443-995-4960   Potomac
E-mail: jeff.rickett@gmail.com
Heart Song Counseling

Ricketts, Daniel Jason – b Tacoma, WA, Oct 11, 45; f Marshall L.; m Maxine R. Cole; w Eileen Jeanette Springer, Wildwood, NJ, Jun 17, 67; chdn D. Jason Jr., Charissa Jeanette, DoriAn Marsha, Dana Jean; HighC 63-65; GlenJC 66; ClrCC 69, BA; FTS 69-71; BibTS 73, MDiv; WTS, grad wk; O Apr 76, Cov Pby (BPC); p Central Bible Ch, No Wildwood, NJ, 73-81; ob fndr, Dir Barnabas House, Wildwood, NJ, 81-96; Chap NJ ANG, 83-; hr; ss Fairfield P Ch, Fairton, NJ, 84-85; USArmy Chap officer adv course, 88; Command and General Staff course, 95; Chap LTC Ret, 95

2165 North East Boulevard, Vineland, NJ 08360 – 856-213-6750   New Jersey
E-mail: punditty45@aol.com
HR

Rico, Sam – b Minneapolis, MN, Feb 12, 77; w Wendy Chantile; chdn Tessa, Samantha, Nick, Francesca; MDiv, 03; ThM, 06; Chap USArmy, 07-; Chap Basic Course, 07; Ft. Drum, NY, 07-10; deployed Afghanistan, 09; Ft. Leonardwood, MO, 10-11; Ft. Carson, 12-14; deployed Afghanistan, 13-14; Chaplain

Rico, Sam, continued
Captains Career Course (C4), 15; Joint Base Lewis McCord, 1-2 Stryker Brigade Combat Team, 1-14th Calvary Reg, 15-; "Thirsting for God: The Levitical Inheritance Motif in the Apocalypse," *Westminster Theological Journal*, Fall 12. Vol 74, No 2

9220 Periwinkle Loop NE, Lacey, WA 98516 – 314-413-0800   Rocky Mountain
E-mail: samuel.rico.mil@mail.mil
United States Army

Riddle, John Randolph – b Burnsville, NC, Dec 14, 40; f Stanley McCormick; m Mary Irene Bailey; w Judith Ann Powell, Anderson, SC, Aug 11, 63; chdn Michael Randolph, John Paul; MHC 59-61, AA; USC 64-66, BS; CBS 73-76, MDiv; O Nov 21, 76, Cal Pby; p Union Mem P Ch, Winnsboro, SC, 76-79; op Cov Ch, Myrtle Bch, 79-80, ob ev 81-83; p Grace P Ch, Conway, SC, 83-06; hr 06

905 Hart Street, Conway, SC 29526 – 843-248-2337   Pee Dee
HR

Riddle, Julian Lee Jr. – b Raleigh, NC, Mar 16, 49; f Julian L Sr.; m Nancy H.; w Deborah L. Fowler, Raleigh, NC, Mar 29, 75; chdn Kelly Rene, Kristen Marie, Joshua Lee; CampU 67-71, BS; CBS 83-88, MDiv; L Apr 89; O Feb 91, Palm Pby; ascp Northeast P Ch, Columbia, SC, 89-96; p Surfside P Ch, Surfside Beach, SC, 96-

1590 Crooked Pine Drive, Myrtle Beach, SC 29575 – 843-215-3083   Pee Dee
E-mail: jriddle4@gmail.com
Surfside Presbyterian Church – 843-650-2020

Ridenhour, David F. – b Greenville, SC, May 30, 80; f James F., Jr.; m Carol Van Auken; w Jennifer Susan Lalewicz, Eatonton, GA, Mar 3, 07; chdn Nathaniel Franklin, Elijah David, Samantha Joy; PC 02, BA; RTSFL 08, MDiv; O Sept 28, 08, CentGA Pby; ascp Lake Oconee P Ch, Eatonton, GA, 08-13; srp Metrocrest P Ch, Carrollton, TX, 13-

7129 Sample Drive, The Colony, TX 75056 – 706-816-1646   North Texas
E-mail: david@metrocrestchurch.org
Metrocrest Presbyterian Church – 972-394-1122

Ridgeway, George A. – b Chicago, IL, Apr 12, 53; f George D.; m Adele Jusczyk; w Kathleen Jean Rieger, Williams Bay, WI, Jan 4, 75; chdn Christopher George, Erika Lynn; MarqU 75, BS; UNC 85, MA; ColGS 83, MDiv; TEDS 96, ThM; O Apr 12, 87, Wcar Pby; Chap USN, 87-06; hr 07

410 Prairie Avenue, Naperville, IL 60540 – 630-815-4262   Western Carolina
E-mail: gridge1@gmail.com
HR

Ridgway, Jeffrey – b Covina, CA, Apr 21, 71; f David; m Linda Mitchell; w Kim Saturnia, New Providence, NJ, Jun 17, 94; chdn Titus, Silas, Isaiah; JMU 93, BS; CTS 01, MDiv; L Jun 8, 02, MNY Pby; O Apr 6, 03, MNY Pby; astp Hope P Ch, Randolph, NJ, 03-09; ascp 09-18, p 18-

145 Baker Avenue, Wharton, NJ 07885-2414 – 973-366-9997   Metropolitan New York
E-mail: jeff@realhope.org
Hope Presbyterian Church – 973-895-9991

Rieger, Joshua Michael – b Tucson, AZ, May 15, 77; f Stanley August; m Susan Elaine Jackson; w Gina Lea Cates, Columbus, SC, Dec 17, 05; chdn Jackson, Riley Cates; UAZ 00, BS; RTS 10, MDiv; O Nov 14, 10, MSVal Pby; astp, int First P Ch, Jackson, MS, 10-12; mis MTW, 10-

c/o Mission to the World   Mississippi Valley
E-mail: joshandgina@gmail.com
PCA Mission to the World

MINISTERIAL DIRECTORY

Rienstra, Robert S. – b Patterson, NJ, Aug 19, 59; f Robert J.; m Marion F. Ver Hage; w Elizabeth Lynne Norton, Northampton, MA, Oct 3, 81; chdn Jacob, Anneka; RutgU 81, BA; WTS 86, MDiv; L Mar 84, NJ Pby; O Oct 86, pby of NJ, OPC; Recd PCA 99, NGA Pby; p Providence OPC, Glassboro, NJ, 86-88; p P Ch of Cape Cod OPC, Cape Cod, MA, 89-99; p Trinity P Ch, Covington, GA, 99-

250 Alcovy Circle, Covington, GA 30014 – 678-863-0455   Metro Atlanta
E-mail: rob@trinitypca.net
Trinity Presbyterian Church – 770-787-7493

Riexinger, Glen A. – Recd PCA Mar 9, 96, Phil Pby; cop Hope Ch, Moosic, PA, 96-00, wc 00-10; hr 10

295 Sampson Street, Old Forge, PA 18518 – 570-357-4543   Philadelphia
HR

Rigg, Bryan – astp Redeemer P Ch, Lynchburg, VA, 12-15; astp Mercy P Ch, Forest, VA, 15-18; ascp 18-

2036 Longwood Road, Lynchburg, VA 24503   Blue Ridge
Mercy Presbyterian Church – 434-386-7045

Riley, Donovan K. – b Washington, DC, Nov 7, 48; f Col. Frederick Frazier R; m Mary Eleanor Kenealy; w Susan Ann Thomas, Memphis, TN, May 30, 81; chdn Daniel Wilson; MempSU 75, BA; TEDS 77-81, MDiv; O Nov 18, 84, PCUSA; Recd PCA Oct 26, 91, NoTX Pby; ascp, mout/evan Highland Pk P Ch (PCUSA), Dallas, TX, 81-91; couns, admin Park Cities P Ch, Dallas, TX, 91-92, astp 92-93, wc 93-96; ss New Cov P Ch, Dallas, TX, 95-96; op Covenant P Ch Msn, Fremont, NC, 96-97, wc 97-06; ob exec dir Discipling Men, Inc, 06-

8726 Pepper Bush Lane, Germantown, TN 38139 – 901-624-8848   Covenant
E-mail: disciplingmeninc@bellsouth.net
Discipling Men, Inc

Riley, James I. Jr. – O Nov 17, 91, Palm Pby; p Lebanon P Ch, Winnsboro, SC, 91-10; hr 10

969 Newberry Road, Winnsboro, SC 29180 – 803-635-5887   Palmetto
E-mail: jriley48@truvista.net
HR

Riley, Leo – astp Coral Ridge P Ch, Ft. Lauderdale, FL, 15-18

Address Unavailable   South Florida

Ritter, Ross – b Marietta, GA, Jun 11, 79; f Victor; m Ruth; w Margaret Anne Pitts, Mar 20, 04; chdn Mary Claire, Julie Anne, Lily Kate; UGA 02, BA; WTS 09; O Feb 19, 10, OPC; ascp Covenant OPC, Reading, PA, 09-12; p Cherokee P Ch, Canton, GA, 13-

1498 Johnson Brady Road, Canton, GA 30115   Northwest Georgia
E-mail: office@cherokee-pca.org
Cherokee Presbyterian Church – 770-704-9594

Rivera, Jeremiah – O Mar 6, 16, Palm Pby; astp New Cov P Ch, Aiken, SC, 16-

715 Winged Foot Drive, Aiken, SC 29803   Palmetto
E-mail: jeremiah@ncpcaiken.org
New Covenant Presbyterian Church – 803-649-5007

Ro, Danny Chang Soo – astp Korean Central P Ch of Wash, Vienna, VA, 02-03; srp 04-12; srp Sa Rang Comm Ch, Anaheim, CA, 14-

Sa Rang Community Church – 714-772-7777   Korean Southwest Orange County

Ro, James Jinjun – b Seoul, Korea, Mar 11, 58; f Young Pal; m Hi Cha Shin; w Sung Mi Hong, Seoul, Korea, Jun 16, 87; chdn Clare Young Woo, Nathan Seung Woo; TowU 82, BA; WTS 85, MDiv; L Sept 88, DMV Pby; O Apr 2, 90, KorSE Pby; ap Emmanuel P Ch, Timonium, MD, 90-91; op Calvary P Ch, Baltimore, MD, 90-91, p 91-10; srp The Way Ch, Los Angeles, CA, 10-; trans into Korean *True Christianity*, Aradt; *Germanica Theologia*; *True Prayer*, Liech; *Introduction to the New Testament*, D. A. Carson ed

E-mail: ro9308@gmail.com Korean Southwest
The Way Church – 323-262-2002

Ro, Stephen J. – b Seoul, Aug 14, 63; f Young Pal Ro; m Hi Cha Shin; w Hyun Joo Lee, Timonium, MD, Jul 28, 90; chdn Christian, Calvin, Prosper; TowU 83-88, BS; WTS 88-91, MDiv; O Apr 6, 93, KAPC; Recd PCA 00, MNY Pby; op Living Faith Comm Ch, Flushing, NY, 00-03, p 03-

43-24 247 Street, Little Neck, NY 11363 – 718-357-4388 Metropolitan New York
E-mail: steve@lfcc.net
Living Faith Community Church – 718-428-0700

Roach, Pat Garner – b Houston, TX, Mar 2, 70; f Pat H. (d); m Joyce Elizabeth Garner (d); w Ashley Danielle, Temple, TX, Jan 11, 97; chdn Mary Ashley, Anna Claire, James David; TXA&M 88-92, BA; WTS 95-99, MDiv; L Apr 24, 99, SoTX Pby; O Aug 22, 99, SoTX Pby; campm RUF, RiceU, 99-07; chp, op Hope P Ch, Portland, OR, 07-13, p 13-14; campm RUF, coord West,14-

2427 SE Tibbetts Street, Portland, OR 97202 – 503-805-0112 Pacific Northwest
E-mail: pat.roach@yahoo.com
PCA Reformed University Fellowship

Roach, Phil – astp Christ P Ch, Nashville, TN, 04-05; astp Covenant P Ch, Nashville, TN, 06-

904 Hawthorne Court, Franklin, TN 37061 – 615-791-6014 Nashville
E-mail: philr@covenantpres.com
Covenant Presbyterian Church – 615-383-2206

Robbins, Carl – b Oklahoma City, OK, Aug 17, 59; f Gordon; m Janice Moore; w Sandy Steinberg, Oklahoma City, OK, Jan 4, 80; chdn John Patrick, James Cameron, Sarah Elizabeth (Holmes), Elizabeth Anne (d); MidSoBC 80-83, BS; CTS 92, MA; L Oct 88, Cal Pby; O Oct 25, 92, Mid-America; astp Mt Calvary P Ch, Spartanburg, SC, 87-89; astp New Cov P Ch, Anderson, SC, 89-91; chmn Anderson CS, Anderson, SC, 89-91; bd mbr Carolina Pregnancy Ctr, Spartanburg, SC, 87-90; astp Heritage P Ch, Edmond, OK, 91-93, ascp 93-95; srp Spring Meadows P Ch, Las Vegas, NV, 95-00; srp Woodruff Road P Ch, Simpsonville, SC, 00-; rm Living Waters, 96-00; bd mbr Piedmont Women's Center, 00-; rm The Presbyterian Pulpit, 02-; contr *The Auburn Avenue Theology, Pros and Cons: Debating the Federal Vision*, 03; contr *Tabletalk*

2519 Woodruff Road, Simpsonville, SC 29681 Calvary
E-mail: pastor@woodruffroad.com
Woodruff Road Presbyterian Church – 864-297-5257

Robbins, Daniel – b Seattle, WA, Jul 29, 84; f Thomas; m Candice Todd; w Bethany Reine Meeks, Seattle, WA, Nov 26, 05; chdn Elijah Forrest Goodnight, Lazarus William Wayne, Ruth Mae Reine; UW 07, BA; CTS 13, MDiv; O Oct 6, 13, PacNW Pby; astp Christ Ch Bellingham, Bellingham, WA, 13-15, ascp 15-18; ob fm Serge, 18-

Mill House, Newmachar, Aberdeen, Aberdeenshire AB21 0RD United Kingdom Pacific Northwest
E-mail: dfrobbins@gmail.com
Serge Global, Inc.
101 West Avenue, #305, Jenkintown, PA 19046

MINISTERIAL DIRECTORY

Robbins, Jerry Robert – b Petersburg, VA, Jul 17, 61; f Marvin; m Beryle Kirkland; w Jan Singletary, Pensacola, FL, Dec 28, 85; chdn Sarah Kathleen, Samuel Kirkland; CC 84, BA; JMU 85, MA; FSU 91, PhD; RTS 89, MDiv; L Jan 14, 92; O Jan 31, 93, Gr Pby; p Waynesboro P Ch, Waynesboro, MS, 92-96; srp First P Ch, Tuscumbia, AL, 96-01, wc 01-03; astp Warrington P Ch, Pensacola, FL, 03-

209 SE Baublits, Pensacola, FL 32507 – 850-455-3094   Gulf Coast
Warrington Presbyterian Church – 850-455-0301

Roberts, Aaron – O Dec 4, 16, BlRdg Pby; astp Covenant P Ch, Harrisonburg, VA, 16-

32 Southgate Court, Harrisonburg, VA 22801   Blue Ridge
E-mail: aroberts@cov-pres.org
Covenant Presbyterian Church – 540-433-3051

Roberts, Charles – Recd PCA 16, Cal Pby; p Reedy River P Ch, Conestee, SC, 16-

124 Meadowbrook Drive, Mauldin, SC 29662   Calvary
E-mail: revdrcr@gmail.com
Reedy River Presbyterian Church – 864-277-5455

Roberts, David Floyd – b Great Falls, SC, Dec 12, 46; f Floyd L; m Ruby Mae Baker; w Sandra Fern Bentley, St. Louis, MO, Jul 29, 72; chdn Heather Rene, Langdon Kyle; CCSC 66; LeeC 70, BA; CTS 75, MRE, MDiv; L 71; O 75, Ch of God; Recd PCA Apr 23, 76, TX Pby; Chap USArmy, 75-99; astp Redeemer P Ch, Evans, GA, 04-08; hr 09

1073 Cumberland Drive, Evans, GA 30809 – 706-855-1584   Savannah River
HR

Roberts, Donald A. – b Highland Park, MI, Sept 13, 56; f William Arthur; m Charlotte Nelle Moore; w Lisa Margaret Buckmiller, Colorado Springs, CO, Mar 18, 95; chdn Matthew Thomas, Ashley Marie, Caleb Michael, Grant Alan; SchoolcraftCC 76, AAS; WmTynC 82, BRE; UMI 84, MBA; NGTS 97, MDiv; O Oct 14, 01, RMtn Pby; astp Village Seven P Ch, Colorado Springs, CO, 01-08; ascp 08-

2645 Tuckerman Court, Colorado Springs, CO 80918 – 719-592-9477   Rocky Mountain
E-mail: droberts@v7pc.org
Village Seven Presbyterian Church – 719-574-6700

Roberts, George Dewey – b Cleveland, MS, Mar 21, 51; f Dillard Iverson; m Nora Alma Byrd; w Teressa Jane Ayers, Winston-Salem, NC, Feb 24, 79; chdn Samuel Davies, Kara Suzanna; BelC 73, BA; RTS 76, MDiv; WhTS 17, PhD; O Jun 16, 76, MSVal Pby; p Mount Carmel P Ch, Bailey, MS, 76-78; p Bailey P Ch, Bailey, MS, 76-80; op Beaumont, TX, 80-82; p First P Ch, Florala, AL, 82-84; exec dir MS Right to Life, 85-86; p First Ref P Ch, Minco, OK, 86-89; sc MidA Pby, 88-92; p Covenant P Ch, Fort Smith, AR, 89-91; Chap OK NatGd, 87-92; Chap Desert Storm, 90-91; Chap USAR, 92-11; p Safe Harbor P Ch, Destin, FL, 92-95; p Cornerstone P Ch, Destin, FL, 95-; exec dir Church Planting Int, Pensacola, FL, 13-

726 Vintage Circle, Destin, FL 32541-1647 – 850-654-7840   Gulf Coast
E-mail: DRob9944@aol.com
Cornerstone Presbyterian Church – 850-654-7133
Church Planting International – 850-444-9889

Roberts, James Thomas – b Highland Park, MI, May 12, 58; f William Arthur; m Charlotte Nelle Moore; w Robin Gale Nesbitt, Miami, FL, Mar 4, 89; chdn Andrew Thomas, Sarah Elizabeth; TayU 78-82, BA; CIU 93-96, MDiv; L Oct 97, Evan Pby; O Feb 8, 98, Evan Pby; ascp Westminster P Ch, Huntsville, AL, 98-05; p Westminster P Ch, Clinton, SC, 05-

56 Mansdale Drive, Clinton, SC 29325 – 864-833-4583   Calvary
E-mail: jim@westminsterpc.net
Westminster Presbyterian Church – 864-833-1275

Roberts, John Christopher – b San Diego, CA, May 12, 60; f John Mack; m Lois Beverly Lennon; w Julie Marie Paulson, Sioux Falls, SD, Jun 2, 84; chdn Johanna Marie, John Samuel Paulson, Marta Julie, Noah Edwin Omie; UIA 84, BS, 86, MA; CTS 99, MDiv; MaryvUStL 14, MEd; O Aug 13, 06, MO Pby; astp Covenant P Ch, St. Louis, MO, 06-

908 Dinard Drive, Manchester, MO 63021 – 314-229-6341   Missouri
E-mail: jroberts@cpcstl.org
Covenant Presbyterian Church – 314-432-8700

Roberts, Linleigh John – b Victoria, Australia, Feb 5, 34; f Leigh; m Verona Rozynski; w Laverne H. Roehl, New Leipzig, ND, Jul 5, 57; chdn Gwen (Westerlund), David, Jonathan, Judith (Shoemaker), Daniel; OtC 53, dipl; MBI 57, dipl; CBC 60, BA, 62, MA; CTS 67, MDiv, 80, MA, 80, ThM; L 65, Midw Pby; O Apr 71, DMV Pby (RPCES); prof CBS, 67-70; p Evangelical P Ch, Newark, DE, 71-73; p Dingley Union Ch, Australia, 73-74; pres ECBS, Melbourne, Austr, 74-81; prof WhitBC, 81-82; ip EP Ch, Colorado Springs, CO, 82-83; p Macon P Ch, Macon, MS, 83-86; p Highline Ref P Ch, Seattle, WA, 86-89; ob t Biblical Foundations Intnl, 89-; *Let Us Make Man*

2907 Nevermind Lane, Colorado Springs, CO 80917 – 719-637-9016   Pacific Northwest
E-mail: bfi4truth@juno.com
Biblical Foundations International

Roberts, Matthew Stephen – b Birmingham, AL, May 3, 79; f Eugene; m Maryln Jones; w Kathryn Ellen Moore, Pittsburgh, PA, Aug 11, 01; chdn Brianna Paige, Brooke Ellen, William Landon; UMW 01, BA; CTS 05, MDiv; O Sep 20, 08, Pot Pby;chp app Grace Fellowship Ch, Chantilly, VA, 05-08; astp Shady Grove P Ch, Derwood, MD, 08-15; op Christ Comm Ch, Germantown, MD, 09-15, p 15-

21201 Owls Nest Circle, Germantown, MD 20876 – 301-768-9700   Potomac
E-mail: matt@cccgermantown.com
Christ Community Church – 301-768-9700

Roberts, Sean Joseph Stessman – b McAllen, TX, Oct 9, 85; f Larry Joseph Stessman; m Sharon Ann Roberts; w Claire Elizabeth Kirkpatrick, Glenside, PA, Mar 17, 12; chdn Lily Grace, Isla Yoshie ; LU 03, BS; WTS 09, MDiv; O Dec 11, 11, Phil Pby; astp New Life P Ch, Glenside, PA, 11-13, ascp 13-14; p Christ the Redeemer P Ch, Portland, ME, 14-

69 Woodmont Street, Portland, ME 04102   Northern New England
E-mail: sroberts@ctrportland.org
Christ the Redeemer Presbyterian Church – 207-878-1211

Robertson, Benjamin – campm RUF, CWM, 06-

102 Black Oak Drive, Williamsburg, VA 23185 – 757-645-8058   Tidewater
E-mail: brobertson@ruf.org
PCA Reformed University Fellowship

Robertson, Don Wayne – b Petersburg, VA, Jan 25, 68; f Don Wayne Sr.; m Brenda Faye Vest; w Cathy Lee Weeks, Richmond, VA, May 13, 89; chdn Micah Wayne; CC 87-90, BA; CTS 90-94, MDiv; L Jul 18, 95; O Oct 17, 95, MO Pby; ydir Good Shepherd P Ch, 90-91; Sunshine Mission, 93-95; ob astp First CRC, 95-98; p Grandcote Ref P Ch, Coulterville, IL, 98-02; srp Faith Comm Ch, Pearland, TX, 02-; cert EE teacher/trainer; *The Christian Sabbath*

1010 North Sunset, Pearland, TX 77581   Houston Metro
E-mail: drob281@sbcglobal.net
Faith Community Church – 281-997-3660

Robertson, J. Stephen – b Jackson, MS, Feb 22, 74; f John William; m Ann Winters McLean; w Amy Elizabeth Hancock, Augusta, GA, Aug 3, 96; chdn Joseph Ransom, Mary Elizabeth, John Anthony; VandU 96, BA; CTS 06, MDiv; O Apr 1, 07, Nash Pby; mis MTW, 07-; p Iglesia Cristo Rey Eterno, 10-15; reg council coord MTW, 16-18; int dir MTW, 18-

Avenida Borgoño 19700, #131, Concón 2510021 CHILE – 615-916-7519   Nashville
E-mail: steve.robertson@mtw.org
PCA Mission to the World

Robertson, John William – b Los Angeles, CA, Nov 18, 43; f Charles Ray R; m Margaret Stephen; w (1) (dv), (2) Ann McLean, Meridian, MS, Aug 28, 71; chdn Marianna McLean (Quinn), John Stephen, David William, Benjamin Donald; UMS 65, BA, 67, MBA; RTS 74, MDiv; O Sept 15, 74, War Pby; ap Carrollton Ch, New Orleans, LA, 72-73; srp Riverwood P Ch, Tuscaloosa, AL, 74-98; admin AC, 98-

3510 Miller Farms Lane, Duluth, GA 30096 – 770-416-0210   Warrior
E-mail: jrobertson@pcanet.org
PCA Administrative Committee – 678-825-1000

Robertson, Mark Allen – b Washington Court House, OH, Mar 21, 82; OHSU 08, BA; CTS 12, MDiv; O Dec 2, 12, MO Pby; moy, mfam Old Orchard Ch, Webster Groves, MO, 11-12; ascp 12-15; astp Harvest P Ch, Medina, OH, 15-; op The Heights P Ch, Shaker Heights, OH, 16-

3609 Glencairn Road, Shaker Heights, OH 44122   Ohio
E-mail: mark.robertson@harvestpca.com
Harvest Presbyterian Church – 330-723-0770
The Heights Presbyterian Church – 314-707-6050

Robertson, Owen Palmer – b Jackson, MS, Aug 31, 37; f John Westbrook R; m Bess Kincannon; w (1) Julia Ruffin (d); (2) Joanna Reilly, Dec 3, 96; chdn Jane Kincannon, Virginia Buchanan, Gwenette Orr, John Murray, David Elliot, Daniel Isaac; BelC 59, BA; WTS 62, BD; UTSVA 66, ThM, ThD; O Jun 13, 65, SMS Pby; p First P Ch, Picayune, MS, 65-67; assoc prof RTS, 67-71; assoc prof WTS, 71-80; prof CTS, 80-85; p Immanuel Ch, West Chester, PA, 78-80; ascp Memorial P Ch, St. Louis, MO, 83-85; p Wallace P Ch, Hyattsville, MD, 85-92; ob prof African Bible College, Malawi, 92-03; ob prof KTS, 95-02; ob Dir, prin African Bible University, Uganda, 03-; contr *Toward A Theology for the Future*; *New Perspectives on Evangelical Theology*; *The Christ of the Covenants*; *The Power of God Unto Salvation*; *Covenants: God's Way with His People*; Nahum, Habakkuk, and Zephaniah in *The New International Commentary on the Old Testament*; *Jonah: A Study in Compassion*; *The Final Word*; *Psalms in Congregational Celebration*; *Prophet of the Coming Day of the Lord (Joel)*; *Understanding the Land of the Bible*; *The Israel of God: Yesterday, Today, and Tomorrow*; *Coming Home to God*; *The Christ of the Prophets*; *The Genesis of Sex*; *God's People in the Wilderness: The Church in Hebrews*; *Sampler from 'A Way to Pray'*; *A Way to Pray*

PO Box 103, Clinton, MS 39060 – 601-922-1962   Potomac
E-mail: opalmerrobertson@gmail.com
African Bible University
PO Box 71242, Kampala, Uganda – 011-256-414-201-037

Robertstad, Arnold John – b Madison, WI, Jun 3, 49; f Gordon W; m Janice M. Lowe; w Edie Coldwell, Dallas, TX, Jun 6, 70; chdn Samuel Gordon, Peter Charles, Janice Michele, Lauren Bethany, John David, Karen Grace, Thomas Arnold; SDSU 67-68; UHou 71, BA; ETXSU 78; DTS 76, ThM; O Nov 81, TX Pby; ap Casa Linda Ch, Dallas, TX, 81-83; p Lakewood P Ch, Dallas, TX, 84-; ed *The Psalter of Lakewood Presbyterian Church*, 17

9322 Forest Hills Boulevard, Dallas, TX 75218-3633 – 214-240-7399   North Texas
E-mail: arnrob@prodigy.net
Lakewood Presbyterian Church – 214-321-2864

Robfogel, William Allen – b Cincinnati, OH, Dec 31, 43; f Charles A; m Thelma Idle; w Edna Wiebe (d), Oct 20, 84; MDJC 68, AA; BelC 71, BA; RTS 76, MDiv; L 75; O 76, 2nd Pby (ARP); p Sandy Plains ARP Ch, 76-80; admin Neely's Creek ARP Ch, 81; mis SIMA, Nigeria, 82-85; mis MTW, Nigeria, 85-03; ob mis SIM USA; hr 10

915 Ivory Coast Street, Sebring, FL 33875 – 863-593-3345   Fellowship
E-mail: wrobfogel@earthlink.net
HR

Robinson, David Wesley – b Chester, PA, Jun 15, 38; f Wesley; m Mabel Atkinson; w Elaine Meeuwsen, Hazelwood, MO, Sept 4, 64; chdn Joanita Elaine (Deen); TempU 59; CC 70, BA; CTS 71, MDiv; L Jan 73; O Jul 73, Midw Pby (RPCES); p Hanna City P Ch, Hanna City, IL, 71-79; p Limestone RP Ch, Hanna Cty, IL, 71-79; p Westminster P Ch, Vincennes, IN, 79-86; ip Westminster P Ch, Atlanta, GA, 91-92, astp 92-93, wc 93; ss Old Peachtree P Ch, Duluth, GA, 94-95; ip Dayspring P Ch, Forsyth, GA, 96; astp Covenant P Ch, Fayetteville, GA, 97-00; ob p St. Johns United Evang. Ch (Ind), Rochester, PA, 01-05; hr 05

2417 Chandawood Circle, Pelham, AL 35104   Ascension
E-mail: davidjo3@earthlink.net
HR

Robinson, Keith – O Oct 10, Pac Pby; astp City-Wide Redeemer P Msn, North Las Vegas, NV, 10-12; op City-Wide Redeemer P Ch - South Valley, Las Vegas, NV, 12-14; min at large, Memorial P Ch, St. Louis, MO, 14-17; astp 17-

26 North Boyle, St. Louis, MO 63108   Missouri
E-mail: keith.robinson@memorialpca.org
Memorial Presbyterian Church – 314-721-0943

Robinson, Kenneth Grant – b Charleston, WV, Nov 12, 42; f Bernard C.; m Dorothy G. Moore; chdn Tammy Lynn, Jennifer Leigh, Cynthia Jo; MorHarC 72-74; BelC 74-76, BA; RTS 76-79, MDiv; O Sept 3, 79, Westm Pby; p King Mem P Ch, Bristol, VA, 79-81; p Lippincott Ch, Bristol, VA, 79-81; Tamassee DAR School, Tamassee, SC, 81-82; ss Pliny P Ch, Pliny, WV, 82-85; Chap PalmHC, 85-88; rep MERF, 88-89; ap Trinity P Ch, New Martinsville, WV, 89-90; p Faith Ref P Ch, Fairmont, WV, 90-99; op Christ Comm Ch, Fairmont, WV, 99-01, p 01-02; hr

3504 Labelle Street, Charleston, WV 25312 – 304-363-8933   New River
HR

Robinson, Mark – astp Redeemer P Ch of New York, New York, NY, 07-09; ob p 12-15

7413 Penn Avenue, Pittsburgh, PA 15208   Metropolitan New York
E-mail: merobinaa@msn.com

Robinson, Thomas – Recd PCA Jul 24, 16, Ecar Pby; Chap USArmy, 16-

137 Frizell Street, Ft. Leavenwood, MO 65473 – 314-681-3271   Eastern Carolina
E-mail: Revtcr@gmail.com
United States Army

Robison, Michael – O May 25, 14, SNE Pby; astp Presbyterian Ch of Manchester, Manchester, CT, 14-

182 Boulder Road, Manchester, CT 06040   Southern New England
E-mail: mrobison@manchesterpca.org
Presbyterian Church of Manchester – 860-643-0906

Robles, Ramon – astp Harbor P Ch - Chula Vista, Chula Vista, CA, 06-10; wc 10-

Address Unavailable   South Coast

Robson, Jonathan – astp Walnut Creek P Ch, Gahanna, OH, 06-08; ascp 08-12; p CenterPoint Ch, Tallahassee, FL, 12- 18; ascp Walnut Creek P Ch, Gahanna, OH, 18-

E-mail: jrobson@wcpc.org   Columbus Metro
Walnut Creek Presbyterian Church – 614-337-9200

Robson, William Bradford – O Feb 22, 15, Cov Pby; astp Independent P Ch, Memphis, TN, 15-

4738 Walnut Grove Road, Memphis, TN 38117 – 901-833-2424   Covenant
E-mail: brobson@indepres.org
Independent Presbyterian Church – 901-685-8206

Rodriguez, Carlos H. – b Alexandria, VA, Jan 18, 71; w Leigh Ellen; chdn Mark, Will, Daniel, Maria; UVA, BA; RTSDC, MDiv; p Redeemer P Ch, Virginia Beach, VA, 11-15, p 15-

873 Old Cutler Road, Virginia Beach, VA 23454 – 757-761-4024   Tidewater
E-mail: carlos@redeemervb.com
Redeemer Presbyterian Church – 757-689-7488

Rodriguez, Charles Quintard Jr. – b Pinehurst, NC, Dec 2, 44; f Charles Q.; m Mary Helen Planchard; w Paula Beth Pennington, Ruston, LA, Mar 5, 76; chdn Laura Beth, LaelAnne, Lola Christine; LATU 72, BA, 76, MA; CTS 84, MDiv; L Sept 84, Siouxl Pby; O Sept 85, LA Pby; p First P Ch, Oakdale, LA, 85-87; ob Chap Fed Detention Ctr, Oakdale, LA, 86-87; mgr RTS Bookstore, Jackson, MS; p Mount Carmel P Ch, Bailey, MS, 91-14; hr 14; owner, Fortress Book Svc; "Understanding the City," *PCA Messenger* Mar, 88

1607 Tanglewood Drive, Clinton, MS 39056-3649 – 601-924-9471   Mississippi Valley
HR

Rodriguez, Demetrio Jr. – b Puerto Rico, Apr 28, 45; f Demetrio Sr.; m Rosa Ruiz; w Dolohiram, Puerto Rico, Dec 17, 61; IAU/UCA, BA; ERS of PR; WTS 97, DMin; O Apr 85, CRC; ev MNA, NY/NJ, Hispanic, 92-; *Teaching for Reconciliation - A Curriculum on Urban Mission Geared to a Non-formal Training Program for the Enabling of Adult Hispanics*; *Por Quien Murio Cristo?*

E-mail: demetriopr@hotmail.com   Metropolitan New York
PCA Mission to North America

Rodriguez, Samuel – O May 7, 10, NoTX Pby; astp Beal Heights P Ch, Lawton, OK, 10; p Mt. Carmoel OPC, Somerset, NJ, 11-13; p First Ref P Ch, Minco, OK, 14-

PO Box 156, Minco, OK 73059   Hills and Plains
E-mail: rodriguezsam6@gmail.com
First Reformed Presbyterian Church – 405-352-4966

Roessler, Gustave Mark – b Memphis, TN, Dec 28, 48; f Gustave T.; m Eleanor Ham; UNC 66-70, BA; UPA 71-74, MBA; WTS 75-77, MAR; RTS 78-79, MDiv; O Aug 26, 79, SFL Pby; mout/evan Kendall P Ch, Miami, FL, 79-81; ap Coral Ridge P Ch, Ft. Lauderdale, FL, 81-90; ascp Briarwood P Ch, Birmingham, AL, 90-94; op Catalina Foothills Ch, Tucson, AZ, 94-96, srp 96-15; hr 15

5920 East Territory Drive, Tucson, AZ 85750 – 520-529-4785   Southwest
HR

Roff, Lawrence Charles – b St Louis, MO, Jun 4, 46; f Norman Charles (d); m Lorene Oleta Goddard (d); w Betty Jane Elliott, Miami, FL, Jun 21, 68; chdn Elliott Lovell, Jennifer Elizabeth (Landreth); BelC 68, BMus; RTS 72, MDiv; PTS 77-78, ThM; WChC 80; WTS 79-81, DMin; PSCE 85-86; O Jun 18, 72, St. And Pby; p Marks P Ch, Marks, MS, 72-73; medu Kendall P Ch, Miami, FL, 73-76; ss Second P Ch,

Roff, Lawrence Charles, continued
Greenville, SC, 76; p Fairfield P Ch, Fairton, NJ, 77-84; p West Hopewell P Ch, Hopewell, VA, 84-88; ascp Key Biscayne P Ch, Key Biscayne, FL, 88-92; adj prof KTS, 91-00; p Covenant P Ch, Steubenville, OH, 92-00; prof KTS, 00-04; ss Cornerstone P Ch, Palm Beach Gardens, FL, 00-01; astp Coral Ridge P Ch, Ft. Lauderdale, FL, 00-04; ascp Lake Osborne Continuing P Ch, Lake Worth, FL, 04-09; ob adj prof KTS, 04-07; srp First P Ch, Schenectady, NY, 09-16; Chap Quarryville P Ret Comm 16-; *The Fairfield Presbyterians: Puritanism in West Jersey from 1680*; *Let Us Sing: The Hymnody of the Christian Church*; ed *Trinity Hymnal*; contr *Leadership Handbooks of Practical Theology*; contr *Complete Library of Christian Worship*

548 Park Avenue, Quarryville, PA 17566 – 717-847-3624   Susquehanna Valley
E-mail: presrevroff@aol.com
Quarryville Presbyterian Retirement Community – 717-786-7321
625 Robert Fulton Highway, Quarryville, PA 17566

Rogers, Brad – w Rachel Meadows; chdn Addie, Andrew, Anna Cate; O Jan 30, 05, OHVal Pby; campm RUF, 05-11; astp Redeemer P Ch, Raleigh, NC, 11-12, ascp 12-

5321 Back Sail Court, Raleigh, NC 27613 – 859-229-4339   Eastern Carolina
E-mail: brad@redeemerpca.net
Redeemer Presbyterian Church – 919-518-2370

Rogers, Christopher J. – campm RUM, MercU, 07-13 astp Ivy Creek Ch, Lawrenceville, GA, 13-16; astp Restoration P Ch, Hoschton, GA, 16-

2335 Hamilton Parc Lane, Buford, GA 30519 – 478-361-0507   Georgia Foothills
E-mail: brogers@restpres.org
Restoration Presbyterian Church – 770-945-7800

Rogers, Daniel – ascp Christ The King P Ch, Cambridge, MA, 08-18; p Christ the King Dorchester, Dorchester, MA, 08-18

22 Upland Avenue, Dorchester, MA 02124   Southern New England

Rogers, David Jeffrey – b Cuba City, WI, May 18, 66; f David; m Ruth Mohlman; w Kelly Ann Koterman, Menomonee Falls, WI, Oct 20, 90; chdn Tianna Marie, Haley Cherith, Celine Elizabeth, Josiah David Fredner, Liliana Grace; MATC 87, AD; UWM 96, BA; CTS 99, MDiv; L 99, NoIL Pby; O Oct 22, 99, GrLks Pby; op Faith Comm Ch, LaPorte, IN, 99-06; ascp Evangelical P Ch, Cape Coral, FL, 06-10; p Town North P Ch, Richardson, TX, 10-

2128 Wheaton Drive, Richardson, TX 75081 – 214-930-1119   North Texas
E-mail: david.rogers@tnpc.org
Town North Presbyterian Church – 972-235-1886

Rogers, Kevin – op Redeemer Comm Ch, Moncton, NB, 11-

24 Devonshire Court, Moncton, NB E1E 2M7 – 506-386-1135   Eastern Canada
E-mail: info@redeemercommunitychurch.ca
Redeemer Community Church – 506-386-1135

Rogers, Michael Allen – b Buffalo, NY, Jun 20, 49; w Carol, Williamsville, NY, May 31, 69; chdn Evelyn, Paul, Daniel, Benjamin; HougC 70, BA; GCTS 73, MTS, 74, ThM; WTS 88, DMin; O Sept 15, 74, WNY Pby (UPCUSA); Recd PCA 80; p Worthington Ch, PA, 74-76; p Hillcrest Ch, Monroeville, PA, 76-77; ap Randall Mem. Ch (Ind), Williamsville, NY, 77-80; op, p Church of the Savior (PCA), Williamsville, NY, 80-88; srp Valley P Ch, Lutherville, MD, 88-94; srp Westminster P Ch, Lancaster, PA, 94-; trustee CTS 01-02; trustee WTS 03-18; *The Covenant of Grace and Baptism*, 10; *What Happens After I Die?* 13

101 Grouse Avenue, Lititz, PA 17543   Susquehanna Valley
E-mail: michaelcarolrogers@gmail.com
Westminster Presbyterian Church – 717-569-2151

Rogland, Edward Alan – b Kingsville, TX, Feb 9, 74; f Robert; m Sharon Minshull; w Mariah Meadow Moncecchi, Cheyenne, WY, Aug 8, 09; chdn Abigail Rose, Caleb Edward; UW 97, BA; CTS 12, MDiv, 13, MAC; O Oct 27, 12, MO Pby; Chap MO ARNG, 13-15; Chap Int St. Louis VAMC (CPE), 13-14; Chap Res St. Louis VAMC (CPE), 14-15; Chap Butler VA Healthcare, 15-; Chap PA ARNG, 15-

105 Fulton Drive, Valencia, PA 16059 – 314-780-3549   Missouri
E-mail: edward.rogland@gmail.com
Pennsylvania Army National Guard

Rogland, Max Frederick – b Tacoma, WA, Oct 9, 68; f Robert; m Sharon Minshull; w Lara Jay Van Dooren, Tacoma, WA, Aug 30, 92; chdn Chalmers Theophilus, Elias Peregrin, Latimer Gilchrist, Solveig Marguerite; UW 86-91, BA, 86-91, BMus; CTS 93-96, MDiv; ULeiden 96-01, PhD; L Nov 15, 01, SiouxI Pby; O Feb 10, 02, SiouxI Pby; p Trinity P Ch, Rochester, MN, 01-07; ob asst prof ErskTS, 07-10; ob assoc prof ErskTS, 10-; p Rose Hill P Ch, Columbia, SC, 13-

937 Riverview Drive, West Columbia, SC 29169-6937 – 803-374-7089   Palmetto
E-mail: rogland@erskine.edu
Erskine Theological Seminary
Rose Hill Presbyterian Church – 803-771-6775

Roldan, William – O Aug 10, 97, SWFL Pby; op Iglesia Berea Msn, Winter Haven, FL, 97-09; p 09-13, hr 13; ss Berea P Msn, Winter Haven, FL, 15-16

1942 Peddlers Pond Boulevard, Lake Wales, FL 33859-5425 – 863-589-5957 S   Southwest Florida
E-mail: pastorbillroldan@yahoo.com
HR

Roley, Scott – b Alexandria, VA, Jan 29, 52; f Robert; m Joan Rea; w Linda Kendall, Flint, MI, Nov 1, 74; chdn Michelle, Matthew, Emily, Jeffrey, Samuel; DePU 70; SArU 73-74; BannockburnC 06, BA; CTS 94; WTS 07; L Mar 93; O Feb 6, 94, TNVal Pby; ydir Christ Comm Ch, Franklin, TN, 89-94, ascp 94-06; ip 06-07; srp 07-11; wc 11-; contemporary Christian music min, 74-89, writing, performing, rec, producing, publ; contr devotional *Morning Light* (with Steve Green); *God's Neighborhood,* IVP; *Hard Bargain; The Will Of The Nation,* Safe House Publishing

2504 Buena Vista Pike, Nashville, TN 37218 – 615-591-1182   Nashville
E-mail: scott@scottroley.com

Rollins, John H. Jr. – b Mullens, WV, Nov 11, 53; f John H Sr.; m Winnie Ruth Mullens; w Kristine Hoagland, Chillicothe, OH, Oct 27, 79; chdn Kara Melissa, Joel Michael, James Ethan, Jothan Daniel, Chloe Elizabeth; WVTech 71-74, BS; GrTS 76-81, MDiv; L Jan 88, NoIL Pby; O Jan 12, 92, GrLks Pby; Cornerstone Bible Ch, Evanston, IL, 82-87; astp Tyrone Cov P Ch, Fenton, MI, 91-93, wc 93-97; p Covenant P Ch, Nitro, WV, 98-

111 Teays Medows, Scott Depot, WV 25560 – 304-757-7319   New River
E-mail: covenantpc@juno.com
Covenant Presbyterian Church – 304-755-2992

Rollman, Marc Jeffrey – b Alexandria, VA, May 4, 68; f John Robert; m Janet Marilyn Williams; w Michelle Louise Del Bene, Columbia, MD, Jan 19, 91; chdn Leila Maria, Hudson Marcus, Xavier Joshua, Austin Jack, Jonah Reinaldo; UMD 90, BA; ChTS 00, MDiv; L Nov 13, 99, Pot Pby; O Jan 20, 01, MNY Pby; astp Comunidade Crista Presbiteriana, Newark, NJ, 01-04; astp Knowlton P Ch, Columbia, NJ, 10-12; wc 12-

937 Toliver Lake Road, Manchester, TN 37355   Metropolitan New York
E-mail: mrollman@msn.com

Rollo, Taylor – ascp Grace Cov P Ch, Blacksburg, VA, 15-

2101 Shadow Lake Road, Blacksburg, VA 24060   Blue Ridge
E-mail: taylor@gracecovenantpca.org
Grace Covenant Presbyterian Church – 540-552-3364

Romaine, Blanchard DeBaun III – b Glen Ridge, NJ, Jan 31, 44; f Blanchard D. Jr; m Margaret Gaillard; w Barbara Blair, Philadelphia, PA, Jun 26, 71; CBC 65, BA; NyC 67-, BS; REpS 70, MDiv; L Jun 70; O Mar 71, Monm Pby (PCUSA); p Oak Grove UP Ch, Portersville, PA, 71-83; ob Dir Camp Sherman Acres, New Castle, PA, 83-98; mgr City Rescue Mission, New Castle, PA, 98-03; hr 06

220 East Englewood Avenue, New Castle, PA 16105 – 724-656-0360   Ascension
E-mail: bromaine3@gmail.com
HR

Romaine, James Gaillard – b Glen Ridge, NJ, Jul 26, 45; f Blanchard D.; m Margret Gaillard; w Karan Koskamp, Ocean City, NJ, Aug 26, 67; chdn James G. Jr., Kathryn Elizabeth, Jonathan Marc; CBC 67, BA; REpS 70, BD, 84, MDiv; CBS 93, DMin; L Oct 10, 70, NoE Pby; O Aug 71, NJ Pby (RPCES);mis TEAM, Istanbul, Turkey, 71-92; ob Intl Friendship House, 92-93; ZIMS, 93-06; Dir Central Asian Study Center, 95-00; adj prof Kazak Evan Christ Sem, 99-; mis International 06-

201 East 18th Street, Apt. 3D, Brooklyn, NY 11226   Metropolitan New York
e-mail: drjimromaine@gmail.com

Roop, Gary Nelson – b Davenport, IA, Apr 23, 50; f George Nelson Jr.; m Dorothy Amelia; w C. Melissa Brackett, Chattanooga, TN, Mar 25, 78; chdn Joshua David, Laura Elizabeth, Gregory Nelson; IAWC 68-72, BA; CBS 76-82, MDiv; O Aug 84, TNVal Pby; dean CBC, 78-84; p Brainerd Hills P Ch, Chattanooga, TN, 84-

9718 Rookwood Circle, Ooltewah, TN 37363-1055 – 423-892-7259   Tennessee Valley
E-mail: pastor@bhpca.org
Brainerd Hills Presbyterian Church – 423-892-5308

Ropp, John Conway Jr. – b Columbia, SC, Mar 20, 49; f John Conway; m Sarah Wilson Beaty; w Linda Lorraine Gaskin, Columbia, SC, Apr 3, 71; chdn Sarah Elizabeth, John Conway III, Emily Lorraine; ErskC 71, BA; RTS 74, MDiv; FulTS, grad wk; RTSNC 97-99, grad wk; O Aug 11, 74, Pdmnt Pby, PCUS; p Honea Path Ch, SC, 74-77; op Westminster P Ch, Sumter, SC, 77-79, srp 80-00; Chap USAFR, Shaw AFB, SC, 79-91, 00-08; Chap USAFR, Langley AFB, VA, 92-95; Chap USAFR, Bolling AFB, Washington, DC, 96-99; p Trinity P Ch, Orangeburg, SC, 00-11; res chap Palmetto Health Hosp, Columbia, SC (CPE), 11-12; astp Northeast P Ch, Columbia, SC, 13-

127 Belleclave Road, Columbia, SC 29223 – 803-764-0120   Palmetto
E-mail: johnropp71@gmail.com
Northeast Presbyterian Church – 803-788-5298

Rosander, Douglas Edward – b Philadelphia, PA, Feb 10, 54; f Norman; m Dorothy Josephson; w Crystal Haag, Havertown, PA, Jun 4, 77; chdn Kyle, Kimberly; PhilCB 72-76, BS; WCBS 78-80, MA; TempUGS 81-82; EBapTS 88; PTS 88; Duke DivS 98-99, ThM; O Jul 85, Conroe Bible Ch; Recd PCA Sept 88; t ODCA, Ft. Washington, PA, 80-83; DCE Rhawhurst Ch (PCUSA), Phila, PA, 83-85; ap Conroe Bible Ch, Conroe, TX, 85-87; ip Albion Bible Ch, Albion, NJ, 87-89; Chap USN, 1st Mar Aircraft Wing, Okinawa, 89-92; Chap USN, USS SOUTH CAROLINA, Norfolk, 92-95; Chap USN, 2d Mar Div, Camp Lejeune, NC, 95-97; Chap USN, CVW THREE, NAS Oceana, VA, 97-98; stu Duke Divinity School, 98-99; Chap USN, NAS Rota, Spain, 99-02; Chap USN, USS KEARSARGE, Norfolk, VA, 02-04; Chap USN Naval Chap Sch, Newport, RI, 04-07; Chap USN, NAF Atsugi, Japan, 07-10; Chap USN, NS Newport, RI, 10-11; Chap USN, US Naval War College, Newport, RI, 11- 16; USNavy ret

47 Island Drive, Middletown, RI 02842 – 401-572-0957   Philadelphia

MINISTERIAL DIRECTORY 543

Rosato, Vincent Anthony – b Birmingham, AL, Aug 10, 42; f Anthony V.; m Mary Jo Donze; w Mary Virginia Torian, Birmingham, AL, Jan 6, 64; chdn Leanne, Mary Jo (Lammert); SEBC 79, BA; BhamTS 89, MDiv; L Apr 15, 87, SEAL Pby; O Nov 15, 87, SEAL Pby; p Providence P Ch, Montgomery, AL, 87-90; p Friendship P Ch, Hope Hull, AL, 87-14; ss Pea River P Ch, Clio, AL, 14; ss Pleasant View P Ch, Clayton, AL, 14

1174 Woodbridge Drive, Montgomery, AL 36116 – 334-284-5391   Southeast Alabama

Rose, Daniel J. – op High Desert Ch (PCA), Albuquerque, NM, 11-

8429 Manuel Cia Place NE, Albuquerque, NM 87122 – 505-821-8314   Southwest
E-mail: revdanieljrose@gmail.com
High Desert Church (PCA) – 505-697-8163

Ross, Michael Frederick – b Columbus, OH, Apr 1, 49; f Robert F.; m Margie Ann; w Jane G. Virden, Jackson, MS, Jul 29, 78; chdn Joanna H., Abigail V., Nathan Gray, Aaron R.; OHSU 67-71, BS; MUOH 73-74, MBA; CBS 79-82, MDiv; RTS 97, DMin; L Jul 82; O Nov 82, Cal Pby; op Surfside P Ch, Surfside Beach, SC, 82-92; srp Trinity P Ch, Jackson, MS, 92-06; srp Christ Covenant P Ch, Matthews, NC, 06-17, p em, 17-19; adj fac RTS, 04-; SJC 04-07; mod CCP, 10, 12, 14; Mod PCAGA, 12; *Preaching for Revitalization*, 05; *The Light of the Psalms*, 06; The PCA's 50 Days of Prayer devotional booklets: *God Our Refuge*, 02; *God Our Redeemer*, 03; *God Our Rejoicing*, 04; *The Parables of Jesus*, 05; *Revive Us Again*, 06; *Faith of Our Fathers*, 07; *Men, Message and Ministry*, 08; *Justice, Mercy and Truth*, 09; *The Gospel of the Kingdom: The Sermon on the Mount*, 10; *Messiah*, 11; *Generations in Community*, 12; *So Great A Salvation*, 13; *Life With God*, 14; *Love: The Third Way*, 15

1254 Millstone Square, Westerville, OH 43081 – 704-989-4740   Columbus Metro
E-mail: mfross4149@gmail.com

Rossi, Luiz Henrique – op Christ is Life P Ch, Fairfield, CT, 06-

2124 North Avenue #1, Bridgeport, CT 06606   Southern New England
Christ is Life Presbyterian Church – 203-345-3957

Rossi, Roberto – Recd PCA Jan 20, 16, ChiMet Pby; astp Crete Ch, Crete, IL, 16-18

E-mail: revrossi1973@gmail.com   Chicago Metro

Roth, Harold W. – p Bullock Creek P Ch, Sharon, SC, 08-11; wc 11-

928 Jefferson Road, Penn Hills, PA 15235 – 412-723-2551   Pittsburgh
E-mail: HRoth7@aol.com

Roth, Kenneth L. – b Victorville, CA, Apr 6, 55; w Connie Marie Thiesen, Anaheim, CA; chdn Lisa Crystalyn, Jenica Joy; CPStU 79, BS; TalTS 79-83, MDiv; RTS 92-95, ThM; L Feb 14, 94, MSVal Pby; O Jul 14, 96, LA Pby; stus Concord P Ch, Pickens, MS, 94-96; p DeRidder P Ch, DeRidder, LA, 96-05; op Grace P Ch, Sierra Vista, AZ, 05, p 05-; "The Psychology and Counseling of Richard Baxter (1615-1691)," *Journal of Psychology and Christianity* 17:1

7637 East Madera Drive, Sierra Vista, AZ 85650 – 520-803-1415   Southwest
E-mail: ps34_ate@hotmail.com
Grace Presbyterian Church – 520-458-0034

Rott, Timothy Donald – b Baltimore, MD, Feb 13, 49; f Frank Joseph; m Anna J. Cizler; w Georgette Yvonne, Baltimore, MD, May 19, 73; chdn Tiffany Anne, Shannon Elizabeth; CC 76, BA; WTS 79, MDiv; TTS 91, DMin; L Sept 78; O Jun 10, 79, MidAtl Pby; p Gethsemane P Chapel, West Grove, PA, 79-82;

Rott, Timothy Donald, continued
Chap USNRet, 83-97; srp Faggs Manor P Ch, Cochranville, PA, 97-00; ob Trinitas CS, Pensacola, 03-10; Reformed Ch of Christchurch; RefCh of NZ 11-14; ss Loxley P Ch, Loxley, AL, 15-

1405 Soundview Trail, Gulf Breeze, FL 32561 – 850-725-6839　　　　　　　　Gulf Coast
E-mail: retiredchap@bellsouth.net
Loxley Presbyterian Church – 251-964-5647

Rountree, T. David – b Augusta, GA, Nov 12, 57; f Richard C.; m Martiel Ellis; w Patti Burton, York, SC, Jul 12, 80; chdn Andrew Burton, Bethany Ann, Timothy David; CC 80, BA; RTS 83, MDiv; FulTS 96, DMin; L Nov 83; O Jan 84, Cal Pby; p Central P Ch, Kingstree, SC, 84-88; srp New Cov P Ch, Anderson, SC, 88-; *No Money Making Ministries: An Evaluation of Modern Day Fund Raising in God's Church*, 89; *Growing Your Church: Preaching First Peter*, 96; *Baptism's Beauty and Benefits*, 12

110 Benfields Ridge, Williamston, SC 29697 – 864-226-5171　　　　　　　　Calvary
E-mail: rountree@ncchurch.net
New Covenant Presbyterian Church – 864-224-8724

Routzahn, John Albert Jr. – b Frederick, MD, Dec 16, 55; f John A. Sr.; m Alma D. Stottlemyer; w Cheryl Lynn; UMD 73-77, BS; WTS 83-87, MDiv; L Oct 89; O Mar 10, 91, NoCA Pby; Chap USAR, 91-92; ev, cop Peninsula Hills P Ch, Mountain View, CA, 91-92; Chap USArmy, Ft Leonard Wood, MO, 92-95; Chap USArmy, Korea, 95-96; Chap USArmy, Savannah, GA, 97-99

Address Unavailable　　　　　　　　　　　　　　　　　　　　Northern California
E-mail: john.routzahn@us.army.mil
United States Army

Row, Robert – ascp Grace P Ch, Cookeville, TN, 10; astp First P Ch, Chattanooga, TN, 10-

308 Ault Road, Chattanooga, TN 37377　　　　　　　　　　　　　　Tennessee Valley
E-mail: robertrow@1stpresbyterian.com
First Presbyterian Church – 423-267-1206

Rowan, Peter James – b Tacoma, WA, Jan 4, 82; f Kenneth; m Nancy; w Kathryn Melise Mullins, Oct 29, 11; chdn Lillie, James; campm RUF, VCU, 10-15; p Second City Ch, Harrisburg, PA, 15-

1624 Green Street, Harrisburg, PA 17102 – 253-720-1454　　　　　　　Susquehanna Valley
E-mail: peter@secondcitychurch.org
Second City Church – 717-232-0604

Rowden, Ryan – O Nov 16, 18, EPA Pby; Chap USArmy, 18-

1240 Pennsylvania Avenue #2, Oreland, PA 19075 – 704-995-7748　　　　Eastern Pennsylvania
United States Army

Rowe, Craig Richard – b Harrisburg, PA, May 19, 47; f Ken; m Dorthy Peterson; w Sue Schenkel, Jenkintown, PA, Aug 4, 73; chdn Andrew, Stephen, Timothy, Suzanne; ElizC 69, BS; WTS 73, MDiv, 96, DMin; L 73, OPC; O Feb 25, 75, Gr Pby; int Point Loma, CA OPC, 73-74; p Magee P Ch, Magee, MS, 75-78; p Vineland, NJ OPC, 79-82; p Cheyenne, WY OPC, 82-92; couns, t Arlington Heights, IL, 93-98; p Gallatin Valley P Ch, Bozeman, MT, 98-06; ascp Trinity P Ch, Statesboro, GA, 06-14; hr 14; "Getting Christ off the Couch," *The Journal of Modern Ministry*, Vol 5, 2, 08

153 Sierra Drive, Bozeman, MT 59718 – 912-536-7568　　　　　　　　Savannah River
E-mail: craigrrowe@frontiernet.net
HR

MINISTERIAL DIRECTORY

Rowe, David – b PA, May 11, 60; f Carleton N; m Marian B.; w Awilda, New York, NY, Dec 19, 98; chdn Ethan, Olivia; Ithaca 82; WTS 01, MDiv; ob ascp Westerly Road Ch, Princeton, NJ, 04-06; op Hope P Ch, Lawrenceville, NJ, 06-

104 Bergen Street, Lawrenceville, NJ 08648 – 609-895-0511   Metropolitan New York
E-mail: drowe@hopechurch-nj.org
Hope Presbyterian Church – 609-896-9090

Rowe, Ronald C. – b Birmingham, AL, Jan 27, 61; f L. Conrad; m Ann Beverly Chancellor; w Claudia Williams Montague, Hattiesburg, MS, Dec 21, 85; chdn Timothy Montague, Daniel Christopher, Melinda Ann; AU 79-80; USM 80-83, BS; CTS 84-87; RTS 88-89, MDiv; L Oct 87, Gr Pby; O Feb 18, 90, SoTX Pby; int Woodland P Ch, Hattiesburg, MS, 87-88; op Reformed P Ch, Beaumont, TX, 89-92, p 92-99; RUM, reg coord, SW Joint Co, 00-08; astp Providence P Ch, Dallas, TX, 08-

2819 86th Street, Lubbock, TX 79423   North Texas
E-mail: ronnie.rowe@providencedallas.com
Providence Presbyterian Church – 214-270-1224

Rowlen, Chandler – astp Faith P Ch, Brookhaven, MS, 15-16; astp Trinity P Ch, Tuscaloosa, AL, 16-18

400 Magee Drive, Brookhaven, MS 39601   Warrior

Royal, Austin – O Apr 22, 18, Nash Pby; campm RUF, APeay, 18-

3484 Brookfield Drive, Clarksville, TN 37043   Nashville
PCA Reformed University Fellowship

Royes, David – w Megan; chdn Joanna, Luke, Karalyn, Micah; RTS, MDiv; O Nov 19, 17, EPA Pby; ob campm DiscipleMakers, 17-; ascp West Valley P Ch, Emmaus, PA, 18-

948 Kressler Road, Allentown, PA 18103   Eastern Pennsylvania
DiscipleMakers
West Valley Presbyterian Church – 610-421-8066

Rubino, Thomas Robert – astp Potomac Hills P Ch, Leesburg, VA, 12-15; astp Wildwood P Ch, Tallahassee, FL, 15-18

6147 Cortina Hills Way, Tallahassee, FL 32312   Gulf Coast

Ruby, Herbert Edgar III – b Baltimore, MD, Aug 5, 48; f Herbert E, Jr; m Helen Early; w Shelley Armacost, Westminster, MD, Jun 9, 68; chdn Michael, Bradley, Mark; GetC 70, BA; CTS 83, MDiv; WTS 93, DMin; L Mar 82; O Mar 83, DMV Pby; op Covenant of Grace P Ch, Reisterstown, MD, 83, srp 83-

2718 Old Westminster Pike, Finksburg, MD 21048 – 410-861-8497   Chesapeake
E-mail: hruby3@comcast.net
Covenant of Grace Presbyterian Church – 410-833-2160

Ruddell, Lawrence Steele – b Charlotte, NC, Nov 10, 51; f Joseph Preston; m Patricia Conaway; w Aylin, chdn Anna, Preston; DavC 74, BA; OHSU 76, MA; WTS 80, MAR; WTSFL 82, MDiv; UHou 89-93, PhD, 10, MBA; L Oct 82; O Nov 83, TX Pby; ap, p Westminster P Ch, Webster, TX, 83-85; ap Oaklawn P Ch, Houston, TX, 85-86; Chap USN, 86-89; astp Bay Area P Ch, Webster, TX, 89-01; Chap USNR 89-06; ascp Oaklawn P Ch, Houston, TX, 01-07; ast prof HoustBaptU, 01-09; ret USN 06; hr 07; Prof, dean fac BelUHou; "Yourself and You," *Journal of Pastoral Practice*, 77; *Business Ethics - Faith That Works*, 04, 2nd ed, 14; *rogers, da*, 18

1319 Indian Autumn Trace, Houston, TX 77062 – 281-286-3578   Houston Metro
E-mail: LRuddell@peoplepc.com
Belhaven University Houston
HR

Rug, John Alex – b Minneola, NY, Mar 20, 52; f Gerard E.; m Zeta I. Banks; w Cathy Irene Foster, Beaver, PA, May 4, 74; chdn Ana Beth, Elena Lois, Benjamin Gray, Juanita; GenC 71-74, BA; CTS 79-84, MDiv; L Jul 83; O Aug 85, MO Pby; mis MTW, Chile, 85-

c/o MTW   Missouri
E-mail: jrug@mtwsa.org
PCA Mission to the World

Ruhl, Richard Wayne – b Ft. Morgan, CO, Feb 8, 38; f David J.; m Catherine Geist; w (1) (dv) (2) Janice Lee Waller, Denver, CO, May 25, 73; chdn Nathan Scott, Elizabeth Anne; YC 57-58; ColCC 59-62, BA; DenTS 62-64; CTS 83-85; L Jan 24, 86; O Oct 4, 87, SW Pby; ap Grace P Ch, Colorado Springs, CO, 85-90; op Crossroads Comm Ch (Msn), Sedalia, CO, 90-93, wc 93-04; hr 04

982 South Dante Drive, Pueblo, CO 81007 – 719-547-0959   Rocky Mountain
E-mail: rwruhl@aol.com
HR

Ruiz Ore, Jesus de Israel – O Sept 25, 16, Pot Pby; astp Emmanuel P Ch, Arlington, VA, 16-

2500 South Walter Reed Drive, Unit C, Arlington, VA 22206   Potomac
E-mail: iruiz@emmanuelarlington.org
Emmanuel Presbyterian Church – 703-525-5605

Russ, Brian – b Wilson, NC, Jul 12, 77; f William L.; m Janet Tart; w Audrey; chdn Eowyn, Leah, Allison, William; ClemU 00, BA; RTS 05, MDiv; O May 06, Wcar Pby; astp Arden P Ch, Arden, NC, 06-16; astp Cornerstone P Ch, Huntsville, AL, 16-

108 Cannes Drive, Brownsboro, AL 35741   Providence
E-mail: brian@cornerstone-pres.org
Cornerstone Presbyterian Church – 256-489-4625

Russell, Daren Lamar – b Charlotte, NC, May 21, 62; f Charles Henry; m Mary Ruth Jones; w Tinnie Wilson, Bristol, TN, Jun 2, 84; chdn Hannah Gray, Zachary Lamar; GBibC 84, BA; CTS 90, MDiv; L Oct 90; O Feb 10, 91, Cal Pby; ap Hazelwood Ref P Ch, St. Louis, MO, 88-89; p Hopewell P Ch, Rock Hill, SC, 91-98; p Rivers Edge Bible Ch, Hopewell, VA, 98-01; p Chapel in the Gardens P Ch, Garden City, GA, 01-

91 Smith Avenue, Garden City, GA 31408   Savannah River
E-mail: darenrussell@bellsouth.net
Chapel in the Gardens Presbyterian Church – 912-964-5734

Russell, Julian Charles – b New Providence, Bahamas, Sept 18, 55; f James W. (d); m Helen Delores Neely; w Christiana Marva , New Providence, Bahamas, Jul 4, 81; chdn Andrew Julian, Jason Christian, Jamila Hadiya; CBahamas; RTS 97, MDiv; CTS 08, ThM, 13, DMin; O Oct 28, 95, Orlando Bapt Temple; Recd PCA Oct 7, 97, Cov Pby, p 84-94; p Orlando Bapt Ch, 95-97; op New Beginnings Comm Ch, Memphis, TN, 97-05, p 05-07; astp Park Cities P Ch, Dallas, TX, 07-16; mis, team ldr Bahamas, MTW, 16-

3167 Shenandoah Street, Dallas, TX 75205 – 214-678-9520   North Texas
E-mail: juefish@msn.com
PCA Mission to the World

Russell, Michael Henry – b Asheville, NC, Mar 23, 62; f Roger LeMar; m Shannon Estelle Arrowsmith; w Catherine Louise Kelly, Prattville, AL, Dec 22, 84; chdn David Michael, Stephen James, Andrew LeMar, Lauren Elizabeth; UAL 80-84, BA; WTS 87-91, MDiv; L Aug 23, 90, Evan Pby; O Oct 27, 91, CentGA Pby; staff CCC, Vancouver, BC, CAN, 84-87; astp First P Ch, Augusta, GA, 91-93; p Northside P Ch, Burlington, NC, 93-94; p Lakewood P Ch, Pell City, AL, 94-98; ss First P Ch, Russellville, AL, 02; ss First P Ch, Gadsden, AL, 09-13; wc; ob ev PEF, 16-

2324 Garland Drive, Birmingham, AL 35216 – 205-822-2706   Evangel
Presbyterian Evangelistic Fellowship – 423-573-5308

MINISTERIAL DIRECTORY 547

Rutherford, Way – campm RUF, ULouisville, 07-14; campm RUF, Baylor, 14-

11004 Trailwood Drive, Woodway, TX 76712   North Texas
E-mail: wrutherford@ruf.org
PCA Reformed University Fellowship

Rutledge, William Eugene Jr. – b El Paso, TX, Jan 19, 64; f W. E.; m Nancy Lee Johnson; w Gena Renee Rhodes, Birmingham, AL, May 12, 90; chdn Katherine Lee, William E III; UAL 86, BA; BDS 93, MDiv; L Sept 21, 93; O May 10, 94, Evan Pby; ms/sa Covenant P Ch, Birmingham, AL, 91-93; op, ev Grace Comm P Ch, Trussville, AL, 94-96, p 96-99, wc 99-01; ss Lakewood P Ch, Pell City, AL, 01-14

5144 Colonial Park Road, Birmingham, AL 35242 – 205-991-7340   Evangel

Ryan, Eric – O Jun 3, 18, GulCst Pby; astp Wildwood P Ch, Tallahassee, FL, 18-

8240 Dancing Shadow Court, Tallahassee, FL 32312   Gulf Coast
Wildwood Presbyterian Church – 850-894-1400

Ryan, James Calvin – b Rockford, IL, Jun 6, 62; f Robert; m Anna; w Sarah Bucknell, Rockford, IL, Jun 25, 89; chdn Christine, Emily, James; WheatC 83, BA; RockfordC 92, MA; PTS 91, MDiv; TEDS; O Jul 14, 91, PCUSA; Recd PCA 01, Ill Pby; p First UPC, Elyria, OH, 91-01; p Marissa P Ch, Marissa, IL, 01-

117 North Hamilton Street, Marissa, IL 62257 – 618-295-1463   Illiana
E-mail: jsryan3@frontier.com
Marissa Presbyterian Church – 618-295-2292

Ryan, Mark – astp Crossroads P Flwsp, Maplewood, MO, 11-13; prof CTS, 13-

2623 Lyle Avenue, Maplewood, MO 63143 – 314-552-1114   Missouri
E-mail: Mark.Ryan@CovenantSeminary.edu
Covenant Theological Seminary – 314-434-4044

Ryken, Philip Graham – b Eugene, OR, Sept 29, 66; f Leland Ryken; m Mary Alice Graham; w Elisabeth Kristen Maxwell, Colorado Springs, CO, Jun 6, 87; chdn Joshua Philip, Kirsten Elisabeth, James Maxwell, Kathryn Elaine, Karoline Jorena; WheatC 88, BA; WTS 92, MDiv; UOxf 95, PhD; L Sept 10, 95, Phil Pby; O Feb 4, 96, Phil Pby; ascp Tenth P Ch, Philadelphia, PA, 95-01, srp 01-10; ob pres WheatC, 10-; *Courage to Stand: Jeremiah's Battle Plan for Pagan Times*, 98; *The Heart of the Cross* (with James Boice), 99; *Thomas Boston as Preacher of the Fourfold State*, 99; *Discovering God in Stories From the Bible*, 99; *Is Jesus the Only Way?* 99; *When You Pray: Making the Lord's Prayer Your Own*, 00; *Jeremiah and Lamentations*, 01; *The Communion of Saints*, 01; *The Message of Salvation*, 01; *The Sovereignty of God's Mercy*, 01; *Jesus on Trial* (with James Boice), 02; *The Doctrines of Grace* (with James Boice), 02; *My Father's World: Meditations on Christianity and Culture*, 02; *The Prayer of Our Lord*, 02; *City on a Hill: Recovering the Biblical Pattern for the Church in the 21st Century*, 03; *What Is a True Calvinist?*, 03; *Written in Stone: The Ten Commandments and Today's Moral Crisis*, 03; *Give Praise to God* (with Ligon Duncan and Derek Thomas). 03; *Tenth Presbyterian Church of Philadelphia*, 04; *He Speaks to Me Everywhere: Meditations on Christianity and Culture*, 04; *Galatians*, 05; *Exodus*, 05; *Ryken's Bible Handbook* (with Leland Ryken), 05; *Art for God's Sake*, 06; *What Is the Christian Worldview?*, 06; *1 Timothy*, 07; *The ESV Literary Study Bible* (with Leland Ryken), 07; *The Incarnation in the Gospels, Luke*, 09; *Ecclesiastes: Why Everything Matters*, 10; *Our Triune God* (with Michael LeFebvre), 11; *1 Kings*, 11; *King Solomon and the Temptations of Money, Sex, and Power*, 11; *Justification*, 11; *Pastors in the Classics* (with Leland Ryken and Todd Wilson), 11; *Loving the Way Jesus Loves*, 12; *Liberal Arts for the Christian Life*, 12 (with Jeffry Davis); *Grace Transforming*, 12; What Is Mercy Ministry? 13 (with Noah Toly); *Kingdom, Come!* 13; *Christian Worldview: A Student's Guide*, 13; *Loving Jesus More*, 14; *Salvation by Crucifixion*, 14; *Why Everything Matters*, 15; *When Trouble Comes*, 16; *The Messiah Comes to Middle Earth*, 17; co-auth *Is God Real?* 18; *Knowing Jesus*, 18; *Who is the Holy Spirit?* 18

Office of the President, Wheaton College   Chicago Metro
501 East College Avenue, Wheaton, IL 60187
E-mail: philip.ryken@wheaton.edu
Wheaton College

Ryman, Matthew – b Minneapolis, MN, Mar 16, 78; w Hana; chdn Noah, Lydia, Hadassah, Elizabeth; SCSU 06, BA; RTSFL 09, MDiv; astp University P Ch, Orlando, FL, 10-13, srp 13-

2562 Rouse Road, Orlando, FL 32817 – 407-782-1696   Central Florida
E-mail: mryman@upc-orlando.com
University Presbyterian Church – 407-384-3300

Ryoo, Eung Yul – p Korean Central P Ch, Centreville, VA, 15-

5105 Grande Forest Court, Centreville, VA 20120   Korean Capital
E-mail: preachchrist@kcpc.org
Korean Central Presbyterian Church – 703-815-1200

Ryor, John Charles – b Battle Creek, MI, Jun 3, 65; f John E.; m Carol Mae Dollinger; w Carolyn Marie Gewecke, Washington, DC, Jul 14, 90; chdn John Nicholas, Holly Ann; WVU 84-87, BS; RTSFL 91-93, MATS; L Feb 9, 99, GulCst Pby; O Nov 14, 99, GulCst Pby; astp Wildwood P Ch, Tallahassee, FL, 99-00, ascp 00-02; op CenterPoint Ch, Tallahassee, FL, 02-07; p 07-08; srp Christ Ch of Pasadena, Pasadena, CA, 08-09; wc 10-

Address Unavailable   Pacific

Sackett, John Gordon – b Ede, The Netherlands, Dec 14, 65; f John W.; m Joyce W. Clark; w Susan Marie Collins, Towson, MD, Jun 12, 93; chdn Isabelle F., Abigail J., Laura E., William D., Samuel D.; WBC 91-94, BA; ChTS 94-95; CTS 95-98, MDiv; ILIFF 10-11, MAPSC; O Mar 7, 99, Pot Pby; ydir Timonium P Ch, Timonium, MD, 94-95; USAFR, chap cand, 96-99; int New Cov P Ch, Abingdon, MD, 98-99, ascp 99-01; Chap USAFR, 512 Air Wing, Dover AFB, 99-01; Chap USAF, 95th AW, Edwards AFB, 01-04; Chap USAF, 35th FW, Misawa AB, Japan, 04-07; Chap USAF, Ft. Warren AFB, WY, 07-11; Chap USAF, Cannon AFB, NM, 11-15; Wing Chap USAF, Vance AFB, Enid OK, 15-

1601 West Broadway, Enid, OK 73703 – 307-287-4678   Rocky Mountain
E-mail: revjohnny@live.com
United States Air Force

Sacks, Stuart David – w Marion; chdn David, Adam, Heather; BosU 63, BS; CrozS 67; FTS 67-68; SWTS 68-73, ThM, ThD; O 73, C&MA; ap Bay Ridge Comm Ch, Brooklyn, NY, 73; ap Tenth P Ch, Philadelphia, PA, 74-77; op Bryn Mawr, PA (PCA), 78-79; p Berith P Ch, Bryn Mawr, PA, 79-92, wc; hr 14; American Missionary Fellowship, 92-02; *When You Haven't Got a Prayer*; *Revealing Jesus as Messiah*; *Hebrews Through a Hebrew's Eyes*

246 Orchid Court, New Holland, PA 17557 – 610-688-7774   Philadelphia Metro West
E-mail: shmah@verizon.net
HR

Sadler, Jonathan Brent – astp Trin Ref P Msn, Germany, 07-08; p 08-11; p Grace P Ch at Jackson, Jackson, TN, 12-18

115 Maywood Drive, Jackson, TN 38305   Covenant
E-mail: bsadler.1982@gmail.com

Saenz, Hernando – astp Christ Cov Ch, Southwest Ranches, FL, 05-06; op Grace Int Ch, Lawrenceville, GA, 08-10; MNA 11-

1251 Providence Drive, Lawrenceville, GA 30045 – 678-620-1347   Georgia Foothills
E-mail: hsaenz@pcanet.org
PCA Mission to North America – 678-825-1200

Sagan, Paul S. – b Mobile, AL, May 24, 57; f Joseph S.; m Peggy Faust; w Denise Barta, Jun 29, 85; chdn Joy Marie, Anna Faye, Joseph Tucker, Christina Mae; UMS 79, BA; RTS 83, MDiv; O Mar 83; op Covenant P Ch, Fayetteville, AR, 83-85, p 85-; Chap USAR, 86-89; ARNG, 89-95; Chap Desert Storm, 91

2112 East Gentle Oaks Lane, Fayetteville, AR 72703 – 479-521-0367   Hills and Plains
E-mail: psagan@sbcglobal.net
Covenant Church – 479-442-5267

Sage, Steven – Wichita, KS, Aug 18, 71; f John; m Barbara Stamm; w Carissa Ezell, Manhattan, KS, May 15, 93; KSU 93, BS; RTS 02, MDiv; O Jun 22, 03, RMtn Pby; astp Rocky Mountain P Ch, Westminster, CO, 03-05; astp Deer Creek Community Ch, Littleton, CO, 05-08, ascp; astp Grace Redeemer Ch, Glen Rock, NJ, 18-

258 Ross Avenue, Hackensack, NJ 07601 – 720.335.0318   Metropolitan New York
E-mail: steve@graceredeemer.com
Grace Redeemer Church – 201-357-4216

Sagnibene, Gary – O Nov 13, 94, CentGA Pby; astp Covenant P Ch, Warner Robins, GA, 94-; English p - Korean P Ch, Macon GA; chap Boland Prosthetics, Warner Robins, GA; t Veritas Classical, Warner Robins, GA

2386 Gwendale Drive West, Lizella, GA 31052 – 478-250-5829   Central Georgia
E-mail: gsagnibene@netzero.net
Covenant Presbyterian Church – 478-929-4770

Salabarria, Carlos M. – b Matanzas, Cuba, Feb 9, 61; f Manuel F; m Elena Hernandez; w Mirtha Rodriguez, Miami, FL, Dec 19, 81; chdn Alejandro Nicolas, Andres Cristobal, Alberto Fe; MDCC 81, AA; FIU 83, BA; GCTS 86, MDiv; O Sept 77, SFL Pby; ap El Redentor P Ch, Miami, FL, 86-88; chp SFL Pby, 88-89; p Shenandoah P Ch, Miami, FL, 90-94, wc 94-98; astp Granada P Ch, Coral Gables, FL, 99-02; p Immanuel P Ch, Miami, FL, 02-05; astp El Redentor P Ch, Miami, FL, 06-07; p 07-

12940 SW 135th Street, Miami, FL 33186-6986 – 954-971-9852   South Florida
E-mail: salcm@aol.com
El Redentor Presbyterian Church – 305-553-7546

Salinas, Guillermo Santiago – b Mexico, D.F., Jul 25, 60; f Guillermo Salinas Sanchez; m Yolanda Padilla Mejia; w Jennie Wilson, Acapulco, MX, Jun 27, 87; chdn Sarah Grace, Amanda Elizabeth, William James, Stephanie Anne; UAGuer 85, dipl; BhamTS 86-90, MDiv, MMiss; L Jan 91; O Jan 30, 93, SoTX Pby; mis, chp MNA, 89; ev SoTX Pby, 93-; op Rios de Agua Viva (Msn), 94-95; ob ev PEF, 95-

APDO #600, ZIHUATANEJO, JRO 40880, MEXICO   South Texas
Presbyterian Evangelistic Fellowship
425 State Street, Bristol, VA 24201 – 276-591-5335

Salsedo, David – O Apr 08, ChiMet Pby; astp Covenant P Ch, Chicago, IL, 08-

1827 West Patterson Avenue #1, Chicago, IL 60613 – 209-247-3345   Chicago Metro
E-mail: dsalsedo@gmail.com
Covenant Presbyterian Church – 773-486-95

Salter, Brian – b Atlanta, GA, Nov 1, 74; f James Edward; m Christine Varnadore; w Kendra Elaine Henderson, Cedartown, GA, May 11, 02; chdn Jeb Henderson, Sutton Christine, Haddon Edward, Simeon Ryle; UGA 93-97, BEd; RTSFL 06, MDiv; O Apr 20, 07, TNVal Pby; astp Lookout Mountain P Ch, Lookout Mountain, TN, 06-11; ascp 11-

1103 Lula Lake Road, Lookout Mountain, GA 30750   Tennessee Valley
E-mail: Brian@lmpc.org
Lookout Mountain Presbyterian Church – 423-821-4528

Salyer, David – b North Platte, NE, Oct 31, 81; w Dawn, Jun 1, 02; chdn Haven, Evelyn, Jocelyn, Peregrine; CTS 10, MDiv; astp Trinity P Ch, Kearney, NE, 11, ascp 11-

1603 West 35th Street, Kearney, NE 68845   Platte Valley
E-mail: davesalyer@gmail.com
Trinity Presbyterian Church – 308-234-3142

Sampson, Donald Wayne – b Oak Park, IL, Apr 10, 60; f Wendell; m Esta Lee Mapes; w Nancy Lee Lueking, Pensacola, FL, May 7, 83; chdn Kathleen (Schoolfield), Christine; SUNYO 82, BS; CTS 00, MDiv; O Dec 2, 01, Pot Pby; chp Harvester P Ch, Springfield, VA, 01, astp 01-02; p Crossroads P Ch, Woodbridge, VA, 02-; comm PRCC, 17-

13531 Pleasant Colony Drive, Manassas, VA 20112 – 703-901-1643   Potomac
E-mail: donsampson@crossroadspca.net
Crossroads Presbyterian Church – 703-794-9431

Sanchez, Adriel – w Ysabel; O 13, SoCst Pby; astp New Life P Ch, La Mesa, CA, 13-14; op North Park P Ch, San Diego, CA, 14-

3925 Illinois Street, San Diego, CA 92104 – 619-855-7162   South Coast
E-mail: pastoradriel@northparkpres.com
North Park Presbyterian Church

Sanders, David Hart – f Rhett; m Virginia; w Linda; chdn Makaria, Charis, Hart, Asher, Raenie; WCU 94; RTSNC 07, MDiv; astp Westminster P Ch, Martinez, GA, 08-11; astp Mount Calvary P Ch, Roebuck, SC, 11-15, ascp 15-

1401 Walnut Grove Road, Roebuck, SC 29376 – 864-345-5225   Calvary
E-mail: david@mtcalvary.org
Mount Calvary Presbyterian Church – 864-576-6156

Sanders, Frank Rhett Jr. – w Ann; chdn Rhett III, Sophie (Nix), Rigsbee; UNCG, BS; RTSNC, MDiv; O Jan 03, Palm pby; ydir Northeast P Ch, Columbia, SC, 87-01, astp 02-10; op Blythewood P Ch, Blythewood, SC, 10-13; p 13-

111 Craigwood Drive, Blythewood, SC 29016 – 803-331-8547   Palmetto
E-mail: rhett@blythewoodpres.com
Blythewood Presbyterian Church – 803-786-2399

Sanders, Mike – astp Church of the Redeemer, Atlanta, GA, 12-

E-mail: mike@redeemeratlanta.org   Metro Atlanta
Church of the Redeemer – 678-298-1150

Sanders, Paul Lambert – b Columbia, SC, Mar 7, 76; f Frank Rhett, Sr.; m Virginia Townsend; w Suzanne Robinson, Hendersonville, TN, Jan 3, 98; chdn Mary Grace, Ainsley Ruth, Robinson Isaiah, Josiah Burgin, Virginia Faith; Solomon; CIU 98, BS; RTSNC 08, MDIV; O Feb 8, 09, Cal Pby; DnStu Sardinia & New Harmony Ch, 96-05; mfam, ydir Mount Cal P Ch, Roebuck, SC, 05-09, astp 09-11; srp Christ Comm Ch, Simpsonville, SC, 11-, Pres PCA IRC, 11, 17; PCA MTW, 14; PCA AC, 15; PCA MNA, 16; Cal Pby MNA, 12-, chmn 14-; Cal Pby Admin Co, 14-; Mod Cal Pby 15; Cal Pby Nom Co, 16-

121 Heritage Point Drive, Simpsonville, SC 29681 – 864-431-6688   Calvary
E-mail: paul@christcommunitychurchonline.org
Christ Community Church – 864-967-2815

Sanders, William Albert III (Tripp) – b Charlotte, NC, Apr 23, 74; f William Albert; m Diane Finlayson; w Jennifer Laine Melton, Clemson, SC, Jun 2, 01; chdn Benjamin, Luke, Elizabeth; UNC 96, BS; CTS 07, MDiv; O Jul 18, 09, PTri Pby; astp Redeemer P Ch, Winston-Salem, NC, 09-10; ascp 10-

1206 Miller Street, Winston-Salem, NC 27103 – 336-473-5785   Piedmont Triad
E-mail: tsanders@redeemerws.org
Redeemer Presbyterian Church – 336-724-2217

Sandford, Ron – Recd PCA Sept 22, 18, Wisc Pby; p Faith Ref Ch, Cedar Grove, WI, 18-

243 South 4th Street, Cedar Grove, WI 53013   Wisconsin
Faith Reformed Church

Sandhoff, Thomas W. Jr. – b Trenton, NJ, Jun 1, 42; f Thomas W; m Ruth Anna Van Marter; w Karen L. Pierce, Trenton, NJ, Jun 15, 68; chdn Jeffrey Alan, Todd Watson, Erin Leigh, Kristen Janel; UC 64, BS; DenTS 68, MDiv; O Mar 28, 69, Bapt; Recd PCA Jan 14, 95, SWFL Pby; DCR Seminole P Ch sch, Tampa, FL, 87-94; ascp Seminole P Ch, Tampa, FL, 95-02, ip 99, astp 02-03; p Grace Comm Ch, Palm Harbor, FL, 03-06; hr

4 North Bougainvillea Court, Apt A, Orange City, FL 32763 – 386-218-0229   Southwest Florida
E-mail: twatsyjr42@gmail.com
HR

Sandifer, Brian Matthew – b Montgomery Co, VA, Nov 18, 74; f Thomas Milton; m Lynette Gay Wooden; w Samara Leeann Martindale, Manassas, VA, Oct 14, 00; chdn Rachel, Roman, Ryleigh, Reston, Rebekah; VPI 97, BS; RTSDC 09, MAR; O Dec 17, 11, Pot Pby; ascp Heritage P Ch, Warrenton, VA, 11-

393 Gale Court, Warrenton, VA 20186   Potomac
E-mail: brian.sandifer@heritage-pca.org
Heritage Presbyterian Church – 540-347-4627

Sandoval, Chris – b Chicago, IL, Aug 26, 77; w Carrie Anne Jurgensen, Nov 16, 13; MIT 00, BS; WSCAL 05, MDiv; O 16, SoCst Pby, ev 16; op Servant Ch of San Diego, San Diego, CA, 16-

2859 Webster Avenue, San Diego, CA 92113 – 708-921-7014   South Coast
E-mail: casandoval77@gmail.com
Servant Church of San Diego – 619-363-1931

Sandvig, Steven Kyle – b Aberdeen, SD, Feb 26, 51; f Alfred C.; m Bette Jean Berg; w Christy Jones, Cincinnati, OH, May 9, 81; chdn Zoe, Mark Christian, Laura, John Bradford; L May 96; O Apr 13, 97, GrLks Pby; mis CCC, 73-93; astp Northwest P Ch, Dublin, OH, 93-98; astp Christ Comm Ch, Carmel, IN, 98-04, ascp 04-14; hr 14; lead dev CentIN pby

1814 North Talbott Street, Indianapolis, IN 46202 – 317-496-4269   Central Indiana
E-mail: sandvigsteve@yahoo.com
HR

Sanford, Shelton Palmer III – b Macon, GA, Feb 14, 50; f S P Jr; m Martha Hill; w Anne Burns, (d); (2) Mary Ann Crowell, Nov 13, 10; chdn Martha (McIntyre), Sara Lucille (Brazzell), Shelton Palmer IV; MerU 72, BA; RTS 78, MDiv, 85, DMin; L Jun 76, MSVal Pby; O May 28, 78, Gr Pby; p Thomson Mem P Ch, Centreville, MS, 78-80; p Faith P Ch, Brookhaven, MS, 80-85; srp Westminster P Ch, Rock Hill, SC, 85-14; hr 14

4 Phillips Lane, Greenville, SC 29605 – 803 984-6803   Fellowship
E-mail: spsanford03@gmail.com
HR

Santos, Carl – O Jun 24, 18, CanW Pby; srp New City Ch, Calgary, AB, 18-

Calgary, AB – 403-461-2763   Canada West
E-mail: carl@newcitychurch.ca
New City Church – 403-354-0525

Santos, Danillo – prof Recife, Brazil, 16-

1640 Quarry Road, Lansdale, PA 19446 – 661-400-6532   Mississippi Valley
E-mail: danilla_santos89@hotmail.com
Recife, Brazil

Sargent, Twig – w Joanna; chdn Luke, Philip, Lily, Lydia; TXTU 95, BMus; CTS 10, MDiv; O May 15, 11, MO Pby; Chap USN, Beaufort, SC, 11-

11118 Ivy Hill Drive, San Diego, CA 92131 – 314-456-7847   Missouri
E-mail: twig.sargent@gmail.com
United States Navy

Sarran, Alex – b Vénissieux, FRANCE, Apr 12, 80; f Robert; m Diana Speirs; w Suzanne Donna Foucachon, Limonest, France, Jun 1, 01; chdn Matthieu, Timothée, Étienne, Vallouise, Augustin, Violette; ULLyon 01, BA, 03, MA; FacJCal 01, ThB; O Aug 14, 18, Evan Pby; p Église Réformée Évangélique, 04-; ob chp Global Outreach

17 chemin du Caillou, Brindas, 69126 FRANCE   Evangel
E-mail: alexsarran@gmail.com
Église Réformée Évangélique

Sartelle, John Prentis – b San Diego, CA, Sept 8, 44; f Preston Orr Sr; m Mary Perry; w Janet Barnes (d), Cobb Cty, GA, Aug 6, 65; chdn Sara Jill, John Prentis Jr, Jamie Lauren Maclaren; KgC 66, MA; ColTS 69, MDiv; O Aug 10, 69, PCUS; p Covenant P Ch, Cedar Bluff, VA, 69-77; srp Independent P Ch, Memphis, TN, 77-05; srp Tates Creek P Ch, Lexington, KY, 05-12; astp Christ P Ch of Fayette Co, Somerville, TN, 12-14; ip 14-15; srp 15-; *Infant Baptism: What Christian Parents Should Know*

60 Augusta Drive, Oakland, TN 38060   Covenant
E-mail: Jpsartelle@att.net
Christ Presbyterian Church of Fayette County – 901-592-9899

Sartelle, Preston Orr Jr. – b Richlands, VA, Nov 28, 40; f P.O. Sr. ; m Mary Ellen Perry; w Mary Ellen Sproles, Ringold, GA, Jun 9, 60; chdn Vic, Mary Beth (Jennings), Cynthia (Cox), Julia Blake (Steed); HSC 59-60; KgC 60-63, BA; ColTS 63-66, MDiv; O Jul 66, PCUS; p Midway Ch, Anderson, SC, 66-70; p Kingston Ch, Conway, SC, 70-83; p Drapers Valley P Ch, Draper, VA, 83-98; mis Caribbean Christian Cent. for Deaf, 99-01; hr 01

100 Sherwood East, Wytheville, VA 24382 – 276-228-6959   Westminster
E-mail: psartelle@emgarymail.com
HR

Sartorius, Arthur – b St. Louis, MO, Oct 8, 54; w Janet, Jacksonville, FL, May 28, 94; MU 76; UFL 82, JD; RTS 07, MDiv; O 08; p Black Hills Comm Ch, Rapid City, SD, 08-

3930 Jackson Boulevard, Rapid City, SD 57702 – 605-716-6723   Siouxlands
E-mail: sportart@aol.com
Black Hills Community Church – 605-341-9090

Sauls, Christopher Scott – b Maryland, Apr 7, 68; f Herbert Rex; m Rebecca Ann Harris; w Patricia Ann Murray, St. Louis, MO, Aug 12, 95; chdn Abigail Lynn, Elizabeth Ann; FurU 90, BA; CTS 96, MDiv;

Sauls, Christopher Scott, continued
L Aug 17, 96; O Dec 1, 96, Hrtl Pby; ascp Woodland Ridge P Ch, Lenexa, 96-98; chp Lee's Summit, MO, 98; op Oak Hills P Ch, Overland Park, KS, 98-02, p 02-03; chp/p RiversideEPC, St. Louis, MO, 03-07; astp Redeemer P Ch of New York, New York, NY, 08-11; upper West Side Lead Pastor, 10-12; ascp Redeemer P Ch of NY, 11-12; srp Christ P Ch, Nashville, TN, 12-; *Jesus Outside the Lines*, 15; *Befriend*, 16, *From Weakness to Strength*, 17; *Irresistable Faith*, 19

703 Roantree Drive, Brentwood, TN 37027　　　　　　　　　　　　　　　　　　Nashville
E-mail: cssauls@gmail.com
Christ Presbyterian Church – 615-373-2311

Saunders, George Michael Sr. – b Wolfboro, NH, Jun 27, 55; f George William Jr.; m Theresa Alice Waterman; w (1) (dv) Deborah (2) Patricia Ann Straley, Winter Park, FL, Mar 8, 92; chdn George Michael Jr., Deborah JoAnne (Zayas), Joseph Adam Baucom, Jennifer Renee (Alvarez), Andrea Marie (Higgins); BerkCC 75, AA; BelC 78, BA; RTS 83, MDiv; MINTS 09, DMin, 12 PhD; L Jul 83; O Nov 13, 83, Evan Pby; p First P Ch, Enterprise, AL, 83-90, ss 90; astp Covenant P Ch, Hammond, IN, 92-97; astp Granada P Ch, Coral Gables, FL, 97-06; ob lect The Holy Land Experience, 06-08; dir A New Beginning Ministries of Grace; astp St. Andrews P Ch, Hollywood, FL, 14-15; ob ev Christian Witness to Israel, 13-15; hr 16; refp CHAIM Min, 15-; dir Village Church Bible Institute, Live Oak, FL, 17-; *God's Promise for Marriage*, 08, rev & exp, 10; *The Picture of Redemption in the Feasts of Israel*, 08, rev 15; *The Picture of Redemption in the Feasts of the Messiah*, 17

PO Box 4124, Dowling Park, FL 32064　　　　　　　　　　　　　　　　　　South Florida
HR

Saunders, Jonathan – Cincinnati, OH, Feb 19, 82; f David; m Laura Gleason; w Vanessa Yvonne, Brighton, MI, Jun 12, 04; chdn Lillian, Eleanor, Henry, Marion; MISU 04, BA; CalvS 15, MDiv; O Jan 17, 16, GrLks Pby; astp University Ref Ch, East Lansing, MI, 16-17; astp Redeemer P Ch Detroit, Detroit, MI, 17-

2545 West Boston Boulevard, Detroit, MI 48206　　　　　　　　　　　　　　Great Lakes
Redeemer Presbyterian Church Detroit – 313-539-5979

Saunders, Stephen Jeffrey – O Mar 13, 16, Cov Pby; mis MTW, 16-

397 Roseland Place, Memphis, TN 38111　　　　　　　　　　　　　　　　　　Covenant
E-mail: jsaunders86@gmail.com
PCA Mission to the World

Savage, Tom J. – w Wendy; chdn Jeannette, Garrison, Nathaniel; CTS, MDiv, MA; UTXA, MA; O Jul 03, NoCA Pby; astp Valley Springs P Ch, Roseville, CA, 03-06, ascp 06-07; srp Ridge P Ch, Paradise, CA, 07-16; wc 16-

615 Pearson Road, Paradise, CA 95969 – 530-327-7194　　　　　　　　　Northern California
E-mail: tomridgepc@gmail.com

Saville, David A. – w Mary Christine; chdn Kara Elizabeth, Mark David, John Robert (Jack), Caleb James; UVA 97, BA; RTSFL 01, MDiv, 01, MA; astp Grace Comm Ch, Charlottesville, VA, 02-05, ascp 05-12; ascp Westtown Ch, Tampa, FL, 13-16; ob 17-

15007 Arbor Hollow Drive, Odessa, FL 33556　　　　　　　　　　　　　　Southwest Florida
E-mail: davidsaville@gmail.com

Sawyer, Charles Frederick Jr. – b Asheville, NC, Dec 15, 50; f Charles Frederick, Sr; m Maxine McCall; w Yvonne Dodd, Oct 11, 98; chdn Ethan Lyon, Claire Germain, Devon McCall, Charles F. III (Trey), Nicolas Carlton; LRC 68-70; UNC 70-72, BA; CBS 76-79, MDiv; O Apr 9, 89, Wcar Pby; chp

Sawyer, Charles Frederick Jr., continued
MTW, Quito,Ecuador, 89-93; chp MTW, Bogota, Colombia, 94-95; chp MTW, Miami, FL, 95-97; ev PEF, Family & Children Faith Coal; ceo Hope for Miami; hr 17

550 NW 42 Avenue, Miami, FL 33126 – 786-223-9698   South Florida
E-mail: info@hopeformiami.org
Hope for Miami – 786-388-3000
HR

Sawyer, Randy K. – b Sheridan, WY, Feb 12, 60; f Thomas; m Loeva Adamson; w Judy Day, Canon City, CO, Jul 3, 93; chdn Caleb K., Katie M.; ShJC 85, AD; UWY 88, BS; SCS 92, MDiv; L Apr 93; O Feb 96, RMtn Pby; p Wetmore Comm Ch, Wetmore, CO, 92-93; ob p Big Horn Comm Ch (non-PCA), Big Horn, WY, 96-97; op New Cov P Ch, Sheridan, WY, 97-00; ob p United for Christ Comm Ch, Blanca, CO, 00-04; op New Cov P Ch, Sheridan, WY, 04-09; Chap USArmy, 09-

1 Country Estates Drive, Sheridan, WY 82801 – 307-674-8372   Rocky Mountain
E-mail: randy.sawyer@us.army.mil
United States Army

Sawyers, Sean – b Memphis, TN, Jan 15, 75; w Nikki; BayU 97, BA; RTS 00, MATS; O Jun 00, non-PCA; O Nov 19, 06, MO Pby; astp Prov Christ Fell, Colorado Springs, 00-01; chp Agkura Fell, Colorado Springs, 01-03; srp Heritage P Ch, Wildwood, MO, 06-11; Chap Eureka Fire Protection Dist, 07-11; p Trinity P Ch, Orangeburg, SC, 11-16; astp Christ The King P Ch, Cambridge, MA, 16-; p Boston North P Ch, Wakefield, MA, 18-

15 1st Street, Melrose, MA 02176   Southern New England
E-mail: pastorsawyers@gmail.com
Christ The King Presbyterian Church – 617-354-8541
Boston North Presbyterian Church – 781-486-4477

Saxon, James – b Gadsden, AL, Nov 11, 51; f Lewis A. (d); m Josie Piazza; w Cindy Myers, Mar 27, 82; chdn Natalie Jean, Adrienne Cecilia; UAL 70-74, BS; RTS 79, MDiv; O Jul 8, 79, CentFL Pby; op Tampa Bay P Ch, Tampa, FL, 79-82, srp 82-00; ob astp Ch of the Apostles, Atlanta, GA, 00-

5518 Sylvania Drive, Mableton, GA 30126 – 770-948-5785   Metro Atlanta
E-mail: jsaxon@apostles.org
Church of the Apostles – 404-842-0200
3585 Northside Parkway NW, Atlanta, GA 30327

Saye, Randy – w Leigh Anne; chdn Jon Walter, Daniel, Jack; BrPJC 96, BA; RTSFL 13, MDiv; O Oct 6, 13, CentGA Pby; ascp Houston Lake P Ch, Kathleen, GA, 13-16; p St. Andrews P Ch, Americus, GA, 16-

236 GA Highway 27 East, Americus, GA 31709 – 478-718-3399   Central Georgia
E-mail: randysaye@gmail.com
St. Andrews Presbyterian Church – 229-924-1772

Sayler, Ethan – Recd PCA Jan 23, 13, Siouxl Pby; p Lennox Ebenezer P Ch, Lennox, SD, 15-

221 West 1st Avenue, Lennox, SD 57039   Siouxlands
E-mail: reveds@msn.com
Lennox Ebenezer Presbyterian Church – 605-647-2659

Sayour, George – O Oct 1, 17, SFL Pby; ascp St. Andrews Park Road P Ch, Hollywood, FL, 17-

St. Andrews Park Road Presbyterian Church – 954-989-2655   South Florida

Scales, Martin W. – b Philadelphia, PA, Feb 20, 53; f Robert D; m Ruth Pennington; w Lee A. Steinstra, Newport Beach, CA, Jun 1, 79; chdn Jennifer Lee, David Martin; PhilCB; TalTS; O 81, Indep; Recd PCA Oct 20, 92, SFL Pby; moa SoCst Comm Ch, (Indep), Irvine, CA, 81-89; exec dir Serendipity House, Denver, CO, 89-91; astp Spanish River P Ch, Boca Raton, FL, 91-95; p Canyon Creek P Ch, San Ramon, CA, 96-

569 Saint George Road, Danville, CA 94526 – 925-735-1118   Northern California
E-mail: mscales@canyoncreekchurch.com
Canyon Creek Presbyterian Church – 925-244-1200

Schaeffer, Rick – op Grace Harbor Ch, Long Beach, CA, 06-13; wc 13-

7800 4th Place, Downey, CA 90241 – 562-621-1048   Pacific

Schafer, Bryan Robert – b Sep 24, 60; f Robert; m Nancy; w Heather; chdn Christopher, Casey; Biola, BS; RTS, MDiv; astp North Coast P Ch, Encinitas, CA, 99-13; Dir North Coast Christian Min, 03-13; ascp Redeemer P Ch of San Diego, Encinitas, CA, 13-; mod SCst pby, 13-

1077 Crest Drive, Encinitas, CA 92024 – 858-442-2678   South Coast
E-mail: bryan@redeemersd.org
Redeemer Presbyterian Church of San Diego – 760-753-2535

Schafer, Jason – O Nov 27, 16, PlVall Pby, mis 16-

2-28-14 Umegaoka, Terrace B, Setagaya, Tokyo 154-0022 JAPAN – (+81) 080-7992-1984   Platte Valley
E-mail: jason.j.schafer@gmail.com

Scharf, Russell Eugene – b Grand Junction, CO, Oct 20, 48; f Wm. H; m Tatman; w Cheryl Ayers, Golden, CO, Sept 18, 68; NEJC 66-67; ASC 68-70; SCS 85-89, MDiv; L 88; O Apr 89, Indep; Recd PCA Sept 27, 90; p Cody Pk Comm Ch, Westcliff, CO , 87-89; mis MTW, 90-02; Chap CO Prison, 02-14; astp Grace P Ch, Colorado Springs, CO, 06-13; hr 14

Address Unavailable   Rocky Mountain
E-mail: thescharfs@ris.net
HR

Scharfenberg, Jay Rynning – O Sep 29, 12, EPA Pby; astp Calvary P Ch, Willow Grove, PA, 12-16; wc 16-

1001 Easton Road, # 513M, Willow Grove, PA 19090 – 215-407-7302   Eastern Pennsylvania

Scheibe, Marc – campm RUF, UNoCO, 05-09; campm RUF, UTulsa, 09-10; p Covenant P Ch at Hot Springs, Hot Springs, AR, 10-15

34 Balcon Estate, St. Louis, MO 63141   Covenant

Schill, Harold Gus – b Ft Dodge, IA, Sept 10, 61; f H. Andrew; m Arline Estlund; w Kay Brown, Cold Spg, MN, Feb 15, 87; chdn Elizabeth Hope, Michael Andrew, David Earl, Jonathan Paul; WartbC 80-84, BS; NWMOSU 85, MEd; RTS 88-91, MDiv; L Jul 90, SFL Pby; O Apr 92, Wcar Pby; int First P Ch, Jackson, MS, 91; astp Arden P Ch, Arden, NC, 92-94, ascp 94-03; astp Grace Comm Ch, Fletcher, NC, 03-10; op Gr Biltmore PCA, Asheville, NC, 05-10; ob 12-

360 Asheville School Road, Asheville, NC 28805   Western Carolina
E-mail: schillg@ashevilleschool.org

Schilling, Matthew L. – b Tampa, FL, Oct 10, 70; f Lester William; m Constance Marshall Worsley; w Katrina Reinee Helman, Jackson, MS, Aug 10, 96; chdn Kathryn Maria, Martin William; LRC 88-92, BA; RTS 93-99, MDiv; L Oct 12, 99, MSVal Pby; O Feb 20, 00, Cov Pby; p Grenada P Ch, Grenada, MS, 00-09; ob t P CS, Hattiesburg, MS, 09-18; chap USN, 18-

3353 Onslow Drive, Camp Lejeune, NC 28547 – 601-408-5580   Grace
E-mail: 4schillings@gmail.com
United States Navy

Schimke, Kurt – mis

14860 County Road 35, Karval, CO 80823 – 719-683-9350   Rocky Mountain
E-mail: kurt@kmschimke.org

Schirmer, James A. – b Saginaw, MI, Sept 13, 56; f Charles Albert; m Jeanne Ashbaugh; w Ann Sims, Memphis, TN, Aug 24, 91; chdn James Andrew, Joseph Allen, Jonathan Ambrose, Joel Adam, Jacob Alexander; AndC 75-78, BA; CBS 89-92, MDiv, MA; RTS 09, DMin; L Jul 22, 93; O Nov 7, 93, Palm Pby; p Heritage P Ch, West Columbia, SC, 93-

319 Morningwood Drive, Lexington, SC 29073 – 803-358-9080   Palmetto
E-mail: jschirmer@windstream.net
Heritage Presbyterian Church – 803-791-1831

Schitter, Damein – w Leah; chdn Olivia, Scarlett, Adeline; CTS 11, MDiv; ascp Grace Renewal Ch, Chula Vista, CA, 12-14; astp NewCity Orlando, Orlando, FL, 14-15, ascp 15-

815 North Magnolia Avenue, Orlando, FL 32803   Central Florida
E-mail: dschitter@newcityorlando.com
NewCity Orlando – 407-872-0883

Schley, John – b West Lafayette, IN, Nov 28, 60; f Arvis Ervin; m Joan Clara Fleck; w Jacquelyn Williams, Morrow, GA, Sept 1, 84; chdn Timothy John, Elizabeth Joanna, Jeremiah Andrew, Stephanie Joy; GATech 84, BIE; WheatGrS 88, MEd; CBS 05, MDiv; O Dec 11, 05, Palm Pby; ascp Metro North P Ch, Goose Creek, SC, 96-

154 Balbriggon Drive, Goose Creek, SC 29445 – 843-824-8511   Lowcountry
E-mail: jschley@metronorthpca.org
Metro North Presbyterian Church – 843-764-0873

Schley, Timothy J. – w Elizabeth Levine, Jul 16, 11; chdn Ransom Timothy, Elizabeth Anastasia; O Jun 14, 15, Tidw Pby; ascvininp Calvary Ref P Ch, Hampton, VA, 15-

403 Whealton Road, Hampton, VA 23666   Tidewater
E-mail: tj@calvaryrpc.org
Calvary Reformed Presbyterian Church – 757-826-5942

Schlichting, Randall – b Milwaukee, WI; w Dorothy; chdn Katherine, Allison, Sarah; UHou, BBA; UTXD, MA; MetAtlSem, MDiv; astp Perimeter Ch, Johns Creek, GA, 03-; *Minority Rules*; *Quoteworthy*; *Re-Start for Marriages*; *All is Calm*; *Like Sheep with a Shepherd*; Podcast: One 4 the Road

421 Sassafras Road, Roswell, GA 30076   Metro Atlanta
E-mail: randys@perimeter.org
Perimeter Church – 678-405-2206

Schmidt, Brad Douglas – p CityChurch, Ft. Lauderdale, FL, 09-

700 SE 8th Street, Ft. Lauderdale, FL 33316 – 954-531-4687   South Florida
CityChurch – 954-634-2489

Schmidt, Kyle – O May 27, 15, MO Pby; ob Chap Caris Healthcare, MO, 15-

7415 Canton Avenue, University City, MO 63130　　　　　　　　　　　Missouri
Caris Healthcare

Schmidtberger, Robert – b Gaylord, MI, Jul 2, 85; f Robert; m Margaret; w Jennifer Howell, May 3, 08; GroCC 08, BA; RPTS 13, MDiv; O Aug 18, 13, Pitts Pby; astp Grace and Peace P Ch, Pittsburgh, PA, 13-15; astp Stillwaters P Ch, PCA, West Grove, PA, 15-16; astp City Ch Wilmington, Wilmington, DE, 16; astp Iron Works West Chester, West Chester, PA, 16-

132 West Chestnut Street, West Chester, PA 19380 – 724-714-3108　　　Philadelphia Metro West
E-mail: robbie@ironworkschurch.org
Iron Works West Chester – 484-883-1951

Schmitt, Thomas Neil – b Pittsburgh, PA, Dec 2, 53; f Raymond W.; m Regina; w Patricia Reynolds, Raleigh, NC, Dec 16, 78; chdn Matthew Thomas, Rachel Marie, Joseph Edward; NCSt 80, BS; WTS 83, MAR, 85, MDiv; L Mar 18, 89; O Jan 6, 91, Wcar Pby; p Emmanuel P Ch, Franklin, NC, 91-99, ascp 99-01; ascp Christ P Ch, Clarkesville, GA, 06-09; p 09-12; wc 12-

1974 Low Gap Road, Lakemont, GA 30552 – 706-212-2070　　　　　　　Georgia Foothills
E-mail: cygnethouse@windstream.net

Schneeberger, Greg – astp Redeemer P Ch of San Diego, 13-14; astp New Valley Ch, Phoenix, AZ, 14- 17; p Christ Ch Santa Fe PCA, Santa Fe, NM, 17-

1307 Lejano Lane, Santa Fe, NM 87501 – 505-620-8547　　　　　　　　Southwest
E-mail: greg@christchurchsantafe.org
Christ Church Santa Fe PCA – 505-982-8817

Schneider, Jeffrey Allen – b Dallas, TX, Jun 24, 76; f Allen Robert; m Elaine Carroll; w Cynthia, Jul 17, 10; chdn Virginia Pinar, Zachary Allen; PU 98, AB; TEDS 04,MDiv, 12, ThM; mis MTW, 06-10; astp Covenant P Ch, Chicago, IL, 10-

2012 West Dickens Avenue, Chicago, IL 60647　　　　　　　　　　　　Chicago Metro
E-mail: jschneider@covenantchicago.org
Covenant Presbyterian Church – 773-486-9590

Schneider, Thomas Glynn – b El Paso, TX, Mar 13, 58; f Robert L.; m Gloria J. Bohn (d); w Carolyn J. Bryan, Atlanta, GA, Sep 6, 80; chdn Christin Joy, Jonathan Robert, Julie Rebekah; BryC 79, BA; RTS 84, MDiv; L Oct 83, MSVal Pby; O Jan 1, 85, SFL Pby; ap Inverness P Ch, Baltimore, MD, 80-82; ap, ip Crossbridge Ch Miami, Miami, FL, 84-86; ev, p West Kendall P Ch, Miami, FL, 86-89; p East Ridge P Ch, East Ridge, TN, 89-95; ascp Covenant Life P Ch, Sarasota, FL, 95-12; p Covenant P Ch, Sebring, FL, 13-

4862 Myrtle Beach Road, Sebring, FL 33872 – 941-228-1599　　　　　　Southwest Florida
E-mail: ccttschneider@hotmail.com
Covenant Presbyterian Church – 863-385-3234

Schoepp, Jed Michael – O Nov 11, 12, Wcan Pby; astp Faith Ref P Ch, Vancouver, BC, 12-13; mis 13-15; ascp Faith Ref P Ch, Vancouver, BC, 15-17; ob 17-

4980 Geer Road, Sechelt, BC V0N 3A2 CANADA – 604-365-4000　　　　Western Canada
E-mail: jed.schoepp@gmail.com

Scholten, Mark A. – b Detroit, MI, Nov 23, 64; f David L.; m C. Faye Howes; w Kathleen S. VanGiessen, Holland, MI, Oct 25, 86; chdn Sarah E., Rachel M., Jason T., Bethany J., Matthew J.; HopeC

Scholten, Mark A., continued
82-86, BA; RTS 89-92, MDiv; L Oct 15, 91, MSVal Pby; O Jul 19, 92, Christian Reformation Ch; Recd PCA May 17, 97, NoE Pby; p Christian Reformation Ch, 92-97; p Presbyterian Ch of Manchester, Manchester, CT, 97-07; srp Faith P Ch, Akron, OH, 07-15; p Westminster P Ch, Martinez, GA, 15-

3149 Alexandria Drive, Grovetown, GA 3083 – 330-208-6027   Savannah River
E-mail: sinnersaint1980@yahoo.com
Westminster Presbyterian Church – 706-863-8978

Schoof, Steven Kendall – b Glen Ridge, NJ, Dec 14, 52; f Robert C.; m Barbara Kendall; w Beth De Troye, Oostburg, WI, Jan 14, 76; RBC 70-71; CC 71-74, BA; WTS 74-79, MDiv, 92, DMin; L May 14, 79; O Jul 1, 79, MidAtl Pby; ap New Cov P Ch, 79-81; op New Life P Ch, 79-81, p 81-85; mis MTW, Australia, 85-; MTW, team ldr, 88-94; MTW, regional dir, 94-03; p Westminster P Ch, Perth, Australia, 96-12; cons on evan/chplant in WestAust, 04-12; MTW HMA, 12; srp Marco P Ch, Marco Island, FL, 13-

875 West Elkam Circle, Marco Island, FL 34145 – 304-261-5250   Suncoast Florida
E-mail: s.b.schoof@gmail.com
Marco Presbyterian Church – 239-394-8186

Schrage, Jeffrey P. – O 17, CentInd Pby; astp Christ P Ch, Richmond, IN, 17-

2514 Locust Lane, Richmond, IN 47374   Central Indiana
Christ Presbyterian Church – 765-966-40

Schreiber, Andy – O May 6, 12, SoCst Pby; astp New Life P Ch, Escondido, CA, 12-; op Ramona Valley P Ch, Ramona, CA, 12-

New Life Presbyterian Church – 760-489-5714   South Coast
Ramona Valley Presbyterian Church – 760-787-1570

Schriver, Walter Jerome – b Louisville, KY, Dec 31, 40; f Walter Bayless; m Marjorie Lucile Wheeler; w Patricia Claire Miller, St. Louis, MO, May 31, 86; chdn Dawn Bridget (McSavaney), Stacey Lynn (Wolf), Elizabeth Lindsey (Coors); ElmC 62, BA; MHA, WashU MedSch72; EdTS 70, MDiv; O Nov 7, 71, UChC; Recd PCA Jan 17, 95, MO Pby; VP Ancillary Svcs, Deaconess Hosp, 71-76; MTW, COO, 95-96; astp Perimeter Ch, dir Bus & Fin Min, Duluth, GA, 97-07; pres Christian Stewardship Network, 06-10; astp area pastor, Perimeter Ch, Johns Creek, GA, (area p, Johns Creek Parish) 10-; bd, PCAF, 00-11; chmn, 04-07; vchair 08-09; chmn 09-10; bd PCA AC, 09-16, chmn 15-16; sec bd PCA AC, 13-14; bd PCAF, 14-17; bd PCA AC, 17-

580 Croydon Lane, Johns Creek, GA 30022 – 770-754-0254   Metro Atlanta
E-mail: jerryschriver@gmail.com
Perimeter Church – 678-405-2110

Schrock, Daniel – O Jun 3, 12, Phil Pby; astp Third Ref P Ch, Philadelphia, PA, 12-13; p 13-

3112 Morning Glory Road, Philadelphia, PA 19154 – 505-793-5405   Philadelphia
E-mail: schrock68@yahoo.com
Third Reformed Presbyterian Church – 215-637-2266

Schubert, Jason Christopher – b Charlotte, NC, Jun 8, 79; f Larry M.; m Patricia Ann Sigmon; w Lindsey Pettit Clerico, Clemson, SC, May 13, 06; chdn Adelaide Elizabeth, Beckett Tillman, Greta Mae; NCSt 01, BS; CTS 09, MDiv; O Nov 7, 10, JR Pby; ascp Grace P Ch, King George, VA, 10-15; op Harbor P Ch, Elizabeth City, NC, 16-

912 West Church Street, Elizabeth City, VA 27909   Tidewater
E-mail: jason@harborecity.com
Harbor Presbyterian Church – 252-679-3088

Schuelke, Michael B. – b Montclair, NJ, Dec 11, 54; f Edwin R.; m Patricia Denne; w Susan Stotler, Penn Hills, PA, Sept 25, 82; chdn Lauren Michal, Gregory Barrett; IUP 77, BS; CTS 87, MDiv; L Oct 86, Asc Pby; O Mar 11, 88, GrLks Pby; ascp Westminster P Ch, Muncie, IN, 87-92; p Fairfield P Ch, Fairton, NJ, 92-

PO Box 68, Fairton, NJ 08320-0068 – 856-451-4249 New Jersey
E-mail: mbs21@comcast.net
Fairfield Presbyterian Church – 856-451-7687

Schuler, Paul F. – b Northridge, CA, Oct 29, 57; f Frederick; m Helen Weis; w Cynthia Raun, Granada Hills, CA, Jun 16, 79; chdn Kurt, Heidi, Anna, Heather, Eric, Elisabeth; UCLA 75-79, MA; WSCAL 85-89, MDiv; L Sept 15, 89; O Feb 18, 93, Indep; Recd PCA Feb 17, 96, PacNW Pby; ascp Peninsula Bible Fellowship, 89-96; op, chp Cross Sound Ch, Bainbridge Island, WA, 96-02, p 02-11; p The City Ch of Honolulu, Honolulu, HI, 11-

2123 Hunnewell Street, Honolulu, HI 96822 Northern California
E-mail: pschuler@cchnl.org
The City Church of Honolulu – 808-946-4720

Schumate, Jonathan – mis

E-mail: jonathan.schumate@gmail.com Houston Metro

Schumpelt, Joash – O Nov 19, 12, Ecan Pby; op Sovereign Comm Ch, Douglastown, NB, 12-

440 Percy Kelly Drive, Miramichi, NB E1V 5V8 – 506-625-2568 Eastern Canada
E-mail: joash.schumpelt@gmail.com
Sovereign Community Church – 506-773-9624

Schuster, Andrew J. – b Wisconsin Rapids, WI, Feb 18, 88; w Kelsey, Jun 12, 10; chdn David Andrew, Josiah, Lukes; UNCC, BA; RTSNC, MDiv; O Oct 12, 14, CentCar Pby; astp Christ Cov Ch, Matthews, NC, 14-17; p Northside P Ch, Winder, GA, 17-

299 Natchez Circle, Winder, GA 30680 – 704-962-4222 Georgia Foothills
E-mail: pastorandynpc@gmail.com
Northside Presbyterian Church – 770-867-4220

Schutter, David H. – b Monterey, CA, Jan 8, 71; f David John; m Ellen Carol Hoffman; w Kimberly Gene Piotrowski, Detroit, MI, Jun 11, 94; chdn David Jonathan, Luke Lawrence, Anika Lynn; WheatC 89-91; MUOH 91-93, BA; CTS 94-97, MDiv; WTSLon 17, ThM; L Jul 97, Siouxl Pby; O Apr 98, Siouxl Pby; p Foothills Comm Ch, Sturgis, SD, 98-01; Chap USAR, 95-06; sc Siouxl Pby, 00-01; astp Naperville P Ch, Naperville, IL, 01-02; Chap USAR, active duty, Afghanistan, 03-04; ascp Naperville P Ch, Naperville, IL, 04-07; srp Northwest P Ch, Dublin, OH, 07-; vol Chap Dublin PD, 14-; PRJC endorsement; mbr MNA co, 15-18; "Doctrine of Adoption," *Jonathan Edwards Encyclopedia*

5426 Haverhill Drive, Dublin, OH 43017 – 614-381-2741 Columbus Metro
E-mail: dschutter@npc-dublin.org
Northwest Presbyterian Church – 614-799-2300

Schwanebeck, Robert Gnann Jr. – b Meridian, MS, Jun 3, 53; f Rev. R. G. Sr. ; m Mary Julia Turk; w Carol Leanne Roberts, Omaha, NE, Jan 4, 75; chdn Jason Robert, David Joseph; ConcU 71-72; CC 72-76, BA; RTS 76-79, MDiv, 85, DMin; O May 27, 79, Gr Pby; p Magee P Ch, Magee, MS, 79-85; p First P Ch, Louisville, MS, 85-00; ob admin, dir Ch rel PalmHC, 01-02; exec dir 02-05; srp Northpointe P Ch, Meridian, MS, 05-18; hr 18

109 Lionheart Lane, Starkville, MS 39759 Mississippi Valley
E-mail: bobschwanebeck@gmail.com
HR

Schwartz, Richard Tunstall – b Richmond, VA, Jul 27, 67; f Donald Malcolm; m Jane Tunstall Adams; w Sarah Elizabeth Murphy, Richmond, VA, Apr 21, 90; chdn Hannah Elizabeth, Richard Alexander, Emma Grace; VPI 89, BA; CTS 96, MDiv; L Nov 3, 96; O Nov 3, 96, Flwsp Pby; astp Bethel P Ch, Clover, SC, 96-98; astp Grace P Ch, Peoria, IL, 98-02; p Christ P Ch of Clarksville, Clarksville, TN, 02-

3483 Brookfield Drive, Clarksville, TN 37043 – 931-358-0599   Nashville
E-mail: rtschwartz@bellsouth.net
Christ Presbyterian Church of Clarksville – 931-906-6650

Schwartzbeck, Robert James – b St. Paul, MN, Aug 31, 58; f Richard Arthur; m Virginia Ann Pile; w Marilyn Yoder, Hutchinson, KS, May 26, 84; chdn Joshua, Justin, Zachary, Kaitlin; UKS 77-81, BS, 81-83, MS; TEDS 85-91, MA, MDiv, ThM; CTS 05, DMin; L Jul 25, 98, SoTX Pby; O Aug 30, 98, SoTX Pby; astp Bay Area P Ch, Webster, TX, 98-99; p Oaklawn P Ch, Houston, TX, 00-01, wc 01-05; astp Oaklawn P Ch, Houston, TX, 05-

6906 Trimstone, Pasadena, TX 77505 – 281-998-9219   Houston Metro
E-mail: bmschw@yahoo.com
Oaklawn Presbyterian Church – 713-921-5635

Schweissing, David – b Westminster, CO, Mar 24, 73; f Richard Emil; m Virginia Mary Baimonte; w Kerri Christina Malloch, Nashville, TN, May 4, 02; chdn Lauren Christina, Ashlyn Kathleen, Carter Andrew; WheatC 95, BA; CTS 99, MDiv; O Jun 1, 03, PacNW Pby; ascp Cascade P Ch, Eugene, OR, 03-05; ascp Presbyterian Ch of Pitcairn, Pitcairn, PA, 06-08; p 08-16; op Indiana Msn, Indiana, PA, 18-

345 Ben Franklin Road North, Indiana, PA 15710 – 412-266-6729   Pittsburgh
E-mail: schweissing@gmail.com
Indiana Mission

Schweitzer, William McCarty – b Tampa, FL, Nov 13, 74; f William Henry; m Norma Jean Palmer; w Pamela Marie, Jul 19, 97; chdn Mark, Bethany, Mary, Anna, James, Rebecca; URoch 97, BA; FCSC 07, ThB; UEdin 05, ThM, 09, PhD; O Jan 23, 09, Palm Pby; USMC, 97-05; mis MTW, England, 09-; *God is a Communicative Being: Divine Communicativeness and Harmony in the Theology of Jonathan Edwards*

310 Waterway Drive, Sneads Ferry, NC 28460   Lowcountry
E-mail: w.m.schweitzer@gmail.com
PCA Mission to the World

Schwenk, David – O Jun 1, 97, Mid-America; p Christ P Ch of Claremore, Claremore, OK, 97-

PO Box 1488, Claremore, OK 74018-1488 – 918-266-1168   Hills and Plains
Christ Presbyterian Church of Claremore – 918-342-5134

Scott, Aaron – w Angie; chdn Barrett, Ainsley, Creed, Wyatt, Gage; CrisC, BS; WTS, MDiv; O Jul 06, SoTX Pby; astp Christ Ch, Katy, TX, 99-00; Park Cities P Ch, Middle School pastor, Dallas, TX, 01-04; chp Christ P Ch, New Braunfels, TX, 05-06; op Church of the Cross, San Marcos, TX, 06-11; p 11-13; astp Faith Cov P Ch, Kalispell, MT, 14-; op Church of the Cross, Whitefish, MT, 15-

PO Box 1382, Whitefish, MT 59937   Rocky Mountain
E-mail: aaron@cotcw.org
Faith Covenant Presbyterian Church – 406-752-2400
Church of the Cross – 406-730-3052

Scott, Arthur Earl – b Collingswood, NJ, Oct 21, 41; f McGregor; m Myrtle Martin; w Sharon Christ, Scranton, PA, Jun 26, 65; chdn Jonathan, Debbi, David, Stephen; CC 63, BA; CTS 68, BD, MA; L Apr 30, 69; O Jun 14, 70, RMt Pby (RPCES); ap, p Grace P Ch, Colorado Springs, CO, 68-81; p Faith P Ch, Myrtle Beach, SC, 82-02, wc 03-05; hr

7610 Glenwood Drive, Myrtle Beach, SC 29572-4154 – 843-449-4905   Pee Dee
E-mail: ascott1941@gmail.com
HR

Scott, Chad – campm RUF, 08-13; astp Faith P Ch, Brookhaven, MS, 13-

114 Hillcrest Drive, Brookhaven, MS 39601   Grace
E-mail: schadscott@gmail.com
Faith Presbyterian Church – 601-833-0081

Scott, David Eugene – b Bellevue, WA, Sept 21, 68; f Wayne; m Jenny Knautz; w Sara Bynum, Seattle, WA, Jan 17, 98; chdn Elizabeth, Rebecca, Hannah, Samuel; BIOLA 87-89; TrinWest 89-91, BA; RTS 94-96, MA; WTS 98-00, MDiv; L Jul 01, PacNW Pby; O Jul 01, PacNW Pby; ascp Covenant P Ch, Issaquah, WA, 01-07; astp Faith P Ch, 07-09; chp Resurrection P Ch, Puyallup, WA, 07-09; p 09-

8423 137th Street, Court E, Puyallup, WA 98373 – 253-468-3448   Pacific Northwest
E-mail: david@resurrectionpc.org
Resurrection Presbyterian Church – 253-256-4183

Scott, Kelly – O Oct 26, 14, BlRdg Pby; ob Campus Crusade, 14-

112 Lewis Mountain Circle, Charlottesville, VA 22903 – 434-249-1761   Blue Ridge
E-mail: kelly.scott@athletesinaction.org
Campus Crusade

Scott, Robert – b Mar 5, 51; f John P.; m Norma C.; w Valerie; chdn Justin, Jessica, Anna; AU 73, BA, 75, MEd; RTS 84, MDiv; O 15, MetAtl Pby; fac BrChS, 76-84; prin West End, Hopewell, VA, 84-86; headm Perimeter Christian sch, Norcross, GA, 86-; astp Perimeter Ch, Johns Creek, GA, 15-; *Children's Membership Guide,* 87; *When Children Love to Learn,* 04; *Probing a Child's Heart,* 10

590 Martin Street SE, Atlanta, GA 30312 – 404-408-8575   Metro Atlanta
E-mail: bscott@perimeter.org
Perimeter Christian School
Perimeter Church – 678-405-2000

Scott, Robert D. – b Kansas City, MO, Jul 15, 28; f Thomas George; m Gladys Esther Davis; w Libby Mainland, Philadelphia, PA, Nov 23, 55; chdn Mike, Terri, Rob, Sandy; ORSU 48-50; HighC 53-55, BA; FTS 55-56; CTS 56-60, MDiv; L 60; O 60, Midw Pby; p Covenant P Ch, Issaquah, WA, 60-65; p Milwaukie OPC, Milwaukie, OR, 69-73; p University P Ch, Las Cruces, NM, 73-82; mis MTW, Australia, 82-94; srp Immanuel P Ch, Mesa, AZ, 95-97; srp Westminster P Ch, Mandurah West Aust, 97-99; astp University P Ch, Las Cruces, NM, 99-03; hr

2593 Scenic Crest Loop, Las Cruces, NM 88011-0849 – 505-556-0185   Southwest
E-mail: roblibscott@aol.com
HR

Scott, Robert J. – b Cedar Rapids, IA, Mar 2, 55; f Albert J; m Margaret E Schroeder; w Anne M. Edeleanu, Cambridge, MA, Jun 4, 77; chdn Jessica M., Melanie A.; MIT 77, BS; CMU 78, MBA; CTS 91, MDiv; L Oct 6, 90; O Jul 14, 91, NoCA Pby; chp, int Canyon Creek P Ch, San Ramon, CA, 90-91, ev, chp 91-92, ascp 91-94; p Grace Ch of Pleasanton, Pleasanton, CA, 94-98, ev 06-08; wc 09-15; hr 16

661 South Stage Road, Medford, OR 97501 – 541-857-5067   Pacific Northwest
E-mail: bs7@charter.net
HR

Scott, Stephen – w Londa Bragdon; chdn Sophia, Josiah, Naomi, Caroline; CC 97, BA; GPTS 05, MA; O Oct 16, 10, GulCst Pby; Chap USN, 10-

PO Box 30800 PMB 182, Honolulu, HI 96820 – 850-602-3400   Gulf Coast
E-mail: sscott5298@gmail.com
United States Navy

Scott, Travis – b Kalamazoo, MI, Mar 18, 76; w Brooke, Grand Rapids, MI, May 13, 00; chdn Sophia, Zoe, Jerram; Kuyper 00, BA; CTS 06, MDiv, 17, ThM; Recd PCA Jan 28, 17, Pitts Pby; p City P Ch, Auckland, NZ, 09-16; lect Grace Theo C, Auckland, 09-16; p Grace and Peace P Ch, Pittsburgh, PA, 17-

1616 Morningside Avenue, Pittsburgh, PA 15206 — Pittsburgh
E-mail: travis@graceandpeacepgh.org
Grace and Peace Presbyterian Church

Scruggs, Chad – campm RUF, SMU, 09- 13; astp Park Cities P Ch, Dallas, TX, 13-15, ascp 15-18; srp Covenant P Ch, Nashville, TN, 18-

5313 Cherry Blossom Trail, Nashville, TN 37215 – 214-714-7805 — Nashville
E-mail: chads@covenantpres.com
Covenant Presbyterian Church – 615-383-2206

Scruggs, John Mark – O 16, TNVal Pby; campm RUF, UTChatt, 16-

E-mail: jmscruggs@gmail.com — Tennessee Valley
PCA Reformed University Fellowship

Seah, Christopher – ob mis Singapore, 08-

SINGAPORE — Philadelphia

Seal, Zachary B. – p Danville P Ch, Danville, CA, 18-

394 Ilo Lane #102, Danville, CA 94526 — Northern California
Danville Presbyterian Church – 510-792-7755

Seale, Daniel Shannon – b Fairfax, VA, Sept 29, 67; f Robert; m Natalie Shannon; w Debora Hurvitz, Harrisonburg, VA, Jun 3, 89; chdn Mary-Brooke, Cassandra, Emmeline, AnGrace; JMU 89, BS; WTS 93, MDiv; L Jan 15, 94; O Jun 26, 94, Phil Pby; int Crossroads Community Ch, Upper Darby, PA, 91-92, astp 93-94, ascp 94-98; p Knollwood P Ch, Sylacauga, AL, 98-06; srp Redeemer P Ch, Raleigh, NC, 06-

11412 Strickland Road, Raleigh, NC 27613 – 919-848-3788 — Eastern Carolina
E-mail: Dan@RedeemerPCA.net
Redeemer Presbyterian Church – 919-518-2370

Sealy, Phillip – b Grove Hill, AL, Jan 19, 63; f Walter L.; m Martha Gaddy; w Lori Grace Mullwee, Dillon, SC, Nov 26, 94; chdn Joshua Garrett, Elizabeth Cameron; AUM 94, BS; GPTS 04, MDiv; O Sept 26, 04, Wcar Pby; int Landis P Ch, Marion, NC, 00-01; stus 01-04, p 04-10, op Redeemer P Ch, Sylva, NC, 10-16, p 16-18; chp 18-

3605 Fernwood Drive, Ocean Springs, MS 39654 — Grace
E-mail: phillipsealy@gmail.com

Searle, Richard Wayne – b Lake Charles, LA, Apr 25, 57; f Joseph W.; m Vera Burnsed; w Kathryn Ruth Richards, Perry, GA, Mar 20, 82; chdn Jonathan, Jacob, Sara Kathryn; VSC 78-81, BMusEd; VanderCook C Mus 91-92; RTS 95-98, MDiv; L Nov 99, Evan Pby; O Nov 99, Evan Pby; astp Decatur P Ch, Decatur, AL, 98-00; astp Westminster P Ch, Johnson City, TN, 00-02; p Faith P Ch, Anniston, AL, 02-

409 Wildwood Road, Anniston, AL 36207 – 256-236-9267 — Evangel
E-mail: rws@faithchristian.info
Faith Presbyterian Church – 256-238-8721

MINISTERIAL DIRECTORY

Sears, Ian Scott – b Quantico, VA, Sept 18, 60; f Walter; m Sally F. Leadeux; w Ann Marie Reidun Knaust, Waterloo, IL; chdn Callum, Connor, Andrew; CC 78-79; VMI 80-83; CTS, MDiv; L Aug 90; O May 26, 91, Cal Pby; ascp Mount Cal P Ch, Roebuck, SC, 90-93; astp Covenant P Ch, Nashville, TN, 93-94, ascp 94-01; p The Ch of Gr Village: A Comm of the PCA, Nashville, TN, 01-

1709 Leaton Court, Franklin, TN 37064 – 615-781-3964   Nashville
The Church of Grace Village: A Community of the PCA – 615-810-9845

Seaton, Scott P. – b Los Angeles, CA, Aug 21, 60; f Philip; m Marcia Claire Huston; w Catherine Christina Church, Atlanta, GA, Nov 28, 92; chdn Catherine Claire, David Philip, Audrey Elizabeth; UVA 82, BA; O Jun 14, 98, NGA Pby; asst, chp MTW/Impact, Japan, 85-87; astp, mout, mfam Intown Comm Ch, Atlanta, GA, 87-01; admin MTW, 01-06; astp McLean P Ch, McLean, VA, 06-09; op Emmanuel P Ch, Arlington, VA, 08-09; p 09-

1911 North Van Buren Street, Arlington, VA 22205 – 703-270-9033   Potomac
E-mail: sseaton@emmanuelarlington.org
Emmanuel Presbyterian Church – 703-270-9163

Secrest, Jonathan – astp Greenwood P Ch, Greenwood, SC, 10-11, ascp 11-15; Chap USAR

1121 Hunt Road, Fort Leavenworth, KS 66027 – 864-538-9948   Calvary
United States Army Reserve

Seda, Jonathan Paul – b Hornell, NY, Apr 10, 52; f Peter; m Marion Spencer; w Dale-Karen Michealsen, Syosset, NY, Jul 19, 75; chdn Michelle Lee, Matthew Lee, Kristen Marie, Mark Phillip; HougC 74, BA; BibTS 79, MDiv; CTS 02, DMin; L Jun 14, 80; O Nov 9, 80, DMV Pby (RPCES); ap Faith P Ch, Wilmington, DE, 79-83; srp Grace Ch PCA, Dover, DE, 83-

251 Mifflin Road, Dover, DE 19904 – 302-734-8502   Heritage
E-mail: jseda@gracedover.com
Grace Presbyterian Church – 302-734-8150

Seder, Scott – wc

6040 Whetstone Drive, Colorado Springs, CO 80923 – 719-640-9589   Rocky Mountain
E-mail: slsederpca@icloud.com

Seivright, David C. – w Pauline, Aug 14, 64; ULvrpl, LLB; WTS 82, MDiv; ob p International Comm Ch OPC, 82-87; CCC, 88-17; hr 17

5461 SW 71st Place, Miami, FL 33155-5618 – 305-321-4511   South Florida
E-mail: dave@seivright.com
HR

Seldal, W. Kent – b Seattle, WA, Aug 30, 47; f Walter E.; m Verna; w Mary Beth; chdn Joshua Kent, Timothy Christian; MuSB 68, ThB; WWSU 73, BA; CTS 82, MDiv; O Mar 20, 83, StLouis Pby; MTW, 83-84; p Bible P Ch, 84-88; ob Chap CPE Geisinger Med Ctr, Danville, PA, 89-91; ob DPC Muncy Vly Hosp, Muncy, PA, 89-91; ob DPC Mem Med Ctr, Ashland, WI, 91-14; hr 14

27705 South Maple Hill Road, Washburn, WI 54891 – 715-373-2964   Wisconsin
E-mail: kseldal@centurytel.net
HR

Sellers, David Robert – b Chattanooga, TN, May 6, 63; f Robert R.; m Linda Tate; w Carrie Lynn Piercy, Apple Valley, CA, Jun 28, 94; chdn Emma Mercy, Elijah David, Grace Julia, Isaac Dayne; FSU 81-

Sellers, David Robert, continued
85, BS; FulTS 90-93, MDiv; O 93, PCUSA; O 01, PacNW Pby; ascp Apple Valley, CA, 93-00; astp Grace Ch Seattle, Seattle, WA, 00-04; ascp Cross Sound Ch, Bainbridge Island, WA, 04-11; srp 11-

6135 Lynwood Center Road, Bainbridge Island, WA 98110 – 425-885-6589   Pacific Northwest
E-mail: dave@crosssound.org
Cross Sound Church – 206-842-6898

Sempier, Scott Leonard – b May 25, 80; SusqU 02, BA; WTS 07, MDiv; O Nov 20, 10, NJ Pby; p Locktown Ch, Flemington, NJ, 10-13; wc 13-18; Chap Thomas Jefferson Hosp, 18-

320 Collins Avenue, Moorestown, NJ 08057 – 856-287-3008   New Jersey
E-mail: scottsempier@yahoo.com
Thomas Jefferson Hospital

Sen, Aniruddha – w Kimberly; chdn Jacob, Lily; UNC 95, BA; RTSFL 02, MDiv; O Nov 02, Ecar Pby; op Grace Comm Ch, Chapel Hill, NC, 02-05, p 05-10; astp NewCity Orlando, Orlando, FL, 11-18

231 Mill Chapel Road, Chapel Hill, NC 27517   Central Florida
E-mail: rusen@mac.com

Seneker, Ben – O Nov 12, 17, Wcar Pby; astp Grace Mills River, Mills River, NC, 17-

1600 Ridgewood Boulevard, Hendersonville, NC 28791   Western Carolina
E-mail: ben.seneker@gmail.com
Grace Mills River – 828-891-2006

Seo, Dong Joo – b Korea, Jun 10, 60; f Sang Kil Seo; m Mal Sun Jung; w Hyun Sook Ha, Korea, Sept 30, 84; chdn Ae Nok, Annah, Yonah; KBNU 83, BA; KorTS 86, MDiv; O Apr 5, 88, PCK; Recd PCA 99, KorCap Pby; op Ellicott City, MD, 99-05; p Korean Jerusalem P Ch, Ellicott City, MD, 05-10

6374 Beechfield Avenue, Elkridge, MD 21075   Korean Capital
E-mail: djs610@hotmail.com

Seo, Kyoo Won – p Ch of Love & Truth, Vienna, VA, 05-

209 Oak Street SW, Vienna, VA 22180 – 703-242-5989   Korean Capital
E-mail: kwseo7@yahoo.com
Church of Love & Truth – 703-242-5989

Seo, Kyung Jae – wc 14-16; op Montgomery Open Kingdom P Ch, Pike Road, AL, 16-

26 Boykin Loop, Pike Road, AL 36117   Korean Southeastern
E-mail: godstori@gmail.com
Montgomery Open Kingdom Presbyterian Church

Serven, Doug – b Detroit, MI, Nov 5, 70; f Daniel; m Donna Waggoner; w Julie Halbert, Springfield, MO, Mar 5, 94; chdn Ruth, Cal, Drew, Anna; UMOC 93; CTS 00, MDiv; L Sept 16, 01, NoTX Pby; O Sept 16, 01, NoTX Pby; Navs, OK, NE, 93-97; Ref Discipleship Ministries, Colorado Springs, CO; CTS, Youth in Ministry dir, 00; campm RUF, UOK, 01-11; op City P Ch, Oklahoma City, OK, 11-14; srp 14-; *TwentySomeone*, 03

1937 NW 17th Street, Norman, OK 73106 – 405-364-4635   Hills and Plains
E-mail: servenator@gmail.com
City Presbyterian Church

Sessions, Richie – b Little Rock, AR, Jun 20, 75; f Leslie; m Nancy Griffin; w Laura Steele, Jackson, MS, Sept 16, 00; chdn Mamie, Griffin, Margaret; BelmC 99, BS; RTS 04, MDiv; O Jun 13, 04, Cov Pby; astp Covenant P Ch at Cleveland, Cleveland, MS, 04-05, ascp 05-07; astp Independent P Ch, Memphis, TN, 07-09; srp 09-15; campm RUF, VandU, 15-

126 Cottonwood Circle, Franklin, TN 37069 – 901-685-8206 Nashville
E-mail: richie.sessions@ruf.org
PCA Reformed University Fellowship

Seto, Raymond – O Jul 1, 18, Pot Pby; ob Child Evangelism Fellowship, 18-

14836 Bodley Square, Centreville, VA 20120 – 571-758-4477 Potomac
E-mail: rayseto@gmail.com
Child Evangelism Fellowship

Seufert, Michael – O Oct 23, 16, Pot Pby; astp Wallace P Ch, College Park, MD, 16-

5100 Dorset Avenue, Chevy Chase, MD 20815 – 760-681-1686 Potomac
E-mail: MichaelJSeufert@gmail.com
Wallace Presbyterian Church – 301-935-5900

Seul, Paul Kyunghwan – srp Raleigh Bethel P Ch, Raleigh, NC, 15-17

Address Unavailable Korean Southeastern
E-mail: paulkseul@gmail.com

Severance, Stacey L. – O Jul 23, 16, PD Pby; op Good Shepherd P Ch PCA, Florence, SC, 16-

705 Bellemeade Cir, Florence, SC 29501 – 843-453-8076 Pee Dee
E-mail: stacey@gsflo.org
Good Shepherd Presbyterian Church PCA – 843-453-8076

Sewell, Chris – O Oct 5, 14, MetAtl Pby; astp Carriage Lane P Ch, Peachtree City, GA, 14-18; p Trinity P Ch, Lancaster, SC, 18-

519 West Barr Street, Lancaster, SC 29720 – 423-385-0809 Fellowship
Trinity Presbyterian Church – 803-283-3305

Sexton, Gary Keith – b Ft. Gordon, GA, Aug 24, 54; f Lionel Francis; m Lorene B. James; w Frances Jo Fuehrer, Augusta, GA, Jun 18, 77; chdn Ryan Daniel, Ian Graham, Colin Andrew, Sara Renee; AugC 77, BA; CTS 78-81, MDiv; L 82; O 83, CentGA Pby; op Covenant P Ch, Milledgeville, GA, 82-84; Chap USArmy, 84-12 (ret); astp New Life in Christ Ch, Fredericksburg, VA, 12-14; hr 17

10218 North Hampton Lane, Fredericksburg, VA 22408 – 540-710-5414 James River
E-mail: sextongk@gmail.com
HR

Seyfert, Kirk Andrew – ascp Evergreen P Ch, Salem, OR, 14-

1660 Jefferson Street NE, Salem, OR 97301-7968 – 503-507-4293 Pacific Northwest
E-mail: kseyfert@hotmail.com
Evergreen Presbyterian Church – 503-371-1177

Shackleford, Dennis W. – b Memphis, TN, Aug 22, 67; f Charles R.; m Paula McDonald; w Shannon LaNell Gordon, Memphis, TN, Aug 17, 91; chdn Grace Elizabeth, John Alan; CriC 92, BS; RTS 96, MDiv;

Shackleford, Dennis W., continued
L Feb 11, 97; O Jun 1, 97, GulCst Pby; ascp First P Ch, Niceville, FL, 97-11; business mgr RUF, 12-15, dir operations, 16-

3094 Brooksong Way, Dacula, GA 30019 – 770-561-4609   Gulf Coast
E-mail: dwshack@gmail.com
PCA Reformed University Fellowship

Shamblin, George – b Columbus, GA, Nov 22, 67; f William R.; m Sandra Bryant; w Jill Dickinson, Birmingham, AL, Feb 27, 93; chdn Sydney, Bailey, Miller, Bryant; AU 91, BA; RTS 98, MDiv; L Apr 99, GulCst Pby; O Oct 99, GulCst Pby; ip Camden & Oak Hill ARP churches, 95-97; astp Pinewoods P Ch, Cantonment, FL, 99-00; op Christ Comm Ch, Pensacola, FL, 00-01, p 01-07; wc; The Center for Exec Leadership

2621 Southminster Road, Birmingham, AL 35243-2155   Evangel
E-mail: george@thecenterbham.org
The Center for Executive Leadership

Shane, John Joseph – b Recife, Brazil, Dec 17, 51; f Robert Clark; m Ruth Marion Hampton; w Susan Elizabeth Austin, Kingsport, TN, Dec 20, 75; chdn Nathaniel Austin, Lindsay Elizabeth; UT 69-70; SCC; NCSt 75-78, BS; CBS 78-83, MA, 78-83, MDiv; L 83; O 83, Cal Pby; mis MTW, Nairobi, Kenya, 85-99; Dir co-ops in Africa, 96; MTW, reg dir, Southern Africa, 99-

c/o MTW   Palmetto
PCA Mission to the World – 678-823-0004

Shank, Andrew David – O May 3, 15, Palm Pby; astp Hilton Head P Ch, Hilton Head Island, SC, 15-17; campm RUF, WCarU, 17-

49 Grove Road, Sylva, NC 28779   Western Carolina
E-mail: andrew.shank@ruf.org
PCA Reformed University Fellowship

Shannon, Nate – O Sept 15, Phil Pby; ob prof Torch Trinity Grad U, Seoul, 15-

Address Unavailable   Philadelphia

Sharpe, Timothy – O Aug 19, 12, Ecar Pby; astp Christ Our Hope Ch, Wake Forest, NC, 12-16, ascp 16-

541 Clifton Blue Street, Wake Forest, NC 27587 – 919-521-7946   Eastern Carolina
E-mail: timmattsharpe@yahoo.com
Christ Our Hope Church – 919-570-9717

Sharrett, Michael Craig – b Baltimore, MD, Feb 22, 56; f Allan Crane (d); m Emily Hastings Hill (d); w Janice Leigh Beechwood, Hartsville, PA, Jul 29, 78; chdn Michael Christopher, Luke Caleb, Laura Caroline; GetC 78, BA; UVA 79, MEd; WTS 88, MDiv; O Oct 23, 88, JR Pby; astp Trinity P Ch, Charlottesville, VA, 82-92; chp, op Fort Worth P Ch, Fort Worth, TX, 92-96, p 96-04; op Redeemer P Ch, Lynchburg, VA, 04-15; bd trust WTS; bd trust Redeemer Sem, 14-16; ip Calvary P Ch, Willow Grove, PA, 16-18; ip Wallace P Ch, College Park, MD, 18-; *Watching Over the Heart; Watching the Path of Your Feet*

201 Merrywood Drive, Forest, VA 24551 – 434-525-6563   Blue Ridge
E-mail: sharrett.mike@gmail.com
Wallace Presbyterian Church – 301-935-5900

Shaw, Ben – campm RUF, USoMS, 08-18; op Christ Comm Ch, St. Francisville, LA, 18-

14003 Sunrise Way, St. Francisville, LA 70775   Southern Louisiana
E-mail: benshaw12@gmail.com
Christ Community Church – 601-540-3624

MINISTERIAL DIRECTORY

Shaw, Benjamin – b Silver City, NM, Oct 18, 53; f Norman; m Irene Lux; w Lynn Ann Hartman, Greenville, SC, May 25, 96; chdn Daniel Dwight McMullen, Sarah Patricia McMullen, Kathyryn Ruth McMullen, Paul Alan McMullen; NMSU 71-74; UNM 74-77, BUS; PittsTS 77-80, MDiv; PTS 80-81, ThM; DukeU, PhD cand; BJU 05, PhD; O Feb 18, 96, Cal Pby; prof GPTS, 91-; *Studies in Church Music*

60 Schulman Street, Sylva, NC 28779– 864-268-9735   Calvary
E-mail: bshaw@gpts.edu
Greenville Presbyterian Theological Seminary – 864-322-2717
PO Box 690, Taylors, SC 29687

Shaw, Geoffrey – b York, PA, Aug 18, 68; f Ronald; m Queta; w Breanne; CalvC 90, BA; CTS 00, MDiv; L 01, Pac Pby; campm RUF, UCSB, 01-05; astp Valley P Ch, North Hills, CA, 05-08; srp Redeemer P Ch, Torrance, CA, 10-14

1480 East Howard Street, Pasadena, CA 91104-2632 – 310-375-3393   Pacific
E-mail: geoffreysshaw@gmail.com

Shaw, Jim – p Unity P Ch, Weogufka, AL; p Redeemer P Ch, Brunswick, GA, 17-

1411 Lanier Boulevard, Brunswick, GA 31520 – 205-451-5433   Savannah River
E-mail: jamesrshaw68@gmail.com
Redeemer Presbyterian Church – 912-466-9915

Shaw, Jay – O Nov 13, 18, Evan Pby; astp Briarwood P Ch, Birmingham, AL, 18-

Briarwood Presbyterian Church – 205-776-5200   Evangel

Shaw, Ronald Lee – b Ipava, IL, May 21, 40; f Don L.; m Emily Parry; w Queta Pope, Hazel Park, MI, Aug 25, 62; chdn Elizabeth, Geoffrey, Rachel; BJU 62, BA; WTS 65, MDiv; GetLS 68; L 66; O 66, OPC; p Faith OP Ch, Fawn Grove, PA, 66-69; p RP Ch, Nashville, TN, 69-78; p Covenant P Ch, Wheat Ridge, CO, 78-84; ap Village Seven P Ch, Colorado Springs, CO, 84-90; p New Cov P Ch, Aiken, SC, 90-93; pal MTW, 93-01, DirSpLi 01-06, asst to DirSpLi, MTW, 06-07; ind cont MTW, 09-14; min sen, Arden P Ch, Arden, NC, 14-17, astp 17; hr 17

4218 Tullamore Drive, Daphne, AL 36526 – 828-550-8955   Western Carolina
E-mail: ronaldleeshaw@gmail.com
HR

Shaw, Rondell B. – b Lebanon, NE, Apr 24, 24; f Lewis C.; m Mary June Welborn; w Dorothy Cole (d) (2) Lou Ann Heft, Manhattan Beach, CA, Aug 15, 98; chdn Mark David, Mary Lydia; UNV 49, BS; FulTS 55, BD; PTS 59, ThM; O Oct 57, New Castle Pby (PCUSA); p Ocean Cty, MD, 57-59; p Military Ave UPC, Detroit, MI, 61-73; p Ch of Our Saviour (Ind), Chicago Hgts, IL, 74-89; hr 89; astp Valley P Ch, North Hills, CA, 90-00; astp Redeemer P Ch, Torrance, CA, 00-16

1908 Lynngrove Drive, Manhattan Beach, CA 90266 – 310-546-2304   Pacific
HR

Shaw, Scott – b Jun 24, 67; w Rebecca Healy, Jul 16, 88; chdn Joshua Aaron, Jacqueline Nicole, Caleb Scott, Andrew Robert; GraceC 89, BS; BallSU 94, MS; MoodyTS 13, MDiv; O Oct 13, 13, GrLks Pby; astp Knox P Ch, Harrison Township, MI, 13-16, ascp 16-18; srp Shore Harvest P Ch, Easton, MD, 18-

Shore Harvest Presbyterian Church – 410-763-7070   Heritage

Shaw, Timothy – astp Independent P Ch, Savannah, GA, 17-

611 East 56th Street, Savannah, GA 31405   Savannah River
E-mail: tshaw@ipcsav.org
Independent Presbyterian Church – 912-236-3346
207 Bull Street, Savannah, GA 31402

Shea, Tyson – astp New Valley Ch, Phoenix, AZ, 17-

E-mail: tysonshea@gmail.com Southwest
New Valley Church – 480-940-5560

Sheahan, Kevin – O Oct 21, 18, SusqV Pby; astp Reformed P Ch, Ephrata, PA, 18-

21 East Locust St., Ephrata, PA 17522 Susquehanna Valley
E-mail: KevinS@ephratarpc.com
Reformed Presbyterian Church – 717-733-0462

Shear, Ben – Chap USN, 13-

2854 South 48th Drive, Yuma, AZ 85364 – 757-771-1035 Tidewater
E-mail: bjshear@gmail.com
United States Navy

Shelby, Steven Tate – b Charlotte, NC, Oct 31, 59; f Milton Guy; m Betty Jo Sisk; w Marti Robbins, Charlotte, NC, Aug 13, 83; chdn Knox Wagner (d), Tate Bradford, Guy Steven, Madeline Ruth; DavC 82, BA; RTS 86, MDiv, MCE; GCTS 02, DMin; L Jul 86; O Apr 87, JR Pby; ascp Stony Point Ref P Ch, Richmond, VA, 86-93; ev, chp, op West End P Ch, Richmond, VA, 93-95, p 95-

9528 Chatterleigh Drive, Richmond, VA 23233-4405 – 804-346-0240 James River
E-mail: steve@wepc.org
West End Presbyterian Church – 804-741-6462

Shelton, Christopher – b Decatur, AL, Mar 22, 63; f Marshall; m Linda Kay Sandlin; w Tracey Leigh Doude, French Camp, MS, Sept 25, 99; chdn Andrew Thomas, Jonathan Mark, Benjamin Luke; UAB 84-87, BA; RTS 96-99, MDiv; O Jun 11, 00, MSVal Pby; p First P Ch, Union, MS, 00-

101 Woodhaven Drive, Union, MS 39365 – 601-774-0604 Mississippi Valley
E-mail: cmshelton@juno.com
First Presbyterian Church – 601-774-9257

Shelton, Jason Brian – b Athens, GA, Feb 5, 57; f Jack D. (d); m Rose L. DeLay (d); w Cindy Danielle Smedberg, Panama, NY, May 26, 79; chdn Hannah Rose (Singer), Jared Alan, Jack Graham, Linnea Ruth (Taylor); PenCC 75-79, BA, 79-81, MA; RTS 84-86, MDiv; L Oct 84; O 86, MSVal Pby; p Edwards P Ch, Edwards, MS, 86-91; p Brandon P Ch, Brandon, MS, 91-99; p Providence P Ch, Salisbury, MD, 99-

5955 Oxbridge Drive, Salisbury, MD 21801 – 410-546-8455 Heritage
E-mail: jason.shelton@providencesalisbury.org
Providence Presbyterian Church – 410-546-0577

Shelton, Ted Leon – b Chicago, IL, Feb 7, 42; f Costy; m Imogene Katrina Wilhoit; w Betty Jane May, Knoxville, TN, Dec 2, 61; chdn Susan Beth (Drennen); UT 73, BS; RutgU 79; BhamTS 94, MBibCoun, 96, MDiv; WTS 04, DMin; L Jan 28, 97; O Mar 9, 97, Evan Pby; DirCouns Briarwood P Ch, Birmingham, AL, 93-03, ascp, modis 97-03; hr 03; exec dir Reconciliation Couns Resource Cent, 03-; *Model and Manual for Lay Counseling in the Local Church*, 94; *Restoring Counseling to the Church*, 04

5408 Woodford Drive, Birmingham, AL 35242 – 205-907-3310 Evangel
E-mail: tedlshelton@bellsouth.net
HR

MINISTERIAL DIRECTORY

Shelton, Wayne – Fernandina Beach, FL, Jun 8, 61; f James C.; m Faye; w Michelle Merritt; chdn Kristen (Fielder), Kelly (Trawick), Keri; BaptCFL 89, ThB; BDS 93, MDiv; RTS 11, DMin; O May 14, Evan Pby; op Redeemer P Msn, Gardendale, AL, 15-

2050 Pinehurst Drive, Gardendale, AL 35071 – 205-514-0199   Evangel
E-mail: wayne@redeemerpca.org
Redeemer Presbyterian Mission

Shepherd, Charles Douglas – O Oct 9, 05, NoTX Pby; mis MTW, Ukraine, 05-

c/o MTW   North Texas
PCA Mission to the World

Sheppard, Craig A. – b Cincinnati, OH, Apr 21, 65; f Charles W; m Marilyn S. Thomas; w Lisa M. Scholz, St. Louis, MO, Jun 6, 87; chdn Jared, Nathan, Luke, Andrew, Abigail; UKS 87, BA; RTS 94, MDiv, 97, ThM; UWales 09, PhD; L Oct 19, 93, MSVal Pby; O Sept 18, 94, Hrtl Pby; mis, chp MTW, Sofia, Bulgaria, 94-09; srp Bethel Ch PCA, Dallas, TX, 09-13; srp Arden P Ch, Arden, NC, 13-

52 King Heights Drive, Fletcher, NC 28732 – 828-702-2813   Western Carolina
E-mail: Craigshep7@gmail.com
Arden Presbyterian Church – 828-684-7221

Shepperson, Sam G. – b Chester, SC, Aug 2, 24; f Flournoy; m Nellie McGill; w Dorothy Lyle, El Dorado, AR; chdn Lyle McGill, John Hampton, Joel Zachary; FurU 46, BA; FTS 49, BD; L 46; O 49, BPC; ob p Marrable Hill Chapel, (non-PCA) El Dorado, AR, 49-95; hr 95; p Scotland P Ch, Junction City, AR, 05; *The Lord's Doing*, 99; *A Word from the Pastor*, 07

903 Marrable Hill Road, El Dorado, AR 71730-8254 – 501-862-1885   Covenant
HR

Sherard, Stewart – b Fairfort, MO, Sept 2, 39; f Stewart L; m Gladys L. Ausmus; w Carolie Potter, Marshall, MO, Jul 1, 62; chdn Jeffrey Blane, Stephen Lee; USMA 62, BS; UMN 68, MA; L Sept 22, 94; O Oct 9, 95, SW Pby; int Desert Springs P Ch, Tucson, AZ, 93-94, p 94-04; sc SW Pby, 98-04; hr 04; p em Desert Springs P Ch, Tucson, AZ

5211 East Hill Place Drive, Tucson, AZ 85712 – 520-322-0195   Southwest
E-mail: stusherard@aol.com
HR

Sherbon, Wallace E. Jr. – b Pittsburgh, PA, Jul 16, 47; f Wallace E.; m Schnarrenberger; w Janet Mucho, Pittsburgh, PA, Jun 6, 70; chdn Kathy, Julie; UPitt 69, BS; ColU 71, MS; BibTS 83, MDiv; L 83, Phil Pby; O Apr 86, JR Pby; p New Life P Ch, Virginia Beach, VA, 86-15; hr 15; *Destined for the Trinity*, 13

4424 Crossings Ridge, Birmingham, AL 35242 – 757-287-2558   Evangel
E-mail: w.sherbon@verizon.net
HR

Sherwood, David Allen – b West Chester, PA, Mar 14, 61; f Laurence Thomas Jr.; m Patricia Ann Bringhurst; w Kimberly Ann Mayhugh, Durham, NC, May 6, 83; chdn Jennifer Ann (Walker), Emily Patricia, Katherine Jeanette (Greer), Ryan Immanuel; DukeU 80-83, BA; GCTS 83-86, MDiv, 11-17, DMin; L Jul 85, NoE Pby; O Nov 13, 88, NoTX Pby; srp Christ P Ch, Flower Mound, TX, 88-04; srp Trinity P Ch, Providence, RI, 05-; art "The Pastor as Attorney"; *No More, No Less: Exploring the Extent and Limits of the Mission of the Visible Church*

16 Telford Road, Barrington, RI 02806   Southern New England
E-mail: david@trinitypresri.org
Trinity Presbyterian Church – 401-272-0766

Shields, Corby – astp New Life P Ch, Dresher, PA, 11-12; astp Christ The King P Ch, Cambridge, MA, 12-13; astp Grace South Shore, 12-13; wc 13-14; astp Rock Creek Flwsp, Rising Fawn, GA, 14-

2008 Durham Road, Rising Fawn, GA 30738 – 781-510-2573　　　　　　　　Tennessee Valley
E-mail: corby@rockcreekfellowship.org
Rock Creek Fellowship – 706-398-7141

Shields, Curtis Jonathan – O Aug 16, 15, CentCar Pby; mis MTW, 15-

3121 Overton Drive, Birmingham, AL 35209 – 205-903-2625　　　　　　　　Central Carolina
E-mail: curtis.j.shields@gmail.com
PCA Mission to the World

Shields, John Thomas – b Moss Point, MS, Sept 23, 54; f Richard V Jr.; m Erma Paschal; w Cynthia Fortenberry, Silver Creek, MS, Sept 27, 75; chdn Laura Beth, Anna Lise; DSU 71-75, BS; RTS 76-80, MDiv; O Aug 20, 80, CMS Pby (PCUS); p Louisville P Ch, Louisville, MS, 76-85; p First EPC, Anna, IL, 86-89; srp Faith P Ch, Brookhaven, MS, 89-95; p Collins P Ch, Collins, MS, 95-; ss First P Ch, Taylorsville, MS, 95-; Presbyterian Christian HS, Hattiesburg, 98-

PO Box 116, Collins, MS 39428-0116 – 601-765-1788　　　　　　　　　　　Grace
E-mail: revtshields@bellsouth.net
Collins Presbyterian Church – 601-765-4977
First Presbyterian Church – 601-785-4696
Presbyterian Christian High School, Hattiesburg

Shields, Jonathan Adam – astp Grace Cov Ch, Las Cruces, NM, 09-14; ascp Providence P Ch, Salisbury, MD, 15-

3993 Trace Hollow Run, Salisbury, MD 21804　　　　　　　　　　　　　　Heritage
E-mail: jashields3@hotmail.com
Providence Presbyterian Church – 410-546-0577

Shields, Thomas L. III – b Charlotte, NC, Mar 25, 50; f Thomas L. Jr.; m Nellie Tarlton; w Lynda Schreck, Mint Hill, NC, Jul 29, 72; chdn Leslie Elizabeth, Philip Andrew; CPCC 70-72, AA; BelC 72-74, BA; GCTS 74-77, MDiv; O Oct 16, 77, PCUS; Recd PCA May 14, 91, Pot Pby; p Ridgecrest P Ch, Stanfield, NC, 77-81; p McGee P Ch, Charlotte, NC, 81-84; srp First P Ch, Rochester PA, 84-91; p Westm Ref P, Westminster, MD, 91-97, wc 97-99; p Castanea P Ch, Stanley, NC, 99-00; wc; ss Faith P Ch, Charlotte, NC, 04; wc 05-

6422 Ridgeview Commons Drive, Charlotte, NC 28269 – 980-297-3330　　　　Catawba Valley
E-mail: clergycop@yahoo.com

Shim, Hyunchan Lloyd – p Naperville First P Ch, 02-04, wc 04-10, ob Trin Inst of Washington, 10-

10287 Quiet Pond Terrace, Burke, VA 22015 – 703-352-5913　　　　　　　Korean Capital
E-mail: lloydshim@sbcglobal.net
Trinity Institute of Washington

Shim, Wonsub – p Korean Central P Ch of Cincinnati, Cincinnati, OH, 18-

11061 Grand Avenue, Blue Ash, OH 45242　　　　　　　　　　　　　　　Korean Central
Korean Central Presbyterian Church of Cincinnati – 513-432-0901

Shin, Dae Hyun – ob

E-mail: daehyun_shin@msn.com　　　　　　　　　　　　　　　　　　　Korean Southwest

Shin, Eugene – b Korea, Jun 22, 54; f Chung Soo; m Keum Wha Lee; w Helen Choi, New York, NY, Nov 26, 83; chdn Susan, Linda; YonU 73-77, BS; TEDS 90-92, MDiv; ascp Chicago, IL, 91-95; srp Arlington Heights, IL, 95-00; srp Siloam Korean Ch of Atlanta, Norcross, GA, 00-

1841 Watford Glen, Lawrenceville, GA 30043 – 770-338-2949   Korean Southeastern
E-mail: yshin@mailcity.com
Siloam Korean Church of Atlanta – 770-846-2600

Shin, Light – b Seoul, Korea, Apr 10, 76; w Diane; chdn Abigail, Kathryn, Hannah; USMA 99, BS; WTS 08, MDiv; Chap USArmy, Ft. Bragg, NC, 08-11; Chap USArmy, Ft. Benning, GA, 11-15; Chap USArmy, Ft. Leavenworth, KS, 15-16; Chap USArmy, Ft. Jackson, SC, 16-18; Chap USArmy, Vicenza, Italy, 18-

CMR 427, Box 3764, APO, AE 09630   Korean Eastern
E-mail: light.k.shin.mil@mail.mil
United States Army

Shin, Sangwon – astp Disciple Comm Ch, Irvine, CA, 16-

Disciple Community Church – 949-502-4923   Korean Southwest Orange County

Shin, Soungkook – b Seoul, Feb 24, 61; f Tae Young; m Bok Soon; w Mi Sun, Seoul, Sept 1, 87; chdn John, Phillip; UWI 85, MS; ORSU 98, PhD; BibTS 04, MDiv; O May 7, 17, JR Pby; op New Life Korean Ch, Fredericksburg, VA, 17-

11118 Dragons Lair Drive, Fredericksburg, VA 22407   James River
E-mail: kookshin@hotmail.com
New Life Korean Church – 540-355-8869

Shin, Sung Jong – b Seoul, Feb 17, 37; f Suk Jun; m Dong Gi Kim; w Jong Sook Lee, Seoul, Feb 23, 67; chdn In Sung, Philip; GATS 67; WTS 71, ThM; TempU 73, MA, 74, PhD; L Oct 74, Gen Assem P Ch; O Oct 75; Recd PCA Nov 22, 96, KorSW Pby; p Daejon Cent Ch, 87-91; srp Choong Hyun P Ch, 91-95; srp Holy Hill Comm Ch, 95-08; hr; *New Testament Introduction*; *New Testament Theology*; numerous books on New Testament

4480 Wawona Street, Los Angeles, CA 90065-5117 – 323-258-9206   Korean Southwest
E-mail: drsjShin@gmail.com
HR

Shin, Sung Uk – p Na Nu Rie P Ch of Lawton, Lawton, OK, 09-10; op Nu Rie Nun Ch, Lawton, OK, 13-15, wc

67-25A 186th Lane #2B, Fresh Meadows, NY 11365 – 580-919-9990   Korean Southern
E-mail: jkshin48@hanmail.net

Shin, Sunghoon – op Areumdown P Ch, Miami, FL, 14-

13715 SW 90th Avenue #M202, Miami, FL 33176   Korean Southeastern
E-mail: sunghoon0925@gmail.com
Areumdown Presbyterian Church – 786-337-0255

Shin, Tae – op Trin P Msn, Orange, CA, 98-06; wc 06-

21159 Via Noriega, Yorba Linda, CA 92887 – 714-961-8377   Pacific

Shin, Wah Rang – mis 14-

E-mail: sys742@hotmail.com   Korean Southeastern

Shin, Young Soo – b Korea, Feb 17, 32; f Shin Ma Tae; m Kim Ki Doung; w Cha Soon Ye, Korea, Nov 11, 58; PGATCS 57; THTS 57; O Apr 62, Kyungki Pby; p Buknae Ch, 62-69; p Sung Won Ch, 69-80; p Hosanna P Ch, San Jose, CA, 84-13; hr 13

Address Unavailable   Korean Northwest
HR

Shin, Young Sun – b Kimpo, Korea, Dec 7, 63; f Hong-Shik; m Soon-Young Lee; HSU 82-86, BS; DTS 86-91, ThM; L Apr 11, 91, KorS Pby; O Apr 6, 92, KorSE Pby, mis; ascp Korean Central P Ch of Wash, Vienna, VA, 92-93; mis Thailand, 93-

GPO Box 1013, Bangkok, 10501 THAILAND – 66-2-398-9839   Korean Capital
E-mail: youngsunshin5@gmail.com

Shipley, James Everett – b Ft. Lewis, WA, Jun 28, 46; f James E.; m Barbara Burgess; w Mary Anne Houser, Macon, GA, Jun 13, 69; chdn James E. Jr., Mary Kathryn, John N.; OKSU 64-65; OKCiU 65-68, BS; CTS 77-80, MDiv; O Jun 20, 80, CentGA Pby; srp Perry P Ch, Perry, GA, 80-98, wc 98-12; sc CGA Pby, 07-12; hr 12

PO Box 6253, Macon, GA 31208 – 478-719-7305   Central Georgia
E-mail: jshipley4@gmail.com; jim@benefit-analysts.com
HR

Shipma, Michael – b Morrison, IL, Dec 29, 70; f Larry R.; m Florence J.; w Adriana Moreno, Jun 25, 94; chdn Cristiana Esther, Michael Peter, James Alexander, Gabriela Lucia; MidARS 98, MDiv; O Apr 99, OPC; p Covenant Comm OPC, Evansville, IN, 99-02; p Knox OPC, OKC, OK, 02-04; astp Heritage P Ch, Edmond, OK, 05-08; admin Veritas Classical Academy, OKC, OK, 08-11; admin Westminster Ch Acad, Huntsville, AL, 11-14; astp Westminster P Ch, Huntsville, AL, 12-15; DirRelEd Redstone Arsenal, 16-; Chap USAR 17-

110 Capote Drive, Harvest, AL 35749   Providence
E-mail: michaelrshipma@gmail.com
United States Army Reserve

Shipman, Alexander Myron – b Metter, GA, Jan 31, 77; f Alexander James; m Imogene Sutton; w Wyketa Walker, Macon, GA, Mar 5, 05; chdn Madison Joy, Treyson Alexander; VSC 01, BFA; RTSNC 08, MDiv; O Nov 08, Prov Pby; int Christ Central Ch, Charlotte, NC, 03; int Redeemer P Ch, Greenville, SC, 05-06; int Decatur P Ch, Decatur, AL, 06-07; astp Southwood P Ch, Huntsville, AL, 08-11; chp The Village Ch, Huntsville, AL, 08-11; srp 11-

2103 Virginia Boulevard, Huntsville, AL 35811   Providence
E-mail: alex@enterthevillage.net
The Village Church

Shirley, Wilson – w Laura; RTS 10, MDiv; astp Highlands P Ch, Ridgeland, MS, 11- 14; p Cornerstone P Ch, Brownsboro, AL, 14-

2956 Elk Meadows Drive SE, Brownsboro, AL   Providence
E-mail: wilsonashirley@gmail.com
Cornerstone Presbyterian Church – 256-489-4625

Shoemaker, Ben – ob p St. Paul Church, Fairbanks, AK, 08-11; wc 11-

653 East Dana Lane, Coeur D'Alene, ID 83815   Pacific Northwest
E-mail: cobblers@hushmail.com

MINISTERIAL DIRECTORY 573

Shope, Ward W. – b Camden, NJ, Feb 24, 57; f R. Wesley; m Katherine Ann Robison; w Debra Kay Yonkey, Sewickley, PA, Nov 21, 87; chdn Wesley Stephen, Jonathan Michael, Emma Katherine; GenC 75-79, BA; GCTS 79-81; DrewTS 81-84, MDiv; L May 17, 97; O Aug 24, 97, SusqV Pby; p UMC, Landenberg, PA, 84-93; mis WHM, Amsterdam, 97-02, US Headquarters 03-10; Harvest USA, Philadelphia, PA, 10-11; wc 11- 17; astp New Life P Ch, Dresher, PA, 17-

2832 Carnation Avenue, Willow Grove, PA 19090 – 215-706-0291   Susquehanna Valley
New Life Presbyterian Church – 215-641-1100

Showers, James Frederick – b Olean, NY, Oct 3, 54; f John Walter (d); m Mary Lee Riddle (d), stepm Dixie Showers; w Kathy Dickerson, Chesapeake, VA, Nov 10, 79; chdn John P, Jennifer M; ODU 72-76, BA; BibTS 80-84, MA, MDiv; L Sept 15, 84, JR Pby; O Jan 27, 91, Pot Pby; astp Loch Raven P Ch, Baltimore, MD, 91-97; p Covenant Life P Ch, Saltillo, MS, 97-08; astp Providence P Ch, Salisbury, MD, 09-; op Shore P Msn, Onancock, VA, 09-11; astp, PRes Eastminster P Ch, Virginia Beach, VA, 11-

957 Cogliandro Drive, Chesapeake, VA 23320   Tidewater
E-mail: revjfshowers@yahoo.com
Eastminster Presbyterian Church – 757-420-8133

Shrimpton, Eric – O Mar 11, 18, OHVal Pby; astp North Cincinnati Comm Ch, Mason, OH, 18-

6170 Irwin Simpson Road, Mason, OH 45040   Ohio Valley
E-mail: eric@northciny.org
North Cincinnati Community Church – 513-229-0190

Shuffield, Danny – b Amarillo, TX, Sept 25, 63; f Loyd L.; m Joy L. Briant; w Janet M. Leon, Petersburg, TX, May 23, 87; chdn Luke, Anne Elise, Daniel, Seth; TXTU 86, BA, 88, cert; RTS 93, MA, 95, MDiv; L Feb 10, 96; O May 26, 96, GulCst Pby; astp Pinewoods P Ch, Cantonment, FL, 96-99; ascp Redeemer P Ch, Austin, TX, 99-15, wc 15-16, ob 16-

4806 Sika Way, Austin, TX 78749 – 512-343-6962   South Texas
E-mail: dshuff25@gmail.com

Shull, James Louis – b Macon, MS, May 5, 50; f William L; m Emily Falkner; w Elizabeth Wingate, Columbus, MS, Jun 25, 72; chdn Katherine Elizabeth (Brunone), Jonathan Wingate; BelC 72, BA; RTS 75, MDiv, 85, DMin; L Nov 1, 74; O Jul 20, 75, Gr Pby; p Bay Springs P Ch, Bay Springs, MS, 75-83; p North Park P Ch, Jackson, MS, 83-96, wc 96-97; p First P Ch, Philadelphia, MS, 97-02; p First P Ch, Crystal Springs, MS, 02-

318 East Marion Avenue, Crystal Springs, MS 39059   Grace
E-mail: shullj@bellsouth.net
First Presbyterian Church – 601-892-2715

Shuman, Steven Brady – b Richwood, OH, May 8, 52; f Marion B; m Margaret Smith Reed; w Sarah Denise Goodwin, Birmingham, AL, Aug 16, 74; chdn Sarah Brady, Steven Michael; BelC 70-74, BA; RTS 75-78, MDiv, 97, DMin; L Apr 14, 78; O Jul 16, 78, Gr Pby; p Leakesville P Ch, Leakesville, MS, 78-81; p First P Ch, Hueytown, AL, 81-85; p Grace P Ch, Cedartown, GA, 85-91; p Covenant P Ch, Laurel, MS, 91-; sc Grace pby, 14-

4519 Forest Drive, Laurel, MS 39440-1169 – 601-425-2614   Grace
E-mail: drsteveshuman@att.net
Covenant Presbyterian Church – 601-649-3683

Shurden, Nathan – astp First P Ch, Jackson, MS, 07-10; astp Parish P Ch, Franklin, TN, 10-11; op, p Cornerstone P Ch, Franklin, TN, 11-

3177 Tristan Drive, Franklin, TN 37064   Nashville
E-mail: nate@cstonepres.org
Cornerstone Presbyterian Church – 615-618-4707

Shurtliff, Will – O Oct 17, 10, GrLks Pby; astp Pathway Comm Ch, 10-17; op Christ Ch Ann Arbor, Ann Arbor, MI, 12-17, p 17-18

2043 Georgetown Boulevard, Ann Arbor, MI 48105 – 734-276-6119   Great Lakes
E-mail: william.shurtliff@gmail.com

Sibley, John Paul – b Columbus, MS, Sept 27, 79; f Danny P.; m Rebecca Cardwell; w Laurie Ingram; chdn Isaiah Daniel, Robert Patrick, Brynn Karis; FurU 02, BA; RTS 09, MDiv; O Aug 22, 09, Cal Pby; astp Redeemer P Ch, Greenville, SC, 09- 14; chp Orangeburg, SC, 14-16; op New City Flwsp Msn, Orangeburg, SC, 16-

835 Stanley Street, Orangeburg, SC 29115 – 864-238-5279   Lowcountry
E-mail: jpsibley@gmail.com
New City Fellowship Mission – 803-747-4935

Sica, Jason – w Katie; chdn Kylie, Naomi; GenC 02, BA; CTS 05, MDiv; O Nov 06, Hrtg Pby; astp Faith P Ch, Wilmington, DE, 05-10; op City Ch Wilmington, Wilmington, DE, 10-

1323 West 8th Street, Wilmington, DE 19806 – 302-409-0229   Heritage
E-mail: jason@citychurchwilmington.com
City Church Wilmington – 302-354-7451

Sickert, Jayme Smith – b Belo Horizonte, Brazil, Jun 21, 47; f Paulo; m Annie Smith; w Mary Elizabeth Gerstung, St. Louis, MO, Aug 17, 68; chdn Jonathan Edward, Joel Perrin, Amy Cecilia; CC 69, BA; CTS 74, MDiv; L , Midw Pby; O 74, SE Pby (RPCES); ap Glen Ridge RP Ch, St. Louis, MO, 74; op First Ref P Ch, Greensboro, NC, 74-76; p Faith P Ch, Myrtle Beach, SC, 76-81; moy Mitchell Road P Ch, Greenville, SC, 82-83; p Westminster P Ch, Clinton, SC, 83-89; MNA, 90-91; ob exec dir Sickert Ministries, Inc, 92-02; hr 02; ip Christ P Ch, Sharpesburg, GA, 10; p 11-

20 Plainfield Place, Newnan, GA 30065 – 678-552-9070   Metro Atlanta
E-mail: jssickert@bellsouth.net
Christ Presbyterian Church

Sicks, Christopher M. – w Sara Sundberg (d), (2) Naomi Moseley, Ellicott City, MD, Nov 5, 17; RTS 10; O Oct 17, 10, Pot Pby; astp Alexandria P Ch, Alexandria, VA, 10-15, ascp 15-; *Tangible-Making God Known Through Deeds of Mercy and Words of Truth*, 13

4502 Holborn Avenue, Annandale, VA 22003 – 703-626-7120   Potomac
E-mail: Chris.sicks@alexandriapres.org
Alexandria Presbyterian Church – 703-683-3348

Sidebotham, Bruce – b Lakeland, FL, Dec 24, 59; f Thomas; m Dorothy; w Theresa Lynn Dixon, Aug 29, 82; chdn Peter, David, Roger, Joseph; WheatC 81, BS; CIU 89, MA, 02, MDiv; NGTS 03, DMin; O 04, RMtn Pby; Chap USAR, 05-

18245 Knollwood Boulevard, Monument, CO 80132-8908 – 719-572-5963   Rocky Mountain
E-mail: bruce.t.sidebotham.mil@mail.mil
United States Army Reserve

Sidebotham, Thomas E. – b Yonkers, NY, Jun 3, 33; f John A.; m Helen Kleybecker; w Dorothy Louise Jacobsen (d) (2) Thelma J. Heagy, Placida, FL, Apr 8, 07; chdn Bruce T., April Radcliffe; BarC 55, BA; CTS 58, MDiv; WebsU 82, MA; L Jun 58, MidSo Pby; O Dec 13, 58, FL Pby (RPCES); ap BP Ch, Lakeland, FL, 58-61; p Faith P Ch, Sarasota, FL, 61-65; Chap USN, 65-82; admin CovCS, Orlando, FL, 82-95; ascp Covenant P Ch, Oviedo, FL, 83-95, wc 95-96; astp Willow Creek Ch, Winter Springs, FL, 96-02; hr 02

2533 Rustic Oak Court, Sarasota, FL 34232 – 941-830-0037   Suncoast Florida
E-mail: tomside@comcast.net
HR

Siegenthaler, Andrew Mercer – b Jackson, MS, Jun 2, 65; f Ronald; m Bertha; w Allison, Delray Bch, FL, Jun 25, 88; chdn Adrienne, Eliza, Will; CC 84-87, BA; CTS 90-92, MDiv; L Jul 14, 92; O Dec 6, 92, SWFL Pby; astp Marco P Ch, Marco Island, FL, 92-93, ascp 93-96; p Christ Cov P Ch, Cullman, AL, 96-

1736 Woodland Street NW, Cullman, AL 35055 – 256-737-5443   Providence
E-mail: Andrew@christcovenantcullman.org
Christ Covenant Presbyterian Church – 256-739-0505

Siegenthaler, Ronald Lynn – b Alliance, OH, Dec 18, 38; f Clyde S; m Marguerite Phillips; w Bertha Littleton, Atlanta, GA, Aug 26, 60; chdn Andrew Mercer, Anna Lee; UFL 57-58; BelC 61, BA; ColTS 64, BD; KTS 09, DD; O Sept 6, 64, CMS Pby; p Mt Hermon Ch, Madison, MS, 64-69; p First P Ch, Tuscumbia, AL, 69-85; ap Seacrest Boulevard P Ch, Delray Beach, FL, 85-89, p 89-97; ap, exec p Coral Ridge P Ch, Ft. Lauderdale, FL, 97-09; hr 10

10 Cotton Creek Circle, Black Mountain, NC 28711 – 754-224-7167   South Florida
E-mail: blsiegenthaler@gmail.com
HR

Siems, Leonard – w Colleen; chdn Albert; BrBC; RTS; O Nov 7, 04, MSVal Pby; Chap USArmy, 05-

2604 Wisser Street, Honolulu, HI 96819 – 814-806-9757   Mississippi Valley
E-mail: dagesh.lenny@gmail.com
United States Army

Siha, Zaka Anees – b Egypt, Mar 25, 42; f Zaka; m Senia; w Fareda Masri, Syria, Oct 22, 76; chdn Albert, Doreen, Alfred; Cairo 70, BA; UIN, grad wk; EvTS 70, MDiv; WTS 88, DMin, 85, ThM; AUBS 99, PhD, 04, Ed.D; O 71, Nile Syn (PCE); ap Egypt, 71-72; p, mis Syria, 72-80; mis USA to Arabic speaking, 81-; op Church Without Walls Msn, Willow Grove, PA; auth *Reformed Faith and Education* (Arabic), *Christology in Islam*; *Principles and Methods of Church Growth in North American Muslim Context*; *Al-Shahada Al Massihia* (in Arabic, trans of JM Boice's teaching on the Bible), 95; *Ten Steps in Witnessing to Muslims*, 98; co-auth *Muslims and Christians at the Table*, 99; *God in the Bible and the Quran*; *Jesus in the Bible and the Quran*; *How to Expain the Diety of Christ to Muslims*; *Moslems and Christians From Conflict to Conversation – Witnessing Without Compromising*; co-auth *The Truth About Islam: In the Light of Scriptures and History*; *It is Written: The use of Van Til's Biblical Apologetics for Doing Missions Among Muslims*, comp by Anees Zaka and Alfred A. Z.Siha; *Christology in Islam and the Biblical Antitheses*, 18

1334 Grovania Avenue, Abington, PA 19001-2511 – 215-887-3710   Eastern Pennsylvania
E-mail: cww.biis@juno.com
Church Without Walls Mission – 215-784-9194

Sikes, Maurice K. – b Atlanta, GA, Jan 15, 55; f Thomas R.; m Evelyn Jean Morris; w JoAnn Tatum, Atlanta, GA, Aug 20, 77; chdn Maurice Keith, Jr, Luke Thomas, James Michael; GSU 77, BS; IST 86, MDiv; L 85, Pac Pby; O 86, DMV Pby; op Lake Ridge Msn, Woodbridge, VA, 86-88; ascp Covenant P Ch, Palm Bay, FL, 88-05; ob ev

ION Alexandru nr. 25, Codlea, BV 505100 ROMANIA – 321-257-9812   Central Florida
E-mail: mauricesikes@gmail.com

Sillaman, Joshua P. – b Annapolis, MD, Nov 8, 84; f Randy; m Diane Battles; w Katrina Hatcher, Huntington, WV, Mar 15, 08; chdn Malachi, Gideon, Obadiah, Alethea; LibBC 07, BS; RTSDC 12, MDiv; O Nov 13, Chspk Pby; p Grace Point P Ch, Severn, MD, 13-

323 Wende Way, Glen Burnie, MD 21061 – 434-665-7099   Chesapeake
E-mail: Josh.sillaman@gmail.com
Grace Point Presbyterian Church – 410-969-2345

Silman, A. Campbell – b St. Louis, May 12, 76; f Henry Andrew; m Eleanor; w Rebecca, Zachary, LA, Jun 7, 97; chdn Andrew Ellis, Benjamin Campbell, Vaiden Mills; CC 99, BA; CTS 03, MDiv; O Jan 05, SoTX Pby; astp Southside Community Ch, Corpus Christi, TX, 03-06; astp Plains P Ch, Zachary, LA, 06-

1350 East Plains Port Hudson Road, Zachary, LA 70791 – 225-654-2089   Southern Louisiana
E-mail: campbell.plains@gmail.com
Plains Presbyterian Church – 225-654-2960

Silman, Henry Andrew – b Athens, GA, Apr 7, 50; f Clarence E; m Sara Grace Yonce; w Eleanor Rucker Vaiden, Augusta, GA, Aug 22, 70; chdn Shannon Elizabeth (Holland), Andrew Campbell; AugC 68-70; CBC 71-75, BA; CTS 75-78, MDiv; RTS 96, DMin; O Aug 6, 78, Cov Pby; ap The P Ch of Columbus, MS, 78-79; p First P Ch, Belzoni, MS, 79-81; p Redlands Comm Ch, Homestead, FL, 81-87; p Plains P Ch, Zachary, LA, 87-94; mid-South reg Coord, MNA, 93-98; srp First P Ch, Hattiesburg, MS, 94-06; GA MNA 92-96, chmn 94-96; bd trust CTS, 97-02; p Cornerstone P Ch, Brevard, NC, 06-; mod LA pby, 90-91; chmn WCar Shep co, 08-11; mod WCar pby, 11-12; brd dir, RidgeHaven, 11-12; chmn WCar RUF co, 12-

594 Gardner Lane, Pisgah Forest, NC 28768 – 828-885-6079   Western Carolina
E-mail: asilman@comporium.net
Cornerstone Presbyterian Church – 828-884-3305

Silverglate, Russell – f Lawrence; m Dale; w Beth Ann Mezzatesta; chdn Dylan Nicholas, Quinn Alexander; UFL 85, BA, 88, JD; RTS 04, MDiv; p Hammock Street Ch, Boca Raton, FL, 09-

22500 Hammock Street, Boca Raton, FL 33428   Gulfstream
E-mail: russell@hammockstreetchurch.com
Hammock Street Church – 561-483-0460

Silvernail, David V. Jr. – b Syracuse, NY, May 19, 58; f David V; m Ann Miller; w Joanne Leslie Marshall, Wayland, MA, Jun 20, 82; chdn David VanBenschoten III, Rebecca Lynn, Sarah Constance, Daniel Marshall, Samuel Miller; AmU 80, BA; GCTS 91, MDiv; CTS 06, DMin; L Sept 23, 91; O Nov 10, 91, SEAL Pby; p First P Ch, Enterprise, AL, 91-96; p Potomac Hills P Ch, Leesburg, VA, 97-; guest lect RTSDC, 10-

714 Catoctin Circle NE, Leesburg, VA 20176-4943 – 703-777-5795   Potomac
E-mail: dsilvernail@potomachills.org
Potomac Hills Presbyterian Church – 703-771-1534

Sim, Bill – w Grace; chdn Joshua, Charissa; CentBC, BA; CTS, MDiv; p New Ch of Atlanta, Atlanta, GA, 04-18, p em 18-

9415 Coleherne Court, Alpharetta, GA 30022 – 770-417-1404   Korean Southeastern
E-mail: bsim@pcanet.org

Sim, Hoseup – op Korean Cov P Msn, Marietta, GA, 03-11; mis Alti Mission, Korea, 11-

1396 Brookcliff Drive, Marietta, GA 30062 – 770-579-0379   Korean Southeastern
E-mail: hoseupsim@msn.com
Alti Mission, Korea

Simmons, Jay – astp Old Orchard Ch, Webster Groves, MO, 05-10; op South City Ch, St. Louis, MO, 06-10, p 10- 14; astp All Saints P Ch, Austin, TX, 14-; op Grace and Peace P Ch of Austin, Austin, TX, 16-17, srp 17-18

3305 Harris Park Avenue, Austin, TX 78705   South Texas
E-mail: simmonsjayd@gmail.com

Simmons, Scott A. – b Ft. Belvoir, VA, Dec 15, 53; f Henry C.; m Marion Gentle; w Valerie A Schilb, Miami, FL, Aug 18, 79; chdn Everet, Calder; UFL 71-75, BS, BA; RTS 78-81, MDiv; O Oct 18, 81, Everglades Pby; p No Miami Bch P Ch, 81-85; p First P Ch, Apopka, FL, 85-87; astp Old Cutler P Ch, Miami, FL, 87-94; p DaySpring P Ch, Spring Hill, FL, 94-04; ob p Covenant Ch (ind), Gainesville, FL, 07-08; Comm P Ch, McIntosh, FL, 08-

3541 NW 23 Place, Gainesville, FL 32605 – 352-246-1639   North Florida
E-mail: cpcscott@cox.net
Community Presbyterian Church – 352-591-1517

Simmons, Scott J. – b Columbus, OH, Jun 29, 68; f Paul; m Nancy Walker; w Sundee Michelle Perkins, Reisterstown, MD, Apr 25, 92; chdn Nathan Marshall, Emily Ruth, Julianna Lee; JMU 87-91, BS; RTS 94-97, MDiv; O Oct 14, 01, Pot Pby; astp Chapelgate P Ch, Marriottsville, MD, 01-05, ascp 05-09; ob 10-

1804 East Cheryl Drive, Winter Park, FL 32792   Central Florida

Simmons, Steven Gregory – b Fayetteville, NC, May 27, 55; f William Belvin; m Alvie Pearl Stewart; w Jane Dorothy Grinton, Columbia, SC, Aug 11, 79; chdn Katie, Betsy, Jenny, Lorrie, Greg, John; CBC 78, BS; MidABTS 83, MDiv; RTS 95, DMin; L 88, Palm Pby; O Aug 8, 82; Recd PCA Jul 10, 90, TNVal Pby; p First P Ch, Crossville, TN, 90-98; ob p Immanuel Fell Ch, Kalamazoo, MI, 99-03; p Fifth Street P Ch, Tyler, TX, 04-

3007 Oak Knob, Tyler, TX 75701 – 903-312-3156   North Texas
E-mail: steve@fifthstreetpca.org
Fifth Street Presbyterian Church – 903-592-1613

Simmons, Wes – w Nancy; chdn Emily Anne, Katherine Grace; RTSFL 06, MABS, MAC; astp Second P Ch, Memphis, TN, 07-10; campm RUF, CarNewC, 10- 14; campm RUF, AubU, 14-

824 Heard Avenue, Auburn, AL 36830   Southeast Alabama
E-mail: wes.simmons@ruf.org
PCA Reformed University Fellowship

Simoneau, James Robert – b Hialeah, FL, Oct 17, 53; f William Arthur; m Jane Montgomery; w Susan Welford Cathey, Columbia, SC, Jun 26, 76; chdn Christopher Welford (d), Beverly Joy, Joel Brian, Jonathan William, Laura Elizabeth; CBC 73-77, BA; RTS 77-80, MDiv, 88-92, DMin; L Apr 21, 77; O Aug 3, 80, Cal Pby; p Scherer Mem P Ch, Lake Wylie, SC, 80-88; p Church Creek Ref P Ch, Charleston, SC, 88-96; srp New Cov P Ch, Aiken, SC, 96-02; srp Young Meadows P Ch, Montgomery, AL, 02-

8619 Rockbridge Circle, Montgomery, AL 36116 – 334-356-6469   Southeast Alabama
E-mail: jsimoneau@ympca.org
Young Meadows Presbyterian Church – 334-244-1385

Simpson, Grady Erskine Jr. – b Birmingham, AL, Dec 6, 27; f Grady Erskine S; m Esther Gary; w Leta Bouck, San Francisco, CA, Aug 1, 46; chdn John M, Patricia E, Mary Lois; BhamSoC 60-61; RolC 62-65; GSU 65-66; ColTS 65-68; O Feb 2, 69, Atl Pby; astp Westminster P Ch, Atlanta, GA, 69-70; p Mount Salus P Ch, Clinton, MS, 71-73; mis Liberia, 73-77; ev MUS Evan Pby, 77-80; p Evangel P Ch, Helena, AL, 80-83; mis Kenya, 84-87; MNA, 87-89; astp Covenant P Ch, Birmingham, AL, 89-92; hr 92; astp Evangel P Ch, Helena, AL, 97-04; ch admin Evangel Ch, Alabaster, AL, 05-10

1967 Riva Ridge Road, Helena, AL 35080 – 205-223-9830   Evangel
E-mail: gsimpson12.06@att.net
HR

Sin, Timothy Tae – GroCC 08; WTS 12, MDiv; O Oct 12, KorE Pby; astp Cornerstone P Ch, Chalfont, PA, 12-15; astp New Life Msn Ch of Colorado, Aurora, CO, 15-

15912 East Dakota Place, Unit C, Aurora, CO 80017   Rocky Mountain
E-mail: ttsin1@gmail.com
New Life Mission Church of Colorado – 303-337-9191

Sinclair, Bruce Alan – b Cleveland, OH, Aug 24, 57; f James Robert; m Evangeline Jane Vahey; w Pamela Dean Messer, Hazelwood, NC, May 26, 79; chdn Timothy Daniel, Celeste Arlene; UNCC 75-76; FBC 76-79, BA; CapBS 79-83, ThM; O Aug 19, 83, Faith Bible Ch; chp CAM Intn'l, Mexico, 84-88; sp Covenant P Ch, 89, p 89-91; p Abingdon P Ch, 91-95; adj prof KgC, 95; chp, op New Song Ch, 96-99, p 99-03; astp Christ Comm Ch, 03-04; mis MTW, 04-; lect Westm Theo C, Kampala, Uganda, 05-; adj prof African Bible College, Kampala, Uganda, 06-; acad dn Westm Theo C, Kampala, Uganda, 06-; prof Westm Theo Sem, Uganda, 07-

c/o MTW   Gulf Coast
E-mail: bpsinclair@gmail.com
PCA Mission to the World

Sinclair, David G. Sr. – b Columbus, GA, Nov 17, 57; f W.G.; m Joy Simpson; w Rebecca Sue Purvis, Union, SC, May 24, 80; chdn David Graham Jr, Laura Catherine, Benjamin Tyler; ClemU 80, BS; CTS 84, MDiv; RTS 97, DMin; O Aug 84, Cal Pby; campm RUM, ClemU, 84-97; srp Lexington P Ch, Lexington, SC, 97-07; srp Clemson P Ch, Clemson, SC, 07-

218 King's Way, Clemson, SC 29631 – 864-654-2106   Calvary
E-mail: david.sinclair@clemsonpres.org
Clemson Presbyterian Church – 864-654-4772

Sinclair, Gary – O Aug 26, 18, MSVal Pby; astp First P Ch, Jackson, MS, 18-

772 Pinehurst Place, Jackson, MS 39202   Mississippi Valley
E-mail: garys@fpcjackson.org
First Presbyterian Church – 601-353-8316

Sinclair, Steven – TTS, PhD; astp Christ the King PCA Ch, Seminole, FL, 08-; prof St. Petersburg College

6797 122 Street North, Seminole, FL 33777 – 727-393-7262   Southwest Florida
E-mail: sdg2323@gmail.com
Christ the King PCA Church – 727-394-0787
St. Petersburg College – 727-244-1973

Singenstreu, Michael A. – b Mt. Gilead, OH, Dec 20, 55; w Leslie Kay Williams, Feb 7, 76; chdn Zachary (d), Laura, Hannah, Clara, Tanner; RBC 87, BRE; CTS 91, MDiv; L May 9, 93; O May 9, 93, Ill Pby; int CV, Ballwin, MO; ip Faith EFC, Cape Girardeau, MO, 92-93; p Marissa P Ch, Marissa, IL, 93-97; op Christ P Ch, Victoria, TX, 98-02; bd trust RBC, 97-04; Chap, Dir Victoria Fire Dep, 01-; p Christ P Ch, Victoria, TX, 02-

541 Springwood, Victoria, TX 77905 – 361-935-4559   South Texas
E-mail: pastordad@nodial.net
Christ Presbyterian Church – 361-935-4559

Singletary, Steve – BDS, MDiv; RTS, DMin; astp Covenant P Ch, Birmingham, AL, 02-09; ob Center for Executive Leadership, 09-

2781 Acton Place, Birmingham, AL 35243 – 205-970-7332   Evangel
E-mail: ssingletary@cfel-al.org
Center for Executive Leadership

MINISTERIAL DIRECTORY

Singleton, James Ellsworth – b Duluth, MN, Mar 26, 43; f Glenn E.; m Margaret M. Brewer; w Beverly J. Kesselring, Underwood, ND, Jul 1, 66; chdn Clay, Kirk, Kendra; CC 65, BA; CTS 69, MDiv; L Apr 6, 68, RMt Pby; O May 28, 69, FL Pby (RPCES); Chap USAR; p Covenant P Ch, Wheat Ridge, CO, 72-78; p P Ch, Calabasas, CA, 78-90; sc Pac Pby; Chap USArmy, 91-03; astp Village Seven P Ch, Colorado Springs, CO, 91-92, ascp 92-99, chap YMCA of the Rockies, 07-08; chap Courtside Min, 08-15; hr 15

35 Woodmen Court, Colorado Springs, CO 80919-2516 – 719-598-9622   Rocky Mountain
E-mail: jsingle419@aol.com
HR

Sink, Jeremy Wayne – b Cape Cod, MA, Apr 5, 71; f Russell Wayne; m Judy Diane; w Regina Perryman, Lexington, NC, Oct 7, 95; chdn Joshua Wayne, Josiah Lee, Garrett Franklin; EmbryR 89-92; UNCC, BS; RTSNC 97-01, MDiv; L Jan 27, 01, CentCar Pby; O Jul 8, 01, PTri Pby; int Meadowview Ref P Ch, Lexington, NC, 97-01, astp 01; op Gr Flwsp Msn, Asheboro, NC, 01-05, p 05-10; mis MTW, Nagoya, Japan, 11-18; fm Serge, Japan, 18-

2358 Lamb Road, Lexington, NC 27295 – 336-308-5359   Piedmont Triad
E-mail: jwsink@gmail.com
Serge

Sinn, Tedrick – astp Trinity P Ch, Lakeland, FL, 04-07; op City Ch Orlando, Orlando, FL, 08-

1222 Latta Lane, Orlando, FL 32804-6380   Central Florida
City Church Orlando

Sinnard, Benjamin – astp Redeemer PCA, Lincoln, NE, 12-13; astp Cornerstone Ch, Delafield, WI, 13-18, ascp 18-

1115 West Sunset Drive, Waukesha, WI 53189 – 262-422-4457   Wisconsin
E-mail: bensinnard@cornerstone-pca.com
Cornerstone Church – 262-646-6445

Siple, Matt – O 15, GAFH Pby; astp Redeemer P Ch, Athens, GA, 15-

165 Pulaski Street, Athens, GA 30601 – 706-714-9916   Georgia Foothills
E-mail: msiple@redeemerathens.com
Redeemer Presbyterian Church – 706-227-3344

Sisco, Abel – O Jan 16, 10; chp; wc 18

613 James Boulevard, Signal Mountain, TN 37377 – 423-544-4011   Platte Valley
E-mail: abelsisco@gmail.com

Sittema, John R. – w Carol Beckham; TCC 71, AB; CalvS 75, MDiv; WSCAL 86, DMin; O Sept 25, 75, CRC; Recd PCA 02, CentCar Pby; srp Sanborn CRC, IA, 75-81; srp First CRC, Pella, IA, 81-89; srp Bethel CRC, Dallas, TX, 89-02; astp, medu, mfam Christ Cov P Ch, Matthews, NC, 02-05; p Christ Ch, Jacksonville, FL, 05- 14, astp; ob pres Mission: Hope, 14-; *With A Shepherd's Heart: Reclaiming the Office of Elder*, 96; *Called to Preach: Pondering God's Commission for Your Life*, 89; *Meeting Jesus at the Feast: The Festivals of Israel and the Gospel*, 10

937 Herrons Ferry Road, Rock Hill, SC 29730 – 904-899-2219   North Florida
E-mail: jrs@sittema.org
Mission: Hope

Skeele, Harrison – Amherst 78, BA; TEDS 86, MDiv, 87, ThM; WTS, PhD cand; Recd PCA Mar 12, 00, MNY Pby; op Crossroads Comm Ch, Hillsborough, NJ, 00-10, p 10-

567 Southwoods Road, Hillsborough, NJ 08844 – 908-431-9674   Metropolitan New York
E-mail: pastor@crossroadsnj.org
Crossroads Community Church – 908-431-4373

Skipper, Gregory C. – astp New Covenant P Ch, Anderson, SC, 08-09; ob Dir Calv Home for Chdn, Anderson, SC, 09-

218 Devon Way, Anderson, SC 29621   Calvary
E-mail: greg@calvaryhome.org
Calvary Home for Children – 864-296-5437
110 Calvary Home Circle, Anderson, SC 29621-1002

Skipper, Jeff – ascp Redeemer Winter Haven, FL, 12-

613 Oak Avenue, Eagle Lake, FL 33839 – 863-287-3840   Southwest Florida
E-mail: jeff.skipper@yahoo.com
Redeemer Winter Haven – 863-298-9849

Sklar, Jay – prof CTS, 06-

12330 Conway Road, St. Louis, MO 63141   Missouri
Covenant Theological Seminary – 314-434-4044

Skogen, Seth – O Nov 11, 18, Palm Pby; astp Rose Hill P Ch, Columbia, SC, 18-

217 South Saluda Avenue, Columbia, SC 29205   Palmetto
Rose Hill Presbyterian Church – 803-771-6775

Skylling, Mark Anders – O Nov 18, 18, CentCar Pby; astp Uptown Church, PCA, Charlotte, NC, 18-

801 Heather Lane, Charlotte, NC 28209 – 224-430-8003   Central Carolina
E-mail: markskylling@gmail.com
Uptown Church, PCA – 704-375-7355

Slack, Dennis Paul – ob 13-

1206 North Petty Road, Muncie, IN 47304 – 765-273-7285   Central Indiana
E-mail: d.slack@munciemission.org

Slate, Shawn – astp Covenant P Ch, St. Louis, MO, 02-05; campm RUF, UVA, 05-15; srp Redeemer Ch of Knoxville, TN, 15-

1012 Thompson Place, Knoxville, TN 37917 – 434-284-1274   Tennessee Valley
E-mail: slate@redeemerknoxville.org
Redeemer Church of Knoxville – 865-524-4552

Slater, Joseph M. – b Sept 21, 67; f James A.; m Joan C.; w Terri L. Brown, Hopewell, VA, Jul 1, 89; chdn Nathan A., Anna R., Austin M., Iain T., Naomi G.; JMU 85-89, BS; RTSFL 92-96, MDiv; L Apr 13, 96; O Oct 13, 96, JR Pby; ydir Covenant P Ch, Harrisonburg, VA, 94-96, ascp, moy 96-14; campm RUF, JamesMadU, 14-

3125 Flint Avenue, Harrisonburg, VA 22801 – 540-383-8321   Blue Ridge
E-mail: joe.slater@ruf.org
PCA Reformed University Fellowship

Slaton, Benjamin – b Sept 23, 75; w Natalie; chdn Elise, Sam, Andrew; SMU, BA; RTS, MDiv; O Feb 1, 04, SoTX Pby; campm RUF, 03-09; astp All Saints P Ch, Austin, TX, 09- 12; astp Redeemer P Ch, San Antonio, TX, 12-15; ascp 15-18; chp 18-

E-mail: benjislaton@gmail.com   Tennessee Valley

MINISTERIAL DIRECTORY 581

Slawter, William Draper III – b Chester, PA, May 16, 48; f William D. Jr.; m Anna Lee Sutcliffe; w Judith Nell Barker, Houghton, NY, Oct 31, 70; chdn Kathryn Eileen, Sarah Beth, Jennifer Nell, William David; HougC 70, BS; BibTS 79, MDiv; CTS 85, DMin; L Jun 11, 80; O May 15, 81, Pitts Pby (RPCES); op Jersey RP, Pataskala, OH, 80-82; p Jersey P Ch, 83-84; MTW, Autsralia, 84-92; p Covenant Community P Ch, Wexford, PA, 92-94; mout First Evangelical P Ch, East Liverpool, OH, 95; p East Ridge P Ch, East Ridge, TN, 96-01; astp First P Ch, Ft. Oglethorpe, GA, 02-06; ob Pastors in Residence, 06; p Hope Ch, Ballston Spa, NY, 06-13; wc 13; hr 14

25 Park Avenue, Newport News, VA 23607 – 757-380-0583   Tidewater
HR

Sleeth, Brian C. – b Baton Rouge, LA, Jul 26, 68; f Larry K.(d); m Betty Jean Smith; w Stacy Marie Spradley, Baton Rouge, LA, Aug 25, 90; chdn Brianna Evangeline, Benjamin Titus, Shepherd Shiloh, Gideon Josiah; LSU 90, BA; MSU 92, cert; RTS 96, MDiv; CTS 08, DMin; L Feb 95, MSVal Pby; O Mar 2, 97, Pot Pby; int Highlands P Ch, Ridgeland, MS, 93-96; ascp Cornerstone P Ch, California, MD, 96-00; op Harvest Flwsp, Lusby, MD, 96-00, p 00-05, chp 05-06; op GracePointe P Ch, Novi, MI, 06-09; srp Covenant P Ch at Greenville, Greenville, MS, 09-10; wc 10-13; exec dir The Christian Outreach Center, Baton Rouge, LA, 13-

10170 Garden Oaks Avenue, Denham Springs, LA 70706 – 225-614-3292   Southern Louisiana
E-mail: briansleeth@me.com

Slimp, Robert Louis – b Inglewood, CA, Feb 15, 29; f Louis Lea; m Anna Alice Weaver; w Urcula Elisabeth Sommer, Nurenburg, Germany, Sept 10, 60; chdn Robert Stephen, Louis Haus, Thomas Jefferson; BayU 46-50, BA; CST 50-53, MDiv; L 51, Meth Ch; O Jun 53, Evan Meth Ch, Altona, PA; Chap USArmy, 53-73; p Calvary Ch, Columbia, SC, 77-84; ob sp First Bible P Ch, Grand Junction, CO, 86-87, wc 88-89; ss Liberty Springs P Ch, Cross Hill, SC, 90-95; hr 96; ss Liberty Springs P Ch, Cross Hill, SC, 00, 05-06; Lt Col USArmy, Bronze Star for valor in combat, Vietnam; Meritorious Service Medal, Army Commendation Medal (3 oak leaf clusters); edtls/art *Christian Observer*; *Christian News*

100 Joseph Walker Drive, Laurel Crest, Room 642-1, West Columbia, SC 29169   Palmetto
803-782-0924
E-mail: ruslimp@bellsouth.net
HR

Sloan, Fred L. – b Birmingham, AL, Mar 3, 48; f Fred F.; m Annie Lee Crump; w Grace Scott Nesbit, Dalton, GA, May 26, 70; chdn Joel Andrew, Michael Asher, John Elliott, Elizabeth Ann; TNTC 70, BA; TEDS 74, MDiv; O Jul 14, 01, JR Pby; ob p Westminster Ref P Ch, 01-03; wc 04-

1805 Capeway Road, Powhatan, VA 23139 – 804-598-7391   James River
E-mail: flsoan@gmail.com

Sloan, Mike – b Richmond, VA, Dec 20, 77; f Fred L.; m Grace Nesbit Sloan; w Emily Ann McCampbell, Sweetwater, TN, Jun 16, 01; chdn Anna Grace, Elanor Martha, Lucy Elizabeth, Matilda Asher, Jane Nesbit; CC 01, BA; CTS 08, MDiv; O Feb 15, 09, GAFH Pby; astp Old Peachtree P Ch, Duluth, GA, 09-11; ascp 11- 14; op New City P Ch, Hilliard, OH, 14-15

6062 Glade Run Road, Hilliard, OH 43026   Columbus Metro
E-mail: mikeasloan@gmail.com

Smalling, Roger – b Seattle, WA, Jul 14, 44; f Duel Cloy; m Doris Pearl Cleeton; w Dianne Powers, London, England, Aug 19, 72; USCA-LB 64-65; BapCU 85-86, BA; UNCO 87-88, BA; BapCU 86-87, MA; MiamiIntSem 02, MTS; Miami Int U, DMin; O Jul 19, 97, Wcar Pby; mis MTW, Quito, Ecuador, 97-16; Dir VisionReal, Miami, 01-; *Unlocking Grace: A Study Guide in the Doctrines of Grace; Si, Jesusz*

Smalling, Roger, continued
(Spanish version of *Unlocking Grace*); *Liderazgo Cristiano; Felizmente Justificados* (Spanish version of *Joyfully Justified*); *El Evangelio de la Prosperidad: Los Neo-Carismáticos* (Spanish version of *The Prosperity Movement: Wounded Charismatics*)

14825 SW 112 Street, Miami, FL 33196 – 305-752-7617   Western Carolina
E-mail: rlsds@bellsouth.net; www.smallings.com
VisionReal, Miami

Smallman, Robert Tibbals – b Suffern, NY, Jan 29, 47; f Frank Edward; m Elizabeth Tibbals; w Linda Douglas, Pontiac, MI, Dec 21, 68; chdn Heather Elizabeth, Robert Scott, Holly Diane; BJU 68, BA; TEDS 72, MDiv, 76-77, grad wk, 85, ThM; L 73; O 73, Midw Pby (RPCES); op Good Shepherd P Ch, Valparaiso, IN, 73-75; p BPC, Merrill, WI, 78-; sc NoIL Pby, 93-99; sc Wisc Pby, 06-11; hr 15; ip Swamp Christian Fell, Reinholds, PA, 16-17

1007 East 3rd Street, Merrill, WI 54452-2529 – 715-536-7863   Wisconsin
E-mail: bob.smallman29@gmail.com
HR

Smallman, Stephen Edward Jr. – b Orlando, FL, Aug 14, 62; f Stephen E.; m Sandra Yoder; w Lutz, Greenville, SC, Aug 4, 84; chdn Isaiah, Paul; CC 85, BA; WTS 91, MDiv; L May 93; O Feb 27, 94, Pot Pby; yp New City Flwsp, Chattanooga, TN, 85-87; yp Spirit & Truth Fellowship (CRC), Philadelphia, PA, 88-92; astp New Song Comm Ch, Baltimore, MD, 94-95, ascp 95-

519 Overdale Road, Baltimore, MD 21229 – 410-371-1600   Chesapeake
New Song Community Church – 410-728-2816

Smallman, Stephen Edward Sr. – b Suffern, NY, May 29, 40; f Frank E.; m Elizabeth Tibbals; w Sandra Yoder, Greenville, SC, May 31, 61; chdn Stephen Jr., Cynthia, Christa, Andrew; BJU 62, BA, 64, MA; CTS 67, MDiv; IHLS 76; L Oct 67; O Jan 68, Phil Pby (RPCES); srp McLean P Ch, McLean, VA, 68-96; ob exec dir WHM, 97-01; srp New Life Northeast P Ch, Philadelphia, PA, 01-05; hr 06; astp New Life P Ch, Glenside, PA, 10-16; ip liberti Fairmount, Philadelphia, PA, 11-12; hr 16; "Understanding the Faith;" "What is a Reformed Church?" "What is True Conversion?" *Beginnings-Understanding How We Experience the New Birth*, 06; *Forty Days on the Mountain*; *How Our Children Come to Faith*; *The Walk-Steps for New and Renewed Followers of Jesus*; *What is Discipleship?*

214 Brookdale Court, Dresher, PA 19025-1516 – 215-793-4112   Philadelphia
E-mail: stephensmallman@mac.com
HR

Smart, Robert Davis – b Columbia, MO, Mar 30, 60; f John Stevenson S.; m Elizabeth Anne Thompson; w Karen Lee Grose, Cleveland, OH, Sept 15, 84; chdn Emily Mae, Nathaniel Chipman, Jonathan William, Ethan Gardiner, Elizabeth Grace; Purdue 82, BS; CTS 93, MDiv; UWales 08, PhD; L Sept 91, GrLks Pby; O Jun 13, 93, NoIL Pby; staff Navs, Purdue & BallSU, 86-90; int Twin Oaks P Ch, Ballwin, MO, 90-93; srp Christ Ch, Normal, IL, 93-; "Jonathan Edwards' Experimental Calvinism: Pastors Learning Revival Harmony of Theology and Experience from a Leader in the Great Awakening," *Reformation and Revival Journal*, vol 12, no. 3 (03); *Jonathan Edward's Aplogetic for the Great Awakening*, 10

1629 Cheyenne Lane, Normal, IL 61761 – 309-862-2405   Northern Illinois
E-mail: rs.revival@frontier.com
Christ Church – 309-452-7927

Smartt, Kennedy – b Lookout Mt, TN, Nov 7, 24; f J E S; m Mary Read; w Mary Van Voorhis (d), Schenectady, NY, Aug 16, 52; chdn Matthew Kennedy, Daniel Arnold, Ellen Maria (Manning), Mary Elizabeth (Carter); DavC 49, BA; WTS 50-52; ColTS 54, BD; AUBS 93, DD; O Jan 54, Atl Pby; p

MINISTERIAL DIRECTORY

Smartt, Kennedy, continued
Ingleside P Ch, Lawrenceville, GA, 54-60; Chap RabGSch, 60-62; p Rabun Gap Ch, 60-62; p West End P Ch, Hopewell, VA, 62-77; assoc, coord MTW, 77-82; MNA, coord ev, 82-92; astp, mout/evan Chestnut Mountain P Ch, Chestnut Mountain, GA, 93-; *I Am Reminded: A History of the PCA*, 94

PO Box 7095, Chestnut Mountain, GA 30502-0001 – 770-967-4695, 770-540-7191   Georgia Foothills
E-mail: kennedy.mary.smartt@gmail.com
Chestnut Mountain Presbyterian Church – 770-967-3440

Smed, John P. F. – b Calgary, AB, Canada, Feb 6, 53; f Kai; m Lydia Jensen; w Caron Harper, Calgary, AB, Mar 8, 74; chdn Teresa, Elisa, Erica, Matthew, Jennifer; UCalg 77-81, BA; WTS 82-85, MDiv; L Nov 20, 85; O Nov 20, 85, PacNW Pby; op, p Woodgreen P Ch, Calgary, AB, 85-91; MNA, coord chp, 91-99; op, chp, ev Grace Vancouver, Vancouver, BC, 99-08, p 08-12; astp 12-

11350 Maddock Avenue, Lake Country, BC V4V 2J6 CANADA – 604-565-9001   Western Canada
E-mail: jfsmed@gmail.com
Grace Vancouver – 604-738-3537

Smit, Joel – b Sioux Center, IA, Feb 4, 80; f David; m Marian Walhof; w Stefanie Coenen, Redding, CA, Oct 18, 03; chdn Peter David, Evelyn Corinne, Alice Claire, Paul Robert; SimpC 02, BA; GPTS 08, MDiv; O Jun 8, 08, NWGA Pby; int Woodruff Road P Ch, Simpsonville, SC, 07-08; astp Midway P Ch, Powder Springs, GA, 08-16; p Smyrna P Ch, Smyrna, GA, 16-

970 Waverly Court SW, Marietta, GA 30064 – 678-363-4865   Northwest Georgia
E-mail: joel.smit@smyrnapres.org
Smyrna Presbyterian Church – 770-435-2251

Smith, Allen – w Sandi; chdn Abigail, Adeline, Mary, Evangline; RTS, MDiv; L Jan 16, 04, Gr Pby; p Ellisville P Ch, Ellisville, MS, 04-05; ob mis Christian Missionary Society, 06-15; astp Perimeter Ch, Johns Creek, GA, 15-17; astp Crossbridge Ch Miami, Miami, FL, 17-18; ob astp Bay Area Comm Ch, Annapolis, MD, 18-

637 Snow Goose Lane, Annapolis, MD 21409 – 501-400-2202   Chesapeake
E-mail: allensmith1976@gmail.com
Bay Area Community Church, Annapolis, MD

Smith, Cameron – b Wyalusing, PA, Jan 1, 86; w Kaela; chdn Zoe, Lucy; PASU 08, BS; CTS 13, MDiv; O 14, TNVal Pby; campm RUF, Car-NewC, 14-

715 West Jefferson Street, Jefferson City, TN 37760   Tennessee Valley
E-mail: cms5019@gmail.com
PCA Reformed University Fellowship

Smith, Carl Eric – b Jackson, MS, Jun 16, 52; f Jacob F.; m Melba Louise Taylor; w Martha Diane Dorroh, Caruthersville, MO, Jun 7, 75; chdn Nathan Alan, Rachel Anne; MSU 70-74, BS; RTS 74-78, MDiv, MCE; O Aug 13, 78, CentGA Pby; ap Vineville P Ch, Macon, GA, 78-81; astp Orangewood P Ch, Maitland, FL, 81-82, ascp 82-08; astp Faith P Ch, Birmingham, AL, 08-

4601 Valleydale Road, Birmingham, AL 35242   Evangel
E-mail: csmith@faith-pca.org
Faith Presbyterian Church – 205-991-5430

Smith, Carl Michael – b Hodgenville, KY, Dec 27, 54; f Otis Ray; m Rita Comer; w Rinda Marie Lockett, Knoxville, TN, May 28, 77; chdn James Michael, Joel Ray, Abigail Marie; WKU 76, BS; GCTS

Smith, Carl Michael, continued
81, MDiv; L Oct 11, 81; O Oct 11, 81, TNVal Pby; ap Cedar Springs P Ch, Knoxville, TN, 81-87; astp Christ Comm Ch, Franklin, TN, 88-95, ascp 95-; *Getting Ready for a Lifetime of Love*; *Six Steps to Prepare for a Great Marriage*, 99

114 Poteat Place, Franklin, TN 37064   Nashville
E-mail: mike.smith@christcommunity.org
Christ Community Church – 615-468-2200

Smith, Chad – b Little Rock, AR, Sept 8, 75; w Jennifer L. Tragesser; chdn Amelia, Benjamin, Elliott; UT, BA; RTS, MDiv; campm RUF, BelhC; campm RUF, EastTNState, 11-16; p Trinity P Ch, Asheville, NC, 16

17 Shawnee Trail, Asheville, NC 28805   Western Carolina
E-mail: chad@trinityasheville.com
Trinity Presbyterian Church – 828-299-3433

Smith, Christopher – b Philadelphia, PA, Apr 12, 68; f Marshall; w Sonja Christine Hopkins, IN, May 16, 92; chdn Abigail, Hannah Grace, Alexander, Andrew; Purdue, BA; CTS, MDiv; O Oct 01, MO Pby; astp Providence Ref P Ch, St. Louis, MO, 01-03, ascp 03-11; op Resurrection P Ch, St. Louis, MO, 09-14; ob 14- 16; astp Covenant P Ch, St. Louis, MO, 16-

965 Briarton Drive, St. Louis, MO 63126 – 314-962-1953   Missouri
E-mail: ctsmith53@gmail.com
Covenant Presbyterian Church – 314-432-8700

Smith, Corey – b Mar 2, 77; w Janet; chdn Tyler, Drew, Luke; CTS, MDiv; O May 22, 11, CentInd Pby; astp Christ Comm Ch, Carmel, IN, 10-15; srp Midtown Ch, Indianaplis, IN, 15-

5140 North Park Avenue, Indianapolis, IN 46205 – 317-869-9044   Central Indiana
E-mail: corey@midtownchurchindy.org
Midtown Church – 317-414-0602

Smith, D. Blair – b Toledo, OH, Dec 20, 75; f J. Douglas; m Lynn Ericson; w Lisa Marie Leafgren, Toledo, OH, Oct 18, 03; chdn Eleanor Corinne, Douglas Blair, Lucile Lynn, John Graham; BJU 97, BS; RTS 03, MDiv; HDS 07, ThM; O Jul 28, 07, GrLks Pby; ob astp Fourth EPC, Bethesda, MD, 07-5; ascp Michiana Cov Ch, Granger, IN, 15-16; asst prof RTSNC, 16-

6608 Gold Wagon Lane, Mint Hill, NC 28227 – 301-542-3083   Central Carolina
E-mail: dblairsmith@gmail.com
Reformed Theological Seminary, NC – 704-366-5066
2101 Carmel Road, Charlotte, NC 28226

Smith, Dale L. – b Pasadena, CA, Mar 6, 49; f Lansing T III; m Carolyn J. Linson; w C. Anne Miller, Pensacola, FL, May 22, 71; chdn Catherine Rozear, Meredith Taylor, Jonathan Edwards, Benjamin Baxter; PerkJC; CC, BA; CTS, MDiv; O Nov 30, 76, TX Pby; srp Colleyville P Ch, Colleyville, TX, 76-14; hr 14

6512 Paula Court, North Richland Hills, TX 76180-4238 – 817-498-6813   North Texas
HR

Smith, Daniel – b Tyler, TX, Mar 23, 83; f Philip; m Dorothy Gracey; w Brittany Lead, Mesquite, TX; UOK 05, BA; CTS 12, MDiv; O Oct 14, 12, NoTX Pby; campm RUF, UTXT, 12-17; campm RUF, UAZ, 17-

3202 E. Pima Street, Tucson, AZ 85716 – 903-360-6316   North Texas
E-mail: dan.smith@ruf.org
PCA Reformed University Fellowship

Smith, Daniel Joseph – b Takoma Park, MD, Jun 26, 65; f W. Harley; m Patricia A. Summers; w Sandra M. Boerum, Annapolis, MD, Feb 23, 91; chdn Grant Daniel, Elliot Warren, Natalie Summers; TowU 88, BS; RTSFL 94, MDiv; L Oct 94; O May 28, 95, Pot Pby; srp Grace Evangelical P Ch, Davidsonville, MD, 95-00; astp Evangelical P Ch, Annapolis, MD, 01-09, ascp 09-

734 LaRue Road, Millersville, MD 21108 – 410-849-3366　　　　　　　　　　Chesapeake
E-mail: dansmith@epannapolis.org
Evangelical Presbyterian Church – 410-266-8090

Smith, Darren – astp Concord P Ch, Waterloo, IL, 06-08; ascp 08-12; astp The Ch of Gr Village: A Comm of the PCA, Nashville, TN, 12-

8300 Oak Knoll Drive, Brentwood, TN 37027　　　　　　　　　　　　　　　　Nashville
E-mail: betterstory.ds@gmail.com
The Church of Grace Village: A Community of the PCA – 615-810-9845

Smith, David B. – b Jasper, AL, Jan 2, 62; f James Lewis; m Carolyn Hayne; w Adelia Russell, Tuscaloosa, AL, Dec 18, 82; chdn Amy A, Brian H; UAB 84, BS; RTS 94, MDiv; Benedictine 14, PhD; L Jan 95; O Mar 12, 95, Evan Pby; chp, mis MTW, Odessa, Ukraine, 95-01, staff 01-03, wc 03-07; consult MTW

1206 Dundee Lane, Lynn Haven, FL 32444　　　　　　　　　　　　　　　　　　Evangel
E-mail: sky.rhino@gmail.com
PCA Mission to the World

Smith, David M. – b Meridian, MS, Sept 30, 48; f E. (d); m Lillian Beatrice Knight (d); w Clara Kathleen Austin, Cleveland, MS, Oct 9, 76; chdn David Nathan, Hilary Kathleen, Amanda Claire; MSU 71, BS, 73, MS; RTS 85, MDiv; L Mar 85, Cov Pby; O Oct 18, 87, Cov Pby; op, p Covenant Life P Ch, Saltillo, MS, 87-90, wc 90-92; p Sardis P Ch, Sardis, MS, 92-06; p Maple Drive P Ch, Pontotoc, MS, 06-

341 Spring Hill Drive, Pontotoc, MS 38863　　　　　　　　　　　　　　　　　　Covenant
E-mail: mapledrivepc@bellsouth.net
Maple Drive Presbyterian Church – 662-488-0401

Smith, E. Kirby – b Beaumont, TX, Aug 3, 50; f E. Kirby; m Connor Baldwin; w Fern Carter, Rolling Fork, MS, Aug 21, 76; chdn Edmund Kirby, Kelly Carter, Zachary Wallace; TCU 72, BA; RTS 79, MDiv; L Jun 78, Evan Pby; O Feb 79, Evan Pby; p Pea River P Ch, Clio, AL, 79-82; p Millbrook P Ch, Millbrook, AL, 82-94; p Faith P Ch, Montgomery, AL, 94-08; prof BhamTS; astp Young Meadows P Ch, Montgomery, AL, 08-

5780 Vaughn Road, Montgomery, AL 36116 – 334-277-5744　　　　　　Southeast Alabama
E-mail: ksmith@ympca.org
Birmingham Theological Seminary
Young Meadows Presbyterian Church – 334-244-1385

Smith, Ethan Andrew – b Ft. Lauderdale, FL, Jan 14, 84; w Holly, May 26, 06; chdn Annaleigh, Addison; FSU 06; RTS 14; O May 1, 16, PTri Pby; astp Hope P Ch, Winston-Salem, NC, 16-18, ascp 18-

4712 Tolley Creek Drive, Winston-Salem, NC 27106　　　　　　　　　　　　Piedmont Triad
E-mail: ethanandrewsmith@gmail.com
Hope Presbyterian Church – 336-768-8883

Smith, Francis – w Bonnie; chdn Matthew; Elon 73, BBA; SEBTS 80, MDiv; astp Meadowview Ref P Ch, Lexington, NC, 09-12; ascp 12-17; hr 17

2509 Newington Court, Clemmons, NC 27012 – 336-309-5182　　　　　　Piedmont Triad
E-mail: francissmith8@gmail.com
HR

Smith, Geoff – p Park Woods P Ch, Overland Park, KS, 17-

Park Woods Presbyterian Church   Heartland

Smith, George William – b Philadelphia, PA, Sept 5, 30; f George; m Lillie Crane; w Martha Manker, Columbus, OH, Jun 25, 55; chdn Glenn, Jacque, Jeff; TempU 53, BS; WTS 59, MDiv; O 59, Phil Pby (RPNAGS); ap Calvary P Ch, Willow Grove, PA, 59-64; p P Ch, Manchester, CT, 64-74; srp Calvary P Ch, Willow Grove, PA, 74-96; pres CTI & Cov House; hr 96; ss Covenant P Ch, Cape May, NJ, 98-05

10620 SW 29th Avenue, C5, Ocala, FL 34476 – 609-263-7948   New Jersey
HR

Smith, Henry Lewis – b Chinquapin, NC, Jun 9, 32; f Rev William Clifford; m Carrie Louise Lewis; w Anna Beth Lynn, Rock Hill, SC, Dec 29, 64; chdn Henry Lewis, Jr, Sara Lynn (SmithT), Timothy Jefferies, Anna Elizabeth (Chapman); PC 53, BA; ColTS 56, MDiv; NCEd 56-57; BhamTS 08, DMin; L Jul 23, 56; O Jul 23, 56, SWGA Pby; p Monroeville, AL, 57-63; p First ARP Ch, Rock Hill, SC, 63-66; p Covenant P Ch, Winter Haven, FL, 66-78; prof BhamTS, 79-; srp First P Ch, Prattville, AL, 78-01; sc SEAL Pby, 85-; astp First P Ch, Prattville, AL, 01-05; ip Camden, Bethel, Prosperity ARP, 01-10; supply Bethel Ch, Union Springs, AL, 15-; Frdm Found Awd for Serm, 76

1315 India Road, Opelika, AL 36801 – 334-745-6494   Southeast Alabama
E-mail: hls0609@charter.net
Birmingham Theological Seminary

Smith, Jack – O Aug 26, 09, SoTX Pby; ascp Redeemer P Ch, Austin, TX, 09-

406 Hidden Brook Lane, Austin, TX 78665 – 512-220-6992   South Texas
E-mail: jsmith@redeemerpres.org
Redeemer Presbyterian Church – 512-708-1232

Smith, James Anderson – b Vineland, NJ, Feb 24, 29; f William Anderson; m Laura Fitzsimmons; w Marilyn Laura Heath (d); (2) Margo, Feb 24, 02; chdn Philip W., Cheryl A., Scott C., Dirk A., Guy B.; Kg'sC 51, BA; FTS 54, BD, 55, ThM; L May 8, 54; O May 27, 55, NJ Pby (BPC); ob p Faith Bible Ch (Ind), Brick Township, NJ, 55-05; sc NJ Pby, 82-; hr 05

236 McGuire Boulevard, Brick, NJ 08724 – 732-206-1138   New Jersey
E-mail: jimtheclerk936@gmail.com
HR

Smith, James Lewis Jr. – b Sylacauga, AL, Jul 27, 55; f James L.; m Mary Elizabeth Machen; w Nancy Patricia Noga, Miami, FL, Jun 24, 78; chdn Andrew James, Megan Claire, Katherine Grace, Nathan Michael; FSU 73-77, BA; RTS 80-84, MDiv; L Jan 83; O May 84, Gr Pby; ap Faith P Ch, Brookhaven, MS, 84-86; op Oak Hill Msn, Spring Hill, FL, 86-88; ap Granada P Ch, Coral Gables, FL, 88-89, p 89-97; srp Westminster P Ch, Butler, PA, 97-03; ob Glade Run Lutheran Serv, 03-; ss Cornerstone P Ch, Youngstown, OH, 08-09

110 Shawnee Drive, Butler, PA 16001 – 724-283-9436   Ascension
E-mail: jsmith@gladerun.org
Glade Run Lutheran Services

Smith, Justin – O Feb 12, 17, MetAtl Pby; astp City Ch - Eastside, Atlanta, GA, 17; campm RUF, 17-

229 Jagoe Street, Denton, TX 76201   North Texas
E-mail: justin.smith@ruf.org
PCA Reformed University Fellowship

MINISTERIAL DIRECTORY

Smith, Kenneth A. – b Yonkers, NY, Nov 12, 47; f Thomas R; m Lucy Kalata; w Carol Springer, Ft Lauderdale, FL, Sept 8, 73; chdn Nathaniel Thomas, Benjamin Joseph, Thomas Roy, Mary Elizabeth; Kg'sC, BA; UNoCL, MA; PTS, MDiv; CTS 95, DMin; O Jul 9, 78, MidAtl Pby; op Princeton P Ch, Princeton, NJ, 78-81, srp 81-; NE Reg Coord for chp, 95-; 1993 Alumnus of the Year, The King's College; art *Witherspoon Review*; rad min "A Firm Foundation" 79-; TVprog "A Firm Foundation" 88-; *Who's Who in Religion*, 88; chmn of bd, Alpha Pregnancy Center; bd ECHO Cuba; *Principles of Worship for the Metro New York Presbytery,* 99; "Christianity and the United States Supreme Court," *Oxford Roundtable*, Oxford, England, 07

PO Box 3003, Princeton, NJ 08543 – 609-452-1918   Metropolitan New York
E-mail: ksmith5678@aol.com
Princeton Meadow Church – 609-987-1166

Smith, Kevin M. – b Philadelphia, PA, May 2, 64; f Willie Howard; m Jeanette Threats; w Sandra Jean Brown, Philadelphia, PA, Aug 1, 87; chdn Tesia, Bethany, Chara, Joanna; PASU 81-82; TempU 89, BS; WTS 91-93; ChTS 98, MATS; L Sept 95, Pot Pby; O Oct 18, 98, Pot Pby; int Tenth P Ch, Philadelphia, PA, 91-94; int Harvester P Ch, Springfield, VA, 98; chp, op Mt. Zion Cov Ch Msn, Glendale, MD, 98-05; p Pinelands P Ch, Miami, FL, 05-12; srp New City Flwshp, Chattanooga, TN, 12-

2412 E 4th Street, Chattanooga, TN 37404   Tennessee Valley
E-mail: REVKEV@newcityfellowship.com
New City Fellowship – 423-629-1421

Smith, Lawrence – Recd PCA 18, Phil Pby; srp New Life Ch of Phil, Philadelphia, PA, 18-

New Life Church of Philadelphia – 215-324-4566   Philadelphia

Smith, Luke Bryant – w Sokha, Jul 2, 11; chdn Hannah, Asa; DTS 09; mis MTW, Cambodia, 09-

c/o MTW   North Texas
E-mail: luke.bryant.smith@gmail.com
PCA Mission to the World

Smith, Luke Townsend – w Joelle; chdn Dale; UMemp, BBA, MS; CTS, MDiv; O Oct 13, 13, SW Pby; astp Rincon Mountain P Ch, Tucson, AZ, 13-

4301A East Fairmount Street, Tucson, AZ 85712-3988 – 520-400-2227   Southwest
E-mail: lsmith@rinconpres.org
Rincon Mountain Presbyterian Church – 520-327-2390

Smith, Malcolm Wilson – b Wauchula, FL, Dec 11, 43; f Malcolm CS; m Patty Arlington; w Betty Davis, Jackson, MS, Jun 6, 68; chdn Deborah, Daniel, Jonathan; BelC 68, BA; RTS 73, MDiv, 98, DMin; L 70, CMS Pby; O Jun 10, 73, SMS Pby; p Bay Springs P Ch, Bay Springs, MS, 70-74; p Midway P Ch, Powder Springs, GA, 74-83; p Vineville P Ch, Macon, GA, 83-89, wc 89-90; p First P Ch, Crystal Springs, MS, 90-02; astp, chp Midway P Ch, Powder Springs, GA, 02-03; op Grace Cov P Ch, Dallas, GA, 02-03, p 03-14; hr 14; *A Study of the Role of Minister's Wives in Selected PCA Churches*

91 Vineyard Drive, Dallas, GA 30132 – 678-363-6350   Northwest Georgia
E-mail: drwilbet@bellsouth.net
HR

Smith, Mark Thomas – w Jayna; chdn Joshua, Megan, Lucas, Samuel; Covenant OPC, Columbia, TN, 95-00; Providence OPC, Huntsville, AL, 00-03; p Covenant OPC, Forest, MS, 03-05; p Forest P Ch, Forest, MS, 05-

103 Village Avenue, Forest, MS 39074 – 601-469-1961   Mississippi Valley
E-mail: forestpresbyteri@bellsouth.net
Forest Presbyterian Church – 601-469-1961

Smith, Nate – w Emily; chdn Clay, Thomas, Henry, Amelia; TXA&M, BA; CTS, MDiv; O Mar 13, 05, Cov Pby; astp Riveroaks Ref P Ch, Germantown, TN, 04-16, ascp 16-

8211 Everwood Cove, Germantown, TN 38138 – 901-754-0998   Covenant
E-mail: natesmith99@bellsouth.net
Riveroaks Reformed Presbyterian Church – 901-755-7772

Smith, Randolph Quin – b Birmingham, AL, Apr 5, 50; f Howard Quin; m Kathryn Jones; w Barbara Britton Gordy, Montgomery, AL, Dec 15, 73; chdn Kathryn, William, Sarah, John, Benjamin; AU 68-69; MBI 70-73, BA; GCTS 77-80, MDiv; O Nov 80, CentGA Pby; mis MTW, NAM, 81-86; ascp First P Ch, Augusta, GA, 86-93; srp Mitchell Road P Ch, Greenville, SC, 93-07; ascp 07-08; hr 16

3448 Paces Ferry Circle SE, Smyrna, GA 30080 – 404-414-1387   Calvary
E-mail: randolphqsmith@gmail.com
HR

Smith, Richard O'Dell Jr. – b Charleston, SC, Sept 18, 58; f Richard O. Sr.; m Ann Lois Sherer; w Lynne Mell, Atlanta, GA, Oct 6, 90; chdn Richard O'Dell III, Evelyn Pearl; WinC 81, BS; RTS 87, MDiv; L Jul 27, 85, Cal Pby; O Nov 8, 87, NGA Pby; BdDir Ridge Haven Conference Center, 90-95; 09-14; 15-; astp Covenant P Ch, Fayetteville, GA, 87-93; ascp 93-96; p First P Ch, Florala, AL, 96-00; p Northgate P Ch, Albany, GA, 00-15; campm RUFI, Penn State, 15-

2529 Zion Rd, Bellefonte, PA 16823 – 229-894-9167   Susquehanna Valley
E-mail: richard.smith@ruf.org
PCA Reformed University Fellowship International

Smith, Richard R. – b Kansas, Apr 24, 49; f Roy H.; m Cleo Mae Clark; w Vicki Hall, CA, Aug 18, 73; chdn Brea Elizabeth, Mesha Lael, Jonathan Erik, Nathaniel Shad; KSU 71, BS; CTS 82, MDiv; L Jul 82, SW Pby; O Jul 82, SW Pby; op First Chapel, Sierra Vista, AZ, 82-83; p Prov Ch, Las Cruces, NM, 83-85; yp University P Ch, Las Cruces, NM, 87-89; p Westminster P Ch, Alamogordo, NM, 90-94; wc 94-95; ob InFaith, 95-

1512 Phoenix Avenue NW, Albuquerque, NM 87107 – 505-859-5500   Rio Grande
E-mail: ricksmith@infaith.org
InFaith

Smith, Robert Lee III – b Miami, FL, Mar 20, 64; f Robert L. Jr; m Paula L. Spiczak; w April D. Bradley, Macon, GA, Aug 11, 87; chdn Robert Bradley, Whitney Dianne, Timothy Edwards, Jacob Douglass; MerU 86, BA; RTS 94, MDiv; O Oct 23, 94, JR Pby; int Coral Ridge P Ch, Ft. Lauderdale, FL, 85; ydir Perry P Ch, Perry, GA, 86-87; int Immanuel P Ch, DeLand, FL, 93-94; ascp New Life in Christ Ch, Fredericksburg, VA, 94-01; p First P Ch, Waynesboro, GA, 01-04; op Christ P Msn, Danville, VA, 04-08; ascp Redeemer P Ch, Lynchburg, VA, 10-

3700 Otter Place, Lynchburg, VA 24503   Blue Ridge
E-mail: tre@redeemerlynchburg.org
Redeemer Presbyterian Church – 434-238-3300

Smith, Robert Todd – b Spartanburg, SC, May 14, 75; f Robert paul Jr.; m Brenda Gail Patterson; w Dora Louise Easler, Roebuck, SC, May 1, 99; SpartMethC 95, AA; ErskC 97, BA; GPTS 03, MDiv; O Oct 31, 03, Cal Pby; p Center Point P Ch, Moore, SC, 03-05; stus 01-03, p 03-05; p Central P Ch, Kingstree, SC, 05-06; Trinity P Ch, Slidell, LA, 06-

220 Bluefield Drive, Slidell, LA 70458 – 985-726-0696   Southern Louisiana
E-mail: todds16@cnonline.net
Trinity Presbyterian Church – 985-641-1507

Smith, Ronald Moore – b Ft Benning, GA, Jan 19, 51; f Anderson Q; m Kittie Moore; w Margaret Allison Yeager, Arlington, VA, Jul 2, 83; chdn Benjamin Ramon, Allison Maria; WBC 85, BA; RTS 95, MDiv; L Oct 19, 93; O Oct 17, 95, MSVal Pby; ss Old Madison P Ch, 95-96; mis, chp MTW/Impact, Guayquil, Ecuador, 95-99; chp MTW, Guayaquil, Ecuador, 00-06; mis MTW, Caribbean, 07-17; p Presbyterian Ch of Boatswain Bay, 09-17; hr 17; *Dios Salve Al Ecuador*

5124 Woodland Trace, Tuscaloosa, AL 35405 South Florida
E-mail: ronypegsmith@hotmail.com
HR

Smith, Samuel A. – w Jodi Dean, Aug 8, 92; chdn Collin, Kaitlynn, Christopher, Kaebrie; AUM 95, BA; RTS 02, MDiv; p First P Ch, Louisville, MS, 02-05; Chap USAF, 05-08; p First P Ch, Yazoo City, MS, 08-; Chap Air Nat'l Guard, 08-15; Chap Air Nat'l Guard, 08-; srp Lake Oconee P Ch, Eatonton, GA, 15-

1021 Liberty Bluff Lane, Greensboro, GA 30642 – 662-590-6361 Central Georgia
E-mail: sam.smith@lopc-pca.org
Air National Guard
Lake Oconee Presbyterian Church – 706-484-0600

Smith, Scott Ward – b Burlington, NC, Feb 1, 50; f Thomas Argo; m Martha Amanda Ward; w Darlene Gale Eakin, Graham, NC, May 5, 72; chdn Kirstin Amanda, Scott Nathaniel; UNC 68-72, BA; WTS 75-77, MAR; O Mar 5, 78, PCUS; p First Ch, Winston-Salem, NC, 78-79; p First Ch, Nashville, TN, 79-80; p Christ P Ch, Nashville, TN, 81-86; op Christ Comm Ch, Franklin, TN, 86, srp 86-06; ascp 07-12; wc; astp West End Comm Ch, Nashville, TN, 14-; *Unveiled Hope*; *Speechless*; *Objects of His Affection*; *The Reign of Grace*; *Restoring Broken Things*

801 Highgrove Circle, Franklin, TN 37069-4117 – 615-373-3901 Nashville
West End Community Church – 615-463-8497

Smith, Thomas Joseph – b York, PA, Jul 17, 65; f Joseph; m Geraldine; chdn Evelyn, Katherine, Kristina; PennSt 87, BS; CTS 02, MDiv; ob p St. Johns Ref Ch (Ind), 06-11; ob mis I.T.E.M. in Croatia, 11-

141 Humphrey Road, Slippery Rock, PA 16457 – 01 385 +098 9767243 Ascension
E-mail: christ4croatia@burryschurch.org
I.T.E.M., Inc.
Ulica Stjepana Radica 38A, 47000 Karlovac, HR

Snapp, Lawrence Byron – b Marion, VA, Oct 1, 48; f Lawrence Byars S; m Rebecca Orr; w Janey Furrow, Callaway, VA, Jun 12, 71; chdn Samuel Byron, Anna Elizabeth (Lindauer), Sarah Ellen (Bradley); KgC 70, BA; RTS 73, MDiv; O Sept 23, 73, Gr Pby; p Leakesville P Ch, Leakesville, MS, 73-78; Salem P Ch, Gaffney, SC, 78-84; astp Covenant P Ch, Cedar Bluff, VA, 84-94; admin CovCS, 84-93; ascp Calvary Ref P Ch, Hampton, VA, 94-14; admin CalCS, 94-00; hr 14; ed *The Presbyterian Witness*; contr *A Comprehensive Faith*; contr *Election Day Sermons*

200 Oneida Court, Kingsport, TN 37664 – 423-212-2604 Tidewater
E-mail: bjsnapp@gmail.com
HR

Snead, Curtis – Recd PCA Nov 9, 17, Palm Pby, ob 17-

380 Eagle Point Drive, Columbia, SC 29206 Palmetto

Sneed, Robert Bryant (Chip) – b Winston-Salem, NC, Feb 12, 69; f Robert Morris; m Carolyn King Goins; w Tina Mendenhall, Winston-Salem, NC, Aug 8, 92; chdn Robert James, Samuel Mendenhall, Laura

Sneed, Robert Bryant (Chip), continued
Elizabeth; WCU 87-89; HCB, BA; ErskTS 93-97, MDiv; O Feb 22, 98, Flwsp Pby; int Covenant P Ch, 97; p Trinity P Ch, Chester, SC, 98-02; astp Christ Cov P Ch, Matthews, NC, 02-10; op NorthCross Ch, Cornelius, NC, 03-10; p 10-18

7807 Chaddsley Drive, Huntersville, NC 28078 – 704-947-0686   Catawba Valley

Sniffin, Peter Raymond – b Heidelberg, Germany, Jul 6, 62; f Charles R.; m Jean Elizabeth Hearn; w Rose Marie Finney; chdn Olivia Caitlin, Amelia Blessing; VMI 81-85, BA; WTS 85-88, MDiv; USACGS 02, MMAS; USAWC 14, MSS; L Mar 90; O Dec 90, Phil Pby; Chap BSA, Goshen, VA, 91; Chap USArmy, 90-91; Chap USArmy, Inf Batt, Ft. Stewart, GA, 91-94; Chap USArmy, 221st BSB, Wiesbaden, Germany, 94-96; Chap USArmy, HQ, Heidelberg, Ger, 96-98; Chap USArmy, 1-377 FAR, Ft. Bragg, NC, 98-00; Chap USArmy, 18 FA BDE, Ft. Bragg, NC, 00-01; stu USArmy, USACGSC, Ft. Leavenworth, 01-02; staff USArmy, Chaplain Sch, Ft. Jackson, SC, 02-05; Chap USArmy, Wiesbaden Germany, 05-09; Chap USArmy, The Pentagon, 09-11; Kabul, Afghanistan, 11-12; The Pentagon, 12-13; US Army Chaplain School, 13-16

441 Park Drive, Carlisle, PA 17015 – 540-656-8434   Eastern Pennsylvania
E-mail: pete.sniffin@us.army.mil
United States Army

Snow, Keith – b Jacksonville, FL, May 25, 79; f William, Jr.; m Wanda Davis; w Kristen Forssell, Bradenton, FL, Dec 15, 02; chdn London, Noël, Adeline, Luke; UNFL 04, BA; RTS 07, MATS; O Apr 9, 15, NFL Pby; ascp Cross Creek P Ch, St. Johns, FL, 15-17, p 17-

70 Calumet Drive, St. Johns, FL 32259 – 904-504-8112   North Florida
E-mail: keithsnow@me.com
Cross Creek Presbyterian Church – 904-287-4334

Snowden, Ralph W. – b Irondale, AL, Feb 19, 28; f Thomas Edward; m Ruby E Willcutt; w Mary W. Caddell, Aug 30, 52; chdn Stephen Edward, Karen Leah; UAL 53-58; CST 68-74; BhamTS 77-82; L Jun 10, 80; O Jun 20, 82, Evan Pby; p Talucah P Ch, Valhermoso Springs, AL, 80-

1019 Clubview Drive NW, Huntsville, AL 35861 – 256-852-4763   Providence
Talucah Presbyterian Church – 256-778-8288

Snyder, Nathan W. – ascp Exeter P Ch, Exeter, NH, 13-16; wc 16-

11 Elm Street, Dover, NH 03820   Northern New England
E-mail: nathanwesleysnyder@gmail.com

Snyder, Will – srp Presbyterian Ch of Coventry, Coventry, CT, 18-

31 Hatch Hill Road, Vernon, CT 06066   Southern New England
Presbyterian Church of Coventry – 860-742-7222

So, Brian – O Oct 22, 10, Ecan Pby; ob p Toronto, 10-

19 Craftsman Lane, Toronto, ON M6H 4J5 CANADA – 416-876-0320   Eastern Canada
E-mail: mingnbrian@gmail.com

Sofield, William – astp Granada P Ch, Coral Gables, FL, 07-10; p Grace Comm Ch, Carrboro, NC, 10-18

108 Ephesus Church Road, #106, Chapel Hill, NC 27517 – 919-699-1679   Eastern Carolina
E-mail: williamsofield@gmail.com

Sojaento, Eddy – ob p Agape Evangelical Ch, South Philadelphia, 08-17; ob ev, 17-

Address Unavailable   Metropolitan New York

Sokol, Drew – O Sept 28, 13, Pac Pby; astp Pacific Crossroads Ch, Los Angeles, CA, 13-16; wc 16-18; astp Redeemer P Ch of New York East Side, New York, NY, 18;

310-927-5350   Metropolitan New York

Soltau, Addison P. – b Seoul, Korea, Dec 14, 26; f Theodore Stanley; m Mary Cross Campbell; w Roselynne Eleanor Moore, Owosso, MI, Aug 24, 49; chdn Marilyn Sue (Wright), Theodore Scott, John Sanders; UMN 44; SWC 45; WheatC 49, BA; FTS 52, BD; CalvS 66, ThM; ConcS 82, ThD; L 52; O 52, So Pby (BPC); mis WPM, Japan, 53-70; prof RBC, 72-77; assoc prof CTS, 77-89; ap, mp Coral Ridge P Ch, Ft. Lauderdale, FL, 89-91; ob VP Evangelism Explosion III Int., Fort Lauderdale, FL, 91-96; astp First P Ch of Coral Springs, Margate, FL, 97-17; adj prof KTS, 89-17; hr 17

100 Scenic Highway #11, Lookout Mountain, TN 37350 – 954-782-7506   South Florida
E-mail: addsoltau@gmail.com
HR

Son, Byung Deuk – mis England, 02-

Address Unavailable   Korean Central

Son, Steve – wc 02-

1310 Saddle Rack Street, Apt. 336, San Jose, CA 95126 – 408-249-3768   Korean Northwest

Song, Daniel – b Los Angeles, CA, Nov 25, 78; f Yong; m Bok Yeah; w Hannah H. Doh, Chicago, IL, Jan 15, 05; chdn Stephen Moses, Renee Karen, Norah Abigail; UIL 01, BA; CTS 09, MDiv; O Nov 8, 09, MO Pby; Grace P Ch of St. Louis, dor coll, St. Louis, MO, 05-09; astp Crossroads P Flwsp, Maplewood, MO, 09-10, ascp 10-14; p Wst Side, 14-18; srp Restoration Comm Ch, St. Louis, MO, 18-

60 Pricewoods Lane, St Louis, MO 63132 – 314-722-6212   Missouri
Restoration Community Church

Song, Daniel Munkyu – astp Columbia P Msn, Columbia, SC, 06-08; ob chp Ch of the Nations, Anchorage, AK 08-

1703 Bellevue Loop, Anchorage, AK 99515-3117   Korean Southeastern
E-mail: Dgjsong@hotmail.com
Church of the Nations, Anchorage, AK – 907-947-1872

Song, David – b Aug 27, 86; f Byoung Il; m Sang; w Lisa; CalvC, BA; TalTS, MDiv; O 15, KorSW Pby; astp, yp Inland Korean P Ch, Pomona, CA, 15-

1101 North Glen Avenue, Pomona, CA 91768   Korean Southwest
E-mail: songdasol@gmail.com
Inland Korean Presbyterian Church – 909-622-2324

Song, Jin Yong – astp Korean Open Door P Ch, Houston, TX, 13-15; op Ye Won Msn Ch, Houston, TX, 15-

2810 Silvervit Trail Lane, Katy, TX 77450   Korean Southern
E-mail: pascalsong37@gmail.com
Ye Won Mission Church

Song, John – ob

208 Lucas Park Drive, San Rafael, CA 94903 — Korean Northwest
E-mail: Jungsik23@gmail.com

Song, Ken K.C. – astp Lamp P Ch of Los Angeles, Gardena, CA, 08- srp Seattle Lamp P Ch, Bellevue, WA, 10-

405 102nd Avenue SE #M, Bellevue, WA 98004 — Korean Southwest
E-mail: kksong1@juno.com
Seattle Lamp Presbyterian Church – 425-999-5293

Song, Philip – srp Antioch Korean Christian Comm Ch, Los Angeles, CA, 04-

14435 Mercado Avenue, La Mirada, CA 90638 – 323-351-0159 — Korean Southwest
E-mail: philipinhosong@gmail.com
Antioch Korean Christian Community Church – 323-930-0678

Song, Sang Chol – b Daechun, Korea, Jun 25, 54; f Chang Kuk; m On Jun Jung; w Dok Kee, Seoul; chdn Peter, David; ChShCS 79, BA; HPTS 82, MDiv; LibU 95, ThM; FulTS, DMin cand; O Oct 1, 84, KPC-Ref; Recd PCA Jul 8, 97, KorSE Pby; srp Church of Truth, Seoul, 91; srp Lynchburg Kor Ch, 95; p Sae Han P Ch of Atlanta, Alpharetta, GA, 96-

3510 Evonvale Glen, Cumming, GA 30041 – 678-566-0103 — Korean Southeastern
E-mail: jcsongsaehan@hotmail.com
Sae Han Presbyterian Church of Atlanta – 770-619-5340

Song, Young-Jae – astp Emmanuel Ch in Phil, Philadelphia, PA, 03-07; wc 08-

144-77 Roosevelt Avenue 5C, Flushing, NY 11465 — Korean Eastern

Sorensen, Carl M. – b Los Angeles, CA, Feb 7, 35; f Rev. Norman Martin; m Pearle Craig; w Evelyn O'Guin, Kansas City, KS, Jun 24, 56; chdn Carla (Banish), Anita (Morton), Stephen; BJU 53-58, BS, grad wk; L 54, BJU; O 59, Grace Bap Ch, Landrum, SC; ap Augusta Street P Ch, Greenville, SC, 65-67; ap Walnut Grove P Ch, Roebuck, SC, 67-70; p Westm Ch, Concord, NC, 70-81; t Mitchell Road P Ch, Greenville, SC, 81-82; p Augusta Street P Ch, Greenville, SC, 82-96, wc 96-03; hr; sp, t various SC churches, 96-

200 Johnson Road, Roebuck, SC 29376-9511 – 864-576-1327 — Calvary
HR

Sorgenfrei, Brian – campm RUF, MSU, 09-17; campm RUF, OleMiss, 17-

403 Allen Cove, Oxford, MS 38655 – 662-418-6928 — Covenant
E-mail: brian.sorgenfrei@ruf.org
PCA Reformed University Fellowship

Southerland, Matthew – O Sept 11, 16, STX pby; astp CrossPointe Ch, Austin, TX, 16-

12931 Marimba Trail, Austin, TX 78729 — South Texas
E-mail: mlsouthland@gmail.com
CrossPointe Church – 512-249-1006

Southworth, John Franklin, Jr. – b Memphis, TN, Oct 16, 49; f John Franklin; m Dorothy Standridge; w Judith Cochran, Sep 6, 75; chdn Jennifer; VandU 71, BA; UT 73, JD; CTS 81, MABS; WTS 03, PhD; O Oct 30, 11, TNVal Pby; astp Hixson P Ch, Hixson, TN, 11-14; wc 14-16; hr 16

1626 Gunston Hall Road, Hixson, TN 37343 – 423-847-6611 — Tennessee Valley
E-mail: johnjudysw@gmail.com
HR

Sowder, Roger I. – b Lawrenceville, GA, Mar 18, 61; f Roger; m Emily Patterson; w Jeanne Marie Etheredge, Tallahassee, FL, Mar 24, 84; FSU 79-83, BA; CIU 85-88, MDiv; L Apr 89, Pac Pby; O Nov 18, 89, SoCst Pby; op Oak Springs P Msn, Temecula, CA, 89-92, wc 92; astp Cornerstone P Ch, Tallahassee, FL, 93; op Foothills P Ch, Boiling Springs, SC, 93-97, p 97-02; astp Christ Comm Ch, Simpsonville, SC, 02-03, ascp 03-

700 Harrison Bridge Road, Simpsonville, SC 29680 – 864-238-9340   Calvary
E-mail: roger@christcommunitychurchonline.org
Christ Community Church – 864-967-2815

Spanjer, Stephen Harold – RTSFL, 04; ev Germany, 06-09; op Neuenberg Int Ch, 07-

Ernst-Eisenlohrstr. 8a, 79410 Badenweiler GERMANY   Southeast Alabama
Neuenberg International Church

Spanjer, William – O Nov 7, 99, NoE Pby; p Affirmation P Ch, Somers, NY, 99-

197 Fleury Road, Pine Bush, NY 12566 – 914-778-1185   New York State
Affirmation Presbyterian Church – 914-232-0546

Sparkman, Joshua – astp Christ P Ch, Mobile, AL, 14-16, p 16-

6616 Gaslight Lane North, Mobile, AL 36695   Gulf Coast
E-mail: josh@cpcmobile.com
Christ Presbyterian Church – 251-633-2002

Speakman, David G. – b Chattanooga, TN, Jun 26, 74; f W. Fred; m Starlet Light; w Margaret Ann Scheu, Jacksonville, FL, Aug 8, 98; chdn Mary Gray, Samuel, Lewis; DavC 96, BA; CTS 02, MDiv; O Jan 18, 04, CentCar Pby; campm RUF, DavC, 04-12; astp Hope P Ch, Winston-Salem, NC, 12-

401 Hearthside Drive, Winston-Salem, NC 27104 – 704-779-1273   Piedmont Triad
E-mail: daspeakman@gmail.com
Hope Presbyterian Church – 336-768-8883

Speaks, Stephen – b Camden, SC, Aug 17, 70; f John Robert; m Nancy Cameron West; w Rebekah Laena Talmadge, Camden, SC, Jan 1, 94; chdn Kathryn Grace, Connor Talmadge; ClemU 93, BS; CTS 98, MDiv; L Jun 14, 98, Cal Pby; O Jun 14, 98, Cal Pby; campm RUF, ClemU, 98- 17; srp Trinity P Ch, Jackson, MS, 17-

5132 Kaywood Circle, Jackson, MS 39211   Mississippi Valley
E-mail: stephen@tpcjackson.org
Trinity Presbyterian Church – 601-977-0774

Speck, Ryan – O Feb 5, 07, JR Pby; ascp Immanuel P Ch, Norfolk, VA, 07- 12; p Redeemer P Ch, Columbia, MO, 12-

3504 Vista Place, Columbia, MO 65202 – 573-990-9343   Missouri
E-mail: speckster2@yahoo.com
Redeemer Presbyterian Church – 573-443-2321

Speece, Lincoln – b Austin, TX, May 24, 71; f Richard E.; m Jean M.; w Melinda Franklin, Nashville, TN, May 31, 03; chdn Halina Bless, Jameson Churchill, Hudson Tyndale; UT 94, BS; VandU 00, MEd; RTS 10, MDiv; O Jun 19, 11, SEAL Pby; p Hayneville P Ch, Hayneville, AL, 11-; p Lowndesboro P Ch, Lowndesboro, AL, 11-; p Good Hope P Ch, Benton, AL, 11-

130 West LaFayette, Hayneville, AL 36840   Southeast Alabama
E-mail: speeces03@gmail.com
Hayneville Presbyterian Church – 334-313-3355
Lowndesboro Presbyterian Church – 334-278-3238
Good Hope Presbyterian Church – 334-874-7878

Spellman, Mark C. – b Nevada, MO, Sept 8, 51; f John Richard; m Bette Ruth Clark; w Dawn Powell, Jackson, MS, Jun 3, 72; chdn Eric N, Page A, Lori A, Joshua Drew; TulU 75, BArch, 77, MArch; RTS 92, MDiv; NGTS 17, DMin; L May 91, MSVal Pby; L Sept 92, Gr Pby; O Jan 24, 93, Gr Pby; p First P Ch, Taylorsville, MS, 92-94; p Marion P Ch, Marion, AL, 94-98; astp Arlington P Ch, Arlington, TX, 98-99; op New Life P Ch, Midland, TX, 98-99, p 99-02; ob Chap, t Evan Chr Acad, CO Springs, 02-08; adj prof NGTS, 04-12; op Cov Ref P Ch Msn, PCA, Pueblo West, CO, 05-12; p 12- 14; p Wynndale P Ch, Terry, MS, 14-; adj prof BelU, 16-

6602 Terry Road, Terry, MS 39170　　　　　　　　　　　　　　　　　　　　　Mississippi Valley
E-mail: wynndalepca@att.net
Wynndale Presbyterian Church – 601-878-6870

Spence, Joel – astp Hill Country PCA Msn, Killeen, TX, 17-18, p 18-

101 S. Twin Creek Drive #2208, Killeen, TX 76543　　　　　　　　　　　　　　North Texas
E-mail: joel.g.spence@hotmail.com
Hill Country PCA Mission – 254-698-4950

Spence, Mark Joel – b Cleburne, TX, Sept 14, 50; f Joel C.; m Marca B.; w Karen, Corpus Christi, TX, Apr 5, 75; chdn Brooke, Joel; TXTU 72, BA; APTS 76, MDiv; O Jun 1, 76, PCUS; First P Ch, Taft, TX, 77-78; First P Ch, Alpine, TX, 86-90; First P Ch, Sweetwater TX, 90-98; First P Ch, Beeville, TX, 98-06; op, p Providence P Ch, Beeville, TX, 06-12, hr 12

208 Skyview Drive, Kerrville, TX 78028 – 830-367-3675　　　　　　　　　　　South Texas
E-mail: markspence50@gmail.com
HR

Spence, R. Neil – b Cleveland, TN, Sept 2, 60; f James F. Jr.; m Bobbie Louis; w Pamelia V. Floyd, Benton, TN, Jan 4, 80; chdn Emily, Nicholas; CNC 84, BA; MempTS 87, MDiv; VandU 91, DMin; NashSchLaw 07, JD; O May 4, 86, CumbPC; Recd PCA Nov 10, 01, Nash Pby; astp Christ P Ch, Nashville, TN, 01-03; op Redeemer P Ch, Dickson, TN, 02-05; p 05-

PO Box 1006, Dickson, TN 37056 – 615-446-9495　　　　　　　　　　　　　　Nashville
E-mail: nspence@rpcdickson.org
Redeemer Presbyterian Church – 615-740-7898

Spencer, Shaun – b Dec 2, 74; w Danielle, May 18, 96; chdn Eva Denise, Lily Grace; MABCS 00, BS; CTS 07, MDiv; O Nov 07, Palm Pby; astp New Cov P Ch, Aiken, SC, 07- 09; ascp 09-10; p Lake Trails P Ch, Madison, WI, 10-

1 Point Place, Suite 1, Madison, WI 53719 – 608-213-2206　　　　　　　　　　Wisconsin
E-mail: shaun@laketrailschurch.org
Lake Trails Presbyterian Church – 608-833-4497

Speyers, Joshua – Arlington, VA, May 23, 82; f Franklin Delano; m Bonnie Jo Duthler; w Hannah Rene Schulert, Lansing, MI, Aug 13, 06; chdn Evangeline Trinity, Gideon Shadrach; CalvC 05, BA; GCTS 13, MDiv; O Jun 5, 16, GrLks Pby; astp New City P Ch, Royal Oak, MI, 16-18

17574 Warrington, Detroit, MI 48221　　　　　　　　　　　　　　　　　　　Great Lakes
E-mail: joshua.speyers@gmail.com

Spink, Peter – b Ridley Park, PA, Aug 3, 51; f William; m Nancy Jane Binns; w Deborah Knowles, Greenville, SC, Jun 10, 72; chdn Jessica Lynn, Peter Bradley; DavC 73, BA; GCTS 76, MDiv; L 76; O 76, SE Pby (RPCES); p Trinity P Ch, Spartanburg, SC, 76-83; p Rainbow P Ch, Rainbow City, AL, 83-85, wc 87; ascp Mitchell Road P Ch, Greenville, SC, 88-06; p Fairview P Ch, Fountain Inn, SC, 06-15, hr 15; p/t coor Pastoral Care, Fellowship P Ch, Greer, SC

221 East Shallowstone Road, Greer, SC 29650-3410 – 864-918-2815　　　　　　Calvary
E-mail: dpspink@charter.net
HR

Spink, William Alan – b Memphis, TN, Oct 6, 82; f William, Jr.; m Marsha Creedle; w Christina Carroll, Lexington, SC, Jul 3, 04; chdn Caitlyn Hope, Allison Jane, Lily Carroll; ClemU 05, BA; CTS 08, MDiv; O Nov 16, 08, Evan Pby; ascp Southwood P Ch, Huntsville, AL, 08-

827 Harrisburg Drive SE, Huntsville, AL 35802 – 256-882-3085   Providence
E-mail: will.spink@southwood.org
Southwood Presbyterian Church – 256-882-3085

Spink, William Jr. – b Decatur, AL, Aug 3, 53; f William; m Nancy Binns; w Marsha Creedle, Atlanta, GA, Jul 24, 76; chdn William Alan, Peter Boykin, Mary Taylor, Kristen Joye; FurU 75, BA; CTS 78, MDiv; L Mar 77, SE Pby; O Oct 78, FL Pby (RPCES); ap Covenant P Ch, Naples, FL, 78-81; srp Riveroaks Ref P Ch, Germantown, TN, 81-

1191 Saddle Ridge Drive, Germantown, TN 38138-1532 – 901-757-1721   Covenant
E-mail: bspinkle@bellsouth.net
Riveroaks Reformed Presbyterian Church – 901-755-7772

Spiritosanto, James Lee – b Philipsburg, PA, Dec 15, 46; f James Vincent; m Phoebe E. Scott; w Mary Katherine Storey, Ruston, LA, Aug 22, 70; chdn Vincent Edgar, Rebecca Ann, Deborah Ruth, Samuel Scott, Mary Elizabeth; LATU 65-71, BA; RTS 78, MDiv; O Jan 28, 79, Evan Pby; ap First P Ch, Gadsden, AL, 79-84; Chap USN, 84-98; Chap Dept of Corrections, NC, 98; hr 13

5907 Sandypine Court, Spring, TX 77379 – 910-938-1422   Evangel
E-mail: giacomo_s@yahoo.com
HR

Spitler, Harrison – b Montgomery, AL, Sept 7, 61; w Sandy Jean West, Atlanta, GA, Aug 27, 88; chdn Rebekah, Sarah, Nathan, Jonathan, Abby, Hannah, Isaac; AU; UAB; BhamTS 96, MDiv; CTS 08, DMin; L Jan 26, 96; O Jun 1, 97, Evan Pby; mis MTW, Lyon, France, 97-99; srp First P Ch, Pike Road, AL, 99-02; astp Christ Cov P Ch, Matthews, NC, 02-04; op Grace Comm Ch, Marvin, NC, 03-05, p 05-17; p Southlake P Ch, Huntersville, NC, 17-

13812 Hagers Ferry Road, Huntersville, NC 28078 – 704-650-4503   Catawba Valley
E-mail: harrisonspitler@gmail.com
Southlake Presbyterian Church – 704-949-2200

Spitzel, James – b Buffalo, NY, Jun 1, 50; f John Francis; m Florence Margaret Hansen; DuqU 69-72, BS; GCTS 74-77, MDiv; QnsC 79; O Nov 80, PCUS; Recd PCA May 88, AscPby; yp, DCE First P Ch of Flushing, Flushing, NY, 77-79; p Woodside P Ch, Roanoke, VA, 80-87; ap Presbyterian Ch of Pitcairn, Pitcairn, PA, 88-90, p 91-08; astp First Ref P Ch, Pittsburgh, PA, 08-11; ascp 11-

109 Elm Drive, Trafford, PA 15085-1319 – 412-372-5543   Pittsburgh
E-mail: jspitzel@gmail.com
First Reformed Presbyterian Church – 412-793-7117

Spokes, Will – b Ann Arbor, MI, Dec 2, 74; w Megan Lorraine McFarland, Jul 29, 00; chdn Liam Mackenzie, Elliot Thomas, Henry Dylan, Oliver Matthew; DukeU 97, BA; WTS 03, MDiv; O Jul 29, 05, Ecar Pby; campm RUF, Duke, 05-12; astp Tenth P Ch, Philadelphia, PA, 12-13; ascp 13-15; p Red Mountain Ch, Birmingham, AL, 15-

2301 Downey Drive, Vestavia Hills, AL 35216 – 205-245-5207   Evangel
E-mail: will@redmountainchurch.org
Red Mountain Church

Spoon, Logan – O Jun 25, 17, MNY Pby; astp Hope P Ch, Randolph, NJ, 17-18; astp Christ Ch Greensboro, Greensboro, NC, 18-

106 Cheyenne Drive #S, Greensboro, NC 27410 – 864-684-9491   Piedmont Triad
Christ Church Greensboro – 336-209-5659

Spooner, Gary Bernhard – b Seminole Co, GA, Jun 10, 50; f Luther Edwin; m Martha Nell Garwood; w Jill Evans, Fulton Co, GA, Jun 1, 74; chdn Caroline, Joy, Stephen, Stuart, Anne; UGA 72, BA; RTS 76, MDiv; WTS 17, DMin; O Aug 8, 76, CMS Pby; p Christ's Comm Ch, Clinton, MS, 76-80; p Trinity P Ch, Dothan, AL, 80-85; srp Covenant P Ch, Auburn, AL, 86-14; exec dir The Owen Center, Auburn, AL, 14-; *The Glory of Christ in Counseling: How Biblical Theology Reforms Biblical Counseling,* 17

670 North College Street, Suite A, Auburn, AL 36830 – 334-329-5259   Southeast Alabama
E-mail: garyspooner@theowencenter.com
The Owen Center, Auburn, AL

Spraberry, Harold – b Grenada, MS, Oct 31, 51; f S.L.; m Helen Cole; w Carolyn Carpenter, Dec 19, 81; chdn Sarah Elizabeth, Samuel Andrew; MidSoBC 79, BS; UMemp 82, MA; MidABTS 93, MDiv; O 08, Cov Pby; p First P Ch at Water Valley, Water Valley, MS, 08-

417 Kimmons Street, Water Valley, MS 38965-2404 – 662-473-0475   Covenant
E-mail: harold.spraberry@gmail.com
First Presbyterian Church at Water Valley – 662-473-1421

Sprinkle, Robert Franklin Jr. – b Norton, VA, Dec 23, 45; f Robert F. Sr. ; m Neva Noreen Riddle; w Judith Elaine Templeton, Knoxville, TN, Aug 17, 69; chdn Sarah Elaine, Rachel Irene; UT 68, BS; ColTS 68-69; RTS 71, MDiv; O Nov 71, Hlst Pby (PCUS); p Newport Ch, Newport, TN, 71-78; chmn Eastern Hgts Chr sch bd, 82-84; chmn Westm Pby Nom Comm, 86-91; p Valley Pike P Ch, Bristol, TN, 78-91; p Temple P Ch, York, SC, 92-; sc Flwsp Pby, 94-; *Presbyterian Theology and Polity*

3248 York Street, P.O. Box 205, Sharon, SC 29742 – 803-927-7640   Fellowship
E-mail: rsprin1313@aol.com
Temple Presbyterian Church – 803-684-0981

Spurgeon, James N. – b Bellingham, WA, Apr 8, 46; f Orville N; m Winifred L. Burkhart; w Linda C. Schraeder, Willow Grove, PA, Jun 12, 71; chdn Lisa, Jeffrey, Christopher; BethlC 64-68, BA; WTS 68-72, BD, MDiv; O Apr 24, 77, Pby of Long Island (PCUSA); ap First P Ch, Babylon, NY, 77-80; Broughton P Ch, Bloomfield, NJ, 80-82; Bethany P Ch, Wichita, KS, 82-88; p Evangel P Ch, Wichita, KS, 89-92, wc 92; p Grace Ref P Ch, Dale City, VA, 93-07; hr 07; ob ss Reformed P Ch, Manassas, VA, 10-11

13326 Nassau Drive, Woodbridge, VA 22193-4107 – 703-680-6774   Potomac
E-mail: jandlspurgeon@verizon.net
HR

St. Clair, Joel Craig II – WTS 09, MDiv; O Mar 7, 10, Pot Pby; astp Emmanuel P Ch, Arlington, VA, 10-13; op Mosaic Comm Ch, Silver Spring, 13-16, p 16-

2415 Seminary Road, Silver Spring, MD 20910 – 240-424-5235   Potomac
E-mail: joel@mosaicsilverspring.org
Mosaic Community Church – 240-424-5235

St. Germain, Jean Dony – b Jeremie, Haiti, May 13, 66; f Bresile; m Andree Caidor; w Sharon Coleen Johnson, Miami, FL, Jun 26, 93; CIU 94, MA; KTS 97, MDiv; JacksonvilleTheoSem 98, DMin; O Apr 30, 95, SFL Pby; op El Shaddai P Ch, Miami, FL, 96-99, p 99-14; El Shaddai Min, Haiti, 14-

319 Andover Drive, Davenport, FL 33897 – 305-688-0344   South Florida
E-mail: donysha@aol.com
El Shaddai Ministries, Haiti

St. Germain, Louis E. – b Haiti, Aug 26, 67; f Bresile; m Andree Caidor; w Martina Cauguste, Canada, Aug 5, 89; chdn Cristopher See, Lyssa Andy, Charles Lloyd, Itzak Lenny; Centre d'Etude theo, ThB; Jaxville Sem, ThM; L Apr 18, 00, SFL Pby; O Aug 13, 00, SFL Pby; astp El Shaddai P Ch, Miami, FL, 00-14; El Shaddai Min, Haiti, 14-

2121 SW 3rd Avenue, #601, Miami, FL 33129   South Florida
El Shaddai Ministries, Haiti

St. John, Russell – w Amy; chdn Reid, Brett, Belle, Mae, Jack, Ben; WAStU 95, BA; CTS 99, MDiv; GCTS 13, DMin; ascp Grace United Ref Ch, Kennewick, WA, 99-05; p Oakwood P Ch, State College, PA, 05-10; Chap 10-14; srp Twin Oaks P Ch, Ballwin, MO, 14-

850 Ivy Trace Drive, Ballwin, MO 63021   Missouri
E-mail: rstjohn@twinoakschurch.org
Twin Oaks Presbyterian Church – 636-861-1870

St. John, Stephen – w Jennifer; chdn Joshua, Andrew, Jacob, Simon Peter, Elijah, Grace; CC, BA; CTS, MA; O May 23, 04, Evan Pby; srp North Hills P Ch, Meridianville, AL, 04-08; mis Jakarta, Indonesia, 08-

104 Pine Street, Black Mountain, NC 28711-3020 – 256-858-0897   Providence

St. Martin, John – O Jun 3, 17, Siouxl Pby; astp Grace P Ch, Sioux Falls, SD, 17-18; op Resurrection Ch, Fargo, ND, 18-

2747 11th Street West, West Fargo, ND 58078 – 507-381-8441   Siouxlands
E-mail: john@resurrectionfargo.org
Resurrection Church – 701-809-3668

Stain, David R. – O Aug 12, 02, MO Pby; admin Twin Oaks P Ch, Ballwin, MO, 95-01; astp 02-04; p Spring Hills P Ch, Fenton, MO, 04-

1008 Balsawood Drive, High Ridge, MO 63049 – 636-376-0408   Missouri
E-mail: davestain@att.net
Spring Hills Presbyterian Church – 636-677-0409

Stakely, Charles Averett IV – b Tuscaloosa, AL, Dec 28, 58; f Charles Averett III; m Carolyn Cowan; w Elise Winter McKay, Anniston, AL, Nov 21, 92; chdn Charles Averett V, Carolyn Ellen, Thomas McKay; UAL 77-82, BA; RTS 89-92, MDiv; L Jan 25, 94; O Jan 25, 94, Evan Pby; ev PEF, Japan, 93-95; astp Trinity P Ch, Montgomery, AL, 95-99, ip 99-99; op Redeemer P Ch, Evans, GA, 00-02, p 02-

8 Woodbridge Circle, Evans, GA 30809 – 706-414-9907   Savannah River
E-mail: charlie@redeemerevans.org
Redeemer Presbyterian Church – 706-854-9707

Staley, Ira McDuell – b Honesdale, PA, Dec 9, 50; f Joseph Lewis; m Edna June Keller; w Deborah Kinney Johnson, Murrysville, PA, Aug 24, 74; chdn Christen, Jenny, Nathan; AllC 72, BA; WTS 78, MDiv; GCTS 98, DMin; L 80; O 80, NE Pby (RPCES); p Covenant Ch, Johnstown, NY, 79-84; ap Hope Ch, Ballston Spa, NY, 86-88; p West Hopewell P Ch, Hopewell, VA, 88-98, wc 99-04; astp Stony Point Ref P Ch, Richmond, VA, 04-08; wc; hr 11

9110 Newcastle Drive, Mechanicsville, VA 23116 – 804-550-9121   James River
E-mail: istaley@comcast.net
HR

Stallard, Larry H. – b Clinchport, VA, Apr 15, 45; f John A.; m Bessie Ann Carter; w Janice Lynn Bailiff, Elizabethton, TN, Dec 23, 72; ETSU 63-67, BS; TEDS 75-78, MDiv; L 80; O Dec 80, Westm Pby; p Arcadia P Ch, Kingsport, TN, 80-96; ss Edgemont P Ch, Bristol, TN, 96-97, p 97-07; ss 07-09; hr 13

3976 Bloomingdale Pike, Kingsport, TN 37660-7004 – 423-288-4604   Westminster
HR

Stamberg, Jonathan – w Crystal Steadham; chdn Elisa, Micah; UNI 98, BA; CIU 10, MDiv; GATech 17, EMBA; O Mar 4, 12, MetAtl Pby; astp Perimeter Ch, Johns Creek, GA; astp Christos Comm Ch, Norcross, GA, 12-

2236 Tahoe Court, Norcross, GA 30071 – 706-294-7985   Metro Atlanta
E-mail: jonathan@christoscommunity.org
Christos Community Church

Stamper, Nathaniel – O 17, SusqV Pby; astp St. Stephen Ref Ch, New Holland, PA, 17-18, ascp 18-

105 East Broad Street, New Holland, PA 17557   Susquehanna Valley
E-mail: nathanielfstamper@gmail.com
St. Stephen Reformed Church – 717-354-7871

Stancil, Jody – astp Cherokee P Ch, Canton, GA, 08-09; ascp 09-10; ascp Grace Ch, Canton, GA, 10-; op Riverside Comm Ch, Cartersville, GA, 14-

14 Moss Way NW, Cartersville, GA 30120 – 404-345-3807   Northwest Georgia
E-mail: jody.stancil@gmail.com
Grace Church – 678-493-9869
Riverside Community Church – 404-345-3807

Standiford, Ronald Dawson – b Baltimore, MD, Jul 2, 49; f Howard W.; m Rosalie M. Burton; w Darby Shaver, Timonium, MD, Sept 7, 85; chdn Leah Dawson, Emily Ashmore; AmU 71, BA; UBSL 75-77; WTS 80, MDiv; O Oct 25, 81, DMV Pby (RPCES); ap P Ch, Timonium, MD, 81-88; op Redeemer P Ch, Kingsville, MD, 86-88, p 88-; fndr Redeemer Classical CS, adj fac, 96-09, chap 09-

6415 Mt. Vista Road, Kingsville, MD 21087 – 410-592-5521   Chesapeake
E-mail: classicdadman@yahoo.com
Redeemer Presbyterian Church – 410-592-9625
Redeemer Classical Christian School

Standridge, John – astp Christ the King P Ch, Cambridge, MA, 08-12; op Christ P Ch - Kerrville, Kerrville, TX, 12-

1049 Creek Run, Kerrville, TX 78028 – 830-792-6804   South Texas
E-mail: johnstandridge@gmail.com
Christ Presbyterian Church – Kerrville

Stanghelle, Matthew – O Aug 12, 18, SEAL Pby, chp 18-

31115 Cedar Ridge Drive, Lindstrom, MN 55045   Southeast Alabama
E-mail: matt@wegoinfaith.org

Stanley, Vaughan – b Charleston, WV, Oct 21, 50; f James Virgil; m Lois Jean Vaughan; w Katheryne May Giles, Jackson, TN, Jun 12, 76; chdn Kara Suzanne, Kelly Amanda, Krista Elizabeth, Jonathan Vaughan; HSC 68-72, BA; RTS 79, MDiv, MMiss; LRTS 82, DMin; O Feb 24, 80, SFL Pby; astp, ascp Seacrest Boulevard P Ch, Delray Beach, FL, 80-88; astp Orangewood P Ch, Maitland, FL, 88-02; astp Westminster P Ch, Ft. Myers, FL, 02-04, ascp 04-10; ob Chap Hope Hospice, 10-17; hr 17

600 West Faith Terrace, Maitland, FL 32751 – 239-822-1956   Suncoast Florida
E-mail: vaughanstanley@gmail.com
HR

Stanton, Allen – O Oct 9, 11, Gr Pby; p Waynesboro P Ch, Waynesboro, MS, 11- 17; p Pinehaven P Ch, Clinton, MS, 17-

109 Primrose Landing, Clinton, MS 39056   Mississippi Valley
E-mail: allenstanton12@gmail.com
Pinehaven Presbyterian Church – 601-708-4653

Stanton, Dallard Jonathon – b St. Charles, IL, Aug 22, 55; f James Dallard; m Mona Joan Tucker; w Beth Jean Hamilton, Burlington, NC, Aug 13, 77; chdn Jonathon David, Jocelyn Ruth, James Hamilton, Josiah Dallard, Johanna Marilyn; BroCC 73-74; CC 74-78, BA; RTS 78-82, MDiv; O Mar 6, 83, PCUS; p Northminster P Ch, Murfreesboro, TN, 83-87; chp/p Providence P Ch, 87-92; chp MTW, Odessa, Ukraine, 92-02, staff 02-04; mis MTW, Madrid, 05-07; mis MTW, tm ldr, chp, Sofia, Bulgaria, 07-

c/o MTW – 678-388-9718 (home phone via Vonage)   Heritage
E-mail: dal.mtwbg@gmail.com
PCA Mission to the World

Stanton, Eldon C. – wc 85; ob Chap Waterfront Msn, Ft Walton Beach, FL, 85-01; hr 01

1235 Bayshore, Valparaiso, FL 32580-1338 – 850-678-0067   Gulf Coast
HR

Stanton, Steven Patrick – O Apr 18, RMtn Pby; astp Forestgate P Ch, Colorado Springs, CO, 18-

7290 Grand Prairie Drive, Colorado Springs, CO 80923 – 719-510-3124   Rocky Mountain
E-mail: stanton.steve@gmail.com
Forestgate Presbyterian Church – 719-495-5672

Stapleton, Curtis A. – b Maryville, TN, Apr 14, 69; f John D.; m Carolyn Beason; w Suzanne Bowen, Marietta, GA, Oct 22, 94; chdn Katherine Grace, Knox Augustus, Kristine Adelle, Kenzi Ruth; MaryvC 89-92; CTS 95-98, MDiv; L Mar 17, 98, Westm Pby; O Aug 23, 98, Westm Pby; int RUF, WinC, 92-94; campm RUF, ETSU, 98-03; astp Westminster P Ch, Johnson City, TN, 03-04, ascp 04-08; chp, op Mercy P Ch, Morgantown, WV, 08-

525 Santa Fe Court, Morgantown, WV 26508-5831 – 304-218-0105   New River
E-mail: mercypreacher@gmail.com
Mercy Presbyterian Church

Stark, James Paul – b Alton, IL, Oct 17, 59; f Paul E; m Carolyn Liley; w Jeanie Holt, Troy, AL, Jun 11, 83; chdn Paul Kenneth, Jonathan Thomas, Jessica Eugenia; TrSU 81-83, BS; CTS 87-91, MDiv; CTS 10, DMin; L Oct 91; O Feb 23, 92, SEAL Pby; mis MTW, MIA, 92-04; admin ICTS, Grenada, W. Indies, 93-04; p Grandcote Ref P Ch, Coulterville, IL, 04-

PO Box 411, Coulterville, IL 62337 – 618-758-2730   Illiana
E-mail: jjstark@frontier.com
Grandcote Reformed Presbyterian Church – 618-758-2432

Stark, Richard A. – w Betsy; chdn Rachel, Kakki, Caroline, Sam; SELAU 81, BA; IST 92, cert; RTS 02, MDiv; O Feb 8, 04, MSVal Pby; staff Athletes in Action, MSU, 82-87; Dir Athletes in Action, SE, Auburn, 87-03; astp Trinity P Ch, Jackson, MS, 03-07; ascp Covenant P Ch, Auburn, AL, 07-09; astpEastwood P Ch, Montgomery, AL, 09-10; op Plains P Msn, Auburn, AL, 09-11; p 11-14; ip Millbrook P Ch, Millbrook, AL, 16; ascp Decatur P Ch, Decatur, AL, 14-17

PO Box 5855, Decatur, AL 35601 – 334-209-0381   Providence
E-mail: rstark8905@gmail.com

Starkes, Monte Thomas – b Atlanta, GA, Dec 25, 68; f Tommy; m Nancy Carol Lawler; w Amy Elizabeth Johnston, Birmingham, AL, May 28, 94; chdn Luke, Charity, Philip, Anna Grace; SamU 92, BS; BDS 94, MTS, 02, MDiv;TalTS 13, DMin; O Oct 26, 03, NGA Pby; yp Oak Mountain P Ch, Birmingham, AL, 92-94;Campus Outreach, 95-02; ascp Westminster P Ch, Gainesville, GA, 02-04; ascp Grace Comm Ch, Marvin, NC, 04-05; ascp Oak Mountain P Ch, Birmingham, AL, 05-08; astp Perimeter Ch, Johns Creek, GA, 08-

100 Halite Drive, Alpharetta, GA 30022   Metro Atlanta
E-mail: montes@perimeter.org
Perimeter Church – 678-405-2000

Starkey, Seth – astp Second P Ch, Greenville, SC, 11-13; campm RUF, BelU, 13-18; astp Madison Heights P Ch, Madison, MS, 18, ascp 18-

415 Bozeman Road, Madison, MS 39110　　　　　　　　　　　　　　　Mississippi Valley
E-mail: seth@madisonheightschurch.com
Madison Heights Presbyterian Church – 601-605-9929

Starnes, Timothy Austin – b Vicksburg, MS, Aug 14, 56; f William Dennis; m Mary Elsie Jones; w Sarah Lynn Spencer, Port Gibson, MS, Dec 27, 75; chdn Sarah Elizabeth, Timothy Austin Jr., Mary Naomi; DSU, BS; RTS, MDiv; O Jun 26, 83, Cov Pby; ap Covenant P Ch, Cleveland, MS, 83-87, srp 87-

1517 Terrace Road, Cleveland, MS 38732-2936 – 662-843-1194　　　　　　　Covenant
E-mail: tastarnes@yahoo.com
Covenant Presbyterian Church – 662-843-9598

Staton, R. Keeth – b St. Augustine, FL, Feb 6, 53; f Van E; m Willie R. Lawrence; w Lauri A. Smith, Ocala, FL, Nov 5, 83; chdn Matthew, Lyndsay, Stephen, Caroline; CFLCC 73, AA; UWFL 75, BS, 80, MS; RTS 93, MDiv, 05, DMin; O Feb 10, 94, CentFL Pby; op Springs P Ch, Dunnellon, FL, 94-95, p 95-

11664 North Kenlake Circle, Citrus Springs, FL 34434-2217 – 352-465-4411　　Central Florida
E-mail: kstaton@bellsouth.net
Springs Presbyterian Church – 352-489-8992

Stava, Jonas – ob min to military, 18-

Address Unavailable　　　　　　　　　　　　　　　　　　　　　　　　Philadelphia

Steel, Ronald Eugene – b Ocala, FL, Jul 22, 48; f James A. Jr.; m Lela Mae Godwin; w Jennifer Christine Bean, Ocala, FL, May 19, 73; chdn Matthew Benjamin, Bryan James, Jonathan Lanier; CFLCC 66-68, AA; UFL 68-70, BS; SWBTS 70-71; RTS 73-76, MDiv; O Nov 21, 76, FL Pby (ARP); ap Cornerstone Bap Ch, Orlando, FL, 80-82; ap Briarwood P Ch, Birmingham, AL, 82-89; prof BhamTS, 82-89; srp Chapelgate P Ch, Marriottsville, MD, 90-04; srp Twin Oaks P Ch, Ballwin, MO, 04-11; p Eastbridge P Ch, Mount Pleasant, SC, 12-

3671 Bagley Drive, Mount Pleasant, SC 29466　　　　　　　　　　　　　Lowcountry
E-mail: ronsteel48@gmail.com
Eastbridge Presbyterian Church – 843-849-6111

Steele, Joseph Henry, III – p Woodland P Ch, Hattiesburg, MS, 12-18; p Westminster P Ch, Huntsville, AL, 18-

108 Stonecroft Drive, Madison, AL 35757 – 843-263-7730　　　　　　　　Providence
E-mail: jhsteele3@gmail.com
Westminster Presbyterian Church – 256-830-5754

Steele, Randy Lane – b Burlington, IA, Jun 10, 53; f Norman Lance; m Lola Arlene Pendarvis; w Linda Anne Hale, Las Cruces, NM, Dec 27, 75; chdn Cody Lane, Raudy Lance, Bethany Anne; COz 71-72; ENMU 73-75, BS; FulTS 76-77; CTS 77-80, MDiv; NGTS 13, DMin; L Nov 25, 79, Ramsey Creek Bap Ch; O Jan 6, 80, Salt Rvr Bap; p Hill Bap Ch, Las Cruces, NM, 80-81; p Hope Ch (PCA), Mesa, AZ, 81-83; op Cornerstone P Ch, Ft. Collins, CO, 83-90; Dir SCS, 90-91; srp Providence P Ch, Albuquerque, NM, 91-

13801 Encantado Road, NE, Albuquerque, NM 87123　　　　　　　　　　Rio Grande
E-mail: rsteele@ppcpca.org
Providence Presbyterian Church – 505-292-2605

Steele, Rick Lynn – b Burlington, IA, Aug 25, 47; f Norman Lance; m Lola Arlene Pendarvis; w Karen Leigh Fell, Norristown, PA, Sept 1, 72; chdn Joanna Leslie, Luke Chandler; COz 65-69, BA; PTS 69-70; FulTS 70-71; PTS 71-72, MDiv; O Sept 12, 72, PCUSA; Recd PCA Oct 23, 93, NoIL Pby; astp First P Ch of Las Cruces, NM (PCUSA), 72-75; p Sunbeam U. P. Ch (PCUSA), Aledo, IL, 76-93; op Trinity P Ch, Aledo, IL, 93-94; p Westminster P Ch, Alamogordo, NM, 95-11; sc SW Pby, 97; rc, SW pby, 99-10; astp Providence P Ch, Albuquerque, NM, 12-

636 Marquis Drive NE, Albuquerque, NM 87123 – 505-323-3568 Rio Grande
E-mail: pastorick1@live.com
Providence Presbyterian Church – 505-292-2605

Steere, Daniel – b Forteleza, Brazil, Oct 16, 53; f David Jason; m J. Ruth Stalker; w Susan Louise Scott, Cedarville, OH, Dec 7, 74; chdn Daniel, Krista, Anna, Jason; CedC 75, BA; Uday 77, MA; GSU 00, PhD; L Apr 15, 97; O Aug 2, 97, NGA Pby; headm, medu Harvester Christian Ac, 90-98; p First P Ch, Summerville, GA, 98-05; ob Equipping Pastors, Int., 05-; ascp Covenant P Ch, Chattanooga, TN, 09-; "For the Peace of Both, For the Humour of Neither," *Sixteenth Century Journal* 27:3 (96)

8905 Hurricane Ridge Road, Chattanooga, TN 37421 – 706-506-0070 Tennessee Valley
E-mail: magister53@gmail.com
Equipping Pastors, International
Covenant Presbyterian Church – 423-899-5377

Stein, Thomas J. Jr. – b Cincinnati, OH, Oct 16, 63; f Thomas J; m Jessie Anna Mountel; w Beth Ann McIlhenny, Bristol, PA, Jun 25, 88; chdn Taylor Borden, Andrew Thomas, Emily Sharon; GenC 86, BA; CTS 88-91, MDiv; INU 96, MA; L Sept 90, GrLks Pby; O May 1, 94, SiouxI Pby; p Christ P Ch, Farmington, MN, 94-99; p Christ P Ch, Richmond, IN, 99-11; ob DAlRel GenC, 11-13; instr GenC, 13-; astp Chapel P Ch, Beaver, PA, 13-14, ascp 14-

110 Poplar Drive, Monaca, PA 15061 – 724-777-1228 Ascension
E-mail: pastortomstein@gmail.com
Chapel Presbyterian Church – 724-495-0297

Steinbarger, Chris – O May 17, 15, Wisc Pby; Chap Providence Acad, Green Bay, WI, 15-

159 North Maple Avenue, Green Bay, WI 54303 Wisconsin
Providence Academy, Green Bay, WI

Stelzig, Douglas Lyndon – b Houston, TX, Dec 23, 59; f Guy W.; m Annabelle Lucille Allen; w Cynthia Marie Robinson, Gastonia, NC, Aug 11, 90; chdn Kurt Stephen; UHou 83, BS; TEDS 89, MDiv, 90, ThM; L Jan 27, 90, SoTX Pby; O Jun 9, 91, NoIL Pby; int Presb Ch of the Covenant, Houston, TX, 89-90; astp, moy North Shore P Ch, Lake Forest, IL, 91-93; lect Emmanuel Bib Inst, Oradea, Romania, 93-94; mis MTW/Impact, 94-97; mis MTW, South Africa, 97-12

967 Busch Street, Montomery, AL 36801 – 704-908-3987 Southeast Alabama
E-mail: dstelzig@gmail.com

Stephan, Michael – b Annapolis, MD, Apr 15, 73; w Barbara Beth; chdn Jenna Elizabeth, Leigha Collette; TowU 96, BS; RTS 02, MAR; Chap USArmy, 06-16; astp Severna Park Evangelical P Ch, Pasadena, MD, 16-

290 Poplar Road, Millersville, MD 21108 – 254-319-5519 Chesapeake
E-mail: mstephan@spepchurch.org
Severna Park Evangelical Presbyterian Church – 410-544-5013

Stephens, Anthony – op Stillwaters P Ch, PCA, West Grove, PA, 07-11, p 11-

408 West Locust Lane, Kennett Square, PA 19348 – 610-444-0499 Heritage
E-mail: pastortony@stillwatersfamily.com
Stillwaters Presbyterian Church, PCA – 610-869-2009

Stephens, Noah – mis MTW, 12-

c/o MTW – 678-617-3927   Georgia Foothills
E-mail: noahstephens1@gmail.com
PCA Mission to the World

Stephenson, Clive Norris – b Kingston, Jamaica, May 3, 40; f Cyril; m Beryl McKenzie; w Hyacinth Yvonne Dixon, Kingston, Jun 26, 65; chdn Avery, Noreen, Clive; RTS; WhTS; O Apr 22, 07, NFL Pby; ascp Ortega P Ch, Jacksonville, FL, 07-08; ob mis Min in Action, Jamaica, 08-10; hr 17

1112 Lake Parke Drive, Jacksonville, FL 32259   North Florida
E-mail: clivestephenson@live.com
HR

Stephenson, James Frank – b Charleston, WV, Jul 6, 53; f Frank; m Margaret Kathleen Williamson; w Debra Kay Hunt, Greenville, SC, Jul 11, 75; chdn Jessica (Taylor), James F. Jr.; BJU 71-75, BS; NIU 81-83, MMus; RTS 95-98, MDiv; O Aug 2, 98, Cal Pby; mmus Mitchell Road P Ch, Greenville, SC, 83-97; op Horizon Ch, Greenville, SC, 98-99, p 99-

116 Terra Lake Drive, Greer, SC 29650 – 864-268-9855   Calvary
E-mail: jim@horizonchurch.org
Horizon Church – 864-286-9911

Stephenson, John David – p Gr P Chelsea, Chelsea, AL, 07-12; astp McLean P Ch, McLean, VA, 12-

1034 Balls Hill Road, McLean, VA 22101   Potomac
E-mail: david@mcleanpres.org
McLean Presbyterian Church – 703-821-0800

Stephenson, Lane – op New Cov P Ch, Summit, MS, 07-08, p 08-15, wc 15-16; astp Westminster P Ch, Gainesville, GA, 16-

4118 Woodcutter Lane, Gainesville, GA 30506 – 470-399-1565   Georgia Foothills
E-mail: lanes@wcpca.org
Westminster Presbyterian Church – 770-534-1078

Sterling, Jason – campm RUF, 06-16; srp Faith P Ch, Birmingham, AL, 16-

4601 Valleydale Road, Birmingham, AL 35242   Evangel
E-mail: jsterling@faith-pca.org
Faith Presbyterian Church – 205-979-6585

Sterling, Richard W. – O Oct 17, 10, NJ Pby; p Covenant P Ch, Cape May, NJ, 10-

9 Westwood Drive, Cape May Court House, NJ 08210-2017 – 609-465-3693   New Jersey
E-mail: sterlingr@mtps.sjtp.net
Covenant Presbyterian Church – 609-886-2448

Stern, William – op Hope P Ch, Chadds Ford, PA, 16-

1216 Painters Crossing, Chadds Ford, PA 19317 – 610-715-7492   Heritage
E-mail: pastorwill@explorehopechurch.org
Hope Presbyterian Church

Stevener, Crawford Michael – O Jun 30, 13, Ecar Pby; campm RUF, DukeU, 13-18; campm RUF, Stanford, 18-

2104 Manzanita Avenue, West Menlo Park, CA 94025   Northern California
E-mail: crawford.stevener@ruf.org
PCA Reformed University Fellowship

Stevens, Carl David – b Sapulpa, OK, Jul 28, 40; f Russel Henry; m Moni Livoni; w Irma Waldesbuhl, Nov 4, 86; chdn Mona E; AZSU 63, BA; DTS 68, ThM; PTS 79; WTS 92, PhD; O Oct 8, 78, Bham Pby (UPCUSA); p Mount Cal P Ch, 74-80; mis MTW, 91-06; t FrTA, 92-99; t Trin Theological College, Aust, 00-06; hr; p/t p Clayton P Ch, Clayton, AL, 06-10; ss Bethel P Ch, Union Springs, AL, 07-10; p/t t Westwood P Ch, Dothan, AL

E-mail: k.stevens@bigfoot.com   Southeast Alabama
HR

Stevens, Chris – b Houston, TX, Oct 3, 83; chdn Phineas, Tobias; UARF 06, BA; WSCAL 11, MDiv; McMasterDiv 19, PhD; O May 20, 18, GrLks Pby; ascp Redeemer P Ch, Traverse City, MI, 18-

520 Wadsworth Street, Traverse City, MI 49684   Great Lakes
E-mail: chris@redeemertraversecity.org
Redeemer Presbyterian Church – 231-946-1700

Stevens, Decherd – b Greenville, SC, Sept 21, 54; f Joseph B.; m Elizabeth Fair Foster; w Sylvia Mae Sterbin, Racine, WI, Sept 23, 78; chdn Krista, David, Victoria; BJU; GPTS 95, BD; L Jul 90; O Apr 30, 95, Cal Pby; int Calvary P Ch, Greenville, SC, 89-90, ss 90-95, p 95-16; astp Carlisle Ref P Ch, Carlisle, PA, 16-

8 Old Coach Lane, Carlisle, PA 17013   Susquehanna Valley
E-mail: pcapastor@bellsouth.net
Carlisle Reformed Presbyterian Church – 717-249-5675

Stevens, Matthew – b Sept 10, 73; w Courtney; chdn Mary, Samuel, Elisabeth, Lydia, John, Abigail, Thomas, Martha; VPI 95, BS; RTS 12, MDiv; O Oct 28, 12, Cal Pby; p Liberty Springs P Ch, Cross Hill, SC, 12-14; p Story Mem P Ch, Marion, NC, 14-

174 Shady Lane, Marion, NC 28752 – 864-538-8284   Western Carolina
E-mail: mattandcc.stevens@gmail.com
Story Memorial Presbyterian Church – 828-652-9683

Stevenson, John T. – b Washington, DC, Sept 1, 53; f Jesse H; m Carmen M; w Paula M. Ryle, Hollywood, FL, Aug 9, 73; chdn Sky Heather (McNeill); FBC 71-77, BA; KTS 90-95, MDiv; RTSFL 07, DMin; L Jan 92; O May 14, 95, SFL Pby; t SW Miami Bib Inst, 77-79; astp St. Andrews P Ch, Hollywood, FL, 95-; t TIU, FL campus, 07-; lect Moldova Bib Sem, 00-07; assoc prof, lect RTS, 03-04; instr, adj prof, lect SFLBC, 05-; *Romans: The Radical Righteousness of God*, 08; *First Corinthians: Striving for Unity*, 08; *Galatians: Our Freedom in Christ*, 08; *Hebrews: The Sufficiency of the Savior*, 08; *Doctrines of the Bible: Outlines in Systematic Theology*, 08; *Luke: In the Footsteps of the Savior, Redeemer*, 09; *Mark: The Servant who Came to Save*, 09; *A Survey of the Old Testament: The Bible Jesus Used*, 09; *Genesis: The Book of Beginnings*, 09; *The Epistle of James: A Faith that Works*, 10; *The Historical Books of the Old Testament: One God, One People, One Land*, 10; *The Epistle to the Ephesians: The Wealth & Walk of the Christian*, 11; *Ecclesiastes: A Spiritual Journey*, 12

301 South 56th Terrace, Hollywood, FL 33023 – 954-962-1687   South Florida
E-mail: johnstevenson@bellsouth.net
St. Andrews Park Road Presbyterian Church – 954-989-2641
South Florida Bible College

Stevenson, Richard Hunter — w Heather Trupia; chdn Mary Rachel, Martha Marie, Joseph Stone, James Hunter; MonC 91, AS; FurU 93, BS; RTS 03, MDiv; astp First P Ch, Macon, GA, 04-10; srp North Macon P Ch, Macon, GA, 10-

617 Saint Ives Place, Macon, GA 31204 – 478-474-1862   Central Georgia
E-mail: hunter@nmpc.net
North Macon Presbyterian Church – 478-477-7777

Stewart, David Lynn – b Spangler, PA, Dec 6, 62; f John Wesley Jr.; m Robena Mae Lee; w Wendy Jeane Robinson, Levittown, PA, Nov 27, 82; chdn Zachary David, Jordan Michael, Kaylie Elizabeth; IUP 84, BMusEd; RTS 96, MDiv; O May 19, 96, Mid-Atlantic (EPC); Recd PCA Jul 10, 99, NR Pby; p Lee Park EPC, Monroe, NC, 95-98; p Faith EPC, Roanoke, VA, 98; astp Westminster P Ch, Roanoke, VA, 99-02; p Covenant P Ch, Vienna, WV, 02-04; ascp Christ the Redeemer Ch, Portland, ME, 07- 14; ob headm Greater Portland CS, 14-15; p Grace P Ch, Lake Suzy, FL-

13275 SW Pembroke Circle North, Lake Suzy, FL 34269   Suncoast Florida
E-mail: pastordave@gracelakesuzy.com
Grace Presbyterian Church

Stewart, Hubert Creswell – b Sparta, IL, Jan 2, 30; f Rev Robert W.S.; m Helen Creswell; w Joan Schrader, Canton, OH, Jul 15, 55; chdn Randy Lynn, Teryl Lynette; BJU 51, BA, 51-52, grad wk; WTS 53-54; REpS 54-55, BD; L 52, RPC; O Jan 56, CMS Pby; ap Oakland Ave Ch, Pontiac, MI, 52-53; p First P Ch, Philadelphia, MS, 56-60; p Carolina P Ch, Philadelphia, MS, 56-60; p Pearl P Ch, Pearl, MS, 60-65; ap Carrollton Ch, New Orleans, LA, 65-71; p First P Ch, Enterprise, AL, 72-74; p Eastside P Ch, Gadsden, AL, 74-83; sc Evan Pby, 76-00; p First P Ch, Russellville, AL, 90-98; hr 98; bd of RH Conf Cent

4013 Wright Circle, Rainbow City, AL 35906-6555 – 256-442-0880   Evangel
E-mail: hubertcstewart@gmail.com
HR

Stewart, James Holland – b Little Rock, AR, Sept 17, 45; f Arthur Talmadge S. Jr.; m Josephine Holland; w Sue Treloar, Raymond, MS, Jun 5, 71; chdn Sarah Ann, Esther Elizabeth, James Holland Jr.; UGA 67, BS; RTS 72, MDiv, 88, DMin; O Nov 18, 73, TX Pby; staff CCC, 67-71; prof Tyler Junior Coll, 72-75; ap Fifth Street P Ch, Tyler, TX, 72-75; p Perry, GA, 75-79; mis Taiwan, 79-85; mis MTW, Hong Kong, 85-88; lect ChinMS, 88-08; DnStu RTS, 91-92; astp First P Ch, Jackson, MS, 93-08; Comm on MTW, 98-01; ed *China News and Church Report*, 88; contr ed *The China Mission Handbook;* reg coord EE, Int, 08-

506 Shalom Way, Flowood, MS 39232 – 601-956-0497   Mississippi Valley
E-mail: JamesHStewart@comcast.net
Evangelism Explosion

Stewart, Joseph Edward – b Mobile, AL, Sept 25, 65; f William Clark S; m Sullivan; w Connie Cawthorn, Memphis, TN, Jun 23, 90; chdn Ashley Grace, Joseph Wesley, Hannah Faith, Jennifer Cawthorn; UMS 88, BA; RTS 88-92, MDiv; L Jun 2, 92; O Jul 5, 92, MSVal Pby; int First P Ch, Yazoo City, MS, 88-92, astp 92-93; astp First P Ch, Crossville, TN, 93-94; ev, op Grace P Ch, Cookeville, TN, 93-94, p 94-07; exec dir Ref Youth Min, 07-

3446 Cloudcrest Trail, Signal Mountain, TN 37377 – 901-581-7579   Nashville
E-mail: joey@rymonline.org
Reformed Youth Ministries

Stewart, Kenneth James – b New Westminster, BC, Can, Oct 20, 49; f John Ray; m Christina Lamont Gowans; w Jane Katherine Grosser, Ridgewood, NJ, Jul 10, 76; chdn Elizabeth Jane, Andrew James, Peter William, Caroline Ruth; UBC 71, BA; WTS 75, MDiv, 76, ThM; UWatO 85, MPhil; NCEd 88-91, PhD; L Aug 76; O Aug 76, PCC; Recd PCA Apr 25, 86, PacNW Pby; p Murray Harbour P Ch, PEI, 76-78; p St.

Stewart, Kenneth James, continued
Andrew's Ch, Parry Sound, Ont, 79-84; p Calvary EFC Ch, Lacombe, Alberta, 84-88, wc 88-91; ob ip Iron Spgs, (Alberta) CRC, 91-92; ob ip First CRC Lethbridge, (AB), 92-93, wc 93-94; prof, PBC&GS, 94-97; prof CC, 97-; auth *Restoring the Reformation*, 06; ed *The Emergence of Evangelicalism*, 08; auth *Ten Myths About Calvinism*, 11; *In Search of Ancient Roots: The Christian Past and the Evangelical Identity Crisis*, 17; contr *Encyclopedia of the Reformed Faith*; *Scottish Dictionary of Church History and Theology*; *Blackwell's Dictionary of Evangelical Biography: 1730-1860*; *God's People: One Hundred and Ten Characters in the Story of Scottish Religion*

1203 Aladdin Road, Lookout Mountain, GA 30750 – 706-820-7146   Tennessee Valley
E-mail: ken.stewart@covenant.edu
Covenant College – 706-419-1653

    Stewart, Michael R. – b Charleston, SC, Apr 9, 58; f DonalM.; m Irene Bernice Magruder; w Jeri Lynn Park, LaGrange, GA, Jun 13, 81; chdn Christie, Mason; Citadel 80, BS; DTS 89, ThM; GCTS 11, DMin; ColumbusSU 94, MS; L Oct 00, CentGA Pby; O Jun 01, CentGA Pby; ob Piedmont Columbus Reg, 00-; comm PRCC, 16-

527 Double Churches Road, Columbus, GA 31904 – 706-571-1795   Central Georgia
E-mail: michael.stewart@crhs.net
Piedmont Columbus Regional

    Stewart, Michael Scott – b Charlotte, NC, Aug 14, 70; f Norman A.; m Jean Mills; w Amy Robinson, Rock Hill, SC, Jan 8, 00; chdn Luke Robinson, Jackson Wiley; ASU 92, BA; RTSNC 02, MDiv; L Jan 18, 04, PTri Pby; O Mar 21, 04, PTri Pby; astp Grace P Ch, Kernersville, NC, 02-05; astp, chp Grace Comm Ch, Fletcher, NC, 07-12; op Gr Foothills, Tryon, NC, 11-12; p 12-15; astp Midtown Flwsp Ch, Nashville, TN, 15-18; p CrossPoint Comm Ch, Boone, NC, 18-

277 Wild Turkey Ridge, Boone, NC 28607 – 828-808-6867   Western Carolina
E-mail: scottstewart25@gmail.com
CrossPoint Community Church – 828-264-5288

    Stewart, Neil – p Second P Ch, Yazoo City, MS, 02-06; p Kirk O the Isles P Ch, Savannah, GA, 06-16

6500 Habersham Street, Savannah, GA 31405 – 912-247-5176   Savannah River

    Stiemann, Tim – srp Oaklawn P Ch, Houston, TX, 06-

207 Lansing Crest Circle, Houston, TX 77015 – 832-741-1190   Houston Metro
E-mail: pastortim@oaklawnpca.org
Oaklawn Presbyterian Church – 713-921-5635

    Stigers, Timothy H. – b Camden, NJ, Jun 18, 48; f Harold G.; m Mary J. Olson; w Patricia Ann Brown, Coulterville, IL, Jun 11, 71; chdn Joshua Timothy, Peter James, Robert Luke; CC 70, BA; CTS 76, MDiv; BallSU 10, MA; L May 76, Midw Pby; O Jun 5, 77, GrLks Pby (RPCES); ap Christ Ch, Grand Rapids, MI, 77-79; p Immanuel Ch, Poland, OH, 79-81; p Cornerstone Ch, Boardman, OH, 81-83; t/tr Chattanooga Christian Sch, 83-91; ap New City Flwsp, Chattanooga, TN, 87-89; p Trinity P Ch, Maryville, TN, 91-96; p New Life P Ch, Yorktown, IN, 96-03, wc 03-05; ob Chap SouthernCare, Muncie, IN, 05-13; Chap Signature HealthCARE, Muncie, IN, 13-17; hr 17

5467 Maple Avenue, St. Louis, MO 63112 – 765-760-7190   Central Indiana
E-mail: timothystigers@gmail.com
HR

    Still, Seth – campm RUF, DeltaSt, 08-17; p Crosstown Fellowship, Cleveland, MS, 17-

300 South Bolivar Ave., Cleveland, MS 38732 – 601-503-7250   Covenant
E-mail: sethstill@gmail.com
Crosstown Fellowship

Stockhaus, Jaimeson – campm RUF, UCSB, 13-16; chp 16-17; op Redeemer San Jose, San Jose, CA, 17-

1127 Fairview Avenue, San Jose, CA 95125   Northern California
Redeemer San Jose

Stockton, William Clinton – b Longview, TX, May 9, 49; f William Eldon (d); m Shirley Ruth Maxson; w Esther L. Pickersgill, Miami, FL, Mar 12, 94; chdn Andrew Jackson, James Clinton; ClarksSTheo 78, ThB, 80, ThM; MINTS 04, MDiv; O Apr 9, 78, Bapt; Recd PCA 07, Palm Pby; p Cole Spring Bapt Ch, Russellville, MO, 76-78; p Hickory Point Bapt, Iberia, MO, 78-80; p First P Ch EPC, Homestead, FL, 02-06; p Andrews P Ch, Andrews, SC, 07-18; wc 18-

106 South Rosemary, Andrews, SC 29510 – 843 325-9760   Pee Dee
E-mail: slint@pastorstockton.com

Stoddard, David Alexander – b West Branch, MI, Jul 10, 74; f Dana L.; m Donna Baumgartner; w Eowyn Genevieve Clowney Jones, Escondido, CA, Dec 27, 97; chdn Jesse Alexander, Liam Edmund, Alethea Grace, Emmanuelle Joy, Ethan Lewis; KgC 92-96, BA; WSCAL 96-99, MDiv WTS 17, ThM; L Jul 98, TNVal Pby; O Oct 17, 99, TNVal Pby; astp New Life P Ch, 99-00; chp, mis MTW, Berlin, Germany, 00-17; int dir Europe, MTW, 17-

c/o MTW – +4901735271710   Tennessee Valley
E-mail: davidinberlin@gmail.com
PCA Mission to the World

Stoddard, Jonathan – b Ithaca, NY, May 29, 82; WTS 13, MDiv; O Feb 14, 14, NoCA Pby; ascp Jordan Valley Ch PCA, West Jordan, UT, 14-16, p 16-; *Computer Science: Discovering God's Glory in Ones and Zeros* 15; *Choosing a Church: A Biblical and Practical Guide*, 16 ebook;

5179 Nokasippi Lane, South Jordan, UT 84095 – 720-256-1177   Northern California
E-mail: jon@chipeta.net
Jordan Valley Church – 801-280-6378

Stodghill, John Wesley – b Crystal Spgs, MS, Aug 23, 34; f Charles Ellis; m H.J. Bordeaux; w Jane Kay, Jackson, MS, Dec 23, 60; chdn John, Jane (Sims), Jim, Justin, Joy (Rancatore); BelC 64; ColTS 70, MDiv; BethS 89, DMin; L Jul 19, 70; O Jul 19, 70, PCUS; Recd PCA Jul 18, 92, CentCar (re-received, orig PCA); p Lebanon P Ch, Abbeville, SC, 70-71; p First P Ch, Indianola, MS, 72-75; p First P Ch, Biloxi, MS, 75-76; p, ip Covenant Ref, Mobile, AL, 77-83; p Odessa Ref, Artas, SD, 83-87; p SW ARP, Little Rock, AR, 87-88; p Pleasant Hill ARP; p Heath Spgs, SC, 88-92; p Shearer P Ch, Mooresville, NC, 92-94; p Grenada P Ch, Grenada, MS, 94-98; p Philadelphus P Ch, Waynesboro, MS, 98-05; Chap Wayne General Hospital/ Hospice, 98-14; hr 07

1310 Highland Drive, Waynesboro, MS 39367 – 601-735-1043   Grace
E-mail: jwstodghill@gmail.com
HR

Stogner, John Phillip Jr. – b Simpsonville, SC, Dec 19, 58; f John P. Sr.; m Barbara Jean Bradshaw; w Wendy Thigpen, Turbeville, SC, Jul 31, 82; chdn John Phillip III, Benjamin Coppedge, Seth Preston, Hannah Kaitlin; Citadel 77-81, BA; CTS 81-84, MDiv; RTS 03, DMin; L 84; O 84, Westm Pby; p Fellowship P Ch, Newland, NC, 84-88; p Frank P Ch, Crossnore, NC, 84-88; op DaySpring P Ch, Spring Hill, FL, 88-91, srp 91-93; ob chp NCA Pby, Park City, UT, 93-96; op Park City P Ch, Park City, UT, 96-98, p 98-06; chp Daniel Island, SC, 06-08; op Two Rivers P Ch, Charleston, SC, 08-11; p 11 18; fm MTW, Scotland, 18-;

305 Creswell Avenue E, Greenwood, SC 29646 – 843-259-4477   Lowcountry
E-mail: stognerphil@gmail.com
PCA Mission to the World

MINISTERIAL DIRECTORY

Stogner, Russell Stuart – b Greenville, SC, Jul 9, 63; f James Robert; m Patricia Ann Everton; w Kimberly Sue Helmintoller, Winston-Salem, NC, Dec 19, 87; chdn Camille Anderson, Tess Everton; WFU 85, BA; WTS 90, MDiv; L Sept 9, 90; O Sept 9, 90, CentCar Pby; int Redeemer P Ch, Winston-Salem, NC, 85-86; ydir New Life Ch of Phil, Philadelphia, PA, 87-90; astp Redeemer P Ch, Winston-Salem, NC, 90-93, ascp 93-00; op Hope P Ch, Winston-Salem, NC, 98-00, p 00-07; staff CCEF, 07-10; astp Hope P Ch, Winston-Salem, NC, 12-

717 Archer Road, Winston Salem, NC 27106 – 336-659-1040   Piedmont Triad
Hope Presbyterian Church – 336-768-8883

Stokes, Simon Hardesty – w Katie; chdn Emory; O Oct 18, 13, Ecar Pby; campm RUF, UNCCH, 13-

3115 Thistlecone Way, Durham, NC 27707 – 314-258-2956   Eastern Carolina
E-mail: simon.stokes@ruf.org
PCA Reformed University Fellowship

Stoms, Jay – w Laura Anne; KTS, MDiv; O Aug 1, 04, PacNW Pby; prof African Bible College, 02-; astp Green Lake P Ch, Seattle, WA, 04-

African Bible College, PO Box 1028, Lilongone Malawi   Pacific Northwest
E-mail: jaystoms@malawi.net
African Bible College
Green Lake Presbyterian Church – 206-789-7320

Stone, Darin – b Fresno, CA, Aug 27, 76; f Terry Lynn; m Karen Lee Slaughter; w Rebecca Anne Linton, Jackson, MS, Mar 13, 04; chdn Sarah Anne; UAZ 99, BA; RTS 05, MDiv; O Feb 17, 07, SoCst Pby; int Pear Orchard P Ch, Ridgeland, MS, 04-05; astp Harbor P Ch, San Diego, CA, 06-09; p First P Ch, Biloxi, MS, 10-12; ob p The Kirk, Greensboro, NC, 15-18; MNA Ministry to State, 18-

4005 Sassafras Court, Greensboro, NC 27410 – 919-238-9228   Piedmont Triad
MNA Ministry to State

Stone, Donald Stewart – b Rockeville Centre, NY, Jan 28, 49; f Walter D. Jr.; m Muriel V. Cleary; w Stacy Strawn, Springtown, PA, Jul 6, 74; chdn Hannah Elisheba, Naomi Keturah, Phoebe Damaris; PASU 67-71, BS; SWBTS 77-80, MDiv; St. Vladimir's Orthodox Theo Sem 98, DMin; L 82; O 82, Phil Pby; p Lehigh Valley P Ch, Allentown, PA, 82-

102 North 13th Street, Allentown, PA 18102 – 610-782-0285   Eastern Pennsylvania
E-mail: donstone@lvpca.org
Lehigh Valley Presbyterian Church – 610-439-0200

Stone, John Simpson IV – b Chester, SC, May 31, 65; f John S. III; m Amelia Beatrice Heckle; w Marisa O'Neil Tate, Memphis, TN, Jul 31, 93; chdn Sarah Amelia, Katherine McMeekin, Mary Simpson; ClemU 88, BA; CTS 92, MDiv; O Jul 18, 93, MSVal Pby; campm RUM, BelC, 93-96; campm RUF, UT, 96-03, asst coord 03-17; srp Catalina Foothills Ch, Tucson, AZ, 18-

Catalina Foothills Church – 520-615-8500   Arizona

Stone, Jordan – O Nov 12, 17, NoTX Pby; srp Redeemer P Ch, McKinney, TX, 17-

5121 Sugarberry Drive, McKinney, TX 75071 – 214-212-6082   North Texas
E-mail: jordan@redeemer-mckinney.org
Redeemer Presbyterian Church – 972-529-1502

Storck, Jon – astp Perimeter Ch, Duluth, GA, 07-09; astp Astoria Comm Ch, Astoria, NY, 10-12; astp Queens P Ch, Long Island City, NY, 12-13; ascp 13- 17; p Grace Flwsp Ch, Sunnyside, NY, 17-18

4601 43rd Avenue 6DW, Sunnyside, NY 11104 – 901-568-0072   Metropolitan New York
E-mail: storckjon@gmail.com

Story, David – w Karen; chdn Daphne, Alice, Thomas; FSU 00, BA; WTS 03, MDiv; O Apr 10, 05, GulCst Pby; int Christ P Ch, Marietta, GA, 03-04; campm RUF, FSU, 04-17

1140 Carissa Drive, Tallahassee, FL 32308   Gulf Coast

Stoudt, Bryan R. – b Philadelphia, PA, Jan 11, 73; f Dwight F.; m Diane Lou Stock; w Sharon L. Hinski, Haddonfield, NJ, May 30, 98; chdn Carissa Elisabeth, B Matthew, Anna Elisabeth, Braedon; LafC 95, BA; WTS 99, MDiv; L May 8, 99, Phil Pby; O Jan 23, 04, Phil Pby; ob campm DiscipleMakers, Lehigh Valley area, 03-07; Dir Medical Campus Outreach, 06-08; area dir CMDA08-

419 Llanerch Avenue, Havertown, PA 19083 – 856-524-2126   Philadelphia
E-mail: stoudtb@gmail.com
Christian Medical and Dental Associations

Stout, Stephen Oliver – b Knoxville, TN, Aug 10, 50; f K. Deane; m Velma Ruth Dynes; w Marlene Frances Hill, Scotland, ONT, Nov 23, 73; chdn Deirdre Michael, Danielle Kirsten, Lydia Meghan; CBC 72, BA; GrTS 76, MDiv; WTS 77, ThM; CTS 88, DMin; L Jan 28, 78, Phil Pby (RPCES); O Mar 18, 79, SE Pby (RPCES); ap Prosperity P Ch, Charlotte, NC, 79-81, p 81-05; prof CBCC, 90-; sc CentCar Pby, 80-91; rc CentCar pby, 91-02; prof HGST, 02-05; p Shearer P Ch, Mooresville, NC, 09-; mem Evan Theo Society

4306 Garvin Drive, Charlotte, NC 28269-1605 – 704-596-2577   Catawba Valley
E-mail: sostout@juno.com
Shearer Presbyterian Church – 704-892-8866

Stovall, John – O May 22, 16, NYS Pby; astp Redeemer Ref P Ch, Queensbury, NY, 16-17; p The Rock P Ch, Stockbridge, GA, 17-

33 White Drive, Stockbridge, GA 30281 – 713-899-7620   Metro Atlanta
E-mail: pastorjohnstovall@gmail.com
The Rock Presbyterian Church – 770-389-8008

Straight, Jerry – op Cov PCA, Rockingham, NC, 05-08; p 09- 12; op Providence Ch Newburgh, Newburgh, IN, 12-

6301 East Oak Street, Evansville, IN 47715   Illiana
E-mail: jerryastraight@yahoo.com
Providence Church Newburgh

Strain, David – b Glasgow, Scotland, Aug 1, 74; f James; m Joyce Lindsay; w Sheena; chdn Euan, Joel; campm UCCF Scotland, 96-98; Glasgow Uni BD, 99-01; Free Church College, 01-02; London City Presbyterian , 02-08; p Main Street P Ch, Columbus, MS, 08-13; astp First P Ch, Jackson, MS, 13-14; srp 14-

229 Hickory Glen, Madison, MS 39110   Mississippi Valley
E-mail: davids@fpcjackson.org
First Presbyterian Church – 601-353-8316

Strawbridge, Theodore R. – b Plant City, FL, Jan 12, 60; f Vincent F.; m Marion Selle; w Mary Lu Harrell, Lakeland, FL, Aug 29, 81; chdn Samuel Jackson, Alice Carey, Knox Frederick, Jennifer Ellen, Anne Charlotte; AugC 83, BS; RTS 89, MDiv; L Oct 16, 87, CentFL Pby; O Jul 23, 89, CentGA Pby; ascp Lakemont P Ch, Augusta, GA, 89-92; chp, op Good Shepherd P Ch, Ocala, FL, 92-94; srp 94-16

89 Kington Lane, Lookout Mountain, GA 30750   Tennessee Valley
E-mail: ted.straw@gmail.com

Strickman, Scott – b Brooklyn, NY, Aug 31, 72; f Stephen; m Alice Storheim; w Kathleen Camphouse, Santa Barbara, CA, Dec 29, 01; chdn Noah Spencer, Orli Storheim, Samuel Asaph; BrooklynC 94, BA; WTS 02; O Jun 8, 03, MNY Pby; ascp Emmanuel P Ch, New York, NY, 03-

371 West 117th Street #2B, New York, NY 10025 – 917-597-5121   Metropolitan New York
E-mail: sstrickman@emmanuelnyc.org
Emmanuel Presbyterian Church – 212-870-3185

Stringer, Kiernan – staff Grace Toronto Ch, Toronto, ON, 12-14, astp 14-

25 Longhope Place, North York, ON M2J 1Y1 CANADA – 416-571-6562   Eastern Canada
E-mail: Kiernan@gracetoronto.ca
Grace Toronto Church – 416-860-0895

Strumbeck, David Mark – b Wilmington, DE, May 12, 53; f Ronald; m Rosa; w Susan Davis, New Castle, DE, Jul 4, 75; chdn Daniel Mark, Megan Ruth, Alison Rosa; UDE 75, BA, 77, MA; WTS 83, MDiv; L May 85; O May 86, DMV Pby; mis MTW, Peru, 86-89; mis MTW, Colombia, SA, 89-96; mis MTW, Ecuador, 97-04; ascp Cornerstone P Ch, Kemblesville, PA, 05-15; wc 15-16; hr 16

7 Hartford Place, Newark, DE 19711 – 302-266-0688   Heritage
HR

Struyk, Kevin – O Nov 6, 11, CentFL Pby; ob ascp Saint Andrew's Chapel, Sanford, FL, 11-

5525 Wayside Drive, Sanford, FL 32771   Central Florida
E-mail: mosteen@sachapel.com
Saint Andrew's Chapel, Sanford, FL

Stryd, Jason – O May 15, 11, Phil Pby; astp Northeast Comm Ch, Philadelphia, PA 11-17; astp Christ The King P Ch, Cambridge, MA, 17

37 Janet Road, Quincy, MA 02170   Southern New England
E-mail: jasonstryd@gmail.com
Christ The King Presbyterian Church – 617-354-8431

Stuart, William Kenneth, III – b Park Ridge, IL, Dec 27, 62; f William Kenneth, Jr.; m Audrey Louise Turner; w Karan Berniece Sorlie, Columbia, SC, Nov 26, 88; chdn William Kenneth IV, Philip Sorlie, Maggie Turner; BroCC 82; FSU 84, BS; CBS&SM 90, MDiv; O Sept 6, 09, Prov Pby; DCE, dir sm grp Cornerstone P Ch, Columbia, SC, 91-92; Lookout Mountain P Ch, Child Min, Lookout Mountain, TN, 98-03; mfam, mp Southwood P Ch, Huntsville, AL, 03-09; ascp 09-12; astp Cahaba Park Ch PCA, Birmingham, AL, 12-6; wc 16-

256-426-9485   Evangel

Stubbs, John Berry – b Atlanta, GA, Dec 28, 64; f William J.; m Barbara Berry; w Denise C. Long (dv); chdn David Berry, Micah Christine; UNC 83-87, BA; RTSFL 91-94, MDiv; O Dec 11, 94, Wcar Pby; ydir New Cov P Ch, Aiken, SC, 90-91; ydir New Hope P Ch, Eustis, FL, 91-94; astp Covenant Ref P Ch, Asheville, NC, 94-99; campm RUF, UNCA, 94-99, wc 00-01; ss Goshen P Ch, Belmont, NC, 01, p 01-03; wc 03-09; p Prosperity P Ch, Charlotte, NC, 09-15

11904 Mountain Crest Circle, Charlotte, NC 28216-9684 – 704-399-6133   Catawba Valley
E-mail: bstubbs26@bellsouth.net

Stubbs, Joseph Olan – SamU, BA; RTS, MAR; BhamTS, MDiv; CTS, DMin; O , Evan Pby; astp Briarwood P Ch, Birmingham, AL, 09-; Campus Outreach, Birmingham, AL, 09-

2008 Little Ridge Circle, Birmingham, AL 35242 – 205-408-7694   Evangel
E-mail: ostubbs@campusoutreach.org
Briarwood Presbyterian Church – 205-776-5200
Campus Outreach, Birmingham, AL

Stulac, George Michael – b Chicago, IL, Aug 18, 44; f Josef Florian; m Dagmar Pakonen; w Barbara Susan Bareford, Plainfield, NJ, Aug 23, 69; chdn Robert Josef, Sara Nicole, David Michael, Daniel John; WashU 67, BA; GCTS 71, MDiv; CTS 93, DMin; O Dec 71, UPCUSA; Recd PCA Apr 83; staff IVCF, Nebraska, 71-74; Dir IVCF, Nebraska/Iowa, 74-76; p Bethany Ch, UPCUSA, Wichita, KS, 76-81; srp Memorial P Ch, St. Louis, MO, 81-14; mod MO Pby, 13-14; ob IVCF, 14-; *James*, IVP New Testament Commentary Series 16

7032 Kingsbury Boulevard, University City, MO 63130-4329 – 314-725-4176   Missouri
E-mail: gmstulac@hotmail.com
Inter-Varsity Christian Fellowship

Stull, Richard Jeffrey – b Chicago, IL, Aug 19, 57; f Richard B.; m Mary K. Jeffries; w Beth Ann DeBra, Ft. Lauderdale, FL, Dec 4, 93; chdn Evan, Charis; FSU 81, BA; WSCAL 86, MAR; ICGU 87, MA; WTS 93, DMin; CarCU 96, PhD; Recd PCA Oct 19, 99, SFL Pby; staff CCC, 80-88, couns, int 88-89; moy New Life P Ch, Dresher, PA, 89-91; couns 89-; astp First P Ch, Plantation, FL, 92-94; astp Rio Vista Comm Ch, Ft. Lauderdale, FL, 99-04; couns Access Christian Couns, Cumming, GA, 94-; astp Big Creek Church, Cumming, GA, 05; ob Church Mult Min

71 Hawks View, Dahlonega, GA 30533 – 770-844-8469   Metro Atlanta
E-mail: drrjstull@hotmail.com
Access Christian Counseling

Sturgis, Smiley – b Atlanta, GA, Aug 3, 54; f Guy K.; m Irene Jacob; w Karen Sue St. John, Ft. Lauderdale, FL, Oct 24, 81; chdn Lydia Anne, Luke Phillip, Nathan Radford, Caleb James, Mark Robert, Mary Lee; SJRJC 74, AA; Flagler C 76, BA; RTS 76-79, MDiv; O Jan 27, 80, SFL Pby, op 80; p WestBoca P Ch, Boca Raton, FL, 80-90; chp, op Good News Ch, St. Augustine, FL, 91-93, p 93-

1357 Wildwood Drive, St. Augustine, FL 32086 – 904-824-8533   North Florida
E-mail: ssturgis@gnpc.org
Good News Church – 904-819-0064

Stutzman, Brent – O Aug 20, 15, ChiMet Pby; ascp Trinity P Ch, Hinsdale, IL, 15-

427 East Walnut Street, Hinsdale, IL 60521   Chicago Metro
E-mail: brent@trinityhinsdale.com
Trinity Presbyterian Church – 630-286-9303

Suffern, Edward W.B. – b Ridgewood, NJ, Nov 20, 57; f Richard; m Eugenia Gibson; w Lois Kooistra, Aug 10, 85; chdn Kathryn, Rachel, Johanna, John; GroCC 80, BS; NewBrunsSem 87, MDiv; O Jun 87, RCA; Recd PCA Sept 19, 09, NYS Pby; ascp Sixth Ref Ch, N.Haledon, NJ, 87-93; p Hope Ref Ch, Clifton, NJ, 93-07; p First Ref Ch, Orange City, IA, 07-09; p Redeemer Ref P Ch, Queensbury, NY, 09-

47 Hidden Hills Drive, Queensbury, NY 12804 – 518-932-1967   New York State
E-mail: nsuffern@gmail.com
Redeemer Reformed Presbyterian Church – 518-798-9794

Suh, Bobby Jin Won – astp Koinos Flwsp Ch, Chantilly, VA, 10-11; ob astp Koinos Young Saeng P Ch, Centreville, VA, 11-14; astp Christ Central P Ch, Centreville, VA, 14-

25870 Clairmont Manor Square, Aldie, VA 20105 – 703-501-1223   Korean Capital
E-mail: bobby.suh@christcentralpc.org
Christ Central Presbyterian Church – 703-815-1300

Suh, Chang Kwon – b Seoul, Apr 17, 58; f Young Chul; m Ae In Shin; w Hyo-Jung Lee, Seoul, May 12, 84; chdn Sun-Ah, Jin-Ah, Paul; KorU 84, BA; BibS 94, MDiv, 94, MA; L Apr 94, KorE Pby;

MINISTERIAL DIRECTORY

Suh, Chang Kwon, continued
O Apr 23, 95, KorE Pby; astp Emmanuel Ch in Phil, Philadelphia, PA, 95-98; p Korean Ch of Chicago, Hoffman Estates, IL, 98-18; hr 18; mis; *Heavenly Father's Heart,* 09; *The Spiritual Discernment,* 15;

1500 West Algonquin Road, Hoffman Estates, IL 60192   Korean Central
E-mail: suhchang12@gmail.com
HR

    Suh, David Younghwan – Chap 07-

United States Air Force   Korean Southeastern

    Suh, Euisoo – srp Washington Evergreen Ch, Mt. Jackson, VA, 08-

644 Windfield Road, Mt. Jackson, VA 22842 – 540-477-2070   Korean Capital
E-mail: euisoosuh@aol.com
Washington Evergreen Church – 540-477-2070

    Suh, John JungKon – b Seoul, Korea, Dec 18, 50; f Kil Won; m Yoo; w Choi, Seoul, Kor, May 13, 78; chdn Anna; Sung Kyun Kwan Univ, Seoul, Kor, BE; UGA 82-90, MBA, PhD cand; CTS 91-94, MDiv; L Jun 21, 94; O Oct 4, 94, KorCent Pby; srp Korean P Ch of St. Louis, St. Louis, MO, 94-151; hr 15

11032 Manchester Road, St. Louis, MO 63122   Korean Central
E-mail: johnsuh1950@yahoo.com
HR

    Suh, Joon Taek – b Korea, Jan 14, 61; f Sung Ryong; m Jung Soon Choi; w Seong Hee Choi, Korea, Jul 2, 94, America, Oct 13, 94; chdn Hannah, Joseph; IHU 87, BS; CapBS 97, MDiv; L Apr 7, 97, KorCap Pby; O Oct 5, 98, KorCap Pby, p Morning Star P Ch, Lutherville, MD, 98-13; ob Kernel Mission Ch, 13-

7854 Marioak Drive, Elkridge, MD 21075 – 443-300-2235   Korean Capital
E-mail: revjoontsuh@gmail.com
Kernel Mission Church – 410-412-3380

    Suh, Jung Soo – w Gye Sook; chdn Hyo Yong, Hee Won, Bong Seok; O, Kor HapDong P Ch; Recd PCA Oct 9, 95, KorS Pby; p First Korean P Ch of Dallas, Carrollton, TX, 95-98; p Korean Ch of the Lord, Carrollton, TX, 98-17; hr 17

1033 Kyan Lane, Carrollton, TX 75006 – 972-478-8370   Korean Southern
E-mail: krchlord@msn.com
HR

    Suh, Mike Eil – astp liberti Fairmount, Philadelphia, PA, 12-13; ob 14-15; chp 15-16; op Missio Dei, Los Angeles, CA, 16-

826 Silver Lake Boulevard #A, Los Angeles, CA 90026   Korean Southeastern
Missio Dei

    Suh, Sam Jung – b Korea, Jan 1, 42; f Suh Cha Gu; m Kim Hae Ja; w Yoon Ok Ja, Korea, Feb 2, 71; chdn Eil Min, Hannah, Daniel; Myung JiU 69, BA; KorPTS 63-67; O Oct 12, 68, Chyung Kyu Sun; p Dong Hyun Ch, Seoul, 68-71; Chap Korean Navy, 71-74; srp Korean First P Ch, Tucker, GA, 76-

5846 Old Stone Mountain Road, Stone Mountain, GA 30087 – 770-923-6801   Korean Southeastern
Korean First Presbyterian Church – 770-934-8282

    Suh, Sam Sun – p First Korean P Ch, Glenview, IL, 02-

5857 North Medina Avenue, Chicago, IL 60646 – 773-792-1118   Korean Central
E-mail: samssuh@hotmail.com
First Korean Presbyterian Church – 847-299-1776

Suh, Seung Il – Chap USArmy, 11-

7243 Cayman Drive, Fayetteville, NC 28306　　　　　　　　　　　　　　　Korean Capital
E-mail: seungilsuh@yahoo.com
United States Army

Suh, Woosuk – p

20611 36th Place West, Lynnwood, WA 98036 – 916-549-4253　　　　　Korean Northwest
E-mail: revwssuh@gmail.com

Suhr, Jeffrey – w Helen; chdn Megan, Noah, Seth; UCSD, BA; WSCAL, MDiv; L Mar 04, Pac Pby; ascp New Life Msn Ch of Burbank, Burbank, CA, 02-04; ascp Anaheim New Life Msn Ch, Fullerton, CA, 04-11; op New Life Msn Ch of Irvine, Irvine, CA, 11-

84 Capricorn, Irvine, CA 92618 – 949-596-9996　　　　　　　　　　　　　　South Coast
E-mail: jeff@newlifeirvine.org
New Life Mission Church of Irvine – 949-439-4346

Suits, R. Kent – b Sept 24, 87; w Kaitlin; chdn Caris, Liza, Audrey; ErskTS 13, MDiv; ydir Willow Creek Ch, Winter Springs, FL, 14-17; op Christ Comm Ch, Batesburg-Leesville, SC, 18-

320 Rawls Drive, Leesville, SC 29090 – 803-849-0378　　　　　　　　　　　　Palmetto
E-mail: kentsuits@gmail.com
Christ Community Church

Suk, David Joonghoon – srp New Sprout P Ch of New York, Whitestone, NY, 09-13; ob 14-

1800 Rocky Brook Road, Opelika, AL 36801　　　　　　　　　　　　　Korean Northeastern
E-mail: solidshiningstone@gmail.com

Suk, Sang Eun – astp Choong Hyun P Ch, Houston, TX, 03-; op Global P Ch, Houston, TX, 09-

1522 Hannington Drive, Katy, TX 77450 – 281-579-9088　　　　　　　　Korean Southern
E-mail: petersuk@gmail.com
Global Presbyterian Church – 713-320-7721

Sukhia, Doug – b Altadena, CA, Mar 9, 48; f Darius; m Mildred Russell; w Nancy Wilson, Grand Island, NY; chdn Leah Elizabeth (Trautz), Adam Wilson; CalCollArts 71, BFA; FTS 76, MDiv; O May 77, BPC; Recd PCA 07, NYS Pby; BPC Grand Island,NY 76-79; BPC Lakeland,FL 79-83; srp Armor Bible P Ch, (PCA 07), Orchard Park, NY, 83-16; ob Union Road UCC, 17-

35 Lawrence Place, Orchard Park, NY 14127 – 716-662-0602　　　　　　　New York State
E-mail: desukhia@gmail.com

Sukhia, Russell Bruce – b Baltimore, MD, Nov 11, 50; f Darius E.; m Mildred A. Russell; w Donna Lee Kilmer, Altamonte Sprgs, FL, Jul 8, 71; chdn Nathan Douglas, Grace Abigail; SemJC 70, AA; UFL; ShelC 75, BA; FTS 73-76, MDiv; L 76; O Mar 17, 77, GrLks Pby; ap NE BPC, Phila, PA, 74-75; p Armor BPC, Orchard Pk, NY, 76-83; op Suncoast BPC, Palm Harbor, FL, 83-88; p Maryville Evangelical Ch, Maryville, TN, 88-01; ob t WesmAc, Ft. Lauderdale, FL, 01-04; astp Coral Ridge P Ch, Ft. Lauderdale, FL, 01-04; p Liberty Ch, PCA, Owings Mills, MD, 04-17; hr 17 *Wry Bread*

711 Branched Antler Court, Midlothian, VA 23112 – 410-795-1521　　　　　　Chesapeake
HR

MINISTERIAL DIRECTORY

Sullivan, Thomas Byron Jr. – b Athens, GA, Jul 26, 48; f Thomas Byron Sr.; m Helen Thompson; w Hope Harman Vaughan, Pulaski, VA, Jul 6, 74; chdn Joshua Thomas; KgC 66-70, BA; ColTS 70-73, MDiv; CCEF, dipl; O Jul 15, 73, Abing Pby; p Seven Mile Ford P Ch, 73-82; p Seven Springs P Ch, Glade Spring, VA, 73-; t GBibC, 86-; mem ACBC (form NANC), 95-

PO Box 457, Chilhowie, VA 24319-0457 – 276-646-5189   Westminster
Seven Springs Presbyterian Church
Graham Bible College – 423-968-4201

Summers, Jeffrey Scott – b Boulder, CO, Apr 13, 68; f Doald; m Jeanne Marrow; w Camie Cole, San Angelo, TX, Jun 8, 91; chdn Tirzah, Jace; UT 95, BA; RTSNC 01, MDiv; L Dec 01, CentCar Pby; O Dec 01, CentCar Pby; astp, yp University City P Ch, Charlotte, NC, 01-03; astp Pinewood P Ch, Middleburg, FL, 03-05, ascp 05-07; astp Perimeter Ch, Johns Creek, GA, 07-

3195 River Summit Trail, Duluth, GA 30097   Metro Atlanta
E-mail: jeffs@perimeter.org
Perimeter Church – 678-405-2000

Summers, Marc – mis MTW, 12-

c/o Mission to the World   Metro Atlanta
E-mail: marcsummers366@msn.com
PCA Mission to the World

Sun, Junho – O Sept 27, 15, KorNE Pby, ob 15-

Address Unavailable   Korean Northeastern

Sun, Seog Woo – ob astp Korean United Ch of Phil, Philadelphia, PA, 09-15; p Sarang Nanum Comm Ch, Ambler, PA, 15-

1502 Basswood Grove, Ambler, PA 19002 – 267-474-0740   Korean Eastern
E-mail: ssahara@hotmail.com
Sarang Nanum Community Church – 267-474-0740

Sun, Young Kwon – astp Lamp P Ch of Los Angeles, Gardena, CA, 09-14

4155 Griffin Trail Way, Cumming, GA 30041   Korean Southwest
E-mail: sunyk12@hotmail.com

Sundberg, Stanley Frank – b Isle, MN, Jun 24, 42; f John; m Jean West; w Eileen Gloria Johnson, Beaubier, SK, Jul 29, 66; chdn John Wesley, Marc Stanley; BrBI 62-65, dipl; L Dec 63, Warman Bap Ch (BGC); O May 66, Mills Comm Ch; p Mills Comm Ch, Mills, NE, 66-67; p Berean Fund Ch, Ainsworth, NE, 68-76; p Berean Fund Ch, Auburn, NE, 77-80; p Grace & Syracuse Bap chs, NE, 81-83; p Germantown P Ch, Chancellor, SD, 83-94; sc Siouxl Pby, 94-00; op, ev Gr P Msn, Sioux Falls, SD, 94-96; op, ev New Cov P Ch, Spearfish, SD, 96-00; wc 00-07; hr 07

PO Box 488, Spearfish, SD 57783 – 605-642-5323   Siouxlands
E-mail: stansundberg@gmail.com
HR

Sung, Daniel – O Jun 10, 18, Pot Pby; astp Mosaic Comm Ch, Silver Spring, MD, 18-

9003 Manchester Road, Silver Spring, MD 20901   Potomac
E-mail: dan@mosaicsilverspring.org
Mosaic Community Church – 240-424-5235

Sung, Samuel Ki-Joong – astp Inland Korean P Ch, Pomona, CA, 03-08; p Hudson Korean P Ch, 08-13; wc 13-16; op Glory Comm Ch, Cliffside Park, NJ, 16-

100 Hickory Avenue #2, Tenafly, NJ 07670 – 201-400-0830 Korean Northeastern
E-mail: pastorsamsung@gmail.com
Glory Community Church – 267-210-8957

Sunu, Aaron – O Sept 13, KorSW Pby; astp Living Faith P Ch, Los Angeles, CA, 13-

9051 Cattaraugus Avenue #3, Los Angeles, CA 90034 Korean Southwest
E-mail: aaronsunu@livingfaithla.com
Living Faith Presbyterian Church – 562-716-3132

Surprenant, Louis – astp Christ Ch, Greensboro, NC; astp New Life Mission Ch, Irvine, CA, 17-

New Life Mission South Coast

Surprenant, Steven Michael – ascp Armor Bible P Ch, Orchard Park, NY, 07-16; ob fndr, exec dir Fresh Water Friends, Inc., 17-

8 Forsythia Court, Orchard Park, NY 14127 – 716-649-7564 New York State
E-mail: quarkmaster@verizon.net
Fresh Water Friends, Inc.

Susabda, Yakub B. – b Indonesia, Jun 13, 46; f I. Tirtaleksana; m Sara; w Esther Magelang, Indonesia; chdn Arlene, Agnes; Jakarta TS 71, BD; RTS 77, MCE; TEDS 79, ThM; TalTS 88, PhD; L Oct 17, 78; O 78, MSVal Pby, mis 78-; AcadDn Ref Theo Sem, Indonesia, 91-07 pres, Ref Theo Sem, Indonesia, 07-; pres Hope Couns and Assess Cent, 07-; *Church Administration*, 81; *Pastoral Counseling*, 2 vols, 85; *Introduction to Modern Theology*, 2 vols, 90, 92; *Evangelicalism*, 91; *Handbook for Married Enrichmen*, (3 vols), 92; *Intro to Reformed Theology*, 93; *Doctrine of God*, 01; *Becoming a Professional Counselor; Handbook for Premarital Counseling*

Jul. Kemang Utara IX/10, Jakarta 2760, INDONESIA – 021-546-1510 Mississippi Valley
E-mail: reformed@idola.net.id
Reformed Theological Seminary, Indonesia
Hope Counseling and Assessment Center

Sutherland, Ryan – b Plattsburgh, NY, Feb 15, 78; f Dennis; m Ellen Houghton; w Rachel Dieter, Brookings, SD, Sept 2, 01; MTStU 00, BA; WTS 06, MDiv; O Feb 4, 07, RMtn Pby; chp, ev Missoula, MT, 07-09; op All Souls Missoula, Missoula, MT, 09-13; srp 13-

2704 Emery Place, Missoula, MT 59804 – 406-529-2468 Rocky Mountain
E-mail: ryan@allsoulsmissoula.org
All Souls Missoula – 406-529-2468

Sutton, David F. – b Newport, TN, Jan 20, 37; f Earl R.; m Zelma Mae O'Neil; w Helen C. Rowe, Enon Valley, PA, Jul 22, 66; chdn Amy E., Merrily B., Christina J., Andrew D.; CBC 59, BA; CTS 62, BD; L 62; O 63, Midw Pby (RPCES); p Reformed P Ch, Cutler, IL, 61-65; ob p Bible P Ch (non-PCA), Enon Valley, PA, 65-

PO Box 262, Enon Valley, PA 16120-0262 – 724-336-5896 Ascension
Bible Presbyterian Church (non-PCA), Enon Valley, PA

Sutton, James – b Richmond, VA, Nov 27, 76; f James Morrison, Sr.; m Cynthia Godwin; w Katie Ann Hanson, Jul 21, 06; chdn Josephine Shannon, James Morrison III, John Randall, Peter Lewis, Marian

Sutton, James, continued
Elyse; NCSt 99, BA, 00, BA; RTSFL 04, MDiv; O Aug 3, 14, Ecar Pby; ascp Christ The King P Ch, Raleigh, NC, 14-

325 Worth Street, Raleigh, NC 27601 – 919-673-0778   Eastern Carolina
E-mail: jsutton@ctkraleigh.org
Christ The King Presbyterian Church – 919-546-0515

Sutton, John – O May 22, 16, MetAtl Pby; ascp Covenant P Ch, Fayetteville, GA, 16-

E-mail: john@covenantpres.net   Metro Atlanta
Covenant Presbyterian Church – 770-460-9450

Svendsen, Daniel – O ChiMet Pby; astp Ethos P Msn, Chicago, IL, 15-16; ob 16-

Address Unavailable   Chicago Metro

Svendsen, Graham Isaac – O Sept 23, 15, Wcar Pby; p Grace Highlands Ch, Boone, NC, 15-

967 Rainbow Trail, Boone, NC 28607 – 828-388-6837   Western Carolina
E-mail: graham.svendsen@gmail.com
Grace Highlands Church – 828-263-1114

Svendsen, Ronald Stener – b Los Angeles, CA, Aug 9, 55; f Donald E; m Segar; w Huddleston, Los Angeles, CA; chdn Andrew, Graham, Sydney; CSULA 73-77, BA; WTS 80, MAR, 81, MDiv; RTS 16, DMin; O Dec 26, 81, RCA; Recd PCA Mar 1, 91, Pac Pby; ip Deep Run Mennonite, Bedminster, PA, 80-81; p Fairfield Ch (RCA), Fairfield, NJ, 81-91; srp Valley P Ch, North Hills, CA, 91-

9649 Columbus Avenue, North Hills, CA 91343-2209 – 818-894-2191   Pacific
E-mail: Ronald.svendsen@gmail.com
Valley Presbyterian Church – 818-894-9200

Swafford, Raun – p New Beginnings Comm Ch, Memphis, TN, 12-13

Address Unavailable   Covenant

Swafford, Ronald Leonard Sr. – b Los Angeles, CA, Jul 27, 43; f J L S; m Norma May Colvin; w Martha Julia Parsons, Buchannan, GA, Dec 30, 60; chdn Ronald Leonard, Jr, Michael David; BelC 61-63; UAL 69, BS; RTS 73, MDiv; O Jun 73, SMS Pby (PCUS); p Taylorsville, MS, 73-74; op Melbourne, FL, 74-78; p Covenant Ch, Melbourne, FL, 78-81; Chap USN, VA Beach, VA, 81-84; Chap USN, Bath, ME, 84-86; Chap USN, Okinawa, Japan, 86-89; Chap USN, Newport, RI, 89-90; Chap USN, CREDO, Mayport, FL, 90-94; Chap USN, RSG, Mayport, FL, 94-96; Chap USN, USCG HQ Washington, DC, 96-99; Chap USN, USCG, Alameda, CA, 99-03; Chap USN, Subase, Kings Bay, GA, 03-05; hr 05; assoc dir Chaplains Min and Presbyterian & Reformed Commission on Chaplains and Military Personnel, 07-14

6324 Marble Head Drive, Flowery Branch, GA 30542 – 850-274-9272   North Florida
E-mail: swaff43@icloud.com
HR

Swagerty, Douglass Eugene – b Long Beach, CA, Jun 26, 54; f Robert; m Mildred Young; w Lois Clough, Manhattan Bch, CA, Aug 14, 76; chdn Ryan, David, Diane; CC 76, BA; VilU 80, MA; WTS 83, MAR, MDiv; L Feb 12, 83; O Jul 1, 84, SoCA Pby (OPC); srp Coastal Comm Ch, Oceanside, CA, 84-98; sc SoCst Pby, 89-98, wc 98-99; ev Harbor P Ch Downtown, San Diego, CA, 99-03; srp Harbor P Ch, San Diego, CA, 03-09; p North Coast P Ch, Encinitas, CA, 09-13; ascp Christ Ch Santa Fe PCA, Santa Fe, NM, 13-15; SW reg dir MNA, 15-

3050 Blenkarne Drive, Carlsbad, CA 92008   Rio Grande
E-mail: dswagerty@pcanet.org
PCA Mission to North America

Swain, Scott – ob pres, prof RTSFL;

1231 Reformation Drive, Oviedo, FL 32765   Central Florida
Reformed Theological Seminary, FL – 407-366-9493

Swain, Stewart – O Nov 5, 15, War Pby; campm RUF, UAL, 15-

1612 Woodridge Road, Tuscaloosa, AL 35406 – 630-310-9150   Warrior
E-mail: stewart.swain@ruf.org
PCA Reformed University Fellowship

Swan, Marc – w Wendy; chdn Samantha, Michaela, Joshua, Jacob; CTS 01, MDiv; O Mar 05, GrLks Pby; astp Greentree Comm Ch, St. Louis, 00-05; op Redeemer Ch Msn, Kalamazoo, MI, 05-06; p Grace Ch, Rochester, NY, 07-

47 Leonard Crescent, Penfield, NY 14526 – 585-764-3564   New York State
E-mail: marc@gracechurchpca.com
Grace Church – 585-445-8225

Swanson, Brent – O May 1, 10, Pac Pby; ascp Grace Harbor Ch, Long Beach, CA, 10-13; wc 13-

335 College Heights Drive, Batesville, AR 72501   Pacific

Swanson, Erik – b Jul 27, 80; f David; m Deborah; w Joy Vaughn, Jul 6, 02; chdn Nathaniel David, Micah Patrick, Jude Zachary; CC 02, BA; CTS 07, MDiv; O Apr 6, 08, MNY Pby; astp Redeemer Ch of Montclair, Montclair, NJ, 08-11; ascp 11- 15; p New Life P Ch, York, PA, 15-

55 Blueberry Lane, Red Lion, PA 17356   Susquehanna Valley
E-mail: erikswanson828@gmail.com
New Life Presbyterian Church – 717-855-2360

Swanson, Mark – ob astp All Angels Church, 07-08; ascp Grace Vancouver, Vancouver, BC, 09-

1696 West 7th Avenue, Vancouver, BC V6J 1S5 CANADA – 778-822-0680   Western Canada
E-mail: watchung5@gmail.com
Grace Vancouver – 604-738-3537

Swartz, Craig A. – b Aurora, IL, Jul 27, 60; f Jack; m Prause; w Frances Barrett, Augusta, GA, Mar 5, 83; chdn John Craig, William Bradford, Laura Livingston, Andrew Barrett; WheatC, BA; CBS&SM, MDiv; L Nov 88; O Nov 88; ascp Seminole P Ch, Tampa, FL, 88-93; ascp Covenant P Ch, Easley, SC, 93-98; op, chp Redeemer P Ch, Riverview, FL, 98-01, p 01-

2223 Eagle Bluff Drive, Valrico, FL 33594 – 813-661-8445   Southwest Florida
E-mail: craig@redeemerprespca.org
Redeemer Presbyterian Church – 813-741-1776

Sweeney, Jacob – astp Christ the King P Ch, Houston, TX, 17-

Christ the King Presbyterian Church – 713-892-5464   Houston Metro

Sweet, John – b Bartow, FL, May 23, 76; f John; m Gretchen Strawbridge; w Kathryn Adams; chdn Micah John, Asher Lee, Kathryn Michelle; SamU 98, BA; RTSFL 04, MDiv; O Sept 05, MNY Pby; astp Park Slope P Ch, 06-07; astp Brooklyn P Ch, Brooklyn, NY, 08-12; astp Grace Ch of Marin, CA, 12-13; ascp 13-

Grace Church of Marin – 415-259-0894   Northern California

Sweney, Jack C. Jr. – b Peoria, IL, May 24, 64; f Jack; m Emma Jean Moore; w Leigh Ann Shields, Atlanta, GA, Jul 28, 90; chdn Anna Caroline, Jack Charles III; DukeU 86, BA; TEDS 96, MDiv; L Jul 96, NGA Pby; O May 97, NGA Pby; astp Perimeter Ch, Johns Creek, GA, 97-

2464 Kingsbrook Court, Duluth, GA 30097 – 770-418-1726   Metro Atlanta
E-mail: chips@perimeter.org
Perimeter Church – 678-405-2000

Swicegood, David B. – b Charlotte, NC, Mar 23, 59; f Graham; m Jean Carter; w Cheryl Smith, LaGrange, GA, Dec 3, 83; chdn Justin Paul, Brian Glenn; TNTU 78-83, BA; DTS 86-91, ThM; O Jul 14, 91; Recd PCA Jan 18, 92, NGA Pby; p Christ P Ch, Marietta, GA, 92-96; ob Samaritans Purse, Marietta, GA, 96-02; ascp Marco P Ch, Marco Island, FL, 02-06; ascp Ponte Vedra P Ch, Ponte Vedra Beach, FL, 06-10; wc 10-

112 Catherine Towers Lane Street, St. Augustine, FL 32092 – 904-273-9247   North Florida
E-mail: dswicegood@bellsouth.net

Swisher, John L. – b Pittsburgh, PA, Nov 14, 38; f Furman L.; m Claire Marie Weber; w Linda Susan Thomas, Ft. Lauderdale, FL, Feb 27, 76; chdn Joseph J.; RTS, MDiv; O Jul 19, 86; Recd PCA Apr 24, 90, SFL Pby; astp Kendall P Ch, Miami, FL, 90-94, ascp 94-95; srp Shenandoah P Ch, Miami, FL, 95-97; mis MTW, 97-99; srp Florida Crossroads Comm Church, 00-03; hr 03; coor missions co, SFL pby, 95-97

17750 SW 139th Court, Miami, FL 33177 – 305-378-4921   South Florida
HR

Sy, Charles – op Foothills Neighborhood Ch, Sierra Madre, CA, 10-18, p 18-

PO Box 1937, Arcadia, CA 91077   Pacific
E-mail: charles@foothillsneighborhoodchurch.com
Foothills Neighborhood Church – 626-243-4720

Sylvia, B. Gabriel – b Springfield, MO, May 1, 69; f Boris; m Marilyn Walling; w Kimberly Ann Floyd, West Point, NY, Jun 3, 91; chdn Kelsey, Luke, Noelle, Liberty, Abigail; USMA, BS; TEDS, MDiv; Recd PCA Jan 08, CentCar Pby; USArmy, 91-97; USAR, ILARNG, 98-00; astp Christ Cov P Ch, Matthews, NC, 07-17; srp Christ Our Hope Ch, Wake Forest, NC, 17-

924 Federal House Avenue, Wake Forest, NC 27587   Eastern Carolina
E-mail: gabe@christourhopechurch.com
Christ Our Hope Church – 919-570-9717

Szelmeczki, Steven T. – b West Allis, WI, Dec 27, 76; f Thomas Edward; m Judith Arlene Litzkow; w Brenda Ann Jenkins, Jackson, MS, Jun 23, 01; chdn Madeline Claire, Owen Geoffrey, Stuart Allen, Zachary James; Ashford 11, BA; RTS 14, MDiv; O Jul 19, 15, NR Pby; ob p Timber Ridge Christian Ch, High View, WV, 15-18; Chap USN, 18-

68 Banyan Drive, Beaufort, SC 29906   New River
E-mail: wims@bellsouth.net
United States Navy

Taaffe, Sam – campm RUF, MTSU, 14-17; campm RUF, UKY, 17-

3125 Montavesta Road, Lexington, KY 40502   Ohio Valley
E-mail: sam.taaffe@ruf.org
PCA Reformed University Fellowship – 678-825-1070

Tabor, Will – O Jun 13, 10, SELA Pby; campm RUF, Tulane, 10-

1401 Henry Clay Avenue, New Orleans, LA 70118   Southern Louisiana
E-mail: will.tabor@ruf.org
PCA Reformed University Fellowship

Taha, Allend – TCU 94, BA; CTS 01, MDiv, 10, DMin; L Aug 18, 01, Hrtl Pby; O Apr 7, 02, Hrtl Pby; astp Trinity P Ch, Kearney, NE, 01-03, ascp 03-05; op Trinity P Ch, Boerne, TX, 05-09; p 09-

31 Ammann Road, Boerne, TX 78015 South Texas
E-mail: info@trinityboerne.org
Trinity Presbyterian Church – 830-815-1212

Takeda, Tsuneyoshi – b Hokkaido, Japan, Jun 7, 36; f Toyogoroo; m Haru Takeshita; w Makimi Ogoshi, Tokyo, Japan, Apr 22, 63; chdn Yukari, Ayumi, Nozomi; JapChrC 56-60, BA; KRTS 60-63, BD; O Dec 5, 66, East Pby (RCin Japan); p Sendai Eikoo Ref Ch, 63-72; p Kasugai Ref Ch, 72-77; p to Japanese in Atlanta; op Westm Japanese Msn, Roswell, GA, 91-13, p em 13-; prof CBTS, 68-72; *Explanation of Directory for Worship*

504 Mirasol Circle #103, #10, Celebration, FL 34747 – 321-939-4095 Metro Atlanta
E-mail: makiba.takeda@gmail.com

Talarico, James Michael – b Sewickley, PA, Nov 4, 56; f James H; m Betty L. Gurcic; w Kelly Jane Zinke, Beaver, PA, Aug 27, 77; chdn Sarah, Jessica, Justin, Rebekah, Christopher; PASU 74-77; GenC 78-80, BS; EIG 81-83; WTS 88-91, MDiv; L Oct 90, SoCst Pby; L Apr 91, SW Pby; O Oct 20, 91, RMtn Pby; p Covenant P Ch, Wheat Ridge, CO, 91-99; op Rocky Mountain P Ch, Westminster, CO, 99-05, p 05-14; ss, ip Christ Comm Ch, Carmel, IN, 16-17

4111 West 149th Avenue, Broomfield, CO 80023 – 303-257-0792 Rocky Mountain
E-mail: jim.talarico@gmail.com

Talley, Chris – w Beth; chdn Emma, Kaley, Nathanael; CumbC, BA; RTS, MDiv; ascp Redeemer Ch of Knoxville, Knoxville, TN, 07-15; astp Atlanta Westside P Ch, Atlanta, GA, 15, ascp 15-

PO Box 93511, Atlanta, GA 30377 – 865-237-1717 Metro Atlanta
E-mail: chrisdtalley@gmail.com
Atlanta Westside Presbyterian Church – 404-567-5428

Talley, Jeffrey Matthew – b Ridley Park, PA, Aug 9, 51; f C. Richard; m Patricia Ann Farrell; w Esther Lois Armes, Lake George, NY, Aug 17, 74; chdn Laura Marie, Matthew Richard, Janet Patricia, Kyle Benjamin; CC 73, BA; WTS 78, MDiv; L 79, Phila Pby (RPCES); O 80, Phila Pby (RPCES); mis WPM, 80-83; mis MTW, AFRICA, 83-03; mis MTW, Slovak Repub, 04-

c/o MTW Philadelphia
E-mail: jeffestalley@hotmail.com
PCA Mission to the World

Talley, Jon – campm RUF, 07-14; op Christ Ch Milwaukee, Shorewood, WI, 14-18, srp 18-

1661 North Farwell Avenue, Milwaukee, WI 53202 – 414-587-1798 Wisconsin
E-mail: jonetalley@gmail.com
Christ Church Milwaukee

Tallman, Brian – w Andria; O Sept 05, SoCst Pby; p New Life P Ch, La Mesa, CA, 05-

5333 Lake Murray Boulevard, La Mesa, CA 91942 – 619-667-5999 South Coast
E-mail: bstallman@newlifelamesa.org
New Life Presbyterian Church – 619-667-5999

Tam, John Ha – astp Chinese Christian Ch, Falls Church, VA, 09-16; hr 16

4915 Gainsborough Drive, Fairfax, VA 22032-2317 – 703-323-5660 Potomac
E-mail: jmtam01@yahoo.com
HR

Tan, John Li Zhou – O Dec 13, 15, Pot Pby; astp Chinese Christian Ch, Falls Church, VA, 15-

3952 Bradwater Street, Fairfax, VA 22031 – 5713462123   Potomac
E-mail: tanlizhou@gmail.com
Chinese Christian Church – 703-820-1010

Tan, Timothy – b Singapore, May 3, 62; f Peh Bah Tan; m Kum Ling Thow; w Euphemia Siu, Eugene, OR, Dec 26, 97; chdn Julian, Dylan; UOR 86, BS, 86, BA; O Dec 16, 12, Nash Pby; chp, ev Crossroads of the Nations, Brentwood, TN, 11-14; op 14-

638 Streamside Lane, Franklin, TN 37064 – 615-482-2787   Nashville
E-mail: juldyl@gmail.com
Crossroads of the Nations

Tan, Wai-Choon – b Singapore, Apr 28, 45; f K. Keng; m P. Choo Low; w Ruby Yee, NY, NY, Jul 30, 77; chdn Timothy, Paul, Anna; TTC 67, dipl; FEBibC 73, ThB; FTS 75, MDiv, 77, STM; CTS 76; GrTS 82, ThD; O Oct 79, Singapore Pby; ap Life Bible P Ch, 79-83; p New Life Bible P Ch, 83-85; p Emmanuel Chr Ch, 86; prof TTC, 87-88; p Singapore Bible Coll, 88-89; Living Water Chr Ch, 88-89; wc 89-90; p Long Island Abundant Life Ch, 90-91; ob sp Chinese Ref Ch of Yonkers, NY, 91; ob fndr, p Asian American Ministries, Syosset, NY, 91; ob fndr, p Asian American Comm Ch, 92-96; ob p Mount Hermon Bible P Ch, 96-01; ob srp New Hope Comm Ch, 01-

2 Herkomer Street, New Hyde Park, NY 11040 – 516-354-7787   Metropolitan New York
E-mail: drtan2004@yahoo.com
New Hope Community Church

Tanzie, Robert Hugh – w Joanne; chdn Kristen, Nathan; GenC 74, BA; WTS 78, MDiv; Immanuel OPC, Bellawr, NJ, 79-86; New Covenant OPC, Boston, 86-05; mis MTW, Spain, 06-

c/o Mission to the World   Gulfstream
E-mail: roberttanzie@gmail.com
PCA Mission to the World

Tarantino, Owen Lee – b NJ, Nov 27, 66; f Paul; m Vera Dean; w Melissa Jane Trent, Huntingburg, IN, Jun 3, 89; chdn Laura, Alysse, Trent; RutgU 89, BA; CTS 95, MDiv, 09, DMin; O Nov 23, 97, MO Pby; ydir Good Shepherd P Ch, St. Louis, MO; astp Chesterfield P Ch, Chesterfield, MO, 95-99, ascp 99-

303 Hill Trail, Ballwin, MO 63011 – 636-227-1692   Missouri
E-mail: owent@chespres.org
Chesterfield Presbyterian Church – 636-394-3337

Tate, David Edward – b Orlando, FL, May 29, 65; f Jerry Glenn; m Marianna Cowley (d); w Cindy Ann Flack, Glenside, PA, Jan 12, 91; chdn (twins) Caleb Davis, Daniel Robert, Andrew Nathan; VandU 83-87, BA; WTS 89-92, MDiv; PTS 00-, doct stu; L May 93, Phil Pby; O Jul 31, 94, Phil Pby; int Christ P Ch, Nashville, TN, 87-89; int New Life P Ch, Glenside, PA, 89-92, yp 92-94, ascp 94-01; srp Manor P Ch, Cochranville, PA, 01-15

2 Linmar Lane, Cochranville, PA 19330 – 610-593-4424   Susquehanna Valley

Tauriello, Vincent J. – b Queens, NY, Jun 30, 65; f Vincent Joseph; m Benvenuta Dorothy LaSala; w Lorraine Anne Bruce, Manhasset, NY, Aug 13, 94; chdn Julia, Jessica, David; QnsC 89, BMus; ConBaptSemEast 96, MDiv; L Jun 98, OPC; L ; p Hope P Ch, Staten Island, NY, 98-00; ascp Franklin Square OPC, NY, 00-02; ascp New Hope P Ch, Frederick, MD, 02-09; op Northeast Comm Ch, Philadelphia, PA, 09-18; ob By Design Coaching, 18-

716 Ripley Street, Philadelphia, PA 19111 – 215-742-1857   Philadelphia
E-mail: vtauriello@gmail.com
By Design Coaching – 267-444-8988

Taylor, Benton Warthen Jr. – b Americus, GA, Nov 7, 61; f B.W., Sr (d); m Ann Emily Beers (d); w Tracy Johnson, Talbotton, GA, Jun 6, 87; chdn Samuel Benton, Joel Warthen, Hannah Elizabeth; VSC 80-84, BBA; RTS 84-87, MDiv; WTS 09, DMin; L Nov 87; O Feb 26, 89, DMV Pby; stu, int Harvester P Ch, Springfield, VA,87-88, astp 88-89, ap 89-90; p Ortega P Ch, Jacksonville, FL, 90-95; op Gr P Msn, St. Marys, GA, 95-99; ascp Timonium P Ch, Timonium, MD, 99-; Thesis: "For the Joy Set Before Us: Grief Counseling in Light of the Kingdom of Heaven"

304 Wellingborough Way, Apt. F, Cockeysville, MD 21030   Chesapeake
E-mail: bwt@timpca.org
Timonium Presbyterian Church – 410-252-5663

Taylor, Braden E. – b Hartford, CT, Nov 12, 61; f Donald S.; m Priscilla Mary Holton; w Colleen Diane Bryan, Charlottesville, VA, Aug 18, 84; chdn Daniel, Christina Hope, Philip Bryan; UVA 83, BA; WTS 89, MDiv; O Feb 18, 90, JR Pby; mis MTW, Madrid, Spain, 90-00; ascp Briarwood P Ch, Birmingham, AL, Hispanic min, 00-17; fm World Reach, 18-

5458 Dover Cliff Circle, Birmingham, AL 35242 – 205-746-0871   Evangel
E-mail: bradetayor61@gmail.com
World Reach, Inc. - 205-979-2400

Taylor, Christopher Paul – O Nov 1, 15, Cov Pby; astp Trinity Gr Ch, Rogers, AR, 15-16, ascp 16-; op Christ Ch Bentonville, Bentonville, AR, 18-

5845 Bellview Road, Rogers, AR 72758   Hills and Plains
E-mail: christaylor@christchurchbentonville.org
Trinity Grace Church – 479-636-9977
Christ Church Bentonville

Taylor, Drew – b FL, Jul 29, 85; w Becky, Winter Springs, FL, Apr 18, 15; UFL 08, BA; RTS 13, MDiv; O May 21, 17, CentFL Pby; astp Willow Creek Ch, Winter Springs, FL, 17-

1583 Canterbury Circle, Casselberry, FL 32707 – 352-442-2880   Central Florida
E-mail: dtaylor352@gmail.com
Willow Creek Church – 407-699-8211

Taylor, Frank – astp Willow Creek Ch, Winter Springs, FL, 02-05; op Westtown Ch, Tampa, FL, 05-09; p 09-

13521 Race Track Road, Tampa, FL 33626   Southwest Florida
E-mail: Frank@westtownchurch.org
Westtown Church – 813-746-8683

Taylor, Jonathan Elliott – b Alexandria, VA, Oct 13, 60; f Marvin Elliott; m Roberta Lou Owen; w Katherine Ann McGill, Clover, SC, Jun 29, 85; chdn Katherine Ruth, Owen Elliott; ClemU 82, BA; CTS 92, MDiv; O Jun 92, First Pby, ARP; Recd PCA Jan 19, 99, MO Pby; ss, stus Mt. Zion ARP, Troy, MO, 88-92; op Grace ARP, Winter Springs, FL, 92-94, p 94-95; ob Dir CTS, regional support, 95-97; ob VP Intl Theological Education Ministries, 97-98; astp Kirk of the Hills P Ch, 98-04; mis MTW, Bulgaria, 04-16; wc 16-; "Raising Shepherds: The 'Whys' and 'Hows' of Elder Preparation," *Faith and Practice*, 97

11 Kings Mountain Street, York, SC 29745   Missouri
E-mail: jetaylor.sc@gmail.com

Taylor, Jonathan P. – b Randolph, VT Apr 2, 70; w Allie; chdn Jonathan Paul, Jr., Jacob Patterson, Charles Dunlap, Hudson Fall; RTSNC 03, MDiv; O Jul 03, Cal Pby; astp Covenant P Ch, Easley, SC, 03; astp First P Ch of Concord, Concord, NH, 04-09; op Ch of the Redeemer of Manchester, Manchester, NH, 04-09; p 09-

150 Tennyson Drive, Manchester, NH 03104 – 603-232-1318   Northern New England
E-mail: jonpaultaylor@comcast.net
Church of the Redeemer of Manchester – 603-622-1881

MINISTERIAL DIRECTORY

Taylor, Lee Roy Jr. – b Birmingham AL, Aug 12, 44; w Donna Wich, McCalla, AL, Aug 16, 65; chdn Rebekah Anne, Timothy Stephen; SEBC 66, BA; GrTS 70, MDiv; grad wk, NOBTS 72-73; FulTS 87, DMin; O Aug 6, 73, Evan Pby, ap 63-65; ap Birmingham Gosp Tabernacle, 70-71; p Alliance Bib Ch, 71-72; p Rainbow P Ch, Rainbow City, AL, 73-78; instr BhamTS, 74-80; asst prof RTS, 78-82; p First P Ch, Hattiesburg, MS, 82-93, ss 93-94; vis lect/prof RTS, 85; rc Evan Pby, 73-80; mod Gr Pby, 84; GAAC, 92-95; GASJC, 93-99; prof RTS, 93-98; vis lect/prof ChShTS, Korea, 97-01; vis lect/prof Highland Theo College, Scotland, 97; vis lect/prof Hong Kong Theo Sem, 97; vis lect/prof Internation Ctr for Theo Stud, Indonesia, 97; sc PCA, 98-; adj prof RTS, 98-; vis lect/prof Ukraine Biblical Seminary, 02; chmn NAPARC, 98, 99; chmn brd NAE, 98-; brd dir World Relief, 98-; adj prof RTS, 98-17; TV min *Master Plan*, 1982-1993; TVmin *Celebration*, 1987-1988; contr *The Practice of Confessional Subscription*; contr *Four Views on Biblical Polity*

6229 Ivy Springs Drive, Flowery Branch, GA 30542   Georgia Foothills
E-mail: ac@pcanet.org
PCA Administrative Committee – 678-825-1000

Taylor, Nate – O Feb 16, MO Pby; astp Trinity P Ch, Kirkwood, MO, 16-

1110 South Glenwood Lane, Kirkwood, MO 63122   Missouri
E-mail: ntaylor.trinity@gmail.com
Trinity Presbyterian Church – 314-821-7311

Taylor, Nathanael – O Apr 3, 16, NoCA Pby; p Hidden Valley P Ch, Draper, UT, 16-

14201 Adobe School Drive, Draper, UT 84020   Northern California
E-mail: nathanael.p.taylor@biola.edu
Hidden Valley Presbyterian Church – 801-553-7144

Taylor, Paul Woolley III – b Wilmington, DE, Jan 3, 44; f Paul W. Jr.; m Emily Mitchell Bent; w Sarah Parks Mahlow, Wilmington, DE, Sept 1, 66; chdn Bonnie Elizabeth, Paul Woolley IV, Sarah Rebecca, Bethany Lynne; TayU 65, BA; TEDS 70, MDiv; FulTS 86, DMin; L Apr 69, RPCES; O Apr 71, RPCES; op Covenant P Ch, 68-69; p Grace P Ch, 70-73; Murrysville Comm Ch, 73-78; ev Pitts Pby (RPCES), 78-80; DChPl NPM, 81-82; mal Upper Midw, 82-84; DirChPl MNA, 84-91; mis MTW, 91-15; admin MTW, int dir, Asia/Pacific, 06-14; hr 15

4266 Lawhon Drive, Tucker, GA 30084 – 770-295-8855   Chicago Metro
E-mail: paulwtaylor3@gmail.com
HR

Taylor, Ro – O Feb 11, SavRiv Pby; campm RUF, GASouU, 11–17; campm RUF, DeltaSt, 17-

308 S Bolivar Avenue, Cleveland, MS 38732   Covenant
E-mail: ro.taylor@ruf.org
PCA Reformed University Fellowship

Tchilinguirian, Berdj – b Cairo, Egypt, Oct 9, 65; w Jennifer Maude Beauchamp; chdn Madison Grace, Hovsep Jayson, Ani Hope, Rafi James Beauchamp; Bernard Baruch, BBA; FAU, MBA; KTS, MDiv; O Jan 18, 05, SFL Pby; astp, modis First P Ch of Coral Springs/Margate, Margate, FL, 04-08; astp Christ P Ch, New Braunfels, TX, 10-

3506 Tilden Trail, New Braunfels, TX 78132   South Texas
E-mail: berdjt@gmail.com
Christ Presbyterian Church – 830-629-0405

Teague, Gary Len – b Knoxville, TN, Sept 12, 53; f Daniel Claude; m Norma Dean Beaty; w Shannon Simpson, Knoxville, TN, Jul 31, 76; chdn Jesse, Marshall, Kathleen; UT 76, BS; FulTS 88; O May 24, 98,

Teague, Gary Len, continued
TNVal Pby; Dir Young Life, Chattanooga, 78-85; Chap Baylor school, Chattanooga, 85-89; ydir Lookout Mountain P Ch, Lookout Mountain, TN, 90-98, ascp, yp 98-; adj prof CC, 89-14

1616 Fairy Dell Trail, Lookout Mountain, GA 30750 – 706-820-1234　　　　Tennessee Valley
E-mail: len@lmpc.org
Lookout Mountain Presbyterian Church – 423-821-4528

Teasley, Kevin Brown – b Jackson, MS, Jul 1, 70; f James A.; m Susan Marie Weldon; w Rosemary McCool Fenwick, Kosciusko, MS, Dec 18, 93; chdn Kennedy Evelyn, Micah Fenwick, Molly Jane; UMS 88-92, BBA; CTS 92-96, MDiv; L Apr 9, 96, Nash Pby; O Oct 13, 96, Nash Pby; campm RUF, TNTU, 96-02; campm RUF, Wake Forest, 02-15; admin RUF, 15-

2330 Wimbledon Circle, Franklin, TN 37069 – 336-774-6779　　　　Piedmont Triad
E-mail: kteasley@ruf.org
PCA Reformed University Fellowship

Tebbano, Patrick – b Cleveland, OH, Sept 17, 79; f Jerry; m Sharon Reuscher; w Nicole Marie, Oct 4, 03; chdn Hannah, Jonah, Zachariah; GroCC 02, BA; CTS 07, MDiv; O Aug 26, 07, SW Pby; astp University P Ch, Las Cruces, NM, 07-09, ascp 09-13, srp 13-

3275 View Drive, Las Cruces, NM 88011 – 505-373-0258　　　　Rio Grande
E-mail: pntebbano@hotmail.com
University Presbyterian Church – 575-522-0828

Tedford, J. Mark – b KS, Mar 12, 49; f James; m Lois Beard; w Linda Laverell, Oreland, PA, Jun 7, 74; chdn Jeffrey Mark, Laurie Anne, David James; KSU 67-68; SterC 71, BA; WTS 74, MDiv; L Apr 74, Phil Pby; O Nov 74, DMV Pby; ap Faith P Ch, Wilmington, DE, 74-76; p Church of the Servant, Palmyra, PA, 78-91, wc 91; ob Chap Hershey Med Ctr, Hershey, PA, 91-92; Chap Church of the Brethren Retirement Comm, 93-06, Dir Past Serv, 06-

135 East Oak Street, Palmyra, PA 17078-2440 – 717-838-8607　　　　Susquehanna Valley
E-mail: mtedford1@verizon.net
Brethren Village Retirement Community – 717-581-4283

Tell, Jeffrey Scott – O Jul 7, 13, Pac Pby; p New Life Burbank, Burbank, CA, 13-

E-mail: jeffreytell@juno.com　　　　Pacific
New Life Burbank – 818-590-0841

Teller, Landman Todd – b Ft. Riley, KS, Jan 24, 68; f Landman Jacob Jr.; m Hossfield; w Story, Memphis, TN, Aug 13, 94; UMS 86-90, BA; CTS 92-96, MDiv; L May 28, 96, Cov Pby; O Jun 30, 96, Cov Pby; astp First P Ch, Clarksdale, MS, 96-00; astp First P Ch, Augusta, GA, 00-02, ascp 02-05; astp Christ P Ch, Nashville, TN, 05-06; ascp 06-

2309 Wimbledon Circle, Franklin, TN 37069 – 615-595-1184　　　　Nashville
Christ Presbyterian Church – 615-373-2311

Temples, David Dwayne – b Houston, TX, Dec 12, 63; f Charles Quincy; m Mary Carolyn Stevenson; w Patricia Elma Cajka, Camp Lejeune, NC, May 9, 92; chdn Rachel Elma, Christopher David, Daniel Anthony, Calvin Robert; UFL 86, BS; RTS 97, MDiv, 11, ThM; L May 23, 99, SEAL Pby; O May 23, 99, SEAL Pby; p Westwood P Ch, Dothan, AL, 99-

5480 West Main Street, Dothan, AL 36305 – 334-796-2163　　　　Southeast Alabama
E-mail: dtemples@westwoodpca.org
Westwood Presbyterian Church – 334-794-4080

MINISTERIAL DIRECTORY

Tenent, Parker – campm PCA RUF, UAZ, 07-10; astp Independent P Ch, Memphis, TN, 10-

4738 Walnut Grove, Memphis, TN 38111 – 901-305-1087   Southwest
E-mail: ptenent@ipcmemphis.org
Independent Presbyterian Church – 901-685-8206

Terrell, Andrew – b Atlanta, GA, May 15, 88; f Bruce; m Melissa Condit; w Olivia Patton, Athens, GA, Dec 19, 09; chdn Asa; UGA 09, BS; RTSNYC 17, MA; cert Practical Theo, CitytoCity; campm RUF, 18-

343 Saint Nicholas Avenue #27, New York, NY 10027 – 917-656-3252   Metropolitan New York
E-mail: andrewterrell@gmail.com
PCA Reformed University Fellowship

Terrell, John – astp Christ Ch, Katy, TX, 11-13

1515 Rio Grande Drive, Apt. 1112, Plano, TX 75075 – 469-387-9415   Houston Metro
E-mail: jetterrel@gmail.com

Terrell, Matthew – b Mar 8, 85; w Megan Lanelle McConkey, May 19, 07; ClemU 07, BS; CTS 11, MDiv; campm RUF, Samford, 12-16; campm RUF, NYC, 16-

250 West 85th Street, Apt. 5G, New York, NY 10024 – 205-504-1484   Metropolitan New York
E-mail: matthew.terrell@ruf.org
PCA Reformed University Fellowship

Terrell, Shane – srp Grace PCA, Danville, KY, 14-

260 East Lexington Avenue, Danville, KY 40422   Ohio Valley
E-mail: sterrell@gracedanville.org
Grace PCA – 859-236-9137

Terwilleger, Isaac – b Dubuque, IA, Mar 27, 78; w Kathee Smith, Dubuque, IA, Jul 31, 99; chdn Gideon, Hope, Esther, Eve; BethlC 00, BA; CTS 17, MDiv; O May 20, 18, PlVall Pby; astp Grace Chapel, Lincoln, NE, 17-

4030 Sheridan Boulevard, Lincoln, NE 68506 – 309-236-9105   Platte Valley
E-mail: isaac@gracepca.com
Grace Chapel – 402-484-8555

Thacker, Robert D. – b Westminster, MD, May 20, 70; f Robert E.; m Carolyn Elaine Ruby; w Elizabeth Ann Clark, Yazoo City, MS, Sept 3, 94; chdn Frederick Clark, Elizabeth Lee, Robert Douglas Jr., Samuel Joseph; CC 88-92, BA; RTS, MDiv; L Feb 21, 95; O Apr 14, 96, MSVal Pby; astp First P Ch, Belzoni, MS, 95-96; p Bailey P Ch, Bailey, MS, 97-99; astp Westminster P Ch, Greenwood, MS, 99-03; p First P Ch, Indianola, MS, 03-11; p Faith P Ch, Goodlettsville, TN, 11-

105 Wallingfort Court, Hendersonville, TN 37075   Nashville
E-mail: revof4@gmail.com
Faith Presbyterian Church – 615-859-1130

Tharp, Douglas – b Houston, TX, Sep 3, 82; f Donald Dean; m Mona Lynn Noble; w Sarah Marie (d); Nicole Christine Alexander, Colorado Springs, CO, Jul 22, 07; chdn Simon Douglas, Jude Alexander; UNCO 03, BA; NGTS 11, MDiv; O Mar 11, 12, RMtn Pby; astp Village Seven P Ch, Colorado Springs, CO, 11-16; srp Cornerstone P Ch, Center Valley, PA, 16-; devotional on Ruth, devotional on Philippians

4488 Glasgow Drive, Center Valley, PA 18034   Eastern Pennsylvania
E-mail: doug@cornerstonepca.net
Cornerstone Presbyterian Church – 610-282-5683

Thiele, Dale – astp Valley Springs P Ch, Roseville, CA, 09-10; ob Cameroon, 10-11; p Oak Hills P Ch, Shawnee, KS, 11-

9909 Oakridge Drive, Overland Park, KS 66212　　　　　　　　　　　　　　　　　Heartland
E-mail: dalethiele@gmail.com
Oak Hills Presbyterian Church – 913-341-4500

Thielman, Frank – b Waynesville, NC, Nov 18, 57; f Calvin; m Dorothy Bell Barnett; w Abigail Barnard Rhines, Quincy, MA, Jul 14, 84; chdn Jonathan Rhines, Sarah Jane, Rebekah Barnett; WheatC 80, BA; UCam 82, BA; GCTS 82-83; UCam 86, MA; DukeU 87, PhD; O Nov 27, 90, ARP; Recd PCA 01, Evan Pby; ob prof BDS, 89-; *Paul and the Law; Philippians; The Law and the New Testament; Theology of the New Testament;* "Ephesians" *Bker Exegetical Commentary on the New Testament;* "Romans" *Zondervan Exegetical Commentary on the New Testament*

415 Woodland Drive, Birmingham, AL 35209 – 205-871-0133　　　　　　　　　　　Evangel
E-mail: fsthielm@samford.edu
Beeson Divinity School

Thomas, Benjamin – O Aug 30, 14, NWGA Pby; astp Midway P Ch, Powder Springs, GA, 14-17; ob 17-

740 Skyview Drive, Marietta, GA 30060　　　　　　　　　　　　　　　　　　　Northwest Georgia

Thomas, Brian – O Aug 24, 13, Wcar Pby; campm RUF, WestCar, 13-17; campm RUF, UFL, 17-

4718 NW 17th Place, Gainesville, FL 32605　　　　　　　　　　　　　　　　　　　North Florida
E-mail: brian.thomas@ruf.org
PCA Reformed University Fellowship

Thomas, Christopher – b Apr 22, 79; w Kandice, Jun 27, 98; chdn Margaret, Christopher, Elizabeth Rose; TXTU 01, BA, 03, MA; RTS 07, MDiv; p Carthage P Ch, Carthage, MS, 07-08; op Redeemer P Msn, Amarillo, TX, 08-12; p 12-

203 Sunset Terrace, Amarillo, TX 79106　　　　　　　　　　　　　　　　　　　　North Texas
E-mail: info@redeemeramarillo.com
Redeemer Presbyterian Mission – 806-358-9001

Thomas, David C. Jr. – b Swarthmore, PA, Nov 26, 45; f David Cooper; m Anne Allen Wilson; w Sherry Lee Hair, Lancaster, PA, Feb 14, 70; chdn David Bradford, Emily Sarah (Croce), Michelle Lynn (Wiegers), Elizabeth Anne (Darlington); TempU 68, BS; ShSU 78, MBA; CTS 03, MDiv; O May 22, 05, NoIL Pby; op All Souls P Ch, Urbana, IL, 07-11; srp 11-14; ob Interim Pastor Min, 14-

45 Parkwood Trail, Hampstead, NC 28443　　　　　　　　　　　　　　　　　　　Eastern Carolina
E-mail: pastordavethomas@gmail.com

Thomas, John Franklin – b Union City, TN, Aug 5, 57; f Jerry H.; m June Burden; w Shari Lynn Thompson, Miami, FL, Jun 12, 82; chdn Michaelanne Marie, Corey Allan, Rebecca Christine; CIU 78, BA; CBS 82, MDiv; TIU 95, PhD; O Jun 82, SBC; Recd PCA Jan 97, NGA Pby; astp Franklin Heights Bap Ch, Rocky Mount, VA, 82-83; astp Trinity Bap Ch, Denver, CO, 83-86; mis World Team, 86-93; VP Program Development, Int. Church Planting Cntr, 93-96; op Church of the Redeemer, Atlanta, GA, 97-02, p 02-07; ob dir glob trng, Redeemer City to City, NYC, NY, 07-

234 Columbus Avenue #2A, New York, NY 10023　　　　　　　　　　　　　Metropolitan New York
E-mail: john@redeemercitytocity.com
Redeemer City to City, New York

MINISTERIAL DIRECTORY

Thomas, Kellett Varnedoe – b Pensacola, FL, Mar 17, 62; f James K. III; m Claire FlowersVarnedoe; w Adrea Anna Morar, Panama City, FL, May 11, 85; chdn William Kellett, Jonathan Heeth, Hudson Varnedoe, Lawson Howard; FSU 85, BS; RTS 88, MDiv; L Jul 96; O May 11, 97, North GA; astp Ivy Creek Ch, Lawrenceville, GA, 97-00; chp Jacksonville, FL, 00-01; op City Hope Ch, Jacksonville, FL, 01-03; astp All Souls Flwsp, Decatur, GA, 10- 12; ascp Ivy Creek Ch, Lawrenceville, GA, 12-15; wc 15-

3434 Cooper's Mill Court, Dacula, GA 30019 – 404-333-4353   Georgia Foothills

Thomas, Richard McIver – b Greenville, SC, Sept 20, 61; f Charles Brannon; m Virginia Mason; w Lisa McCall, Greenville, SC, May 3, 86; chdn Richard McIver Jr., Janie McKinnon, Payton McCall, William Wallace; ClemU, BS; RTS, MDiv; L Nov 90; O Jul 14, 91, NR Pby; ss Providence Ref P Ch, Barboursville, WV, 90-91; mis MTW/Impact, 91-92; astp Woodruff Road P Ch, Simpsonville, SC, 92-93, ascp 93-01; srp Mount Calv P Ch, Roebuck, SC, 01-

337 Swamp Fox Road, Spartanburg, SC 29306   Calvary
E-mail: rmt@mtcalvary.org
Mount Calvary Presbyterian Church – 864-576-6156

Thomas, Tony – ob

708 Luria Lane, Champaign, IL 61822   Korean Central
E-mail: tonythomas@cfchome.org

Thompson, Chris – w Lynn; chdn Megan, Ross; O Oct 19, 97, Evan Pby; astp Briarwood P Ch, Birmingham, AL, 97-98, ascp, mpc 99-

1149 Bristol Way, Birmingham, AL 35242 – 205-980-8166   Evangel
E-mail: cthompson@briarwood.org
Briarwood Presbyterian Church – 205-776-5239

Thompson, Daniel Keith – b Placetas, Cuba, Nov 30, 57; f Leslie James; m Carolyn Anne Backlund; w Margaret Douglas Harvey, Beaufort, SC, Jun 23, 84; chdn Carolyn Grace, Daniel Keith, Margaret Dargan, William Harvey; MBI 75-78, dipl; UMiami 78-79, BA; RTS 79-82, MDiv, 88, DMin; O Oct 82, Cal Pby; ap Westminster P Ch, Rock Hill, SC, 82-85; p First P Ch, Hazlehurst, MS, 85-88; op Christ Comm Ch, Titusville, FL, 88-90, p 90-18

3950 Hidden Hills Drive, Titusville, FL 32796 – 321-269-1125   Central Florida
E-mail: dant1130@gmail.com

Thompson, Frederic Delong Jr. – b Mobile, AL, Jun 22, 32; f Frederic D T; m Ruth Hurst; w Betty Danielsen, Charleston, SC, Jun 6, 64; chdn Rachel Louise; GATech 49-52; PC 53-55, BA; UTSVA 55-57; ColTS 64-66, MDiv; ErskTS 90, DMin; O Jun 26, 66, Atl Pby; p Villa Rica, GA, 64-67; Chap USN, 67-70; p First Ch, Woodruff, SC, 70-73; p Roebuck P Ch, Roebuck, SC, 73-86; ss McCutchen Mem P Ch, Union, SC, 86-92; ss Zion P Ch, Chester, SC, 93-00, wc 00-01; ss Powell P Ch, Spartanburg, SC, 01-03; hr 03

PO Box 161, Roebuck, SC 29376-0161 – 864-576-1394   Calvary
HR

Thompson, Greg – b Greenville, SC, Sept 14, 73; f Bruce Wilson; m Barbara Jane Malone; w Courtney Ann McLean, Florence, SC, Sept 30, 95; chdn Caroline Brown, Margaret Bell, Ann McLean, Harold Ames; USC 95, BA; CTS 00, MDiv; L Apr 9, 00, JR Pby; O Nov 11, 01, JR Pby; campm RUF, UVA, 00-05; astp Trinity P Ch, Charlottesville, VA, 05-06, srp 06-17

831 Village Road, Charlottesville, VA 22903   Blue Ridge

Thompson, J. Allen – b Placetas, Cuba, Oct 27, 32; f Elmer V.; m Evelyn McElheran; w Marilyn Corey, Port Angeles, WA, Sept 7, 54; chdn Debi, Shari; PraBibI 48-53, dipl; CBC 53-55, BA; DenTS 60-

Thompson, J. Allen, continued
63, MDiv, 79, DD; TEDS 90-91, PhD; Recd PCA Oct 16, 90, NGA Pby; mis Cuba, 56-60; mis Dom Rep, 63-67; pres WorldTeam, Inc., 67-81, Dir 85-89; p Trin B Ch, Denver, CO, 82-85; MNA, Multicultural Ch Plant Coord, 90-98; MNA Sr. Assoc, 99-02; pres International Church Planting Center, 91-; hr 06; coauth w/ Tim Keller *Church Planter Manual*, 02; Coaching Urban Church Planters, 08

56 Glezen Street, Worcester, MA 01604 – 770-856-3077   Pacific Northwest
E-mail: jallenth5@gmail.com
HR

Thompson, Jeffrey Lee – b Hollywood, FL, Jul 27, 65; f Leland Earl; m Linda Ann Jones; w Caroline Marshall Kerr, Nov 13, 99; chdn George Leland, Caroline Marshall; MHC 87, BS; RTS 91, MDiv; O Jun 4, 95, Wcar Pby; chp, campm MTW, Toyko, Japan, 95-01; campm RUF, UGA, 01-

189 Hardin Drive, Athens, GA 30605 – 706-296-8676   Georgia Foothills
E-mail: rufiuga@gmail.com
PCA Reformed University Fellowship – 678-825-1070

Thompson, John Robert Jr. – b Atlanta, GA, Feb 21, 50; f John Robert Sr.; m Frances Shirley Sanders; w Wanda Jean McCarty, Snellville, GA, Feb 2, 73; chdn Amanda Jean, Rebecca Elizabeth, Sarah Ellen; ErskC 68-70; DeKCC 70-71; USC 76-80, BS; CTS 83-86, MDiv; L Oct 65, CentCar Pby; O Feb 5, 89, NGA Pby; int, yp, headm Second Street P Ch, Albemarle, NC, 86-88; ss The Rock P Ch, Stockbridge, GA, 88-89; ss Rock of Ages P Msn, Atlanta, GA, 89-90; ev PEF, 88-; srp Pilgrim P Ch, Martinsburg, WV, 90-97; ob admin PEF, 98-03; p Chapel Woods P Ch, Snellville, GA, 03-

2541 Poplar Street, Snellville, GA 30078 – 770-978-4172   Georgia Foothills
E-mail: jrtwjt@bellsouth.net
Presbyterian Evangelistic Fellowship
Chapel Woods Presbyterian Church – 770-978-1445

Thompson, Kenneth Allan – b Placetas, Cuba, Apr 2, 56; f Leslie J.; m Mary Louise Doty; w Kimberly Lee Coven, Lansing, MI, Aug 11, 79; chdn Mary Louise, Benjamin James, Nathan Allan; MBI, dipl; TCIL, BA; BhamES; RTS, MDiv; O Apr 83, SFL Pby; mis Logoi, Mexico, 84-86; mis MTW, Miami, FL, 86-95; mis Logoi, Miami, FL, 86-95; ob MTW, Int Ch Planting Ctr, 95-96, admin 96-13; wc 13-15; hr 15

344 Bailey Walk, Alpharetta, GA 30009 – 770-402-8606   Metro Atlanta
E-mail: ken@kakthompson.net
HR

Thompson, Michael E. – w Robin; chdn Ginny, Tara, Michael; WrightSt 91; RTSNC 06; O May 21, 06, Wcar Pby; CCC, 93-96; moy Faith P Ch, Morganton, NC, 96-06, ascp 06-07; srp 07-

1591 Piedmont Road, Morganton, NC 28655 – 828-438-1716   Western Carolina
E-mail: xmikep@gmail.com
Faith Presbyterian Church – 828-433-1052

Thompson, Nathanael – O Feb 28, 16, NYS Pby; p Hope Ch, Ballston Spa, NY, 16-

208 Greenfield Avenue, Ballston Spa, NY 12020 – 518-885-7442   New York State
E-mail: natethompson81@gmail.com
Hope Church – 518-885-7442

Thompson, Nathaniel – b Bellevue, WA, Apr 25, 80; f James Wood; m Linda Lee Remington; w Suzanne Cheryl Norcliffe, St. Louis, MO, Jun 27, 08; chdn Iain Remington, Adelaide Elise, Owen Daniel; UAZ; UW 04, BA; CTS 10, MDiv; O May 11, NoCA Pby; astp Trinity P Ch, Kailua, Oahu, HI, 11-16; campm RUF, WWAU, 16-

2231 King Street, Bellingham, WA 98225   Pacific Northwest
E-mail: nathaniel.thompson@ruf.org
PCA Reformed University Fellowship

MINISTERIAL DIRECTORY 627

Thompson, Randy Edward – b Charleston, WV, Feb 11, 54; f Alvin E; m Vivian Pauline Young; w Catherine Sue Imhoff, South Charleston, WV, May 20, 78; chdn Matthew James, Andrew Cameron, Amanda Paige, Alexander Edward; VPI 76, BS; MorHarC 76-77, grad wk; CTS 80, MDiv; WSCAL 94, DMin; L Jan 80, Midw Pby (RPCES); O Sept 80, FL Pby (RPCES); op Evangelical P Ch, Cape Coral, FL, 80-81; srp 81-95; sc SWFL Pby, 94-95; srp Westminster P Ch, Greenwood, MS, 95-02; p First P Ch, Tuscumbia, AL, 02-

401 East 5th Street, Tuscumbia, AL 35674 – 256-381-0406   Providence
E-mail: randyethompson@gmail.com
First Presbyterian Church – 256-383-2412

Thompson, Ryan – O Jul 25, 10, Wcar Pby; astp Covenant P Ch, Hendersonville, NC, 10-12; ascp Redeemer P Ch, Waco, TX, 12-

204 Trailwood Drive, Waco, TX 76712   North Texas
Redeemer Presbyterian Church – 254-776-7292

Thompson, Walter Eugene – b Savannah, GA, May 14, 46; f Walter C.; m Virginia Ruth Chapin; w Krista Ann Jacobson, Monmouth, OR, Jul 31, 71; chdn Mellisa Kim (Michelson), Heidi Joy, David Eugene, Andrew Josiah; BJU 72, BA; RTS 77-80, MDiv; O Jul 82, CentCar Pby; Recd PCA 98, Flwsp Pby; p South Point P Msn, Gastonia, NC, 82-86; p Emmanuel P Ch, Wilmington, NC, 86-88; p Covenant P Ch, Grass Valley, CA, 89-94; p Redeemer P Ch, Auburn, CA, 94-95; p Salem Ref Ch, 96-98; p Bullock Creek P Ch, Sharon, SC, 98-02; p White Oak P Ch, Fremont, NC, 02-

3206 Nahunta Road, Pikeville, NC 27863 – 919-242-1008   Eastern Carolina
E-mail: gk5solas@gmail.com
White Oak Presbyterian Church – 919-284-4196

Thomson, James Allen – b St. Paul, MN, Feb 5, 48; f Robert Mapes; m Barbara Monroe Allen; w (1) Shirley Irene Doutt (d) (2) Beth Davies, Jan 8, 82; chdn Elisabeth Dawn, Amy Rebecca; HougC 66-70, BA; GCTS 70-74, MDiv; L Jul 13, 74, National Capitol Union Pby UPCUSA; O Aug 11, 74, Shenango Pby UPCUSA; p Bethel UP Ch, Enon Valley, PA, 74-78; p Eastminster Ch, Cincinnati, OH, 78-81; p Faith P Ch, Cincinnati, OH, 81-84; p First Evangelical P Ch, East Liverpool, OH, 84-03; p Covenant P Ch, Hammond, IN, 03-

6939 Baring Avenue, Hammond, IN 46324 – 219-554-0017   Chicago Metro
Covenant Presbyterian Church – 219-844-7028

Thornton, James William Sr. – b Johnson City, TN, Jul 30, 52; f Smith Patton; m Livingston; w Melissa Carolyn Howard, Elizabethton, TN, Jan 3, 81; chdn Lauren, James Jr, Justin; CBC, BA; CBS&SM, MDiv; ETNStU, MAcc; L Oct 89, Palm Pby; O Mar 25, 90, TNVal Pby; Chap Rikard Nursing Homes, Lexington, SC, 85-90; p Chattanooga Valley P Ch, Flintstone, GA, 90-92, wc 92; p Meadow Creek P Ch, Greeneville, TN, 93-01, wc 01-06; astp Memorial P Ch, Elizabethton, TN, 06-11; wc; hr 14

2310 Abbott Drive, Johnson City, TN 37601 – 423-926-7587   Western Carolina
HR

Thornton, Jamie – mis MTW, 05-

c/o MTW   Ohio
PCA Mission to the World

Thorpe, James S. – b Columbia, SC, Mar 15, 56; f Archie Steele (d); m Mary Joe Wylie (d); w Mary Lynn Frances Milhizer, Midlothian, VA, Jun 18, 93; chdn Steven Robert Penny, Julia Renee, David Franklin; USC 80, AS, 83, BA; CTS 96-00, MDiv; O Aug 6, 00, SEAL Pby; int Kirk of the Hills, St. Louis,

Thorpe, James S., continued
MO, 97-00; astp Covenant P Ch, Montgomery, AL, 00-01, ascp 01-03; p Aimwell P Ch, Ridgeway, SC, 03-07; p First P Ch, Atmore, AL, 07-

1002 South Pensacola Avenue, Atmore, AL 36502 – 251-368-2522   Gulf Coast
E-mail: jnmthorpe@frontiernet.net
First Presbyterian Church – 251-368-5453

Thrailkill, William – b Dillon, SC, Jul 4, 60; f Benjamin E Jr.; m Peggy Braddy; w Angela Hood, Mar 27, 93; chdn William (Will) Robert Jr., Daniel Hood, Anna Grace; CCSC 78-82, BS; USC 82-85, JD; RTS 89-92, MDiv; L Oct 2, 90, Cov Pby; O Feb 7, 93, Cal Pby; ss Oak Ridge P Ch, Water Valley, MS, 90-92; int Powell P Ch, Spartanburg, SC, 92-93, p 93-01; p Back Creek P Ch, Mount Ulla, NC, 01-

2180 Back Creek Church Road, Mt. Ulla, NC 28125 – 704-278-9549   Catawba Valley
E-mail: thrailkill1@juno.com
Back Creek Presbyterian Church – 704-278-2798

Threatt, Erwin – b Lancaster, SC, Jul 29, 66; f Ralph; m Cornelia; w Roxann, Scottsbluff, NE, Jan 7, 89; chdn Luke, Nadia, Charis, Victoria; USC 88, BS; RTS 09, MDiv; O May 14, 95, Bapt; Recd PCA Aug 4, 13, Palm Pby; astp Aimwell P Ch, Ridgeway, SC, 13; p Adams Farm ARP, 13-16; chp Christ Community Ch, Batesburg-Leesville, SC, 16-17; p Aimwell P Ch, Ridgeway, SC, 17-

13 Ashley Place Court, Columbia, SC 29229 – 803-381-3109   Palmetto
E-mail: erwin.threatt@gmail.com
Aimwell Presbyterian Church – 803-337-2386

Thumpston, Kevin Wayne – b Jackson, MS, Aug 19, 69; f Charles Wayne; m Janet Clara Madden; w Andrea Jane Penland, Aiken, SC, Apr 17, 93; chdn Andrew, Allison, Emma; USC 89-92, BA; CTS 95-98, MDiv; O Oct 14, 98, Ecar Pby; chp Ecar Pby, Raleigh, 98-00; op Christ Our Comfort P Ch, Raleigh, NC, 00-02, p 02-05; astp Redeemer P Ch, Charleston, SC, 05-07; ss Longtown P Ch, Ridgeway, SC, 09-10; astp Lexington P Ch, Lexington, SC, 11- 14; op Watershed Flwsp, Lexington, SC, 11-13, p 14-; chp coor Palm Pby, 14-15, Palm, Lowc, PD Pby, 16, Palm and PD Pby, 17

229 Circleview Drive, Lexington, SC 29072 – 803-738-5335   Palmetto
E-mail: kevint@watershedfellowship.org
Watershed Fellowship – 803-738-5335

Thurman, James Kenneth Jr. – b Shreveport, LA, Aug 23, 51; f James K. Sr.; m Gladys Maurell Burson; w Linda Susan Dahmer, Shreveport, LA, Jun 4, 71; chdn Laura Ellen (Wimberly), Lindsay Michelle; LSU 69-73, BS; RTS 91-94, MDiv; L Apr 26, 03, SoTX Pby; O Aug 22, 03, SoTX Pby; ascp Southwest P Ch, Bellaire, TX, 03-

7407 Fall Creek Bend, Humble, TX 77396-3760 – 281-608-6823   Houston Metro
E-mail: jktldt2016@gmail.com
Southwest Presbyterian Church – 713-432-0040

Tietje, Benjamin – O May 18, PTri Pby; astp New Hope P Ch, Clemmons, NC, 18-

1701 Harper Spring Dr, Clemmons, NC 27012 – 336-708-6947   Piedmont Triad
New Hope Presbyterian Church – 336-778-1556

Tilley, Douglas Brian – b Waynesville, NC, Apr 4, 50; f Arley A.; m Wanda Jean Wollard; w Catherine J. Mroczek, Paw Paw, MI, Jul 26, 74; chdn Rachel Catherine (Witherow), Sarah Ranell, Hannah Marie (Broecker); CBC 72, BA; RTS 72-73; GrTS 75, MDiv; WheatGrS 77-78; CTS 03, DMin; O Sept 12, 76, UPCUSA; stus First United P Ch, Columbia City, IN, 74-75; ip Ligonier United P Ch, Ligonier, IN, 75-

MINISTERIAL DIRECTORY

Tilley, Douglas Brian, continued
76; p Pine Street P Ch, (rec'd PCA 1980), Hammond, IN, 76-86; sc NoIL Pby, 85-86; p Westminster P Ch, Columbus, GA, 87-99; p Malvern Hills P Ch, Asheville, NC, 00-11; hr 11

2 Auburndale Drive, Asheville, NC 28806 – 828-670-5254   Western Carolina
E-mail: douglasbtilley@gmail.com
HR

Tilley, Mike – op Lake Baldwin Comm Ch, Orlando, FL, 09-

2884 Stanfield Avenue, Orlando, FL 32814 – 407-970-4152   Central Florida
E-mail: Mike.Tilley@lakebaldwinchurch.com
Lake Baldwin Community Church

Timberlake, Darol Craig – O Jun 14, 15, CentCar Pby; astp Church of the Redeemer, Monroe, NC, 15-

1107 Willow Oaks Trail, Matthews, NC 28104 – 704-847-4845   Central Carolina
E-mail: timbersdt@live.com
Church of the Redeemer – 704-225-0161

Timmons, Matt – O Dec 11, 05; op Cov Ref Flwsp Msn, Ashland, OH, 05-10; ob Providence Ch, Mifflin, OH, 12-

1010 Chestnut Street, Ashland, OH 44805 – 937-947-8086   Ohio
E-mail: timmons.m1@gmail.com
Providence Church

Timms, Grover Brown Jr. – b Winnsboro, SC, Jan 8, 60; f G. B. Sr.; m Frances Boyd; w Lisa Bergmanis, St. Louis, MO, Jun 7, 86; chdn John Grover, Preston Everett, David Lymon; CBC 78-82, BA; CTS 82-85, MDiv; L Jul 85, Cal Pby; O Nov 86, Palm Pby; p Longtown P Ch, Ridgeway, SC, 86-88; p Fulton P Ch, Greer, SC, 89-

1028 Abner Creek Road, Greer, SC 29651-9042 – 864-877-8739   Calvary
E-mail: pastor@fultonpca.org
Fulton Presbyterian Church – 864-879-3190

Tindall, Stephen – ascp Hillcrest P Ch, Volant, PA, 05-07; p New Life P Ch, Middletown, NJ, 07-12; wc 12-

34 Heather Circle, Jefferson, MA 01522 – 732-533-7844   New Jersey
E-mail: stindall77@yahoo.com

Tinsley, H. Wallace Jr. – b Chester, SC, Oct 16, 51; f H. Wallace Sr.; m Ruth Neil; w Ruth Robeson, Chester, SC, Jun 9, 73; chdn H. Wallace III, E. Robeson, Clara A., Averett M.; DavC 73, BA; WTS 77, MDiv, 79, ThM; O Oct 9, 77, Cal Pby; ap Second P Ch, Greenville, SC, 77-81; p Filbert P Ch, York, SC, 81-; chmn membshp co, Flwshp Pby, 94-97; GA CEP com, 96-; contr wkly nwscol "Bible Basics," 89-91; *View From The Top: Studies In The Life Of Joseph*, CEP Bible Study for WIC, 95; contr wkly nwscol "Y3B: Read the Bible in 3 Years," 00

1399 Filbert Highway, York, SC 29745-9776 – 803-684-3600   Fellowship
E-mail: hwtjr@comporium.net
Filbert Presbyterian Church – 803-684-6881

Tinsley, Timothy Edward – b St. Louis, MO, Mar 26, 57; f Mel; m Doryle Arlene Counts; w Laura J.; chdn Jordan David, Sarah Marie, Carter Andrew; WheatC 80, BA; BhamTS 90-91; DTS 01, MA; L Jan

Tinsley, Timothy Edward, continued
97; O Nov 97, NoTX Pby; ydir Calvary Ch, Charlotte, NC, 83-88; ydir Cedar Springs P Ch, Knoxville, TN, 88-91; astp, yp, mfam Park Cities P Ch, Dallas, TX, 91-00, ascp, mfam 01-10; srp First P Ch, Chattanooga, TN, 10-

509 Rock House Court, Signal Mountain, TN 37377 – 423-468-3303   Tennessee Valley
E-mail: tim.tinsley@1stpresbyterian.com
First Presbyterian Church – 423-267-1206

Tippetts, Jason Edward – b Feb 11, 72; w Kara Lynne Thewlies (d), (2) Sara Lynn, Mar 12, 17; chdn Eleanor Grace, Harper Joy Sonnet, Lake Edward, Story Jane; SDSU 98, BS; RTSNC 11, MDiv; O Nov 25, 12, RMtn Pby; int Marin Covenant Ch, San Rafael, CA, 93-94; yp First Baptist Ch, Golden, CO, 98-99; asst Story Mem P Ch, Marion, NC, 03-11; stus Landis P Ch, Marion, NC, 11; astp Village Seven P Ch, Colorado Springs, CO, 12- 14; op Westside Ch, Colorado Springs, CO, 14-

745 Saddlemountain Road, Colorado Springs, CO 80919 – 719-306-2361   Rocky Mountain
E-mail: jason@westsidechurchpca.org
Westside Church – 719-306-2361

Tipton, Stephen B. – O Sept 26, 10, Asc Pby; p Hillcrest P Ch, Volant, PA, 10-

250 South New Castle Street, New Wilmington, PA 16142 – 724-946-2510   Ascension
Hillcrest Presbyterian Church – 724-533-4315

Tircuit, Nathan Charles – b Ellsworth AFB, SD, Sept 16, 74; f Col Elwood C.; m Zilphia Elizabeth Switzer; w Jennifer Ann Kennedy, Memphis, TN, Sept 15, 01; chdn Kennedy Ann, William Charles, Caroline Elizabeth, Emma Grace; BelC 97, BS; RTS 01, MDiv; L Oct 2, 01, Cov Pby; O Oct 7, 01, Cov Pby; ydir First P Ch, Prattville, AL, 97-98; ydir First P Ch, Crystal Springs, MS, 98-01; campm RUF, UTMartin, 01-06; campm RUF, MSState, 06- 09; srp Grace Comm Ch, Cordova, TN, 09-18; srp South Baton Rouge P Ch, Baton Rouge, LA, 18-

1456 Beckenham Drive, Baton Rouge, LA 70808   Southern Louisiana
E-mail: nathan.tircuit@gmail.com
South Baton Rouge Presbyterian Church – 225-768-9999

Tiscione, Louis – VilU 73, BEEn; Trin Epis 94, MDiv; O Deac Jun 18, 94; O Dec 21, 94, Dio of CFL, PECUSA; Recd Feb 6, 05, NoTX Pby; St. James Epis Ch, Ormond Beach, FL, 94-96; St. Christophers Epis Ch, Orlando, 96-02; St. Andrews Epis Ch, Ft. Worth, TX, 02-04; op Weatherford P Ch, Fort Worth, TX, 05-

2205 Brandy Drive, Weatherford, TX 76087 – 817-594-1347   North Texas
E-mail: weatherfordpca@att.net
Weatherford Presbyterian Church – 817-598-1277

Tisdale, Adam – b Memphis, TN, Aug 17, 76; w Lydia Wyn, Aug 8, 98; chdn Ethan Scott, Kara Elise; UGA 98, BA; CTS 03, MDiv; L Jan 15, 05, JR Pby; O Apr 30, 05, JR Pby; astp Calvary P Ch, Norfolk, VA, 05-06, ascp 06- 09; p North Hills P Ch, Meridianville, AL, 09-; *Outdo One Another: Fostering Honor Among Pastoral Colleagues*

135 Castlehill Drive, Meridianville, AL 35759   Providence
E-mail: adamtisdale@hotmail.com
North Hills Presbyterian Church – 256-829-0333

Todd, David L. – b Ashland KY, Feb 27, 43; f Joseph J; m Jean Hardin Johnson; w L. Murray Woodson, Ft. Lauderdale, FL, Jun 9, 73; chdn David James, Jessica Leigh, Joanna Elizabeth; WFU 61-65,

Todd, David L., continued
BS; DukeU 65-66; RTS 72-75, MDiv; LRTS 77-78, DMin; O Jun 29, 75, SFL Pby; p Bethany Ch, Ft. Lauderdale, 75-86; Evangelism Explosion III Int., Fort Lauderdale, FL, 86-87; op North Macon P Ch, Macon, GA, 87-88, p 88-01, wc 01-07; hr 07

159 Tattershall Court, Macon, GA 31210-2174 – 478-335-3058   Central Georgia
HR

    Toledo, Pablo – astp Christ Cov Ch, Southwest Ranches, FL, 05-11; op Principe de Paz, Davie, FL, 08-11; astp First P Ch of Coral Springs, Coral Springs, FL, 11-

13140 SW 7th Place, Davie, FL 33325 – 954-424-0673   South Florida
First Presbyterian Church of Coral Springs – 954-752-3030

    Tolson, Aaron – astp Lookout Mountain P Ch, 06-

1113 Lula Lake Road, Lookout Mountain, GA 30750 – 706-820-7539   Tennessee Valley
E-mail: aaron@lmpc.org
Lookout Mountain Presbyterian Church – 423-821-4528

    Tomberlin, John – O 16, TNVal Pby; astp North Shore Flwsp, Chattanooga, TN, 16-

1074 Tiftonia View Road, Chattanooga, TN 37419   Tennessee Valley
E-mail: jctomberlin@gmail.com
North Shore Fellowship – 423-266-3757

    Tompkins, Ryan – w Jennifer; chdn Molly, Charlotte, Lewis; UBuf, BA; WTS, MDiv, TruettTheoSem, DMin; O Jun 13, 03, MNY Pby; astp Redeemer P Ch of New York, New York, NY, 03-06; p Rockwall Ch, Rockwall, TX, 06-

400 Lago Circle, Heath, TX 75032   North Texas
E-mail: rtompkins@rockwallpres.org
Rockwall Presbyterian Church – 972-772-8208

    Tonnessen, Gareth Eugene – b Wilmington, DE, Jun 20, 44; f Thorvald Eugene (d); m Marion (d); w Nelly Elisabeth Moret, Aigle, Switzerland, Jul 20, 69; chdn Claire Danielle (Barthelmess), Rachel Elisabeth (Peters), Lynette Marion (McKee); UDE 66, BA; SIL 72; CTS 70, MDiv; RETS Elect sch 86; L 69; O 70, PacNW Pby (RPCES); yp First EP Ch, Seattle, 70-71; mis WPM, 72-75; p Reformed P Ch, Boothwyn, PA, 76-81; case wk, Del Co, (PA), Srv for Aging, 81-86, wc 90-91; astp Grace P Ch, Dover, DE, 91-94; astp Eastgate P Ch, Millsboro, DE, 94-05; ob staff UDE Coll of Marine Stu; astp New Cov P Ch, Lewes, DE, 05-15; wc 15-16; hr 16; Built on the Rock catechism course (software); various speaking and teaching engagements: Quarryville P Ret Comm; Harvest PC in Willow Street, PA; RUFI, UDE; seminaries in Bangalore and Chennai, India; Genesis course material translated into Telugu and Tamil

527 Park Avenue N503, Quarryville, PA 17566 – 302-645-9479   Heritage
E-mail: LuvTruth@msn.com
HR

    Toombs, Jon Marq – p Christ Cov Ch, Mesquite, TX, 16-

E-mail: marq@christcovenantc.com   North Texas
Christ Covenant Church

    Torrens, Alister – ob mis International Theol Ed Min, Ukraine, 07-

ul. Dekabristov 12/37 kv.208, Kiev 02121 UKRAINE – +380989795664   Eastern Pennsylvania
E-mail: alistert@gmail.com
International Theological Education Ministries, Ukraine

Torres, Timothy – astp Christ Cov Ch, Southwest Ranches, FL, 07-17; astp Spanish River Ch, Boca Raton, FL, 17-

16440 Del Palacio Court, Delray Beach, FL 33484 – 754-234-9794   Gulfstream
Spanish River Church – 561-994-5000

Townsley, Chad – b Huntsville, AL, Jan 12, 83; w Annaliese Gilman , Jun 18, 05; chdn Lyla Adeline, Teller Clayton, Worth Tindall; CTS 10, MDiv; O Feb 5, 12, Prov Pby; ascp Southwood P Ch, Huntsville, AL, 13-15; astp Seven Rivers P Ch, Lecanto, FL, 15-

5730 West Paul Bryant Drive, Crystal River, FL 34429   Central Florida
E-mail: ctownsley@sevenrivers.org
Seven Rivers Presbyterian Church – 352-746-6200

Trapp, John – O Sept 10, 16, SoTX Pby; campm RUF, 16-

311 Westhaven Drive, Austin, TX 78746   South Texas
E-mail: john.trapp@ruf.org
PCA Reformed University Fellowship

Traub, William C. – b Wilkes-Barre, PA, Jul 17, 50; f George B.; m Ethel C. Thompson; w Judith L. VanSice, Elkton, MD, Aug 14, 76; chdn William C. Jr., Dietrich A.; HougC 68-69, 70-72, BA; RutgU 69-70; WTS 72-76, MDiv; L 76; O 76, Eureka Clas (RCUS); p Peace Ref Ch, Loveland, CO, 76-82; ss Valley Ref P Ch, Cloverdale, VA, 82-83; p Grace Cov P Ch, Blacksburg, VA, 84-86; mis MTW, Germany, 86-00; coor theo ed, MTW Europe, 01-12; mis MTW, Scotland, 12-; "Die Lehre von der Schrift in den reformierten Benkenntnisschriften," *Bibel und Gemeinde*, Apr-Jun (97); "Karl Barth and the Westminster Confession of Faith" in: *The Westminster Confession Into the 21st Century – Essays in Remembrance of the 350th Anniversary of the Westminster Assembly*, J. Ligon Duncan III (ed.), vol. 3, (Ross-shire: Christian Focus Publ, 09)

7106 Wessynton Drive, Charlotte, NC 28226 – 704-752-3818   Blue Ridge
E-mail: willtraub@mac.com
PCA Mission to the World

Treat, Chris – w Jana; chdn Grayson, Madison, Jackson, Bryson; UCAR 94, BS; RTS 04, MDiv; O Apr 05, Cov Pby; Dir Student Mobilization, Delta State, 95-98; p Saline Comm Ch, Benton, AR, 99-02; ob p Delta Fell Ch, Helena, AR, 04-07; astp Independent P Ch, Memphis, TN, 07- 08; p Christ P Ch of Fayette Co, Somerville, TN, 08-14; op Hope Ch PCA, Bryant, AR, 14-

4708 Augusta Drive, Benton, AR 72019 – 501-249-5971   Covenant
E-mail: c.treat@yahoo.com
Hope Church PCA

Tree, Iho K. – w Adna; chdn Esther, Philip; VPI 79, BS, 86, PhD; IAStateU 81, MS; DenTS 95, MA; CTS 08, ThM, O Mar 3, 96, Chinese Discipleship Grace Ch; p Galilee Chinese Bapt Ch, Denver, CO, 94-96; ascp Chinese Discipleship Grace Ch, Phoenix, 96-00; astp Chinese Christian Ch, Falls Church, VA, 00-01, ascp 01-06, doct stu CTS, 08-14; ob p Madison Chinese Christian Ch (non-PCA), Madison, WI, 10-16; op Madison Chinese Christian Ch (PCA), 16-

2754 Richardson Street, Fitchburg, WI 53711 – 608-819-2936   Potomac
E-mail: ihotree@aol.com
Madison Chinese Christian Church

Trefsgar, Theodore W. Jr. – b Philadelphia, PA, Jun 17, 61; f Theodore W. Sr.; m Joyce C. Messick; w Sheryl Anne Duffy, Philadelphia, PA, Sept 17, 88; chdn Elisabeth Gabrielle, Sarah Danielle, Isaac James, Joshua Luke, Christopher Jude; PASU 84, BS; REpS 88, MDiv; O Sept 9, 90, Grace Ch of Harmony,

MINISTERIAL DIRECTORY 633

Trefsgar, Theodore W. Jr., continued
Harmony, PA; Recd PCA Apr 20, 96, Ecar Pby; ascp Grace Ch of Harmony, 91-96; chp, op Grace P Ch, Fuquay-Varina, NC, 96, p 96-00; p Village P Ch, Mount Laurel, NJ, 01-14; srp Grace P Ch, Mount Laurel, NJ, 14-

550 Union Mill Road, Mount Laurel, NJ 08054 – 856-313-3228   New Jersey
E-mail: pastorted@gpml.org
Grace Presbyterian Church – 856-778-5472

    Treichler, Gary – b Lockport, NY, Feb 1, 48; f Luther Elmer; m Esther Mae Tolhurst; w Kim, Erie, PA, Aug 4, 70; chdn Christy Lyn, Geoff Michael; RWC, BA; FulTS; KTS 91, grad wk; RTS 03, MDiv; O Aug 25, 73, ECA; Recd PCA Nov 13, 94; area dir YL, Mont Com MD, 70-80; reg dir YL, Columbus, OH, 80-87; dir sm grp Grace Fellowship Ch, Baltimore, MD, 87-90; nat trng dir Serendipity, Wheaton, IL, 90-91; astp Spanish River Ch, Boca Raton, FL, 91-03; ob exec p Orchard Hill Church, Wexford, PA, 03-07; Vista Comm Ch, Dublin, OH; ob 16-

475 Damascus Road, Marysville, OH 43040   Gulfstream
E-mail: garytreichler@gmail.com

    Treick, Donald William – b Manitowoc, WI, Aug 2, 41; f Edward Peter William; m Erna Alma Rodewald; w Myrene Kay Larson, Aberdeen, SD, Sept 12, 70; chdn Rachel Elizabeth, Joel Donald; CarrC 63, BA; WTS 66, MDiv; L May 66; O May 66, RCUS; p Aberdeen & Leola, SD, 66-74; p Hastings, NE, 74-79; p Bismark, ND, 80-83; p Bakersfield, CA, 83-87; sc RCUS, 67-77, sc Pac Pby 91-92; ascp Covenant P Ch, Bakersfield, CA, 89-91; wc 91-92; p Campbell P Ch, Campbell, CA, 92-99; chap Campbell, CA PD, 92-99; wc 99-01; chap Asheville, NC PD, 00-03; astp Malvern Hills P Ch, Asheville, NC, 01-02, wc 02-05; hr 05; ip First P Ch, Summerville, GA, 05-06; Chap Dalton Police Dept, 04-16

3181 Creekwood Drive, Cantonment, FL 32533 – 706-820-8259   Gulf Coast
E-mail: dtreick@gmail.com
HR

    Treick, Joel – b Hastings, NE, Oct 27, 76; f Donald; m Myrene; w Katharine Brown, Santa Barbara, CA, Jul 9, 03; chdn Lilia Marie, James Donald; PepU 99, BA; WSCAL 07, MDiv; O 07; astp First P Ch, Chattanooga, TN, 07-12; p Pinewoods P Ch, Cantonment, FL, 12-

1318 Soaring Boulevard, Cantonment, FL 32533   Gulf Coast
E-mail: joel@pinewoodschurch.org
Pinewoods Presbyterian Church – 850-968-9342

    Trexler, Matthew – O May 3, 16, Pac Pby; campm RUF, UCLA, 16-

6330 San Vicente Boulevard, Suite 102, Los Angeles, CA 90048   Pacific
E-mail: matthewtrexler88@gmail.com
PCA Reformed University Fellowship

    Trinkle, Elbert Lee III – b Crewe, VA, Jan 4, 35; f Elbert L T Jr; m Dorothy Kidd; w Catherine Gibbs, Staunton, VA, Jun 13, 59; chdn Leta Sue, Mary Elizabeth, Virginia Lee; USMA 54-56; VPI 60, BS; RTS 73, MDiv; L Jun 73; O Jun 73, GulCst Pby; p Fairfield P Ch, Pensacola, FL, 73-73; mis Taiwan, 76-81; p Covenant P Ch, Panama City, FL, 81-84; p West End P Ch, Hopewell, VA, 84-86; p Knollwood P Ch, Sylacauga, AL, 86-89; PCA IFBD, 89-90; chp, ev Evan Pby, 90-05; hr 90

3090 Healthy Way, Apt. 233, Vestavia Hills, AL 35243 – 205-706-6618   Evangel
E-mail: ltrinkle@ltrinkle.com
HR

Triolo, Andrew – O Aug 7, 16, MSVall pby; astp First P Ch, Jackson, MS, 16-17; astp Westminster P Ch, Bryan, TX, 18-

2603 Briar Oaks Drive, Bryan, TX 77802   South Texas
E-mail: treetriolo@gmail.com
Westminster Presbyterian Church – 979-776-1185

Tripp, French Walter – b Chattanooga, TN, Jan 5, 37; f Hiram Glennwood; m Margaret Ellen Buckner; w Ruth Doris Schooling, Perryville, KY, Sept 1, 57; chdn Mark Glennwood, John Davidson (d); UChat 56; KgC 57; BelC 58-60, BA; ColTS 62-63; NOBTS 65, ThM; IntSem 81, ThD, 91, PhD; O Jul 65, SMissPby; p Prentiss P Ch, Prentiss, MS, 64-; p Sleigo P Ch, Prentiss, MS, 64-01

1859 John, Prentiss, MS 39474-0561 – 601-792-5879   Grace
E-mail: drfwtripp@windstream.net
Prentiss Presbyterian Church – 601-792-5879

Tripp, Paul – b Toledo, OH, Nov 12, 50; f Bob; m Fae; w Luella Jackson; chdn Justin, Ethan, Nicole, Darnay; CIU 72, BA; PhilTS 75, MDiv; WTS 88, DMin; astp Whaley Street UMC, Columbia, SC, 71-72; astp Lejune P Ch, Coral Gables, FL, 72-74; p Scranton Bapt Fell, Scranton, PA, 77-87; prin Northeastern CS, Scranton, PA, 78-85; lect PhilTS, 89; lect BibTS, 89-94; staff Family Bible Ch, Willow Grove, PA, 90-99; couns, fac CCEF, 97-06; adj prof WTS, 97-07; astp Tenth P Ch, Philadelphia, PA, 07-11; pres Paul Tripp Ministries, 07-; prof RedTS, Dallas, TX, 09-; Dir Center for Pastoral Life and Care, Ft. Worth, TX, 09-; *Instruments in the Redeemer's Hands*, 02; *War of Words: Getting to the Heart of Our Communication Struggles*, 00; *Age of Opportunity: A Biblical Guide to Parenting Teens* , 97; *Lost in the Middle: Midlife and the Grace of God*, 04; *How People Change* (co-author), 06; *Relationships: A Mess Worth Making* (co-author), 06; *A Quest for More*, 07; *Whiter Than Snow*, 08; *Broken Down House*, 09; *What Did You Expect: Redeeming the Realities of Marriage*, 10; "Homework and Biblical Counseling, Part 2," *The Journal of Biblical Counseling* 11, no. 3, 93; *Whiter Than Snow: Meditations on Sin and Mercy,* 08; *A Shelter in the Time of Storm: Meditations on God and Trouble*, 09; *Broken Down House: Living Productively in a World Gone Bad,* 09; *Forever: Why You Can't Live Without It*, 11

7214 Frankford Avenue, Philadelphia, PA 19135   Philadelphia
E-mail: paultripp@paultrippministries.org
Paul Tripp Ministries
Redeemer Theological Seminary
Center for Pastoral Life and Care, Ft. Worth, TX

Trombetta, Joseph – b Philadelphia, PA, Nov 1, 57; f Joseph N.; m Lillian F. Sanguinetti; w Ellen Marie Teti, Cape May, NJ, Jan 8, 83; GBibC 76-80, BBE; BibTS 80-83, MA, 80-83, MDiv; L Nov 19, 83; O Dec 9, 84, NJ Pby; Recd PCA 98, NoE Pby; p Trinity OPC, 83-97; p Christ P Ch, Nashua, NH, 98-99, wc 00-01; ob Chap HCR Manor Care, NJ, 01- 09; ob Chap Care Alternatives Hospice, 09-; chap Our Lady of Lourdes PACE Prog. 09-; chair MNANJ 02-

326 Springfield Terrace, Haddonfield, NJ 08033 – 856-857-1172   New Jersey
E-mail: revvv1@juno.com
Care Alternatives Hospice
Our Lady of Lourdes PACE

Trostle, Jeffrey – w Deborah; chdn Jennifer, Andrew; USF 75, BA; CTS 96, ThM; WhTS 12, PhD; ascp Comm of Christ, Lutz, FL, 82-85; ascp Covenant Comm, Tallahassee, 92-95; astp Wildwood P Ch, Tallahassee, FL, 06-14

E-mail: toopilgrims@gmail.com   Gulf Coast

Trott, Richard H. – b Oconomowoc, WI, May 27, 41; w Joyce Anne Mills, Charlotte, NC, Aug 28, 64; chdn John Philip, Mary Rebecca (Campbell Jr.), Elizabeth Anne, Michael Arthur; CIU 59-63, BA;

MINISTERIAL DIRECTORY   635

Trott, Richard H., continued
Purdue 68-69, grad wk; CTS 63-66, grad wk; O Mar 27, 83, CentCar Pby; p Darlington CongCC, Darlington, In, 66-68; p Friends Union Ch, Turkey Run, IN, 68-69; p Westminster Ref P Ch, Concord, NC, 83-02; hr 02

838 Cherokee Road, Charlotte, NC 28207-2111 – 704-375-9110   Central Carolina
E-mail: ricktr2@gmail.com
HR

Trotter, Andrew Hugh Jr. – b Maryville, TN, Oct 10, 50; f Andrew Hugh; m Hazel Ann; w Marie Goforth Cochran, Lookout Mountain, TN, Jul 1, 72; chdn Andrew Hugh III, Christopher Robert, Michael Willis; UVA 68-72, BA; GCTS 72-75, MDiv; UCam 87, PhD; UMunst 81; O Aug 2, 81, TNVal Pby; Dir Elmbrook Chr Study Ctr, Elmbrook Ch, 81-87; ob Dir/Pres Ctr for Christian Stdy, 87-09; Exec Dir Consortium Christian Stdy Ctrs, 09-; *Interpreting the Epistle to the Hebrews*

1530 Rugby Avenue, Charlottesville, VA 22903 – 434-295-8323   Blue Ridge
E-mail: drew@studycentersonline.org
Consortium of Christian Study Centers – 434-296-3333
485 Hillsdale Drive, Suite 300, Charlottesville, VA 22901

Trotter, Lawrence Calvin – b Springfield, OH, Mar 9, 61; f Wallace D.; m Suzanne Nagley; w Sandra L. Martin, Ft. Lauderdale, FL, Aug 17, 85; chdn Whitney Martin, Natalia Catherine; DukeU 83, BS; WTS 85, MAR, 86, MDiv; RegU 07, PhD; L Sept 86; O Jun 7, 87, DMV Pby; ap Glen Burnie Evangelical P Ch, 87-89; ev MTW, Mexico, 89-16; op Florida Coast Ch, Pompano Beach, FL, 16-; "Triple Defense: Robert Lewis Dabney on Stonewall Jackson," *The Journal of Communication and Religion*, Nov (04); "Blasting Rocks: The Extemporaneous Homiletic of Robert Lewis Dabney"

5555 North Ocean Boulevard #30, Lauderdale-by-the-Sea, FL 33308 – 954-299-1238   South Florida
E-mail: larry@floridacoastchurch.org
Florida Coast Church

Trouten, Timothy – O May 12, 15, NoIL Pby; astp, exec p Christ Ch, Normal, IL, 14-

125 South Orr Drive, Normal, IL 61761   Northern Illinois
E-mail: tim@christchurchpca.org
Christ Church – 309-452-7927

Troutman, William S. – b Statesville, NC, Apr 14, 47; f Victor C.; m doris Levan; w Harriet Henderson, Atlanta, GA, Jun 9, 73; chdn William Donald, Sarah Lanelle; JPershing 70, BA; ColTS 73, MDiv; O 73, PCUS; p Summerton P Cc, SC, 73-78; ss Pinewood P Ch, SC, 73-78; p John Calvin P Ch, Greenville, SC, 78-87; p John Knox P Ch, Shelby, NC, 88-02; ss Ellenboro P Ch, NC, 94-02; op McBrayer Springs Ch, Shelby, NC, 02-; instr Cleveland Comm College, 94-16

257 Cornwell Road, Shelby, NC 28150 – 704-472-5023   Catawba Valley
E-mail: bill.troutman@carolina.rr.com
McBrayer Springs Church – 704-484-0927

Troxell, Thomas Edward – b Philadelphia, PA, Aug 12, 46; f Charles E.; m Kathryn C. MacDonald; w Jean Annette Holliday, Pittsburgh, PA, Jun 26, 70; chdn Thomas Charles, David Scott; UKY 64-65; CC 69, BA; WTS 73, MDiv; L Apr 73, Phil Pby; O Nov 4, 73, Pitts Pby (RPCES); p Chapel RP Ch, Beaver, PA, 73-77; op Hope RP Ch, Mesa, AZ, 77-80; instr RedTS, 79-85; campm AZSU, 80-85; Chap AZNG, 82-04; astp Hope P Ch, Gilbert, AZ, 92-94; ascp 94-95; astp Covenant P Ch, Sun City West, AZ, 99-00, p 00-16, pem 17-; hr 17; "Civil Disobedience and the Christian," *The Presbyterian Journal* (78); "Humor as a Preaching Tool," *Military Chaplain's Review*, Winter (86); "A Brief History of the Arizona National Guard," *Arizona Historical Society Convention* (98); Arizona Military Museum, 02; "A Theology of Aging," "A Theology of Dying," *Serving and Challenging Seniors* (05)

13215 West Copperstone Drive, Sun City West, AZ 85375 – 623-544-6808   Arizona
E-mail: tetroxell@cox.net
HR

Troyer, Arlin – b Goshen, IN, Jul 21, 61; f Owen R.; m Katie Mae Miller; w Catherine Lee Ingram, Franklin, TN, May 6, 89; chdn Clara Pauline, Samuel Chancey, Owen Ingram, Maia Abagail; TayU, BA; WTS, MDiv; L Mar 6, 96; O Aug 25, 96, Wcar Pby; astp Grace Comm Ch, Fletcher, NC, 96-98; ascp West End Comm Ch, Nashville, TN, 98-02; op New City Flwsp of Chicago, Chicago, IL, 02-04; exec dir City Sem of Chicago, 05-08; exec dir Hope for Chicago, 06-08; p Gr Flwsp PCA, Thompson's Station, TN, 08-11; wc 11-

2518 IL West Road, Columbia, TN 38401   Nashville

Trucks, Richard Carlton – b Birmingham, AL, May 21, 49; f Warren; m Louise Wright; w Mary Eleanor Cantrell, Birmingham, AL, Jul 31, 71; chdn MaryRebekah, LauraBeth, Richard Jr., James Allen; SamU 75, BA; RTS 78, MDiv, 87, DMin; O Jun 25, 78, Bham Pby (PCUS); p Third P Ch, Birmingham, AL, 78-; sc Evan Pby, 01-03

3537 Laurel View Lane, Birmingham, AL 35216-3859 – 205-979-9898   Evangel
E-mail: trucks.richard@gmail.com
Third Presbyterian Church – 205-322-1404

Truell, Jason Richard – b Claremont, NH, Nov 17, 80; f Richard; m Claudia Geno; w Kristie Lynn Southall, Roanoke, VA, Feb 5, 81; chdn Eleanora Belle, Abram Asher, John Amos, Gabrielle Joy; UVA 03, BA; ChinES 11, MDiv; O Dec 11, 16, CanW Pby; ob astp Immanuel CRC, 16-

3651 Bowen Drive, Richmond, BC V7C 4C8 CANADA – 778-680-4416   Canada West
E-mail: jasontruell@gmail.com
Immanuel Christian Reformed Church

Truong, Hung – O Feb 20, 16, MetAtl Pby; astp St. Paul's P Ch, Atlanta, GA, 16-

915 Geddy Way, Alpharetta, GA 30022   Metro Atlanta
E-mail: hung@stpaulsatlanta.com
St. Paul's Presbyterian Church – 404-709-2264

Tsui, Brian – b Danbury, CT, Nov 3, 84; f David; m Suzanne; w Nicole, Pismo Beach, CA, Sept 16, 11; UCSB, BS; RTS, MDiv; astp Bethel Ch PCA, Dallas, TX, 13-16; campm RUF, SanJoseSU, 16-

88 East San Fernando Street #503, San Jose, CA 95113   Northern California
E-mail: brian.tsui@ruf.org
PCA Reformed University Fellowship

Tu, Chi Derek – op Chinese PCA Msn, Plano, TX, 12-15; astp Trinity P Ch, Plano, TX, 15-18; astp Redeemer P Ch, McKinney, TX, 18-

7820 Silverado Trail, McKinney, TX 75070 – 972-529-1502   North Texas
E-mail: derek@redeemer-mckinney.org
Redeemer Presbyterian Church – 972-529-1502

Tubbesing, Bradley Evan – b St. Louis, MO, Oct 19, 80; f John; m Janet Sue Bradley; w Caroline Beatrice Taylor, St. Louis, MO, Jun 14, 03; chdn Elizabeth Allison, Adelaide Beatrice, Jane Taylor, John Richard; MUOH 02, BA; CTS 06, MDiv; O Jul 9, 07, Evan Pby; campm RUF, UAHuntsville, 07-12; campm RUF, IndianaU, 12-18; astp Redeemer P ch, San Antonio, TX, 18-

15822 Eagle Cliff Street, San Antonio, TX 78232 – 812-361-2122   South Texas
Redeemer Presbyterian Church – 210-930-4480

Tubley, David Alan – San Diego, CA, Mar 27, 54; f George F.; m Barbara Tromans; w Alice Grace Rice, Tulsa, OK, Jul 10, 76; chdn Andrew David, Peter Robert; ObC 76, BA; WTS 80, MDiv; L Jan 16,

Tubley, David Alan, continued
90; O Jun 10, 90, CentFL Pby; ap Willow Creek Ch, Winter Springs, FL, 90-91; sc CentFL Pby, 90-92, wc 91-92; Chap Orlando reg Healthcare System, Orlando, FL, 92-93; Chap USN, 93-15; assoc dir PRJC, 15-

6867 Pennington Road, Columbia, SC 29209 – 360-471-5665   Central Florida
E-mail: dtubley@pcanet.org
Presbyterian and Reformed Chaplain Commission

Tuck, Tag – b Martinsville, IN; w Gina; chdn Nora, Ian; CTS 12, MDiv; O 13, BlRdg Pby; astp Grace Community Ch, Charlottesville, VA, 13-17; op Word and Table PCA, Charlottesville, VA, 17-

1926 Asheville Drive, Charlottesville, VA 22911 – 314-422-5395   Blue Ridge
E-mail: tagtuck@wordandtable.org
Word and Table PCA – 434-234-4593

Tucker, Mark – w Alice Belz; chdn Levi, Isaiah, Abel, Sol; astp Old Orchard Ch, Webster Groves, MO, 05-07, ascp 07-11; op Midtown Ch, St. Louis, MO, 12-

4148 Botanical Avenue, St. Louis, MO 63110   Missouri
E-mail: maltucker@gmail.com
Midtown Church

Tucker, Ray – O Aug 14, 18, Evan Pby; astp Briarwood P Ch, Birmingham, AL, 18-

205-677-8798   Evangel
E-mail: rtucker@briarwood.org
Briarwood Presbyterian Church – 205-776-5200

Tuckett, James – hr 08

1301 East Captain Dreyfus Avenue, Phoenix, AZ 85022 – 602-374-7403   Heartland
E-mail: Jameset@aol.com
HR

Turner, Benjamin James – O Oct 13, 13, SWFL Pby; ascp Trinity P Ch, Lakeland, FL, 13-; op Strong Tower Msn, Lakeland, FL, 14-

613 North Vermont Avenue, Lakeland, FL 33801 – 863-670-0484   Southwest Florida
E-mail: ben@strongtower.org
Trinity Presbyterian Church – 863-603-7777
Strong Tower Mission – 863-940-9777

Turner, Chad – O Jan 21, 17, CentGA Pby; campm RUF, ValSU, 17-

2202 North Sherwood Drive, Valdosta, GA 31602   Central Georgia
PCA Reformed University Fellowship

Turner, Charlie McCoy – O Aug 18, 13, SavRiv Pby; p Redeemer P Ch, Brunswick, GA, 13-16; astp Grace Ch of the Islands, Savannah, GA, 16-17, ascp 17-18

6901 Concord Road, Savannah, GA 31410 – 912-230-6493   Savannah River

Turner, James Albert – b Philadelphia, MS, Jan 23, 37; f James R.; m Katherine McMillin; w Ellen White, Mebane, NC, Jun 3, 67; chdn Elizabeth Landis, David Alexander, Mary Katherine; BelC 58, BA; ColTS 64; O Aug 2, 64, CMS Pby; moy First P Ch, Jackson, MS, 64-72; ap First Ch, Columbus, MS, 72-74; Trinity P Ch, Montgomery, AL, 74-78; campm UMS, Oxford, MS, 78-87; astp First P Ch, Clarksdale, MS, 91-94, ascp 94-95; ob coord CMDS, Jackson, MS, 95-14; hr 14

1106 Lyncrest Avenue, Jackson, MS 39202 – 601-212-4526   Mississippi Valley
HR

Turner, Mark W. – w Shari; chdn Michael, Lauren, Toby, Savannah; RTSFL, MDiv; O Apr 05, Palm Pby; ascp Armor BPC, 97-05; srp Oakbrook Comm Ch, Summerville, SC, 05-

409 Murray Boulevard, Summerville, SC 29483-9027 – 843-224-9337   Lowcountry
E-mail: mturner@oakbrookpca.org
Oakbrook Community Church – 843-851-1900

Turner, Nick – astp Westminster P Ch, Rock Hill, SC, 16-

1118 Evergreen Circle, Rock Hill, SC 29732 – 803-325-6729   Fellowship
E-mail: nturner@wpcgo.com
Westminster Presbyterian Church – 803-366-3107

Turner, Tyson – O Mar 17, 13, Ohio Pby; astp Christ the Word Ch, Sylvania, OH, 13–17; p Grace Redeemer PCA, Crestview, FL, 17-

2577 Isle of Capri, Crestview, FL 32536 – 419-490-6864   Gulf Coast
E-mail: pastortyson@outlook.com
Grace Redeemer PCA – 850-797-8849

Turpin, Michael – astp Covenant P Ch, Columbia, SC, 05-06; ascp 06-07; Chap USArmy, Ft. Jackson, SC, 07-

Address Unavailable   Palmetto
E-mail: michael.d.turpin@us.army.mil
United States Army

Tweeddale, John W. – srp First Ref P Ch, Pittsburgh, PA, 09-15; ob LigMin, Sanford, FL, 15-; ob adj prof Reformation Bible College, Sanford, FL, 15-

465 Ligonier Court, Sanford, FL 32771   Central Florida
E-mail: jtweeddale@ligonier.org
Ligonier Ministries – 407-333-4244
Reformation Bible College

Twit, Kevin John – b Omaha, NE, Aug 4, 64; f Kenneth John; m Kay Jean Capps; w Wendy Morgan, Feb 28, 98; chdn Cooper McCheyne, Isaac Morgan, Amelia Mei Evans; Berklee C of Music, Boston 86, BA; CTS 95, MDiv; L Nov 19, 95; O Nov 19, 95, Nash Pby; astp Christ Comm Ch, Franklin, TN, 95-98, ascp 98-02; campm RUF, BelmU, 98-

4805 Hall Court, Nashville, TN 37211 – 615-473-5826   Nashville
E-mail: kevintwit@comcast.net
PCA Reformed University Fellowship

Twitty, Hunter – astp Third P Ch, Birmingham, AL, 15-

3709 Spring Valley Road, Birmingham, AL 35223   Evangel
E-mail: hunter.twitty@gmail.com
Third Presbyterian Church

Tyson, James David – b Norristown, PA, Nov 22, 60; f Robert James; m Eileen Patricia Baird; w Mildred Jean Raeburn, Bridgeport, PA, Oct 18, 80; chdn Joshua David, Daniel James, Caleb John, Jonathan Aaron, Nathaniel Josiah; VFCC 90, BS; WTS 97, MDiv; L Sept 9, 00, Phil Pby; O Feb 24, 02, SusqV Pby; DCE Proclamation P Ch, Bryn Mawr, PA, 97-01; p Immanuel P Ch, Shrewsbury, PA, 02-08; ip City Ch York, York, PA, 15-

2880 Bradley Avenue, Dallastown, PA 17313 – 717-246-7438   Susquehanna Valley
E-mail: JimT601@comcast.net
City Church York

Tyson, Richard Wayne – b Abington, PA, Oct 5, 49; f Earl J; m Thelma M. Gakenheimer; w Elisabeth Ann Nicholas, Glenside, PA, Jun 29, 71; chdn Daniel Aaron, Peter Nicholas; CC 71, BA; CTS 74, MDiv; L Apr 75; O Feb 76, NE Pby (RPCES); p Grace RP Ch, Ballston Spa, NY, 76-77; p Hope Ch, Ballston Spa, NY, 78-81; p Immanuel P Ch, Exton, PA, 81-92; ascp Calvary P Ch, Willow Grove, PA, 92-96, srp 96-16; hr 16

1348 Arline Avenue, Abington, PA 19001 – 215 840-8736   Eastern Pennsylvania
HR

Tyson, William Howard – b Jackson, MS, Oct 13, 48; f William L, Jr; m Georgia Neal Boswell; w Mary Ann Cappel, Knoxville, TN, Aug 14, 70; chdn Mary Kristin, Lisa Joy, Heidi Lynn, David William; BelC 66-70, BA; RTS 70-73, MDiv; FulTS 87, DMin; O Aug 5, 73, SW GA Pby (PCUS); p Steam Mill Rd Ch (PCUS), Columbus, GA, 73-76; p Assoc Ref Ch, Bartow, FL, 76-80; p Boyce Mem Ch (ARP), Kings Mtn, NC, 80-89; srp Westminster P Ch, Ft. Walton Beach, FL, 89-18, astp 18; hr 18

6178 Christmas Drive, Nolensville, TN 37135 – 850-651-9845   Gulf Coast
E-mail: tysonb1048@gmail.com
HR

Uc, Isaias – b Becal Campeche, Mexico, Dec 3, 27; f Valerio; m Colli Petrona; w Ruth, Mexico, Sept 6, 58; chdn Juan Carlos, Isai, Idida, Jemimah, Isaias Jr.; ColAm 58, STM; L Jan 57; O Nov 58, PNUG; p Ch, Mexico City, 3 yrs; p group, 18 yrs; t Mex-s, 2 yrs; op Dios Con Nosotros Ch, Edinburg, TX, 82-02, p 02-09; hr 09

3113 North 27th Street, McAllen, TX 78501 – 210-687-6460   South Texas
HR

Udouj, Timothy Joseph – campm RUF, 04-07; campm RUF, Furman, 07-14; astp Downtown P Ch, Greenville, SC, 14-16; op Grace and Peace P Ch, Greenville, SC, 16-

12 Northwood Avenue, Greenville, SC 29609 – 864-991-7630   Calvary
E-mail: tim@graceandpeacepres.com
Grace and Peace Presbyterian Church – 864-283-6603

Uhall, Michael A. – b California, May 30, 55; w Vicky Grier, Jun 12, 76; chdn Joshua, Bethel, Benjamin; Trident TechC, SC, AD; WoffC, BS; CBS&SM, MDiv; O Jun 8, 86, Cal Pby; sp Cal Pby, 86; Chap USN, MAG, 2nd MAW Cherry Point, NC, 86-89; Chap USN, NSGA, Adak, Alaska, 89-91; CmdChap USN, CMDESRON, San Diego, CA, 91-94; CmdChap USN, USNAS, Bermuda, 94-95; Chap USN, 2/5 Mar, Camp Pendleton, CA, 95-96; Chap USN, 1stMarDiv, Camp Pendleton, CA, 96-97; Chap USN, USS Enterprise, Norfolk, VA, 97-99; Chap USN, TBS Quantico, VA, 99-01; Chap FBI Academy, 99-01; Chap USN, H&S Bn, Quantico, VA, 01-03; Chap USN, Marine Corps U, Quantico, VA, 01-03; Chap USN, Navy Supply Corps Sch, GA, 03-04; Chap USN, Cent for Serv Support, GA, 04-06; ret USN 06; wc 07-

5319 Highway 184 East, Donalds, SC 29638 – 864-379-2832   Calvary
E-mail: duewest@wctel.net

Uldrich, Matthew – w Cheri; chdn Elle, Skye, Bailey; UMOC, BA; CTS, MDiv, MAC; DMin; O Oct 04, SW Pby; astp Catalina Foothills Ch, Tucson, AZ, 04-08; ascp 08-13; ob University City Ch, Tucson, AZ, 13-14; astp Valley Springs P Ch, Roseville, CA, 15-16; wc 16-

13693 SE State Route CC, Faucett, MO 64448   Northern California
E-mail: matt.uldrich@gmail.com

Ulrich, Dean Richard – b Pittsburgh, PA, Apr 19, 63; f John Richard (d); m Ann Louise Lanicker; w Dawn Sigrid Errickson, Washington, NJ, Aug 17, 91; chdn Cynthia Louise, John Gordon; Grace Coll 85, BA; RPTS 88, MDiv; WTS 96, PhD; DuqU 01, MA; N-WU (SAfr) 14, PhD; L Mar 89, Asc Pby; O Feb 11,

Ulrich, Dean Richard, continued
96, Pitts Pby; p Covenant Comm P Ch, Wexford, PA, 96-01; wc 01-02; ob assoc prof Trinity Episcopal School, 02-07; ob mis China Ref Theo Seminary, 08-13; wc 14-

601 Lee Avenue SW #5, Rome, GA 30161 – 470-439-5021   Ascension
E-mail: ulrichx4@gmail.com

Um, Junsub – astp Korean Bethel P Ch of Jacksonville, Jacksonville, FL, 07-10; chap USN

PSC 485 Box 276, FPO, AP 96321   Korean Southeastern
United States Navy

Um, Stephen – b Seoul, Mar 15, 67; f Kwi Whan Um Kim; w Kathleen Chang, Orange, NJ, Jan 1, 92; chdn Noel, Adeline, Charlotte; BosU 90, BA; GCTS 94, MDiv, 98, ThM; UStAnd(Scot) 01, PhD; O Nov 94, KAPC; Recd PCA Sept 01, SNE Pby; astp Christ The King P Ch, Cambridge, MA, 01-08; chp, op Citylife P Ch of Boston, Boston, MA, 04-08; srp 08-; *The Theme of Temple Christology in John's Gospel*; *The Library of New Testament Studies*; *The Kingdom of God (TGC Booklets)*, 11; *Why Cities Matter*, 13

3 Lawnwood Place, Charlestown, MA 02129 – 617-216-4420   Southern New England
E-mail: pastor@citylifeboston.org
Citylife Presbyterian Church of Boston – 617-292-0990

Up De Graff, Morse DeWitt – b New Castle, IN, Jan 18, 43; f L A U; m Jane DeWitt; w Janie Lanier, Savannah, GA, Jul 22, 67; chdn Stacey Marie (VanVoorhis), Deborah Jane (Ertel), Stephen Morse; BelC 66, BA; CTS 69, MDiv; O Jun 69, Athens Pby; p Chestnut Mountain P Ch, Chestnut Mountain, GA, 69-75; p Edgemont P Ch, Bristol, TN, 75-87; p Presbyterian Ch East, Birmingham, AL, 87-94; admin/ceo Ridge Haven Conference Center, 94-07; exec dir/ceo Ridge Haven Conference Center, Brevard, NC, 07-09; wc 10; ss Malvern Hills P Ch, Asheville, NC, 11-12; ss Covenant P Ch, Hendersonville, NC 13-14; ss Story Memorial P Ch, Marion, NC, 14; hr 16

1316 Afternoon Sun Road, Matthews, NC 28104 – 828-508-2662   Central Carolina
E-mail: mo1udg@gmail.com
HR

Upchurch, David Emerson – b Atlanta, GA, Aug 7, 46; f Jerry E.; m Kathleen Cox; chdn Nathanael; UKS 68, BA; GCTS 75, MDiv; L 81; O 81, Midw Pby (RPCES); p Christ Ch, Topeka, KS, 79-85, wc 85; ob t Cair-Paravel Latin School, Topeka, KS, 86-88, wc 88-89; Chap USAR, 89-06; Grace EPC, Lawrence, KS, 07-; hr 07

E-mail: daveupchurch@lycos.com   Heartland
HR
Grace EPC, Lawrence, KS

Upton, Mark Edward – b Columbus, MS, Mar 1, 69; f C. Harry; m Jackie Johnson; w Holly Love Hillsman, Montreat, NC, May 28, 94; chdn Laurel Love, Charles Davis; WFU, BS; RTSNC, MDiv; L Nov 26, 00, CentCar Pby; O Nov 26, 00, CentCar Pby; astp, mout Uptown Christ Cov Ch, Charlotte, NC, 00-02; op Hope Comm Ch, Charlotte, NC, 02-04; srp 04-

5936 Colchester Place, Charlotte, NC 28210 – 704-564-8183   Central Carolina
E-mail: markupton@hopecommunity.com
Hope Community Church – 704-521-1033

Urish, James Everett – b Rockford, IL, May 23, 47; f Robert A.; m Lucy Alice Strawbridge; w Anne Penny, Green Mountain Falls, CO, Mar 27, 77; chdn Luke Michael, Mimi Marie, Abigail Ruth; StOlC 69, BA; UAZ 72, MBA; CTS 79, MDiv, 94, DMin; L Feb 79, Midw Pby; O Dec 79, RMtn Pby (RPCES);

Urish, James Everett, continued
p Covenant P Ch, Lander, WY, 79-01; p Forestgate P Ch, Colorado Springs, CO, 01-14; hr 14; contr *A Peaceable Plea About Subscription: Toward Avoiding Future Divisions in The Practice of Confessional Subscription*, ed D. Hall; contr "By What Authority? The Logic of Humanism" in *Election Day Sermons*

PO Box 855, Green Mountain Falls, CO 80819 – 719-488-4425   Rocky Mountain
E-mail: jimurish@gmail.com
HR

    Vahle, Joshua – campm RUF, UIA, 08-14; astp Chapin P Ch, Chapin, SC, 14-18; ob p Quincy, IL, 18-

1704 South 46th Street, Quincy, IL 62305   Palmetto

    Van Bemmel, Jason – b Oklahoma City, OK, Mar 26, 74; f John Albin; m Randi Schoch; w Beth Anne, Columbia, MD, Jun 20, 98; chdn Andrew, Jeremiah, Kathryn; UMD 96, BA; CC 09, MEd; RTSDC 09, MAR; p Faith P Ch, Cheraw, SC, 11-13; ob prin Whitefield Acad, Mableton, GA, 13-15; p Forest Hill P Ch, Forest Hill, MD, 15-

305 Cherokee Place, Bel Air, MD 21015   Chesapeake
E-mail: jason.vanbemmel@gmail.com
Forest Hill Presbyterian Church – 410-838-7674

    van Blerk, J.A.T. (Theo) – b Bloemfontein, South Africa, Jan 12, 63; f Gert Maartin; m Catharina Susanna; w Lidia, Durban, South Africa, Dec 15, 84; chdn Gert Maartin, Ferdinand, Rina-Mari; NWU, South Africa 83, BA; PUCHE 84 Honns, 90, MDiv; L Jan 11, 91, South Africa; p Ref Ch Magol, Ellisras, SA, 91-00; Ref Ch Wapadrant, Pretoria, SA, 00-02; p Meadow Creek P Ch, Greeneville, TN, 02-07; p Harvestwood Cov P Ch, Floyd, VA, 08-

226 Pine Street, Floyd, VA 24091 – 540-745-5697   Blue Ridge
E-mail: jatvanberk@swva.net
Harvestwood Covenant Presbyterian Church – 540-745-3614

    Van Der Pol, Doug – b Pella, IA, Feb 24, 64; f Howard; m Betty Blom; w Joni Lynn Randall, Pella, IA, Dec 22, 90; chdn Kristina Grace, Jenna Faith, Olivia Hope; CentC 86, BA; CTS 96, MDiv; L Jul 23, 96; O Aug 11, 96, Pac Pby; p Covenant P Ch, Bakersfield, CA, 96-01; ascp Redeemer P Ch, Torrance, CA, 01-04; mod Pac Pby, 02-03; p Bethany Evangelical & Ref Ch, Ledyard, IA, 04-12; ob Bethel CRC, 13-

101 Kirkwood Street, Pella, IA 50219 – 515-646-2022   Iowa
E-mail: djvdp08@hotmail.com
Bethel Christian Reformed Church

    van der Westhuzien, Johan – b Barberton, South Africa, Jan 21, 52; f Roelof Christoffel; m Maria Labuschagne; w Stephanie Marian Teubes, Durban, South Africa, Jan 20, 78; chdn Lycia, Lionel, Brendon; FlorBeaconBC 91, BA; LogosGS 97, MDiv; mis, chp MTW, Chile, 85-

c/o MTW   Evangel
PCA Mission to the World

    Van Devender, John Arch – b Hattiesburg, MS, Aug 15, 46; f Willard Sterrett Sr.; m Wilhemina Estelle Donovan; w Judith Trapier O'Neal, Tampa, FL, Jun 7, 69; chdn John Archie Jr., William Richard, Robert Keith, Stephen Prentiss; USM 68, BS, MS; USNPGS 76; ChTS 94; L Feb 91; O Mar 5, 95, Pot Pby; stus, chp, op Severn Run Evangelical P Ch, Millersville, MD, 94, srp 95-16, hr 16; ss Inverness P Ch, Baltimore, MD, 16-18

109 Sherburn Road, Severna Park, MD 21146-3016 – 410-544-3726   Chesapeake
E-mail: pastorarch@gmail.com
HR

Van Dyke, John Carden – b Newport News, VA, Jan 23, 64; f James F.; w Lisa Welch, Charlottesville, VA, Aug 2, 86; chdn Rachel Elaine, Samuel James; KgC 86, BA; RTS 92, MDiv; GlasgowU 97, PhD; O Oct 92, EPC; Recd PCA Oct 5, 99, Wcar Pby; astp Fellowship P Ch, Newland, NC, 99-02; srp Grace P Ch of the Western Reserve, Hudson, OH, 02-04; Chap USN, 06-

505 Oak Grove Road, Norfolk, VA 23505   Western Carolina
E-mail: drjohn97@gmail.com
United States Navy

Van Eck, Stephan – b Chicago, IL, Dec 9, 53; f Herman; m Gertrude; w Gabriela, Southfield, MI, Jul 30, 77; chdn Joshua Stephan, Abigail Margaret (Deenik), Nathan Paul, Joshua Gabriel; Detroit Bible 76, BRE; WTS 80, MDiv; KTS 12, DMin; O Oct 12, 82, Bible Fell; ascp Bible Fell Ch, Sunbury, PA, 80-83; p Bible Fell Ch, Denville, NJ, 83-88; p Iowa Falls CRC, Iowa Falls, IA, 88-91; p Sunnyslope CRC, Salem, OR, 91-95; p East Martin CRC, Martin, MI, 95-01; p Second CRC, Highland, IN, 01-06; astp Coral Ridge P Ch, Ft. Lauderdale, FL, 06-09; brd Dir KTS 07-09; op Trin P Msn, DeMotte, IN, 09-11, p 11-

11122 West Drive, DeMotte, IN 46310 – 219-987-4822   Great Lakes
E-mail: statedclerkofglp@gmail.com
Trinity Presbyterian Church – 219-863-8484

van Eyk, Bernie – b Red Deer, Alberta, Canada, Dec 29, 64; f Arie; m Frances Meinen; w Patricia Wilma Van der Maarl, Dundas, Ontario, Canada, May 11, 91; chdn Stephanie, Emberlee, Melissa, Matthew, Calvin, Ryan Arie; St.ClairC 84, dipl; UWindsor 87, Bcomm; UWOntario 94, BA; WSCAL 99, MDiv; L Apr 24, 99, SoCst Pby; O Oct 6, 00, CentFL Pby; chp apparent Kirk O' the Isles, Savannah, 99-00; op Indian River P Ch, Vero Beach, FL, 00-05; p Grace P Ch, Stuart, FL, 05-

2975 NW Stoney Creek Avenue, Jensen Beach, FL 34957 – 772-532-4374   Gulfstream
E-mail: tcoaks@gmail.com
Grace Presbyterian Church – 772-692-1995

Van Gilst, Mark – b Oskaloosa, IA, Aug 24, 47; f Bass; m Harriet; w Lola Sharpe, Kalamazoo, MI, May 27, 69; chdn Amy, Tonya, Heidi, Michael; CalvC 69, BA; ILSU 75, MEd; L May 90; O Dec 90, Hrtg Pby; admin ChSch, 75-88; ydir Evangelical P Ch, Newark, DE, 88-90, ascp 90-94; chp, op Cornerstone P Ch, Kemblesville, PA, 94-96, srp 96-16; hr 16

604 Gypsy Hill Road, Landenberg, PA 19350 – 610-255-3301   Heritage
E-mail: vangilst@aol.com
HR

Van Lant, Timothy L. – b Lynden, WA, Dec 19, 74; f Jay; m Fran; w Robin, Boulder, CO, Jul 8, 06; CalvC 99, BA; CalvS 03, MDiv; O 03, CRC; Recd PCA 08, RMtn Pby; int Community CRC, Wyoming, MI, 01-03; p Cedar CRC, Cedar, IA, 03-06; Chap Swedish Med Cntr, Denver, 06-07, wc 07-

303 Pheasant Run, Louisville, CO 80027 – 303-879-8434   Rocky Mountain
E-mail: ptvanlant@msn.com

Van Marel, Brandon – b Orange City, IA, Sept 23, 79; w Kelly, Jan 4, 03; chdn Joanna, Eliana, Makayla, Titus; NWC, BS; GenC, MHED; CTS, MDiv; O Mar 12, 17, PlVall Pby; astp Grace Ch PCA, Fremont, NE, 17-

1774 Austin Lane, Fremont, NE 68025 – 712-737-7944   Platte Valley
E-mail: bvanmarel@yahoo.com
Grace Church PCA – 402-721-6260

Van Meerbeke, David Alan – b Redbank, NJ, Jun 10, 63; f Ronald; m Joan Thomas; w Cynthia Kane, Kennett Square, PA, Sept 24, 88; chdn Rebecca, Katelyn, Joshua David; UDE 85, BS; WTS 94, MDiv; L

Van Meerbeke, David Alan, continued
Mar 18, 95; O Aug 27, 95, Hrtl Pby; astp, yp New Hope P Ch in America, Olathe, KS, 95-99; astp Crossroads Comm Ch, Upper Darby, PA, 99-02, ascp 02-

121 West Stratford Avenue, Lansdowne, PA 19050 – 610-804-2788   Philadelphia Metro West
E-mail: pastordavidvan@gmail.com
Crossroads Community Church – 610-352-3130

Van Ness, Dale Thomas – b Corning, NY, Jul 23, 52; f Thomas Maxwell; m Donna Belle Yessa; w Joanne Marie Greer, Pittsburgh, PA, Apr 4, 81; chdn Abigail, Mollie Kate, Sarah, Peter; Corning CC 71-72; VCU 73-82, BA; CalvC 84-85, MATS; RTS 88-91, MDiv; L Oct 90; O Nov 1, 92, MSVal Pby; stus Smyrna P Ch, Kosciusko, MS, 90-91; int First P Ch, Lexington, MS, 91-92, p 92-05; p Olive Street P Ch, Coatesville, PA, 05-

110 Milbury Road, Coatesville, PA 19320 – 610-466-9359   Philadelphia Metro West
E-mail: casiodorus@aol.com
Olive Street Presbyterian Church – 610-466-7640

Van Schouwen, Andrew – w Joan; chdn Paul, Mary, David; O Sept 19, 58, CRC; p CRC Hawarden, IA, 58-63; p CRC Chandler, MN, 63-68; p CRC Oakland, MI, 68-79; p Grace CRC, Kalamazoo, MI, 79-83; p CRC Hartley, IA, 83-92; p CRC Ackley, IA, 92-95; hr 95

2652 Gay Paree Drive, Zeeland, MI 49464 – 616-748-1390   Great Lakes
HR

Van Vlake, John Marcus – b Columbia, SC, Aug 25, 72; w Shelly; chdn Jackson Lee, Julia, John Richard, Jessie; astp Bethel P Ch, Clover, SC, 12; p New Cov P Ch, Manning, SC, 12-15; p Bethel P Ch, Clover, SC, 15-

2445 Highway 557, Clover, SC 29710   Fellowship
E-mail: mvanvlake@hotmail.com
Bethel Presbyterian Church – 803-222-7166

Vance, John Lloyd – b Rainelle, WV, Jun 25, 41; f Lloyd L.; m Icie I. Gwinn; w Marlene Ann Malcolm, Winter Haven, FL, Oct 7, 68; chdn Gwyneth Lisbeth, Meredith Lee; MorHarC 60-62; WVSC 59-60; BJU 67, BA; CTS 72, MDiv; ConcS 72-73; PTS 76, ThM; DrewU 86, MPhil, 90, PhD; L 73; O 73, NE Pby (RPCES); p Westminster P Ch, Rock Tavern, NY, 73-88, ss 88-90, p 90-13; hr 14; adj prof SUNY; *The Ecclesiology of James Henley Thornwell: An Old South Presbyterian Theologian*; "The Care of the Souls in the 1990's: A Strategy for the Care of the Souls through the Ministry of the Church," *Presbyterion*

253 Aretta Drive, Meadow Bridge, WV 25976 – 304-484-7759   New York State
E-mail: jlloyd41@frontiernet.net
HR

Vanden Brink, Kevin Jay – b Holland, MI, May 22, 69; f Donald; m Joyce Van Drunen; w Stephene Ann Sexton, Upland, IN, Aug 3, 91; chdn Samuel, Benjamin, Alia; TayU 91, BA; CTS 96, MDiv; L Oct 3, 03, PacNW Pby; O Feb 22, 04, PacNW Pby; VP/Enrollment CTS, 96-02; ascp CrossPoint Green Lake, Seattle, WA, 04-07; ascp/lead pastor New City Flwsp South City, St. Louis, MO, 07-18; ob Langham Parnership, 18-

3919 Hartford Street, St. Louis, MO 63116 – 314-488-0256   Missouri
E-mail: kevin.vandenbrink@langham.org
Langham Parnership

Vanden Brink, Paul Martin – O Feb 9, 05; op Grace Valley Ch, Dundas, ON, 15-

59 James Street, Dundas, ON L9H 2J8 CANADA – 905-517-0936   Eastern Canada
E-mail: paul@gracevalleychurch.ca
Grace Valley Church – 905-517-0936

Vanden Heuvel, Thomas C. – b Grand Rapids, MI, Apr 5, 36; f Christian; m Anne De Haan; w Dolores Mae Van Putten, Grand Rapids, MI, Nov 26, 58; chdn Geoffrey, Jane (Jelgerhuis), Joel, James, Jonathan; CalvC 58, BA; CalvS 61, MDiv; LVBCS 78, DD; L Jun 59, CRC; O Sept 61, Classis WI, CRC; Recd PCA Oct 12, 96, GrLks Pby; p Bethel CRC, Waupun, WI, 61-64; p First CRC, Milwaukee, 64-67; p Central Ave CRC, Holland, MI, 67-75; p First CRC, Chino, CA, 75-79; p First CRC, Orange City, IA, 79-85; p First CRC, Byron Center, MI, 85-97; op Covenant P Ch, Holland, MI, 96-98, p 98-06; hr 06

1220 Canal Boulevard, Ripon, CA 95366   Great Lakes
E-mail: tomlaur@aol.com
HR

Vander Maas, Andrew – b Grand Rapids, MI, Feb 8, 69; f Henry; m Sandra Lee Perkins; w Lisa Lyn Vander Roest, Kalamazoo, MI, May 31, 91; chdn Josiah John, Lydia Grace, Sophia Marie, Malachi, Isaiah, Gabriella, Zoe; CalvC 87-91, BA; CalvS 94-97; CTS 97-99, MDiv, 09, DMin; L Apr 18, 99, MO Pby; O Oct 24, 99, MO Pby; ydir Seventh Ref Ch, Grand Rapids, MI, 93-97; astp Covenant P Ch, St. Louis, MO, 98-03; op Crossroads P Flwsp, Maplewood, MO, 03-04; p 04-14; srp Christ Ch, Grand Rapids, MI, 14-

4211 Holyoke Drive SE, Grand Rapids, MI 49508   Great Lakes
E-mail: andrew.vandermaas@gmail.com
Christ Church – 616-949-9630

Vanderveen, Garry – Recd PCA Oct 15, 16, Wcan Pby; p Christ Covenant Church, Langley, BC, 16-

21670 Maxwell Crescent, Langley, BC V2Y 2P9 CANADA – 604-309-3116   Western Canada
E-mail: grvdveen@gmail.com
Christ Covenant Church

VanGemeren, Willem Arie – b Boskoop, Holland, Apr 7, 43; f Jacobus Johannes; m Sarah Cornelia Langeveld; w Evona Leslie Adkins, Bassett, VA, Jun 15, 66; chdn Nurit Tabitha, Tamara Shulamit, Shoshanna Sharon; UIL, BA; HebUJ; WTS, BD; UWI, MA, PhD; L Mar 4, 74; O Nov 19, 76, OPC; ss Concord P Ch, Pickens, MS, 79-91; ob asst prof GenC 74-78; asst, assoc, prof RTS Jackson, 78-92; ob prof TEDS, 92-12; TEDS, dir PhD prog, 00-10; prof em TEDS, 13; prof, Logos EvSem, 13-; prof Chongshin Theo Sem, Seoul, 16-; *The Progress of Redemption: The Story of Salvation From Creation to the New Jerusalem*, 88; *Interpreting the Prophetic Word*, 90; *Expositor's Bible Commentary: Psalms*, 91; ed *The New International Dictionary of Old Testament Theology and Exegesis*, 97; listed in *Who's Who in Religion*, 92

1251 County Road 2500 E, El Paso, IL 61738-9284 – 309-527-2025   Northern Illinois
Logos Evangelical Seminary

VanLandingham, Frank D. – b El Paso, TX, Oct 31, 49; f Clarence A.; m Hazel M. Stokely; w Carole Jeanne Hancock, Tucumcari, NM, Dec 31, 70; chdn Kelly, Christine (Woerner), Shelly (Waggoner); EPCC 85-86; GCTS 90, MDiv; L Apr 26, 91, SW Pby; O Nov 10, 91, RMtn Pby; int Trinity Ref P Ch, Montrose, CO, 90, srp 91-14

66132 Cottonwood Drive, Montrose, CO 81401 – 970-249-0368   Rocky Mountain
E-mail: frankvan49@gmail.com

Vannoy, John Robert – b Wilmington, DE, Mar 3, 37; f Wesley G.; m Margaret D. Bruce; w Kathe M. Polder, Amsterdam, Netherlands, May 11, 65; chdn Margaret Anna, Robert Bruce, Mark Alexander, Jonathan Peter; ShelC 53-57, BA; BosU 59; FTS 57-60, MDiv; BranU 60; FTS 60-62, STM; FrUAmst 62-65; UHeid 64; FrUAmst 77, ThD; L Apr 24, 71; O Apr 24, 71, Phila Area Pby (BPC); Recd PCA 80, Phil Pby; instr ShelC, 61-62; instr FTS, 65-68, asst prof 68-71; assoc prof BibTS, 71-77; lect WTS, 76-77; prof BibTS, 77-05; hr 05; prof em BibTS; *Covenant Renewal at Gilgal*, 78; contr *The Law and The Prophets*, 74; *NIV Study Bible*, 85; contr ed *Interpretation and History: Essays in Honor of Allan A. MacRae*,

MINISTERIAL DIRECTORY 645

Vannoy, John Robert, continued
86; contr *BEB*, 88; contr *New Geneva Study Bible*, 95; *Evangelical Dictionary of Biblical Theology*, 95; *The New Living Translation*, 96; contr *New International Dictionary of Old Testament Theology and Exegesis*, 97; "1-2 Samuel," *Cornerstone Biblical Commentary*, Tyndale House Publishers, Dec.09

218 West Walnut Street, Souderton, PA 18964-1618 – 215-692-2120   Philadelphia Metro West
E-mail: jrobertvannoy@hotmail.com
HR

Vasholz, Robert Ivan – b Kansas City, MO, Sept 27, 36; f Frank J.; m Mollie A. Goldstein; w Julia E. Martin, Baton Rouge, LA, Jun 15, 63; chdn Rachel Kay; BJU, BA, MA, BD; CTS, ThM; StLU 76, MA; UStel, ThD; admin, prof CTS, 74-79, prof 79-07; past asst First P Ch, Augusta, GA, 07-; hr 07; adj prof ErskTS; *Hebrew Exercises: a Programmed Approach*; *Data for the Sigla of the BHS*; *Old Testament Canon in the Old Testament Church*; *The Rationale for Old Testament Canonicity*; *Pillars of the Kingdom*, 97; *Benedictions*, 07; *Calls to Worship*, 07; *Commentary on Leviticus*, 07; *Gilgamesh Revisited;The Future of Israel inLlight of the Abrahamic and Mosaic Covenants*; *Greek Exercises: A Programmed Approach*; *When the Trinity Shook Hands*; *Hosea and Atonement*; *Sayings from our Pulpit*

3433 Heather Drive, Augusta, GA 30909-2707   Missouri
E-mail: Vasholri@comcast.net
HR

Vasquez, Rick – b San Jose, CA, Apr 16, 58; f Manuel; m Celia Guzman; w Melinda Albarian (d); (2) Kathleen McFadden, San Francisco, CA, Jul 17, 04; chdn Victoria, Jeremy, Monica, Jason, Caleb, Leo, Lydia, Elliot; W. Valley C 79, AS; LibBapC 82, BS; BIOLA 86, MA; WSCAL 97, MDiv; L Apr 97, RMtn Pby; O Feb 98, RMtn Pby; astp Covenant P Ch, Wheat Ridge, CO, 97-99; op Skyview P Ch, Centennial, CO, 98-00, p 00-

7607 South Emerson Court, Centennial, CO 80122 – 303-791-8791   Rocky Mountain
E-mail: skyviewpres@gmail.com
Skyview Presbyterian Church – 303-797-9000

Vaughn, Jeff – O Nov 26, 00, Hrtl Pby; astp Heartland Comm Ch, Wichita, KS, 00-05; mis MTW, 05-

625 Buckingham Drive, Oviedo, FL 32765 – 915-781-5847 Heartland
E-mail: jandhv@protonmail.com
PCA Mission to the World

Vaughn, Peter R. – b Three Rivers, MI, May 28, 47; f Russell Lyle; m Mary Alice Brown DeLong; w Linda Ann Cromer, Las Cruces, NM, Jun 7, 69; chdn Eleanor Rose, Katharine Ruth, Peter DeLong; UTXAu 69, BA; WebsU 72, MA; CTS 76, MDiv; L Jan 76, Midw Pby (RPCES); O May 1, 77, Union Ch of Guatemala; ap Union Ch, Guatemala; ap University P Ch, Las Cruces, NM, 77-78; p Providence Ch, Las Cruces, NM, 78-83; prin CovCS, Cranford, NJ, 83-85; ss Covenant P Ch, Short Hills, NJ, 85-86; p Covenant P Ch, Macomb, IL, 86-93; astp Spring Meadows P Ch, Las Vegas, NV, 93-95; ob ascp Ch of the Redeemer (Indep), Mesa, AZ; ob prin Redeemer CSch, Mesa, AZ, 95-00; ob headm Cov Ch Acad, Colleyville, TX, 00-01; MTW, Lyon, France, 01-03; ob Chap Friendship Village, St. Louis, MO, 03-12; hr 12

2002 12th Street, East Moline, IL 61244 – 309-798-2530   Missouri
E-mail: peterrvaughn@gmail.com
HR

Veazey, Lee – b Hendersonville, NC, Jun 25, 66; f Alexander H. Jr.; m Ruth Anne Fisher; w Michelle Renee Aust, Rochester, MN, Jun 28, 97; chdn Mary Lauren, Matthew James; DukeU 88, BA; WTS 05, MDiv; O Jun 9, 07, OHVal Pby; op Grace and Peace P Ch, Fort Mitchell, KY, 07-16, p 16-

256 Watch Hill Road, Ft. Mitchell, KY 41011 – 859-331-6163   Ohio Valley
E-mail: veazey@zoomtown.com
Grace and Peace Presbyterian Church – 859-757-8644

Veazey, Robert Foster – b Alexander City, AL, Jul 21, 84; f Louis F.; m Barbara Lindsey; w Nora Foshee, Alexander City, AL, Jul 21, 84; chdn Foster Kennedy, Weathers Lindsey; UAL 77-80, BA; ColTS 88-91, MDiv; O Aug 4, 91, WestKY (PCUSA); Recd PCA Jan 15, 00, CentGA Pby; p First PCUSA, Mayfield, KY, 91-96; srp Trinity PCUSA, Meridian, MS, 96-97; srp Elkin PCUSA, Elkin, NC, 97-99; op Grace Comm Ch, Macon, GA, 99-02, p 02-

205 Alexandria Drive, Macon, GA 31210 – 478-731-3313   Central Georgia
E-mail: VeazeyBob@aol.com
Grace Community Church – 478-731-3313

Veerman, Erik – b Chicago, IL, Mar 8, 1973; f Paul; m Darian Faull; w Amy Downing, Lake Osborne, FL, Apr 01; chdn Marguerite Lynn, Nathan Philip, Katherine Downing, Caleb James; WheatonCol 95, BA; RTS ATL 10, MDiv; O Feb 2015, MetAtl; astp Westminster P Ch, Atlanta, GA, 15-

3065 Four Oaks Drive, Atlanta, GA 30360   Metro Atlanta
E-mail: e.veerman@wmpca.org
Westminster Presbyterian Church – 404-636-1496

Veiga, Luis – b Havana, Cuba; w Suzanne Barber Veiga; chdn Daniel, Michael; UMiami 77, BEEn; Xavier 81, MBA; GPTS 08, MDiv; dir dev GPTS, 06-08; srp Covenant P Ch, Houston, TX, 09-

11910 Valley Vista Court, Houston, TX 77077 – 281-881-3512   Houston Metro
E-mail: pastorveiga@yahoo.com
Covenant Presbyterian Church – 281-870-0349

Veinott, Laurence – b Sydney, NS, Oct 6, 52; f Dean William; m Ann Furdas; w Margaret MacGibbon, Cornerbrook, Newfoundland, Aug 9, 75; chdn Heather, Patricia, Natalia; Dalhousie 74, BA; WTS 80, MAR; FCSC 81, dipl; L Oct 26, 82, OPC; p Lisbon OPC, Lisbon, NY, 82-04; p New Life P Ch, Canton, NY, 04-

125 Judson Street Road, Canton, NY 13617 – 315-379-0717   New York State
E-mail: larrynlpc@gmail.com
New Life Presbyterian Church – 315-379-1578

Veleber, Todd – O Nov 15, 09, GulCst Pby; astp Wildwood P Ch, Tallahassee, FL, 09-

3450 Paces Ferry Road, Tallahassee, FL 32309 – 850-228-5275   Gulf Coast
Wildwood Presbyterian Church – 850-894-1400

Venable, Adam Paul – O May 27, 15, Evan Pby; campm RUF, UAB, 15-

1529 Alford Avenue, Hoover, AL 35226   Evangel
PCA Reformed University Fellowship

Vick, Craig Ralph – b Van Nuys, CA, Feb 2, 55; f Ralph; w Kelly Patricia Carmean, Sepulveda, CA, Jun 11, 83; chdn Nathaniel, Michelle; CSUN 82-88, BA; ClGS 87-88, grad wk; L 81; O Jul 82, Pac Pby; astp Valley P Ch, North Hills, CA, 82-88; p Covenant P Ch, Issaquah, WA, 89-95; Chap Resource Cntr, Handicapped Tech Inst, Bothell, WA, 92-; astp Bellewood P Ch, Bellevue, WA, 95-16

6311 SE 2nd Street, Renton, WA 98059 – 425-868-6519   Pacific Northwest
E-mail: craig_vick@msn.com

Victa, Francisco – astp Trinity P Ch, Harrisburg, PA, 16-; astp Hershey P Ch, Hummelstown, PA, 18-

36 E. Penn, Cleona, PA 17042 – 717-769-9627   Susquehanna Valley
Trinity Presbyterian Church – 717-545-4271
Hershey Presbyterian Church – 717-489-1535

MINISTERIAL DIRECTORY

Vidal, Lauris Glen – b Gainesville, FL, Nov 3, 48; f A Pierre; m Betty Helen Watson; w Janice A Leopold, Gainesville, FL, Mar 27, 71; chdn Sarah Catherine, Lauris Glen, Jr, John-David Pierre; CBC 74; RTS 77, MDiv; O Jun 19, 77, CentGA Pby; p Faith P Ch, Gainesville, FL, 77-80; p West Hills P Ch, Harriman, TN, 80-84; op Coquina P Ch, Ormond Beach, FL, 84-85, p 85-94; ss Grace P Ch, Palm Coast, FL, 94-95; ob area dir CentFL for Christian Ldrshp Concepts, 94-98; ob dir disc Motor Racing Outreach, 98-03; ob, pres and fndr, Legacy Ministry Intl., Inc., 03-; srp Faith P Ch, Gainesville, FL, 08-13; hr 13

PO Box 328, Evinston, FL 32633 – 352-591-2001   North Florida
E-mail: gatorbball70@gmail.com
Legacy Ministry International
HR

Viehman, David – O Mar 10, 13, SusqV Pby, wc 13-15; astp Cresheim Valley Ch, Chestnut Hill, PA, 15-

79 High Gate Lane, Blue Bell, PA 19422 – 215-628-3543   Philadelphia
E-mail: d.viehman@gmail.com
Cresheim Valley Church – 215-740-3759

Viera, Michael – b Topeka, KS, Mar 9, 71; f Ruben; m Julie Acosta; w Andrew June French, New Hartford, NY, Dec 23, 95; chdn Kyla Marisol, Jacob Michael, Nathan Alexander, Joshua Christopher; USMA 93, BS; RTS 13, MDiv; O Jul 30, 16, NNE Pby, mis 13-15; mis MM&I, 16-

1386 Lincoln Gap Road, Lincoln, VT 05443   Northern New England
E-mail: mikeanj1223@hotmail.com

Vigil, Mark P. – b Denver, CO, Dec 27, 51; f Armando; m Lavinia Lucero; w Laurie Tipton, St. Louis, MO, Aug 25, 79; chdn Christopher, Andrew; WestC 71-72; CC 74, BA; CTS 79, MDiv; L Apr 78, RMt Pby; O Nov 25, 79, SE Pby (RPCES); ap Mitchell Road P Ch, Greenville, SC, 79-81; p Providence P Ch, Springfield, MO, 81-89; op Hope P Ch, Collinsville, IL, 89-92, p 93-98; ascp Memorial P Ch, St. Louis, MO, 98-02; p Westminster P Ch, Godfrey, IL, 02-04; hr 10; chmn MO pby MNA, 88-89; chmn Ill pby MNA, 94-

122 Echo Lake Circle, Eureka, MO 63025 – 636-326-9466   Illiana
E-mail: wpcgodfrey@tcip.net
HR

Villarreal, Bryan – O Feb 9, 14, SoTX Pby; astp Trinity P Ch, Boerne, TX, 14-16; astp Lakemont P Ch, Augusta, GA, 16-

1950 Bolin, North Augusta, SC 29841   Savannah River
E-mail: bryan@lakemontpca.org
Lakemont Presbyterian Church – 706-736-5011

Villasana, Alejandro – srp Oaklawn P Ch, Houston, TX, 02-06; astp Perimeter Ch, Johns Creek, GA, 06-17; op Cristos Comm Ch, Norcross, GA, 09-17, p 17-

4888 Duncan Wood Drive, Duluth, GA 30096   Metro Atlanta
E-mail: alex@christoscommunity.org
Cristos Community Church

Vining, Dale H. Jr. (Chip) – b Tampa, FL, Dec 30, 64; f Dale Hubert; m Sylvia Elizabeth Stringer; w Karen Liane Larsen, Gainesville, FL, Jul 23, 88; chdn Jonathan Taylor, Elisabeth Margaret; UFL 87, BS; RTS 91, MAMFT; O Aug 02, SoTX Pby; private practice, Marriage & Family Therapy, 90-93; t Mt. Salus Christian School, 90-93; adj fac Hinds Community College, 91-93; astp Spring Cypress P Ch, Spring, TX,

Vining, Dale H. Jr. (Chip), continued
93-05; t Spring Cypress Presbyterian Schools, 98-05; princ Spring Cypress Presbyterian Schools, 00-05; dir Spring Cypress Presbyterian Early Childhood Program, 93-05; srp Covenant P Ch, Hendersonville, NC, 05-13; mod WCar Pby, 13-14; adj prof MonC, 13-; hr 17

540 Walnut Loop Road, Hendersonville, NC 28739 – 828-699-4410   Western Carolina
E-mail: chipvining@gmail.com
HR

Vinson, Daniel Paul – O Dec 4, 16, CentCar Pby; astp Grace Comm Ch, Waxhaw, NC, 16-18, p 18–

124 Maple Grove Church Road, Matthews, NC 28104 – 704-491-4812   Central Carolina
E-mail: danielpvinson@gmail.com
Grace Community Church – 704-650-4503

Viramontes, Adam – astp Hill Country PCA Msn, Killeen, TX, 11-15; op Mosaic Ch, Albuquerque, NM, 15-

10444 Rayner Drive NW, Albuquerque, NM 87114 – 505-269-2114   Rio Grande
E-mail: adam@mosaicabq.com
Mosaic Church – 505-269-2114

Vise, Richard Martin Jr. – b Jackson, MS, Aug 28, 73; f Richard Martin Sr.; m Mary Elizabeth Brookshire; w Amy Ruth Stork, Kosciusko, MS, Jun 14, 97; chdn William Thompson, Elizabeth Ruth, Paul Brookshire; VandU 92-96, BS; CTS 98-01, MDiv, 18, DMin; O Oct 14, 01, SEAL Pby; campm RUF, AU, 01-13; srp Trinity P Ch, Tuscaloosa, AL, 13-

1628 Greystone Drive, Tuscaloosa, AL 35406   Warrior
E-mail: rvise@trinitytuscaloosa.org
Trinity Presbyterian Church – 205-391-2111

Vogel, Christopher Paul – b Lancaster, PA, Mar 19, 60; f Andrew H. III; m Suzanne Banks; w Janet Jolly, Lancaster, PA, Sept 4, 82; chdn Jennifer Suzanne, John Andrew, Michael Ryan; MBI 78-81; UDE 81-82, BA; CBS 87, MDiv; MarqU; L Jan 26, 91; O May 1, 92, NoIL Pby; op Cornerstone Ch, Waukesha, WI, 92-94, p 94-18; pal/ dir OnWisconsin Network, 17-; dir NXTGEN Pastors, 18-

2309 Melody Lane, Waukesha, WI 53186-2816 – 262-501-1161   Wisconsin

Volpitto, Perry Paul Jr. – b Augusta, GA, Apr 4, 42; f Perry P.; m Mary Elizabeth Stevens; w Barbara Elizabeth Ramsey, Ft. Lauderdale, FL, Jun 13, 69; chdn Gregory Paul, Christine Elizabeth; UGA 60-62; CC 72-74, BA; AUBS 82, MDiv; L Apr 81; O May 27, 84, NGA Pby; p Grace P Ch, Cedartown, GA, 84-85; ev PEF, (C.A.R.E.), 87-; ss ARP and PCA chs, 88-89; ss Johnston ARP Ch, SC, 87-; coord AugSBS, 92-

610 Carlton Drive, Augusta, GA 30909-3506 – 706-736-7495   Metro Atlanta
E-mail: asbs@gabn.net
Johnston ARP Church
Augusta School of Biblical Studies – 706-736-7711

Volz, Edward L. – b Los Angeles, CA, Mar 4, 44; f John L; m Aleda King; w Kathleen Alice Good, Manhattan Beach, CA, Aug 19, 67; chdn Heather Ann, Michael Edward; USCA 66, BA; WTS 69, BD; WestTS 02, MAC; L Aug 68; O Jun 70, OPC; Recd PCA 90, PacNW Pby; ap First OPC, Long Bch, CA, 69-75; GCP, Philadelphia, PA, 75-76; p Covenant OPC, Pittsb, PA, 76-79; ap Bellewood P Ch, Bellevue, WA, 90-91, wc 91-97; astp Green Lake P Ch, Seattle, WA, 97-

415 240th Street SW, Bothell, WA 98021-8619 – 425-483-8094   Pacific Northwest
E-mail: firstlightwa@msn.com
Green Lake Presbyterian Church – 425-697-0579

MINISTERIAL DIRECTORY

von Drehle, James Brewster – b Tylertown, MS, Jul 30, 49; f Harold C.; m Anna R. Belcher; w Cheryl Jeanne Matheson, Saratoga, CA, Sept 15, 73; chdn Ryan James, Alyssa Kristine; SJSU 71, BA; CTS 79, MDiv, 80, MA; L Jan 81, Midwy Pby; O Apr 81, GrLk Pby (RPCES); Chap St. Vincent Hosp, Toledo, OH, 81-85; Chap St. Jos Mrcy Hosp, Pontiac, MI, 85-00; chap St. John Oakland Hosp, Madison Heights, MI, 00-12; board cert chap, Assoc of Prof Chap; hr 12

545 Riverine Drive #205, Traverse City, MI 49684   Great Lakes
E-mail: jamesvondrehle@gmail.com
HR

Vos, David R. – b Dearborn, MI, Jan 12, 47; f Osborne R.; m Kathleen Baker; w Rachel Marie Huttar, Holland, MI, Dec 30, 78; chdn Rebecca Anne, Sarah Joy; SFSC 65-68; UCSB 69-70, BA; WestTS 75-78, MDiv; WTS 96, ThM; L May 23, 78; O Jul 19, 78, Classis of Holland, MI; Recd PCA Sept 21, 96, SusqV Pby; p Ref Dutch Ch, Prattsville, NY, 78-90; ob mis AWM/Pioneers, 96-12; hr 73

131 3rd Street #C, Aston, PA 17501 – 717-588-4070   Susquehanna Valley
E-mail: davidv4523@gmail.com
HR

Vosseller, David A. – b Plainfield, NJ, Feb 11, 69; f Eldon Richard Jr.; m Jane Ann Hedges; w Allegra Jeanne Smith, Roselle, IL, Aug 26, 06; chdn Nathan David, Matthew Jin Shan; BucknU 87-91, BA; CTS 94-98, MDiv; O Apr 25, 99, CentGA Pby; int Grace Community Ch, Bridgewater, NJ, 97; ydir St. Andrews P Ch, Midland, GA, 98, astp, yp 99-05; ascp Spring Valley P Ch, Roselle, IL, 05-12; srp Lakemont P Ch, Augusta, GA, 12-

765 Chinaberry Court, Martinez, GA 30909 – 706-945-2567   Savannah River
E-mail: davhoops@me.com
Lakemont Presbyterian Church – 706-736-5011

Vroom, Paul – b Pella, IA, Dec 20, 69; f Howard Wayne; m Cathy Sue De Nooy; w Laura Van Dyken, Orland Park, IL, Nov 24, 01; chdn Grace Anne, Isaac Allen; TCC 92, BA; TEDS, grad wk; WestTS, grad wk; O Oct 18, 11, RCA; Recd PCA Dec 18, 14, ChiMet Pby; moy Peace Comm Ch, 03-06; srp Missio Dei, New Lenox, IL, 06-

8122 West Sauk Trail, Frankfort, IL 60423 – 708-846-6133   Chicago Metro
E-mail: paul@mdchurch.us
Missio Dei – 815-717-8006

Vuksic, Andrew A. – b Pittsburgh, PA, Jul 15, 64; f Vlatko; m Radmilla Ilich; St. ThomasU 86, BA; RTS 03, MDiv; O Oct 21, 03, SFL Pby; astp Spanish River P Ch, Boca Raton, FL, 03-07; ob chp, mis Gospel on the Go Ministries, Croatia, 07-

3901 NW 6th Street, Deerfield Beach, FL 33442   Gulfstream
E-mail: vuksic@gospelonthego.net
Gospel on the Go Ministries, Croatia

Wade, Anthony R. – b Kalamazoo, MI, Sept 5, 61; f Vern L; m Carole Elaine Herr; w Elizabeth Kay Nelson, Wilmington, DE, May 28, 94; chdn Margaret A., Miriam A., Nathanael K.; GtwnU 83, BS; WTS 94, MDiv; L Dec 4, 96; O Dec 4, 96, Hrtg Pby; srp Manor Ref P Ch, New Castle, DE, 96-03; Chap USAF, Little Rock AFB, AR, 03-08; Thule AB, Greenland, 08-09; Arlington National Cemetery, VA, 09-11; Andrews AFB, MD, 11-14; Wright-Patterson AFB, OH, 14-16; Incirlik AB, Turkey, 16- 17; Travis AFB, CA, 17-18; Wright-Patterson AFB, OH, 18-

78 Bradstreet Road, Centerville, OH 45459   Heritage
E-mail: the_wade_family@msn.com
United States Air Force

Wagner, James Richard – b Lancaster, PA, Nov 4, 31; f Charles Earl; m Anna Elizabeth May; w Geneva Windsor Weston (d), Pensacola, FL; chdn Ruthann (Holt), James Richard, Jr; BelC 60, BA; WTS 64, MDiv; O Jan 65, SMS Pby (PCUS); p Waynesboro P Ch, Waynesboro, MS, 65-67; p Edwards P Ch, Edwards, MS, 67-69; lib RTS, 69-77; p, mis St. Andrews Ch, Belize City, CAm, 77-79; p Forest P Ch, Forest, MS, 79-96; State Chap American Legion, 83-90, 91-96; Nat'l Chap Amer Legion, 92-93; hr 96; ss First P Ch, Sandersville, GA, 98-10; chap Post 6 American Legion, 01-11; chap Milledgeville Police Dept, 08-12; asst to pastor, Cov P Ch, Milledgeville, GA, 12-16

300 Charter Boulevard #214, Macon, GA 31210 – 478-812-8162   Central Georgia
HR

Wagner, John Douglas – b Sentinel, OK, Sept 5, 51; f William Clarence; m Ernestine Faulkner; HCC 93, AA; Free Church College 05, BTh; O Sept 28, 05, Free Pby of Inv, Loch & Ross (FCS); astp Free North Ch, Inverness, Scotland, 05-11; Recd PCA Aug 12, MSVal Pby; p Edwards P Ch, Edwards, MS, 12-16; ip Ref P Ch, Beaumont, TX, 08-16, astp 17-18

5640 Clinton Street, Beaumont, TX 77706 – 769-234-3004   Mississippi Valley
E-mail: jdwagnerx2@aol.com

Wagner, Martin – b Tuscaloosa, AL, Mar 3, 82; f Thomas Michael; m Cindy; w Hallie Bourland; chdn Walter Russell, William Thomas, John Martin; UAL 04, BS; BDS 07, MDiv; O Aug 26, 07, Evan Pby; astp Faith P Ch, Birmingham, AL, 07-; sc Evan Pby, 16-

4601 Valleydale Road, Birmingham, AL 35242 – 205-454-0617   Evangel
E-mail: mwagner@faith-pca.org
Faith Presbyterian Church – 205-991-5430

Wagner, Robert A. – b Peoria, IL; w Michelle; chdn Jonathan, Rebekah, Justin; UTXAu 94, BS; UHou 98, MS; WTS 05, MDiv; astp Trinity P Ch, Statesboro, GA, 05-06, ascp 06-15; astp Denton P Ch, Denton, TX, 15-17, ascp 17-

2204 Woodbrook Street, Denton, TX 76205 – 912-690-4379   North Texas
E-mail: robert.wagner9@gmail.com
Denton Presbyterian Church – 940-783-7097

Wahlman, Donald – b Huntington, WV, Jul 26, 58; f Donald A.; m Virginia Mae McClure; w Mary Beth McNutt, Charleston, WV, Jun 20, 81; chdn Matthew, Martha, Benjamin, Philip, Rachel; WVU 80, BS; MarU 90, MA; RTS 95, MDiv; L 95, MSVal Pby; O Oct 25, 98, Nash Pby; astp Zion P Ch, Columbia, TN, 98-18; ob admin BrChS, 18-

3517 Cahaba Valley Road, Birmingham, AL 35242 – 931-797-0745   Evangel
E-mail: wahlmandon@gmail.com
Briarwood Christian School

Wainwright, Kevin – Chap USArmy, Ft. Campbell, KY

1713 Wolverton Drive, Ft. Campbell, KY 42223   Potomac
E-mail: wharchangel91@gmail.com
United States Army

Wakefield, Jason – w Allison; chdn Victoria, Andrew, Nicole; GroCC, BA; RegC, MDiv; O Dec 4, 05, NNE Pby; p Christ P Ch, Nashua, NH, 05-

17 Wethersfield Road, Nashua, NH 03062 – 603-888-2802   Northern New England
E-mail: jason@nashuapca.org
Christ Presbyterian Church – 603-889-3105

Wakeland, David L. – b Hattiesburg, MS, Sept 25, 54; f John Levi; m Margaret E. Street; w Melinda W. Montague, Hattiesburg, MS, Jul 14, 79; chdn Jonathan David, Joseph William, James Montague, Jess Lee; USM, BS; CTS, MDiv; L Mar 84; O Feb 2, 86, TN-AL Pby, ARP; Recd PCA Feb 23, 92, SoTX Pby; p First P Ch of Muscle Shoals, AL (ARP), 86-92; p Southwest P Ch, Bellaire, TX, 92-

5815 Braesheather Drive, Houston, TX 77096 – 713-728-8359   Houston Metro
E-mail: dlwakeland@sbcglobal.net
Southwest Presbyterian Church – 713-432-0040

Walch, Jason – b San Antonio, TX, Mar 26, 71; f Thomas F.; m Mary Frances Young; w Nina Gaynelle Mullis, Atlanta, GA, Feb 17, 96; chdn Elliot Mullis, Livingstone True; UTXAu 94, BFA; DTS, stu; CTS 99, MDiv; L Jul 30, 99, SoTX Pby; O Feb 6, 00, SoTX Pby; astp Grace P Ch, The Woodlands, TX, 99-00, wc 00-02; astp Perimeter Ch, Duluth, GA, 02-07; astp Chesterfield P Ch, Chesterfield, MO, 07-14; astp Denver P Ch, Denver, CO, 14-

2069 Uinta Street, Denver, CO 80238   Rocky Mountain
E-mail: jason@denverpres.org
Denver Presbyterian Church – 720-441-3981

Waldecker, Gary Thomas – b Minneapolis, MN, Apr 17, 54; f Thomas C.; m E. Lillian Roath (d); w Phyllis Ann Hagerty, Wilmington, DE, Jun 14, 81; chdn Micah Joel, Seth Jason, Andrea Megan, Audrey Apryl; CC 76, BA; CTS 80, MDiv; WTS 97, DMin; GWU 10, EdD; L 80; O 80, Ill Pby (RPCES); mis MTW, Latin America, 80-16

92 Tucker Branch Road, Rising Fawn, GA 30738 – 706-406-4279   Illiana
E-mail: gary@waldecker.net

Waldo, Mark – O Jan 29, 17, BlRdg Pby, Chap 17-

1014 Blenheim Avenue, Charlottesville, VA 22902   Blue Ridge

Waldron, Shane – astp Rocky Mountain Comm Ch, Billings, MT, 11-12; ascp Faith Cov P Ch, Kalispell, MT, 12- 17; p Rocky Mountain P Ch, Westminster, CO, 17-

12247 Cook Court, Thornton, CO 80241 – 720-697-8881   Rocky Mountain
E-mail: shane.waldron99@rmpca.org
Rocky Mountain Presbyterian Church – 303-404-3200

Walicord, Sacha – b Linz, Austria, Mar 19, 71; f Ali; m Margit Strasser; w Martina, Neuhofen, Austria; chdn David, Hannah, Stefan, Michael, Jacob, Sarah; ULinz 92, BA, 99, LLB, 03, PhD; GPTS 08, MA; O Mar 22, 09, GrLks Pby; prof Austria, 01-08; prof Mt. Vernon Nazarene Univ, 08-; srp Christ Cov Ref (PCA), Reynoldsburg, OH, 09-10, p Knox OPC, Mt. Vernon, OH, 11-14; p Grace Ref P Ch PCA, Orange City, IA, 17-; "Staat und Kirche in Oesterreich" *Reformatorischer Verlag Beese*, 05; "Gott oder Pharao" *Reformationsbund*, 16

107 4th Avenue NE, Sioux Center, IA 51250 – 712-578-2023   Iowa
E-mail: Reformation@Bulloch.net
Grace Reformed Presbyterian Church PCA – 712-395-0983

Walker, Bryan James – Chap USArmy, 09-

12840 Beaver Dam Road, Des Peres, MO 63131 – 314-882-0633   Missouri
United States Army

Walker, Chad – CTS 17, MDiv; O Aug 14, 18, Evan Pby; astp Oak Mtn Ch, Birmingham, AL, 18-

256-856-2630   Evangel
E-mail: chad@ompc.org
Oak Mountain Church – 205-995-9265

Walker, Christopher – b Kettering, OH, Oct 14, 84; f Robert; m Carol; w Kathryn; chdn Alana Grace, Andrew Earl, Annette Leigh, Kristiana Beth; HDC 06, BA; WTS 08, MAR; O Oct 13, SusqV Pby; astp, yp Westminster P Ch, Lancaster, PA, 13-15, ascp 15-

279 Robin Dale Drive, Leola, PA 17540   Susquehanna Valley
E-mail: walker@westpca.com
Westminster Presbyterian Church – 717-569-2151

Walker, Douglas – astp Willow Creek Ch, Winter Springs, FL, 02-05; wc 05-

Address Unavailable   Central Florida

Walker, Nate – op Christ Ch Bellingham, Bellingham, WA, 09-13; p 13-

4205 Springland Lane, Bellingham, WA 98226-6864 – 425-533-4340   Pacific Northwest
E-mail: nateswalker@gmail.com
Christ Church Bellingham – 425-533-4340

Walker, Paul Cameron – b Toronto, Ont, Can, Aug 29, 39; f James Coutts; m Elizabeth Grieves Robson; w Bernace Ruth Nute, Orangeville, Ont, Aug 18, 62; chdn Ruth, Cameron, Margaret, Sarah; UTor 61, BA; WTS 66, MDiv; L Jun 19, 66; O Jun 19, 66, ETor Pby (PCC); p P Ch, Chambly, Quebec, Can, 66-68; p St.Paul's P Ch, Glace Bay, NS, Can, 68-72; p Fairview P Ch, Vancouver, BC, Can, 73-77; t CS, Vancouver, 77-80; spec, Can Assoc for Pastoral Ed; Chap Chilliwack Gen Hosp, 81-94; Chap Royal Columbian Hospital, 94-04; astp Faith P Ch, Vancouver, BC, 95-02; sc WCan Pby 09-15; hr 15; co-auth *Savior and King, and All that Jesus Began to Say and Teach*

3683 Borham Crescent, Vancouver, BC V5S 3X2 CANADA – 604-438-1151   Western Canada
E-mail: pbwalker65@shaw.ca
HR

Walkup, Clay – O Nov 21, 10, PTri Pby; ascp New Hope P Ch, Clemmons, NC, 10-12; astp Grace Flwsp P Ch, Albertville, AL, 12-14; astp Chattanooga Valley P Ch, Flintstone, GA, 14-17

105 Claire Street, Rossville, GA 30741   Tennessee Valley
E-mail: claywalkup@gmail.com

Walkup, James Robert – b Greenwood, SC, Feb 8, 25; f John Belk Sr.; m Lucy Miller Keister; w Martha Elizabeth McKemie, Clay County, GA, Aug 14, 54; chdn John Mark, David James, Mary Elizabeth; UFL 52, BS; ColTS 57, MDiv; L Jul 57; O Jul 57, Suw Pby (PCUS); Recd PCA Nov 83, CentFL Pby; p First Ch, Live Oak, FL, 57-82; p Comm P Ch, Live Oak, FL, 82-93, p em 93-; hr 93; ss Comm P Ch, McIntosh, FL, 95-06

PO Box 648, McIntosh, FL 32664-0648 – 352-591-1512   North Florida
HR

Wallace, Kenneth I. – w Evelyn; chdn Ruth (Matthews), Paul, Peter, Lois (d); WTS 65, MDiv; L 65; O 66, Phil Pby; t PBI, 60-61; t Philmont CHS, 68-70; fndr, prin PACS, 71-79; p Calvary Ref P Ch, Media, PA, 79-82; staff Comm to Reach Muslims in Phil, PA, 83-; ip Third Ref P Ch, Philadelphia, PA, 89-90, wc 90-00; hr 00

1330 Grovania Avenue, Abington, PA 19001-2511 – 215-887-8072   Philadelphia
HR

Wallace, Mark Stephen – b Atlanta, GA, Oct 10, 51; f Matthew Mark; m Willene Hayes; w Deborah Elizabeth DeYoung, Tuscumbia, AL, Sept 9, 78; chdn Mary Eleanor, Stephen Corson; MerU 73, BA; RTS 78, MDiv; O Aug 13, 78, Gr Pby; p Philadelphus P Ch, Waynesboro, MS, 78-80; p First P Ch, Madison, MS, 80-87; ascp Second P Ch, Greenville, SC, 87-92; srp Christ P Ch, Mobile, AL, 92-00; ob t Covenant

MINISTERIAL DIRECTORY

Wallace, Mark Stephen, continued
CS, Tuscumbia, AL, 00-01; ss First P Ch, Russellville, AL, 01-02; ss Redeemer P Ch, Florence, AL, 02-03; astp, exec p First P Ch, Chattanooga, TN, 03-08; ob COO RTS 08-11; COO/COS RTS 11-13; Acting CEO RTS 13; COO RTS 13-15; Exec Dir RTS Global Ed, & Dir RTS NYC, 15-16; Exec Dir RTS NYC, 16-18; ast brd sec RTS, 08-18

2645 Lori Lane, Charlotte, NC 28226 – 423-240-5488   Tennessee Valley
E-mail: swallace@rts.edu; mstevewallace@gmail.com

Wallace, Peter J. – b Sunnyvale, CA, Aug 29, 70; f William; m Lorna Loram; w Virginia Shank, Augusta Co, VA, Aug 1, 98; chdn Lena, Robert, William, Fiona, Lorna, Peter, Geneva; WheatC 93, BA; WTS 96, MDiv; UNotD 04, PhD; O Apr 26, 97, OPC; Recd PCA Apr 30, 16, GrLks Pby; p Grace Ref, Walkerton, IN, 97-98; ss Michiana Cov Ch, Granger, IN, 01-16, srp 16-

52775 Arbor Drive, South Bend, IN 46635   Great Lakes
Michiana Covenant Church – 574-273-5906

Wallace, Seth – b Douglasville, GA, Feb 24, 74; w Leslie Rundles, Gainesville, GA, Dec 12, 98; chdn Micah, AnnaGrace, Esther; ClaySU 00, BA; BhamTS 07, MA; O May 4, 14, GAFH Pby; fm MTW, 14-18; p Christ the King P Ch, Vero Beach, FL, 18-

5865 39th Lane, Vero Beach, FL 32966 – 678-943-0912   Central Florida
E-mail: jsethwallace@gmail.com
Christ the King Presbyterian Church – 772-978-5848

Waller, Bryce – b Houston, TX, May 28, 80; f Michael Rex; m Diane Uthlaut; w Lisa Madrid, Aug 12, 06; chdn Liam Christopher, Michael Ryan, Emma Grey; UTXAu 02, BA; WSCAL 08, MDiv; O May 24, 09, RMtn Pby; astp Rocky Mountain Comm Ch, Billings, MT, 09-10; astp Fort Worth P Ch, Fort Worth, TX, 10; op Christ P Ch, Mansfield, TX, 10-14; dir RedTS, 14-16; astp Redeemer P Ch, Austin, TX, 17-; *Come to Worship, Anchor Devotional* Vol 35, No. 10; *Images of Christ, Anchor Devotional*, Vol. 37, No. 11

8800 Golden Rain Cove, Austin, TX 78735 – 512-590-2206   South Texas
E-mail: bwaller@redeemerpres.org
Redeemer Presbyterian Church – 512-708-1232

Waller, Jack Henry – b Pensacola, FL, Jul 12, 52; f Clyde; m M Virginia Whitlock; w Christina Cooley, Jun 18, 77; chdn Jacob Whitlock, Rachel Grace, Caleb Daniel, Abigail Joy; UWFL 80, BA; RTS 80-83, MDiv; L May 14, 82, Gr Pby; O Jun 26, 83, GulCst Pby; op, p Northeast P Ch, Pensacola, FL, 83-85, p 85-92; p Good Hope P Ch, Fulton, MD, 92-

15009 Timberlake Drive, Silver Spring, MD 20905-4331 – 301-384-5772   Potomac
E-mail: jwaller6@comcast.net
Good Hope Presbyterian Church – 301-236-4151

Wallover, David Beatty – b Beaver Falls, PA, Jul 25, 58; f James Irwin; m Marjean Wilson; w Lisa Jo Nuss, Brooklyn, NY, May 19, 84; chdn James Irwin II, Robert Lockard, Katherine Anne; WJC 76-77; WFU 77-80, BA; GCTS 80-83, MDiv; RTS 98, DMin; O Jan 6, 85, PCUSA; Recd PCA Mar 93, Phil Pby; Petersburg PCUSA, 84-93; op Hope Ch, Moosic, PA, 93-96, cop 96-00, wc 00; p Harvest Ch of Medina, Medina, OH, 00-; *The Majesty of Christ Study Guide*; *A Shattered Image: Facing Our Human Condition Study Guide*

158 Essex Lane, Medina, OH 44256 – 330-721-1467   Ohio
E-mail: david.wallover@harvestpca.com
Harvest Church of Medina – 330-723-0770

Walter, Eric – b Wiesbaden, Germany, Nov 12, 66; f Eugene LeRoy, Jr. (d); m Dawn Uglum; w Frances M., Jun 10, 95; chdn Edward Leighton, Ethan Lawrence, Allison Grace, Olivia Caitlin; LibU 88, BS; RTSNC 05, MDiv; O Oct 22, 09, Palm Pby; astp Hilton Head P Ch, Hilton Head Island, SC, 09-12; astp Northeast P Ch, Columbia, SC, 12-

512 Great North Road, Columbia, SC 29223 – 803-629-2313 Palmetto
E-mail: reformedhoss@gmail.com
Northeast Presbyterian Church – 803-788-5298

Waltermyer, Donald Franklin Jr. – b York, PA, Aug 10, 56; f Donald; m Betty Martin; w Patricia Burris, West Chester, PA, May 28, 77; chdn David Andrew, Joel Timothy, LeahElizabeth; WChSC 78, BS; WTS 81, MAR, 83, MDiv; L 83, SFL Pby; O Jan 84, Phil Pby; op Providence P Ch, York, PA, 84-86, p 86-94; astp Faith P Ch, Wilmington, DE, 94-97; chp, op Redeemer P Msn, Morristown, TN, 97-00, wc 00-01; PRes Chattanooga Valley P Ch, Flintstone, GA, 01, astp 01-02; p Washington P Ch, Washington, PA, 02-

429 Burton Avenue, Washington, PA 15301 – 724-809-9298 Pittsburgh
E-mail: thewaltermyers@gmail.com
Washington Presbyterian Church – 724-228-4776

Walters, Michael – w Rachel, Jul 8, 06; chdn Thomas, Jonathan; O Nov 7, 04, Palm Pby; astp Church Creek Ref P Ch, Charleston, SC, 04-07; p Faith P Ch, Florence, SC, 07-13; wc 13-16; astp Church Creek P Ch, Charleston, SC, 16-

210 Factors Walk, Summerville, SC 29485 – 843-209-3659 Lowcountry
E-mail: mwalters@jonesford.com
Church Creek Presbyterian Church – 843-766-1381

Walton, Charles P. – Bethesda, MD, Dec 12, 59; f John; m Harriet; w Erin Marie McKenna, Malvern, PA, Feb 2, 91; chdn Abigail, John, Daniel, Peter; TempU 84, BArch; CIU 89, MDiv; O Jun 16, 97, SusqV Pby; Bucks Central Ch, 89-95; ap Westminster P Ch, Lancaster, PA, 95, ascp 98-00; p Wright CRC, Kanawha, IA, 00-09; p Grace P Ch, Pardeeville, WI, 09-

W6144 Haynes Road, Pardeeville, WI 53954 – 608-745-8255 Wisconsin
E-mail: pastorchuck@gracepresinfo.com
Grace Presbyterian Church – 608-429-9086

Walton, Steven – b Jun 9, 67; f Kent; m Alda; w Hilary Smyth, Dec 30, 94; chdn Samuel Kent, John Branch; UHou 89, BMus; Julliard 92, MMus; GPTS 12, MDiv; O Aug 21, 12, SEAL Pby; op Covenant Flwsp Ch, 12-; chap USAR, 12-

CMR Box 1256, APO, AE 09128 – 864-214-3784 Southeast Alabama
E-mail: walton.steven.k@gmail.com
Covenant Fellowship Church – 011-49-176-8418-5896
United States Army Reserve

Wanaselja, Larry Wayne – b North Canton, OH, Jul 20, 49; f Oley; m Lulu May Embree; w Phyllis Adelle Wann, Baltimore, MD, Oct 23, 71; chdn Rachel Lynn, Timothy Isak, Amy Joy, Benjamin David; Kg'sC 71, BS; RTS 78, MDiv; L Oct 78; O Nov 79, DMV Pby (RPCES); op New Cov P Ch, Abingdon, MD, 79-82,p 82-99, wc 99-02; ss New Cov P Ch, Rehoboth, DE, 02-03, p 03-10; wc 10-16; ss Shore Harvest P Ch, Easton, MD, 16-18; astp Eastgate P Ch, Millsboro, DE, 18-

209 Heronwood Lane, Milton, DE 19968 – 302-381-4981 Heritage
E-mail: larrywana@gmail.com
Eastgate Presbyterian Church – 302-945-5498

Wang, Frank Yu-Chieh – b Morgantown, WV, Apr 21, 16; w Sarah Marie Booth, Dec 21, 13; chdn Nathaniel; PU 08, BA; RTSDC 16, MDiv; O Sept 24, 17, Pot Pby; astp Potomac Hills P Ch, Leesburg, VA, 17-

1089 Smartts Lane NE, Leesburg, VA 20176   Potomac
E-mail: fwang@potomachills.org
Potomac Hills Presbyterian Church – 703-771-1534

Wang, Peter – w Cedar; chdn Matthew, Kaylyn, Mitchell; UPA 94, BS, 94, BA; RTS 02, MDiv; O Nov 2, 02, Hrtg Pby; astp Faith P Ch, Wilmington, DE, 02-04; op Grace Redeemer Ch, Teaneck, NJ, 04-06, p 06-

21 Harristown Road, Glen Rock, NJ 07452   Metropolitan New York
E-mail: peter@graceredeemer.com
Grace Redeemer Church – 201-357-4216

Wang, Zhiyong Paul – p Grace Christian Ch, Herndon, VA, 10-

13712 Frankford Circle, Centreville, VA 20120 – 703-437-8430   Potomac
E-mail: onelaw1@yahoo.com
Grace Christian Church – 703-471-4046

Ward, Donald Henry Jr. – b Hampton,VA, Oct 14, 59; f D.H. Sr.; m Ada Lee Mitchell; w Caron Lisa Scharp, Towson, MD, Jun 4, 83; chdn Emily Elizabeth (Masengill), Anna Catherine; JMU 81, BBA; RTS 85, MDiv; RTSFL 03, DMin; L Oct 83, MSVal Pby; O Aug 85, NGA Pby; ap Midway P Ch, Powder Springs, GA, 85-88; op South Dayton P Ch, Centerville, OH, 88-91, p 91-97; astp, ev Trinity P Ch, Charlottesville, VA, 97-00; ev, op Grace Comm Ch, Charlottesville, VA, 97-00, p 01-

5146 Dickerson Road, Charlottesville, VA 22911 – 434-978-4371   Blue Ridge
E-mail: dward@cvillegrace.org
Grace Community Church – 434-975-2259

Ward, Gregory Allen – ascp Three Rivers P Ch, Covington, LA, 03-06; astp Redeemer P Ch, Austin, TX, 13-14; ascp 14-17; p Emmanuel P Ch, Cedar Park, TX, 17-

2401 Granite Creek Drive, Austin, TX 78641   South Texas
E-mail: gward@emmanuelcedarpark.church
Emmanuel Presbyterian Church – 512-690-2577

Ward, Herbert D. Jr. – b St. Louis, MO, Mar 4, 54; f Herbert D Sr.; m Margaret Rose Lauck; w Kathleen Decker, Midland, Jul 17, 76; chdn Laura Elizabeth, Herbert David III; WheatC 75, BA; UMO 79, JD; CTS 90, MDiv, 91, ThM; UStel 09, DTh; L Oct 89; O Oct 13, 91, MO Pby; int Covenant P Ch of St. Louis, St. Louis, MO, 89-90; DCE Twin Oaks P Ch, Ballwin, MO, 90-91; mis MTW, Tanzania, EAfr, 92-95; mis MTW, Kenya, 96; mis MTW, Soth Africa, 97-01; astp Twin Oaks P Ch, Ballwin, MO, 01-02, ascp 02-05; assoc prof Bib Stud CC, 05-10; prof Bib Stud CC, 10-

685 Hidden Oaks Drive, Flintstone, GA 30725 – 706-820-8267   Missouri
E-mail: hward@covenant.edu
Covenant College – 706-820-1560

Ward, Lewis Albert Jr. – b Bethesda, MD, Feb 1, 69; w Allison Ponder, Fairhope, AL, Apr 30, 94; chdn Jeremy Lewis, Joseph Albert, Samuel Reade, Sarah Anne; AU 92; RTS 06, MDiv; int Providence P Ch, Clinton, MS, 02-07, astp 07-09; p Zion P Ch, Chester, SC, 09-

2459 Old York Road, Clinton, SC 29706 – 803-385-6667   Fellowship
E-mail: aandaward@yahoo.com
Zion Presbyterian Church – 803-581-6071

Ware, Brister Hagaman – b Jackson, MS, Oct 4, 36; f Marvin Brister W; m Anna Rosina Hagaman; w Marian Elizabeth Clarke, Johnson City, TN, Jul 8, 60; chdn Clarke Brister, Evelyn Elizabeth; MillsC 54-56; BelC 56-58, BA; USM 65-67; ColTS 58-61, BD, 72, MDiv; L Jul 30, 61; O Jul 30, 61, CMS Pby, PCUS; p First P Ch, Philadelphia, MS, 61-64; p Carolina P Ch, Philadelphia, MS, 61-64; p USM, 64-67; p Lookout Valley P Ch, Chattanooga, TN, 67-69; p North Park P Ch, Jackson, MS, 70-83; astp First P Ch, Jackson, MS, 83-

48 Westridge Drive, Brandon, MS 39047-9022 – 601-992-6669   Mississippi Valley
E-mail: brister@fpcjackson.org
First Presbyterian Church – 601-353-8316

Warhurst, Steven Edward – w Susan; chdn Jordan, Mackenzie, Audra, Alden, Lindsay, Kara, Owen, Knox; RTSFL 92, MA; O Mar 31, 02, NR Pby; astp Providence Ref P Ch, Barboursville, WV, 02; astp Westminster P Ch, Kingsport, TN, 02-04, ascp 04-

1748 Harmony Road, Jonesborough, TN 37659 – 423-390-9070   Westminster
E-mail: reforming@yahoo.com
Westminster Presbyterian Church – 423-247-7341

Warmath, Thomas – wc

555 East Roosevelt Avenue, Salt Lake City, UT 84105   North Texas

Warner, Drue – O Oct 26, 17, MetAtl Pby; astp Perimeter Ch, Johns Creek, GA, 17-

E-mail: druew@perimeter.org   Metro Atlanta
Perimeter Church – 678-405-2000

Warren, Douglas D. – b Winter Park, FL, Jul 1, 68; f Harry Joe; m Sue Ellen Donnelly; w Kristen Anne Houltberg, Orlando, FL, Jun 17, 95; chdn D. Donnelly, Karis A., Elisabeth G., Colby R.; JMU 90, BS; RTS 97, MDiv; L Oct 25, 97, NoTX Pby; L Oct 31, 98, SoTX Pby; O May 16, 99, SoTX Pby; ob campm CCC, Houston, TX, 99-00; chp, op Christ the Redeemer Ch, Portland, ME, 00-05, p 05-13; astp Bay P Ch, Bonita Springs, FL, 13-17; op Gulf Coast P Msn, Estero, FL, 15-17; ob p Woodstock, VT, 18-

41 Elm Street, Woodstock, VT 05091   Northern New England

Warren, James Paul – b Ft Worth, TX, Jun 21, 61; f John Arch; m Shirley Joyce Carpenter; w Phyllis E. Moore, Lookout Mtn, GA, Jul 29, 89; chdn Stephen Arnold, John Arch II, Zoë Grace (Harrison), William Carpenter, David Shepherd, Glory Joy; CC, BA; RTSFL 95, MDiv; L Jul 16, 95; O Jul 16, 95, NGA Pby; astp Parkview Ch, Lilburn, GA, 95-97; p Abbott Mem P Ch, Baltimore, MD, 97-

3426 Bank Street, Baltimore, MD 21224-2301 – 410-534-6246   Chesapeake
E-mail: polowarren@gmail.com
Abbott Memorial Presbyterian Church – 410-276-6207

Warren, John Arch – b Paris, TX, Dec 2, 33; f John D; m Mamie Jewel Smith; w Shirley Joyce Carpenter, Dallas, TX, May 3, 52; chdn Brenda (Ferrell), J Andrew, J Paul, Rebecca Ruth (Carter), David Beau, Barbara Ann (Vreeland), Rose Carol (Prater); ACU 54, BS; TCU 58-60; L Jan 88; O May 88, TNVal Pby; Ch of Christ, Three Rvrs, TX, 54-56; Ch of Christ, Longview, WA, 56-57; p Sweetwater Valley P Ch, Sweetwater, TN, 88-91; p Zion P Ch, Columbia, TN, 91-09; p em 10; astp Covenant P Ch, Nashville, TN, 14-16

435 Eddy Lane, Franklin, TN 37064   Nashville
E-mail: Jarchw@gmail.com

Warren, John McKnight Jr. – b Miami, FL, Nov 12, 46; f John McKnight Sr.; m Lillian Charlotte Havlicek; w Mary Beth Owens, Purvis, MS, Jun 12, 69; chdn Mary Lydia (Roberts), John Howard (d), David Wesley; BelC 68, BA; USM 72, MEd; RTS 80, MDiv; O Feb 81, Ashv Pby (PCUS); stus Ruth Mem

MINISTERIAL DIRECTORY

Warren, John McKnight Jr., continued
P Ch, Poplarville, MS, 78-80; ast to p, Clover P Ch, Clover, SC, 78; p First P Ch, Weaverville, NC, 81-87; p Calvary P Ch, Raleigh, NC, 87-93; p Faith P Ch, Mooresville, NC, 94-98; t Mooresville Middle sc, 95-98; p Grace P Ch, Aiken, SC, 98-04; p First P Ch, Eutaw, AL, 04-13; p Boligee P Ch, Boligee, AL, 06-13; hr 13; astp New Life Comm Ch, Fayetteville, NC, 14; Award: *The American Christian Leadership Council of Atlanta Georgia - Who's Who in American Christian Leadership*, 89

3028 Brookcrossing Drive, Fayetteville, NC 28306 – 910-551-0846, 205-496-0994   Warrior
E-mail: johnmwarrenjr@att.net
HR

Watanabe, Gary I. – b Okinawa, Japan, 54; w Lois C. , Columbia, SC, 81; chdn Rachel, Amanda, Mark; CBC 76-80, BA; WTS 83-86, MAR, 83-86, MDiv; L Sept 85; O Nov 85, Pac Pby; mis MTW, Mexico, 86-01; mis MTW, Philippines, 01-06; mis MTW, NYC, 06-; City to City Asia Pacific, Nagoya, Japan, 15-

c/o Mission to the World   South Coast
E-mail: giw_296@gmail.com
PCA Mission to the World – 678-823-0004
City to City Asia Pacific

Waters, Brian – b Roanoke, VA, Jna 18, 74; w Danielle, Harrisonburg, VA; chdn Jack, Kayla, Samuel, Lucy; JMU 96, BS; RTSNC 08, MDiv; O Nov 08, BlRdg Pby; ascp Grace Cov P Ch, Blacksburg, VA, 08-15; op Providence P Ch, Christiansburg, VA, 12-15; p 15-

85 Massie Drive, Christiansburg, VA 24073 – 540-382-3207   Blue Ridge
E-mail: brian@providencechristiansburg.org
Providence Presbyterian Church – 540-250-2925

Waters, Guy Prentiss – b Washington, DC, Jan 20, 75; f Elzberry; m Karen Louise Volland; w Sarah Anne Vasaly, Philadelphia, PA, May 31, 97; chdn Phoebe Louise, Lydia Anne, Thomas Edward Elzberry; UPA 95, BA; WTS 98, MDiv; DukeU 02, PhD; L Apr 17, 99, Ecar Pby; O May 18, 03, MSVal Pby; asst prof BelC, 02-07; adj prof BelC, 07-; assoc prof RTS, 07-12; James M. Bair Prof of NT, 12-; *Justification and the New Perspectives on Paul: A Review and Response*, 04; *The Federal Vision and Covenant Theology*, 06; *The End of Deuteronomy in the Epistles of Paul*, 06; co-ed (with Gary L.W. Johnson), *By Faith Alone: Answering the Challenges to the Doctrine of Justification*, 07; *A Christian's Pocket Guide to Justification: Being Made Right With God?* 10; *How Jesus Runs the Church*, 11; co ed *Children and the Lord's Supper*, 11; *What is the Bible?* 13; *The Acts of the Apostles*, 15; *The Life and Theology of Paul*, 18; *The Lord's Supper as the Sign and Meal of the New Covenant*

308 Westwood Court, Madison, MS 39110 – 601-853-1915   Mississippi Valley
E-mail: gwaters@rts.edu
Belhaven University
Reformed Theological Seminary – 601-923-1697

Watkins, Chad – b Austell, GA, Aug 31, 79; f Mike; m Judy; w Michelle Ivette; chdn Esther Ivette, Isabelle Anne, Molly Grace; BerryC 01, BMus; RTSA 11, MDiv; L Sept 12, 09, NWGA Pby; L May 25, 10, Cov Pby; O Mar 25, 11, Cov Pby; astp Main Street P Ch, Columbus, MS, 10-14; astp Arden P Ch, Arden, NC, 14-17; srp Westminster P Ch, Ft. Walton Beach, FL, 18-

1020 Pineview Boulevard, Ft. Walton Beach, FL 32547 – 828-702-1562   Gulf Coast
E-mail: michaelchadwatkins@icloud.com
Westminster Presbyterian Church – 850-862-8825

Watkins, JB – b Ft. Leonardwood, MO, Oct 20, 79; f Victor W. (d); m Angelika Anita; w Stephanie Lynette, Memphis, TN, Jan 14, 06; chdn Bryant Michael, Sydney Victoria, Langston Len; TNWeslyan 03, BS; RTS 07, MDiv; op St. Roch Comm Ch, New Orleans, LA, 07-13; p 13-

1738 St Roch Avenue, New Orleans, LA 70117 – 504-460-0655   Southern Louisiana
E-mail: jb@strochcc.org
St. Roch Community Church – 504-906-2469

Watlington, Alex – b Lookout Mountain, GA, Dec 15, 79; w Rebecca Stewart Ballard, Aug 24, 02; chdn Alexander Whitfield, Miles Manning, William Monroe; GASoU 02, BBA; WTS 08, MDiv; campm RUF, PennSt, 08-14; campm RUF, SoCal, 14-

3047 Stoneley Drive, San Marino, CA 91107 – 814-441-5090   Pacific
E-mail: awatlington@ruf.org
PCA Reformed University Fellowship

Watson, Emory Olin Jr. – b Conway, SC, Mar 17, 46; f Emory O. Sr.; m Patricia S. Scoggin; w Frankie Anne Rhodes, N. Charleston, SC, Jun 8, 69; chdn Frances Patricia (Parsons), Bryan David, Grace Elizabeth; Citadel 68, BA; CBS 79, MDiv; O May 82, FIE; p Augusta St Ch, Columbia, SC, 82-86; astp St. Andrews P Ch, Columbia, SC, 86-92; p First P Ch, Greenville, AL, 92-00; astp St. Andrews P Ch, Columbia, SC, 00-06; hr

117 Schooner Lane, Columbia, SC 29212 – 803-407-3003   Palmetto
E-mail: eowatsonjr@yahoo.com
HR

Watson, James Benjamin – b Monroeville, AL, Aug 20, 45; f Emeris Carlton; m Margaret Simmons; w Mary Nell Black, Beatrice, AL, Aug 6, 83; chdn James Carlton, Mary Margaret; UAL 67, BA, 70, JD; RTS 86, MDiv; L Aug 12, 86; O Jun 7, 87, Gr Pby; p Leakesville P Ch, Leakesville, MS, 87-93; p Linden P Ch, Linden, AL, 93-97; p First P Ch, Ellerbe, NC, 97-12; hr 12; ss Covenant P Ch, Rockingham, NC, 14-

4133 Seven Lakes West, West End, NC 27376 – 910-400-5441   Central Carolina
E-mail: jbwatson45@gmail.com
HR

Watson, James Edward – b Dade City, FL, Mar 24, 44; f Leslie; m Tommie O'Steen; w Linda Fain, Jun 23, 67; chdn Ashleigh Lauren, James Edward Jr., Jonathan David, Jeremy Matthew; KgC 62-66, BA; ColTS 67-70, MDiv; O Jul 70, Knoxv Pby (PCUS); p Chattanooga Valley P Ch, Flintstone, GA, 70-75; ap Cedar Springs P Ch, Knoxville, TN, 75-80; p Westminster P Ch, Tallahassee, FL, 80-86; p Cornerstone P Ch, Tallahassee, FL, 86-18; hr 18

3784 Sally Lane, Tallahassee, FL 32312-1015 – 850-668-2178   Gulf Coast
HR

Watson, James Edward – b Madison, IN, Nov 9, 47; f F Edward; m Margaret K Webb; w Lynn Beth Kneisley, Mt Nebo, PA, Aug 28, 70; chdn Jennifer Lynn, Susan Margaret; AsbC 65-69, BA; ColTS 69-72, MDiv; RegC 73-74, 79 MCS; FAU 80, MEd; OHSU 83, PhD; O Jul 2, 72, PCUS; p New Dublin Ch, Dublin, VA, 72-73; ap Coral Ridge P Ch, Ft. Lauderdale, FL, 74-81; ob asst, supt Grace Brethren Chr Schs, Worthington, OH, 83-85; ob headm Wheaton Ch HS, Wheaton, IL, 85-89; ob assoc prof AsbC, Wilmore, KY, 89-93; ob ap Comm Ch of Greenwood, IN (non-PCA), 93-98; ob admin Christian Acad of Greenwood, 98-00; ob prof CIU, 00-; "Integrating a Biblical Worldview into Bible College Teacher Education Programs," *Christian Higher Education*, Jan (08); co-auth "Preparing Tomorrow's Classroom Leaders: Challenges for Christian Higher Education," *Christian Perspectives in Education* (07); "The Inclusion of Intentional Ethos Enablers in Electronic Distance Learning Opportunities of Christian Institutions," *The American Journal of Distance Education*, Dec (08)

826 Tara Trail, Columbia, SC 29210 – 803-750-9790   Palmetto
E-mail: dockwatt@gmail.com
Columbia International University – 803-807-5320

Watson, JonPaul Dee – w Carrie Ann Stallings; chdn Lucy Ann, Judah Dee, Luke Claud, Jane Murphy; O May 11, 14, Ecar Pby; astp Christ P Ch, Winterville, NC, 14-16, ascp 16-

417 Crestline Boulevard, Greenville, NC 27834-6819 – 252-565-6964   Eastern Carolina
E-mail: jpwatsoncpc@gmail.com
Christ Presbyterian Church – 252-355-9632

MINISTERIAL DIRECTORY

Watson, Loren Vaught – b Chattanooga, TN, Aug 20, 24; f Karl Brantley W; m Lena Seagle; w Mary Lois Dixon, Muncie (d), IN, Oct 30, 43; chdn Judith Kay (Bowers), David Randolph, James Stephen; UChat 42, 46-48, BBA; ColTS 59, MDiv; L Jul 26, 59; O Jul 26, 59, PCUS; p First Ch, Appalachia, VA, 59-64; ap McIlwain Mem P Ch, Pensacola, FL, 64-68; p John Calvin Ch, Greenville, SC, 68-73; p Fulton P Ch, Greer, SC, 73-81, wc 81; p McCutchen Mem P Ch, Union, SC, 82-85; RBI, 86-89, ob 89-94; hr 94

3546 Valley High Lane, Chattanooga, TN 37415-3918 – 423-877-4657   Tennessee Valley
E-mail: watsonchatt@juno.com
HR

Watson, Thom – O 17, Wcar Pby; astp Grace Blue Ridge, Hendersonville, NC, 17-18

4941 Howard Gap Road, Flat Rock, NC 28731   Western Carolina

Watson, Richard G. – b Roanoke, VA, Jan 23, 30; f Haile Otto; m Epsie Baldwin; w Jeanette Lovell, Pensacola, FL, Aug 7, 54; chdn Suzanne Elaine, Patricia Annette, Alexis Caren; HSC 47-51, BS; ColTS 54-57, MDiv; USF 76-77, MA; USM 78-82, PhD; L Jun 57; O Jun 57, Fl Pby; p First Ch, Crestview, FL, 57-61; p Seminole P Ch, Tampa, FL, 61-77; prof RTS, 77-95, AcadDn 82-94; ob p West Union Ch, Louisville, MS, 85-00; VP RTS, 88-95; exec dir Ukraine Partnership, 95-01; Dir Ukraine Theo Sem, 95-; p King's Bay P Ch, Panama City Beach, FL, 00-03; ip First P Ch, Panama City, FL, 03-04, p 04-14; *God Made Me Laugh*, 74

7215 Resota Lane, Panama City, FL 32409 – 850-271-4609   Gulf Coast

Wattley, Daryl – O Hrtg Pby; campm RUF, DEStU, 16-

1415 S Farmview Drive, Dover, DE 19904   Heritage
E-mail: daryl.wattley@ruf.org
PCA Reformed University Fellowship

Watts, Robert Raymond – b Greenville, AL, Jan 3, 48; f Robert M W; m Emily Roberts; w Betty Wilson, Shreveport, LA, Oct 26, 74; chdn Joy Wentworth, Hayley McCormack; MarI 68, AA; BelC 70, BS; RTS 74, MDiv; FulTS 75; O Jul 5, 74, Evan Pby; mis Taejonk Korea, 74-78, HMA 78-80; p St. Andrews Ch, Belize City, Belize, CentAmer, 80-90, HMA 90-91; ss Sandy Ridge P Ch, Fort Deposit, AL, 92-18

942 Sherling Lake Road, Greenville, AL 36037 – 334-382-6568   Southeast Alabama
E-mail: rwatts004@centurytel.net

Weathers, Mark – b Homestead, FL, Dec 30, 69; f Dr. William T.; m Nancy A. Walker; w Tara M. Byler, St. Louis, MO, Oct 31, 98; chdn Walker, Liam, Stephen; CC 92, BA; CTS 98, MDiv; O Feb 27, 00, MO Pby; mis MTW, Guayaquil, Ecuador, 01-03; astp Prosperity P Ch, Charlotte, NC, 03-05; op Providence P Ch, Concord, NC, 03-05, ascp 05-08; srp 08-; *How to Pray for your Wife: a 31-Day Guide*, 06

5883 Misty Forest Place, Concord, NC 28027 – 704-721-0051   Catawba Valley
E-mail: mark@ppcnet.net
Providence Presbyterian Church – 704-796-6560

Weaver, Craig E. – b Los Angeles, CA, May 27, 51; f Bernard E.; m Jo Ellen; w Arlo M. Granlund, Whitehall, WI, Aug 18, 79; chdn Matthew Aaron, Jonathan Bernard, JoAnna Christine, Rebecca Danielle; UCLA 74, BA; FulTS 76-77; ORUGST 80, MDiv; L Mar 20, 81; O Oct 4, 81, SW Pby (RPCES); sc Mid-A Pby, 83-85; ascp Christ P Ch, Tulsa, OK, 81-14; hr 15

2577 Paul Poole Drive, Tracy, CA 95377   Northern California
E-mail: craigeweaver@gmail.com
HR

Weaver, Dan – b Lancaster, PA, May 4, 33; w Marilou Pittman, Wheaton, IL, Jun 6, 59; chdn Lori Kay, Daniel Scott, Terence Richard; PhilBibU 54, dipl; WheatC 56, BA; UPitt 67, MEd; O Jun 8, 58; ob mis WBT; ip Trinity P Ch, Lancaster, SC, 08-10

13600 Kenwanda Drive, Snohomish, WA 98296 – 704-843-6836 Fellowship
E-mail: dan_weaver@wycliffe.org
Wycliffe Bible Translators

Weaver, William James Jr. – b Wilmington, DE, Jul 22, 72; f William J. Sr.; m Janet Emily Buker; w Karen Lee Emerson, Newark, DE, Jun 18, 94; chdn Kaitlyn Emerson, Megan Elizabeth, Lauren Emily, Georgia Ann; UDE 94, BS; ChTS 99, MATS; L Feb 99, Hrtg Pby; O Jan 00, Hrtg Pby; p Crossroads P Ch, Middletown, DE, 99-

205 Karins Boulevard, Townsend, DE 19734-3028 – 302-378-6105 Heritage
E-mail: jweaver@crossroadsfamily.com
Crossroads Presbyterian Church – 302-378-6235

Webb, Andrew James – b Rochford, Essex, England, Jul 29, 69; f Victor G.; m Wendy M. Cook; w Rhonda Joy Moore, Falls Church, VA, Nov 6, 93; chdn Margaret Abigail; UStAndr, Scotland 87-91, MA; WTS 97-01, MDiv; L May 97, Pot Pby; O Dec 2, 01, CentCar Pby; astp Cross Creek P Ch, Fayetteville, NC, 01-05; op Providence P Ch, Fayetteville, NC, 01-05, p 05-

223 Early Street, Fayetteville, NC 28311 – 910-482-8226 Central Carolina
E-mail: ajwebb@providencepca.com
Providence Presbyterian Church – 910-630-1215

Weber, Ben – b Vicksburg, MS, Nov 10, 84; f Stanley Dale; m Alice Jane Veluw; w Leah Marie Handermann, Birmingham, AL, Dec 15, 14; chdn Ellie Row; SamU 07, BS; BhamTS 17, MDiv; O Feb 26, 17, NWGA Pby; astp King's Chapel P Ch, Carrollton, GA, 17-; campm Campus Outreach, WestGA, 17-

416 Cedar Street, Carrollton, GA 30117 Northwest Georgia
E-mail: bweber@campusoutreach.org
King's Chapel Presbyterian Church – 770-834-0729
Campus Outreach

Webster, Brent – campm RUF, UCB, 07- 17; op Resurrection Oakland Ch, Oakland, CA, 17-

5837 Chabot Court, Oakland, CA 94618 – 415-317-7111 Northern California
Resurrection Oakland Church

Webster, Brian S. – b Feb 6, 47; f Raymond S.; m Nancie D. Edwards; w (1) dv; (2) Diane H. Muller, Charlottesville, VA, Sept 7, 85; chdn Hilary Jane, Andrew Stuart, Sterling James; BSIndEng, VPI 69; JMU 80, MBA; WTS 95, MDiv; L Jul 95; O Jul 28, 96, NR Pby; p Valley Ref P Ch, Cloverdale, VA, 95-98; astp Fort Worth P Ch, Fort Worth, TX, 98-00, ascp 00-05; p Christ Ch of Arlington, Arlington, VA, 05-

3008 Federal Hill Drive, Falls Church, VA 22004 – 571-481-8838 Potomac
E-mail: brian@ccapca.org
Christ Church of Arlington – 703-527-0420

Weckerly, Bill – w Sheila; chdn Bill, Eric, Erin, Brian; PittsTS 67, MDiv; ChrTS 87, DMin; hr

1845 Summit Oaks Circle, Minneola, FL 34715 – 352-988-5307 Central Florida
E-mail: wsweckerly@aol.com
HR

Weeber, Robert Christian – b New Castle, PA, Aug 26, 45; f Robert C. Sr.; m Doris Rosamond Cooke; w Elizabeth Ann LoBuono, North Huntingdon, PA, Aug 25, 67; chdn Kristin, Scott, Molly; ThielC 67, BA; CTS 70, MDiv; L Oct 70, Pitts Pby; O Jun 6, 71, DMV Pby (RPCES); p EP Ch, Elkton, MD,

Weeber, Robert Christian, continued
70-76; p Christ Ref P Ch, New Castle, PA, 77-83; p Calvin P Ch, North Huntingdon, PA, 83-06; astp Murrysville Comm Ch, Murrysville, PA, 06-10; hr 10

2601 Robbins Station Road, North Huntingdon, PA 15642 – 412-370-0033   Pittsburgh
E-mail: weeber.bob@comcast.net
HR

Wegener, David Jonathan – b Hartford, CT, Jun 23, 57; f Dr. Jonathan G.; m Eleanore M. Zimmerman; w Terrianne Elizabeth Wood, Bloomington, IN, May 7, 83; chdn Elizabeth, Mary, John, Sarah; INU 81, BS; UWI 90, MA; UGS 90-91; TEDS 86, MDiv, 89, MA; L Mar 13, 93; O Nov 13, 94, GrLks Pby; astp Geneva Campus Ch (CRC), Madison, WI, 91-92; astp Grace Cov P Ch, 93-98; ob astp Church of the Good Shepherd (Ind), 99-00; mis MTW, Zambia, 01-

c/o MTW   Central Indiana
E-mail: djwegener@gmail.com
PCA Mission to the World

Wegener, Jason T. – RTS 17, MDiv; O Sept 17, 17, HouMet Pby; ascp Christ Ch, Katy, TX, 17-

28903 Hollycrest Drive, Katy, TX 77494 – 281-381-9941   Houston Metro
E-mail: jason.wegener@cckpca.org
Christ Church – 281-392-0002

Weidenaar, James – b Dec 8, 65; w Deborah Ann Klaasen, Jun 15, 91; chdn Abigail; CalvC 89, BA; CalvS 95, MTS; WTS 11, PhD; O Feb 21, 16, Pitts Pby; ob Harvest USA, Dresher, PA, 16-; astp First Ref P Ch, Pittsburgh, PA, 17-

159 Spring Grove Road, Pittsburgh, PA 15235-1805 – 215-385-4390   Pittsburgh
E-mail: jdweidenaar@gmail.com
Harvest USA – 215-482-0111 715
Twining Road, Suite 200, Dresher, PA 19025
First Reformed Presbyterian Church – 412-793-7117

Weinman, Robert Edward – b Pittsburgh, PA, Jun 22, 26; f Clarence Edward; m Mary Elizabeth Newell; w Vonda Louise Bradshaw, Chicago, IL, Apr 24, 65; chdn Timothy Robert; UPitt 46-50, BS; DTS 50-54, ThM; ChiLuS 61-62, grad wk; PittsTS 68-69, grad wk; L Sept 54; O Sept 5, 55, Great Falls Pby (PCUSA); p First Ch, Harlem, MT, 54-60; ap First Ch, River Forest, IL, 60-67; p First Ch, Columbiana, OH, 67-78; p Cov Ch, San Diego, CA (IND), 78-86, wc 86; Bridge Assoc West; ip Carmel Comm Evang P Ch (non-PCA), San Diego, CA, 88-90; hr 91

6459 Lake Tahoe Court, San Diego, CA 92119-2534 – 619-464-7216   South Coast
E-mail: rweinbdg@cox.net
HR

Weir, Jeffrey Robert – b Toledo, OH, Aug 26, 51; f Joseph R.; m Gloria A. Bennett; w Dorcas M. Miller, Mansfield, OH, Nov 17, 73; chdn Katherine Joanne, Stephen Jeffery, David Robert; OHSU, BS; CTS, MDiv; Udall 10, MHum; L Jun 26, 82, StLou Pby; O Nov 14, 82, Evan Pby; int Reformed P Ch, Cutler, IL; ap First P Ch, Montgomery, AL, 82-84; p First P Ch, Union, MS, 84-86; Chap USN, 86-94; Officers' Christian Fellowship, 95-97; srp New Cov P Ch, Dallas, TX, 97-03, wc 03-07; ss Bethel Ch PCA, Dallas, TX, 07; ob CPE Chaplain Resident, 07; Chap Lion Hospice, Hurst, TX, 08; VA Chap Marion, IN, 09-13; chief of Chap, VA, Marion, IN, 10-13; chief of Chap, Temple, TX, 13-17; hr 18

3821 Sky Lane, Round Rock, TX 78681 – 254-534-9130   North Texas
E-mail: weirjr51@gmail.com
HR

Welborn, Mitch – astp Spring Cypress P Ch, Spring, TX, 14-17; ascp CityLife Ch, St. Paul, MN, 17-

CityLife Church – 612-559-4505   Siouxlands

Welch, Toby – astp Southwest P Ch, Bellaire, TX, 06-11

937 SW 96th Place, Seattle, WA 98106   Houston Metro
E-mail: twelch07@gmail.com

Welden, Dale B. – b Frankfurt, Germany, Jun 29, 55; f James Wesley; m Irene Johnson; w Connie Lynn Lattner, St. Louis, MO, May 22, 76; chdn Nathan Matthew, Rachel Christine, Benjamin James, Abigail Cathleen; MOBC 76, BA; CTS 80, MDiv, 01, DMin; L Mar 9, 79, Midw Pby; O Jul 18, 80, Pitts Pby (RPCES); ap First Ref P Ch, Pittsburgh, PA, 80-83; p Greene Valley P Ch, Carmichaels, PA, 83-88; srp Covenant P Ch, Fayetteville, GA, 88-06; srp St. Andrews P Ch, Columbia, SC, 06-

318 Ridge Run Trail, Irmo, SC 29063 – 803-760-6285   Palmetto
E-mail: welden@sapc.net
St. Andrews Presbyterian Church – 803-732-2273

Weldon, Timothy P. – astp Grace Ch, Harrisburg, NC, 09-11; ARP, 11-13; astp Lake Osborne P Ch, Lake Worth, FL, 13-18; wc

1752 13th Avenue North, Lake Worth, FL 33460   Gulfstream

Wellman, Mark R. – b Dhahran, Saudi Arabia, May 10, 68; f Mark Robert; m Magda Persa; w Tami Johnson, Hawaii, Dec 15, 90; chdn Emily Kristine, Elizabeth Kari, Esther Katherine, Ellie Joy; WestC 86-90, BA; RTS 90-93, MDiv; L Oct 9, 93; O Feb 6, 94, SWFL Pby; int Westminster P Ch, Brandon, FL, 93-94, astp 94-98; op, ev Hope P Ch, Randolph, NJ, 98-02, p 02-14; wc 14-16; astp Redeemer Hoboken, Hoboken, NJ, 16-; op Redeemer Jersey City Msn, Jersey City, NJ, 17-

236 VanHorne Street #2a, Jersey City, NJ 07304 – 973-219-3720   Metropolitan New York
E-mail: revmarkwellman@gmail.com
Redeemer Hoboken – 917-554-7181
Redeemer Jersey City Mission – 973-219-3720

Wells, Cecil M. – b Rosedale, MS, Oct 28, 49; f Thurman Cecil; m Elinor Glenn Caffey; w Genie Kathleen Caldwell, Pontotoc, MS, Jun 3, 72; chdn Kelly Kathleen, Marcy Michele, Morgan Robert, Clark Houston, Cecily Clare, Wallace Martin; MSU 67-71, BA; RTS 84-87, MDiv; O Feb 18, 86, MSVal Pby; ydir Brandon P Ch, Brandon, MS, 84-86; astp Pear Orchard P Ch, Ridgeland, MS, 86-89; chp Ft. Worth, TX, 89-91; p Hickory Withe P Ch, Hickory Withe, TN, 96-97; wc 97-

PO Box 156, Brandon, MS – 601-519-9349   Covenant
E-mail: re4md1@gmail.com

Wells, Daniel – b Tampa, FL, Aug 26, 85; f Ralph Franklin; m Janet Elaine Huffman; w Ashlee Rene Willeke, Medina, OH, Jun 5, 10; chdn Ralph Franklin II, Simon Patrick, Grace Elizabeth; ErskC 08, BA; RTSNC 11, MDiv, 18, MACC; Recd PCA Jun 30, 17, NYS Pby; p Hill City ARP, Rock Hill, SC, 15-17; srp Church of the Redeemer, Cortland, NY, 17-; co-auth *Countdown to Launch: Ten Church Planting Rules Worth Breaking*;

6 Duane Street, Cortland, NY – 514-767-3165   New York State
E-mail: danielfwells@gmail.com
Church of the Redeemer

Wells, Derek – Recd PCA 17, CentCar Pby; astp Christ Cov Ch, Matthews, NC, 17-

8217 Glamorgan Lane, Matthews, NC 28104 – 704-698-6707   Central Carolima
E-mail: dwells@christcovenant.org
Christ Covenant Church – 704-847-3505

Wells, Kyle – DurhamU, MATR, PhD; O Feb 28, 10, Pac Pby; p Christ P Ch, Santa Barbara, CA, 10-; "The Vindication of Agents, Divine and Human: Paul's Reading of Deuteronomy 30.1-14 in Romans" in *'What Does the Scripture Say?' Studies in the Function of Scripture in Early Judaism and Christianity, Volume 2: The Letters and Liturgical Traditions*; "Grace and Agency in Paul and Second Temple Judaism: Interpreting the Transformation of the Heart," *Novum Testamentum Supplements* 157, 14; "4 Ezra and Romans 8:1–13: The Liberating Power of Christ and the Spirit" in *Reading Romans in Context: Paul and Second Temple Judaism*, 15; *Grace and Agency in Paul and Second Temple Judaism: Interpreting the Transformation of the Heart*, 15

36 East Victoria Street, Santa Barbara, CA 93101 – 805-452-8101 Pacific
E-mail: Kyle@cpcsb.org
Christ Presbyterian Church – 805-957-4200

Wells, Scott – b Lockport, NY, Mar 9, 72; f Douglas Call ; m Jill Grace ; w Jennifer McLeod Johnson, Waynesboro, VA, Mar 23, 96; chdn Karisa Sheila, Harrison Conley; JMU 95, BBA; RTS 01, MDiv; L , JR Pby; O Apr 2, 06, TNVal Pby; astp Hixson P Ch, Hixson, TN, 06-08; wc 09-11; ob Harvest USA, Chattanooga, TN, 11-15; campm RUF, CC, 15-

8001 Woodstone Drive, Hixson, TN 37343 – 423-847-6497 Tennessee Valley
E-mail: scott.wells@ruf.org
PCA Reformed University Fellowship

Weltin, Michael – astp First P Ch of Coral Springs, Margate, FL, 06-17; p Inverness P Ch, Dundalk, MD, 17-

Inverness Presbyterian Church – 410-282-3143 Chesapeake

Wendland, Kenneth Lynn – b Ft. Lauderdale, FL, Jul 14, 53; f Robert Paul; m Donna Copeland; w Lisa Rim, Philadelphia, Mar 9, 90; chdn Daniel Paul, Kimberly Hannah; FSU 75, BA; WTS 84, MAR, 85, MDiv; L Nov 14, 87; O Jun 10, 90, Phil Pby; astp Korean United Ch of Phil, Philadelphia, PA, 90-93; p Berea P Ch, E. Providence (Barrington), RI, 93-97; ip Christ Cov P Ch, Warminster, PA, 97; srp Trinity P Ch, Escondido, CA, 98-; astp Proclamation P Ch, Bryn Mawr, PA, 16-

5 Henley Drive, Glen Mills, PA 19342 Philadelphia Metro West
Proclamation Presbyterian Church – 610-520-9500

Wenger, Theodore Thomas – b W. Reading, PA, Apr 14, 70; f William Vernon; m Virginia Mae Ziehl; w Melyna Irene Hoover, Oklahoma City, OK, Nov 26, 94; chdn Joshua Avery, Daniel Harold, Abigail Irene, Caleb Thomas, Sarah Katherine, Benjamin Brandt, William Bert; UCin 88-89; MUOH 89-93, BA; RTS 95-99, MDiv; O Jul 4, 99, MSVal Pby; astp First P Ch, Jackson, MS, 99-02, campm PCA RUF, UAR, 02-12; op Redeemer P Ch, Siloam Springs, AR, 12-

2405 Villa View Street, Siloam Springs, AR 72761 – 479-466-9449 Covenant
E-mail: ted@redeemersiloam.org
Redeemer Presbyterian Church – 479-466-9449

Wenger, Thomas L. II – ap Evangelical P Ch, Annapolis, MD, 07-11; ascp 11-15; op Trinity P Ch, Crofton, MD, 14-15, p 15-

1666 Village Green, Crofton, MD 21114 – 410-224-0998 Chesapeake
E-mail: thomas.l.wenger@gmail.com
Trinity Presbyterian Church – 443-302-9645

Wenger, Thomas Lynn, Sr. – b Ephrata, PA, Apr 11, 47; f Eli; m Dorothy Gamber; w Joanne T. Hammond, Grantham, PA, Aug 22, 70; chdn Thomas L. II, John F., Jami Beth, Joshua D., Kadi M., Jodi Christine, Timothy Joel; LanBC 69, BS; REpS 73, dipl, 84, MDiv; O Mar 83, DMV Pby; astp Aisquith P

Wenger, Thomas Lynn, Sr., continued
Ch, Baltimore, MD, 83-85; ascp Severna Park Evangelical P Ch, Pasadena, MD, 85-02; p Pasadena Evangelical P Ch, Pasadena, MD, 02-

7717 Suitt Drive, Pasadena, MD 21122-3233 – 410-437-1120   Chesapeake
E-mail: twenger@pasadena-ep.org
Pasadena Evangelical Presbyterian Church – 410-255-0003

Wenzler, Michael – O Aug 18, 13, Wisc Pby; campm RUF, UWI, 13-18; campm RUF, COStU, 18-

3015 Cortez Street, Fort Collins, CO 80525   Rocky Mountain
E-mail: mike.wenzler@ruf.org
PCA Reformed University Fellowship

Werner, John Clayton – w Liz; chdn Isaac, Claire, David, Andrew, Noah; WSCAL 07, MDiv; astp First P Ch, Chattanooga, TN, 07-09; p Lexington P Ch, Lexington, SC, 09-14; op Good Shepherd P Msn, Athens, GA, 15-

128 Lenox Place, Athens, GA 30606 – 803-604-7691   Georgia Foothills
E-mail: claywerner@gmail.com
Good Shepherd Presbyterian Mission – 803-604-7691

Werner, John R. – b Philadelphia, PA, Sept 28, 30; f John H.; m Bess Turner; w Helen Booras (d), Athens, Greece, May 26, 58; chdn John C., Elisabeth H. (Lee); DrexU 47-48; ShelC 49-51, BA; FTS 51-54, BD; UPA 54-57, MA, 59-62, PhD; ASCS 57-58; LSA 67 & 68 (summers); O Jun 54, NJ Pby (BPC); instr FTS, 54-55; instr CC, 62; instr CTS, 62; prof TCC, 62-72; op RP Ch of West Shore, Harrisburg, PA, 72-73; WBT, 75-86, wc 86; ss Westminster P Ch, Bedford, TX, 87; coord of research, Chr. Leadership Min, Dallas, TX, 87-88; chmn HINTS Int'l, 89-11; vis lect/prof IGST, 89-94; astp Bethel Ch, Dallas, TX, 06-08; t numerous seminaries internat'l, 94-09; hr 08; *Greek: A Programmed Primer*, 80; *I Corinthians: An Expanded Paraphrase*; *Romans: An Expanded Paraphrase*; notes on Philemon, *New International Version Study Bible*

1505 West Pine Avenue, Lompoc, CA 93436 – 805-618-8404   North Texas
E-mail: JohnRWerner@yahoo.com
HR

Werson, Jan Paul – b Tokyo, Japan, Jan 29, 51; f Bert Landers W.; m Trula Mildred (Freeman); w Dorothy Diane McCants, Pensacola, FL, Aug 27, 77; chdn Jana Lynn, Matthew James; CSUH 72, BA; RTS 88, MDiv; O Nov 20, 88, MSVal Pby; mout/evan First P Ch, Jackson, MS, 85-90; Chap USN, 90-02; astp Christ Ch, Jacksonville, FL, 01-02, ascp 02-07; astp Christ Comm Ch, Walnut Creek, CA, 07-09; astp Fairfield P Ch, Pensacola, FL, 09; ascp Cross Creek P Ch, Jacksonville, FL, 09-12; ascp Marco P Ch, Marco Island, FL, 12-18; mis 18-

310 Treasure Harbor Drive, Ponte Vedra, FL 32081   North Florida

Wessel, Hugh S. G. – b Brooklyn, NY, Jan 30, 47; f Bertil Stig; m Woods; w Martine Pelet, Ollon, Switzerland, Apr 28, 73; chdn Laurence Kathleen Madeleine, Damaris Suzanne, Nils Bertil Maurice; NYU 65-66, 68-69; UMD 67-68; NSSR 69-70; WTS 79, MDiv; L Jan 79; O May 80, Phila Pby (RPCES); MTW, Marseille, France, 80-

23 Rue de Cluny, 13008 Marseille, FRANCE – 011 491 81 12 33   Philadelphia Metro West
E-mail: hughwessel@gmail.com
PCA Mission to the World – 678-823-0004

West, Byron – O Jan 18, 15, SucstFL Pby; astp Westminster P Ch, Ft. Myers, FL, 15-16, p 16-

15330 Cricket Lane, Fort Myers, FL 33919   Suncoast Florida
E-mail: byron@wpcfortmyers.org
Westminster Presbyterian Church – 239-481-2125

West, Tracey Coburn – O Mar 6, 16, MetAtl Pby; campm RUFI, GATech, 16-

11101 Collier Road NW # D1, Atlanta, GA 30318 – 912-658-2216   Metro Atlanta
E-mail: tracey.west@ruf.org
PCA Reformed University Fellowship International

Weston, Patrick – O Aug 4, 13, MO Pby; astp Grace P Ch of St. Charles Co, MO, 13-16; op True Comm Flwsp, Kirksville, MO, 16-

1225 North Frankin Street, Kirksville, MO 63501   Missouri
E-mail: patrick@truecommunitykv.org
True Community Fellowship

Weston, Tim – w Rosamma; chdn Jessica, Suzanne, Michael; CTS 02, MDiv; astp Providence Ref P Ch, St. Louis, MO, 11-18; Dir International Students, Inc.

3916 Cottage Place, Anacortes, WA 98221 – 314-814-2019   Pacific Northwest
E-mail: stltimweston@gmail.com
International Students, Inc.

Whang, Peter – ascp Eun Sung P Ch, Rowland Heights, CA, 16-

1826 Wellspring Drive, Diamond Bar, CA 91765   Korean Southwest
E-mail: kanghwan.whang@gmail.com
Eun Sung Presbyterian Church – 626-854-0306

Wheat, Anthony Joseph III – b Quincy, FL, Apr 17, 62; f Anthony J, Jr; m Carol Ann Brown; w Gina Dawn Smith; AU 84, BS; RTS 87, MDiv; L Sept 87, Evan Pby; O Feb 19, 89, CentGA Pby; ap Raymond P Ch, Raymond, MS, 86-87; ap First P Ch, Augusta, GA, 89-91; op Trinity P Ch, Tuscaloosa, AL, 91-93, p 93-98; srp Village Seven P Ch, Colorado Springs, CO, 98-05; srp Highlands P Ch, Ridgeland, MS, 05-

125 Adderley Boulevard, Madison, MS 39110 – 601-605-1792   Mississippi Valley
E-mail: ajwheat@highlandspca.org
Highlands Presbyterian Church – 601-853-0636

Wheatley, Sam – b Augusta, GA, Aug 25, 65; f Lenward Avery; m Wanda Lee Findley; w Katherine Anderson, Augusta, GA, Dec 13, 87; chdn Bennett Andrew, Zoe Grace, Julia Faith; ClemU 89, BS; WTS 97, MDiv; L Apr 15, 97; O Feb 21, 98, NGA Pby; astp ChristChurch P, Atlanta, GA, 97-00; p New Song P Ch, Salt Lake City, UT, 00-16; astp Redeemer P Ch of New York, New York, NY, 16-

100 West 18th Street #5E, New York, NY 10011   Metropolitan New York
E-mail: sam.wheatley@redeemer.com
Redeemer Presbyterian Church of New York – 212-808-4460

Wheeler, Benjamin – b Tyler, TX, Feb 23, 74; f Don R.; m Janet K.; w Rachel Leigh Pearson, Corpus Christi, TX, Dec 28, 96; chdn Caleb Reid, Joshua Keegan, Abigail Carolene, John Benjamin; TXA&M 96, BS, 98, MS; WTS 08, MDiv; O Dec 09, SoTX Pby; astp Southside Comm Ch, Corpus Christi, TX, 09- 11; op Christ the King Msn, Duncanville, TX, 11-12; op Redeemer P Ch, Tyler, TX, 15-

3314 Pollard Drive, Tyler, TX 75701   North Texas
E-mail: Ben@redeemertyler.com
Redeemer Presbyterian

Wheeler, Richard John – p Trinity P Ch, Chester, SC, 03-

664 Pineview Lakes Road, Chester, SC 29706 – 803-385-2738   Fellowship
E-mail: rjwheeler@truvista.net
Trinity Presbyterian Church – 803-385-5724

Whipkey, Jeremy Reid – b Somerset, PA; w Vanessa; chdn Joseph, Carena; TriangleTech 95, AS; RPTS 10, MDiv; O Feb 26, 12, Pitts Pby; ascp New Life P Ch, Harrison City, PA, 12-17; srp Presbyterian Ch of Pitcairn, Pitcairn, PA, 17-

1010 Shantytown Court, Jeannette, PA 15644 – 724-433-8102   Pittsburgh
E-mail: jeremy@pitcairnpca.org
Presbyterian Church of Pitcairn – 412-372-7707

Whipple, Mark – w Jen; chdn Mercy, Micah, Luke, Sophia; O Mar 03, Wcar Pby; ascp Trinity P Ch, Asheville, NC, 03-08; op Westside Ch, Asheville, NC, 08-17; astp Church of the Good Shepherd, Durham, NC, 17-

4210 Peachway Drive, Durham, NC 27705   Eastern Carolina
E-mail: markwhipple@cgsonline.org
Church of the Good Shepherd – 919-490-1634

Whitaker, Andrew – Christianna; chdn Vivian Noelle; MBI 99; CTS 14; O Mar 13, 16, Wisc Pby; astp Cornerstone Ch, Delafield, WI, 16-17; astp Lexington P Ch, Lexington, SC, 18-

214 Beltrees Drive, Lexington, SC 29072   Palmetto
E-mail: awhitaker@gmail.com
Lexington Presbyterian Church – 803-359-9501

White, Bo Michael – b Clinton, IA, Dec 19, 71; f Donald; m Marcia Huizenga; w Tamara Kae Spence, St. Louis, MO, Jun 28, 97; CentC 89-93, BA; CTS 94-98, MDiv; O Mar 00, NoIL Pby; int Twin Oaks P Ch, Ballwin, MO; astp Westminster P Ch, Elgin, IL, 98-01; astp Twin Oaks P Ch, Ballwin, MO, 01-05; ob

Address Unavailable   Missouri

White, Dale R. – O Feb 21, 16, Pitts Pby; op Pilgrim P Msn, Scottdale, PA, 16-

804 Walnut Avenue, Scottdale, PA 15683 – 724-887-4722   Pittsburgh
E-mail: drwhite@zoominternet.net
Pilgrim Presbyterian Mission

White, David Carlton – b Tarboro, NC, Jun 17, 35; f Louis P W; m Sarah Eure; w Barbara Mayhew, Davidson, NC, Jun 14, 58; chdn Rebecca Gail, Lisa Marie, David Carlton Jr; DavC 57, BA; WTS 57-59, 88, DMin; ColTS 61, MDiv, 61, ThM; Taipei Lang Inst 75-79, cert; O Aug 27, 61, KgMt Pby; p Castanea P Ch, Stanley, NC, 61-67; ap West End P Ch, Hopewell, VA, 67-69; p New Hope Ch, Gastonia, NC, 69-73; Admin Sec ECOE, 73; Admin Sec MTW, 73-75; MTW, Taiwan, 75-90; pres Christ's Coll, Taiwan, 81-84, pres 87-89; mis MTW, Hong Kong, 90-91; p Roebuck P Ch, Roebuck, SC, 91-96, wc 96-98, mis 98-12(MTW 00-12); hr 12

No 51 Ziqiang Road, Tamsui Dist., New Taipei City, 29162 TAIWAN   Calvary
E-mail: wdpca@aol.com
HR

White, David M. – ob ev 04-

1661 Cavan Drive, Dresher, PA 19025 – 215-885-2099   Philadelphia
E-mail: davew@harvestusa.org

White, J. Wesley – b Lynchburg, VA, May 31, 77; w Melinda; chdn Anna, David, Geneva, Hope, Leah, Rochelle, Virginia; MidARS, MDiv; GPTS, ThM; O Jan 23, 04, Siouxl Pby; p New Cov P Ch, Spearfish, SD, 05-15; p Evergreen P , Sevierville, TN, 15-; "'On Justification' by Leonard Rijssen," MARS

White, J. Wesley, continued
JT 16 (05); "Saying 'Justification by Faith Alone' Isn't Enough," MARS JT 17 (06); "Piscator on Justification," *Confessional Presbyterian*, 07

325 Beal Woods Drive, Sevierville, TN 37862 – 865-567-6763   Tennessee Valley
E-mail: weswhite.net@gmail.com
Evergreen Presbyterian Church – 865-428-3001

White, James Andrew – b Kingsport, TN, May 7, 47; f Andrew John; m Mary Hunter Johnston; w Kay McConnell, Kingsport, TN, Dec 21, 68; chdn Hunter Hope; KgC 66-70, BA; TEDS 73-76, MDiv; CTS 86-91, DMin; O Sept 12, 76, PCUS; p Meadowview Ch, Bristol, TN, 76-81; p N. Miami Ch, N. Miami, FL, 81-82; op, p No Dade Ch, No Miami, FL, 82-86; srp Northside P Ch, Burlington, NC, 86-92, wc 92-95; MTW, 95-06; p Princeton P Ch, Johnson City, TN, 06-12; hr 12; brd RH, 12-, Pres 16-; "Abortion: A Christian Response", *Trinity Journal [TEDS]*, Vol 5, Spring 76; "Darkness in the Pasture: Clergy Depression in the Presbyterian Church in America", *Covenant Theological Seminary dissertation*, 91

484 Wyndham Drive, Gray, TN 37615 – 423-477-3204   Westminster
E-mail: jandrewwhite1@gmail.com
HR

White, Jeffrey Douglas – O Sept 21, 17, SW Pby; astp Las Tierras Comm Ch, El Paso, TX, 17-

3218 Richmond Avenue, El Paso, TX 79930 – 915-258-5213   Southwest
E-mail: whitejd89@gmail.com
Las Tierras Community Church – 915-740-9207

White, Jeffrey – b Memphis, TN, Oct 15, 70; f Sammy; m Dorris; w Susan Keil, New York, NY, May 14, 05; chdn Gabrielle Alexandra, Lydia Opal, Rosemary Samantha; UMemp 92, BBA; RTS 97, MDiv, 97, MA; DrexU 11, PhD; O Jul 20, 08, NoTX Pby; astp Park Cities P Ch, 08- 17; astp Christ P Ch, New Haven, CT, 17-

89 Killdeer Road, Hamden, CT 06517   Southern New England
Christ Presbyterian Church – 203-777-6960

White, Jeffrey O. – b Akron, OH, Nov 8, 60; f Harry Owens; m Clara Droppleman; w Rebecca Detwiler, Havertown, PA, Mar 30, 85; chdn Kirsten Renee, Corina Grace, Andrew Owens; UDE 83, BS; WTS 89, MDiv; L Sept 9, 89; O Nov 19, 89, Phil Pby; ap Tenth P Ch, Philadelphia, PA, 89-90; chp MNA, NYC, 90-91; ascp Redeemer P Ch of New York, New York, NY, 91-99; op New Song Comm Msn, New York, NY, 99-12; astp Redeemer P Ch of New York, NY, 12-17; astp Redeemer P Ch Downtown, New York, NY, 17-

220 West 123rd Street, New York, NY 10027   Metropolitan New York
Redeemer Presbyterian Church Downtown

White, Joe – O May 1, 10, Pac Pby; campm RUF, UCLA, 10-16; astp Lake Baldwin Ch, Orlando, FL, 16-

Lake Baldwin Church   Central Florida

White, Randall Fowler – b Nashville, TN, Jun 22, 54; f Vernon R; m Sally M; w Joann A Sharrock, Dallas, TX, Aug 18, 79; chdn Collin R, Hilary E; VandU 76, BA, 86, MA; DTS 80, ThM; WTS 87, PhD; O Jan 8, 95, SFL Pby; assoc prof KTS, 94-99, prof 99-08, admin 98-07; ob pres Ligonier Acad of Bib and Theo Studies, 08-10; vpres acad aff, prof/chair Bib Stud, 10-11; srp Valley P Ch, Lutherville, MD, 12-; "Reexamining the Evidence for Recapitulation in Rev 20:1-10," *Westminster Theological Journal* 51 (89); "Richard Gaffin and Wayne Grudem on 1 Cor 13:10: A Comparison of Cessationist and Noncessationist Argumentation," *Journal of the Evangelical Theological Society* 35, no. 2 (92); "Gaffin and Grudem on

White, Randall Fowler, continued
Eph 2:20: In Defense of Gaffin's Cessationist Exegesis," *Westminster Theological Journal* 54 (92); "Making Sense of Rev 20:1-10? Harold Hoehner Vs. Recapitulation," *Journal of the Evangelical Theological Society* 37, no. 4 (94); "The Sparrow in the Hurricane: A Review of Jack Deere's *Surprised by the Power of the Spirit*," *Reformation & Revival* 4, no. 3 (95); Book Chapter, "Does God Speak Today Apart from the Bible?" in John H. Armstrong, ed., *The Coming Crisis in Evangelicalism: Modern Challenges to the Authority of the Gospel*, 96; "On the Hermeneutics and Interpretation of Rev 20:1-3: A Preconsummationist Perspective," *Journal of the Evangelical Theological Society* 42, no. 1 (99); "Agony, Irony, and Victory in Inaugurated Eschatology: Reflections on the Current Amillennial-Postmillennial Debate," *Westminster Theological Journal* 62 (00); "O Conceito do 'Ensino Autoritativo' e o Papel da Mulher no Culto Congregacional," *Os Puritans* IX (Abril/Maio/Junho) 2001; Book, co-editor (with Gary L. W. Johnson) and contributor, *Whatever Happened to the Reformation?* 01; Book Chapter (with Richard B. Gaffin), "Eclipsing the Canon? The Spirit, the Word, and 'Revelations of the Third Kind'," in Gary L. W. Johnson and R. Fowler White, eds., *Whatever Happened to the Reformation?* 01; "Contrary to What You May Have Heard: On the Rhetoric and Reality of Claims of Continuing Revelation," in Gary L. W. Johnson and R. Fowler White, eds., *Whatever Happened to the Reformation?* 01; "Covenant and Apostasy" and "A Response to 'Trinitarian Anthropology" in E. Calvin Beisner, ed., *The Auburn Avenue Theology, Pros & Cons: Debating the Federal Vision,* 04; "Covenant, Inheritance, and Typology: Understanding the Principles at Work in God's Covenants" (with E. Calvin Beisner) in Guy Prentiss Waters and Gary L. W. Johnson, eds., *By Faith Alone: Answering the Challenges to the Doctrine of Justification,* 07; "A Megashift in Time," *Tabletalk*, Dec 09; "The Letter to the Church in Thyratira," *Tabletalk*, May 09; "Designed for Dignity," *Tabletalk*, July 05; devotions for the book of Numbers, *ESV Men's Devotional Bible*, 15

2200 West Joppa Road, Lutherville, MD 21093 – 954-782-4953 — Chesapeake
E-mail: rfwhite@valleypca.org
Valley Presbyterian Church – 410-828-6234

White, S. Knox – O Jun 28, 15, GulCst Pby; astp Westminster P Ch, Ft. Walton Beach, FL, 15-

223 Moriarty Street NW, Ft. Walton Beach, FL 32548 — Gulf Coast
E-mail: sknoxwhite@gmail.com
Westminster Presbyterian Church – 850-862-8825

Whited, Brian – b Ft. Belvoir, VA, Jun 18, 81; f Brian Michael; m Susan Baker; w Krisha Nicole Jay, Harrisonburg, VA, Jan 8, 05; chdn Chase Alexander, Sophia Elizabeth; JMU 03, BS; RTSFL 07, MDiv; ob Chap Hospice, 10-

1037 Welton Avenue SW, Roanoke, VA 24015 — Blue Ridge
E-mail: briancwhited@gmail.com

Whited, Rodney Wilford – b East McKeesport, PA, Oct 21, 35; f Stanley E.; m Emma Rowand; w Margaret McKelway, Wilkinsburg, PA, Feb 22, 57; chdn David, Mindy, Janice; GenC 57, BA; LRTS 81, MDiv; O Aug 16, 81, CentFL Pby; srp Pinewood P Ch, Middleburg, FL, 81-05; hr 05

225 West Seminole Boulevard #308, Sandford, FL 32771 – 904-728-8011 — North Florida
E-mail: whitedrp@yahoo.com
HR

Whitenack, Sean James – w Julie; chdn Liam, Grace, Madeleine, Jonathan; CSU 96, BS; CCC 96-97; NGTS 04, MDiv; O May 15, 05, JR Pby; astp New Life in Christ Ch, Fredericksburg, VA, 05-08; ascp 08-; adj prof NGTS, 08-

11719 Eisenhower Lane, Fredericksburg, VA 22407 – 540-898-8677 — James River
E-mail: seanwhitenack@msn.com
New Life in Christ Church – 540-786-4848

MINISTERIAL DIRECTORY 669

Whitfield, Russell Douglas – O Sept 25, 10, Pot Pby; astp Grace P Ch of Wash, D.C., Washington, DC, 10-13; ascp 13-

637 Indiana Avenue NW Suite 300, Washington, DC 20004   Potomac
E-mail: russ@gracemosaic.org
Grace Presbyterian Church of Washington, D.C. – 202-386-7637

Whitham, Michael Craig – b Tulsa, OK, Mar 17, 88; f Kenton; m Jean Palmer; w Anna McDowell, Huntsville, AL, May 223, 10; chdn Eleanor Katherine; UOK 10, BA; RTS 13, MDiv; O Jan 5, 14, CentCar Pby; campm RUF, J&W, 14-

310 Lima Avenue, Charlotte, NC 28208 – 918-513-2703   Central Carolina
E-mail: mcwhitham@gmail.com
PCA Reformed University Fellowship

Whitley, Eric – b Lexington, KY, May 31, 84; f Ron; m Janet; w Stephanie, Lexington, KY, Nov 24, 07; chdn Anna Katherine, Callan, Lawson, Cora Grace; INU 06, BMus; CTS 11, MDiv; O Feb 26, 12, MO Pby; astp Covenant P Ch, St. Louis, MO, 12-18; campm RUF, IU, 18-

3532 South Tudor Lane, Bloomington, IN 47401 – 314-630-1711   Central Indiana
E-mail: eric.whitley@ruf.org
PCA Reformed University Fellowship

Whitley, Jonathan – Recd PCA Jul 8, 17, Wisc Pby; astp Jacob's Well P Ch, Green Bay, WI, 17-18, ascp 18-

1427 Springdale Lane, Green Bay, WI 54304   Wisconsin
Jacob's Well Presbyterian Church – 920-264-9564

Whitlock, Luder Gradick Jr. – b Jacksonville, FL, Jun 20, 40; f Luder G; m Juanita O. Nessmith; w Mary Louise Patton, Miami, FL, Aug 29, 59; chdn Frank Christopher, Alissa Ann, Beth LaVerne; BelC 58-59; UFL 62, BA; WTS 66, MDiv; VandU 73, DMin; ErskTS, DD; Hon: SterlC, DD; BelhU LittD; L Jun 2, 66; O Nov 4, 66, Pby of South (OPC); p Sharon Ch, Hialeah, FL (OPC), 66-69; p West Hills P Ch, Harriman, TN, 69-75; vis lect/prof RTS, 74-78, pres 78-01; ss Park Cities P Ch, Dallas, TX, 91; ip Christ Cov PCA, 05; ip Pinewood PCA, 08-09; ip Westm P Ch, Ft. Myers, FL, 09-10; ob pres Found for Ref/Excelsis, 01-; pres Telios, 05-09; exec dir The Trinity Forum, 03-08, Sr. Fellow, 08-; int pres ErskTS, 05-06; Exec Comm, Assoc of Theo Schools, 94-02, pres, 98-00; Trustee, Schloss Mittersill, 07-15; Board of Governors, The Geneva School, 08-17; Board of Governors, John Jay Institute, 08-; Trustee, Montreat College, NC, 09-; Trustee, KTS, 09-; Dir, The CNL Charitable Foundation; Ex Dir, The Seneff Family Foundation; Dir of Strategic Development, Redeemer City to City, 10-13; brds: Ligonier Ministries, 88–95, Ex Com 93-95; CC 73–79, Ex Com. 77-79; WTS 73–76; The Church Planting Center, 89–95; Lifework Leadership 89-92; WEF 1992 -96, Ex Com 94–96; NAE 1992, Chair Theology Committee 1994 -96; International Reformed Fellowship, Co president 92-00; Key Life 95-06; Alliance of Confessing Evangelicals 94-96; The Barna Institute 95-02; CareNet 98-02; World Reformed Fellowship 00-10, Ex Com 00-06; Institute for Worship Studies 01-10, Vice Chairman 08-10; Graduate Institute for Advanced Studies in Linguistics 02-06, 09-; The Lausanne Committee for World Evangelization, 01-05; Greater Europe Mission 04–07; Institute for Classical Schools 10-; Desire Street Ministries 10-17, Chairman, 11; Knox Theological Seminary 09-14, Chairman 09; The Christian Study Center, Gainesville, FL 08-10; Trinity Forum Europe 05-; National Commission on Higher Education, NAE 95-03; int pres KTS, 12-13; hr 17 exec dir *The New Geneva Study Bible*; exec dir, *The Spirit of the Reformation Study Bible*; contr *Evangelical Dictionary of Theology*; contr *Reformed Theology in America*; *Southern Reformed Theology*; contr *Baker Encyclopedia of the Bible*; contr *The Westminster Shorter Catechism in Modern English*; contr *The Changing of the Evangelical Mind; The Dictionary of Twentieth Century Christian Biography*; contr *Blackwell's Dictionary of Evangelical Biography; The Spiritual Quest; Divided We Fall; Overcoming a*

Whitlock, Luder Gradick Jr., continued
History of Christian Disunity; contr *The Practice of Confessional Subscription, The Westminster Shorter Catechism in Modern English, A Mighty Long Journey: On the Way to Racial Reconciliation, A Theology of Sexuality, A Code of Ethics for Pastors, A Code of Ethics for Churches*

1700 Spring Lake Drive, Orlando, FL 32804 – 407-872-0450　　　　　　　　　Central Florida
E-mail: lwhitlock@cnl.com
HR

　　Whitman, H. Morton – b New York, NY, Sept 15, 39; f H. Motley; m Jetteke Tjaarda; w Jennifer A. Davoud, Coventry, UK, Dec 7, 74; chdn Henri Marcus, Jillian Tandy; LycomingC 64, BA; WTS 68, MDiv; L'Abri, Swit 73; CTS 85, DMin cand; L 69; O 70, Phil Pby; op, p Grace Cov P Ch, Williamsburg, VA, 70-84; p Murphy-Blair Comm Ch, St. Louis, MO, 84-90; ob mis, staff mis appt for staff, ISI, St. Louis, MO, 90-91; ob staff, campm ISI, 90-; Chap Forest Park Hosp, 98-99; Psych Tech, 99-01; Chap St.Alexius Hosp, 02-04; mis Greater Europe Mission, Romania, 04-; CPE, 99

Address Unavailable　　　　　　　　　　　　　　　　　　　　　　　　　　　　　Missouri
E-mail: isi6@juno.com
Greater Europe Mission, Romania

　　Whitner, John Addison III – b Atlanta, GA, Apr 12, 34; f Joseph W. (d); m Dorothy Coffin (d); w Geraldine Jones, Huntsville, AL, Feb 22, 58; chdn John Randall, Richard Bennett, Stephen Andrew, Jerri Ann (d); GATech 56, BS; ColTS 64, BD, 93, MDiv; O Aug 9, 64, SC Pby; p Todd Mem Ch, Laurens, SC, 64-67; p Dickenson First P Ch, Haysi, VA, 67-74; Dir Appalachian Mtn Presb Msn, 75-80; p Sandlick P Ch, Birchleaf, VA, 80-86; op Bartlick P Ch, Haysi, VA, 86-96, p 96-12; hr 12

115 Whitner Lane, Haysi, VA 24256-9750 – 276-865-4680　　　　　　　　　　Westminster
E-mail: mommaw13@yahoo.com
HR

　　Whitner, Stephen – w Tracy; chdn Stephanie, Michael, Rachel; KgC, BA; SamU, MA; BDS, MDiv; CTS 14, DMin; O Oct 13, 02, Evan Pby; ascp Altadena Valley P Ch, Birmingham, AL, 02-

514 Caldwell Mill Circle, Birmingham, AL 35242 – 205-981-2756　　　　　　　　Evangel
E-mail: steve@avpc.org
Altadena Valley Presbyterian Church – 205-967-0680

　　Whitney, Peter Joseph – O Aug 25, 13, SavRiv Pby; astp Kirk O the Isles P Ch, Savannah, GA, 13-16, p 16-

5415 Reynolds Street, Savannah, GA 31405 – 912-655-3823　　　　　　　　Savannah River
Kirk O' the Isles Presbyterian Church – 912-355-3141

　　Whittle, James Ivan – b Louisville, KY, Oct 12, 60; f Noah; m Ann McNeely; w Shari Dengg, Louisville, KY, Aug 22, 81; chdn Matt, Josh, Alan, Alicia, Rebecca; CCK 82, BS; GATech 84, BS; RTSFL 93, MDiv; L Oct 90; O Jan 10, 93, CentFL Pby; chp, op Northside P Ch, Melbourne, FL, 93-95, p 95-00; p Chapel Hill P Ch, Douglasville, GA, 01-12; ob proj dir Equipping Leaders, Int, 12-

9889 Live Oak Court, Douglasville, GA 30135 – 770-363-7464　　　　　　　Northwest Georgia
E-mail: jimwhittle.eli@gmail.com
Equipping Leaders International – 770-363-7464

　　Whitwer, William Nick – b Tilden, NE, Jul 23, 30; f Theodore Gottfried W; m Bertha Kossman; w Carol Sue Colley, Pensacola, FL, Jul 10, 71; chdn Karla Elaine, Karen Lynne; SUNY 53, BA; FulTS 56, BD; O Jan 58, MS Pby; ap First P Ch, Jackson, MS, 56-57; p Wdvlle & Gloster, MS, 58-61; p Edwards P

Whitwer, William Nick, continued
Ch, Edwards, MS, 61-65; p Bethesda P Ch, Edwards, MS, 61-65; ap First P Ch, Gadsden, AL, 65-74; ap First P Ch, Jackson, MS, 74-78; p Pear Orchard P Ch, Ridgeland, MS, 78-86; ap First P Ch, Jackson, MS, 87-91; p Lakeland P Ch, Brandon, MS, 91-95; p Rainbow P Ch, Rainbow City, AL, 95-02; hr 02

262 Geneva Boulevard, Madison, MS 39110   Evangel
HR

Wichlan, Michael – b Paris, TN, Jan 4, 68; f Felix J.; m Carol Ann Hobbs; w Cherri Denise Lassiter, Hazel, KY, Dec 21, 91; chdn Madeline Grace, Baylee Elizabeth; UT 90, BS; CTS 08, MDiv; O Nov 22, 09, NoTX Pby; astp Trinity P Ch, Plano, TX, 09-12; ascp 12-18; astp Briarwood P Ch, Birmingham, AL, 18-

5875 Shades Run Lane, Hoover, AL 35244 – 972-740-4330   Evangel
E-mail: mwichlan@briarwood.org
Briarwood Presbyterian Church – 205-776-5200

Wikner, Benjamin – astp McLean P Ch, McLean, VA, 15-; op Cross Comm Ch, Rockville, MD, 15-

17 Jefferson 5, Rockville, MD 20850   Potomac
E-mail: bwik2010@gmail.com
McLean Presbyterian Church – 703-821-0800
Cross Community Church

Wilbanks, JB – w Allison Christine; chdn Lillian Joy, John Lewis; O Feb 12, 17, NoTX Pby; astp Christ Ch Mansfield, Mansfield, TX, 17; campm RUF, UTTyler, 17

3114 Summer Grove Court, Mansfield, TX 76063 – 903-224-5764   North Texas
E-mail: jb.wilbanks@ruf.org
PCA Reformed University Fellowship

Wilbourne, Rankin – astp First P Ch, Chattanooga, TN, 03-06; srp Pacific Crossroads Ch, Los Angeles, CA, 06-

1169 South Crescent Heights Boulevard, Los Angeles, CA 90035 – 310-551-0081   Pacific
E-mail: rankin@pacificcrossroads.org
Pacific Crossroads Church – 310-551-0081

Wilcher, David Jack – b Macon, GA, Aug 15, 60; f Elbert Talmadege Jr.; m Barbara Jean Hamm; w Vicki Arleen Yaughn, Macon, GA, Jun 6, 80; chdn Lauren Elizabeth, Barbara Ashley, Hannah Michelle, Jonathan David; CTS 92-96, MDiv; L Jul 27, 96, SoTX Pby; O Jul 27, 96, SoTX Pby; op Grace P Ch, The Woodlands, TX, 96-98, p 98-

145 Riverbend Way, Montgomery, TX 77316 – 832-928-8222   Houston Metro
E-mail: david@gracewoodlands.org
Grace Presbyterian Church – 281-296-0911

Wilcke, Clinton Harris – b Delray Beach, FL, Apr 7, 69; f Ralph Gardner; m Allian Harris Hoover; w Kathy Lynn Roberts, Oxford, MS, Jul 24, 96; chdn Kendall, Caleb, Robert, Benjamin, Zachery; UMS 92, BA; RTS 01, MDiv; L Sept 11, 01, Gr Pby; O Sept 30, 01, Gr Pby; ydir Covenant P Ch, Nashville, TN, 95-97; int First P Ch, Jackson, MS, 97-01; campm RUF, USM, 01-08; astp Christ P Ch at Olive Branch, Olive Branch, MS, 08-10; op Christ Cov Ch, Hernando, MS, 09-10, srp 10-

2550 Oak Woods Drive East, Hernando, MS 38632 – 662-449-4903   Covenant
E-mail: cwilcke@lovetrainserve.org
Christ Covenant Church – 901-907-9575

Wilcox, Clifton David – b DeFuniack Spgs, FL, Mar 3, 58; f Richard Lee; m Kitty Jean Wooten; w Julie Linton, Brookhaven, MS, Aug 1, 81; chdn Kathryn Linfield, Janie Cameron, Zachary David; BelC 79-81, BA; CTS 89-92, MDiv; L Jul 20, 92; O Feb 21, 93, CentFL Pby; ydir Lake Forest P Ch, Knoxville, TN, 81-83; ydir McIlwain Mem P Ch, Pensacola, FL, 83-89; int Kirk of the Hills P Ch, St. Louis, MO, 89-92; campm RUF, UFL, 92-03; asst coord RUM, 03-09; chp FL, 09-10; op Circle PCA, Pensacola, FL, 10-

4285 Woodbine Road, Pace, FL 32571   Gulf Coast
E-mail: cwilcox@circlepca.org
Circle PCA – 850-748-3939

Wildeman, Robert A. Jr. – b Newark, NJ, Jun 23, 43; f Robert A Sr.; m Eva M. McCombs; w Nancy J. Kramer, St Louis, MO; chdn Stephen, Anna (Miller), Daniel; CC 65, BA; CTS 69; EBapTS 95, DMin; L Mar 69; O Nov 69, MO Pby (RPCES); p Westminster P Ch, Vincennes, IN, 69-72; p BPC, Merrill, WI, 73-78; Chap USArmy, 78-02; Chap USArmy, Inf Cntr Chap, Ft. Benning, GA, 95-97; Chap USArmy, Ft. Clayton, Panama, 97-99; Chap USArmy, Korea, 99-02; ss Christ Comm Ch, Fairmont, WV, 03-05, p 05-10; hr 10

477 Ann Marie Drive, Bridgeport, WV 26330 – 304-842-3855   New River
E-mail: thewildemans@hotmail.com
HR

Wiley, Alan – O Feb 15, 15, Flwsp Pby; astp Redeeming Gr PCA, Lake Wylie, SC, 15-17, ascp 17-

1222 Winding Path Road, Clover, SC 29710 – 724-309-5870   Fellowship
E-mail: ar.wiley@gmail.com
Redeeming Grace PCA – 803-831-7133

Wiley, C. R. (Christopher) – p Presbyterian Ch of Manchester, Manchester, CT, 08-; *Man of the House: A Handbook for Building a Shelter That Will Last in a World That is Falling Apart* (Wipf and Stock); articles in *Touchstone Magazine, Modern Reformation, Sacred Architecture, The Imaginative Conservative, Front Porch Republic, Scenes Media, Kuyperian Commentary, National Review Online, First Things*; blog on Patheos, Evangelical Channel

127 Gehring Road, Tolland, CT 06084 – 860-871-9539   Southern New England
E-mail: crwiley62@msn.com
Presbyterian Church of Manchester – 860-643-0906

Wiley, Matt – O May 7, 17, NoTX Pby; astp City P Ch, Oklahoma City, OK, 17-; op Shawnee P Ch, Shawnee, OK, 17-

18 Northridge Road, Shawnee, OK 74804 – 405-612-2784   Hills and Plains
E-mail: jmatt.wiley@gmail.com
City Presbyterian Church
Shawnee Presbyterian Church – 405-612-2784

Wilhelm, Carl – Recd PCA 15, MetAtl Pby; ob admin Metro Atlanta Seminary, 15-

1700 North Brown Road, Lawrenceville, GA 30043   Metro Atlanta
Metro Atlanta Seminary

Wilkerson, James Daniel – astp Golden Isles P Ch, St. Simons Island, GA, 05-06; p Redeemer P Ch, Brunswick, GA, 06-13; ob p Christ Ch of the Carolinas, 13-18; p Christ Cov Ch, Columbia, SC, 18-

1617 Edgehill Road, Columbia, SC 29204 – 803-413-7529   Palmetto
E-mail: jim@ccotc.org
Christ Covenant Church – 803-782-2442

Wilkes, Larry – b Atlanta, GA, Nov 27, 59; f Roy D.; m Ruth Emma Frazier; w Amanda Shifa Ahmed; chdn Hannah, Elise; SCS 11, MDiv; O May 22, 16, RMtn Pby; mis MTW, 16-

2309 North Nevada Avenue, Colorado Springs, CO 80907 – 719-201-6183   Rocky Mountain
E-mail: larry.wilkes@yahoo.com
PCA Mission to the World

Wilkes, Lennon Craig – b Vidalia, GA, Apr 25, 53; f George Lennon; m Marion Aleta Witt; w Vicki Maree Wingate, Columbia, SC, Mch 31, 01; chdn George Craig, Susannah Kate; BrPJC, AA; UGA, BEd; RTS 79-80; ColTS 81-82, MDiv; O Jan 1, 83, Cong Pby (PCUS); p Rose Hill P Ch, Columbia, SC, 83-93; admin MNA, ch relations, 94; admin MTW, partner relations; wc p First P Ch (ARP), Columbia, SC, 04-17

417 Dean Hall Lane, Columbia, SC 29209 – 803-331-9745 Palmetto
E-mail: vwilkes@bellsouth.net

Wilkes, Terry – O Aug 6, 00, Palm Pby; op Covenant Comm Ch, Lexington, SC, 00-02; p 02-06; wc 07-

1081 Shady Grove Road, Irmo, SC 29063 – 803-732-4399   Palmetto

Wilkie, Brant Edward – b Evansville, IN, Mar 13, 53; f Bruce Edward; m Jane Augusta Laubscher; w Juliane Strasburger, Evansville, IN, Jun 3, 78; chdn Janelle Grace, Lorin Juiet, Brock Edward, Jacob Brant, Caleb Joseph; VinU 73; CTS 94, MDiv; L Jan 4, 97; O Jan 17, 98, NR Pby; p Faith P Ch, Charleston, WV, 98-06; hr 16

158 Pearson Circle, Lake Lure, NC 28746 – 828-625-2716   New River
HR

Wilkins, Jeff – b Honolulu, HI, May 2, 64; f Dan B.; m Laura Ann Davis; w Catherine Anna Green, Dyersburg, TN, Jul 7, 91; chdn Micah Davis, Asher Green, Anna Grace; Hendrix 82-86, BA; MTS, VandU 88-90; WTS 90-95, MDiv; L Jul 26, 97, NoTX Pby; O Oct 15, 00, NoTX Pby; ascp Fort Worth P Ch, Fort Worth, TX, 96-04; campm RUF, 04-10, campm RUF, 10-15; p City Ch of East Nash, Nashville, TN, 15-

1101 Lischey Avenue, Nashville, TN 37207 – 919-889-9230   Nashville
E-mail: jeffersondwilkins@gmail.com
City Church of East Nashville – 615-262-3246

Wilkins, John Langley – b Philadelphia, PA, Aug 27, 23; f John; m Leah; w Anne Entriken, Havertown, PA, Apr 27, 46; chdn Glenn, Bruce, David; UPA 52; REpS 70, BD; O Mar 13, 75, Ref Epsi Ch; rec Ref Epis Ch of the Reconciliation, Phil, PA, 72-75; p Bethany P Ch, New Castle, DE, 76-89; ip New Life OPC, Lampeter, PA, 89; ascp Heritage P Ch, New Castle, DE, 90-98, p em 98-; hr 98

300 Willow Valley Lakes Drive #B-203, Willow Street, PA 175848 – 717-464-3155   Heritage
HR

Wilkins, R.R. Andrew – mis MTW, 12-14; astp Northwest P Ch, Dublin, OH, 14-18; astp Trinity Park Ch, Cary, NC, 18-

525 Abbey Fields Loop, Morrisville, NC 27560 – 719-271-1714   Eastern Carolina
E-mail: drew@trinityparkchurch.org
Trinity Park Church – 919-439-3718

Wilkinson, Billy Scott – b Mooresville, NC, Sept 25, 60; f Bill J.; m Sarah Casey; w Amelia Diane, Mooresville, NC, Apr 11, 15; chdn Joshua Scott, Sarah Elizabeth, John Isaac; UNCC 78-82, BS; RTSFL 92-94, MDiv; L Aug 28, 94; O Aug 28, 94, CentFL Pby; int Southlake P Ch, Huntersville, NC, 93; int River

Wilkinson, Billy Scott, continued
Oaks P Ch, Lake Mary, FL, 94; p Northshore P Ch, Jacksonville, FL, 94-97; srp Westminster P Ch, Bryan, TX, 97-02; p New Hope P Ch, Clemmons, NC, 02-08; wc 09; ip Summer Oaks P Ch, Greensboro, NC, 11-17, p 17-

1980 Landover Drive, Clemmons, NC 27012-9217 – 336-712-8128 Piedmont Triad
E-mail: scott@nbfsa.com
Summer Oaks Presbyterian Church – 336-671-0427

Wilks, Nathanael – b Martinsburg, WV, Jan 29, 79; f Lowell; m Rebecca; w Bethany Jagoditsch, Augusta, GA, Jul 26, 03; chdn Kayleigh, Hayden, Elise; GenC 01, BA; CTS 10, MDiv; O Mar 11, SusqV Pby; astp Manor P Ch, Cochranville, PA, 10-13; p Calvary P Ch, Raleigh, NC, 13-

4512 Cobbler Place, Raleigh, NC 27613 – 919-917-0601 Eastern Carolina
E-mail: nwilks@calvarypca.org
Calvary Presbyterian Church – 919-781-9015

Willborn, C. Nixon – b Gadsden, AL, Jul 6, 55; f Louis C.; m Frances Nadine Hilley; w Carol Bell, Kingston, TN, Aug 11, 84; chdn Sophie Caroline, William Cas, Iain Boice; TNTU 84, BS; MidABTS 88, MDiv; WTS 03, PhD; L Mar 85; O Mar 85, SBC; Recd PCA Mar 12, 94, Phil Pby; p Stanton Bap Ch, 85-87; ascp Open Door Bible Ch, 89-91; ob cand dir AWM, 91-96; p Reformed Hrtg P Ch, Birmingham, AL, 96-99, wc 99-00; ob prof GPTS, 00-09; srp Covenant P Ch, Oak Ridge, TN, 09-; adj prof GPTS, 09-; co-ed The Confessional Presbyterian 05-; vis prof RTS, 12-; contr *Sanctification: Growing in Grace*; ed, contr *Confessing Our Hope*; co-ed *The Covenant*, 05; co-ed *The Worship Of God* 05; "The 'Ministerial and Declarative' Power of the Church and In Thesi Declarations," *The Confessional Presbyterian*" (05); contr ed *The Confessional Presbyterian*; "Presbyterians in the South and the Slave: A Study in Benevolence," *The Confessional Presbyterian* (07); "Gilbert Tennent: Pietist, Preacher, and Presbyterian" in *Colonial Presbyterianism*, 07; "Biblical Theology in Southern Presbyterianism" in *The Hope Fulfilled*, 08; "Eschatology in the Westminster Standards," *The Confessional Presbyterian*; ed *A Christian Worldview: Essays from a Reformed Perspective*, 08; co-ed *Covenant: God's Voluntary Condescension*, 05; "The Deacon: A Divine Right Office with Divine Uses" in *The Confessional Presbyterian*, 09; "Hodge-Thornwell: Princes in Israel" in *The Confessional Presbyterian,* 12; "James Henley Thornwell: An American Theologian," in *The Confessional Presbyterian*, 13; *The Selected Writings of Benjamin Morgan Palmer*, 14; "The Gospel Work of the Diaconate," in *The Confessional Presbyterian*, 14; "Sanctification and the American Reformed Tradition" in *The Confessional Presbyterian*, 15; B.M. Palmer's "Broken Home: Lessons in Sorrow," *The Confessional Presbyterian,* 16; "Disciples Love Sound Doctrine" in *Tabletalk*, Jun 18; "A Children's Book about God's Hesed" in *The Confessional Presbyterian,* 18

8305 Burchfield Drive, Oak Ridge, TN 37830 – 865-765-6761 Tennessee Valley
E-mail: cnwillborn@gmail.com
Covenant Presbyterian Church – 865-483-9888
Greenville Presbyterian Theological Seminary

Willett, Christopher Bruce – O Apr 24, 16, NFL Pby; astp Pinewood P Ch, Middleburg, FL, 16-17; srp Columbia P Ch, Columbia, MS, 17-

1609 Orchard Drive, Columbia, MS 39429 Grace
E-mail: chris@columbiapca.org
Columbia Presbyterian Church – 601-736-4728

Willetts, Robert Alexander – b Silver Spring, MD, Oct 16, 71; w April Maureen Pierce, Bristol, PA, Dec 17, 94; chdn Alex, Jeff, Bailey; UMD 94, BS; WTS 02, MDiv; L Nov 01, Phil Pby; O Jun 02, Phil Pby; ascp New Life Northeast P Ch, Philadelphia, PA, 02-05; p New Life Northeast P Ch, Philadelphia, PA, 06-07; astp Trinity P Ch, Norfolk, VA, 07-08; ascp 08-13; op Grace P Msn, Chesapeake, VA, 09-13; p 13-

715 Hill Point Court, Chesapeake, VA 23322 Tidewater
E-mail: bob@gracechesapeake.com
Grace Presbyterian Church – 757-773-0014

MINISTERIAL DIRECTORY 675

Williams, Buster – Chap USN, 09-

134 Noke Street #6, Kailua, HI 96734   Northwest Georgia
E-mail: buster.williams@uscm.mil
United States Navy

Williams, Charles Ernest – hr

18626 North Spanish Garden Drive #334, Sun City West, AZ 85375 – 509-572-7498   Southwest
E-mail: erniewil@msn.com
HR

Williams, Charles Scott – O 05, CentFL Pby; Chap USArmy, 05-

7433 Wilkins Drive, Ft. Bragg, NC 28311   Central Florida
United States Army

Williams, David C. – O UPCUSA; Recd PCA Mar 23, 83, NoIL Pby; srp Covenant P Ch, Chicago, IL, 85-05; pal 06-08; p Westminster P Ch, Elgin, IL, 08-16; hr 17

230 South Taylor Avenue, Oak Park, IL 60302-3526 – 708-524-0470   Chicago Metro
HR

Williams, Dean – astp First P Ch of Coral Springs, Coral Springs, FL; ascp Pear Orchard P Ch, Ridgeland, MS, 18-

831 Rice Road, Apt. 198, Ridgeland, MS 39157   Mississippi Valley
E-mail: dean1643@comcast.net
Pear Orchard Presbyterian Church – 601-956-3283

Williams, Ford Smith Jr. – b Columbia, SC, Jul 13, 45; f Ford S; m Anne Ella Fugate; w Martha Marian Caldwell, Jackson MS, Mar 15, 75; chdn Ford Smith III, Mary Catherine, Douglas Fugate Caldwell; MillsC 63-65; UMS 65-68, BA; RTS 68-71, MDiv; O Jun 27, 71, St And Pby (PCUS); ap First Ch, Cleveland, MS, 71-74; campm DSU, 71-74; campm MSSU, 75-84; p Grace P Ch, Starkville, MS, 84-89; p Grace P Ch, Jackson, TN, 90-94; astp Riveroaks Ref P Ch, Germantown, TN, 94, ascp 95-14; ss Covenant P Ch at Jackson, Jackson, TN, 14-15; ob Trinity Ref Ch, Rossville, TN, 16-17

1684 Hapano Drive, Germantown, TN 38138 – 901-848-8284   Covenant
E-mail: fordandmartha@gmail.com

Williams, Forrest Todd – b Baltimore, MD, Jul 22, 66; f Forrest Henry; m Carole Elaine Connelly; w Cynthia Ruth Hoffman, Baltimore, MD, Jan 2, 88; chdn Forrest David, Jacob Raymond, Samuel Calvin, Hope Mallory; UB 89, BS; RTS 93, MDiv; L Jan 9, 94; O Aug 28, 94, Pitts Pby; ascp Providence P Ch, Robinson Township, PA, 94-97; astp Evangelical P Ch, Annapolis, MD, 97-98; op Safe Harbor P Ch, Stevensville, 98-99, srp 99-

307 Bay City Road, Stevensville, MD 21666-2781 – 410-604-1703   Chesapeake
E-mail: todd@safeharborpca.org
Safe Harbor Presbyterian Church – 410-604-1700

Williams, Hubert – mis MTW, 11-

1610 Memorial Avenue SW #A, Roanoke, VA 24015 – 410-777-8950   Chesapeake
PCA Mission to the World

Williams, James Adam – b Columbia, SC, May 8, 80; f John Cashion; m Debra Satterfield; w Lauri Elizabeth McCallum, Columbia, SC, May 25, 02; chdn Cayden Elizabeth, Tucker Adam, John Logan, Claire Lindsay; USC 02, BA; LAMP Theo Sem 17, MDiv; O May 26, 17, Palm Pby; op Rivercrest P Ch, Lexington, SC, 17-

202 Collins Court, Columbia, SC 29212   Palmetto
E-mail: adam@rivercrestpca.org
Rivercrest Presbyterian Church – 803-920-8497

Williams, James Edward – w Barbara; chdn Collette, Christopher, Casey, Courtney, Caylund; RTS, MDiv; O Mar 3, 96, MO Pby; ascp New City Flwsp, University City, MO, 96-01; srp New Life P Ch, Florissant, MO, 01-10; ob Ministries in Action, 11- 17; p 2Cities Ch, Montgomery, AL, 17

3528 Reserve Circle, Apt C, Montgomery, AL 36116 – 314-921-5188   Southeast Alabama
2Cities Church – 334-294-1226

Williams, John Kirby – b Murray, KY, Mar 14, 55; f Herbert Lee; m Mary Elizabeth Roberts; w Kaye Dover McFarling, Memphis, TN, Jul 2, 75; chdn Elizabeth Anne, Ashley Kaye; UMemp 77, BA; KTS 06; O Oct 16, 07, SFL Pby; ob srp New Hope Comm Church, 05-

6550 NE 21st Drive, Ft. Lauderdale, FL 33308 – 954-351-7667   South Florida
New Hope Community Church

Williams, Jonathan – Recd PCA Jul 26, 14, Palm Pby; astp Two Rivers P Ch, North Charleston, SC, 14-16; p Fairview P Ch, Fountain Inn, SC, 16-

505 Scarlet Oak Drive, Fountain Inn, SC 29644   Calvary
E-mail: Pastor@fairviewpca.com
Fairview Presbyterian Church – 864-862-2403

Williams, Lindsey Taylor – b Raleigh, NC, Apr 25, 75; f James Oliver; m Julia Kendall; w Kara Lauren Whiteside, Rocky Mount, NC, Aug 1, 98; chdn Austin Laurence, Marion Blair, Ann Lauren; UNC 97, BA; RTS 03, MDiv; O Aug 24, 03, CentCar Pby; astp Uptown Christ Cov Ch, Charlotte, NC, 03-05; ascp 05-08; op Midtown Comm Ch, Raleigh, NC, 08-

2417 Basil Drive, Raleigh, NC 27612-2875   Eastern Carolina
E-mail: Lindsey@midtown-church.org
Midtown Community Church – 919-601-3903

Williams, Michael D. – prof CTS, 99-

833 Pebblefield, Ballwin, MO 63021 – 636-227-0163   Missouri
Covenant Theological Seminary – 314-434-4044

Williams, Michael Rhodes – b Anniston, AL, Jan 20, 49; f Austin Richard; m Mittie Inez Bowman; w Kim Ann Moffett; chdn Michael Rhodes Jr., Anna Leigh, Holly Catherine, Alexander Burch; SamU 67-73, BA; CTS 73-77, MDiv; GrTS 86, MA; L Jun 28, 77; O Jun 28, 77, TNVal Pby; p Westminster Ch, Louisville, KY, 77-78; ap Briarwood P Ch, Birmingham, AL, 79-81; p Mount Cal P Ch, Pinson, AL, 81-85; ap Good Shepherd P Ch, Valparaiso, IN, 85-86; fndr, Dir Immanuel Couns Min, 86-97, sus 97-01; ob couns, Dir Immanuel Counseling Min, Birmingham, 01-

5085 Caldwell Mill Road, Birmingham, AL 35242 – 205-969-6488   Evangel
E-mail: icmin87@gmail.com
Immanuel Counseling Ministries, Birmingham

Williams, Randy Edward – b Melbourne, AR, Dec 15, 58; f Otto; m Audrey Womack; w Susan; chdn Clayton; NOBTS 92-94, MDiv; L Oct 12, 97; O Oct 12, 97, NoCA Pby; moy Northside Bapt Ch,

Williams, Randy Edward, continued
Slidell, LA, 88-89; p Airport Rd Bapt Ch, Slidell, LA, 89-94; Chap USN, USS DUBUQUE, 96-98; Chap USN, Naval Station, Pascagoula, MS, 98-02; Chap USN, Commander Destroyer Squad Six, 02-04; Chap USN, NAS, Patuxent River, MD, 04-07; Chap Dist Comm 9th Coast Guard District Cleveland, OH , 07-10; ob Chap VA Med Center, Memphis, 17-

2672 Dibrell Trail Drive, Collierville, TN 38017   Northern California
E-mail: rewilliams3830@gmail.com

    Williams, Roger Neil – b Macomb, IL, Jun 17, 72; f Fred Roger; m Donna Jo Utsinger; w Carmen Lee Antle, Bushnell, IL, May 27, 95; chdn Luke Adam, Elizabeth Marie, Rebekah Grace, Sarah Christine, Joshua David; UStateNY 93, BA; CTS 98, MDiv; L Oct 98, GrLks Pby; O Feb 21, 99, GrLks Pby; astp Christ Community Ch, Carmel, IN, 98-02; op New City Ch, Indianapolis, IN, 02-07; p 07-

1044 North Audubon Road, Indianapolis, IN 46219 – 317-322-0692   Central Indiana
E-mail: roger@newcityindy.org
New City Church – 317-352-1479

    Williams, Ronald – b Memphis, TN, Mar 1, 49; f Riley; m Elizabeth Johnson; w Paula Chunn, Dallas, TX, May 30, 71; chdn Randy; DBU 71, BA; SWBTS 74, MDiv; O Aug 03, NoTX Pby; astp Park Cities P Ch, Dallas, TX, 03-

3883 Turtle Creek Boulevard, Apt 1604, Dallas, TX 75219-4431 – 972-333-7588   North Texas
E-mail: ron.williams@pcpc.org
Park Cities Presbyterian Church – 214-224-2500

    Williams, Thurman Lenard – b Aug 17, 67; f Edwin W.; m Dorothy L. Ford; w Evanthia Adele Philippides, Timonium, MD; TowU 87-90; ChTS 94-00, MDiv; L May 99, Pot Pby; O Feb 20, 00, Pot Pby; int Faith Christian Flwsp Ch, Baltimore, MD, 95-99; srp New Song Comm Ch, Baltimore, MD, 00-13; astp Gr & Peace Flwsp, St. Louis, MO, 13-

5920 Etzel Avenue, St. Louis, MO 63112 – 314-300-8344   Missouri
E-mail: thurmanwi@gmail.com
Grace & Peace Fellowship – 314-367-8959

    Williams, Warren E. – b Bimidji, MN, Jan 9, 25; f John Leo W; m Annette; w Cecelia Bourdeaux, Minneapolis, MN, Apr 12, 47; chdn Warren Scott; BIOLA 55-57; LVBCS 66-67; BerBI 74, GrT; O May 74, Pac Pby; p Comm Congr Ch, San Ysidro, CA, 70-73; p Chapel Del Sol Comm Ch, 73-94; p New Cov Ch (non-PCA), 85-94; hr 94

Address Unavailable   South Coast
HR

    Williamson, Walter Cecil Jr. – b Montgomery, AL, May 15, 40; f Walter Cecil W; m Jane Owen; w Peggy Duke, Selma, AL, Sept 17, 66; chdn Kimberly Lynn, Richard Brian, Jennifer Leigh; AU 62, BA; ColTS 65, BD; WTS 81, DMin; Jones SchLaw 04, JD; O Jun 6, 65, Tusc Pby; p AL Ave Ch, Selma, AL, 65-68; p Crescent Hill P Ch, Selma, AL, 69-15; hr 15

221 Cone Drive, Selma, AL 36701-7112 – 334-872-7327   Warrior
HR

    Willis, Clayton – w Kristi; chdn Calvin, Alexandra, Joshua, Elizabeth; BIOLA, BA; WSCAL, MATS; O 06, SoCst Pby; p Providence P Ch, Palm Desert, CA, 05-18; ip Christ Ch P, Irvine, CA, 18-

17065 Branco Drive, Chinio Hills, CA 91705 – 760-880-5621   South Coast
E-mail: pastorclayton@christchurchpres.net
Christ Church Presbyterian – 949-407-9227

Willis, Shawn – b San Antonio, TX, Jan 18, 76; f David; m Linda House; w Melissa Boyce, Sparta, IL, Feb 16, 08; SIU 01, BA; CTS 10, MDiv; O Feb 20, 11, Iowa Pby; p West Friesland P Ch, Ackley, IA, 11-17; p Faith P Ch, Ackley, IA, 11-17; p Cornerstone P Ch, Ackley, IA, 16-18

410 South Main Street, PO Box 6, Cutler, IL 62238 Iowa
E-mail: shawndwillis@gmail.com

Wills, Tolivar – w Samantha; chdn Hailey Paige, Riley Benson, Anthony Graham; WittU 91, BS; GCTS 05, MDiv; O Nov 05, SNE Pby; astp Christ P Ch, New Haven, CT, 06-14; op Christ P Ch in the Hill, New Haven, CT, 13-14; srp St. Paul's P Ch, Atlanta, 14-

163 Ponce De Leon Avenue NE, Atlanta, GA 30308 Metro Atlanta
E-mail: twills02@gmail.com
St. Paul's Presbyterian Church – 404-709-2264

Willson, Bruce – b Paris, France, Jan 5, 56; f Bruce; m Martha Ann Albritton; w Kathy Ann Kiper, Monroe, LA; chdn Bruce G. III, Rachel Renaud (Lane), Abigail Kiper (Anderson); LATU 78, BS; DTS 82, ThM; RTS 95, DMin; O 82, SBC; Recd PCA 16, MSVal Pby; astp Forest Meadow Bapt Ch, Dallas, TX, 82-85; p Audubon Drive Bible Church, Laurel, MS, 85-93; srp Grace Bible Church, Nacogdoches, TX, 93-00; p Alabama Baptist Church, Arcadia, LA, 02-12; ss John Knox P Ch, Ruston, LA, 12-16, p 16-

133 Mayfield Road, Ruston, LA 71270 Mississippi Valley
E-mail: bgwillson@gmail.com
John Knox Presbyterian Church

Wilmhoff, Marshall Ray – O Aug 24, 14, OHVal Pby; astp Tates Creek P Ch, Lexington, KY, 14-

463 Johnson Avenue, Lexington, KY 40508 – 205-616-3248 Ohio Valley
E-mail: mwilmhoff@tcpca.org
Tates Creek Presbyterian Church – 859-272-4399–

Wilson, Andrew S. – w Jonelle; chdn Bryna, Emmett, Henry; UPitt 93, BA; GCTS 01, MDiv, 02, ThM; O May 25, 03, SNE Pby; astp, int Redeemer P Ch, Concord, MA, 01-03; medu First EPC, Renton, WA, 03-05; p Grace P Ch, Laconia, NH, 05-; bk rvw "The Shallows," *Modern Reformation*, Jul/Aug 11

363 Pleasant Street, Laconia, NH 03246 – 603-524-1325 Northern New England
E-mail: pastorandy@grapcanh.org
Grace Presbyterian Church – 603-528-4747

Wilson, Carl William – b Montgomery, AL, Jul 17, 24; f Carl William; w Sara Jo Kiger, Maryville, TN, Aug 17, 48; chdn Mary Linda, David Carl, Stephen Alan, Sharon Ruth, Joy Marie; MaryvC 46-49, BA; FulTS 50-53, MDiv, 57, ThM; ETSU 60-61, stu; L Apr 22, 54; O May 2, 54, EAL Pby (PCUS); ev EAL Pby, 54-56; p New Bethel, Piney Flats chs, Piney Flats, TN, 56-60; p Rocky Spgs Ch, Piney Flats, TN, 56-60; p Central Ch, Athens, GA, 61-63; p Perry P Ch, Perry, GA, 64-65; ydir CCC, 65-74, wc 74; t WDA, 74-98; op Carriage Lane P Ch, Peachtree City, GA, 88-90; ob dir Ch rel, t RTSFL, 99-03; hr; *With Christ in the School of Discipleship Building*; *Our Dance Has Turned to Death*; *From Uncertainty To Fulfillment*; *Man Is Not Enough*; *Essentials for Training Leaders*, 00; *True Enlightenment: From Natural Chance to Personal Creator*; *Essentials for Training Leaders*, 00; *Fulfillment: The Life and Ministry of Jesus the Christ*; Rev *With Christ In School Of Disciple Building*; *Liberty in an Evil Age*, 08; *The Power of New Covenant Love: Revealing God's Image by Marriage Union of Man and Woman*, 13

223 Blue Creek Drive, Winter Springs, FL 32708 – 407-971-6831 Metro Atlanta
E-mail: andragathia@bellsouth.net; www.bravegoodmen.org
HR

Wilson, Dan – b Memphis, TN, Aug 20, 70; w Heather R. Garrison, Memphis, TN, Jul 28, 95; chdn Mikaela Elizabeth, Emmalyn Joy, Lydia Grace, Daniel Graham; UMemp 93, BA; MidABTS 96, MDiv, 01,

Wilson, Dan, continued
PhD; O Jul 10, 07, TNVal Pby; asst prof BryC, 01-05; ob Harvest USA Mid-South Region, Chattanooga, TN, 05-; diss "Jesus' Rhetoric of Authority in the Temple Conflict Narrative: A Rhetorical Analysis of Matthew 21-23;" rvw "Greek for the Rest of Us: Mastering Bible Study without Mastering Biblical Languages," *Journal of the Evangelical Theological Society. 47.3*, 04; "Hermeneutical Adequacy: A Brief Case for Reading Scripture as Scripture." *Christ and Culture: Proceedings of the 2001 Christianity in the Academy Conference*; " 'Pornified"Men In the Church: How Bad Is It?" *Pulpit Helps*, Oct 09; "Why So Many Men are Pornified: Sexual Idolatry, Sexual Wasteland" *Pulpit Helps*, Nov 09; "Shepherding 'Pornified' Men: Leading Strugglers Out of the Wasteland," *Pulpit Helps*, Dec 09

1203 Osbourne Avenue, Abington, PA 19001 – 423-775-8786　　　　　　　　Tennessee Valley
E-mail: dan@harvestusa.org
Harvest USA Mid-South Region

Wilson, David Andrew – b Ft Lauderdale, FL, Oct 16, 65; f James Hamilton; m Mary Eunice Hard; w Angela Renee Tymon, Mt Carmel, TN, Jun 18, 88; chdn Nathaniel James, Samuel Barrett, Emma Kate, Benjamin David, Calvin Jack; KgC 87, BA; RTSFL 92, MDiv; L Apr 93, Westm Pby; O Jan 28, 96, CentGA Pby; campm RUF, GASoU, Statesboro, GA, 95-06; chp Denton, TX, 06-07; op Denton P Ch, Flower Mound, TX, 07-11; p 11-

157 Chaparral Est, Shady Shores, TX 76208-5738 – 940-498-1881　　　　　　　　North Texas
E-mail: david@dentonpres.org
Denton Presbyterian Church

Wilson, Gary Michael – b St. Louis, MO, Mar 17, 45; f Cecil Galen (d); m Bernice Davis (d); w Michele McCartan, St. Louis, MO, May 22, 71; chdn Christopher Garrett, Jennifer Nicole (Ostan); GrnvC 68, BS; TEDS 79, MDiv; O Jan 12, 80, TNVal Pby; mis MTW, Germany, 81-85; mis OCI, Germany, 81-85; Dir OCI, 85-98; Dir Barnabas Int, Colorado Springs, CO, 98-07; assoc Paraclete Mission Group, CO Springs, CO, 07-

8012 Corn Mountain Place NW, Albuquerque, NM 87114-6082 – 719-964-6216　　　Tennessee Valley
E-mail: wilsonmick@gmail.com
Paraclete Mission Group – 719-964-6216

Wilson, John W. – p New Cov P Ch, Monroeville, PA, 09-

3 Manorfield Circle, Delmont, PA 15626 – 724-468-6946　　　　　　　　　　　Pittsburgh
E-mail: jwilson@newcovpca.org
New Covenant Presbyterian Church – 412-856-5717

Wilson, Kenneth Douglas – b Pensacola, FL, Jul 25, 42; f James Roland W (d); m Mary Claire Jordan (d); w Leslie Ann Hall, Ft Lauderdale, FL, Sept 11, 65; chdn Nathan Allen, Benjamin Scott, Rachel Claire (Radbill); PenJC 60-62; BelC 62-64, BA; ColTS 64-67, BD; O Jun 67, Bham Pby, PCUS; astp Briarwood Pch, Birmingham, AL, 67-69, ascp 69-05; hr 05

4001 Meadowview Circle, Birmingham, AL 35243-5637 – 205-967-1452　　　　　　Evangel
E-mail: kwilsoncare@bellsouth.net
HR

Wilson, Larry Wright – b Asheville, NC, Oct 31, 47; f Lionel W; m Oleta Wright; w Charlotte Massie, Tazewell, VA, Dec 9, 72; chdn Lionel William, Rebekah Pace, Caroline Melissa, Kirsty Alice; WCU 69, BA; ColTS 73, MDiv; O Oct 73, PCUS; p Maple Grove & Sprg Creek chs, 73-74; p Alta Vista & Fork Creek, 74-79; p Murphy P Ch, NC, 79-82; p Providence P Ch, Murphy, NC, 82-92; instr TriCCC, 91-; p Hazelwood P Ch, Hazelwood, NC, 92-10; instr Haywood Comm College, 04-12, hr 12; ss Providence P Ch, Murphy, NC, 12-13; p Andrews P Ch, Andrews, NC, 18

PO Box 2295, Robbinsville, NC 28771 – 828-926-7503　　　　　　　　　Western Carolina
E-mail: dudelarry@charter.net
Andrews Presbyterian Church

Wilson, Louis H. – b Chicago, IL, Jun 28, 53; f Clifford E.; m Diana Murphy; w Ella C., Chicago, IL, May 25, 82; chdn Kameron, Christopher Morgan; MBI 82; Emmus Bible Sch 84; DBU 92, BA; NTSU 95, MS; DTS 92, ThM; L Aug 82; O Apr 84; Recd PCA Jul 15, 95, North GA; ydir Greater St Mis Bap Ch, Chicago, Il, 82-84; Dir, ev Bibleway Bib Ch, 85-89; Bap; UEM, Dallas, TX, 89-92; chp Perimeter Ministries, Atlanta, GA; op Redemption Flwsp P Ch, Fayetteville, GA, 95-99, p 99-00; srp New Song Comm Ch, Baltimore, MD, 15-

1601 North Calhoun Street, Baltimore, MD 21217   Chesapeake
E-mail: pastorwilson@nscommunity.org
New Song Community Church – 410-728-2816

Wilson, Matthew Edward – b Omaha, NE, Sep 26, 66; f Dale Edward; m Katherine Rae Watters; w Rebecca Sue Carey, Ellicott City, MD, Dec 28, 90; chdn Stephanie Ann, Tessa Kahri, Sarah Kate; TowU 88, BS; ChTS 00, MTS; O Aug 11, Glfstrm Pby; astp Wellington P Ch, Wellington, FL, 11-13; p New City Ch, Palm Beach Gardens, FL, 13-

4097 Catalpha Avenue, Palm Beach Gardens, FL 33410   Gulfstream
Email pastor@newcitychurchpbg.org
New City Church – 561-389-4382

Wilson, Robert Curtis – b Concord, NC, Apr 13, 44; f Earl Jackson; m Vivian Key; w Joyce Gattis, Dillon, SC, Jun 12, 65; chdn Jack, Lynette; CPCC 70-72, AD; BelC 72-74, BA; RTS 74-77, MDiv, 87, DMin; L Jan 21, 75, MSVal Pby; O Jun 26, 77, CentCar Pby; op Fayetteville, NC, 77-80; p Cross Creek P Ch,Fayetteville, NC, 81-82; p Westminster P Ch, Ft. Walton Beach, FL, 82-88; BdDir PEF, 88, ev 95-; p West End P Ch, Hopewell, VA, 88-01, wc 01-04; hr 04

4784 Styers Ferry Road, Winston-Salem, NC 27104   James River
HR

Wilson, Scott – O Nov 16, 14, EPA Pby, Chap Spring House Estates, Lower Gwynedd, PA, 14-

217 Cornwall Drive, Chalfont, PA 18914 – 267-664-6066   Eastern Pennsylvania
E-mail: scottwilson217@comcast.net
Spring House Estates – 215-628-8110

Wilson, Stephen R. – b Schenectady, NY, Oct 18, 52; f Robert E.; m Nina Fess; w Cheryl Fuchs, West Chester, PA, Dec 27, 75; chdn Sarah, Mark, Michael; WChSC 75, BS; WTS 82, MAR, 85, MDiv; L Nov 95; O Jun 2, 96, SusqV Pby; moy Evangelical P Ch, Newark, DE, 77-79; moy Bala Cynwyd, PA, 80-82; IVCF, Philadelphia, PA, 82-93; astp Lancaster, PA, 93-96; astp Westminster P Ch, Lancaster, PA, 96-99, wc 00; p Hope Ch, Moosic, PA, 00-

25 Frothingham Street, Pittstown Township, PA 18640 – 570-655-3330   Eastern Pennsylvania
E-mail: pastor@hopenepa.org
Hope Church – 570-451-7460

Wilson, Timothy – O Sept 30, 18, GrLks Pby; ev, mis MTW, 18-

c/o MTW   Great Lakes
PCA Mission to the World – 678-823-0004

Wiltse, Jason – O Nov 7, 10, Ohio Pby; astp Christ the Word Ch, Toledo, OH, 10-16; p Liberty P Ch, Sylvania, GA, 16-

1451 Savannah Highway, Sylvania, GA 30467 – 419-578-0732   Savannah River
E-mail: pro2720@gmail.com
Liberty Presbyterian Church – 912-564-5915

MINISTERIAL DIRECTORY

Wiman, Richard Payne – b Brandon, MS, Jul 31, 50; f James; m Williams; w Caulfield, Water Valley, MS, Jun 8, 74; chdn Lydia Ruth, Joy Elizabeth, Lindsay Caroline; USM 72, BA; RTS 76, MDiv; L Jul 9, 76; O Oct 17, 76, Gr Pby; p Calvary P Ch, Mize, MS, 76-81; p First P Ch, Belzoni, MS, 82-; *Tired Tubes and Ten-Speed Turkeys*; contr *The Christian Observer*

503 Holmes Street, Belzoni, MS 39038-3809 – 662-580-4151   Mississippi Valley
E-mail: fpc@belzonicable.com
First Presbyterian Church – 662-247-3326

Winchester, H. Scott – Dover, DE, Jun 27, 74; f William Robert; m Gerlinde Emelia Merovitz; w June Belle Schafer, Bear, DE, Mar 3, 01; chdn Cecilia Belle, Lydia June, Julia Alice, Sofia Marie; DETech 96, AAS; GoldBeacC 02, BS; RTS 15, MA; O Jun 11, 17, Hrtg Pby; astp The Town, Middletown, DE, 17-

3 Jersey Court, Middletown, DE 19709 – 302-588-4717   Heritage
E-mail: pastorscott@thetown.org
The Town – 302-464-5782

Winder, Keith Alan – O Sept 19, 17, SusqV Pby; astp Wheatland P Ch, Lancaster, PA, 17-18, ascp 18-

736 Barrcrest Lane, Lancaster, PA 17603 – 717-390-2021   Susquehanna Valley
Wheatland Presbyterian Church – 717-392-5909

Windham, John – O Aug 6, 17, MSVal Pby; astp Madison Heights P Ch, Madison, MS, 17-18; p Trinity P Ch, Corinth, MS, 18-

4175 North Harper Road, Corinth, MS 38834   Covenant
E-mail: johnwindhamtpc@gmail.com
Trinity Presbyterian Church – 662-603-3332

Windish, Michael Walter, Jr. – astp Sandhills P Ch, Southern Pines, NC, 11-12

548 Marshalls Way, Jefferson, NC 28640 – 910-528-1309   Central Carolina
E-mail: mwwindishjr@yahoo.com

Windt, Jeffrey – O Jan 21, 17, SavRiv Pby; ascp Trinity P Ch, Statesboro, GA, 17-18; astp Second P Ch, Greenville, SC, 18-

324 Meadowmoor Road, Greer, SC 29651 – 864-979-1623   Calvary
E-mail: jeffwindt@gmail.com
Second Presbyterian Church – 864-232-7621

Winebrenner, Mike – w Roxanne Dawn; chdn Eli Jackson, Edward Jude, Leo Edward, Andi Marie; UMS 01, BA; RTS 07, MA; astp Christ P Ch at Olive Branch, Olive Branch, 01-14; op Christ Flwsp, Horn Lake, MS, 14-

5805 Alta Jean Cove, Horn Lake, MS 38637 – 901-359-1220   Covenant
E-mail: mike@hornlakepca.org
Christ Fellowship – 901-609-6174

Winfree, Ambrose – O Nov 3, 13, JR Pby; mis MTW, 13-

8631 Gem Street, Richmond, VA 23235-4109 – 804-323-6077   James River
E-mail: awinfree@comcast.net
PCA Mission to the World

Winfree, Jonathan – astp Trinity P Ch, Lakeland, FL, 08; astp Ch of the Redeemer, Winter Haven, FL, 08-

295 White Ibis Lane, Winter Haven, FL 33884 – 863-297-9767   Southwest Florida
E-mail: jonathan@redeemerwinterhaven.org
Church of the Redeemer

Wingard, Charles M. – w Lynne Shockley; chdn Thomas Dowd Prettyman, Charles Andrew Wingard, John Howlett Prettyman, Clayton Thomas Wingard; USo 80, BA; VandDivS 84, MDiv; GPTS 92, DMin; O 85, Wcar Pby; p Faith P Ch, Morganton, NC, 85-91; srp First P Ch North Shore OPC, Ispwich, MA, 91-00; srp P Ch of Cape Cod OPC, 02-05; srp Westminster P Ch, Huntsville, AL, 05-14; ob prof RTS, 14-; p First P Ch, Yazoo City, MS, 16-

670 Dogwood Drive, Yazoo City, MS 39194   Mississippi Valley
E-mail: cwingard@rts.edu
First Presbyterian Church – 662-746-1226
Reformed Theological Seminary

Wingard, John Calvin – b Montgomery, AL, Sept 30, 26; f George Thomas; m Dorinda Thompson; w Betty Jo Soyars, Mason, TN, Apr 4, 61; chdn John Calvin, George Clifton; Lyons College 48, BA; ColTS 51, BD, 61, ThM; L Jul 51; L Nov 74; O Jul 51, AR Pby; O Nov 74, Gr Pby; p Paragould Ch, AR, 51-53; p Handsboro Ch, MS, 54-57; p Union Ch, Memphis, TN, 58-61; p Liberty P Ch, Liberty, MS, 62; p Ripley Ch, TN, 63-73, ss 73-74; p Liberty P Ch, Liberty, MS, 74-76; p Westminster P Ch, Milton, FL, 76-78; p McDonald P Ch, Collins, MS, 78-86; p First P Ch, Water Valley, MS, 86-93; ss Oak Ridge P Ch, Water Valley, MS, 91-93; rc Cov Pby, 93-95; ss New Life Ref P Ch, Munford, TN, 96-98, p 98-15; p First P Ch, Ripley, TN, 15-; ed "The Covenant Herald," presbytery newssheet, 00-02; radio min, WTRB, 16-

500 Payne Avenue, Covington, TN 38019-3016 – 901-476-3316   Covenant

Wingfield, S. Blake – astp Hope P Ch, Smithfield, VA, 17-

111 Cary Street, Smithfield, VA 23430   Tidewater
E-mail: blake.wingfield@hopepca.com
Hope Presbyterian Church – 757-542-3733

Winkler, Ben – O Otc 18, 15, Cov Pby; astp Redeemer P Ch, Memphis, TN, 15-

651 South Cooper Street, Memphis, TN 38104   Covenant
E-mail: ben@redeemermemphis.org
Redeemer Presbyterian Church – 901-721-8057

Winkler, Charles L. – EPUL, MS; RPTS 76, MDiv; WTS 04, DMin; L 74; O 75, Pitts Pby (RPCES); p Reformed P Ch of Slate Lick, Kittanning, PA, 75-79; p Ref P Ch, Murrysville, PA, 79-96; astp New Hope P Ch, Monroeville, PA, 97-98, ascp 98-05; astp Hillcrest P Ch, Volant, PA, 05-07; p Grace Ref P Ch, DuBois, PA, 07-11; p em, hr 12

1897 Sher De Lin Road, Du Bois, PA 15801-6091 – 814-371-1246   Ascension
E-mail: clwinkler@aol.com
HR

Winston, Richard – ob Geneva Ref Sem, Greenville, SC, 15-; p Roebuck P Ch, Roebuck, SC, 15-; "Christ the End of the Law: The Interpretation of Romans 10:4," *Puritan Reformed Journal*, 15

2169 East Blackstock Road, Roebuck, SC 29376   Calvary
Roebuck Presbyterian Church – 864-576-5717
Geneva Reformed Seminary

MINISTERIAL DIRECTORY   683

Winter, Richard – prof CTS, 02-

12330 Conway Road, St. Louis, MO 63141   Missouri
Covenant Theological Seminary – 314-434-4044

Winton, Mark – CTS 03; O Jul 03, Nash pby; Chap USArmy, 05-

225 Winder Way, Carthage, NC 28327   Nashville
E-mail: mark.t.winton.mil@mail.mil
United States Army

Wirebaugh, Brett Michael – b Jackson, MI, Mar 18, 69; f Larry; m Julie Reichow; w Holly Bult, Spring Arbor, MI, Aug 14, 93; chdn McKenna Joy, Carson Brad, Allayna Grace, Brooklyn Faith; Oakland U 91, BA; RTSFL 95, MDiv; WaybC 05, MA; RTSFL 15, DMin; L Jan 11, 97; O Apr 26, 97, Pitts Pby; ascp Providence P Ch, Robinson Township, PA, 95-03; ob Chap, t, hdmstr Robinson Township Ch Sch, 03-10; ascp Harvest P Ch of Medina, OH, 10-

2770 Sunburst Drive, Medina, OH 44256 – 330-636-1653   Ohio
E-mail: brett.wirebaugh@harvestpca.com
Harvest Presbyterian Church – 330-723-0770

Wise, Norman R. – w Terry; chdn Alex, Justina, Gregory; KTS, MDiv; O Sept 18, 94, SFL Pby; astp Coral Ridge P Ch, Ft. Lauderdale, FL, 94-96; srp First Ch West, Plantation, FL, 96-17, ascp 17-

221 SW 57th Avenue, Plantation, FL 33317 – 954-916-1563   South Florida
E-mail: normwise@bellsouth.net
First Church West – 954-452-4404

Wissel, Larry – b Richmond, IN, Oct 31, 54; f Leo J.; m Loretta C. Weiss; w Terri Noble, Jackson, MS, Oct 19, 91; XavU 74, BS; FuITS 82, MA; RTS 91, MDiv; L Feb 16, 99, MSVal Pby; O Mar 5, 00, MSVal Pby; ss Hollandale P Ch, Hollandale, MS, 91-97; ss Wynndale P Ch, Terry, MS, 98-00, p 00-02, wc 02-04; ss Oldenburg P Ch, Meadville, MS, 04-07; ob p West Union P Ch, Louisville, MS, 08-

201 Winsmere Way, Ridgeland, MS 39157 – 601-605-2230   Grace
West Union Presbyterian Church

Witherington, Will – astp Tates Creek P Ch, Lexington, KY, 15-

773 Rainwater Drive, Lexington, KY 40515   Ohio Valley
E-mail: wwitherington@campusoutreach.org
Tates Creek Presbyterian Church – 859-272-4399

Witmer, Timothy Zimmerman – b New Holland, PA, Sept 5, 53; f Robert John; m Mary Myers Zimmerman; w Barbara Simmers, New Holland, PA, Jul 26, 75; chdn Sara Michelle, Rebecca Anne, Nathan Timothy; WChSC 75, BA; WTS 79, MDiv; RTSFL 98, DMin; O Nov 11, 79, MidAtl Pby; ap Berith Ch, Bryn Mawr, PA, 79-86; srp Crossroads Comm Ch, Upper Darby, PA, 86-15, p em 15-; prof WTS, 97-17, prof em 17-; fndr, Dir Shepherd's Institute; p St. Stephen Ref Ch, New Holland, PA, 15-; *The Shepherd Leader*, 10; *The Shepherd Leader at Home.* 12; *Mindscape: What to Think About Instead of Worrying,* 14

106 Lynwood Drive, Box 486, Terre Hill, PA 17581 – 610-733-1659   Susquehanna Valley
E-mail: twitmer@wts.edu
St. Stephen Reformed Church – 717-354-7871

Witten, Kevin – astp Crossgate Ch, Seneca, SC, 16-18; astp Trinity P Ch, Boerne, TX, 18-

413 Hickman Street, Boerne, TX 78006 – 864-710-7971   South Texas
E-mail: kevin@trinityboerne.org
Trinity Presbyterian Church – 830-815-1212

Wohlers, Tim John – b St. Charles, IL, Jun 9, 74; f Gerald L.; m Cheryl J. Young; w Nicole Marie Clack, IL, Jan 19, 96; chdn Megan, Amaya, Eliana; MBI 94-97, ThB; RTSFL 98-99, MDiv; O Sept 2, 00, NoCA Pby; astp Oak Hills P Ch, Concord, CA, 00-01, wc 01-02; ob p Indianola Comm Ch, Indianola, WA, 02-03; ascp Calvary P Ch, Allentown, NJ, 14-15, ascp 15-16; p Faith P Ch, Akron, OH, 16-

1526 Basswood Drive, Uniontown, OH 44685 – 848-232-9387   Ohio
E-mail: pastorwohlers@gmail.com
Faith Presbyterian Church – 330-644-9654

Wojohn, Robert Edward Jr. – b Mobile, AL, Mar 19, 54; f Robert E.; m Willie Pearl Becton; w Christina Ellen Moller, Jonesboro, AR, Sept 27, 80; chdn Corrie Elizabeth, Anna Caroline, William Hunter, Robert Elijah, Luke Mills; AU 77, BS; RTS 90, MDiv; O Aug 12, 90, CentGA Pby; campm WDA, 78-87; ms/sa Trinity P Ch, Jackson, MS, 87-90; astp First P Ch, Macon, GA, 90-93; p First P Ch, Yazoo City, MS, 93-99; srp Perry P Ch, Perry, GA, 99-08; srp Plains P Ch, Zachary, LA, 09-17; hr 17

4930 Myrtle Hill Drive, Zachary, LA 70791 – 478-951-3148   Southern Louisiana
E-mail: bobwojohn@gmail.com
HR

Wolcott, Michael P. – b Troy, NY; w Sharon Meiners ; chdn Joseph, Anna, Daniel, Eden; HougC 94; RTSDC 09, MDiv; O Apr 11, 10, SusqV Pby; astp Trinity P Ch, Harrisburg, PA, 10-

3609 Salem Road, Harrisburg, PA 17019 – 717-526-2174   Susquehanna Valley
E-mail: mwolcott@trinityhbg.com
Trinity Presbyterian Church – 717-545-4271

Wolfe, Joe Arthur – b Minneapolis, KS, Jan 16, 29; f Joseph John; m Daisy Hester Babb; w Dorothy Margaret Magnus, Minneapolis, KS, Aug 22, 59; chdn Darrell Duane (d); BrBI 56-59; L 56, Bap Ch, Minneapolis, KS; O Apr 66, Berean Fund Ch; p Berean Fund Ch, Burwell, NE, 63-72; p Northwest Berean Fund Ch, 72-83; p Seven Mile Ford P Ch, 83-89; p Asbury P Ch, Johnson City, TN, 89-94, ss 94; hr 94; op New Cov P Ch, Sheridan, WY, 00-02; hr 04

2101 Snow Drive, Alamogordo, NM 88410 – 575-439-8013   Rio Grande
E-mail: joewolfe@q.com
HR

Wolfe, Luke – b MN, Nov 11, 86; w Aimee Noelle Meunier, Jan 2, 09; chdn Caleb, Katie Grace; UWI 10, BA; CTS 15, MDiv; O Jun 3, 18, SWFL Pby; ascp Trinity P Ch, Lakeland, FL, 18-

512 Wwst Maxwell Street, Lakeland, FL 33803 – 763-670-7337   Southwest Florida
E-mail: luke@trinitylakeland.org
Trinity Presbyterian Church – 863-603-7777

Wolfe, Paul David – b Pittsburgh, PA, Feb 4, 71; f Richard Alan; m Anne Marie Fisher; w Christine Lynne Olson, Alexandria, VA, May 23, 98; chdn Henry Fisher, Philip Campbell, Charlotte Lillian ; UVA 93, BA; WTS 00, MDiv, 17, ThM; L May 8, 99, Pot Pby; O Sept 24, 00, Pot Pby; ascp New Hope P Ch, Fairfax City, VA, 00-17; srp 18-; *My God Is True! Lessons Learned Along Cancer's Dark Road; Setting our Sights on Heaven: Why It's Hard and Why It's Worth It*

4007 Woodland Drive, Fairfax, VA 22030 – 703-267-6542   Potomac
E-mail: Paul@NewHopeFairfax.org
New Hope Presbyterian Church – 703-385-9056

Wolfe, Richard McPherren – b Milwaukee, WI, Mar 11, 58; f Harve; m Bonnie McPherren; w Lori Kauffman, Wayne, PA, Dec 28, 83; chdn Katelyn Joy, Christopher McPherren, Caleb Thomas; SRU 81, BA; WTS 86, MDiv; LTSPA 90, STM; CIU 01, DMin; L Jan 10, 87; O Nov 29, 87, Phil Pby; ap Tenth P Ch, Philadelphia, PA, 87-89; astp Village Seven P Ch, Colorado Springs, CO, 89-92; mis MTW, Manila,

Wolfe, Richard McPherren, continued
Phillipines (tm ldr), 92-99; mis MTW, Mexico, 99-03; MTW, reg dir Caribbean/Cent Amer, 04-16; astp Village Seven P Ch, Colorado Springs, CO, 16-; "Foundations in the Christian Life" and "Discovering & Using Your Spiritual Gifts" in *Tagalog*; *Growing in Leadership* (training man); *Leading the Way: Training Elders and Deacons; Character of a Christian Leader*

4610 Bridle Pass Drive, Colorado Springs, CO 80923 – 719-380-9127   Rocky Mountain
E-mail: rwolfe@v7pc.org
Village Seven Presbyterian Church – 719-574-6700

Wolfgang, William Ralph – b Youngstown, OH, May 3, 37; f Ralph Edgar; m Carrie Alexander; w Judith Williams (d), Youngstown, OH, Jun 12, 64; chdn Linda, Amy Beth; CC 67, BA; CTS 70, MDiv; L Apr 69; O Apr 71, Pitts Pby; p Fairview Ref P Ch, Industry, PA, 71-72; p Robinwood RP Ch, Youngstown, OH, 72-81; p Cornerstone P Ch, Youngstown, OH, 81-05; hr 05

9691 Country Scene Lane, Mentor, OH 44060 – 440-579-5835   Ohio
HR

Womack, Patrick Joseph – b Waynesville, NC, Apr 17, 67; f Charles J; m Norma Jean Winchester; w Kathleen Anne Farley, Mt. Holly, NC, Mar 13, 93; chdn Joseph Sutton, Sarah Grace; WCU 85-89, BA; RTS 89-92, MDiv; L Jul 18, 92; O Feb 7, 93, CentCar Pby; ydir Hazelwood P Ch, Hazelwood, NC, 87-89; stus Cuba Ch, Cuba, AL, 90-92; int Westview P Ch, Mount Holly, NC, 92-93, p 93-96; p Carolina P Ch, Locust, NC, 96-10; p Hazelwood P Ch, Waynesville, NC, 10-

PO Box 67, Hazelwood, NC 28738 – 828-550-0240   Western Carolina
E-mail: pwomack@hazelwoodchurch.com
Hazelwood Presbyterian Church – 828-456-3912

Won, Hoon Sang – p Panama City Korean Ch, Panama City, FL, 04-13; astp Korean American Ch of Jackson, Raymond, MS, 13-

E-mail: hsw316@hotmail.com   Korean Southeastern
Korean American Church of Jackson – 601-922-8459

Won, Peace Junghoon – p Oregon Eden P Ch, 06-

Oregon Eden Presbyterian Church – 503-848-8168   Korean Northwest

Wong, David – b Hong Kong, Nov 27, 53; f Kenneth; m Yun Juen Ong; w Judy Hui, New York, NY, Aug 22, 76; chdn Joseph David, Jonathan David, Deborah Judith, David Jacob; BrkPI 74, BS; WTS 89, MDiv; L Sept 9, 89; O Jun 2, 90, NoE Pby; srp Covenant Ch, Whitestone, NY, 90-

400 Chelsea Avenue, Paramus, NJ 07652-3436 – 201-599-0083   Metropolitan New York
Covenant Church – 718-352-8646

Wong, Didi – b Hong Kong, May 21, 75; f Andrew; m Rita; w Amber; chdn Elijah Jackson, Shiloh Isaac, Tristan Josiah; UMD, BA; RTSFL, MDiv; O Jul 30, 06, RMtn Pby; astp Deer Creek Community Ch, Littleton, CO, 06-10; astp Church of the Good Shepherd, Durham, NC, 10-13, ob; p One Ancient Hope P Ch, Iowa City, IA, 16-

PO Box 305, Iowa City, IA 52244   Iowa
E-mail: pilgrimdd@hotmail.com
One Ancient Hope Presbyterian Church – 319-512-7264

Woo, Luke Heewon – astp Renewal Church of the Main Line, Devon, PA, 16-

65-08 Drexelbrook Drive, Drexel Hill, PA 19026   Philadelphia Metro West
E-mail: lukewoo@renewalmainline.org
Renewal Church of the Main Line

Woo, Sundong – wc

E-mail: woosd66@hotmail.com   Korean Capital

Wood, Andy – b Richmond, VA, Nov 16, 76; f Roy; m Susan Seaman; w Amy Rickman, Richmond, VA, Aug 9, 03; chdn Josiah Archer, Cooper Simeon, Sadie Jane, Benjamin Sutton; VPI 99, BS; CTS 07, MDiv; O May 25, 08, Ecar Pby; astp Redeemer P Ch, Raleigh, NC, 08-09, ascp 09-11; campm RUF, VATech, 11-

206 Fincastle Drive, Blacksburg, VA 24060   Blue Ridge
PCA Reformed University Fellowship

Wood, Brian C. – ascp New Life Ch of Phil, Philadelphia, PA, 00-05, ob 05-12; srp Berachah Ch, Cheltenham, PA, 08-12; ascp Grace Christian Ch, Herndon,VA, 12-18; p City of Hope Ch, Columbia, MD, 18-

5174 Downwest Ride, Columbia, MD 21044 – 443-546-4066   Chesapeake
E-mail: pbcw@live.com
City of Hope Church – 443-583-4265

Wood, Britton – campm RUF, USCarolina, 07-11; campm RUF, Stanford, 11-18; admin RUF, area coord, 18-

6509 Radcliff Drive, Nashville, TN 37221   Northern California
E-mail: bwood@ruf.org
PCA Reformed University Fellowship

Wood, Hobie – w Hannah; ClemU 05, BA; RTS 11, MDiv; O Apr 12, GAFH Pby; p Christ P Ch, Clarkesville, GA, 12-

643 Washington Street, Clarkesville, GA 30523 – 706-490-2065   Georgia Foothills
E-mail: hobie.wood@gmail.com
Christ Presbyterian Church – 706-490-2065

Wood, James – O Mar 1, 16, SoTX Pby; astp All Saints P Ch, Austin, TX, 16; astp Grace and Peace P Ch of Austin, Austin, TX, 16-17

501 Farber Road, 116, Princeton, NJ, 08540   South Texas
E-mail: james.wood1218@gmail.com

Wood, Matthew – O Mar 4, 12, NoTX Pby; op Grace and Peace P Ch, Anna, TX, 12-17, p 17-

4304 Ridgewood Road, Melissa, TX 75454   North Texas
E-mail: matt@graceandpeace-pca.org
Grace and Peace Presbyterian Church – 972-529-1502

Wood, P. Thomas – w Rachel Frye, Columbia, SC, Sept 10, 77; chdn Anne, Julie, Amy; FIU; MCU; CBC, BA; CBS 81-84, MDiv; RTSFL 09, DMin; L Jul 83, Cal Pby; O Feb 85, SW Pby; op, p Northeast P Ch, Albuquerque, NM, 84-89; bd mbr Albuquerque YFC; Chap Goose Crk PD; VP alum assoc, CIU; op Metro North P Ch, Goose Creek, SC, 89-93, p 93-00; admin, ev Perimeter Ministries, Atlanta, GA, 00-03; ob pres Church Multiplication Ministries, 03-; co-auth *Gospel Coach*, 12*; Church Planter Field Manual: Exploring*, 13*; Church Planter Field Manual: Climbing* , 13

7115 Dressage Way, Cumming, GA 30040 – 770-619-3089   Metro Atlanta
E-mail: Tom@cmmnet.org
Church Multiplication Ministries

MINISTERIAL DIRECTORY

Wood, Vincent Lee – b Amarillo, TX, Jul 6, 64; f Jerry; m Shirley Jones; w Robin Carlson, Ft. Collins, CO, Dec 28, 85; chdn Patrick Ryan, Michael Scott; Aims Comm Coll; SCS 90-91; GPTS 92-94, BD; TTS 15, MA, PhD; L Sept 93; O Sept 25, 94, SW Pby; int Hope P Ch, Gilbert, AZ, 93-94, p 94-96; ascp Imm-anuel P Ch, Mesa, AZ, 96-97, p 97-08; sc SW Pby, 98; mis MTW 08-11; ob 11-12; srp Providence P Ch, York, PA, 12-; *The Train: A Model for Transforming the Heart*

2182 Narnia Drive, York, PA 17404 Susquehanna Valley
E-mail: vwood@yorkpca.org
Providence Presbyterian Church – 717-767-4772

Wood, Walter W. Jr. – b Mobile, AL, Feb 10, 52; f Walter W Sr.; m Barbara Ann Brown; w Rebecca Ann Esch, May 27, 78; chdn Walter III, Elisabeth Ann (Ball); UAL 74, BA; RTS 82, MDiv, 92, DMin; L Aug 1, 82; O Aug 1, 82, NGA Pby; ms/sa First P Ch, Jackson, MS, 80-82; vis lect/prof RTSFL, 94; astp Perimeter Ch, Duluth, GA, 82-94; chp North Cincinnati Comm Ch, Mason, OH, 94-96, srp 96-15, p em 15-; US dir Redeemer City to City, 15-17; Redeemer City to City, sr catalyst, West Eur, asst dir, North Amer, 17-; vis lect/prof RTS, 98; mod OHV pby, 08; chm OHV MNA co, 02-08, 10-14; *Ministry to the Never Married Single Adult*; 2 art in *Messenger* (Feb 91)

3436 Surrey Lane, Mason, OH 45040 – 513-459-1258 Ohio Valley
E-mail: walter@redeemercitytocity.com
Redeemer City to City

Wood, William P. – b Pittsburgh, PA, Oct 3, 38; f W. Paul; m Margaret A. Taylor; w Dr. Christel Baer, Jan 12, 91; UChi 56-58; UPitt 62-63; GenC 64-68, BS; RPTS 74, MDiv; WTS 80-89, PhD; L 83; O 83, Phil Pby; ap Presbyterian Ch (Ind), Coatesville, PA, 83-85; mis MTW, Liebenzell Msn, Pac Is BibC, 86-04; hr

Address Unavailable Philadelphia
HR

Woodall, Justin Conner – O Aug 15, 10, Palm Pby; astp Surfside P Ch, Myrtle Beach, SC, 10-14; astp Westtown Ch, Tampa, FL, 14-; op City Ch St. Petersburg Msn, St.Petersburg, FL, 16-

2411 14th Avenue North, St. Petersburg, FL 33713 – 727-201-7626 Southwest Florida
E-mail: justwoodall@gmail.com
Westtown Church – 813-855-2747
City Church St. Petersburg Mission – 727-201-7625

Woodard, Luther Paul – b Woodland, WA, Jan 30, 38; f M. Luther; m Margaret E. Griffith; w Kathy E. Brown, Norfolk, VA, Jun 15, 68; chdn Kimberly, Kelly, Jonathan; CBC 66-70, BA; CTS 77-81, MDiv; L Jan 89; O May 7, 89, MO Pby; ascp Memorial P Ch, St. Louis, MO, 89-94, wc 95; Chap Friendship Village, St. Louis, MO, 95-11; hr 11; astp New City Flwsp, St. Louis, MO, 13-

6012 Cates Avenue, St. Louis, MO 63112 – 314-780-5252 Missouri
E-mail: woodardlup@gmail.com
HR
New City Fellowship

Woodham, Michael Charles – b Dothan, AL, Oct 10, 47; f Charles Henderson; m Opal Jowers; w Deborah Dee Rabe, Jackson, MS, Jul 8, 72; chdn Michael Titus, Hannah Leah; BelC 71, BA; RTS 75, MDiv; UAL 96, DEd; O Aug 3, 75, NGA Pby; ap Smyrna P Ch, Smyrna, GA, 75-77; mis MTW, Ecuador, 77-84; mis, coord ISC, Mandeville, Jamaica, 84-88; mis, Int Dir IONA Centres/Theo Study, Caribbean, 88-06; mod SFL Pby, 05-06; astp, exec p Granada P Ch, Coral Gables, FL, 06-12*;* sc SFL pby, 11-17; ob Alive Again Ministries, 12-15; hr 15; *Attitudes of Church Members Toward a Commitment to Biblical Absolutes and the Exercise of Social Tolerance as Related to Changes in Church Membership*, 96

22055 SW 194th Avenue, Miami, FL 33170 – 305-256-1536 South Florida
E-mail: doctorwoody@mac.com
HR

Woods, Alex – O Oct 29, 17, MetAtl Pby; astp Church of the Redeemer, Atlanta, GA, 17-

E-mail: awoods@intown.org   Metro Atlanta
Church of the Redeemer – 678-298-1150

Woods, Jeff – p Southwood P Ch, Talladega, AL, 14; Chap UAB Hosp

180 Stonebrier Drive, Calera, AL 35040   Evangel
E-mail: woodsjw1@gmail.com
UAB Hospital

Woods, Philip – O EPC; Recd PCA 13, SWFL Pby; p Cornerstone of Lakewood Ranch, Bradenton, FL, 13-

14306 Covenant Way, Lakewood Ranch, FL 34202 – 314-703-7699   Southwest Florida
E-mail: phil@cornerstonelwr.org
Cornerstone of Lakewood Ranch – 941-907-3939

Woodson, Robert Coyle – b St. Louis, MO, Sept 11, 35; f Karl B.; m Orva Burns; w Shirley Elizabeth Heyes, Levittown, PA, Jun 10, 61; chdn Robert Mark, Elizabeth Ann, Stephen James, Kathryn Ruth; NWU 57, BA; CTS 60, BD; L Nov 60; O Nov 60, Midw Pby (RPCES); p BP Ch, Affton, MO, 60-63; mis MTW, Peru, SA, 64-; team ldr Cusco, 84-92; chp Lima, Peru, 93-10; hr 10; *Oh, What God Has Done, The History of the Presbyterian Mission in Peru*, 18

2529 Alnwick, Duluth, GA 30096   Missouri
HR

Woolard, Gordon Thomas – b Richmond, VA, Mar 10, 51; f James F; m Dorothy Cumming; w Marilyn Marlene Wigand, Wisconsin, Jun 3, 72; chdn Ian Gordon, Jillian Kate, Allison Blake, Jocelyn May; UWI 73, BA; WTS 76, MDiv; Chambre de Commerce, Bruxelles, Belgique 90, dipl; L 76; O Jul 8, 77, OPC; Recd PCA May 93, Pac Pby; int Bethel OPC, Ostburg, WI, 76-77; p Westminster OPC, Santa Cruz, C, 77-80; p Calvary OPC, Tallahassee, FL, 81-83; ev IFES, Brussels, Belgium, 84-92; p Grace Cov P Ch, Blacksburg, VA, 93-04; mis MTW, French-speaking Caribbean and Africa, 04-17; reg dir MTW, Indigenous Ministries of North America, 17-; *Une Résidence Royale*, 14

2520 Van Buren Street #10, Hollywood, FL 33020 – 954-925-7576   Blue Ridge
E-mail: gtwoolard@gmail.com
PCA Mission to the World

Woolner, Barry Scott – b Philadelphia, PA, Sept 30, 50; f Jack; m Alma Ziesch; w Kathleen Mitchell, Windham, NH, Aug 29, 72; chdn Rebekah (Arnold), Jonathan, Christopher, Elizabeth; BerkCC, BA; PittsTS, MDiv; O Aug 76, UPCUSA; Recd PCA 01, Asc Pby; p Glade Run UPC, Valencia, PA, 76-80; ip Meridian UPC, 81-82; op Westminster OPC, 93-98; astp Gospel Flwsp P Ch, Valencia, PA, 01-15; wc

342 Glade Mill Road, Valencia, PA 16059 – 724-898-2805   Ascension
E-mail: kathywoolner@hotmail.com

Wooten, Clay – ascp Redeemer P Ch, Edmond, OK, 16-

Redeemer Presbyterian Church – 405-550-1464   Hills and Plains

Wootton, Robert Lee – b Richmond, VA, Jun 26, 72; f Robert; m Patricia Black; w Robin Jester; chdn Abigail, Nathaniel, Naomi, Miriam; VCU 95, BFA; CTS 08, MDiv; O Oct 15, PacNW Pby; p CrossPoint Queene Anne, 08-10, wc 11-12, PRes 13, wc 14-16; p River's Edge Bible Ch, Hopewell, VA, 16-18; ip West Hopewell P Ch, Hopewell, VA, 18-

7420 Trailing Rock Road, Prince George, VA 23875 – 757-577-2420   James River
E-mail: rob@rebcpca.org
West Hopewell Presbyterian Church – 804-458-4008

Worstall, Edwin L. Jr. – b Philadelphia, PA, Mar 7, 33; f E Lawrence; m Margorie Volker; w Virginia McCool, Lansdowne, PA, May 14, 55; chdn Timothy L., Lynda L., David M.; NAC 56, BS; ColTS 63, BD; O Jul 7, 63, Atl Pby; p Bethany & Gum Creek chs, Covington, GA, 63-65; p Friendship P Ch, Laurens, SC, 66-70; p Lookout Valley P Ch, Chattanooga, TN, 70-73; p Fuller Mem P Ch, Durham, NC, 73-77; p Hopewell P Ch, Rock Hill, SC, 77-81; p Trinity Ch, Rock Hill, SC, 77-81; ss Hopewell P Ch, Rock Hill, SC, 82-83, wc 84; ss Rock Bridge P Ch, Clinton, SC, 87-91; p Fairview P Ch, Fountain Inn, SC, 91-02; hr 02; ss Bullock Creek P Ch, Sharon, SC, 02-07

719 Morningside Drive, Rock Hill, SC 29730 – 86803-329-8455　　　　　　　　　　Fellowship
HR

Woznicki, Andy – b Wausau, WI, Jul 24, 77; f Daniel P.; m Jacquelyn Jean Doyle; w Melisa Ann Penland, Augusta, GA, Mar 10, 01; chdn Abigail Kate, Caleb Randall, Stephen Samuel, Joseph Andrew; GASoU 00, BA; MetAtlSem 16, MDiv; O Mar 5, 17, MetAtl Pby; astp Creekstone Ch, Dahlonega, GA, 17-

481 Morgan Lane, Dawsonville, GA 30533　　　　　　　　　　　　　　　　Metro Atlanta
E-mail: ajwoznicki@gmail.com
Creekstone Church – 678-807-9164

Wreyford, Jeff – O 15, GAFH Pby; astp ChristChurch Suwanee, Suwanee, GA, 15-16; op Christ Redeemer PCA, Jonesboro, AR, 16-

1002 Villa, Jonesboro, AR 72401 – 770-714-0214　　　　　　　　　　　　　Covenant
E-mail: jeff@thewreyfords.com
Christ Redeemer PCA

Wright, Albert Melvin III – b Columbia, SC, Oct 25, 51; f A.M. Jr.; m Bobbie Steedley; w Teresa Pela, Florence, SC, Nov 30, 74; chdn Katie, Sally; USC 73, BA; GCTS 78, MDiv; O Jul 78, SC Pby (PCUS); ap First P Ch (PCUS), Clinton, SC, 78-80; p First Ch (PCUS, PCUSA), Orangeburg, SC, 80-86; p Trinity P Ch, Orangeburg, SC, 86-90; chp MNA, Palm Pby, 91-93; op Grace Cov Ch, Blythewood, SC, 91-93, wc 93-02; ss St. Andrews P Ch, Columbia, SC, 02, ss 05-06; ss Gracepoint P Ch, Irmo, SC, 09; wc

125 Tam O Shanter Drive, Blythewood, SC 29016-9457 – 803-786-4434　　　　　　Palmetto

Wright, Bradley – b Mesquite, TX, Mar 29, 76; f larry Glen; m Melinda Ann Moore; w Jamie June Hudson, Houston, TX, Aug 22, 98; chdn Avery Elaine, William Bradley, Walker James; UTXAu, BA; CTS, MDiv; O Jul 03, BlRdg Pby; int Kirk of the Hills P Ch, St. Louis, MO, 98-02; astp Trinity P Ch, Charlottesville, VA, 02-04; astp Grace P Ch, The Woodlands, TX, 04-07; op Redeemer Sugar Land, Sugar Land, TX, 07-16; astp Christ the King P Ch, Houston, TX, 16-

7118 Greatwood Trails Drive, Sugar Land, TX 77479　　　　　　　　　　　　Houston Metro
Christ the King Presbyterian Church – 713-892-5464

Wright, Christopher – Aug 21, 74; w Kerry Lynn; chdn Jennifer Karleene, Lisa Katherine; CC, BA; RTSNC, MDiv; O Jul 11, 05, War Pby; p Linden P Ch, Linden, AL, 04-08; p North Park P Ch, Jackson, MS, 08-13; p Delhi P Ch, Delhi, LA, 16-

111 4th Street, PO Box 368, Delhi, LA 71232　　　　　　　　　　　　　Mississippi Valley
E-mail: ckwright51@hotmail.com
Delhi Presbyterian Church – 318-878-2358

Wright, Joseph Grady IV – b Anderson, SC, May 14, 74; f Joseph G. III; m Rebecca Ann Stephens; w Summer Marie Kent, Anderson, SC, Aug 8, 98; chdn Joseph Grady V, Owen Nathan, Murray Jonathan; MerU 97, BA; RTS 01, MDiv; O Aug 26, 01, MSVal Pby; campm RUM, MSColl, 01-12; Chap 12-

RAF Mildenhall, PSC 37 Box 3197, APO, AE 09459　　　　　　　　　　Mississippi Valley
E-mail: joey4w@gmail.com

Wright, Lee – O Jun 15, CentFL Pby; campm RUF, UCentFL, 14-

4533 Northern Dancer Way, Orlando, FL 32826　　　　　　　　　　　Central Florida
E-mail: lee.wright@ruf.org
PCA Reformed University Fellowship

Wright, Scott R. – b Kalamazoo, MI, Feb 22, 60; f John P; m Nancy Joan Pritchard; w Linda Susan Lex, New Hope, PA, May 26, 90; chdn Sarah Catherine, Hannah Lindsay, Emily Elizabeth, Samuel Davies, Taylor Grace, Madison Anna, Chelsea Joy; PU 82, BA; GCTS 91, MDiv; WTS 99, PhD; L Sept 93, Phil Pby; O Oct 1, 95, Asc Pby; astp Faith P Ch, Akron, OH, 95-96; op Redeemer Ch, Hudson, OH, 96, p 96-

7565 Deerpath Trail, Hudson, OH 44236 – 330-653-9544　　　　　　　Ohio
E-mail: scott.wright@redeemerohio.org
Redeemer Church – 330-656-5787

Wright, Steven C. – w Allegra , Jackson, MS, Nov 30, 02; chdn Hannah, Lydia, Matthew, Abigail; WFU 87, BA; WSCAL 93, MAR; O Mar 18, 07, LA Pby; p Bethel P Ch, Lake Charles, LA, 07-15; p Covenant P Ch at Jackson, Jackson, TN, 15-

PO Box 10385, Jackson, TN 38308　　　　　　　　　　　　　　　　Covenant
E-mail: pastor@cpcjackson.org
Covenant Presbyterian Church at Jackson – 731-300-7351

Wrigley, Paul Riley – b Tulsa, OK, May 22, 54; f Pat Riley; m Nadine Elizabeth Koerner; w Kay Janeen Kelly, Virginia Beach, VA, Apr 10, 82; chdn Gabrielle Janeen, Philip Riley, Alicia Meredith; USNA 72-76, BS; BibTS 83-87, MDiv; NavWC 95, MA; L Sept 10, 88; O Oct 30, 88, Phil Pby; Chap USN, 89-11; astp, exec p Covenant Ch of Naples, Naples, FL, 11-12, ascp 12-16

1784 Legare Lane, Virginia Beach, VA 23464　　　　　　　　　　　Suncoast Florida
E-mail: pwrigley@juno.com

Wroughton, James Francis – b Yarinachocha, Peru, SA, Oct 16, 54; f James Orville; m Gloria Gray; w Lynn Ellen Kelly, May 7, 83; chdn Katherine Lynn, Elizabeth Anne; WheatC 76, BA; UTXA 88, MA; GCTS 79, MDiv; FTSSWM 96, ThM; L 79; O 79, Pac Pby; mis MTW, WBT, 83-

7500 West Camp Wisdom Road, Dallas, TX 75236-5629 – 972-809-4370　　Pacific
PCA Mission to the World

Wyatt, Andrew Lee – astp Christ Ch PCA, Trussville, AL, 12-14; astp First P Ch, Macon, GA, 14-

3710 Overlook Drive, Macon, GA 31204 – 478-787-1050　　　　　　　Central Georgia
E-mail: awyatt@fpcmacon.org
First Presbyterian Church – 478-746-3223

Wymond, William Kenneth – b Louisville, KY, Jan 26, 42; f Chess Bond W; m Grace Shackleton; BelC 67, BA; RTS 70, BD, 88, DMin; O Jul 26, 70, CMS Pby PCUS; ap First P Ch, Jackson, MS, 70-73; prof BelC, 73-78; ap First P Ch, Jackson, MS, 78-88; ob mmus Independent P Ch, Memphis, TN, 89-93; ob astp Independent P Ch, Savannah, GA, 93; astp First P Ch, Jackson, MS, 93-

10 C Park Avenue, Jackson, MS 39202　　　　　　　　　　　　　　Mississippi Valley
E-mail: billw@fpcjackson.org
First Presbyterian Church – 601-353-8316

Wynja, Stephen – w Dawn; chdn Kayla Ann, Noah Nicholas; ob p Holland CRC, Holland, MN, 07-

450 Sioux Street, Holland, MN 56139 – 507-347-3344　　　　　　　Siouxlands
E-mail: swynja@woodstocktel.net
Holland Christian Reformed Church, Holland, MN

MINISTERIAL DIRECTORY

Wynne, Carlton – w Linley, Jul 5, 03; chdn Robert Carlton, Connor David, Anderson Reed; astp Providence P Ch, Dallas, TX, 08-10; wc 10-15; ob prof WTS, 15-

720 Pine Hill Road, Wayne, PA 19087   Philadelphia Metro West
E-mail: cwynne35@yahoo.com
Westminster Theological Seminary

Wynne, Carroll L.G. – b Markdale, Ontario, Apr 7, 56; f Thomas Laurence; m Margret Ruth Ellis; w Kimberly Sue Wise, Philadelphia, PA, Jul 7, 84; chdn David Laurence, Jonathan Alistair, Rachel Grace; MesC 78, BA; TEDS 81, MDiv; L Mar 81; O Jan 24, 93, Phil Pby; astp St. Andrews P, Ontario, 81-82; asst, Dir Whosoever Gospel Mis, 83-84; exec dir Scripture Gift Msn (USA), 85-89; ascp Tenth P Ch, Philadelphia, PA, 89-

234 Congress Avenue, Lansdowne, PA 19050   Philadelphia
E-mail: cwynne@tenth.org
Tenth Presbyterian Church – 215-735-7688

Yaegashi, Kazuhiko – b Sendai, Miyagi, Japan, Aug 15, 47; f Tadao; m Eiko Kikuchi; w Katherine Alun Moore, Sendai, Miyagi, Japan, Mar 25, 72; chdn James Kazuhiko, David Tadahiko, Megumi Jane, Morris Yoshihiko, Emi Katrina; Tohoku Gakuin U 67-71, BA; RTS 74-77, MDiv; O Oct 18, 77, MSVal Pby; ev Yamagata Chapel (OPC Japanese msn) ob t Yamagata Gakuin HS, 77-08; ob lect Extension Seminary of Tohoku Pby, 81-97; wedding couns, 94-; brd trust, Yamagata Gakuin HS, 97-01; *Confessing Christ* – the revised Japanese translation

1-14-12 Kagota, Yamagata Shi, 990-2484 JAPAN   Mississippi Valley
E-mail: uhk54026@nifty.com

Yagel, Gary Wayne – b Washington, D.C., Apr 25, 50; f Clair C.; m Sara Elisabeth Barnitz; w Sandra Elaine Jones, Fairfax, VA; chdn Kimberly Ellen & Karen Suzan (twins), Brian Scott, Timothy George, Joshua Thomas; PASU, BA; GCTS, MDiv; RTSFL 12, DMin; L May 23, 82; O May 23, 82, MidAtl Pby; op Shady Grove P Ch, Derwood, MD, 82-84, p 84-02; op Mount Airy P Ch, Mount Airy, MD, 92-95, ss 95-98; ob Family Builders, Inc, Olney, MD, 02-; PCA CEP, cons. to Men's Min, 08-; *Forging Bonds of Brotherhood*, *Grace Transformed Sexuality*, *Allegiance: Building a Foundation of Loyalty to God*

18211 Bluebell Lane, Olney, MD 20832-3106 – 301-570-0033   Potomac
E-mail: gyagel@forgingbonds.org
Family Builders Inc.

Yancey, Robert Anthony, Jr. – O Pot Pby; astp McLean P Ch, McLean, VA, 17-

9332 Glenbrook Road, Fairfax, VA 22031   Potomac
E-mail: rob@mcleanpres.org
McLean Presbyterian Church – 703-821-0800

Yancie, Remargo S. – O Jan 7, 18, Pot Pby; astp Grace P Ch of Washington, DC, Washington, DC, 18-

807 Decatur Street NW, Washington, DC 20011 – 678-925-6516   Potomac
E-mail: ryancie@gmail.com
Grace Presbyterian Church of Washington, DC – 202-386-7637

Yang, Daniel – Recd PCA 15, MetAtl Pby, chp 15-16

425 Williams Drive, Apt. 724, Marietta, GA 30066   Metro Atlanta
E-mail: yang.mksn@live.com

Yang, David Woo Gwang – b Namwon, South Korea, Mar 10, 66; w Haesook; chdn Soohwan, Sooin; STU 89, BA; STU 89, MDiv; ACTS 99, MDiv; FTS 06, DMin; srp Sierra Vista P Ch, Sierra Vista, AZ, 09-

2875 Sierra Bermeja Drive, Sierra Vista, AZ 85650 – 520-803-9102   Korean Southwest Orange County
E-mail: woogwangyang@hanmail.net
Sierra Vista Presbyterian Church – 520-378-2466

Yang, Seong Gil – ob

E-mail: Gil0720@hotmail.com   Korean Northwest

Yang, Solomon D. – op New Life Msn Ch of Glendale, Burbank, CA, 07-

19364 Laroda Lane, Santa Clarita, CA 91350 – 661-297-4234   Korean Southwest
E-mail: solomondyang@yahoo.com
New Life Mission Church of Glendale – 661-714-7607

Yang, Stephen Daehyun – b Los Angeles, CA, Sept 28, 81; f Samuel; m Eunice; w Kendra Jeannette Scouten, Chambersburg, PA, Sept 29, 07; UCLA 04, BA; GCTS 07, MDiv; astp, yp Intown Comm Ch, Atlanta, GA, 09-11, astp, moya 11-13; wc 13-17; asst Christ The King P Ch, Cambridge, MA, 17-

67 Day Street, Apt. 3, Jamaica Plain, MA 02130   Southern New England
E-mail: stevedyang@gmail.com
Christ The King Presbyterian Church – 617-354-8431

Yang, Tae Seog – b Korea, Aug 18, 43; f Gyu Bok Yang; m Keum Yeo Park; w Song Cha, Korea, Oct 3, 70; chdn Soo Jung (Choe), Jee Woon, Jee Ho; KorNavalAc 68, BA; Seoul P Sem 74; HGST 99, MDiv; L Apr 6, 92, Kor Seoul Pby; O Apr 28, 93, Kor Seoul Pby, mis 83-95; ob Chap Houston Intnat'l Seafarer's Center, 95-00; p Houston Ye Darm P Ch, 95-97; Chap Internat'l Maritime Center, Oakland, 00; hr

322 West MacDonald Avenue, Richmond, CA 94801 – 510-886-8010   Korean Northwest
HR

Yang, Woo Jun – srp Starkville Korean Ch, Starkville, MS, 14-17; srp Korean Comm Ch of Ft. Myers, North Ft. Myers, Fl, 17-

2801 Rustic Lane, North Fort Myers, FL 33917   Korean Southeastern
E-mail: heekyeol@gmail.com
Korean Community Church of Ft. Myers

Yarbrough, Robert Wayne – b St. Louis, MO, Oct 12, 53; f Lewis E.; m Dolores B. Benson; w Bernadine Ann Boemler, High Ridge, MO, Aug 10, 73; chdn Luke Benson, Micah Logan; SWBC 79, BA; WheatC 82, MA; AberU 85, PhD; L 76; O 80, Bap; Recd PCA Apr 26, 91, NoIL Pby; p Bap & Bible chs, 77-89; assoc prof Liberty U, 85-87; assoc prof WheatC, 87-91; sp Scotland, Germany & Romania, 83-91; assoc prof CTS, 91-96; TEDS, 96-10; pastoral assistant St. Mark Lutheran, Lindenhurst, IL 01-; prof Emanuel U, Oradea, Romania, 95-06; prof CTS 10-; trans *Historical Criticism of the Bible*, 90; auth *The Gospel of John*, 91; trans *Is There a Synoptic Problem?*, 92; trans *Bible Hermeneutics*, 94; trans *Adolf Schlatter*, 96; co-auth (w/Walter Elwell) *Encountering the New Testament*, 98, 2nd ed, 05, 3rd ed, 13; co-auth (w/Walter Elwell) *Readings from the First Century World*, 98; *The Salvation Historical Fallacy?* 04; co-trans (w/Andreas Koestenberger) *Do We Know Jesus?* 05; *Kregel Pictorial Guide to the New Testament*, 08; *1, 2, and 3 John*, 08; *The Letters to Timothy and Titus*, 18

PO Box 1034, High Ridge, MO 63049 – 847-687-0813   Chicago Metro
E-mail: bob.yarbrough@covenantseminary.edu
Covenant Theological Seminary – 314-434-4044

Yarbrough, William – b Hobbs, NM, May 21, 53; f Richard William (d); m Helen Gail Elson (d); w Susan Lyn Crow; chdn Richard Clay, Elisabeth Ann, Audrey Eva, Nathanael Lee; UnAmer, Mexico 81, cert; InstLing, Mexico; TechMexico 94, AD; SpurgeonC, London 95, cert; CTS 99, MDiv, 11, DMin; UStFran, 16, cert; O Apr 18, 00, MO Pby; p Anchor Point Chapel, AK, 73-80; Comunidad Crisitana de Puebla, Mex, 80-85; srp Alance Leon, Mexico, 86-96; astp, mp New City Flwsp, University City, MO, 97-03; mis MTW, 03-; cert spiritual dir, Aquinas Institute of Theology, 14-

1703 Arctic Court, Columbia, MO 65202 – 404-326-1917   Missouri
E-mail: fdb11821226@gmail.com
PCA Mission to the World

Yates, Christopher Dodson – b Baltimore, MD, Mar 15, 60; f Richard Andrew; m Majorie Bullard; w Kristine Ann Gabriel, Timonium, MD, Jan 3, 87; chdn Jason Andrew, Marissa Anne, Benjamin Robert; YCPA 78-82, BS; CTS 83-87, MDiv; L Jul 85, MO Pby; O Aug 30, 87, SoTX Pby; campm RUM, Texas A&M, 87-98; chp, ev Redeemer P Ch, Indianapolis, IN, 98-01; p Bay Area P Ch, Webster, TX, 01-04; srp Arden P Ch, Arden, NC, 04-12; fndr, Dir, couns, W Carolina Bibl Couns Ctr, Fletcher, NC, 13-14; astp Bay Area P Ch, Webster, TX, 15-17, ascp 18-

2030 Hillside Oak Lane, Houston, TX 77062   Houston Metro
E-mail: cyates@bapc.org
Bay Area Presbyterian Church – 281-280-0713

Yates, Stephen Philip – b Jacksonville, FL, Jul 16, 86; w Kristine Elisa James, Aug 9, 08; chdn Julianna Merenda; FSU 08, BA; CTS 13, MDiv, 13, MA; O Oct 27, 13, SW Pby; astp University P Ch, Las Cruces, NM, 13-17; astp Intown Comm Ch, Atlanta, GA, 17-

905 Conway Avenue #51, Las Cruces, NM 88005 – 904-635-2230   Metro Atlanta
E-mail: stephenpyates@gmail.com
Intown Community Church – 404-633-8077

Yates, Timothy Paul – b Endicott, NY, Dec 31, 61; f Donald W; m Doris M. Harris; w Barbara L. Lawson, Butler, PA, May 13, 84; chdn Valerie Ann, Natalie Jane, Jonathan Edward, Janine Marie, Karen Beth, Trisha Joy, Nathan James; GenC 84, BS, BA; DuqU 85-86; WTS 89, MDiv, 97, DMin; L Feb 17, 90; O Jun 23, 91, SusqV Pby; yp Trin Ch, 81-84; yp Holy Family Ins, 84-86; yp Ref P Ch, 87-91; mis MTW/Impact, Christ's Coll, 91-94, mis 94-95; ob Dir CMI, Mission Training Center, 95-01; t/tr CMI, discipleship trainer, 97-01; lect, China Ref Sem, 98-; p Friendship P Ch, Taipei , 01-08; ed, China Prayer Letter, CMI, 1997-01; mis Friends of CRTS, 02-; dean BibCouns CRTS, 01-; dean DistLearn, CRTS, 08-; AcadDean CRTS, 08-; *Doxological Counselor Training: Visually Mapping an Applied Systematic Theology as an Aid for a Counselor Hermeneutic*, 97; *Journal of Biblical Counseling*: "What is Biblical Counseling?" "Eleven Principles for Biblical Counseling," "Comfort from God for Single Parents Psalm 23," 05; "Sex Education and Psalm 16," "What's Wrong with Pornography?" "Kids' School Grades and the Gospel,". 06; "Pre-Marital Counseling for Your Adult Children" Let the Children Come to Me: Mark 10:13-16", 07; "Building a Christian Marriage that will Last: Hebrews 3," "Introduction to Biblical Counseling," 08; "Family of Origin from a Gospel Perspective," "A Biblical View of Other's Expectations," 09; "Ten Signs of Sickness and Health in Dating or Engaged Relationship," 10; "God's Providential Goal in Marriage: Strengthening Your Faith by Trials," "James' Preparations for the Joys and Trials of Growing Old," 11; "Renewing Our Commitment to Marriage compared with Homosexuality," "Hebrews 12 Encouragements & Warning Facing Loss of Spouse," 13; "Depression Related Counseling," 14; "Mercy & Care for the Homosexually Tempted," 15; *China Reformed Theological Seminary Bulletin*: "A Biblical Perspective on Suffering in the World," pp. 1-3; "Vision for CRTS from Psalm 111" 11; "Biblical Counselor Qualifications for Properly Critiquing Psychological Theories" 12; "A Summary of Westminster Confession Theological Themes," 13; "Defining Denominational Differences and Comparing with 1 Corinthians 1-4, Part 1, 13; "Denominations, NT Essentials and Acceptance in Minor Differences, Part 2," 14; "Six Solas of Reformation Christianity" 15; "Five Christ-Imaging Mandates of the Christian Life" 15; bklt *Sharing in Chinese trans Foundations*, 17; art *Chinese Journal of Biblical Counseling*: Vol 22, Jul 15: "Counseling Kids in the E-generation" "Counseling from Themes in Colossians"; Vol 23, Jan 16: "Problems of Self-

Yates, Timothy Paul, continued
Deception in Religious Self-Identity from James"; Vol. 24, Jul 16: "Imaging the Attributes of God in our Internet Use from Ephesians"; Vol. 25, Jan 17: "Biblical Reflections on AIDS and God's Purposes" and "Using Time Wisely from Ephesians 5:16"; Vol. 26, Jul 17: "Romans: An Eternal Perspective on Work"; Vol 27, Jan 18 "A Biblical Perspective on Suffering with Dementia"; Vol 28, Jul 18: "God-Centered Counsel in the Book of Job"; Vol. 29 "Model of Evangelism for Outsiders: 1 Cor. 14:23-26 in context of mute idol Worship 1 Cor. 12:2"; art in *China Reformed Theological Seminary Bulletin*: Fall 15: "Vision for a Reformed Movement"; Spring 16: "The Church and Marketplace Ministry"; Fall 17: "Topical Symphonic Theology"

Jing Feng Street, Lane 48, Alley 11 #7 3F Susquehanna Valley
Taipei 11687, TAIWAN – 886-912-578-984
E-mail: tpyates@gmail.com
China Reformed Theological Seminary – 886-22-718-1110

Yeager, Larry Jon – b Bethlehem, PA, Apr 5, 52; w Dale Trumbore, Sept 7, 74; chdn Rebecca, David, Matthew Henry, Rachel; GroCC 74, BA; GCTS 78, MDiv; O Sept 79, UChC; yp Church of Good Samaritan, Paoli, PA, 79-81; yp Eastminster Ch, Wichita, KS, 81-86; astp McLean P Ch, McLean, VA, 86-93, wc 94; srp Liberty Ref P Ch, Owings Mills, MD, 94-03; ascp Heritage P Ch, Warrenton, VA, 03-11; srp 11-

11287 Cardinal Drive, Remington, VA 22734 – 540-439-3721 Potomac
E-mail: larry.yeager@heritage-pca.org
Heritage Presbyterian Church – 540-347-4627

Yelverton, Randall Jerome – b Laurel, MS, Sept 13, 43; f Coburn Henry; w Dianne Corson DeYoung, Prattville, AL, Jul 25, 69; chdn Adrian Carey, Terrell Mark, Randall Jerome Jr; BelC 61-65, BA; ColTS 66; RTS 67-69, MDiv; O Jul 20, 69, Cent MS Pby (PCUS); p Brandon P Ch, Brandon, MS, 69-70; p Southwest Ch, Little Rock, AR, (ARP), 70-77; p Ozark P Ch, Ozark, AL, 77-11; hr 11

103 Fern Cove, Florence, AL 35634 – 256-263-9071 Providence
E-mail: randallyelvertonsr@gmail.com
HR

Yenchko, John V. D. – b Greensburg, PA, Jan 30, 57; f John; m Sue Van Dyck; w Nina Lari, Philadelphia, PA, Dec 19, 81; chdn Andrew Lari, Charlotte Anne; UVA 79, BA; WTS 82, MDiv, 84, DMin; L Dec 84; O May 85, Phil Pby, (OPC); srp New Life P Ch, Glenside, PA, 84-03; p North Shore Comm Ch, Oyster Bay, NY, 03-

213 South Street, Oyster Bay, NY 11771 – 516-558-7362 Metropolitan New York
E-mail: jvyenchko@gmail.com
North Shore Community Church – 516-922-7322

Yeo, John J.W. – astp New Life Msn Ch of Buena Park, Buena Park, CA, 08-14

427 Shady Court, Brea, CA 92821 Korean Southwest
E-mail: johnyeo@yahoo.com

Yeo, Toon Hang – b Malaysia, Apr 2, 62; f Ah-long; m Nyok-Moi Lu; w Ju-Ping Chiao, Malaysia, Jun 3, 89; chdn Zephaniah, Anna, Praisye; SUA&M 85-88, BS; RTS 89-92, MDiv, 06, DMin; GCTS 15, ThM; O Jun 8, 96, Pot Pby; astp Chinese Christian Ch, Falls Church, VA, 96-98; p Grace Chinese Christian Ch, Herndon, VA, 98-09; ob China Ref Theological Sem, 09-

No. 32 Guilin RD, 11F-1, Wanhua Dist, Taipei, TAIWAN Potomac
886-2-2364-3542
E-mail: tyeo.crts@gmail.com
China Reformed Theological Seminary – 886-22-718-1110

Yi, David – b Hattiesburg, MS, Dec 18, 69; f Walter C.; m Haengja Chang; w Jane Hae Won Chung, Jackson Heights, NY, Oct 8, 07; chdn Kayla, Joshua; NyC 09, BS; WTS 13, MDiv; O Oct 21, 14, KorNE Pby, chp 14 -16; op Gospel Center Ch, Little Neck, NY, 16-

233-14 39th Road, Douglaston, NY 11363 – 917-807-6700   Korean Northeastern
E-mail: thetruthsetmefree@gmail.com
Gospel Center Church – 347-801-0123

Ying, Daniel – YU 89, BA; TEDS 94, MDiv; WTS 99, ThM; CTS 11, DMin; ob p North Shore Chinese Christian Ch, 01-10; srp Redeemer Ch of Montclair, Montclair, NJ, 12-

72 Park Avenue, Verona, NJ 07044 – 973-857-1715   Metropolitan New York
E-mail: dan@redeemermontclair.com
Redeemer Church of Montclair – 973-233-0388

Yohannan, Jacob – b Feb 16, 70; f Chacko; m Sara; w Jaya; chdn Elijah Jedidiah, Jesse Philip, Josephine Sarala, Noah Yaakov, Judah-Benjamin Christian; NYU 91, BA; WTS 96, MDiv; O Oct 25, 02, NoTX Pby; Park Cities P Ch, Dallas, TX, 00-02; astp Trinity P Ch, Plano, TX, 02-03, ascp 04-06; chp Redeemer P Ch, NYC, 06-07; op Grace Village Msn, Englewood, NJ, 07-09; Chap Fairleigh-Dickinson U, CrossPoint Ch, NJ, 12-18; astp Trinity P Ch, Plano, TX, 18-

4701 Hedgcoxe Road, Plano 75024 – 201-889-7232   North Texas
E-mail: jake.yohannan@trinityplano.org
Trinity Presbyterian Church – 972-335-3844

Yom, Daniel Kwang Yol – b Korea, Mar 11, 45; f Byung Whan; m Koo Nam Lee; w Ai Ja Choi, Philadelphia, PA, Feb 16, 74; chdn John, Gina, Daniel; TempU 85, MEd, 85, DEd; WTS 81, MAR, 85, MDiv; L Jun 84; O Jul 86, KorE Pby; ap Emmanuel Ch in Phil, Philadelphia, PA, 86-87, ap, medu; srp Korean Westm P Ch, Orange, CA, 88-01; p Trin P Ch, Anaheim, CA, 01-07; prof, AcadDn, CAGradSch, Garden Grove, CA 07-

242 Rose Arch, Irvine, CA 92620 – 714-996-4393   Korean Southwest
E-mail: dkyyom@gmail.com
California Graduate School of Garden Grove – 714-636-1722

Yoo, Do Hyun – b Jun-Nam, Korea, Mar 27, 61; f Ki Won; m Duk Lim Kim; w Tae Ran Kim, Jun-Nam, Korea, Jul 17, 89; chdn Tabitha, Philemon, Lydia, Priscilla; AUTC 89, ThB; RTSK 93, MDiv; L Apr 12, 94; O Jun 2, 96, KorSE Pby; astp Sung Yahk P Ch (msn), 96, wc 97-00; p Hanmaum P Ch, Norcross, GA, 00-03

7340 Lytham Trace, Cumming, GA 30041 – 678-339-0690   Korean Southeastern

Yoo, Dwight – astp Emmanuel Ch in Phil, Philadelphia, PA, 04-08; ascp Renewal P Ch, Philadelphia, PA, 08-12; srp 12-

5016 Catharine Street, Philadelphia, PA 19143 – 215-490-3695   Philadelphia
E-mail: dwightyoo@gmail.com
Renewal Presbyterian Church – 215-476-0330

Yoo, Eung Yeon – b Hwang Hae Do, Korea, Feb 9, 31; f Jong Seop; m In Soon Park; w Keun Sil Kye, Seoul, Kor, Oct 4, 58; chdn James J., Paul S, Hyun Mi Chon; KPGACTS 67; L Sept 26, 75; O Oct 14, 76, P Ch of Kor denom; Sam Sung P Ch, Seoul, Kor, 73-81; op Korean Jerusalem Ch Msn, Santa Clara, CA, 81-00; hr 00

17100 South Park Lane #103, Gardena, CA 90247 – 310-532-7679   Korean Southwest
HR

Yoo, James – astp, pEng Vineyard P Ch, Elmhurst, IL

1305 Ansley Court, Mundelein, IL 60060   Korean Central
E-mail: jamyoo@gmail.com
Vineyard Presbyterian Church – 630-279-1199

Yoo, James J.B. – ob 09-

E-mail: jyou@hotmail.com   Korean Southwest

Yoo, Sam – b Korea, Oct 21, 62; f Suk hee; m Sun Jae Son; w Soo Yeon Kim, Irvine, CA, Jan 6, 90; chdn Hannah, Amy; UCI 82-87, BS; WTS 90-93, MDiv; O Oct 93, KorSW Pby; astp Buena Park New Life Msn Ch, Buena Park, CA, 94-03, op 03-17

17003 Jeanette Avenue, Cerritos, CA 90703 – 562-802-7823   Korean Southwest Orange County
E-mail: samyoo@integrity.com

Yoo, Seesun – b Ichon, So Korea, Oct 5, 65; f Jae Choon; m Choon, Ji Namkung; w Renee Yi, Chicago, IL, Mar 12, 94; UWIM 84-88; YRFD 89-90; NPTS 91-94, MDiv; L Apr 94; O May 21, 95, KorCent Pby; yp, pEng Korean Bethel P Ch, Chicago, IL, 89-94; op Bethel Christian Ch Msn, Chicago, IL, 95-06; p 06-

1009 Midway, Northbrook, IL 60062 – 847-498-5158   Korean Central
E-mail: seesunu@gmail.com
Bethel Christian Church – 773-202-7900

Yoo, Yong W. – ob KorS Pby, 02-

Address Unavailable   Korean Southern

Yoon, Daniel – Recd PCA 18, NoCA Pby; p Grace Sacramento, Sacramento, CA, 18-

Grace Sacramento – 916-737-5190   Northern California

Yoon, Jooho – astp Bethel P Ch of Chicago, Palatine, IL, 17-

998 Church Street, Apt 249, Glenview, IL 60025   Korean Central
E-mail: joohoyoon@gmail.com
Bethel Presbyterian Church of Chicago – 773-545-2222

Yoon, Mike – mis Pusan, Korean, 92-

Address Unavailable   Korean Central

Yoon, Sung Eun – op Korean Ch of the Lord, Carrollton, TX, 17-

3900 Swiss Avenue #211, Dallas, TX 75204 – 407-497-8808   Korean Southern
Korean Church of the Lord – 972-242-1104

Yoran, David Andrew – O Feb 17, 08, CentCar Pby; astp Church of the Redeemer, Monroe, NC, 08-09, ascp 09-14; ip Carolina P Ch, Locust, NC, 14-15, p 15-

404 Renee Ford Road, Locust, NC 28097 – 704-681-0608   Central Carolina
E-mail: dyoran@carolinapca.org
Carolina Presbyterian Church – 704-888-4435

York, Jesse – p Heritage P Ch, Wildwood, MO, 13-

2410 Lake Tekawitha Road, Pacific, MO 63069   Missouri
E-mail: jesse@heritagewildwood.org
Heritage Presbyterian Church – 636-938-3855

York, Joe Wilbum – b Cartersville, GA, Oct 27, 36; f Preston Rudolph Y; m Violet Dupree; w Jacqueline Chandler, Bartow Cty, GA, Jul 7, 56; chdn Bobby Joe, Jeffery Rudolph, Mary Jacqueline, Sharon Elizabeth; ErskC 67, BA; RTS 71, dipl; O Apr 23, 72, CMS Pby; p Ebenezer P Ch, Huntsville, AL, 71-72; mis Brazil, 72-75; p Ebenezer P Ch, Huntsville, AL, 75-77; CNEC, 77-86, wc 86; ob mis PEF, 88-98; ob Chap Marietta, GA, 98-01; hr 01; ss Grace P Ch, Cedartown, GA, 03-07

3651 Highland Drive, Acworth, GA 30101-5100 – 770-975-0037   Evangel
E-mail: jaquln2004@yahoo.com
HR

York, W. Tucker – b Houston, TX, Sept 28, 74; w Stacy, Feb 14, 98; chdn William Tuck, Jr., Marriaye Helen, Titus Owen, Slayton James, Silas Matthew, Justus Andrew, Jonathan Michael; VandU 97, BE; CTS 03, MDiv; WTS 16, DMin; O Mar 14, 04, SusqV Pby; astp Westminster P Ch, Lancaster, PA, 03-05, ascp 05-; sc SusqVal Pby, 16-

1825 Old Farm Lane, Lancaster, PA 17602 – 717-327-4163   Susquehanna Valley
E-mail: york@westpca.com
Westminster Presbyterian Church – 717-569-2151

Yost, Gerald E. – b Fairport, NY, Sept 20, 34; f Melvin; m Edna Miller; w Mary E. Wood, Brockton, MA, Jan 22, 61; chdn Donna, David; BucknU 52-56, BA; ANTS 56-60, BD; NCEd 61; O Jun 12, 60, CCCC; p South Congr Ch, Brockton, MA, 59-61; p First Congr Ch, St. Albans, VT, 61-75; p Trinity P Ch, St. Albans, VT, 75-00; hr 00

106 Messenger Street, Saint Albans, VT 05478-1549 – 802-524-3956   Northern New England
HR

Young, Albert – O Oct 30, 16, KorCap Pby; astp Christ Central P Ch, Centreville, VA, 16-

13944 Malcolm Jameson Way, Centreville, VA 20120   Korean Capital
E-mail: urepalal@gmail.com
Christ Central Presbyterian Church – 703-815-1300

Young, Bruce D.L. – b Kingston, PA, May 17, 47; f John M. L.; m Jean Elder; w Susan Henson, St. Louis, MO, Aug 17, 74; chdn Nancy Elizabeth, Brian Douglas, John Lawrence; CC 70, BA; CTS 74, MDiv, 91, ThM; L 74; O 75, So Pby (RPCES); mis WPM, Japan, 75-84; chp MTW, Nagoya, Japan, 85-95; chp MTW, Tokyo, Japan, 96-04, MTW office 04-

20 Lantern Cove Road, Chicamauga, GA 30707 – 678-699-7678   Tennessee Valley
E-mail: bruce.young@mtw.org
PCA Mission to the World – 678-823-0004

Young, Corey – b Wichita Falls, TX, Sep 12, 77; f Lawrence Yau Hoon; m Patricia Anne; w Jessica; chdn Noah Isaac; WheatC 00, BA; DukeU 03, MATS; O Jun 11, NoTX Pby; mis MTW, 03-06; min dir Park Cities P Ch, 06-09; mis MTW, Cambodia, 11-16; ob mis English Language Institute, 16-

3711 Cedar Elm Lane, Wichita Falls, TX 76308   North Texas
E-mail: coreytyoung@gmail.com
English Language Institute

Young, Daniel J. – w Rebecca K; chdn Benjamin James, William Arthur, Rachel Catherine, Lisa Kristine; O May 4, 86, SW Pby; ap University P Ch, Las Cruces, NM, 86-87; chp MTW/Impact, Peru, 87-90; chp MTW, BEAMM, El Paso, TX/Juarez, Mex, 90-; p Oasis P Msn, El Paso, TX, 04-05; mis MTW/BEAMM, 05-12; mis MTW North Mexico, border, 12-

10312 North 12th Street, McAllen, TX 78504 – 915-309-1619   South Texas
E-mail: danyoung4@me.com
PCA Mission to the World

Young, David S. – b Montgomery, AL, Jan 20, 61; f Charles Benjamin; m Euris Scott; w Sandy Leigh Morrison, Montgomery, AL, Jul 21, 84; chdn Scott, Catie, Ben; AU 79-83, BS; CTS 93-96, MDiv; L Oct 96; O Feb 9, 97, GrLks Pby; astp Christ P Ch, Richmond, IN, 96-99; srp Lennox Ebenezer P Ch, Lennox, SD, 99-09; chp/op Grace Redeemer Msn, Crestview, FL, 10-15, p 15-17; ch, op Riverside Ch, Beaumont, TX, 17-

4550 North Mayor Drive #2016, Beaumont, TX 77513 – 409-730-3198   Houston Metro
E-mail: riversidechurch.david@gmail.com
Riverside Church – 409-730-3198

Young, James Ross III – b Memphis, TN, Jan 14, 48; f J R Jr; m Cornelia Hendrick; w Sue Ann Betzelberger, Memphis, TN, Jul 2, 70; chdn Grace Ann, Meghan Holman, Emily Elizabeth; UT 66-70, BS; RTS 72-75, MDiv, 87, DMin; O Jul 15, 75, SFL Pby; p Grace P Ch, Ocala, FL, 75-85; ap Central Ch, Memphis, TN, 85-91; ob p Grace Evangelical Ch, Germantown, TN, 91-

9365 Wheatland, Germantown, TN 38139 – 901-629-3618   Covenant
Grace Evangelical Church (non-PCA) – 901-756-7444

Young, Jon – astp West End Community Ch, Nashville, TN, 17-18; astp Parks Ch PCA, Nashville, TN, 18-

7238 Willow Creek Road, Nashville, TN 37221   Nashville
E-mail: jon@parkschurchpca.com
Parks Church PCA – 629-255-4337

Young, Martin – w Sandy; chdn James, Amanda, David, Daniel; USMA 93, BS; GATech 01, MS; GCTS 06, MDiv; NYU 07, MBA; GCTS 09, ThM, 15, DMin; Chap USArmy, 11-

585 Winterford Drive, West Chester, PA 19382 – 617-501-8004   Philadelphia Metro West
E-mail: marty.young@me.com
United States Army

Young, Randall G. – astp First Ch West, Plantation, FL, 00-05; hr 16

1332 Mt. Pitt Street, Medford, OR 97501   South Florida
HR

Young, Richard R. – b Ellwood City, PA, Jun 8, 52; f Richard E.; m Lois A. Thompson; w Sandra L. Thompson, Ellwood City, PA, Sept 2, 72; chdn Casey, Kelly; SEBC 77, BA; AndSTh 81, MDiv; O Mar 15, 81, Church of God; Recd PCA Oct 13, 00, NoCA Pby; Chap USArmy, 81-06; hr

8434 Magdalena Run, Helotes, TX 78023-4504 – 210-687-0880   Northern California
HR

Young, Seth – O Oct 11, 15, PTri Pby; ascp Friendly Hills Ch PCA, Jamestown, NC, 15-16; ob ascp Christ Comm Ch, Huntington, WV, 16-

601 11th Avenue, Huntington, WV 25701   New River
E-mail: sethyoung@mac.com
Christ Community Church, Huntington, WV

Young, Shawn – w Jennifer; chdn Easton, Jonas, Selah, Lucy, Gemma, Asher; CTS 02, MDiv; O Sept 02, NoTX Pby; astp Heritage P Ch, Edmond, OK, 02-07; ascp 07-09; p Cornerstone P Ch, Castle Rock, CO, 10-

3225 Arroyo Verde Court, Castle Rock, CO 80108 – 303-668-1239   Rocky Mountain
E-mail: shawn@cornestonepc.org
Cornerstone Presbyterian Church – 303-660-0267

Young, Stephen Thomas – b Tokyo, Japan, Jan 1, 50; f John M. L.; m Jean Elder; w Sarah Kelly, Richmond, VA, Jun 18, 77; chdn Stephanie Elizabeth, Eric Thomas; CC 72, BD; CTS 76, MDiv; L 76; O 76, So Pby (RPCES); op RP mis, Terre Haute, IN, 76-77; mis Japan, 77-90; mis MTW, Melbourne, Aust (Japanese chp), 90-00; mis MTW, Perth, Aust, 01-14; fm MTW 14-18; astp Crossroads of the Nations, Nashville, TN, 18- *From Frozen Rage to Inner Peace - The Ex-POW's Journey Toward Healing*

6015 Wellesley Way, Brentwood, TN 37027 – 615-635-2543   Nashville
E-mail: s2young@iinet.net.au
Crossroads of the Nations

Youngblood, Eric – w Cathy S.; chdn W. Kahler; UTC, BS; RTSFL, MDiv; L Sept 01, TNVal Pby; O Feb 02, TNVal Pby; astp Lookout Mountain P Ch, Lookout Mountain, TN, 01-02; op Rock Creek Flwsp, Lookout Mtn, GA, 02, p 02-

2008 Durham Road, Rising Fawn, GA 30738 – 706-398-0886   Tennessee Valley
E-mail: eric@rockcreekfellowship.org
Rock Creek Fellowship – 706-398-7141

Youngblood, James Benjamin Jr. – astp Eastern Shore P Ch, Fairhope, AL, 06; astp Briarwood P Ch, Birmingham, AL, 06-

800 Hillshire Drive, Birmingham, AL 35244 – 205-739-9023   Evangel
E-mail: byoungblood@briarwood.org
Briarwood Presbyterian Church – 205-776-5321

Yu, John T. – ap Han-Maum P Msn, Chicago, IL, 91-92; p, ss Korean P Ch of St. Louis, St. Louis, MO, 91-92, ob p 92-03; hr 03

2107 West Downer Place #103, Aurora, IL 60506 – 630-264-6970   Korean Central
E-mail: jtjyu4283@sbcglobal.net
HR

Yu, Joseph – astp Redeemer P Ch of New York, New York, NY, 16-

1055 River Road #404, Edgewater, NJ 07020   Metropolitan New York
E-mail: joseph.yu@redeemer.com
Redeemer Presbyterian Church of New York – 212-808-4460

Yu, Young Jae – mis 08-

E-mail: youngjaeyu@hotmail.com   Korean Capital

Yuan, Ted – O Jun 12, 16, Pot Pby, ob 16-

25674 South Village Drive, South Riding, VA 20152   Potomac
E-mail: Ted.Yuan@gmail.com

Yun, Young Min – b Seoul, Jan 15, 29; f Hak Hyun; m Jung Nim Kim; w Teon Hyang Lim, Korea, Jan 3, 53; chdn Jung Jin, Ae Kyung (Cho), Nam Sik, Seung Sik, Nami Yun (Son), Koo D, Soomi; HUFS 77-81, MDiv; L 81; O 81; op Korean Msn Ch, San Jose, CA, 98-3; hr 13

26185 Pierce Road, Los Gatos, CA 95030 – 408-353-9489   Korean Northwest
HR

Yurik, Michael – w Katherine; chdn Claire; O 16, Hrtg Pby; astp Faith P Ch, Wilmington, DE, 16-

3072 Savannah East Drive, Lewes, DE 19958 – 585-703-4410　　　　　　　　Heritage
E-mail: mtyurik@gmail.com
Faith Presbyterian Church – 302-764-8615

Yurus, Edward J. – b Yonkers, NY, Nov 13, 59; f John Edward; m Margaret Mary O'Brien; w Linda Ann Langley, Ft. Lauderdale, FL, Nov 11, 82; chdn Matthew Charles, Lauren; FAU 82, BA; KTS 99, MDiv; L Oct 99, SFL Pby; O Jan 18, 00, SFL Pby; West Boca P Ch, Boca Raton, FL, 98-00; Chap USArmy, 00-

816 Mimosa Drive, Vass, NC 28394-9650 – 931-647-2262　　　　　　　　South Florida
United States Army

Zapata-Ruiz, Aaron – b Yucatan, Mexico, Oct 12, 47; f Francisco Zapata-Monge; m Maria Luisa Ruiz-Cruz; w Leticia Gonzalez-Perez, Merida, Yucatan, Feb 10, 76; chdn Aaron Adan, J. Marcos, Ana Leticia; UY 76, BCEng; RTS 85, MDiv, 86, MCE, 88, MEd; L Jun 86; O Mar 21, 87, Peninsular Pby, Mexico; Recd PCA Sept 19, 96, SW Pby; astp Jesus P Ch, Yucatan, 86; prof San Pablo Theo Sem, 86-94; p Antioch Ch, Merida, Siloe Ch, El Divino Maestro, 87-93; p Jesus P Ch, Yucatan, 93-94; p Shalom P Ch, Yucatan, 94; pres San Pablo Theo Sem, 91-94; chp Hillside P Msn, El Paso, TX, 96-98; op Oasis P Msn, El Paso, TX, 98-04; ob San Pablo Theo Sem, Juarez, 03-

353 Belvidere Street, El Paso, TX 79912-2135 – 915-587-7605　　　　　　　　Rio Grande
E-mail: azapata@flash.net
San Pablo Theological Seminary, Juarez

Zarlenga, Dale – b York, PA, Apr 16, 79; w Beth Cox; chdn Emma Grace, Madelyn Hope; JMU 01, BM; CTS 09, MDiv; O Nov 15, 09, MO pby; astp Twin Oaks P Ch, Ballwin, MO, 09-11; astp Carriage Lane P Ch, Peachtree City, GA, 11-13; ascp 13-

19 Bridgewater Drive, Newnan, GA 30265 – 770-755-8335　　　　　　　　Metro Atlanta
E-mail: dzarlenga79@gmail.com
Carriage Lane Presbyterian Church – 770-631-4618

Zavadil, David Wayne – b Niantic, NC, Dec 21, 63; f John L; m Deborah Anne Freedman; w Catherine Frances Jurgens, Birmingham, AL, Aug 16, 86; chdn Kristen, Joshua, Daniel, Sara-Catherine; UMonte 85, BA; RTS 93, MDiv; L Apr 93; O Jun 20, 93, War Pby; Presbyterian Home for Child, 85-88; moy First P Ch, Atmore, AL, 88-90; ydir Grace P Ch, 91-92; p Covenant P Ch, York, AL, 93-96; p Orleans P Ch, New Orleans, LA, 96-98; p Grace Flwsp Ch, Kingston, TN, 98-04; ss Grace P Ch, Dalton, GA, 05-06; p Eastminster P Ch, Virginia Beach, VA, 06-

3249 MacDonald Road, Virginia Beach, VA 23464 – 757-309-4606　　　　　　　　Tidewater
E-mail: david.zavadil@eastminsterpca.org
Eastminster Presbyterian Church – 757-420-8133

Zehnder, Jeff K. – w Joanna, Greenville, SC, Feb 17, 07; FurU 03, BA; CTS 09, MDiv, 11, ThM; O May 20, 12, Asc Pby; ascp Fairview Ref P Ch, Industry, PA, 12-16, srp 16-

6364 Tuscarawas Road, Midland, PA 15059　　　　　　　　Ascension
E-mail: pastorjeff@fairviewpca.org
Fairview Reformed Presbyterian Church – 724-643-8104

Zeigler, Ronald W. – b West Chester, PA, Aug 8, 58; w Kathleen S., Baltimore, MD, Dec 23, 89; ESSC 76-78; UMD 78-80; TowU 80-84; ChTS 90-95; L Feb 95, Pot Pby; O Dec 10, 95, SusqV Pby; ascp New Cov Flwsp, Mechanicsburg, PA, 95-01; p Church of the Servant, Palmyra, PA, 01-15; co-chair, ed & conf co, SusqV pby, 97-99

187 Macintosh Drive, Palmyra, PA 17078 – 717-838-9462　　　　　　　　Susquehanna Valley
E-mail: ronzeigler@juno.com

Zekveld, Richard – b Ingersoll, Ontario, Oct 7, 74; f Jacob; m Ada Hengeveld; w Nancy VanderMeer, Winnipeg, Manitoba, May 29, 04; chdn Anton, Annika, Autumn, Augustin, Adamina; RedC 96, BA; MidARS 01, MDiv; CalvS; O Jun 11, 16, ChiMet Pby, int 02-03, p 03-08, p 08-15; p Covenant Flwsp Ch of South Holland, South Holland, IL, 15-

E-mail: rhzekveld@gmail.com   Chicago Metro
Covenant Fellowship Church of South Holland

Zelaya, Andres – O Nov 15, 17, HouMet Pby; astp Redeemer Sugar Land, Sugar Land, TX, 16-17; astp Christ the King P Ch, Houston, TX, 18-

Christ the King Presbyterian Church – 713-892-5464   Houston Metro

Zeller, Andrew Scott – b Sasebo, Japan, Jun 6, 59; f Dwight F.; m Lois A. Clark; w Beth Ann Piske, Salem, OR, Jul 30, 83; chdn Hannah Bess, Marie Elise, Heidi Evangeline, Clara Faith, James Clark, Katherine Grace, Peter Dwight, Bennet Scott, Noelle Caroline, Elizabeth Joy, Elias Achamo, Micah Batamo, Laurel Annelise ; UCO; CC 82-84, BA; SCS 79-81, MDiv; CTS 84-86, ThM; GCTS 98-01, DMin; L Sept 83, TNVal Pby; O Mar 86, Ill Pby; chp First P Ch, West Frankfort, IL, 86-87; Chap USArmy, Ft. Lewis, WA, 87-90; Chap USArmy, Wertheim, Germany, 90-91; Chap USArmy, Babenhausen, Germany, 91-92; Chap USArmy, Ft Mommouth, NJ, 93; Chap USArmy, Ft. Benning, GA, 93-94; Chap USArmy, Ft. Leavenworth, KS, 94-96; Chap COANG 96-11; ob Pres Sangre de Cristo Sem, 00-;

6160 County Road #130, Westcliffe, CO 81252-9619 – 719-783-2463   Rocky Mountain
Sangre de Christo Seminary

Zeller, Dwight F. – b Monmouth, IL, Sept 15, 29; f Frederick S; m Bertha Jane Fullerton; w Lois A. Clark, Indianapolis, IN, Oct 17, 56; chdn Joel F; Andrew S; Rebecca E (van der Linden), Lydia R (Robertson), Jerry D, William E, Daniel G, Paul M; BJU 50, BA; CPTS 54, BD; MempTS 69, MDiv; ChiGST 70, ThM; EBapTS 77, DMin; BBDS; CBTS; WLST; L 54; O 54, CPC; Recd PCA Apr 23, 93, RMtn Pby; Chap USN, 54-74; prof REps, 74-78; ob Dir SCS, 78-09; hr; *Workbook for Reviewing the Essentials of Greek Grammar & Syntax*

5100 County Road 130, Westcliffe, CO 81252 – 719-783-9095   Rocky Mountain
HR

Zellner, Eric – b Nashville, TN, Dec 4, 73; f Cordelle Wayne; m Dorothy Almy; w Susan Grainger, Birmingham, AL, Dec 19, 98; chdn Olivia Grace; Emma Frances; John Cordelle, Lucy Elizabeth; AU 96, BS; CTS 06, MDiv; O Jun 3, 07, Evan Pby; ascp Westminster P Ch, Huntsville, AL, 07-12; p First P Ch at Indianola, Indianola, MS, 12-18, op Christ P Ch of Auburn, Auburn, AL, 18-

1795 Lauren Lane, Auburn, AL 36803   Southeast Alabama
E-mail: ericzellner@yahoo.com
Christ Presbyterian Church of Auburn – 334-310-1007

Zepp, Renfred E – b York, PA; RTSNC 09, MAR; O Oct 11, 12, NFL Pby; rep Navigators, 81-; astp Pinewood P Ch, Middleburg, FL, 12-; "Covenant Theology from the Perspective of Two Puritans" in *A Puritan Theology*

624 Morgan Street, Orange Park, FL 32073   North Florida
E-mail: renzepp@aol.com
Pinewood Presbyterian Church – 904-272-7177
The Navigators

Zetterholm, Paul Ellison – b St. Charles, IL, Aug 8, 42; f Earl E.; m Helen E. Paul; w Mary L. Bowen, Fallon, NV, Aug 10, 62; chdn Michele (Case), Rhonda (Roush), Eric, Deborah (Roush), Joanna (Murphy), Rebecca, Matthew, Nathan; PalC 71-73, AA; ColC 79-81, BA; RTS 81-84, MDiv; O Jul 84, MSVal Pby;

Zetterholm, Paul Ellison, continued
p Clinton P Ch, Clinton, MS, 84-89, wc 89; p Tchula P Ch, Tchula, MS, 90-95, wc 95; astp Alta Woods P Ch, Pearl, MS, 97-99; p Harvest P Ch, Jacksonville, NC, 00-11; hr 11

610 East Abbey Place, Brandon, MS 39047 – 910-265-1347   Eastern Carolina
E-mail: pzetter2@gmail.com
HR

   Zhang, Jinan – p Orlando Chinese Evangelical Christian Ch, Casselberry, FL, 15-

5535 Canteen Court, Orlando, FL 32765   Central Florida
E-mail: zjinan@gmail.com
Orlando Chinese Evangelical Christian Church – 407-331-1477

   Zhang, Ryan – O Aug 24, 17, OHVal Pby; astp New City P Ch, Cincinnati, OH, 17-

4311 Allison Street, Cincinnati, OH 45212   Ohio Valley
E-mail: ryan.zhang@newcitycincy.org
New City Presbyterian Church – 513-512-5759

   Zhuravlev, Aleksey – Recd PCA Sept 11, 18, SucstFL Pby; p Covenant of Gr P Ch, North Port, FL, 18-

2546 Lancaster Lane, North Port, FL 34286   Suncoast Florida
Covenant of Grace Presbyterian Church – 941-225-3945

   Ziegler, Geoff M. – b Boston, MA, Sept 27, 74; f Michael; m Celia Atkins; w Jennifer McCullough, Wheaton, IL, Sept 7, 96; chdn Timothy, Daniel, Joel; WheatC 96, BA; MTC 01, BD; WheatC, PhD; O Sept 27, 09, ChiMet Pby; p Trinity P Ch, Hinsdale, IL, 09-; p Trinity P Ch Palos Heights, Palos Heights, IL, 14-18

202 Phillippa Street, Hinsdale, IL 60521 – 630-286-9303   Chicago Metro
E-mail: gziegler@trinitypreschurch.com
Trinity Presbyterian Church – 630-286-9303

   Zink, Daniel W. – b Madison, WI, Feb 17, 53; f Charles Edward; m Dorothea Carroll; w Carolanne Burger, Mt. Vernon, OH, Mar 22, 75; chdn Laurianne Margaret; Bethanne Coeur; ENazC 75, BA; OHSU 77, MSW; CTS 89, MDiv; StLU 00, PhD; L Oct 28, 89; O May 6, 90, NoTX Pby; ap New Cov P Ch, Dallas, TX, 89-90; dir Stu Serv CTS, 90-95, asst prof 95-06, assoc prof 07-18, prof 18-, int dir couns, 16-18, dir couns 18-; "Grace-shaped Counseling" in *All for Jesus: A Celebration of the 50th Anniversary of Covenant Theological Seminary*; "The Practice of Marriage and Family Counseling and Conservative Christianity" in *The Role of Religion in Marriage and Family Counseling*

1574 Eagle Hill Lane, St. Charles, MO 63304 – 314-960-8887   Missouri
Covenant Theological Seminary – 314-434-4044

   Zoeller, Fred L. Jr. – b Portsmouth, VA, Mar 24, 50; f Fred L.; m Norma May Broaddus; w Nancy Reed; chdn Anna Elizabeth, Laura Alice, John Frederick, Reed Louis; CBC 68-72, BA; TEDS 73-76, MDiv; O Mar 25, 79, Cal Pby; p Grace P Ch, Aiken, SC, 79-84; ap First P Ch, Gadsden, AL, 84-86; p St. Andrews P Ch, Americus, GA, 86-91; p Westminster P Ch, Everett, WA, 91-

2531 Hoyt Avenue, Everett, WA 98201   Pacific Northwest
E-mail: fzoeller@verizon.net
Westminster Presbyterian Church – 425-252-3757

   Zoellner, John Garnet – b Grand Forks, BC, Apr 4, 55; f William; m Dorothy Whitham; w Daryl Martin, Edmonton, AB, Dec 31, 75; chdn Sara (Ludwig), Kira (Boule'), Erin (Gretillat), Martin, Daniel,

Zoellner, John Garnet, continued
Andrea; UAlb 76, BA; WTS 78, MAR; McGU 87, STM; L 83; O 83, NoE Pby; mis MNA assigned to FAREL, Canada, 83-; p Eglise reformee de Beauce, 83-89; inst Institut Farel, 89-92; p Eglise reformee St-Jean, Montreal, 92-15; Chap (LCol) Canadian Army Reserve, 91-15; dir Institut Farel, 15-

6160 J-A-Cousineau, Montreal, QB H4E 4L7 CANADA   New York State
514-767-3165, 514-831-3138
FAREL, Faculté de théologie réformée, Montréal, Canada

    Zoller, Jacob – b Sherman, TX, Feb 27, 86; f Jay; m Catherine Louise Ihrig; w Leigh Carroll Douglas, Columbus, GA, Dec 18, 10; chdn George; UOK 08, BS; RedTS 15, MDiv; O Feb 14, 17, GulCst Pby; campm RUF, USoAL, 17-

1959 Myrtle Avenue, Mobile, AL 36606   Gulf Coast
E-mail: jacobzoller@gmail.com
PCA Reformed University Fellowship

    Zugg, Julian Michael – UCTSA 86, BS; Buckingham 00, LLB; RTS 01, MDiv; O 02, HouMet Pby; astp Covenant P Ch, Houston, TX, 02-08; ob Belize P Sem, Central America, 08-11; astp Covenant P Ch, Houston, TX, 11- 18; dean MINTS, 11-18

14502 Piping Rock, Houston, TX 77077 – 281-493-1675   Houston Metro
E-mail: jzugg@mac.com

ABBREVIATIONS USED WITH MINISTERIAL BIOGRAPHICAL DATA

AA	Associate in Art Degree	AIHLS	American Institute of Holy Land Studies, Jerusalem, Israel
AACC	Anne Arundel Community College		
AACPC	Abortion Alternative & Crisis Pregnancy Center	AIM	Auburn International Ministries
AAM	Army Achievement Medal	AirNG	Air National Guard
AB	Alberta, Canada	AiShU	Ain Shams University
ABAC	Abraham Baldwin Agricultural College	AKBC	Alaska Bible College
		AkBI	Akron Bible Institute
ABCA	American Baptist Church of America	AlbJC	Albany Junior College
		AldBC	Alderson Broaddus College
ABCC	Atlanta Biblical Counseling Center	AllBS	Allahabad Bible Seminary (India)
ABCKor	Atlanta Bible College (Korean)	AllC	Allehgeny College
		AllgCC	Allegheny Community College
ABD	Anchor Bible Dictionary	AmbC	Ambassador College
AberU	Aberdeen University, Scotland	AmC	American College
		AmCLU	American College of Life Underwriters
Abgd	Abingdon Presbytery (PCUS)	AmU	American University
ABMJ	American Board of Mission to the Jews	AmUB	American University, Beirut, Lebanon
ABR	Associates for Biblical Research	AndC	Anderson College, Indiana
		AndJC	Anderson Junior College, SC
Ac	Academy	AndrU	Andrews University
ac dir	Acting Director	ANG	Army National Guard
acad	academic	ANTS	Andover Newton Theological School
AcadDn	Academic Dean		
ACC	Adirondack Community College	Apr	April
		ap	Assistant or Associate Pastor
ACM	Army Commendation Medal	APC	Arkansas Polytechnic College
ACSC	Air Command & Staff College	APTS	Austin Presbyterian Theological Seminary
ACT	Australian College of Theology	ARC	Arkansas College
ACTS	Association of Canadian Theological Schools	ArcBI	Arctic Bible Institute, BI
		ARDM	Alliance for Reformed Disciplemaking Ministries
ACU	Abilene Christian University		
AD	Associates Degree	ARI	Annenberg Research Institute
adj fac	Adjunct Faculty	ArmSC	Armstrong State College
adj prof	Adjunct Professor	ARP	Associate Reformed Presbyterian Church
admin	Administrator; Administration	art	Article(s)
adv	Advisor	AS	Associate in Science
advbd	Advisory Board	ASARB	Association of Statisticians of American Religious Bodies
AEF	Africa Evangelical Fellowship		
AES	Association of Evangelical Studies	AsbC	Asbury College
		ASBS	Atlanta School of Biblical Studies
AF	Air Force		
AFC	Ambassadors for Christ	AsbTS	Asbury Theological Seminary
AffEv	Affiliate Evangelist		
AfrBC	African Bible Colleges	ASC	Adams State College
AG	Assemblies of God	Asc	Ascension
AIA	Archaeological Institute of America	ascp	Associate Pastor
		ASCS	American School of Classical Studies, Athens, Greece
AIBS	Albany Institute of Biblical Studies		

ABBREVIATIONS

AshC	Ashland College	BBDS	Berkley Baptist Divinity School
AshTS	Ashland Theological Seminary	BBE	Bachelor of Bible Education
Ashv	Asheville	BC	British Columbia, Canada
ASM	American Society of Missionaries	BCE	Bachelor of Christian Education
ASMT	Atlanta Seminary of Ministry & Theology	BCEng	Bachelor of Civil Engineering
assoc	Associate/Association	BChE	Bachelor of Chemical Engineering
asst	Assistant	BD	Bachelor of Divinity
astp	Assistant Pastor, Assistant to the Pastor	Bd	Board
ASU	Appalachian State University	bd adm	Board of Administrators
ATA	Asia Theological Association	BdDir	Board of Directors
AtCC	Atlantic Christian Bible College	BDS	Beeson Divinity School
AtlU	Atlanta University	BDT	Baker's Dictionary of Theology
AtManU	Ateneo de Manila University	BEAMM	Border Evangelism and Mercy Ministry
ATS	Alliance Theological Seminary	BEB	Baker Encyclopedia of the Bible
attd	Attended	BECB	Baker's Evangelical Commentary on the Bible
AU	Auburn University	BEE	Biblical Education Extension
Aug	August	BEEn	Bachelor of Electrical Engineering
Aug	Augusta		
AugC	Augusta College	BelAbC	Belmont Abbey College
AugJC	Augusta Junior College	BelC	Belhaven College
AugSBS	Augusta School of Biblical Studies (extension of ASBS)	BelEx	Bellahouston Extension (Scotland)
AUM	Auburn University, Montgomery	BelmC	Belmont College
AurU	Aurora University	BerBI	Berean Bible Institute
AusC	Austin College	BerC	Berea College
Aust	Australia	BerCC	Berean Christian College
AUTC	Asia United Theological College	BerkCC	Berkshire Christian College, MA
auth	Author	BerryC	Berry College
AvC	Averett College	Beth	Bethany
AVI	American Vision, Inc.	BethBI	Bethany Bible Institute
AWM	Arab World Ministries	BethC	Bethany College
AzPU	Azusa Pacific University	BethCS	Bethany Christian Services
AZSU	Arizona State University	BethlC	Bethel College
b	Born	BethlTS	Bethel Theological Seminary
BA	Bachelor of Arts	BethS	Bethany Seminary
BabsC	Babson College	BethTS	Bethany Theological Seminary
BaC	Barry College, Miami, FL		
BahnS	Bahnsen Seminary	BFA	Bachelor of Fine Arts
BallSU	Ball State University	BfBC	Belfast Bible College
Balt	Baltimore Presbytery (UPCUSA)	BFC	Bible Fellowship Church
Bap	Baptist	BGBU	Bowling Green Business University
BapBC	Baptist Bible College	BGEA	Billy Graham Evangelistic Association
BapBI	Baptist Biblical Institute		
BapCC	Baptist College of Charleston	BGS	Bachelor of General Studies
BapCU	Baptist Christian University	BGSU	Bowling Green State University
BarC	Barrington College	Bham	Birmingham
BarMin	Barnabas Ministries	BhamES	Birmingham Extension Seminary of Theological Education
BasU	Basel University		
BatesC	Bates College		
BayU	Baylor University	BhamSoC	Birmingham Southern College

BhamTS	Birmingham Theological Seminary	BS	Bachelor of Science
BHC	Black Hawk College	BSA	Boy Scouts of America
BHM	Board of Home Ministries	BSC	Buffalo State College
BibEv	Bible Evangelism, Inc.	BST	Biblical School of Theology
BibS	Biblical Seminary, New York	BucknU	Bucknell University
BibTS	Biblical Theological Seminary, Hatfield, PA	BUS	Bachelor of University Studies
BIE	Bachelor of Industrial Engineering	ButGSR	Butler Graduate School of Religion
Biola	Biola College	ButU	Butler University
BIOLA	Bible Institute of Los Angeles	BW	Baldwin Wallace
BIPA	Biblical Institute of Pennsylvania	BWI	British West Indies
BITX	Bible Institute of Texas	BWM	Biblical Wellness Ministries
BJU	Bob Jones University	ByzOrthS	Byzantine Orthodox Seminary
bklt	Booklet	C&MA	Christian & Missionary Alliance Church
BLA	Bible Language Academy	CaBS	Capernwray Bible School
BlC	Bluefield College	CAc	Christian Academy
BlueMC	Blue Mountain College	CAC	Christian Action Council
Blues	Bluestone	CACC	California Christian College
BME	Bachelor of Mechanical Engineering	CACI	California Christian Institute
BMin	Bachelor of Ministry	CAJ	Christian Academy in Japan
BMus	Bachelor of Music	Cal	Calvary
BMusEd	Bachelor of Music Education	CalBC	Calvary Bible College
BosU	Boston University	CalNo	California Northern
BosUST	Boston University School of Theology	CalSt	California State University
BowSt	Bowie State	CalvC	Calvin College
BPC	Bible Presbyterian Church	CalvS	Calvin Seminary
BPC&E	Broward Professional Counseling and Education	CAm	Central America
BradU	Bradley University	CampLf	Campus Life
BRAMA	Baton Rouge Area Ministerial Association	campm	Campus Minister/Ministry
BranU	Brandeis University	CampU	Campbell University
BrBI	Briercrest Bible Institute	CamU	Cameron University
BrC	Bryant College, Rhode Island	Can	Canada
BRCC	Blue Ridge Community College	CanBC	Canadian Bible College
BrChS	Briarwood Christian School	cand	Candidate
BrCS	Briarwood Continuing Seminary	CanPL	Canadian Protestant League
BrCTech	Brighton College of Technology, England	CanSC	Canadian Services College
BreCC	Brevard Community College, Florida	CanTS	Canadian Theological Seminary
BreJC	Brevard Junior College	CAP	Civil Air Patrol
BrkPI	Brooklyn Polytechnic Institute	CapBS	Capital Bible Seminary
BroCC	Broward Community College	Car	Carolina
BroCJC	Broward County Junior College	CarBC	Carver Bible College
BrPJC	Brewton Parker Junior College	CargIT	Carnegie Institute of Theology
BrU	Brown University	CarrC	Carroll College, Waukesha, WI
BryC	Bryan College	CASSS	Combined Arms and Services Staff School
		CatC	Catawba College
		CatCC	Catonsville Community College
		CathUAm	Catholic University of America
		CatonCC	Catonsville Community College
		CAU	Chung-Ang University
		CBapTS	Central Baptist Theological . Seminary

ABBREVIATIONS

CBC	Columbia Bible College	CEP	Christian Education and Publications (now CDM)
CBCC	Columbia Bible College (Charlotte)	cert	Certificate
CBCE	Center for Biblical Counseling and Education	CES	Christian Educational Society
CBI	Cedine Bible Institute	CFLCC	Central Florida Community College
CBS	Columbia Biblical Seminary		
CBS&SM	Columbia Biblical Seminary School of Missions	CFP	Christian Focus Publications
		CGST	California Graduate School of Theology
CBTS	Conservative Baptist Theological Seminary, Denver	ch	Church
		ChamU	Chaminade University, Honolulu
CC	Covenant College		
CCA	Christian Counseling Associates	Chan	Chancellor
		Chap	Chaplain, Chapel
CCAc	Christian Center Academy	ChBC	Christian Brothers College, Memphis
CCC	Campus Crusade for Christ		
CCCC	Conservative Congregational Christian Conference	ChBI	Chattanooga Bible Intstitute
		ChC	Chapman College
CCCCI	Centralia Christian Communications Cooperative, Inc.	CHC	College of the Holy Cross
		chdn	Children
		ChdnBS	Children's Bible in Story
CCCU	City College of City University, NY	CHerC	Christian Heritage College
		Chero	Cherokee
CCDS	Cuttington College & Divinity School	ChHC	Chestnut Hill College
		ChicI	Chicago Institute
CCEF	Christian Counseling and Educational Foundation	ChiGST	Chicago Graduate School of Theology
CCK	Centre College of Kentucky	ChiLuS	Chicago Lutheran Seminary
CCL	Center for Christian Leadership	ChinBS	China Bible Seminary
		ChinMS	Chinese Mission Seminary
CCLA	Centenary College of Louisiana	ChIU	Christian International University
CCM	Combs College of Music, PA	ChJC	Chipola Junior College
CCM	Caribbean Christian Ministries	ChMI	China Ministries International
CCO	Coalition for Christian Outreach	chmn	Chairman
		ChosunU	Chosun University
CCPhil	Community College of Philadelphia	chp	Church Planter/Church Planting
CCS	Center for Christian Study	ChrBC	Christian Bible College
CCSC	College of Charleston, South Carolina	ChrC	Christ's College, Aberdeen, Scotland
CCServ	Christian Counseling Service	ChrCns	Christian counseling
CDM	Committee on Discipleship Ministries (formerly CEP)	ChrTS	Christian Theological Seminary, Indianapolis, IN
CE	Christian Education	CHS	Christian High School
CedC	Cedarville College	ChShC	Chong Shin College
CEF	Child Evangelism Fellowship	ChShCS	Chong Shin College and Seminary
CentAZ	Central Arizona College		
CentBC	Central Bible College	ChShTS	Chong Shin Theological Seminary
CentC	Central College, Iowa		
CentCar	Central Carolina	ChSoU	Charleston Southern University
CentFL	Central Florida		
CentGA	Central Georgia	ChStTI	Chattanooga State Technical Institute
CentStU	Central State University		
CentTS	Central Theological Seminary	ChTI	Chicago Theological Institute
		ChTS	Chesapeake Theological Seminary

ChungCE	Chungjoo College of Education	cons	Consultant
CIM	China Inland Mission	cont/ed	Continuing Education
CIT	California Institute of Technology	contr	Contributor
		contr ed	Contributing editor
Citadel	Citadel, the Military College of South Carolina	coord	Coordinator
		cop	Co Pastor
		CornU	Cornell University
CIU	Columbia International University (formerly CBC)	CoS	Church of Scotland
		COSM	Colorado School of Mines
ClarkU	Clark University	couns	Counselor, counseling
ClarU	Clarion University	Cov	Covenant
CLCC	Christian Life Care Centers, Inc.	CovCS	Covenant Christian School
ClemU	Clemson University	COz	College of the Ozarks
ClGS	Claremont Graduate School	CPC	Cumberland Presbyterian Church
CLJC	Copiah-Lincoln Junior College	CPCC	Central Piedmont Community College
ClrCC	Clearwater Christian College		
CLS	Christian Legal Society	CPE	Clinical Pastoral Education
CMA	Centre Missionnaire, Albertville, France	CPStU	California Polytechnical State University
CmdChap	Command Chaplain	CPTS	Cumberland Presbyterian Theological Seminary
CMDS	Christian Medical & Dental Society	CPU	Columbia Pacific University
CMEC	Christian Methodist Episcopal Church	CRC	Christian Reformed Church
		CRDS	Colgate Rochester Divinity School
CMF	Central Missionary Fellowship	CriC	Crichton College
		CrisC	Criswell College
CMI	Children's Ministry International	CRM	Church Resource Ministries
		CrownC	Crown College
CMS	Central Mississippi	CrozS	Crozier Seminary
CMU	Carnegie-Mellon University	CS	Christian School
CNC	Carson Newman College	CSB	Christian Service Brigade
CNEC	Christian Nationals Evangelism Commission	CSCC	Cleveland State Community College
Co	County	CSCS	Coral Springs Christian School
COBS	Colorado Bible Seminary		
CoeC	Coe College, Cedar Rapids, IA	CSMC	Christian Service Men's Center
ColAm	Colegio Americano		
ColC	Columbus College	CSq	College of Sequoias
ColCC	Colorado Christian College	CST	Candler School of Theology (Emory University)
ColCU	Colorado Christian University		
		CSU	Colorado State University
ColGS	Columbia Graduate School	CSUF	California State University, Fullerton
ColgU	Colgate University		
CollD	College Director/Minister	CSUFr	California State University, Fresno
ColStCC	Columbia State Community College		
		CSUH	California State University, Hayward
ColTS	Columbia Theological Seminary		
		CSULA	California State University, Los Angeles
ColU	Columbia University		
ConcCI	Concordia Collegiate Institute	CSULB	California State University, Long Beach
ConcS	Concordia Seminary	CSUN	California State University - Northridge
ConcU	Concordia University		
Cong	Congaree	CTI	Christian Training, Inc.
CongCC	Congregational Christian Church	CTM	Comunidad Teologica de Mexico
Congr	Congregational	CTS	Covenant Theological Seminary
ConoCS	Cono Christian School		

ABBREVIATIONS

CU	Cambridge University	DirCouns	Director of Counseling
CUNY	City University of New York	DirSpLi	Director of Spiritual Life
CUTS	Center for Urban Theological Studies	dirStSvs	Director of Student Services
		disc	Disciple(s), Discipleship
CV	Churches Vitalized	DisChr	Disciples of Christ
CWC	Central Wesleyan College	dism	Dismissed
CWE	Committee on World Evangelization	Div	Divinity
		DKU	Dan Kook University
CWM	College of William and Mary	DLI	Defense Language Institute
CWoos	College of Wooster	DLipsC	David Lipscomb College
CZ	Canal Zone	DMin	Doctor of Ministry
d	Deceased	DMiss	Doctor of Missiology
DAlRel	Dean of Alumni Relations	Dmv	Delmarva
DAS	Director of Advanced Studies	DnAc	Dean of Academics
DavC	Davidson College	DnFac	Dean of Faculty
DBU	Dallas Baptist University	DnStu	Dean of Students
DC	District of Columbia	doct stu	Doctoral Studies
DCC	District of Columbia College	DordtC	Dordt College
DCE	Director of Christian Education	DPC	Director of Pastoral Care
		DrakU	Drake University
DChPl	Director of Church Planting	DRCSA	Dutch Reformed Church, South Africa
DCR	Director of Christian Resources	DRCSL	Dutch Reformed Church, Sri Lanka
DD	Doctor of Divinity	DRE	Doctor in Religious Education
Dec	December		
DEC	Davis & Elkins College	DrewTS	Drew Theological Seminary
DEd	Doctor of Education	DrewU	Drew University
DefS	Defenders Seminary	DrexU	Drexel University
DeKCC	DeKalb Community College	Drs	Doctorandus
DelC	Delta College, MI	DrU	Dropsie University (formerly Dropsie College for Hebrew & Cognate Learning)
den	denomination		
DenBI	Denver Bible Institute		
DenTS	Denver Theological Seminary	DSIPS	Dynamic Springs Institute of Professional Studies
DenU	Denison University	DSU	Delta State University
DenvU	Denver University	DTS	Dallas Theological Seminary
DePU	DePauw University	DubTS	Dubuque Theological Seminary
DEStHosp	Delaware State Hospital		
DEStU	Delaware State University	DubU	Dublin University, Erie
Det	Detachment	DukeU	Duke University
DetIMA	Detroit Institute of Musical Arts	DuqU	Duquesne University
		Dur	Durant
DHTS	Dae Han Theological Seminary	dv	Divorced
		EAfr	East Africa
DicC	Dickinson College	EAL	East Alabama
DICCS	Daniel Iverson Center for Christian Studies	EB&CE	Encyclopedia of Biblical & Christian Ethics
DictChHist	Dictionary of Church History	EBapTS	Eastern Baptist Theological Seminary
dipl	Diploma		
Dir	Director	EbenTS	Ebenezer Theological Seminary
dir cand	Director of Candidates		
dir ch rel	Director of Church Relations	EBFBC	Evangelical Baptist Fellowship Bible College
dir dev	Director of Development	EC	Earlham College
dir disc	Director of Discipleship	ECA	Evangelical Church Alliance
dir pers	Director of Personnel	ECan	Eastern Canada
dir sm grp	Director of Small Groups	ECar	Eastern Carolina
dir trng	Director of Training	ECarU	Eastern Carolina University
dirAdm	Director of Admissions	ECB	Evangelical Commentary on the Bible
dirC&S	Director of College & Singles		

ECBC	East Coast Bible College	ESR	Emmanuel School of Religion
ECBS	Evangelical College of Biblical Studies	ESSC	East Stroudsburg State College
ECC	Essex Community College	EStHosp	Eastern State Hospital
ECentU	East Central University	ESU	Emporia State University
ECJC	East Central Junior College	ETS	Eastern Theological Seminary
ECol	Eastern College, St. Davids, PA	ETSU	East Tennessee State University
ECU	East Carolina University		
ed	editor/edition(s)	ETXSU	East Texas State University
Ed.D	Education Doctorate	EU	Eastern University
edtl	editorial	EUB	Evangelical United Brethren
EdTS	Eden Theological Seminary	ev	Evangelist, Evangelism
Educ	Educator	Evan	Evangel, Evangelical
EE	Evangelism Explosion	EvBI	Evangelical Bible Institute, Savannah, GA
EFC	Evangelical Free Church		
EFMA	Evangelical Fellowship of Mission Agencies	EvC	Evangel College
EFMA	Evangelical Fellowship of Mission Agencies	EvCC	Evangelical Covenant Church
EICR	Escuela de Idiomas de Costa Rica	EvCU	Evangelical Christian University
EIG	Evangelical Institute of Greenville, SC	Evgld	Everglades
		EvTC	Evangelical Theological College
EKCC	East Korean Christian College		
EKYU	Eastern Kentucky University	EvTS	Evangelical Theological Seminary
ElizC	Elizabethtown College		
ElizU	Elizabethtown University	EWU	Eastern Washington University
ElmC	Elmhurst College		
em	Emeritus	exec comm	Executive Committee
EMenC	Eastern Mennonite College	exec dir	Executive Director
EMenS	Eastern Mennonite Seminary	exec p	Executive Pastor
EMIU	Eastern Michigan University, Ann Arbor	exec sec	Executive Secretary
		ExposB	Expositor's Bible
EMS	East Mississippi	ExposBC Commentary	Expositors Bible
EmU	Emory University		
ENazC	Eastern Nazarene College	ext	Extension
EncyChr	Encyclopedia of Christianity	f	Father
ENMU	Eastern New Mexico University	fac	Faculty
		FAHSS	Faith Academy Higher Secondary School
enr	Enrolled		
Enre	Enoree	FATP	Faculté Autonôme de théologic protestante, University of Geneva, Switzerland
EPC	Evangelical Presbyterian Church		
EPCC	El Paso Community College		
Epis	Episcopal	FAU	Florida Atlantic University
EpTS	Episcopal Theological Seminary, Kentucky	FBBI	Fruitland Baptist Bible Institute
EPUL	Ecole Polytechnique de l'Univ de Lausanne	FBC	Florida Bible College
		FBIBTS	Fredericksburg Bible Institute & Brown Theological Seminary
equiv	Equivalent		
ERC	Evangelical and Reformed Church		
		FCAc	French Camp Academy
ErCC	Erie Community College	FCCJ	Florida Community College, Jacksonville (formerly Florida Junior College)
ERS	Evangelical Reformed Seminary		
ErskC	Erskine College		
ErskTS	Erskine Theological Seminary	FCS	Free Church of Scotland
		FCSC	Free Church of Scotland College
ESM	Eastman School of Music, Rochester, NY		
		FeatiU	Feati University, Philippines
		Feb	February
		FEBC	Far East Broadcasting Company

ABBREVIATIONS

FEBibC	Far Eastern Bible College, Singapore	GCCC	Gulf Coast Community College
fel	Fellow	GCP	Great Commission Publications
FELS	Faith Evangelical Lutheran Seminary	GCTS	Gordon Conwell Theological Seminary
FGEA	Fred Guthrie Evangelistic Association	GEM	Greater European Mission
FIE	Fellowship of Independent Evangelicals	GenAs	General Assembly
		GenC	Geneva College
FieldI	The Fielding Institute	GenTC	Geneva Theological College
FIU	Florida International University	GetC	Gettysburg College
		GetLS	Gettysburg Lutheran Seminary
FLET	Facultad Latinoamericana de Estudios Teologicos	GETS	Garrett Evangelical Theological Seminary
FLTechU	Florida Technical University		
FLTR	Faculté Libre de Theologie Reformee	GFA	Grace Fellowship Atlanta
		GFM	Gospel Fellowship Missions
FLTR/Aix	Faculté Libre de Theologie Reformee, Aix en Provence, France	GGSB	Golden Gate Baptist Theological Seminary
		GidTC	Gideon Theological College
Flwsp	Fellowship	GlasSU	Glassboro State University
FMarC	Francis Marion College	GlenCC	Glendale Community College
FMC	Franklin and Marshall College		
fndr	Founder	GlenJC	Glendale Junior College
FOCUS	Fellowship of Christians in Universities and Schools	GMCUVA	George Mason College of University of Virginia
FredC	Frederick College	GMF	Global Missionary Fellowship
FrlCT	Freelanda College of Theology	GNHS	Glasgow Northern Hospitals, Scotland
FrSC	Frostburg State College	GOM	Global Outreach Missions
FrTA	Freie Theologische Akademie	GordC	Gordon College
		GPCT	George Peabody College for Teachers
FrUAmst	Free University of Amsterdam		
FSC	Florida Southern College	GPD	Global Partners for Delopment
FSU	Florida State University		
FSWM	Fuller School of World Mission	GPTS	Greenville Presbyterian Theological Seminary
FTS	Faith Theological Seminary	Gr	Grace
FTSSWM	Fuller Theological Seminary School of World Missions	grad	Graduate
		grad wk	Graduate Studies, Graduate Work
FtWBC	Ft. Wayne Bible College	GrBC	Grace Bible College
FU	Friends University	GRBS	Grand Rapids Baptist Seminary
FulJC	Fullerton Junior College		
FulTS	Fuller Theological Seminary	GrCC	Grand Canyon College
FurU	Furman University	GrinC	Grinnell College
FWBC	Free Will Baptist College	GrLks	Great Lakes
GannU	Gannon University	GrnvC	Greenville College
GAPC	Georgia Association for Pastoral Care	GroCC	Grove City College
		grp	Group
GarC	Garland College	GrPl	Great Plains
GASoC	Georgia Southern College	GrT	Graduate of Theology
GASoU	Georgia Southern University	GrTech	Greenville Technical
GASW	Georgia Southwestern	GrTS	Grace Theological Seminary
GATech	Georgia Institute of Technology	GSBS	Gastonia School for Biblical Studies
GATS	General Assembly Theological Seminary	GSC	Good Samaritan Colony
		GSJC	Gadsden State Junior College
GBC	Grace Brethren Church	GSM	Graduate School of Missions
GBibC	Graham Bible College	GSU	Georgia State University
GC	Gospel Crusade		
GCC	Garrett Community College		

GTS	German Theological Seminary	HU	Harding University
GtwnU	Georgetown University	HudR	Hudson River
GU	Greenwich University	HUFS	Hankuk University of Foreign Studies, Seoul Korea
Guer	Guerrant	ia	Interim Administrator
GuilC	Guilford College	IAI	Israel American Institute
GulCst	Gulf Coast	IALCC	Iowa Lakes Community College
GWC	Gardner Webb College		
GWSJC	George C. Wallace State Junior College	IASTC	Iowa State Teacher's College
		IAU/UCA	Interamerican University, (Universidad Cristiana de las Americas)
GWU	George Washington University		
HahnHosp	Hahnamen Hospital, Philadelphia	IAWC	Iowa Wesleyan College
		IBAR	Instituto Biblico Abierto Reformado
HanU	Hanyang University, Seoul, Korea	IBCS	International Bible College & Seminary
HarvU	Harvard University		
HavC	Haverford College	IBPFM	Independent Board for Presbyterian Foreign Missions
HBI	Hindustan Bible Institute, Madras, India	IC	Iona College
HBU	Houston Baptist University	ICAF	Industrial College of the Armed Forces
HCAR	Hebron Center for Alcoholic Rehabilation	ICCI	International Cross Culture Institute
HCB	Holmes College of the Bible		
HDC	Hillsdale College	ICGU	International Christian Graduate University
HDS	Harvard Divinity School		
headm	Headmaster	ICM/NA	Instituto Cultural Mexicano/Norte Americano
HebUC	Hebrew Union College		
HebUJ	Hebrew University, Jerusalem, Israel	ICS	Institute for Christian Studies
		ICTS	IONA Centres for Theological Studies
HeC	Hesser College		
HGST	Houston Graduate School/Theology	ICV	International Children's Verson
HighC	Highland College		
HJC	Hinds Junior College	ICWE	International Congress World Evangelization, Lausanne, Switzerland
HLC	Hawaii Loa College		
HLIC	Here's Life Inter-City/Citihope		
		IDEA	International Discipleship & Evangelization Association
Hlst	Holston		
hm	Home Missions; Home Mission Assignment	IFCA	Independent Fundamental Churches of America
HMISI	Henry Martyn International School of Islamics, India	IFES	International Fellowship of Evangelical Students
HntC	Huntingdon College	IGST	International Graduate School of Theology, Seoul, Korea
HongU	Hong-Ik University, Korea		
HopeC	Hope College		
HougC	Houghton College	IHLS	Institute of Holy Land Studies
HowC	Howard College		
HPtC	High Point College	IHU	In Ha University
HPTS	Hapdong Presbyterian Theological Seminary	IICS	International Institute of Christian Studies
hr	Honorably Retired	IIT	Illinois Institute of echnology
Hrmny	Harmony	Ill	Illiana
Hrtg	Heritage	ILSU	Illinois State University
Hrtl	Heartland	IMCS	International Mission College & Seminary, New York
HSC	Hampden-Sydney College		
HsinBS	Hsinchu Bible School		
HSU	Hardin-Simmons University		
HTC	Hebrew Theological College, Skokie	IMPACT	International Mission Programs and Cross Cultural/Career Training
HTS	Hansung Theological Seminary		
		InchU	Incheon University, Korea

ABBREVIATIONS

instr	Instructor	KBNU	Kyung Book National University
INStU	Indiana State University		
int	Intern, Intern year	KCC	Keimyung Christian College
Int	International	KCT	Knox College, Toronto
IntSem	International Seminary (formerly International Bible Inst. & Seminary)	KeioU	Keio University, Tokyo
		KEMAN	Korean Evangelical Mission to All Nations
INU	Indiana University	KenC	Kennesaw College
ip	Interim Pastor	KETS	Korea Evangelical Theological Society
IPC	International Presbyterian Church	Kg'sC	The King's College
is	Interim Supply	KgC	King College
ISBE	International Standard Bible Encyclopedia	KGITM	Karolyi Gaspar Institute of Theology and Missions
isc	Interim Stated Clerk	KgMt	Kings Mountain
ISC	Iona Study Center, Jamaica	KHU	Kyung Hee University
ISCF	International Students Christian Fellowship	KKU	Kon Kuk University, Seoul, Korea
ISH	International Seamen's House	KMS	Kemper Military School
ISI	International Students, Inc.	Knoxv	Knoxville
ISS	International Seamen's Service	KookC	Kookjae College
		KOR	Korea
IST	International School of Theology (affiliated with CCC)	KorBC	Korean Bible College
		KorCap	Korean Capital
		KorCC	Korean Christian College
		KorCent	Korean Central
ISU	State University of Iowa	KorCPPTS	Korea Christian Pure Presbyterian Theological Seminary
ITSLA	International Theological Seminary, Los Angeles, California		
		KorE	Korean Eastern
IUP	Indiana University of Pennsylvania	KorNW	Korean Northwest
		KorPTS	Korean Presbyterian Theological Seminary
IVBI	Illinois Valley Bible Institute		
IVCF	Inter Varsity Christian Fellowship	KorS	Korean Southern
		KorSE	Korean Southeastern
Jan	January	KorSW	Korean Southwest
J & W	Johnson & Wales University	KorTS	Korea Theological Seminary
JAXSU	Jacksonville State University	KorU	Korean University
JBC	Jamaica Bible College	KosU	Kosin University
JBS	Japanese Bible Seminary	KPGACTS	Korea Presbyterian General Assembly College & Theological Seminary
JBU	John Brown University		
JCBC	Johnson City Business College		
		KRTS	Kobe Reformed Theological Seminary
JCJC	Jones County Junior College		
JCS	John Calvin Seminary, Chile, SA	KSC	Keene State College
		KSJL	Kobe School of Japanese Languages
JCTS	Japan Christian Theological Seminary		
		KStU	Kent State University
JCU	John Carroll University	KSU	Kansas State University
JD	Doctor of Jurisprudence	KTS	Knox Theological Seminary
JerCit	Jersey City	KTSCO	Knox Theological Seminary, CO
JFC	John Fletcher College	L	Licentiate; Licensure
JHU	Johns Hopkins University	L&O	Licensed and Ordained
JMU	James Madison University	L'Abri	L'Abri Fellowship, Switzerland
JR	James River		
JSJC	Jefferson State Junior College	LA	Louisiana
JSM	Jaffray School of Missions	LaelU	Lael University
JSU	Jackson State University	LafC	Lafayette College
Jul	July	LaGC	LaGrange College
Jun	June	LAM	Latin American Missions
Kan	Kanawha	LambC	Lambuth College

LanBC	Lancaster Bible College	LTS	Lexington Theological Seminary
lang stdy	Language study		
Lans	Lansing	LTSPA	Luthern Theological Seminary of Pennsylvania
LanTS	Lancaster Theological Seminary	LTU	Lamar Technical University
LaSU	LaSalle University	LutC	Luther College
LATU	Louisiana Tech University	LVBCS	Linda Vista Bible College & Seminary
LawrIT	Lawrence Institute of Technology	LVSC	Ligonier Valley Study Center
LBC	Long Beach College, CA	m	Mother
LBTS	Liberty Baptist Theological Seminary	MABCS	Mid-Atlantic Bible College & Seminary in Systematic Theology
LC	Louisiana College		
LCAAT	Lambton College of Applied Arts & Technology	MABS	Master of Arts in Biblical Studies
LCD	London College of Divinity	MaC	Macalester College
LCGS	Lesley College Grad School	MAC	Master of Arts in Counseling
LCS	Lincoln Christian Seminary	MacC	Macon College
lect	Lecturer	MACE	Master of Arts in Christian Education
LeeC	Lee College		
LehU	Lehigh University	MAF	Missionary Aviation Fellowship
LeTC	Le Tourneau College		
lgdn	Legal guardian	magz	Magazine
LHD	Doctor of Humanities	mal	Minister at large
lib	Librarian	MAMFT	Master of Arts, Marriage & Family Therapy
LibBC	Liberty Bible College		
LibU	Liberty University	ManhSM	Manhattan School of Music
LICC	London Institute for Contemporary Christianity	ManSC	Mankato State College
		MaPr	Maritime Provinces
LicTh	Licence en theologie	Mar	March
LigMin	Ligonier Ministries	MAR	Master of Arts in Religion
LimeC	Limestone College	MarC	Marion College
LinC	Linfield College	MarI	Marion Institute
LincU	Lincoln University	MariC	Marietta College
Lit	Literature	MarqU	Marquette University
LittD	Doctor of Letters	MarU	Marshall University
LIU	Long Island University	MaryvC	Maryville College
LivU	Livingston University	MATC	Milwaukee Area Technical College
LLB	Bachelor of Laws		
LLSI	Landour Language School, India	MATS	Master of Arts in Theological Studies
LM	Loyola Marymount	May	May
LMJC	Lees-McRae Junior College	MBA	Master of Business Administration
Louisv	Louisville		
lpc	Licensed Professional Counselor	MBC	Martha Berry College
		MBI	Moody Bible Institute
LPTS	Louisville Presbyterian Theological Seminary	MBibCoun	Master in Biblical Counseling
LRBC	Luther Rice Bible College	MBICS	Moody Bible Institute Correspondence School
LRC	Lenoir-Rhyne College		
LRTS	Luther Rice Theological Seminary	mbr	Member
		MCC	Miami Christian College
LSA	Linguistic Society of America	MCCC	Macomb County Community College
LSB	Lynn School of the Bible	MCDE	Medical Center of Delaware
LSU	Louisiana State University	MCE	Master of Christian Education
LTh	Licence en Theologie		
LTI	Lowell Technological Institute	McGU	McGill University
		McNSU	McNeese State University
		mcouns	Minister of Counseling

ABBREVIATIONS

MCSC	Morningside College, Sioux City, IA	miss	Missiology
MCU	Miami Christian University	MISU	Michigan State University
MCVA	Medical College of Virginia	MIT	Massachusetts Institute of Technology
MDCC	Miami Dade Community College	MitC	Mitchell College
mdis	Medically disabled	MJC	Montgomery Junior College
MDiv	Master of Divinity	MlvSC	Millersville State College
MDJC	Miami Dade Junior College	MlvU	Millersville University, PA
ME	Master of Engineering	MM	Mercy Ministry
MEd	Master of Education	MMin	Master of Ministry
medu	Minister of Education	MMiss	Master of Missiology
Mem	Memorial	mmus	Minister of Music
Memp	Memphis	MMus	Master of Music
MempSU	Memphis State University	MNA	Mission to North America
MempTS	Memphis Theological Seminary	mng ed	Managing Editor
		MNW	Moody Northwest
MercAc	Mercersburg Academy	MO	Missouri
MERF	Middle East Reformed Fellowship	moa	Minister of Adults
		MOBC	Missouri Baptist College
Merid	Meridian	moc/ym	Minister of Career and Young Married
MerU	Mercer University		
MesaC	Mesa College	mocg	Minister of Church Growth
MesC	Messiah College	Mod	Moderator
mev	Minister of Evangelism	mod	Minister of Discipleship
mfam	Minister to Families	MonC	Montreat College
MFM	Mercy Field Ministry	Monm	Monmouth
MFT	Marriage and Family Therapy	MonSC	Montclair State College
		MorC	Moravian College
MGAC	Middle Georgia College	MorCC	Morris County College
MGCJC	Mississippi Gulf Coast Junior College	MorHarC	Morris Harvey College
		MorS	Moravian Seminary
MGPCC	Middle Georgia Pastoral Counseling Center	MorSU	Morgan State University
		mout	Minister of Outreach
mgr	Manager	mov	Minister of Visitation
mgt	Management	moy	Minister of Youth
MHC	Mars Hill College	moya	Minister of Young Adults
MhdSU	Morehead State University	mp	Missions Pastor
MHJC	Mary Holmes Junior College	mpc	Minister of Pastoral Care
MIA	Men in Action	MRA	Master of Religious Arts
MidA	Mid-America	MRE	Master of Religious Education
MidABTS	Mid-America Baptist Theological Seminary	ms	Minister to Seniors
		ms/sa	Minister to Singles/Single Adults
MidAC	Mid-America College		
MidANU	Mid-America Nazarene University	MSAT	Morrisville State Agriculture & Technical
MidARS	Mid-America Reformed Seminary	MSB	Master of Science in Bible
		MSBC	Mississippi Baptist Convention
MidAtl	Mid-Atlantic		
MidSo	Mid South	MSC	Mississippi College
MidSoBC	Mid-South Bible College	MSM	Merchant Seamen's Mission, SC
Midw	Midwestern	MSM	Meritorious Service Medal
MillsC	Millsap College	MSMC	Mount St. Mary College
min	Ministry/Ministries	Msn	Mission
min assim	Minister of Assimilation	MSRCN	Missions Seminary of the Reformed Churches in the Netherlands
min c/c	Minister of College/Career		
min dir	Ministry Director		
MinAct	Ministries in Action	MSS	Missionary Sending Service
mis	Missionary/Missionaries	MSSC	Mississippi Southern College
misal	Missionary at Large	MST	Methodist School of Theology
miscand	Missionary Candidate	MSU	Mississippi State University

MSVal	Mississippi Valley	NCBC	North Central Bible College
MSW	Master of Social Work	NCC	Nationally Certified Counselor
MtAlU	Mount Allison University		
MTC	Moore Theological College, Sydney Australia	NCCIL	North Central College, Naperville, IL
MTS	McCormick Theological Seminary	NCEd	New College, Edinburgh
		NCP	National Conference on Preaching
MTSK	Methodist Theological Seminary, Korea	NCSt	North Carolina State College/University
MTSU	Middle Tennessee State University	NCTS	North China Theological Seminary
MTW	Mission to the World	NCWC	North Carolina Wesleyan College
MuhC	Muhlenberg College		
MUOH	Miami University, Ohio	NDSU	North Dakota State University
mus	Music		
MuSB	Multnomah School of the Bible	NEBC	Northeastern Bible College
		NECC	Northeastern Correctional Center
MuskC	Muskingum College		
MWBTS	Midwestern Baptist Theological Seminary	NEJC	Northeastern Junior College
		NELSC	Northeast Louisiana State College
MWCC	Midwest Christian College		
MWCPA	Midwest Church Planting Association	NELU	Northeast Louisiana University
MWTS	Midwest Theological Seminary	NEMOSTC	Northeast Missouri State Teacher's College
MX	Mexico		
NA	North America	NEMSJC	Northeast Mississippi Junior College
NAC	National Agricultural College		
		NEOKAM	Northeastern Oklahoma A&M
NACCC	National Association of Congregational Christian Churches	NESAJ	Near East School of Archaeology, Jerusalem
		NEST	Near East School of Theology, Beirut, Lebanon
NACFT	National Academy of Counselors and Family Therapists	NewbC	Newberry College
		NewU	Newport University
NAE	National Association of Evangelicals	NFSRE	National Foundation for the Study of Religion & Economics
NAM	North Africa Mission		
NANC	National Association of Nouthetic Counselors	NGA	North Georgia
		NGJC	North Greenville Jr. College
NAS	Naval Air Station	NGSB	New Geneva Study Bible
NASD	North America School of Drafting	NGTS	New Geneva Theological Seminary, CO
Nash	Nashville	NHBH	New Haley's Bible Handbook
NatGd	National Guard		
NatU	National University, Korea	NISBE	New International Standard Bible Encyclopedia
Navs	Navigators		
NavWC	Naval War College	NIU	Northern Illinois University, Aurora
NazTS	Nazarene Theological Seminary		
		NJ	New Jersey
NAZU	Northern Arizona University	NMSU	New Mexico State University
NB	New Brunswick, Canada	NNE	Northern New England Presbytery
NBI	National Bible Institute		
NBS	Navajo Bible School		
NBTS	Northern Baptist Theological Seminary	NOBTS	New Orleans Baptist Theological Seminary
NCAC	National Christian Action Council	NoCA	Northern California Presbytery
NCACC	Northampton County Area Community College	NoE	Northeast Presbytery
		NoIL	Northern Illinois Presbytery

ABBREVIATIONS

NoIre	North Ireland		University
NorC	Norman College	OCI	Overseas Crusades International
NoTX	North Texas		
Nov	November	Oct	October
NP&RYLC	National Presbyterian & Reformed Youth Leadership Conference	ODU	Old Dominion University
		oe	Organizing Evangelist
		OgleU	Oglethorpe University
NPC	National Presbyterian Church	OHNU	Ohio Northern University
NPM	National Presbyterian Missions	OHSPA	Ohio State Police Academy
		OHSU	Ohio State University
NPMRPC	National Presbyterian Missions of the Reformed Presbyterian Church	OHWU	Ohio Wesleyan University
		OKBU	Oklahoma Baptist University
		OKSU	Oklahoma State University
NPRF	National Prebyterian and Reformed Fellowship	om	Office manager
		OMF	Overseas Missionary Fellowship
NPTS	North Park Theological Seminary	ONT	Ontario, Canada
		op	Organizing Pastor
NPU	New Paltz University	OPC	Orthodox Presbyterian Church
NR	New River		
NRCC	New River Community College	OpResc	Operation Rescue
		Or	Orange
NS	Nova Scotia, Canada	ORSU	Oregon Statue University
NSSR	New School for Social Research	ORU	Oral Roberts University
		ORUGST	Oral Roberts University Graduate School of Theology
NT	New Testament		
NTSU	North Texas State University	OSTC	Oshkosh State Teacher's College
NU	Nova University		
NWBS	Northwestern Bible School		
NWC	Northwestern College	OT	Old Testament
NWCC	Northwest Christian College	OtC	Otira College
NWES	Northwestern Evangelical Seminary	OU	Ohio University
		p	Pastor
NWMOSU	Northwest Missouri State University	P	Presbyterian
		Pac	Pacific
NWNC	Northwest Nazarene College	PaC	Patton College
nwsltr	Newsletter	PacLU	Pacific Lutheran University
nwspr col	Newspaper Column	PacNW	Pacific Northwest
NWSTS	Northwestern Schools Theological Seminary	PACS	Philadelphia Association for Christian Schools
NWSU	Northwestern State University	PacSR	Pacific School of Religion
		PadCC	Paducah Community College
NWU	Northwestern University	pal	Pastor at Large
NyC	Nyack College (formerly Nyack Missionary College)	PalC	Palomar College (CA)
		Palm	Palmetto
NYS	New York State Presbytery	PalmHC	Palmer Home for Children
NYSATI	New York State Agricultural & Technical Institute	PalmJC	Palmer Junior College
		PasC	Pasadena College
NYSCF	New York State College of Forestry	PASU	Pennsylvania State University
		PBAC	Palm Beach Atlantic College
NYTS	New York Theological Seminary	PBC	Piedmont Bible College
		PBC&GS	Prairie Bible College and Graduate School
NYU	New York University		
O	Ordained	PBI	Prairie Bible Institute
o&e	Outreach & Evangelism	PBJC	Palm Beach Junior College
OakCC	Oakland City College, IN	PBTS	Practice Bible Training School
ob	Laboring out of bounds		
ObC	Oberlin College		
OBU	Ouachita Baptist University, NC	Pby	Presbytery
		PC	Presbyterian College
OCEU	Oxford College of Emory		

PCA	Presbyterian Church in America	PLF	Philadelphia Leadership Foundation
PCAGA	Presbyterian Church in America General Assembly	PMC	Presbyterian Medical Center
PCAust	Presbyterian Church of Australia	PMI	Presbyterian Mission International
PCBBC	Pacific Coast Baptist Bible College	PNFS	Pensacola Navy Flight School
PCC	Presbyterian Church of Canada	PNG	Papua New Guinea
PCE	Presbyterian Church in Egypt	PNUG	Presbiterio Nacional Uuvias de Gracia
PCNZ	Presbyterian Church of New Zealand	PolkJC	Polk Junior College
PCTSUSA	The Presbyterian College &Theological Seminary of the USA Synod	Pot	Potomac
		PPC	Point Park College
		PR	Puerto Rico
PD	Police Department	PRCC	Presbyterian and Reformed Commission on Chaplains and Military Personnel
PeabC	Peabody College, Nashville		
PEF	Presbyterian Evangelistic Fellowship	pres	President
		PRes	Pastor in Residence
PEI	Prince Edward Island	prin	Principal
PenCC	Pensacola Christian College	PRJC	Presbyterian and Reformed Joint Commission on Chaplains and Military Personnel (now PRCC)
pEng	pastor of English services		
PenJC	Pensacola Junior College		
PennSt	Pennsylvania State University		
		prof	Professor
PepU	Pepperdine University	prof em	Professor Emeritus
PerkJC	Perkinston Junior College	proflg	Professor at Large
PFA	Prison Fellowship Association, Columbia, SC	PSC	Paul Smith's College
		PSCE	Presbyterian School for Christian Education
PGATCS	Presbyterian General AssemblyTheological College & Seminary		
		PST	Perkins School of Theology
		PSU	Portland State University
pgs	Post graduate studies	pt	Part-time
PhC	Phoenix College	PTS	Princeton Theological Seminary
PHCC	Pasco-Hernando Community College		
		PTSDD	Presbyterian Theological Seminary, Dehra Dun, India
PhD	Doctorate		
PhD cand	Doctorate candidate	PU	Princeton University
Phil	Philadelphia	publ	publisher/publication(s)
PhilCB	Philadelphia College of the Bible	PUCHE	Potchefstroom University for Christian Higher Education
PhilCC	Philadelphia Community College	Purdue	Purdue University
		PXTS	Pittsburgh-Xenia Theological Seminary
PhilChrU	Philippines Christian University		
		PYA	Presbyterian Youth in America
PhilTS	Philadelphia Theological Seminary		
		QB	Quebec, Canada
PhM	Master of Philosophy	QnsC	Queens College
PHSJC	Patrick Henry State Junior College	QPH	Quarryville Presbyterian Home
PhU	Phillips University, OK	QUB	Queens University of Belfast, N. Ireland
PhUG	Phillips University, Germany		
PI	Philippine Islands	QUCC	Queens University/Conestoga College, Canada
PineJC	Pinebrook Junior College		
Pitts	Pittsburgh		
PittsTS	Pittsburgh Theological Seminary	RabI	Rabello Institute
		RadC	Radford College
PJC	Presbyterian Junior College	RAP	Reformed Academic Press
PLC	Point Loma College		

ABBREVIATIONS

RBC	Reformed Bible College, Grand Rapids	RPTS	Reformed Presbyterian Theological Seminary
RBI	PCA Retirement and Benefits, Inc.	RPTSW	Reformed Presbyterian Theological Seminary, Wilkinsburg, PA
rc	Recording Clerk	RTS	Reformed Theological Seminary, Jackson, MS
RCA	Reformed Church in America		
RCC	Rockland Community College	RTSFL	Reformed Theological Seminary, Orlando, FL
RckmC	Rockmont College		
RCM	Reformation Christian Ministries	RTSK	Reformed Theological Seminary, Korea
RCUS	Reformed Church in the U.S.	RTSNC	Reformed Theological Seminary, Charlotte, NC
re	Ruling Elder		
REC	Reformed Episcopal Church	RU	Rice University
rec	Rector	RUF	Reformed University Fellowship
Recd	Received		
recgn	recognized in/for	RUM	Reformed University Ministries
RedC	Redeemer College		
RedTS	Redeemer Theological Seminary	RutgU	Rutgers University
		RWC	Roberts Wesleyan College
Ref	Reformed	SA	South America
reg	Regional	SAC	South America Crusades
Reg	Registrar	SacBC	Sacramento Baptist College
RegC	Regent College	SacBTS	Sacramento Baptist Theological Seminary
RegU	Regent University, VA		
rep	Representative	SacHU	Sacred Heart University
REpS	Reformed Episcopal Seminary	SACS	Southern Association of Christian Schools
RES	Reformed Ecumenical Synod	SamU	Samford University
res	Resident	SanJoa	San Joaquin
resrch	Research	SanJoseSU	San Jose State University
ret	Retired	SArC	Spring Arbor College
rf	Research Fellow	SBA	Seminario Biolico Alianza, Ecuador
RGNS	Rabun Gap Nacoochee School		
RhC	Rhodes College	SBap	Southern Baptist
RhU	Rhodes University	SBC	Southern Baptist Convention
RiC	Richland College	SBI	Stregic Bible Institute
RiCC	Riverside Community College	SBTS	Southern Baptist Theological Seminary
RIPHF	Rotary International Paul Harris Fellow	sc	Stated Clerk
		SCAD	Savannah College of Art & Design
RISD	Rhode Island School of Design		
RIT	Rochester Institute of Technology	SCBC	Southern California Bible College
RLMI	Right to Life of Michigan	SCC	Sandhills Community College
rm	Radio Ministry		
RMI	Reformed Ministries International	sch	School
		SCS	Sangre de Christo Seminary
RMtn	Rocky Mountain	SCTSC	Southern Connecticut State College
RoanC	Roanoke College, Salem, VA		
RolC	Rollins College	SDSU	San Diego State University
RosGS	Rosemead Graduate School	SE	South East
RPCES	Reformed Presbyterian Church, Evangelical Synod	SEAL	Southeast Alabama
		SeaWTS	Seabury-Western Theological Seminary
RPCNA	Reformed Presbyterian Church of North America	SEBC	Southeastern Bible College
RPI	Rensselaer Polytechnic Institute	SEBTS	Southeastern Baptist Theological Seminary

sec	Secretary	SpoBC	Spokane Bible College
SEC	Southeastern College	SprC	Springfield College
SECC	Southeastern Community College	SPS	South Presbyterian Seminary, Sao Paulo, Brazil
SELA	Southeast Louisiana	SpT	Spartanburg Tech
sem	Seminary	SPU	Seattle Pacific University
SemJC	Seminole Junior College	srp	Senior Pastor
SEMOStC	Southeast Missouri State College	SRU	Slippery Rock University
		ss	Stated Supply
Sept	September	SSC	Salem State College
SETS	Southeastern Theological Seminary	SSCU	Soong Sil Christian University
		StAnd	St. Andrews
SFAU	Stephen F. Austin University	StAndC	St. Andrews College
SFBC	San Francisco Baptist ollege	StanU	Stanford University
SFC	Sioux Falls College	STB	Bachelor of Sacred Theology
SFL	Southern Florida	STC	Sungkyul Theological College
SFSC	San Francisco State College	StCCCC	St. Clair County Community College
SFTS	San Francisco Theological Seminary	STCNJ	State Teacher's College, New Jersey
SGA	Slavic Gospel Association		
ShBC	Shenandoah Bible College	StCS	St. Charles Seminary
ShelC	Shelton College	STD	Doctor of Sacred Theology
ShepC	Shepherd College	SterC	Sterling College
ShJC	Sheridan Junior College	StFrC	St. Francis College
SHSU	Sam Houston State University	StJosC	St. Joseph College
		StLawU	St. Lawrence University
ShSU	Shippensburg State University	StLou	St. Louis
		StLU	St. Louis University
SIL	Summer Institute of Linguistics	STM	Master Of Sacred Theology
		StOlC	Saint Olaf College
SIM	Serving in Mission	STPC	Seminario Teologico Presbiteriano de Campinos
SIMA	Servants in Missions Abroad (IMPACT as of 1991)	StPJC	St. Petersburg Junior College
SimpC	Simpson College	STPM	Seminario Teologico Presbiteriano de Mexico
SiouC	Sioux City		
SiouxI	Siouxlands	StrathU	Strathclyde University
SIU	Southern Illinois University	StrC	Strayer College, Washington, DC
SJBC	Sumerland Junior Bible College	STS	Seoul Theological Seminary
		stu	Student, Studies
SJC	Standing Judicial Commission	stu int	Student Intern
SJCC	San Jose City College	stus	Student Supply
SJRJC	St. John's River Junior College	StVC	Saint Vincent College
		StVdP	St. Vincent de Paul
SJSU	San Jose State University	SU	Scripture Union
SK	Saskatchewan, Canada	SUA&M	Southern University A & M
sm	Step Mother	SUDS	Silliman University Divinity School
SMBC	Sydney Missionary and Bible College		
		sum int	Summer Intern
SMS	Southern Mississippi	SUNY	State University of New York
SMU	Southern Methodist University	SUNYB	State University of New York (Brockport)
SNE	Southern New England Presbytery		
SNU	Seoul National University, Korea	SUNYM	State University of New York (Morrisville)
SoCst	South Coast	supt	Superintendent
SogangU	Sogang University	sus	Suspended; Suspension
SoTC	Soundwell Tech College, UK	SusqU	Susquehanna University
SoTX	South Texas	SusqV	Susquehanna Valley
sp	Supply Pastor	Suw	Suwannee
SPC	Seattle Pacific College	SW	Southwest
SPN	Seminario Presbiteriano Do Norte		

ABBREVIATIONS

SwarC	Swarthmore College	TIIR	Townsend Institute of International Relations
SWBC	Southwest Baptist College		
SWBTS	Southwestern Baptist Theological Seminary	TIU	Trinity International University, Deerfield, IL
SWBU	Southwest Baptist University	TJU	Thomas Jefferson University
SWC	Southwestern College	TMcC	Truett-McConnell College
SWCPLN	Southwest Church Planting Network	TMS	The Master's Seminary
		TMTS	Trinity Marathon Theological Seminary
SWFL	Southwest Florida		
SWTU	Southwest Texas University	TNSU	Tennessee State University
SWU	Southwest University	TNTC	Tennessee Temple College
SWUM	Southwestern University, Memphis	TNTU	Tennessee Technological University
Syn	Synod	TNVal	Tennessee Valley
SyU	Syracuse University	TokCU	Tokyo Christian University
t	Teacher	TokUFS	Tokyo University of Foreign Studies
t/tr	Teacher/Trainer		
Tab	Tabernacle	TorST	Toronto School of Theology
TabC	Tabor College	TowU	Towson University
TalTS	Talbot Theological Seminary	TPC	Taejon Presbyterian College
TarkC	Tarkio College	TPCDRC	Turning Point Christian Drug Rehabilitation Center
Tasm	Tasmania Presbytery		
TayU	Taylor University	trans	Translated, Translator
TBC	Trinity Baptist College	transf	Transferred
TBTS	Temple Baptist Theological Seminary	TRBI	Thomas Road Bible Institute, Lynchburg, VA
TC	Trinity College	TrenSC	Trenton State College
TCC	Trinity Christian College	TriCCC	Tri-County Community College
TCE	Trinity College, Bristol, England	Trin	Trinity
		TRM	Tidewater Reformed Ministries
TCIL	Trinity College, Deerfield, IL		
TCIN	Trinity College, Newburg, IN	TrPS	Trinity Presbyterian School
TCRCN	Theological College of the Reformed Churches of the Netherlands (Kampen)	TrSU	Troy State University
		trus	Trustee; Trustees
		TS	Theological Seminary
		TSIL	Trinity Seminary, IL
TCRCNV	Theological College of the Reformed Churches of the Netherlands (Vrijgmaakt)	TTC	Teacher's Training College, Singapore
		TThC	Trinity Theological College, Singapore
TCS	Thornwell Christian School		
TCU	Texas Christian University	TTS	Trinity Theological Seminary, Newberg, IN
TEAM	The Evangelical Alliance Mission		
		TueU	Tuebingen University
TEDS	Trinity Evangelical Divinity School	TufC	Tufts College
		TulU	Tulane University
TEE	Theological Education by Extension	Tusc	Tuscaloosa
		TusC	Tusculum College
TempU	Temple University	TVMin	Television Ministry
TempUGS	Temple University Graduate School	Twnsh	Township
tf	Teaching Fellow	TXA&M	Texas A & M University
TFBC	Toccoa Falls Bible College	TXA&MC	Texas A & M - Commerce
Th	Theology	TXTU	Texas Technological University
th res	Theologian-in-Residence		
ThB	Bachelor of Theology	TXTUL	Texas Tech – Lubbock
ThC	Thomas College, ME	TynC	Tyndall College
ThD	Doctor of Theology	UAB	University of Alabama, Birmingham
ThielC	Thiel College		
ThM	Master of Theology	UAGuer	Universidad Autonoma de Guerrero
THTS	Tai Han Theological Seminary, Korea		
		UAK	University of Alaska

UAkr	University of Akron	UGue	University of Guelph, Ontario
UAL	University of Alabama		
UAlb	University of Alberta	UHeid	University of Heidelberg, Germany
UAR	University of Arkansas		
UARF	University of Arkansas, Fayetteville	UHH	University of Hawaii at Hilo
		UHou	University of Houston
UARLR	University of Arkansas, Little Rock	UIA	University of Iowa
		UID	University of Idaho
UAuck	University of Auckland	UIL	University of Illinois
UAZ	University of Arizona	UInd	University of Indianapolis
UAZT	University of Arizona at Tucson	UKar	University of Karachi
		UKS	University of Kansas
UB	University of Baltimore	UKY	University of Kentucky
UBas	University of Basil, Switzerland	ULanE	University of Lancaster, England
UBF	University of Biarritz, France	ULon	University of London
UBSL	University of Baltimore School of Law	ULV	University of Louisville
		ULvrpl	University of Liverpool
UBuf	University of Buffalo	UMA	University of Massachusetts
UC	Ursinus College	UMC	United Methodist Church
UCalg	University of Calgary	UMD	University of Maryland
UCam	University of Cambridge, England	UME	University of Maine (Portland)
UCAR	University of Central Arkansas	UMemp	University of Memphis
		UMI	University of Michigan
UCB	University of California, Berkeley	UMiami	University of Miami
		UMN	University of Minnesota
UCBWM	United Church Board for World Missions	UMO	University of Missouri
		UMOC	University of Missouri, Columbia
UCD	University of California, Davis		
UCDS	University of Chicago Divinity School	UMOKC	University of Missouri, Kansas City
UCF	University of Central Florida	UMonte	University of Montevallo
UChat	University of Chattanooga	UMOSL	University of Missouri at St. Louis
UChC	United Church of Christ		
UChi	University of Chicago	UMS	University of Mississippi
UCI	University of California, Irvine	UnC	Union College
		UNC	University of North Carolina
UCin	University of Cincinnati	UNCA	University of North Carolina, Asheville
UCLA	University of California, Los Angeles		
		UNCC	University of North Carolina, Charlotte
UCO	University of Colorado		
UCSB	University of California, Santa Barbara	UNCCH	University of North Carolina, Chapel Hill
UCSD	University of California, San Diego	UNCG	University of North Carolina, Greensboro
UCT	University of Connecticut	UNCO	University of Northern Colorado
UCTSA	University of Cape Town, South Africa		
		UNCW	University of North Carolina, Wilmington
Uday	University of Dayton		
UDE	University of Delaware	UND	University of North Dakota
UDet	University of Detroit	UNE	University of Nebraska
UDub	University of Dubuque	UNFL	University of North Florida
UEdin	University of Edinburgh	UNH	University of New Hampshire
UFL	University of Florida		
UGA	University of Georgia	UNIA	University of Northern Iowa, Cedar Falls
UGS	Université de Genève, Switzerland		
		UniTC	Unity Theological Center
UGST	United Graduate School of Theology	UniTS	United Theological Seminary
		unk	Unknown

ABBREVIATIONS

UNM	University of New Mexico	USNA	United States Naval Academy
UNotD	University of Notre Dame	USNPGS	United States Naval Post Graduate School
UNTX	University of North Texas		
UNV	University of Nevada		
UOK	University of Oklahoma	USNR	United States Navy Reserve
UOR	University of Oregon	USo	University of the South
UOxf	University of Oxford, England	UStel	University of Stellenbosch
		UStrF	University of Strassburg, France
UPA	University of Pennsylvania		
UPac	University of Pacific	USU	Utah State University
UPar	University of Paris	USusx	University of Sussex, England
UpC	Upsala College		
UPCUSA	United Presbyterian Church in the United States of America	USWLA	University of Southwestern Louisiana
UPEI	University of Prince Edward Island, Canada	UT	University of Tennessee, Knoxville
UPI	University of the Philippines	UTamp	University of Tampa
UPitt	University of Pittsburgh	UTC	University of Tennessee, Chattanooga
UPR	University of Puerto Rico		
UPre	University of Pretoria	UTol	University of Toledo
UPTC	United Presbyterian Theological College	UTor	University of Toronto
		UTSNY	Union Theological Seminary, New York
UPugS	University of Puget Sound		
URed	University of Redlands	UTSVA	Union Theological Seminary, Virginia
UReg	University of Regina		
URich	University of Richmond	UTul	University of Tulsa
URoch	University of Rochester	UTXA	University of Texas, Arlington
USACGS	United States Army Command and Graduate School		
		UTXAu	University of Texas, Austin
USAF	United States Air Force	UTXT	University of Texas, Tyler
USAf	University of South Africa	UUJ	University of Ulster, Jordanstown, N. Ireland
USAFA	United States Air Force Academy		
		UUT	University of Utah
USAFIT	United States Air Force Institute of Technology	UUtr	University of Utrecht
		UVA	University of Virginia
USAFR	United States Air Force Reserve	UVT	University of Vermont
		UW	University of Washington
USAL	University of Southern Alabama	UWA	United Wesleyan, Allentown, PA
USanCris	University of San Cristoba	UWales	University of Wales
USAR	United States Army Reserve	UWatO	University of Waterloo, Ontario
USArmy	United States Army		
USask	University of Saskatchewan	UWFL	University of West Florida
USC	University of South Carolina	UWI	University of Wisconsin
USCA	University of Southern California	UWIM	University of Wisconsin, Madison
USCGA	United States Coast Guard Academy	UWO	University of Western Ontario, London, Ontario, Canada
USCWM	U. S. Center For World Missions	UWM	University of Wisconsin, Milwaukee
USF	University of Southern Florida	UWY	University of Wyoming
		UY	Universidad de Yucatan, Mexico
USIU	United States International University		
		v	Vacant
USM	University of Southern Mississippi	ValpU	Valparaiso University
		VandU	Vanderbilt University
USMA	United States Military Academy	Vang	Vanguard
		VATech	Virginia Tech
USMC	United States Marine Corps	VCC	Virginia Commercial College
USN	United States Navy		

VCSTC	Valley City State Teacher's College, North Dakota	WFU	Wake Forest University
		WGAC	West Georgia College
VCU	Virginia Commonwealth University	WheatC	Wheaton College
		WheatGrS	Wheaton Graduate School
VFCC	Valley Forge Christian College	WhitBC	Whitworth Bible College
		WhitC	Whitworth College
VilU	Villanova University	WHM	World Harvest Mission
VinU	Vincennes University	WhTS	Whitefield Theological Seminary
vis	Visiting		
VMI	Virginia Military Institute	WI	Wisconsin
vol	Volunteer	WichSU	Wichita State University
VP	Vice President	WiLaU	Wilfred Laurier University
VPI	Virginia Polytechnic Institute	WilC	Wilkes College
VSC	Valdosta State College	WIM	West Indies Mission
VTS	Virginia Theological Seminary, Alexandria	WIMI	Western Indian Ministries, Incorporated
W	Western	WinC	Winthrop College
w	Wife	Winch	Winchester
WabRPby	Wabash River Presbytery	WinJC	Wingate Junior College
WaC	Waldorf College	WittU	Wittenburg University
War	Warrior	WJBC	William Jennings Bryan College
WartbC	Wartburg College		
Wash	Washington	WJC	Washington and Jefferson College
WashTS	Washington Theological Seminary		
		wk	Work
WashU	Washington University, St. Louis	wkbk	Workbook
		wksh ldr	Workshop Leader
WASU	Washington State University	WKU	Western Kentucky University
WaybC	Waynesburg College		
WaySU	Wayne State University	WLBI	Word of Life Bible Institute
WBC	Washington Bible College	WLibStC	West Liberty State College
WBibC	Word Biblical Commentary	WLST	Winona Lake Summer School of Theology
WBM	Westminster Biblical Missions		
WBT	Wycliffe Bible Translators	WLU	Washington and Lee University
wc	Without Charge/Without Call		
WCar	Western Carolina	WmCC	William Carter College, SC
WCarC	West Carolina College	WMDC	Western Maryland College
WCBS	Western Conservative Baptist Seminary-Oregon	WmsC	Williams College
		WmTynC	William Tyndale College
WChC	Westminster Choir College	WMU	Western Michigan University
WChSC	West Chester State College	WoffC	Wofford College
WCPA	Westminster College, PA	WonK	Won Kwang University
WCU	Western Carolina University, NC	WooSU	Woo Suck University, Korea
WCUTor	Wycliffe College, University of Toronto	WorPL	Worcester Polytechnic Institute, MA
WDA	Worldwide Discipleship Association	WPM	World Presbyterian Missions
		WPMA	West Point Military Academy
WEAA	World Evangelical Aids Association	WPRF	World Presbyterian and Reformed Fellowship
WebsU	Webster University		
WeC	Westmar College	wr	Writer
WEF	World Evangelical Fellowship	WResU	Western Reserve University
WesC	Westman College	WRHCC	William Rainy Harper Community College
WeslCh	Wesleyan Church		
WesmAc	Westminster Academy	WRS	Westminster Reformed Seminary
WestC	Westmont College		
Westm	Westminster	WSal	Winston Salem
WestmC	Westminster College, Missouri	WSC	Western State College
WestmCAc	Westminster Christian Academy	WST	Westminster School of Theology
WestmCTX	Westminster College, Texas		
WestTS	Western Theological Seminary		

ABBREVIATIONS

WTC	Westminster Theological College, Perth, Australia	Ybk	Yearbook
		YC	Yankton College
WTS	Westminster Theological Seminary	YCPA	York College of Pennsylvania
WTSCA	Westminster Theological Seminary, California	ydir	Youth Director
		YDS	Yale Divinity School
WTSFL	Westminster Theological Seminary, Florida	YFC	Youth for Christ
		YL	Young Life
WTSTX	Westminster Theological Seminary, Dallas	YLI	Young Life Institute of Youth Ministry
WTSU	West Texas State University	YonU	Yonsei University
WVC	Wenatchee Valley College	yp	Youth Pastor
WVNCC	West Virginia Northern Community College	YSU	Youngstown State University
		YU	Yale University
WVSC	West Virginia State College	YUE	Yeung nam University of Engineering
WVTech	West Virginia Tech		
WVU	West Virginia University	YuSU	YuenShe University of Seoul
WWA	Western Washington University	ZIMS	Zwemer Institute of Muslim Studies
WWC	West Washington College	ZPEB	Zondervan Pictorial Encyclopedia of the Bi
WWCL	Woodrow Wilson College of Law, Atlanta		
WWSU	Western Washington State University		
WyBibC	Wycliffe Bible Commentary		
WyBibE	Wycliffe Bible Encyclopedia		
y	Youth		
YAP	Youth Advocate Programs		